Introduction to Color Imaging Science

Color imaging technology has become almost ubiquitous in modern life in the form of color photography, color monitors, color printers, scanners, and digital cameras. This book is a comprehensive guide to the scientific and engineering principles of color imaging. It covers the physics of color and light, how the eye and physical devices capture color images, how color is measured and calibrated, and how images are processed. It stresses physical principles and includes a wealth of real-world examples. The book will be of value to scientists and engineers in the color imaging industry and, with homework problems, can also be used as a text for graduate courses on color imaging.

HSIEN-CHE LEE received his B.S. from National Taiwan University in 1973 and Ph.D. in electrical engineering from Purdue University in 1981. He then worked for 18 years at Kodak Research Laboratories in Rochester, New York. There he did research on digital color image processing, color science, human color vision, medical imaging, and computer vision. He is now Senior Vice President of Advanced Imaging at Foxlink Peripherals, Inc., Fremont, California. With more than 20 years of research and product development experience in imaging science, he has given many lectures and short courses on color imaging, color science, and computer vision at various universities and research institutes. He has published many technical papers and has 14 US patents in inventions related to color imaging science.

Introduction to
Color Imaging Science

HSIEN-CHE LEE

CAMBRIDGE
UNIVERSITY PRESS

CAMBRIDGE UNIVERSITY PRESS
Cambridge, New York, Melbourne, Madrid, Cape Town, Singapore, São Paulo, Delhi

Cambridge University Press
The Edinburgh Building, Cambridge CB2 8RU, UK

Published in the United States of America by Cambridge University Press, New York

www.cambridge.org
Information on this title: www.cambridge.org/9780521103138

© Cambridge University Press 2005

This publication is in copyright. Subject to statutory exception
and to the provisions of relevant collective licensing agreements,
no reproduction of any part may take place without the written
permission of Cambridge University Press.

First published 2005
This digitally printed version 2009

A catalogue record for this publication is available from the British Library

ISBN 978-0-521-84388-1 hardback
ISBN 978-0-521-10313-8 paperback

Cambridge University Press has no responsibility for the persistence or accuracy of
URLs for external or third-party Internet websites referred to in this publication, and
does not guarantee that any content on such websites is, or will remain, accurate or
appropriate.

This book is dedicated with love and gratitude to my mother,
my wife Hui-Jung, and my daughter Joyce
for their many, many years of help, support, patience, and understanding

Contents

Preface

To understand the capturing, the processing, and the display of color images requires knowledge of many disciplines, such as image formation, radiometry, colorimetry, psychophysics, and color reproduction, that are not parts of the traditional training for engineers. Yet, with the advance of sensor, computing, and display technologies, engineers today often have to deal with aspects of color imaging, some more frequently than others. This book is intended as an introduction to color imaging science for engineers and scientists. It will be useful for those who are preparing to work or are already working in the field of color imaging or other fields that would benefit from the understanding of the fundamental processes of color imaging.

The sound training of imaging scientists and engineers requires more than teaching practical knowledge of color signal conversion, such as YIQ to RGB. It also has to impart good understanding of the physical, mathematical, and psychophysical principles underlying the practice. Good understanding ensures correct usage of formulas and enables one to come up with creative solutions to new problems. The major emphasis of this book, therefore, is to elucidate the basic principles and processes of color imaging, rather than to compile knowledge of all known systems and algorithms. Many applications are described, but they serve mainly as examples of how the basic principles can be used in practice and where compromises are made.

Color imaging science covers so many fields of research that it takes much more than one book to discuss its various aspects in reasonable detail. There are excellent books on optics, radiometry, photometry, colorimetry, color science, color vision, visual perception, pigments, dyes, photography, image sensors, image displays, image quality, and graphic arts. Indeed, the best way to understand the science of color imaging is to read books on each of these topics. The obvious problem is the time and effort required for such an undertaking, and this is the main motivation for writing this book. It extracts the essential information from the diverse disciplines to present a concise introduction to the science of color imaging. In doing so, I have made unavoidable personal choices as to what should be included. I have covered most of the topics that I considered important for a basic understanding of color imaging. Readers, who want to know more on any topic, are strongly encouraged to study the books and articles cited in the reference list for further information.

I would like to thank Professor Thomas S. Huang of University of Illinois, for his wonderful lectures and his suggestion of writing a book on color imaging. I would also like to thank Professor Thomas W. Parks of Cornell University for his numerous suggestions on how to improve the presentation of the material and for his help in constructing homework problems for students. During the time he and I cotaught a course on color imaging science at Cornell, I learned a lot from his many years of teaching experience. My career in imaging science began under Mr. James S. Alkofer and Dr. Michael A. Kriss. They let me wander around in the interesting world of color imaging under their experienced guidance. I appreciate their encouragement, friendship, and wisdom very much. I am also very grateful to my copy-editor, Maureen Storey, for her patient and meticulous editing of my manuscript.

During the preparation of this book, my wife took care of the family needs and all the housework. Her smiles brightened my tired days and her lively description of her daily activities kept me in touch with the real world. She loves taking pictures and her casual comments on image quality serve as reality checks of all the theories I know. My book-writing also required me to borrow many weekends from my daughter. Her witty and funny remarks to comfort me on my ever increasing time debt just made it more difficult for me to figure out how much I owe her. Certain things cannot be quantified.

1 Introduction

1.1 What is color imaging science?

Color imaging science is the study of the formation, manipulation, display, and evaluation of color images. Image formation includes the optical imaging process and the image sensing and recording processes. The manipulation of images is most easily done through computers in digital form or electronic circuits in analog form. Conventional image manipulation in darkrooms accounts only for a very small fraction of the total images manipulated daily. The display of color images can use many different media, such as CRT monitors, photographic prints, half-tone printing, and thermal dye-transfer prints, etc. The complete imaging chain from capture, through image processing, to display involves many steps of degradation, correction, enhancement, and compromise. The quality of the final reproduced images has to be evaluated by the very subjective human observers. Sometimes, the evaluation process can be automated with a few objectively computable, quantitative measurements.

The complexity of color imaging science stems from the need to understand many diverse fields of engineering, optics, physics, chemistry, and mathematics. Although it is not required for us to be familiar with every part of the process in detail before we can work in and contribute to the color imaging science field, it is often necessary for us to have a general understanding of the entire imaging chain in order to avoid making unrealistic assumptions in our work. For example, in digital image processing, a frequently used technique is histogram-equalization enhancement, in which an input image is mapped through a tonal transformation curve such that the output image has a uniformly distributed histogram of image values. However, the technique is often applied without knowing what the units of the digital images really are. The same image can be digitized in terms of film density or image exposure. Depending on which way it is digitized, the resulting histogram can differ widely. Writing that an image has been processed by the "histogram-equalization" technique without saying in which metric the histogram was equalized does not allow the reader to draw any meaningful conclusion. If we have a general understanding of the practice of image scanning and display, we can easily avoid this type of error. Sometimes, causes of errors can be more subtle and it requires understanding of a different kind to avoid them. For example, the geometrical theory of optical imaging tells us that the out-of-focus point spread function is a uniform disk. However, if we understand that the fundamental assumption of geometrical optics is not valid around the image focus area, we are more careful in using the uniform disk as a blur model. In this case, basic knowledge of the assumptions underlying various approximations made by theories lets us watch out for potential pitfalls. For these

1

reasons, this book aims at providing the needed general understanding of the entire color imaging chain whilst making the various assumptions and approximations clear.

1.2 Overview of the book

This book is written based on the belief that for a beginning color imaging scientist or engineer, a basic, broad understanding of the physical principles underlying every step in the imaging chain is more useful than an accumulation of knowledge about details of various techniques. Therefore, on the one hand, some readers may be surprised by many of the topics in the book that are not traditionally covered by textbooks on color science and imaging science. On the other hand, some readers may be disappointed that no comprehensive surveys are provided for various algorithms or devices. If we truly understand the nature of a problem, we can often come up with very creative and robust solutions after some careful thinking. Otherwise, even if we know all the existing tricks and methods to solve a problem, we may be at a loss when some critical constraints are changed. The following is an overview of the book.

1.2.1 Measurement of light and color

Since color images are formed by light, we first describe, in Chapter 2, the nature and properties of light as we understand them today. The history of how we came to achieve that understanding is fascinating, but it would take up too much space to give a full account of the intellectual struggle which involved some of the brightest minds in human history. However, properties of light, such as the wave train, its quantum nature, coherence, and polarization, come up in color imaging frequently enough that we have to at least understand these basic concepts involved in characterizing the light. Before we explain in Chapter 5 how light interacts with matter, we have to understand how we quantify and measure the energy propagation of light.

The scientific basis of color imaging starts from the defining concepts of how light can be measured. These are the topics of radiometry (Chapter 3) and photometry (Chapter 4). In these two chapters, we describe how the flow of light energy can be quantified in a physical system and how our "brightness" sensation can be related to the measurement. With proper knowledge of radiometry, we then come back to study the light–matter interaction, which is often very complex from a theoretical point of view and, in its full detail, not easy to comprehend. We, therefore, have to treat many aspects of the interaction phenomenologically. Thus, in Chapter 5, we discuss dispersion, refraction, reflection, scattering, transmission, absorption, and diffraction, basically following the traditional and historical development.

In Chapter 6, we cover the topic of colorimetry, which starts with the physical specification of stimuli that our visual system perceives as colors. The word color, as we use it in our daily conversation, implicitly refers to human color vision. In studying color imaging systems, a spectrum of incident light can be specified with respect to any physical sensing system that can sense more than one spectral component. Colorimetry can be established for any such system. For example, when we wish to study how other animals or insects see the world, separate colorimetric systems can be constructed according to their spectral sensing mechanisms. From this perspective, we can appreciate how color imaging can be thought of as a branch of science that relates different physical systems with the same basic laws. For human color perception, the colorimetry system established by the Commission Internationale de l'Eclairage (CIE) is the most widely accepted system today. Much of Chapter 6 is devoted to explaining what the CIE system is and how it was derived. It is of fundamental importance that we understand this system thoroughly.

Since the spectral composition of the light reflected from an object surface is the product of the spectral composition of the light incident on the surface and the spectral reflectance factor of the surface, the spectral characteristics of light sources directly (through direct illumination) or indirectly (through mutual reflection) affect the spectral composition of the optical image formed at the sensor(s) of a color imaging system. Therefore, it is necessary for us to have a good knowledge of the nature of the various light sources that are involved in color imaging applications. This is the subject of Chapter 7.

The colorful contents of natural scenes are the results of the complex interaction of light and objects. The quantitative description of such interactions is called scene physics, and is the subject of Chapter 8. It is important to note that such quantitative description is a very difficult problem to formulate. The concept of the bidirectional reflectance distribution function (BRDF) is one formulation that has been widely accepted because of its practical applicability and usefulness, although it certainly is not valid for every conceivable light–matter interaction. Various models for reflective and transmissive materials are discussed following this basic concept. In addition to color imaging applications, these models often find use in color image synthesis, colorant formulation, the printing industry, and computer vision. These fields are closely related to color imaging and color imaging research benefits from ideas and results from them. The chapter also includes a general overview of the physical and optical properties of some of the common materials that we encounter in color imaging applications. The chapter ends with a summary of some statistical properties of natural scenes. These properties are empirical, but they are useful for at least two purposes: (1) Many practical color imaging problems, such as white balance and exposure determination, are open research problems that seem to have no provable, deterministic solutions. Statistical properties of natural scenes can be used as *a priori* knowledge in any Bayesian estimate. (2) The statistical properties reveal certain regularities in the natural scenes and thus form a very rich source of research topics that will increase our understanding of how the physical world behaves.

1.2.2　Optical image formation

The next component in the events of an imaging chain is the formation of the optical images on the sensor. Within the visible wavelength range, optical imaging can be very well described by treating light as rays, neglecting its wave and photon characteristics most of the time. Such an approximation is called geometrical optics, in which Snell's law plays the most important role. However, when discontinuous boundaries exist, such as an aperture stop in a camera, light's wave nature (diffraction) becomes an important factor to consider. For example, in geometrical optics, the image of an object point in an aberration-free system is always assumed to be an ideal image point, independently of the aperture size. This is simply not true. From electromagnetic wave theory, we can derive the so-called "diffraction-limited" point spread function, which turns out to have a fairly complicated spatial distribution. The description of the optical image formation through wave theory is called wave optics or physical optics. Chapters 9 and 10 cover the basic concepts in both geometrical optics and physical optics. The geometrical theory of optical imaging is quite general and, as far as color imaging science is concerned, the most interesting result is that the mapping between the object space and the image space is a projective transformation. This leads naturally to the matrix method for paraxial ray tracing that allows us to do quick and simple calculations of the basic characteristics of most optical imaging systems. The most fundamental tool for analyzing the image quality of an imaging system is the optical transfer function (OTF). The relationship between the OTF and the wavefront aberration can be derived from diffraction theory, which is the foundation of physical optics for image formation.

In the sensing and recording of optical images, it is very important to calculate how much light (image irradiance) is collected on the sensor plane, as a function of focal length, object distance, and aperture size. In Chapter 10, the image irradiance equations, like the theory of radiometry, are derived from geometrical optics. These equations are very important for all practical optical imaging systems and should be understood well. A more detailed desciption of the light distribution in the image space has to be derived from physical optics. The results from geometrical optics and physical optics are compared using a case study of the blur caused by defocus. The conclusion is that when the defocus is severe, the predictions of both theories are quite similar. However, when the defocus is slight, the predictions are very different. Physical optics even predicts, against our intuition, that the center of the point spread function can become zero at a certain defocus distance. This rather counterintuitive prediction has been confirmed by experiments.

1.2.3 *In the eye of the beholder*

The beauty of color images is in the eye of the beholder. Thus, it is necessary for us to understand the function and the characteristics of the human visual system, so that color imaging systems can be efficiently optimized. We examine the optics of the eye in Chapter 11. Basic anatomical structures and optical models of the eye are described. Its optical properties, such as the modulation transfer function (MTF), acuity, and accommodation, are summarized. A computational model of the OTF of the eye as a function of viewing parameters is then discussed, based on the wavefront aberrations of the pupil function. This type of approach is very useful when we want to model the optical performance of the eye under viewing conditions very different from the laboratory settings. In Chapter 12, we discuss how the visual signal is sensed and processed in our visual pathways from retina to brain. The physiology and the anatomy of the visual system presented in this chapter help us to understand the practical constraints and the general features of our visual perception. In Chapter 13, we shift our attention to the basic issues in the psychophysics of visual perception. Here we try to clarify one of the most confused areas in color imaging. The basic approach is to describe how psychophysical experiments are conducted, so that color imaging scientists and engineers will think more carefully about how to apply the psychophysical data to their work. In this chapter, we have chosen to discuss the concepts of brightness and lightness in some detail because they show us how complicated the computation can be even for some things that sound intuitively obvious. We also discuss at length the perception of images when they are stabilized on our retinas. The finding that the perceived images quickly fade when they are stabilized on the observer's retina clearly demonstrates that the visual perception is more a task of reconstruction from visual features than a job of mapping the optical images directly to our mind.

After we have studied the human visual system in Chapters 11–13, we are well prepared to explore the basic ideas and theories behind the various color order systems in Chapter 14. We have delayed the discussion of this subject until now so that we can appreciate the motivation, the limitations, and the difficulties involved in any color order system. (For example, the concept of opponent color processes was developed to explain many psychophysical observations, and therefore it also plays an important role in the Ostwald and the NCS color order systems.) The idea of using a color atlas for everyday color specification seems an intuitive thing to do, but from the perspective of colorimetry, a color atlas may be a useless thing to have because the everyday illuminants are almost never as specified by the atlas. It is the powerful color processing of our visual system that does all the "auto" compensations that make a color atlas of any practical use.

1.2.4   Tools for color imaging

The practice of color imaging science requires physical and perceptual evaluation of color images. The tools for physical evaluation are spectroradiometers, spectrophotometers, densitometers, and other electrical and optical instruments. Chapter 15 covers physical color measurement tools and Chapter 16 mathematical tools.

The tools for perceptual evaluation are less well developed, but they fall into the general categories of tone reproduction (Chapter 17), color reproduction (Chapter 18), and image quality (mostly *ad hoc* measures of sharpness, resolution, noise, and contrast, as discussed in Chapter 21). There have been quite extensive studies of tone and color reproduction, and some general principles can be systematically summarized. Good tone reproduction is the number one requirement in the perceived image quality. In the past, research has been focused on the tone reproduction characteristics of an imaging system as a whole. As digital processing becomes common practice for most imaging applications, a general theory of image-dependent tone reproduction is needed. On the subject of color reproduction, there are fewer definitive studies. The major effort seems to be in working out a usable color appearance model. Although the current model is incomplete because it does not explicitly take spatial and temporal variations into consideration, it seems to produce reasonable measures for color reproduction.

1.2.5   Color image acquisition and display

Tremendous progress has been made since the 1970s in the development of new image acquisition and display devices. Photographic films and papers are still quite important, but in many applications, they are being replaced by digital cameras, scanners, and many printing/display devices. Chapter 19 discusses various color image acquisition media, devices, and systems, while Chapter 20 covers those for color image display. Basic understanding of the characteristics and working principles of the various input/output systems is very important in the practice of color imaging science. Even if we do not directly work on a particular device or medium, it is very likely we will encounter images that are acquired by that device or are to be displayed on that medium. Often, the solution to a color imaging problem for a given device may have been worked out for other devices. Understanding the problems and technology behind one type of system often helps us to solve problems in another type of system. A good example is the unsharp masking method for image enhancement, which has long been practised in photographic dark rooms. The same technique is now used extensively in digital imaging as well.

1.2.6   Image quality and image processing

Every imaging system, from its design to the finished product, involves many cost, schedule, and performance trade-offs. System optimization and evaluation are often based on the image quality requirements of the product. The metrics that are used to evaluate image quality, therefore, play a very important role in the system design and testing processes. In Chapter 21, we present the basic attributes and models for image quality. Objective measures, such as camera/sensor speed, image noise, and spatial resolution, are quickly becoming standardized. Subjective measures, such as contrast, sharpness, tone, and color reproduction, are less well defined physically and rely more on psychophysical experiments with human observers. It is necessary to understand what procedures can be used and what precautions we need to take.

Digital image processing can be used to correct some deficiencies in current imaging systems, such as noise reduction, image sharpening, and adaptive tone adjustment. Furthermore, algorithms can be used to increase the system performance, such as autofocus, autoexposure, and auto-white-balance. Basic algorithms in digital image processing are very well covered in existing textbooks. Unfortunately, some algorithms are too slow to be practical, and many others too fragile to be useful. Most good and fast algorithms tend to be proprietary and not in the public domain. They also tend to be hardware specific.

Color image processing is not simply repeating the same processing for three monochromatic images, one for each color channel. There are many new concepts and new problems that we do not encounter in gray scale images for two basic reasons: (1) color images are vector fields, and (2) our color vision has its own idiosyncracy – color information is represented and processed by our visual system in a specific way. In Chapter 22, we concentrate on only a few selected concepts, such as color space design, vector gradient, color segmentation, and statistics of directional data. These are concepts that have not received much discussion in the literature, but are very important for many practical applications to take into account. It is easy to be misled if we have not thought about the various issues by ourselves first.

1.3   The International System of Units (SI)

In this book, we use the terminology and units in the International System of Units (SI) and those recommended by the Commission Internationale de l'Eclairage (CIE). When there are

Table 1.1. *SI prefixes (from [942])*

Factor	Prefix	Symbol	Factor	Prefix	Symbol
10^{24}	yotta	Y	10^{-1}	deci	d
10^{21}	zetta	Z	10^{-2}	centi	c
10^{18}	exa	E	10^{-3}	milli	m
10^{15}	peta	P	10^{-6}	micro	μ
10^{12}	tera	T	10^{-9}	nano	n
10^{9}	giga	G	10^{-12}	pico	p
10^{6}	mega	M	10^{-15}	femto	f
10^{3}	kilo	k	10^{-18}	atto	a
10^{2}	hecto	h	10^{-21}	zepto	z
10^{1}	deca	da	10^{-24}	yocto	y

conflicts in symbols, we will use the CIE symbols for the units in radiometry, colorimetry, and photometry. The International System of Units is described in many standard documents (such as [942]) and the book by Ražnjević [787] provides good explanations. The CIE system is well described in its publication: *International Lighting Vocabulary* [187]. The International System of Units (SI) adopted by CGPM[1] is composed of basic units, derived units, and supplementary units. There are seven basic units: meter [m] for length, kilogram [kg] for mass, second [s] for time, ampere [A] for electric current, kelvin [K] for temperature, candela [cd] for luminous intensity, and mole [mol] for amount of substance. The meter is defined as the length of the path traveled by light in vacuum during a time interval of 1/299 792 458 second. The unit of plane angle, radian [rad], and the unit of solid angle, steradian [sr], are two of the supplementary units. Since they are dimensionless derived units, they do not need to be defined as a separate class of unit. Many SI derived units, such as watt [W], volt [V], hertz [Hz], and joule [J], are quite familiar to us. Other SI derived units, such as lux [lx] and lumen [lm], that we are going to use frequently in the book will be defined in detail later. When the numerical values are too large or too small, the SI prefixes in Table 1.1 can be used to form multiples and submultiples of SI units. It is a convention that a grouping formed by a prefix symbol and a unit symbol is a new inseparable symbol. Therefore, cm (centimeter) is a new symbol and can be raised to any power without using parentheses. For example, 2 cm^2 = 2 (cm)^2. Convention also requires that unit symbols are unaltered in the plural and are not followed by a period unless at the end of a sentence.

Unfortunately, there are many instances when one standard symbol could represent more than one physical quantity. For example, E is used both for the electric field strength [V m^{-1}] and for irradiance [W m^{-2}]. Similarly, H is used for the magnetic field strength [A m^{-1}] and also for exposure [J m^{-2}]. Since this happens very frequently and since changing standard symbols for various physical quantities can create more confusion, we decided that the best way to avoid ambiguity is to specify the units when it is not clear from the context which physical quantity is used. This will free us to use the same, widely accepted, standard symbol for different physical quantities in our discussion throughout the book. In

---

[1]   CGPM stands for Conférence Générale des Poids et Measures. Its English translation is: General Conference on Weights and Measures. It is the decision-making body of the Treaty of the Meter, signed in 1875. The decisions by CGPM legally govern the international metrology system among all the countries that signed the Treaty.

Table 1.2. *Some important physical constants used in this book*

Quantity	Symbol	Value
speed of light in vacuum	c	$299\,792\,458$ m s^{-1}
permeability of vacuum	μ_0	$4\pi \times 10^{-7}$ m kg s^{-2} A^{-2}
permittivity of vacuum	ϵ_0	$\dfrac{1}{\mu_0 c^2}$ m^{-3} kg^{-1} s^4 A^2
Planck constant	h	$6.626\,075\,5 \times 10^{-34}$ J s
Boltzmann constant	k	$1.380\,658 \times 10^{-23}$ J K^{-1}
electron volt	eV	$1.602\,177\,33 \times 10^{-19}$ J

almost all cases, the context and the name of the physical quantity will make the meaning clear. The physical constants shown in Table 1.2 will be useful in our later discussion.

1.4 General bibliography and guide to the literatures

Color imaging science cuts across many different disciplines. For further details on any specific topic, the reader is encouraged to consult books and papers in that field. There are many excellent books in each field. Since every person has a different style of learning and a different background of training, it is difficult to recommend books that will be both useful and interesting to everyone. A short bibliography is compiled here. No special criteria have been used for selection and the list represents only a tiny fraction of the excellent books available on the various topics. Hopefully, it may be useful for you. If you know some experts in the field you are interested in, you should ask them for more personalized recommendations.

Radiometry and photometry

Radiometry and the Detection of Optical Radiation, by R.W. Boyd [127].
Optical Radiation Measurements, Volume I, by F. Grum and R.J. Becherer [369].
Reliable Spectroradiometry, by H.J. Kostkowski [525].
Illumination Engineering – From Edison's Lamp to the Laser, by J.B. Murdoch [687].
Self-Study Manual on Optical Radiation Measurements, edited by F.E. Nicodemus [714].
Geometrical Considerations and Nomenclature for Reflectance, by F.E. Nicodemus, J.C. Richmond, J.J. Hsia, I.W. Ginsberg, and T. Limperis [715].
Thermal Radiation Heat Transfer, by R. Siegel and J.R. Howell [872].
Introduction to Radiometry, by W.L. Wolfe [1044].

Color science

Billmeyer and Saltzman's Principles of Color Technology, 3rd edition, by R.S. Berns [104].
Principles of Color Technology, 2nd edition, by F.W. Billmeyer and M. Saltzman [111].
Measuring Colour, by R.W.G. Hunt [430].
Color: An Introduction to Practice and Principles, by R.G. Kuehni [539].
Color Measurement, by D.L. MacAdam [620].
Colour Physics for Industry, 2nd edition, edited by R. McDonald [653].

Handbook of Color Science, 2nd edition, edited by Nihon Shikisaigakkai (in Japanese) [716].
The Science of Color, 2nd edition, edited by S.K. Shevell [863].
Industrial Color Testing: Fundamentals and Techniques, by H.G. Völz [989].
Color Science, 2nd edition, by G. Wyszecki and W.S. Stiles [1053].

Human visual perception

The Senses, edited by H.B. Barlow and J.D. Mollon [54].
Handbook of Perception and Human Performance, Volumes I and II, edited by K.R. Boff, L. Kaufman, and J.P. Thomas [118, 119].
Vision, by P. Buser and M. Imbert [153].
The Visual Neurosciences, edited by L.M. Chalupa and J.S. Werner [167].
Visual Perception, by T.N. Cornsweet [215].
The Retina: An Approachable Part of the Brain, by J.E. Dowling [264].
An Introduction to Color, by R.M. Evans [286].
Color Vision: From Genes to Perception, edited by K.R. Gegenfurtner and L.T. Sharpe [337].
Eye, Brain, and Vision, by D.H. Hubel [418].
Color Vision, by L.M. Hurvich [436].
Human Color Vision, 2nd edition, by P.K. Kaiser and R.M. Boynton [480].
Visual Science and Engineering: Models and Applications, by D.H. Kelly [500].
Vision: A Computational Investigation into the Human Representation and Processing of Visual Information, by D. Marr [636].
Images of Mind, by M.I. Posner and M.E. Raichle [774].
The First Steps in Seeing, by R.W. Rodieck [802].
Visual Perception: The Neurophysiological Foundations, edited by L. Spillmann and J.S. Werner [892].
Foundations of Vision, by B.A. Wandell [1006].
A Vision of the Brain, by S. Zeki [1066].

Optics

Handbook of Optics, Volumes I and II, edited by M. Bass [84].
Principles of Optics, 7th edition, by M. Born and E. Wolf [125].
Introduction to Matrix Methods in Optics, by A. Gerrard and J.M. Burch [341].
Statistical Optics, by J.W. Goodman [353].
Introduction to Fourier Optics, by J.W. Goodman [354].
Optics, 2nd edition, by E. Hecht [385].
Lens Design Fundamentals, by R. Kingslake [508].
Optics in Photography, by R. Kingslake [509].
Optics, 2nd edition, by M.V. Klein and T.E. Furtak [512].
Physiological Optics, by Y. Le Grand and S.G. El Hage [580].
Aberration Theory Made Simple, by V.N. Mahajan [626].
Optical Coherence and Quantum Optics, by L. Mandel and E. Wolf [631].
Geometrical Optics and Optical Design, by P. Mouroulis and J. Macdonald [682].

Introduction to Statistical Optics, by E.L. O'Neil [729].

Elements of Modern Optical Design, by D.C. O'Shea [733].

Applied Photographic Optics, 3rd edition, by S.F. Ray [786].

States, Waves and Photons: A Modern Introduction to Light, by J. W. Simmons and M.J. Guttmann [877].

The Eye and Visual Optical Instruments, by G. Smith and D.A. Atchison [884].

Modern Optical Engineering, 3rd edition, by W.J. Smith [887].

The Optics of Rays, Wavefronts, and Caustics by O.N. Stavroudis [899].

Scene physics

Absorption and Scattering of Light by Small Particles, by C.F. Bohren and D.R. Huffman [120].

The Cambridge Guide to the Material World, by R. Cotterill [217].

Light by R.W. Ditchburn [258].

Sensory Ecology, by D.B. Dusenbery [269].

Seeing the Light, by D.S. Falk, D.R. Brill, and D.G. Stork [297].

Color in Nature, by P.A. Farrant [301].

Color and Light in Nature, by D.K. Lynch and W. Livingston [615].

The Colour Science of Dyes and Pigments, by K. McLaren [654].

Light and Color in the Outdoors, by M. Minnaert [667].

The Physics and Chemistry of Color, by K. Nassau [693].

Light and Color, by R.D. Overheim and D.L. Wagner [736].

Introduction to Materials Science for Engineers, 4th edition, by J.F. Shackelford [853].

Colour and the Optical Properties of Materials, by R.J.D. Tilley [952].

Light and Color in Nature and Art, by S.J. Williamson and H.Z. Cummins [1036].

Color Chemistry, 2nd edition, by H. Zollinger [1071].

Image science

Foundations of Image Science, by H.H. Barrett and K.J. Meyers [64].

Image Science, by J.C. Dainty and R. Shaw [232].

Principles of Color Photography, by R.M. Evans, W.T. Hanson, and W.L. Brewer [289].

The Theory of the Photographic Process, 4th edition, edited by T.H. James [459].

Handbook of Image Quality, by B.W. Keelan [494].

Science and Technology of Photography, edited by K. Keller [495].

Image Technology Design: A Perceptual Approach, by J.-B. Martens [642].

Handbook of Photographic Science and Engineering, 2nd edition, edited by C.N. Proudfoot [779].

Fundamentals of Electronic Imaging Systems, 2nd edition, by W.F. Schreiber [841].

Imaging Processes and Materials, edited by J. Sturge, V. Walworth, and A. Shepp [923].

Photographic Sensitivity: Theory and Mechanisms, by T. Tani [936].

Digital image processing

Digital Image Processing: A System Approach, 2nd edition, by W.B. Green [363].

Digital Image Processing, by R.C. Gonzalez and R.E. Woods [351].

Digital Image Processing: Concepts, Algorithms, and Scientific Applications, 4th edition, by B. Jähne [456].

Fundamentals of Digital Image Processing, by A.K. Jain [457].

Two-dimensional Signal and Image Processing, by J.S. Lim [594].

A Wavelet Tour of Signal Processing, by S. Mallat [628].

Digital Pictures: Representation and Compression, by A.N. Netravali and B.G. Haskell [708].

Digital Image Processing, 2nd edition, by W.K. Pratt [776].

Digital Picture Processing, 2nd edition, by A. Rosenfeld and A.C. Kak [807].

The Image Processing Handbook, by J.C. Russ [814].

Digital Color Imaging Handbook, edited by G. Sharma [857].

Color reproduction

Color Appearance Models, by M.D. Fairchild [292].

Color and Its Reproduction, by G.G. Field [309].

Digital Color Management, by E.J. Giorgianni and T.E. Madden [347].

Colour Engineering, edited by P.J. Green and L.W. MacDonald [362].

The Reproduction of Colour in Photography, Printing, and Television, 5th edition, by R.W.G. Hunt [433].

Color Technology for Electronic Imaging Devices, by H.R. Kang [483].

Colour Imaging: Vision and Technology, edited by L.W. MacDonald and M.R. Luo [622].

Colour Image Science: Exploiting Digital Media, edited by L.W. MacDonald and M.R. Luo [623].

Introduction to Color Reproduction Technology, (in Japanese) by N. Ohta [726].

Colour Science in Television and Display Systems, by W.N. Sproson [895].

Principles of Color Reproduction, by J.A.C. Yule [1065].

Color imaging input/output devices

Television Engineering Handbook, edited by K.B. Benson [97].

CCD Astronomy: Construction and Use of an Astronomical CCD Camera, by C. Buil [147].

Scientific Charge-Coupled Devices, by J.R. Janesick [461].

Digital Color Halftoning, by H.R. Kang [484].

Handbook of Print Media, edited by H. Kipphan [511].

Display Systems: Design and Applications, edited by L.W. MacDonald and A.C. Lowe [621].

Digital Video and HDTV: Algorithms and Interfaces, by C. Poynton [775].

Flat-Panel Displays and CRTs, edited by L.E. Tannas Jr. [938].

Solid-State Imaging with Charge-Coupled Devices, by A.J.P. Theuwissen [948].

Color in Electronic Displays, edited by H. Widdel and D.L. Post [1029].

1.5 Problems

1.1 Let $X = g(Y)$ be the input/output characteristic response function of an image capture device (say, a scanner), where Y is the input signal (reflectance) and X is the output response (output digital image from the scanner). Let $y = f(x)$ be the input/output characteristic function of an image display device (say, a CRT monitor), where x is the input digital image and y is the luminance of the displayed image. Assume that both g and f are one-to-one functions. If our objective is to make the displayed image y proportional to the scanned target reflectance Y, what should be the functional transformation on X before it is used as the input, x, to the display?

1.2 A monitor has two gray squares, A and B, displayed on its screen. When the room light is on, the amounts of light from the two squares are L_A and L_B, where $L_A \geq L_B$. When the room light is off, the amounts of light become D_A and D_B, where $D_A \geq D_B$. Which of the contrast ratios is higher, L_A/L_B or D_A/D_B?

1.3 The Poynting vector, $\mathbf{E} \times \mathbf{H}$, is a very useful quantity in the study of electromagnetic waves, where $\mathbf{E}$ is the electric field strength $[V\,m^{-1}]$ and $\mathbf{H}$ is the magnetic field strength $[A\,m^{-1}]$. By analyzing its unit, can you guess the physical meaning of the Poynting vector?

2 Light

Within our domain of interest, images are formed by light and its interaction with matter. The spatial and spectral distribution of light is focused on the sensor and recorded as an image. It is therefore important for us to first understand the nature and the properties of light. After a brief description of the nature of light, we will discuss some of its basic properties: energy, frequency, coherence, and polarization. The energy flow of light and the characterization of the frequency/wavelength distribution are the subjects of radiometry, colorimetry, and photometry, which will be covered in later chapters. The coherence and the polarization properties of light are also essential for understanding many aspects of the image formation process, but they are not as important for most color imaging applications because most natural light sources are incoherent and unpolarized, and most imaging sensors (including our eyes) are not sensitive to polarization. Therefore, we will discuss these two properties only briefly. They are presented in this chapter. Fortunately there are excellent books [208, 631, 871] covering these two topics (also, see the bibliography in *Handbook of Optics* [84]). From time to time later in the book, we will need to use the concepts we develop here to help us understand some of the more subtle issues in light–matter interaction (such as scattering and interference), and in the image formation process (such as the OTFs).

2.1 What is light?

The nature of light has been one of the most intensively studied subjects in physics. Its research has led to several major discoveries in human history. We have now reached a stage where we have an extremely precise theory of light, quantum electrodynamics (QED) [307, 602, 760] that can explain all the physical phenomena of light that we know about and its interaction with matter, from diffraction, interference, blackbody radiation, the laser, and the photoelectric effect, to Compton scattering of x-rays [211]. However, the nature of light as described by QED is quite abstract. It is so different from our everyday experience that no simple mental model or intuition, such as waves or particles, can be developed in our understanding to comprehend its nature. A fair statement to make about the nature of light is that we do not really "understand" it, but we have a very precise theory for calculating and predicting its behavior. Since the nature of light is literally beyond our comprehension, the most fundamental description of light has to rely on experimental facts – phenomena that are observable. For example:

1. Due to its wave nature, light has different temporal frequencies. By saying this, we are implying that light is described as periodic functions, at least over a very short period of time. The spectrum of a beam of sunlight as produced by a prism has many different colors, each associated with light of different frequency v. The word "light" usually refers to the frequency range that is visible (approximately, from 4.0×10^{14} Hz to 7.8×10^{14} Hz).

2. Light carries energy (we feel heat from sunlight) and when it is absorbed, it is always in discrete amounts. The unit energy of the discrete amounts is hv, where h is Planck's constant and v is the frequency of the light.

3. Light (photon) has linear momentum, hv/c, and therefore exerts force on a surface it illuminates.

4. Light of the same frequency can have different characteristics (called polarizations) that can be separated out by certain materials called polarizers. In quantum mechanics, a photon can have one of two different spins (angular momentum): $\pm h/(2\pi)$.

Because of its complexity and its nonintuitive nature, QED theory is rarely used to explain "simpler" light behavior, such as interference, or to design optical imaging systems, such as a camera or a scanner. Fortunately, for these applications, we have alternative theories or models. The two most valuable ones are the ray model (geometrical optics) and the wave model (physical optics). Both models are incapable of explaining or predicting certain phenomena, but within their domains of validity, they are much simpler and more intuitive, and therefore, very useful.

The wave model is based on the Maxwell equations for classical electromagnetic theory. The velocity of the electromagnetic wave was shown to be the same as that of light. By now, it is well accepted (with the knowledge that the description is not complete) that light is an electromagnetic wave, as are the microwave used for cooking, the radio-wave used for communications, and the x-ray used for medical imaging. The light ray in the simpler geometric optics is often thought of as the surface normal to the wavefront of the electromagnetic wave, although this simple interpretation does not always work well, especially when the wave is not a simple plane wave or spherical wave. The connection between the electromagnetic wave and the photon in QED theory is not as straightforward to make. Quantum theory uses two objects to describe a physical system: the *operator* for the physical variables, such as the electric field intensity, and the Schrödinger *wave function*, ψ, for the state of the system. The Schrödinger wave function, ψ, is usually a complex function and its product with its complex conjugate, $\psi\psi^*$, gives the probability of finding photons at a point in space and time. It should be pointed out that the Schrödinger wave function, ψ, as solved in QED is not the electromagnetic wave as described by the Maxwell equations. The connection between the two waves is a statistical one: for classical phenomena, such as interference, the time-averaged Poynting vector, $\langle \mathbf{E} \times \mathbf{H} \rangle$ [W m^{-2}] as calculated from the Maxwell equations, predicts the average number of photons per unit time per unit area at that point in space, as calculated from QED.

For the majority of the optical applications that are of interest to us in this book, we will treat light as electromagnetic waves described by the Maxwell equations. The wavelength (in vacuum) range of the light that is visible to our eyes is approximately from 380 nm

(7.89 × 10^{14} Hz) to 740 nm (4.05 × 10^{14} Hz). The sources of light relevant to color imaging are mostly thermal sources, such as the sun, tungsten lamps, and fluorescent lamps. For these sources, light is incoherent and unpolarized – these two concepts can be treated within the electromagnetic wave model.

2.2   Wave trains of finite length

When we treat light as electromagnetic waves, we need to realize that the waves are of finite length. When we turn on a light lamp at time t_1, light is emitted from the lamp, and when we turn off the lamp at time t_2, the emission of light stops (approximately, because the tungsten filament does not cool down instantly). In this case, the duration of each of the trains of electromagnetic waves cannot be much longer than $t_2 - t_1$. In fact, they are all many orders of magnitude shorter than $t_2 - t_1$. When an electron of an atom or a molecule makes a transition from a higher energy state to a lower one, a photon is emitted. The time it takes for the electron to make the transition is very short and so is the length of the wave train of the light emitted. Although we have not measured the transition time directly, there are measurements that give us good estimates of the approximate length of the wave train for several light sources (e.g., [258, Chapter 4]). If the transition is spontaneous, the phase is often random, and the length of the wave train is short (on the order of 10^{-8} s [258, p. 93, 306, Volume I, p. 33–2, 631, p. 150]). If the transition is induced by an external field, such as in a laser, then the wave train can be much longer (as long as 10^{-4} s). However, for light with a wavelength of 500 nm, even a 10^{-8} s wave train contains 6 million wave cycles! There are two implications from the result of this simple calculation. (1) For most theoretical derivations concerning phase relations on a spatial scale in the range of a few wavelengths, such as light reflection from a smooth surface, we can approximate the light as a sinusoidal wave (such as a plane wave). (2) For most measurements of light, the integration time for sensing is much longer than 10^{-8} s, and the finite length of a wave train cannot be neglected. From the theory of Fourier analysis, a sine wave of duration Δt has a frequency bandwidth $\Delta \nu \approx 1/\Delta t$. Therefore, there is no such thing as a monochromatic (single-frequency) light wave. When the frequency bandwidth of radiation is very narrow, $\Delta \nu / \nu \ll 1$, we call it a quasi-monochromatic wave.

Conventional wave analysis relies heavily on Fourier analysis, which has the disadvantage of having a very sharp frequency resolution, but very poor spatial or time resolution (i.e., the sine and cosine functions can have a single frequency, but then they extend to infinity spatially or temporally). A new mathematical tool called wavelet analysis allows us to decompose any signal into wavelets that are more localized in time. It can be shown that wavelet solutions to the Maxwell equations can be found [478] and they may provide a more natural description for wave trains of finite length.

2.3   Coherence

The electromagnetic fields at two different points in space-time can fluctuate completely independently. In this case, we can say that they are completely incoherent. If the fluctuations of the fields at these two points are not completely independent of each other, then they are partially or completely coherent with each other. The degree of independence or the degree of coherence can be measured by statistical correlation [631, Chapters 4 and 6, 742]. Two special cases of coherence theory are temporal coherence (field fluctuation measured at the same spatial location) and spatial coherence (field fluctuation measured at the same time instant). Let us first consider the case of the temporal coherence in the famous Michelson interferometer.

2.3.1 Temporal coherence

Figure 2.1 shows a schematic diagram of a Michelson interferometer [661]. Let us use a partially silvered mirror, M, to split a light wave train into two components: one transmitted through the mirror and the other one reflected away from the mirror. In electromagnetic theory, a wave train, W, of finite duration, ΔT, is split into two finite-length wave trains, W_a and W_b, of smaller amplitudes. If these two wave trains are then brought back together (say, by two other mirrors, A and B, properly positioned), the two wave trains combine into a single wave train, W'. If there is no relative time delay between the two wave trains, the resulting combined wave, W', looks like the original wave train, W (assuming little loss and distortion in between the splitting and the recombination). In this case, at the spatial point of combination, the two wave trains are said to be temporally coherent. Now let us introduce a time delay Δt in one of the wave trains, say W_a, by making it travel a slightly longer distance. If $\Delta t < \Delta T$, the two wave trains, W_a and W_b, partially overlap and the resulting wave train, W', looks different from W. If $\Delta t > \Delta T$, the two wave trains, W_a and W_b, have no overlap and they are incoherent. Instead of a single wave train as the source, we can use

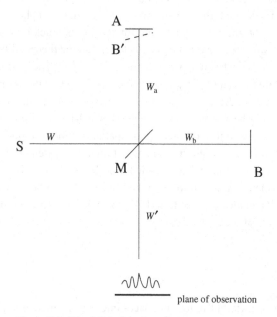

Figure 2.1. The Michelson interferometer.

a light source that generates line spectra, such as a sodium lamp or a mercury arc lamp. For these sources, we can imagine that many wave trains are emitted randomly, but each wave train, W, is split into a pair of trains, W_a and W_b, which are later brought back together at the plane of observation, which is set up somewhere along the path that the combined light beam travels. Instead of making the reflecting mirrors, A and B, perfectly parallel with respect to the images as seen by the beam splitter M, we introduce a minutely small tilt angle on mirror B. As a result of this tilt, the wave trains arriving at different points on the plane of observation are out of phase by different amounts and thus produce interference fringes. At the points where the pair of wave trains W_a and W_b differ in relative phase by integer multiples of the wavelength, the field amplitudes add exactly constructively and the radiant flux density $[\mathrm{W} \cdot \mathrm{m}^{-2}]$ reaches the maximum, $E_{\max}$. At the points where the relative phase differs by an odd multiple of half the wavelength, the field amplitudes cancel each other, and the light flux density falls to the minimum, $E_{\min}$. Michelson [661, p. 36] defined the fringe visibility (also known as Michelson contrast), V, as:

$$V = \frac{E_{\max} - E_{\min}}{E_{\max} + E_{\min}} \qquad (2.1)$$

and he showed that it varies as a function of the time delay Δt introduced between the two paths for W_a and W_b, or equivalently as a function of the optical path difference, $d = v\Delta t$, where v is the velocity of the light in the medium. By analyzing the visibility V as a function of d, he was able to estimate the spectral distribution of the light source. For example, the cadmium red line at 643.8 nm was shown to have a half-width (at the half-height) of 0.000 65 nm [258, p. 80], which can be used to deduce that the duration of the wave train emitted by the cadmium is on the order of 10^{-8} s.

Our immediate interest is that Michelson interference as described above occurs only when the relative time delay between the two wave trains is less than the duration of the original wave train. This time duration, ΔT is called the coherent time of the light. Its corresponding optical path difference, $\Delta l = v\Delta T$, is called the longitudinal coherence length [631, pp. 148–9]. For the cadmium red line at 643.8 nm, the coherent time is about 10^{-8} s and the corresponding longitudinal coherence length is about 3 m in the air.

There is another interesting aspect of Michelson interference. If we consider a wave train as a sine wave of frequency ν windowed (multiplied) by a rectangle function of width ΔT, from Fourier analysis, the resulting frequency spectrum of the wave train is a sinc function, centered at ν, whose main lobe has a half-width of $1/\Delta T$. If the sine wave is windowed by a Gaussian function with a standard deviation of ΔT, the resulting frequency spectrum is also a Gaussian function, centered at ν, with a standard deviation of $1/(2\pi\Delta T)$. Experimentally, one finds that the Michelson interference fringes appear only when $\Delta\nu\Delta T \leq 1$ approximately, where $\Delta\nu$ is the bandwidth of the light source. Therefore, the coherent time ΔT is approximately inversely proportional to the bandwidth of the light beam $\Delta\nu$.

2.3.2 Spatial coherence

Young's famous two-slit interference experiment demonstrates spatial coherence. Figure 2.2 shows a schematic drawing of the typical setup of such an experiment. According to

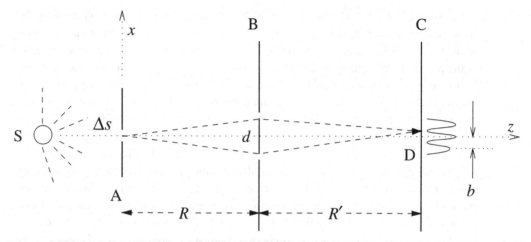

Figure 2.2. Young's two-slit interference experiment.

Ditchburn [258, p. 119], Grimaldi was among the first to attempt to observe interference. He used a (thermal) light source S (without screen A) in front of a screen (B) with two slits and observed fringes on a screen (C) some distance behind the slits. However, it was Young who discovered that the light source size had to be made very small for the interference fringes to be observed. He used an additional screen (A) with a small hole (Δs) to let the light through and projected the light onto the two slits. This small hole thus serves to reduce the size of the light source. In our later analysis, we will see that this was the critical modification that made him successful. Young reported his results in 1802 in front of the Royal Society, but was met with great ridicule because Newton's particle model of light was the dominant theory at that time. However, regardless of how the phenomenon should be explained, the experiment was a very important one in presenting the very basic nature of light (see the interesting discussion in [306, Volume III]).

The two light beams that pass through the two slits to produce the interference are separated spatially although they come from the same small thermal source. The fact that the spatially separated light beams can produce interference means that the field fluctuations in the two spatially-separated slits are correlated. This is easy to imagine if one thinks of a spherical wave propagating from the small source towards the two slits on the screen. However, this is only a mental model and in reality we know that this wave model is not true because it does not explain many phenomena, such as the photoelectric effect. Therefore, the experimental facts alone force us to describe the light going through the two slits as having spatial coherence.

Experiments have shown that whether interference fringes are observed or not depends critically on some of the experimental parameters. Let the source (the tiny hole on the screen A) be at the origin of the coordinate system, and the positive z-axis go through the middle of the two slits on the screen B, intersecting with the observation screen C at the point D. (The widths of the two slits affect the modulation of the interference pattern because of diffraction, but as long as they are very narrow compared with the distance between them, we can ignore this in what we would like to discuss below. We can make sure that the fringe pattern that we are seeing is due to interference, not diffraction, by covering one of the slits when the pattern should disappear.) Let the x-axis be parallel with the line connecting the two slits on the screen B. As mentioned above, the size of the source along the x-direction, Δs, should be small, because different points on the source along that direction generate interference fringes that are offset from each other and therefore smear out the interference pattern. Also, R, the distance from screen A to screen B, and R', the distance from screen B to screen C, both should be much larger than d, the distance between the two slits on the screen B, because the angular subtenses from the source to the slits and from the slits to the observation screen determine the optical path difference. If the optical path difference is too long (say, longer than the typical duration of the wave train of the light), the interference does not occur. Experiments (as well as theoretical calculation based on optical path difference [258, pp. 120–1]) show that the interference fringes are observable when

$$\Delta s \frac{d}{R} \approx \Delta s \, \Delta\theta \leq \lambda, \qquad (2.2)$$

where $\Delta\theta \approx d/R$ is the angle formed by d the distance between the two slits relative to the source, and λ is the wavelength of the light from the source. The width of the interference band, b (the distance from maximum to maximum), on the observation plane C can also be calculated from the optical path difference between the two slit paths: $b = R'\lambda/d$ [208, Section 2.3]. In a typical experiment, the two slits are separated by about 1 mm, the screen distances, R and R', are about 1 m, and the wavelength is about 500 nm. Therefore the width of the interference band, b, is about 0.5 mm, which is observable by the naked eye.

The above experimental results allow us to define a few terms regarding spatial coherence. The two beams passing through the two slits are separated by a distance d and they are located at a distance R away from the source of dimension Δs. In order for the interference fringes to be observable, the spatial separation d has to satisfy the following relation:

$$d \leq \frac{R\lambda}{\Delta s}. \qquad (2.3)$$

Therefore, we can define $R\lambda/\Delta s$ as the transverse coherence length, and its square, $R^2\lambda^2/(\Delta s)^2$, as the coherence area, ΔA. If we take the product of the longitudinal coherence length Δl and the coherence area, ΔA, we get the coherence volume, $\Delta V = \Delta l \Delta A$. From the uncertainty principle of quantum mechanics, we can show that photons in the coherence volume are not distinguishable from each other [631, pp. 155–9]. Although we have derived the concepts of coherence length, coherence area, and coherence volume from the electromagnetic wave models, they are consistent with quantum theory as well.

It is instructive to calculate the coherence area of some common light sources that we see in our imaging applications. The sun has an angular subtense ($\Delta s/R$) of about 0.5°. The middle of the visible spectrum is at about 500 nm. Therefore, the coherence area of sunlight at 500 nm is about 3.3×10^{-3} mm^2 and the transverse coherence length is about 0.057 mm. This is so small that we can treat sunlight reflected from any two points of an object surface as incoherent for all practical purposes. On the other hand, light from a distant star has a relatively large coherent area on the earth's surface and starlight needs to be treated with its coherence property in mind. For example, the red giant star Betelgeuse in the constellation of Orion has an angular subtense of 0.047 arcsec [660]. Assuming that its effective wavelength is 575 nm, then its transverse coherence length is about 2.52 m! Images of the stars do look like images of coherent sources.

2.4 Polarization

The constraints imposed by Maxwell's equations require that far from their source electric and magnetic fields are orthogonal to each other and to the direction of the propagation. Since the magnetic field can be determined from the electric field, we will discuss only the behavior of the electric field. The electric field, ξ, of the electromagnetic wave is a vector that has a magnitude as well as a direction, which can vary in the plane perpendicular to the vector of wave propagation. Therefore, there are two degrees of freedom in the direction of the electric field and these can be represented by two basis vectors. The variation of the electric vector direction as a function of time is called the polarization.

2.4.1 Representations of polarization

Referring to Figure 2.3, let us assume that a monochromatic light beam is traveling along the z-axis towards the positive z-direction and that we are looking at the beam directed towards us. The x-axis is directed horizontally to the right and the y-axis directed vertically to the top. Let us further assume that the electromagnetic wave has an electric field vector with the following x- and y-components at a given position on the z-axis:

$$\begin{aligned} \xi_x(t) &= A_x \cos(2\pi vt + \delta_x), \\ \xi_y(t) &= A_y \cos(2\pi vt + \delta_y), \end{aligned} \tag{2.4}$$

where v is the frequency $[s^{-1}]$, A_x and A_y are the amplitudes $[V\,m^{-1}]$, and δ_x and δ_y are the phases [rad]. For the following discussion, the important parameter is the phase difference $\delta = \delta_y - \delta_x$.

From electromagnetic theory [512, p. 70], the radiant flux density $[W\,m^{-2}]$ of the wave is given by the magnitude of the Poynting vector, $\mathbf{P}$:

$$P(t) = \frac{n}{c\mu}\xi^2(t), \tag{2.5}$$

where $\xi^2(t) = \xi_x^2(t) + \xi_y^2(t)$, n is the index of refraction, μ is the magnetic permeability, and c is the velocity of light in vacuum. For visible light, the frequency is on the order of 10^{14} Hz, too fast to be measured by almost all instruments that measure energy flux. What is measured is the time-averaged radiant flux density, $\langle P(t) \rangle$, $[W\,m^{-2}]$. Since the averaged value of cosine squared is $1/2$,

$$\langle P(t) \rangle = \frac{n}{2c\mu}(A_x^2 + A_y^2) = \eta(A_x^2 + A_y^2), \tag{2.6}$$

where $\eta = n/(2c\mu)$.

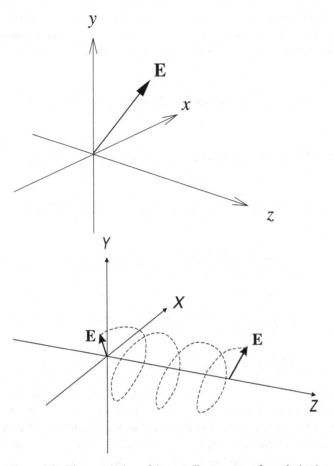

Figure 2.3. The convention of the coordinate system for polarization.

The electric field vector varies continuously as a function of the phase of the wave within the duration of the wave train. When $\delta = 0$, the direction of the vector remains constant, the light is said to be linearly polarized (or plane polarized). When $\delta = \pm\pi/2$ and $A_x = A_y$, the direction of the vector varies and traces out a circle, and the light is said to be circularly polarized. In the most general case, the direction of the vector traces out an ellipse and the light is said to be elliptically polarized. The circularly (or elliptically) polarized light is further divided into the right-hand circular (RHC) (or elliptic) polarization and the left-hand circular (LHC) (or elliptic) polarization. The handedness convention is to observe the light coming to us. If the electric field vector rotates in the clockwise direction, i.e., $\delta > 0$, the light is said to be right-hand circularly (or elliptically) polarized. If the electric field vector rotates in the counterclockwise direction, i.e., $\delta < 0$, then the light is said to be left-hand circularly (or elliptically) polarized.

Another important representation of polarization is to use the the RHC polarization and the LHC polarization as the two basis vectors. It can be shown that the electric field vector represented by Eqs. (2.4) can be expressed as the sum of a RHC wave with amplitude A_R and phase δ_R and a LHC wave with amplitude A_L and phase δ_L. At the same point on the z-axis as in Eqs. (2.4), the RHC wave is represented as

$$\xi_x = A_R \cos(\delta_R - 2\pi \nu t), \tag{2.7}$$

$$\xi_y = A_R \sin(\delta_R - 2\pi \nu t), \tag{2.8}$$

and the LHC wave as

$$\xi_x = A_L \cos(\delta_L + 2\pi \nu t), \tag{2.9}$$

$$\xi_y = A_L \sin(\delta_L + 2\pi \nu t). \tag{2.10}$$

The parameters in the (x, y) and the (RHC, LHC) representations are related by the following equations:

$$A_R^2 = \frac{1}{4}(A_x^2 + A_y^2 + 2A_x A_y \sin\delta), \tag{2.11}$$

$$A_L^2 = \frac{1}{4}(A_x^2 + A_y^2 - 2A_x A_y \sin\delta), \tag{2.12}$$

$$\tan\delta_R = \frac{A_y \cos\delta_y - A_x \sin\delta_x}{A_x \cos\delta_x + A_y \sin\delta_y}, \tag{2.13}$$

$$\tan\delta_L = \frac{A_x \sin\delta_x + A_y \cos\delta_y}{A_x \cos\delta_x - A_y \sin\delta_y}. \tag{2.14}$$

It should be pointed out that at a given point on the z-axis, the magnitude of the electric field of the circularly polarized wave remains the same for the duration of the wave train, but its direction is changing around a circle. The averaged radiant flux density of a circularly polarized wave thus does not have the $1/2$ factor from the averaged value of cosine squared, and the magnitude of the Poynting vector is $2\eta A_R^2$ for the RHC wave, and $2\eta A_L^2$ for the LHC wave. The total radiant flux density $[\mathrm{W\,m^{-2}}]$ for the wave is

$$\langle P(t)\rangle = 2\eta A_R^2 + 2\eta A_L^2 = \eta(A_x^2 + A_y^2). \tag{2.15}$$

As we discussed in the previous section, light emitted from thermal sources consists of short wave trains of duration on the order of 10^{-8} s. Each wave train has its polarization, but it varies so rapidly (10^8 times a second) and randomly that most instruments cannot detect any effects due to polarization (assuming they average out in all directions). This type of light is said to be completely unpolarized. If the averaged polarization does not completely cancel out in all directions and the light is not of any single polarization, the light is said to be partially polarized. These concepts will be defined more quantitatively later.

The polarization of light is treated in the quantum theory in a very different way conceptually. A photon is a two-state system. The two base states are often taken as the RHC polarization and the LHC polarization. The reason is that each base state is then associated with a spin number $+1$ or -1, with an angular momentum of $h/2\pi$ or $-h/2\pi$, where h is Planck's constant. The state of a given photon can be any linear combination of these two base states. For the linearly polarized light, the coefficients (or amplitudes) of the two states are equal. For the elliptically polarized light, one coefficient is greater than the other.

2.4.2 Stokes parameters

Among the various polarizations discussed above, elliptic polarization is the most general case. Linear polarization corresponds to a zero eccentricity and circular polarization to unit eccentricity. To characterize the polarization of a quasi-monochromatic light wave, we can specify its eccentricity, handedness, and azimuth angle. However, there are two drawbacks in using these parameters: (1) they are not easily measurable, and (2) they are not additive when many independent wave trains of light are mixed together. For these reasons, we will introduce the Stokes parameters [913] as a means for characterizing polarized light. One of the major advantages of using the Stokes parameters is that they are directly measurable and can be defined operationally with simple linear and circular polarizers. Let us first introduce these polarizers.

An ideal linear polarizer is an optical element that has a transmission axis. Light linearly polarized along this axis is transmitted without any attenuation. If the incident light is linearly polarized at a $90°$ angle from this axis, the transmittance is 0. If the incident light is linearly polarized at an angle θ from this axis, the transmittance is $\cos^2\theta$ because the electric field component projected onto the axis is reduced by $\cos\theta$ and the transmitted light is proportional to the square of the electric field. This is called the law of Malus. Very-high-quality linear polarizers are commercially available. A retarder is an optical device that resolves an incident polarized beam of light into two orthogonally polarized components, retards the phase of one component relative to the other, and then recombines the two components into one emerging light beam. The polarization state of the two resolved components can be linear, circular, or elliptical depending on the type of the retarder. A retarder transmits the two components without changing their state of polarization. It just changes their relative phases. For example, an ideal linear retarder is an optical element that resolves an incident beam into two linearly polarized components, one along a fast axis and the other along a slow axis. Light that is polarized in the direction of the fast axis is transmitted faster than light polarized along the slow axis. As a consequence, the phase of the slow-axis component is retarded relative to that of the fast-axis component. If the thickness of the retarder is such that a phase shift of a quarter cycle is introduced between the two components, the retarder is called a quarter-wave plate. A quarter-wave plate can convert linearly polarized light into circularly polarized light. As will be shown shortly, a quarter-wave plate followed by a linear polarizer can be used to measure the circularly polarized component of an incident ray. A linear polarizer followed by a quarter-wave plate can be used to turn incident light into circularly polarized light.

With an ideal linear polarizer, an ideal quarter-wave plate, and a light flux detector, we can make the following six radiant flux density [$W\,m^{-2}$] measurements:

1. E_h: radiant flux density measured with a horizontal linear polarizer;
2. E_v: radiant flux density measured with a vertical linear polarizer;
3. E_{45}: radiant flux density measured with a $45°$ linear polarizer;
4. E_{135}: radiant flux density measured with a $135°$ linear polarizer;
5. E_R: radiant flux density measured with a right circular polarizer;
6. E_L: radiant flux density measured with a left circular polarizer.

The Stokes vector consisting of the four Stokes parameters, s_0, s_1, s_2, and s_3, is defined as

$$
\mathbf{S} = \begin{bmatrix} s_0 \\ s_1 \\ s_2 \\ s_3 \end{bmatrix} = \begin{bmatrix} E_h + E_v \\ E_h - E_v \\ E_{45} - E_{135} \\ E_R - E_L \end{bmatrix}.
\tag{2.16}
$$

The Stokes vector depends on the measurement geometry and the wavelength. If the polarizers are not ideal, corrections and transformations can be performed to calculate the desired Stokes vector. Let us see how light of different polarizations is represented by the Stokes vector. For a monochromatic light beam, using the same notation as before, we have

$$
\xi_x = A_x \cos(2\pi \nu t + \delta_x),
\tag{2.17}
$$
$$
\xi_y = A_y \cos(2\pi \nu t + \delta_y).
\tag{2.18}
$$

The horizontal linear polarizer only passes the ξ_x component, and therefore, $E_h = \eta A_x^2$ where $\eta = n/(2\mu c)$. Similarly, $E_v = \eta A_y^2$. For the 45° linear polarizer, the x- and y-components of the electric field have to be projected onto the 45° axis, and the electric field amplitude, ξ_{45}, is $\xi_x \cos(\pi/4) + \xi_y \cos(\pi/4)$, and the radiant flux density $E_{45} = n/(\mu c)\langle \xi_{45}^2 \rangle$, where $\langle \dots \rangle$ represents the time-averaged value. Carrying out the computation for the 45° polarizer and similarly for the 135° polarizer, we have

$$
E_{45} = \frac{\eta}{2}(A_x^2 + A_y^2 + 2A_x A_y \cos\delta),
\tag{2.19}
$$
$$
E_{135} = \frac{\eta}{2}(A_x^2 + A_y^2 - 2A_x A_y \cos\delta).
\tag{2.20}
$$

For the RHC and LHC polarizers, we have, from the previous section,

$$
E_R = 2\eta A_R^2 = \frac{\eta}{2}(A_x^2 + A_y^2 + 2A_x A_y \sin\delta),
\tag{2.21}
$$
$$
E_L = 2\eta A_L^2 = \frac{\eta}{2}(A_x^2 + A_y^2 - 2A_x A_y \sin\delta).
\tag{2.22}
$$

Therefore, we can express the Stokes vector for a monochromatic light wave as

$$
\mathbf{S} = \begin{bmatrix} s_0 \\ s_1 \\ s_2 \\ s_3 \end{bmatrix} = \eta \begin{bmatrix} A_x^2 + A_y^2 \\ A_x^2 - A_y^2 \\ 2A_x A_y \cos\delta \\ 2A_x A_y \sin\delta \end{bmatrix}.
\tag{2.23}
$$

The first Stokes parameter, $s_0 = \eta(A_x^2 + A_y^2) = \langle P(t) \rangle$, is the radiant flux density [W m^{-2}] associated with the light wave. The other three parameters, s_1, s_2, and s_3, can be positive, zero, or negative. For a completely polarized light wave, the four Stokes parameters are not linearly independent because $s_0^2 = s_1^2 + s_2^2 + s_3^2$, as can be verified from Eq. (2.23). Since the definition of the Stokes vector is in terms of energy flux density, the Stokes vector of an incoherent light beam is the sum of all the Stokes vectors representing each individual wave component in the beam. The Stokes vector can be written as

$$
\mathbf{S} = \begin{bmatrix} s_0 \\ s_1 \\ s_2 \\ s_3 \end{bmatrix} = \begin{bmatrix} \sum_i s_0^{(i)} \\ \sum_i s_1^{(i)} \\ \sum_i s_2^{(i)} \\ \sum_i s_3^{(i)} \end{bmatrix},
\tag{2.24}
$$

where the index i denotes each individual wavetrain in the beam. If the relation $s_0^2 = s_1^2 + s_2^2 + s_3^2$ holds true for a light beam as in the case of the monochromatic light wave described in Eq. (2.23), we say that the light beam is completely polarized. If the light is completely unpolarized, the positive and the negative contributions to s_1, s_2, and s_3 from all the individual wavetrains cancel each other to make all three parameters zero. Therefore, $s_1^2 + s_2^2 + s_3^2 = 0$ for completely unpolarized light. It can be proved that $s_0^2 \geq s_1^2 + s_2^2 + s_3^2$ for all possible mixtures of polarized light [168, p. 32]. When $s_0^2 > s_1^2 + s_2^2 + s_3^2 > 0$ for a light beam, we call it partially polarized. We can now define the degree of polarization, p, as

$$
p = \frac{\sqrt{s_1^2 + s_2^2 + s_3^2}}{s_0}.
\tag{2.25}
$$

It can be shown that for completely polarized light, $p = 1$; for unpolarized light, $p = 0$; and for a mixture of polarized light and unpolarized light, $0 < p < 1$. Furthermore, the degree of polarization can be shown to represent a measure of the coherence (statistical correlation) between two different components (such as the x- and y-components) of the electromagnetic field at the same point in space [877, pp. 199–200].

Let us see how the different polarizations can be represented using the Stokes vector. Let E denote the radiant flux density [W m^{-2}] of the light beam, i.e., $E = s_0$. First, as discussed just now, the unpolarized light is represented as $[E, 0, 0, 0]^{\mathrm{T}}$. Light linearly polarized parallel to the x-axis is $[E, E, 0, 0]^{\mathrm{T}}$ and light linearly polarized parallel to the y-axis is $[E, -E, 0, 0]^{\mathrm{T}}$. What about the light that is linearly polarized at an angle θ relative to the x-axis? This can be represented by projecting the electric field vector to the x-axis and to the y-axis (similarly to what is done in deriving the law of Malus). The resulting Stokes vector is $[E, E \cos 2\theta, E \sin 2\theta, 0]^{\mathrm{T}}$. For the circularly polarized light, the representation is straightforward from the operational definition of the Stokes vector in Eq. (2.16): $[E, 0, 0, E]^{\mathrm{T}}$ for RHC and $[E, 0, 0, -E]^{\mathrm{T}}$ for LHC .

It should be noted that although a given light beam is represented by a unique Stokes vector, the converse is not true. Two light beams with the same Stokes vector are not necessarily the same optically [742], i.e., there are ways to tell them apart by using optical elements, such as polarizers. Because the Stokes vector is a function of frequency and a light wave train is of finite duration and hence consists of many frequencies, the exact spectral content of a light beam is quite important when we use the Stokes vector. In general, Stokes vectors should be expressed as Stokes vector functions of frequency. This is necessary when we consider how an optical element, a surface, or even the air, changes the polarization state of a light beam, because these light–matter interactions are all functions of spectral content.

2.4.3 The Mueller matrix

When light beams are represented by Stokes vectors, the behavior of many types of optical element can be described by a 4×4 matrix, relating the four-component Stokes vector of the incident light beam to the four-component Stokes vector of the exiting light beam. This 4×4 matrix is called the Mueller matrix of the corresponding optical element (or cascaded elements). For example, a polarizer (a rotator) that rotates a linearly polarized beam by an angle θ can be represented by the following matrix:

$$
M = \begin{bmatrix} 1 & 0 & 0 & 0 \\ 0 & \cos 2\theta & \sin 2\theta & 0 \\ 0 & -\sin 2\theta & \cos 2\theta & 0 \\ 0 & 0 & 0 & 1 \end{bmatrix}.
\tag{2.26}
$$

Let us consider a polarizer (diattenuator) which is an optical element that attenuates the orthogonal components of an optical beam differently. Let us assume that the attenuation factors are a_x and a_y, for the two orthogonal components, A_x and A_y, as in Eq. (2.23). The exiting Stokes vector $\mathbf{S_e}$ is related to the incident Stokes vector $\mathbf{S_i}$ by

$$
\mathbf{S_e} = \eta \begin{bmatrix} a_x^2 A_x^2 + a_y^2 A_y^2 \\ a_x^2 A_x^2 - a_y^2 A_y^2 \\ 2a_x A_x a_y A_y \cos \delta \\ 2a_x A_x a_y A_y \sin \delta \end{bmatrix} = \frac{1}{2} \begin{bmatrix} a_x^2 + a_y^2 & a_x^2 - a_y^2 & 0 & 0 \\ a_x^2 - a_y^2 & a_x^2 + a_y^2 & 0 & 0 \\ 0 & 0 & 2a_x a_y & 0 \\ 0 & 0 & 0 & 2a_x a_y \end{bmatrix}
$$

$$
\times \eta \begin{bmatrix} A_x^2 + A_y^2 \\ A_x^2 - A_y^2 \\ 2A_x A_y \cos \delta \\ 2A_x A_y \sin \delta \end{bmatrix} = M\mathbf{S_i},
\tag{2.27}
$$

where

$$
M = \frac{1}{2} \begin{bmatrix} a_x^2 + a_y^2 & a_x^2 - a_y^2 & 0 & 0 \\ a_x^2 - a_y^2 & a_x^2 + a_y^2 & 0 & 0 \\ 0 & 0 & 2a_x a_y & 0 \\ 0 & 0 & 0 & 2a_x a_y \end{bmatrix}
\tag{2.28}
$$

is the Mueller matrix of the polarizer.

Two other useful Mueller matrices are the matrix for the ideal linear polarizer and the matrix for the ideal linear retarder. Both matrices are discussed in articles and books on polarized light (e.g., [869]).

As mentioned above, an ideal linear polarizer has a polarization axis. Light linearly polarized in this direction will pass through the polarizer with a transmittance equal to 1. Light linearly polarized in the perpendicular direction will not pass through the polarizer, i.e., the transmittance is equal to 0. A Nicol-prism polarizer comes close to this ideal. Let α be the angle between the polarization axis of the ideal polarizer and the x-axis. The Mueller matrix for an ideal linear polarizer is

$$
M_p = \frac{1}{2} \begin{bmatrix} 1 & \cos 2\alpha & \sin 2\alpha & 0 \\ \cos 2\alpha & \cos^2 2\alpha & \sin 2\alpha \cos 2\alpha & 0 \\ \sin 2\alpha & \sin 2\alpha \cos 2\alpha & \sin^2 2\alpha & 0 \\ 0 & 0 & 0 & 0 \end{bmatrix}. \tag{2.29}
$$

A linear retarder is usually made of a birefringent material, such as calcite or quartz. A birefringent material has a fast axis and a slow axis (the latter is usually perpendicular to the former). Light linearly polarized to the fast axis travels faster than the light linearly polarized to the slow axis. As a result, when light emerges from the material, the relative phase along one axis is retarded relative to the other axis. The phase shift is called the retardance, δ, which is a function of the thickness, d, and the difference of the refraction indices of the fast and the slow direction, $n_f - n_s$, i.e., $\delta = 2\pi d(n_f - n_s)/\lambda$. Let β be the angle between the fast axis and the horizontal x-axis. The Mueller matrix for an ideal linear retarder is

$$
M_r = \begin{bmatrix} 1 & 0 & 0 & 0 \\ 0 & \cos^2 2\beta + \sin^2 2\beta \cos \delta & \sin 2\beta \cos 2\beta(1 - \cos \delta) & -\sin 2\beta \sin \delta \\ 0 & \sin 2\beta \cos 2\beta(1 - \cos \delta) & \sin^2 2\beta + \cos^2 2\beta \cos \delta & \cos 2\beta \sin \delta \\ 0 & \sin 2\beta \sin \delta & -\cos 2\beta \sin \delta & \cos \delta \end{bmatrix}. \tag{2.30}
$$

When $\delta = \pi/2$, the retarder is called a quarter-wave plate. When $\delta = \pi$, the retarder is called a half-wave plate. An ideal circular polarizer can be constructed using an ideal linear polarizer (with the polarization axis at an angle α) followed by an ideal quarter-wave plate (with the fast axis at an angle β), then its Mueller matrix, M_c, is the product of the two matricies, M_p and M_r:

$$
M_c = M_r M_p \tag{2.31}
$$

$$
= \frac{1}{2} \begin{bmatrix} 1 & \cos 2\beta & \sin 2\beta & 0 \\ \cos 2\alpha \cos 2(\alpha - \beta) & \cos 2\alpha \cos 2\beta \cos 2(\alpha - \beta) & \cos 2\alpha \sin 2\beta \cos 2(\alpha - \beta) & 0 \\ \sin 2\alpha \cos 2(\alpha - \beta) & \sin 2\alpha \cos 2\beta \cos 2(\alpha - \beta) & \sin 2\alpha \sin 2\beta \cos 2(\alpha - \beta) & 0 \\ \sin 2(\alpha - \beta) & \cos 2\beta \sin 2(\alpha - \beta) & \sin 2\beta \sin 2(\alpha - \beta) & 0 \end{bmatrix} \tag{2.32}
$$

When $\alpha - \beta = \pm\pi/4$,

$$
M_c = \frac{1}{2} \begin{bmatrix} 1 & \cos 2\beta & \sin 2\beta & 0 \\ 0 & 0 & 0 & 0 \\ 0 & 0 & 0 & 0 \\ \pm 1 & \pm \cos 2\beta & \pm \sin 2\beta & 0 \end{bmatrix} \tag{2.33}
$$

and the output light is circularly polarized.

2.4.4 The interference of polarized light

In the two-slit interference experiment described in the previous section, the light source is a thermal source and therefore unpolarized. Fresnel and Arago repeated Young's two-slit interference experiments with polarized light by placing polarizers in front of the light source, behind the two slits, and the observation plane. By varying the orientations of these polarizers, they could experiment with the effects of different polarization states on the interference patterns. Their results were summarized in the following four statements by Collett [208, Chapter 12] (called the interference laws of Fresnel and Arago):

1. Two beams of light linearly polarized in the same plane can produce interference patterns.
2. Two beams of light linearly polarized perpendicularly to each other cannot produce interference patterns.
3. Two beams of linearly polarized light, derived from an *unpolarized* light beam in perpendicular directions, cannot produce interference patterns even if they are brought back to the same polarization plane by polarizers.
4. Two beams of linearly polarized light, derived from a *linearly polarized* light beam in perpendicular directions, can produce interference patterns if they are brought back to the same polarization plane by polarizers.

The first law is easy to understand. The second law can also be understood because in a general case perpendicular electric fields of the linearly polarized light add up to elliptically polarized light. Different light paths have different phase delays and they create elliptically polarized light with different phase angles, but do not cancel each other. Therefore, interference patterns are not seen with light beams linearly polarized in perpendicular directions. The third and fourth laws can be shown [208, Chapter 12] to be true by using Stokes vectors and Mueller matrices. This is, in fact, a very good example that shows the usefulness of Stokes vectors in analyzing polarized light.

2.5 Problems

2.1 A laser beam has a coherent time of 10^{-4} s. What is its approximate frequency bandwidth $\Delta \nu$?

2.2 A quasi-monochromatic light source has an angular subtense of 30 arcsec. If the wavelength is 500 nm, what is its coherent area at the point of observation?

2.3 Let E be the radiant flux density [$\mathrm{W\,m^{-2}}$] of a light beam. If it is a linearly polarized light beam with a polarization angle of $30°$ relative to the x-axis, what is its Stokes vector?

2.4 What is the Mueller matrix of a $30°$ polarizer (relative to the x-axis)?

3 Radiometry

If we are given an optical imaging system, one thing we would like to know is how much light will be available to our sensors. Because all sensors have limited operating ranges, controlling the amount of light irradiating the sensors is very important to obtain the best usage of the sensors and for the best quality of our images. In order to study the energy flow of light through the various stages of image formation, we have to carefully define the concepts and terms that we are going to use. The study and measurement of optical energy flow are the subject of radiometry.

Over the years several nomenclature systems have been proposed for light measurement and although there is still some debate on the subject, the units and terms proposed by the CIE have gained general acceptance. These units and terms are described in detail in the CIE publication *International Lighting Vocabulary* [187]. They have also been adopted by the American National Standards Institute (ANSI Z7.1-1967) and recommended by the publications of the (US) National Bureau of Standards [700, p. 8]. We will describe the radiometric concepts using CIE units and terms.

3.1 Concepts and definitions

The concepts and measurements of optical energy flow in radiometry are traditionally defined using geometrical optics. For example, optical rays are used to define the cone associated with a light beam and the path by which a ray is transmitted from one medium to another is determined by Snell's law. As a consequence of this idealization, many concepts lose their meanings when the spatial dimension is reduced to an infinitely small distance. For example, in an imaging system, rays cannot converge to an ideal image point, and the physical optics of diffraction has to be considered. However, this difficulty does not make these concepts useless because, in practice, we never measure things in infinitely small spatial extents. Similar problems exist in other fields of physics as well. For example, we often say that the humidity of the air is such and such percent, but in a volume smaller than a hydrogen atom, the definition of humidity loses its meaning completely. This does not make humidity a useless concept in a weather report.

It should be pointed out that one can also formulate the concepts of radiometry from physical optics and take into account the coherence property of the light [598, 631, Chapter 5, 1041]. Conventional radiometry has been mainly developed for thermal sources that have incoherent radiation. It can be shown [631, Chapter 5] that for a general class of sources, called quasi-homogeneous sources[1] (to which thermal sources usually belong), a radiometric model can be developed from physical optics. However, the treatment becomes unnecessarily complicated for most color imaging applications where light is almost always incoherent.

In the description of optical energy flow, there are quantities, such as radiance, which are associated with light rays and they are functions of both position and direction. Other quantities, such as radiant exposure, which are associated with surfaces or volumes, are functions of only position or only direction, but not both. Of course, there are also quantities, such as energy, that are not associated with geometry. Also, there are quantities that are sometimes associated with rays and other times are associated with surfaces. For this last class of quantities, the exact meaning can often be understood from the context in which they are used. It is therefore not necessary to create separate terms for these quantities when used in different ways. The *International Lighting Vocabulary* [187] usually follows this principle. For example, irradiance is defined as the radiant flux per unit area of a surface. It can mean the radiant flux from a given direction, or it can mean the total radiant flux integrated over the hemisphere of the surface. The irradiance is thus a function of both position and direction in the former, but it is only a function of position in the latter.

The unit of radiant light energy, Q, is the joule. The energy flow per unit time through a point (x, y, z) in space in a direction (θ, ϕ) is called the radiant flux, $\Phi(x, y, z, \theta, \phi)$ [W]. It is important to realize that the radiant flux is a function of both the position and direction, and, in this sense, it is a quantity associated with a light beam.

At a distance very far away from the light source, we can treat the light source as a point source. A point source is an idealization which has a spatial location but no physical dimension. Although there is no such thing as a point source, it is a good approximation in many real-world problems. For example, a star can be treated as a point source even if it is much larger than the earth. As a rule of thumb, if the physical dimension of the source is smaller than one-tenth of the distance between the source and the object, the source can be treated as a point source and the error in the radiometric calculation is on the order of 10% (see Example 3.1).

Projected area A_{proj}

In a radiometric calculation, it is often necessary to compute the foreshortened area as seen from a direction different from the surface normal. For example, if we look at a circular disk from an oblique angle, it appears to be an elliptical disk with an apparent area smaller than its real physical area. Figure 3.1 shows an area A with a surface normal $\mathbf{N}$. Let $\mathbf{V}$ be the direction of viewing. The area A_{proj} is the projected area of A in the direction of $\mathbf{V}$. It can be calculated as $A_{\text{proj}} = A \cos \theta$ where θ is the angle between $\mathbf{N}$ and $\mathbf{V}$.

Solid angle

Since a cone of rays radiating from a point source diverges at a rate proportional to the inverse of the square of the distance from the source, we need a measure of the spatial

---

[1]   Quasi-homogeneous sources are sources whose linear dimensions are much larger than the coherence length of their radiation.

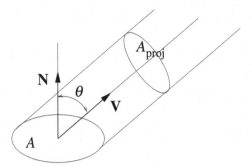

Figure 3.1. The definition of projected area.

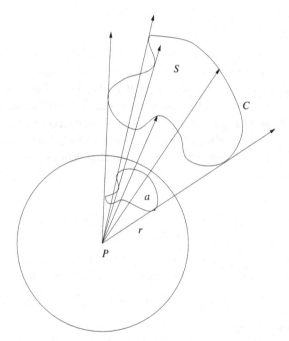

Figure 3.2. The definition of a solid angle.

extent of the cone angle. The concept for this measure is called the *solid angle* (in contrast with the plane angle we use in two-dimensional space). The solid angle of a cone is defined as the area cut out by the cone on a unit sphere (radius $= 1$) that is centered at the apex of the cone (see Figure 3.2). If the intersection of a cone and the unit sphere has an area ω, we say that the cone has a solid angle of ω. A sphere thus has a solid angle of 4π. If the intersection is between the cone and a sphere of radius r, the solid angle is equal to the intersection area divided by r^2. The concept of a solid angle is more general than a regular cone. In Fig. 3.2, a patch of surface, S, of arbitrary shape, bounded by a closed curve, C, in space, forms a solid angle with a point, P. If all the lines connecting P and

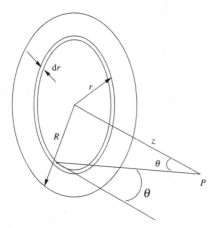

Figure 3.3. The solid angle subtended by a disk.

every point on C cut off an area a on the sphere centered at P with a radius of r, then the surface patch S forms a solid angle of a/r^2 with the point P. The unit of solid angle is called the steradian, because the measure of the intersection area is relative to the radius of a sphere. The steradian is the solid angle that, having its vertex at the center of a sphere with radius r, cuts off an area of the surface of the sphere equal to r^2. To calculate the solid angle subtended by an area of arbitrary shape, the differential definition of the solid angle is

$$d\omega = \frac{dA_{\text{proj}}}{r^2},$$ (3.1)

$$\omega = \int_A d\omega = \int_A \frac{dA_{\text{proj}}}{r^2},$$ (3.2)

where dA_{proj} is the elemental area dA projected to the direction of the ray connecting dA and the point source.

Example 3.1 Calculation of solid angle
Calculate the solid angle subtended by a circular disk to the point source P (see Fig. 3.3). The radius of the disk is R and the distance from P to the center of the disk is z.

Solution   Since points on the disk are not equal distances away from P, we will divide the disk into ring-shaped elemental areas so that the solid angle can be calculated by integration. If the area of a ring has a radius of r, its distance from P squared is $r^2 + z^2$. Since the area of the ring, dA, is not perpendicular to the view from P, we have to use its projected area dA_{proj}. Therefore the solid angle ω can be calculated as

$$\omega = \int_0^R \frac{dA_{\text{proj}}}{r^2 + z^2} = \int_0^R \frac{(2\pi r\,dr)\cos\theta}{r^2 + z^2} = \int_0^R \frac{2\pi r z\,dr}{(r^2 + z^2)^{3/2}} = 2\pi \left(1 - \frac{z}{\sqrt{R^2 + z^2}}\right).$$ (3.3)

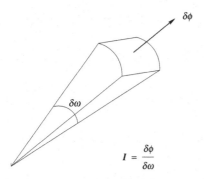

Figure 3.4. The intensity of a point source.

Comment When $z \ll R$, $\omega \to 2\pi$. Note that when $z \gg R$, $\omega \to \pi R^2/z^2$, and the solid angle falls off with the inverse of the square of the distance, z.

Intensity I

If the radiant flux leaving a point source through a cone of solid angle $d\omega$ [sr] is $d\Phi$ [W] (see Fig. 3.4), the quantity that describes the light output from the point source at this cone is called the radiant intensity, I, which is defined as the radiant flux per unit solid angle, i.e.,

$$I(x, y, z, \theta, \phi) = \frac{d\Phi(x, y, z, \theta, \phi)}{d\omega} \; \text{W sr}^{-1}. \tag{3.4}$$

It should be pointed out that, in theory, light from a source of very small dimension has a very large coherent area. Therefore, images of stars taken by well-corrected telescopes often exhibit certain features of diffraction patterns that are characteristic of coherent light source [631, p. 154]. This will be discussed in Chapter 9 when we derive the OTF of an ideal lens. The concept of intensity is an idealization and it is useful mostly in developing other terms in radiometry.

Radiance L

If the light source is nearby, we can no longer treat it simply as a point source. If we divided the area of the source into very small elements dA, each one can be treated as a point source, but now the amount of light coming from that element is proportional to its area dA. Furthermore, if that elemental surface is not perpendicular to the direction of the cone of rays, its projected area $dA \cos\theta$ has to be used, where θ is angle between the cone and the surface normal of the element. The quantity that describes the amount of light coming from a surface is called the radiance, L [W sr^{-1}m^{-2}], which is the light flux per solid angle per projected surface area (see Fig. 3.5):

$$L(x, y, z, \theta, \phi) = \frac{d^2\Phi(x, y, z, \theta, \phi)}{dA \cos\theta d\omega} \; \text{W sr}^{-1}\,\text{m}^{-2}. \tag{3.5}$$

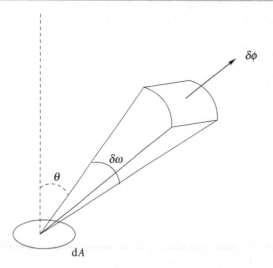

Figure 3.5. The radiance of a surface element.

Therefore, we use radiance to describe how much light is reflected from a wall, or how much light is coming from the sun.

Radiant flux density W, irradiance E, and radiant exitance M

To describe how much light passes through a surface area, we use the term radiant flux (surface) density, $W(x, y, z, \theta, \phi)$ [W m^{-2}]. When the radiant flux is irradiating on a surface, we use the term irradiance, $E(x, y, z, \theta, \phi)$ [W m^{-2}], for incident radiant flux per unit area. When the radiant flux is leaving the surface, we use radiant exitance, $M(x, y, z, \theta, \phi)$ [W m^{-2}], for exiting radiant flux per unit area. In these definitions, W, E, and M are functions of both position and direction. Very often, we are interested in the total power irradiated on the sensor surface. In that case, the incident flux is integrated over all the angles and is no longer a function of direction. The *International Lighting Vocabulary* still uses the same term, irradiance E, for this integrated radiant flux per unit area. A similar practice holds for radiant exitance M.

Lambertian sources

Most reflecting surfaces appear to be approximately equally bright, independently of the viewing angle. As we will discuss in later chapters, there are two reasons for this, one physical and one psychophysical. The physical reason is that the retinal image irradiance is proportional to the scene radiance, and most object surfaces reflect light (excluding the specular highlight) with approximately equal radiance in all directions. A radiation source (either self-emitting, transmitting, or reflecting) whose radiance is completely independent of the viewing angle is called a Lambertian source (self-emitting) or a Lambertian surface (reflecting or transmitting). A Lambertian surface that reflects (transmits) 100% of the incident light is called a *perfect reflecting (transmitting) diffuser*. This idealized reflector (transmitter) is important because it is used in the definition of *radiance factor*, which describes how bright a surface looks to an imaging system.

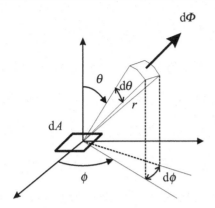

Figure 3.6. The spherical coordinate system used to integrate the total radiant flux from an area dA.

Example 3.2 Radiant exitance of a Lambertian source
If the radiance from a planar Lambertian surface is L, then what is its radiant exitance M?

Solution   To find the radiant exitance, we first calculate the total amount of flux radiated from the surface. The integration of the total flux, Φ, is best done in the spherical coordinate system as shown in Fig. 3.6.

$$\Phi = \int d\Phi = \int L \cdot dA \cdot \cos\theta \cdot d\omega,$$

$$= L \cdot dA \int_{\theta=0}^{\pi/2} \int_{\phi=0}^{2\pi} \cos\theta \cdot [(r\,d\theta)(r\sin\theta\,d\phi)/r^2],$$

$$= L \cdot dA \int_{\theta=0}^{\pi/2} \int_{\phi=0}^{2\pi} \cos\theta \sin\theta\,d\phi\,d\theta = \pi L \cdot dA.$$

Therefore, $M = \Phi/dA = \pi L$. This is a very useful relation when we want to estimate the radiance (or luminance in photometry) from the surface illumination. For example, if a perfect Lambertian surface (i.e., reflectance $= 1$) is illuminated with 7π W m^{-2}, then we know that its reflected radiance will be 7 W m^{-2} sr^{-1}. (Note that the dimension of exitance M is [W m^{-2}], while the dimension of radiance L is [W m^{-2} sr^{-1}].)

Example 3.3 Calculation of on-axis surface irradiance
Calculate the surface irradiance at dA from a Lambertian source of a circular disk with a radius r, located at a perpendicular distance z away from dA (see Fig. 3.7). The Lambertian source has a radiance of L.

Solution   All points on a ring with a radius of s on the disk source have the same distance and orientation relative to the elemental area dA, which forms a solid angle of $d\omega$ to any point on the ring, where

$$d\omega = \frac{dA \cdot \cos\theta}{z^2 + s^2}.$$

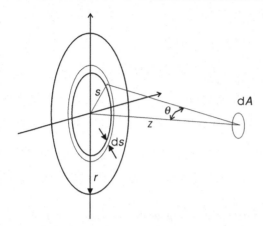

Figure 3.7. The on-axis surface irradiance.

The radiant flux, $d\Phi$, illuminating dA from the ring dA' can be calculated as

$$d\Phi = L \cdot dA' \cdot \cos\theta \cdot d\omega = L \cdot (2\pi s\,ds) \cdot \cos\theta \cdot d\omega.$$

The total radiant flux illuminating dA can be computed by integrating the ring over the entire disk:

$$\Phi = \int d\Phi = \int L \cdot (2\pi s \cos\theta\,ds) \cdot d\omega = L \cdot dA \cdot \int_0^r \frac{2\pi s \cos^2\theta}{z^2 + s^2}\,ds$$

$$= L \cdot dA \cdot \int_0^r \frac{2\pi s z^2}{(z^2 + s^2)^2}\,ds = \pi L \cdot dA \cdot \frac{r^2}{z^2 + r^2}.$$

Therefore, the irradiance on dA is

$$E = \frac{\Phi}{dA} = \frac{\pi r^2}{z^2 + r^2} L.$$

Note that when $z \gg r$, $E \to (\pi r^2 / z^2)L$, and the irradiance at a plane far away from a circular, Lambertian source is simply the radiance L of the source times the solid angle of the source.

In this example, the irradiated plane element dA is located on the axis of symmetry and that makes the integral simple. What happens if we shift dA off the axis by an amount h? As expected, the integral becomes much more complicated. It is derived in Section 10.2. Here we show the result for completeness of this discussion.

Example 3.4 Calculation of off-axis surface irradiance

Calculate the surface irradiance at dA from a Lambertian source of a circular disk with a radius r, located at a perpendicular distance z away from dA (see Fig. 3.8). The off-axis angle is θ and the radiance from the source is L.

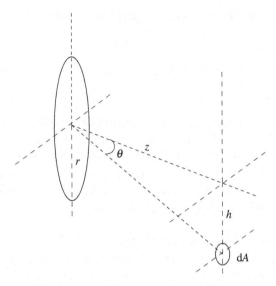

Figure 3.8. The off-axis surface irradiance.

Solution   The derivation is lengthy and is given in Section 10.2.

$$E = \frac{\pi L}{2} \left[1 - \frac{(z^2 + h^2 - r^2)}{\sqrt{(z^2 + h^2 + r^2)^2 - (2rh)^2}} \right] \tag{3.6}$$

$$= \frac{\pi L}{2} \left[1 - \frac{(z^2 - r^2 \cos^2 \theta)}{\sqrt{(z^2 - r^2 \cos^2 \theta)^2 + 4z^2 r^2 \cos^4 \theta}} \right]. \tag{3.7}$$

Comment   When $z \gg r$, $E \to (\pi r^2 / z^2) L \cos^4 \theta$. This is called the cosine-to-the-fourth-power fall-off. The result will be very useful when we discuss the radiometry of image formation. It is important to recognize that this fall-off has nothing to do with the properties of the lens. It is purely a property of geometry. Both the source and the receiver have to be projected onto the line connecting them and that accounts for $\cos^2 \theta$. The distance between the center of the source and the receiver is $z / \cos \theta$. Since the radiant flux density falls off with the inverse of the square of the distance, that accounts for another $\cos^2 \theta$. Therefore, the $\cos^4 \theta$ fall-off is a consequence of geometrical projection.

Radiant exposure

For sensors from which time-dependent signals cannot be read out continuously, a shutter has to be used to control the time interval during which the sensors are exposed to the image signals. Basically, these sensors respond to the energy per unit area, rather than the power per unit area. All photographic·films and most CCD sensors function this way.[2] Therefore, the proper quantity for these sensors is the integrated product of image irradiance and time,

---

[2]   The human eye is different because the image signal is processed continuously in real time.

which gives energy per unit area. This quantity is called the radiant exposure, H. Let Δt be the exposure time, then

$$H = \frac{dQ}{dA} = \int_{\Delta t} E \, dt \quad [\text{J m}^{-2}]. \tag{3.8}$$

Reflectance ρ

Light illuminating an object surface is partially reflected, partially absorbed, and partially transmitted. The ratio of the radiant flux of the reflected light to that of the incident light is called the reflectance, ρ. In general, the value of reflectance depends on the geometry, the polarization, and the spectral composition of the incident and reflected light. Since energy cannot be created in a passive material, reflectance cannot be greater than 1. A Lambertian surface with reflectance equal to 1 is called a perfect (reflecting) diffuser.

Reflectance factor, transmittance factor, and radiance factor β

Reflectance is a measure of how strongly a material reflects the light. However, in calculating the reflectance, the *total* amount of reflected light is used regardless of how it is distributed angularly. Reflectance thus does not correspond well with the visual appearance of a reflecting surface. For example, a mirror in a dark room illuminated by a spot light does not look bright from the off-specular angle, even if its reflectance is very high. In order to characterize the visual appearance of a surface, we have to introduce the concept of the *reflectance factor*, which is defined as the ratio of the radiant flux reflected in the direction delimited by the measurement cone to that reflected in the same direction by a perfect reflecting diffuser identically irradiated. When the measurement cone is very small and the measured quantities are radiances, the ratio is called the *radiance factor*. In practice, the terms reflectance factor and radiance factor are sometimes used interchangeably. When the sample is a transmissive material, we compare the transmitted radiant flux within the measurement cone with that of a perfect transmitting diffuser and call the ratio the *transmittance factor*. Again, when the measurement cone is small and the measured quantities are radiances, we call the transmittance ratio the radiance factor. In this sense, the radiance factor applies to both reflection and transmission. The *radiance factor* thus is a relative measure that correlates better with what we see than the *reflectance* does. Some material surfaces (such as safety reflectors for bicycles) reflect light strongly in certain directions, and they may have reflectance factors greater than 1 for that lighting and reflecting geometry. Perceptually, they look more like self-luminous sources than reflecting surfaces because their reflectance factors in the normal direction are greater than 1.0!

Example 3.5 Calculation of reflectance factor

A safety reflector reflects 60% of the incident light uniformly into a cone of 0.4π sr. What is its reflectance factor in that cone direction?

Solution   Let L be the reflected radiance of a perfect reflecting diffuser identically irradiated. The total radiant flux from the surface is πL, which is equal to the total flux irradiated on the surface. The radiance from the safety reflector is *approximately* $0.6\pi L/(0.4\pi)$, i.e., $1.5L$. Therefore, the reflectance factor in the cone direction is $1.5L/L = 1.5$. This example shows that the surface reflectance, ρ, is always less than 1, but its reflectance factor, R, from a certain viewing geometry, can be greater than 1. In Chapter 10, we will show that the image irradiance is proportional to the surface radiance, which, in turn, is proportional to its reflectance factor. Therefore, the brightness of an object in an image is proportional to its surface reflectance factor, not its reflectance. The image of a safety reflector appears brighter than that of a Lambertian white object. Things that look brighter than white often appear to be self-luminous sources.

Responsivity (sensitivity) s

The responsivity of a detector is defined most generally as the ratio of the output signal to the input power (light flux). Its unit depends on the form of the electrical response exhibited by a given detector (see [127, p. 109]). However, there are detectors (such as photographic films) that respond to the total light energy (exposure), and the responsivity can be defined as the ratio of the output signal to the input light energy. If the output signal is measured as a function of the wavelength of the input light, the spectral responsivity is denoted by s_λ. The term sensitivity is often used interchangeably with responsivity. However, in vision science, sensitivity is defined as the inverse of the input power required for the system to produce a thresold response. If the system response is a nonlinear function of the input power, measured sensitivity is a function of the threshold response that is chosen for the measurement.

Although most radiometric measurements are simple to describe, they are very difficult to perform accurately. The problem is that there are many factors that have to be taken into account and uncertainty in each one of them introduces errors [1043]. For example, the responsivity of a detector is often a function of the wavelength of the radiation, the temporal variation of the radiation, the direction of the incident radiation, the position on the detector, the temperature of the instrument, the polarization of the radiation, and the degree of coherence of the radiation, etc.

3.2 Spectral radiometry

The concepts and terms we described above are defined without reference to the spectral composition of the light that we are measuring. In practice, the instrument's response as a function of wavelength has to be specified when reporting those quantities. When our interest is in quantifying light energy flow as a function of spectral wavelength or frequency, the quantities we have defined so far have to be measured within a small wavelength or frequency interval. The resulting quantities are called by the same names but the adjective "spectral" is added in front of the terms, and their units become per unit wavelength interval (e.g., nanometer) or per unit frequency interval. For example, spectral radiance is $L_\lambda = d^3\Phi/(d\omega d\lambda dA \cos\theta)$ if a wavelength interval is used, or $L_\nu = d^3\Phi/(d\omega d\nu dA \cos\theta)$ if a frequency interval is used. The relation between L_λ and L_ν can be derived from the relation $c/n = \nu\lambda$, where c is the velocity of light in the vacuum, and n is the index of refraction of the medium, and

$$L_\nu = \frac{n\lambda^2}{c}L_\lambda. \tag{3.9}$$

Table 3.1. *Comparison of three measures of light energy flow*

Energy	Visual	Photon
radiant flux Φ_e	luminous flux Φ_v	photon-flux Φ_p
radiant intensity I_e	luminous intensity I_v	photon-flux intensity I_p
radiance L_e	luminance L_v	photon-flux sterance L_p
irradiance E_e	illuminance E_v	photon-flux density E_p

3.3 The *International Lighting Vocabulary*

So far, we have covered some of the most basic concepts and terms in radiometry. The *International Lighting Vocabulary* contains 950 terms, which are well annotated. Obviously, it is not appropriate to discuss all the terms here. Some of the terms that are related to our interests in this book can be found in the Glossary at the end of the book. The reader should consult the Glossary whenever an unfamiliar term is encountered.

In 1987, the International Electrotechnical Commission (IEC) and the CIE issued the fourth edition of the *International Lighting Vocabulary* [187]. The aim of the publication is to promote international standardization of quantities, units, symbols, and terminology in the field of radiometry, photometry, and lighting engineering.

In Section 3.1, we discussed the concepts and definitions of radiant flux, radiance, and irradiance, etc. These quantities are measured in terms of radiant energy, which is usually denoted by a subscript e so that their symbols become Φ_e, L_e, and E_e. When different wavelengths are weighted by their visual efficiency in producing the "brightness" sensation, the resulting terms are the luminous flux, luminance, and illuminance, and they are denoted by Φ_v (unit: lumen), L_v (unit: candela per square meter), and E_v (unit: lux). These will be defined later when we discuss photometry. Sometimes, it is desirable to measure the radiation in terms of number of photons. In this case, the symbols have the subscript p. The corresponding terms are the photon flux Φ_p, photon radiance L_p, and photon irradiance E_p. Table 3.1 shows the correspondence of these different measures.

3.4 Radiance theorem

In geometrical optics, light is treated as rays, and tracing rays from one point in space to another is an operation carried out in diverse applications, such as lens design, thermal radiative transfer, scanner engineering, and computer graphics. An implicit assumption in ray tracing is that each ray carries with it some measure of energy flux through space and time. The radiometric quantity associated with each ray is the so-called "basic radiance" [700] which is L/n^2, the radiance divided by the index of refraction squared. It can be proved that the basic radiance is conserved when light is propagated through nonabsorbing and nonscattering media. This conservation property of the basic radiance is called the *radiance theorem*.

Figure 3.9 shows the propagation of the basic radiance along a light ray through two different media. Let dA be an elemental area of the interface between two media, with refractive indices, n_1 and n_2. From Snell's law, a ray, with an incident angle θ_1 relative to

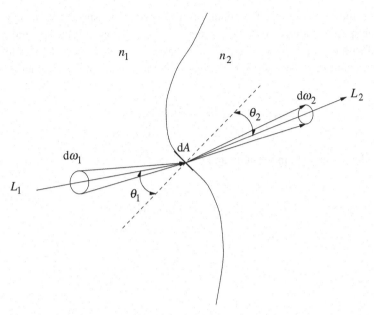

Figure 3.9. The propagation of the basic radiance along a ray.

the surface normal, is refracted to a transmission angle of θ_2, and

$$n_1 \sin \theta_1 = n_2 \sin \theta_2. \tag{3.10}$$

If we take derivatives of both sides, we have

$$n_1 \cos \theta_1 d\theta_1 = n_2 \cos \theta_2 d\theta_2. \tag{3.11}$$

Light incident on the interface between the two media is partially reflected back to medium 1 and partially transmitted into medium 2. Let the radiant flux of the part of the incident ray that is transmitted into the second medium be $d\Phi_1$, and the radiant flux of the transmitted ray in the second medium be $d\Phi_2$, then

$$d\Phi_1 = L_1 \cdot dA \cdot \cos \theta_1 \cdot d\omega_1 = L_1 \cdot dA \cdot \cos \theta_1 \cdot \sin \theta_1 \cdot d\theta_1 \cdot d\phi_1, \tag{3.12}$$
$$d\Phi_2 = L_2 \cdot dA \cdot \cos \theta_2 \cdot d\omega_2 = L_2 \cdot dA \cdot \cos \theta_2 \cdot \sin \theta_2 \cdot d\theta_2 \cdot d\phi_2. \tag{3.13}$$

Since Snell's law also requires that the incident light and the transmitted light be on the sample plane, any angular quantity perpendicular to the plane of incidence will be preserved, and $d\phi_1 = d\phi_2$. Assuming that there is no loss of energy in the interface, i.e., $d\Phi_1 = d\Phi_2$, then from Eqs. (3.10), (3.11), (3.12), and (3.13), we have

$$\frac{L_1}{n_1^2} = \frac{L_2}{n_2^2}. \tag{3.14}$$

Therefore, the basic radiance, L/n^2, is preserved. In fact, it can be shown that the radiance theorem is true for a ray traversing a nonuniform, nonisotropic medium in which the refractive index changes continuously [592].

It should be pointed out that the arguments used in the proof of the radiance theorem are relative to energy flux. When dealing with spectral radiance, there are two possible measures: L_ν and L_λ. If the spectral radiance is measured with respect to frequency ν interval, the basic spectral radiance remains the same, L_ν/n^2. However, if the spectral radiance is measured with respect to wavelength, L_λ, the basic spectral radiance changes to L_λ/n^3, because the radiant flux is measured per wavelength interval and the wavelength has to be scaled by n:

$$L_{\lambda_1} = dL_1/d\lambda_1 = dL_1/(d\lambda_0/n_1), \tag{3.15}$$
$$L_{\lambda_2} = dL_2/d\lambda_2 = dL_2/(d\lambda_0/n_2), \tag{3.16}$$

where λ_0 is the wavelength in vacuum, and therefore,

$$dL_1/n_1^2 = (L_\lambda)_1 d\lambda_0/n_1^3, \tag{3.17}$$
$$dL_2/n_2^2 = (L_\lambda)_2 d\lambda_0/n_2^3. \tag{3.18}$$

Since $dL_1/n_1^2 = dL_2/n_2^2$, we have

$$\frac{L_{\lambda_1}}{n_1^3} = \frac{L_{\lambda_2}}{n_2^3}. \tag{3.19}$$

3.5   Integrating cavities

In many applications, it is necessary to integrate nonuniform radiant fluxes to produce a source of uniform radiant flux. This is often achieved by using integrating cavities. An integrating cavity is a physical cavity enclosed by reflecting surfaces. Integrating cavities are a cost-effective means of providing the uniform illuminating sources needed by scanners [486]. The study of the radiant flux distribution in an integrating cavity involves radiometric calculation of the mutual reflection of surfaces. Finite element analysis is most efficient in solving the problem for Lambertian surfaces, while Monte Carlo ray tracing is slower, but can handle arbitrary types of reflecting surface.

One of the best-known integrating cavities is the integrating sphere, which is a spherical enclosure of a uniform diffuse reflecting surface, such as a surface coated with pressed PTFE (polytetrafluoroethylene) [58, 1020]. An integrating sphere has the useful property that if an area dA_1 on the sphere is illuminated by a light beam, the irradiance at any other area dA_2 on the sphere due to the light reflected from dA_1 is independent of their relative locations. This property, known as the theory of the integrating sphere, can be shown as follows. Referring to Fig. 3.10, let dA_1 and dA_2 be two elemental areas on the interior surface of the sphere, and D be the distance between them. Since the surface normals of dA_1 and dA_2 both point to the center of the sphere, the two angles θ_1 and θ_2 are equal, $\theta_1 = \theta_2 = \theta$ and $D = 2R\cos\theta$, where R is the radius of the sphere. Let L be the radiance from dA_1 and $d\omega$ be the solid angle that dA_2 subtends at dA_1. The radiant flux received on dA_2 from dA_1 is

$$d\Phi = L \cdot \cos\theta_1 \cdot dA_1 \cdot d\omega \tag{3.20}$$
$$= L \cdot \cos\theta_1 \cdot dA_1 \cdot dA_2 \cdot \cos\theta_2/D^2 \tag{3.21}$$
$$= L \cdot dA_1 \cdot dA_2/(4R^2) \tag{3.22}$$

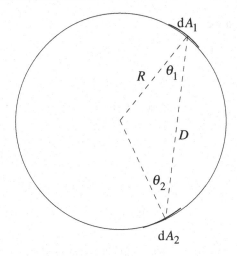

Figure 3.10. The integrating sphere.

and

$$dE_2 = \frac{d\Phi}{dA_2} \cdot = \frac{L \cdot dA_1}{4R^2},$$ (3.23)

which is independent of the location of dA_2 if dA_1 is a perfect diffuser, i.e., L is a constant for all directions.

An integrating sphere is an elegant way to achieve uniform diffuse lighting for measuring reflectances. A reflectance sample can be positioned inside the sphere and an incident beam is then directed at the sample. The light is reflected to and integrated by the sphere. Since every point inside the sphere is uniformly illuminated, one can place the detector wherever convenient to measure the irradiance which is proportional to amount of reflected light. The same principle can be applied to the measurement of the radiant flux of a large beam of nonuniform cross-section, because the sphere turns the beam into uniform surface irradiance proportional to the incident radiant flux, and a small aperture detector can then be used for the measurement. Figure 3.11 shows an example of how an integrating sphere can be used to measure surface irradiance due to an extended source. The entrance port of the sphere is positioned at the location of interest and the measurement is taken at the exit port. The integrating sphere can be only a few centimeters in diameter. The entrance port allows it to collect over a wide solid angle formed by the extended source, and the exit port provides a fairly uniform area for measurement.

3.6 Blackbody radiation

Natural and artificial light sources are often compared with the idealized concept of blackbody radiation for good reasons. Sunlight and its scattered portion, skylight, are the most important sources of optical radiation on earth. Their combination, called daylight, varies greatly according to different humidity, dust, cloud conditions and the angle of the sun.

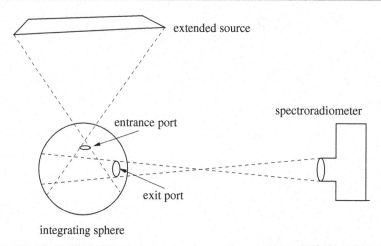

Figure 3.11. Using an integrating sphere to measure the spectral irradiance on a surface illuminated by an extended source.

However, the color quality (chromaticity) of daylight is very similar to that of blackbody radiation at various temperatures. In addition, the spectral compositions of artificial tungsten light sources are very close to those of blackbody radiation. For these reasons, light source colors are often compared with those of blackbody radiators at different temperatures, and are often specified by their "correlated color temperatures" which will be formally defined later.

3.6.1 Planck's radiation law

A blackbody is an idealized object that absorbs all incident radiant energy, i.e., no energy is reflected from or transmitted through it. Since visible light is one form of radiant energy, no light is reflected from such an object, and it looks black (assuming that it is at a very low temperature). Hence it is called a blackbody. A blackbody is an idealized concept because no known material actually absorbs all the incident radiant energy. Only a small number of surfaces, such as carbon black and gold black (which consists of fine metal particles), absorb radiant energy to an extent close to a blackbody.

The temperature of an object that absorbs all the incident radiant energy rises higher and higher, unless the absorbed energy is transferred to the ambient environment. When the rate of energy absorption is equal to the energy dissipation, the object is said to reach thermal equilibrium with its environment. One path for thermal energy dissipation is through thermal radiation heat transfer. The thermal radiative properties of a blackbody have been studied extensively for many years. In 1901, Max Planck [763] derived the theoretical energy spectrum of blackbody radiation. Planck's blackbody radiation law can be expressed in many forms. Here we express the spectral radiance as a function of wavelength and absolute temperature, when the blackbody is emitting into a medium with an index of refraction n:

$$L_\lambda(\lambda, T) = \frac{2C_1}{n^2\lambda^5(e^{C_2/n\lambda T} - 1)}, \qquad (3.24)$$

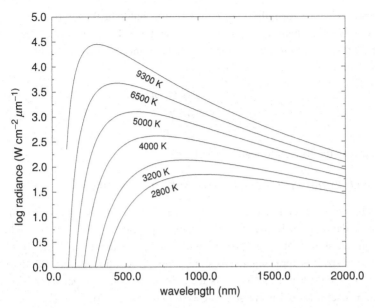

Figure 3.12. The spectral radiance functions of blackbody radiators at different temperatures.

where $C_1 = hc^2 = 0.595\,52 \times 10^{-16}$ W m^2, $C_2 = hc/k = 1.438\,769 \times 10^{-2}$ m K, h $(=$ $6.626\,075\,5 \times 10^{-34}$ J s) is Planck's constant, k $(= 1.380\,658 \times 10^{-23}$ J K$^{-1})$ is the Boltzmann constant, c $(= 2.997\,924\,58 \times 10^8$ m s$^{-1})$ is the velocity of light in vacuum, λ is the wavelength in the medium, and T is the absolute temperature. Figure 3.12 shows the spectral radiance of the blackbody at several temperatures. It should be noted that the spectral radiance of a blackbody is independent of the angle of radiation. A blackbody is thus a Lambertian radiator – it looks equally bright (or dark) from all angles. From Eq. (3.24), we can calculate the wavelength, λ_{max}, at which the spectral radiance is maximum:

$$\lambda_{max} = \frac{C_3}{nT}, \tag{3.25}$$

where $C_3 = 2.8978 \times 10^{-3}$ m K. This is called Wien's displacement law. It shows that the peak wavelength is shifted to a shorter wavelength as the temperature of the blackbody increases. For example, a blackbody at 5221.3 K has the peak wavelength at 555 nm, while that at 5715.6 K has the peak wavelength at 507 nm. As will be discussed in Section 4.2, 555 nm is the wavelength of the peak photopic luminous efficiency of our eyes and 507 nm is that of the peak scotopic luminous efficiency. The effective radiating surface temperature of the sun is approximately 5750–5780 K [687, p. 88, 872, p. 24] with the peak wavelength located at about 501 nm.

Planck's radiation law can be simplified when the temperature is very low ($C_2 \gg n\lambda T$) or very high ($C_2 \ll n\lambda T$). When the temperature is very low ($C_2 \gg n\lambda T$),

$$e^{C_2/n\lambda T} - 1 \approx e^{C_2/n\lambda T}, \tag{3.26}$$

$$L_\lambda(\lambda, T) \approx \frac{2C_1}{n^2\lambda^5}e^{-C_2/n\lambda T}, \tag{3.27}$$

which is known as Wien's formula. $T \ll C_2/(n\lambda)$ turns out to be the temperature range that is most relevant to color imaging. For $\lambda = 550$ nm and $n = 1$, $C_2/(n\lambda) = 26\,160$ K, which is much higher than the color temperatures of most commonly available light sources.

When the temperature is very high ($C_2 \ll n\lambda T$),

$$e^{C_2/n\lambda T} \approx 1 + C_2/n\lambda T, \tag{3.28}$$

$$L_\lambda(\lambda, T) \approx \frac{2C_1 T}{n C_2 \lambda^4}, \tag{3.29}$$

which is known as the Rayleigh–Jeans formula.

3.6.2 Blackbody chromaticity loci of narrow-band systems

The fact that blackbody radiation can be described analytically and that its color variation is similar to that of daylight can be used to derive some empirical rules for imaging applications. In this section, we show that for a narrow-band imaging system, the blackbody locus in a logarithmic color space is approximately a straight line. If we allow the blackbody radiation to be scaled to account for attenuation, its locus is on a plane in logarithmic space. This property can be useful for color image processing [314, 561, 565].

For $T \ll 25\,000$ K, blackbody radiation can be approximated by Wien's formula (assuming $n = 1.0$):

$$L_\lambda(\lambda, T) \approx \frac{mC_1}{\lambda^5} e^{-C_2/\lambda T}, \tag{3.30}$$

where m is a scale factor. Within a narrow spectral bandwidth (say less than 100 nm), we can approximate $L_\lambda(\lambda, T)$ by a first degree polynomial: $L_\lambda(\lambda, T) \approx P(T)\lambda + Q(T)$. Let $\hat{s}_i(\lambda)$ be the spectral responsivity function of the ith (narrow-band) channel of a color imaging system. Without loss of generality, we will assume that $\hat{s}_i(\lambda)$ has been normalized so that $\int \hat{s}_i(\lambda)d\lambda = 1$. The image irradiance, E_i, can be expressed as

$$E_i = \int L_\lambda(\lambda, T)\hat{s}_i(\lambda)d\lambda$$

$$\approx P(T)\int \lambda\hat{s}_i(\lambda)d\lambda + Q(T)\int \hat{s}_i(\lambda)d\lambda$$

$$= P(T)\lambda_i + Q(T)$$

$$\approx L_\lambda(\lambda_i, T),$$

where $\lambda_i = \int \lambda\hat{s}_i(\lambda)d\lambda$. Thus, within the degree of the first order approximation, the image irradiance as determined by a narrow-band spectral responsivity function can be represented by the mean wavelength in the band. We can therefore approximate the red, green, and blue image irradiances as

$$E_r \approx L_\lambda(\lambda_r, T) \approx \frac{mC_1}{\lambda_r^5} e^{-C_2/\lambda_r T},$$

$$E_g \approx L_\lambda(\lambda_g, T) \approx \frac{mC_1}{\lambda_g^5} e^{-C_2/\lambda_g T},$$

$$E_b \approx L_\lambda(\lambda_b, T) \approx \frac{mC_1}{\lambda_b^5} e^{-C_2/\lambda_b T},$$

and, letting $R = \log E_r$, $G = \log E_g$, and $B = \log E_b$, we have:

$$R = \log E_r \approx \log m + \log C_1 - 5 \log \lambda_r - \frac{C_2}{\lambda_r T} = a + R_0 + c_r/T,$$

$$G = \log E_g \approx \log m + \log C_1 - 5 \log \lambda_g - \frac{C_2}{\lambda_g T} = a + G_0 + c_g/T,$$

$$B = \log E_b \approx \log m + \log C_1 - 5 \log \lambda_b - \frac{C_2}{\lambda_b T} = a + B_0 + c_b/T,$$

where $a = \log m$, $R_0 = \log C_1 - 5 \log \lambda_r$, $G_0 = \log C_1 - 5 \log \lambda_g$, $B_0 = \log C_1 - 5 \log \lambda_b$, $c_r = -C_2/\lambda_r$, $c_g = -C_2/\lambda_g$, and $c_b = -C_2/\lambda_b$. Therefore, for a constant m, the blackbody locus is on a straight line which passes through $(a + R_0, a + G_0, a + B_0)$ in the direction of (c_r, c_g, c_b). If we also allow the scale factor to vary, the blackbody locus is on a plane spanned by the vectors (c_r, c_g, c_b) and $(1,1,1)$.

3.7 Problems

3.1   In vision literature, a visual angle is often used to describe the size of an object. If the visual angle of a circular disk is α (rad), what is the solid angle (sr) subtended by the disk relative to the eye?

3.2   Given a square plate of frosted glass which is a cm on a side (see Fig. 3.13) and can be considered to be a Lambertian source with radiance L [W m^{-2} sr^{-1}], calculate the irradiance E at a point P on a plane parallel to the plane of the source, and separated from the source by z meters.

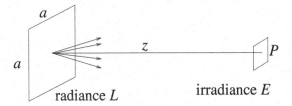

Figure 3.13.

3.3   There are two ways to express the spectral radiance: radiance per unit wavelength, L_λ, and radiance per unit frequency, L_ν. How is L_λ related to L_ν?

3.4   For an application, it is necessary to provide a uniform illumination for a planar test target with a size of 25 cm $\times$ 25 cm. Suppose we position one spherical source directly above each of the four corners at a distance d from the target plane. Assuming that each spherical source is 5 cm in diameter and is uniformly bright (i.e., has equal radiance) in all directions, what is the minimum distance d that will produce an illumination uniform to within 10%, i.e., the maximum illuminance is no larger than 1.1 times the minimum illuminance on the test target? (Hint: For a Lambertian sphere source of radius r and luminance L, a surface perpendicular to the source direction will have an illuminance E. It can be shown from spherical symmetry that $E = \pi L(r^2/d^2)$.)

The symmetry argument is: since the flux from a unit area on the sphere is πL (from Example 3.2), the total flux of the sphere is $4\pi r^2(\pi L)$ which is distributed uniformly to an area of $4\pi d^2$ at a distance of d.)

3.5   The surface of many traffic signs is made to reflect light more strongly in the direction perpendicular to the surface. Suppose that some snow happens to cover part of a STOP sign. The snow on the STOP sign looks white in daylight, but looks dark gray in the evening when it is illuminated by car headlights. How do you explain such a perceptual difference?

4 Photometry

In our discussion of radiometry, light flux is measured in terms of power or energy. However, even under identical viewing conditions, equal power of light of different wavelengths does not produce equal brightness sensation in our visual perception. (In an extreme case, even a kilowatt infrared source will not help us to see.) Therefore, radiometric quantities are not always meaningful in our visual world, especially in the field of illumination engineering. For example, in order to illuminate a library reading room, we need to know "how much" visible light our chosen light sources will provide for reading. For these types of applications, we need to measure light flux in quantities that are representative of its visual impact, such as brightness. Photometry deals with measurements of visible light in terms of its effectiveness to produce the "brightness" sensation in the human visual system. Given two stimuli of different spectral compositions, the basic goal of photometry is to set up a quantitative procedure for determining which stimulus will appear "brighter" or more luminous to an average observer.

Measuring visual quantities of light is complicated because light stimuli of different spectral compositions produce complex perceptions of light, such as bright red or dark green. It is not easy (if not impossible) to order these different color sensations along a single, intensive scale. In fact, years of research have not produced a completely satisfactory solution. However, the applications are so important that an agreed-upon, incomplete solution is better than no solution at all. It is important to point out that we should not be surprised if, once in a while, object A appears to be brighter than object B when the photometric measurements tell us that object B is more luminous than object A.

4.1 Brightness matching and photometry

There are two types of photoreceptor, rods and cones, in our retinas and they operate under different illumination levels. In the low-illumination range, only rods are responsible for seeing and we call this range of vision *scotopic vision*. In the high-illumination range, only cones are responsible, and we call this range of vision *photopic vision*. In the transition between these two ranges, both rods and cones are responsible for vision, and we call the transition range of vision *mesopic vision*. The peak luminous sensitivity changes from 555 nm for photopic vision to 507 nm for scotopic vision (see Fig. 4.1). This shift is called the Purkinje shift. As the ambient light level becomes dimmer (as in the twilight), objects that reflect mostly long wavelength light (such as red flowers) look darker compared with

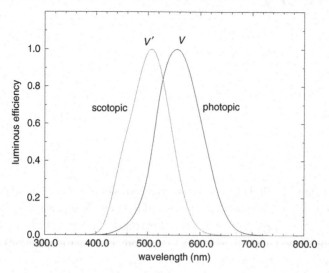

Figure 4.1. The CIE luminous efficiency functions: $V(\lambda)$ for the photopic vision, $V'(\lambda)$ for scotopic vision.

other objects that reflect mostly short wavelength light (such as blue flowers). This is due to the difference in spectral absorption in the photopigments in cones and rods.

Monochromatic lights of different wavelengths, but the same power, do not produce equal brightness or luminous sensation. For example, in the photopic range, it is found that light of around 555 nm wavelength requires the least radiant power to produce a given level of luminous sensation. The problem of quantifying the photopic luminous sensation is that there is no single photoreceptor that is responsible for it. Instead, in the photopic range, the sensation is produced from the quantum catches of the three cone mechanisms. The exact dependence of the luminous sensation on the three cone photoreceptions is unknown, and probably will remain so for some time to come. In the scotopic range, there is only a single type of photoreceptor (the rods) that actively responds to light at this low level, and the measured luminous sensation as a function of wavelength does correspond to the spectral sensitivity of rod, as measured *in vitro*, with correction for the absorption of the optical media in the eye.

The difficulty of comparing the brightness of objects of very different colors is immediately clear to anyone who has tried to do so. To deal with the problem, measurement procedures have been proposed and the quantitative specifications of luminous sensation are thus defined by the results from these procedures [479]. A typical procedure involves matching the brightness of one wavelength against that of another wavelength. In order to reduce the difficulty in matching the brightness of different colors, the two wavelengths under comparison are chosen to be similar. Therefore, one compares the brightness of 500 nm light with that of 505 nm light, then one compares 505 nm light with 510 nm light, and so on. This procedure is called step-by-step brightness matching. Another brightness matching procedure involves temporal comparison. Lights of two different wavelengths are presented at the same spatial location in quick succession temporally at a certain frequency. If the two wavelengths differ a lot in brightness, one sees flickers. When the radiant power of the darker of the wavelengths is adjusted upward, the perceived flickering sensation is reduced. When the ratio of the radiant powers of the two wavelengths is such that the flickering sensation is at a minimum, the two wavelengths are said to be of equal luminance. This is called minimum-flicker brightness matching. The setting of the alternating frequency is somewhat involved. If the frequency is too high (e.g., higher than 30 Hz), one cannot see any flicker. If it is too low (say lower than 2 Hz), one always sees the two alternating stimuli. Therefore the frequency has to be adjusted so that a small amount of flicker is always perceived (about 12–15 Hz).

In addition to the minimum-flicker and step-by-step brightness matching methods, there are other methods for determining the relative efficiency of different wavelengths to produce luminous sensation. Some of these alternative methods are: direct heterochromatic brightness matching, absolute thresholds, increment thresholds, minimally distinct border, and visual acuity [185]. It is important to point out that different brightness matching procedures do not produce the same luminous efficiency curve, and even within the same procedure, data may vary a lot from observer to observer. The range of interobserver variation in the luminous efficiency function as measured by flicker photometry can be as large as one log unit in the short wavelength region, although the standard deviation of the variation is much smaller (on the order of $0.1 \log_{10}$ unit) [614]. A good discussion of the various methods and issues can be found in [479].

Empirical findings of brightness matching are summarized in the forms of laws [1053, p. 252] as:

1. Symmetry law: If stimulus A matches stimulus B, then stimulus B matches stimulus A. (It does not matter how you move them around.)
2. Transitivity law: If A matches B and B matches C, then A matches C.
3. Proportionality law: If A matches B, then αA matches αB, where α is any positive factor by which the radiant power of the stimulus is increased or decreased, while its spectral composition is kept the same.
4. Additivity law: If A matches B and C matches D, then $(A \oplus C)$ matches $(B \oplus D)$, where the operator "$\oplus$" means additive color mixture. (By "additive mixture", we mean a color stimulus of which the radiant power at any wavelength is equal to the sum of the powers at the same wavelength of the constituents of the mixture.) Also, if A matches B and $(A \oplus C)$ matches $(B \oplus D)$, then C matches D.

The four laws are similar to the four laws in color matching to be described in Chapter 6. Although the four laws in color matching are intuitively acceptable from the point of view of equivalent quantum catches by photoreceptors, the similar laws in brightness matching do not have the same foundations based on receptor-level matching. In particular, the proportionality law and the additivity law, sometimes referred as Abney's laws, have been questioned many times, and there is plenty of evidence to show their failure [185]. Among the different brightness matching methods, it is found that the minimum-flicker method, the minimally distinct border method, and the visual acuity method yield results that follow the additivity law well. Other methods of determining brightness matches do not do as well. In particular, chromatic stimuli generally require less luminance to match their brightness to that of the achromatic stimuli. This effect is called the *Helmholtz–Kohlrausch* effect. A number of systematic studies have been conducted to quantify this effect [973]. However, the deviations of luminous quantities calculated using these two laws are often acceptable for many applications (e.g., illumination engineering) for which the convenience in computation often outweighs concern about the resulting inaccuracy. Applications, such as color reproduction, that are much more sensitive to the perceptual errors have to model brightness more accurately. One of the obvious problems with flicker photometry is that the measurement involves temporal variations that are faster than our everyday color perception. The other problem is that the spatial frequency has not been treated as a measurement variable. The discrepancy between different brightness matching methods has been attributed to the fact that certain perceptual information processing channels (the red–green and yellow–blue chromatic channels) cannot respond (or respond with attenuated amplitudes) to the flicker frequency used in the flicker photometry. As a consequence, the measured brightness only represents the response from the achromatic channel. Brightness perception in a static scene consists of contributions from the chromatic channels as well as the achromatic channel. This "explanation" seems to be in general agreement with the experimental data.

4.2   The spectral luminous efficiency functions

If we are willing to assume that the luminous sensation is additive, one of the important tasks in photometry is to measure the relative efficiency of light of various wavelengths in producing the luminous sensation. The resulting function, called the spectral luminous efficiency function, can then be used as a weighting function for calculating the luminous sensation for stimuli of any spectral compositions.

Let us denote the wavelength of the maximal efficiency by λ_m. A spectral luminous efficiency function gives the ratio of the radiant power of a monochromatic stimulus at wavelength λ_m to that of a monochromatic stimulus at wavelength λ, when the two stimuli produce luminous sensations that are judged to be equivalent under some given viewing conditions and according to certain specified criteria. In 1924, the CIE adopted the standard spectral luminous efficiency function for *photopic vision*, $V(\lambda)$, which was derived from the results of several independent experiments. The final result was not an average of the experimental data, but a weighted assembly of the different sets of data [1053, p. 395]. In all the experiments, a 2° test field was used. The luminance level of the experiments was around 1.5 cd m^{-2}. Finally, it should be noted that because of the age-related increase of optical density of the eye lens, especially in the short-wavelength region, there is a gradual reduction of luminous efficiency with age in the corresponding wavelength region [817].

In 1951, the CIE adopted the standard spectral luminous efficiency function for *scotopic vision*, $V'(\lambda)$, which was based on experimental data from subjects all under 30 years of age. Both $V(\lambda)$ and $V'(\lambda)$ are shown in Fig. 4.1. The photopic luminous efficiency function, $V(\lambda)$, has its maximum value, 1.0, at 555 nm, and the scotopic luminous efficiency function, $V'(\lambda)$, at 506–508 nm. A detector whose relative spectral responsivity curve conforms to the $V(\lambda)$ function (or to the $V'(\lambda)$ function) may be referred to as a CIE Standard Photometric Observer for photopic (or scotopic) vision. Because of the complexity of the problem, CIE has not recommended standards for the mesopic luminous efficiency function yet [188].

The $V(\lambda)$ function is recommended for a visual field of 2°. For large fields, the luminous efficiency is higher at short wavelengths. Recognizing the difference, CIE also provisionally provided a $10°$ luminous efficiency function, $V_{10}(\lambda)$ (which is the same as $\overline{y}_{10}(\lambda)$ for the CIE 1964 $10°$ color matching functions) [1053, p. 397]. For field sizes larger than $10°$, the luminous efficiency function remains quite close to the $10°$ data. However, $V(\lambda)$ remains the official recommendation for photometric calculations.

Compared with the photopic $V(\lambda)$, the scotopic $V'(\lambda)$ is relatively free from difficulties. Since only one type of photoreceptor (rods) is responsible for scotopic vision, the additivity law holds well. The interobserver variation for $V'(\lambda)$ is also small. At the opposite end of the case of standardization, the luminous efficiency function for mesopic vision (from about 10^{-3} cd m^{-2} to 3 cd m^{-2}) is a sensitive function of the luminance level. Empirical formulas have been suggested for calculating mesopic luminance from photopic luminance and scotopic luminance [185, p. 21, 188]. From the above discussion, we can also predict that the luminous efficiency function of color-deficient (color-blind) observers is quite different from that of color-normal observers. For example, protanopia observers (those missing the long-wavelength sensitive cones) have abnormally low luminous efficiency at the long-wave end of the spectrum. Their peak luminous efficiency wavelength is shifted from the 555 nm of the normal observer to 540 nm. The totally color-blind observer, missing all three types of cone, has a luminous efficiency function identical to the scotopic $V'(\lambda)$.

Not long after CIE published its 1924 recommendation for $V(\lambda)$, experimental data began to show that the recommended luminous efficiency value was too low in the short-wavelength range. In 1951, Judd proposed a modified luminous efficiency function to correct the deficiency. Judd's modified function became widely used by the vision research community and was finally published by CIE, with some slight modification, as one of the optional luminous efficiency functions. It is called the CIE 1988 Modified Two Degree Spectral Luminous Efficiency Function for Photopic Vision, $V_M(\lambda)$ [190]. This modification is a supplement to, not a replacement of, the CIE 1924 $V(\lambda)$. Figure 4.2 shows the comparison between $V(\lambda)$ and $V_M(\lambda)$.

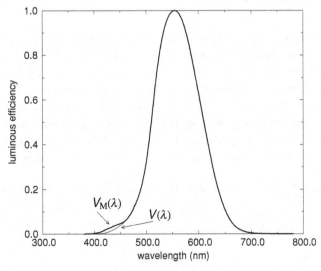

Figure 4.2. Comparison between CIE 1924 $V(\lambda)$ and Judd's modified version $V_M(\lambda)$ for photopic vision.

4.3 Photometric quantities

The terms radiant flux and radiant power (symbol: Φ_e; unit: watt, W) are synonyms for power emitted, transferred, or received in the form of radiation. The spectral concentration of radiant flux, called the spectral radiant flux, is represented as $\Phi_{e,\lambda}$. For photopic vision, the luminous flux Φ_v (unit: lumen) of a radiation whose spectral distribution of radiant flux is $\Phi_{e,\lambda}(\lambda)$ can be expressed by the equation:

$$\Phi_v = K_m \int_{360\,\text{nm}}^{830\,\text{nm}} \Phi_{e,\lambda}(\lambda)V(\lambda)\,d\lambda, \tag{4.1}$$

where the scaling factor, K_m, is known as the maximum spectral luminous efficacy of radiation for photopic vision. Its value is defined to be 683.002 lumens per watt [lm W^{-1}]. For scotopic vision the luminous flux Φ'_v is given by:

$$\Phi'_v = K'_m \int_{360\,\text{nm}}^{830\,\text{nm}} \Phi_{e,\lambda}(\lambda)V'(\lambda)\,d\lambda, \tag{4.2}$$

where the scaling factor, K'_m, is known as the maximum spectral luminous efficacy of radiation for scotopic vision. Its value is defined to be 1700.06 lm W^{-1}. K_m and K'_m are defined so that the wavelength 555.016 nm has the same value of luminous flux for both photopic and scotopic vision.

**Example 4.1 Calculating reflected luminous flux from skin under
a daylight illuminant**
Given the spectral reflectance $\rho(\lambda)$ of a sample skin illuminated by a daylight source $L(\lambda)$ in Table 4.1, calculate the luminous flux illuminating the skin, the reflected luminous flux from the skin, and the reflectance of the skin.

Solution   Measurement data are often given at discrete wavelengths. Therefore, it is important to determine how the data are measured before we can calculate the spectral radiant flux, $\Phi_{e,\lambda}(\lambda)$. In this example, the data points are given at discrete wavelengths at every 10 nm. For example, $L(720\,\text{nm}) = 0.6160$ W means that the total radiant power illuminating the sample skin, from $\lambda = 715$ nm to $\lambda = 725$ nm, is 0.6160 W. Sometimes, $L(\lambda)$ is given as power per nanometer, then $L(\lambda)$ needs to be multiplied by 10 for the 10 nm interval. Here, we will assume that $L(\lambda)$ values are power per 10 nm interval. Using the discrete sum to replace the integral, we can find the source luminous flux illuminating the skin:

$$\Phi_v(\text{illumination}) = K_m \sum_\lambda L(\lambda)V(\lambda) = 683.002\ [\text{lm W}^{-1}] \times 10.571\ [\text{W}] = 7220\ [\text{lm}],$$

and the luminous flux reflected from the skin:

$$\begin{aligned} \Phi_v(\text{skin reflection}) &= K_m \sum_\lambda L(\lambda)\rho(\lambda)V(\lambda) \\ &= 683.002\ [\text{lm W}^{-1}] \times 4.649\ [\text{W}] = 3175\ [\text{lm}]. \end{aligned}$$

Table 4.1. *Example of a photopic luminous flux calculation*

λ (nm)	$L(\lambda)$ (W)	$\rho(\lambda)$	$V(\lambda)$	$L(\lambda)V(\lambda)$ (W)	$L(\lambda)\rho(\lambda)V(\lambda)$ (W)
390	0.5467	0.230	0.0001	5.47E-05	1.257E-05
400	0.8278	0.232	0.0004	3.31E-04	7.616E-05
410	0.9151	0.221	0.0012	1.098E-03	2.427E-04
420	0.9346	0.224	0.0040	3.738E-03	8.374E-04
430	0.8670	0.236	0.0116	1.006E-02	2.374E-03
440	1.0488	0.267	0.023	2.412E-02	6.441E-03
450	1.1703	0.307	0.038	4.447E-02	1.365E-02
460	1.1783	0.340	0.060	7.070E-02	2.404E-02
470	1.1488	0.363	0.091	0.1045	3.795E-02
480	1.1594	0.380	0.139	0.1611	6.124E-02
490	1.0882	0.395	0.208	0.2264	8.941E-02
500	1.0936	0.406	0.323	0.3532	0.1434
510	1.0781	0.416	0.503	0.5423	0.2256
520	1.0480	0.415	0.710	0.7440	0.3088
530	1.0769	0.406	0.862	0.9283	0.3769
540	1.0441	0.389	0.954	0.9961	0.3875
550	1.0405	0.394	0.995	1.0353	0.4079
560	1.0000	0.401	0.995	0.9950	0.3990
570	0.9633	0.399	0.952	0.9171	0.3659
580	0.9579	0.408	0.870	0.8333	0.3400
590	0.8868	0.465	0.757	0.6713	0.3122
600	0.9000	0.540	0.631	0.5679	0.3067
610	0.8959	0.592	0.503	0.4507	0.2668
620	0.8769	0.622	0.381	0.3341	0.2078
630	0.8428	0.641	0.265	0.2233	0.1432
640	0.8369	0.655	0.175	0.1465	9.593E-02
650	0.8002	0.667	0.107	8.562E-02	5.711E-02
660	0.8021	0.676	0.061	4.893E-02	3.307E-02
670	0.8227	0.683	0.032	2.633E-02	1.798E-02
680	0.7827	0.692	0.017	1.331E-02	9.208E-03
690	0.6971	0.698	0.0082	5.716E-03	3.990E-03
700	0.7160	0.704	0.0041	2.936E-03	2.067E-03
710	0.7434	0.704	0.0021	1.561E-03	1.099E-03
720	0.6160	0.704	0.0010	6.16E-04	4.336E-04
730	0.6988	0.704	0.0005	3.49E-04	2.460E-04
740	0.7508	0.704	0.0003	2.25E-04	1.586E-04
750	0.6359	0.704	0.0001	6.36E-04	4.476E-05
sum				$\sum = 10.571$	$\sum = 4.649$

Therefore, the reflectance of the sample skin is about 0.44, which is typical of fair Caucasian skin in a body area not exposed to sun. In this example, the reflectance is calculated with respect to $V(\lambda)$ and a daylight source (D65). In other applications, it may be calculated with other system spectral response functions. Therefore, when we use the phrase "reflectance" or "reflectance factor" in color imaging applications, it is important, wherever appropriate, to specify the light source, the imaging geometry, and the system spectral response function [563]. Let us illustrate this point by recalculating in Table 4.2 all the numbers with respect to the scotopic luminous efficiency function $V'(\lambda)$. Using the discrete sum to replace the integral, we can find the scotopic luminous flux of the source illuminating

Table 4.2. *Example of a scotopic luminous flux calculation*

λ (nm)	$L(λ)$ (W)	$ρ(λ)$	$V'(λ)$	$L(λ)V'(λ)$ (W)	$L(λ)ρ(λ)V'(λ)$ (W)
390	0.5467	0.230	2.21E-03	1.208E-03	2.778E-04
400	0.8278	0.230	9.29E-03	7.690E-03	1.769E-03
410	0.9151	0.221	3.48E-02	3.188E-02	7.046E-03
420	0.9346	0.224	9.66E-02	9.028E-02	2.022E-02
430	0.8670	0.236	0.1998	0.1732	4.088E-02
440	1.0489	0.267	0.3281	0.3441	9.189E-02
450	1.1703	0.307	0.4550	0.5325	0.1635
460	1.1783	0.340	0.5670	0.6681	0.2272
470	1.1488	0.363	0.676	0.7766	0.2819
480	1.1594	0.380	0.7930	0.9194	0.3494
490	1.0882	0.395	0.9040	0.9837	0.3886
500	1.0936	0.406	0.9820	1.0739	0.4360
510	1.0781	0.416	0.9970	1.0749	0.4471
520	1.0480	0.415	0.9350	0.9799	0.4067
530	1.0769	0.406	0.8110	0.8734	0.3546
540	1.0441	0.389	0.6500	0.6787	0.2640
550	1.0405	0.394	0.4810	0.5005	0.1972
560	1.000	0.401	0.3288	0.3288	0.1318
570	0.9633	0.399	0.2076	0.2000	7.979E-02
580	0.9579	0.408	1.21E-01	0.1161	4.737E-02
590	0.8868	0.465	6.55E-02	5.808E-02	2.701E-02
600	0.9000	0.540	3.32E-02	2.984E-02	1.611E-02
610	0.8959	0.592	1.59E-02	1.427E-02	8.449E-03
620	0.8769	0.622	7.37E-03	6.463E-03	4.020E-03
630	0.8428	0.641	3.34E-03	2.811E-03	1.802E-03
640	0.8369	0.655	1.50E-03	1.253E-03	8.206E-04
650	0.8002	0.667	6.77E-04	5.417E-04	3.613E-04
660	0.8021	0.676	3.13E-04	2.510E-04	1.697E-04
670	0.8227	0.683	1.48E-04	1.2176E-04	8.316E-05
680	0.7827	0.692	7.15E-05	5.596E-05	3.873E-05
690	0.6971	0.698	3.53E-05	2.463E-05	1.719E-05
700	0.7160	0.704	1.78E-05	1.274E-05	8.972E-06
710	0.7434	0.704	9.14E-06	6.795E-06	4.783E-06
720	0.6160	0.704	4.78E-06	2.944E-06	2.073E-06
730	0.6988	0.704	2.55E-06	1.779E-06	1.253E-06
740	0.7508	0.704	1.38E-06	1.035E-06	7.289E-07
750	0.6359	0.704	7.60E-07	4.833E-07	3.402E-07
sum				$\sum = 10.469$	$\sum = 3.996$

the skin:

$$\Phi'_v(\text{illumination}) = K'_m \sum_λ L(λ)V'(λ)$$

$$= 1700.06 \text{ [scotopic lm W}^{-1}] \times 10.469 \text{ [W]} = 17978 \text{ [scotopic lm]},$$

and the scotopic luminous flux reflected from the skin:

$$\Phi'_v(\text{skin}) = K'_m \sum_λ L(λ)ρ(λ)V'(λ)$$

$$= 1700.06 \text{ [scotopic lm W}^{-1}] \times 3.996 \text{ [W]} = 6793 \text{ [scotopic lm]}.$$

Table 4.3. *Comparison of radiometric and photometric quantities*

Radiometry (energy)	Photometry (visual)
radiant flux Φ_e [W]	luminous flux Φ_v [lm]
radiant intensity I_e [W sr^{-1}]	luminous intensity I_v [cd] or [lm sr^{-1}]
radiance L_e [W sr^{-1} m^{-2}]	luminance L_v [cd m^{-2}] or [lm sr^{-1} m^{-2}]
irradiance E_e [W m^{-2}]	illuminance E_v [lx] or [lm m^{-2}]
radiant exposure H_e [W m^{-2} s]	luminous exposure H_v [lx s]

The reflectance of the sample skin with respect to $V'(\lambda)$ is now reduced to 0.38 (from 0.44). This is easy to see because, comparing with $V(\lambda)$, the weight of $V'(\lambda)$ is shifted to the shorter-wavelength region, where $\rho(\lambda)$ has a smaller value.

The above example also shows that the value of scotopic lumen and that of photopic lumen are quite different. In this example, the former is larger than the latter, but this is not always true. It is dependent on the spectral distribution of radiant flux and the spectral reflectance function. The convention is that when the scotopic function is used in calculating the photometric quantities, it has to be explicitly stated; otherwise, the photopic function is assumed.

We are now in a position to define the various quantities in photometry that correspond to those we have learned in radiometry. The basic conversion formula is the same as that used to convert radiant flux to luminous flux (i.e., Eq. (4.1) or (4.2)). Luminous flux corresponds to radiant flux, luminous intensity corresponds to radiant intensity, luminance corresponds to radiance, and illuminance corresponds to irradiance. There is a one-to-one correspondence in the two systems, with the understanding that the energy or power in the radiometry is always weighted by the luminous efficiency function when we want to calculate the corresponding photometric quantities. The base unit of photometry is the *candela* (cd), which was defined by CGPM in 1979 as the luminous intensity in a given direction of a source that emits monochromatic radiation of frequency 540×10^{12} Hz (i.e., 555.016 nm) and that has a radiant intensity in that direction of 1/683 W sr^{-1}. The *lumen* (lm) is the unit of luminous flux emitted in unit solid angle by an isotropic point source having a luminous intensity of 1 cd. The *lux* (lx) is the unit of illuminance (luminous flux per unit area incident on a surface) and it is the illuminance produced by 1 lm of luminous flux over the area of 1 m^2. Table 4.3 lists the corresponding units in radiometry and photometry.

Example 4.2
A spherical Lambertian source has a radius of 10 cm. It radiates a total luminous flux of 1000 lm. What is the luminance of the source?

Solution   From Example 3.2, we know that the luminous exitance [lm m^{-2}] of a Lambertian surface with luminance L is πL. Since the radius of the source is $r = 0.1$ m, the total surface area is $A = 4\pi r^2 = 0.04\pi$ m^2. Therefore, 1000 lm $= A(\pi L)$, and $L = 2533$ cd m^{-2}.

CIE recommended a level of 3 cd m^{-2} for photopic color matching [185], the rods' contribution being considered negligible above this luminance level. For most practical

Table 4.4. *Typical lighting levels in terms of illuminance, luminance and EV*

Lighting	Illuminance (lux)	Luminance (cd m^{-2})	EV (ISO-100 B/W film)
bright sun	50 000–100 000	3000–6000	18.17–19.17
hazy sun	25 000–50 000	1500–3000	17.17–18.17
cloudy bright	10 000–25 000	600–1500	15.85–17.17
cloudy dull	2000–10 000	120–600	13.52–15.85
very dull	100–2000	6–120	9.20–13.52
sunset	1–100	0.06–6	2.56–9.20
full moon	0.01–1	0.0006–0.006	−4.08–−0.76
star light	0.0001–0.001	0.000 006–0.000 06	−10.73–−7.41
operating theater	5000–10 000	300–600	14.85–15.85
shop windows	1000–5000	60–300	12.52–14.85
drawing offices	300–500	18–30	10.79–11.52
offices	200–300	12–18	10.20–10.79
living rooms	50–200	3–12	8.20–10.20
corridors	50–100	3–6	8.20–9.20
good street lighting	20	1.2	6.88
poor street lighting	0.1	0.006	−0.76

Table 4.5. *Photometric unit conversion*

1 footcandle (fc) = lm ft^{-2} = 10.763 91 lux
1 footlambert (fL) = π^{-1} cd ft^{-2} = 3.426259 cd m^{-2}
1 lambert (L) = π^{-1} cd cm^{-2} = $(10^4/\pi)$ cd m^{-2}
1 phot (ph) = 1 lm cm^{-2} = 1.0×10^4 lx
1 stilb (sb) = 1.0×10^4 cd m^{-2}

purposes, we can say that the scotopic vision is below 10^{-3} cd m^{-2} [1053, p. 406], when only rods are responsible for seeing. Mesopic vision is from luminances of approximately 10^{-3} cd m^{-2} to 3 cd m^{-2}, when rods and cones are both contributing to the perception of visual contrasts. Typical levels of illumination and luminance of a 20% reflectance surface are shown in Table 4.4 [198, 429, p. 617].

The photometric units that we introduce in this chapter are based on the SI base unit of luminous intensity, the candela (cd), as defined by the International System of Units (SI), and other derived units as used in the CIE vocabulary. Over the years, many other units have been used. They have not been accepted as international standards and should not be used in the future. For the purpose of converting the old units into the standard units, the conversion factors in Table 4.5 can be consulted [714, 942].

4.4 Photometry in imaging applications

In designing cameras, it is often necessary to specify several photometric parameters related to camera performance characteristics. These parameters are mostly groupings of some fundamental variables to provide good, but not precise, quantitative estimates of exposure, lighting, etc. They are so commonly used in photography and imaging in general that some knowledge of them will be useful to help us understand products and literature related to color imaging. We introduce some of them in this section.

4.4.1 Exposure value (EV)

A camera can control its film/sensor exposure by changing either its aperture size or its shutter speed. A given exposure can usually be achieved by different combinations of these two variables. For example, we can increase the size of the aperture by a factor of 2 and reduce the exposure time by a factor of 2, and the resulting exposure will remain the same. Of course, this is true only when focal length is not changed. In fact, to a fairly good approximation, it is the ratio of focal length f to aperture diameter D, i.e., $F = f/D$, that determines the exposure. This ratio F is called the f-number of the camera (or the lens). It is written in various forms, e.g., $f/4$, $f4$, $F/4$, etc. The exposure setting of a camera can thus be expressed as a function of the f-number and the shutter speed (exposure time). Therefore, a measure of exposure called the exposure value (EV) is often used in camera exposure control.

The exposure value (EV) is defined as:

$$EV = \log_2 \frac{F^2}{\Delta t},\qquad(4.3)$$

where F is the f-number (relative aperture) of the lens and Δt is the exposure time. For distant objects on the optical axis of a camera, the image illuminance E' is approximately related to the scene luminance L by the following equation:

$$E' = \frac{\pi L}{4F^2}.\qquad(4.4)$$

Therefore, the exposure $H = E'\Delta t$ [lx s] is related to the exposure value by:

$$H = E'\Delta t = \frac{\pi L \Delta t}{4F^2}\qquad(4.5)$$

$$\log_2 H = \log_2\left(\frac{\pi}{4}\right) + \log_2 L - EV = \log_2 L - EV - 0.3485\qquad(4.6)$$

$$EV = \log_2 L - (\log_2 H + 0.3485).\qquad(4.7)$$

The last equation shows that to obtain a certain exposure H on the film or CCD sensor, the exposure value is proportional to the base 2 logarithm of the scene luminance. Let us take $H = 0.008$ [lx s], which is the exposure required for an ISO 100 speed black-and-white film to develop to a density of 0.1 above the minimum density of the film. Then, $EV = \log_2 L + 6.6173$. The tables in the previous section show the exposure value for the various lighting conditions.

4.4.2 Guide number

Different flashbulbs produce different light outputs. In order to help the users to set the correct aperture, manufacturers often provide a guide number for their flashbulbs. For a given film/sensor speed, the guide number is defined as the product of the f-number and the subject distance. The product makes sense only if we assume that the camera exposure is inversely proportional to the square of the f-number and the light reaching the subject is also inversely proportional to the square of the subject distance. The following derivation requires some knowledge of the imaging photometry to be covered later, but it will give us an idea of how the concepts of photometry can be used for this practical problem. As we mentioned in the above, the image illuminance E_i of a camera is related to the scene luminance L by the following simplified relation:

$$E_i = \frac{\pi L}{4F^2},\qquad(4.8)$$

where F is the f-number of the camera. The ISO speed, S, of a film is related to the exposure H_m required to develop the film to a certain density by $S = k/H_m$, where the constant k depends on the type of film of interest. The flash light is assumed to be a point source with an intensity I. At a distance r, the illuminance of an object surface can be calculated as $E_r = I/r^2$. Assuming that the surface is a Lambertian reflector with a reflectance of ρ, we can calculate the luminance L of the surface as seen by the camera from the relation $M = \rho E_r = \pi L$, where M is the luminant exitance of the surface. Therefore,

$$L = \frac{\rho I}{\pi r^2}.\qquad(4.9)$$

The image exposure H_m is related to the image illuminance E_i by $H_m = E_i \Delta t$, where Δt is the exposure time. Therefore,

$$S = \frac{k}{H_m} = \frac{k}{E_i \Delta t} = \frac{4kF^2}{\pi L \Delta t} = \frac{4kF^2 r^2}{\rho I \Delta t}$$

and the guide number, GN, is given by:

$$GN = Fr = \frac{1}{\sqrt{4k}}\sqrt{S\rho I \Delta t}.\qquad(4.10)$$

If the film is a black-and-white film, then according to the ISO standard [920, Section 2.11] $k = 0.8$. The H_m in the speed definition corresponds to a density of 0.1 above the film base density and therefore it is from a very dark object. Let us assume that $\rho = 0.018$, then we have $GN = 0.075\sqrt{SI\Delta t}$.

For a given photographic situation that requires the use of a strobe, the lens aperture (f-number) can be found by dividing the given guide number of the flashbulb by the subject distance. This is based on the assumption that the duration of the flash light is shorter than the exposure time during which the shutter is open. The definition of the guide number does not consider the effect of the ambient lighting, nor mutual reflection among ambient surfaces. Therefore, it is at best an approximate guide. If the flash is used in a small room with light walls, the amount of reflected light from the walls significantly increases the exposure on the film/sensor. The aperture should be properly stopped down to avoid overexposing the film/sensor. It should also be noted that guide number has the unit of length, which can be either in feet or meters, and the subject distance should be measured in the same unit.

How much exposure is appropriate for a film/sensor is determined by how sensitive the film/sensor is with respect to the flash light. Therefore, the guide number is specified for a particular type of film/sensor and its ISO speed. The dependence of the guide number of a flash unit on the film/sensor type is usually assumed to be small, i.e., the standard source used in ISO speed determination should not be too different from the spectrum of the flash light.

4.4.3 Additive system of photographic exposure (APEX)

A system of expressing camera exposures can be summarized in the equation:

$$AV + TV = BV + SV = EV, \tag{4.11}$$

where $AV = \log_2 F^2$ (F is the aperture or f-number of the lens), $TV = \log_2(1/\Delta t)$ (Δt is the exposure time in seconds), $BV = \log_2(B/6)$ (B is the lighting illuminance in footcandles, where 1 footcandle = 10.76 lx), $SV = \log_2 S$ (S is the exposure index of film or sensor), and EV is the exposure value. Note that $AV + TV = EV$ is basically the definition of the exposure value, EV. The other part of the system, $BV + SV = EV$ defines the quantity called the exposure index, which is proportional to the ISO film speed or digital camera speed. The proportionality constant depends on the type of film or camera speed. To see this connection, let us recall the relation derived in Section 4.4.1: $EV = \log_2(\pi/4) + \log_2 L - \log_2 H$. Furthermore, the illuminance, E_s [lx], of a Lambertian surface with reflectance ρ is related to its luminance, L, by $\rho E_s = \pi L$. Therefore, we have:

$$
\begin{aligned}
SV &= EV - BV = [\log_2(\pi/4) + \log_2 L - \log_2 H] - \log_2(B/6) \tag{4.12} \\
&= [\log_2(\pi/4) + \log_2 L - \log_2 H] - \log_2[E_s/(10.76 \times 6)] \tag{4.13} \\
&= [\log_2(\pi/4) + \log_2 L - \log_2 H] - \log_2[\pi L/(10.76 \times 6 \times \rho)] \tag{4.14} \\
&= \log_2 \frac{16.14 \times \rho}{H} = \log_2 S \tag{4.15}
\end{aligned}
$$

and the exposure index, S, can be determined by

$$S = \frac{k}{H} = \frac{16.14 \times \rho}{H}, \tag{4.16}$$

which is of the same form as the ISO speed. For example, if $\rho = 0.05$, then the exposure index $= 0.8/H$, which is the definition of the ISO speed for black-and-white film (see Section 19.2.7). For digital camera applications, S is defined as: $S = 0.32 \times REI$, where REI stands for recommended exposure index of the camera [195].

This system is called the additive system of photographic exposure (APEX). The equation is useful for finding different combinations of aperture, shutter speed, film speed, and scene illuminance for a given camera exposure. In particular, the brightness value, BV, is often used to specify the level of lighting for a given scene or for a given object in the scene.

4.5 Problems

4.1 Give the commonly used metric units for the following radiometric and photometric quantities:

(a) radiant flux, Φ_e;

(b) radiant intensity, I_e;

(c) radiance, L_e;

(d) irradiance, E_e;

(e) radiant exposure, H_e;

(f) luminous flux, Φ_v;

(g) luminous intensity, I_v;

(h) luminance, L_v;

(i) illuminance, E_v;

(j) luminous exposure, H_v.

4.2 Let d be the distance between two small disks (disk 1 and disk 2) whose radii are r_1 and r_2, respectively (see Fig. 4.3). The distance d is much larger than the sizes of the disks, i.e., $d \gg r_1$ and $d \gg r_2$. Disk 1 is a Lambertian source with a luminance of $L_1 = 1000$ cd m^{-2}. Disk 1 is tilted at an angle of 30° and disk 2 is tilted at an angle of 45°, relative to the axis connecting the centers of the two disks. Let $r_1 = 0.1$ m, $r_2 = 0.2$ m, and $d = 10$ m. What is the illuminance on disk 2 from the illumination of disk 1? (Since $d \gg r_1$ and $d \gg r_2$, any solid angle can be approximated by projected area divided by the distance squared.)

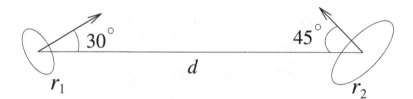

Figure 4.3.

4.3 Objects A and B look equally bright at noon, but object A looks brighter than object B at sunset. What can we say about the spectral reflectance factors of the two objects?

4.4 For the same radiant power, some lamps look brighter than others. Why?

4.5 What is the maximum intensity (cd) that can be produced by a 100 W lamp? Is this maximum efficiency lamp good for general lighting?

4.6 Let us assume that the sky is a uniform hemisphere with a luminance of 1500 cd m^{-2}. Let us further assume that the sun is at a 30° angle from the zenith and has a luminance of 1.2×10^9 cd m^{-2}. The sun is approximately a uniform disk with a diameter of 30 arcmin in visual angle as viewed on the earth's surface.

a. What is the solid angle subtended by the sun?

b. What is the illuminance on a horizontal plane due to the sunlight?

c. What is the illuminance on a horizontal plane due to the skylight?

5 Light–matter interaction

The interaction between light and matter is often very complicated. The general description of the resulting phenomena often uses empirical measurement functions, such as the bidirectional spectral reflectance distribution function (BSRDF) to be discussed in the next chapter. However, the optical properties of a homogeneous material in its simple form (such as gas or crystal) can be calculated from physical principles. Understanding the basic optical properties of material is important because it serves as a foundation for understanding more complex phenomena. In this chapter, we will first discuss the physical properties of light, matter, and their interaction for simple cases. We will then derive the optical "constants" of material that characterize the propagation of light in the material.

5.1 Light, energy, and electromagnetic waves

For color imaging applications, light can be defined as the radiant electromagnetic energy that is visible either to our visual system, or to the image capture devices of interest. (When discussing visual systems of different species, we have to vary its range accordingly.) In optics, the scope of definition of light is larger, including other wavelengths for which the behavior of optical elements (such as lenses) can be described by the same laws as used for the visible spectrum. In physical chemistry, light is sometimes used to denote electromagnetic waves of all frequencies.

The electromagnetic spectrum that is visible to our eyes is from about 360 nm to about 830 nm in the air (according to the CIE specifications), corresponding to the frequency range of 3.61×10^{14}–8.33×10^{14} Hz. This range is dependent on the intensity of the stimulus. For the wavelengths below 400 nm or above 700 nm to become easily visible, their radiant power has to be very high. At the short-wavelength end, the optic media before the retina block the ultraviolet radiation, while at the long-wavelength end, the photon energy is too low to be absorbed by the photoreceptors in the retina. The two regions neighboring visible light in the electromagnetic spectrum are the infrared and the ultraviolet. The infrared region extends roughly from 3×10^{11} Hz ($\lambda = 1$ mm) to about 4×10^{14} Hz ($\lambda = 750$ nm), while the ultraviolet region extends from about 8×10^{14} Hz ($\lambda = 375$ nm) to 3.4×10^{16} Hz ($\lambda = 8.8$ nm). Many image sensors are responsive to radiation from these two spectral regions and care must be taken to exclude them so that color reproduction will not be adversely affected. Against a completely dark background, light of various wavelengths is seen as having a distinct color. Table 5.1 roughly shows the common color names for

Table 5.1. *The spectral colors as seen in the dark*

Wavelength range (nm)	Color name
360–430	blue–purple
430–480	blue
480–490	green–blue
490–510	blue–green
510–530	green
530–570	yellow–green
570–580	yellow
580–600	orange
600–720	red
720–830	red–purple

different wavelength regions when viewed against a completely dark background for an average color-normal observer. (It should be pointed out that the spectral composition at a given spatial location does not uniquely determine the color we perceive at that location. Color perception will be discussed in detail in later chapters.) The convenient energy unit for photons is the electron volt (eV), which is $1.602\,177\,33 \times 10^{-19}$ J, and which corresponds to a wavelength of 1239.84 nm in vacuum or a frequency of $2.417\,75 \times 10^{14}$ Hz. A 2 eV photon has a wavelength of 619.92 nm in vacuum (that 620 nm corresponds to 2 eV is worth remembering). The visible photon energy, $h\nu$, therefore is approximately from 1.49 eV to 3.44 eV. Typically, the number of photons emitted by a light source is very large. For example, a hypothetical 100 W light bulb might emit 5 W of visible light, which contain 1.5×10^{19} photons per second at 600 nm. Let us assume that the light source subtends a visual angle of 1° by 1°. There will then be about 3.6×10^{14} photons per second coming on to the cornea. Even if only 1% of these photons is captured by one million cones in the fovea, each cone will receive 3.6 million photons per second!

5.2 Physical properties of matter

In terms of structural complexity, material can exist as free atoms (such as helium gas), free molecules (such as hydrogen gas), atom clusters (a few hundreds of atoms), molecule clusters, atomic crystals, ionic crystals, molecule crystals, polycrystals, glasses, molecular liquid crystals, atomic or molecular liquids, and other forms. Before we discuss physical properties, it is useful to have a good feeling for the relative scale of things that we will talk about. Table 5.2 gives the order of magnitude of the size of various things.

Gas, liquid, and solid are commonly referred to as the three states of pure elements and compounds. Gases and liquids are collectively called fluids, while liquids and solids are referred to as condensed matter. A material exists in one or more of these states at a given temperature, pressure, and volume.

In gas, the atoms or molecules collide with each other about 10^9–10^{10} times per second. At room temperature and atmospheric pressure, the mean free path length between

Table 5.2. *Relative sizes of object dimensions*

Object	Size	Object	Size
hydrogen atom (radius)	0.529 Å	H–H bond length	0.74 Å
C=C bond length	1.33 Å	C–C bond length	1.54 Å
Si–Si bond length	2.35 Å	Ge–Ge bond length	2.45 Å
NaCl (Na–Na distance)	5.64 Å	DNA threads (diameter)	~2 nm
cell membrane (thickness)	~5 nm	medium-sized protein	~10 nm
bacteria cell wall (thickness)	10–80 nm	virus	~100 nm
light wavelength	360–830 nm	red blood cell (diameter)	~5 μm
medium-sized human body cell	~10 μm	crystal grain (metal)	~0.01–1.0 mm

collisions is about 50–100 nm (corresponding to about 100–1000 times the size of the atom or molecule). Therefore, each particle can be considered as independent of the others. The optical properties of a gas can thus be derived from that of the individual atoms or molecules that are present in the gas.

Both liquid and solid are forms of condensed matter. The density of a liquid is usually only about 5% less than that of the solid (water is one of the exceptions). When the atoms and molecules in a solid are arranged in a very orderly periodic lattice structure, the solid is called a crystal. When they are arranged without a regular, periodic structure, the solid is called a glass. (Note that here glass refers to a state of matter. Window glass is one of the best-known materials in this state. Also, the common use of the name crystal glass to denote certain clear glasses is not compatible with the terms we define here.) Typically a 1 cm^3 crystal contains about 10^{23} atoms. The distance between atoms or molecules is on the order of the size of the atom or molecule. For example, the sodium atom has a radius of 1.9 Å (at the valence electron shell) and the distance between the centers of nearest neighbors in a sodium crystal is about 3.7 Å (neighbors actually overlap slightly!). Therefore, the optical properties of solids or liquids cannot be derived from the individual atoms or molecules alone – the interactions between all of them have to be considered.

In the simplest case of a crystal, atoms or molecules are well ordered in a lattice. According to the lattice geometry, there are 14 possible lattices (the Bravais lattices) and they are grouped into seven crystal systems according to characteristic symmetry elements: triclinic, monoclinic, orthorhombic, tetragonal, cubic, trigonal, and hexagonal. For example, the cubic system consists of the simple cubic lattice, the body-centered cubic (bcc) lattice, and the face-centered cubic (fcc) lattice. Many metal crystals are bcc (such as Fe(α), Li, Na, and K) or fcc (such as Au, Al, Ag, Fe(γ) and Pb). If there is more than one atom at each lattice site, then considering all possible symmetries and the translational invariance of a lattice, the total number of the so-called space groups is only 230. This is a surprisingly small number, showing that the requirement to produce the spatially repeating patterns of a lattice is a very severe constraint. The major consequence of the lattice structure is that the optical properties of most crystals are anisotropic [124, Chapter 14, 1048]. An exception is the cubic system – its lattice symmetry also makes it optically isotropic [381, pp. 14–15]. The natural vibrational frequency in crystals is at around 10^{12} Hz, i.e., in the infrared region.

Most natural crystals are rather small in size (less than a few millimeters). A large piece of metal consists of many small crystals bound together. Each of the tiny crystals is called a grain, and the piece of metal is called a polycrystal. The metal crystal grains are usually very small. This is why metals are not seen to have the characteristic shapes exhibited by other crystalline materials, such as calcite.

As the temperature or pressure increases, the thermal vibrations reach a point at which the crystal structure of the solid begins to break down. The empty spaces between atoms or molecules may be large enough for an atom or molecule to move around without too much force. The atoms or molecules lose their ordered structure and the substance becomes liquid and optically isotropic. There are substances that can exist in a state that seems to be between crystal and liquid. These are called liquid crystals; they are anisotropic liquids, in the sense that molecules can move around, but they more or less maintain their orientations relative to their neighbors (these molecules are rod-like or disk-like in shape [209]).

The majority of the everyday materials around us are more complicated than pure elements and compounds. For example, stones, bricks, paints, paper, leaves, wood, and soils are mixtures of many types of elements and compounds. Many of them are also mixtures of materials in different phases. For example, an aerosol is liquid or solid dispersed in gas, and shaving cream is gas dispersed in liquid. There are two consequences of this structural and compositional complexity. (1) Calculation of the optical properties of everyday objects, such as a ceramic vase, from first principles is impractical if not impossible. It is necessary to measure the properties directly or indirectly. (2) Light reflected from most everyday objects is not as sensitive to viewing angle as that reflected from a pure and highly ordered crystalline solid. Structural and compositional randomness tend to make the optical properties more isotropic, because there is no orderly interference or diffraction from all the atoms and molecules. Of course, everyday objects do not exactly reflect or transmit light isotropically, i.e., independently of the incident and viewing angles. Nevertheless, this randomization towards optical isotropy helps our eyes and brains solve the visual perception problem. Although the reflected radiance from an object surface does not stay constant as we move around and look at it from slightly different angles, it does not change drastically either. Otherwise, it would be very difficult to maintain a constant appearance of that object in our visual perception.

5.3 Light and matter

Electromagnetic radiation, of which visible light is one form, comes from the nonuniform motion of charged particles. Conversely, electromagnetic radiation can change the motion of charged particles. The interaction between light and matter is that between the electromagnetic field associated with light and the charged particles associated with matter. In the classical model, an electromagnetic wave passing through a medium introduces forced oscillations of the charged particles in the array of atoms or molecules. From quantum mechanics, electrons can absorb quanta of light energy and be excited to a higher energy state. The energy required for state transitions for the outer electrons of an atom is typically from 1 to 10 eV, corresponding to the visible and ultraviolet ranges. Infrared radiation is absorbed in the energy transitions between different states of molecular vibrations and rotations. The microwave region, which extends roughly from 10^9 Hz to 3×10^{11} Hz, is also effective in causing state transitions in the vibrations and rotations of polar molecules, such as water. The interaction between light and matter can be quite complicated. For example, some nonlinear optical materials, such as quartz, can change the frequency of the incident light. If we shine a high-energy beam from an infrared laser at quartz, we can see a green light beam coming out of the crystal [131]. This is called frequency-doubling and is used in laser optics quite often. However, nonlinear optical interaction is rare or weak in most color applications and we will not treat it here.

5.3.1 Optical properties of matter

For most (dielectric or conducting) materials, the complex index of refraction, $\hat{n}(v) = n(v) + i\kappa(v)$, where v is the frequency, is most useful for describing the effects of a medium on the propagation of light through it. Its real part, n, is the index of refraction which, by tradition, is defined as the ratio of the phase velocity of light in vacuum (free space) to that in the medium. However, this definition can often cause considerable difficulty in understanding mathematical results (e.g., n can be zero or negative in some cases [859, 1040]). It is better to think about n as a response function of the material to the incident electromagnetic wave [121, p. 6.14]. The imaginary part, κ, is related to the absorption coefficient of the medium. For certain materials, the complex index of refraction is also a function of light polarization (e.g., left circular or right circular) and its direction of propagation. In order to understand these complicated interactions, we have to study what happens when an electromagnetic wave travels through a material.

The interaction of an electromagnetic field with a medium is usually described by macroscopic characteristics that are readily measurable, directly or indirectly. Among these are the electric polarization (dielectric constant, permittivity), the magnetization (permeability), and the electric conductivity. Materials are often classified as insulators (dielectric), semiconductors, and conductors, based of their electric properties. They are also classified as ferromagnetic, paramagnetic, or diamagnetic, based on their magnetic properties. The general theory that relates the material structures to their electromagnetic properties is very interesting, but will not be covered here. We concentrate only on the optical properties of common materials.

For conducting materials, such as metals, charges (mainly electrons) are free to move under the influence of the incident electric field. As a result, the electromagnetic field is very strongly and quickly attenuated in the conductor (i.e., the electric field is neutralized by the charge motion and redistribution). Most of the energy of the light is reflected back and conductors are very good reflectors. The depth that an electromagnetic wave can propagate into a conductor is called the skin depth and this decreases with increasing frequency (at high frequencies, the skin depth can be less than a wavelength).

For nonconducting materials, there are no free charges. The electrons are bound to the nuclei. An electric field will pull apart the negative charge (the electrons) and the positive charge (the nucleus) until their mutual attractive force balances out the external field. If the field is strong enough, the charges can be separated and the atom (or the molecule) is ionized. Otherwise, the atom (or the molecule) is said to be polarized. Two electric charges, q and $-q$, separated by a distance d is called an electric dipole. It is represented by a vector whose direction is from the negative charge to the positive charge, and whose magnitude $p = qd$, is called the dipole moment. An electromagnetic wave traveling through matter induces dipole moments in the material. In a linear homogeneous material, when the electric field is not too strong, the induced dipole moment per unit volume, $\mathbf{P}$, is proportional to the electric field, $\mathbf{E}$:

$$\mathbf{P} = \epsilon_0 \chi_e(\nu)\mathbf{E}, \tag{5.1}$$

where $\epsilon_0 = 8.8542 \times 10^{-12}\,\mathrm{m^{-3}\,kg^{-1}s^{-4}A^2}$ is the permittivity of free space and $\chi_e(\nu)$ is the electric susceptibility of the material. For many materials, the induced polarization $\mathbf{P}$ is not even in the same direction as the electric field $\mathbf{E}$, and the relation has to be expressed as a 3×3 matrix. Values of χ_e can be quite large for materials that consist of polar molecules, such as water ($\chi_e = 79.4$ at zero frequency, but drops to about 0.78 at optical frequencies, because its permanent dipole moments cannot oscillate that fast). Glass has a $\chi_e(0)$ between 3 and 7, while polyethylene has a $\chi_e(0)$ of 1.26. The permittivity ϵ of a material is $\epsilon = \epsilon_0(1 + \chi_e)$. For most dielectric materials, the permittivity is often larger than that of free space, and, as we will see later, this is the major parameter that makes the speed of light much slower in the dielectric material than in free space. It should be pointed out that permittivity need not be a real number, meaning that an electromagnetic wave is attenuated and/or delayed in phase when it propagates through the material.

The interaction of a magnetic field with matter is much weaker than that of an electric field, except for certain ferromagnetic materials, such as iron, nickel, and cobalt, that retain a substantial magnetization indefinitely after the external field is removed. In the presence of an external magnetic field, materials become magnetized. There are two types of magnetization: paramagnetization (the magnetization is in the same direction as the external field) and diamagnetization (the magnetization is in the opposite direction). Both phenomena require quantum mechanical explanations. One can define magnetization in a similar way to electric polarization. Thus, a magnetic dipole moment $\mathbf{m}$ (a vector) can be defined as the contour integral of the current along a curved loop. For a planar loop, the definition becomes the product of the current I and the area of the loop, a, i.e., $m = Ia$, with the vector direction normal to the area and the current running in the counterclockwise direction when we look towards the vector. In a linear homogeneous material, when the magnetic field is not too strong, the induced magnetic dipole moment per unit volume, $\mathbf{M}$, is proportional to the magnetic field, $\mathbf{H}$:

$$\mathbf{M} = \chi_m(\nu)\mathbf{H}, \tag{5.2}$$

where $\chi_m(\nu)$ is called the magnetic susceptibility of the material and is usually a function of the frequency of the magnetic field. The permeability μ of a material is $\mu = \mu_0(1 + \chi_m)$, where $\mu_0 = 1.2566 \times 10^{-6}\,\mathrm{m\,kg\,s^{-2}A^{-2}}$ is the permeability of free space. For most materials, typical values of χ_m are 10^{-5}, and we can assume that $\mu \approx \mu_0$.

5.3.2 Light wave propagation in media

Now, let us consider how an electromagnetic wave propagates in a material. First, we will restrict our discussion to temporal harmonic (sinusoidal) waves because all the time derivatives can be done very simply by representing a sinusoidal wave as a complex function, with the understanding that the real part of the complex function has to be used to calculate what is physically observable. Fourier transform theory allows us to decompose most finite energy signals into sums or integrals of harmonic functions. Therefore, in principle, if we understand how a sinusoidal wave of any given frequency propagates in a material, we should be able to find out how any wave of arbitrary waveform will propagate through the material.

The representation of a sinusoidal wave by a complex function is not unique and a chosen convention has to be used consistently throughout the analysis [408]. Here we choose to represent a plane wave traveling to the direction of the vector $\mathbf{k}$ as

$$\mathbf{E}(\mathbf{r}, t, \omega) = \mathbf{E}_0 e^{i(\mathbf{k} \cdot \mathbf{r} - \omega t)}, \tag{5.3}$$

where $\mathbf{E}_0$ is a constant complex vector independent of time, t, and the position vector, $\mathbf{r}$, $\omega = 2\pi \nu$ is the angular frequency, and $\mathbf{k}$ is the wave vector.

From the Maxwell equations,

$$\nabla \cdot \mathbf{D} = \rho, \tag{5.4}$$

$$\nabla \cdot \mathbf{B} = 0, \tag{5.5}$$

$$\nabla \times \mathbf{E} = -\frac{\partial \mathbf{B}}{\partial t}, \tag{5.6}$$

$$\nabla \times \mathbf{H} = \mathbf{J} + \frac{\partial \mathbf{D}}{\partial t}, \tag{5.7}$$

where $\mathbf{E}$ is the electric field vector, $\mathbf{B}$ is the magnetic induction vector, $\mathbf{H}$ is the magnetic field vector, $\mathbf{D}$ is the electric displacement vector, $\mathbf{J}$ is the current density vector due to the "free charge", and ρ is the density of the "free charge". The charged particles (mostly electrons and holes) that are free to move around in the material are called the free charges, in contrast with the bound charges (such as valence electrons that are bound to atoms or molecules). The effects due to the bound charges are accounted for by the polarization vector and the magnetization vector. However, this distinction between free charges and bound charges becomes quite arbitrary when the frequency of the external fields is very high, as in optical radiation. In a high-frequency oscillating field the free charges do not move very far, and the bound charges also oscillate with the field. When the free charges do not move further than the bound charges in a given oscillating cycle, the distinction between them is difficult to make. Therefore, the definitions of the permittivity $\epsilon(\nu)$ and the conductivity $\sigma(\nu)$ of a material at optical frequencies tend to become a matter of convention [38, pp. 776–9]. In general, the convention is to lump the response of all charged particles into the permittivity $\epsilon(\nu)$. This will be discussed further shortly.

For a linear, homogeneous, isotropic material, the electric displacement vector and the magnetic field vector are related to the electric field vector and the magnetic induction vector by

$$\mathbf{D} = \epsilon_0 \mathbf{E} + \mathbf{P}, \tag{5.8}$$

$$\mathbf{H} = \frac{1}{\mu_0} \mathbf{B} - \mathbf{M}, \tag{5.9}$$

where $\mathbf{P}$ is the electric polarization vector and $\mathbf{M}$ is the magnetization vector. These quantities are further related by

$$\mathbf{J} = \sigma \mathbf{E}, \tag{5.10}$$

$$\mathbf{P} = \epsilon_0 \chi_e \mathbf{E}, \tag{5.11}$$

$$\mathbf{D} = \epsilon_0 \mathbf{E} + \mathbf{P} = \epsilon_0 (1 + \chi_e) \mathbf{E} = \epsilon \mathbf{E}, \tag{5.12}$$

$$\mathbf{B} = \mu_0 (\mathbf{H} + \mathbf{M}) = \mu_0 (1 + \chi_m) \mathbf{H} = \mu \mathbf{H}. \tag{5.13}$$

Substituting Eqs. (5.10), (5.12), and (5.13) into Eqs. (5.4)–(5.7), we have

$$\nabla \cdot \mathbf{E} = \frac{\rho}{\epsilon}, \tag{5.14}$$

$$\nabla \cdot \mathbf{H} = 0, \tag{5.15}$$

$$\nabla \times \mathbf{E} = -\mu \frac{\partial \mathbf{H}}{\partial t}, \tag{5.16}$$

$$\nabla \times \mathbf{H} = \sigma \mathbf{E} + \epsilon \frac{\partial \mathbf{E}}{\partial t}. \tag{5.17}$$

Almost all the materials we encounter every day are electrically neutral, i.e., there is no (or negligible) net charge on them, and we have $\rho = 0$. For typical conductors in the presence of an external field, any electric charge density will decay exponentially with a time constant on the order of 10^{-18} s [124, p. 612]. From Eqs. (5.16), (5.17), and the vector identity $\nabla \times (\nabla \times \mathbf{E}) = \nabla(\nabla \cdot \mathbf{E}) - \nabla^2 \mathbf{E}$,

$$\nabla^2 \mathbf{E} = \mu \sigma \frac{\partial \mathbf{E}}{\partial t} + \mu \epsilon \frac{\partial^2 \mathbf{E}}{\partial t^2}. \tag{5.18}$$

Substituting Eq. (5.3) into Eq. (5.18), we have:

$$\mathbf{k} \cdot \mathbf{k} = \omega^2 \mu \epsilon + i \omega \mu \sigma = \omega^2 \mu \left(\epsilon + i \frac{\sigma}{\omega} \right) = \omega^2 \mu \hat{\epsilon}, \tag{5.19}$$

where $\hat{\epsilon} = \epsilon + i(\sigma/\omega)$ is called the complex permittivity. (At optical frequencies, the definition of ϵ and σ is not unique, as will be discussed later. We will relate the complex permittivity to the complex index of refraction.) Therefore, the wave vector $\mathbf{k}$ is also a complex vector. We now express the wave vector as:

$$\mathbf{k} = \mathbf{k}_1 + i \mathbf{k}_2 \tag{5.20}$$

and Eq. (5.3) becomes:

$$\mathbf{E}(\mathbf{r}, t, \omega) = \underbrace{\mathbf{E}_0 e^{-\mathbf{k}_2 \cdot \mathbf{r}}}_{\text{amplitude}} \overbrace{e^{i(\mathbf{k}_1 \cdot \mathbf{r} - \omega t)}}^{\text{phase}}. \tag{5.21}$$

Substituting Eq. (5.20) into Eq. (5.19), we can solve for the magnitudes of $\mathbf{k}_1$ and $\mathbf{k}_2$ in terms of the material optical constants (which are functions of frequency). The directions of $\mathbf{k}_1$ and $\mathbf{k}_2$ have to be solved from boundary conditions. It should be noted that $\mathbf{k}_1$ and $\mathbf{k}_2$ are not necessarily pointing in the same direction. The vector $\mathbf{k}_1$ is perpendicular to the surface of constant phase, while the vector $\mathbf{k}_2$ is perpendicular to the surface of constant amplitude. When $\mathbf{k}_1$ and $\mathbf{k}_2$ are in the same direction (or when $k_2 = 0$), the wave is said to be homogeneous. Otherwise, it is said to be inhomogeneous. For example, a plane wave entering an absorbing material (such as a metal) at an oblique angle will be attenuated according to the distance perpendicular to the interface (i.e., $\mathbf{k}_2$ is normal to the interface), while its wave vector $\mathbf{k}_1$ is at an oblique angle with the interface. Therefore, the wave is inhomogeneous. On the other hand, a wave propagating in a vacuum is homogeneous.

The surface of constant phase ($\mathbf{k}_1 \cdot \mathbf{r} - \omega t =$ constant) travels at a velocity v:

$$v = \frac{dr}{dt} = \frac{\omega}{k_1}. \tag{5.22}$$

By definition, the index of refraction, n, of a medium is the ratio of the phase velocity of light in vacuum (free space) to that in the medium:

$$n = \frac{c}{v} = \left(\frac{c}{\omega}\right) k_1. \tag{5.23}$$

The complex wave vector $\mathbf{k} = \mathbf{k}_1 + i\mathbf{k}_2$ is used to define the complex index of refraction $\hat{n}$:

$$\hat{n} = \left(\frac{c}{\omega}\right) k = \left(\frac{c}{\omega}\right) k_1 + i \left(\frac{c}{\omega}\right) k_2 = n + i\kappa. \tag{5.24}$$

The optical properties of a material are usually characterized by the complex index of refraction, because it can be derived from quantities that are directly measurable by experiments [120, p. 41]. There are published tables and books of n and κ for many different materials [739, 740].

The amplitude of the wave is attenuated in an absorbing material. The rate of attenuation α (the absorption coefficient) is defined as:

$$\alpha = -\frac{1}{I} \frac{dI}{dr}, \tag{5.25}$$

where I is the radiance of the light beam and is proportional to the square of the amplitude of the electric field. Therefore,

$$\alpha = 2k_2 = \frac{2\omega\kappa}{c}. \tag{5.26}$$

In a nonconducting material for which $\sigma = 0$, Eq. (5.19) gives us: $k_1 = \omega\sqrt{\mu\epsilon}$ and $k_2 = 0$. Therefore, from Eq. (5.22), we have

$$v = \frac{1}{\sqrt{\epsilon\mu}}, \tag{5.27}$$

where ϵ and μ are the permittivity and the permeability of the material. Thus, the speed of light in vacuum is $c = 1/\sqrt{\epsilon_0\mu_0}$. These two are the special cases that we are most familiar with. In general, the expression for phase velocity (Eq. (5.22)) is more complicated.

From Eqs. (5.24) and (5.19), we can derive expressions for ϵ and σ in terms of n and κ:

$$\epsilon = \frac{\mu_0 \epsilon_0}{\mu} (n^2 - \kappa^2), \tag{5.28}$$

$$\sigma = \left(\frac{\omega \mu_0 \epsilon_0}{\mu} \right) (2n\kappa). \tag{5.29}$$

As we discussed before, ϵ accounts for the effect due to the bound charges and σ for that of the free charges. At optical frequencies, the distinction between the two effects becomes blurred. One can continue to think of the electrons in the conduction band as the free charges and the electrons in the valence band as the bound charges. In terms of external measurable optical properties, they are not easy (if it is possible at all) to distinguish and it is customary to lump the two together and define a complex permittivity $\hat{\epsilon}$ to account for their combined effect on the propagation of a light wave:

$$\hat{\epsilon} = \hat{n}^2 \epsilon_0 \mu_0 / \mu = \epsilon_1 + i\epsilon_2. \tag{5.30}$$

The real part ϵ_1 and the imaginary part ϵ_2 of $\hat{\epsilon}$ can be expressed in terms of n and κ:

$$\epsilon_1 = \frac{\mu_0 \epsilon_0}{\mu} (n^2 - \kappa^2), \tag{5.31}$$

$$\epsilon_2 = \left(\frac{\mu_0 \epsilon_0}{\mu} \right) (2n\kappa). \tag{5.32}$$

This pair of equations will be important when we discuss optical dispersion in the next section. The dispersion relation will be derived for $\hat{\epsilon}$ and then be related back to the measurable quantities n and κ through these two equations.

5.3.3   Optical dispersion in matter

The majority of light sources relevant to color imaging are polychromatic. The light they radiate is composed of electromagnetic waves (or photons) of many frequencies (continuous or discrete). Since the optical properties of a material are functions of optical frequency, it is very important for us to understand this frequency-dependent behavior. A fundamental explanation of optical dispersion will ultimately require the use of the theory of quantum mechanics. Fortunately, classical models based on electromagnetic theory are much easier to understand and they also give us an adequate description of the phenomena, with the correct forms of formulas (using empirical parameters). The physical meanings of these parameters are often quite involved and their details have to be explained by quantum mechanics theory. In this section, we will base our discussions on Drude–Lorentz theory.

An electromagnetic wave propagating in a material can be modified in a complicated way. The interaction between the charged particles in the material depends on the frequency, the wave polarization, and the direction of the propagation. The frequency dependence of the interaction is called the dispersion relation. The best-known example is a beam of "white" light being dispersed by a glass prism into a spectrum of light seen as "rainbow" colors: the high frequencies (the "blue" light) are refracted (or bent) more than low frequencies (the "red" light). The prism absorbs very little of the incident light and, for most practical purposes, can be considered as nonabsorbing, transparent material. Its optical properties can be characterized by the index of refraction, n. However, the nonabsorbing, transparent material is an idealization and most materials absorb some of the visible light and are not completely transparent. To characterize the optical properties of an absorbing medium, we have introduced in the last section the concept of the complex index of refraction, $\hat{n}$:

$$\hat{n}(\nu) = n(\nu) + i\kappa(\nu), \tag{5.33}$$

in which both the real part, $n(\nu)$, and the imaginary part, $\kappa(\nu)$, are functions of optical frequency ν. For a typical glass, the imaginary part $\kappa(\nu)$ is quite small for most visible frequencies, and the real part, $n(\nu)$, the index of refraction, is greater than 1. In this case, n can be comfortably related to our familiar concept, the ratio of the phase velocity of light in vacuum to that in the medium. As it turns out, for some materials, n can be less than 1 (meaning that the speed of light in the medium is greater than that in vacuum), or can even be negative. We may feel quite uncomfortable about the idea that the phase velocity of light in the medium is greater than c, the speed of light in vacuum, since this seemingly contradicts the fundamental assumption of the theory of relativity. However, it can be proved that this is not so [120, p. 236]. It can be shown that as long as $n(\nu)$ and $\kappa(\nu)$ satisfy the following Kramers–Kronig relations, signals cannot be propagated with a speed greater than c. The Kramers–Kronig relations are derived from the causality principle:

$$n(\omega) - 1 = \frac{2}{\pi} \int_0^\infty \frac{\omega' \kappa(\omega')}{\omega'^2 - \omega^2} \, d\omega', \tag{5.34}$$

$$\kappa(\omega) = \frac{-2\omega}{\pi} \int_0^\infty \frac{n(\omega')}{\omega'^2 - \omega^2} \, d\omega', \tag{5.35}$$

where $\omega = 2\pi\nu$ and the integral is understood to be the Cauchy principal value [402, pp. 592–6], meaning that the integral is taken excluding a small circle of ω' around ω with the radius of the circle approaching zero. The Kramers–Kronig relations are valid for all causal systems (and for that matter, all the optical phenomena we are interested in) and therefore are frequently used to compute $n(\nu)$ from $\kappa(\nu)$, or vice versa.

The classical Drude–Lorentz model of optical dispersion assumes that an electron moves under the influence of the electromagnetic field of the incident light wave. The motion also experiences some resistive or frictional energy loss. The resulting equation for the forced motion can be expressed as

$$m\frac{d^2 r}{dt^2} + m\Gamma\frac{dr}{dt} + m\omega_0^2 r = q E_1 e^{-i\omega t}, \tag{5.36}$$

where r, m, and q are the position, the mass, and the electric charge of the electron, E_1 is the local electric field, Γ represents a damping mechanism, and the term $m\omega_0^2 r$ represents a spring-like Hooke's law restoring force. Now let us solve the equation for a steady state solution. The solution r is

$$r = \frac{q E_1/m}{(\omega_0^2 - \omega^2) - i\Gamma\omega}. \tag{5.37}$$

As we discussed before, the forced motion of a charged particle induces an oscillating electric dipole moment, p:

$$p = qr = \frac{q^2 E_1/m}{(\omega_0^2 - \omega^2) - i\Gamma\omega} = \hat{\alpha} E_1, \tag{5.38}$$

where $\hat{\alpha}$ is called the complex polarizability:

$$\hat{\alpha} = \frac{q^2/m}{(\omega_0^2 - \omega^2) - i\Gamma\omega}. \tag{5.39}$$

The average induced dipole moment per unit volume, P, is proportional to the number of electrons, N, in the unit volume, and therefore, $P = N\langle p \rangle = N\hat{\alpha}\langle E_1 \rangle$. In general, among the N electrons, there are various fractions f_j of them in different states, corresponding to different resonant frequencies ω_j and damping factors Γ_j. The general expression for $\hat{\alpha}$ is the sum of all these components:

$$\hat{\alpha} = \frac{q^2}{m} \sum_j \frac{f_j}{(\omega_j^2 - \omega^2) - i\Gamma_j\omega}. \tag{5.40}$$

We now have to relate the averaged local electric field back to the externally applied macroscopic electric field E. The resulting dispersion function will be different for gas, solid, and liquid, with metal as a special case.

Dispersion in gases

In a gas, atoms or molecules are so far apart that the local field is essentially the same as the macroscopic electric field. Therefore, we have

$$P = N\hat{\alpha}E \equiv \epsilon_0 \chi_e E \tag{5.41}$$

and

$$\hat{\epsilon} = \epsilon_0(1 + \chi_e) = \epsilon_0 \left(1 + \frac{N\hat{\alpha}}{\epsilon_0}\right) = \epsilon_0 \left[1 + \frac{Nq^2}{\epsilon_0 m} \sum_j \frac{f_j}{(\omega_j^2 - \omega^2) - i\Gamma_j\omega}\right]. \tag{5.42}$$

Recall that the complex index of refraction, $\hat{n} = n + i\kappa$, is related to the complex permittivity by $\hat{\epsilon} = \hat{n}^2 \epsilon_0 \mu_0 / \mu$. Therefore,

$$\hat{n}^2 = \frac{\mu}{\mu_0} \left[1 + \frac{Nq^2}{\epsilon_0 m} \sum_j \frac{f_j}{(\omega_j^2 - \omega^2) - i\Gamma_j\omega}\right]. \tag{5.43}$$

Dispersion in condensed matter without free electrons

In condensed matter (solids or liquids) without free electrons, the local electric field is not the same as the macroscopic electric field (i.e., the externally applied field) because the dipole moments of the surrounding atoms also contribute to the local field. For an isotropic material, these two fields are related by a term called the Lorentz local field correction [512, pp. 109–11]:

$$E_1 = E + \frac{P}{3\epsilon_0}. \tag{5.44}$$

Therefore we arrive at the following equation:

$$P = N\hat{\alpha}\langle E_1 \rangle = N\hat{\alpha}\left(E + \frac{P}{3\epsilon_0}\right), \tag{5.45}$$

which can be rearranged to become

$$P = \left(\frac{N\hat{\alpha}}{1 - N\hat{\alpha}/3\epsilon_0}\right)E \equiv \epsilon_0 \chi_e E. \tag{5.46}$$

We can now express the complex permitivity as:

$$\hat{\epsilon} = \epsilon_0(1 + \chi_e) = \epsilon_0 \left(\frac{1 + 2N\hat{\alpha}/3\epsilon_0}{1 - N\hat{\alpha}/3\epsilon_0}\right). \tag{5.47}$$

Therefore,

$$\frac{(\mu_0/\mu)\,\hat{n}^2 - 1}{(\mu_0/\mu)\,\hat{n}^2 + 2} = \frac{\hat{\epsilon}/\epsilon_0 - 1}{\hat{\epsilon}/\epsilon_0 + 2} = \frac{N\hat{\alpha}}{3\epsilon_0} = \frac{Nq^2}{3\epsilon_0 m} \sum_j \frac{f_j}{(\omega_j^2 - \omega^2) - i\Gamma_j \omega}. \tag{5.48}$$

For a dielectric material, in the frequency region where ω is slightly lower than one resonant frequency ω_j, but much higher than the next lower resonant frequency, the index of refraction, n, is an increasing function of frequency. For example, glasses have natural resonant frequencies (around 3×10^{15} Hz) in the ultraviolet region, and their indices of refraction are higher for blue light than for red light.

Dispersion in metals as a special case

There are both free electrons and bound electrons in metals (in the condensed state). The optical properties of metals show the effects from both types of electron. There are two unique features. (1) The free electrons do not experience a spring-like Hooke's law restoring force, and therefore have no resonant frequencies, i.e., $\omega_0 = 0$. (2) The free electrons move rapidly to effectively shield the bound electrons from electric fields caused by neighboring atoms. The local electric field is essentially the same as the externally applied field. As a result, the complex permitivity of a metal consists of a term from the conducting electron with $\omega_0 = 0$, and other terms similar to those in the complex permitivity of a gas. Therefore,

$$\hat{\epsilon} = \epsilon_0 \left[1 + \frac{N_f q^2}{\epsilon_0 m} \frac{1}{-\omega^2 - i\Gamma_f \omega} + \frac{Nq^2}{\epsilon_0 m} \sum_j \frac{f_j}{(\omega_j^2 - \omega^2) - i\Gamma_j \omega}\right] \tag{5.49}$$

and

$$\hat{n}^2 = \frac{\mu}{\mu_0} \left[1 + \frac{N_f q^2}{\epsilon_0 m} \frac{1}{-\omega^2 - i\Gamma_f \omega} + \frac{Nq^2}{\epsilon_0 m} \sum_j \frac{f_j}{(\omega_j^2 - \omega^2) - i\Gamma_j \omega}\right]. \tag{5.50}$$

If we neglect all the terms associated with the bound electrons and the effect due to friction Γ_f, we can simplify the expression for n to

$$n^2(\omega) \approx \frac{\mu}{\mu_0}\left(1 - \frac{\omega_p^2}{\omega^2}\right), \tag{5.51}$$

where $\omega_p = \sqrt{(N_f q^2)/(\epsilon_0 m)}$ is called the plasma frequency. The charge on an electron, q, is 1.602×10^{-19} C. The electron mass is 9.109×10^{-31} kg. The free electron density N_f

is about 10^{23} cm^{-3} for metals and typical values of plasma frequency for metals are in the ultraviolet region ($\omega_p > 10^{15}$ Hz). When the incident wave frequency is far above the plasma frequency, the index of refraction approaches 1 and the metal is transparent. At frequencies below ω_p, the index of refraction for a metal is a complex number and electromagnetic waves can only penetrate a fraction of the wavelength into the metal. The majority of metals reflect almost all the incident light regardless of wavelength and are therefore essentially colorless. If a metal has a particular color, it means that the bound electrons of the atoms are participating in the absorption process, in addition to the free electrons. For example, in copper, the d-bands absorption begins at $\lambda = 600$ nm (about 1.93 eV) and the metal looks reddish.

5.3.4   Quantum mechanics and optical dispersion

Although the Drude–Lorentz theory of dispersion describes experimental data surprisingly well, the meaning of its parameters remains quite vague. For example, what is the nature of the damping force (Γ_j) and what are the natural resonant frequencies (ω_j)? The theory also has two serious difficulties that eventually require quantum mechanics to resolve. (1) The mean free path length of an electron in a crystal, as calculated by the Drude–Lorentz theory, turns out to be on the order of hundreds of angstroms long. For example, the radius of a copper atom is about 1.41 Å and the mean velocity of a conduction electron is around 1.5×10^8 cm s^{-1}. The mean time between collisions at 273 K is about 2.7×10^{-14} s. It is difficult to imagine that an electron can travel through hundreds of atoms without a collision. The Drude–Lorentz theory cannot explain the dependence of conductivity on the absolute temperature either. (2) The Drude–Lorentz theory treats the conduction electrons as free particles, and cannot predict the heat capacity of crystals. Fermi–Dirac statistics, which is based on Pauli's exclusion principle, has to be used to resolve this difficulty.

In quantum mechanics, the behavior of electrons is very different from the classical model used in Drude–Lorentz theory. An electron can only have discrete energy states in atomic or molecular orbitals. The natural resonant frequencies correspond to the energy required for transitions from the lower-energy states to the higher ones. The damping force corresponds to collisions with neighboring atoms, vibrations of the crystal lattice, and some other perturbing processes, such as lattice defects. What is remarkable is that the dispersion functions derived from quantum mechanics have essentially the same functional forms as those derived from Drude–Lorentz theory.

5.4   Light propagation across material boundaries

Although QED describes the atomic, molecular, and crystal levels of light–matter interaction very well, practical applications in radiometry, photometry, colorimetry, and color imaging involve light–matter interaction on a much larger scale where the detailed spatial structures of the matter are too complicated for the quantum mechanical calculation to be feasible. Descriptions that are based on electromagnetic theory of simplified models of matter are thus widely used for light–matter interaction on this macroscopic scale. Five such descriptions that are particularly relevant to color imaging are reflection, refraction, transmission, absorption, and scattering. These processes are usually described in terms of monochromatic, time-harmonic electromagnetic plane waves, not only because the analytical solution is easier, but more importantly because: (1) a monochromatic field can be regarded as a Fourier component of an arbitrary field; and (2) in general, at a distance far from the source and on a scale such that variations in the electromagnetic field are small, the field behaves locally as a plane wave (see, e.g., [135, p. 121]). It should be emphasized that the analytic descriptions of these "laws" are true only for single-wavelength, monochromatic light, and the optical parameters of a material, such as reflectance, refraction index, and absorption coefficients, are functions of wavelength. Proper scales of material homogeneity and surface smoothness relative to the wavelength of light of interest should also be considered when interpreting the optical properties of a material.

In studying the optical scene formation processes, it should be noted that although we use different terms (such as reflection, scattering, etc.) to describe the various aspects of light–matter interaction, the reason for doing so is mostly historical. All their underlying causes are actually the same – they are all the result of the interaction of light and the charged particles (mainly the electrons) in matter. Reflection, refraction, scattering, diffraction, absorption, transmission, polarization, and interference were studied empirically long before any comprehensive theory of light was available. The distinctions between these phenomena are mostly artificial and we should not try to classify them too rigidly.

Even after the classical electromagnetic theory of light was developed, phenomenological derivation of various optical laws, such as Snell's law of refraction and Fresnel's formula for reflection, often relies on solving the Maxwell equations with surface boundary conditions, as if light is refracted or reflected only by the object surface and the rest of the matter beneath it is irrelevant. In fact, the reflected light should be treated as the interference of the secondary radiation from all the matter the surface encloses [121]. It just happens that these secondary waves cancel out so neatly that the electromagnetic field solution can be derived from the surface boundary conditions. If we were to remove most matter from under the surface, the reflection would be quite different. With the right thickness of material left, the reflected component of the light may disappear completely.

With these warnings and qualifiers, we will discuss the various aspects of light–matter interaction in traditional terms. They offer us a common language with the current literature and often a conventional list of topics to study.

5.4.1 Reflection and refraction

In this section, we will review reflection and refraction at an interface plane between two linear, isotropic, homogeneous media. We will first describe the case where both media are nonabsorbing (i.e., $\kappa = 0$), and the complex index of refraction, $\hat{n} = n$, is a real number. We will then discuss the general case when either or both media may be absorbing. In that general case, the formulas for the relations between the incident, the reflected, and the transmitted electric field still have the same forms as in the nonabsorbing case, except that physical intuition can only be gained from sorting out the magnitude and the phase of the complex numbers in the formula. The definition of the function of complex variables can

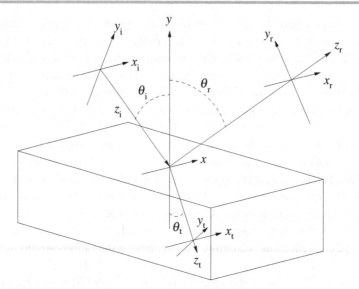

Figure 5.1. The convention for the coordinate systems for the Fresnel equations.

be found in many books on calculus or complex variables (e.g., [402, Chapter 10]). The relations describing the incident, reflected, and transmitted electromagnetic fields are called the Fresnel equations. The coordinate systems (see Fig. 5.1) we will be using are the same as the one we used in the previous chapter for describing the light polarization.

Nonabsorbing media
When a monochromatic plane wave encounters a boundary between two homogeneous media of different optical properties, part of it is reflected back into the first (incident) medium and part of it is transmitted through the second medium. If the boundary between the two media is "ideally smooth", the reflected wave vector is on the same plane (plane of incidence) as the surface normal and the incident wave vector. The angle of reflection is equal to the angle of incidence. The transmitted wave does not propagate in the same direction as the incident wave unless the wave is normal to the boundary. The change in direction is called refraction. The transmitted wave is also on the plane of incidence. The incident angle, the reflected angle, and the transmitted angle are denoted by θ_i, θ_r and θ_t. Snell's law states that

$$n_i \sin \theta_i = n_t \sin \theta_t, \tag{5.52}$$

where n_i and n_t are the indices of refraction of the incidence medium and the transmittance medium, respectively. The proportions of energy in the reflected and refracted components depend on the polarization of the plane wave, which is usually decomposed into a component parallel (∥) to the plane of incidence and a component perpendicular (⊥) to it. We will denote the parallel component of the amplitude of the electric field of the incident wave by $E_{i\parallel}$, and the perpendicular component by $E_{i\perp}$, and so on. Let the permeability of the first medium be μ_i, and that of the second medium be μ_t, then the amplitude reflection coefficients $r_\|$, $r_\perp$, and the amplitude transmission coefficients $t_\|$, $t_\perp$, are [385, pp. 94–6]:

$$r_\perp = \left(\frac{E_r}{E_i}\right)_\perp = \frac{(n_i/\mu_i)\cos\theta_i - (n_t/\mu_t)\cos\theta_t}{(n_i/\mu_i)\cos\theta_i + (n_t/\mu_t)\cos\theta_t}, \tag{5.53}$$

$$t_\perp = \left(\frac{E_t}{E_i}\right)_\perp = \frac{2(n_i/\mu_i)\cos\theta_i}{(n_i/\mu_i)\cos\theta_i + (n_t/\mu_t)\cos\theta_t}, \tag{5.54}$$

$$r_\| = \left(\frac{E_r}{E_i}\right)_\| = \frac{(n_t/\mu_t)\cos\theta_i - (n_i/\mu_i)\cos\theta_t}{(n_t/\mu_t)\cos\theta_i + (n_i/\mu_i)\cos\theta_t}, \tag{5.55}$$

$$t_\| = \left(\frac{E_t}{E_i}\right)_\| = \frac{2(n_i/\mu_i)\cos\theta_i}{(n_t/\mu_t)\cos\theta_i + (n_i/\mu_i)\cos\theta_t}. \tag{5.56}$$

These coefficients are called Fresnel reflection and transmission coefficients. At the normal incident angle, $\theta_i = 0$,

$$r_\| = -r_\perp = \frac{n_t - n_i}{n_t + n_i}, \tag{5.57}$$

$$t_\| = t_\perp = \frac{2n_i}{n_t + n_i}. \tag{5.58}$$

For a glass with $n_t = 1.5$ in air (i.e., $n_i \approx 1.0$), the amplitude reflection coefficient is 0.2. Since the radiant power is proportional to the amplitude squared, the radiant flux (power) reflection coefficient is $0.2 \times 0.2 = 0.04$.

It is interesting to note that since the perpendicular and parallel components are attenuated differently, the reflected light beam and the transmitted light beam have different polarizations from the incident light beam. We can use the Stokes vectors for these beams and derive the input–output relations between them. These relations are the Mueller matrices for the planar dielectric interface. Let S_i, S_r, and S_t be the Stokes vectors for the incident, reflected, and transmitted beams, respectively. Since the Mueller matrix will be determined on the interface plane, all observables (radiant flux density) in the Stokes vector should be projected onto the plane. Therefore,

$$S_i = \frac{n_i\cos\theta_i}{2\mu_i c}\begin{bmatrix} (E_i)_\perp^2 + (E_i)_\|^2 \\ (E_i)_\perp^2 - (E_i)_\|^2 \\ 2(E_i)_\perp(E_i)_\|\cos\delta \\ 2(E_i)_\perp(E_i)_\|\sin\delta \end{bmatrix}, \tag{5.59}$$

$$S_r = \frac{n_r\cos\theta_r}{2\mu_r c}\begin{bmatrix} (E_r)_\perp^2 + (E_r)_\|^2 \\ (E_r)_\perp^2 - (E_r)_\|^2 \\ 2(E_r)_\perp(E_r)_\|\cos\delta \\ 2(E_r)_\perp(E_r)_\|\sin\delta \end{bmatrix}, \tag{5.60}$$

$$S_t = \frac{n_t\cos\theta_t}{2\mu_t c}\begin{bmatrix} (E_t)_\perp^2 + (E_t)_\|^2 \\ (E_t)_\perp^2 - (E_t)_\|^2 \\ 2(E_t)_\perp(E_t)_\|\cos\delta \\ 2(E_t)_\perp(E_t)_\|\sin\delta \end{bmatrix}, \tag{5.61}$$

where δ is the phase difference between the perpendicular and parallel components, $(\delta_\perp - \delta_\parallel)$. Since $n_r = n_i$, $\mu_r = \mu_i$, and $\theta_r = \theta_i$, the Mueller matrix for reflection, M_r, is:

$$S_r = M_r S_i = \frac{1}{2} \begin{bmatrix} r_\perp^2 + r_\parallel^2 & r_\perp^2 - r_\parallel^2 & 0 & 0 \\ r_\perp^2 - r_\parallel^2 & r_\perp^2 + r_\parallel^2 & 0 & 0 \\ 0 & 0 & 2r_\perp r_\parallel & 0 \\ 0 & 0 & 0 & 2r_\perp r_\parallel \end{bmatrix} S_i, \tag{5.62}$$

and the Mueller matrix for transmission, M_t, is:

$$S_t = M_t S_i = \frac{n_t \mu_i \cos \theta_t}{2 n_i \mu_t \cos \theta_i} \begin{bmatrix} t_\perp^2 + t_\parallel^2 & t_\perp^2 - t_\parallel^2 & 0 & 0 \\ t_\perp^2 - t_\parallel^2 & t_\perp^2 + t_\parallel^2 & 0 & 0 \\ 0 & 0 & 2t_\perp t_\parallel & 0 \\ 0 & 0 & 0 & 2t_\perp t_\parallel \end{bmatrix} S_i. \tag{5.63}$$

Absorbing media

In our discussion of reflection and refraction involving absorbing media, we will use the complex index of refraction $\hat{n}$. All the formulas presented above remain the same in form, but with all the ns replaced by $\hat{n}$s. The meaning of the sine and cosine of a complex number thus needs a new interpretation. The definitions of elementary functions of a complex variable can be given in terms of polynomials once the products of two complex numbers are defined [402]. The following functions will serve our purpose here:

$$e^z = 1 + z + \frac{1}{2!}z^2 + \frac{1}{3!}z^3 + \cdots; \tag{5.64}$$

$$\sinh z = \frac{1}{2}(e^z - e^{-z}); \tag{5.65}$$

$$\cosh z = \frac{1}{2}(e^z + e^{-z}); \tag{5.66}$$

$$\sin z = \sin(x + iy) = (\sin x \cosh y) + i(\cos x \sinh y); \tag{5.67}$$

$$\cos z = \cos(x + iy) = (\cos x \cosh y) - i(\sin x \sinh y). \tag{5.68}$$

With the above mathematical definitions of complex functions, let us present the formulas for the absorbing media. Snell's law can still be derived from the boundary conditions that the tangential components of $\mathbf{E}$ and $\mathbf{H}$ are continuous across the interface and so are the normal components of $\epsilon\mathbf{E}$ and $\mu\mathbf{H}$. We obtain the following Snell's law:

$$\hat{n}_i \sin \hat{\theta}_i = \hat{n}_t \sin \hat{\theta}_t, \tag{5.69}$$

where $\hat{n}_i$ and $\hat{n}_t$ are the complex indices of refraction for the incidence medium and the transmittance medium, respectively. The incident angle $\hat{\theta}_i$ and the transmission angle $\hat{\theta}_t$ can both now be complex numbers. The physical interpretation of complex angles requires us to go back to the wave vector and find out how the surface of constant phase and the surface of constant amplitude propagate through the second medium. An example of such derivation can be found in [124, Section 13.2].

The amplitude reflection coefficients, $\hat{r}_\parallel$, $\hat{r}_\perp$, and the amplitude transmission coefficients, $\hat{t}_\parallel$, $\hat{t}_\perp$, become:

$$\hat{r}_\perp = \left(\frac{E_r}{E_i}\right)_\perp = \frac{(\hat{n}_i/\mu_i)\cos\hat{\theta}_i - (\hat{n}_t/\mu_t)\cos\hat{\theta}_t}{(\hat{n}_i/\mu_i)\cos\hat{\theta}_i + (\hat{n}_t/\mu_t)\cos\hat{\theta}_t}, \tag{5.70}$$

$$\hat{t}_\perp = \left(\frac{E_t}{E_i}\right)_\perp = \frac{2(\hat{n}_i/\mu_i)\cos\hat{\theta}_i}{(\hat{n}_i/\mu_i)\cos\hat{\theta}_i + (\hat{n}_t/\mu_t)\cos\hat{\theta}_t}, \tag{5.71}$$

$$\hat{r}_\parallel = \left(\frac{E_r}{E_i}\right)_\parallel = \frac{(\hat{n}_t/\mu_t)\cos\hat{\theta}_i - (\hat{n}_i/\mu_i)\cos\hat{\theta}_t}{(\hat{n}_t/\mu_t)\cos\hat{\theta}_i + (\hat{n}_i/\mu_i)\cos\hat{\theta}_t}, \tag{5.72}$$

$$\hat{t}_\parallel = \left(\frac{E_t}{E_i}\right)_\parallel = \frac{2(\hat{n}_i/\mu_i)\cos\hat{\theta}_i}{(\hat{n}_t/\mu_t)\cos\hat{\theta}_i + (\hat{n}_i/\mu_i)\cos\hat{\theta}_t}. \tag{5.73}$$

The reflectances are defined as: $R_\parallel = \|\hat{r}_\parallel\|^2$ and $R_\perp = \|\hat{r}_\perp\|^2$, both being real numbers. The interpretation of these complex reflection and transmission coefficients is simple. They represent the amplitude as well as the phase change of the complex, incident electric field vector, $\mathbf{E}_i$, upon reflection and transmission. An important special case is that of the normal incident angle, $\hat{\theta}_i = 0$:

$$\hat{r}_\parallel = -\hat{r}_\perp = \frac{\hat{n}_t - \hat{n}_i}{\hat{n}_t + \hat{n}_i}, \tag{5.74}$$

$$\hat{t}_\parallel = \hat{t}_\perp = \frac{2\hat{n}_i}{\hat{n}_t + \hat{n}_i}. \tag{5.75}$$

The reflectance at the normal incidence is:

$$R_\parallel = R_\perp = \frac{(n_t - n_i)^2 + (\kappa_t - \kappa_i)^2}{(n_t + n_i)^2 + (\kappa_t + \kappa_i)^2}. \tag{5.76}$$

Equation (5.76) shows that when κ_t is very much greater than κ_i, i.e., when the absorption is very high (κ is proportional to the absorption coefficient), the reflectance is also very high. This is very typical for metals. They are strong reflectors and also strong absorbers (so strong that light cannot travel through more than a wavelength or so before it disappears). Actually, most light energy is reflected back.

5.4.2 Scattering

Scattering is the process in which energy is removed from a beam of light and reemitted with a change in direction, phase, or wavelength. This definition is general, but not universally accepted. In fact, the term scattering as used in optical phenomena refers to many different special cases of light–matter interaction [120, Chapter 1]. In the most general meaning, scattering is the excitation of charged particles by, and the subsequent reradiation of, electromagnetic waves. The key point is that the reradiated waves are in all directions and the sum of the reradiated waves that emerge at a given spatial position is very much dependent on the physical composition and structure of the material and medium involved. The specular reflection of a plane wave by a mirror is not typically considered to be a scattering process, but the excitation and reradiation process is no different from diffuse reflection from a rough surface. The unique feature in the former is that the mirror because it is so smooth produces a very directional path of constructive interference, so that the reflected wave propagates "only" in that direction [307]. We will not adopt this broad definition of scattering here, but instead opt for a narrower and more traditional phenomenological definition.

For our applications, it is simpler to say that due to the presence of particles of index of refraction different from the surrounding medium, light changes its direction and phase. If the frequency is not changed, this is called elastic scattering, if it is, it is called inelastic scattering. One of the best-known examples of scattering is that by particles much smaller than the wavelengths of the light (known as Rayleigh scattering [921]), such as the scattering of sunlight by air molecules to produce blue skies and red sunsets. The general problem of scattering by a spherical particle has been solved several times independently [600]. A well-known publication is that by Gustav Mie [662] and published in 1908, about the scattering of a plane monochromatic wave by a homogeneous sphere in a homogeneous medium. The scattering of light by multiple spheres can be found by applying the Mie solution to each of the spheres and summing the scattered light from each sphere. When the radius of the sphere is much smaller than the wavelength, Mie's solution approaches Rayleigh scattering. In that case, the scattered energy is inversely proportional to the fourth power of the wavelength. Light at 450 nm will be scattered 4 times more than that at 650 nm. Without air, the sky would look dark but with air, blue light is scattered more than green or red light and the sky looks cyan blue. For particles that are much larger than the wavelength, the scattering is less dependent on the wavelength. Transparent materials such as glass when ground into small particles become white and opaque, because light is scattered at the many interfaces of the particles and is diffusely directed to all angles, instead of going through the material in a regular direction. Sugar, salt, clouds, and snow appear white because their particles or crystals are much larger than the visible wavelengths.

Scattering not only redistributes energy from a beam of light in different directions, but it can also change the state of polarization of the scattered light. It is a well known that skylight is polarized even though sunlight is unpolarized. The description of light scattering thus requires the use of a *scattering matrix*, which is a Mueller matrix that transforms the Stokes vector of the incident light beam to that of the scattered light beam as a function of the scattering angle. The conventional coordinate system takes the propagation direction of the incident ray as the z-axis, which is called the forward direction (see Figure 5.2). A scattered

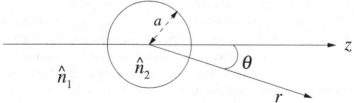

Figure 5.2. The convention for the coordinate systems for scattering.

ray r and the incident ray form a plane, called the scattering plane for that scattered ray. The angle between the scattered ray and the incident ray is called the scattering angle, θ. The Stokes vectors are then defined relative to the scattering plane. The incident and scattered electric field vectors are both decomposed into one component that is perpendicular to the scattering plane and another component that is parallel to the scattering plane.

The quantitative description of Rayleigh scattering can be derived from the induced dipole field of the air molecules and is given by the following equation [453, p. 423] in terms of the total scattering cross-section per molecule of the gas, σ_s:

$$\sigma_s \approx \frac{32\pi^3}{3N^2\lambda^4}\|n-1\|^2,\tag{5.77}$$

where N is the number of molecules per unit volume, λ is the wavelength in vacuum, and n is the index of refraction of the air, assuming $\|n-1\|\ll 1$. A somewhat simplified calculation given by Jackson [453, p. 423] shows that in typical conditions, the percentages of transmission through the atmosphere for the wavelengths 650 nm and 410 nm are 96% and 76% for the sun at zenith, and 21% and 0.0065% for the sunrise/sunset. Rayleigh scattering greatly contributes to the red sky of the beautiful sunset.

Alternatively, Rayleigh scattering can also be derived from the Mie scattering by summing up the first few terms in a series expansion, under the assumption that the particle size is much smaller than the wavelength. The relation can be expressed by the scattering matrix [120, p. 132]:

$$I_s = \frac{16\pi^4 a^6}{\lambda^4 r^2}\left\|\frac{m^2-1}{m^2+2}\right\|^2
\begin{bmatrix}
\frac{1}{2}(1+\cos^2\theta) & \frac{1}{2}(\cos^2\theta-1) & 0 & 0 \\
\frac{1}{2}(\cos^2\theta-1) & \frac{1}{2}(1+\cos^2\theta) & 0 & 0 \\
0 & 0 & \cos\theta & 0 \\
0 & 0 & 0 & \cos\theta
\end{bmatrix}
I_i,\tag{5.78}$$

where I_i (the radiant flux density) is the Stokes vector of the incident light beam, I_s (the radiant flux density) is the Stokes vector of the scattered light beam, λ is the wavelength in the medium, a is the radius of the particle, m is the ratio of $\hat{n}_2$, the (complex) index of refraction of the particle, to $\hat{n}_1$, the index of refraction of the medium, and r is the distance from the center of the particle to the observation point of the scattered beam, It should be noted that Rayleigh scattering is not strictly proportional to λ^{-4} because the index of refraction is also a function of λ.

5.4.3 Transmission and absorption

Light traveling in an optical medium is attenuated by absorption and scattering. The energy that is transmitted along the regular path is reduced more the longer it propagates in the medium or when the concentration of the absorbing ingredient in the medium is higher. The energy removed from the transmitted light beam is either absorbed or scattered to other directions. For a medium that does not cause significant multiple scattering, the radiant flux density of the transmitted light, I_t, is related to the radiant flux density of the incident light, I_i, by two laws [1053, pp. 30–1]:

1. The Lambert–Bouguer law: $I_t(\lambda) = I_i(\lambda)e^{-\alpha(\lambda)d}$, where $\alpha(\lambda)$ is absorption coefficient and d is the thickness of the medium. If the law is expressed to base 10, i.e., $I_t(\lambda) = I_i(\lambda)10^{-k(\lambda)d}$, then k is called the extinction coefficient.

2. Beer's law: $I_t(\lambda) = I_i(\lambda)e^{-\beta(\lambda)c}$, where c is the concentration of the absorbing medium.

The two laws can be combined into a law called the Beer–Lambert law: $I_t(\lambda) = I_i(\lambda)10^{-\epsilon(\lambda)cd}$, where the concentration is in moles per liter, and the constant $\epsilon(\lambda)$ is called the molar extinction coefficient. The Beer–Lambert law is true only when the effect of multiple scattering is negligible because the energy scattered once away the forward direction by one particle can be scattered back into the forward direction by a second particle. Of course this can only happen if there is a large number of particles along the path, either because the concentration of particles is high or because the path is long.

Where do the photons go?

Once a photon is absorbed by a medium, there are several forms into which the energy may be converted. It may be converted to motion (thermal) energy through collision between atoms and molecules, and later reradiated as a lower-energy (invisible) photon. In this case, the process is called dissipative absorption. Alternatively, the energy may be reradiated immediately as a photon at the same frequency (reflection, refraction, and scattering). In other cases, the reemission persists for some time after the incident light has been turned off. If the decay time constant is about 10^{-9}–10^{-5} s, this is called fluorescence. If the time constant is from about 10^{-3} to several seconds, it is called phosphorescence. These processes correspond to transitions through different paths of energy states (see [44, pp. 598–9, 1053, p. 235]). Phosphorescence has important applications in image display (CRT monitors). It involves intersystem crossing from a singlet excited state (electrons are paired and have opposite spins) to a triplet excited state (electrons have parallel spins). Once an excited electron reaches a triplet state, it cannot quickly radiate its energy and return to the ground state (singlet) because the transition does not preserve the angular momentum. Only through the spin–orbit coupling (it requires a heavy atom that has strong spin–orbit coupling) can it accomplish the transition. It is a slow process, and the radiative emission of energy can take a long time. For fluorescent materials color measurements are more difficult to specify and it is necessary to determine whether there is any fluorescence when making any color measurements. For example, many glass filters fluoresce when irradiated by ultraviolet radiation. Use of these filters in color measurement may require prefilters to block the ultraviolet radiation.

5.4.4 Diffraction

In our everyday experience, a beam of light in air seems to travel in a straight line. Thus, we can draw lines from the light source to predict the shape of the shadow that is cast by an object. This type of shadow is called the geometrical shadow and the approximation of the propagation of a light beam in a uniform medium by a straight line is called geometrical optics. However, there are several areas where the approximation does not give us a reasonable answer. Two of these areas in imaging applications are: (1) areas around material discontinuities, such as the boundary of the shadow we mentioned above, and (2) areas where many light rays concentrate together, such as near the focus point. In traditional terms, deviation from a straight line in light propagation (due to an obstacle) is called diffraction.

Diffraction problems in optics are very difficult to solve exactly. In principle, we can solve the Maxwell equations with proper boundary conditions on the surfaces of obstacles. In practice, only a small number of problems, which involve obstacles of very simple shape and ideal properties have been solved rigorously [124, Chapter XI]. The most famous one is the diffraction by a half-plane infinitely-conducting infinitely-thin sheet, solved by Sommerfeld in 1896. Even for the simple geometry of an aperture in a planar screen of finite width and of finite conductivity, the solution to the diffraction problem becomes too complicated. An approximate solution to the diffraction problem can be calculated using the Huygens–Fresnel principle formulated mathematically by Kirchhoff in 1882. Kirchhoff's approximation expresses the electromagnetic wave as a scalar function (i.e., neglects its polarization) and assumes that the field and its first derivative normal to the surface of the screen are everywhere zero, except in the aperture where the field is the same as the incident field (see Fig. 5.3). This zero field and normal derivative boundary condition is mathematically inconsistent with the Helmholtz wave equation that describes the electromagnetic wave. If the boundary condition is true, the field should be zero everywhere. This inconsistency can be removed by assuming different boundary conditions to allow either the

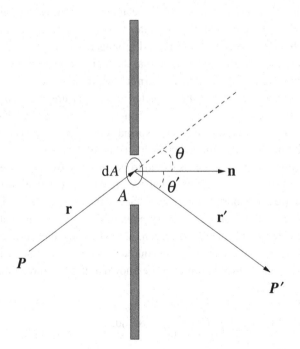

Figure 5.3. Diffraction from an aperture: the Huygens–Fresnel principle.

field or its normal derivative to be nonzero on the screen surface. These different boundary conditions result in different approximations, but in the domains in which we are interested (the source and the observation points are far away from the screen, relative to the size of the aperture, which in turn is very much larger than the wavelength of the light), they give very similar results. The vector theory of the approximation can also be derived when the screen is assumed to be perfectly conducting [888, Section 12.18].

Despite all the idealistic assumptions, Kirchhoff's approximation works remarkably well for many cases of practical interest. We will use it to calculate the optical transfer function for a diffraction-limited lens. The Huygens–Fresnel principle formulated by Kirchhoff can be expressed in the following form:

$$E(P') = \frac{1}{i\lambda} \iint_A E(P)\frac{e^{ikr}}{r}\frac{e^{ikr'}}{r'}\frac{1}{2}(\cos\theta + \cos\theta')dA, \tag{5.79}$$

where $E(P)$ is the known electric field at point P, and $E(P')$ is the diffracted electric field at point of observation, P'; λ is the wavelength of the incident light, A is the aperture, $\mathbf{r}$ is the vector from P to a small surface element dA at the aperture A, $\mathbf{r}'$ is the vector from dA to P', $\mathbf{n}$ is the unit normal vector to the surface element dA, pointing to the opposite side from P (see Fig. 5.3), θ is the angle between $\mathbf{r}$ and $\mathbf{n}$, and θ' is the angle between $\mathbf{r}'$ and $\mathbf{n}$. The term which involves the two angles is called the inclination factor. In the distance range where the theory is valid, the inclination factor is very close to a constant.

From Eq. (5.79), if we know the source field distribution, $E(P)$, we can compute the diffraction field at any point in the space. The physical meaning of the Huygens principle can be seen in Eq. (5.79): the source field at P propagates to the aperture element dA as a spherical wave, e^{ikr}/r, which then acts as a source and propagates as a spherical wave, $e^{ikr'}/r'$, to the observation point, P'. It should be noted that the input field at the aperture is assumed to be a diverging sphere as indicated by the term e^{ikr}/r, implying that the lateral spatial coherence length is at least as large as the diameter of the aperture. Therefore, the source has to be far away from the aperture, or the aperture has to be smaller than the transverse coherence length of the source (see (2.3)). Normally, the integral is calculated over a planar surface over the aperture (assuming that the boundary of the opening is a planar curve). However, since the observation point is assumed to be far away from the aperture, we can use any smooth surface over the opening that will make our calculation of the integral easier. For example, we can choose a spherical surface with the center located at the observation point P', so that r' will be constant at every point of the surface. Alternatively, if the source is a point on the left hand side of the screen, we can choose the surface to be a spherical surface with the center located at the point source P, so that r will be constant. In many imaging applications, the field is assumed to be known at the aperture A and the Huygens–Fresnel integral is expressed as:

$$E(P') = \frac{1}{i\lambda} \iint_A E(P)\frac{e^{ikr'}}{r'}(\cos\theta')dA, \tag{5.80}$$

where P is now a point in the aperture. The inclination factor has now been modified. Although it is not consistent with the original form, this rarely matters because the integral is an approximation anyway and is valid only for a far-away observation point, leading to similar results for different forms of the inclination factor [453, p. 143].

Calculation of the diffraction pattern from Eq. (5.79) or (5.80) is done for far-away observation points. The factor r' in the denominator can be treated as approximately constant for every point on the aperture. However, the r' in the numerator $e^{ikr'} = e^{i2\pi r'/\lambda}$ determines the phase of the field and cannot be approximated as a constant because a minute difference of half a wavelength in the radial distance r' can change the wave from constructive to destructive, or vice versa. Two different approximations are often used for calculating this phase factor, depending on the observation distance. The Fraunhofer approximation is valid for the far field and the resulting diffraction patterns are called Fraunhofer diffraction patterns. For the near field (still many, many wavelengths away), the Fresnel approximation is used, and the resulting patterns are called Fresnel diffraction patterns. These two approximations will be discussed in later chapters when we deal with the wave optics of image formation.

Diffraction is a consequence of the "wave" nature of light and the resulting diffraction pattern is often complicated and nonintuitive in the sense that it can be quite different from what the light ray model (the geometric shadow) would predict. For example, from the Huygens–Fresnel integral, Poisson showed that an opaque circular disk at a certain distance can cast a shadow with a bright spot in the center of the shadow. This is so "counterintuitive" that Poisson used it as evidence to object to Fresnel's theory of diffraction. However, a careful experiment performed later confirmed the prediction of the diffraction theory. Similarly, a circular opening in a screen can transmit a bright disk of light with a dark spot right in the center. In both cases, the diffraction patterns show numerous, alternating, dark and bright, concentric rings.

5.5 Problems

5.1 The peak sensitivity of $V'(\lambda)$ is at 507 nm. What is the photon energy in eV at this wavelength?

5.2 The silicon substrate in a CCD sensor has a band gap of about 1.1 eV. Which part of the visible wavelengths can be readily absorbed by the silicon?

5.3 When an external electric field, **E**, is applied to a material, the molecules in the material are polarized (due to charge displacement). If the molecules are themselves polar (such as water molecules), the induced dipole moment per unit volume, **P**, can be quite large because the molecules will align with the external electric field. **P** is often proportional to **E**. The proportionality constant is found to be a function of frequency. Give a qualitative explanation of why this is so.

5.4 The index of refraction of a material is a function of frequency. Within the visible wavelength range, the index of refraction of some materials, such as glasses, is higher for shorter wavelengths and lower for longer wavelengths. For other materials, the trend is reversed, i.e., the index of refraction is lower for shorter wavelengths. What causes this difference? For a given material, does the index of refraction continue to increase or decrease when the optical frequency is increased?

5.5   Due to the presence of free electrons in their conduction bands, most metals reflect light of different visible wavelengths equally well and therefore appear gray. However, some metals such as copper and gold have characteristic colors, why?

5.6   In order to detect submarines under the sea surface, polarization filters are often used in the optical imaging devices on an airplane. To which direction should the filters be turned?

5.7   Although sunlight is unpolarized, skylight can be completely polarized at a certain angle from the sun. This can be seen from Eq. (5.78). What is this angle and what is the direction of polarization? Can you give an intuitive explanation of why this polarization occurs?

5.8   It is well known that if the aperture size of a camera is reduced, the depth of field (the range of depth in which objects appear sharp) is increased. However, the amount of available light is also decreased. Therefore, we cannot always use as small an aperture as we would like. Even if we have plenty of light, there are two other factors to consider: coherence and diffraction. Discuss their effects on image formation.

6 Colorimetry

The beauty of the golden sky at sunset, the splendor of peacock feathers, and the glorious spectacle of fireworks are displays of changing color. Our visual sense is greatly enriched by our perception and appreciation of colors. Although our color perception seems to be direct and effortless, it is a very interesting subject of immense complexity, as are other aspects of our visual perception. In the last 70 years, we have made a lot of progress in understanding the physics, chemistry, optics, physiology, psychophysics, anatomy, neural science, and molecular biology of human color vision, but we are still very far from being able to describe exactly how it works. Therefore, practical use of color requires certain empirical rules. These rules, which are by no means perfect, are based on many years of experimentation and observation, and they form the empirical foundation of *colorimetry*, the science of measuring color.

The basic measurement of a color stimulus is its spectral power distribution as a function of wavelength (or frequency). The spectral power distribution of a reflecting surface is the product of the spectral power distribution of the illumination and the spectral reflectance factor of the surface. Although the same spectral power distribution may produce different color sensations, depending on its surroundings, background, illumination, and viewing geometry, all physical specifications of color stimuli start from their spectral power distributions. The link between the objective physics and the subjective perception is provided by photometry and colorimetry. These two fields of scientific study attempt to quantify the capacity of light stimuli to produce color sensation. Because of the incomplete knowledge we have of the total process of color perception, the initial goals of photometry and colorimetry have been intentionally limited to the physical specifications of colors, without addressing the problems of the appearance of color. However, even with this limited scope of study, their applications to practical problems have been widely accepted and the results have been quite useful. In this chapter, we will review the basis of colorimetry and describe some of its applications.

6.1 Colorimetry and its empirical foundations

Colorimetry is a scientific field in which the physical specifications of light stimuli that produce a given color sensation under restricted viewing conditions are studied. In particular, it seeks to represent the spectral power distribution of any incident light with a much reduced number of parameters (almost always three, and sometimes four, corresponding to the number of photoreceptor types we believe are facilitating the sensation of color under the given conditions). Colorimetry is mainly concerned with color matching and predicting small color differences when two stimuli do not match. It should be pointed out from the beginning that colorimetric data alone do not specify what color we will see. The objective of colorimetry is to specify the physical aspects of color stimuli, not the color appearance.

Long before the current, direct evidence for the four types of photoreceptor (rod and three types of cone) in the retina of our eyes was available, psychophysical data had suggested the experimental laws of color matching. In the luminance range in which the rods are mostly saturated and by restricting the visual angle to a small subtense around the fovea, it was found that many, but not all, visual stimuli can be completely matched in color by additive mixtures of three fixed, independent stimuli (called primaries) with their radiant powers properly adjusted. ("Independent" here means that none of the three stimuli can be matched by any additive mixture of the other two.) The empirical observations were summarized by Grassman [359, 861]. A stronger form of Grassman's laws was given by Wyszecki and Stiles [1053] as follows:

1. Symmetry law: If color stimulus A matches color stimulus B, then color stimulus B matches color stimulus A. (It does not matter how you move them around.)
2. Transitivity law: If A matches B and B matches C, then A matches C.
3. Proportionality law: If A matches B, then αA matches αB, where α is any positive factor by which the radiant power of the color stimulus is increased or decreased.
4. Additivity law: If A matches B and C matches D, then $(A \oplus C)$ matches $(B \oplus D)$, where the operator "$\oplus$" means the additive color mixture. Also, if A matches B and $(A \oplus C)$ matches $(B \oplus D)$, then C matches D.

These laws hold true only if the matching color stimuli are observed under the same viewing conditions (including the surround and the background) and by the same observer. The laws are very similar to the definition of a vector space, and indeed, Grassman did express them in terms of vector operations. These empirical laws become easy to understand if we assume that the light incident on our retinas is absorbed by three types of photoreceptor and color matching between two color stimuli is achieved when the photoreceptor responses to both stimuli are equal. This interpretation is called the receptor-level theory of color matching.

6.2 The receptor-level theory of color matching

One of the main goals of colorimetry is to derive a concise numerical representation of any given color stimulus from its spectral power distribution. A spectral power distribution may take more than 40 numbers to specify. Knowing that we have only three types of (cone) photoreceptor responsible for color vision, we would expect that only three numbers are necessary to specify the "visual effects" that the given spectral power distribution exerts on our visual system. Therefore, the main task of colorimetry is to determine the three cone response functions. However, until the 1980s [837], it was not technically possible to measure the cone response functions directly from the photoreceptors themselves. Before that the best available method for estimating the cone spectral response functions was the

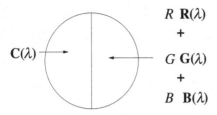

Figure 6.1. The bipartite field used in color matching experiments.

psychophysical color matching experiment which was developed in the 1920s. As will be shown shortly, this method cannot give us the cone response functions themselves, but only some of their linear combinations. For the purpose of specifying a color stimulus, linear combinations are good enough. The only need then was to standardize a set of linear combinations of the cone spectral response functions to be used for color specifications. The standardized functions are the CIE color matching functions, $\bar{x}(\lambda)$, $\bar{y}(\lambda)$, and $\bar{z}(\lambda)$, to be described below.

The basic procedure for measuring a color matching function is to use a bipartite visual field of a certain angular subtense, where the three primaries and the test monochromatic stimulus are projected onto two separate halves (see Figure 6.1). The observer adjusts the radiant powers R, G, B of the three primaries (R), (G), (B) until the color produced by the additive mixture of the three primaries matches that of the test stimulus. The unit for the radiant power of the primaries is chosen so that the mixture of one unit from each of the three primaries will match the color of the equal-energy white. The term, equal-energy white,[1] refers to a stimulus that has equal radiant power per wavelength interval at every wavelength. The test stimulus is ideally a single-wavelength light of unit power. The wavelength is varied over the range to be measured. The amounts of the unit power for the three primaries are then recorded as the *tristimulus values* of the test stimulus. For example, if (R), (G), and (B) are the unit amounts of the three primaries, and the test stimulus (C) is matched by additively mixing R units of (R), G units of (G), and B units of (B), then R, G, B are the *tristimulus values* of (C) with (R), (G), and (B) as the primaries. The CIE recommends expressing this color matching as

$$(\mathbf{C}) \equiv R(\mathbf{R}) + G(\mathbf{G}) + B(\mathbf{B}), \tag{6.1}$$

where $\equiv$ means color matching. Bold upper case letters inside (), such as (C), (R), (G), and (B), represent color stimuli or lights. Italic upper case letters, such as R, G, and B, represent scalar multipliers, meaning the amounts of light. For example, if the radiant power of the light (R) is t W, the radiant power of R(R) is Rt W.

Let us assume that there are three types of cone photoreceptor in our retinas: L, M, and S, each of which has a different and relatively broad (about 100 nm) spectral sensitivity function (see Figure 6.2). Let (R), (G), and (B) be our unit primaries. Let L_r, L_g, and

---

[1]   A more accurate term would be equal-power white because it is the radiant power that is our concern in continuous viewing. However, by tradition the term equal-energy white has been used in colorimetry and we will follow this tradition.

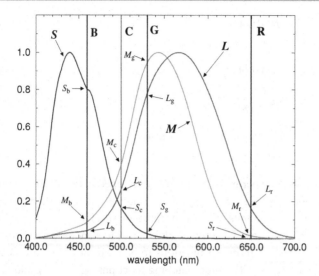

Figure 6.2. An imaginary example experiment for the receptor-level theory of color matching using monochromatic primaries, **R**, **G**, and **B**, and a monochromatic test stimulus, **C**. The three curves represent the normalized spectral sensitivity functions of L, M, and S cones. (The vertical axis is arbitrarily scaled.)

L_b be the number of photons that the L cone absorbs when it is stimulated by one unit of **(R)**, one unit of **(G)**, and one unit of **(B)**, respectively. Let M_r, M_g, M_b and S_r, S_g, S_b be the number of absorbed photons for the M cone and the S cone, corresponding to stimulation by the unit **(R)**, **(G)**, **(B)** primaries. Now when the eye is stimulated by a color stimulus **(C)**, let L_c, M_c, and S_c be the number of photons absorbed by the L, M, and S cones respectively. The receptor-level theory maintains that if the photon catch of each cone system is identical for two color stimuli, the two colors should match each other regardless of any other difference in their physical parameters, such as their spectral compositions. In a color matching experiment, the observer adjusts the radiant power of the three primaries so that the color of their mixture matches the color of the test stimulus. Mathematically, the observer is trying to find the three coefficients a_r, a_g, and a_b by adjusting the primaries so that

$$(\mathbf{C}) \equiv a_r(\mathbf{R}) + a_g(\mathbf{G}) + a_b(\mathbf{B}) \tag{6.2}$$

if and only if

$$\begin{aligned}
L_c &= a_r L_r + a_g L_g + a_b L_b, \\
M_c &= a_r M_r + a_g M_g + a_b M_b, \\
S_c &= a_r S_r + a_g S_g + a_b S_b.
\end{aligned} \tag{6.3}$$

In matrix form, this is

$$\begin{bmatrix} L_c \\ M_c \\ S_c \end{bmatrix} = \begin{bmatrix} L_r & L_g & L_b \\ M_r & M_g & M_b \\ S_r & S_g & S_b \end{bmatrix} \begin{bmatrix} a_r \\ a_g \\ a_b \end{bmatrix} = P \begin{bmatrix} a_r \\ a_g \\ a_b \end{bmatrix} \tag{6.4}$$

and

$$\begin{bmatrix} a_r \\ a_g \\ a_b \end{bmatrix} = \begin{bmatrix} L_r & L_g & L_b \\ M_r & M_g & M_b \\ S_r & S_g & S_b \end{bmatrix}^{-1} \begin{bmatrix} L_c \\ M_c \\ S_c \end{bmatrix} = P^{-1} \begin{bmatrix} L_c \\ M_c \\ S_c \end{bmatrix}. \tag{6.5}$$

As long as the matrix P is nonsingular (i.e., none of the three primaries can be matched by the linear combination of the other two), a_r, a_g, and a_b will always have a unique solution (i.e., the test color can be matched by some algebraic mixture of the three primaries). However, the solution may require that some of a_r, a_g, and a_b be negative, a requirement that has to be satisfied by moving the negative-valued primaries to, and mixing with, the test stimulus. It is also interesting to note that multiplying both sides of Eq. (6.4) by any nonsingular 3×3 matrix from the left does not change the solution of a_r, a_g, and a_b. This means that color matching experiments can determine the cone spectral sensitivity functions only up to their linear combinations. When the test stimulus (**C**) is an ideal, monochromatic (single-wavelength) light of unit power and its wavelength is varied over the visible range, the measured functions: $a_r(\lambda)$, $a_g(\lambda)$, and $a_b(\lambda)$, are called the color matching functions of the chosen **(R)**, **(G)**, **(B)** primaries.

The receptor-level theory of color matching is quite logical and intuitively "true". However, it needs further refinements and qualifications. Firstly, it is assumed that a photon once absorbed by a visual pigment produces the same "neural" signal independent of what its wavelength is. This assumption is called the principle of univariance [1053, p. 586], which has been shown to be consistent with experimental data. Secondly, it is implicitly assumed that the stimuli have to be large enough so that signals sensed by the three types of cones can be compared reliably. For example, if the stimulus when projected on the retina is less than the cross-section of a single cone, the perceived color must be unstable because a slight eye movement is likely to shift the image to a different type of cone. Thirdly, it is also assumed that the neural circuits of our color vision system can compare signals sensed at spatially separated photoreceptors. The same composition of light is sensed by three different types of cone, and the cone output signals are compared to determine the color sensation. Fourthly, it is assumed that the perceived color at a given spatial position is uniquely determined by the receptor photon catches at that location alone. This has been shown many times in the past to be false [139, 344]. The perceived color also depends on the surroundings, the luminance level, and the chromatic adaptation. Therefore, color matches hold true from this point of view only when two stimuli are presented under the "same" viewing conditions, including the surrounding background, the visual angle, the illumination intensity, and the adaptation state of the eyes.

Color matching results have been found to hold over a wide range of illumination level, except when it is very bright (due to response saturation or self-screening: see [1053, p. 588]) or very dim (into the mesopic or scotopic range when rods come into play).

6.3 Color matching experiments

As we mentioned before, in order to set up a physical color specification system such that receptor-level color matching can be achieved whenever two color stimuli have the same numerical representation, the spectral sensitivity curves of the L, M, and S cones are clearly the major functions to be measured. However, due to technical difficulties in direct recording from the photoreceptor cells, in the 1920s and 1930s indirect psychophysical measurements were the only possibility. Direct measurements on the cone spectral absorption curves have since been accomplished [90, 236, 837, 838], and the results agree very well with those from psychophysical color matching experiments [838]. The series of experiments that eventually led to the CIE standard color matching functions (which were "believed" to be linear combinations of the spectral sensitivity functions of the cones) was based on the idea of matching all monochromatic stimuli wavelength by wavelength with three chosen primaries. Since any spectral power distribution can be considered as the sum of monochromatic light at all wavelengths, if we can measure the tristimulus values of monochromatic light at every wavelength, we can calculate the tristimulus values of light of any spectral composition. Therefore, we have a system for specifying all color stimuli. This idea can be most easily understood by using a discrete approximation of the spectral power distribution, $P_\lambda(\lambda)$, of a given color stimulus, $(\mathbf{C})$:

$$(\mathbf{C}) = \sum_i P_\lambda(\lambda_i)\Delta\lambda. \tag{6.6}$$

If unit power (per unit wavelength) of a monochromatic light at wavelength λ_i can be matched by $a_r(\lambda_i)$ units of $(\mathbf{R})$, $a_g(\lambda_i)$ units of $(\mathbf{G})$, and $a_b(\lambda_i)$ units of $(\mathbf{B})$, then by the additivity of color matching, the color stimulus $(\mathbf{C})$ can be matched by A_r units of $(\mathbf{R})$, A_g units of $(\mathbf{G})$, and A_b units of $(\mathbf{B})$, where

$$A_r = \sum_i P_\lambda(\lambda_i)a_r(\lambda_i)\Delta\lambda,$$

$$A_g = \sum_i P_\lambda(\lambda_i)a_g(\lambda_i)\Delta\lambda,$$

$$A_b = \sum_i P_\lambda(\lambda_i)a_b(\lambda_i)\Delta\lambda.$$

Therefore, if we measure the color matching functions, $a_r(\lambda_i)$, $a_g(\lambda_i)$, and $a_b(\lambda_i)$ for a given set of primaries, $(\mathbf{R})$, $(\mathbf{G})$, and $(\mathbf{B})$, any given color stimulus with spectral power distribution $P_\lambda(\lambda)$ can be specified by A_r, A_g, and A_b which are the amounts of the primaries required to match the given color stimulus. Therefore, the basic task of colorimetry is to agree upon a set of color primaries and a set of color matching functions based on that set of primaries.

In order to specify the attributes of a color stimulus independent of its radiant power, we would like to define quantities called chromaticity coordinates. Let R, G, and B be the tristimulus values of a given color, then its chromaticity coordinates (r, g, b) are defined as:

$$r = \frac{R}{R+G+B},$$

$$g = \frac{G}{R+G+B}, \tag{6.7}$$

$$b = \frac{B}{R+G+B}.$$

Since $r + g + b = 1$, it is only necessary to specify any two of r, g, and b. The convention in colorimetry is to use lower case letters r, g, b for chromaticity coordinates, and lower case letters with overbars $\bar{r}(\lambda)$, $\bar{g}(\lambda)$, $\bar{b}(\lambda)$ for color matching functions. In summary, **(R)**, **(G)**, **(B)** are the primaries, R, G, B are the tristimulus values, r, g, b are the chromaticities, and $\bar{r}(\lambda)$, $\bar{g}(\lambda)$, $\bar{b}(\lambda)$ are the color matching functions, which are actually the tristimulus values of a monochromatic light of unit radiant power at wavelength λ.

In a color matching experiment, it is not always possible to match the test color stimulus with an additive mixture of the three primaries. Sometimes, one of the primaries has to be moved to the test stimulus side to achieve a color match. In this case, the radiant power of the primary that has been switched to the test stimulus side is recorded as a negative amount. The experimental results are the spectral tristimulus curves with respect to a particular set of chosen primaries. There are experimental variations for each individual at different trials and also between individuals. Therefore, averages over many sets of measurements are necessary to smooth out the differences within and between individuals to obtain results that are representative for the group of people who have normal color vision. The representative results can then be agreed upon as from an ideal "standard observer". The international standard adopted for the standard observer is that of the CIE. Before we learn about the details of the derivation of the CIE Standard Observers, we have to know how to transform the tristimulus values measured with one set of primaries to those measured with another set of primaries.

6.4 Transformation between two sets of primaries

In the applications of colorimetry, it is often necessary to transform the tristimulus values in one set of primaries to those in another set of primaries. For example, color reproduction on CRT monitors usually requires transformation between RGB and XYZ.

Let **(R)(G)(B)** and **(X)(Y)(Z)** be two sets of primaries. A color stimulus **(C)** can be expressed by the following two color matching relations:

$$(\mathbf{C}) \equiv C_R(\mathbf{R}) + C_G(\mathbf{G}) + C_B(\mathbf{B}), \tag{6.8}$$

$$(\mathbf{C}) \equiv C_X(\mathbf{X}) + C_Y(\mathbf{Y}) + C_Z(\mathbf{Z}). \tag{6.9}$$

If we determine the tristimulus values of **(X)**, **(Y)**, and **(Z)** using the primaries **(R)**, **(G)**, and **(B)**, we have the following relations:

$$\begin{bmatrix} (\mathbf{X}) \\ (\mathbf{Y}) \\ (\mathbf{Z}) \end{bmatrix} \equiv \begin{bmatrix} X_R & X_G & X_B \\ Y_R & Y_G & Y_B \\ Z_R & Z_G & Z_B \end{bmatrix} \begin{bmatrix} (\mathbf{R}) \\ (\mathbf{G}) \\ (\mathbf{B}) \end{bmatrix} \tag{6.10}$$

and, from Eqs. (6.8), (6.9) and (6.10), we have

$$\begin{bmatrix} C_R \\ C_G \\ C_B \end{bmatrix} = \begin{bmatrix} X_R & Y_R & Z_R \\ X_G & Y_G & Z_G \\ X_B & Y_B & Z_B \end{bmatrix} \begin{bmatrix} C_X \\ C_Y \\ C_Z \end{bmatrix}. \tag{6.11}$$

Equation (6.11) shows the transformation of tristimulus values from one set of primaries to another set by a 3×3 matrix. Since there are only nine elements in the transformation matrix, any three linearly independent pairs of tristimulus values are sufficient to determine the unique transformation.

There are situations in which it is desirable to specify the transformation between two sets of primaries by pairs of *chromaticity* coordinates, rather than tristimulus values in both spaces. One example is the transformation of spectral chromaticity functions from a set of physical primaries to a set of imaginary primaries in order to make the color matching functions nonnegative for all wavelengths. This is exactly what was done when the CIE specified its 1931 Standard Colorimetric Observer, as will be described in the following section. Another example is the NTSC specification of color signals, where the chromaticities of the three monitor phosphors and the illuminant are specified for TV color reproduction. Here we will show how the transformation of chromaticity coordinates can be done. Numerical examples will be given in later sections.

Let R, G, B be the tristimulus values for the **(R)**, **(G)**, **(B)** primaries and X, Y, Z be the tristimulus values for the **(X)**, **(Y)**, **(Z)** primaries. Their chromaticity coordinates are denoted by r, g, b and x, y, z. As we have just shown, the transformation from R, G, B to X, Y, Z can be done by a 3×3 matrix, A:

$$\begin{bmatrix} X \\ Y \\ Z \end{bmatrix} = A \begin{bmatrix} R \\ G \\ B \end{bmatrix} = \begin{bmatrix} a_{11} & a_{12} & a_{13} \\ a_{21} & a_{22} & a_{23} \\ a_{31} & a_{32} & a_{33} \end{bmatrix} \begin{bmatrix} R \\ G \\ B \end{bmatrix}. \tag{6.12}$$

Since, by definition, $X = x(X + Y + Z)$, $Y = y(X + Y + Z)$, $Z = z(X + Y + Z)$, $R = r(R + G + B)$, $G = g(R + G + B)$, and $B = b(R + G + B)$, the above equation can be expressed as

$$\begin{bmatrix} x \\ y \\ z \end{bmatrix} = \left(\frac{R + G + B}{X + Y + Z} \right) \begin{bmatrix} a_{11} & a_{12} & a_{13} \\ a_{21} & a_{22} & a_{23} \\ a_{31} & a_{32} & a_{33} \end{bmatrix} \begin{bmatrix} r \\ g \\ b \end{bmatrix}. \tag{6.13}$$

From Eq. (6.12) and the definition of chromaticity, we have

$$X + Y + Z = (a_{11} + a_{21} + a_{31})R + (a_{12} + a_{22} + a_{32})G + (a_{13} + a_{23} + a_{33})B$$
$$= (R + G + B)$$
$$\times [(a_{11} + a_{21} + a_{31})r + (a_{12} + a_{22} + a_{32})g + (a_{13} + a_{23} + a_{33})b]$$

and

$$\frac{R + G + B}{X + Y + Z} = \frac{1}{(a_{11} + a_{21} + a_{31})r + (a_{12} + a_{22} + a_{32})g + (a_{13} + a_{23} + a_{33})b}. \tag{6.14}$$

Substituting the above relation into Eq. (6.13), we have

$$x = \frac{a_{11}r + a_{12}g + a_{13}b}{(a_{11} + a_{21} + a_{31})r + (a_{12} + a_{22} + a_{32})g + (a_{13} + a_{23} + a_{33})b},$$
$$y = \frac{a_{21}r + a_{22}g + a_{23}b}{(a_{11} + a_{21} + a_{31})r + (a_{12} + a_{22} + a_{32})g + (a_{13} + a_{23} + a_{33})b}, \tag{6.15}$$

and z can be computed as $1 - x - y$. Since all the numerators and the denominators can be divided by a nonzero constant, there are only eight unknowns in Eq. (6.15). Therefore, given four pairs of corresponding chromaticity coordinates in both spaces, the transformation can be uniquely determined by solving a system of linear equations in eight unknowns. Alternatively, we can solve the transformation by the following matrix operations. The (somewhat tedious) derivation is left as an exercise.

Let (x_1, y_1, z_1), (x_2, y_2, z_2), (x_3, y_3, z_3), (x_4, y_4, z_4) be four points in the chromaticity space of the primaries $(\mathbf{X})$, $(\mathbf{Y})$, $(\mathbf{Z})$, and (r_1, g_1, b_1), (r_2, g_2, b_2), (r_3, g_3, b_3), (r_4, g_4, b_4) be their corresponding points in the chromaticity space of the primaries $(\mathbf{R})$, $(\mathbf{G})$, $(\mathbf{B})$. Any three points in each space should not be collinear. The transformation of tristimulus values from R, G, B to X, Y, Z is given by Eq. (6.12). It can be shown that $A = cVDU^{-1}$, where c is a constant proportional to $(X + Y + Z)/(R + G + B)$, and

$$V = \begin{bmatrix} x_1 & x_2 & x_3 \\ y_1 & y_2 & y_3 \\ z_1 & z_2 & z_3 \end{bmatrix}, \quad U = \begin{bmatrix} r_1 & r_2 & r_3 \\ g_1 & g_2 & g_3 \\ b_1 & b_2 & b_3 \end{bmatrix}, \tag{6.16}$$

and D is a diagonal matrix:

$$D = \begin{bmatrix} \beta_1/\alpha_1 & 0 & 0 \\ 0 & \beta_2/\alpha_2 & 0 \\ 0 & 0 & \beta_3/\alpha_3 \end{bmatrix}, \tag{6.17}$$

where

$$\begin{bmatrix} \alpha_1 \\ \alpha_2 \\ \alpha_3 \end{bmatrix} = U^{-1} \begin{bmatrix} r_4 \\ g_4 \\ b_4 \end{bmatrix} \quad \text{and} \quad \begin{bmatrix} \beta_1 \\ \beta_2 \\ \beta_3 \end{bmatrix} = V^{-1} \begin{bmatrix} x_4 \\ y_4 \\ z_4 \end{bmatrix}. \tag{6.18}$$

6.5 The CIE 1931 Standard Colorimetric Observer (2°)

In 1931, the CIE adopted the color matching functions $\bar{x}(\lambda)$, $\bar{y}(\lambda)$, $\bar{z}(\lambda)$ of the standard observer for 2° viewing. The functions were based on the chromaticity coordinates of monochromatic stimuli $r(\lambda)$, $g(\lambda)$, and $b(\lambda)$ measured by Guild and Wright and the CIE 1924 luminous efficiency function $V(\lambda)$.

Guild's color matching results were from seven observers using color-filtered primaries of relatively broad wavelength bands. Wright's data were from ten observers using monochromatic stimuli at 650 nm, 530 nm, and 460 nm as primaries. Both of them limited their experiments to between 400 and 700 nm, using 2° bipartite matching fields. Both sets of data were converted to that of monochromatic primaries at wavelengths of 700.0, 546.1, and 435.8 nm. The three primaries are designated as $(\mathbf{R})$, $(\mathbf{G})$, and $(\mathbf{B})$. The reason for choosing these wavelengths was that the last two correspond to two strong mercury spectral lines, which had served as standards for the National Physical Laboratory in England, and the 700 nm wavelength was chosen because its hue is very stable to slight wavelength variations. The units of the three primaries were scaled so that the mixture of unit quantities of the three spectral stimuli matches the equal-energy spectrum. Their radiant powers were in the ratios 72.0962:1.3791:1.0000. This ratio was selected so that equal quantities of the three primaries would match the equal-energy spectrum. The two sets of data after being

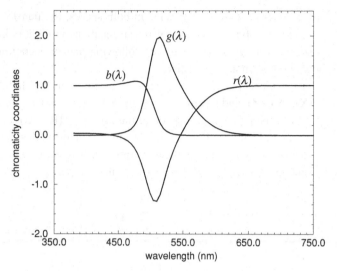

Figure 6.3. The chromaticity coordinates, $r(\lambda)$, $g(\lambda)$, and $b(\lambda)$, of the CIE 1931 *RGB* system with respect to three real primaries: **(R)** at 700 nm, **(G)** at 546.1 nm, and **(B)** at 435.8 nm.

carefully calibrated and converted were averaged and smoothed to produce the chromaticity coordinates of monochromatic stimuli $r(\lambda)$, $g(\lambda)$, and $b(\lambda)$, as shown in Fig. 6.3. It should be pointed out that variations among individual observers were fairly marked, especially in the blue–green region [289, p. 59]. The chromaticities alone do not specify the radiant powers required to achieve a color match (because $r(\lambda) + g(\lambda) + b(\lambda) = 1$ and the absolute radiant power for the match is lost). It would have been possible to derive the color matching functions if all the radiant powers of the monochromatic test stimuli had been recorded in the experiments. In order to derive the color matching functions for the **(R)**, **(G)**, **(B)** primaries, the CIE made a strong assumption that the photopic luminous efficiency function $V(\lambda)$ is a linear combination of the color matching functions $\bar{r}(\lambda)$, $\bar{g}(\lambda)$, and $\bar{b}(\lambda)$:

$$V(\lambda) = L_R \bar{r}(\lambda) + L_G \bar{g}(\lambda) + L_B \bar{b}(\lambda), \tag{6.19}$$

where L_R, L_G, and L_B are the luminances of the three primaries, which can be obtained from the products of the relative radiant power and the luminous efficiency function $V(\lambda)$. The calculated ratio is 1:4.5907:0.0601. Dividing both sides of the equation by $s(\lambda) = \bar{r}(\lambda) + \bar{g}(\lambda) + \bar{b}(\lambda)$, we have

$$\frac{V(\lambda)}{s(\lambda)} = L_R \frac{\bar{r}(\lambda)}{s(\lambda)} + L_G \frac{\bar{g}(\lambda)}{s(\lambda)} + L_B \frac{\bar{b}(\lambda)}{s(\lambda)}$$

$$= L_R r(\lambda) + L_G g(\lambda) + L_B b(\lambda). \tag{6.20}$$

Therefore,

$$s(\lambda) = \frac{V(\lambda)}{L_R r(\lambda) + L_G g(\lambda) + L_B b(\lambda)} \tag{6.21}$$

and the color matching functions can be obtained as $\bar{r}(\lambda) = s(\lambda) r(\lambda)$, $\bar{g}(\lambda) = s(\lambda) g(\lambda)$, and $\bar{b}(\lambda) = s(\lambda) b(\lambda)$, which are shown in Fig. 6.4. Since the units of the primaries are chosen

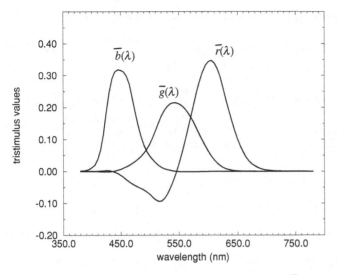

Figure 6.4. CIE 2° color matching functions, $\bar{r}(\lambda)$, $\bar{g}(\lambda)$, $\bar{b}(\lambda)$ with 435.8, 546.1 and 700 nm as primaries.

so that equal quantities of the primaries match the color of the equal-energy spectrum, the areas under the three curves are equal to each other.

The color matching functions, $\bar{r}(\lambda)$, $\bar{g}(\lambda)$, and $\bar{b}(\lambda)$, have negative values at some wavelengths, which is inconvenient for hand calculation. The CIE hence adopted a transformation from the trichromatic system based on the primary stimuli (R), (G), and (B) to one based on new primary stimuli (X), (Y), and (Z). The new primaries (X), (Y), and (Z) were chosen so that [183]:

1. The new color matching functions $\bar{x}(\lambda)$, $\bar{y}(\lambda)$, $\bar{z}(\lambda)$ have only positive values. This means that the new primaries are not physically realizable. (Why? Try to answer this question *after* you finish studying this chapter.)
2. In the new (x, y)-chromaticity diagram, the spectrum locus is bounded, as closely as possible, by the three lines: $x = 0$; $y = 0$; and $x + y = 1$, so that the area inside the (x, y)-chromaticity triangle occupied by the real colors is maximized.
3. In the (r, g)-chromaticity diagram, the locus of spectrum colors from 570 nm to 700 nm is virtually a straight line (see Fig. 6.5). Since $r(\lambda = 700$ nm$) = 1.0$, $g(\lambda = 700$ nm$) = 0.0$ and $r(\lambda = 600$ nm$) = 0.847$, $g(\lambda = 600$ nm$) = 0.154$, the equation of this line is $r + 0.99g = 1.00$. If one axis of the new primaries is chosen on this line, only two primaries are needed in this spectral region.
4. The tristimulus value Y is chosen to be equivalent to the luminance of the color stimuli, and the luminances of the (X) and (Z) primaries are set to zero. Therefore, the (X) and (Z) primary stimuli are located on the alychne (which is Greek for "line without light" [620, p. 189]). The alychne on the (r, g, b)-chromaticity diagram (see Fig. 6.5) is defined by

$$L_R r + L_G g + L_B b = 0,\tag{6.22}$$

Table 6.1. *The chromaticity coordinates for four stimuli of well-defined spectral distributions*

Stimulus	r	g	b	x	y	z
(R) 700.0 nm	1	0	0	0.734 69	0.265 31	0.000 00
(G) 546.1 nm	0	1	0	0.273 68	0.717 43	0.008 90
(B) 435.8 nm	0	0	1	0.166 54	0.008 88	0.824 58
Source B	0.362 30	0.343 05	0.294 65	0.348 42	0.351 61	0.299 97

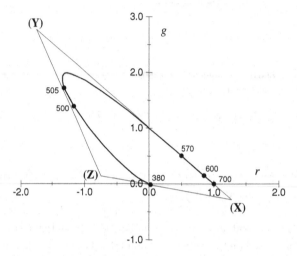

Figure 6.5. The (r, g)-chromaticity coordinates of the X, Y, and Z primaries.

where $L_R : L_G : L_B = 1 : 4.5907 : 0.0601$. The intersection point of the above two lines, $(r, g) = (1.275, -0.278)$ is the new primary X.

5. The third line (see Fig. 6.5) is chosen to be tangential to the spectrum locus at about 504 nm with a very small gap [895].

The above guidelines do not uniquely specify the required transformation. The transformation recommended by the CIE was through the specification of corresponding chromaticity coordinates of four stimuli of well-defined spectral distributions: see Table 6.1.

The CIE 1931 Standard Colorimetric Observer is defined by first transforming the r, g, b chromaticity coordinates to the x, y, z chromaticity coordinates by the following relations, which can be derived from the above four cardinal stimuli:

$$x(\lambda) = \frac{0.490\,00r(\lambda) + 0.310\,00g(\lambda) + 0.200\,00b(\lambda)}{0.666\,97r(\lambda) + 1.132\,40g(\lambda) + 1.200\,63b(\lambda)},$$

$$y(\lambda) = \frac{0.176\,97r(\lambda) + 0.812\,40g(\lambda) + 0.010\,63b(\lambda)}{0.666\,97r(\lambda) + 1.132\,40g(\lambda) + 1.200\,63b(\lambda)}, \qquad (6.23)$$

$$z(\lambda) = \frac{0.000\,00r(\lambda) + 0.010\,00g(\lambda) + 0.990\,00b(\lambda)}{0.666\,97r(\lambda) + 1.132\,40g(\lambda) + 1.200\,63b(\lambda)}.$$

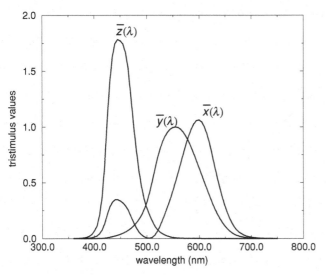

Figure 6.6. CIE 1931 2° color matching functions, $\bar{x}(\lambda)$, $\bar{y}(\lambda)$, $\bar{z}(\lambda)$.

These x, y, z chromaticity coordinates are then converted to spectral tristimulus values (the color matching functions) $\bar{x}(\lambda)$, $\bar{y}(\lambda)$, $\bar{z}(\lambda)$ as follows:

$$\bar{x}(\lambda) = [x(\lambda)/y(\lambda)]V(\lambda), \quad \bar{y}(\lambda) = V(\lambda), \quad \bar{z}(\lambda) = [z(\lambda)/y(\lambda)]V(\lambda), \qquad (6.24)$$

where $V(\lambda)$ is the CIE photopic luminous efficiency function. Figure 6.6 shows the resulting $\bar{x}(\lambda)$, $\bar{y}(\lambda)$, $\bar{z}(\lambda)$ color matching functions, and Fig. 6.7 shows the CIE 1931 (x, y)-chromaticity diagram. It should be pointed out that Guild and Wright's experiments did not actually determine spectral tristimulus values. They determined only matching chromaticities for spectral stimuli. The function $\bar{y}(\lambda)$ was not measured in their experiments. This has three very important consequences: (1) use of $V(\lambda)$ as $\bar{y}(\lambda)$ makes the colorimetric luminance Y consistent with the photometric luminance; (2) errors in the original data of $V(\lambda)$ are now incorporated into the colorimetric standards; and (3) in theory, all color matching functions can be regarded as linear combinations of the three cone spectral sensitivity functions. However, the experimental procedures used to measure $V(\lambda)$, such as the flicker photometry, are not explicitly founded on this hypothesis. By using $V(\lambda)$ as $\bar{y}(\lambda)$, the CIE 1931 color matching functions $\bar{x}(\lambda)$, $\bar{y}(\lambda)$, $\bar{z}(\lambda)$ can be regarded as linear combinations of the three cone spectral sensitivity functions only to the extent that $V(\lambda)$ is itself a linear combination of the three cone spectral sensitivity functions.

The color matching functions $\bar{x}(\lambda)$, $\bar{y}(\lambda)$, $\bar{z}(\lambda)$ recommended in 1986 [186] agree closely with those defined originally in 1931. Three minor changes have been introduced. At $\lambda = 775$ nm the new value of $\bar{x}(\lambda)$ is 0.0001 instead of 0.0000; at $\lambda = 555$ nm the new value of $\bar{y}(\lambda)$ is 1.0000 instead of 1.0002; and at $\lambda = 740$ nm the new value of $\bar{y}(\lambda)$ is 0.0002 instead of 0.0003.

When the visual angle is between 1° and 4°, the CIE 1931 2° Standard Observer color matching functions are recommended. When it is greater than 4°, the CIE recommend use of the 1964 Supplementary Standard Colorimetric Observer, which is described below.

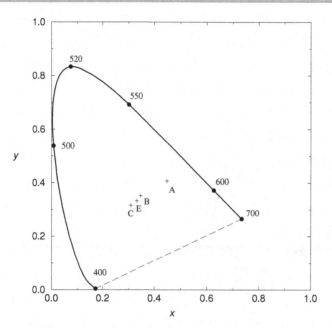

Figure 6.7. CIE 1931 (x, y)-chromaticity diagram. The four crosses show the chromaticity loci of the CIE standard illuminants, A, B, and C, and the equal-energy white E.

6.6 The CIE 1964 Supplementary Standard Colorimetric Observer (10°)

For a visual target larger than 2°, a new set of color matching functions is needed because the ratio of different cone types varies as a function of retina location and because the macula yellow pigments cover the area around the fovea (see Section 11.1). The CIE recommended its 1964 Supplementary Standard Colorimetric Observer for 10° viewing based on the data measured by Stiles and Burch (49 observers), and by Speranskaya (18 observers). In these two experiments, the color matching functions, $\bar{r}_{10}(\lambda)$, $\bar{g}_{10}(\lambda)$, and $\bar{b}_{10}(\lambda)$ were measured directly with no appeal to $V(\lambda)$. In order to reduce possible rod intrusion, the luminance of the matching field of the Stiles–Burch experiment was kept high. The three primaries used were 645.2 nm, 526.3 nm, and 444.4 nm. Figure 6.8 shows the mean data measured by Stiles and Burch. The CIE wanted to construct its 10° color matching functions using a general plan that was as close as possible to that followed in deriving the 1931 CIE(X, Y, Z) 2° color matching functions. The following equations were finally adopted to transform the original $\bar{r}_{10}(\lambda)$, $\bar{g}_{10}(\lambda)$, $\bar{b}_{10}(\lambda)$ data to the color matching functions, $\bar{x}_{10}(\lambda)$, $\bar{y}_{10}(\lambda)$, and $\bar{z}_{10}(\lambda)$ of the CIE 1964 Supplementary Standard Colorimetric (10°) Observer:

$$\bar{x}_{10}(\lambda) = 0.341\,080\bar{r}_{10}(\lambda) + 0.189\,145\bar{g}_{10}(\lambda) + 0.387\,529\bar{b}_{10}(\lambda),$$

$$\bar{y}_{10}(\lambda) = 0.139\,058\bar{r}_{10}(\lambda) + 0.837\,460\bar{g}_{10}(\lambda) + 0.073\,316\bar{b}_{10}(\lambda), \qquad (6.25)$$

$$\bar{z}_{10}(\lambda) = 0.000\,000\bar{r}_{10}(\lambda) + 0.039\,553\bar{g}_{10}(\lambda) + 2.026\,200\bar{b}_{10}(\lambda).$$

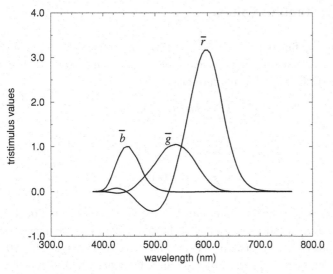

Figure 6.8. The mean 10° color matching function in the Stiles–Burch (1959) experiment. The three primaries used were 645.2 nm, 526.3 nm, and 444.4 nm.

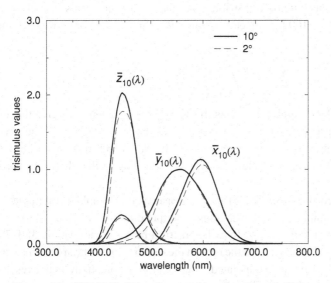

Figure 6.9. CIE 1964 10° color matching functions (solid curves): $\bar{x}_{10}(\lambda)$, $\bar{y}_{10}(\lambda)$, and $\bar{z}_{10}(\lambda)$. The dashed curves are the CIE 1931 2° color matching functions, $\bar{x}(\lambda)$, $\bar{y}(\lambda)$, and $\bar{z}(\lambda)$, for comparison.

The units of the X_{10}, Y_{10}, Z_{10} primaries are again chosen so that the equal-energy white has a chromaticity point (x_{10}, y_{10}) at $(1/3, 1/3)$. The $\bar{y}_{10}(\lambda)$ is to be used for calculating luminances when the size of stimuli is greater than 4°. Figure 6.9 shows the $\bar{x}_{10}(\lambda)$, $\bar{y}_{10}(\lambda)$, and $\bar{z}_{10}(\lambda)$ color matching functions.

6.7 Calculation of tristimulus values

Once the color matching functions, $\bar{x}(\lambda)$, $\bar{y}(\lambda)$, and $\bar{z}(\lambda)$, are defined, the tristimulus values, X, Y, and Z, of a color stimulus, $\phi_\lambda(\lambda)$, can be calculated by the additivity law of color matching, as expressed by the following formulas:

$$X = k \sum_\lambda \phi_\lambda(\lambda)\bar{x}(\lambda)\Delta\lambda, \tag{6.26}$$

$$Y = k \sum_\lambda \phi_\lambda(\lambda)\bar{y}(\lambda)\Delta\lambda, \tag{6.27}$$

$$Z = k \sum_\lambda \phi_\lambda(\lambda)\bar{z}(\lambda)\Delta\lambda. \tag{6.28}$$

The summation should be over the entire range of the visible spectrum, 360–830 nm in 1 nm increments. For most practical purposes, the summation may be approximated by using wavelength intervals, $\Delta\lambda$, equal to 5 nm over the wavelength range 380–780 nm. For a reflecting or transmitting object, the color stimulus function, $\phi_\lambda(\lambda)$, is replaced by the relative color stimulus function, evaluated as $\phi_\lambda(\lambda) = R(\lambda)S_\lambda(\lambda)$, or $\phi_\lambda(\lambda) = \tau(\lambda)S_\lambda(\lambda)$, where $R(\lambda)$ is the spectral reflectance factor (or spectral radiance factor or spectral reflectance) of the object color, $\tau(\lambda)$ is the spectral transmittance of the object color, and $S_\lambda(\lambda)$ is the relative spectral power distribution of the illuminant. In this case, the constant, k, is chosen so that $Y = 100$ for objects for which $R(\lambda)$ or $\tau(\lambda) = 1$ for all wavelengths, and hence

$$k = 100 \left/ \left[\sum_\lambda S_\lambda(\lambda)\bar{y}(\lambda)\Delta\lambda \right] \right. . \tag{6.29}$$

For self-luminous objects and illuminants, if the Y value is required to give the absolute value of a photometric quantity, the constant, k, must be put equal to K_m, the maximum spectral luminous efficacy (which is equal to 683 lm W^{-1}) and $\phi_\lambda(\lambda)$ must be the spectral concentration of the radiometric quantity corresponding to the photometric quantity required.

If some of the needed values of $\phi_\lambda(\lambda)$ are not measured, they should be interpolated from a third-degree polynomial or by the Lagrange interpolation formula (see [430, p. 122]). When the measurement range is less than the practical range of summation, 380–780 nm, the missing values may be set equal to the nearest measured value of the appropriate quantity in question. Methods that use extrapolated values can give potentially better results (see, for example, [620, pp. 64–70]). The CIE specifies that the range of the summation is an essential part of the tristimulus specification.

6.8 Some mathematical relations of colorimetric quantities

There are a few useful mathematical relations between some of the colorimetric quantities. These relations are often used in proving certain statements in colorimetry and frequently have important consequences in applications. They are described in this section.

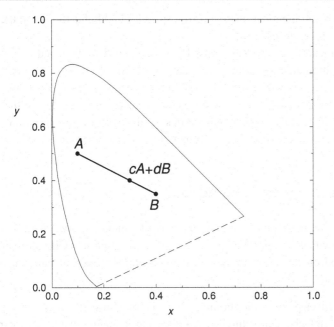

Figure 6.10. The locus of the additive mixture, $cA + dB$, is on the line segment AB.

1. The areas under the curves $\bar{r}(\lambda)$, $\bar{g}(\lambda)$, $\bar{b}(\lambda)$ are equal because of the way the units of the primaries are chosen. The tristimulus values of the equal-energy white are matched by unit amounts of the three primaries. The areas under $\bar{x}(\lambda)$, $\bar{y}(\lambda)$, and $\bar{z}(\lambda)$ are also equal because of the way the transformation is defined in Eq. (6.23).

2. Let A and B be two color stimuli, and c and d be two constants. On a chromaticity diagram, the chromaticity point of the additive mixture of cA and dB is on the line connecting the chromaticity point of A and the chromaticity point of B (see Fig. 6.10). Let the tristimulus values of A be (X_a, Y_a, Z_a), and those of B be (X_b, Y_b, Z_b). Their chromaticity coordinates are (x_a, y_a) and (x_b, y_b). Define k_a and k_b by

$$k_a = \frac{c(X_a + Y_a + Z_a)}{c(X_a + Y_a + Z_a) + d(X_b + Y_b + Z_b)},$$

$$k_b = \frac{d(X_b + Y_b + Z_b)}{c(X_a + Y_a + Z_a) + d(X_b + Y_b + Z_b)}.$$

The tristimulus values of the additive mixture of cA and dB are $(cX_a + dX_b, cY_a + dY_b, cZ_a + dZ_b)$ and the chromaticity coordinates of the mixture, (x, y), are:

$$x = \frac{cX_a + dX_b}{c(X_a + Y_a + Z_a) + d(X_b + Y_b + Z_b)} = k_a x_a + k_b x_b,$$

$$y = \frac{cY_a + dY_b}{c(X_a + Y_a + Z_a) + d(X_b + Y_b + Z_b)} = k_a y_a + k_b y_b.$$

Since $k_a + k_b = 1$, (x, y) is on the line segment connecting (x_a, y_a) and (x_b, y_b). This collinearity of additive color mixing is very useful. For example, it has been used in determining the illuminant chromaticity from specular highlights [560] and the color gamut of reflecting surfaces [617].

3. The chromaticities of all physically possible stimuli must be bounded in a convex region by the chromaticities of the spectrum colors. Since all physically realizable color stimuli are composed of light of different wavelengths in various proportions, their chromaticity loci must fall on the line segments connecting the loci of the single wavelength lights. Therefore, the chromaticities of all physically possible stimuli must be bounded in a convex region by the chromaticities of the spectrum colors.

6.9   Cautions on the use of colorimetric data

Misuse of colorimetric data is quite common. The major problem arises when one confuses color specifications with color appearance. For example, one often sees CIE diagrams with pretty colors painted on them. As Breneman pointed out, this type of painting can be misleading in two ways:

1. It implies that a given point on the chromaticity diagram represents one perceived color. This is not true. In fact, a color stimulus at a given chromaticity point can appear to be almost any color, depending on the illumination, the spectral reflectance, the surround, and the viewing and lighting geometry.
2. It implies that a given perceived color should fall at a certain point on the chromaticity diagram. This is not true, either. A perceived color can come from almost any point on the diagram.

It should also be pointed out that a color matching experiment itself has its inherent difficulties:

1. Adjusting three knobs to match a color cannot always be done accurately. Some people stop short of getting an exact match and give up (humans do not have infinite patience).
2. Certain colors are more difficult to match than others. We are not equally sensitive to color differences at all wavelengths.
3. It is not known how much influence adaptation has when the subject is fixated on the test fields.

Other problems that are worth noting are as follows:

1. $V(\lambda)$ has been found to be too low in the short wavelength region (see Section 4.2).
2. The assumption that $V(\lambda)$ is a linear combination of color matching functions is of unknown validity, although this assumption is accepted as true by many researchers in the vision community [863, 885].
3. Cone sensitivities are not uniform even within $2°$ of the fovea area, and are even less so for the $10°$ area. Fovea cones are slender and parafovea cones are shorter. The shape of the cone may affect its spectral sensitivity.
4. The CIE Standard Observers represent "averaged" sensitivities. Every individual has slightly different sensitivities [134, 515, 702, 703]. For some people, the difference can

be significant. If one plots the chromaticity loci of the spectrum, it generally has the same kind of shape as the standard observer. However, differences tend to be in the yellow direction.

5.   The additivity law in colorimetry fails at very high and very low luminance levels.

6.   The facts that color matching functions vary with field size, that many objects are larger than 2 degrees, and that our eyes are constantly moving, projecting the same object point onto different locations on the retina, all make us wonder how the CIE system of colorimetry can be so useful in so many applications. Evidence shows that our color perception is more of a reconstructed impression than a point-by-point mapping of tristimulus values.

7.   Although there is a high correlation between the colorimetric specification of a color stimulus and its perceptual appearance under normal viewing conditions, it would be a major misuse of the colorimetry if we did not keep in mind that the colorimetric specification of color stimuli only expresses the equivalence relation up to the photoreceptor signal level and not much beyond that. It has been well established that color perception involves many more complex, spatial, and temporal, processes after the photoreceptors in the retina and up into the visual cortex and other parts of the brain.

6.10   Color differences and uniform color spaces

The CIE 1931 XYZ tristimulus values were not defined with explicit consideration of color differences. Two colors with a small difference in the tristimulus values may look very different or virtually indistinguishable depending on where the two colors are located in the XYZ space. For example, MacAdam [618] measured the precision of color matching, under constant luminance, in a 2° matching field surrounded by a 42° surround field of a chromaticity similar to that of CIE source C and a luminance of about 24 cd m^{-2}. His data showed that the just-noticeable color differences varied greatly over the CIE 1931 (x, y) chromaticity diagram. Figure 6.11 shows the contours of 10/3 just-noticeable difference for many chromaticities on the (x, y) diagram at a constant luminance of about 48 cd m^{-2}. These elliptic contours are known as the MacAdam ellipses. It should be pointed out that the MacAdam ellipses were derived from data from only a single observer, and therefore cannot be considered as representative for the average observer. Other research groups repeated MacAdam's measurements and the general finding was that the sizes and the orientations of the ellipses are in good agreement between different experiments. However, there were considerable variations in the shape of the ellipses (the ratio of the major axis to the minor axis) for different observers.

Since then, there have been many attempts to find some transformation that will map these ellipses into circles of the same radius. A transformation with this ideal property can then be said to have mapped the CIE 1931 (x, y)-chromaticity diagram into a uniform chromaticity scale. If luminance variation is also considered, an ideal mapping should produce a uniform color space. It was (and probably still is) believed by many people that a uniform color space would be most useful for applications where perceptual errors are to be minimized.

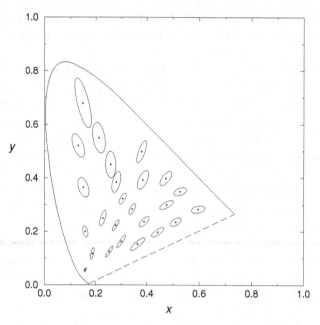

Figure 6.11. MacAdam ellipses showing 10/3 just-noticeable difference contours for stimuli of constant luminance (about 48 cd m^{-2}).

After a long series of studies, proposals, and revisions, in 1976 the CIE recommended the CIE 1976 UCS (uniform chromaticity scale) diagram, the CIELUV color space, and the CIELAB color space. None of these recommended transformations succeeded in making the MacAdam ellipses truly circles of uniform size. However, they all make the transformed spaces nearly uniform. These uniform color spaces are intended for comparisons of small color differences between object colors of the same size and shape, viewed in identical white to mid-gray surroundings, by an observer photopically adapted to a visual field of chromaticity not too different from that of average daylight. Two of the terms that require special attention here are white and neutral. These two terms are often used interchangeably. However, some subtle, but important differences exist. Strictly speaking, white refers to perception and neutral refers to physical specification. For example, in calibrating a CRT monitor, it is important to adjust the monitor circuits so that equal R,G,B values produce the same chromaticity (this is called color tracking, i.e., the three colors track each other to maintain the same chromaticity throughout the whole luminance range). The (physical) chromaticity that is so maintained is called the neutral point. However, it is often impossible to obtain perfect color tracking and therefore the chromaticity at the maximal R,G,B values is commonly taken as the neutral point (it is often called the white point of the monitor because it has the maximum luminance and also often appears to be white). As we mentioned, white refers to perception. For example, the bright snow on an image displayed on the monitor often appears to be white. However, color appearance is often influenced by the colors of the immediately neighboring regions and also by almost everything else in the visual field. Therefore, a color stimulus can appear white, but its physical measurement can be quite different from the physical specification of the neutral chromaticity. The three uniform color spaces recommended by the CIE are all based on normalization to neutral for accounting for the effect of chromatic adaptation. For reflection samples, a neutral point can be defined as the color stimulus from a perfect reflecting diffuser. Since it reflects 100% of the light uniformly into all directions, we will call it the *neutral white* or *reference white* to distinguish it from other reflection samples that have the same chromaticity but different luminances. Although the term "neutral white" seems to be mixing physical and perceptual concepts together, we use it for lack of another more commonly accepted term. The term "reference white" seems to be more widely accepted because the adjective "reference" appears to take away the subjective part in the term " white".

6.10.1 CIE 1976 UCS diagram

The CIE 1976 UCS diagram is recommended whenever a projective transformation of the (x, y) diagram yielding color spacing perceptually more nearly uniform than that of the (x, y) diagram is desired. The chromaticity diagram is produced by plotting u' as the abscissa and v' as the ordinate, where

$$u' = \frac{4X}{(X + 15Y + 3Z)},\tag{6.30}$$

$$v' = \frac{9Y}{(X + 15Y + 3Z)}.\tag{6.31}$$

The third chromaticity coordinate w' is equal to $1 - u' - v'$. The color spacing provided by this chromaticity diagram is known to be more nearly uniform than that of the CIE (x, y)-chromaticity diagram for observation of specimens having negligibly different luminances. Figure 6.12 shows the spectrum loci in the CIE 1976 UCS diagram.

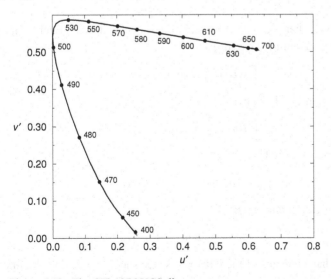

Figure 6.12. The CIE 1976 UCS diagram.

6.10.2   CIELUV color space

The CIE 1976 L^*, u^*, v^* space (recommended abbreviation: "CIELUV") is defined as follows:

$$L^* = 116(Y/Y_\mathrm{n})^{1/3} - 16 \quad \text{for } Y/Y_\mathrm{n} > 0.008\,856, \tag{6.32}$$

$$L^* = 903.3(Y/Y_\mathrm{n}) \qquad\quad \text{for } Y/Y_\mathrm{n} \leq 0.008\,856, \tag{6.33}$$

$$u^* = 13L^*(u' - u'_\mathrm{n}), \tag{6.34}$$

$$v^* = 13L^*(v' - v'_\mathrm{n}), \tag{6.35}$$

where Y_n is the luminance of the reference white and $(u'_\mathrm{n}, v'_\mathrm{n})$ is the chromaticity of the neutral point (or the reference white). Note that the CIELUV space attempts to adjust to different illuminants by a translation of the origin to $(u'_\mathrm{n}, v'_\mathrm{n})$ in (u', v') space. Since u' and v' are ratios of XYZ tristimulus values and since differences in ratios, such as $u' - u'_\mathrm{n}$, do not follow any known models of chromatic adaptation, it is not clear why such an illuminant adjustment procedure was chosen by the CIE. For this reason, we suspect that the CIELUV space should only be used for illuminants that are close to that used in the original experiments that produced the data from which the CIELUV formulas were derived.

For viewing reflection samples, the reference neutral point can be taken as the chromaticity of the lighting illuminant. For viewing self-luminous displays, the definition is less clear. The usual practice is to take the calibrated neutral (white) point. For example, CRT monitors are calibrated to chosen neutral (white) points of various color temperatures and therefore, each monitor should have its white point as $(u'_\mathrm{n}, v'_\mathrm{n})$. For direct viewing of transparency materials, such as photographic reversal (slide) films, a common practice is to use light transmitted through the minimum density of the film as the reference white. For viewing a projection, the screen radiance projected by the film minimum density as measured at the viewing position is taken as the reference white. However, this is problematic because the experimental data used to derive the color space were collected from experiments that used reflection samples.

The difference ΔE^*_{uv} between two color stimuli is calculated as the Euclidean distance between the points representing them in space:

$$\Delta E^*_{uv} = [(\Delta L^*)^2 + (\Delta u^*)^2 + (\Delta v^*)^2]^{1/2}. \tag{6.36}$$

CIE 1976 u,v saturation is defined by:

$$s_{uv} = 13[(u' - u'_\mathrm{n})^2 + (v' - v'_\mathrm{n})^2]^{1/2}. \tag{6.37}$$

CIE 1976 u,v chroma is defined as:

$$C^*_{uv} = (u^{*2} + v^{*2})^{1/2} = L^* s_{uv}. \tag{6.38}$$

CIE 1976 u,v hue-angle is defined by:

$$h_{uv} = \arctan(v^*/u^*). \tag{6.39}$$

Two important characteristics of the CIELUV space should be noted. The first is that the (u^*, v^*) coordinates are proportional to the lightness L^* and so is the chroma C^*_{uv}.

However, the saturation s_{uv} does not depend on the lightness. The distinction between chroma and saturation in CIELUV is an attempt to distinguish the physical correlates of two perceptual quantities. These color perception terms will be described in Chapter 18 when we discuss color appearance. For now, we will clarify the difference in these two quantities by referring to the following common experience. Assume that we are in a room equipped with multiple lamps of the same physical characteristics. For example, in an office environment, fluorescent lamps are arranged in sections, each of which has several lamps that can be controlled by different switches. First, let us turn on only some of the lamps and observe and try to remember the colors of the objects in the room. Next, we turn on all the lamps and the room looks much more brighter. The same objects now look more colorful than before, although the basic physical properties such as the spectral reflectances of the objects have not changed. We say that the chroma has increased with the higher illuminance, but the saturation remains the same. Whether the "perceived" chroma is proportional to the lightness is still an open question.

The second important characteristic of the CIELUV space is that u' and v' are projective transforms of the CIE XYZ space and therefore a straight line in the CIE XYZ space is also a straight line in the u', v' space. For color stimuli of the same luminance, a straight line in the CIE XYZ space is again a straight line in the CIELUV space. This property is important for some applications in additive color reproduction (such as television).

6.10.3 CIELAB color space

The CIE 1976 L^*, a^*, b^* space is abbreviated as "CIELAB". It is defined as follows:

$$L^* = 116 f(Y/Y_n) - 16, \tag{6.40}$$

$$a^* = 500[f(X/X_n) - f(Y/Y_n)], \tag{6.41}$$

$$b^* = 200[f(Y/Y_n) - f(Z/Z_n)], \tag{6.42}$$

where $f(t) = t^{1/3}$ if $t > 0.008\,856$, else $f(t) = 7.787t + 16/116$. (X_n, Y_n, Z_n) are the tristimulus values of the reference (neutral) white point. Note that the adjustment for the illuminant is by taking ratios of tristimulus values relative to the reference white. This type of adjustment is similar to the von Kries model of chromatic adaptation, which is found to describe experimental data quite well. However, the von Kries model requires ratios to be taken for each cone response. The CIELAB space does not follow that model because it takes ratios in XYZ tristimulus values which are linear combinations of the cone responses. Despite this theoretical difficulty, the CIELAB space is found to be adequate in many practical applications.

For viewing reflection samples, the reference white can be taken as the reflection from a perfect reflecting diffuser under the same lighting illuminant. However, this is often unsatisfactory if the target is a photographic reflection print or reflection print of an image. The reason is that the picture on the reflection print is a scene in itself and our visual system makes some adjustment in its judgment regarding the "perceived" lightness, depending on the illumination geometry in the scene. The best density balance for typical reflection prints also leaves some reflectance dynamic range to accommodate for specular highlights so that they are printed "brighter than white". Therefore, the common recommendation for the reference white in a reflection print is to adjust the density to its scene-dependent optimum and then back calculate what the ideal reflecting diffuser will be on that print and use that as the reference white. In this case, the Y_n in (X_n, Y_n, Z_n) for the reflection print is often darker than the paper white, and the chromaticity of the reference white can also be different from that of the viewing illuminant.

For viewing self-luminous displays, the definition of reference white is also problematic. Again, one practice is to take the calibrated white point of the display as the reference white. This is fine if the content of the displayed material is color graphics. If the content is an image, a better result is often obtained when the reference white is taken to be the ideal white object in the image. For direct viewing of transparency materials, such as photographic reversal (slide) films, a common practice is to use light transmitted through the minimum density of the film as the reference white. For viewing a projection, the screen radiance projected by the film minimum density as measured at the viewing position is taken as the reference white. Again, this is fine when the content is color graphics. A better practice is to choose the ideal white in the image. In summary, the application of CIELAB to color image displays is not a straightforward calculation. It involves a subjective adjustment of the color and density balance for each image first before the reference white can be estimated or back calculated.

CIE 1976 a,b chroma is defined by

$$C_{ab}^* = (a^{*2} + b^{*2})^{1/2}. \tag{6.43}$$

CIE 1976 a,b hue-angle is defined as:

$$h_{ab} = \arctan(b^*/a^*). \tag{6.44}$$

The CIELAB space is designed for computing small color differences. The color difference between two stimuli, 1 and 2, are defined as follows. The CIE 1976 lightness difference ΔL^*, chroma difference ΔC^*, and total color difference ΔE_{ab}^* are:

$$\Delta L^* = L_1^* - L_2^*, \tag{6.45}$$

$$\Delta C_{ab}^* = C_{ab,1}^* - C_{ab,2}^*, \tag{6.46}$$

$$\Delta E_{ab}^* = [(\Delta L^*)^2 + (\Delta a^*)^2 + (\Delta b^*)^2]^{1/2}. \tag{6.47}$$

CIE 1976 a,b hue difference is defined by

$$\Delta H_{ab}^* = [(\Delta E_{ab}^*)^2 - (\Delta L^*)^2 - (\Delta C_{ab}^*)^2]^{1/2}. \tag{6.48}$$

Among the various "uniform" color spaces, CIELAB is the most widely used. However, it should be pointed out again that the CIELAB color difference was derived from observing flat reflection samples on a light gray to white background. This type of color judgment is quite different from typical color imaging applications, where colors appear in a complex context and with cognitive interpretation of illumination, texture, shading, shadow, and surface shapes. Two of the important attributes missing in designing the CIELAB and CIELUV spaces are the spatial–temporal variations of the color stimuli and the interplay between the object properties and the "interpreted" color perceptions. There are also attempts to apply the CIELAB metric to the original three-dimensional scenes. This raises two serious questions: what is the reference white and can the metric be applied to stimuli more luminous than the reference white? This type of application is obviously stretching the validity of the CIELAB space too far beyond what it was originally designed for.

6.10.4 The CIE 1994 color-difference model (CIE94)

Developments in color-difference research since 1976 indicated that it is possible to weight the differences in lightness, chroma, and hue differently to achieve better prediction of the experimental data. It was also realized that inconsistency between various field trials of the 1976 CIELAB was largely due to differences in experimental conditions. Therefore, the 1994 color difference model includes a specification of reference conditions under which the color difference experiments are to be conducted. These reference conditions are: illumination: D_{65}; illuminance: 1000 lx; observer: normal color vision; background field: uniform gray with $L^* = 50$; viewing mode: object; sample size: greater than $4°$; sample separation: side by side with edges in direct contact; sample color difference magnitude: 0–5 CIELAB units; sample structure: homogeneous color without visually apparent pattern or nonuniformity.

The new CIE 1994 total color difference ΔE_{94}^* between two color samples is defined by:

$$\Delta E_{94}^* = \left[\left(\frac{\Delta L^*}{k_L S_L}\right)^2 + \left(\frac{\Delta C_{ab}^*}{k_C S_C}\right)^2 + \left(\frac{\Delta H_{ab}^*}{k_H S_H}\right)^2\right]^{1/2}, \tag{6.49}$$

where

$$S_L = 1, \tag{6.50}$$

$$S_C = 1 + 0.045 C_{ab}^*, \tag{6.51}$$

$$S_H = 1 + 0.015 C_{ab}^*, \tag{6.52}$$

where C_{ab}^* is the chroma of the standard sample. If neither sample is considered as the standard, then C_{ab}^* is the geometric mean chroma of the two samples. For the defined reference conditions, k_L, k_C, and k_H are set to 1. In the textile industry, k_L is usually set to 2.0. The complete color-difference model is denoted as the CIE 1994 (ΔL^*, ΔC_{ab}^*, ΔH_{ab}^*) color-difference model with symbol ΔE_{94}^*. The color-difference model is abbreviated as CIE94. When the k_L, k_C, and k_H used are different from unity ($k_L : k_C : k_H$) should be included after the symbol or abbreviation, e.g. CIE94(2:1:1) or $\Delta E_{94}^*(2 : 1 : 1)$ in the textile industry.

6.10.5 CIE2000 color-difference formula: CIEDE2000

The development of a better color-difference formula did not stop with the publication of CIE94. Field tests showed that CIE94 still has large errors in the saturated blue colors and for near-neutral colors [613]. In 2001, CIE recommended an improved color-difference formula, called CIEDE2000 [194], which includes two new features: (1) an interactive term between chroma and hue differences to improve the prediction of blue color differences, and (2) a scaling factor for the CIELAB a^* scale to improve the prediction of the near-neutral color differences. The formula is still based on CIELAB and the CIEDE2000 color differences are calculated as follows: let $\overline{L'}$, $\overline{C_{ab}^*}$, and $\overline{h_{ab}'}$ be the arithmetic means of the L', C_{ab}^*, and h_{ab}' values for a pair of samples denoted by subscripts 1 and 2, and

$$G = 0.5 \left(1 - \sqrt{\frac{\overline{C_{ab}^*}^7}{\overline{C_{ab}^*}^7 + 25^7}} \right), \tag{6.53}$$

$$L' = L^*, \tag{6.54}$$

$$a' = (1 + G)a^*, \tag{6.55}$$

$$b' = b^*, \tag{6.56}$$

$$C_{ab}' = \sqrt{a'^2 + b'^2}, \tag{6.57}$$

$$h_{ab}' = (180°/\pi)\tan^{-1}(b'/a') \ [\text{degree}], \tag{6.58}$$

$$\Delta L' = L_1' - L_2', \tag{6.59}$$

$$\Delta C_{ab}' = C_{ab,1}' - C_{ab,2}', \tag{6.60}$$

$$\Delta h_{ab}' = h_{ab,1}' - h_{ab,2}', \tag{6.61}$$

$$\Delta H_{ab}' = 2\sqrt{C_{ab,1}' C_{ab,2}'} \sin\left(\frac{\Delta h_{ab}'}{2}\right) \tag{6.62}$$

$$\Delta E_{00} = \sqrt{\left(\frac{\Delta L'}{k_L S_L}\right)^2 + \left(\frac{\Delta C_{ab}'}{k_C S_C}\right)^2 + \left(\frac{\Delta H_{ab}'}{k_H S_H}\right)^2 + R_T \left(\frac{\Delta C_{ab}'}{k_C S_C}\right)\left(\frac{\Delta H_{ab}'}{k_H S_H}\right)}, \tag{6.63}$$

where

$$S_L = 1 + \frac{0.015(\overline{L'} - 50)^2}{\sqrt{20 + (\overline{L'} - 50)^2}}, \tag{6.64}$$

$$S_C = 1 + 0.045\overline{C_{ab}^*}, \tag{6.65}$$

$$S_H = 1 + 0.015\overline{C_{ab}^*}T, \tag{6.66}$$

with

$$T = 1 - 0.17\cos(\overline{h_{ab}'} - 30°) + 0.24\cos(2\overline{h_{ab}'}) + 0.32\cos(3\overline{h_{ab}'} + 6°)$$
$$- 0.20\cos(4\overline{h_{ab}'} - 63°) \tag{6.67}$$

and

$$R_T = -\sin(2\Delta\theta)R_C \tag{6.68}$$

where

$$\Delta\theta = 30\exp\left[-\left(\frac{\overline{h_{ab}'} - 275°}{25°}\right)^2\right] \ [\text{degree}], \tag{6.69}$$

$$R_C = 2\sqrt{\frac{\overline{C_{ab}^*}^7}{\overline{C_{ab}^*}^7 + 25^7}}. \tag{6.70}$$

In computing h'_{ab} and $\overline{h'_{ab}}$, the unit used is the degree rather than the radian. All final angles are made positive by an addition of $360°$ if necessary. Since hue angle is a periodic function of $360°$, the convention for computing the average hue angles $\overline{h'_{ab}}$, is to check whether the absolute difference between the two angles is less than $180°$. If yes, $\overline{h'_{ab}}$ is simply the arithmetic mean. If no, $360°$ is subtracted from the larger angle and the arithmetic mean is then taken. For example, if the two angles are $90°$ and $300°$, the correct arithmetic mean is computed by first subtracting $360°$ from $300°$ to get $-60°$ and then taking the arithmetic mean with $90°$ to get the correct mean of $(-60° + 90°)/2 = 15°$.

As one can see, many changes have been made to CIE94 to derive the new CIEDE2000. The color-difference formula is no longer a vector-space distance measure because it depends on the two colors being compared. The increased complexity of the new formula is definitely worthwhile for many applications where a small color difference is of large importance. However, it also brings with it a heavier mathematical burden to maintain its own internal consistency. For example, angle is a periodic function, but Eq. (6.69) contains an exponential function, which is not a periodic function. Here it might be more appropriate to use the von Mises function [318, p. 81–3, 633]: $f(\theta) = A \exp[k \cos(\theta - \alpha)]$. It is very possible that problems will be found and revision will be needed in the future, but for the time being, the formula does improve the prediction of small color-differences significantly [613]. This in itself is a great contribution to many critical applications.

6.11 CIE terms

In order to specify the color coordinates relative to those of an illuminant, the CIE recommends the following terms. Figure 6.13 shows how they are defined relative to an illuminant W for any given stimulus, such as A or B.

- Dominant wavelength (of a color stimulus, A) λ_d: The wavelength of the monochromatic stimulus that, when additively mixed in suitable proportions with the specified achromatic stimulus, matches the color stimulus considered. For stimuli whose chromaticities lie between those of the specified achromatic stimulus and the two ends of the spectrum, the complementary wavelength is used instead of the dominant wavelength.
- Complementary wavelength (of a color stimulus, B) λ_c: The wavelength of the monochromatic stimulus that, when additively mixed in suitable proportions with the color stimulus considered, matches the specified achromatic stimulus.
- Colorimetric purity: Let the dominant wavelength of a given color stimulus, A, be λ_d. The color stimulus, A, can be matched by additively mixing the monochromatic light of λ_d and the specified achromatic light, W. Then the colorimetric purity, p_c is defined by $p_c = L_d/(L_w + L_d)$ where L_d is the luminance of the monochromatic light, and L_w the luminance of the achromatic light. In the case of stimuli specified by the complementary wavelength, suitable mixtures of light from the two ends of the spectrum are used instead of the monochromatic stimuli.
- Excitation purity: $p_e = (y - y_w)/(y_d - y_w)$ or $(x - x_w)/(x_d - x_w)$, where (x, y), (x_w, y_w), and (x_d, y_d) are the (x, y) chromaticity coordinates of the color stimulus considered, the specified achromatic stimulus, and the dominant wavelength.

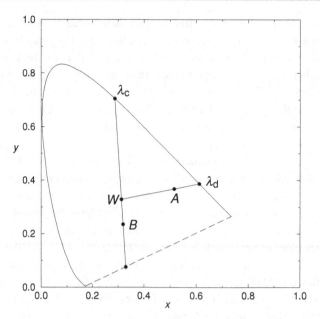

Figure 6.13. CIE 1931 (x, y) chromaticity diagram showing how dominant wavelength, complementary wavelength, colorimetric purity, and excitation purity are defined, all relative to an illuminant W.

- Correlated color temperature: To describe the color quality of an illuminant, the correlated color temperature is often used. The correlated color temperature of a given stimulus is the temperature of the Planckian (blackbody) radiator whose perceived color most closely resembles that of the stimulus at the same brightness, and under the same viewing conditions. The recommended method of calculating the correlated color temperature of a stimulus is to determine on a chromaticity diagram the temperature corresponding to the point on the Planckian locus that is intersected by the agreed isotemperature line containing the point representing the stimulus. The isotemperature lines presently recommended are those normal to the Planckian locus in the now out-dated CIE 1960-UCS (u,v) diagram or equivalently in a chromaticity diagram in which $2v'/3$ is plotted against u', where v' and u' are the coordinates of the CIE 1976 uniform chromaticity scale diagram. One can determine the correlated color temperature of a given light source by calculating its (x, y) chromaticity and graphically interpolating from an existing isotemperature chart [1053, p. 225], or by using a computer to numerically calculate the answer from the definition [1053, pp. 226–7].

6.12 The CIE standard light sources and illuminants

The spectral composition of the light reflected from a surface depends not only on the reflecting properties of the surface, but also on the illumination incident on the surface. The specification of color measurements thus requires the specification of the illumination. To

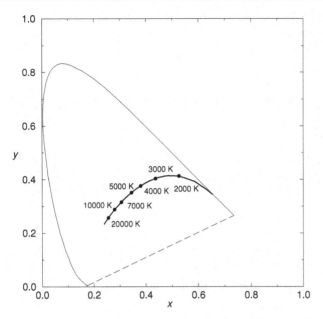

Figure 6.14. The chromaticity loci of a blackbody radiator at different temperatures.

avoid use of a large number of light sources, the CIE has recommended "sources" which it calls A, B, C, and "illuminants", called A, B, C, D, and E. By source is meant the specification of the actual physical setup that can produce the desired light. By illuminant is meant the specification of a spectral power distribution which may or may not be realizable physically. For example, CIE Source A is realized by a gas-filled tungsten filament lamp operating at a correlated color temperature of 2856 K, while CIE Illuminant A is defined to be the light from the blackbody radiator at 2856 K, whose spectral radiant exitance [W m^{-3}], $M_{e,\lambda}$, is given by Planck's radiation law:

$$M_{e,\lambda}(\lambda, T) = \frac{c_1}{\lambda^5(e^{c_2/\lambda T} - 1)}, \tag{6.71}$$

where $c_1 = 3.74183 \times 10^{-16}$ W m^2 and $c_2 = 1.4388 \times 10^{-2}$ m K. The chromaticity loci of a blackbody radiator at different temperatures are shown in Fig. 6.14. CIE illuminant B was intended to represent direct sunlight with a correlated color temperature of 4874 K. CIE Illuminant C was intended to represent daylight (sunlight plus skylight) of a correlated color temperature of 6774 K. Figure 6.15 shows their spectral power distributions.

CIE illuminants D, which were intended to represent various phases of daylight, are specified by the following formulas. The relative spectral power distribution, $S_D(\lambda)$, of a CIE daylight illuminant is defined by

$$S_D(\lambda) = S_0(\lambda) + M_1 S_1(\lambda) + M_2 S_2(\lambda), \tag{6.72}$$

where $S_0(\lambda)$, $S_1(\lambda)$, and $S_2(\lambda)$, are the mean and the two most important "eigenvectors" of a large set of measured daylight distributions (see [1053, p. 762]). Figure 6.16 shows the

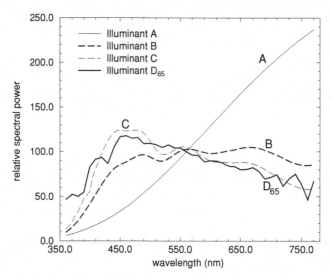

Figure 6.15. The spectral power distributions of CIE standard illuminants.

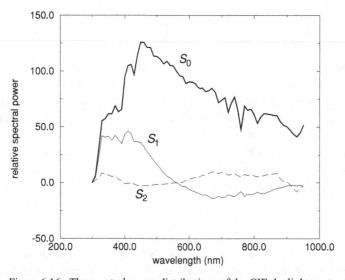

Figure 6.16. The spectral power distributions of the CIE daylight vectors, $S_0(\lambda)$, $S_1(\lambda)$, and $S_2(\lambda)$.

spectral power distribution of the three vectors. M_1 and M_2 are scalar multipliers that are related to the chromaticity coordinates (x_D, y_D) of the illuminant by the following functions [1053, p. 146]:

$$M_1 = \frac{-1.3515 - 1.7703x_D + 5.9114y_D}{0.0241 + 0.2562x_D - 0.7341y_D}, \qquad (6.73)$$

$$M_2 = \frac{0.0300 - 31.4424x_D + 30.0717y_D}{0.0241 + 0.2562x_D - 0.7341y_D}. \qquad (6.74)$$

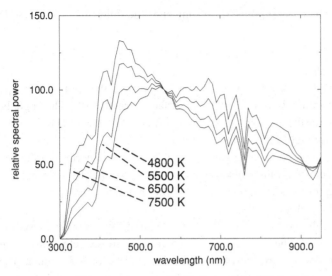

Figure 6.17. The spectral power distributions of the CIE daylights.

The chromaticity coordinate y_D is computed from x_D by

$$y_D = -3.000x_D^2 + 2.870x_D - 0.275, \tag{6.75}$$

which defines the "CIE daylight locus" in the CIE 1931 chromaticity diagram [1053, p. 146]. For correlated color temperatures T_c from approximately 4000 K to 7000 K:

$$x_D = -4.6070\frac{10^9}{T_c^3} + 2.9678\frac{10^6}{T_c^2} + 0.099\,11\frac{10^3}{T_c} + 0.244\,063. \tag{6.76}$$

For correlated color temperatures T_c from approximately 7000 K to 25 000 K:

$$x_D = -2.0064\frac{10^9}{T_c^3} + 1.9018\frac{10^6}{T_c^2} + 0.247\,48\frac{10^3}{T_c} + 0.237\,040. \tag{6.77}$$

Figure 6.17 shows the spectral power distributions of the CIE daylight illuminant at several correlated color temperatures.

In order to reduce the number of illuminants used in colorimetry, the CIE recommends that D_{65} ($T_c = 6504$ K) be used as the preferred illuminant. When it is not convenient to do so, D_{55} ($T_c = 5503$ K) or D_{75} ($T_c = 7504$ K) should be used. CIE illuminant E is defined as a stimulus whose spectral power distribution is constant at all wavelengths. It is also referred to as the equal-energy white or the equal-energy spectrum.

6.13 Illuminating and viewing conditions

Few, if any, physical samples transmit or diffuse light in an isotropic manner. It is, therefore, necessary to specify the illuminating and viewing conditions when making colorimetric measurements. For this purpose, the CIE recommends the following conditions [186] for reflecting specimens:

1. 45°/normal (symbol, 45/0)
   The specimen is illuminated at an angle of 45° ± 2° from the normal to the specimen surface. The specimen is viewed from the surface normal ±10°. The angle between the illuminating (or the viewing) axis and any ray should not exceed 8°.
2. Normal/45° (symbol, 0/45)
   The specimen is viewed at an angle of 45° ± 2° from the normal to the specimen surface. The specimen is illuminated from the surface normal ±10°. The angle between the illuminating (or the viewing) axis and any ray should not exceed 8°.
3. Diffuse/normal (symbol, d/0)
   The specimen is illuminated diffusely by an integrating sphere. It is viewed from the surface normal ±10°. The integrating sphere may be of any diameter provided the total area of the ports does not exceed 10% of the internal reflecting sphere area. The angle between the axis and any ray of the viewing beam should not exceed 5°.
4. Normal/diffuse (symbol, 0/d)
   The specimen is illuminated by a beam whose axis is at an angle not exceeding 10° from the normal to the specimen. The reflected flux is collected by means of an integrating sphere. The angle between the axis and any ray of the illuminating beam should not exceed 5°. The integrating sphere may be of any diameter provided the total area of the ports does not exceed 10% of the internal reflecting sphere area.

The CIE recommends the following conditions [186] for transmitting specimens:

1. Normal/normal (symbol, 0/0)
   The specimen is illuminated by a beam whose effective axis is at an angle not exceeding 5° from the normal to its surface and the angle between the axis and any ray of the illuminating beam does not exceed 5°. The geometric arrangement of the viewing beam is the same as that of the illuminating beam. The specimen is positioned so that only the regular transmitted flux (meaning specular transmission component) reaches the detector. This condition gives the regular transmittance, τ_r.
2. Normal/diffuse (symbol, 0/d)
   The specimen is illuminated by a beam whose effective axis is at an angle not exceeding 5° from the normal to its surface and the angle between the axis and any ray of the illuminating beam does not exceed 5°. The hemispherical transmitted flux is usually measured with an integrating sphere. If the positions of the light source and the detector are interchanged, the method gives the equivalent diffuse/normal (symbol, d/0) quantities.
3. Diffuse/diffuse (symbol, d/d)
   The specimen is illuminated diffusely with an integrating sphere and the transmitted flux is collected in a second integrating sphere. This condition gives the double diffuse transmittance, τ_{dd}.

6.14 The vector space formulation of color calculations

As Grassman recognized in the early 1850s [359, 861], vector space operations are very convenient for describing color matching experiments and colorimetry in general. Indeed, a number of elegant solutions to certain colorimetric problems are successfully derived only after the vector space formulation is adopted [201, 202, 413, 965, 1005]. Interest in the vector space formulation of color calculation is also partially due to the wide use of computers.

The notation used for the vector space formulation is very concise, making it possible to express a very complicated colorimetric statement in a very short mathematical relation. Because of this power of expression and the large knowledge base in linear algebra and set-theoretical methods, the vector space formulation will surely become very important in colorimetry. Since vectors of finite-dimensional spaces are almost always used in computers, we have to be careful about the potential errors resulting from the discrete sampling of spectral distribution functions. Our understanding of this type of error is not quite adequate at present and further research is needed. With this word of caution, we can now introduce the vector space formulation of colorimetry.

Let the spectral sensitivities of the eye at wavelength λ be $s_r(\lambda), s_g(\lambda)$, and $s_b(\lambda)$. Since the visible range of wavelength is finite (roughly from 380 nm to 780 nm), and since most integration is done by summation with small increments, we can sample all functions of wavelength at N discrete equally spaced wavelengths and represent them as finite-dimensional vectors. (Depending on the required accuracy, N can be as many as 401 or more, or as few as 41.) The three cone-sensitivity functions, $s_r(\lambda), s_g(\lambda)$, and $s_b(\lambda)$, can thus be written as $N \times 1$ vectors S_r, S_g, and S_b. We can construct an $N \times 3$ matrix S such that S_r, S_g, and S_b are its three column vectors. Let L, an $N \times 1$ vector, represent the color stimulus incident on the eye, and let R, a 3×1 vector, represent the response (or quantum catches) of the three types of cones. Then we can express the relation between R and L as: $R = S^{T}L$. Given two color stimuli L_1 and L_2, a color match between them simply means $S^{T}L_1 = R_1 = R_2 = S^{T}L_2$. Let A, B, C, and D be four color stimuli, and $R_A = S^{T}A, R_B = S^{T}B, R_C = S^{T}C$, and $R_D = S^{T}D$ be their cone-response vectors. Understanding that additive mixture of two stimuli A and B, i.e., $A \oplus B$, is simply $A + B$ in vector notation, the four laws of colorimetry can now be stated as follows:

1. Symmetry law: If color stimulus A matches color stimulus B, i.e., $R_A = R_B$, color stimulus B matches color stimulus A, i.e., $R_B = R_A$.
2. Transitivity law: If $R_A = R_B$ and $R_B = R_C$, then $R_A = R_C$.
3. Proportionality law: If $R_A = R_B$,

$$R_{\alpha A} = S^{T}(\alpha A) = \alpha S^{T}A = \alpha R_A = \alpha R_B = \alpha S^{T}B = S^{T}(\alpha B) = R_{\alpha B}, \qquad (6.78)$$

where α is any positive factor.

4. Additivity law: If $R_A = R_B$ and $R_C = R_D$,

$$R_{(A+C)} = S^{T}(A + C) = S^{T}A + S^{T}C = R_A + R_C \qquad (6.79)$$
$$= R_B + R_D = S^{T}B + S^{T}D = S^{T}(B + D) = R_{(B+D)}. \qquad (6.80)$$

Also, if $R_A = R_B$ and $R_{(A+C)} = R_{(B+D)}$,

$$R_C = S^T C = S^T(A + C) - S^T A = S^T(B + D) - S^T B = S^T D = R_D. \tag{6.81}$$

Let us select three primaries P_1, P_2, and P_3, each one being an $N \times 1$ vector. Let P be an $N \times 3$ matrix such that P_1, P_2, and P_3 are its three column vectors. A given color stimulus A can be matched by proper mixture of the three primaries if there exists a 3×1 coefficient vector $C_P = [c_1, c_2, c_3]^T$ such that

$$S^T A = S^T(c_1 P_1 + c_2 P_2 + c_3 P_3) = S^T P C_P. \tag{6.82}$$

Obviously, C_P has a unique solution if and only if $S^T P$ is nonsingular, and then

$$C_P = (S^T P)^{-1} S^T A. \tag{6.83}$$

Since S has a rank of 3, it is only necessary to pick a set of three primaries that are mutually independent to guarantee the full rank of the matrix P and the nonsingularity of $S^T P$. This proves that any set of three independent color stimuli can be used as primaries to match any test stimuli. However, the solution vector C_P may have negative component(s), in which case the primary with the negative component is mixed with the test stimulus, instead of with the other primaries. A very interesting and important property of color matching is that the coefficient vector C_P depends on the cone spectral sensitivity function S only up to its linear transformation. In other word, if we construct a new visual system whose cone spectral sensitivity functions, S', are linear combinations of S, i.e., $S' = SW$, where W is any nonsingular 3×3 matrix, it can be shown that the coefficient vector C_P for the new system will remain the same. This means that it is not possible to determine the exact cone spectral sensitivity functions purely by color matching experiments.

By definition, the ith row vector of the color matching functions M_P (an $N \times 3$ matrix) with respect to the primaries P is the coefficient vector C_P^T when the test stimulus A is monochromatic light with the ith element equal to 1 and the rest of the elements 0. From Eq. (6.83),

$$C_P^T = A^T S (P^T S)^{-1}. \tag{6.84}$$

By stacking up N row vectors of C_P^T (1×3), corresponding to the N row vectors, A^T ($1 \times N$), one for each single wavelength stimulus, we have the following expression for the color matching functions M_P (an $N \times 3$ matrix):

$$M_P = S(P^T S)^{-1}. \tag{6.85}$$

Since $(P^T S)^{-1}$ is a 3×3 matrix, the color matching functions M_P are linear combinations of the cone spectral sensitivity functions. Multiplying both sides of Eq. (6.85) on the left by P^T, we can obtain an interesting relation:

$$P^T M_P = I, \tag{6.86}$$

where I is the 3×3 identity matrix. Therefore, the spectra of the primaries, P, and their corresponding color matching functions, M_P, are related in a special way.

If another set of primaries Q is chosen to match the same stimulus A, the coefficient vector C_Q can be related to C_P by:

$$C_Q = (S^TQ)^{-1}S^TA \qquad \text{from Eq. (6.83)}$$

$$= (S^TQ)^{-1}S^TPC_P \quad \text{from Eq. (6.82)} \qquad (6.87)$$

and

$$C_Q^T = C_P^TP^TS(Q^TS)^{-1}. \qquad (6.88)$$

Again, by stacking up C_Q^Ts and C_P^Ts for single wavelength stimuli, we have

$$M_Q = M_PP^TS(Q^TS)^{-1}$$

$$= M_PP^TM_Q, \qquad (6.89)$$

and therefore

$$M_P = M_Q(P^TM_Q)^{-1}. \qquad (6.90)$$

Similarly, $M_Q = M_P(Q^TM_P)^{-1}$, and using this relation, we can also derive the following equation:

$$C_Q = (S^TQ)^{-1}S^TPC_P$$

$$= M_Q^TPC_P$$

$$= (M_P^TQ)^{-1}M_P^TPC_P$$

$$= (M_P^TQ)^{-1}C_P, \qquad (6.91)$$

which is the transformation of tristimulus values between two sets of primaries, as has been shown in Eq. (6.11).

One area in colorimetry is the study of metameric color stimuli (stimuli that have different spectral power distributions, but appear to be the same color visually). An interesting question is that given a spectral power distribution, how can we generate its various metamers systematically? This question is difficult to answer in the continuous domain, but if cast in the finite-dimensional vector space formulation, it becomes quite easy as was first pointed out by Cohen and Kappauf [201]. The basic solution is based on the observation by Wyszecki that if a spectral function, B, produces zero integrals with all three cone-sensitivity functions, s_r, s_g, and s_b, it is invisible to the eye, and when it is added to any spectral power distribution, A, the resulting spectral power distribution, $A + B$, will be a metamer of A. The invisible spectral function B is therefore called a metameric black.

If we treat the three spectral-sensitivity functions of the cones as an $N \times 3$ matrix, S, we can imagine that in N-dimensional space, all vectors that are perpendicular to the three cone vectors will not be visible to our eyes because the inner products between them and the cone spectral-sensitivity functions will be zero. If we can find a projection matrix, V, that will project any N-dimensional vector, A, into the three-dimensional subspace that is spanned by the three cone vectors, the difference, $A - VA$ will be a metameric black. A projection matrix of this nature is well known in matrix algebra [350] to be:

$$V = S(S^TS)^{-1}S^T. \qquad (6.92)$$

Since any nonsingular linear transform of the three cone vectors spans the same subspace, the projection operator V can be constructed from any measured color matching functions as well (see Eq. (6.85)). This can be easily shown as follows: for any $S' = SW$, where W is any nonsingular 3×3 matrix,

$$\begin{aligned}
V' &= S'[(S')^T S']^{-1}(S')^T \\
&= SW[(SW)^T(SW)]^{-1}(SW)^T \\
&= SW[W^T S^T SW]^{-1}W^T S^T \\
&= SWW^{-1}(S^T S)^{-1}(W^T)^{-1}W^T S^T \\
&= S(S^T S)^{-1}S^T = V.
\end{aligned}$$

The elegant simplicity resulting from the vector space formulation is thus clearly demonstrated in the example of computing metameric black and proving its invariance under nonsingular linear transform.

6.15   Applications of colorimetry

The applications of colorimetry are numerous. We will present three examples in this section. The first example shows how the National Television Systems Committee (NTSC) color signals are defined by its choice of phosphor primaries and reference white. The second example shows how a realistic scene should be generated in computer graphics. The third example discusses various issues in digital color image processing.

6.15.1   The NTSC color signals

TV signals decoded at the receiver end are used to drive the R, G, B guns of the TV monitor. The color that will be produced on the monitor obviously depends on the spectral emission curves of the three phosphors in the monitor. To ensure a faithful color reproduction of the original scene on the receiver monitor, it is necessary to define the colors of the monitor phosphors for the transmitted and decoded color signals. However, signal encoding, transmission, and decoding include a nonlinear transformation that makes an exact analysis fairly complicated. The color standard that the NTSC adopted is based on the empirical observation that the effect of the nonlinear transformation on color reproduction is negligible. The following discussion will therefore assume that all signal transformations are linear.

The official NTSC specifications include the definitions of the phosphor primaries and the reference illuminant. Any given color in the original scene can be specified by the CIE XYZ tristimulus values. If the receiver monitor can produce the same XYZ tristimulus values, we can say that a faithful color reproduction has been achieved. However, flicker considerations, phosphor operating characteristics, and other limitations of technology often prevent the luminance of the monitor displays from exceeding 100–200 cd m^{-2} [895, p. 25]. This luminance level is far below that of typical outdoor scenes (more than 1000 cd m^{-2}) and

Table 6.2. *The chromaticity coordinates of the NTSC standard phospors*

Stimulus	r	g	b	x	y	z
red phosphor	1	0	0	0.67	0.33	0.00
green phosphor	0	1	0	0.21	0.71	0.08
blue phosphor	0	0	1	0.14	0.08	0.78
white (illuminant C)	1/3	1/3	1/3	0.310	0.316	0.374

also less than studio lighting (200 cd m^{-2} or more). Therefore, it is not practical to require the TV monitor to reproduce the same XYZ tristimulus values as the original scene. Thus typically the signals of a "white object" with 60% reflectance are scaled to the maximum amplitude but chromaticities are generally reproduced correctly.

The NTSC chromaticity transformation between the phosphor primaries and the CIE XYZ primaries is shown in Table 6.2. Using the relations developed in Section 6.4, we have

$$V = \begin{bmatrix} x_1 & x_2 & x_3 \\ y_1 & y_2 & y_3 \\ z_1 & z_2 & z_3 \end{bmatrix} = \begin{bmatrix} 0.67 & 0.21 & 0.14 \\ 0.33 & 0.71 & 0.08 \\ 0.00 & 0.08 & 0.78 \end{bmatrix}, \tag{6.93}$$

$$U = \begin{bmatrix} r_1 & r_2 & r_3 \\ g_1 & g_2 & g_3 \\ b_1 & b_2 & b_3 \end{bmatrix} = \begin{bmatrix} 1.0 & 0.0 & 0.0 \\ 0.0 & 1.0 & 0.0 \\ 0.0 & 0.0 & 1.0 \end{bmatrix}, \tag{6.94}$$

$$\begin{bmatrix} \alpha_1 \\ \alpha_2 \\ \alpha_3 \end{bmatrix} = U^{-1} \begin{bmatrix} r_4 \\ g_4 \\ b_4 \end{bmatrix} = \begin{bmatrix} 1.0 & 0.0 & 0.0 \\ 0.0 & 1.0 & 0.0 \\ 0.0 & 0.0 & 1.0 \end{bmatrix} \begin{bmatrix} 1/3 \\ 1/3 \\ 1/3 \end{bmatrix} = \begin{bmatrix} 1/3 \\ 1/3 \\ 1/3 \end{bmatrix}, \tag{6.95}$$

$$\begin{bmatrix} \beta_1 \\ \beta_2 \\ \beta_3 \end{bmatrix} = V^{-1} \begin{bmatrix} x_4 \\ y_4 \\ z_4 \end{bmatrix} = \begin{bmatrix} 0.67 & 0.21 & 0.14 \\ 0.33 & 0.71 & 0.08 \\ 0.00 & 0.08 & 0.78 \end{bmatrix}^{-1} \begin{bmatrix} 0.310 \\ 0.316 \\ 0.374 \end{bmatrix} = \begin{bmatrix} 0.286\,283 \\ 0.260\,999 \\ 0.452\,718 \end{bmatrix}, \tag{6.96}$$

and

$$D = \begin{bmatrix} 0.858\,849 & 0 & 0 \\ 0 & 0.782\,997 & 0 \\ 0 & 0 & 1.358\,15 \end{bmatrix}. \tag{6.97}$$

The transformation matrix $A = cVDU^{-1}$ is determined up to a constant factor:

$$A = c \begin{bmatrix} 0.67 & 0.21 & 0.14 \\ 0.33 & 0.71 & 0.08 \\ 0.00 & 0.08 & 0.78 \end{bmatrix} \begin{bmatrix} 0.858\,849 & 0 & 0 \\ 0 & 0.782\,997 & 0 \\ 0 & 0 & 1.35\,8\,15 \end{bmatrix} \begin{bmatrix} 1.0 & 0.0 & 0.0 \\ 0.0 & 1.0 & 0.0 \\ 0.0 & 0.0 & 1.0 \end{bmatrix}$$

$$= c \begin{bmatrix} 0.575\,429 & 0.164\,429 & 0.190\,141 \\ 0.283\,42 & 0.555\,928 & 0.108\,652 \\ 0.000 & 0.062\,639\,8 & 1.05\,936 \end{bmatrix}.$$

The convention is to choose the constant c so that Y is equal to 1.0 when R, G, and B are set to 1.0. By doing so, we obtain the transformation matrix A as

$$A = \begin{bmatrix} 0.607 & 0.173 & 0.200 \\ 0.299 & 0.586 & 0.115 \\ 0.000 & 0.066 & 1.117 \end{bmatrix}. \tag{6.98}$$

The numbers are subject to errors due to rounding and matrix inversion. The matrix matches the familiar NTSC signal specifications to the degree of accuracy in our computation:

$$X = 0.607R + 0.174G + 0.200B,$$
$$Y = 0.299R + 0.587G + 0.114B,$$
$$Z = 0.000R + 0.066G + 1.111B.$$

In order to compensate for the nonlinear characteristics of the CRTs used as television receivers, the (R, G, B) signals are predistorted to (R', G', B') so that when (R', G', B') are applied to the CRTs, the displayed images are proportional to (R, G, B). This predistortion step is called "gamma correction":

$$R' = R^{1/\gamma},$$
$$G' = G^{1/\gamma},$$
$$B' = B^{1/\gamma},$$
$$Y' = 0.299R' + 0.587G' + 0.114B',$$

where $\gamma = 2.2$ for the NTSC standard. The (R', G', B') signals are then converted to color difference signals:

$$U = 0.493(B' - Y'), \tag{6.99}$$
$$V = 0.877(R' - Y'), \tag{6.100}$$
$$I = V \cos 33° - U \sin 33°, \tag{6.101}$$
$$Q = V \sin 33° + U \cos 33°, \tag{6.102}$$
$$I = 0.596R' - 0.275G' - 0.322B', \tag{6.103}$$
$$Q = 0.211R' - 0.523G' + 0.312B'. \tag{6.104}$$

From the TV transmitter, Y' is the luminance signal and (I, Q) are the chrominance signals that are broadcasted. Based on our visual sensitivity, Y' is transmitted with the highest bandwidth: 4.2 MHz; I with the next highest bandwidth: −1.3 MHz to +400 kHz about the chrominance subcarrier frequency; and Q with the lowest bandwidth: −400 kHz to +400 kHz about the chrominance subcarrier.

6.15.2 Computer graphics

Pictorial synthesis of realistic images of real or imaginary objects has become an important tool in many applications. For example, to decide what type of paint to use on an automobile, it is faster and more economical to use computer graphics to synthesize the images of the car painted with the different paints that we are considering, than to build models and actually paint them.

In order that the synthesized images be as close to the real scene as possible, careful modeling of surface reflection and accurate color rendering are very important. The traditional shading model represents Lambertian surface reflection by only three reflectance factors ρ_r, ρ_g, and ρ_b, such as:

$$
\begin{aligned}
R &= E_r\rho_r(\mathbf{N} \cdot \mathbf{L}), \\
G &= E_g\rho_g(\mathbf{N} \cdot \mathbf{L}), \\
B &= E_b\rho_b(\mathbf{N} \cdot \mathbf{L}),
\end{aligned}
\tag{6.105}
$$

where R, G, and B are the three image irradiances, and r, g, and b indicate the conventional red, green, and blue channels. E_r, E_g, and E_b are the red, green, and blue incident irradiances of the surface illumination, and ρ_r, ρ_g, and ρ_b are the diffuse (body) reflectance factors. $\mathbf{N}$ and $\mathbf{L}$ are the surface normal and light source direction vectors. Although this model has been widely used and produces seemingly acceptable images, it is physically incorrect [320, p. 733]. The correct way to generate the R, G, B signals for a color monitor is to use the full spectral energy distribution of the light source and the spectral reflectance function of the surface to calculate the CIE XYZ tristimulus values and then convert them to the CRT RGB values with a 3×3 matrix determined from the CRT phosphor chromaticities and luminances. In general, any reflection model of product forms in R, G, B, such as Eq. (6.105), is physically correct only under very restricted conditions, such as a single light source without ambient illumination (see [320, 563, 567] for more detailed discussions).

6.15.3   Digital color image processing

Colorimetric calibration is one of the most neglected areas in digital color image processing. As a consequence, many images with very poor tone and color reproduction can be seen. Only a small part of the problem is actually due to the limitation of the printing process. The major reason is lack of attention to the underlying colorimetric calibration.

Digital images can be acquired directly from a video or CCD camera, or indirectly from scanning photographic film that has been exposed and developed. In this image acquisition process, it is important to establish two types of calibration: (1) the radiometric relation between the digital values of the image and the scene radiances; and (2) the colorimetric relation between the digital color values and the scene spectral distributions or CIE XYZ values. In the process of image display, similar calibrations also have to be established for the radiometric and the colorimetric relations between the image values and the displayed spectral distributions of light. These calibrations do not in themselves produce the most pleasing output images, but they serve as the basis for any further improvements. In later chapters, we will study how color calibration should be done for input and output devices.

6.16   Default color space for electronic imaging: sRGB

With the increased popularity of electronic imaging devices comes a need for a default standard color space. For example, images captured with a digital camera have to be calibrated so that they can be displayed on a color monitor with good color and tone reproduction. Since cameras and monitors are manufactured by many different companies, the only way to make color reproduction feasible in the open system environment is to set up a common, default, color space on which color images can be exchanged over different devices. For this purpose, sRGB was accepted by the International Electrotechnical Commission (IEC) and the International Standards Organization (ISO) as the default color space for multimedia applications.

The sRGB color space is based on the ITU-R BT.709 reference primaries: see Table 6.3.

Applying the color transformation as discussed for the NTSC system, we can obtain the following matrix for the color transformation between the linear R, G, B of sRGB and CIE XYZ:

$$X = 0.4124R + 0.3576G + 0.1805B,$$
$$Y = 0.2126R + 0.7152G + 0.0722B,$$
$$Z = 0.0193R + 0.1192G + 0.9505B,$$

where R, G, B are assumed to be in the range [0,1]. The inverse transformation can be performed through the following equations:

$$R = 3.2410X - 1.5374Y - 0.4986Z,$$
$$G = -0.9692X + 1.8760Y + 0.0416Z,$$
$$B = 0.0556X - 0.2040Y + 1.0570Z.$$

Most CRT monitors have nonlinear input/output characteristic functions as described by a power function with a power (gamma) equal to about 2.2. Since most color images are viewed on monitors, the RGB signals have to be precorrected by a power 0.45 ($=1/2.2$). Therefore, the RGB signals of the sRGB color space are encoded with this gamma correction. In order to compensate for some viewing flare from the ambient light, the gamma correction is not defined as a pure power function, but as a combination of a linear function when the signal is small and a power function when the signal is large. If $R, G, B \leq 0.003\,040$,

Table 6.3. *The chromaticity coordinates of the ITU-R BT.709 standard phosphors*

Stimulus	r	g	b	x	y	z
red phosphor	1	0	0	0.64	0.33	0.03
green phosphor	0	1	0	0.30	0.60	0.10
blue phosphor	0	0	1	0.15	0.06	0.79
white (illuminant D65)	1/3	1/3	1/3	0.3127	0.3291	0.3583

then

$$r = R/12.92,$$
$$g = G/12.92,$$
$$b = B/12.92;$$

otherwise,

$$r = 1.055R^{1/2.4} - 0.055,$$
$$g = 1.055G^{1/2.4} - 0.055,$$
$$b = 1.055B^{1/2.4} - 0.055.$$

In most applications, the signals are then encoded as eight-bit nonlinear $R'G'B'$.

$$R' = 255.0 \times r,$$
$$G' = 255.0 \times g,$$
$$B' = 255.0 \times b.$$

The sRGB standard allows $R'G'B'$ to be encoded into different numbers of bits and offsets to match different monitor interfaces. The conversion is done simply by adding offsets and applying different scale factors.

If the encoded nonlinear $R'G'B'$ signals are eight-bit/color/pixel, they can be converted to linear RGB as follows:

$$r = R'/255.0,$$
$$g = G'/255.0,$$
$$b = B'/255.0.$$

If $r, g, b \leq 0.039\,28$,

$$R = r \times 12.92,$$
$$G = g \times 12.92,$$
$$B = b \times 12.92;$$

otherwise,

$$R = [(r + 0.055)/1.055]^{2.4},$$
$$G = [(g + 0.055)/1.055]^{2.4},$$
$$B = [(b + 0.055)/1.055]^{2.4}.$$

It should be pointed out that the initial linear segment serves two purposes: (a) to avoid the large quantization of a pure 0.45-power function, and (b) to compensate for viewing flare by making a small signal darker than it is with a pure 0.45-power function. The power 2.4 is to produce a good approximation to the rest of the 2.2-power function after the initial linear segment.

6.17 Problems

6.1 In a color matching equation: $(\mathbf{C}) \equiv R(\mathbf{R}) + G(\mathbf{G}) + B(\mathbf{B})$, $(\mathbf{C})$ represents the color stimulus of the test field, and $(\mathbf{R})$, $(\mathbf{G})$, and $(\mathbf{B})$ are the three primaries.
   (a) What do we call the coefficients R, G, and B?
   (b) When $(\mathbf{C})$ is a monochromatic light (single wavelength) whose wavelength is varied through the entire visible spectrum, what do we call the resulting coefficients R, G, and B as functions of wavelength and what are the standard notations for these functions?
   (c) What are the chromaticity coordinates for the color stimulus $(\mathbf{C})$?

6.2 Let $(\mathbf{R})(\mathbf{G})(\mathbf{B})$ and $(\mathbf{X})(\mathbf{Y})(\mathbf{Z})$ be two sets of primaries. Given:

$$\begin{bmatrix} (\mathbf{X}) \\ (\mathbf{Y}) \\ (\mathbf{Z}) \end{bmatrix} \equiv \begin{bmatrix} X_R & X_G & X_B \\ Y_R & Y_G & Y_B \\ Z_R & Z_G & Z_B \end{bmatrix} \begin{bmatrix} (\mathbf{R}) \\ (\mathbf{G}) \\ (\mathbf{B}) \end{bmatrix},$$

what is the transformation of the tristimulus values from one set of primaries $(\mathbf{X})(\mathbf{Y})(\mathbf{Z})$ to another set of primaries $(\mathbf{R})(\mathbf{G})(\mathbf{B})$?

6.3 Let the chromaticity coodinates of a given color stimulus be $(x, y) = (0.3, 0.5)$, and its luminance be 100, what are the tristimulus values, X, Y, Z, of this color stimulus?

6.4 In the CIE 1931 (x,y)-chromaticity diagram, the spectrum locus is a convex curve of a horse-shoe shape. Knowing that the chromaticity coordinates of any mixture of two color stimuli, $c(\mathbf{A}) + d(\mathbf{B})$, always fall on the straight-line segment connecting the two points representing $(\mathbf{A})$ and $(\mathbf{B})$, prove that no three physically realizable primaries can be chosen to match all physically possible color stimuli (without moving one or more of the primaries to the test field).

6.5 Calculate the CIE 1931 chromaticity coordinates of the daylight illuminant at 6500 K.

6.6 A color sample under illuminant C has a dominant wavelength of 530 nm and an excitation purity of 50%. Calculate its coordinates on the CIE 1931 (x, y) chromaticity diagram.

6.7 On the CIE 1931 (x, y)-chromaticity diagram, additive mixtures of two color stimuli fall on a straight-line segment. Is this property still true for CIE 1976 (u',v'), (u^*,v^*), and (a^*,b^*)?

6.8 How many crossing points must a pair of metameric spectral power distributions have?

6.9 Show that $C_P = (S^T P)^{-1} S^T A$ is invariant under any linear transformation of S, i.e., for any $S' = SW$, where W is any nonsingular 3×3 matrix.

6.10 If a TV color monitor does not use the NTSC standard phosphors, what type of electronic circuits should be put in to correct it?

6.11 How do we generate a color image of a human face that is illuminated by two illuminants of different spectral compositions? Can we use three reflectance factors, ρ_r, ρ_g, and ρ_b, to represent the skin color?

6.12 Histogram equalization is a standard technique for image enhancement. Since the image code value can always be mapped to a different output metric, such as CIEXYZ, CIELUV, or CIELAB, what is the histogram that should be equalized?

6.13 Let (X, Y, Z) be the tristimulus values of color sample 1 and $(8X, 8Y, 8Z)$ be those of color sample 2. Both color samples are identically illuminated reflection samples. Let (a^*, b^*) of color sample 1 be $(12, 7)$. What are the (a^*, b^*) values for color sample 2? Assume that X/X_n, Y/Y_n, and Z/Z_n are all greater than 0.1 and (X_n, Y_n, Z_n) are the tristimulus values of the reference white.

6.14 Two color samples, A and B, are illuminated by a light source W. The chromaticity coordinates of A are $(x, y) = (0.3016, 0.5724)$ and those of B are $(x, y) = (0.4822, 0.3725)$. The dominant wavelength of A is 550 nm and its chromaticity coordinates are $(x, y) = (0.3016, 0.6923)$. The dominant wavelength of B is 600 nm and its chromaticity coordinates are $(x, y) = (0.6270, 0.3725)$. What are the chromaticity coodinates of the light source W? What is the excitation purity of the color stimulus from color sample A?

6.15 A screen is illuminated by the additive mixture of the light beams from three projectors, A, B, and C. When projected with each projector alone, the light reflected from the screen has the chromaticity coordinates $(x_A, y_A) = (0.62, 0.24)$, $(x_B, y_B) = (0.23, 0.64)$, and $(x_C, y_C) = (0.21, 0.25)$, for projectors A, B, and C, respectively. If the luminances of the projectors are adjusted so that $Y_A = 100\,\mathrm{cd\,m^{-2}}$, $Y_B = 200\,\mathrm{cd\,m^{-2}}$, and $Y_C = 300\,\mathrm{cd\,m^{-2}}$, what are the chromaticity coordinates (x, y) of the mixture of light reflected from the screen?

6.16 Room A and room B are two separate rooms illuminated by different light sources. The tristimulus values of the reference white are $(X_n, Y_n, Z_n)_A = (80, 100, 128)$ for room A and $(X_n, Y_n, Z_n)_B = (128, 100, 80)$ for room B. A reflection color sample S in room A has tristimulus values $(X_s, Y_s, Z_s) = (16, 20, 16)$. Another reflection color sample T in room B also has tristimulus values $(X_t, Y_t, Z_t) = (16, 20, 16)$.

(a) Color samples S and T have the same tristimulus values. Do they look the same color in the separate rooms?

(b) Calculate the CIELAB values for color samples S and T.

(c) What color will you see in color sample S? What color will you see in color sample T?

(d) Do you think that color samples S and T have the same or different spectral reflectance factors? If you think their spectral reflectance factors are different, what kind of difference is most likely to exist?

7 Light sources

7.1 Natural sources

7.1.1 Sunlight and skylight

The sun is our major light source. Its visible surface has a radius of about 6.95×10^8 m. The sun's average surface temperature is 5750 K. The earth's orbit around the sun (see Fig. 7.1) is an ellipse with the sun located at one of the foci. (The numerical eccentricity ε of the orbit is very small, $\varepsilon = 0.0167$, and therefore, the orbit shape is almost a circle.) The distance from the earth to the sun varies with the time of the year. The average distance is $R = 1.5 \times 10^{11}$ m (1 astronomical unit). At that distance, the solar irradiance, E_0, outside the earth's atmosphere is $(1.367 \pm 0.07) \times 10^3$ [W m^{-2}]; this is called the solar constant. The solar irradiance falls off with the inverse of the distance squared. On any Julian day, J ($J = 1, 2, \ldots, 365$), the solar irradiance, E_{0J}, can be approximatedly calculated [189] as:

$$E_{0J} = E_0 \left(\frac{R}{R_J} \right)^2 = E_0 \{ 1 + 2\varepsilon \cos[\omega(J - 1) - \phi] \} \qquad (7.1)$$

where R_J is the actual sun–earth distance on day J, $\omega = 360°/365.25$ days $= 0.9856°$/day is the mean angular velocity of the earth around the sun, $\phi = 1.735°$ is an offset angle, J is the number of Julian days, counted from $1 =$ January 1, and $\varepsilon = 0.0167$ is the numerical eccentricity of the earth's orbit. The solar irradiance, thus varies from $1.0334E_0$ at perigee (its near point) to $0.9666E_0$ at apogee (its far point). The top curve of Fig. 7.2 shows the solar spectral irradiance above the earth's atmosphere. The spectral radiance distribution can be approximated as a blackbody radiator at 5750 K.

The daylight that reaches the earth's surface from the sun consists of direct sunlight (solar radiation attenuated by the earth's atmosphere) and skylight (solar radiation scattered by the earth's atmosphere). At sea level on a clear day, the average irradiance received by the earth's surface is about 1200 W m^{-2}. Only about 40% of this power is in the visible wavelength range. The angular size of the solar disk viewed from the earth varies from 31.5 to 32.5 minutes of arc. The peak wavelength of the sunlight spectrum outside the atmosphere is 475 nm (corresponding to a blackbody of 6101 K). It is shifted to a wavelength longer than 500 nm at sea level, depending on the time of the day and the atmospheric conditions. The illuminance and spectral composition of the sunlight are modified by absorption and scattering by ozone, gas molecules, water droplets, dust, and other particles in the atmosphere. Figure 7.2 shows spectral and amplitude modification by a particular atmospheric condition [189]

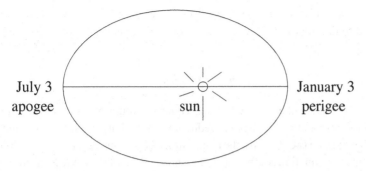

Figure 7.1. The earth's orbit around the sun is an ellipse with the sun at one of the foci. The numerical eccentricity is only 0.0167, very close to a circle. The drawing is exaggerated to show the elliptic shape.

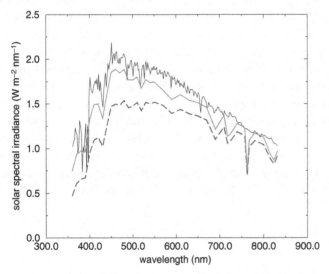

Figure 7.2. The solar spectral irradiance above the earth's atmosphere (the top curve) and at sea level on the earth's surface (the bottom two curves). The bottom curve is the irradiance from direct sunlight on a plane normal to the sun beam. The middle curve (the global solar radiation) shows the direct sunlight plus the scattered sunlight from the atmosphere.

(relative air mass = 1; water vapor content = 1.42 cm precipitable water; ozone content = 0.34 cm STP; spectral optical depth of aerosol extinction = 0.1 at wavelength 500 nm).

Let E be the solar illuminance at sea level and $E_s = 1.275 \times 10^5$ lx be the solar illuminance above the atmosphere, both measured at a surface normal to the sun's rays. From the Beer–Lambert law, we can estimate E by [687, p. 352]:

$$E = E_s e^{-\alpha m}, \tag{7.2}$$

where α is the optical atmospheric extinction coefficient, and m is the relative optical air mass, which is defined as the ratio of the air mass from the actual sun–earth path to the mass when the sun is directly overhead at sea level, i.e., zenith angle = 0. The relative air mass is related to the solar altitude h, which is the angle of elevation of the sun above the horizon:

$$m \approx 1.0/\sin h. \tag{7.3}$$

If the earth and its atmosphere were flat, the equation would be exactly true. In reality, the curvature of earth and its atmosphere reduces the actual air mass. For example, when the sun is on the horizon (i.e., $h = 0$), the actual air mass is about 38, instead of infinity. The optical atmospheric extinction coefficient, α, varies a lot depending on the local atmospheric conditions. An average value is about 0.21 for a clear sky. From Eqs. (7.1), (7.2), and (7.3), we can obtain a very rough estimate of the solar illuminance at sea level on a clear day for the time and location of interest to us.

The relative contribution of the two components of daylight (direct sunlight and skylight) to the illumination of an object varies as a function of the object's surface orientation with respect to the sun's position. For example, for a horizontal plane on a clear day, the skylight contributes about 26% of the surface illuminance when the sun's elevation angle is 20°, and its contribution drops to about 15% when the solar elevation is 50°. When the sun is directly overhead (90°), the skylight contributes about 13% of the surface illuminance of a horizontal plane. Because of the optical path and scattering, the spectral compositions of sunlight and skylight are both functions of the solar altitude. Skylight has more relative energy in the short wavelength region (400–500 nm) and direct sunlight has an overall flat spectrum (from 450 to 700 nm), but it contains less energy at the shorter wavelengths and more energy at the longer wavelengths due to scattering when the solar altitude is low. Figure7.3 shows the relative spectral energy distributions of sunlight and skylight at a solar altitude of 40° on a clear day. In everyday language, the sky is bluish and the sun

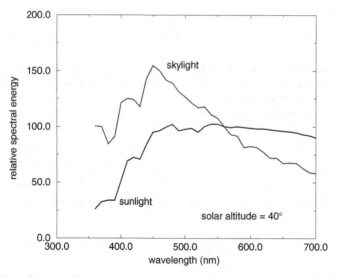

Figure 7.3. The relative spectral energy distributions of sunlight and skylight at a solar altitude of 40°.

is yellowish white. The consequence of this complex variation of illuminance and spectral composition of daylight as a function of solar altitude and object surface orientation is that in a digital image of an outdoor scene the pixels of a curved object surface have different color values depending on its local surface orientations. This is a very basic fact with which all color image segmentation algorithms have to deal. Fortunately, this color variation has a characteristic yellow–blue direction that can be used to our advantage. What is remarkable is that our visual system often perceives a curved surface of a homogeneous material as having a uniform color, when physically every point on the surface is illuminated with a different spectral energy composition!

Judd, MacAdam, and Wyszecki [476] compiled an extensive set of 622 measurements of daylight spectral power distributions, and used principal component analysis to extract several vectors which can be used to reconstruct the typical daylight spectral power distribution from a given correlated color temperature. The CIE has since recommended a method for calculating the daylight illuminant based on their results [1053, pp. 145–6]. This is discussed in Section 6.12.

The luminance and chromaticity of the sky are not uniform. The luminance of the sky depends on the number of scatterers in the line-of-sight. Therefore, the sky looks darker when we are on a very high mountain because there are fewer air molecules to scatter the sunlight into our eyes. For the same reason, the zenith sky also looks darker than the sky near the horizon. This luminance variation can be approximately modeled as $I_0(1 - e^{-\tau})$, where τ is the optical depth of the scattering medium (the air) [615, pp. 24–6]. Near the horizon, the optical depth (air mass) is so large that light of all wavelengths is scattered back (due to multiple scattering), and the horizon sky looks like white, instead of blue.

7.1.2 Moonlight

Moonlight is mainly sunlight reflected by the lunar surface. The luminance of the moon depends on the moon's phase angle, its distance from the earth, its angular elevation from the horizon, etc. The lunar surface reflects light in a manner quite different from that of a Lambertian surface [276, pp. 152–61]. The full moon looks much brighter than the half-moon because the strong retroreflectance of the lunar surface [276, Chapter VII]. The moon at any phase also looks very different from a Lambertian sphere generated by computer graphics. Except for the visible shadowing in some parts of the lunar surface, all points on the moon seem to look equally bright. A Lambertian surface receives light (surface irradiance) according to the cosine of the incident angle and distributes the reflected light in all directions with the same radiance (flux per solid angle per projected area). Therefore, a Lambertian surface looks darker as the surface normal points angularly further away from the light source. This is not what we see from the lunar surface. Since our retinal image irradiance is approximately proportional to the surface radiance, the lunar surface appears to reflect light in such a way that the reflected radiance increases with greater reflection angle so that the effect of the cosine incident angle is cancelled. It is as if the lunar surface distributes the reflected light uniformly per solid angle in all directions, regardless of the angle of reflection. This type of light-reflecting property is not unique to the lunar surface. For example, Hawaiian volcanic cinder exhibits the same property [276, pp. 158–9].

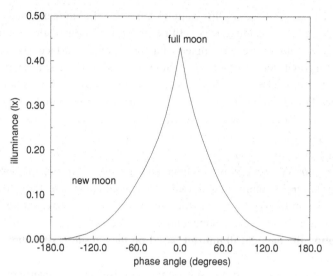

Figure 7.4. The illuminance (on a plane at normal incidence to the moon) due to moonlight plus night skylight as a function of the lunar phase angle.

The illuminance (on a plane at normal incidence to the moon) due to moonlight plus night skylight on a clear night at sea level under full moon is about 0.4 lx. Under a half moon, the average illuminance is only 0.05 lx. This illuminance falls off rapidly as the phase angle increases or decreases from the full moon. The phase angle is defined as the angle between the vector from the object surface to the light source and the vector from the object surface to the viewing observer. Therefore, the phase angle of a full moon is approximately 0°. Let us define the phase angle before full moon as negative and after it as positive. Figure 7.4 shows the illuminance as a function of the lunar phase angle. The curve is not symmetric. The illuminance is generally slightly higher before the full moon for the same phase angle because the visible part of the moon after the full moon has a larger proportion of large dark areas [212].

7.1.3   Starlight

The total illuminance due to starlight is approximately 2×10^{-3} lx for a clear sky night. Although a star is a good example of a point source, its brightness is not traditionally measured in terms of luminous intensity. The visual brightness of a star is measured in apparent magnitude m, which is defined by $m = m_0 - 2.5 \log(E/E_0)$, where E is the illuminance produced by the star on a plane at the earth's surface and normal to the direction of the star, m_0 and E_0 are constants based on the magnitudes ascribed to certain standard stars that are frequently measured by photoelectric instruments [667, p. 96, 772]. E_0 is approximately 2.15×10^{-6} lx for a 0th magnitude star, $m_0 = 0$ [212]. The coefficient 2.5 is chosen so that a magnitude 1 star is exactly 100 times more luminous than a magnitude 6 star. Sirius, which is the brightest star in the sky, the full moon, and the sun have apparent magnitudes of -1.45, -12.73, and -26.74, respectively.

7.2 Artificial sources: lamps

There are many different types of lamps for everyday lighting and for color imaging lighting. Six of the major categories for everyday lighting are incandescent, tungsten halogen, fluorescent, mercury, metal halide, and sodium. For color imaging (photography), the major category is the electronic flash lamp. Two general characteristics of lamps that are important for color imaging are their spectral power distribution as a function of their life time and operating conditions. The light output of a lamp decreases during its life. Also, the spectral power distribution of a tungsten lamp depends on the voltage at which it is operated. Therefore, for critical color calibration or measurement, we cannot always assume that the spectral power distribution of a lamp will remain the same after hours of use or at various operating temperatures. Light sources for laboratory use are reviewed in Chapter 10 of *Handbook of Optics* [84], and will not be covered here.

Radiant spectra from solid thermal sources (such as the tungsten lamps) are continuous. On the other hand, the emission or absorption spectra of electronic transitions from isolated atoms and molecules are quite narrow (they can be less than 10^{-3} nm); therefore, they are called spectral lines. When plotting the spectral power distribution of a light source, such as a fluorescent lamp, which emits a mixture of a continuous spectrum and several spectral lines, the power densities of the spectral lines have to be plotted separately. For example, if the continuous spectral radiance is measured at 5 nm intervals and expressed in $[\text{mW sr}^{-1} \text{ m}^{-2} \text{ nm}^{-1}]$, a spectral line containing 100 mW is plotted as a rectangle of height 20 and width 5 centered at the correct wavelength on a graph for which the unit on the x-axis is the nanometer and the unit along the y-axis is the milliwatt. The area of the finite-width rectangle is equal to the power of the spectral line it is representing. This rectangular bar is raised on top of the continuous spectral radiance so that the total height is their sum. An example is shown in Fig. 7.6.

7.2.1 Incandescent lamps

As an object is heated to higher and higher temperature, the spectral power distribution of its thermal radiation peaks at a shorter and shorter wavelength. This behavior can be completely predicted for the ideal blackbody radiator as discussed in the previous chapter. Since the luminous efficiency for different wavelengths peaks at 555 nm, the maximum luminous efficacy of a blackbody radiator occurs at the temperature of about 6800 K. Heated objects to be used as light sources should operate as close to this temperature as possible. However, most solid materials melt before reaching this temperature. Tungsten has a high melting point (3650 K) and can be produced with high mechanical strength. It is therefore used in most common household incandescent lamps. However, tungsten is not a blackbody radiator. At the same temperature, tungsten does not emit as much radiation energy as the ideal blackbody. The ratio of the radiant exitance of a thermal radiator to that of a blackbody radiator at the same temperature is called the emissivity, ε, of the thermal radiator. Tungsten has an emissivity of about 0.451 at 500 nm when operated at a temperature of 2600 K. The emissivity decreases towards the longer wavelengths (0.423 at 700 nm) and increases towards the shorter wavelengths (0.464 at 400 nm). Therefore, a tungsten source looks

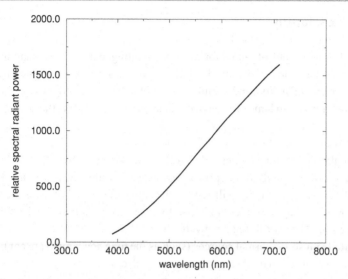

Figure 7.5. An example of the spectral power distribution of a tungsten lamp.

the same color as a blackbody radiator at a slightly higher temperature. (This is called the correlated color temperature of a light source.) Linear interpolation of the emissivity as a function of wavelength gives a fairly good approximation in the visible wavelength range (400–700 nm). The emissivity decreases as the temperature is raised (for example, ε drops to 0.448 at 500 nm when the temperature is raised to 2800 K). A standard 120 V, 100 W tungsten lamp operates at a filament temperature of about 2860 K. If the operating voltage is changed, its filament temperature also changes. Figure 7.5 shows an example of the spectral power distribution of a tungsten lamp. The color temperature of tungsten lamps is a few percent higher than the true temperature. For example, a 3000 K filament radiates light of a correlated color temperature of 3121 K [162]. In general, the spectral power distribution of a tungsten lamp is very well approximated by that of the blackbody at the same color temperature.

Only about 10% of the electric power is converted to visible light in a 100 W light bulb [162]. In an ordinary tungsten lamp, evaporated tungsten atoms are deposited on the inside wall of the bulb which is much cooler than the filament. This results in the blackening of the bulb during its life. Filling the bulb with gases such as argon and nitrogen greatly reduces the blackening effect. However, the gases also reduce the filament temperature and therefore its luminous efficacy. In lamps less than 40 W, the heat loss is greater than the gain in light output by operating the filament at a somewhat higher temperature. Therefore, filling gas is used only for lamps of 40 W or above. The reduction in filament temperature due to the filling gas is less severe when the area of the filament is larger. Therefore, most tungsten lamps today use double-, and even triple-, coiled filaments.

Tungsten lamps have a heating time to 90% of the steady-state luminance of the order of 0.1 s (for a 60 W gas-filled lamp), and a cooling time to 10% of the steady-state luminance around 0.04 s. If one defines the percentage flicker as the ratio of the difference of the maximum and minimum light levels to their sum, multiplied by 100, then for a 60 Hz power source, the percentage flicker of tungsten lamps is about 5%.

Introducing halogen gases (such as iodine) was found (in 1958) to increase the number of lumens per watt and also maintain the luminance level better during a lamp's life. This beneficial effect is caused by the halogen regenerative cycle in which the halogen gas combines with the evaporated tungsten atoms to form tungsten halide; tungsten iodide molecules do not deposit on the bulb wall if the wall temperature is kept between 500 and 1500 K. Tungsten iodide molecules dissociate near the filament where the temperature is high (2800 K) and deposit the tungsten atoms back on the filament. In order to maintain the high wall temperature, quartz is used instead of ordinary glass. The resulting lamps are called the tungsten halogen lamps and have a longer life and better light output. Most such lamps today use bromine instead of iodine because bromine allows a lower wall temperature and it is almost colorless.

7.2.2 Fluorescent lamps

The inside of the tube of a fluorescent lamp is coated with a mixture of phosphors, such as calcium halophosphate and magnesium tungstate. The tube is filled with an inert gas (such as argon) and mercury vapor. Fluorescent lamps produce light by using a high voltage to excite the major gas (argon), which in turn passes the excitation energy to the minor gas (mercury), which radiates its excitation energy mostly in the ultraviolet region with four visible spectral lines at 404.7, 435.8, 546.1, and 577–579 nm. The radiated ultraviolet energy from mercury (4.88 eV or 253.7 nm) in turn stimulates the phosphor to emit visible light. The spectral composition of the emitted light thus depends on the phosphor or the mixture of phosphors coated on the tube. By varying the type of phosphors, fluorescent lamps can be made to produce different spectral power distributions, ranging from "warm white" (with a correlated color temperature of about 2700 K) to "cool white" (about 7500 K).

The spectral distributions from fluorescent lamps are quite different from those of incandescent lamps. They are characterized by a few very narrow, intense concentrations of power superimposed on a continuum. They are less than 0.1 nm wide but have a lot of power. Because their amplitudes are so much higher (tens or hundreds times) than the continuum, they are usually drawn as bars whose areas represent the total power in the spectral line. The width of the bar is equal to the interval that is usually used for weighted-ordinate calculation. If a 10 nm interval is used, the power in the spectral line should be split into the two neighboring intervals according to the wavelength distances. A typical spectral power distribution of a fluorescent lamp consists of a continuous spectrum from the phosphors and the spectral lines (313, 365, 405, 436, 546, and 577–579 nm) from mercury vapor. An example of the spectral power distribution of a fluorescent lamp is shown in Fig. 7.6. The introduction of rare-earth activated phosphors, such as $(Sr,Ca,Ba)_5(PO_4)_3Cl:Eu^{2+}$, $BaMg_2Al_{16}O_{27}:Eu^{2+}$, $CeMgAl_{11}O_{19}:(Ce^{3+}):Tb^{3+}$, $Y_2O_3:Eu^{3+}$, etc., makes the spectral shape of some fluorescent lamps look even more spiky because these phosphors produce narrow-band emission [866, Chapter 5]. The popular three-band fluorescent lamps use rare-earth phosphors with emission spectra in the short-, middle-, and long-wavelength bands to achieve a high color-rendering index. Similarly some CRTs using rare-earth phosphors for light efficiency have very spiky spectral power distributions. The sharp spectral lines may contain very significant energy in some color imaging systems (depending on their spectral responsivities),

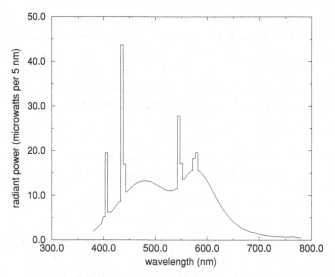

Figure 7.6. An example of the spectral power distribution of a fluorescent lamp.

and often cause difficulties in color reproduction. For example, most photographic color negative films have peak spectral sensitivities at about 430 nm, 550 nm, and 650 nm [924, p. 551]. Images taken under fluorescent lighting often show unusually high "green" and "blue" signals. This effect of course depends on the spectral reflectance factor of the object and therefore it is not possible to correct the problem by simple shifts in log exposures in the three color layers when printing the color negatives. For digital cameras, fluorescent lamps also cause problems in color reproduction and a separate color correction matrix is needed to make the colors of many familiar objects look right.

7.2.3 Electronic flash lamps

An electronic flash lamp produces light by electric discharge through a gas, usually xenon, which is contained in a chamber made of glass or quartz. The discharge spectrum of xenon contains a continuous part and a few spikes (spectral lines) in the infrared region. The spectral composition of the flash light is mainly dependent on the xenon discharge current density. The distribution of the continuous part of the spectrum is close to that of a daylight. The gas pressure in a flash lamp is very high, from 50 to 1500 Torr and the discharge current density is around 1000 to 10 000 A cm^{-2}. Therefore, only some special types of glass and quartz can be used to make the flashtube. There are three electrodes: one at each end of the arc chamber and one which is used to trigger the flash. The electronic triggering circuit consists of a DC power supply, a charging impedance, a large capacitor, and a high-voltage triggering pulse circuit. The time it takes to fully charge the capacitor is often the limiting factor in the shot-to-shot interval for indoor photography.

Light output per flash of a flashtube is measured in lumen seconds. The efficiency of a flashtube is measured as the ratio of light output in lumen second to the energy input in watt seconds. For average photographic applications, 25–45 lm s W^{-1} s^{-1} is quite typical for flashtubes. The flash duration can be as short as 1 μs or as long as 20 ms. The spectral power distribution of a flash lamp consists of a continuous spectrum and a number of discrete xenon lines. The overall shape of the distribution depends (weakly) on several operating parameters, such as the gas pressure and applied voltage, but it is, in general, similar to the daylight spectrum of a correlated temperature of about 6000 K. At the long-wavelength end (greater than 650 nm), the power depends on the operating voltage range. The low-voltage types produce much more infrared than the high-voltage types.

Since the flash duration is often very short compared with the exposure time, the image exposure is controlled by the aperture size or the *f*-number. The amount of light illuminating the subject from the flash is proportional to the inverse of the squared distance between the flash and the subject. Flash manufacturers publish exposure guide numbers for the flash units they make to help users to set the exposure. The guide number is the subject distance (usually in feet) multiplied by the *f*-number for a given film speed. For example, if the guide number of a flash unit is 120 and the subject distance is 15 feet, then an aperture of $f/8$ should be used. However, these numbers are not always very accurate because of variations both in flash power due to manufacturing and in the luminance levels of the ambient lighting. Therefore, some calibration for each flash unit is needed in applications, such as digital cameras.

There are three types of flash unit used in cameras: (1) a manual flash, (2) a self-quenching flash, and (3) a dedicated through-the-lens flash. The manual flash unit discharges a fixed amount of light each time and it is up to the camera user to adjust the aperture for different subject distances. The self-quenching flash unit has a sensor to integrate the total light bounced back to the camera and automatically turns off the flash when enough light has been collected. This type of unit is often used in digital cameras so that the proper exposure can be obtained for flash pictures. The dedicated through-the-lens flash unit works with a particular camera. It links up with the camera's through-the-lens metering system to control the exposure (flash power or aperture) automatically [518, p. 114].

7.2.4 Mercury lamps, sodium lamps, and metal halide lamps

Mercury lamps, sodium lamps, and metal halide lamps are high-intensity discharge lamps. They all require auxiliary electric ballast units to provide high voltages to start and then maintain the current during the lamp operation. They generate light by passing electric current through various metal vapors. The spectral powers of these lamps come mainly from the spectral lines of the metal vapors used. Therefore, a mercury lamp emits most energy at the four mercury spectral lines (404.7 nm, 435.8 nm, 546.1 nm, and 577–579 nm) and a sodium lamp produces most visible light energy around the sodium double lines at 589.0 nm and 589.6 nm. When the lamp is first switched on, it takes a few minutes for the metal and compounds to warm up and build up the temperature and pressure before the lamp can produce full light output. When the lamp is turned off, it also takes from a few seconds to a few minutes for the lamp to cool before it can be turned on again.

7.2.5 Light emitting diodes (LEDs)

Light emitting diodes have been commercially available since 1968, but their colors were initially restricted to red, yellow, and green. In 1993, high efficiency blue LEDs were produced using GaN and related III–V nitride semiconductors [931, pp. 291–2]. This made it possible to use LEDs to produce "white" light sources by combining different color LEDs or by coating certain phosphors, such as yttrium aluminum garnet (YAG), on top of the blue LEDs. The latter approach has the advantage of being more compact and robust. The phosphors on top of the blue LED serve a similar purpose to phosphors coated on fluorescent lamp tubes, i.e., to convert the blue light into light of other wavelengths.

It is now possible to use white-light LEDs as light sources [843, 1072, 1073]. The luminous efficiency of such LEDs approaches 15 lm W^{-1}, about 8 times that of tungsten lamps and 2 times that of fluorescent lamps. Since an LED is quite small, a large array of LEDs can be used to provide the light needed. White-light LEDs only require a low current 15–20 mA, and can produce light with a color temperature close to 8000 K. Many traffic lights now use LEDs. They are low-cost, small in size, very bright, and very energy-efficient. They also last a long time (more than 100 000 hours). CIE is working on standardizing the methods for specifying and measuring LED and LED cluster array characteristics [219].

7.3 Color-rendering index

It is an everyday experience that the illumination in a work environment or a shopping area can strongly affect our perception of colors of objects. As an extreme example, we cannot identify a car by color if the entire parking lot is illuminated by sodium lamps which emit light in only two closely spaced wavelengths. For many applications when color judgement is important (such as the selection of textile or paint color), it is desirable to have a quantitative index, which helps us to select light sources that are suitable for illuminating the spaces where such applications take place. For this purpose, the CIE has defined a color-rendering index for light sources [184]. The objective is for the perceived colors of objects that are illuminated by light sources that have higher color-rendering indices to look more similar to those when the same objects are illuminated by a "reference" source, such as some phase of natural daylight or some incandescent lamp. Several issues are involved in defining such a color-rendering index: (1) What should be used as the reference source? (2) Which objects should be used for comparison? (3) How should chromatic adaptation be accounted for when we view objects under different illuminants? (4) How are the color differences to be quantified? The CIE 1974 color-rendering index is defined by setting standards for answering these four questions.

For a test source with a correlated color temperature below 5000 K, the reference illuminant is a Planckian radiator at the same temperature. For higher color temperatures, the CIE standard daylight illuminant should be used. For calculating the general color-rendering index, a set of eight test-color samples (see Fig. 7.7) are specified in terms of spectral reflectance factors. The CIE *XYZ* tristimulus values of these eight samples are then calculated under both the test source and the reference source. In 1974 when the index was proposed, the recommended color difference formula was the CIE 1964 UCS. Today, it may be more appropriate to use CIELUV or CIELAB formulas, but a study later than 1976 by the CIE concluded that the difference is not large enough to warrant a change in the recommendation.

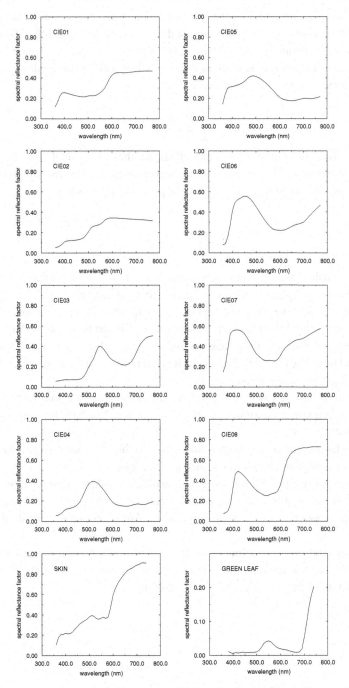

Figure 7.7. The spectral reflectance factors for the eight test-color samples to be used for calculating the CIE general color-rendering index. (The bottom two curves are not CIE recommended color samples – they are from a sample of human skin and a sample from a plant leaf.)

For test-color sample i, let $(\Delta E)_i$ be the color difference between the test source and the reference source expressed in CIE 1964 UCS color difference formula. Then the CIE special color-rendering index is defined by $R_i = 100 - 4.6(\Delta E)_i$. The CIE general color-rendering index R_a is defined as the arithmetic mean of the eight CIE special color-rendering indices R_i for the eight standard test-color samples, i.e.,

$$R_a = \frac{1}{8} \sum_{i=1}^{8} R_i. \tag{7.4}$$

The factor 4.6 in the definition of R_i was chosen so that the CIE general color-rendering index is equal to 50 when a CIE defined standard "warm white" fluorescent lamp is used as a test source in comparison with an incandescent lamp as the reference source.

7.4 Problems

7.1   The earth is further away from the sun in July than in January. For the people living in the northern hemisphere, why is it hotter in July than in January?

7.2   On a cloudless day, if the spectral power distributions of the sunlight and the skylight remain constant throughout the day, what will be the daylight locus in the 1931 CIE chromaticity diagram? Of course, the spectral power distributions do not remain constant. What are the factors that cause the spectral power distributions of the sunlight and the skylight to change throughout the day?

7.3   As we saw in this chapter, the various natural and man-made light sources have quite different spectral power distributions. What impact does this have on color imaging applications?

7.4   Fluorescent lamps have a few spectral lines that have high radiant power. Why is this particularly troublesome for color imaging applications?

7.5   Many digital cameras provide a manual color balance setting for flurescent lightings. Since there are many different types of fluorescent lamp, each with a different color, does it make sense to provide a separate color balance setting just for fluorescent lightings?

7.6   Since the spectral power distribution of the electronic flash lamp that comes with a camera is known to the manufacturer, does it make sense for a digital camera to provide a separate color balance setting for flash pictures?

8 Scene physics

8.1 Introduction

Color images are formed by optical imaging systems from physical scenes that are composed of three-dimensional matter interacting with light. Light radiated from light sources is reflected, refracted, scattered, or diffracted by matter. As a result of all these light–matter interactions, light is redistributed spatially and temporally to create the physical scenes that we see and take pictures of. The study of color imaging science, thus, should begin with the light-field formation process of the physical scenes. This is what we mean by scene physics. The necessity for studying such a subject arises not simply to generate realistic color images by computer graphics. It is also driven by our need to understand and model the scene physics to develop computational algorithms that can adjust the color balance and tone scale of color images automatically so that optimal reproduction and display can be achieved.

8.2 General description of light reflection

Our discussion of reflection (Fresnel equations) in Section 5.4.1 assumes that the object surface is perfectly smooth, flat, and isotropic. However, the surfaces of real objects are almost never like that. In order to characterize light reflection and scattering from surfaces, we need a more general way to describe the optical property of surface reflection.

Although surface reflection is a well-studied subject, the terms used in the literature have not yet been standardized. Difficulties arise not only with the definitions, but also with the underlying concept of measurement and the models of the assumed physical processes. Let us start by treating light as rays (geometric optics) and see what can happen as light interacts with a rough surface.[1] Figure 8.1 shows two light rays (ray 1 and ray 2) undergoing refraction, reflection, scattering, and absorption. Let us assume that the top half of the diagram is air and the bottom half is an object of some inhomogeneous material, say a painted surface. When light (ray 1 and ray 2) is incident on the rough surface, part of its energy is reflected (ray 3 and ray 7) and part of it penetrates into the surface (ray 4 and ray 6). The reflected light can undergo more than one reflection (ray 7). The penetrating light can undergo multiple

---

[1] There are several problems with this type of treatment, and we will discuss them later. For most applications, it is a useful approximation.

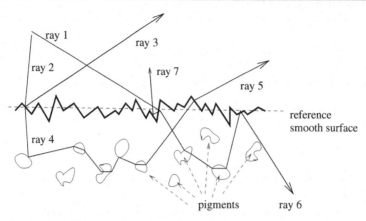

Figure 8.1. Different components of reflected and refracted light beams.

scattering by pigment particles in the surface material, and eventually is absorbed (ray 6) or reflected back into the air (ray 5). The first reflection at the interface (ray 3 and ray 7) has several names: surface reflection, interface reflection, or specular reflection. Reflection coming from under the surface (ray 5) also has several names: subsurface reflection, body reflection, bulk reflection, or diffuse reflection. Strictly speaking, there are problems with all these names and they come from the very basic fact that light cannot be treated as being reflected *only* at the interface [120, p. 5, 307], but rather the incident light interacts with all the atoms and molecules in the object. Only in the ideal situation of a perfectly smooth surface of homogeneous material with infinite spatial extent, can the reflected and refracted electromagnetic fields be neatly treated by the Fresnel equations discussed previously. For nonideal (rough, nonhomogeneous, and finite-size) surfaces, the actual physical description is much more complicated. The geometric ray description is no longer valid. If the surface roughness is small compared with the wavelength of the incident light, it can be treated by the perturbation method for the ideal solution for smooth surfaces. If the scale of the surface roughness or material inhomogeneity is of about the same order as the light wavelength, the problem becomes very difficult to deal with theoretically. Only numerical calculations can handle it satisfactorily. When the surface irregularity is of a scale much larger than the wavelength, it is again possible to develop a method of approximation by treating the surface as composed of many micro-facets, each of which is larger than many wavelengths.

   In this book, we use the name *interface reflection* for the first surface reflection, and the name *body reflection* for the rest. Surface reflection will be used to describe the general process of light being reflected from a surface and therefore includes both interface reflection and body reflection. The term subsurface reflection poses no confusion and can be used interchangeably with body reflection. The terms *diffuse* and *specular* will be used to refer to the angular or directional distribution of the reflected light. If the angular distribution is well concentrated in a narrow angle range, we will call it specular reflection. Otherwise, it will be called diffuse reflection. This is mostly a qualitative distinction and it seems that it is not necessary to be more quantitative than this in our application of these two terms. The following pseudo-equations summarize these terms:

$$\text{surface reflection} = \text{interface reflection} + \text{body reflection};$$
$$\text{interface reflection} = \text{specular component} + (\text{diffuse component})_i;$$
$$\text{body reflection} = (\text{diffuse component})_b;$$
$$\text{surface reflection} = \text{specular component} + \text{diffuse component};$$
$$\text{diffuse component} = (\text{diffuse component})_i + (\text{diffuse component})_b.$$

The subscript i denotes the component from the interface reflection and b that from the body reflection. The diffuse component can come from either the interface reflection (due to surface roughness) or the body reflection. The specular component is almost entirely from the interface reflection and for a smooth surface this component is often perceived as the specular highlight of surface reflection. The other component of the interface reflection is more diffuse and is due to the roughness and/or the inhomogeneity of the surface that cause the scattering of the reflected light into all directions. In comparison, body reflection is always quite diffuse in direction, unless there is strong internal regularity in the material structures. The major differences between the diffuse component from the interface reflection and the diffuse component from the body reflection are: (1) the former is more dependent on the surface roughness, and (2) the spectral composition of the latter is more strongly modified by the pigments or dyes in the subsurface material.

8.2.1 The bidirectional reflectance distribution function (BRDF)

For most applications, the BRDF proposed by Nicodemus *et al.* [715] is a general and useful concept to use. Let us discuss how to define the general description of light reflection with respect to the spatial, spectral, and polarization variables.

1. Geometric consideration
    Referring to Fig. 8.2, the BRDF, f_r, is defined as the ratio of the reflected radiance dL_r in the viewing direction to the irradiance dE_i in the direction of the incident light [412, 715]:

    $$f_r(\theta_i, \phi_i; \theta_r, \phi_r) = dL_r(\theta_i, \phi_i; \theta_r, \phi_r; E_i)/dE_i(\theta_i, \phi_i), \qquad (8.1)$$

    where (θ_i, ϕ_i) and (θ_r, ϕ_r) are the incident and reflected direction angles with respect to the surface normal.

2. Spectral consideration
    The original definition of the BRDF f_r can be extended to include the light wavelength as a variable [715, p. 31]. The resulting function is called the bidirectional spectral-reflectance distribution function (BSRDF), which is defined by

    $$f_r(\theta_i, \phi_i; \theta_r, \phi_r; \lambda) = dL_r(\theta_i, \phi_i; \theta_r, \phi_r; \lambda; E_i)/dE_i(\theta_i, \phi_i; \lambda), \qquad (8.2)$$

    where dL_r and dE_i are the reflected *spectral* radiance and the incident *spectral* irradiance.

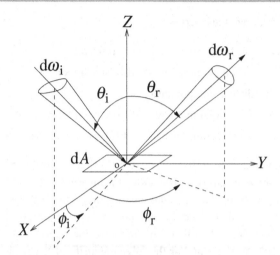

Figure 8.2. The definition of the BRDF.

3. Polarization consideration

    If the incident light is polarized, we can use the Stokes vector to describe the incident
    and reflected light beams. Surface reflection will then have to be described by a 4×4
    Mueller matrix, whose elements are BSRDFs. This Mueller matrix is called the bidi-
    rectional surface scattering spectral-reflectance distribution function (BSSSRDF). The
    BSSSRDF is an extension of the bidirectional surface scattering reflectance distribution
    function (BSSRDF) proposed by Richard Anderson [25] with the additional spectral
    wavelength as a variable.

Although the concept of the BRDF and its extension to the spectral and polarization
cases is quite general and useful, we should point out its limitations as well:

*   The concept is based on the approximation that light propagation can be treated as rays
    (geometrical optics). Wherever and whenever this approximation breaks down (e.g. in
    interference and diffraction), so does the concept of the BRDF. For modeling everyday
    scenes for imaging, this does not pose too much of a problem because we can handle
    those exceptions separately.
*   Using the ratio of reflected radiance L_r to incident irradiance E_i assumes that these
    two quantities are proportional, meaning that if E_i is increased by a factor of 2, then
    L_r will be increased by a factor of 2. This may not be true for all object surfaces.
    One difficulty arises from the practical question of how we measure the BRDF with
    an instrument. An instrument for measuring the BRDF is called a goniophotometer. In
    order to measure the BRDF, we have to illuminate the surface from each incident angle,
    and detect the reflected light at each reflection angle. The aperture for illumination and
    the aperture for detection of any real instrument have a finite size. The definition of the
    BRDF is a ratio of differentials and the basic problem with practical measurement is
    the question of instrument resolution. This is discussed in the literature [715, Section
    IV]. Let us use illumination apertures of different sizes to measure the BRDF. If we get
    a constant BRDF independent of the illumination aperture, there is no difficulty. This

is indeed the case for a Lambertian surface because the detected light (and hence L_r) increases in proportion to the illumination aperture, and so does the surface irradiance (E_i). However, if using a different illumination aperture size gives us a different BRDF measurement, what should we do? Experiments show that this difficulty is most serious when the reflection angle is equal to the incident angle and the surface has a mirror-like reflection [674]. The difficulty arises because the mirror-like reflection component does not vary much with the illumination aperture, but the diffuse reflection component is proportional to the illumination aperture. Therefore, in our imaging applications, this problem has to be kept in mind when we deal with specular reflections.

- The definition of the BRDF assumes that the reflected radiance depends only on the irradiance on the infinitely small area to which the sensor is pointing. This means that light illuminating the near-by surface area should not affect our measurement. This is not true if there is significant subsurface scattering. The light from the neighboring area can be scattered below the surface and then emerge at the point at which we are measuring. As a result, our measured value will differ depending on how large the illuminated area is. This is called the edge effect. A useful (bidirectional surface scattering distribution function) model for such subsurface light transport is described in [466]. One solution in practical measurements is to illuminate (uniformly) an area that is much larger than the extent of the subsurface scattering for the material we are measuring.

There are other minor difficulties too. For example, fluorescent material cannot be treated by the BSRDF concept as presented here. Despite of these difficulties, the BRDF and its extensions are quite general and they are widely used.

Let us look at two special cases of the application of the BRDF. In the first case, we derive the BRDF for a perfectly diffuse reflecting surface (ideal Lambertian surface). Here, L_r is the same for all directions and the total radiant reflected flux, Φ_r, from a small area dA, is

$$\Phi_r = \int L_r \cdot dA \cdot \cos\theta_r \cdot d\omega_r = L_r \cdot dA \cdot \pi. \tag{8.3}$$

Therefore, the BRDF for a perfectly diffuse reflector is

$$f_r = \frac{L_r}{E_i} = \frac{L_r}{\Phi_i/dA} = \frac{L_r}{\Phi_r/dA} = \frac{1}{\pi}. \tag{8.4}$$

In the second case, we derive the BRDF for a perfect mirror, which reflects 100% of the incident light according to Snell's law. The description of such a reflection will require the use of the $\delta()$ function, which can be considered as an intense unit area pulse whose spatial width is below the resolution of the instrument used to measure its radiant power. The mathematical properties of such a generalized function are reviewed in many books (see [129, Chapter 5] for a very good introduction). Let us assume that the incident light flux, Φ_i, illuminates a small elemental area, dA, with an incident angle of (θ_i, ϕ_i) in a spherical coordinate system centered at dA (see Fig. 8.2). According to Snell's law, the reflected light is only in the direction $(\theta_r, \phi_r) = (\theta_i, \phi_i + \pi)$, and no other direction. Therefore, the BRDF of a perfect mirror is proportional to $\delta(\theta_r - \theta_i) \cdot \delta(\phi_r - \phi_i - \pi)$. The proportionality constant has to be determined by energy conservation, as follows. The total reflected flux,

Φ_r, can be calculated by integrating L_r over the half-sphere over the surface element dA:

$$\Phi_r = \int L_r \cdot dA \cdot \cos\theta_r \cdot d\omega$$

$$= \iint L_r dA \cdot \cos\theta_r \cdot \sin\theta_r d\theta_r d\phi_r$$

$$= \iint f_r E_i dA \cdot \cos\theta_r \sin\theta_r d\theta_r d\phi_r$$

$$= \iint f_r \Phi_i \cos\theta_r \sin\theta_r d\theta_r d\phi_r.$$

Since a perfect mirror reflects 100% of the incident light, the reflected flux Φ_r is equal to the incident flux Φ_i. Thus, we have the relation

$$1 = \iint f_r \cos\theta_r \sin\theta_r d\theta_r d\phi_r, \qquad (8.5)$$

and therefore the BRDF for a perfect mirror is:

$$f_r = \delta(\theta_r - \theta_i) \cdot \delta(\phi_r - \phi_i - \pi)/(\sin\theta_r \cos\theta_r) = 2 \cdot \delta(\sin^2\theta_r - \sin^2\theta_i) \cdot \delta(\phi_r - \phi_i - \pi).$$

$$(8.6)$$

The last equals sign follows from the theorem [129, p. 100]: $\delta(f(x)) = \Sigma_k \delta(x - a_k)/|f'(a_k)|$, where $f(a_k) = 0$ and $f'(a_k) \neq 0$ exists within the domain of interest.

8.2.2 Interface reflection

In our previous discussion of surface reflection, we separated the total reflection into two components: interface reflection and body reflection. Because the physical processes involved are quite different, these two components will be discussed separately. Interface reflection so far has received much more research attention than body reflection. In order to discuss the various interface reflection models, we need to understand the different surface structures (roughness) and compositions (material) first, because their physical properties determine the construction of the various surface reflection models.

An ideally smooth, homogeneous surface reflects light specularly, i.e., the reflection angle is equal to the incident angle. Light that is reflected from a nonideal surface spreads out in directions other than the specular reflection angle. This is often called surface scattering – light is scattered into all directions upon reflection from a nonideal surface. Surface scattering has two main mechanisms: (1) topographic scattering caused by surface roughness, defects, scratches, or structures, and (2) material scattering caused by inhomogeneous material composition or density fluctuations on or near the surface. These two mechanisms do not deal with the subsurface reflection for the portion of light that penetrates below the surface and is scattered back out of the surface. Here we will mainly discuss topographic scattering from rough surfaces. Surface scattering caused by material inhomogeneity (material scattering) has not been studied as much as that caused by topographic roughness. Theoretical results for slightly inhomogeneous material have been obtained with the Rayleigh–Rice perturbation method [182, 280, 912].

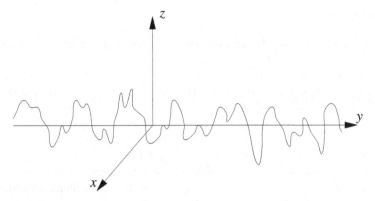

Figure 8.3. An example of a rough surface. The reference surface is on the x–y plane.

Figure 8.3 shows a rough surface. We will define a reference smooth surface $z = 0$, on top of which the random fluctuations in height $z(x, y)$ represent the surface profile of the rough surface. In the following discussion, the reference surface is taken to be a plane (the mean surface) located at the x–y plane. For any given rough surface, it is possible to measure its surface profile with a light beam or a mechanical stylus. In principle, from these surface profile measurements we can calculate the surface scattering. However, all profile measurements are limited by the instrument bandwidth. Even if we know the exact surface profile, we still have to know the precise location of the light beam relative to the surface before we can calculate the exact light scattering numerically. Practically, for almost all applications, we are only interested in the statistical properties of the roughness and their effect on light scattering. A given type of rough surface is often treated as a stationary, isotropic two-dimensional stochastic process (a random field). For example, the surface profiles of all surfaces that are polished by a mechanical polishing machine are considered as belonging to the same random process. There are three functions that are often used to characterize a random rough surface: (1) $S(f_x, f_y)$, the power spectrum (spectral density) of the surface profiles, or equivalently $C(\tau_x, \tau_y)$, the autocorrelation function of the surface profiles; (2) the single-point or multiple-point joint surface height distribution; and (3) the surface slope distribution. Conceptually, the power spectrum of a random field, $Z(x, y)$, can be thought of as the ensemble average of the square of the amplitude of the Fourier transform of every possible realization of the random field $Z(x, y)$. However, there is a serious theoretical difficulty in doing so because a stationary random field extends to infinity with the same property and its Fourier transform does not converge. One way to avoid this difficulty is to define the power spectrum of a random field through the autocorrelation function of the random field. Another method for defining the power spectrum is the generalized harmonic analysis of Wiener [743, Chapter 12]. The autocorrelation function, $C(\tau_x, \tau_y)$, is defined by

$$C(\tau_x, \tau_y) = E\left[\iint Z(x, y)Z(x + \tau_x, y + \tau_y)dx\,dy\right], \qquad (8.7)$$

where $E[\ldots]$ represents the expected value over the entire ensemble of the random field. The power spectrum of the random field is then defined as the Fourier transform of the autocorrelation function:

$$S(f_x, f_y) = \iint C(\tau_x, \tau_y) \exp[-i2\pi(f_x\tau_x + f_y\tau_y)]dx\,dy. \tag{8.8}$$

Since we are assuming that the reference mean surface is on the x–y plane, $E[Z(x, y)] = 0$, and the autocorrelation function is the same as the covariance function. Therefore, the mean-square height h^2 can be expressed as:

$$h^2 = E\left[\iint Z^2(x, y)dx\,dy\right] = C(0, 0). \tag{8.9}$$

Alternatively, a rough surface is often specified by its height distribution function, $p_{\text{height}}(Z)$, or two-point joint distribution function $p_{\text{height}}(Z_1, Z_2)$. The height distribution function gives less complete information about a rough surface than the power spectrum because it does not say anything about the rate of height change as we traverse the rough surface. A third function that has often been used is the surface slope distribution, $p_{\text{slope}}(z_x, z_y)$, where (z_x, z_y) is the surface slope. In practice, the slope probability density function is quite difficult to measure.

One of the most frequently used metrics in quantifying the roughness of a surface is the root-mean-square height, h, in surface fluctuation. It is the standard deviation of the height distribution. As we mentioned before, h does not tell us the rate of change in surface height, i.e., the slope. Therefore, another quantity, called the correlation length, l, is used together with h. The correlation length for a nonperiodic random rough surface is defined as the offset distance over which the autocorrelation function falls to $1/e$ of its height at zero offset (assuming that the random field is isotropic). The correlation length of a rough surface is quite difficult to measure because of its sensitivity to instrument bandwidth [181].

Surface scattering has been studied extensively in radar and optics. Although the wavelength of interest in the two fields differs by many orders of magnitude, the underlying analysis is quite similar because the wavelength can be scaled with the roughness. A rough surface in optics is a very smooth surface for radar. All roughness measures are scaled by the wavelength of interest. Assuming that the incident light is in air or vacuum, a good parameter for the classification of surface roughness is kh, where $k = 2\pi/\lambda$ is the wavenumber, λ is the wavelength in air or vacuum, and h is the root-mean-square height of the roughness. As a general rule of thumb, a *slightly rough* surface is a surface with $kh < 1$, a *very rough* surface is one with $kh > 5$, and a *moderately rough* surface is something in between. However, the light scattering behavior also depends on the incident and scattering angles in question. Therefore, when we describe scattering from a rough surface, we need to specify the lighting and viewing geometry as well as the surface topographic irregularity.

The general problem of surface scattering is quite complicated. One of the successful theories of scattering by a *slightly rough* surface treats the rough surface as a smooth surface with perturbations in height which are smaller than a wavelength. This type of treatment was first used by Lord Rayleigh for sound waves and later extended by Rice to electromagnetic waves. It is called the first order Rayleigh–Rice vector perturbation theory [62, 182, 789, 891, 916] because only the first term in the series expansion of the solution is used for approximation. At the other extreme, the analysis of scattering by a *very rough* surface usually treats the surface as a collection of small (but still much larger than a wavelength), random, planar facets (tangent-plane approximation), each reflecting light according to Fresnel reflection [66, 92]. The light scattered to a point A in space is the sum of the light reflected from all those micro-facets whose surface normals are positioned so that the angle of incidence is equal to the angle of reflection as viewed from point A. We will call this analysis the specular-point tangent-plane approximation. There are three further refinements that have been proposed: (1) self-shadowing: some tangent planes are positioned correctly, but are occluded by the neighboring planes [883, 957]; (2) multiple scattering: the incident wave is scattered several times on the rough surface before it is scattered to the far distance; and (3) small perturbation of the tangent plane: each tangent plane is treated as a slightly rough surface and the Rayleigh–Rice perturbation theory is applied to calculate its scattering [926]. For surfaces that are between slightly rough and very rough, there is no convenient approximation or theory for easy calculation, although their measured light scattering behavior is shown to be between those predicted by the first order Rayleigh–Rice vector perturbation theory and the specular-point tangent-plane approximation.

The qualitative effect of surface roughness on light reflection can be described as follows. For a perfectly smooth planar surface of infinite extent, the reflected light is in a single specular direction $\theta_r = \theta_i$ and $\phi_r = \phi_i + \pi$. Its BRDF is a delta function. If the planar surface has only a finite area, the reflected light (far away) is now spread into a major (very narrow) lobe around the specular angle and many very small lobes around it. This is due to diffraction and the light distribution can be calculated from the Fourier transform of the shape of the area. Now, if a very slight roughness is introduced into the surface, the reflected radiance of the specular main lobe is decreased and that at other scattering angles is increased. The specular main lobe is also called the coherent component (because a perfectly smooth plane reflects a plane wave with a coherent phase), and the nonspecular component is called the incoherent component. The average reflected power in the coherent component decreases exponentially with the mean-square roughness height h^2. As the roughness continues to increase, the specular lobe continues to decrease until it is dominated by the incoherent component and is no longer discernible when $kh > 5$.

We will now present some quantitative descriptions of surface scattering based on the theories and approximations discussed above. As defined in Fig. 8.4, the mean surface is located at the x–y plane and the height fluctuations $z(x, y)$ is in the z-direction. The plane of incidence, defined by the incident beam and the surface normal, is the x–z plane. Similarly, the plane of scattering is defined by the scattered beam and the surface normal. The incident beam is specified by $(\theta_i, \phi_i = \pi)$ and the scattered beam by (θ_s, ϕ_s). As we described in Section 5.4.1, the polarization of an incident plane electromagnetic wave is specified with respect to whether its electric field vector is perpendicular ($\perp$) or parallel ($\parallel$) to the plane of incidence. Similarly, the polarization of the scattered beam is defined relative to the plane of scattering. The BRDF now has to be defined for the different polarizations for the incident and the scattered light. We will use the notation $BRDF_{ab}(\theta_i, \phi_i, \theta_s, \phi_s)$, where a denotes the polarization of the incident light and b that of the scattered light. For example, $BRDF_{\perp\parallel}$ represents the bidirectional reflectance distribution for the perpendicular component of the incident beam and the parallel component of the scattered beam.

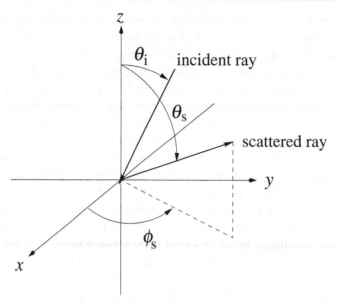

Figure 8.4. Definition of surface scattering angles. The incident ray is assumed to be on the x–z plane and therefore its azimuth (horizontal) angle, ϕ_i is equal to π.

Scattering from "slightly rough" surfaces

For a slightly rough surface, its $(BRDF)_{ab}$ can be expressed as the sum of two components: the coherent component (the specular lobe), $(BRDF)_{ab}^C$, and the incoherent component (the diffuse lobe), $(BRDF)_{ab}^I$:

$$(BRDF)_{ab} = (BRDF)_{ab}^C + (BRDF)_{ab}^I, \tag{8.10}$$

where a and b denote the polarizations of the incident and the scattered light. For a very slightly rough surface of infinite extent (i.e., its surface slopes are everywhere less than 1 and the radii of curvature everywhere are greater than the incident wavelength), it can be shown that the coherent component is approximately a specular spike and

$$(BRDF)_{\perp\perp}^C = r_\perp^2(\theta_i)\exp[-4(kh\cos\theta_i)^2] \cdot \delta(\sin^2\theta_s - \sin^2\theta_i) \cdot \delta(\phi_s - \phi_i - \pi), \tag{8.11}$$

$$(BRDF)_{\|\|}^C = r_\|^2(\theta_i)\exp[-4(kh\cos\theta_i)^2] \cdot \delta(\sin^2\theta_s - \sin^2\theta_i) \cdot \delta(\phi_s - \phi_i - \pi), \tag{8.12}$$

where k is the wavevector, h is the root-mean-square roughness height, and $r_\perp$ and $r_\|$ are the Fresnel reflection coefficients for the ideal, smooth surface, as described in Section 5.4.1. Therefore, the coherent component amplitude is reduced exponentially by the surface mean-square roughness. If the surface is of finite extent and its height distribution is a Gaussian function, its BRDF for the coherent component of the scattered light can be derived as [66, p. 702]:

$$(BRDF)_{ab}^C = \frac{A(f_x, f_y, L_x, L_y)}{\cos\theta_i \cos\theta_s}|B_{ab}|^2 \exp[-(2\pi)^2 h^2 f_z^2], \tag{8.13}$$

where $A(f_x, f_y, L_x, L_y)$ is a factor that is determined by the shape and size (L_x, L_y) of the area illuminated, f_x, f_y, and f_z are defined by

$$f_x = \frac{1}{\lambda}(\sin\theta_i - \sin\theta_s \cos\phi_s),$$

$$f_y = \frac{1}{\lambda}(\sin\theta_s \sin\phi_s), \tag{8.14}$$

$$f_z = \frac{1}{\lambda}(-\cos\theta_i - \cos\theta_s),$$

and B_{ab} are given by

$$B_{\perp\perp} = \cos\theta_i \cos\theta_s r_\perp(\theta_i), \tag{8.15}$$
$$B_{\perp\parallel} = \sin\phi_s r_\parallel(\theta_i), \tag{8.16}$$
$$B_{\parallel\perp} = \cos\theta_i \cos\theta_s \sin\phi_s r_\perp(\theta_i), \tag{8.17}$$
$$B_{\parallel\parallel} = -\cos\theta_s \cos\phi_s r_\parallel(\theta_i). \tag{8.18}$$

The BRDF for the incoherent component of the scattered light can be derived from first-order Rayleigh–Rice vector perturbation theory:

$$(BRDF)_{ab}^{\mathrm{I}} = \frac{16\pi^2}{\lambda^4}\cos\theta_i \cos\theta_s F_{ab}S(f_x, f_y), \tag{8.19}$$

where F_{ab} is a dimensionless quantity, representing a polarization (a, b) dependent reflection coefficient:

$$F_{\perp\perp} = \left|\frac{(\mu-1)(\mu\sin\theta_i\sin\theta_s - \cos\phi_s\sqrt{\mu\epsilon - \sin^2\theta_s}\sqrt{\mu\epsilon - \sin^2\theta_i}) + \mu^2(\epsilon-1)\cos\phi_s}{(\mu\cos\theta_i + \sqrt{\epsilon\mu - \sin^2\theta_i})(\mu\cos\theta_s + \sqrt{\epsilon\mu - \sin^2\theta_s})}\right|^2,$$
$$\tag{8.20}$$

$$F_{\perp\parallel} = \left|\frac{[\epsilon(\mu-1)\sqrt{\epsilon\mu - \sin^2\theta_i} - \mu(\epsilon-1)\sqrt{\epsilon\mu - \sin^2\theta_s}]\sin\phi_s}{(\mu\cos\theta_i + \sqrt{\epsilon\mu - \sin^2\theta_i})(\epsilon\cos\theta_s + \sqrt{\epsilon\mu - \sin^2\theta_s})}\right|^2, \tag{8.21}$$

$$F_{\parallel\perp} = \left|\frac{[\mu(\epsilon-1)\sqrt{\epsilon\mu - \sin^2\theta_i} - \epsilon(\mu-1)\sqrt{\epsilon\mu - \sin^2\theta_s}]\sin\phi_s}{(\epsilon\cos\theta_i + \sqrt{\epsilon\mu - \sin^2\theta_i})(\mu\cos\theta_s + \sqrt{\epsilon\mu - \sin^2\theta_s})}\right|^2, \tag{8.22}$$

$$F_{\parallel\parallel} = \left|\frac{(\epsilon-1)(\epsilon\sin\theta_i\sin\theta_s - \sqrt{\epsilon\mu - \sin^2\theta_s}\sqrt{\epsilon\mu - \sin^2\theta_i}\cos\phi_s) + \epsilon^2(\mu-1)\cos\theta_s}{(\epsilon\cos\theta_i + \sqrt{\epsilon\mu - \sin^2\theta_i})(\epsilon\cos\theta_s + \sqrt{\epsilon\mu - \sin^2\theta_s})}\right|^2,$$
$$\tag{8.23}$$

where μ and ϵ are the relative permeability and permitivity, $S(f_x, f_y)$ is the power spectrum of the surface height as a two-dimensional random field, and f_x and f_y are the "spatial frequency" as defined in Eqs. (8.14).

Scattering from "very rough" surfaces

Different approximations and assumptions have been used to derive the angular distribution of surface scattering from very rough surfaces. Most theories are based on the assumptions that the surface radii of curvature at all points are much larger than the wavelength. A rough surface is approximated as a collection of randomly oriented planar facets, each of which is tangent to the local surface fluctuation. The total scattered field at a given observation point is the sum of all the reflected fields from those tangent planar facets that are correctly oriented so that the incident angle is equal to the reflection angle. An additional refinement of the tangent plane approximation is to allow each tangent plane to be a slightly rough surface and use the Rayleigh–Rice vector perturbation theory to calculate its contribution to the final scattered field. Two complications arise from the tangent plane approximation: self-shadowing and multiple scattering between planar facets. These two factors are usually dealt with as a multiplication factor that modifies the scattered field strength. The self-shadowing has two effects: (1) some of the planar facets are occluded from incident illumination (shadowing), and (2) some of the reflected light is occluded by its neighboring facets from reaching the observation point (masking). Using the geometric optics approximation, these effects are treated as a correction factor (the geometrical attenuation factor) that attenuates the scattered radiance as a function of incident and scattering angles. This type of approximation is valid only for the case in which the local planar facets are much larger than the wavelength.

Without considering self-shadowing and multiple scattering, Barrick [65] showed that the BRDF of a very rough surface is approximately proportional to the probability density function of its surface slopes, p_s:

$$BRDF_{ab} = \frac{4\pi |\beta_{ab}|^2}{\lambda^2 f_z^2 \cos \theta_i \cos \theta_s} p_s \left(-\frac{f_x}{f_z}, -\frac{f_y}{f_z}\right), \qquad (8.24)$$

where β_{ab} is a factor that is not a function of the surface roughness, but is a complicated function of the incident angle and scattered angle, θ_i, θ_s, and ϕ_s, and the incident and scattered polarizations (a, b) [66, p. 722].

Beckmann and Spizzichino [92] used Kirchhoff theory to derive a general expression for scattering by a rough surface. They discussed the case of a perfect conductor in detail. Ogilvy's book [723] offers a more up-to-date account of the derivation. This approach gives a formal integral for surfaces of finite conductivity and the integral needs to be evaluated numerically. Beckmann and Spizzichino give a closed form expression of the scattered field for the case of a rough surface with a Gaussian height distribution. The reflectance of every micro-facet on the local tangent plane of the rough surface is assumed to be 1.0 (for a perfect conductor) or a local average "reflectance" of $R(\theta_i)$ (this is a fudge factor because the original derivation is valid only for a constant reflectance). The Beckmann–Spizzichino model is well known, but there is some uncertainty about its exact form (see the discussion in [404, p. 2854]). Here we use the form presented in [404, p. 2853] (note that we have changed their formula into the BRDF by dividing $dI/(I_0 d\Omega)$ by $\cos \theta_s$ and modifying the delta functions into the correct form):

$$BRDF = \frac{R(\theta_i)}{\cos \theta_s} \exp[-g]\delta(\sin^2 \theta_s - \sin^2 \theta_i) \cdot \delta(\phi_s - \phi_i \pm \pi)$$

$$+ \frac{R(\theta_i)}{\cos \theta_s} \exp[-g]\frac{1}{\lambda^2} F \sum_{m=1}^{\infty} \frac{g^m}{m!} W_m, \qquad (8.25)$$

$$g = k^2 h^2 (\cos \theta_i + \cos \theta_s)^2, \qquad (8.26)$$

$$F = \frac{1 + \cos \theta_i \cos \theta_s - \sin \theta_i \sin \theta_s \cos \phi_s}{\cos \theta_i (\cos \theta_i + \cos \theta_s)^2}, \qquad (8.27)$$

and

$$W_m = \frac{\pi}{m} l^2 \exp[-(2\pi)^2(f_x^2 + f_y^2)l^2/4m] \tag{8.28}$$

for a Gaussian autocorrelation function, or

$$W_m = \frac{2\pi(l/m)^2}{[1 + (l/m)^2(2\pi)^2(f_x^2 + f_y^2)l^2]^{3/2}} \tag{8.29}$$

for an exponential autocorrelation, where h is the root-mean-square height, l is the correlation length, and f_x and f_y are as defined in Eqs. (8.14). The first term represents a specular spike at $\theta_s = \theta_i$ and it is reduced by the surface roughness exponentially, as we discussed in the previous section on scattering by slightly rough surfaces.

Torrance and Sparrow [957] developed a theory to account for off-specular reflection observed in both metal and nonmetal surfaces. The theory is based on the random planar facet model of the rough surface. For each micro-facet plane, scattering is modeled simply as the Fresnel reflection factor, F. The self-shadowing and masking effects are modeled with geometric optics, and the total effect is represented as a geometrical attenuation factor, G. The micro-facet model of the rough surface is described with a slope distribution, D. The resulting expression, $BRDF = cFGD$ (where c is a constant), is found to agree with experimental data quite well for very rough surfaces ($kh \gg 1$). The factor G is given as [213]:

$$G = \min\left[1, \frac{2(\mathbf{N} \cdot \mathbf{H})(\mathbf{N} \cdot \mathbf{V})}{(\mathbf{V} \cdot \mathbf{H})}, \frac{2(\mathbf{N} \cdot \mathbf{H})(\mathbf{N} \cdot \mathbf{L})}{(\mathbf{V} \cdot \mathbf{H})}\right], \tag{8.30}$$

where $\mathbf{N}$ is the unit normal of the mean surface, $\mathbf{V}$ is the unit vector of the scattered beam (pointing to the observer), $\mathbf{L}$ is the unit vector of the incident beam (pointing to the light source), and $\mathbf{H}$ is the unit angular bisector of $\mathbf{L}$ and $\mathbf{V}$:

$$\mathbf{H} = \frac{\mathbf{V} + \mathbf{L}}{|\mathbf{V} + \mathbf{L}|}. \tag{8.31}$$

Comments on theoretical models and experimental data

Many assumptions were made in deriving the surface scattering models. Models can be useful in several ways. They can give us insight into the relationship between the statistical properties of a rough surface and the angle-resolved scattering (ARS) distribution of the reflected light. Knowing the surface profiles allows us to predict the ARS, and conversely, knowing the ARS allows us to infer the statistics of the surface profile. However, reality is much more complicated. For one thing, all surface profile measurements are subject to errors (sometimes quite large) mainly due to the bandwidth of the measuring device. For example, surface slope distribution is very ill defined because it is very sensitive to the spatial resolution of the measurements. Surface power spectra are more robust to estimate from the measured data (the surface power spectrum multiplied by the amplitude squared of the frequency response of the device).

The surface height distribution is often modeled with a Gaussian distribution. This seems to be a good approximation for many surfaces polished by random mechanical scratchings. It is not adequate for certain surfaces with large digs, scratching lines, or fixed-pattern polishing, such as diamond-turned surfaces. The surface autocorrelation function for most surfaces can be better described by exponential distributions or fractal distributions. Only very rarely is a Gaussian correlation function adequate [95].

Various numerical and experimental studies have established some ranges of parameters within which different models are accurate. For slightly rough surfaces ($kh \leq 0.5$), the Rayleigh–Rice vector perturbation theory is known to be valid for $kl < 4$. The Kirchhoff approximation (from which the Beckmann–Spizzichino model is derived) seems to be accurate for $kl > 6$ and $kh \ll 1$ for surfaces that have a Gaussian roughness spectrum, except at high incident angles [950]. Numerical studies also show that for very rough surfaces (e.g., $kh = 9$ and $kl = 12$), significant backscattering ($\theta_s = \theta_i$ and $\phi_s = \phi_i$) can occur at an incident angle not far from normal, say $10°$. The BRDF for a certain range of incident angles shows two peaks, one at some off-specular angle and the other at a backscattering angle. The backscattering seems to be the consequence of multiple scattering and cannot be predicted from the approximation methods discussed so far.

8.2.3 Body reflection

Body reflection (or subsurface reflection) has received relatively little attention. An intuitive model of body reflection is that it has no preferred direction, i.e., it is completely diffuse. The intuition is based on the argument that once light penetrates below the air–material interface boundary, most of it will be scattered many times before it is scattered back out of the surface. Being scattered so many times by randomly distributed particles or nonhomogeneous compositions in the material body, this component of the reflected light becomes quite random in its direction. Therefore, body reflection may be modeled as a perfectly diffuse component (Lambertian reflection). We will call this model the Lambertian body reflection (LBR) model. The LBR model has been used for many years without detailed experimental verification. This is because it is very difficult (if not impossible) to separate the measured reflected light into the interface reflection component and the body reflection component. For good conductors, light does not penetrate more than a few wavelengths beyond the interface boundary and therefore there is virtually no body reflection. Light reflection from typical metal surfaces is usually quite directional and there have been very good empirical models, as discussed in the previous section. For dielectric materials (poor conductors or insulators), light reflected from a surface almost always has a diffuse component (nonzero value in all directions) in it. This component comes both from the scattering from the surface roughness (interface reflection) and from the scattering of light back out of the surface by subsurface material (body reflection). From a single measurement of the reflected light, we cannot separate the sources of these two diffuse components. It is, therefore, permissible (at least numerically) to attribute the "DC" component to body reflection. There are at least two situations in which this arbitrary decomposition does not work: (1) when color measurements are involved because interface reflection and body reflection may have different wavelength dependences; and (2) when the "DC" component is zero for some viewing or lighting geometry and there is no Lambertian "DC" component to account for body reflection (in this case, we can almost be sure that the LBR model is not correct for the surface we are observing). Both cases have been encountered in practice and we are forced to examine the details of how the two diffuse components should be modeled.

The dichromatic reflection model

The simplest model for accounting for the spectral difference between interface reflection and body reflection is the dichromatic model proposed by Shafer [854]. In terms of the BSRDF, the dichromatic model can be expressed as

$$BSRDF(\theta_i, \phi_i; \theta_r, \phi_r; \lambda) = a(\lambda)g(\theta_i, \phi_i; \theta_r, \phi_r) + b(\lambda)h(\theta_i, \phi_i; \theta_r, \phi_r), \qquad (8.32)$$

where the functions g and h are normalized to 1 at their maximum values. The basic assumption is that the spectral and geometrical factors can be separated as products. Furthermore, the spectral factor is assumed to be independent of the lighting and viewing geometry. For many types of material, the interface reflection component is close to nonselective, and therefore, we can set the coefficient $b(\lambda)$ to a constant, s, and call the resulting model the neutral interface reflection (NIR) model. The NIR model [563] can expressed as

$$BSRDF_{NIR}(\theta_i, \phi_i; \theta_r, \phi_r; \lambda) = a(\lambda)g(\theta_i, \phi_i; \theta_r, \phi_r) + sh(\theta_i, \phi_i; \theta_r, \phi_r). \qquad (8.33)$$

The physical meaning of the NIR model as expressed in Eq. (8.33) is that the surface reflects light in two components: the first term represents the wavelength-selective reflection, and the second term, the nonselective reflection. This model has been used widely in computer graphics. It is also used to estimate the scene illuminant chromaticity [560].

The Chandrasekhar–Wolff body reflection model for smooth surfaces

Chandrasekhar [168] developed a radiative transfer theory to calculate light propagation through multiple scattering media, such as air. The theory is expressed as a set of equations. He derived some approximating solutions to the equations. Wolff [1045] used Chandrasekhar's results to derive a reflectance model for body reflection. In order to simplify the model, Wolff assumed that: (1) the surface is smooth and (2) the individual scattering of light from inhomogeneities within dielectric material is isotropic. The second assumption is based on the observation that body reflection is often symmetric with respect to the azimuth (horizontal) angle, i.e., ϕ_r. Chandrasekhar has shown that azimuth-symmetric distributions arise from multiple scattering only when individual scatterers scatter light isotropically. The resulting body reflection model can be expressed as

$$BRDF = \rho[1 - F_1(\theta_i, n)][1 - F_2(\theta_r, n)], \qquad (8.34)$$

where ρ is the total diffuse reflectance, θ_i is the incident angle, θ_r is the scattering angle, n is the index of refraction of the surface material, $F_1(\theta, n)$ is the Fresnel reflection coefficient for incident angle θ and index of refraction n, as discussed in Section 5.4.1, and

$$F_2(\theta_r, n) = F_1\left[\sin^{-1}\left(\frac{\sin\theta_r}{n}\right), \frac{1}{n}\right]. \qquad (8.35)$$

Strictly speaking, ρ is a function of the lighting and viewing geometry. However, its value does not change too much over a large range of angles, and it can therefore be approximated as a constant [1045]. It is interesting to see that the first Fresnel factor, $[1 - F_1]$, accounts for how much light is transmitted from the air into the surface body for the given incident angle, θ_i, and the second Fresnel factor, $[1 - F_2]$, accounts for how much light escapes back into the air from the surface body for the given incident angle, θ, which is related to the reflection angle θ_r by Snell's law, $\sin \theta_r = n \sin \theta$.

The Chandrasekhar–Wolff model predicts that for a normal incident angle, the reflected radiance is relatively constant for θ_r less than $50°$, but falls off rapidly when the reflection angle is increased above $50°$. This is in sharp contrast with the prediction by the Lambertian model which predicts a constant radiance for all reflection angles. Wolff has shown that the Chandrasekhar–Wolff model is in good agreement with the limited experimental data from smooth surfaces.

The Oren–Nayar body reflection model for rough surfaces

As we mentioned before, a very rough surface may be approximated as a collection of random tangent planes. If we treat each facet as a smooth planar surface, we can use any body reflection model for each facet to derive a body reflection model for such a rough surface. Oren and Nayar [732] used the Lambertian body reflection model for each micro-facet. The rough surface is assumed to be composed of long symmetric V-cavities, as proposed by Torrance and Sparrow [957]. The Oren–Nayar model requires knowledge of the slope-area distribution function of the rough surface. Their measured data show that their model is a good approximation. The complete model is in integral form and has to be evaluated numerically. Nayar and Oren [697] give an approximate, qualitative model as:

$$BRDF = \frac{\rho}{\pi}(A + BC \sin \alpha \tan \beta), \tag{8.36}$$

where $\alpha = \max(\theta_i, \theta_r)$, $\beta = \min(\theta_i, \theta_r)$, and

$$A = 1.0 - \frac{0.5\sigma^2}{\sigma^2 + 0.33}, \tag{8.37}$$

$$B = \frac{0.45\sigma^2}{\sigma^2 + 0.09}, \tag{8.38}$$

$$C = \max[0, \cos(\phi_r - \phi_i)], \tag{8.39}$$

where σ is the standard deviation of the probability density function of the facet tilt angle, which is assumed to be normally distributed with zero mean.

One of the most interesting observations from the Oren–Nayar model is that the shading of a matte surface depends on its roughness and therefore the observed radiance from a given area of a surface is in general greater when the observation distance is shorter [697].

8.2.4 Empirical surface reflection models

From the above discussion, it is clear that for many rough surfaces that we see in everyday life, the BRDFs are not easily predictable from other measurable surface quantities,

such as the root-mean-square roughness, the correlation length, or the surface power spectrum. The only reliable way to describe reflection from these surfaces is to measure their
BRDFs directly. However, measuring the BRDF, BSRDF, or BSSSRDF requires a complex
instrument, such as a goniophotometer or a goniospectrophotometer, that is not generally
available, requires skill to operate and calibrate, and with which it takes a long time to
measure a sample (because many angles and wavelengths have to be measured). Therefore,
many empirical surface reflection models have been proposed and they are widely used in
computer graphics, computer vision, and illumination engineering. The simplest model is
the Lambertian surface which has the same reflected radiance independent of the viewing
angle. This model is popular not only because it is simple, but also because it seems to
confirm our observation that most object surfaces look approximately equally bright from
different angles. Of course, near the specular highlight, the Lambertian model does not
work well. So, the next simplest model adds a specular component as a function of the
incident angle to the basic Lambertian reflection model. A popular model in the early years
of computer graphics was that of Phong [757], which models surface reflection as the sum
of a specular lobe and a diffuse (Lambertian) lobe. The specular lobe peaks at the specular
reflection angle and falls off as a power function of the cosine of the off-specular angle.

From the above discussion, we can see that an empirical surface reflection model may
consist of two components, one from interface reflection and the other from body reflection
[384, 696]. Interface reflection of a slightly or moderately rough surface usually has a
specular spike (coherent field) and a specular lobe (incoherent field). For a very rough
surface, the specular spike is often quite small and indistinguishable from the specular lobe.
Body reflection is comparatively less directional, and is called the diffuse lobe. As more
and more BRDF data are measured in the future, we may hope that someday the shapes
of the spike and lobes can be described by families of function that are easy to use. One
example of such an easy-to-use model was proposed by Ward [1012].

Ward's general reflection model is called the anisotropic (elliptical) Gaussian model.
The incident and reflecting geometry is shown in Fig. 8.5. The model assumes that the
surface has two perpendicular (uncorrelated) slope distributions, characterized by σ_x and

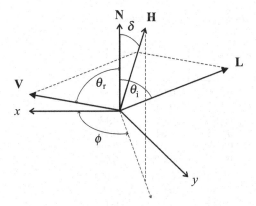

Figure 8.5. The incident and reflecting geometry for the anisotropic (elliptical) Gaussian model
proposed by Ward.

σ_y, where x and y are the two major axes of the elliptical anisotropic surface. Let $\mathbf{N}$ be the unit surface normal, $\mathbf{V}$ be the viewing vector (pointing to the observer), $\mathbf{L}$ be the incident vector (pointing to the source), and $\mathbf{H}$ be the unit angular bisector of $\mathbf{L}$ and $\mathbf{V}$:

$$\mathbf{H} = \frac{\mathbf{V} + \mathbf{L}}{|\mathbf{V} + \mathbf{L}|}. \tag{8.40}$$

The angle δ is the angle between $\mathbf{N}$ and $\mathbf{H}$. The angle ϕ is the angle between the x-axis and the projection of $\mathbf{H}$ on the tangent plane (x–y plane) of the surface. The empirical BRDF function is

$$f(\theta_i, \phi_i; \theta_r, \phi_r) = \frac{\rho_d}{\pi} + \rho_s \frac{1}{\sqrt{\cos\theta_i \cos\theta_r}} \frac{\exp[-\tan^2\delta(\cos^2\phi/\sigma_x^2 + \sin^2\phi/\sigma_y^2)]}{4\pi\sigma_x\sigma_y}, \tag{8.41}$$

where ρ_d is the diffuse reflectance, ρ_s is the specular reflectance, $\rho_d + \rho_s$ is less than 1 and σ is not much greater than 0.2. An isotropic reflection model can be obtained by setting $\sigma = \sigma_x = \sigma_y$:

$$f(\theta_i, \phi_i; \theta_r, \phi_r) = \frac{\rho_d}{\pi} + \rho_s \frac{1}{\sqrt{\cos\theta_i \cos\theta_r}} \frac{\exp[-\tan^2\delta/\sigma^2]}{4\pi\sigma^2}. \tag{8.42}$$

This empirical model has been found to describe measured BRDF data quite well. Its advantages over other models are: (1) the parameters are physically intuitive, (2) the BRDF is properly normalized, and (3) it is quite simple to use. Therefore, the model is often used in computer graphics to generate photorealistic images. Table 8.1 shows the parameters from the model fits to the measured data of some object surfaces [1012, p. 272].

Having discussed the surface reflection models, let us examine some measured BRDF data for the surfaces of nonconductors and conductors. The body reflection constitutes a major portion of the reflection from a nonconductor and therefore its BRDF is less directional. In contrast, there is almost no body reflection from a conductor surface and interface reflection is more directional. Figure 8.6 shows an example of measured BRDF data along the plane of incidence for a surface painted with latex paint [321]. The length of each arrow represents the magnitude of the BRDF in that direction. The incident angle is

Table 8.1. *Measured parameters of Ward's empirical reflection model for some objects*

Material	ρ_d	ρ_s	σ_x	σ_y
rolled brass	0.10	0.33	0.05	0.16
rolled aluminum	0.10	0.21	0.04	0.09
lightly brushed aluminum	0.15	0.19	0.088	0.13
varnished plywood	0.33	0.025	0.04	0.11
enamel finished metal	0.25	0.047	0.080	0.096
painted cardboard box	0.19	0.043	0.076	0.085
white ceramic tile	0.70	0.050	0.071	0.071
glossy paper	0.29	0.083	0.082	0.082
ivory computer plastic	0.45	0.043	0.13	0.13
plastic laminate	0.67	0.070	0.092	0.092

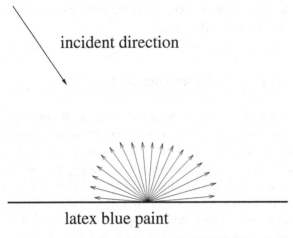

latex blue paint

Figure 8.6. An example of measured BRDF data for a surface painted with latex paint. The length of each arrow represents the magnitude of the BRDF in that direction. All the arrows shown are on the plane of incidence and the incident wavelength is 550 nm. The angle of incidence is 35°.

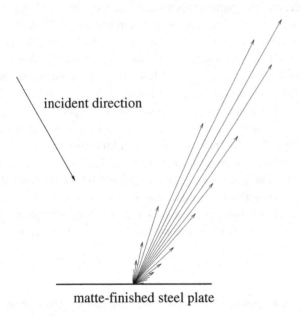

matte-finished steel plate

Figure 8.7. An example of measured BRDF data for a steel plate surface with a matte finish. The length of each arrow represents the magnitude of the BRDF in that direction. All the arrows shown are on the plane of incidence and the incident wavelength is 550 nm. The angle of incidence is 30°.

35°. The overall shape of the BRDF is close to that of a Lambertian reflector, except that there is noticeable backscattering at the incident angle and some off-specular reflection at $\theta_r = 75°$.

Figure 8.7 shows an example of measured BRDF data along the plane of incidence for a steel plate surface with a matte finish [321]. The incident angle is 30°. We now see that the overall shape of the BRDF is very different from that of a Lambertian reflector. The reflection is strongest for $\theta_r = \theta_i$. However, there is significant spread around this ideal reflection angle, due to the rough finish of the surface.

8.3 Radiative transfer theory and colorant formulation

In the previous section, we briefly discussed how body (subsurface) reflection can be modeled through radiative transfer theory. In fact, this is a topic that is of great interest in the paint, textile, paper, plastic, and publishing industries. The central question is how to mix different amounts of dyes and/or pigments to obtain products of a desired color. This is an important part of a process called colorant formulation, which also includes the selection of dyes and pigments for the application requirement, the study of color matching criteria, and the minimization of production cost. An interesting example of such applications is called shading in paint manufacturing. Pigments are ground and dispersed in the liquid solvent and binder (called the vehicle) by milling equipment to produce paint of the desired color. Because of batch to batch differences, the correct color is reached by successive approximations. First, about 80% of the required pigments is ground into the vehicle. Then the color is measured and the additional amount of each pigment required to match the desired color is calculated. Somewhat less than the calculated amount is added and the color checked again. Using repeated trials with visual inspection and comparison it usually takes as many as ten trials to come up with a good color match. With the help of computational models and color measurement, it is now possible to make the match in one or two trials.

The physics of colorant formulation is also of interest in color imaging science because certain color reproduction problems in color imaging share similar types of calculation and modeling. An example is the prediction of reflection density from known dye transmittance functions. Other examples will be discussed in later chapters. The basic physical model is simple for a transparent medium, but can be quite complicated for a turbid (translucent or opaque) medium. A simple classification is that a transparent medium does not contain appreciable numbers of particles or inhomogeneities that produce significant scattering, while a turbid medium does. These two types of medium are discussed separately as follows.

8.3.1 Transparent media

The major optical effect of a transparent medium on light propagation is absorption. Light absorption by a medium depends on several factors, such as the electronic structures of the atoms and molecules in the medium, the concentration of colorants, the thickness of the medium, the temperature of the medium, the polarization and the wavelength of the light. For our applications, the two major dependences are the thickness and the concentration. The effect of the thickness of a medium on the absorption of light is described by the Lambert–Bouguer law (also known as Lambert's law or Bouguer's law). Let $L_\lambda(z)$ be the radiance of light in the medium at position z, and $L_\lambda(z + t)$ be the radiance after it travels a distance t in the medium, then

$$L_\lambda(z + t) = L_\lambda(z)e^{-\alpha(\lambda)t}, \tag{8.43}$$

where $\alpha(\lambda)$ is called the absorption coefficient. If we express the relation in base 10:

$$L_\lambda(z+t) = L_\lambda(z)10^{-k(\lambda)t}, \tag{8.44}$$

then $k(\lambda) = \alpha(\lambda)/2.303$ is called the extinction coefficient. The corresponding law regarding the dependence of absorption on colorant concentration c is called Beer's law:

$$L_\lambda(z+t) = L_\lambda(z)10^{-k'(\lambda)c}, \tag{8.45}$$

for a fixed thickness t. Beer's law can be combined with the Lambert–Bouguer law to give the Beer–Lambert–Bouguer law (usually, called Beer's law):

$$L_\lambda(z+t) = L_\lambda(z)10^{-\epsilon(\lambda)ct}, \tag{8.46}$$

where $\epsilon(\lambda)$ is called the molar extinction coefficient (or the molar absorption coefficient) and c is the molar concentration of the absorbing colorant. In general, the extinction coefficient also includes the effect of scattering. Unfortunately, the names and symbols of these terms are not standardized across different fields and we have to pay attention to the meaning and units of these terms when reading the literature.

The Bouguer–Lambert law can also be written in differential form when the extinction coefficient is not constant throughout the medium. Within a transparent medium, the differential amount of spectral radiance attenuation, $dL_\lambda(z)$, is proportional to the differential distance it travels in the medium, dz, i.e.,

$$dL_\lambda(z) = -\alpha_\lambda(z)L_\lambda(z)dz, \tag{8.47}$$

where $\alpha_\lambda(z)$ is the absorption coefficient at spatial location z. Integrating over a finite thickness, t, we have

$$L_\lambda(z+t) = L_\lambda(z)\exp\left[-\int_z^{z+t}\alpha_\lambda(z)dz\right] = L_\lambda(z)10^{-\int_z^{z+t}k_\lambda(z)dz}. \tag{8.48}$$

The transmittance inside the medium, T_λ, is defined by

$$T_\lambda = \frac{L_\lambda(z+t)}{L_\lambda(z)} = 10^{-k_\lambda t}. \tag{8.49}$$

The optical density inside, the medium, D_λ, is defined by

$$D_\lambda = -\log T_\lambda = k_\lambda t. \tag{8.50}$$

It is important to remember that most of the radiative transfer quantities, such as k_λ, T_λ, and D_λ, are functions of wavelength. They are, of course, also functions of other variables, such as temperature and polarization, but for simplicity, we shall drop the subscript λ and the dependence on other variables in the following discussion.

Within a limited range of concentration, the combined effect of several colorants in a medium can be described by expressing the extinction coefficient as

$$k = k_s + \epsilon_1 c_1 + \epsilon_2 c_2 + \cdots, \tag{8.51}$$

where k_s is the extinction coefficient for the substrate alone, and ϵ_i and c_i are the molar absorption coefficient and molar concentration of the ith colorant.

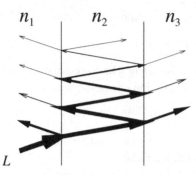

n_1 n_2 n_3

L

Figure 8.8. Calculation of transmittance through a transparent film.

All the above discussion of absorption and transmission applies only to the interior of a transparent medium. In many applications, the medium has a finite thickness and the effect of the discontinuity in the index of refraction at the surface boundaries has to be considered. This effect is usually called the surface correction. Let us consider the example of such a calculation shown in Fig. 8.8. Assume that we have a transparent film of thickness t and index of refraction n_2. On one side of the film is a medium with the index of refraction n_1 and, on the other side, a medium with index of refraction n_3. A beam of light with radiance L is incident on the film from medium 1. At the boundary of the interface, part of the light is reflected back. A portion of the light that is transmitted into the film will be partially absorbed. As the attenuated beam reaches the second surface boundary, part of it is reflected back into the film and the rest is transmitted into medium 3. The reflected beam then goes through the same process again. If the incident beam is perpendicular to the film, the reflection coefficients at the two interfaces are

$$r_1 = \left(\frac{n_1 - n_2}{n_1 + n_2}\right)^2, \tag{8.52}$$

$$r_2 = \left(\frac{n_2 - n_3}{n_2 + n_3}\right)^2. \tag{8.53}$$

It should be noted that when the beam is perpendicular to the interface, the reflection coefficient is the same no matter which way the beam is traveling (from medium 1 to medium 2 or from medium 2 to medium 1). Our problem is to calculate how much light is transmitted from medium 1 to medium 3. The internal transmittance T_i can be calculated from the extinction coefficient, k, of the film, i.e., $T_i = 10^{-kt}$. The total amount of light transmitted through the film is

$$
\begin{aligned}
L_t &= L(1 - r_1)T_i(1 - r_2) + L(1 - r_1)T_i r_2 T_i r_1 T_i(1 - r_2) \\
&\quad + L(1 - r_1)T_i r_2 T_i r_1 T_i r_2 T_i r_1 T_i(1 - r_2) + \cdots \\
&= L(1 - r_1)T_i(1 - r_2) + L(1 - r_1)r_1 r_2 T_i^3(1 - r_2) + L(1 - r_1)r_1^2 r_2^2 T_i^5(1 - r_2) + \cdots \\
&= L(1 - r_1)T_i(1 - r_2)[1 + r_1 r_2 T_i^2 + (r_1 r_2 T_i^2)^2 + \cdots] = \left(\frac{(1 - r_1)T_i(1 - r_2)}{1 - r_1 r_2 T_i^2}\right) L.
\end{aligned}
$$

$$\tag{8.54}$$

Therefore, the externally measured film transmittance, $T = L_t/L$, may be significantly different from the internal transmittance, because of the multiple interface reflections. For example, let us assume that $n_1 = n_3 = 1.0$, $n_2 = 1.5$, and $T_i = 0.8$. Then $r_1 = r_2 = 0.04$, and $T = 0.738$. Because of the finiteness of the film thickness, the reflectance is also different. The total amount of light reflected from the film is

$$
\begin{aligned}
L_r &= Lr_1 + L(1 - r_1)T_i r_2 T_i(1 - r_1) + L(1 - r_1)T_i r_2 T_i r_1 T_i r_2 T_i(1 - r_1) + \cdots \\
&= Lr_1 + L(1 - r_1)^2 r_2 T_i^2 [1 + r_1 r_2 T_i^2 + (r_1 r_2 T_i^2)^2 + \cdots] \\
&= \left[r_1 + \frac{(1 - r_1)^2 r_2 T_i^2}{1 - r_1 r_2 T_i^2} \right] L.
\end{aligned}
\tag{8.55}
$$

Therefore for the same medium, the measured reflectance is $R = L_r/L = 0.0636$, which is significantly larger than $r_1 = 0.04$.

8.3.2 Turbid media

When light propagates through a turbid medium, it is not only partially absorbed, but also partially scattered. The scattered light is not lost and its final destination needs to be accounted for. The classical treatment of light propagation through random, absorbing and scattering media is based on the energy transport equation. The theory of radiative energy transfer is built on geometrical optics and shares many of the same assumptions as classical radiometry. The major assumptions in radiative transfer theory are incoherence of the light, weak scattering, and the infinite horizontal extent of the medium. Recent advances in the theory of multiple wave scattering in random inhomogeneous media have made better connection between radiative transfer theory and rigorous statistical wave theory [529].

Early work on light propagation through turbid media by Schuster [844] was based on the approximation of two diffuse fluxes moving in opposite directions through a random, absorbing, scattering, and self-emitting medium, such as the foggy atmosphere of a star. He assumed that the backward scattering is equal to the forward scattering, which is true only for particles very small compared with the wavelength. Silberstein [168] pointed out that, in a turbid medium, directional fluxes are needed in addition to the two diffuse fluxes to account for the collimated light beam illuminating the medium externally. Therefore, a four-flux theory was used for more general calculation of radiative transfer equations. It was later recognized by others that the absorption coefficients for the directional fluxes could also be different from those for the diffuse fluxes. A general radiative transfer theory was described by Chandrasekhar in his book [168]. On the application side, Kubelka and Munk [536] and Kubelka [537, 538] published a two-flux theory and its formula for various conditions. Mainly because of its simplicity, the Kubelka–Munk theory has become the most widely used theory in colorant formulation. However, its assumption that the propagation of light fluxes in turbid media is perfectly diffuse is not quite realistic in many applications. A more general analysis, called the many-flux theory, was described by Mudgett and Richards [683] for calculating color formulation in the paper, plastics, textile, and protective coating industries.

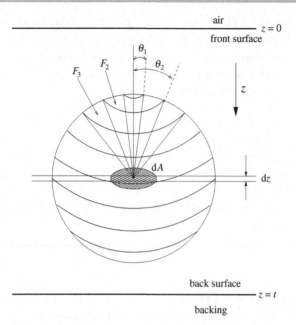

Figure 8.9. The partition of the space around an elemental area dA in the medium into many channels. The solid angle delineated by the cone θ_1 is the first channel. The solid angle between the cones θ_1 and θ_2 is called channel 2, and so on.

Many-flux theory

Let us assume that the scattering medium is bounded by parallel planes and extends over a region very large compared with its thickness, and that the medium is homogeneous and isotropic. The many-flux theory partitions the space around an elemental area dA in the medium into many concentric cone shells, each called a channel. The elemental area dA is parallel to the surface of the medium. Figure 8.9 shows the partition. The z-axis is normal to the interface between the air and the medium. The scattering medium is placed on top of a backing. The thickness of the turbid medium is t. The air–medium boundary plane is located at $z = 0$ and the backing is located at $z = t$. Let F_i be the flux going into channel i. We will assume that there are m channels, where m is an even integer, such that $m/2$ channels (index $1 \leq i \leq m/2$) are going down and $m/2$ channels (index $m/2 < i \leq m$) are going up. Let s_{ij} be the scattering coefficient that describes the scattering from channel j into channel i when $i \neq j$. When $i = j$, s_{jj} represents the total scattering and absorption that occur in channel j.

$$\frac{dF_i}{dz} = \sum_{j=1}^{m} s_{ij} F_j, \quad i \leq m/2, \tag{8.56}$$

$$-\frac{dF_i}{dz} = \sum_{j=1}^{m} s_{ij} F_j, \quad i > m/2, \tag{8.57}$$

where the negative sign for $i > m/2$ is to account for the fact that these channel fluxes are going in the negative z direction. The above radiative transfer equations can be written in matrix form. Let the matrix Λ be defined by $\Lambda_{ij} = s_{ij}$ when $i \leq m/2$, and $\Lambda_{ij} = -s_{ij}$ when $i > m/2$. Let $\mathbf{F}$ be the vector of $[F_1, F_2, \ldots, F_m]^T$, then

$$\frac{d\mathbf{F}}{dz} = \Lambda\mathbf{F}. \tag{8.58}$$

The general solution of this equation is:

$$F_i = \sum_{j=1}^{m} A_{ij}C_j e^{\lambda_j z}, \tag{8.59}$$

where λ_j are the eigenvalues of the matrix Λ, A_{ij} is the ith component of the eigenvector corresponding to the eigenvalue λ_j, and C_j are constants to be determined from the boundary conditions at the front and back surfaces.

The many-flux theory provides a computational method for dealing with any type of illumination and material scattering. However, it is not very practical to experimentally measure so many coefficients in the matrix Λ. In fact, the most useful theory has been the two-flux (Kubelka–Munk) theory. One problem with the two-flux theory is that it deals with only diffuse illumination and diffuse reflection/transmission of the surfaces. With advances in computing power, the four-flux theory should become more useful because it can deal with more realistic illumination.

Four-flux theory

If the external light is collimated and is perpendicular to the material surface, we can expect that a major component of the transmitted light just beneath the surface of a turbid material will be a directional flux. As light penetrates deeper into the material, it is scattered more and the intensity of the directional flux is reduced while the intensity of the scattered diffuse flux is increased. Therefore, a useful model for light propagation in a turbid material can be developed by using only four fluxes: two directional fluxes (one forward and one backward) and two diffuse fluxes (again, one forward and one backward). Figure 8.10 shows the setup of the four-flux theory.

Let F_1, F_2, F_3, and F_4 be the forward directional flux, the backward directional flux, the forward diffuse flux, and the backward diffuse flux, respectively. The scattering and absorption coefficients are defined as follows:

$$k = -\frac{1}{F_1}\frac{dF_1}{dz} = \frac{1}{F_2}\frac{dF_2}{dz}\bigg|_{\text{directional–absorption}} ;$$

$$s_f = -\frac{1}{F_1}\frac{dF_1}{dz} = \frac{1}{F_2}\frac{dF_2}{dz}\bigg|_{\text{directional–forward–scattering}} ;$$

$$s_b = -\frac{1}{F_1}\frac{dF_1}{dz} = \frac{1}{F_2}\frac{dF_2}{dz}\bigg|_{\text{directional–backward–scattering}} ; \tag{8.60}$$

$$K = -\frac{1}{F_3}\frac{dF_3}{dz} = \frac{1}{F_4}\frac{dF_4}{dz}\bigg|_{\text{diffuse–absorption}} ;$$

$$S = -\frac{1}{F_3}\frac{dF_3}{dz} = \frac{1}{F_4}\frac{dF_4}{dz}\bigg|_{\text{diffuse–scattering}} .$$

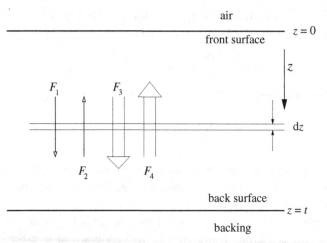

Figure 8.10. The four-flux theory assumes that there are two directional fluxes (F_1 and F_2) and two diffuse fluxes (F_3 and F_4).

Radiative transfer equations are set up by accounting for energy fluxes being transferred from one flux to another or absorbed by the medium. For example, the forward-scattered flux from F_1 is added to the forward diffuse flux F_3, while the backward-scattered flux from F_1 is added to the backward diffuse flux F_4. With these coefficients, we can write the radiative energy transport equations as follows:

$$
\begin{aligned}
\mathrm{d}F_1 &= -kF_1\mathrm{d}z - s_f F_1 \mathrm{d}z - s_b F_1 \mathrm{d}z; \\
-\mathrm{d}F_2 &= -kF_2\mathrm{d}z - s_f F_2 \mathrm{d}z - s_b F_2 \mathrm{d}z; \\
\mathrm{d}F_3 &= s_f F_1 \mathrm{d}z + s_b F_2 \mathrm{d}z - (K+S)F_3\mathrm{d}z + SF_4\mathrm{d}z; \\
-\mathrm{d}F_4 &= s_b F_1 \mathrm{d}z + s_f F_2 \mathrm{d}z + SF_3\mathrm{d}z - (K+S)F_4\mathrm{d}z.
\end{aligned}
\tag{8.61}
$$

Let $\mu = k + s_f + s_b$ and $a = 1 + (K/S)$, then we can simplify the above equations to:

$$
\begin{aligned}
\frac{\mathrm{d}F_1}{\mathrm{d}z} &= -\mu F_1; \\[4pt]
\frac{\mathrm{d}F_2}{\mathrm{d}z} &= \mu F_2; \\[4pt]
\frac{\mathrm{d}F_3}{\mathrm{d}z} &= s_f F_1 + s_b F_2 - aSF_3 + SF_4; \\[4pt]
\frac{\mathrm{d}F_4}{\mathrm{d}z} &= -s_b F_1 - s_f F_2 - SF_3 + aSF_4.
\end{aligned}
\tag{8.62}
$$

These equations can be solved in many different ways, depending on the boundary conditions chosen. One solution based on the boundary conditions at the air–medium interface is:

$$F_1(z) = F_1(0)e^{-\mu z};$$

$$F_2(z) = F_2(0)e^{\mu z} = F_2(t)e^{-\mu(t-z)};$$

$$F_3(z) = F_1(0)\left(Ae^{-\mu z} - A\cosh Sbz + \frac{s_f + \mu A}{Sb}\sinh Sbz\right)$$

$$+ F_2(0)\left(Be^{\mu z} - B\cosh Sbz + \frac{s_b - \mu B}{Sb}\sinh Sbz\right)$$

$$+ F_3(0)\left(\cosh Sbz - \frac{a}{b}\sinh Sbz\right) + F_4(0)\left(\frac{1}{b}\sinh Sbz\right); \tag{8.63}$$

$$F_4(z) = F_1(0)\left(Be^{-\mu z} - B\cosh Sbz + \frac{s_b + \mu B}{Sb}\sinh Sbz\right)$$

$$+ F_2(0)\left(Ae^{\mu z} - A\cosh Sbz + \frac{s_f - \mu A}{Sb}\sinh Sbz\right) - F_3(0)\left(\frac{1}{b}\sinh Sbz\right)$$

$$+ F_4(0)\left(\cosh Sbz + \frac{a}{b}\sinh Sbz\right),$$

where $b = \sqrt{a^2 - 1}$ and

$$A = \frac{S(as_f + s_b) + \mu s_f}{S^2 b^2 - \mu^2},$$

$$B = \frac{S(as_b + s_f) - \mu s_b}{S^2 b^2 - \mu^2}.$$

Kubelka–Munk theory: two-flux model

If we set the the two directional fluxes F_1 and F_2 to zero in the four-flux theory, we have the famous Kubelka–Munk two-flux theory [18, 276, 477, 536, 537, 538, 989]. From Eqs. (8.62), the two relevant equations become:

$$\frac{dF_3}{dz} = -(S + K)F_3 + SF_4;$$

$$\frac{dF_4}{dz} = -SF_3 + (S + K)F_4. \tag{8.64}$$

These can be solved by using the Laplace transform [128, Chapter 11] and the general solutions are

$$F_3(z) = \left(\cosh Sbz - \frac{a}{b}\sinh Sbz\right)F_3(0) + \left(\frac{1}{b}\sinh Sbz\right)F_4(0), \tag{8.65}$$

$$F_4(z) = \left(\cosh Sbz + \frac{a}{b}\sinh Sbz\right)F_4(0) - \left(\frac{1}{b}\sinh Sbz\right)F_3(0), \tag{8.66}$$

where $a = 1 + (K/S)$ and $b = \sqrt{a^2 - 1}$, as frequently used in the Kubelka–Munk formula. We are often interested in determining the (internal) diffuse reflectance, R_i, of the surface, when the medium of thickness t is placed against a backing of diffuse reflectance R_g. Since F_3 represents the downward flux and F_4 the upward flux, then by definition, we have $R_i = F_4(0)/F_3(0)$ and $R_g = F_4(t)/F_3(t)$. Note that the reflectance R_i is at the boundary of the air–medium interface, but still internal to the medium. We can solve for R_i by noting that

$$F_3(t) = \left(\cosh Sbt - \frac{a}{b}\sinh Sbt\right)F_3(0) + \left(\frac{1}{b}\sinh Sbt\right)F_4(0), \qquad (8.67)$$

$$F_4(t) = \left(\cosh Sbt + \frac{a}{b}\sinh Sbt\right)F_4(0) - \left(\frac{1}{b}\sinh Sbt\right)F_3(0), \qquad (8.68)$$

and therefore

$$R_i = \frac{F_4(0)}{F_3(0)} = \frac{1 - R_g(a - b\coth Sbt)}{a - R_g + b\coth Sbt}. \qquad (8.69)$$

There are two cases of special interest here. The first is when there is no scattering, i.e., $S \to 0$. Then,

$$\begin{aligned}
R_i &= \frac{1 - R_g(1 + K/S) + R_g b\coth Sbt}{(1 + K/S) - R_g + b\coth Sbt} \\[2mm]
&= \frac{S - R_g(K + S) + R_g Sb\coth Sbt}{(K + S) - R_g S + bS\coth Sbt} \\[2mm]
&\approx \frac{-R_g K + R_g Sb\coth Sbt}{K + bS\coth Sbt} \approx \frac{-R_g K + R_g K\coth Kt}{K + K\coth Kt},
\end{aligned}$$

and therefore

$$\lim_{S \to 0} R_i = R_g e^{-2Kt}, \qquad (8.70)$$

which is what we expect from the Bouguer–Lambert law because the flux travels through the thickness twice (going down and coming up). However, it should be noted [1056] that the absorption coefficient K here refers to the diffuse flux, while in the Bouguer–Lambert law, the extinction coefficient k refers to directional flux. The other special case is when the thickness t approaches infinity, i.e., $\coth Sbt \to 1$. From the definition of a and b, it follows that $(a + b)(a - b) = a^2 - b^2 = 1$, and we have:

$$R_i = \frac{1 - R_g(a - b)}{a - R_g + b} = \frac{(a + b)(a - b) - R_g(a - b)}{(a + b) - R_g} = a - b.$$

This means that when the layer is very thick, the background reflectance, R_g, no longer affects the layer reflectance, R_i. This result is usually expressed as

$$R_\infty = 1 + \frac{K}{S} - \left[\left(\frac{K}{S}\right)^2 + 2\left(\frac{K}{S}\right)\right]^{1/2}. \qquad (8.71)$$

Solving for K/S, we have

$$\frac{K}{S} = \frac{(1 - R_\infty)^2}{2R_\infty}. \qquad (8.72)$$

This provides a way to determine K/S experimentally by measuring R_∞. The remaining task is to determine the relationship between the internal diffuse reflectance R_i and the externally measurable diffuse reflectance R. The difference between R_i and R is due to the discontinuity in the index of refraction between the air and the medium. The correction for this difference is known as the Saunderson correction [828]. This correction is similar to the calculation given for a transparent film in the previous section, except that the light passing from the medium to the air is now diffuse and the reflectance at the medium–air interface is very different from that at air–medium interface.

Depending on the external illumination and measurement geometry, there are different formulas for the Saunderson correction. In order to calculate the correction, we need to define a number of quantities. Let r_x and r_i represent the external and internal reflection factors for diffuse light, respectively. From the Fresnel reflection equation, it can be shown that [268]

$$r_x = \frac{1}{2} + \frac{(n-1)(3n+1)}{6(n+1)^2} + \left[\frac{n^2(n^2-1)^2}{(n^2+1)^3}\right]\ln\left(\frac{n-1}{n+1}\right) - \frac{2n^3\left(n^2+2n-1\right)}{(n^2+1)(n^4-1)}$$
$$+ \left[\frac{8n^4(n^4+1)}{(n^2+1)(n^4-1)^2}\right]\ln n. \tag{8.73}$$

It is also possible to derive a similar theoretical equation for r_i. However, such a theoretical value is often not useful because of the complication caused by the total internal reflection when the incident angle in the medium is larger than the critical angle. This makes the real internal reflection factor r_i very sensitive to the actually angular distribution of the upward emergent flux. For example, the theoretical value of r_i is 0.596 for $n = 1.5$, but backward calculation from experimental data often indicates a smaller value of around 0.4–0.5. Therefore, in practice, r_i is treated as an additional constant to be estimated.

If the external illumination is diffuse and the sensing geometry is also diffuse, we can determine the relation between R_i and R as follows. Let L be the incident flux. The reflected flux, L_r, leaving the medium is

$$L_r = Lr_x + L(1-r_x)R_i(1-r_i) + L(1-r_x)R_ir_iR_i(1-r_i) + \cdots$$
$$= Lr_x + L(1-r_x)R_i(1-r_i)[1 + r_iR_i + r_i^2R_i^2 + \cdots]$$
$$= L\left[r_x + \frac{(1-r_x)R_i(1-r_i)}{1-r_iR_i}\right] \tag{8.74}$$

and

$$R = \frac{L_r}{L} = r_x + \frac{(1-r_x)(1-r_i)R_i}{1-r_iR_i}. \tag{8.75}$$

Now, let us calculate an ideal case in which $R_i = 0.5, n = 1.5, r_x = 0.0918$, and $r_i = 0.596$. The externally measured reflectance is $R = 0.353$ which is significantly different from R_i. If instead of the ideal value, r_i is only 0.4, then $R = 0.432$.

8.4 Causes of color

The spectral composition of the light emitted from a light source undergoes various changes in the process of scattering, reflection, refraction, transmission, and absorption. As a consequence, objects under one illumination send light of different spectral compositions to our visual system and they produce our perception of various colors. There are many ways materials or light sources can modify or generate light of different spectral compositions (see, e.g., [276, 391, 693, 1038], for more details).

According to Nassau [693], color can be produced by: (1) incandescence (light emitted by heated bodies), (2) gas excitation, (3) atomic or molecular vibration and rotation, (4) transition metals in a ligand field, (5) orbital transitions in organic molecules, (6) charge transfer, (7) energy bands and impurities in metals and semiconductors, (8) color centers, (9) dispersive refraction and polarization, (10) scattering, (11) nonlinear optical effects, (12) interference, (13) diffraction, etc. It is clear that causes of color are many. However, it should be noted that this classification of different causes is a matter of convenience and different causes should not be taken as mutually exclusive. After all, light–matter interaction can be described on a very fundamental level by a single theory called quantum electrodynamics. The following sections discuss some of the common causes of color.

8.4.1 Selective absorption

The majority of surface colors are due to the selective absorption by the pigments embedded in the surface material. Although photons of visible light (1.7–3.1 eV) have energy on the low side for ordinary energy gaps of electron orbitals, and on the high side for molecular vibration and rotation, the molecules that we associate with pigments and dyes all have resonance frequencies within the visible light range.

Many organic dyes have alternate single and double bonds (called a conjugated system) in their long chain molecules. As more double bonds are added to the (polyene) chains the peak absorption wavelength is shifted towards the red [654]. For molecules of the form, $CH_3 (-CH=CH)_n-CH_3$, the peak absorption wavelength is at 230 nm when $n = 2$, and it is shifted to the visible region when $n = 7$ or 8. Table 8.2 shows an example of such shifts [918, p. 596]. Conjugated systems like this have a number of π electrons which are very mobile over the entire chain of the molecule. As the chain becomes longer, the number of possible resonant configurations increases, and the energy of the lowest excited level is reduced. Examples of molecules with conjugated systems include carotene (in carrot, orange, feather, skin), chlorophyll (in plant leaves), and heme (in blood). In fact, the photopigment (rhodopsin) of the photoreceptors in the retina contains a conjugated chromophore (retinal).

Inorganic compounds containing metal ions with unpaired electrons also show very vivid colors. Examples are red ruby (chromium), green emerald (chromium), green or yellow or brown jade (iron), cobalt salt, and other minerals.

Table 8.2. *The peak absorption wavelength as a function of the number of double bonds*

Aldehyde	λ_{max} (nm)
$CH_3(-CH=CH)-CHO$	220
$CH_3(-CH=CH)_2-CHO$	270
$CH_3(-CH=CH)_3-CHO$	312
$CH_3(-CH=CH)_4-CHO$	343
$CH_3(-CH=CH)_5-CHO$	370
$CH_3(-CH=CH)_6-CHO$	393
$CH_3(-CH=CH)_7-CHO$	415

8.4.2 Scattering

Scattering gives rise not only to the blue color of the sky but also to the blue color seen on many animals. Small particles overlying a dark layer give a blue color because the portion of light that is not scattered is absorbed by the underlying dark layer. If the underlying layer has some color in it, the color will combine with the blue to produce various hues. The blue feathers in the blue jay birds, the blue neck coloration of turkeys, and blue eyes in humans (scattering from the pigments in the iris) are all examples where colors are produced by structural scattering.

8.4.3 Interference

Thin films and regular fine structures can produce colors by interference. The colors we see on soap bubbles, peacocks, butterflies, beetles, and opals are the results of light interference [878]. The colors of these objects change when we shift our angle of view.

8.4.4 Dispersion

The index of refraction is a function of wavelength and as a result light of different wavelengths is refracted to different angles, producing spectrum-like colors. Diamond has the highest dispersion power of any naturally occurring gem material, and it also gives a beautiful play of color as it is turned. A rainbow is produced when sunlight is dispersed by water droplets through internal reflection.

8.5 Common materials

In the study of color imaging, it is always helpful to model the underlying physics as much as we can. This often means that some basic understanding of material structures is required. In this section we will give a brief description of the composition and structure of several major classes of common materials: water, minerals, ceramics, metals, glass, polymers, plants, and animals. Books on materials science (e.g., [217, 853]) can be consulted for further details.

8.5.1 Water

A water molecule consists of two hydrogen atoms bonded to one oxygen atom. The oxygen–hydrogen bond length is about 0.096 nm, and the angle between the two oxygen–hydrogen bonds is 101.52°. The attractive forces between water molecules, in both the liquid and solid states, are mainly provided by hydrogen bonds. The positive charge on a hydrogen atom of one water molecule is attracted to the negative charge on an oxygen atom of another water molecule. The two hydrogen bonds and the two covalent (oxygen–hydrogen) bonds form an approximate tetrahedron. This symmetry is found in ice crystals. However, in liquid water at room temperature, a molecule oscillates within a surrounding cage of other molecules for about 4 ps, before jumping out of this position and into an adjacent cage [217, p. 89]. Water molecules can spontaneously break up to form H^+ and OH^- at a rate of 2.5×10^{-5} per second, resulting in a concentration of H^+ (and also OH^-) of about 10^{-7} mole per liter. The hydrogen ion concentration is measured by pH values ($-\log_{10}$ moles per liter). If the hydrogen ion concentration is higher than 10^{-7} mole per liter due to the presence of other chemicals (i.e., when the pH value is lower than 7), the solution is considered acidic, and otherwise, it is considered basic. Changing the pH value of a solution can change the solution's color dramatically. For example, the same molecule, cyanidin, is responsible for the red of the poppy and the blue of the cornflower [43]. In the poppy, the sap is acid and the cyanidin acquires a hydrogen ion and its color is red. In the cornflower, the sap is alkaline, and the cyanidin loses a hydrogen ion and its color is blue!

The color of pure water is pale blue because the hydrogen bonds tend to drag and push neighboring water molecules when they are vibrating, causing a slight absorption at the long-wavelength end of the visible spectrum.

8.5.2   Metals

Metals consist of polycrystals. Each crystal is called a grain. The grain size is typically in the range of 10 μm to 1 mm. Since each grain has a different orientation of its crystal planes, a metal surface exhibits grain boundaries under microscope examination using polarized light. Most metals reflect all wavelengths of visible light nonselectively and appear to be silvery gray; exceptions are the red–yellow of copper and the yellow of gold. In both copper and gold, electrons in the filled d band can be transferred to vacant s and p bands, resulting absorption in the visible wavelength range.

8.5.3   Minerals

In terms of percentages of the whole by weight, about 45% of the earth is oxygen and about 28% of it is silicon. The outer crust of the earth consists of three types of rock: igneous, metamorphic, and sedimentary. Most rocks are formed from aggregates of mainly minerals and a small amount of nonmineral substances. In a restricted sense, a mineral is a homogeneous inorganic crystalline solid occurring in the earth's crust, although the term "mineral" is often used more loosely as anything that is not animal or plant. In our discussion here, we will use the term in the restricted sense. Of all the earth's minerals, more than 90% are silicates which are composed of silicon and oxygen.

Most minerals have quite complex chemical compositions and their crystal structures are also very complicated. Table 8.3 shows the composition of some common minerals. Crystal size ranges from smaller than a millimeter to a few centimeters.

8.5.4   Ceramics and cements

The term ceramic is often used loosely to cover many varieties of natural and man-made materials. It includes stone, brick, concrete, window glass, and clay. A narrower usage is often restricted to pottery or porcelain. A general working definition is that a ceramic is a

Table 8.3. *Compositions of*
some common materials

Mineral	Composition
talc	$Mg_3Si_4O_{10}(OH)_2$
gypsum	$CaSO_4 \cdot 2H_2O$
calcite	$CaCO_3$
quartz	SiO_2
topaz	$Al_2SiO_4F_2$

solid composed of a mixture of metallic (or semi-metallic) and nonmetallic elements, in such a structure and proportion that the resulting material is mechanically hard, and resistant to heat, electricity, and corrosion. With this definition, we can also include tungsten carbide and silicon nitride (used for turbine blades).

A ceramic consists of many fine grains of crystal (about 1 μm in size). These small solid grains are fused together by a heat treatment that causes sintering (a process of adhesion of adjacent particles by an exchange and interpenetration of their atoms). The most commonly found component in natural ceramics is silicate, which is a combination of silicon and oxygen. The silicon atom, after lending its four outermost electrons to four oxygen atoms, has a very small radius of 0.41 Å, and the oxygen atom, after borrowing an electron, is relatively large with a radius of 1.4 Å. The four oxygen atoms form a tetrahedron with a tiny silicon atom filling the gap in the center. Each of the four oxygen atoms can further form another bond to a neighboring silicon atom, resulting in many tetrahedra sharing corners. Therefore, in this case, the chemical formula for silica is SiO_2, not SiO_4. The tetrahedra can be arranged as one-dimensional chains (such as in asbestos), as two-dimensional arrays (such as mica), as three-dimensional lattices (such as cristobalite, one form of quartz), or as random branches (such as window glass). The optical properties of these different forms of silica are different. Ceramics are usually opaque or translucent because they contain many pores among the crystal grains (i.e., they are porous). If these pores are removed, ceramics can become transparent.

A very important class of ceramics is cements. Modern cement is made from limestone (about 80%, mostly $CaCO_3$) and clays (about 20%, mostly aluminosilicates). The final product is a fine powder with particle sizes around 15–60 μm. Portland cements are commonly used in modern concrete. There are five types of Portland cement. They vary in their proportions of the following components: $3CaO \cdot SiO_2$, $2CaO \cdot SiO_2$, $3CaO \cdot Al_2O_3$, $3CaO \cdot Al_2O_3 \cdot Fe_2O_3$, and other minor components such as MgO, CaO, and $CaSO_4$. Concrete is an aggregate composite, combining sand (on the order of mm in size) and gravel (on the order of cm in size) with cement, that forms a matrix that bonds all the aggregate particles into a rigid solid. The hardening process in cement involves the growth of several types of crystal (such as $3CaO \cdot Al_2O_3 \cdot CaSO_4 \cdot 12H_2O$ and $3CaO \cdot Al_2O_3 \cdot 3CaSO_4 \cdot 32H_2O$), each of a different size and shape, interlocking with each other [217, pp. 127–130].

Our understanding of ceramics is still quite limited. When, in 1986, Bednortz and Müller discovered that the ceramic LaBaCuO was a superconductor at 35 K, it was a total surprise to the world of materials science.

8.5.5 Glass

The word glass is usually used to refer to a certain type of material, such as window glass made of silicate oxides. As our understanding of the common glass material increased, it was realized that the key characteristic of glass is its lack of long-range (distance longer than a few hundred atoms) order. Therefore, glass is also used to denote a state of solid that does not have specific order. The chemical elements that form glass are the same as those that form ceramics. Ceramics contain polycrystals, but glass does not. The structure in glass lacks the periodic regularity of ceramics. Instead of a regular arrangement of atoms repeated over a distance of a few thousand or more atoms as in a crystal, glass consists of a random arrangement of the same basic building blocks (such as Al_2O_3) randomly connected, a structure called random network.

Glasses that are used in large quantities for windows, bottles, and other containers are mixtures of oxides. They are the soda-lime–silica glasses, consisting of 70–75% silica (SiO_2), 13–17% sodium oxide (Na_2O), 5–10% lime (CaO), 1–5% magnesia (MgO), and other oxides in minor quantities.

Two of the most significant optical properties of glasses are their transparency and their dispersion power to visible light. The transparency is primarily due to the random arrangement of atoms and the lack of long-range order, which causes the electrons to be trapped in localized wave states. The electrons do not receive sufficient energy from visible light to enable them to jump to the next energy state.

Colored glass is produced by adding a very small amount of impurity to the glass. For example, Fe^{3+} ions give the glass a green color, while a small amount of copper gives it a blue color. An element produces different colors in different glasses because the absorption bands of the color center depend on the local electronic environment. Cobalt gives a pink color to a borosilicate glass, a purple color to potash–silica glass, and a blue color to a soda-lime–silica glass. These impurity color centers are usually the transition metals, which have unfilled d-orbitals. Another way of producing color in glass is to have small aggregates of impurity atoms, which have diameters comparable with or smaller than the wavelengths of visible light. For example, the presence of gold colloidal particles of about 40 nm diameter in lead-silicate glass gives the glass a beautiful red color.

8.5.6 Polymers

The word polymer means many (poly) parts (meros). Polymers are formed by combining (chaining) together many smaller units. These smaller units are called monomers and most polymers consist of repetitions of only a few kinds of monomers. For example, polyethylene consists of only one monomer, $-C_2H_4-$. The elements associated with commercial polymers are H, C, N, O, F, and Si. Most polymers are organic materials (containing carbon). Polymer chains are produced by inducing chemical reactions between monomers so that they are joined by chemical bonds in a long chain. The polymer molecules are so long (several hundred nanometers) that it is difficult for them to form crystals. For example, single crystals of polyethylene are difficult to grow. They tend to be produced as thin platelets about 10 nm thick, with chains folded back and forth in a small volume.

Cellulose and amylose (starch) are the two most abundant biopolymers in plants. Both have the same monomer, glucose, and their structural difference arises from the way the glucose units are connected together.

Most known commercial polymers are plastics and synthetic fibers which are not colored. In order to produce colored plastics, it is necessary to add color pigments in the manufacturing process. Color pigments are not soluble in the plastics or synthetic fibers, and they have to be dispersed in appropriate carrier media which can be solid or liquid. Polyethylene, polypropylene, polyvinyl chloride (PVC), and polystyrene are some of the major types of plastic. Polyester, polyamide, acrylic, and polyolefin (olefin: hydrocarbons with a double bond) are some of the major types of synthetic fiber.

Conventional textile dyeing uses water-soluble or dispersed dyes applied from an aqueous bath. Therefore dye molecules are adsorbed onto the fiber surfaces. Modern mass coloration introduces colorants during or after the formation of the fiber-forming polymers. Dye molecules or pigments are thus dispersed into the fiber filament, rather than adsorbed onto its surface. Interface reflection from plastics and mass-colored synthetic fibers is mostly nonselective, while the spectral composition of their body reflection is determined by the pigments used to color the plastics. Therefore, reflection from plastics materials can be described quite well by the dichromatic reflection model or, more specifically, by the NIR model.

8.5.7 Plants

The green color of plant leaves comes from the pigment chlorophyll. There are several forms of chlorophyll, each with its own characteristic peaks in its absorption spectrum. The most abundant form is chlorophyll a. Chlorophyll is the photopigment that is responsible for photosynthesis. In the green alga, Chlorella, the most effective light for photosynthesis is in two wavelength ranges: long-wavelength light (650–680 nm) and short-wavelength (400–460 nm) light. Therefore the reflected as well as the transmitted light consists of mainly middle wavelength light. There are three major classes of photosynthesis pigments found in plants and algae: the chlorophylls, the carotenoids, and the phycobilins (in some algae). The carotenoids and the phycobilins are called accessory photosynthetic pigments because the light energy absorbed by these pigments can be passed on to chlorophyll. The number of carotenoid molecules is smaller than that of the chlorophyll (about 1:3). A dark green leaf has more carotenoids than a light green leaf. Table 8.4 shows the peak wavelengths of the absorption spectra of these pigments in organic solvents, such as ether. The carotenoids are yellow or orange pigments found in most photosynthesizing leaf cells. In the fall when the chlorophyll breaks down, the color of carotenoids and other pigments, such as anthocyanins and flavonols, can be seen in the colorful leaves.

Carotene ($C_{40}H_{56}$) and its derivatives are also found in many other plants, fruits, and vegetables. They are wholly or partially responsible for the orange–yellow color in carrot, mango, persimmon, butter, etc. Lecopene is a molecule of carotene with its two terminal rings open. It is responsible for the red color of tomato. Carotene and lecopene are both present in and produce the color of apricots. The yellow color of corn is caused by carotene and zeaxanthin ($C_{40}H_{56}O_2$), which is carotene with an oxygen added at each end ring.

Table 8.4. *The peak absorption wavelengths of some natural pigments*

Pigments	Peak absorption wavelength (nm)
chlorophyll a	420 660
chlorophyll b	435 643
vhlorophyll c	445 625
chlorophyll d	450 690
α-carotene	420 440 470
β-carotene	425 450 480
luteol	425 445 475
phycoerhthrins	490 546 576
phycocyanins	618
allophycocyanins	650

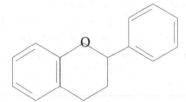

Figure 8.11. The basic framework of flavonoids.

Flavonoids are a class of molecules that have a common structure as shown in Fig. 8.11, with two benzene-like rings and another one in the middle that includes an oxygen. Most of the flavonoids occur in combination with a sugar molecule. Flavonoids are present in leaves and flower petals. They absorb ultraviolet light to protect plant DNAs. Substitution of the hydrogen atoms on the rings produces various classes of flavonoid, such as quercetin (the color of Dyer's oak), peonidin (the colors of peony, cherry, and grape), pelargonidin (the color of red geranium), cyanidin (the colors of raspberry, apple, and grape), and many other red, purple, and blue colors in plants [43, Chapter 5].

8.5.8 Animals

The external, visible surfaces of animals are covered with exoskeleton (insect, crab, and scorpion), feather (bird), hair/wool (sheep, monkey), or skin (human). The structural material of the flexible inner parts of the exoskeletons of insects and arthropods is chitin, which is the same as cellulose except that an –OH group on each glucose unit is replaced by an –NH(CO)CH$_3$ group. The carapaces of crabs, lobsters, and shrimps contain astaxanthin (C$_{40}$H$_{56}$O$_4$), which is liberated from its protein chains when cooked. Astaxanthin is related to carotene with two oxygens added at each of the two end rings, resulting in a pink–red color.

Animal hair and wool consist of α-keratin, which is a protein formed by three right-handed polypeptide α-helices that wrap around each other in a left-handed coil like a triple-stranded rope. Nine of these coils surround two more in the center and form a microfibril of eleven coils. A hair or wool cell consists of a stack of macrofibrils, each of which is a bundle of hundreds of microfibrils. The color of hair or wool is caused by the pigments (mostly melanins) in the hair or wool cells.

In the higher animals, collagens are the main structural molecules. Taking the human body as an example, collagens form the basic structures of tendon, skin, bone, teeth, blood vessel, cartilage, and even the cornea of the eye. Collagen fibers in the dermis of human skin are one of the main structures that scatter light back from the skin, as will be discussed shortly.

Melanins are one of the most common natural pigments in animals. They are responsible for the color of skin, feathers, hair, etc. Sometimes, melanins form structures that produce interference colors, such as those found in peacock feathers. Natural melanins consist of a protein (peptide) portion and a chromophoric polymer portion. The monomers that form the chromophoric polymer are different for different melanins. For example, eumelanin contains single nitrogen monomers such as indoles, indolines, pyrroles, and others, while pheomelanin contains monomers that have two nitrogen atoms.

8.5.9 Humans

People are often the most important subjects in color images. The color reproduction of a closed imaging system (meaning one that uses a known sensor and a known display medium, such as an AgX photographic system from film to paper) is often fine-tuned so as to insure a good reproduction of skin color. Therefore, we will discuss the origin and distribution of skin colors in some detail. We will also touch on the color of eyes and hair because they may be important for computer algorithms that attempt to detect and locate faces in color images.

Skin color

The human skin consists of a series of layers. The top layer is the epidermis, which is about 0.10–0.15 mm thick. It is composed of two types of cell: keratinocytes and melanocytes (which manufacture the pigment melanin). The epidermis consists of four layers. From the top down these are stratum corneum (dead keratinized cells), stratum granulosom (several layers of flat cells, partially keratinized), stratum spinosum (several layers of irregular polyhedral cells), and the basal layer (a single layer of keratinocytes and melanocytes interspersed, with melanin pigments present in both types of cell). Through cell divisions, new keratinocytes are formed in the basal layer and they are shifted upward and gradually keratinized. The top stratum corneum consists of dead cells that are constantly shed. Next to the epidermis is the dermis layer which is a connective tissue with collagen, elastic, and reticular fibers. Within this layer, blood and lymphatic vessels form complex networks. Also present are sweat and sebaceous glands, hair follicles, hairs, nerves, and minute muscles. Under the dermis layer are subcutaneous fat and muscle.

Light impinging on the skin propagates through these layers, and is partially absorbed and scattered by each layer. The absorption of light is mainly due to the various pigments present in the skin. There are several types of pigment in the human skin: melanin and its derivatives (present in the epidermis), bilirubin (reddish-yellow pigments present in the blood), β-carotene (present in the top layer of epidermis, in the blood, and in the subcutaneous fat), and hemoglobin (in the blood). In the epidermis of human skin, melanin (in the form of discrete granules, called melanosomes) is the dominant light absorber. For Caucasian skins, there is little melanin present in the epidermis, except in the basal melanocytes. For darker skins, the number and the size of melanin granules increase and they are present in keratinocytes as well. This accounts for the major difference in skin color among different races. In the dermis, the dominant absorbers of the visible light are oxygenated and deoxygenated hemoglobin [836]. Female skin has less melanin and blood, but more carotenes, and therefore, appears 3–4% lighter than male skin [452, p. 79]. The indices of refraction for most soft tissues are in the 1.38–1.41 range, except for the adipose (fat) tissue which has a refractive index of about 1.46. Secretions from the sweat and sebaceous glands are shown to be quite neutral in their spectral absorption. Therefore, the sweat and sebum that cover the skin surface typically contribute an NIR component to the total reflected light from the skin. Light scattering in skin is caused mostly by collagen fiber bundles and red blood cells, both being much larger than the visible wavelength.

The evolution of human skin coloration depends strongly on the the distribution of ultraviolet radiation on the earth [68, 452]. The color of human skin varies from race to race and from individual to individual. It also varies within an individual, e.g., the forearm is darker and less reddish than the forehead. For example, in one case study of Caucasian skins using the CIELAB space, the skin color of the forearm of an average white male is $L^* = 69.9$, $a^* = 7.9$, and $b^* = 11.6$, while that of the forehead is $L^* = 66.3$, $a^* = 11.2$, and $b^* = 12.3$ [246]. The color difference within an individual is due to exposure to sunlight irradiation as well as the inherent pigment distribution [274, 275, 797]. Figure 8.12 shows the effect of exposure to sunlight on the skin spectral reflectance. The sunlight irradiation

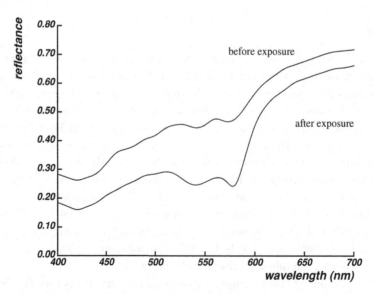

Figure 8.12. The effect of exposure to sunlight on skin color.

Table 8.5. *CIE1931 (Y, x, y) for skins of different racial types*

Race	(Y, x, y) under D40	(Y, x, y) under D65
(reference white)	(100.00, 0.3825, 0.3839)	(100.00, 0.3129, 0.3292)
white blond	(45.26, 0.4356, 0.3925)	(43.98, 0.3637, 0.3575)
white brunet	(40.93, 0.4424, 0.3930)	(39.63, 0.3709, 0.3608)
Japanese	(34.87, 0.4524, 0.3986)	(33.58, 0.3831, 0.3704)
Hindu	(22.06, 0.4564, 0.3991)	(21.17, 0.3873, 0.3706)
mulatto	(13.32, 0.4582, 0.3916)	(12.73, 0.3863, 0.3602)
negro	(7.54, 0.4219, 0.3917)	(7.37, 0.3501, 0.3487)

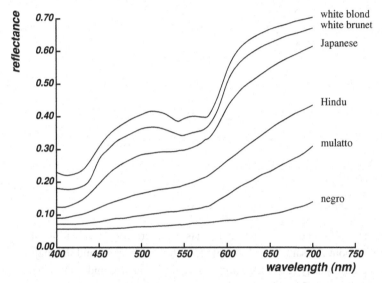

Figure 8.13. The spectral reflectances of different skins (from Edwards and Duntley, *American Journal of Anatomy*, 1939).

makes white skin become darker (e.g., reflectance drops from 0.48 to 0.32). Two types of skin reaction occur after exposure to sun radiation: an immediate erythema and a persistent tanning. Increased blood flow in erythema makes the skin redder (and also darker). After a few days, the red shift gradually disappears. In a study reported by Edwards [275], the chromaticity change is mainly in dominant wavelength (e.g., from 580 nm to 592 nm relative to CIE Illuminant C), and only slightly in excitation purity (e.g., from 20.2% to 20.9%). The effect of exposure to sunlight is less on darker skin. The most significant difference in skin color is across the different races. Figure 8.13 shows six samples of skin spectral reflectance curves measured from the buttocks of people with varying pigmentation [274]. Since the buttock is the area least exposed to sunlight, the measured difference represents purely the difference in race. From this set of data, we can calculate the CIE1931 (Y, x, y) for skins of different racial types illuminated by CIE daylight illuminants with correlated color temperatures of 4000 K and 6500 K. The results are shown in Table 8.5. The major difference is mainly in the lightness (reflectance), ranging from 7.37% in negro to 45.26% in white blond. Figure 8.14 plots the chromaticity loci of the different skins under D65

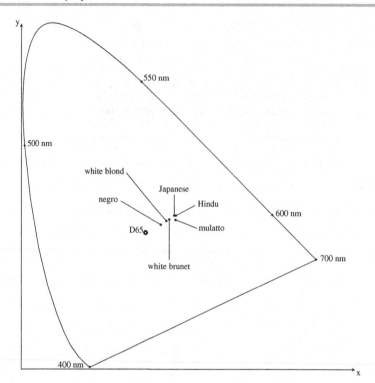

Figure 8.14. The chromaticity loci of six different skins.

Illuminant. The difference in chromaticity has an interesting distribution: the dominant wavelength is about the same for all people (583.6 nm for D65), and the major difference is in the excitation purity (33% for Hindu vs. 17% for negro, under D_{65}). The excitation purities under D_{65} for white blond, white brunet, and Japanese skins, are 23%, 26%, and 31%, respectively.

In the color reproduction of images of human subjects, the preferred skin color is more saturated and reddish than the real, average skin color. It seems that the preferred skin color is also different for different races. For example, studies [823, 1058] have shown that the preferred skin color for Caucasian women has a much higher saturation than the average skin color for Caucasian women, while the preferred skin color for Japanese women has only a slightly higher saturation than the average skin color for Japanese women, although the preferred hue is shifted toward more reddish color.

Hair color

The portion of a hair external to the skin surface consists of tightly packed dead keratinized cells. Under an electron microscope, the surface of a hair fiber is covered with overlapping scales [793]. The root of the hair (the hair bulb) contains melanocytes that synthesize melanins and transfer them to the neighboring keratinocytes, which are then pushed outward to form the hair shaft. Hair color is determined by the absorption, reflection (external and internal), and scattering of incident light [155, 896], and these processes are dependent on the size, density, and distribution of the melanin-containing organelles, melanosomes. A simple light-reflection model of human hair consists of a transparent circular cylinder with a colored interior and a surface composed of rough tilted scales [638]. Human hair follicles often contain various proportions of two major types of melanin: eumelanins and pheomelanins. The correlation between human hair color and melanin types is not very good. For example, while some human red hairs contain mostly pheomelanins, other red hair types contain both eumelanins and pheomelanins [164, p. 221], and some other red hairs contain a different pigment, trichosiderin, that contains iron [43, p. 92].

Although there have been studies showing a high correlation between skin color and hair color [797, p. 113], there is evidence that these two are controlled by different genes. Empirical observation from image databases seems to indicate that hair chromaticity is fairly close to that of the skin. Since the physical process involved in the light interaction with hair is very different from that with skin, we probably should not expect to find a simple relationship between their chromaticities (in addition, think about how people may dye their hair).

Eye color

As far as imaging is concerned, there are two regions in the eye where colors are of immediate interest: the iris and the pupil. The iris consists of the anterior border layer, the stroma, and the posterior, double epithelial layers [962, p. 39]. The posterior epithelial layers contain a large amount of melanin pigment, with the amount not varying much for eyes of different colors [797, p. 75]. In blue eyes, the anterior layer and the stroma contain very little melanin pigment, and the incident short wavelength light is scattered back, while middle and long wavelength light is absorbed by the posterior heavily pigmented layers [693, p. 240]. If there are also yellowish pigments to absorb the short wavelength light, the iris then looks green. If the anterior layer and the stroma contains a large amount of melanin pigment, then the iris looks black. If the amount of melanin is less, then the iris looks brown.

The light that is reflected back through the pupil of the eye has several components, one from the front surface of the retina, one from the pigment epithelium layer behind the retina, and one from the choroid tissue (richly vascular) behind the pigment epithelium. The first two components are not strongly colored. The reflection component from the choroid tissue represents the "fundus" color that one sees when looking through the pupil. The fundus color, as seen by ophthalmologists, is closely related to the skin pigmentation, being orange in Caucasoids and dark-brown in negroids [797, p. 75]. In typical photographs, the color is most distinctly red (the red-eye problem). However, the red-eye problem is rarely seen in the photographs of Mongoloid or negroid people, presumably the red reflection from hemoglobin is mostly masked by the melanin pigments (in the pigment epithelium and the choroid).

8.5.10 Pigments and dyes

A pigment is a colorant that is usually not soluble in the medium in which it is applied and it is incorporated into the medium in particle form. In contrast, dyestuff is usually soluble in the medium in which it is applied, and it exists in the medium as molecules.

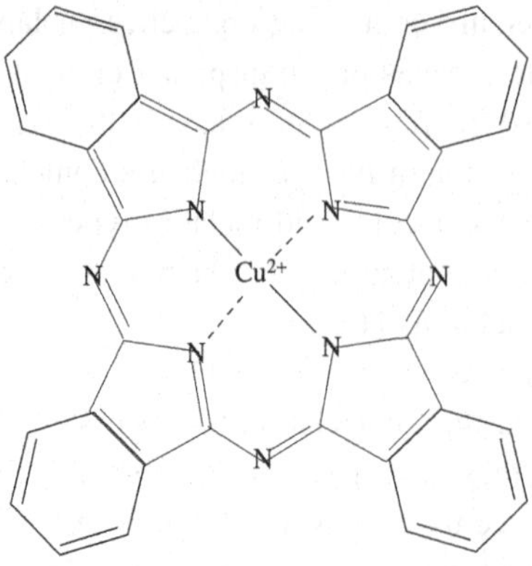

Figure 8.15. Copper phthalocyanine.

Both inorganic and organic pigments are widely used, with inorganic pigments being more common. Inorganic pigments are usually oxides, sulfides, silicates, sulfates, and carbonates. The pigment that is used in the largest quantity is titanium dioxide, which is produced at a particle size of about 200 nm diametre to give effective light scattering. Titanium dioxide (TiO_2) is used as a white pigment in paints, plastics, inks, paper, cosmetics, foodstuffs, and pharmaceuticals, etc. Pure titanium dioxide crystals are colorless. It imparts whiteness by scattering, due to its very high index of refraction ($n = 2.71$ for the rutile crystal form). The yellow and red pigments (such as iron oxides) come next in the quantity of consumption. There is a large variety of organic pigments. Some of them have been used for many decades, such as monoazo pigments, disazo pigments, and copper phthalocyanine pigments (see Fig. 8.15). More recent pigments are mainly of two classes: azo and polycyclic pigments. Azo pigments constitute about 50% of the overall world volume of organic pigments, with polycyclic pigments and copper phthalocyanine pigments constituting about 25% each. High degrees of opacity cannot usually be achieved by organic pigments alone, because their indices of refraction are not very different from that of the organic polymer matrix in the binder.

8.5.11 Paints

A large number of man-made objects have painted surfaces. These surfaces show up very frequently in color images. It is therefore useful to understand the material and optical properties of paints. The major function of a paint is to coat the surface of objects. Depending on the intended use of the surface material to be coated, the ingredients in the paint vary significantly. Therefore, there is no such thing as a "universal paint". A paint intended for a wood surface is quite different from one for an automobile finish.

Paint is a colloidal system because it contains solids (pigment particles) dispersed in liquid (the polymer solution known as the binder). In an oil-based paint, the polymer is dissolved in solvent (oil), and therefore it is called a polymer solution. However, in a latex paint, the polymer itself is also in the form of small particles suspended in water. A typical paint composition consists of about 33% pigments (including filler or extender), 24%

polymer (film-former), 41.8% solvent or water, and 1.3% additives (such as driers, anti-skinning, anti-settling, plasticizers, dispersants, etc.) by weight [261]. Pigments are mainly used to introduce color to the polymer matrix (which is colorless) by scattering and/or absorption. Fillers (also known as extenders) are used to fill the polymer matrix. They are also colorless. The index of refraction of a filler is selected to be close to the polymer matrix used, so that they do not participate in light scattering. Many different polymers are used as the binder (film-former), for example, alkyds, polyesters, vinyls, acrylics, epoxides, polyurethanes, and cellulosics. When the polymer solution dries, the solvent evaporates. The polymer matrix is formed either by chemical reactions, producing cross-linking, or by physical packing together. Therefore, the choice of polymer determines the properties of the paint film. Since the polymer binder of paint is colorless, the spectral composition of light reflected from a painted surface is often very well described by the NIR model.

Two factors determine the color of a paint: absorption and scattering. Both factors are dependent on the pigment particle size and its distribution. The term particle size is usually applied only to sphere-like particles, because not all pigment particles have similar shapes. Most of them (such as titanium dioxide) are more spherical in shape, but some are more needle-like (such as iron oxide yellow) and others are flake-like (such as some metallic pigments). When the particles are elongated in shape, it is the minor dimension that matters most. Roughly speaking, light absorption is inversely proportional to particle size, d, because the number of particles per volume is proportional to d^{-3} and the cross-section of a particle is proportional to d^2. Light scattering by a particle depends on its size relative to the wavelength of the light. The optimum scattering size depends on its concentration, but in general, it is about half of the wavelength. Therefore, most mean particle sizes of pigments are about 200–500 nm. The higher the scattering power a pigment has, the more opaque the surface will be.

8.5.12 Paper

Paper is produced from various kinds of fibers, some synthetic, some cotton, but mostly derived from wood. The bark is removed from the trunk of a tree and the remaining wood is made into chips. Woodchips can be converted into paper pulp in two ways: (1) mechanical grinding, and (2) chemical treatment. Wood contains about 50% cellulose fibers that are bound by a polymer, a phenolic compound called lignin (about 25% of the wood content). The other 25% is hemicellulose (polysaccharide formed from many different sugar molecules with extensive branching). The lignin contained in the wood turns yellow and has to be removed from the paper pulp by chemical reactions. Because of its inherent yellowness, paper brightness is defined as its reflectance at a wavelength of 457 nm. To increase the brightness, paper pulp is often bleached and TiO_2 or fluorescent dyes are added. Newsprint paper has a reflectance of about 60%, while many white printing papers have a reflectance of about 70–80%, with some very bright papers reaching about 90%.

Both internal and surface sizing (to cover or stiffen with glutinous material to fill the pores in surfaces) are used in paper making. Rosin (from pine trees) is often added to the fibers for internal sizing. In the drying process, the tiny rosin globules are melted or fused together. Surface sizing (for example, with starch) is applied to the surface of paper to seal the surface fibers, and thereby, increase its strength.

A paper making machine (such as a fourdrinier machine) uses a fine screen (called a wire) to spread out the fibers to give a flat surface. The side of the paper that touches the wire is called the wire side, and the other side is called the felt side. These two sides have different mechanical properties. The fibers on the wire side are more aligned with the machine coating direction than those on the felt side. For some printing applications, it may be important to know which is the wire side and which is the felt side, because the paper feeder mechanism may work better on one side of the paper than the other side. More recent paper making machines (such as the twin-wire machines) are often designed to reduce the difference between the two sides of a paper.

The basis weight of paper used in the USA is the weight in pounds of 500 sheets. However, sheets are not the same size. A better basis weight is grams per square meter. For example, a 20 lb bound paper ($75.2 \mathrm{~g~m}^{-2}$) is only a little heavier than a 50 lb offset paper ($74.0 \mathrm{~g~m}^{-2}$), because the size of the bond paper is 17″ by 22″, while that of the offset paper is 25″ by 38″.

The surface structural fibers of an uncoated paper are about 20–40 μm wide. When coated with pigment particles, such as clay (kaolin) or chalk (calcium carbonate) of a mean size about 2 μm, the paper surface becomes much smoother and brighter. The adhesive used to bind the pigments together is also an important factor in the properties of paper. Examples of adhesive are starch derivative, protein derivative, cellulose derivative, polyvinyl alcohol, and polymers in latex form, such as styrene–butadiene copolymers. The structure of paper coatings is complicated because of the many ingredients and the various drying process [586]. The print quality on a coated paper is much higher and more consistent than on an uncoated paper. Lightweight coated papers are typically coated with 4–$7 \mathrm{~g~m}^{-2}$ of coating on each side. Heavierweight coated paper has about 12–$15 \mathrm{~g~m}^{-2}$ of coating on each side. Typical coating mixes have several ingredients, such as pigments, binders, modifiers, and other additives. In paints, pigments are distributed in the binder polymer matrix and light scattering is produced at the pigment/polymer interfaces. On a coated paper, the situation is quite different. The amount of binder used is relatively small and light scattering occurs at the air/pigment interfaces. It is the size of the air holes that has to be controlled on a coated paper, rather than the size of the pigment particles.

Uncoated paper is often somewhat acidic because of the rosin and the aluminum sulfate used for internal sizing. The sodium silicate used to disperse the pigments in the starch for coating makes coated paper slightly alkaline. Since acids often depolymerize cellulose and thus weaken the paper, coated paper or acid-free paper lasts much longer. The drying time for inks also decreases as the paper or the coating becomes more alkaline. In addition to the brighter surface, coated paper also makes inks appear more saturated than the uncoated paper. Therefore, color images printed on coated paper look much better than those on uncoated paper.

8.5.13   Printing inks

Printing inks are also colloidal systems with pigments dispersed in liquid media. The liquid medium of an ink is commonly called the varnish (or vehicle). It contains solvent, polymers (binder), and other additives, such as wetting agents, coalescing agents, biocides, siccatives, and agents that prevent peeling off. The choice of varnish depends on the type of printing, the substrate, the method of drying, etc. Ink drying processes vary according to the solvent used. Typical drying processes are evaporation, absorption, oxidative polymerization, and radiation curing. For example, in evaporation drying, the solvent evaporates as the ink is dried, leaving the pigment particles bound by the polymer matrix (the resin). There are five major types of ink: liquid, paste, news, screen, and radiation-curable. Inks are formulated differently for different applications. For example, liquid inks (low viscosity) are used for gravure and flexo printing, while paste inks are used for lithography and letter press printing. Low-viscosity nitrocellulose is a very commonly used resin in solvent-based liquid inks. Other varnishes, such as polyamides, urethane, maleic, and acrylic varnishes, are often used in mixtures for printing inks. Table 8.6 (from [279, p. 226]) shows some representative components in inks for various printing applications.

Many varieties of pigment are used in printing inks. Most of them can be used in different types of printing. Carbon black (mostly in the form of graphite) is the most used black pigment in printing inks. Colored pigments are mostly organic because of their high color strength. The pigments used in printing ink for white surfaces have to be small (15–25 nm in the minor dimension) and transparent. Because the light has to go through a few thin ink layers (about 1–3 μm) and be reflected from the white paper substrate, scattering by the pigment particles (and hence opacity) is not a desired feature as it is in the paint application. For printing on a nonwhite surface (such as brown cartons), ink opacity is also important. In that case, opaque pigments (such as TiO_2) have to be added. Inorganic pigments are usually opaque because their indices of refraction are quite different from that of the organic varnish that carries them. Inkjet printing often uses inks that are solutions of dyes and they dry by absorption into the paper substrate. There is also a trend to use pigments in the inks used in inkjet applications to give lightfastness and less bleeding on the paper.

In multicolor press, inks of different colors are printed on top of each other. Two physical properties are important in this type of printing: tack and trapping. Tack is the resistance of a thin film of ink to breaking up. If the tack of an ink is too low, the half-tone dot will not be sharp. If it is too high, then it may cause picking of paper or pulling of the coating from the coated paper. Trapping is the transfer of ink from one surface to another. Since a high-tack ink on the paper will trap a lower-tack ink from the blanket, in a multicolor press the first-down ink needs to have the highest tack, and the succeeding inks have less and less tack.

Table 8.6. *Some representative ink compositions for various printing applications*

	Heatset web offset	Sheetfed offset	Sheetfed letterpress	Flexography	Rotogravure	Screen
binder	rosin ester long-oil alkyd hydrocarbon resin waxes	long-oil alkyd phenolic resin hydrocarbon resin drier, waxes	long-oil alkyd phenolic resin hydrocarbon resin drier, waxes	polyamide nitrocellulose shellac acrylic resin	rosin ester metallated rosin cellulose ester hydrocarbon resin	long-oil alkyd epoxy resin nitrocellulose cellulose ester
solvent	hydrocarbon oil vegetable oil	hydrocarbon oil vegetable oil	hydrocarbon oil vegetable oil	alcohol water glycol ether	ester/ketone toluene aliphatic hydrocarbon	hydrocarbon alcohol ester/ketone
products	publications	general commercial	general commercial	packaging	packaging/ publication	textiles/posters/ signs

Therefore, a printing process that uses the same inks, but different ink-down sequences, will produce different colors. The other cause of color difference due to ink-down sequence is that inks are not completely transparent. Therefore, the ink-down sequence is also part of the specification for a multicolor press. The most commonly used color sequence seems to be cyan, magenta, and yellow (C–M–Y) with the black before, after, or in between [142, p. 64].

8.6 Statistics of natural scenes

It is often argued [636] that vision is not possible if the physical world does not have enough regularity, because visual tasks are ambiguous and the underlying inverse problems are ill posed [765]. Although certain regularities can be found by experiment [308, 416, 879], the source of any given regularity of natural scenes can be difficult to identify [48, 813]. Most regularities of natural scenes discovered so far are statistical and therefore cannot be applied to any individual scene. However, many practical problems (e.g., the color and density balance problems in image printing and display) do not currently have a reliable, deterministic solution. Most color image processing algorithms today rely on some types of Bayesian estimation and prior statistics are used either explicitly or implicitly. It is thus useful for us to learn about some of the regularities of natural scenes. The important thing to keep in mind here is that, before the cause or the source of a regularity is identified, we should use it with great care. It is always a good practice to build in some error checking steps in the algorithms when using statistical assumptions.

8.6.1 Colors tend to integrate to gray

The integrated color of photographic scenes was found to distribute close to the black-body locus [762], with a cluster around 4800 K. Measurements taken over the course of the day showed that the overall integrated color remains quite constant, until about 30 minutes before sunset. The color turns bluer near sunset (color temperature increases) and remains approximately constant after sunset. The color temperature then rapidly decreases at sunrise. The fact that the integrated color turns bluer at sunset seems to go against our observation that objects look more reddish at sunset. However, the majority of the areas in the scene are illuminated mainly by the blue sky, and the overall integrated color turns bluer.

More quantitative evaluation using consumer images [575] shows that in the log space, the average color of a natural scene is normally distributed around the dominant scene illuminant. The three eigenvectors of the covariance matrix of the distribution are functions of the spectral responsivities of the imaging system. For typical color negative films, they are approximately

$$L = \frac{1}{\sqrt{3}}(\log R + \log G + \log B), \tag{8.76}$$

$$s = \frac{1}{\sqrt{2}}(\log R - \log B), \tag{8.77}$$

$$t = \frac{1}{\sqrt{6}}(\log R - 2\log G + \log B). \tag{8.78}$$

The standard deviations of L, s, and t are 0.273, 0.065, and 0.030 for an image database of 2697 images. The composition of the image database is fairly close to a typical consumer image population: (1) about 60% are indoor scenes and 40% outdoor scenes; (2) about 70% have faces in them; (3) about 28% have sky in them; (4) about 43% have visible green vegetation; and (5) about 23% have sky and green vegetation. From these statistics, it seems that the integrated color of a natural scene is reasonably close to neutral most of the time.

8.6.2 Log luminance range is normally distributed

Let us define the luminance range of a scene as the ratio of its highest luminance to its lowest luminance for a given spatial and luminance resolution of an instrument. For their instruments (films and densitometer), Jones and Condit [471] found that the log luminance range is normally distributed with a mean of approximately 160:1. A more recent study (using color negative films and a scanner) shows data that agree well with that estimate [575, p. 126]. In both studies, camera flare is difficult to correct because strictly speaking, it cannot be treated as a uniform veiling flare. However, a large number of scenes contain enough spatial variations in each scene so that the effect of flare on the estimated range is quite small.[2]

8.6.3 Log radiances tend to be normally distributed

Under a single dominant illumination, the log scene radiance of the *modulated parts* of a natural scene is found to be normally distributed [16, 790]. (Note that the phrase "modulated parts" means that the interior of a uniform area in a scene is excluded from the statistics.) When there is more than one dominant light source in the scene, the histogram of the log scene radiance can be bi-modal, or the sum of two Gaussian distributions.

8.6.4 Color variations span a low-dimensional space

Analysis of spectral reflectance factors for a large number of objects in natural scenes shows that the eigenvalue of the covariance matrix decays very fast and it does not take too many principal components to account for most of the variances [200, 531]. Analysis of the daylight spectra also shows similar results [476]. From these two results, it seems that the majority of the color spectra of natural scenes can be represented in a low-dimensional space [629]. It is estimated that (seven–eight)-dimensional space will be sufficient [630]. This result is somewhat surprising and currently there is no good explanation based on first (physical or chemical) principles.

8.6.5 Power spectra tend to fall off as $(1/f)^n$

The (spatial) power spectra of natural scenes are found to fall off as $(1/f)^n$, where f is the spatial frequency and n varies from about 1.5 to 3.0 [48, 152, 266, 308, 813]. When $n = 2$,

---

[2] If the estimated luminance range is affected by the camera flare, one would not be able to find a scene luminance range as wide as the data show.

the power spectra are said to be scale-invariant. It should be noted that this is true only at the high frequency end [548] and it is not isotropic in all directions. Because the earth's gravity dictates how things should grow or be built, the horizontal and the vertical frequencies tend to have higher energy contents. In a carpentered environment,[3] it is also found that there is more spatial frequency energy in 1–25 cycles per degree along the horizontal and the vertical directions than other directions [929].

8.7 Problems

8.1 Why does the color of a piece of dyed fabric look more saturated when it is wet?

8.2 Why does the sky look red during sunset?

8.3 The BRDF for a perfect Lambertian reflector is $f_r = dL_r/dE_i = 1/\pi$. A Lambertian sphere when illuminated by a collimated light source (all rays are parallel) does not appear as a uniform disk because different areas on the sphere are oriented at different angles from the light source and the surface irradiance E_i falls off as $\cos\theta_i$, where θ_i is the angle between the surface normal and the incident light beam. A full moon looks like a uniform bright disk (neglecting the somewhat random dark spots for the moment). Therefore, the moon surface is not a Lambertian reflector. Since the distance from the moon to the sun is much larger than the radius of the moon, we can assume that the moon is illuminated by parallel light rays coming from the sun. Let us further assume that the moon is a uniform, smooth spherical surface which reflects light as a function of the vertical angle, θ_r, but independent of the horizontal (azimuth) angle, ϕ_r. (The vertical angle, θ_r, is the angle between the reflected ray and the surface normal.) If the reflectance of the lunar surface is ρ, what is its BRDF, $f_r(\theta_r)$?

8.4 Equation (8.55) shows the relationship between the internal transmittance T_i of a transparent film and the externally measurable reflectance factor L_r/L. Typically, r_1 depends on the film material. Let us assume that $r_1 = 0.04$. If the film is placed in contact with a perfect, reflecting white base (i.e., $r_2 = 1.0$), plot the reflection density $D_r = -\log_{10}(L_r/L)$ as a function of the (internal) transmission density $D_t = -\log_{10} T_i$. What is the slope when D_t is large?

8.5 Computer detection and recognition of human faces are an important area of research with many possible applications. One of the key features in such a task is the skin color. Based on what we described in this chapter, list the factors that need to be considered when designing a skin-color detection program. For example, what color space would you use and why?

---

[3] A carpentered environment is an indoor environment in which there are plenty of wooden structures (window frames, door frames, cabinets, desks, chairs, etc.). It can also refer to an outdoor environment where wooden structures are abundant.

9 Optical image formation

Imaging is a mapping from some properties of the physical world (object space) into another representation of those properties (image space). The mapping can be carried out by changing the propagation of various types of physical signals. For example, medical ultrasound imaging is the mapping of the acoustic properties of the body tissue into their representation in the transmitted or reflected intensity of the acoustic field. The mapping is carried out by the absorption, scattering, and transmission of the acoustic energy. Optical imaging, the formation of an optical representation separate from the original objects, is a mapping carried out mostly by changing the directions of the electromagnetic waves coming from the objects. Insofar as light can be treated as rays, the spatial mapping from a point in the object space to a point in the image space can be studied geometrically. This field is called the geometrical theory of optical imaging. Situations arise when the wave nature of the light has to be dealt with explicitly. This field is called the physical (or wave) theory of optical imaging. Of course, there are other cases where the quantum nature of the light is the dominant characteristics to be considered.

In this and the next chapter we will study only the basic concepts and processes of optical imaging. The three main subjects to be studied are geometric optics, physical optics, and the radiometry of imaging. Since the literature on these subjects is voluminous and the underlying principles and theories are very well presented in many books on physics, electromagnetics, and optics [51, 124, 352, 385, 453, 510, 657, 733, 1021], our approach is to build upon the fundamental results that can be derived from first principles such as the Maxwell equations and concentrate on developing the concepts and relations in optical imaging that will be useful in engineering applications.

9.1 Geometrical and physical optics

As we have already discussed, our understanding of the nature of light and its interaction with matter has changed many times in history. The current theory is known as quantum electrodynamics, which describes very accurately both the wave-like character of electromagnetic radiation, such as in diffraction, and the discrete character of light, such as in quantum light absorption. Electromagnetic theory based on the Maxwell equations can be regarded as a special case in which the quantum effect can be neglected. Maxwell's theory describes the wave-like character very well for electromagnetic waves with the wide range of wavelength of 10^{-9}–10^3 m. The wavelength of visible light is less than a micron. Since the object sizes we are dealing with in an optical imaging system are often many orders of magnitude larger than that, the laws of electromagnetic wave propagation can often be very well approximated by completely neglecting the finiteness of the wavelength. In practice, this simplifies a lot of computations and produces very adequate results. The limiting case of making $\lambda \to 0$ allows us to treat light as rays following certain geometric laws, and the optics so developed is called geometrical optics. The basic assumption of geometric optics is that the magnitudes of the changes in the electric and magnetic fields are much smaller than the magnitudes of the two fields over a distance of the order of the wavelength. This assumption is obviously not true where there is strong spatial or temporal discontinuity, such as around the occlusion boundary of an aperture. The other important case where geometric optics is not quite adequate is at the point of focus. For these cases, diffraction theory has to be used and they are considered later in the discussion of physical optics. However, these are exceptions, not rules. For most optical problems, geometric optics provides at least a very good starting point for more refined and in depth analysis.

Many of the results in optics have been derived under further simplification, which leads to linear optics and Gaussian optics. Linear optics is an approximation of geometrical optics. It assumes that all angular quantities are so small that only the linear terms are required for the calculation, e.g., $\sin\theta \approx \theta$, $\tan\theta \approx \theta$, and $\cos\theta \approx 1$. Gaussian optics deals with a special case of linear optics, where all optical surfaces are rotationally symmetric about a central axis (the optical axis). Since most imaging systems are designed to be as close to rotational symmetry as cost permits, we will develop the basic mathematical descriptions of optical imaging in terms of Gaussian optics. Wherever it is necessary, we will provide more accurate descriptions based on more general geometrical optics or physical optics.

9.2   The basis of geometrical optics

In geometrical optics, light is treated as rays that are infinitely small compared with all the components in the optical system. Obviously, light cannot propagate as a single ray, otherwise many optical phenomena, such as interference and diffraction, could not occur. However, from the Maxwell equations, it is possible to derive Fermat's principle, Snell's law, the eikonal equation, and the ray equation, which form the basis of geometrical optics [510, 608]. Here we follow the arguments used by Sommerfeld and Runge [510, p. 11] and Born and Wolf [124] to show that the constant-phase surface of an electromagnetic (EM) wave can be described by the eikonal equation. The optical rays represent the normals of the phase surface. As pointed out by Kline and Kay [510, Chapter 1], the arguments are not completely satisfactory. Our purpose in presenting it here is only to provide some hints for how the Maxwell equations can be linked to geometrical optics. This is based on the belief that the former is more basic than the latter. On the other hand, we can take the completely opposite position that we accept the basic laws in geometrical optics and try to derive the Maxwell equations. It was shown by Stavroudis [899, Chapter XI] that we can indeed come very close to deriving Maxwell's electromagnetic equations from the basic laws of geometrical optics. Interested readers should consult the books by Kline and Kay [510], Stavroudis [899], and Luneburg [608].

An arbitrary complex time function of the EM field can be decomposed into Fourier components of time harmonics. Therefore it is useful to study first the simple case of a general time-harmonic field.

$$\mathbf{E}(\mathbf{r}, t) = \mathbf{E}_0(\mathbf{r})e^{-i\omega t}, \tag{9.1}$$

$$\mathbf{H}(\mathbf{r}, t) = \mathbf{H}_0(\mathbf{r})e^{-i\omega t}. \tag{9.2}$$

In the regions free of currents and charges, the vectors $\mathbf{E}_0$, and $\mathbf{H}_0$, will satisfy the time-free Maxwell equations. By defining $k_0 = 2\pi/\lambda_0$, where λ_0 is the wavelength in the vacuum, we may represent the fields many wavelengths away from the source by the following general types of fields:

$$\mathbf{E}_0(\mathbf{r}) = \mathbf{e}(\mathbf{r})e^{-ik_0\psi(\mathbf{r})}, \tag{9.3}$$

$$\mathbf{H}_0(\mathbf{r}) = \mathbf{h}(\mathbf{r})e^{-ik_0\psi(\mathbf{r})}. \tag{9.4}$$

Under the assumptions that $\lambda_0 \to 0$ and the terms that contain the factor of $1/k_0$ can be neglected, one can derive the following equation from Maxwell's equations [124, p. 112]:

$$\nabla\psi \cdot \nabla\psi = \left(\frac{\partial\psi}{\partial x}\right)^2 + \left(\frac{\partial\psi}{\partial y}\right)^2 + \left(\frac{\partial\psi}{\partial z}\right)^2 = n^2(x, y, z), \tag{9.5}$$

where n is the index of refraction. The function ψ is called the eikonal, and the equation is called the eikonal equation. The surfaces $\psi =$ constant are where the phases of the fields are constants, and are called the geometrical wavefronts. The energy of the EM wave can be shown to propagate, with a velocity of $v = c/n$, in the direction of the surface normal of these wavefronts. Geometrical *light rays* are thus defined as the orthogonal trajectories to the geometrical wavefronts. The electric and magnetic vectors are orthogonal to the rays at every point

Let $\mathbf{r}(s)$ denote the position vector of a point on a light ray, and s the arc length of the ray, then $d\mathbf{r}/ds$ is a unit vector pointing to the direction of the light ray. The eikonal equation can then be written as

$$n\frac{d\mathbf{r}}{ds} = \nabla\psi. \tag{9.6}$$

Since the distance between the two neighboring wavefronts, $d\psi$, can be expressed as

$$d\psi = d\mathbf{r} \cdot \nabla\psi = n\,ds, \tag{9.7}$$

the integral, $\int_{P_1}^{P_2} n\,ds$, taken along a curve, from point P_1 to point P_2, is thus called the optical path length between the points. The shortest distance between two points may not be the shortest optical path between them because light travels slower in the material of higher index of refraction. In many cases, a light ray travels along the path of the shortest optical length (or the path that takes the minimum time). However, this is not always true. It can be shown [682, p. 11] that a light ray always travels along the path that has a zero derivative with respect to time or with respect to optical path length (meaning that it can be a minimum, a maximum or an inflection point). This is called Fermat's principle.

One of the consequences of the ray being the gradient vector of a scalar field is that if the ray vector is operated on by a curl operator, the result is zero ($\nabla \times \nabla\psi = 0$). This leads

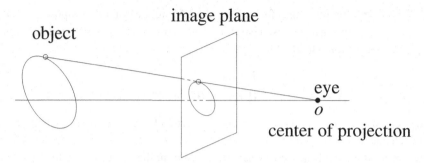

Figure 9.1. The technique of perspective drawing.

to the proof of Snell's law [124, p. 125] which says that the incident ray, the refracted ray, and the surface normal are all on the same plane. Furthermore, the ratio of the sine of the refracted angle to the sine of the incident angle is equal to the ratio of the refractive index of the incident medium to that of the refracted medium. In optical imaging, Snell's law allows us to trace rays through the various refracting surfaces in the optical system and many lenses are designed with computer programs that do ray tracings based on Snell's law.

9.3 Projective geometry

Before we discuss the geometrical theory of optical imaging, we need to be acquainted with some of the transformations used in projective geometry, which has its origin in early Renaissance artists' efforts to understand how we see [135]. Those artists realized that if a plane is placed between the eye and an object (see Fig. 9.1), the intersections between the plane and all the lines that connect the eye (as a point) and points on the object will form a very realistic drawing of what we see. This drawing technique is generally known as perspective projection. The eye serves as the center of projection (or the perspective center). The key observation is that every point in the space that falls on a line radiating from the center of projection is projected onto the same image point. Each line-of-sight in space is therefore identified with a point in the image (on the plane). This forms the basis of the definition of a new geometry called projective geometry. There are two important things to notice here: (1) a three-dimensional space is mapped to a two-dimensional space because of the identification of a space line with an image point; and (2) a line going through the center of projection in a direction parallel to the image plane does not intersect with the image plane and has no corresponding image point. Before we discuss projective geometry and its associated transformation, we should note that in the above discussion, the plane that is placed between the eye and the object has not been specified in terms of its position or orientation. In fact, if two different planes are used, then we obtain two drawings from different perspectives. The two drawings are related by the same lines-of-sight. This relation can be considered as a functional mapping from one image plane to another image plane. This type of mapping is called a perspective transform. It is a special case of the projective transform that will be discussed shortly.

Geometry, in a broad sense, is the study of properties and relations of given elements, such as points, lines, curves, and surfaces, that remain invariant under specified transformations. Modern geometry [135, 394] adopts the definition, proposed by Christian Felix Klein (1849–1925), that geometry consists of a set of elements and a transformation *group* associated with the set. Here the term *group* is a mathematical entity that has a set with a binary operation defined on the set, satisfying closure, identity, inverse, and associativity. For our present purpose, the transformations are linear and represented by matrices and the binary operation simply means matrix multiplication. According to this view, n-dimensional projective geometry (S,T) consists of a set, S, of elements in $(n + 1)$-dimensional space (excluding the center of projection) and all the invertible $(n + 1) \times (n + 1)$ matrices as the transformation group, T. An element in the set, S, is called an image point, which is in fact a space line going through the origin. By convention, the origin is taken as the center of projection. Note that it is not necessary to specify any image plane in this definition. This avoids the awkward problem associated with the space points lying on the plane that passes through the center of projection in a direction parallel to the image plane. Those points are not mapped to any points on the image plane if one is assigned.

Let us look at the case of two-dimensional projective geometry. Let (x_i, y_i, z_i) be an image point in S. By definition, all space points (kx_i, ky_i, kz_i), $k \neq 0$, also belong to the same image point (x_i, y_i, z_i). Recall that an image point is actually a space line passing through the origin $(0, 0, 0)$. Any space plane that contains the space line can be described as $ax_i + by_i + cz_i = 0$, where a, b, and c, are real numbers and $a^2 + b^2 + c^2 \neq 0$. The coordinates of the image point (x_i, y_i, z_i) are called the homogeneous coordinates, because the equation $ax_i + by_i + cz_i = 0$ is a homogeneous equation. When an image plane is chosen, say at $z = f$, then the space line specified by (kx_i, ky_i, kz_i) intersects with the image plane at $(fx_i/z_i, fy_i/z_i, f)$. Since all points on the image plane have the same z coordinate, we can use the inhomogeneous coordinates, $(fx_i/z_i, fy_i/z_i)$, as the two-dimensional coordinates of the image point (x_i, y_i, z_i). This reduction in dimensions is the basic nature of projective geometry in which a space line is identified with an image point. That is why we call this two-dimensional (instead of three-dimensional) projective geometry because the image points can in fact be specified with two-dimensional coordinates if an image plane is chosen. Thus, one advantage of using the homogeneous coordinates is that we do not have to specify an image plane.

The important properties of projective geometry are: (1) a straight line is mapped to a straight line; (2) incidence relations are preserved (e.g., a point on a line will be mapped to a point on the image on that line); and (3) the cross-ratio is preserved [135]. Other familiar properties are: the images of parallel space lines intersect at a vanishing point and the images of parallel space planes intersect at a vanishing line [482]. The fundamental theorem of projective geometry says that $n + 2$ independent points are sufficient to determine a unique projective transformation in n-dimensional projective geometry. This theorem, when applied to colorimetry, tells us that we need four chromaticity points to determine the transformation between two color systems that use two different sets of primaries. All these properties are proved in many textbooks on geometry (see, e.g., [135, 394]).

Since we will be developing the geometrical theory of optical imaging for images in three-dimensional space, we will use three-dimensional projective geometry. The transformation

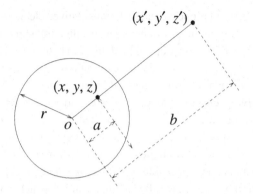

Figure 9.2. The inversion transformation relative to a sphere centered at o, with a radius of r. The point (x, y, z) is mapped to the point (x', y', z') with $a \cdot b = r^2$.

group of three-dimensional projective geometry consists of all invertible 4×4 matrices. For example, one image point (x, y, z, t) is transformed to another image point (x', y', z', t') by matrix M:

$$\begin{bmatrix} x' \\ y' \\ z' \\ t' \end{bmatrix} = \begin{bmatrix} m_{11} & m_{12} & m_{13} & m_{14} \\ m_{21} & m_{22} & m_{23} & m_{24} \\ m_{31} & m_{32} & m_{33} & m_{34} \\ m_{41} & m_{42} & m_{43} & m_{44} \end{bmatrix} \begin{bmatrix} x \\ y \\ z \\ t \end{bmatrix} = M \begin{bmatrix} x \\ y \\ z \\ t \end{bmatrix}.$$

By definition, we can divide the homogeneous coordinates by any nonzero scale factor, we can write (x', y', z', t') as $(x'', y'', z'', 1)$, where $x'' = x'/t'$, $y'' = y'/t'$, and $z'' = z'/t'$, and

$$x'' = \frac{m_{11}x + m_{12}y + m_{13}z + m_{14}t}{m_{41}x + m_{42}y + m_{43}z + m_{44}t},$$

$$y'' = \frac{m_{21}x + m_{22}y + m_{23}z + m_{24}t}{m_{41}x + m_{42}y + m_{43}z + m_{44}t},$$

$$z'' = \frac{m_{31}x + m_{32}y + m_{33}z + m_{34}t}{m_{41}x + m_{42}y + m_{43}z + m_{44}t}.$$

The above equations are often called the projective transformation. We will use this transformation in the next section in the development of the geometrical theory of optical imaging.

It should be pointed out that, from Klein's point of view, projective geometry is the most general type of geometry. It includes Euclidean geometry, affine geometry, inversive geometry, and non-Euclidean geometry as special cases [135] and we now apply the inversion operation used in the inversive geometry (see Fig. 9.2). The transformation group in this geometry maps points inside a sphere to points outside of the sphere, and vice versa. The sphere is mapped into itself. The inversion transformation is defined as follows. Let the sphere C be centered at the origin and its radius be r. A point (x, y, z) is mapped to (x', y', z'), which is on the line connecting the origin and the point (x, y, z), i.e., $x' = kx$, $y' = ky$, and $z' = kz$, and

$$\left(\sqrt{x^2 + y^2 + z^2}\right) \cdot \left(\sqrt{x'^2 + y'^2 + z'^2}\right) = r^2. \tag{9.8}$$

Substituting $x' = kx$, $y' = ky$, and $z' = kz$ into the above equation, we obtain

$$k = r^2/(x^2 + y^2 + z^2)$$

and

$$x' = \frac{r^2 x}{x^2 + y^2 + z^2}, \quad y' = \frac{r^2 y}{x^2 + y^2 + z^2}, \quad z' = \frac{r^2 z}{x^2 + y^2 + z^2}.$$

9.4 The geometrical theory of optical imaging

The geometrical theory of optical imaging can be formulated without referring to any optical components such as lenses or mirrors. The theory is purely abstract, but its beauty is that real optical imaging systems are well described by it in the region near the optical axis. The theory can be proved with rigorous but lengthy mathematics. Here we shall only summarize the main results from the theory. Readers who are interested in more details should consult the discussion in [124, Chapter IV].

First, let us consider what we want to achieve in an optical imaging system. An "ideal" imaging system should be able to form a sharp image from an object. Ideally, the sharp image should also preserve the exact geometrical shape of the object. If it is a three-dimensional object, it will be ideal if the three-dimensional image is an exact duplicate of the original object (except for scale and mirror image). Therefore, sharpness and similarity are the two desired geometrical attributes of an ideal optical imaging system. How do we define these two attributes mathematically?

If all the rays that radiate from a point in the object space can be so refracted as to converge to a point in the image space, we have indeed created a truly sharp point image for that point object. If an imaging system can do this for all the points in the object space, we can say that this system produces sharp images. However, it is not practical to collect all the rays in any direction and it is not necessary to do so to form an image. Therefore we arrive at the following definition:

Stigmatic (sharp) image
If an infinite number of rays from a point source P_0 in the object space pass through a point P_i in the image space, then P_i is said to be a stigmatic (sharp) image of P_0. The infinite number of rays are in a cone intercepted by the pupil of the imaging system. The object space need not be the entire three-dimensional space. It can be defined as a finite volume or region in the three-dimensional space. The set of all its image points will then be the image space. The corresponding points in these two spaces are called conjugate points.

Regarding the similarity between the object and the image, we can allow for the mirror image to be accepted as being similar. If every curve in the image space is similar to its conjugate curve in the object space, we say the image is a *perfect image*, and the imaging is *perfect imaging*. It should be noted that the object space and the image space are both in three-dimensional domains.

An optical imaging instrument producing images that are stigmatic (sharp) and perfect (similar) is called an absolute instrument. The following theorems state important properties of an absolute imaging instrument:

Maxwell's theorem for an absolute instrument [125, pp. 153–156]

The optical length of any curve in the object space is equal to the optical length of its image.

Carathéodory's theorem [125, pp. 156–157]

The mapping of an absolute imaging instrument between the object space and the image space is a projective transformation, an inversion, or a combination of the two.

The above two theorems combined put very serious constraints on what types of images can be produced by an absolute imaging instrument. If we would like to have an imaging system that is both stigmatic (sharp) and perfect (the three-dimensional image is geometrically similar to the three-dimensional object), and the object space and the image space to be in the same homogeneous space (i.e., same index of refraction), since the optical length of any curve in the object space is the same as the optical length of its image, we can only have an imaging system that reproduces an image that is exactly the same size as the object. Such a system is just like a plane mirror and it is not a very intersting system to have. In order to change the image size in the same homogeneous space, we have to drop either the requirement of stigmatism or that of exact similarity. It can further be shown [124, p. 149] that no more than two surfaces may be sharply imaged by a rotationally symmetric system (except the degenerate case, such as a mirror). In most real optical imaging systems, constructed from lenses and mirrors, three-dimensional similarity is never achieved. Images are sharp and similar to the object only on a small region of only one plane or curved surface (i.e., the image plane or surface conjugate to the object).

The above mathematical arguments suggest that we could approximate the imaging process as a projective transformation even though we cannot achieve it exactly. This is indeed true for Gaussian optics, where the off-axis distances and angles are assumed to be small. As will be described later, analysis of the elementary properties of lenses, mirrors, and their combinations under the assumptions of Gaussian optics shows that imaging with a refracting or reflecting surface of revolution is a projective transformation. It can also be proved that the combination of two successive projective transformations which are rotationally symmetrical about the same axis is also a projective transformation. We can therefore conclude that, within the approximation of Gaussian optics, imaging by a centered system is a projective transformation. We now show that a projective transformation under rotational symmetry can be characterized by only four variables.

A general projective transformation is described by the following relations between a point (x, y, z) in object space and a point (x', y', z') in image space (see Fig. 9.3). Both are referred to the same Cartesian coordinate axes.

$$x' = \frac{m_{11}x + m_{12}y + m_{13}z + m_{14}}{m_{41}x + m_{42}y + m_{43}z + m_{44}}, \tag{9.9}$$

$$y' = \frac{m_{21}x + m_{22}y + m_{23}z + m_{24}}{m_{41}x + m_{42}y + m_{43}z + m_{44}}, \tag{9.10}$$

$$z' = \frac{m_{31}x + m_{32}y + m_{33}z + m_{34}}{m_{41}x + m_{42}y + m_{43}z + m_{44}}. \tag{9.11}$$

Let us take the z-axis as the axis of symmetry. Because of rotational symmetry, we only

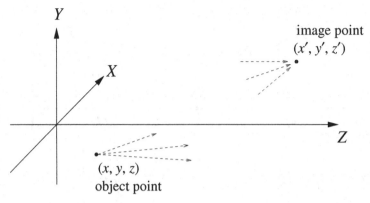

Figure 9.3. Coordinates for projective transformation from an object point (x, y, z) to an image point (x', y', z').

need to consider points on the $x = 0$ plane. The projective transformation becomes

$$y' = \frac{m_{22}y + m_{23}z + m_{24}}{m_{42}y + m_{43}z + m_{44}}, \tag{9.12}$$

$$z' = \frac{m_{32}y + m_{33}z + m_{34}}{m_{42}y + m_{43}z + m_{44}}. \tag{9.13}$$

Furthermore it follows from symmetry that, if we change y to $-y$, z' should remain unchanged and y' should become $-y'$. Therefore, m_{42}, m_{32}, m_{23}, and m_{24} should all be equal to zero, and the transformation further simplifies to

$$y' = \frac{m_{22}y}{m_{43}z + m_{44}},$$

$$z' = \frac{m_{33}z + m_{34}}{m_{43}z + m_{44}}. \tag{9.14}$$

Let $z_0 = -m_{44}/m_{43}$, $z'_0 = m_{33}/m_{43}$, $f = m_{22}/m_{43}$, and $f' = (m_{33}/m_{22})(m_{34}/m_{33} - m_{44}/m_{43})$, we then have

$$y' = \frac{fy}{z - z_0}, \tag{9.15}$$

$$z' - z'_0 = \frac{ff'}{z - z_0}. \tag{9.16}$$

Therefore, we need only four parameters, z_0, z'_0, f, and f' to specify the projective transformation for a rotationally symmetric imaging system. Equation (9.16) is known as *Newton's equation*. Equation (9.15) is the well-known formula for the *perspective transformation of a pinhole camera*. It should be noted that the equations derived here are for an arbitrary symmetric system. They are applicable to any rotationally-symmetric system within the domain of Gaussian optics.

From Eq. (9.16), we know that, if the object is located at $z = z_0$, its absolute image distance, z', will be infinity. This point is called the *object focal point F* (also called the first focal point or the front focal point). Similarly, if the image is located at $z' = z'_0$, the absolute

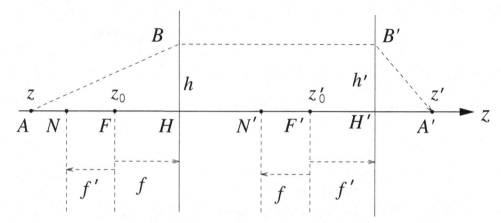

Figure 9.4. Coordinates for projective transformation from an object point (x, y, z) to an image point (x', y', z') for a rotationally symmetric system. The six cardinal points of an imaging system are the focal points (F and F'), the principal points (H and H'), and the nodal points (N and N').

value of its conjugate object distance, z, is also infinity. This point is called the *image focal point F'* (also called the back focal point or the image focal point). The lateral magnification m_y can be calculated as

$$m_y = \frac{dy'}{dy}\bigg|_z = \frac{f}{z - z_0} = \frac{z' - z_0'}{f'}.$$

(9.17)

If the object is located at $z = z_0 + f$, then the lateral magnification is equal to 1. The plane $z = z_0 + f$ is called the *object principal plane* (also called the first principal plane or the front principal plane). Similarly, the plane $z' = z_0' + f'$ is called the *image principal plane*. The object and image principal planes intersect with the axis at the object and image principal points, H and H' (see Fig. 9.4). The distance from the object focal point F to the object principal point H is f, and this is called the object focal length. Similarly, f' is called the image focal length. We can now conclude with the following statement.

Projective property of rotationally symmetric system
The projective transformation of a general, rotationally-symmetric system can be characterized by four parameters: its two focal points and two focal lengths.

Now, we can ask the question: is a rotationally-symmetric system a perfect imaging system? The answer is clearly "NO" as can be seen in the following calculation of its longitudinal magnification m_z:

$$m_z = \frac{dz'}{dz} = -\frac{ff'}{(z - z_0)^2} = -\frac{f'}{f}\frac{f^2}{(z - z_0)^2} = -\frac{f'}{f}m_y^2.$$

(9.18)

The longitudinal magnification is, in general, not equal to the lateral magnification, and the three-dimensional image is not similar to the three-dimensional object.

Another important magnification factor is the angular magnification. Let a point object A be located on the axis at z and a ray radiating from this point object intersect the object principal plane (at $z_0 + f$) at a point B, which is at a distance h from the axis. By the definition of the principal planes, B', the image of B, is on the image principal plane (at $z_0' + f'$) at a distance $h' = h$ away from the axis. The emerging ray intersects the axis at a point A', located at z'. The incident angle θ of this ray at the object principal plane is given by $\tan \theta = h/(z_0 + f - z)$. The exit angle θ' of the emerging ray at the image principal plane is given by $\tan \theta' = h'/(z_0' + f' - z')$. Since $h = h'$, the angular magnification m_a can be calculated as

$$m_a = \frac{\tan \theta'}{\tan \theta} = \frac{z_0 + f - z}{z_0' + f' - z'}. \tag{9.19}$$

From Eq. (9.16), if $z = z_0 - f'$, then $z' = z_0' - f$, and $m_a = 1$. This means that if a ray passes through a point N at $z = z_0 - f'$ in the object space, it will emerge at a point N' at $z' = z_0' - f$ in the image space at an exit angle exactly equal to its incident angle. These two points, N and N', are called the *object nodal point* and the *image nodal point*, respectively. The two focal points, the two principal points, and the two nodal points are called the cardinal points of an optical imaging system (see Fig. 9.4). Their locations are as follows:

$$z_F = z_0, \tag{9.20}$$
$$z_{F'}' = z_0', \tag{9.21}$$
$$z_H = z_0 + f, \tag{9.22}$$
$$z_{H'}' = z_0' + f', \tag{9.23}$$
$$z_N = z_0 - f', \tag{9.24}$$
$$z_{N'}' = z_0' - f. \tag{9.25}$$

Another useful relation expresses the distance, s', between the image plane and the image principal point as a function of f' and m_y. From Eqs. (9.17) and (9.23), we have[1]

$$s' = z' - z_{H'}' = (m_y - 1)f'. \tag{9.26}$$

Example 9.1

The object focal point F and the image focal point F' of an imaging system are located at $z_F = 40$ and $z_{F'} = 120$. It is also known that the object nodal point N and the image nodal point N' are located at $z_N = 80$ and $z_{N'} = 100$. What are the object focal length f and the image focal length f' of this system? Where are the principal points, H and H'? If an object is located at $z = -800$, then where is its image location z'? What is the lateral magnification in this imaging condition?

Solution From Eqs. (9.20)–(9.25), $f = z_{F'} - z_{N'} = 20$ and $f' = z_F - z_N = -40$. The principal points H and H' are located at $z_H = z_F + f = 60$ and $z_{H'} = z_{F'} + f' = 80$. If an object is located at $z = -800$, then from Eq. (9.16) the image is located at $z' = z_{F'} + ff'/(z - z_F) = 120 + (20)(-40)/(-800 - 40) = 120.952$. The lateral magnification $m_y = f/(z - z_F) = 20/(-800 - 40) = -0.023\,81$.

---

[1] Under many imaging conditions, m_y and f' are both negative numbers. Therefore, we might see the relation expressed as $s' = (1 + m)f$, where m is the absolute value of m_y and $f = -f'$ if both the object space and the image space are in the same medium, such as air.

It is clear that if we use the two focal points as the origins for the object and image spaces, all the equations are simplified. One minor inconvenience in doing so is that the focal points are usually located at some intangible surfaces and therefore it is not easy to measure the distances from them. For a thin lens, the principal points lie very close to the lens vertices (the intersection point between the optical axis and the lens surface). Therefore, formulas that relate distances measurable from the principal points have obvious convenience. For example, Newton's equation (9.16) can be cast into a form that is expressed in distances measured from the principal points. Let the object distance from the object principal point be $s = z - (z_0 + f)$ and the image distance from the image principal point be $i = z' - (z_0' + f')$, then

$$z' - z_0' = \frac{ff'}{z - z_0},$$

$$i + f' = \frac{ff'}{s + f},$$

$$(i + f')(s + f) = ff',$$

$$i(s + f) = -sf',$$

$$\frac{1}{i} = -\frac{s + f}{sf'} = -\frac{1}{f'} - \frac{f}{sf'},$$

and therefore we arrive at the *Gauss equation*:

$$\frac{f}{s} + \frac{f'}{i} = -1. \tag{9.27}$$

9.5 Conventions and terminology in optical imaging

In the above analysis of general optical imaging systems, we have employed a coordinate system that is used in most textbooks on optics and will continue to be used in this book. We therefore should take a moment to specify it more clearly here.

The z-axis is always pointing to the right and is the axis of symmetry if the system is rotationally symmetric. This axis is called the *optical axis* of the system. The distance is positive if measured from left to right and negative if measured from right to left. For example, the object focal length $f = z_H - z_0$ is measured from the object focal point F to the object principal point H. If H is located to the right of F, then f is positive. Very often, in contrast to the object space, the image principal point H' is located to the left of the image focal point F', and therefore, the image focal length $f' = z_{H'}' - z_0'$ is negative. It is always important to know the reference point or surface from which distances are measured.

We will use a right-handed coordinate system with the x-axis pointing perpendicularly into the page, and the y-axis pointing upward vertically on the page. For a rotationally symmetric system, an object point can be specified by only its y coordinate, assuming that $x = 0$. In other words, the y-axis is (defined to be) on the plane that passes through the object point and the optical axis. This plane is called the *meridional plane* (it is also called the tangential plane). Any ray that is on this plane is called a *meridional ray*. In a

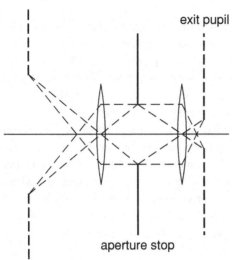

Figure 9.5. The entrance pupil is the image of the aperture formed by the optical components between the aperture and the object. The exit pupil is the image of the aperture formed by the components behind it.

rotationally-symmetric system, a meridional ray stays on the meridional plane all the way through the system. Any ray which is not on the meridional plane is called a *skew ray*.

In any physically realizable imaging system, light can only pass through a finite aperture (see Fig. 9.5). The aperture can be formed by the opening of a physical plane (called the *aperture stop*), or it can represent the narrowest cross-section in the light path through the system. This aperture as seen from the object side is called the *entrance pupil*, and when seen from the image side is called the *exit pupil*. In other words, the entrance pupil is the image of the aperture stop formed by all the optical components in front of it (i.e., on the object side). Similarly, the exit pupil is the image of the aperture stop formed by all the optical components behind it (i.e., on the film side). Therefore, the size of the entrance pupil and the size of the exit pupil are often different from the actual size of the aperture. For example, the pupils in my eyes as seen by you are larger than their actual sizes because you are seeing the images of my pupils as formed by my corneas.

Knowledge of the size and position of the entrance pupil and the exit pupil is very important in analyzing an imaging system. The entrance pupil forms the base and the object point forms the apex of the cone of light rays that are accepted by the imaging system. Similarly, the exit pupil forms the base and the image point forms the apex of the cone of light rays that are focused to the image point by the imaging system. In general, the size of the entrance pupil and the size of the exit pupil are not the same. The ratio of the diameter of the exit pupil, a_{ex}, to that of the entrance pupil, a_{en}, is called the pupil magnification (or pupil factor), m_p, i.e.,

$$m_p = \frac{a_{ex}}{a_{en}}.$$
(9.28)

This parameter is important when we discuss the radiometry and photometry of an imaging system.

The meridional ray which is directed toward the center of the entrance pupil is called the *chief ray*. The ray is important in the sense that it represents approximately the center of the cone of rays going through the optical system. It passes through the center of the aperture stop. Any ray which passes the margin of the entrance pupil is called a *marginal ray*.

The plane which contains the chief ray and is perpendicular to the meridional plane is called the *sagittal plane*. Any ray which is on the sagittal plane is called a *sagittal ray*.

Rays which make small angles, θ, with the optical axis are called paraxial rays. A small region around the optical axis is called the paraxial region. The paraxial approximation assumes that $\sin\theta \approx \theta$ and $\cos\theta \approx 1$. As mentioned before, optical calculation using the paraxial approximation for a rotationally-symmetric system is called Gaussian optics.

The points where the optical axis intersects the front and back surfaces of the lens are called the front and back vertices of the lens. These are tangible points and many optical distances of a lens are specified with respect to the two vertices.

9.6   Refraction at a spherical surface

Having explored the geometrical theory of optical imaging, we will now look at the analysis of real imaging systems, constructed from lenses and other optical components. Although the basic tools of optical analysis are very simple (Snell's law is often said to be the only thing needed), the complete mathematical analysis of any practical system is almost always not practical. Lens designers rely heavily on tracing many, many rays through various optical components in the system to get a feeling of how well the system might work. For example, if we trace many rays from an object point through the system to the image plane and all the rays converge to a single image point, we know that our optical design will work well for this object point. We can then trace rays from other points in the object space to find their image quality in the image space. Obviously, the more object points we check, the better the idea we have about the optical performance.

The ray tracing operation is mostly performed by computers, and experience, insight, and knowledge are required to set up the initial designs to be given to the computers for further modification and optimization. An optical system can be considered as consisting of a number of refracting surfaces spaced apart from each another. The ray tracing operation is to propagate the ray from an object point through one surface to another and trace it through the entire system. There are two basic processes involved in the operation: transfer and refraction [899, 1021]. The transfer process involves propagating the ray until it intersects with a refracting surface. The major problem to solve here is the determination of the intersection point. The refraction process involves finding the direction of propagation after the ray is refracted at the refracting surface. These two processes are repeated again and again until we have traced the ray to the desired image space. In this section, we will study how these two processes are carried out using a spherical surface as an example. Spherical surfaces have been the most important type of surface for lenses made by grinding, because they are the only type of surface that can be produced by grinding two surfaces

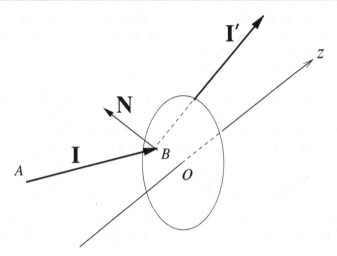

Figure 9.6. Ray tracing of an arbitrary ray through a spherical refracting surface.

repeatedly [385]. Aberrations of spherical lenses are well studied for their wide use in imaging optics.

Referring to Fig. 9.6, a spherical surface $\phi(x, y, z) = x^2 + y^2 + (z - r)^2 - r^2 = 0$ intersects the optical axis at point O, where $x = y = z = 0$. Here we will assume $r > 0$. A ray radiating from point A is propagating along the direction of the unit vector $\mathbf{I}$, and it intersects the sphere at the point B. The surface normal of the sphere at B is the unit vector $\mathbf{N}$ pointing to the center of the sphere. The incident ray is refracted by the sphere into the direction of the unit vector $\mathbf{I}'$. The transfer process is to determine the intersection point B and the refraction process is to determine the vector $\mathbf{I}'$. In the following we will let $\mathbf{A}$ and $\mathbf{B}$ be the positional vectors from the origin O to the points A and B, respectively.

First, let us solve the transfer process. Since B is a point on the ray, it can be expressed as $\mathbf{B} = \mathbf{A} + k\mathbf{I}$, where k is a scalar. Let $\mathbf{U}$ be a unit vector along the z-axis, i.e., $\mathbf{U} = [0, 0, 1]^{\mathrm{T}}$. Thus, the center of the sphere is represented as $r\mathbf{U}$. Let $\mathbf{R} = [x, y, z]^{\mathrm{T}}$ be a point on the sphere, then

$$\phi(\mathbf{R}) = x^2 + y^2 + (z - r)^2 - r^2 = x^2 + y^2 + z^2 - 2rz = \mathbf{R} \cdot \mathbf{R} - 2r\mathbf{R} \cdot \mathbf{U} = 0. \quad (9.29)$$

Since point B is on the sphere,

$$\phi(\mathbf{B}) = \mathbf{B} \cdot \mathbf{B} - 2r\mathbf{B} \cdot \mathbf{U} \quad (9.30)$$

$$= (\mathbf{A} + k\mathbf{I}) \cdot (\mathbf{A} + k\mathbf{I}) - 2r(\mathbf{A} + k\mathbf{I}) \cdot \mathbf{U} \quad (9.31)$$

$$= \mathbf{A} \cdot \mathbf{A} + 2k\mathbf{A} \cdot \mathbf{I} + k^2 - 2r\mathbf{A} \cdot \mathbf{U} - 2kr\mathbf{I} \cdot \mathbf{U} \quad (9.32)$$

$$= k^2 + 2(\mathbf{A} \cdot \mathbf{I} - r\mathbf{I} \cdot \mathbf{U})k + \mathbf{A} \cdot \mathbf{A} - 2r\mathbf{A} \cdot \mathbf{U} \quad (9.33)$$

$$= 0. \quad (9.34)$$

Solving for k,

$$k = -(\mathbf{A} \cdot \mathbf{I} - r\mathbf{I} \cdot \mathbf{U}) \pm [(\mathbf{A} \cdot \mathbf{I} - r\mathbf{I} \cdot \mathbf{U})^2 - \mathbf{A} \cdot \mathbf{A} + 2r\mathbf{A} \cdot \mathbf{U}]^{1/2}. \quad (9.35)$$

The two solutions represent two intersection points. Since the ray is refracted at the first intersection point, we have to determine which is the solution we need. This can be done by choosing A to be a point on the axis, say $\mathbf{A} = -\mathbf{U}$, and $\mathbf{I}$ to be along the axis, i.e. $\mathbf{I} = \mathbf{U}$. The intersection point B will now be at the vertex O, i.e., $\mathbf{B} = \mathbf{A} + k\mathbf{I} = -\mathbf{U} + k\mathbf{U} = O$ and $k = 1$. Therefore we should use the negative sign in Eq. (9.35) and

$$k = -(\mathbf{A} \cdot \mathbf{I} - r\mathbf{I} \cdot \mathbf{U}) - [(\mathbf{A} \cdot \mathbf{I} - r\mathbf{I} \cdot \mathbf{U})^2 - \mathbf{A} \cdot \mathbf{A} + 2r\mathbf{A} \cdot \mathbf{U}]^{1/2}. \qquad (9.36)$$

Having found the intersection point B, we can proceed to the refraction process to determine the refracted ray vector $\mathbf{I}'$. First, we find the surface normal vector $\mathbf{N}$:

$$\mathbf{N} = -\frac{\nabla \phi}{|\nabla \phi|} = -\frac{2\mathbf{B} - 2r\mathbf{U}}{2r} = \mathbf{U} - \frac{1}{r}\mathbf{B}. \qquad (9.37)$$

From Snell's law, the refracted vector $\mathbf{I}'$ is on the plane of incidence spanned by the incident vector $\mathbf{I}$ and the surface normal $\mathbf{N}$. Therefore, we can express $\mathbf{I}'$ as a linear combination of $\mathbf{N}$ and $\mathbf{I}$:

$$\mathbf{I}' = \alpha \mathbf{N} + \beta \mathbf{I}, \qquad (9.38)$$

$$\mathbf{I}' \times \mathbf{N} = \alpha \mathbf{N} \times \mathbf{N} + \beta \mathbf{I} \times \mathbf{N}, \qquad (9.39)$$

$$\sin \theta' = \beta \sin \theta. \qquad (9.40)$$

Therefore $\beta = n/n'$, where n' is the index of refraction of the sphere and n is that of the space outside the sphere. Since $\mathbf{I}'$ is a unit vector, we have:

$$1 = \mathbf{I}' \cdot \mathbf{I}' = (\alpha \mathbf{N} + \beta \mathbf{I}) \cdot (\alpha \mathbf{N} + \beta \mathbf{I}) \qquad (9.41)$$

$$= \alpha^2 \mathbf{N} \cdot \mathbf{N} + 2\alpha\beta \mathbf{N} \cdot \mathbf{I} + \beta^2 \mathbf{I} \times \mathbf{I} \qquad (9.42)$$

$$= \alpha^2 + 2\beta(\mathbf{N} \cdot \mathbf{I})\alpha + \beta^2 \mathbf{I}. \qquad (9.43)$$

Solving for α, we have

$$\alpha = -\beta(\mathbf{N} \cdot \mathbf{I}) \pm [1 - \beta^2 + \beta^2(\mathbf{N} \cdot \mathbf{I})]^{1/2}. \qquad (9.44)$$

In order to determine the sign, let the incident ray be normal to the surface, i.e., $\mathbf{I} = \mathbf{N}$, then $\mathbf{I}' = \mathbf{I}$, and $\alpha + \beta = 1$. Therefore, the positive sign should be used,

$$\alpha = -\beta(\mathbf{N} \cdot \mathbf{I}) + [1 - \beta^2 + \beta^2(\mathbf{N} \cdot \mathbf{I})]^{1/2}, \qquad (9.45)$$

and the refracted vector $\mathbf{I}' = \alpha \mathbf{N} + \beta \mathbf{I}$ can be determined.

By now, we should be convinced that although the basic rule, Snell's law, is simple, the equations that describe the path of a ray can easily become complicated even for a simple refracting surface like the sphere. Computers can handle all the calculations quickly, but for our human minds to grasp what is happening in optical imaging, we need much simpler formulas for our intuition. This is why the Gaussian approximation is made in practice – it is out of necessity, not because we do not care about the exact solution.

We have solved the general problem of ray tracing for the case of a spherical surface. It is interesting to actually trace several rays through this single refraction surface. Let us study the following two cases: (1) on-axis imaging and (2) off-axis imaging.

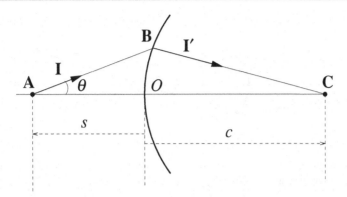

Figure 9.7. On-axis ray tracing through a spherical surface.

9.6.1 On-axis imaging by a spherical surface

Refering to Fig. 9.7, let us assume that the object point $\mathbf{A}$ is located on the optical axis and at a distance s away from the vertex O, i.e., $\mathbf{A} = [0, 0, s]^{\mathrm{T}}$. Since $\mathbf{A}$ is located to the left of the vertex, s is a negative number. Let a ray be propagating in the direction $\mathbf{I}$ which makes an angle θ with the axis, and $\mathbf{I} = [0, \sin\theta, \cos\theta]^{\mathrm{T}}$. From Snell's law, the refracted ray $\mathbf{I'}$ should intersect with the axis. Let that intersection point be $\mathbf{C} = [0, 0, c]^{\mathrm{T}}$. Let us first look at the image distance, c, as a function of the incident angle θ. If the spherical surface is a sharp imaging device, then c should only depend on the object distance s, but not on the incident angle θ. As we will see this is not the case.

From Eqs. (9.36), (9.37), and (9.45), we can calculate c as a function of θ. The derivation is lengthy but straightforward. The result is a relatively complex function:

$$c = s + k\cos\theta + \frac{kr\alpha}{k\alpha - r\beta}\left(1 - \frac{s}{r} - \frac{k}{r}\cos\theta\right) + \frac{kr\beta}{k\alpha - r\beta}\cos\theta, \qquad (9.46)$$

where α is given in Eq. (9.45), and

$$\beta = \frac{n}{n'}, \qquad (9.47)$$

$$k = (r - s)\cos\theta - [(r - s)^2\cos^2\theta - s^2 + 2rs]^{1/2}, \qquad (9.48)$$

$$\mathbf{N}\cdot\mathbf{I} = -\frac{k}{r}\sin^2\theta + \left(1 - \frac{s}{r} - \frac{k}{r}\cos\theta\right)\cos\theta. \qquad (9.49)$$

The values of $\sin\theta$ and $\cos\theta$ can be approximated by their power series expansion:

$$\sin\theta = \theta - \frac{\theta^3}{3!} + \frac{\theta^5}{5!} - \cdots; \qquad (9.50)$$

$$\cos\theta = 1 - \frac{\theta^2}{2!} + \frac{\theta^4}{4!} - \cdots. \qquad (9.51)$$

For small angles, if the first order approximation is used, $\sin\theta \approx \theta$ and $\cos\theta \approx 1$. All terms which involve powers of θ higher than 1 are neglected. (Again, we remind ourselves here

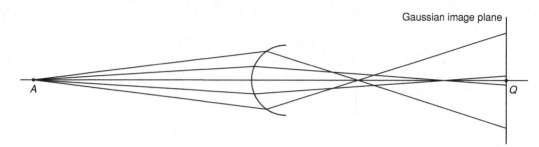

Figure 9.8. On-axis imaging: rays that diverge farther away from the axis are focused at a shorter distance. This is called spherical aberration.

that the first order approximation is called linear optics. If the system is also rotationally symmetric, the approximation is called Gaussian optics.)

If we use the Gaussian approximation, we can simplify Eqs. (9.45)–(9.49) to the following: $k = -s$, $\mathbf{N} \cdot \mathbf{I} = 1 + s\theta^2/r$, $\alpha = 1 - \beta$, and

$$c = \frac{sr}{s + r\beta - s\beta}, \tag{9.52}$$

which can be put into the form of the Gauss equation (9.27):

$$\frac{f}{s} + \frac{f'}{c} = -1, \tag{9.53}$$

where

$$f = \frac{\beta r}{1 - \beta} = \frac{nr}{n' - n}, \tag{9.54}$$

$$f' = \frac{r}{\beta - 1} = \frac{n'r}{n - n'}, \tag{9.55}$$

$$\frac{f}{f'} = -\frac{n}{n'}. \tag{9.56}$$

Therefore, under the Gaussian optics approximation, a spherical surface of radius r has an object focal length f and an image focal length f'. If $n' > n$, as in the case of a glass sphere in air, $f > 0$ and $f' < 0$. Since s and c are both measured from the vertex O, the object and image principal points are both located at the vertex of the surface, i.e., $z_H = 0$ and $z'_{H'} = 0$. The object focal point is located at $z_0 = z_H - f = -f$, and the image focal point is located at $z'_0 = z'_{H'} - f' = -f'$. The object nodal point N is located at $z_N = z_H - f - f' = -(f + f') = r$, and the image nodal point is located at $z'_{N'} = z'_{H'} - (f + f') = r$. The two nodal points are both located at the center of the sphere. This simply means that a ray that is directed towards the center of the sphere is perpendicular to the spherical surface and its direction is not changed by refraction. Also of interest are the intersection point B and the refracted ray vector $\mathbf{I'}$. The Gaussian approximation leads to $B = [0, -s\theta, 0]^T$ and $\mathbf{I'} = V/|V|$, where $\mathbf{V} = [0, [s(1 - \beta)/r]\theta + \beta\theta, 1]^T$. These will be used in the next section, where we develop the matrix method for Gaussian optics.

For rays that are at a large angle from the axis, the Gaussian optics approximation does not apply. Figure 9.8 shows that the various rays radiating from the object point A do

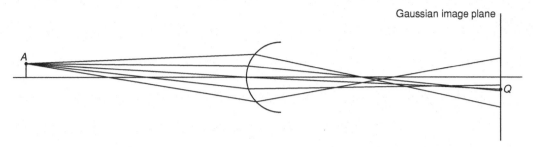

Figure 9.9. Off-axis imaging: different cones of rays converge at different distances and different heights.

not converge to the same point. Rays that diverge further away from the axis are focused at a shorter distance. This is called spherical aberration. The point Q is the image point calculated from Gaussian optics. One can see that most rays converge at a much shorter distance on the axis. If we move the image plane closer to the spherical surface, the image actually becomes sharper, but it is never an ideal point image. The image looks like a blurred circle (called the circle of confusion). When we move the image plane closer to the lens, we reach the position at which the blurred circle is the smallest, we can then say that this is the best focus position. Obviously, this position depends on our definition of the circle of confusion, but in general, when an imaging system has some aberrations, the best focus position is often not at the Gaussian image plane.

9.6.2   *Off-axis imaging by a spherical surface*

If the object point A is located at a distance h away from the axis, the mathematical expressions from ray tracing become too complex to be interesting. The concentric cones of rays converge not only at different distances from the lens, but also at different heights off the axis. Figure 9.9 shows the ray tracing result on the plane containing the optical axis and the object point (the meridional plane). If we place a diffusing surface at the Gaussian plane, we will see a coma-like flare image. Figure 9.10 shows the intersection contours of the various concentric cones of rays from the object point A. We have assumed that the spherical surface has a radius of 5.56 mm (the radius of a reduced human eye model). The object is located at 35.94 mm from the vertex of the eye and at 2.22 mm off the optical axis on the positive y-axis. The outermost contour is from a cone of rays whose center is aimed at the vertex of the eye. The angular subtense of the cone is about 1.1°. As we can see, the blur pattern is not symmetric with respect to the Gaussian image point. The coma's tail is spread out toward the optical axis (in the positive y-direction).

9.7   **Matrix method for paraxial ray tracing**

In Gaussian optics, ray tracing can be very efficiently carried out by matrix multiplications. For rays that are coplanar with the optical axis (meridional rays), the operation can be represented by 2×2 matrices. For other rays, 4×4 matrices are required. The general

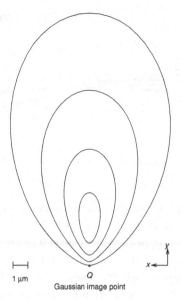

Figure 9.10. Coma-like patterns resulting from cones of rays from an off-axis object point, as seen on the Gaussian image plane.

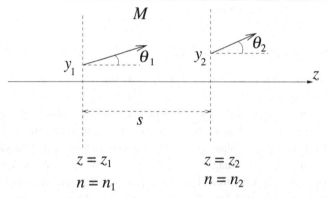

Figure 9.11. Paraxial ray tracing by matrix transformation of ray vectors. The ray vector at the reference plane at $z = z_1$ intersects the plane at a height $y = y_1$ and at an angle $\theta = \theta_1$. The index of refraction at $z = z_1$ is $n = n_1$. After traveling a distance s along the optical axis, the ray vector intersects the second reference plane at $z = z_2$ at a height $y = y_2$ and at an angle $\theta = \theta_2$. The index of refraction at $z = z_2$ is $n = n_2$. The ray vector transition from z_1 to z_2 can be represented by a matrix M.

properties of these matrices are discussed under the subject of (linear) simplectic transformation in various books [50, 371]. The 2×2 matrices lead to a special case of projective transformation and to a "proof" that a rotationally symmetric, optical imaging system can be approximated by a projective transformation characterized by four parameters. This is the subject we will study in this section.

Let us take a plane, perpendicular to the optical axis and located at $z = z_1$, as a reference plane (see Fig. 9.11). A meridional ray which intersects the reference plane at a height of

$y = y_1$ (the x-coordinate is irrelevant for such a ray) and at an angle θ_1 can be characterized by a 2×1 vector, $\mathbf{V}_1 = [y_1, n_1\theta_1]^T$, where n_1 is the index of refraction at (y_1, z_1). We trace this ray to a second reference plane located at $z = z_2$ and represent that ray with the vector $\mathbf{V}_2 = [y_2, n_2\theta_2]^T$, where n_2 is the index of refraction at (y_2, z_2). We would like to determine the transition matrix M that maps $\mathbf{V}_1$ to $\mathbf{V}_2$, i.e., $\mathbf{V}_2 = M\mathbf{V}_1$.

As we described before, there are two processes in the ray tracing: transfer and refraction. Let the distance between the two reference planes be $s = z_2 - z_1$. If there are no refracting surfaces between the two reference planes, the ray should propagate in a straight line. Therefore, $n_1 = n_2 = n$, $\theta_1 = \theta_2 = \theta$, $y_2 = y_1 + s\tan\theta \approx y_1 + s\theta$, and

$$\mathbf{V}_2 = \begin{bmatrix} y_2 \\ n\theta_2 \end{bmatrix} = \begin{bmatrix} 1 & s/n \\ 0 & 1 \end{bmatrix} \begin{bmatrix} y_1 \\ n\theta_1 \end{bmatrix} = M_s^t \mathbf{V}_1. \tag{9.57}$$

Therefore the matrix M_s^t is the transition matrix of the *transfer* process for a distance s. The matrix for the refraction process can be determined from our discussion on refraction from a spherical surface under Gaussian optics. First let us assume that the refraction surface is very thin, i.e., $z_2 \approx z_1$, and therefore, $y_2 = y_1$, meaning that the height of the ray is the same before and after the refraction. From the results in Section 9.6.1, we have the following relations:

$$\tan\theta_2 = \beta\theta_1 - \left(\frac{1-\beta}{R}\right)y_1, \tag{9.58}$$

$$\theta_2 \approx \frac{n_1}{n_2}\theta_1 - \left(\frac{n_2 - n_1}{n_2 R}\right)y_1, \tag{9.59}$$

$$n_2\theta_2 \approx n_1\theta_1 - \left(\frac{n_2 - n_1}{R}\right)y_1, \tag{9.60}$$

where R is the radius of the refracting spherical surface. Therefore,

$$\mathbf{V}_2 = \begin{bmatrix} y_2 \\ n\theta_2 \end{bmatrix} = \begin{bmatrix} 1 & 0 \\ -(n_2 - n_1)/R & 1 \end{bmatrix} \begin{bmatrix} y_1 \\ n\theta_1 \end{bmatrix} = \begin{bmatrix} 1 & 0 \\ -K & 1 \end{bmatrix} \begin{bmatrix} y_1 \\ n\theta_1 \end{bmatrix} = M_R^r \mathbf{V}_1. \tag{9.61}$$

Thus, the matrix M_R^r is the transition matrix of the *refraction* process for a surface of radius R. The quantity $K = (n_2 - n_1)/R$ is often referred to as the power of the refracting surface. It should be pointed out that the radius of the spherical surface R is positive when the surface is convex to the left. Otherwise, it is negative.

Since the refraction process plays a central role in image formation, we will give an alternative derivation of the refraction matrix here, which will give us a more intuitive feeling of how and where paraxial approximations are made in the matrix method of ray tracing. Figure. 9.12 shows a diagram of the various angles involved in the calculation. A ray, intersecting the spherical surface at a height y and an angle θ_1, is refracted at the interface to a direction of angle θ_2. From the diagram, we can write down the following equations:

$$n_1\sin\sigma = n_2\sin\phi \quad \text{(Snell's law)}; \tag{9.62}$$

$$\sigma + \left(\frac{\pi}{2} - \theta_1\right) + \psi = \pi; \tag{9.63}$$

$$\theta_2 = \psi + \phi - \frac{\pi}{2}. \tag{9.64}$$

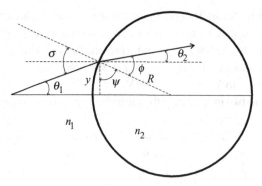

Figure 9.12. Refraction at a spherical surface.

Since $\psi = \cos^{-1}(y/R)$ is known, we can express θ_2 in terms of θ_1 and ψ:

$$\sin\theta_2 = \sin\left(\psi + \phi - \frac{\pi}{2}\right) = -\cos(\psi + \phi) = \sin\psi\sin\phi - \cos\psi\cos\phi; \qquad (9.65)$$

$$\sin\phi = \frac{n_1}{n_2}\sin\sigma = \frac{n_1}{n_2}\sin\left(\frac{\pi}{2} + \theta_1 - \psi\right) = \frac{n_1}{n_2}\left(\cos\theta_1\cos\psi + \sin\theta_1\sin\psi\right). \qquad (9.66)$$

It is clear, from the above equations, that θ_2 is a very nonlinear function of θ_1 and y. The paraxial approximations are such that $\sin\theta_1 \approx \theta_1$, $\cos\theta_1 \approx 1$, $\sin\psi \approx 1$, $\cos\psi \approx y/R$, $\sin\theta_2 \approx \theta_2$, and $\cos\phi \approx 1$. Therefore,

$$\sin\phi \approx \frac{n_1}{n_2}(\cos\psi + \theta_1) = \frac{n_1}{n_2}\left(\frac{y}{R} + \theta_1\right), \qquad (9.67)$$

$$\sin\theta_2 = \sin\psi\sin\phi - \cos\psi\cos\phi \approx \sin\phi - \cos\psi, \qquad (9.68)$$

$$\theta_2 \approx \frac{n_1}{n_2}\left(\frac{y}{R} + \theta_1\right) - \frac{y}{R} = \left(\frac{n_1}{n_2} - 1\right)\frac{y}{R} - \frac{n_1}{n_2}\theta_1. \qquad (9.69)$$

Thus, under the paraxial approximation, we arrive at the same relation that gives us the desired refraction matrix: $n_2\theta_2 = -(n_2 - n_1)y/R + n_1\theta_1$. However, if we use the exact equations (9.65) and (9.66) to calculate the refraction for larger θ_1 and y, we find that paraxial ray tracing becomes quite inaccurate. The vector ray tracing based on Snell's law has to be used. It should always be kept in mind that the matrix method for ray tracing we develop here is valid only for Gaussian optics.

With matrices M^t and M^r, we can perform ray tracings simply by matrix multiplication. Let us assume that we are given a ray vector $\mathbf{V}_0 = [y_0, n_0\theta_0]$ at $z = z_0$, that there are m refracting surfaces located at $z = z_i$ with radii R_i, $i = 1, 2, \ldots, m$, and that the image plane is located at $z = z_p$. We can calculate the ray vector $\mathbf{V}_p$ as it intercepts the image plane by

$$\mathbf{V}_p = M^t_{z_p-z_m} M^r_{R_m} M^t_{z_m-z_{m-1}} M^r_{R_{m-1}} \cdots M^r_{R_1} M^t_{z_1-z_0} \mathbf{V}_0. \qquad (9.70)$$

One important property of the transition matrix (transfer or refraction) is that its determinant is 1:

$$|M^t_s| = \begin{vmatrix} 1 & s/n \\ 0 & 1 \end{vmatrix} = 1; \qquad (9.71)$$

$$|M^r_R| = \begin{vmatrix} 1 & 0 \\ -(n_2 - n_1)/R & 1 \end{vmatrix} = 1. \qquad (9.72)$$

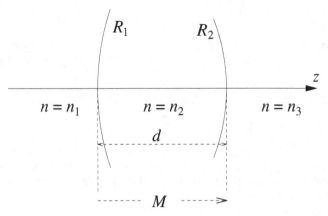

Figure 9.13. A thick biconvex lens with thickness d, index of refraction n_2, and radii of curvature R_1 and R_2 can be represented by a matrix M. The indexes of refraction on either side of the lens are n_1 and n_3.

Since $|M_1 M_2| = |M_1| \cdot |M_2|$, it follows that a system transition matrix, being the product of transition matrices of individual components, also has a determinant of 1. Therefore we conclude that the determinant of the 2×2 transition matrix of any Gaussian optical imaging system constructed by refracting surfaces is 1.

Let us look at some examples. A thick biconvex lens (see Fig. 9.13) consists of two refracting surfaces separated by a distance d. Let R_1 and R_2 be the radii of the front and back surfaces. By convention, $R_1 > 0$ and $R_2 < 0$. Assume that the indices of refraction are n_1, n_2, and n_3 for the object space, the lens, and the image space, respectively. Let us take the vertices of the two surfaces as the two reference planes, then the transition matrix M of the thick lens is

$$
\begin{aligned}
M &= \begin{bmatrix} 1 & 0 \\ -(n_3 - n_2)/R_2 & 1 \end{bmatrix} \begin{bmatrix} 1 & d/n_2 \\ 0 & 1 \end{bmatrix} \begin{bmatrix} 1 & 0 \\ -(n_2 - n_1)/R_1 & 1 \end{bmatrix} \\
&= \begin{bmatrix} 1 & 0 \\ -K_2 & 1 \end{bmatrix} \begin{bmatrix} 1 & d/n_2 \\ 0 & 1 \end{bmatrix} \begin{bmatrix} 1 & 0 \\ -K_1 & 1 \end{bmatrix} \\
&= \begin{bmatrix} 1 - dK_1/n_2 & d/n_2 \\ -(K_1 + K_2) + dK_1 K_2/n_2 & 1 - dK_2/n_2 \end{bmatrix}.
\end{aligned}
\tag{9.73}
$$

In the thin lens approximation, $d \to 0$, and

$$
M = \begin{bmatrix} 1 & 0 \\ -K & 1 \end{bmatrix} = \begin{bmatrix} 1 & 0 \\ -(K_1 + K_2) & 1 \end{bmatrix}.
\tag{9.74}
$$

The optical power of a thin lens is the sum of the powers of its two refracting surfaces and

$$
K = K_1 + K_2 = \frac{n_2 - n_1}{R_1} + \frac{n_3 - n_2}{R_2},
\tag{9.75}
$$

which simplifies to:

$$
K = (n_2 - n_1) \left(\frac{1}{R_1} - \frac{1}{R_2} \right)
\tag{9.76}
$$

when $n_3 = n_1$ and is called the lens-maker's formula.

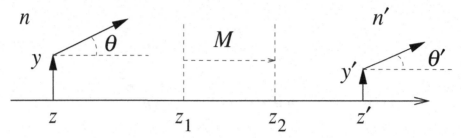

Figure 9.14. Diagram of a general imaging system with a transition matrix from z_1 to z_2. It forms an image y' at z' of an object y at z. A ray from the object forms an angle θ with the optical axis and is refracted to a ray at an angle θ' at the image. The indices of refraction are n and n' for the object space and the image space, respectively.

Can we calculate imaging parameters from these transition matrices? The answer is yes. Here we show how these can be computed for a general optical imaging system (see Fig. 9.14). Let M be the transition matrix of an optical imaging system from z_1 to z_2. An object located at z forms an image at z'. Let M be a general matrix:

$$M = \begin{bmatrix} a & b \\ c & d \end{bmatrix}, \qquad (9.77)$$

where $c \neq 0$. The transformation of a ray-vector $[y, n\theta]^T$ from z to $[y', n'\theta']^T$ at z' is given by

$$\begin{bmatrix} y' \\ n'\theta' \end{bmatrix} = \begin{bmatrix} 1 & (z'-z_2)/n' \\ 0 & 1 \end{bmatrix} \begin{bmatrix} a & b \\ c & d \end{bmatrix} \begin{bmatrix} 1 & (z_1-z)/n \\ 0 & 1 \end{bmatrix} \begin{bmatrix} y \\ n\theta \end{bmatrix}. \qquad (9.78)$$

Therefore,

$$y' = \left[a + \frac{c}{n'}(z'-z_2) \right] y + \left[a(z_1-z) + bn + \frac{c}{n'}(z_1-z)(z'-z_2) + \frac{n}{n'}d(z'-z_2) \right]\theta, \qquad (9.79)$$

$$n'\theta' = cy + [c(z_1-z) + nd]\theta. \qquad (9.80)$$

To find the principal points H and H', we let $y' = y$ for all θ because they are a conjugate pair (i.e., H' is the image of H) with unit lateral magnification. The coefficient of y in the first term of Eq. (9.79) should be unity and we have

$$a + \frac{c}{n'}(z'-z_2) = 1 \quad \rightarrow \quad z'_{H'} = z' = z_2 + \frac{n'}{c}(1-a). \qquad (9.81)$$

Since y' is the image of y, it is independent of θ. The coefficient of θ in Eq. (9.79) should be zero and since $ad - bc = 1$, we have

$$z_H = z = z_1 - \frac{n}{c}(1-d). \qquad (9.82)$$

To find the nodal points N and N', we let $y' = y = 0$ and $\theta = \theta'$ because they are a conjugate pair (i.e., N' is the image of N) with unit angular magnification. From Eq. (9.80), we have

$$z_N = z = z_1 - \frac{n}{c}\left(\frac{n'}{n} - d \right). \qquad (9.83)$$

From Eqs. (9.79) and (9.83), we have

$$z'_{N'} = z' = z_2 + \frac{n'}{c}\left(\frac{n}{n'} - a\right).$$

(9.84)

In order to find the focal points, F and F', we use the property that parallel rays in object space converge to the image focal point, and rays from the object focal point become parallel in image space. Let $\theta = 0$ and $y' = 0$ in Eq. (9.79) to obtain

$$z'_{F'} = z' = z_2 - \frac{n'}{c}(a),$$

(9.85)

and let $\theta' = 0$ and $y = 0$ in Eq. (9.80) to obtain

$$z_F = z = z_1 + \frac{n}{c}(d).$$

(9.86)

The focal lengths f and f' can be found as follows:

$$f = z_H - z_F = -\frac{n}{c};$$

(9.87)

$$f' = z'_{H'} - z'_{F'} = \frac{n'}{c}.$$

(9.88)

These results are very general and useful. For example, when $n = n'$, we have $z_N = z_H$, $z'_{N'} = z'_{H'}$, and $f = -f'$. Therefore, the nodal point and the principal point are the same when the object space and the image space have the same index of refraction, and the object focal length and the image focal length are the same length, but of opposite sign. Since the focal length is measured from the corresponding principal point, this simply means that the two focal points F and F' are located on opposite sides of H and H'. Thus, if F is on the left of H, then F' is on the right of H'. However, when $n \neq n'$, the nodal points are different from the principal points, and the two focal lengths are no longer equal in length (but are still of opposite signs).

If we now use F and F' as the origins to measure the object and image distances, we can greatly simplify the imaging conditions. If z' is the image location of an object located at z, the coefficient of the θ term in Eq. (9.79) is zero because the image height is independent of the ray angle leaving the object (i.e., all rays should converge to the image point). Using z_F, $z'_{F'}$, f, and f', we can simplify the expression to $(z - z_F)(z' - z'_{F'}) = ff'$, which is Newton's equation.

In a special case when z_H is located at z_1 (i.e., $d = 1$) and $z'_{H'}$ is located at z_2 (i.e., $a = 1$), the matrix M simplifies to

$$M = \begin{bmatrix} 1 & 0 \\ -K & 1 \end{bmatrix},$$

(9.89)

where $K = -c$, and $b = 0$ because the determinant of M has to be 1. Therefore, if we use the principal points H and H' as the reference planes for an imaging system, the system transition matrix is very simple and very easy to interpret. Between H and H', the system can be treated as a thin lens. Thus all the ray-tracing diagrams that we use for a thin lens can still be applied to an arbitrary complex system, provided that we trace the rays from an object to H and then continue from H' to its image. The object and image distances are now related by

$$\frac{f}{z - z_H} + \frac{f'}{z' - z'_{H'}} = -1 \tag{9.90}$$

or

$$\frac{n}{z_H - z} + \frac{n'}{z' - z'_{H'}} = K. \tag{9.91}$$

Equation (9.91) shows that distance is often divided by the index of refraction in the imaging equation. For this reason, we call the "normalized" distances, such as $(z_H - z)/n$ and $(z' - z'_{H'})/n'$, the *reduced distances*.

Example 9.2
A biconvex thick lens is made of a glass with index of refraction $n = 1.5$. Its frontal surface is located at $z_1 = 40$ with a radius of curvature $R_1 = 20$. Its back surface is located at $z_2 = 43$ with a radius of curvature $R_2 = -30$. What is the focal length of this lens? Assuming that the lens is in the air, what is the transition matrix from $z = 10$ to $z' = 63$?

Solution   The transition matrix A of the lens (from z_1 to z_2) is

$$A = \begin{bmatrix} 1 & 0 \\ -\frac{(1.0-1.5)}{(-30)} & 1 \end{bmatrix} \begin{bmatrix} 1 & \frac{(43-40)}{1.5} \\ 0 & 1 \end{bmatrix} \begin{bmatrix} 1 & 0 \\ -\frac{(1.5-1.0)}{20} & 1 \end{bmatrix} = \begin{bmatrix} 0.950 & 2.000 \\ -0.041 & 0.967 \end{bmatrix}.$$

The focal length f can be found by $f = 1.0/0.041 = 24.39$. The transition matrix M from z to z' can be determined by

$$M = M^t_{z'-z_2} A M^t_{z_1-z} = \begin{bmatrix} 1 & 20 \\ 0 & 1 \end{bmatrix} A \begin{bmatrix} 1 & 30 \\ 0 & 1 \end{bmatrix} = \begin{bmatrix} 0.133 & 25.333 \\ -0.041 & -0.258 \end{bmatrix}.$$

Example 9.3
Let M be the transition matrix of an optical imaging system from z_1 to z_2, where

$$M = \begin{bmatrix} 1 & 0 \\ -K & 1 \end{bmatrix},$$

$z_1 = 120$, and $z_2 = 125$. The object space and the image space are both in the air, i.e., the index of refraction $n \approx 1$. The image of an object located at $z = 20$ is formed at $z' = 135$. What is the power K of this imaging system?

Solution   The transition matrix M from z to z' can be written as

$$M = \begin{bmatrix} 1 & 135 - 125 \\ 0 & 1 \end{bmatrix} \begin{bmatrix} 1 & 0 \\ -K & 1 \end{bmatrix} \begin{bmatrix} 1 & 120 - 20 \\ 0 & 1 \end{bmatrix} = \begin{bmatrix} 1 - 10K & 110 - 1000K \\ -K & 1 - 100K \end{bmatrix}.$$

Therefore, $y' = (1 - 10K)y + (110 - 1000K)\theta$. Since y' at z' is the image of y at z, it cannot depend on θ. We conclude that $110 - 1000K = 0$ and $K = 0.11$.

Example 9.4
Let M be the transition matrix of an optical imaging system from the object nodal point N (in the object space) to the image nodal point N' (in the image space):

$$M = \begin{bmatrix} a & b \\ -0.06 & d \end{bmatrix}.$$

Let $n = 1$ be the index of refraction of the object space, and $n' = 4/3$ be that of the image space. Determine the values of a, b, and d. What are the object focal length f and the image focal length f'?

Solution   Let us write the ray-tracing equation between the two nodal points:

$$\begin{bmatrix} y' \\ n'\theta' \end{bmatrix} = \begin{bmatrix} a & b \\ -0.06 & d \end{bmatrix} \begin{bmatrix} y \\ n\theta \end{bmatrix}.$$

Therefore, $y' = ay + bn\theta$ and $n'\theta' = -0.06y + dn\theta$. From the definition of nodal points, at N ($y = 0$) and N' ($y' = 0$), the angles θ and θ' should be equal for all rays. Therefore, we have $b = 0$ and $d = n'/n = 4/3$. Since the determinant of the matrix should be 1, $a = n/n' = 3/4$. The refracting power of the system is $K = -c = 0.06$. The object focal length is $f = n/K = 1.0/0.06 = 16.67$ and the image focal length is $f' = -n'/K = -22.22$.

9.8   Matrix description of Gaussian optical imaging systems

In the last section, we concluded that the determinant of the 2×2 transition matrix of any Gaussian optical imaging system constructed by refracting surfaces is 1. We can prove that the converse is also true: any 2×2 transition matrix with determinant 1 can be constructed from refracting surfaces.

Given a 2×2 matrix M with determinant 1,

$$M = \begin{bmatrix} a & b \\ c & d \end{bmatrix}, \tag{9.92}$$

where $ad - bc = 1$. If $c \neq 0$, it is easy to verify that M can be expressed as the product of three matrices, each implementable optically:

$$M = \begin{bmatrix} a & b \\ c & d \end{bmatrix} = \begin{bmatrix} 1 & t \\ 0 & 1 \end{bmatrix} \begin{bmatrix} 1 & 0 \\ -K & 1 \end{bmatrix} \begin{bmatrix} 1 & s \\ 0 & 1 \end{bmatrix}, \tag{9.93}$$

where $t = (a - 1)/c$, $K = -c$, and $s = (d - 1)/c$. This decomposition was used by Gauss as a very powerful tool for analyzing a general imaging system. It is therefore called the Gauss decomposition.

If $c = 0$, then $a \neq 0$ and M can be expressed as the product of four matrices, each implementable optically:

$$M = \begin{bmatrix} a & b \\ 0 & d \end{bmatrix} = \begin{bmatrix} 1 & 0 \\ p/a & 1 \end{bmatrix} \begin{bmatrix} 1 & t \\ 0 & 1 \end{bmatrix} \begin{bmatrix} 1 & 0 \\ -K & 1 \end{bmatrix} \begin{bmatrix} 1 & s \\ 0 & 1 \end{bmatrix}, \tag{9.94}$$

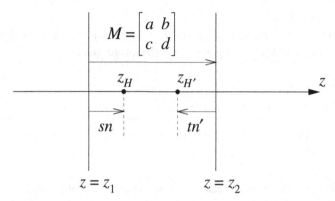

Figure 9.15. From the Gauss decomposition, a general imaging system represented by a transition matrix M from z_1 to z_2 is equivalent to a thin lens transition between two principal planes, z_H and $z_{H'}$.

where $t = (1 - a)/p$, $K = p$, $s = (1 - d)/p + (b/a)$, and p is any nonzero real number. This case of $c = 0$ represents a telescope because

$$\begin{bmatrix} y_2 \\ n_2\theta_2 \end{bmatrix} = \begin{bmatrix} a & b \\ 0 & d \end{bmatrix} \begin{bmatrix} y_1 \\ n_1\theta_1 \end{bmatrix} \tag{9.95}$$

and $\theta_2 = (n_1 d/n_2)\theta_1$ is independent of y_1. The rays from an object located at a far away distance are parallel and the object is represented by its angle relative to the optical axis.

The transition matrix M of a nontelescopic system can be represented as a product of three matrices:

$$M = \begin{bmatrix} a & b \\ c & d \end{bmatrix} = \begin{bmatrix} 1 & t \\ 0 & 1 \end{bmatrix} \begin{bmatrix} 1 & 0 \\ -K & 1 \end{bmatrix} \begin{bmatrix} 1 & s \\ 0 & 1 \end{bmatrix}. \tag{9.96}$$

If M represents the transition matrix from $z = z_1$ to $z = z_2$ (see Fig. 9.15), the equation

$$\begin{bmatrix} 1 & -t \\ 0 & 1 \end{bmatrix} M \begin{bmatrix} 1 & -s \\ 0 & 1 \end{bmatrix} = \begin{bmatrix} 1 & 0 \\ -K & 1 \end{bmatrix} \tag{9.97}$$

tells us that there are two planes located at $z_H = z_1 + sn$ and $z_{H'} = z_2 - tn'$ (where n and n' are the refraction indices of the object and image spaces) such that the transition matrix of the system from z_H to $z_{H'}$ is simply a thin lens transition matrix. These two planes are what we called the principal planes. They are usually two different planes in a general imaging system, while in the thin lens, they are the same. Let us take the thick lens as an example. Decomposing M in Eq. (9.73), we have:

$$\begin{aligned} M &= \begin{bmatrix} 1 - dK_1/n_2 & d/n_2 \\ -(K_1 + K_2) + dK_1K_2/n_2 & 1 - dK_2/n_2 \end{bmatrix} \\ &= \begin{bmatrix} 1 & -dK_2n_2/K \\ 0 & 1 \end{bmatrix} \begin{bmatrix} 1 & 0 \\ -K & 1 \end{bmatrix} \begin{bmatrix} 1 & -dK_1n_2/K \\ 0 & 1 \end{bmatrix}, \end{aligned} \tag{9.98}$$

where $K = (K_1 + K_2) - dK_1K_2/n_2$. The object principal plane is located at $dK_1n_2n_1/K$

in front of the vertex of the first refracting surface, while the image principal plane is at $dK_2n_2n_3/K$ behind the second surface. The separation of the two principal planes is $d[1 + n_2(n_1K_1 + n_3K_2)/K]$.

The idea of principal planes allows us to model a general imaging system, no matter how complex, as a black box. Let us summarize the results we have derived so far. Let n and n' be the refraction indexes of the object space and the image space, respectively. Let the object be located at z and the image at z'.

- A general, rotationally-symmetric, imaging system has two principal planes located at z_H and $z_{H'}$. The transition matrix M between these two planes is given by that of a thin lens with refractive power K:

$$M = \begin{bmatrix} 1 & 0 \\ -K & 1 \end{bmatrix}. \tag{9.99}$$

- The object focal length f and the image focal length f' are:

$$f = \frac{n}{K}, \tag{9.100}$$

$$f' = -\frac{n'}{K}. \tag{9.101}$$

- Let the object distance $s = z_H - z$, the image distance $i = z' - z_{H'}$, the object height be y, and the image height be y. They are related by:

$$y' = -\left(\frac{f}{s-f}\right)y, \tag{9.102}$$

$$\frac{n}{s} + \frac{n'}{i} = K. \tag{9.103}$$

- The object nodal point and the image nodal point are located at s_N and i_N:

$$s_N = (n - n')/K, \tag{9.104}$$

$$i_N = (n' - n)/K. \tag{9.105}$$

The six cardinal points – two focal points, two principal points, and two nodal points – plus entrance and exit pupils can replace an extremely complex optical system in many design studies. The principal points coincide with the nodal points if the index of refraction in the object space is the same as that of the image space.

9.9 Generalized ray tracing

As we pointed out earlier in this chapter, light rays are simply vectors normal to the wavefront that propagates through an optical system. So far, we have discussed methods of tracing a ray through space and the refracting surfaces. Although these methods are very important in the analysis and the design of practical optical systems, they do not directly tell us how the shape of the wavefront associated with the ray is transformed as it propagates through the system. In order to trace the wavefront deformation through an optical system, we have to characterize the local properties of the wavefront surface and find out how the properties are changed during the transfer and refraction processes.

The study of local surface properties is the subject of a branch of mathematics called differential geometry [730]. On a small neighborhood of any given point on a smooth (differentiable) surface, we can describe its shape with two principal vectors. The local surface shape is characterized by the two principal curvatures, k_1 and k_2, along these two vectors, i.e., the shape is approximately $z = (k_1 x^2 + k_2 y^2)/2$ [730, p. 202]. For a given ray, the local surface shape of its associated wavefront will, in general, have two principal vectors and two principal curvatures along these directions. (For spherical surfaces, there is only one curvature for all directions.) The question we would like to ask here is what happens to the principal vectors and curvatures of the wavefront after it goes through the transfer and refraction processes? The answer to this question was obtained by Gullstrand in 1906 and then worked out again in vector notation by Kneisly [514]. Interested readers can also find the derivation in the book by Stavroudis [899, pp. 136–179]. He called the process of tracing these wavefront parameters through an optical system, generalized ray tracing.

9.10   Physical optics

In geometrical optics, the propagation of light is described using rays that are surface normals of the wavefronts. In a region of space, we can imagine that, in general, there is a single ray passing through a given point in that region. The system of space-filling rays is called a congruence. The rays can be curves or straight lines. If, in a congruence, every ray is a straight line, we call it a rectilinear congruence. Light propagation in a homogeneous medium forms such a congruence. A collection of rays possessing an orthogonal wavefront is called a normal congruence. For example, rays coming from a point source form a normal rectilinear congruence in a homogeneous medium and the wavefronts are concentric spheres centered at the point source. It can be shown that a normal congruence remains normal after any number of refractions or reflections. This is called the Malus and Dupin theorem [1021, p. 18].

There are situations in which the light propagation deviates from its typical rectilinear path. This deviation is called *diffraction*. For example, if light propagates through a hole in an otherwise opaque screen, using geometrical optics, we can trace a straight line for any given ray passing through the hole. However, this leads to the prediction of a very sharp shadow boundary which contradicts experimental observation. In reality, the shadow boundary is a little blurry over an angular region of $\theta < \lambda/d$, where λ is the wavelength and d is the diameter of the hole, and the shadow transition exhibits dark and light bands in its fine structure. This cannot be described by geometrical optics.

In an optical imaging system, the aperture stop constricting the passage of light is a very important case where diffraction through an aperture limits the ultimate performance of the system. In order to understand how light propagates through an aperture, we have to treat light as wave functions and the resulting optical calculation is called *physical* (or wave) *optics*. For imaging applications, the most important subject in physical optics is the study of diffraction through an aperture.

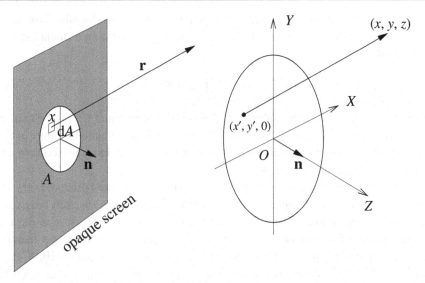

Figure 9.16. Diffraction by an aperture in an opaque screen.

9.10.1 Scalar and vector theories of diffraction

In 1678, Huygens proposed a concept of light wave propagation to the French Academy of Science. He suggested that the wavefront at time $t + \Delta t$ can be computed by considering each point on the wavefront at time t as a new secondary (point) source and calculating the envelope of all the wavefronts from these secondary sources. This concept of wave propagation is called the Huygens principle. More than 130 years later, by heuristically modifying the amplitude and phase of the secondary wavefronts, Fresnel was able to calculate the diffraction pattern very accurately. Although the empirical procedures proposed by Huygens and Fresnel work well, rigorous formulations from more basic theories were needed to "explain" why they worked. There were several attempts to put the Huygens–Fresnel principle on a firm theoretical ground, such as deriving it from Maxwell's equations. Kirchhoff was the first one to formulate a diffraction theory. His theory treated the electromagnetic field as a scalar function. Kirchhoff's formulation was shown to involve inconsistent boundary conditions. Rayleigh and Sommerfeld later modified the formulation to remove the inconsistency. The Kirchhoff–Rayleigh–Sommerfeld scalar diffraction theory works very well for optical applications because the wavelength is very small compared with the sizes of aperture in the system. Referring to Fig. 9.16, the theory can be summarized by the Kirchhoff–Rayleigh–Sommerfeld diffraction formulas [453, p. 431]:

$$V(\mathbf{r}) = \frac{k}{2\pi i} \int_A \frac{e^{ikr}}{r}\left(1 + \frac{i}{kr}\right)\frac{\mathbf{n}\cdot\mathbf{r}}{r}V(\mathbf{x})dA, \tag{9.106}$$

where V is the scalar electric or magnetic field, $\mathbf{r}$ is a vector from a point $\mathbf{x}$ on the aperture to an observation point in the diffracted region, r is its length, dA is an element of the aperture A, and $\mathbf{n}$ is the unit vector pointing to the diffraction region and perpendicular to the aperture at point $\mathbf{x}$. Since electromagnetic fields are vectors fields, the scalar approximation should be extended to deal with the vector nature of the fields, because each vector component is coupled with other components and cannot be treated as a scalar. Symthe formulated such a vectorial diffraction theory and the Symthe–Kirchhoff diffraction formula [453, p. 438] is as follows:

$$E(r) = \frac{1}{2\pi} \nabla \times \int_A [n \times E(x)] \frac{e^{ikr}}{r} dA, \tag{9.107}$$

where $E(x)$ is the total tangential electric field in the aperture and $E(r)$ is the total electric field in the diffraction region. Experiments showed that for a diffraction aperture of diameter d, the Symthe–Kirchhoff formula is quite accurate for $\lambda/d < \pi$, but it breaks down seriously when λ/d is larger than π (see [453, p. 446]).

In spite of its simplistic assumption, the scalar diffraction theory produces very accurate results for optical imaging applications if the diffraction aperture is relatively large compared with the wavelength and if the diffraction field is not observed too close to the aperture, i.e., the distance from the observation point to the aperture is much larger than the size of the aperture [352, p. 32]. This is supported by experimental data [420, 874]. Let us consider diffraction through an aperture on a planar screen of infinite extent. Let the z-axis be perpendicular to the screen and the aperture be located at $z = 0$. Therefore, a point on the aperture is specified by (x', y'). Light illuminating the aperture is coming from the negative z-direction and the half-space corresponding to $z > 0$ is called the diffraction region where light has propagated through the aperture opening. We can calculate the field at a point (x, y, z) in the diffraction region $z > 0$ by Eq. (9.106):

$$V(x, y, z) = \frac{k}{2\pi i} \int_A \frac{e^{ikr}}{r} \left(1 + \frac{i}{kr}\right) \frac{n \cdot r}{r} V(x', y') dx' dy', \tag{9.108}$$

where $r = [x - x', y - y', z]^T$, $r = \sqrt{(x - x')^2 + (y - y')^2 + z^2}$ and $n = [0, 0, 1]^T$. In order to use scalar diffraction theory, we assume that the diffraction field is only observed from such a far distance from the aperture that

$$n \cdot r/r = z/r \approx 1. \tag{9.109}$$

We also have to assume that the wavelength is much smaller than the aperture size and therefore much smaller than r. Therefore, $1 + i/kr = 1 + i\lambda/2\pi r \approx 1$, and

$$V(x, y, z) \approx \frac{k}{2\pi i} \int_A \frac{e^{ikr}}{r} V(x', y') dx' dy'. \tag{9.110}$$

It is interesting to see that except for the scale factor $k/2\pi i$, Eq. (9.110) is clearly an expression of the Huygens principle. Each point (x', y') on the aperture emits a spherical wave e^{ikr}/r that linearly adds up in the diffraction field. We can further simplify Eq. (9.110) by substituting $1/r \approx 1/z$:

$$V(x, y, z) \approx \frac{k}{2\pi i} \int_A \frac{e^{ikr}}{z} V(x', y') dx' dy'. \tag{9.111}$$

Note that e^{ikr} cannot be replaced by e^{ikz} because k is a very large number and the smaller difference between r and z is amplified so much that it will introduce a large error in the phase of the scalar field.

The exact evaluation of diffraction fields through Eq. (9.111) can be done quickly by computers. However, for many imaging applications, there are some approximate evaluation methods that can lead us to very interesting results, and they will be discussed here. The first approximation is called the *Fresnel approximation* and it assumes that

$$r = \sqrt{(x - x')^2 + (y - y')^2 + z^2} \tag{9.112}$$

$$= z\sqrt{1 + \left(\frac{x - x'}{z}\right)^2 + \left(\frac{y - y'}{z}\right)^2} \tag{9.113}$$

$$\approx z\left[1 + \frac{1}{2}\left(\frac{x - x'}{z}\right)^2 + \frac{1}{2}\left(\frac{y - y'}{z}\right)^2\right]. \tag{9.114}$$

With this approximation, Eq. (9.111) becomes:

$$
\begin{aligned}
V(x, y, z) &\approx \frac{e^{ikz}}{i\lambda z} \int_A V(x', y') \exp\left\{i\frac{k}{2z}\left[(x - x')^2 + (y - y')^2\right]\right\} dx'dy' \\
&\approx \frac{e^{ikz}}{i\lambda z} \exp\left[i\frac{k}{2z}(x^2 + y^2)\right] \int_A V(x', y') \exp\left[i\frac{k}{2z}(x'^2 + y'^2)\right] \\
&\quad \times \exp\left[-i\frac{k}{z}(xx' + yy')\right] dx'dy'.
\end{aligned} \tag{9.115}
$$

The region where Eq. (9.114) is a good approximation is called the region of Fresnel diffraction, and the diffraction field calculated with Eq. (9.115) is called Fresnel diffraction. The Fresnel diffraction region extends from a certain distance (approximately 10 times of the diameter of the aperture) to infinity and its range is dependent on the degree of accuracy required.

Equation (9.115) can be further simplified by another approximation (the *Fraunhofer approximation*) when the observation distance is further away from the aperture (z very large) and

$$\frac{k}{2z}(x'^2 + y'^2) \approx 0 \tag{9.116}$$

for any (x', y') on the aperture. Since $k = 2\pi/\lambda$ is very large for visible wavelengths, the distance z at which the approximation is good is indeed very long. For example, if $\lambda = 500$ nm and the radius of the aperture is 1 cm, then z has to be tens or hundreds of kilometers. Using the Fraunhofer approximation, Eq. (9.115) becomes:

$$V(x, y, z) \approx \frac{e^{ikz}}{i\lambda z} \exp\left[i\frac{k}{2z}(x^2 + y^2)\right] \int_A V(x', y') \exp\left[-i\frac{k}{z}(xx' + yy')\right] dx'dy' \tag{9.117}$$

$$\approx \frac{e^{ikz}}{i\lambda z} \exp\left[i\frac{k}{2z}(x^2 + y^2)\right] \int_A V(x', y') \exp\left[-i2\pi(f_x x' + f_y y')\right] dx'dy', \tag{9.118}$$

where $f_x = x/(\lambda z)$ and $f_y = y/(\lambda z)$. This means that the diffraction field $V(x, y, z)$ at a plane normal to the z-axis is proportional to the Fourier transform of the aperture field $V(x', y')$.

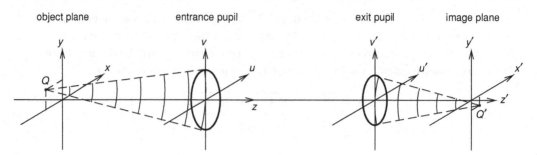

Figure 9.17. A diffraction-limited imaging system converts a diverging spherical wave incident on the entrance pupil into a converging spherical wave leaving the exit pupil.

9.10.2 The field impulse response of an imaging system

According to geometrical optics, a stigmatic (sharp) imaging system will take diverging rays emanating from any point source (in object space) and bend them in such a way that an infinite number of these rays will converge to a single point (in image space). In physical optics, light emanating from any point source is treated as a perfect, diverging, spherical wave, and the function of an ideal imaging system is to convert that into a perfect, converging, spherical wave. Such an ideal imaging system is called a diffraction-limited system for the reason soon to be explained. Figure 9.17 shows the conceptual diagram of such a system. In any physically realizable imaging system, light can only pass through a finite aperture. If we look back into the exit pupil from the image plane, the converging spherical wave will be diffracted when it passes through the finite exit pupil. The diffracted field on the image plane can be calculated from the Huygens–Fresnel principle in Eq. (9.110). The result of this type of calculation reveals that the image of a point source by the ideal imaging system is not a single point, but a fairly complex diffraction pattern. For this reason, the performance of an ideal imaging system is limited by wave diffraction through the aperture and the system is said to be diffraction-limited. When the aperture has a circular shape, at the image plane where the spherical wave is "supposed" to converge to a single point, the pattern is a bright central disk, surrounded by many rings of diminishing intensity. The pattern is called the Airy pattern. In this section, we will study how to calculate the image of a point source from scalar diffraction theory. The image of a point source of unit intensity is called the point spread function of the imaging system. The Fourier transform of the point spread function is the transfer function of the optical imaging system.

Referring to Fig. 9.17 a point source Q, located at (x_0, y_0, z_0) on the object plane, is imaged to Q' located at (x'_0, y'_0, z'_0) on the image plane. The mapping is calculated according to Gaussian optics. The planes u–v and u'–v' are the entrance pupil plane and the exit pupil plane, respectively. If the optical imaging system is an ideal (diffraction-limited) system, the wavefront surface on the exit pupil will be a perfect spherical wave converging to the point Q'. In a real imaging system, the aperture stop is usually not the first limiting aperture. A rigorous solution for the diffraction field at point Q' thus requires a detailed description of the optical structures of the system. However, even if the description is available, the calculation will be very complicated and time consuming. Empirical data seem to show that

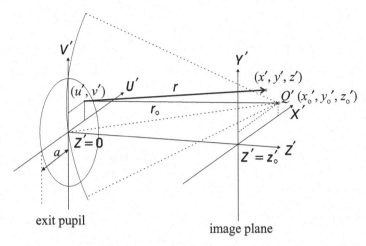

Figure 9.18. The coordinates of the exit pupil and the image plane for OTF calculation.

it is possible to obtain an adequate answer by assuming that diffraction occurs only from the exit pupil to the image plane and that light propagation in other parts of the system can be treated by geometrical optics [352, p. 103]. This is the approach we use in the following calculation.

From Eq. (9.110), the diffracted field $V(x', y', z', x_0, y_0, z_0)$ at any point (x', y', z') in the image space can be calculated from the aperture field $V(u', v', x_0, y_0, z_0)$ at the exit pupil, assuming that the exit pupil is located at $z' = 0$ (see Fig. 9.18). It should be noted that both fields are functions of the location of the point object source (x_0, y_0, z_0).

$$V(x', y', z', x_0, y_0, z_0) \approx \frac{k}{2\pi i} \int_{\text{exit pupil}} \frac{e^{ikr}}{r} V(u', v', x_0, y_0, z_0) du' dv', \quad (9.119)$$

where $r = \sqrt{(x' - u')^2 + (y' - v')^2 + z'^2}$ is the distance from a point (u', v') on the exit pupil to the point at (x', y', z') in the image space. For a diffraction-limited system, the aperture field is a spherical wave converging to Q' at (x'_0, y'_0, z'_0) on the image plane. Therefore, we express the aperture field $V(u', v', x_0, y_0, z_0)$ as a product of an ideal converging spherical wave $\exp(-ikr_0)/r_0$ (see Fig. 9.18) and P that represents the departure from the ideal wavefront:

$$V(u', v', x_0, y_0, z_0) = U(x_0, y_0, z_0)P(u', v', x_0, y_0, z_0)\frac{e^{-ikr_0}}{r_0} \quad (9.120)$$

where $r_0 = \sqrt{(x'_0 - u')^2 + (y'_0 - v')^2 + z'^2_0}$ is the distance from a point (u', v') on the exit pupil to the ideal image point Q' at (x'_0, y'_0, z'_0), and $U(x_0, y_0, z_0)$ is a constant proportional to the intensity of the point source, its magnitude being chosen so that $P(0, 0, x_0, y_0, z_0) = 1$. If the system is diffraction-limited, $P(u', v', x_0, y_0, z_0) = 1$ for (u', v') on the exit pupil, and $P(u', v', x_0, y_0, z_0) = 0$ elsewhere. If the exit pupil is a circular aperture with a radius of a, then $P(u', v', x_0, y_0, z_0) = 1$ for $u'^2 + v'^2 \leq a^2$ and $P(u', v', x_0, y_0, z_0) = 0$ for $u'^2 + v'^2 > a^2$. Thus P is a uniform disk of amplitude 1 inside the circle and 0 outside. The function $P(u', v', x_0, y_0, z_0)$ is therefore called the (generalized) pupil function. If P is not a constant, we can express it as

$$P(u', v', x_o, y_o, z_o) = A(u', v', x_o, y_o, z_o) \exp[ikW(u', v', x_o, y_o, z_o)], \quad (9.121)$$

where A is its magnitude and W is its phase. A is called the apodization function and W is the *wavefront aberration*. Equation (9.119) becomes:

$$V(x', y', z', x_o, y_o, z_o) \approx \frac{k}{2\pi i} \int \frac{e^{ik(r-r_o)}}{rr_o} U(x_o, y_o, z_o) P(u', v', x_o, y_o, z_o) du' dv'. \quad (9.122)$$

Let d be the distance from the point (x', y', z') in the image space to the ideal image point Q', i.e., $d^2 = (x' - x_o')^2 + (y' - y_o')^2 + (z' - z_o')^2$, the phase function $ik(r - r_o)$ can be simplified as follows:

$$r^2 = (x' - u')^2 + (y' - v')^2 + z'^2 \quad (9.123)$$

$$= (x' - x_o' + x_o' - u')^2 + (y' - y_o' + y_o' - v')^2 + (z' - z_o' + z_o')^2 \quad (9.124)$$

$$= [(x_o' - u')^2 + (y_o' - v')^2 + z_o'^2] + [(x' - x_o')^2 + (y' - y_o')^2 + (z' - z_o')^2] \quad (9.125)$$

$$+ 2(x' - x_o')(x_o' - u') + 2(y' - y_o')(y_o' - v') + 2(z' - z_o')z_o' \quad (9.126)$$

$$= r_o^2 + d^2 + 2(x' - x_o')x_o' + 2(y' - y_o')y_o' + 2(z' - z_o')z_o'$$

$$- 2[(x' - x_o')u' + (y' - y_o')v'] \quad (9.127)$$

$$= r_o^2 + d^2 + 2b - 2[(x' - x_o')u' + (y' - y_o')v'], \quad (9.128)$$

where $b = (x' - x_o')x_o' + (y' - y_o')y_o' + (z' - z_o')z_o'$ is independent of the integration variables, u' and v'. For (x', y', z') not too far from (x_o', y_o', z_o'), we can make the approximation:

$$r = r_o \sqrt{1 + \frac{d^2}{r_o^2} + \frac{2b}{r_o^2} - \frac{2[(x' - x_o')u' + (y' - y_o')v']}{r_o^2}} \quad (9.129)$$

$$\approx r_o \left\{ 1 + \frac{d^2}{2r_o^2} + \frac{b}{r_o^2} - \frac{[(x' - x_o')u' + (y' - y_o')v']}{r_o^2} \right\} \quad (9.130)$$

$$= r_o + \frac{d^2}{2r_o} + \frac{b}{r_o} - \frac{[(x' - x_o')u' + (y' - y_o')v']}{r_o}. \quad (9.131)$$

We will also assume that the field is not observed too close to the aperture and the Fresnel approximation of Eq. (9.114) is valid:

$$\frac{e^{ik(r-r_o)}}{rr_o} \approx \frac{e^{ikd^2/2z_o'} e^{ikb/z_o'}}{z' z_o'} e^{-ik[(x'-x_o')u'+(y'-y_o')v']/z_o'}. \quad (9.132)$$

Equation (9.122) then becomes

$$V(x', y', z', x_o, y_o, z_o)$$

$$\approx \frac{U k e^{ikd^2/2z_o'} e^{ikb/z_o'}}{i2\pi z' z_o'} \int P(u', v', x_o, y_o, z_o) e^{-ik[(x'-x_o')u'+(y'-y_o')v']/z_o'} du' dv', \quad (9.133)$$

In imaging applications, the physical quantity we actually measure is the energy flow of the imaging light, rather than the electromagnetic field strength itself. It can be shown [124,

Section 8.4] that the radiant flux density[2] of natural light (incoherent) source for an imaging system of moderate (not too small) aperture is proportional to $|V|^2 = VV^*$, where V^* is the complex conjugate of V. Therefore, the two phase factors, $e^{ikd^2/2z_0'}e^{ikb/z_0'}$, will not affect the image irradiance if we restrict the object domain to be around a small neighborhood of (x_0, y_0, z_0) and consider only the imaging between a plane $z = z_0$ in object space and a plane at z' in image space. Under this condition, Eq. (9.133) shows that the imaging system has a "space-invariant" point spread function because the field distribution in image space depends approximately on the distance to the ideal image point, $\xi = x' - x_0'$ and $\eta = y' - y_0'$. Except for the proportionality factor (denoted as s), the point spread function $\tilde{g}(\xi, \eta)$ of the eletromagnetic *field* is simply the Fourier transform of the scaled pupil function evaluated for (x_0, y_0, z_0):

$$\tilde{g}(\xi, \eta) \approx \frac{s}{\lambda z' z_0'} \int P(u', v')e^{-ik[\xi u' + \eta v']/z_0'}du'dv' \tag{9.134}$$

$$= (s\lambda z_0'/z') \int P(-\lambda z_0' f_x, -\lambda z_0' f_y)e^{i2\pi(f_x\xi + f_y\eta)}df_x df_y. \tag{9.135}$$

The system transfer function $\tilde{G}(f_x, f_y)$ is therefore a scaled version of the pupil function $P(-\lambda z_0' f_x, -\lambda z_0' f_y)$. We can further simplify the expressions to make them more convenient to use. First, we can define the pupil function in a reflected coordinate system, i.e., reversing the u'- and v'-axes in Fig. 9.17 and removing the negative signs. Second, the pupil function is usually defined to be equal to 1.0 at the origin; if we assume that the zero spatial frequency (the DC component) is always transferred through the system, we can define the system transfer function as $G(f_x, f_y)$, where $G(0, 0) = 1.0 = P(0, 0)$, then

$$G(f_x, f_y) = P(\lambda z_0' f_x, \lambda z_0' f_y) \tag{9.136}$$

and the corresponding field impulse response function is

$$g(\xi, \eta) = \int P(\lambda z_0' f_x, \lambda z_0' f_y)e^{i2\pi(f_x\xi + f_y\eta)}df_x df_y. \tag{9.137}$$

9.10.3 The optical transfer function (OTF)

Having derived the impulse response function for the electromagnetic *field*, our next task is to derive the point spread function for the image *irradiance* (radiant flux per unit area). In order to do so, we have to consider the coherence property of incident light. There are two aspects of coherence to be considered: temporal coherence and spatial coherence. Light coming from a source at different time instants can be well correlated or can be uncorrelated (temporal coherence). For example, if the source is a thermal source, the radiant intensity being subject to random thermal fluctuation, the source can be regarded as an incoherent source over the time interval in which most image sensors integrate the signals. At the other extreme, if the source is from a continuous-wave laser, it might have to be considered as a coherent source because the phase variation can be a fairly predictable function of

---

[2] The radiant flux has to be measured as a time-averaged quantity. The measurement time is assumed to be much, much longer than a period of the highest frequency of the light considered.

time. The other type of coherence is spatial coherence. Light coming from two spatial locations can be well correlated in their phase. For example, in the last section, we assumed that a light wave leaving the exit pupil is a perfect spherical wave for a diffraction-limited system. The electromagnetic fields at any two spatial points on the exit pupil are thus assumed to be perfectly correlated. This is a consequence of the source being an ideal point source. If instead, we use a back-illuminated pinhole of finite size as the "point source", the electromagnetic field on the exit pupil will become partially coherent, and the irradiance on the image plane will be different [868].

From Eq. (9.133), we can calculate the point spread function, h, in image irradiance. First, let us simplify the notation by rewriting Eq. (9.133) as:

$$V(\xi, \eta) \approx V_0 \iint P(u', v') \exp\left[-i\frac{2\pi}{\lambda z_0'}(u'\xi + v'\eta)\right] du'dv', \qquad (9.138)$$

where the dependence of V, V_0, and P on (x_0, y_0, z_0) is understood and omitted. The coordinates $\xi = x' - x_0'$ and $\eta = y' - y_0'$ are centered at the Gaussian image point (x_0', y_0'):

$$h(\xi, \eta) = VV^* = V_0V_0^* \iiiint P(u, v)P^*(u', v')$$

$$\exp\left\{i\frac{2\pi}{\lambda z_0'}[(u' - u)\xi + (v' - v)\eta]\right\} du\,dv\,du'\,dv'. \qquad (9.139)$$

Making the changes of variables, $s = u' - u$, $t = v' - v$, $v_x = s/(\lambda z_0')$, and $v_y = t/(\lambda z_0')$,

$$h(\xi, \eta) = V_0V_0^* \iint \left[\iint P(u, v)P^*(u + s, v + t)du\,dv\right] \exp\left[i\frac{2\pi}{\lambda z_0'}(s\xi + t\eta)\right] ds\,dt \qquad (9.140)$$

$$= h_0 \iint \left[\iint P(u, v)P^*(u + \lambda z_0'v_x, v + \lambda z_0'v_y)du\,dv\right] \exp\left[i2\pi(v_x\xi + v_y\eta)\right] dv_x\,dv_y, \qquad (9.141)$$

where $h_0 = \lambda^2 z_0'^2 V_0'V_0^*$. The image irradiance function $h(\xi, \eta)$ is the image of a point object Q. If the light coming from any other point in object space is not correlated with that from Q, then $h(\xi, \eta)$ can be treated as the point spread function of the system because the radiant flux from different object points can be added together to find the image irradiance. This is almost always the case in imaging applications involving natural lighting. However, light coherence is a continuum, ranging from complete incoherence to complete coherence. A general treatment should consider all light sources as characterized by partial coherence, which is a subject that will take us too far away from our immediate interest here. Readers who are interested in the subject can consult to references [98, 124, 353, 631].

The system transfer function $H(v_x, v_y)$ of the optical imaging system is the Fourier transform of $h(\xi, \eta)$:

$$H(v_x, v_y) = \lambda^2 z_0'^2 V_0V_0^* \iint P(u, v)P^*(u + \lambda z_0'v_x, v + \lambda z_0'v_y)du\,dv. \qquad (9.142)$$

Again, it is often more convenient to normalize the transfer function with respect to the

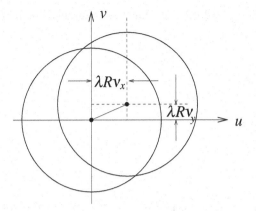

Figure 9.19. The autocorrelation of the pupil function.

zero frequency component. The normalized transfer function is called the OTF:

$$OTF(v_x, v_y) = \frac{H(v_x, v_y)}{H(0, 0)} = \frac{\iint P(u, v)P^*(u + \lambda R v_x, v + \lambda R v_y) du\, dv}{\iint P(u, v)P^*(u, v) du\, dv}, \qquad (9.143)$$

where $R = z_0'$ is the distance from the exit pupil to the Gaussain image plane. In the diffraction-limited system, the wavefront emerging from the exit pupil is a perfect sphere centered at the Gaussian image point (x_0', y_0', z_0'). This sphere is called the reference sphere and its radius is R. Equation (9.143) shows that the OTF is simply the autocorrelation of the pupil function, P, and its complex conjugate, P^*. If the pupil is a circular aperture of radius a, any frequency v, such that $\lambda R v > 2a$, will be completely cut off by the imaging system because the autocorrelation of the pupil will be zero once P and P^* are separated by a distance greater than twice its radius (see Fig. 9.19).

The cut-off frequency, v_c of the system is:

$$v_c = \frac{2a}{\lambda R} \approx \frac{2a}{\lambda f} = \frac{1}{\lambda F}, \qquad (9.144)$$

where f is the focal length of the system and F is the ratio of focal length to the diameter of the pupil. F is known as the f-number of the lens. If the focal length is eight times the pupil diameter, we say the f-number is $f/8$. As we will see later, the f-number is a key parameter in determining the light-collecting capacity or "image brightness" of an optical system.

9.11 Problems

9.1 What are the names and definitions of the six cardinal points, H, H', F, F', N, and N', of an imaging system?

9.2 Let M be the transition matrix of an optical imaging system from z_1 to z_2, where

$$M = \begin{bmatrix} 1.0 & 0.0 \\ -0.02 & 1.0 \end{bmatrix},$$

$z_1 = 20$ and $z_2 = 30$. The object space and the image space are both in the air, i.e., the index of refraction $n \approx 1$ (see Fig. 9.20). Where are the six cardinal points, H, H', F, F', N, and N'?

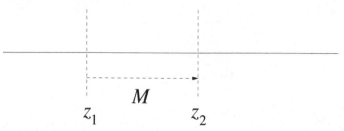

Figure 9.20.

9.3   A spherical surface with a radius of 0.5 is located at $z_2 = 22$ (see Fig. 9.21). The index of refraction on the left is $n = 1.0$ and on the right is $n = 1.5$. Find the transition matrix from $z_1 = 10$ to $z_3 = 40$. Where are the object focal point and the image focal point?

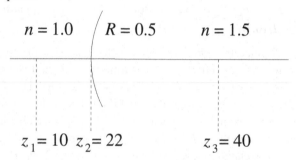

Figure 9.21.

9.4   The nodal points, N, N', and the principal points, H, H', of an optical imaging system are located at $z_N, z_{N'}, z_H$, and $z_{H'}$, respectively. Let n and n' be the indices of refraction of the object space and the image space. Given that $z_N - z_H = z_{N'} - z_{H'} = u > 0$, find the transition matrix M from z_N to $z_{N'}$, with the elements of M expressed only in terms of u, n and n'.

9.5   The object space and the image space of a given Gaussian imaging system are both in the air. Let the z-axis be the optical axis of the system. An object with height $y = 1$ is located at z. Its image is formed at z' with height $y' = -0.1$. A ray radiated from (z, y), at an angle of 0.01 radians relative to the z-axis, arrives at (z', y') at an angle of -0.12 radians. Determine the transition matrix M from z to z'.

9.6   A telescope has an objective lens, a field lens, and an eye lens, with focal lengths f_1, f_2, and f_3, respectively (the telescope is used in the air) (see Fig. 9.22). All three lenses are considered as thin lenses. The objective lens is the outermost lens facing the objects. The field lens is located at a distance of f_1 behind the objective lens, and the eye lens is at a distance of f_3 behind the field lens. The objective lens is known to be the limiting aperture of the telescope, and therefore its image formed by the field lens and the eye lens is the exit pupil. If a user's eye is placed at the exit pupil, he/she can see the entire field of view visible by the telescope.

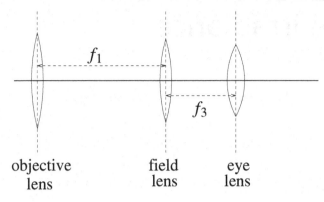

objective
lens

field
lens

eye
lens

Figure 9.22.

(a) Find the location of the exit pupil of the telescope.
(b) The distance from the eye lens to the exit pupil is called the eye distance (or eye relief). It is often desirable to have a longer eye distance so that users with eye glasses can see the entire field of view through the telescope without having to place their eyes too close to the eye lens. In order to increase the eye distance, should we choose a field lens with a longer or shorter focal length?
(c) Prove that the size of the exit pupil does not depend on the focal length of the field lens, f_2.
(d) What is the angular magnification of the telescope?
(Hint: Let the exit pupil be located at a distance r behind the eye lens. Write the transition matrix from the objective lens to the exit pupil. Since the exit pupil is the image of the objective lens, we can solve for r in terms of f_1, f_2, and f_3. To find the angular magnification, we can write the transition matrix from an object to the exit pupil and the ratio θ'/θ is the angular magnification. Note that the telescope is an instrument that is not meant to produce a real image of the scene. Therefore, you will find the the the focal length of the telescope is infinity and you should not try to find the angular magnification from the formula that uses the system focal length.)

10 Lens aberrations and image irradiance

10.1 Introduction

In this chapter, we will study lens aberrations and their effects on light distributed on the image plane. We would like to calculate the image irradiance for a given optical imaging system, especially when there is defocus because this is the most frequent problem in consumer images. First, we derive the relation between the scene radiance and the image irradiance for an ideal optical imaging system which has no lens aberrations and is in perfect focus. Next, we study how the distribution of light on the image plane is affected by some defects in the optical imaging process. The theory of wavefront aberrations is formulated and it is used to calculate the point spread function (PSF) and the OTF in the presence of focus error. Results from geometrical optics and physical optics are compared.

Some terms are used very often in the discussion of image light distribution. Sometimes, however, they are defined differently by different authors. We will define some of these terms here based on the international standard as specified in ISO 9334. The image of an ideal point object is a two-dimensional function, $f(x,y)$, on the image plane, on which the coordinates (x,y) are defined. If we normalize this function so that it integrates to 1, the normalized $f(x,y)$ is the PSF of the imaging system. The Fourier transform of the PSF is the OTF, $F(v_x,v_y)$, where v_x and v_y are the horizontal and vertical spatial frequencies in the image plane. By the definition of the PSF, the OTF is equal to 1 at zero frequency, i.e., $F(0,0) = 1$. An OTF can be a complex function. The modulus (i.e., the absolute value) of the OTF is called the modulation transfer function (MTF), and the argument (i.e., the phase) is called the phase transfer function (PTF). The normalized image of an ideal line (infinitely long with no width) is called the line spread function (LSF). It is defined as the integral of the PSF along the line direction. For example, if the ideal line is along the y-direction, then

$$LSF(x) = \int_{-\infty}^{\infty} PSF(x, y)\mathrm{d}y. \tag{10.1}$$

The normalized image of an ideal step edge (0 on one side and 1 on the other side, after normalization) is called the edge spread function (ESF). It is defined as the integral of the LSF. For example, if the step edge is along the y direction, then the $ESF(x)$ is defined as

$$ESF(x) = \int_{-\infty}^{x} LSF(x')\mathrm{d}x'. \tag{10.2}$$

Strictly speaking, these functions are most useful and meaningful only for linear, shift-invariant systems. However, for a fixed operating point and signals with small to moderate modulation (say, 35% contrast), the concept of the MTF is often used to characterize a nonlinear system as well. For example, the photographic MTF (ANSI/PIMA IT2.39-1988) of a film is often given in product data sheets. For these applications, it is very important to compare data using a comparable measurement procedure.

10.2   Radiometry of imaging

One of the most important relations in imaging is the radiometric relation between the scene radiance, L, and the image irradiance, E'. We will call this relation the *image irradiance equation*. Because it is so useful, we will first summarize some of the key points in this relation before we derive it from Gaussian optics. When the object distance is much larger than the focal length of the system, we have the following relations:

- For a given imaging system, the image irradiance, E', is proportional to the scene radiance, L.
- For a Lambertian surface parallel to the lens, the image irradiance falls off as $\cos^4 \theta$, where θ is the off-axis angle of the object.
- The image irradiance is proportional to the size of the entrance pupil of the imaging system. (The larger the entrance pupil is, the more light a camera collects.)
- The image irradiance is inversely proportional to the square of the focal length of the imaging system. (The lateral magnification is proportional to the focal length. The longer the focal length is, the larger the image area is over which the collected light flux is distributed.)

An imaging system collects a cone of rays radiating from an elemental area dA in the object space of the entrance pupil. Figure 10.1 shows the geometry of radiant energy flowing through an imaging system. The elemental area dA is assumed to be a Lambertian source

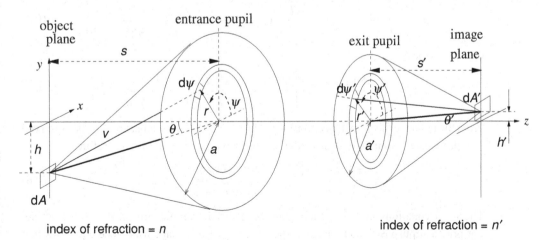

Figure 10.1. Radiant flux through an imaging system.

with radiance L and its surface normal is parallel to the optical axis of the system. The elemental area dA is located at a distance h away from the optical axis. Its image dA' is located at a distance h' off axis. Let s be the distance from dA to the entrance pupil, and s' be the distance of dA' from the exit pupil. Let n and n' be the indices of refraction of the object space and the image space, respectively. Let θ and θ' be the angle between the chief ray and the optical axis in the object space and the image space. Let a and a' be the radii of the entrance pupil and the exit pupil. The total flux, $d\Phi_{en}$, collected by the entrance pupil from dA can be calculated by integrating the small area on the ring over ψ and r. The vector, $\mathbf{v}$, from dA to the small ring area is $[r\cos\psi, r\sin\psi - h, s]^T$. Therefore, the cosine of the angle β between the z-axis (normal to the pupil plane and dA) and the vector $\mathbf{v}$ can be calculated from $\cos\beta = s/\|\mathbf{v}\|$, where $\|\mathbf{v}\|$ is the length of the vector $\mathbf{v}$. The total collected flux, $d\Phi_{en}$, is:

$$\begin{aligned}
d\Phi_{en} &= L \int_{r=0}^{a} \int_{\psi=0}^{2\pi} \frac{r\,d\psi\,dr \cdot \cos\beta}{\|\mathbf{v}\|^2} \cdot dA \cdot \cos\beta \\
&= L \cdot dA \cdot \int_{r=0}^{a} \int_{\psi=0}^{2\pi} \frac{r s^2 d\psi\,dr}{[r^2 \cos^2\psi + (r\sin\psi - h)^2 + s^2]^2} \\
&= L \cdot dA \cdot \int_{r=0}^{a} \frac{2\pi(s^2 + h^2 + r^2)r s^2 dr}{[(s^2 + h^2 + r^2)^2 - 4h^2 r^2]^{3/2}} \\
&= \frac{\pi L}{2}\left[1 - \frac{s^2 + h^2 - a^2}{\sqrt{(s^2 + h^2 + a^2)^2 - 4h^2 a^2}}\right]dA.
\end{aligned}$$

We can also write a similar equation in image space:

$$d\Phi_{ex} = \frac{\pi L'}{2}\left[1 - \frac{s'^2 + h'^2 - a'^2}{\sqrt{(s'^2 + h'^2 + a'^2)^2 - 4h'^2 a'^2}}\right]dA'. \tag{10.3}$$

Assuming that there is no loss in the imaging system, $d\Phi_{ex} = d\Phi_{en}$ and the image irradiance, E', at dA' is

$$E' = \frac{d\Phi_{ex}}{dA'} = \frac{d\Phi_{en}}{dA'} = \frac{\pi L}{2}\left[1 - \frac{s^2 + h^2 - a^2}{\sqrt{(s^2 + h^2 + a^2)^2 - 4h^2 a^2}}\right]\frac{dA}{dA'}, \tag{10.4}$$

or, equivalently,

$$E' = \frac{d\Phi_{ex}}{dA'} = \frac{\pi L'}{2}\left[1 - \frac{s'^2 + h'^2 - a'^2}{\sqrt{(s'^2 + h'^2 + a'^2)^2 - 4h'^2 a'^2}}\right]. \tag{10.5}$$

From the radiance theorem in Section 3.4, we know that the basic radiance L/n^2 is conserved as it propagates through lossless media, and we have $L/n^2 = L'/n'^2$. Therefore,

$$E' = \frac{\pi L}{2}\left(\frac{n'}{n}\right)^2\left[1 - \frac{s'^2 + h'^2 - a'^2}{\sqrt{(s'^2 + h'^2 + a'^2)^2 - 4h'^2 a'^2}}\right]. \tag{10.6}$$

The above equations are quite general, but the required quantities are not easily measurable. For practical purposes, there are two special cases of the image irradiance equations that are more useful. These are discussed in the next two sections.

10.2.1 On-axis image irradiances

The first special case of Eq. (10.6) is when the object is located on axis, i.e., $h = 0$ and $h' = 0$:

$$E' = \pi L \left(\frac{n'}{n}\right)^2 \left[\frac{a'^2}{s'^2 + a'^2}\right] = \pi \left(\frac{L}{n^2}\right) (n' \sin \alpha')^2, \tag{10.7}$$

with

$$\sin \alpha' = \frac{a'}{\sqrt{s'^2 + a'^2}}, \tag{10.8}$$

where α is the half-angle of the cone of light rays from the exit pupil to the image point on axis. From Eq. (10.7), we can see that the image irradiance is proportional to the square of the quantity, $n' \sin \alpha'$. This quantity is called the *numerical aperture* (NA) of the system:

$$NA = n' \sin \alpha'. \tag{10.9}$$

The larger the numerical aperature, the brighter the image. Therefore, it is often used to specify the speed of the optical imaging system. The other quantity that is also often used to quantify the speed is the relative aperture, $\mathcal{F}$, commonly known as the f-number. It is defined as

$$\mathcal{F} = \frac{1}{2n' \sin \alpha'} = \frac{1}{2(NA)}. \tag{10.10}$$

When the object point is located at infinity, the distance, s', between the exit pupil and the image point is often assumed to be f', the image focal length, and

$$F = \frac{1}{2n' \sin \alpha'} \approx \frac{1}{2n' \sin[\tan^{-1}(a'/f')]} \approx \frac{1}{n'} \left(\frac{f'}{2a'}\right) = \frac{1}{m_p n} \left(\frac{f}{2a}\right), \tag{10.11}$$

where $m_p = a'/a$ is the pupil magnification. (Note that we use $\mathcal{F}$ for the relative aperture of the general case, and F for the special case when the object is located at infinity.) For an imaging system in which the index of refraction of the object space and the image space are both in the air, $n = n' \approx 1$ and $F \approx f'/D'$, where $D' = 2a'$ is the diameter of the exit pupil. It should be noted that it is also often defined as $F = f/D$, where D is the diameter of the entrance pupil. Clearly, this is acceptable only when $m_p \approx 1$, which may not be true for many imaging systems (for examples, see [786, p. 104]). The implicit assumption is that m_p is treated as yet another proportionality constant to be calibrated for the system.

It should also be pointed out that the numerical aperture and the relative aperture as defined above are properties of the light beam converging at the image point, rather than the imaging system itself. The reason is that the size of the cone of rays focusing on an image point is a function of the object distance. In order to avoid such ambiguities, the numerical aperture and the relative aperture are often defined for an object located at infinity. Using such definitions, we can write Eq. (10.7) for an object located at infinity as

$$E' = \pi \left(\frac{L}{n^2}\right) (NA)^2 = \frac{\pi}{4F^2} \left(\frac{L}{n^2}\right) = \left(\frac{\pi D^2}{4}\right) \left(\frac{m_p}{f}\right)^2 L. \tag{10.12}$$

Therefore, E' is proportional to the scene radiance L and the area of the entrance pupil, $\pi D^2/4$. Also, the longer the focal length we use in imaging, the darker our image will be.

For a close object, the distance, s', between the exit pupil and the image point deviates from f' significantly, and we need to use Eq. (10.7) to calculate the image irradiance. If the location of the exit pupil is not known, s' is often approximated by the distance from the image plane to the image principal plane, and from Eq. (9.26), $s' \approx (m-1)f'$, where m is the lateral image magnification (note: m and f' are often negative numbers). Equation (10.7) can then be expressed as

$$E' = \frac{\pi}{4F^2(m-1)^2 q}\left(\frac{L}{n^2}\right) \approx \frac{\pi}{4F^2(m-1)^2}\left(\frac{L}{n^2}\right), \tag{10.13}$$

where $q = 1 + 1/[4(m-1)^2 F^2 n'^2]$ is a factor close to 1. For example, at $f/2.8$ (i.e., $F = 2.8$), $q \approx 1.03$ when $n' = 1$.

10.2.2 Off-axis image irradiances

Another special case of Eq. (10.4) is when the object distance s is much greater than the radius of the entrance pupil, a, i.e., $s \gg a$. Equation (10.4) can be simplified to

$$E' \approx \pi L \frac{s^2 a^2}{(s^2 + a^2 + h^2)^2}\frac{\mathrm{d}A}{\mathrm{d}A'} \approx \pi L \frac{s^2 a^2}{(s^2 + h^2)^2}\frac{\mathrm{d}A}{\mathrm{d}A'}. \tag{10.14}$$

The off-axis angle θ is related to the above equation as follows:

$$\cos\theta = \frac{s}{\sqrt{s^2 + h^2}}. \tag{10.15}$$

Therefore,

$$E' \approx \pi L \frac{a^2}{s^2}(\cos^4\theta)\frac{\mathrm{d}A}{\mathrm{d}A'}. \tag{10.16}$$

Let m be the lateral image magnification of the imaging system. We have $\mathrm{d}A'/\mathrm{d}A = m^2$. Furthermore, $ms = (s'/s)s = s' = (m-1)f'$, and therefore,

$$E' \approx \pi L \frac{a^2}{(m-1)^2 f'^2}\cos^4\theta = \frac{\pi \cos^4\theta}{4F^2(m-1)^2 m_p^2}\left(\frac{L}{n'^2}\right). \tag{10.17}$$

The cosine-to-the-fourth-power fall-off can be significant and quite noticeable. For a 35 mm negative (24 mm × 36 mm) and a 50 mm lens, a corner will receive less than 71% of the light received by the center, assuming 100% lens transmission and no vignetting for all θ. However, lens manufacturers often compensate for the fall-off by adjusting the lens surface shapes. Therefore, we cannot expect light fall-off in typical cameras to follow the $\cos^4\theta$ law exactly.

10.2.3 General image irradiances

Equations (10.13) and (10.17) were derived under the assumption that all the light that enters the entrance pupil exits at the exit pupil and converges on the image point. This is not generally true due to a number of lossy processes including: (1) reflection and scattering from lens and other surfaces, (2) absorption by lens materials, and (3) vignetting [507, pp. 212–213]. The first two affect image points at all locations, but the third process affects the image irradiance more when it is further away from the optical axis. Vignetting occurs because part of the imaging aperture is occluded by mechanical parts from image points that are off the optical axis. The image is darker than can be accounted for by the $\cos^4 \theta$ fall-off. A general image irradiance equation takes these factors into account:

$$E'(x', y') = \frac{k\pi T V(x', y')\cos^4 \theta}{4F^2(m-1)^2}\left[\frac{L(x, y)}{n'^2}\right] + g(x', y'),\qquad(10.18)$$

where (x, y) and (x', y') are the object and image coordinates, T is the transmittance of the lens, $V(x', y')$ is the vignetting attenuation factor, $g(x', y')$ is the stray light (flare, glare) component due to scattering from lens, camera body, sensor, etc., and the proportionality constant, k, can be calibrated to include the pupil magnification and other factors. Another popular form of the equation can be derived from Eq. (10.16):

$$E'(x', y') = \frac{k\pi T V(x', y')f^2 \cos^4 \theta}{4F^2 v^2}\left[\frac{L(x, y)}{n'^2}\right] + g(x', y'),\qquad(10.19)$$

where f is object focal length and v is the image distance.

10.3 Light distribution due to lens aberrations

In Chapter 9, we showed that the OTF can be calculated from the autocorrelation of the (generalized) pupil function, P. For an ideal diffraction-limited system, the pupil function is equal to 1.0 within the exit pupil and 0 elsewhere. However, for real lenses, the pupil function is often a complicated function, consisting of various aberrations. The shape of the pupil function is traditionally approximated by a polynomial and different terms in the polynomial are given different names. Deviations of the pupil function from a constant for a given wavelength are called monochromatic aberrations. The other type of aberration is caused by lens dispersion and is called chromatic aberration.

10.3.1 *Monochromatic aberrations*

Let us review the definition of wavefront aberrations. For a diffraction-limited system, the emerging wave on the exit pupil should be a perfect sphere converging to the image point which is the center of the sphere. The sphere is called the reference sphere. Let the radius of the reference sphere be R. The emerging spherical wave on the exit pupil is then of the form $e^{(-ikR)}/R$. If the emerging wave is not a perfect sphere, the wavefront function can be written as

$$P(\xi, \eta; x', y')\frac{e^{-ikR}}{R}\qquad(10.20)$$

where $P(\xi, \eta; x', y')$ represents the deviation of the wavefront from the reference sphere centered at the point (x', y') on the image plane, and ξ and η are the coordinates on the exit pupil (see Fig. 10.2). The function $P(\xi, \eta; x', y')$ therefore is called the generalized pupil function. Its phase is called the wavefront aberration function, W, of the system (see Fig. 10.3), while its amplitude (also called the apodization function), A, is a

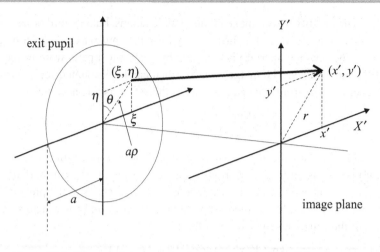

Figure 10.2. The coordinates system for the generalized pupil function.

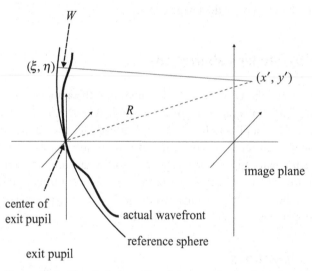

Figure 10.3. The deviation, W, of the actual wavefront from the reference sphere is called the wavefront aberration.

measure of the nonuniformity of the emerging wave. For a lens with aberration function W, $P(\xi, \eta; x', y') = A(\xi, \eta; x', y') \exp[ikW(\xi, \eta; x', y')]$. The apodization function, $A(\xi, \eta; x', y')$, is usually equal to 1 for camera lenses. For an aberration-free lens, $P(\xi, \eta; x', y')$ equals 1 if $\xi^2 + \eta^2 \leq a^2$, where a is the radius of the exit pupil.

For a rotationally symmetric system, the image position on the image plane may be specified by a single variable $r = \sqrt{(x')^2 + (y')^2}$ and points in the exit pupil by the radial and azimuthal coordinates ρ and θ, where $\xi = a\rho \sin\theta$, $\eta = a\rho \cos\theta$, and $0 \leq \rho \leq 1$. Without loss of generality, we assume that the image point of interest is on the y'-axis, i.e., $x' = 0$. Therefore, θ is defined relative to the image point and the η-axis is parallel to the y'-axis. From considerations of symmetry the wavefront aberration function exhibited by such a system is a function of three variables: r^2, ρ^2, and $r\rho \cos\theta$. (For a discussion of this symmetry argument, see, e.g., [682, pp. 206–7]). The wavefront aberration function, W, may be expanded as a power series in the above three variables. An alternative is also possible using the Zernike circle polynomials to expand the function W (see [124, pp. 464–8]). The power series expansion gives us:

$$
\begin{aligned}
W(r^2, \rho^2, r\rho\cos\theta) = \ & W_{020}\rho^2 + W_{111}r\rho\cos\theta \\
& + W_{040}\rho^4 + W_{222}r^2\rho^2\cos^2\theta + W_{220}r^2\rho^2 + W_{131}r\rho^3\cos\theta \\
& + W_{311}r^3\rho\cos\theta + W_{060}\rho^6 + \cdots
\end{aligned}
\tag{10.21}
$$

where the subscripts represent the powers of r, ρ, and $\cos\theta$. The first two terms represent the defocus and the tilt respectively. The next five terms represent the five third order (Seidel) aberrations: spherical aberration, astigmatism, curvature, coma, and distortion. Higher orders are also considered in lens design programs. By careful adjustment of a system's physical parameters (e.g. the shapes, thicknesses, separations of the lenses, glass types, and the locations of the stops), these aberrations can often be minimized.

We now briefly describe the five Seidel aberrations and their corresponding characteristic image patterns which can be derived from their respective polynomial terms. Let $(\xi, \eta) = (a\rho\sin\theta, a\rho\cos\theta)$ be a point on the exit pupil and (x', y') be a point on the image plane. Then, let us trace an arbitrary ray from the object point and assume that it emerges from the exit pupil at (ξ, η). If there is no aberration, this ray will go through the Gaussian image point at $G(x', y')$. If there is an aberration, the ray will intersect with the image plane at a different point $Q(x' + \Delta x', y' + \Delta y')$. The distance between G and Q is called the ray aberration. It can be shown [682, pp. 212–20] that the ray aberration $(\Delta x', \Delta y')$ can be approximately related to the wavefront aberration function, $W(\xi, \eta; x', y')$, by the following equations:

$$
\Delta x' = -\frac{R}{n'}\frac{\partial W}{\partial \xi},
\tag{10.22}
$$

$$
\Delta y' = -\frac{R}{n'}\frac{\partial W}{\partial \eta},
\tag{10.23}
$$

where R is the radius of the reference sphere (i.e., the distance from G to the center of the exit pupil) and n' is the index of refraction of the image space. From these two equations, we can roughly determine the image pattern caused by the aberration. (These patterns are the results of ray tracing and therefore are the predictions of geometrical optics.) In Figs. 10.4–10.8, which explain the five Seidel aberrations, a single lens is used for illustration in place of the exit pupil to show how different rays from an object point may deviate from the Gaussian optics due to the aberrations. In practice, the exit pupil should replace the lens in the diagrams.

Spherical aberration ($W_{040}\rho^4$)

Ideally, rays parallel to the optical axis of a lens should be refracted to converge at a single point, called the image focal point. In a lens with (undercorrected) spherical aberration, rays that are further away from the optical axis converge at a shorter distance than rays that are closer to the optical axis (see Fig. 10.4). Therefore, the image is not sharply focused. The image can be made sharper by stopping down (reducing) the aperture. In portrait photography, a large aperture may be used intentionally to allow more spherical aberration to occur so that the image will look softer.

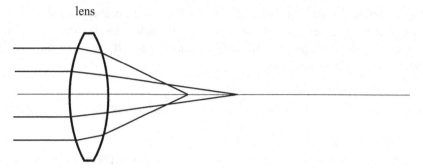

lens

Figure 10.4. Spherical aberration.

The image pattern due to spherical aberration can be derived as follows.

$$\Delta x' = -\frac{R}{n'}\frac{\partial W}{\partial \xi} = -\frac{R}{n'}\frac{\partial(W_{040}\rho^4)}{\partial \xi} = -\frac{W_{040}R}{n'a^2}4\rho^2\xi, \tag{10.24}$$

$$\Delta y' = -\frac{R}{n'a^2}\frac{\partial W}{\partial \eta} = -\frac{R}{n'a^2}\frac{\partial(W_{040}\rho^4)}{\partial \eta} = -\frac{W_{040}R}{n'a^2}4\rho^2\eta. \tag{10.25}$$

Therefore, $(\Delta x')^2 + (\Delta y')^2 = [4W_{040}R/(n'a)]^2\rho^6$. The rays from a circle with a radius of ρ on the exit pupil will intersect the image plane at another circle with a radius of $[4W_{040}R/(n'a)]\rho^3$.

Astigmatism $(W_{222}r^2\rho^2\cos^2\theta)$

In a lens with astigmatism, the meridional rays (rays on the plane of the object point and the optical axis) from an off-axis object point are focused at a point (tangential focal point) and the sagittal rays (rays on the plane perpendicular to the meridional plane) are focused at a different point (sagittal focal point), i.e., the meridional rays and the sagittal rays have different focal lengths (see Fig. 10.5). At the tangential focal point, the image is a horizontal line segment, while at the sagittal focal point, the image is a vertical line segment. Between the two focal points, there is a point where the image is a circle; this is called the circle of least confusion. Astigmatism is zero on axis and becomes increasingly obvious as the object point is moved away from the axis.

The image pattern due to astigmatism can be appreciated better if we consider the effects of defocus together, i.e., $W = W_{020}\rho^2 + W_{222}r^2\rho^2\cos^2\theta$.

$$\Delta x' = -\frac{R}{n'}\frac{\partial W}{\partial \xi} = -\frac{R}{n'a^2}\frac{\partial[W_{020}(\xi^2+\eta^2)+W_{222}r^2\eta^2]}{\partial \xi} = -\frac{RW_{020}}{n'a^2}(2\xi), \tag{10.26}$$

$$\Delta y' = -\frac{R}{n'}\frac{\partial W}{\partial \eta} = -\frac{R}{n'a^2}\frac{\partial[W_{020}(\xi^2+\eta^2)+W_{222}r^2\eta^2]}{\partial \eta} = -\frac{R(W_{020}+W_{222}r^2)}{n'a^2}(2\eta). \tag{10.27}$$

Therefore,

$$\left(\frac{n'a\Delta x'}{2R\rho W_{020}}\right)^2 + \left[\frac{n'a\Delta y'}{2R\rho(W_{020}+W_{222}r^2)}\right]^2 = 1. \tag{10.28}$$

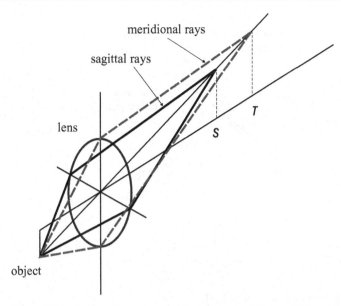

Figure 10.5. Astigmatism: the meridional rays and the sagittal rays have different focal points, T and S.

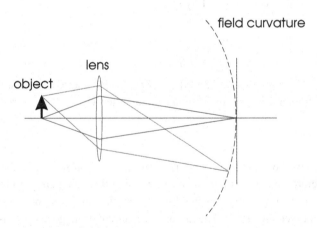

Figure 10.6. Field curvature.

The rays from a circle with a radius of ρ on the exit pupil intersect with a defocused image plane at an ellipse. The semi-axes of the ellipse depend on the position of the image plane, i.e., the amount of defocus, W_{020}.

Field curvature ($W_{220}r^2\rho^2$)

Ideally, the image of a vertical, planar object is also a plane, so that an image will be in focus everywhere on a planar film or a planar CCD sensor. For a lens with field curvature aberration, the sharp image is on a curved surface (see Fig. 10.6).

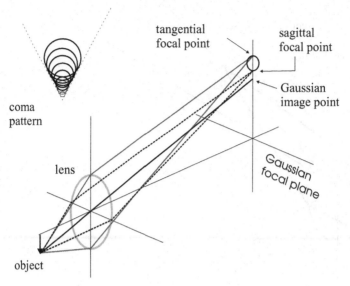

tangential
focal point

sagittal
focal point

Gaussian
image point

coma
pattern

Gaussian
focal plane

lens

object

Figure 10.7. Coma (modified from [779, p. 101]).

The image pattern due to field curvature can be derived as follows.

$$\Delta x' = -\frac{R}{n'}\frac{\partial W}{\partial \xi} = -\frac{R}{n'}\frac{\partial(W_{220}r^2\rho^2)}{\partial \xi} = -\frac{W_{220}Rr^2}{n'a^2}2\xi, \tag{10.29}$$

$$\Delta y' = -\frac{R}{n'}\frac{\partial W}{\partial \eta} = -\frac{R}{n'}\frac{\partial(W_{220}r^2\rho^2)}{\partial \eta} = -\frac{W_{220}Rr^2}{n'a^2}2\eta. \tag{10.30}$$

Therefore, $(\Delta x')^2 + (\Delta y')^2 = [2W_{220}Rr^2/(n'a)]^2\rho^2$. Rays from a circle with a radius of ρ on the exit pupil intersect the image plane at another circle with a radius of $[2W_{220}Rr^2/(n'a)]\rho$.

Coma ($W_{131}r\rho^3\cos\theta$)

For a lens with coma aberration, the meridional rays and the sagittal rays have the same focal distance, but different image positions. The rays passing through a circle in the exit pupil are focused on a circle at the image plane, but the circular image is not centered at the Gaussian image point (see Fig. 10.7). The radius of the circular image and its distance from the Gaussian image point are functions of the radius of the circle on the exit pupil. The image of an off-axis object point is thus a superposition of a continuous series of circles with decreasing radii towards the Gaussian image point. Its shape is like a comet and hence the name of the aberration.

The image pattern due to coma can be derived as follows.

$$\Delta x' = -\frac{R}{n'}\frac{\partial W}{\partial \xi} = -\frac{R}{n'}\frac{\partial(W_{131}r\rho^3\cos\theta)}{\partial \xi} = -\frac{W_{131}Rr}{n'a^3}\frac{\partial \eta(\xi^2+\eta^2)}{\partial \xi} = -\frac{W_{131}Rr}{n'a^3}2\xi\eta,$$

$$\tag{10.31}$$

$$\Delta y' = -\frac{R}{n'}\frac{\partial W}{\partial \eta} = -\frac{R}{n'}\frac{\partial(W_{131}r\rho^3\cos\theta)}{\partial \eta} = -\frac{W_{131}Rr}{n'a^3}\frac{\partial \eta(\xi^2+\eta^2)}{\partial \eta}$$

$$= -\frac{W_{131}Rr}{n'a^3}(\xi^2+3\eta^2). \tag{10.32}$$

images of a square object

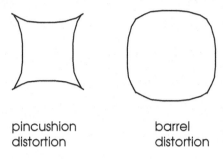

pincushion   barrel
distortion   distortion

Figure 10.8. Distortion.

Therefore,

$$(\Delta x')^2 + \left(\Delta y' + \frac{W_{131}\,Rr}{n'a}\rho^2\right)^2 = \left(\frac{2W_{131}\,Rr\rho\eta}{n'a^2}\right)^2. \tag{10.33}$$

Rays from a circle with a radius of ρ on the exit pupil intersect the image plane at another circle with a radius of $2W_{131}\,Rr\rho\eta/(n'a^2)$. However, the center of the circle on the image plane is shifted by an amount proportional to ρ^2.

Distortion ($W_{311}r^3\rho\cos\theta$)

For a lens with distortion aberration, the lateral magnification is a function of the image height. Therefore, the image of a square object is no longer a square. It can become a pincushion (positive distortion) or a barrel (negative distortion) (see Fig. 10.8). If the magnification gradually increases from the center axis to the corners of the image field, a square is imaged as a pincushion. On the other hand, if the magnification decreases towards the corners, it is a negative distortion and the image of a square becomes a barrel. If a lens system produces a positive distortion, then using the lens system in reverse will produce a negative distortion. In lens design, a symmetrical lens is often used to minimize the distortion. A symmetrical lens is one in which the lens elements are symmtetrically arranged about a central aperture stop.

The image pattern due to distortion can be derived as follows.

$$\Delta x' = -\frac{R}{n'}\frac{\partial W}{\partial\xi} = -\frac{R}{n'}\frac{\partial(W_{311}r^3\rho\cos\theta)}{\partial\xi} = -\frac{R}{n'a}\frac{\partial(W_{311}r^3\eta)}{\partial\xi} = 0, \tag{10.34}$$

$$\Delta y' = -\frac{R}{n'}\frac{\partial W}{\partial\eta} = -\frac{R}{n'}\frac{\partial(W_{311}r^3\rho\cos\theta)}{\partial\eta} = -\frac{R}{n'a}\frac{\partial(W_{311}r^3\eta)}{\partial\eta} = -\frac{R}{n'a}(W_{311}r^3). \tag{10.35}$$

The five Seidel aberrations are only one way to expand the wavefront aberration into polynomials of r, ρ, and $\cos\theta$. Even in a well-designed lens, small amounts of all these five as well as higher order terms are present at the same time. We now turn our attention to a case study of focus error as an example of how to calculate the OTF and the PSF from the wavefront aberration function. It is a very instructive case study because focus error is

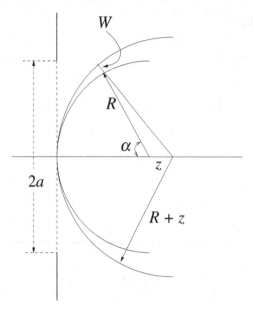

Figure 10.9. The wavefront aberration function W for a focus defect.

one of the major problems in consumer imaging applications. We will also use this case to compare the results from wave optics and from geometrical optics to show that one of the assumptions in geometrical optics is violated when the rays converge to an ideal point, because the spatial dimension of interest is no longer much larger than the wavelength.

Defocus ($W_{020}\rho^2$) as wavefront aberration (wave optics)

As an example, let us calculate the OTF of a defocused diffraction-limited system.[1] For a focus defect, the wavefront aberration function W can be calculated (Fig. 10.9) as follows [915]:

$$W = R + z - (R^2 + z^2 + 2Rz \cos\alpha)^{\frac{1}{2}}, \tag{10.36}$$

where R is the radius of the actual wavefront, $R + z$ is the radius of the reference sphere, and z is the out-of-focus distance. (We will assume that z is much smaller than R in the following discussion.) If we approximate $\cos\alpha$ by $1 - \alpha^2/2$ and neglect any terms that contain α of order higher than 2, we get the expression $W = \frac{1}{2}z\alpha^2[R/(R + z)]$. For the small-angle approximation, $\alpha^2 = a^2\rho^2/R^2$, thus

$$W = \frac{a^2\rho^2 z}{2R(R + z)}, \tag{10.37}$$

and from Eq. (10.21)

$$W_{020} = \frac{a^2 z}{2R(R + z)}. \tag{10.38}$$

---

[1]   Sections 10.3 and 10.4 are a slightly modified version of part of a paper [564] published in *Optical Engineering*. Readers interested in more details should read the paper.

Before we compute the OTF of a defocused perfect lens, we have to normalize the units in pupil coordinates and spatial frequencies so that the results will be independent of focal length and aperture size. Let us define the following variables; f, focal length; a, radius of exit pupil; $F = f/(2a)$; ϕ, the half-angle of the cone subtended by the exit pupil at the image point; v_x, v_y, horizontal and vertical spatial frequency in image plane; u_x, u_y, normalized horizontal and vertical spatial frequency; and $\Delta = W_{020}/(\lambda/4)$, a measure of the degree of defocus. Since we are only interested in the circularly symmetric system, we can specify the spatial frequency by v and u (normalized v), without specifying the angular orientation. The normalized spatial frequency u is defined as $u = \lambda v/2 \sin \phi$, where $v = \sqrt{v_x^2 + v_y^2}$.

Assuming that ϕ is small so that ϕ^n can be neglected for all $n > 2$, that the out-of-focus distance z (Fig. 10.9) is small compared with R, and that the image distance R is approximately equal to the focal length, the following relations can be derived:

$$u = \lambda F v, \tag{10.39}$$

$$\Delta = z/(2\lambda F^2). \tag{10.40}$$

It should be emphasized that the above approximation is good only for small values of z. In fact, $\Delta = W_{020}/(\lambda/4)$ is not symmetric with respect to z, as implied by Eq. (10.40). That is, the magnitude of W_{020} will differ at equal distances either side of the true Gaussian image plane, as can be seen from Eq. (10.38). The absolute values of W_{020} and Δ are larger when z is negative than when it is positive. That is, at equal distances the OTF deteriorates much faster when the film is moved towards the lens than it does if the film is moved away from the lens. This is observed in experimental measurements.

It can be shown that for a defocused perfect lens, the OTF can be computed from the following equation which is derived from Eq. (9.143) by considering only v_x and making an appropriate change of variables (for details, see [410, 588]):

$$H(u, \Delta) = \frac{4}{\pi} \int_u^1 (1 - x^2)^{\frac{1}{2}} \cos[2\pi u \Delta(x - u)] dx. \tag{10.41}$$

When the lens is in perfect focus, $\Delta = 0$ and

$$H(u, 0) = \frac{2}{\pi}[\cos^{-1} u - u(1 - u^2)^{1/2}] \quad \text{for } 0 \le u \le 1, \tag{10.42}$$

which is the diffraction-limited OTF (see Fig. 10.12). From Eq. (10.41), we can compute the OTFs of the lens at various degrees of defocus, and from the computed OTFs we can compute the PSFs by using the Fourier–Bessel transform:

$$h(\tau, \Delta) = 2\pi \int_0^1 H(u, \Delta) J_0(2\pi u \tau) u du, \tag{10.43}$$

where J_0 is the Bessel function of the first kind of order 0. It should be noted that τ is the normalized spatial distance in the image plane, and is related to the real distance r by the relation $r = \lambda F \tau$. For a diffraction-limited system, $\Delta = 0$ and

$$h(\tau, 0) = \frac{\pi}{4} \left[\frac{2J_1(\pi \tau)}{\pi \tau} \right]^2, \tag{10.44}$$

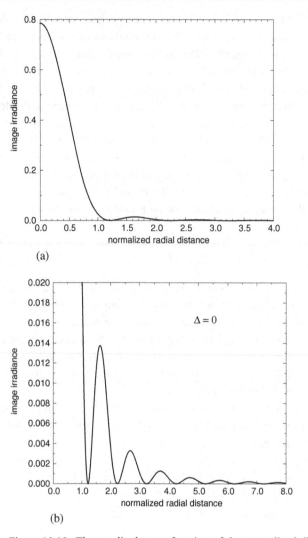

Figure 10.10. The amplitude as a function of the normalized distance of the Airy pattern: (a) the amplitude profile; (b) a magnified view of the details of the ring structure.

where J_1 is the Bessel function of the first kind of order 1. The diffraction-limited PSF has a central bright disk, surrounded by many rings. It is called the Airy pattern, after G.B. Airy who published the result in 1835. Figure 10.10 shows the profile of the Airy pattern. The function $J_1(x)/x$ has a first zero at $x = 3.833$ and therefore the first dark ring occurs at a normalized distance of $\tau = 3.833/\pi = 1.220$, which translates into the real distance r at the image plane as $r = \lambda F \tau = 1.220 \lambda F$. This distance is often used as a measure of the resolving power of an imaging system, and is called the Rayleigh criterion: this says that if the images of two object points are separated by a distance r in the image plane, i.e., if the brightest center of one point image is at the first dark ring of the other point image, the two points can be resolved by the imaging system [881, Chapter 9]. This is a reasonable, but somewhat arbitrary, criterion for at least two reasons: (1) most imaging systems are not

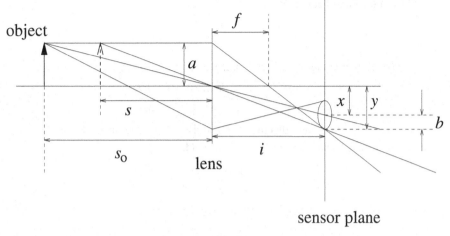

Figure 10.11. The geometric diagram of blur circle.

diffraction limited, and (2) whether two points can be resolved depends on the local image contrast. If the two points are to be resolved by a human observer, human contrast sensitivity has to be taken into consideration. The Rayleigh criterion can also be expressed as angular resolution:

$$\theta \approx \frac{r}{f} = 1.220\frac{\lambda}{D}, \qquad (10.45)$$

where f is the focal length and D is the diameter of the aperture.

Blur circle from defocus (geometrical optics)
The above equations have been derived from wave optics. It is interesting to compare these results with those derived from simple geometrical optics, which approximates the out-of-focus blur by a uniform disk. Geometrical optics treats light as rays that are refracted and reflected at places where the indices of refraction change. An ideal imaging system would map a point in the object space to a point in the image space. A defocused lens will produce, for a point object, a uniformly bright circle (blur circle) on the image plane. The radius of the blur circle, b, can be calculated as follows.

Refering to Fig. 10.11, let s be the object distance at which the camera is focused and s_0 be the true object distance. The image point of s_0 is focused in front of the sensor plane and it becomes a blur circle by the time it reaches the sensor plane. The radius, b, of the blur circle can be calculated as follows. Here we let all symbols, such as s, s_0, i, f, and b, represent absolute distances, i.e., they are all positive values. From similarity, we have $y/i = a/s$ and $x/i = a/s_0$, where a is the radius of the aperture (we have drawn the figure such that the object height is the same as a, but the result is valid in general. It should also be pointed out that in this simplification, the entrance pupil and the exit pupil are assumed to be the same). Now,

$$b = y - x = ai\left(\frac{1}{s} - \frac{1}{s_0}\right), \qquad (10.46)$$

and from the Gauss equation,

$$\frac{1}{s} + \frac{1}{i} = \frac{1}{f}. \tag{10.47}$$

Let p be the percentage focus error, i.e. $p = (s_0 - s)/s_0$, then

$$b = \frac{asf}{s - f} \frac{s_0 - s}{ss_0} = \frac{afp}{s - f}. \tag{10.48}$$

Let i and i_0 be the image distance for s and s_0. Then the out-of-focus distance z can be computed from Gauss' law, $(1/s) + (1/i) = (1/f)$:

$$z = i - i_0 = \frac{f^2(s_0 - s)}{(s - f)(s_0 - f)} \approx \frac{f^2(s_0 - s)}{ss_0} = \frac{f^2}{s} p. \tag{10.49}$$

From Eqs. (10.40), (10.48), and (10.49), we have

$$\Delta = f^2 p/(2\lambda F^2 s), \tag{10.50}$$

$$b \approx \frac{a}{f} z = \frac{z}{2F} = \lambda F \Delta. \tag{10.51}$$

From Eq. (10.51), if we express the PSF from geometrical optics, $h_{geo}(r)$, in terms of the normalized distance τ, where $r = \lambda F \tau$, then $h_{geo}(\tau)$ becomes a uniform disk with radius Δ and magnitude $1/(\pi \Delta^2)$. The OTF from geometrical optics becomes

$$H_{geo}(u, \Delta) = \frac{J_1(2\pi \Delta u)}{\pi \Delta u}. \tag{10.52}$$

Comparison of the defocus models from wave optics and geometrical optics

Now let us compare the results from wave optics and geometrical optics. Because the PSF from geometrical optics is so much simpler than that from wave optics, one would like to see if the former is a good approximation of the latter. The answer is that geometrical optics is a good approximation when the blur circle is large (say, $\Delta > 100$). Otherwise, we have to carefully specify what our error tolerance is. Figures 10.12–10.17 show the comparison of the results from geometrical optics and wave optics. The PSF and the OTF at various degrees of defocus, Δ, are compared.

It is interesting to note that the low-frequency part of the OTFs from wave optics and geometrical optics move closer and closer to each other as the defocus Δ becomes more and more severe. The low-frequency responses (frequencies below the first zero crossing) from these two models are almost identical to each other for $\Delta > 20$ (see Fig. 10.15). However, the high-frequency parts of the OTFs are never similar to each other. Two questions naturally arise: (1) In consumer photography, is a typical focus error, Δ, often greater than 20? (2) Are the differences in the high-frequency response visible in the final scanned images? The answer to the first question is "not very often". The answer to the second question has to take into consideration the image blur introduced by other system components, e.g. the film and the scanner.

Let us consider the case of a typical camera for 35 mm film. Let the focal length of the lens be 50 mm, the f-number, F, be 8.0, and the subject be 3 m away, i.e., $s = 3$ m. Let us assume that the average effective wavelength is 500 nm. From Eq. (10.50), we have $\Delta = 13.02p$. In order to have $\Delta > 20$, the focus error p has to be greater than 150%,

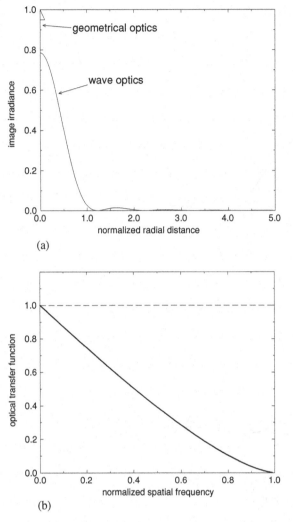

Figure 10.12. The PSF and the OTF computed from wave optics and geometrical optics at focus error $\Delta = 0$; (a) the geometrical PSF is an impulse at the origin with unit amplitude; the wave PSF is the solid curve; (b) geometrical OTF (dashed curve), wave OTF (solid curve).

meaning that we have to mistakenly focus the camera at a distance closer than 1.2 m, when the subject is actually 3 m away. Focus error of this magnitude does occur, but only rarely. Most errors are more likely to be less than 40%, i.e., $p < 0.4$, and the corresponding Δs are less than 5.2. Clearly, the use of geometrical approximation is often not justified in consumer photography. Even for a serious focus error, say $\Delta = 40$, it is not clear whether geometrical optics is good enough for a high-resolution digital image. The two outermost rings within the blur circle of the PSF as predicted by the wave optics in this case have a peak-to-peak spacing of 28.8 μm, with a contrast, $(I_{max} - I_{min})/(I_{max} + I_{min})$, of more than 25%. A digital image scanned from a 34 mm by 22 mm area of a 35 mm negative with a resolution of 2000 pixels per line (longer dimension) has a pixel spacing of 17 μm, which could be capable of resolving the outer rings of the PSF.

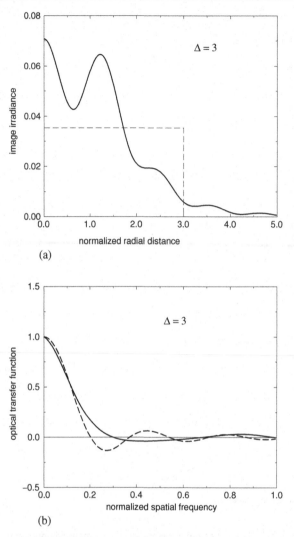

Figure 10.13. The PSF and the OTF computed from wave optics and geometrical optics at focus error $\Delta = 3$; (a) the geometrical PSF (dashed curve) is a uniform disk centered at the origin; the wave PSF is the solid curve; (b) geometrical OTF (dashed curve), wave OTF (solid curve).

10.3.2 Depth of field

An image often contains many objects at different distances. Although only one distance is in best focus, objects around the best focus distance also often look reasonably sharp. They are said to be within the depth of field of the best focus position. The depth of field is defined with respect to what can be regarded as acceptable blur.

For a normal eye, the limiting angular separation is about 1 minute of arc. If we assume that an image on a 35 mm negative is to be printed on photographic paper with 3.8× magnification, and the viewing distance is 14 inches (355 mm), then 1 minute of arc corresponds to 0.103 mm on the print and 0.027 mm on the negative. According to this simple calculation,

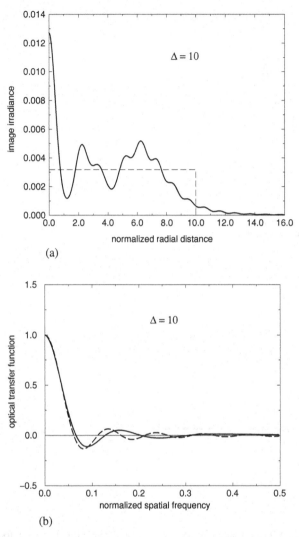

image irradiance

normalized radial distance

(a)

optical transfer function

normalized spatial frequency

(b)

Figure 10.14. The PSF and the OTF computed from wave optics and geometrical optics at focus error $\Delta = 10$; (a) the geometrical PSF (dashed curve) is a uniform disk centered at the origin; the wave PSF is the solid curve; (b) geometrical OTF (dashed curve), wave OTF (solid curve).

it is usually assumed that if a point object is imaged into a disk with a diameter less than 0.027 mm on the negative, it is an acceptable focus. From this point of view, the term, depth of field can be defined as the range of depth in the field around the focused object distance for which a point object will produce a disk image of diameter less than 1 minute of arc on the final print under standard viewing conditions.

Assuming our eyes cannot resolve two points closer than $2b$ on the image plane, i.e. if we can tolerate a blur circle of radius b, and the camera is focused at the object distance s_o, then any point at a distance between S_{near} and S_{far} is imaged into a circle with radius less than b. From Eq. (10.48), assuming $a \gg b$, we can calculate the depth of field DF from

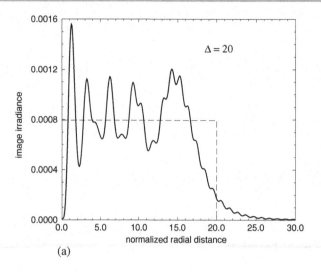

(a)

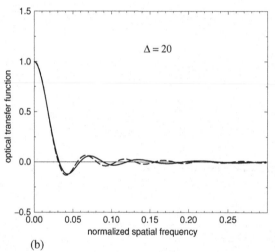

(b)

Figure 10.15. The PSF and the OTF computed from wave optics and geometrical optics at focus error $\Delta = 20$; (a) the geometrical PSF (dashed curve) is a uniform disk centered at the origin; the wave PSF is the solid curve; (b) geometrical OTF (dashed curve), wave OTF (solid curve).

the following equations:

$$S_{\text{near}} = \frac{s_0 f}{f + \frac{b}{a}(s_0 - f)}, \tag{10.53}$$

$$S_{\text{far}} = \frac{s_0 f}{f - \frac{b}{a}(s_0 - f)}, \tag{10.54}$$

$$DF = S_{\text{far}} - S_{\text{near}}. \tag{10.55}$$

It is easy to see from Eqs. (10.53) and (10.54) that if one keeps the focal length and the

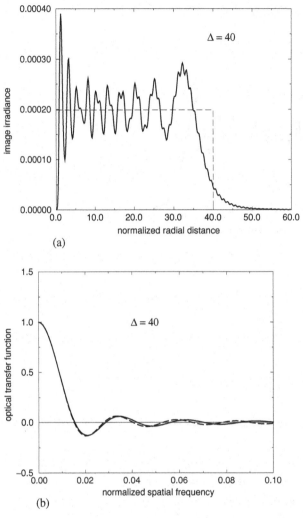

Figure 10.16. The PSF and the OTF computed from wave optics and geometrical optics at focus error $\Delta = 40$; (a) the geometrical PSF (dashed curve) is a uniform disk centered at the origin; the wave PSF is the solid curve; (b) geometrical OTF (dashed curve), wave OTF (solid curve).

subject distance constant, increasing the aperture radius a has the effect of reducing the depth of field, as is well known in photography. If the camera is focused at an object distance $s_o = (1 + a/b)f$, then S_{far} becomes ∞, and S_{near} becomes $\frac{1}{2}(1 + a/b)f$. This distance, $s_o = (1 + a/b)f$, is called the hyperfocal distance [365]. A fixed-focus camera can be made to focus at $s_o = (1 + a/b)f$ and any object from a distance of $s_o/2$ to infinity will be "well" in focus.

In digital camera applications, one is often tempted to define the depth of field using the sensor pixel size as the blur circle. This practice is not meaningful when the pixel size is smaller than the size of the Airy disk ($d = 2.44\lambda F$). For example, if the camera uses an $f/2.8$ lens and a CCD sensor with a pixel size of 2.6 μm, the blur circle cannot be the pixel size because the Airy disk diameter for $\lambda = 500$ nm would be 3.4 μm. A correct definition

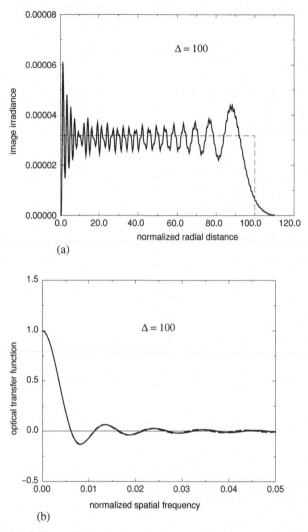

Figure 10.17. The PSF and the OTF computed from wave optics and geometrical optics at focus error $\Delta = 100$; (a) the geometrical PSF (dashed curve) is a uniform disk centered at the origin; the wave PSF is the solid curve; (b) geometrical OTF (dashed curve), wave OTF (solid curve).

of the depth of field has to start from the intended image magnification as viewed by an observer with one minute of arc visual resolution. We can then calculate the size of the blur circle on the sensor plane. Only when the calculated blur circle is smaller than a pixel can we use the pixel size as the blur circle.

10.3.3 Sine condition

In Chapter 9 and Sections 10.1–10.3, the paraxial approximations $\sin\theta \approx \theta$ and $\cos\theta \approx 1$ have been used to derive most of the imaging equations. The approximations are necessary so that we can simplify the relations and obtain a good intuitive understanding. In reality, we have to consider those rays that make moderate angles with the optical axis. For example, a 35 mm camera with a focal length of 50 mm has to produce good images on the 24 mm × 36 mm film area. The diagonal corners form angles up to 23.4°, which is about 0.4083 radians. The sine value of that angle is 0.3970 and the cosine is only 0.9178. The error of the paraxial approximation is from 2.8% to 8.9% even at this moderate angle. If the object point is located off-axis, rays coming from it can make even larger angles. In order for these rays to converge at the same image point, the optical system has to satisfy the sine condition [682, pp. 112–14]: $ny \sin \theta = n'y' \sin \theta'$, where n, y, and θ are the index of refraction, the off-axis distance of the object point, and the angle that the ray makes with the axis, all in the object space, while n', y', and θ' are the corresponding quantities in the image space. The sine condition is an important requirement for an optical imaging system to form a sharp image of an extended object near the optical axis.

10.3.4 Chromatic aberration

Another type of aberration is chromatic aberration, which arises from the fact that the index of refraction of a material is often a function of the lightwave frequency (dispersion). The main consequence of chromatic aberration in imaging is that light of different wavelengths is focused at different image distances (longitudinal chromatic aberration) and at different locations in the image (lateral chromatic aberration). The problem of chromatic aberration is usually corrected by using combinations of positive and negative lenses [385].

Longitudinal chromatic aberration has the same magnitude over the entire field and increases with aperture size. Lateral chromatic aberration does not depend on aperture [675]. Optical correction of chromatic aberration usually aims at correcting either the longitudinal or the lateral chromatic aberration, depending on the aperture and the field size of the system. Systems that have large apertures are usually corrected for longitudinal chromatic aberration, while those that have a small field of view are corrected for lateral chromatic aberration. If the system is corrected only for longitudinal chromatic aberration, rays of different wavelengths will come to a focus at the same plane, but the magnification may not be constant over the focal plane. On the other hand, if the system is corrected only for lateral chromatic aberration, the magnification will be the same, but the images may not all lie on the same plane.

For the simple case of two thin lenses, with focal lengths $f_1(\lambda)$ and $f_2(\lambda)$, located a distance d apart on the optical axis, the combined focal length $f(\lambda)$ is given by:

$$\frac{1}{f} = \frac{1}{f_1} + \frac{1}{f_2} - \frac{d}{f_1 f_2}. \tag{10.56}$$

Assuming that the index of refraction for lens 1 is n_1 and that for lens 2, n_2, and that the medium surrounding the lens is air with a refractive index close to 1, the focal length of a thin lens is inversely proportional to the difference in index of refraction between the medium and the lens, i.e.,

$$\frac{1}{f_1} = k_1(n_1 - 1),$$

$$\frac{1}{f_2} = k_2(n_2 - 1).$$

(10.57)

If we require that the combined focal length f be the same at two different wavelengths λ_r and λ_b, then solving for d we obtain

$$d = \frac{1}{k_1 k_2} \frac{k_1[n_1(\lambda_b) - n_1(\lambda_r)] + k_2[n_2(\lambda_b) - n_2(\lambda_r)]}{[n_1(\lambda_b) - 1][n_2(\lambda_b) - 1] - [n_1(\lambda_r) - 1][n_2(\lambda_r) - 1]}.$$

(10.58)

For a chosen focal length f at some wavelength d is fixed, and the refractive indices of the two lenses have to be different (Newton did not know that glasses can have different refractive indices and he concluded that an achromatic lens system was not possible). Actually, Eq. (10.58) imposes a very serious constraint on the design of the achromatic lens because a pair of glasses with indices of refraction satisfying the constraint may be very costly and difficult to obtain.

10.4   Optical blur introduced by the camera

Light distribution on the image plane is also affected by factors other than the optics. These factors are related to the mechanical structure of the camera and its relative motion with respect to the objects and the scene. Here, we will examine these other factors.[2]

A camera is basically a light-tight box with a lens to form an image, a diaphragm to control the aperture size, a shutter to limit the exposure time, and a means of holding the sensors and/or the medium (e.g. film) to record the image. The lens, the diaphragm, and the shutter, together, are responsible for producing the optical image on the film. They are tightly coupled in their optical effects and usually cannot be analyzed as independent components.

10.4.1   The real lens

The above discussion on the defocus blur function is true only for a perfect lens. In practice, camera lenses are not diffraction-limited, but suffer from various kinds of aberration, which are usually carefully balanced to achieve good performance at a reasonable cost. Photographic lens designs have changed considerably since the 1960s, with the maturing of computer optimization programs and the extensive use of the MTF as a design tool. Photographic lenses are now designed to function over a larger focusing range, typically at a magnification of 0–0.1 [109]. They are optimized at different focusing positions at the same focal length simultaneously. Classical aberrations in terms of series expansions are convenient for lens design optimization programs but not for quantitative descriptions of system performance. For this reason, the so-called through-focus MTF analysis has become

---

[2]   This section is a slightly modified version of part of a paper [564] published in *Optical Engineering*.

widely used. The MTF responses of several selected spatial frequencies and azimuth angles are computed as functions of the out-of-focus distances. The OTF of a real lens depends on many other variables than just the out-of-focus distance z. To completely characterize a lens, a set of OTFs have to be used for the following reasons [741]:

1. The incident light for imaging is almost never monochromatic, and it is necessary to specify the light source for the MTF measurement.
2. The best focus position is almost impossible to determine exactly because of the aberrations. For a given spatial frequency, there is a flat maximum on the transfer function magnitude vs. focusing distance curve. Furthermore, the maximum does not occur at the same focusing distance for different spatial frequencies.
3. The OTF is a function of the field position. It depends on the angle between the chief ray for the object and the optical axis. It is, therefore, necessary to measure the MTF for a number of field positions (usually three or four) to cover the range of interest.
4. It is also necessary to measure the MTF at various distances around the best focus, because aberrations prevent the direct calculation of the curves from the "best focus" MTF curves.
5. Optical image formation for extra-axial rays is more or less astigmatic and therefore the tangential and radial spatial frequencies have different transfer responses. Separate MTFs have to be measured along these two directions.
6. Objects at different distances are imaged at different magnifications. The MTF measured with the lens focused on infinity is different from that obtained when the lens is focused on a nearby object. It is necessary to measure the lens MTF at several magnifications.

The above discussion raises the question of the number of MTFs necessary for the complete description of a photographic lens. Assuming that four field positions, three apertures, five focusing distances, two magnifications, and three illuminants are required, then a total of 360 MTF curves have to be measured. Unfortunately, individual curves cannot be deduced from the others but must be measured separately. This clearly shows how difficult it is to model the image blur accurately, even if the blur is caused only by the lens optics. For digital image restoration, one does not know the exact depth of an object, the individual lens aberrations, the spectral distribution of the incident light, or any manufacturing defects associated with the system with which the image was taken. It is not realistic to assume that one can have complete knowledge of the lens blur. A reasonable approach to modeling is to use the functions derived from the diffraction-limited lens and adjust certain parameters, such as aperture size and defocus distance, to approximate the real blur functions.

The MTF of a real camera system under a small degree of defocus is quite difficult to predict accurately unless the exact wavefront aberration function of the lens is known. However, when the defect of focus is severe, its effect tends to dominate other aberration terms, and thus becomes more susceptible to analytic approximation. Since information about the exact wavefront aberration function of a camera lens is often unknown, we can only model the blur function for a diffraction-limited lens under the various focus errors. This serves as the best case study for small focus defects.

It has been proposed that the MTF of a very good camera lens at a given aperture may be approximated by reducing the aperture diameter of the corresponding diffraction-limited lens by a factor of 1.4–2. For example, the MTF of a good photographic lens at $f/5.6$ is about equivalent to that of an $f/12$ diffraction-limited lens. If one tests this idea, one finds it necessary to have different factors for a lens at different defocus distances. A better approximation of a good quality lens is to use the OTF of a stopped-down diffraction-limited lens with a slight focus error, say $\Delta = 1$. When the defocus error is severe (Δ larger than 5), the real aperture size can be used and the MTF computed from Eq. (10.41) is a good approximation to the measured one. This seems to confirm one's intuition that when the defocus error, W_{020}, is large, it will dominate all other aberration terms, as can be seen from Eq. (10.21).

10.4.2   The diaphragm

A diaphragm or stop is a device used to limit the diameter of the bundle of light rays that passes through a lens. It is used to control the exposure of the film and the sharpness of the image by partially reducing many of the lens aberrations. Virtually all good quality lenses today have built-in iris diaphragms that provide continuous control over the diameter of the aperture. The iris consists of a series of overlapping curved blades that move in unison as a setting ring or lever is moved, forming a circle of any desired diameter. In some automatic cameras, a twin-bladed shutter also serves to form the aperture stops, the blade travel distance being limited so as to form an opening of the correct size for the shutter speed in use [785, p. 64].

When taking a picture, it is often true that multiple combinations of aperture and speed can be used to get the proper exposure. In addition to the effect of depth of field, a camera often has an aperture setting which gives the best sharpness of the image. Because spherical aberration is decreased by stopping down, the sharpness of definition is increased as the lens is stopped down until an aperture is reached at which the effect of decreasing spherical aberration is counteracted by the increasing effect of diffraction; this is known as the critical aperture. From a modeling point of view, the smaller the aperture is, the closer the system is to the diffraction-limited case, and the easier it is to model.

Another effect of the aperture stop is to modify the vignetting behavior of the lens. As we mentioned before, vignetting is the progressive darkening of the image towards the periphery, due to the fact that parts of the lens may receive no light at all from certain regions of the scene [124]. This phenomenon worsens the light fall-off from the image center to the image periphery, in addition to the cosine fourth power fall-off. One way to reduce the vignetting effect is to reduce the size of the aperture. In modeling the image formation process, it is, therefore, important to consider all these factors which affect the relationship between the radiance L of the object and the irradiance E' of the object image [785, p. 65].

10.4.3   The shutter

In a camera, there is a shutter (Fig. 10.18) which is placed in the optical path before the sensing/recording medium (see [271, 406, 490, 785, 845] for more details). A shutter can

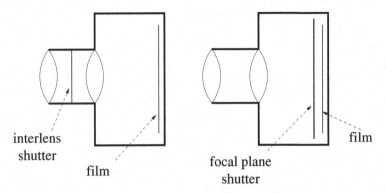

Figure 10.18. The two major types of shutter: the interlens shutter and the focal plane shutter.

be placed before a lens, between the lens components, or at any point between the lens and the focal plane of the camera. There are two major types of shutter: the interlens shutter and the focal plane shutter. Both types of shutter affect the effective camera OTF. In fact, some shutters have been intentionally designed to shape the camera OTF in a desirable manner [764].

The interlens shutter
In the center-opening shutter, light is usually prevented from passing into the camera by two or more overlapping leaves of opaque material. When the shutter is operated, the leaves part to permit passage of light for the specified time, and then return to their original positions. A center-opening shutter is usually placed between the lens components. This is called the interlens or between-the-lens shutter. The leaves of an interlens shutter are usually placed as close as possible to the diaphragm, where the light beam cross-section is smallest. Most interlens shutters change shape and size while they open and close, making the effective aperture of the camera a function of time. The time-varying aperture makes the effective system transfer function more complicated, especially at high shutter speeds, because the opening and closing phases of the shutter motion are a significant fraction of the total exposure time.

To consider the effect that this type of shutter has on the MTF of the lens, we have to know the shutter function, i.e. the light flux on the image plane as a function of time while the shutter opens, remains open, and closes (Fig. 10.19). The shutter function can be approximated as a function having a linear opening phase, a flat fully-open phase, and a quick linear closing phase [271, 490]. Let $L_{a(t)}(u)$ be the OTF of the lens at time t and the radius of the exit pupil $a(t)$. We can therefore compute the time-averaged OTF of a lens, $\bar{L}(u)$, with shutter function $S(t)$ as follows:

$$\bar{L}(u) = \frac{1}{T} \int S(t) L_{a(t)}(u) \mathrm{d}t, \tag{10.59}$$

where $T = \int S(t) \mathrm{d}t$. If one assumes that the shape of the opening remains a circle at all times, the radius of the exit pupil is proportional to the square root of the light flux. During the fully-open phase, let the light flux S be 1 (to make the normalized cut-off frequency

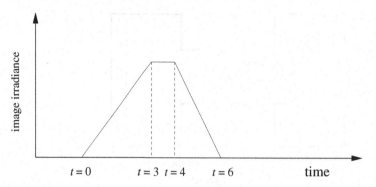

Figure 10.19. An example of a shutter function $S(t)$ of an interlens shutter.

equal 1.0 at the full aperture) and the OTF be $L(u)$. Then Eq. (10.59) becomes:

$$\bar{L}(u) = \frac{1}{T} \int S(t) L[u/\sqrt{S(t)}] dt. \tag{10.60}$$

The focal plane shutter

Another major type of shutter, frequently used in SLR (single-lens reflex) cameras, is called the focal plane shutter. This type of shutter usually consists of two curtains, one moving ahead of the other, forming a slit of variable width w, just in front of the film plane. If we assume that the shutter is almost at the film plane, there is little diffraction due to the shutter, and the OTF of the lens should not be affected. However, for mechanical reasons the so-called focal plane shutter is always at a small distance, d, in front of the focal plane.

The effect of the focal plane shutter on the lens OTF can be analyzed by using the Huygens–Fresnel principle. However, this is difficult to do and a simpler approximation method has been proposed by Shack [852]. He solved the problem by starting from Eq. (9.143) with the assumption that the shutter is sufficiently removed from the focal plane for its effect to be virtually identical to that of an equivalent shutter in the pupil. His analysis showed that, when the object is not moving relative to the camera, the net effect of the focal plane shutter is to act as an independent component with its own transfer function.

Assuming that the shutter is a vertical slit moving in a horizontal direction (Fig. 10.20), let $\bar{L}(u_x, u_y)$ be the combined OTF of the lens and the shutter, and $L(u_x, u_y)$ be the OTF of the lens alone, then

$$\bar{L}(u_x, u_y) = \begin{cases} L(u_x, u_y)(1 - |u_x|/c) & 0 < |u_x| < c, \\ 0 & \text{otherwise,} \end{cases} \tag{10.61}$$

where $c = wf/ad = 2wF/d$ and w is the width of the shutter opening. This derivation makes the assumption, which was not pointed out in Shack's paper [852], that $w < w_f - (d/F)$, where w_f is the film width. This assumption is not always true in photography. For example, if the shutter is traveling at $6\ \mathrm{m \cdot s^{-1}}$, and the exposure time is set at $1/100$ s, the shutter slit width is 60 mm which is wider than the film width for a 35 mm negative. In this case, the second curtain will not start moving until some time after the first one has already traveled all the way to the other side of the film. To compute the combined shutter and lens

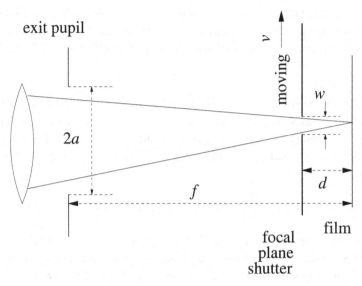

Figure 10.20. The effect of a focal plane shutter on the lens OTF can be modeled as a modification of the shape of the exit pupil.

OTF, the exact integral as shown in Eq. (10.71) has to be evaluated numerically with $p(t)$ and $q(t)$ set to 0. In practice, for the case of $w > w_f - (d/F)$, the shutter effect on the total system transfer function is negligible because the shutter slit is wide open compared with the diaphragm and does not limit the passage of any imaging light.

It is not clear whether Shack's assumption that the focal plane shutter can be treated as a pupil plane shutter is valid in practice because the distance d between the image plane and the shutter plane is about 5 mm, while the shutter slit is usually wider than 10 mm (the field is observed too close to the aperture). It is necessary to gather experimental data in order to verify Eq. (10.61). Obviously, the OTF can no longer be rotationally symmetric when the camera uses a focal plane shutter. The question is how much effect it has on the final OTF. The majority of today's designs have a slit of variable width, traveling at a constant speed. The speed can be as high as $6.7\,\mathrm{m\,s^{-1}}$, as in the Nikon FM-2 camera, while other cameras may have a lower speed. Assuming that the speed is $6\,\mathrm{m \cdot s^{-1}}$ and the exposure time is set to 1/500 s, the slit width will then be 12 mm. If d is 5 mm, f is 50 mm, then $c = 13.44$ for $f/2.8$, and $c = 76.8$ for $f/16$. Recall that the normalized cut-off frequency is 1.0 when the OTF of an ideal lens drops to zero, and, therefore, the effect of the focal plane shutter is indeed negligible in most cases when there is no object motion. When the exposure time is reduced to 1/4000 s, the slit width becomes 1.5 mm, and $c = 1.68$ for $f/2.8$. The effect of the shutter on the system OTF then has to be considered. For more information about typical shutter operations, Chapter 13 of [365] has a good but not too rigorous discussion.

10.4.4 Effects of object motion

If the object or the camera is moving while the shutter is open, the recorded image has additional blur caused by motion. The image of a point on the object will be the convolution of the instantaneous lens OTF with the projected image of the motion trajectory. The analysis of object motion in the presence of shutter motion is simple for the interlens shutter, but fairly complex for the focal plane shutter when the diffraction effect has to be considered.

The interlens shutter
First, let us consider the motion blur for the interlens shutter. To continue using the normalized spatial frequencies, we again let the cut-off frequency of the full opening aperture be 1.0. Let the projected object motion trajectory on the image plane be described by the parametric functions: $p(t)$ and $q(t)$ for the x and y motion components. The PSF of the motion blur is

$$g(x, y) = \frac{1}{T} \int S(t)h_t(x - p(t), y - q(t))dt, \tag{10.62}$$

where $S(t)$ is the same shutter function used in Eqs. (10.59) and (10.60), and $h_t(x, y)$ is the instantaneous PSF of the camera at time t. (In this case we have assumed a space-invariant PSF, at least over the region covered by the object motion.) Taking the Fourier transform of Eq. (10.62), we have:

$$G(u_x, u_y) = \frac{1}{T} \int S(t)H_t(u_x, u_y) \exp\{-i2\pi[u_x p(t) + u_y q(t)]\}dt, \tag{10.63}$$

where $H_t(u_x, u_y)$ is the Fourier transform of $h_t(x, y)$. Assuming that the interlens shutter has a circular aperture with the radius being a function of time, then

$$H_t(u_x, u_y) = L\left(u_x/\sqrt{S(t)}, u_y/\sqrt{S(t)}\right) \tag{10.64}$$

and

$$G(u_x, u_y) = \frac{1}{T} \int S(t)L\left(u_x/\sqrt{S(t)}, u_y/\sqrt{S(t)}\right) \exp\{-i2\pi[u_x p(t) + u_y q(t)]\}dt. \tag{10.65}$$

For the simplified case in which $S(t)$ is a rectangle with amplitude 1.0, and the motion is a linear uniform motion, i.e. $p(t) = v_x t$ and $q(t) = v_y t$, Eq. (10.65), after normalization with $G(0, 0)$, becomes

$$G(u_x, u_y) = \text{sinc}[(v_x u_x + v_y u_y)T]L(u_x, u_y), \tag{10.66}$$

where $\text{sinc}(x) = \sin(\pi x)/(\pi x)$. Since $d_x = v_x T$ and $d_y = v_y T$ are the normalized distances traveled by the image point during the entire exposure time T, Eq. (10.66) can be simplified to

$$G(u_x, u_y) = \text{sinc}(d_x u_x + d_y u_y)L(u_x, u_y). \tag{10.67}$$

Equation (10.66) is a familiar simple model often used for motion blur. For a high-efficiency interlens shutter (i.e., $S(t)$ close to a rectangle function), this tends to be a very good approximation. It should be pointed out that Eqs. (10.63) and (10.66) are derived for the region inside the moving object. They are also useful for translational camera motion when the scene is stationary.

The focal plane shutter

The motion blur in a focal plane shutter camera is more complex than that in an interlens shutter camera. In addition to the complexity arising from the relative motion between the object image and the shutter slit, the diffraction effect due to the finite opening of the shutter is more complicated than we could model accurately.

The major geometrical effect of the focal plane shutter is the partial occlusion of the light cone converging to the ideal image point (see Fig. 10.20). If we use geometrical optics to approximate the motion blur, when the image plane is in focus the effect of the shutter is to modify the image irradiance at a point on the image plane as a function of time, depending on the relative position between the object point and the shutter. If the image plane is out of focus, the instantaneous PSF is a uniform disk, truncated by the shutter slit. Imagine that we are sitting just behind and moving with the center of the moving shutter slit, looking at the moving ray cone coming from a moving object point through the lens. What we see is a uniform disk of light appearing on the edge of the slit, tracing along a certain path of motion, and then disappearing again from the edge (at which edge it disappears depends on the relative motion between the object image point and the shutter). By using the shutter-slit-centered coordinate system, one can compute the relative motion as a function of time and also the truncated uniform disk as the instantaneous PSF, based on geometrical optics. However, instead of using geometrical optics from the spatial domain, let us use wave optics to approach the problem from the frequency domain as Shack did for the stationary object. Assume that the projected object motion trajectory on the image plane is described by the parametric functions: $p(t)$ and $q(t)$ for the x and y motion components. The motion blur PSF $g(x, y)$ can therefore be derived as

$$g(x, y) = \frac{1}{T} \int h_t(x - p(t), y - q(t))\mathrm{d}t, \tag{10.68}$$

where $h_t(x, y)$ is the instantaneous PSF of the camera at time t.

For objects moving parallel to the film plane, the pupil function (unmodified by the shutter) is not a function of time. If the object motion has a component perpendicular to the film plane, the camera focus position for the object becomes a function of time. In that case, detailed knowledge of the three-dimensional motion is necessary for blur computation. Since this type of knowledge is often unknown, the following discussion will focus on the case when the motion is parallel to the film plane. Assume that the shutter slit is moving with a projected speed v on the exit pupil in the direction of negative x. Let $P(x, y)$ be the unmodified pupil function, $s(x + vt)$ the shutter slit function projected on the exit pupil plane, and T the total time for the shutter slit to travel across the film. Then by applying Eq. (9.143) to the normalized frequency domain we can compute the transform of $h_t(x, y)$ as:

$$H_t(u_x, u_y) = \iint s(x + vt + \tfrac{1}{2}u_x)P(x + \tfrac{1}{2}u_x, y + \tfrac{1}{2}u_y)s^*(x + vt - \tfrac{1}{2}u_x)$$
$$\times P^*(x - \tfrac{1}{2}u_x, y - \tfrac{1}{2}u_y)\mathrm{d}x\mathrm{d}y. \tag{10.69}$$

Taking the Fourier transform of Eq. (10.68), we have

$$G(u_x, u_y) = \frac{1}{T} \int H_t(u_x, u_y) \exp\{-\mathrm{i}2\pi[u_x p(t) + u_y q(t)]\}\mathrm{d}t. \tag{10.70}$$

By grouping time related terms, we have

$$G(u_x, u_y) = \iint K(u_x, u_y, x)P(x + \tfrac{1}{2}u_x, y + \tfrac{1}{2}u_y)P^*(x - \tfrac{1}{2}u_x, y - \tfrac{1}{2}u_y)dxdy,$$
(10.71)

where

$$K(u_x, u_y, x) = \frac{1}{T}\int s(x + vt + \tfrac{1}{2}u_x)s^*(x + vt - \tfrac{1}{2}u_x)\exp\{-i2\pi[u_x p(t) + u_y q(t)]\}dt.$$
(10.72)

For the case of a linear uniform motion (say, $p(t) = v_x t$ and $q(t) = v_y t$), if $w < w_f - (d/F)$, one can show that after normalization with $G_s(0, 0)$, Eq. (10.72) becomes:

$$K(u_x, u_y, x) = G_s(u_x, u_y)\exp[i2\pi x(v_x u_x + v_y u_y)/v],$$
(10.73)

where

$$G_s(u_x, u_y) = (1 - |u_x|/c)\text{sinc}[(v_x u_x + v_y u_y)(c - u_x)/v]$$
(10.74)

for $|u_x| < c$ and 0 otherwise. It is interesting to note that the factor $(1 - |u_x|/c)$ which represents the basic effect of the focal plane shutter on the stationary object still appears in the same form for the moving object case. Furthermore, for most cases, $c \gg u_x$ and $(c - u_x)/v \approx c/v$ which is roughly the exposure time. The second term of Eq. (10.74) is therefore very similar to the first term of Eq. (10.66) for the interlens shutter.

Equation (10.71) can now be written as:

$$G(u_x, u_y) = G_s(u_x, u_y)L_s(u_x, u_y),$$
(10.75)

where

$$L_s(u_x, u_y) = \frac{1}{\pi}\iint P(x + \tfrac{1}{2}u_x, y + \tfrac{1}{2}u_y)P^*(x - \tfrac{1}{2}u_x, y - \tfrac{1}{2}u_y)$$
$$\times \exp[i2\pi x(v_x u_x + v_y u_y)/v]dxdy.$$
(10.76)

The factor $\frac{1}{\pi}$ is the normalization factor. It should be pointed out that because we have used the normalized frequencies in the derivation, v_x and v_y are in the normalized image coordinate space, while v is the shutter slit speed projected onto the exit pupil and normalized with the pupil radius. The ratio v_x/v is equal to $[d/(2\lambda F^2)](V_x/V)$, if the unnormalized speeds V_x and V are used. For a defocused perfect lens, $P(x, y) = \exp[ikW_{020}(x^2 + y^2)]$, and its OTF is given by:

$$L(u_x, u_y, \Delta) = \frac{1}{\pi}\iint P(x + \tfrac{1}{2}u_x, y + \tfrac{1}{2}u_y)P^*(x - \tfrac{1}{2}u_x, y - \tfrac{1}{2}u_y)dxdy$$
$$= \frac{1}{\pi}\iint_A \exp\{ikW_{020}[(x + \tfrac{1}{2}u_x)^2 + (y + \tfrac{1}{2}u_y)^2 - (x - \tfrac{1}{2}u_x)^2$$
$$- (y + \tfrac{1}{2}u_y)^2]\}dxdy$$
$$= \frac{1}{\pi}\iint_A \exp[ikW_{020}2(u_x x + u_y y)]dxdy,$$
(10.77)

where $\Delta = W_{020}/(\lambda/4)$ and the integrals are only evaluated on the intersection area A of the pupil functions $P(x + \frac{1}{2}u_x, y + \frac{1}{2}u_y)$ and $P^*(x - \frac{1}{2}u_x, y - \frac{1}{2}u_y)$. This equation is the same as Eq. (10.41) which, because of circular symmetry, has been simplified to a one-dimensional integral.

If we let $a_x = \lambda v_x/v$ and $a_y = \lambda v_y/v$, Eq. (10.76) becomes:

$$L_s(u_x, u_y) = \frac{1}{\pi} \iint_A \exp[ik(a_x u_x + a_y u_y + 2W_{020}u_x)x + ik2W_{020}u_y y]dx dy.$$

$$(10.78)$$

If the lens is in perfect focus, then $W_{020} = 0$ and,

$$L_s(u_x, u_y) = \frac{1}{\pi} \iint_A \exp[ik(a_x u_x + a_y u_y)x]dx dy. \qquad (10.79)$$

If $W_{020} \neq 0$, let $u_m = u_x + (a_x u_x + a_y u_y)/(2W_{020})$, then

$$L_s(u_x, u_y) = \frac{1}{\pi} \iint_A \exp[ikW_{020}2(u_m x + u_y y)]dx dy. \qquad (10.80)$$

Both integrals could be evaluated by rotating the x–y coordinates by an angle θ, where $\tan\theta = u_y/u_x$, and then integrating over A numerically. For typical system parameters, $d = 5$ mm, $F = 8$, $\lambda = 500$ nm, and a large motion $V_x/V = 0.01$ (i.e. the image point moves 20 pixels in a 2000 pixel wide image), v_x/v is about 0.78 and a_x is 0.78λ, which is three times the commonly acceptable aberration of 0.25λ. For a smaller amount of motion, say $V_x/V = 0.002$, $a_x = 0.156\lambda$ becomes comparable with or smaller than the aberration of a good camera lens.

10.5 Camera flare

When a light ray enters the front surface of the camera lens, it can be refracted to form part of the optical image and it is called the imaging light. Alternatively, it can be reflected between the lenses, the camera body, and the sensor, and eventually absorbed at a sensor location very far away from its intended image position. In the latter case, it is called the flare light and it does not contribute usefully to the intended image formation. Obviously, this definition of flare light is not good enough for a quantitative analysis because strictly speaking, even the image of a point object formed by a diffraction-limited lens has a very large spread over the image plane. Conventionally the term flare is used to refer to light that has a spread that is more than ten times greater than that caused by aberrations of the lens. Again this is a vague concept because there is an implicit assumption that the spread of image-forming light is finite, which is true only when we put a threshold on the irradiance level. For example, if we define the size of a PSF as the smallest radius that contains 99% of the power, the above definition can begin to make sense. If one searches through the literature, one comes to the conclusion that there is no quantitative definition of flare that is commonly agreed upon. In fact, camera flare is often defined operationally by its measurement instruments and procedures [522, 809, 1008, 1054]. A common simplifying assumption is that flare light tends to spread so widely that it covers the entire image plane uniformly. This is called

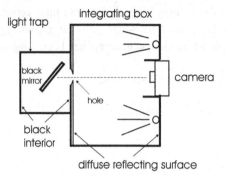

light trap

integrating box

black mirror

camera

hole

black interior

diffuse reflecting surface

Figure 10.21. An experimental setup for measuring camera flare.

uniform veiling flare. Of course, the flare light distribution is not really uniform because one can easily see more flare around light sources. The experimental setup [645, 940, 1008] to measure the veiling flare usually consists of a black hole (a light trap) surrounded by a uniformly illuminated background with luminance L (the uniform background is usually part of the interior surface of an integrating sphere). Figure 10.21 shows an example of such a flare measurement setup. The design of the black hole is such that no light is emitted from the hole (other than the negligible blackbody thermal radiation at room temperature). The hole typically subtends about $1°$ at the camera. If it is too small, the measurement will be sensitive to focus error. If it is too big, the flare may not be uniform inside the image area of the hole. The camera under test is used to take an image of the black-hole target and the exposure in the center of the black hole is measured as a percentage of the exposure of the bright background in the image. Good photographic cameras have less than 3% flare [645]; however, the measured value depends somewhat on the size of the black hole because of the local nature of camera flare [1008]. Since a large portion (as much as 30%) of the incident light is reflected from the film or the sensor, flare measurement is a function of not only the camera, but also the film or the sensor used in the camera.

Zoom lenses with many lens surfaces tend to have much more flare, especially at long focal lengths. The data also show that flare is a function of aperture size. At large apertures, lens aberration, lens edge scattering, and reflection from lens inner surfaces and the camera interior all contribute to flare. As the aperture is stopped down, the total flare light from these sources is reduced. However, the relative area of the diaphragm edge that is exposed to light increases and reflection from it creates a new source of flare. As a result, flare as a function of aperture size (f-number) is usually a U-shaped curve. For color photography, flare has to be measured for the red, green, and blue components separately because lens transmission and film-surface reflection are functions of wavelength. The green component of the flare is usually the smallest of the three. The differences in the red, green, and blue components of flare also contribute to the color cast in the film image and therefore, a well-color-balanced flare is preferred.

The most visible effect of camera flare is that a dark area on the image does not appear black, especially a dark area near a bright object. The minimum image illuminance is raised by the flare and the apparent image contrast is reduced. Jones and Condit [473] defined the flare factor as the ratio of the scene luminance range (L_{max}/L_{min}) to the image illuminance range (E_{max}/E_{min}). Obviously, the flare factor depends on the scene contents as well as the instrument used to measure the scene luminance range because the instrument itself might have flare. A better model of camera flare is to treat it as a PSF that has a large support [643, 1008]. Thus, it can be estimated from a knife-edge target by computing the MTF from the image. In this case, flare shows up as a very-low-frequency component superimposed on top of a smooth MTF. One can often see that in the very-low-frequency region, there is a discontinuity in the curve. The frequency where the discontinuity occurs is near where the image-forming MTF intersects with the flare MTF.

10.6 Problems

10.1 The exit pupil of an imaging system is located at $z_1 = 10$ and its radius is $a' = 4$. The image plane is located at $z_2 = 18$. What are the numerical aperture and the relative aperture (f-number) of this imaging condition? Assuming that there is no light loss in the system, what is the on-axis image illuminance of a Lambertian object that has a luminance of 100 cd m^{-2}? The object is a plane perpendicular to the optical axis. The object space and the image space are both in the air.

10.2 A camera is equipped with a flash lamp. The camera is used to take a picture of a painting on a wall (see Fig. 10.22). Let us assume that the flash lamp is a point source with equal intensity in all directions (although this is not true in reality). If the painting and the wall are Lambertian surfaces, what is the dependence of the image illuminance on $\cos\theta$, where θ is the off-axis angle of the camera? Although many museum visitors take pictures this way, it is less than ideal. What are the potential problems?

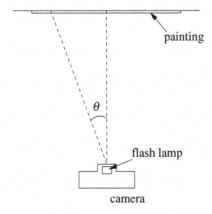

Figure 10.22.

10.3 In order to take a good picture of a painting that is placed on a flat wall, we set up four point sources. The painting is a square, 2 m long on each side. Let A, B, C, and D be the four corners of the painting, and P be its center. The camera is 4 m away and pointing at the center of the painting. In order to illuminate the painting as uniformly as possible, the four point sources are placed on a plane parallel to the wall and at the same distance away from the wall as the camera (i.e., 4 m). Each of the point sources is directly aligned with one of the corners of the painting (i.e., the line connecting the source and the corresponding corner of the painting is perpendicular to the wall). The intensity of each of the point sources is 1000 cd and it is uniform in all directions. The camera lens is set at $f/8$ (i.e., the f-number is 8.0) and the shutter at 0.1 second. The lateral magnification, m, is much smaller than 1 (i.e., $1 + m \approx 1$). Assume that the painting is a Lambertian surface and there is no light loss in the camera. (You can assume that the reflectances are all equal to 1.0 or you can use $\rho_A, \rho_B, \rho_C, \rho_D, \rho_P$ for the reflectances.)

(a) What are the illuminances at the center P and the corners, A, B, C, and D, of the painting?

(b) What are the exposures at the center P' and the corners, A', B', C', and D', of the film image of the painting, where P', A', B', C', and D' are images of P, A, B, C, and D, respectively?

10.4 Assume that the maximum acceptable blur circle is 10 μm in diameter on the image plane. If the lens has a focal length of 16 mm and an f-number of 4, what is the hyper focal distance of this camera? If the camera specifications call for a focus range from 0.8 m to infinity, at least, how many focus points have to be calibrated to cover that range?

10.5 A camera lens has a focal length of 50 mm. What is the size of the Airy disk (for $\lambda = 500$ nm) when the aperture is set at $f/8$? (The size of the Airy disk is defined as the radius of the first dark ring.)

11 Eye optics

The optics of the eye imposes the upper bound on the image details that can be seen by the visual system. It is important to understand and be able to model this limit of image quality under various viewing conditions, so that the performance by imaging systems can be properly optimized. However, it should be pointed out that the optical characteristics of the human eye are constantly changing throughout life, and there are also very significant variations among individuals. In this chapter, we will first describe the important features of the anatomy of the eye. Since the anatomy shows a structure too complicated to model in detail, we will then describe two simplified optical models of the eye: the reduced eye and the schematic eye. These models are very useful because they allow us to make good estimates of geometrical metrics for our retinal images. We will discuss some optical properties of the ocular media and the eye as a whole. We will also touch on the mechanism of accommodation and pupil control. Finally, we will describe how to put together a computational model of the eye optics for calculating the optical quality of the retinal image. Such a model will allow us to perform more detailed analyses under various viewing conditions and for different stimuli.

Before our discussion on visual optics, we need to define "visual angle" as a measure of image size and retinal distance. Since the image size of an object on the retina depends on its distance from the eye, it is often more convenient to use visual angle to specify object size or retinal distance. The visual angle formed by two image points on the retina is the angle between two points relative to the image nodal point of the eye. The visual angle of two points in the visual field is the angle between the two points relative to the object nodal point of the eye (see Fig. 11.1).

11.1 Anatomy of the eye

The average dimensions of an adult human eye are about 24 mm from the anterior pole to the posterior pole, 23 mm vertically, and 23.5 mm horizontally [962, p. 5]. The eyeball consists of, approximately, segments of two spheres placed one in front of the other (Fig. 11.1). The radius of the anterior sphere is 8 mm and that of the posterior sphere is 12 mm. Thus, the centers of the two spheres are separated by 4 mm.

The eyeball has three coats, the sclera (with the cornea), the choroid (with the ciliary body and the iris), and the retina. The outside radius of curvature of the cornea is about 8 mm, but the horizontal radius is about 0.05–0.25 mm flatter than the vertical radius [822]. The margin of the cornea is nearly, circular about 6 mm in radius. The iris is heavily pigmented and

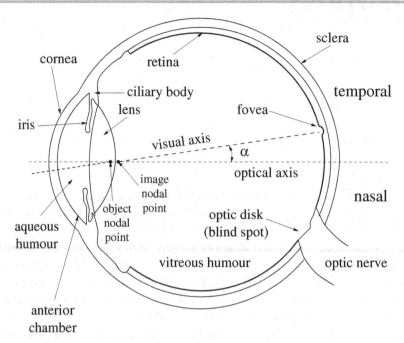

Figure 11.1. Diagram of the horizontal section of the human eye. (To make it easier to label, the positions of the fovea and the optic disk are drawn a little further away from the optical axis. See the text for more accurate dimensions.)

contains muscles that constrict and dilate the pupil from 2 to 8 mm in diameter, depending on the light level and the adaptation state of the eye. The entrance pupil, defined as the image of the aperture stop as seen from the object side, is the pupil that one observes in a person's eye. It is the image of the real pupil magnified by the cornea. The exit pupil, defined as the image of the aperture stop as seen from the image side, is the real pupil magnified by the lens. The sizes of the entrance pupil and the exit pupil are about 1.125 and 1.05 times that of the real pupil.

The sclera has a radius of curvature of about 12 mm, and comprises five-sixths of the surface area of the eye, with the remaining one-sixth being the cornea [962, p. 4]. The anterior cornea portion is more curved than the posterior sclera. The unit of the refracting power for a lens is usually expressed in diopter (D), which is the inverse of focal length or object distance in meters.[1] A lens with a focal length 1 m is said to have a refracting power of 1 D. A lens with a focal length 0.5 m is said to have a refracting power of 2 D. The refracting power of the combination of two lenses is simply the sum of their individual refracting powers. The relaxed eye as a whole has a refracting power of about 60 D, of which the cornea is responsible for about 70%, and the remaining 30% is accomplished by the lens behind it.

The retina, which contains the light-sensing photoreceptors, which is the innermost layer (with respect to the center of the eyeball) in the posterior sclera portion. The photoreceptors are located at the outermost layer of the retina. All the optical media preceding the

---

[1]   Using this unit is convenient because of the relation $\frac{1}{s} + \frac{1}{i} = \frac{1}{f}$, where s is the subject distance, i is the image distance, and f is the focal length.

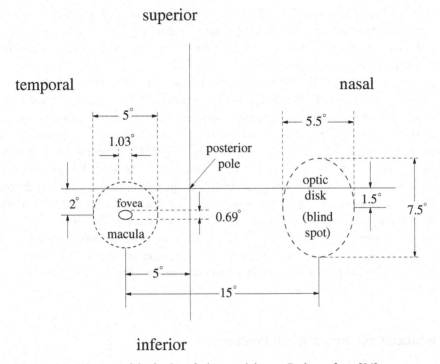

Figure 11.2. Diagram of the fundus of a human right eye. Redrawn from [94].

photoreceptors absorb more of the short-wavelength energy than the long-wavelength energy of the incident light. Furthermore, its optical density depends markedly on the age of the eye, being much denser when it gets old. This is a significant factor to consider when comparing colorimetric measurements [1053, pp. 108–112].

There is a shallow, rounded pit about 1.85 mm in diameter (about 5° of visual field) on the temporal side of the optical axis of the eye (see Fig. 11.1). This area is called the fovea centralis. In its center, there is an area, approximately 0.35 mm in diameter (about 1° of visual field), which is only 0.13 mm thick, much thinner than the surrounding retina region (about 0.2–0.5 mm thick). This area is called the foveola. Around the foveola are the parafovea (0.5 mm wide) and the perifovea (1.5 mm wide). The fovea region contains mostly cones (with rod-free region about 0.5–0.6 mm, or 1.7–2°), and the central region of foveola contains almost no S (short-wavelength sensitive) cones.

Strictly speaking, the eye is not a rotationally symmetric structure and therefore, does not have an optical axis. The center of curvature of the cornea is slightly shifted, relative to the axis of the crystalline lens [580, p. 58]. Therefore, there is an ambiguity of 1–2° in defining the best fit of an optical axis. The line connecting the center of the fovea with the image nodal point is called the visual axis. The angle, α, between the visual axis and the optical axis is about 5°. The visual axis extends from the object nodal point in the same direction outward towards the point of fixation. The lens has a flatter front surface and a more curved back surface. Its curvatures change as the eye accommodates for seeing objects at a short distance.

Figure 11.2 shows the spatial locations of the various structures when we look into the fundus of a human right eye. Surrounding the foveola is a yellow-colored region, called the macula lutea (or yellow spot), of about 3–5 mm diameter. The yellow coloration is probably due to the presence of the carotenoid pigment xanthophyll in the ganglion and the bipolar cells. The foveola region itself, having no bipolar and ganglion cells, does not have the yellow coloration [962, p. 43].

Another significant structure on the retina is the optic disk, where all the nerve fibers from the retina exit to the brain. The optic disk is about 7.5° high and 5.5° wide. The size of the optic disk varies from individual to individual and also varies with race, age, gender, and refractive error [986]. Typically its size is from 1.8 to 3.4 mm^2. Its center lies 1.5° below the horizontal meridian, and its nasal boundary is about 13° temporal to the fixation point [659, p. 179]. It is located about 4 mm from the fovea. The optic disk does not have any photoreceptors, i.e., the portion of the optical image falling on that region of the retina is not sensed at all, and the optic disk is also called the blind spot. One interesting problem to think about is why our visual image does not have a blank hole in it, if the blind spot does not detect image signals at all. This is a very intriguing question which leads us to rethink very carefully how "visual images", as we perceive them, are actually "synthesized" in our brain. The optical retinal images and our mental images generated from them are two very different sets of images!

11.2   Reduced eye and schematic eyes

For various applications, we need different levels of approximation of the eye optics. As we discussed in the last section, the eye is not rotationally symmetric, nor is the fovea located on the "optical axis". Furthermore, the index of refraction of the lens of the eye varies considerably from the center (highest) to the edge (lowest). This helps to reduce the spherical aberration of the eye. However, in oversimplified models, we simply treat it as a centered system with uniform indices of refraction in all the ocular media. The simplest form of approximation is the reduced eye, which consists of a single spherical surface with a radius R of 5.55 mm. The apex of the equivalent spherical surface is located about 1.67 mm behind the apex of the cornea. The reduced eye ball is filled with the vitreous humour, which has an index of refraction equal to 4/3 and a dispersion similar to water. The image focal length can be calculated as $n_2 R/(n_2 - n_1) = 22.22$ mm, with the resulting image focal point located at the retina [1025]. Since the nodal point is at the center of the sphere, the retina is therefore at 16.67 mm behind the node point. For this reduced eye, a distant ray directed at the node point will not be refracted and the visual angle is calculated with 16.67 mm as the radius of curvature. For example, near the optical axis, 1 mm on the retina corresponds to 3.437°.

The next level of complexity of an eye model is a paraxial schematic eye that has more than one refracting surface. There are several models that have been widely used for paraxial approximation. Here we will not give the parameters for these models. They can be found in many books (for example, [884] has a very good summary). Instead, for our applications, the positions of the six cardinal points are more valuable. As we have already learned in the previous chapters, a general imaging system can be characterized by four parameters (e.g., the two focal points and the two focal lengths). In visual optics, we often assume that

Table 11.1. *Parameters of Le Grand's theoretical eye*

Surface	n	Radius (relaxed)	Distance	Radius (accommodated)	Distance
cornea (front)	1.3771	7.800	0.000	7.800	0.000
cornea (back)	1.3374	6.500	0.550	6.500	0.550
lens (front)	1.4200	10.200	3.600	6.000	3.200
lens (back)	1.3360	−6.000	7.600	−5.500	7.700
retina			24.197		21.932

one medium is air and the refractive indexes of the optical media of the eye are known. The two focal lengths are thus related. Therefore, there are only three more parameters to be specified. A convenient choice is to specify its focal length, f (when the index of refraction is 1), and the two principal points, H_1 and H_2. Other cardinal points can be calculated from these. For example, let F_1 and F_2 be the object (front) focal point and the image (back) focal point, N_1 and N_2 be the object nodal point and the image nodal point, n_1 and n_2 be the indices of refraction of the object space and the image space, and f_1 and f_2 be the object and image focal lengths.[2] It can be shown that they are related by:

$$F_1 H_1 = f_1 = n_1 f, \tag{11.1}$$

$$H_2 F_2 = f_2 = n_2 f, \tag{11.2}$$

$$H_1 N_1 = (n_2 - n_1) f, \tag{11.3}$$

$$H_2 N_2 = (n_2 - n_1) f. \tag{11.4}$$

It follows that $N_2 F_2 = n_1 f = f_1$, which is an important relation for calculating the visual angle.

As a first example, let us describe Le Grand's theoretical eye which has four refracting surfaces: two for the cornea and two for the lens (see Table 11.1). All distances are measured in millimeters from the apex of the cornea. The index of refraction, n, is for the medium immediately next to the surface towards the retina. The aperture stop (iris) of Le Grand's theoretical eye is at the front surface of the lens. For the relaxed state, the entrance pupil has a radius of 4.000 mm (magnification 1.131) and is located at 3.038 mm. The exit pupil has a radius of 3.682 mm (magnification 1.041) and is located at 3.682 mm. The total refractive power is 59.940 D. For the accommodated state, the entrance pupil has a radius of 4.000 mm (magnification 1.115) and is located at 2.660 mm. The exit pupil has a radius of 3.785 mm (magnification 1.055) and is located at 3.255 mm. The total power is 67.677 D. The cardinal points of Le Grand's theoretical eye are given in Table 11.2.

Another frequently used model of the eye optics is the Gullstrand–Emsley schematic eye. It has three refracting surfaces: one for the cornea and two for the lens. The positions (again, measured from the front surface of the cornea) and curvatures are given in Table 11.3 [884, 94]. For the relaxed state, the aperture stop (iris) is located at the first lens surface.

---

[2] Note that, following the traditional usage in eye optics, f_1, f_2, and f in this chapter are all positive numbers. If we use the convention in the previous chapters, the image focal length $f' = -f_2$.

Table 11.2. *Cardinal points of Le Grand's theoretical eye*

Symbol	Relaxed eye (mm)	Accommodated eye (mm)
AH_1	1.595	1.819
AH_2	1.908	2.192
AN_1	7.200	6.784
AN_2	7.513	7.156
AF_1	−15.089	−12.957
AF_2	24.197	21.932

Table 11.3. *Parameters for the Gullstrand–Emsley schematic eye*

Surface	n	Radius (relaxed)	Distance	Radius (accommodated)	Distance
cornea	1.3333	7.80	0.00	7.80	0.00
lens (front)	1.416	10.00	3.60	5.00	3.20
lens (back)	1.3333	−6.00	7.20	−5.00	7.20
retina			23.89		21.25

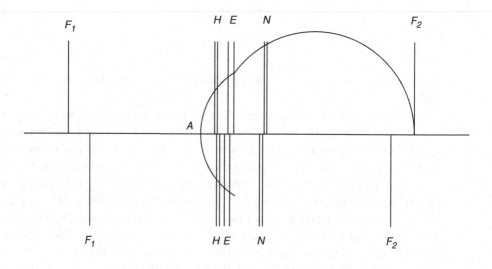

Figure 11.3. The cardinal points of the Gullstrand–Emsley schematic eye.

For the accommodated state, it is located at the second lens surface. Figure 11.3 shows the cardinal points of the schematic eye in the relaxed and the accommodated state. A is the vertex of the cornea. For the sake of clarity, the two pupil locations are marked as E, where E_1, the entrance pupil, is located in front of E_2, the exit pupil. The principal points, H_1 and H_2, are marked only with H, with the understanding that H_1 is in front of H_2. Similarly, N_1

Table 11.4. *Cardinal points of the Gullstrand–Emsley schematic eye*

Symbol	Relaxed eye (mm)	Accommodated eye (mm)
AH_1	1.55	1.78
AH_2	1.85	2.13
AN_1	7.06	6.56
AN_2	7.36	6.91
AE_1	3.05	2.67
AE_2	3.69	3.25
AF_1	−14.98	−12.56
AF_2	23.89	21.25

Table 11.5. *Cardinal points of the revised Gullstrand–Emsley schematic eye*

Symbol	Relaxed eye (mm)
AH_1	1.51
AH_2	1.82
AN_1	7.11
AN_2	7.42
AF_1	−15.16
AF_2	24.09

is in front of N_2. The distances between these points are listed in Table 11.4. The relaxed state of the Gullstrand–Emsley schematic eye has an equivalent power of 60.49 D. The index of refraction of the air, n_1, is assumed to be 1.0 and that of the eye, n_2, is 1.333. The object (front) focal length is 14.98 mm +1.55 mm = 16.53 mm, and the image (back) focal length is 23.89 mm −1.85 mm = 22.04 mm. The radius of the entrance pupil is 4.000 mm (magnification 1.130), and that of the exit pupil is 3.667 mm (magnification 1.036). The accommodated state of the Gullstrand–Emsley schematic eye has an equivalent power of 69.72 D. The object (front) focal length is 14.34 mm, and the image (back) focal length is 19.12 mm. The radius of the entrance pupil is 4.000 mm (magnification 1.114), and that of the exit pupil is 3.766 mm (magnification 1.049).

After reviewing some more recent data, Bennett and Rabbetts [94, p. 253] suggested changing the value of n_2 to 1.336 and the equivalent power of the relaxed eye to 60.0 D, which corresponds to an object (front) focal length of 16.67 mm. The image (back) focal length is $n = 1.336$ times that, i.e., 22.27 mm. For the revised model of a relaxed eye, the cardinal points are given in Table 11.5. If the eye is accommodated, the equivalent power increases and the focal length decreases. For example, if the eye is accommodated at an object distance of 66.67 cm, i.e., 1.5 D, the equivalent power of the eye becomes 61.5 D and the front focal length is 16.26 mm. In the computational eye-optics model we will develop shortly, the revised values of n_2 and f_1 will be used.

11.3 Conversion between retinal distance and visual angle

Visual angles are often used in specifying spatial dimension in visual perception. When relating the distance between two points on the retina to the visual angle, we have to convert between these two quantities. The relation between the retinal distance and the visual angle can be derived from the reduced eye or the schematic eye. For small visual angles, the paraxial eye model is adequate, and the relation is a simple proportionality. For example, in the relaxed state of the original Gullstrand–Emsley schematic eye, the image nodal point is located 16.53 mm from the retina. For a region near the optical axis, the visual angle $d\theta$ [degree] is then related to the retinal distance dx [mm] by $d\theta = 3.466dx$. In the accommodated state, it becomes $d\theta = 3.996dx$. However, these approximations do not apply a distance away from the optical axis because they do not take into account the actual radius of curvature of the real retina (about 11 mm), which is significantly smaller than the distance from the image nodal point to the retina. Let r be the radius of curvature of the retina and R be the distance from the image nodal point to the retina. Then,

$$\theta = \frac{180}{\pi} \sin^{-1}\left[\frac{r}{R} \sin\left(\frac{x}{r}\right)\right] \quad [\text{degree}], \tag{11.5}$$

where x is the arc distance on the retinal surface from the point where the retina intersects with the optical axis.

The above discussion is based on the paraxial eye model. To derive the conversion relation for retinal points far away from the optical axis, we need to use a wide-angle model of the eye optics and do ray tracing through the refracting surfaces of the cornea and the lens. Currently, there is no agreed-upon wide-angle model of the eye optics. To convert between retinal distance and visual angle, the curves published by Drasdo and Fowler [265] have quite often been used. They calculated their numerical results based on their schematic human eye, which has an equivalent power of 63.72 D, with the radii of curvature for the cornea, the anterior lens surface, the posterior lens surface, and the retina being 7.80 mm, 10.0 mm, 6.0 mm, and 11.06 mm, respectively. The first lens surface is located 3.6 mm from the apex of the cornea, while the object nodal point is at 6.95 mm and the image nodal point is at 7.32 mm. The retina is located 23.01 mm from the apex of the cornea. The unique feature of their schematic eye is the cornea, which is an ellipsoid. An empirical equation of the nonlinear relation between the retinal distance and the visual angle is given by

$$\theta = 0.1 + 3.4x + 0.035x^2, \tag{11.6}$$

where θ is eccentricity in degrees and x is eccentricity in millimeters, both measured from the optical axis. Obviously, the equation does not apply near the optical axis (when $x = 0$), but this is not a problem because we can then use the linear approximation for the model (the distance from the image nodal point to the retina is 15.69 mm): $\theta = 3.65x$ for $x < 0.425$ mm. According to this nonlinear formula, we find that the fovea is about 1.42 mm away from the optical axis (assuming that the angle $\alpha = 5°$), and the distance-to-angle conversion is about 286 μm/degree in the fovea. This is only an estimate. Other methods of estimation produce slightly different values. For example, another good estimate puts the value at 291 μm/degree [1033]. A simple number to remember is that 1 mm retinal distance corresponds to about 3.5°.

11.4 Retinal illuminance

From Eq. (10.17),[3] the retinal irradiance, E', is related to the scene radiance, L, by

$$E' \approx L \frac{\pi a^2}{(1+m)^2 f'^2} = \frac{L \cdot p}{(1+m)^2 f'^2} \approx \frac{L \cdot p}{f'^2},$$

where a is the radius of the entrance pupil, m is the lateral magnification,[4] f' is the image (back) focal length, and p is the entrance pupil area. Since the lateral magnification, m, of the eye is typically much smaller than 1, the retinal irradiance is proportional to the product of the scene radiance L and the pupil area p. In most imaging applications, scene radiances or luminances are measured. In order to calculate the retinal irradiance or illuminance when the eye is viewing an external object of a known luminance, we need to know the pupil size. Conventionally, retinal illuminance is given in trolands. A *troland* is defined as the retinal illuminance when a surface of luminance 1.0 cd m^{-2} is viewed through a pupil of 1 mm^2. The troland value of an eye with a p mm^2 pupil is simply the product of the luminance and p. If the luminance is calculated with the CIE 1924 photopic luminous efficiency function $V(\lambda)$, the unit is called the photopic troland, or simply the troland. If the scotopic luminous efficiency function, $V'(\lambda)$, is used, the unit is called the scotopic troland.

11.5 Depth of focus and depth of field

The central bright area of the PSF of a diffraction-limited system is called the Airy disk and its radius (the first dark ring) is equal to $1.22\lambda f/d$, where f is the image focal length and d is the diameter of the pupil. For example, if the pupil diameter is 2.5 mm, the wavelength is 550 nm, and the image focal length is 22.22 mm, then the diameter of the Airy disk is 11.9 μm. The minimum cone spacing in the fovea is about 0.5 minutes of arc, which is about 2.42 μm. The eye with a 2.5 mm pupil is close to the diffraction-limited system and even under this condition the Airy disk still covers several cones. The best MTF for a group of subjects seems to occur at a pupil size of 3 mm [35]. From these simple calculations, we know that our focus detection mechanism cannot detect image blur on a single-cone basis. Charman and Whitefoot [170] found that for a 2 mm pupil diameter, the mean depth of field is about 0.6 D, and it drops to about 0.3 D at a 7 mm pupil diameter. Other studies using subjective methods [41] and objective methods [632] showed similar numbers. These numbers are compatible with the reported threshold of perceptual blur being about 0.15 D [665, p. 57]. The depth of field of our visual system is not as sensitive as the ideal diffraction-limited lens to the change in the pupil size.

---

[3] Here, the $\cos^4 \theta$ fall-off factor is not considered for the eye because the retinal surface is curved.
[4] Here, $m = |m_y|$ is the absolute value of the lateral magnification, m_y, which is a negative number for our eyes, i.e., our retinal images are inverted.

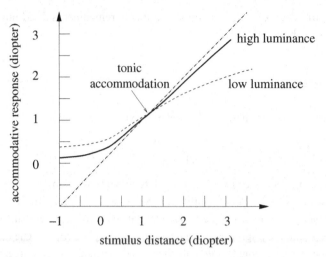

Figure 11.4. Examples of eye accommodation response functions. At a high luminance level with a stimulus with good luminance contrast details, the eye accommodates better and the response curve (thick solid curve) quite closely follows the ideal diagonal line (chain line). At a low luminance level or without good contrast details, the response function (dashed curve) deviates far from the ideal line.

11.6   Focus error due to accommodation

Experiments [174, 584] show that when the eye is presented with a uniform visual field without a high-contrast target to focus at, it is accommodated to a tonic level (reflecting the tonic level of neural activity when the accommodation system has no input signal to drive it). This is often called the tonic accommodation or resting accommodation [857]. The tonic accommodation appears to decrease with age [196]. The average tonic accommodation for young college-age observers is about 1.52 D (corresponding to an object distance of 25.9 inches) with a standard deviation of about 0.77 D [584].

Figure 11.4 shows two examples of the eye accommodation response as a function of stimulus distance; both are measured in diopters. Zero diopter means that the object is located at infinity, and 1 D means at 1 m away, etc. The chain diagonal line represents an ideal response, i.e., the eye is always focused at exactly the distance where the stimulus is located. The real eye response deviates from this ideal. If the object is located at a distance further or closer than the distance of the tonic accommodation of the observer, the eye tries to accommodate to the correct distance, but the accommodative response seems always to fall short of the amount needed, and thus creates a focus error. For example, if the tonic accommodation is 1.5 D and the object vergence calls for a 3.0 D accommodation, the eye typically responds with only a 2.85 D accommodation, resulting in a ΔD of 0.15 D. If the object vergence calls for a 0.8 D accommodation, the eye usually responds with a 0.87 D accommodation, resulting in a ΔD of -0.07 D. The general behavior of the accommodative response system is therefore to respond with a lag behind the needed change from its tonic level. This behavior is true for polychromatic as well as monochromatic light [172]. If we model the accommodative mechanism as a feedback control system, we can identify the tonic accommodation as the open loop output. The accommodation error results in image blur which is detected by the sensing mechanism to generate the control signal. If the blur-sensing mechanism has an inherent threshold, the accuracy of the accommodative response depends on the form of the target and the depth of focus of the eye. Experimental data show that the accommodative error is a function of the spatial frequency content of the target [169, 196, 737], the luminance [468], and the pupil size [360, 395]. The accuracy of accommodation is best for intermediate spatial frequencies (4–6 cycles per degree) and deteriorates at higher and lower frequencies, following the general trend in the contrast sensitivity function.

The accommodation response function is generally an S-shaped curve with a near straight-line portion around the tonic accommodation level with a slope about 0.86 for a Snellen target [171]. The variation of slope among individuals is fairly significant, e.g., from 0.72 to 0.92 for a 4.3 cycles per degree square wave target at 311 cd m^{-2} [737]. The slope decreases very slightly as the luminance of the target is reduced from bright daylight level. The rate of decrease accelerates greatly when the luminance falls below about 0.5 cd m^{-2} [468]. The slope also decreases when the pupil diameter is reduced [395].

For targets of polychromatic light, a question arises as to which wavelength the eye will accommodate to and bring to focus. Evidence suggests that the wavelength in focus on the retina is a function of the viewing distance. It has been shown [664] that the eye focuses at the long wavelengths (about 680 nm) when looking at infinity, and it focuses at shorter wavelengths (484 nm) when looking at an object 25 cm away. This observation is consistent with the data from the accommodation response curve. Suppose that the eye is trying to focus at a middle wavelength (say, 540 nm) when it is at a tonic accommodation level of 1.5 D (65.8 cm). If the object is now moved to infinity, i.e., 0.0 D, the eye responds with an accommodation to 0.6 D for 543 nm. This focus error means the 543 nm wavelength image is out of focus and the wavelength in focus is shifted to a longer wavelength (about 660 nm). Conversely, if the object is moved closer to 25 cm (4.0 D), the eye responds with an accommodation to 3.6 D, and the wavelength in focus is shifted to about 485 nm. We can therefore account for the change of wavelength in focus by using the accommodative response function, without invoking an additional empirical relation. However, this still leaves a question unanswered: how do we calculate the wavelength that the eye is trying to focus on? In fact, it seems that, with proper practice, the eye can focus on monochromatic light of any wavelength [172]. There are two types of information that seem to suggest that, to a good approximation, the sustained accommodation component focuses at the luminance contrast. First, it was shown that accommodation was essentially unresponsive to the isoluminant edge and exhibited increasing focusing accuracy with increased luminance contrast [1042]. Second, it was found that for a white light stimulus, the accommodative response curve matches that of the luminance-weighted average wavelength [172]. Because of the accommodation error, the average wavelength is usually not the wavelength in focus. If the object is closer than the tonic accommodation, the wavelength in focus is shorter than the average wavelength. Conversely, if the object is further than the tonic accommodation, the wavelength in focus is longer.

11.7   Pupil size

For imaging applications, it is important to be able to calculate the natural pupil size from the image viewing condition. However, the pupillary response seems to be determined by many complicated variables, such as changes in luminance [1053, p. 106], chromaticity [1062], attitude [398], spatial pattern [975], accommodation [949, p. 418], and others [603]. The natural pupil size of an eye looking at images is thus expected to change constantly with time. Studies on pupillary response reveal that there are two components of the response: transient and sustained. For imaging applications, a practical solution is to calculate the sustained component from the viewing condition, knowing that this is a somewhat compromised approach.

The spectral sensitivity of the sustained component of the pupillary response is close, but not identical, to the luminance efficiency function. Several empirical formulas have been proposed for calculating the pupil diameter from the luminance level of the viewing condition [1053, p. 106]. The following relation proposed by de Groot and Gebhard [243] is a useful approximation:

$$\log d = 0.8558 - 4.01 \times 10^{-4}(\log L + 8.6)^3, \tag{11.7}$$

where d is the pupil diameter (in millimeters) and L is the luminance level (in candelas per square meter) of the adapting visual field.

The lighting level for image viewing controls the pupil size, which in turn affects the contrast sensitivity and visual acuity [100, 582], presumably because the optical aberration of the eye worsens when the pupil size becomes larger than about 3 mm in diameter. However, the lighting level can be measured with either photopic luminance or scotopic luminance. It is somewhat surprising that the pupil size in indoor viewing has been shown to correlate much better with scotopic luminance than with photopic luminance [101], even in the luminance range between 20 cd m^{-2} and 300 cd m^{-2}, at which level rod response seems to have long reached saturation [13]. Regression on the experimental data showed that log pupil area is linearly related to log scotopic illuminance measured in the plane of the viewer's eye:

$$\ln A \approx 4.32 - 0.33 \ln S, \tag{11.8}$$

where A is the pupil area in square millimeters and S is the illuminance at the eye in scotopic lux.

11.8   Stiles–Crawford effect

Light entering the pupil at different distances from the optical axis is perceived as having different brightnesses. This effect is called the Stiles–Crawford effect of the first kind. It is attributed to the directional sensitivity of the photoreceptors [283]. The effect reduces the adverse influence of the marginal rays entering the pupil and improves the OTF of the eye slightly.

Table 11.6. *The parameter p as a function of wavelength in a model of the Stiles–Crawford effect*

wavelength λ (nm)	430	500	540	580	620	660
coefficient p	0.067	0.060	0.048	0.046	0.052	0.056

Stiles [908] first proposed using the following formula to fit the luminous efficiency data, η, of the Stiles–Crawford effect:

$$\eta = 10^{-pr^2}, \tag{11.9}$$

where r is the distance (in millimeters) on the pupil from the peak location of η, and p is a function of the wavelength of the incident light. Table 11.6 [1053, p. 427] lists the value of p as a function of wavelength. Although later studies [816] found that a Gaussian function fits log η better than the simple quadratic function in Eq. (11.9), the difference is very small for a pupil size smaller than 6 mm, which corresponds to a field luminance of less than 0.002 cd m^{-2}. Also, it was found [29] that η is not rotationally symmetric, but the deviation is again not large. The Stiles–Crawford effect can be modeled as an apodization function $A(x, y)$ for the OTF computation using the generalized pupil function $P(x, y)$.

Studies performed on large populations [29] showed that the peak position of the Stiles–Crawford effect is located at nasal 0.51 mm and superior 0.20 mm. Using the nodal points in the Gullstrand–Emsley schematic eye, the peak location is approximately mapped to 4.46° temporal and 1.78° inferior on the retina when the eye is accommodated. That position is about where the fovea is located.

11.9 Visual acuity

The capability of the eye to see spatial details is called the visual acuity. Depending on the type of spatial details that are used for measuring the acuity, we can roughly classify acuity into five types [884]:

1. Grating acuity (about 2 minutes of arc): this measures the highest sinusoidal frequency that the eye can resolve. It is usually between 30 and 60 cycles per degree.
2. Snellen (letter) acuity (about 5 minutes of arc): this measures the smallest size of letter that can be recognized.
3. Vernier acuity (about 10 seconds of arc): this measures the minimum detectable amount of mis-alignment between two line segments.
4. Point discrimination acuity (about 1 minute of arc): this measures the discrimination of two point white sources on a black background or vice versa.
5. Stereo-depth acuity (about 5 seconds of arc): this measures the minimum stereo disparity that can be resolved.

These are single number measures. In the next sections, we discuss the MTF and OTF, which are functions of spatial frequencies.

11.10 Measurements and empirical formulas of the eye MTF

Currently there are four ways to determine the eye MTF:

1. the double-pass method, which measures the point image reflected from the retina [158, 695];
2. the psychophysical method, which measures the visual contrast sensitivity of an observer with and without the degradation of the eye optical degradation; the ratio between the two is an estimate of the eye MTF [157]. The eye optics is bypassed by using laser sources to create interference gratings on the retina;
3. the objective aberroscope method, which measures the wavefront aberration of the eye [821, 1004];
4. the computational method, which calculates the eye OTF from eye aberration data [984].

Each of these methods has its shortcomings. The double-pass method assumes that the retina is a perfect diffuser and that it contributes the major reflection component. In reality, the retina is not a perfect diffuser, and there may be many other reflection components. Psychophysics measurement is sensitive to noise at high frequencies and chromatic aberration is not included because lasers are monochromatic sources. The aberroscope relies on the reflected image from the eye and therefore suffers the same drawbacks as the double-pass method. The computational method is very flexible, but data are not available on all aspects of eye aberrations.

So far there is no internationally accepted standard eye MTF. Campbell and Gubisch's data [158] are usually used for comparison. Vos, Walraven, and van Meeteren [993] combined those data with other flare measurement data to produce a numerical table of the eye PSF at six pupil sizes. Charman [173] considered this set of data the most useful currently available in 1982.

Improvements in instrumentation have made it possible to measure a large number of eye MTFs [34, 36, 632, 695, 1004]. As a result, several empirical formulas for eye MTF have been proposed [37, 242, 338, 438, 465, 695, 994].

An analytical expression for the PSF of the eye was proposed by Geisler [338]:

$$h(r) = \frac{a_1}{2s_1} \exp\left[-0.5\left(\frac{r}{s_1}\right)^2\right] + \frac{a_2}{2s_2} \exp\left[-0.5\left(\frac{r}{s_2}\right)^2\right]. \tag{11.10}$$

For a 2 mm pupil, $a_1 = 0.684$, $a_2 = 0.587$, $s_1 = 0.443$ minutes of arc, and $s_2 = 2.035$ minutes of arc.

Evidence suggests that there is a flare (stray-light) component in addition to the normal image forming component in the combined total PSF of the eye [993, 994]. Since the eye flare affects only very-low-frequency signal (less than 1 cycle per degree), it is not very important in most imaging applications because the visual contrast sensitivity below 1 cycle per degree is very small. Nevertheless, it is included in the computational model so that its effect can be simulated when the image viewing calls for it. X-ray image viewing may be such an application. The formulas proposed to model the eye MTF usually use linear

Table 11.7. *Parameters of the two-exponential*
model for eye MTF as a function of pupil size

Pupil diameter (mm)	A	B	C
2.5	0.16	0.06	0.36
3.0	0.16	0.05	0.28
4.0	0.18	0.04	0.18
6.0	0.31	0.06	0.20
8.0	0.53	0.08	0.11

combinations of multiple terms of exponential functions to approximate the experimental data. In particular, the following two-term formula was found to fit data from different retinal eccentricities and pupil sizes [37, 695]:

$$MTF(v) = (1 - C)\exp(-Av) + C\exp(-Bv) \qquad (11.11)$$

where the parameters are determined by curve fitting to the experimental data measured by a double-pass method using 632.8 nm monochromatic laser beams. Table 11.7 lists some of the parameter values.

IJspeert, van den Bug and Spekreijse [438] proposed a four-component model:

$$MTF(v) = c_1 \exp(-\beta_1 v) + c_2 \exp(-\beta_2 v) + c_3 \exp(-\beta_3 v) + c_4 \exp(-\beta_4 v), \qquad (11.12)$$

where $c_1 + c_2 + c_3 + c_4 = 1.0$. The first two terms approximate the eye MTF without flare, and the last two terms represent the flare. The empirical flare model here includes an age factor AF and the eye pigmentation, m:

$$AF = 1.0 + (\text{age}/70.0)^4; \qquad (11.13)$$

$$c_{\text{la}} = \frac{1}{1 + (m^{-1} - 1)/AF}; \qquad (11.14)$$

$$c_3 = \frac{c_{\text{la}}}{(1 + 25m)(1 + AF^{-1})}; \qquad (11.15)$$

$$c_4 = c_{\text{la}} - c_3; \qquad (11.16)$$

$$\beta_3 = \frac{360.0}{10 + 60m - 5/AF} \ (\text{c/deg})^{-1}; \qquad (11.17)$$

$$\beta_4 = 360.0 \ (\text{c/deg})^{-1}. \qquad (11.18)$$

For the mean blue Caucasian eye, $m = 0.16$. For the mean brown Caucasian eye, $m = 0.106$. For the mean pigmented-skin dark-brown eye, $m = 0.056$. For the mean Caucasian eye (blue and brown), $m = 0.142$. No information was provided by these authors regarding to the effects of pupil size, accommodation and color on the eye flare.

One common problem with all the empirical analytical expressions is that their parameters have to be determined for each application condition. For example, the parameters in the double-exponential formula were determined for monochromatic light of a specific wavelength. Imaging applications which typically require polychromatic lighting will not be able to make good use of these data. Other formulas developed for white-light viewing [438] cannot be adapted for the effect of accommodation and color. In particular, we are

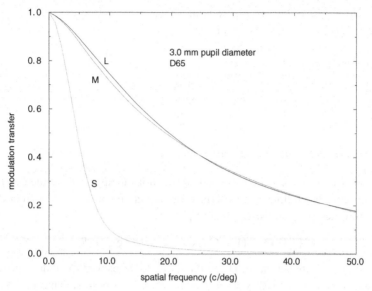

Figure 11.5. The model MTFs as seen by the L, M, and S cones with a 3.0 mm pupil.

interested in the optical image quality as seen by the three human cone systems, each having a different spectral sensitivity.

11.11   Method of eye MTF calculation by van Meeteren

In 1974, van Meeteren used eye aberration data to calculate the average eye MTF [984]. This is a very flexible tool for estimating the eye MTF under various application conditions. Figure 11.5 shows an example of such a calculation. The spectrum of the incident light is D65 and the LMS cone spectral sensitivity functions are used to compute the wavelength-weighted average MTF for each cone type.

In order to compute the eye OTF, we have to determine the pupil function[5] $P(x, y)$ for the eye, which is expressed as:

$$P(x, y) = A(x, y) \exp[ikW(x, y)] = A(x, y) \exp\left[i\frac{2\pi n_2}{\lambda} W(x, y)\right], \quad (11.19)$$

where λ refers to the light wavelength in the air. Since the image space of the eye has an index of refraction, $n_2 = 1.336$, which is different from that of the air ($n_1 = 1.0$), the wavelength parameter λ has to be divided by n_2. However, most eye aberrations are measured external to the eye and expressed in diopters. The index of refraction is automatically absorbed into the aberration coefficients in the experimental data. It is therefore better to cast the pupil function into the following form:

$$P(x, y) = A(x, y) \exp\left[i\frac{2\pi}{\lambda} \overline{W}(x, y)\right], \quad (11.20)$$

---

[5]   The pupil function here refers to the generalized pupil function as defined in Eq. (10.20).

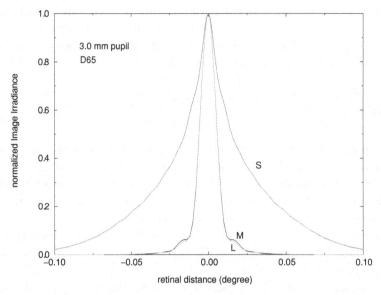

Figure 11.6. The model point spread functions as seen by the L, M, and S cones with a 3.0 mm pupil.

where $\overline{W}(x, y)$ is introduced to express the eye aberrations in terms of the externally measured data, and thus

$$\overline{W}(x, y) = n_2 W(x, y) = W_f(x^2 + y^2) + W_s(x^2 + y^2)^2 + W_a y^2 + W_c(x^2 + y^2)y + W_d y, \tag{11.21}$$

where W_f represents the defocus, due to either accommodation error or chromatic focus error, W_s is the spherical aberration, W_a represents the astigmatism, W_c the coma, and W_d the distortion. The dependence of the image coordinate Y is absorbed into the respective aberration coefficients, because we are only interested in the fovea vision and therefore Y is approximately a constant. Also the field curvature aberration, $W_{220} Y^2 (x^2 + y^2)$, is neglected because the retina is approximately "concentric" with the curved image surface and the error is quite small. The OTF of the eye can be calculated as the autocorrelation of the generalized pupil function as shown in Eq. (9.143).

If we can collect the aberration data for the average subjects that we are interested in modeling, we can then compute the MTF of their eyes. Furthermore, the spectral composition of the color stimulus, the spectral sensitivity functions of the cone, the focus error, etc. can all be simulated to see their effects on the eye MTF.

One of the advantages of the computational model is its flexibility. For example, Vos, Walraven, and van Meeteren's data [993] do not allow us to calculate the MTFs as seen by the L, M, and S cones. Figure 11.5 shows an example of the MTFs as seen by the three photoreceptors from the model calculations. The flare is not included. The figure shows the horizontal frequencies at a 3.0 mm pupil size. The half-height frequencies of the MTF as seen by the fovea cones are found to be 19.6, 19.1, and 4.7 cycles per degree for the L, M, and S cones.

The profiles of the corresponding PSF can also be computed. They are shown in Fig. 11.6. The half-height widths of the PSF as seen by the L, M, and S cones in the fovea are found to be 42.0, 42.2, and 108.4 seconds of arc, respectively. The foveal cone diameter is about 30 seconds of arc, smaller than the half-height width of the L-cone point spread function.

11.12 Problems

11.1 What is the size of retinal image of the sun in terms of visual angle? Assume that the sun has a radius of 6.95×10^8 m and its distance from the earth is 1.5×10^{11} m.

11.2 Use the matrix method in Section 9.7 to calculate the positions of the six cardinal points for the Le Grand theoretical eye with four refracting surfaces as given in Section 11.2. Verify the results with the numbers given in the same section.

11.3 Let the luminance of a surface be 100 cd m^{-2} and the eye be fully adapted to it. What is the retinal illuminance in terms of the troland? Use Eq. (11.7) to calculate the pupil size.

11.4 If a light source is a blackbody radiator at 2800 K, what is the ratio of the scotopic troland to the photopic troland?

12 From retina to brain

Although our interest in the human visual system is mainly in the role it plays as the observer in a color imaging system, we cannot completely treat it as a big black box, because the system is nonlinear and far too complicated to be characterized as such. There have been many attempts to apply linear system theory to the human visual system and characterize it with a system transfer function. That approach may serve some purposes in a few applications, but it is inadequate for most color imaging applications. Another possible approach is to treat it as many medium-sized black boxes, one for each special aspect in image perception. This is a more practical approach and it has been used very well for many applications. For example, we can measure the human contrast sensitivity as a function of luminance, field size, viewing distance, noise level, and chromatic contents, and the results can be used to design the DCT quantization tables for color image compression. However, the medium-sized black box approach does not give us much insight or guidance when our problem becomes more complicated or when we have a new problem. The size of the black boxes has to be reduced. An extreme limit is when each box corresponds to a single neuron in the visual pathway. Even then, some details inside the neuron may still be important to know. In general, how much detail we need to know is highly application-dependent, but the more we know the better we are equipped to deal with image perception related questions. For example, it is often desirable to build a computer model to predict if the results of certain image processing operations, such as image compression/decompression in medical imaging, will produce visible artifacts. A special-purpose computer model of this kind (such as fixed luminance level, fixed noise level, and fixed target patterns) is not too difficult to build because we can string together several medium-sized black boxes to get what we want. But to build a general-purpose model for varying conditions and application domains, we need to know more details about how the black boxes interact with each other. It also helps to know if certain operations make sense in a visual model in terms of the possibility of their being feasible in the human neural system. Yet another reason for studying such a subject is the hope that we may gain some insight into how we might attempt to solve very difficult vision problems by learning from the best system we know. For these reasons, we will study, in this chapter, some of the known neural structures in the visual signal processing.

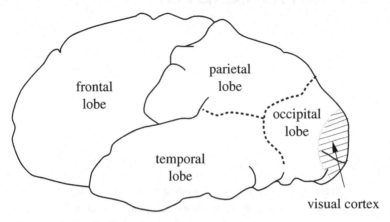

Figure 12.1. The four lobes of a human brain (a side view).

12.1 The human visual system

Vision is one of the five sensory functions that we have for collecting information about the world we live in. The optic nerve contains about one million neural fibers transmitting information from the retina to the brain. In comparison, the auditory nerve contains only about 30 000 fibers, and the number of all the dorsal root fibers entering the entire spinal cord is less than one million. Visual input thus accounts for about 40% of the total sensory input to our brain. The complexity and importance of our visual signal processing are quite obvious. Most of that processing is performed in our brain.

The human brain is a very complicated organ. On the average, it weighs about 1400 g. Structurally, the brain is composed of the cerebrum, the cerebellum, and the brainstem. The cerebrum contains two cerebral hemispheres (the left brain and the right brain). A very distinctive feature of human cerebral hemispheres is their convoluted and folded surfaces. A ridge on these heavily folded surfaces is called a gyrus, and a groove between ridges is called a sulcus (however, a very deep groove is called a fissure). Although the appearance of these gyri and sulci varies from one brain to another, certain major features are reasonably constant in human brains. For example, four prominent sulci – the central sulcus, the lateral sulcus, the parieto-occipital sulcus, and the calcarine sulcus (in junction with the preoccipital notch) – are used to divide each cerebral hemisphere into four regions: the frontal lobe, the parietal lobe, the temporal lobe, and the occipital lobe, which occupy roughly the front, the top, the side, and the back parts of the hemisphere, respectively. Figure 12.1 shows the locations of these four regions. In the discussion of the brain anatomy, we often have to refer to the direction of a structure. The directional terms are of two types. Terms such as anterior, posterior, superior, and inferior are relative to the normal upright orientation of the body as a whole. Thus, we say that the frontal lobe is anterior to the parietal lobe. Terms such as dorsal (top) and ventral (bottom) are relative to the center of the structure in discussion. If the brain is treated as a sphere, then the northern hemisphere (the top part) is the dorsal direction and the southern, the ventral direction. Note that surface normals at various points on the northern hemisphere are not all pointing in the same direction. The only thing we can say is that all of them have a positive "north" component. In comparison, the superior direction is strictly north and has no horizontal component. Of course, no structure in the brain has the shape of a sphere, but the dorsal/ventral convention roughly corresponds to such an analogy. Thus, we can say that the visual pathway going from the occipital lobe to the parietal lobe is the dorsal pathway (relative to the center of the brain) and the visual pathway going from the occipital lobe to the bottom of the temporal lobe is the ventral pathway.

One of the major achievements in neural science is the establishment of the functional localization of various brain areas (see [1066] for some very interesting historical accounts). Various sensory and motor functions are performed in different localized cortical areas. For example, Broca's area in the frontal lobe is the first area so identified. It was hypothesized by Pierre Paul Broca in 1861 to be involved in speech [1066]. The area that is mainly dedicated to processing visual signals (the visual cortex) is located on the occipital lobe at the back of the brain (the shaded area in Fig. 12.1). The visual cortex is further divided into the primary visual cortex (V1) and the visual association cortex (V2, V3, V4, and V5) surrounding the primary visual cortex [981, 982].

Visual perception begins at the photoreceptors (rods and cones) in the retina. The visual signals are then processed and sent to the visual cortex and other areas in the brain. Figure 12.2 shows a schematic diagram of the visual pathway from the retina to the brain. There are several important features that should be pointed out in this figure. The first is

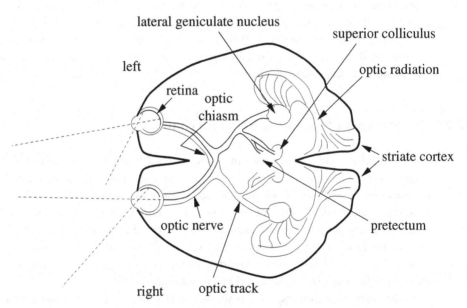

Figure 12.2. Schematic diagram of the visual pathway from the retina to the visual cortex. This diagram is a bottom view (looking up from below the brain). The main path of the visual signal transmission is from the retina to the lateral geniculate nucleus and then from there to the striate cortex. The thick lines represent the visual signals of the right visual field from each half of the two eyes. Therefore the right visual field is projected to the left brain and the left visual field to the right brain. There are other projections from the retina. For example, one of the projections is to the superior colliculus and another to the pretectum.

that the optic nerve leaving the retina carries information about the whole visual field of that retina, but the neurons that carry the visual signals from the right half of the visual field separate out from those carrying the signal from the left half at the optic chiasm and join with the neurons that carry the right visual field from the retina of the other eye. The combined optic tract goes to the lateral geniculate nucleus on the left side of the brain, and from there projects to the visual cortex of the left brain. Similarly, the visual signals from the left visual field are projected to the right brain. The major communication between the left brain and the right brain is through the corpus callosum (which is a huge fiber bundle, serving the equivalent function of computer cables). The second notable feature is that the visual cortex is not the only brain area that receives visual signals from the retina. There are also other projections from the retina, such as: (1) to the superior colliculus (for control of eye movement), (2) to the pretectal area (for control of pupillary light reflex), and (3) to the hypothalamus (for light related control of the biological clock). Projections also exist from the visual association cortex to the superior colliculus and/or the pretectal area (for the accommodation reflex) and from the visual cortex to the superior colliculus (possibly for visual attention).

The main pathway for visual information transmission and processing (see Figs. 12.3 and 12.4) is from the photoreceptor to the bipolar cells, the ganglion cells, the lateral geniculate nucleus (LGN), the primary visual cortex (V1) and the visual association cortex (V2, V3, V4, and V5) both sequentially and in parallel. Further projections are made to the temporal lobe and the parietal lobe. The primary visual cortex is also called the striate cortex (because of its visible layer structures) or area 17 (according to Brodmann's chart [1066, p. 69]). The visual association cortex is also called the prestriate cortex and it includes areas 18 and 19. The details of the visual information processing in the brain are mostly unknown and remain areas of intensive research.

12.2   The concepts of receptive field and channel

The physiological correlations with the various visual functions are established through numerous measurements from various neurons in the visual pathway. However, such a connection between perception and neural responses is not easy to make. Imagine how difficult it would be to understand how computers work by measuring electrical waveforms at different points in the complex circuits and chips. Fortunately, certain higher-level concepts in visual information processing have emerged from some early physiological and psychophysical studies. We will explain two such important concepts, receptive field and channel, before we discuss the neural structures and signal processing.

In the study of neuron response to various input stimuli, it is found that a neuron (especially that in the early processing stage of a sensory signal) only responds to stimuli presented in a certain spatial region of limited extent. For example, a fovea ganglion cell responds (changes its discharge rate) to a small spot moving across the central region of the visual field, but does not respond to stimuli that are presented in the peripheral region of the visual field. The region of the visual field within which a neuron responds to any input stimuli is called the receptive field of that neuron. Since the external visual field can be mapped to the retina, the receptive field of a neuron is often specified in terms of the region on the retina where some projected image of an external stimulus causes the neuron to respond. An important thing to point out is that neural connections rely on some threshold mechanisms to communicate with each other and therefore the measured size of the receptive field of a retina cell may be a function of several variables, such as the level of the illumination and the state of the visual adaptation. We should not constrain ourselves with a preconceived notion that the receptive fields are fixed structures. For example, the area for the spatial summation of rod signals seems to grow larger when the luminance level is reduced. This signal pooling works to improve the signal-to-noise ratio when there is little light available for seeing.

If the response of a neuron to a light pattern presented to its receptive field is determined by the weighted sum of the image illuminance over the entire receptive field, the neuron is said to have a linear response and this property is called the linearity of spatial summation. In this case, the neuron can be modeled as a (linear) filter and the weighting factor as a function of the spatial position in its receptive field can be treated as the correlation kernel of the filter. If the weighting function is circularly symmetric, it can also be treated as a convolution kernel. (It should be understood that when we say that a neuron, other than a photoreceptor, responds to some light stimulus, we mean that the light is sensed by the photoreceptors and the responses of the photoreceptors are transmitted through various intermediate neurons to the neuron that we are discussing.) For a small input dynamic range (signal of low contrast), many neurons can indeed be approximated as linear filters. A fairly-well-studied example is the center-surround receptive field of the ganglion cell. Light illuminating the central circular region of the receptive filed evokes a response (increased rate of action potentials) in the (on-center) ganglion cell, while light illuminating an annular region surrounding the central circular region evokes a response with an opposite polarity (decreased rate of action potentials). This center-surround receptive field response profile can be well approximated as the difference of two Gaussian functions with different spreads and heights.

If we consider visual signal processing by a neuron with its receptive field as computing a filtered output of the input image at a certain spatial location, we need a sampling grid of neurons covering the entire visual field so that a complete filtered image can be properly sampled and represented [333]. Such a set of neurons having the same (or very similar) receptive field structure, and covering the entire visual field, is called a channel, because their output as a whole represents the visual scene processed in a certain way (such as an image filtered through a bandpass filter in digital image processing). Of course, the filter analogy is only an approximation for human visual signal processing because the photoreceptors in the human retina are not linear in their response to light, their sampling grids are not exactly regular, and their sampling intervals are functions of eccentricity. It is not known to great accuracy how the filtered images are represented in the early visual processing. The concept of the channel is just a convenient way of imagining how the human visual signal can be modeled. It should also be pointed out that the concept of the channel can often oversimplify the actual complexity, interaction, and mixing of various types of signal along the visual pathways. Visual signals most likely are not neatly partitioned into channels [802, p. 269]. The concept of the channel is a useful one, but has to be taken cautiously until we understand exactly what is going on in our visual signal processing.

12.3   Parallel pathways and functional segregation

There have been many documented clinical cases that described patients who have suffered selective loss of visual functions (such as color discrimination, face recognition, and motion perception) while other functions (such as form perception) remained intact. For example, an artist lost his color vision in an accident. After the injury, he could only see things in black-and-white. Other aspects of his vision did not seem to suffer much. Therefore, he could still paint and draw well, but the colors he used to paint were all wrong. Another patient lost her capability to perceive motion. When she poured tea into a cup, the tea seemed to be frozen. She could not see the tea filling up the cup in continuous motion, and before she realized it, the tea had overflowed the cup. Such very selective loss of a certain visual function can now be correlated with findings through various brain imaging methods, such as x-ray computed tomography (CT), positron emission tomography (PET), and magnetic resonance imaging (MRI). The cortical areas that are damaged can be located quite well. Furthermore, it was discovered that a change in the amount of oxygen carried in our blood flow has a remarkable effect on the blood's magnetic properties, and these changes can be picked up clearly by MRI. When performing certain tasks, the brain areas that are involved show increased blood flow and these functional activities in the brain can be mapped out by MRI. Such techniques in imaging the brain are referred to as functional MRI (fMRI), and they have allowed us to see the brain's activities while we are carrying out some psychophysics experiments [774, 979]. Since the 1970s, anatomical, physiological, and psychophysical evidence has clearly shown that the primate visual system consists of several parallel visual pathways that analyze different aspects of the retinal images more or less independently [585, 599, 666, 774, 1066]. Figure 12.3 shows how some of these parallel visual pathways may be wired. It should be pointed out that such a clean partition of different visual functions into separate neural pathways is most likely an oversimplification. Exchange of information among these pathways cannot be ruled out.

Our current knowledge about these parallel pathways indicates that there are at least four of them: one color pathway, one motion pathway and two form pathways (dynamic form and static form). Segregation of these different aspects of visual signals seems to start in the retina, especially in the ganglion cells. They are called the P and M pathways because these ganglion cells have different sizes and shapes, and they terminate in the different layers of the LGN. New discoveries are continually made by researchers and more detailed structures will undoubtedly emerge in the near future. In the following sections, let us trace the visual signals from the retina to the brain through various neural connections.

12.4   The retina

The human retina extends about $1100 \, mm^2$ and its average thickness is about 250 μm. Under a microscope, the human retina can be seen as a many-layered structure. It is made up of the following identifiable layers as shown in Fig. 12.4: (1) the pigment epithelium, (2) the outer segments of photoreceptors, (3) outer limiting membrane, (4) outer nuclear layer, (5) outer

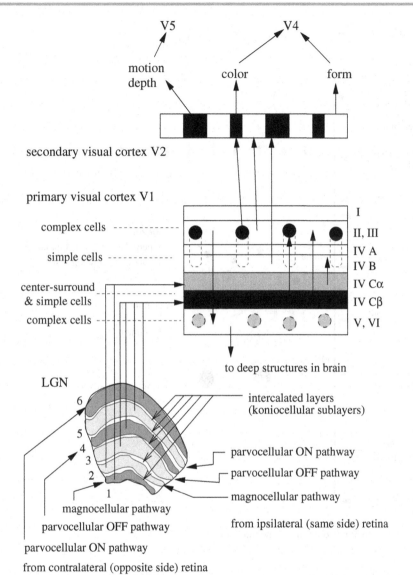

Figure 12.3. Schematic diagram of the parallel visual pathways according to our current understanding.

plexiform layer, (6) inner nuclear layer, (7) inner plexiform layer, (8) ganglion cell layer, (9) optical nerve fibers, and (10) inner limiting membrane. As can be seen from the names of these layers, the term *nuclear* refers to cell bodies and the term *plexiform* refers to synaptic connections. The terms *outer* (or *distal*) and *inner* (or *proximal*) are used relative to the order of synaptic connection to the brain. Therefore, the photoreceptors are *outer* relative to the ganglion cells.

From the signal transmission point of view, the direct path through the retina consists of the photoreceptors (rods and cones), the bipolar cells, and the ganglion cells (Fig. 12.4).

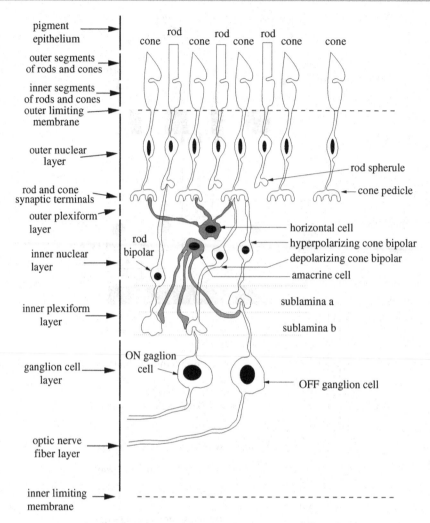

Figure 12.4. Schematic diagram of the human retina.

There are horizontal cells that make contact with many photoreceptors. There are also amacrine cells that make contact with bipolar cells and ganglion cells. The nuclei of the horizontal and the amacrine cells are located in the inner nuclear layer. Some nuclei of the amacrine cells are also found in the ganglion cell layer. Over the past 100 years, there have been extensive studies on the structure and functions of the retina. Its complexity is now much more appreciated than before. The five major classes of cells mentioned so far are greatly oversimplified. We now know that there are at least 10 types of bipolar cells, 20–25 types of ganglion cells, 3 types of horizontal cells, and 20–40 types of amacrine cells. Most of these cells have not been studied in detail, and the number of possible micro-circuits formed by them is potentially very large. The current research effort is directed towards the isolation and understanding of each of these micro-circuits [229, 231, 644].

12.4.1 Photoreceptors: rods and cones

There are two kinds of photoreceptors in the human retina: rods and cones. Their names came from their morphological shapes. Both rods and cones have four distinguishable parts: the outer segment (with many disk-shaped structures that contain visual pigments), the inner segment (with mitochondria and other cellular organelles), the nucleus, and the synaptic terminal. The outer segments of rods are generally cylinder-shaped (like a rod), while the outer segments of cones are broader at the base and tapering to their distal ends (like a cone). However, it is not always easy to discriminate between the two types of photoreceptors based on the shape alone, because rods and cones vary in size and shape at different eccentricities on the retina. For example, the outer segments of rods near the edge of the retina are about 20 μm long and 2.5 μm in diameter, while those at about 5° from the fovea are longer and thinner, about 30 μm long and 1 μm in diameter. In comparison, the outer segments of fovea cones measure 40 μm long and 0.9–1.0 μm in diameter (as skinny as rods), but those in the periphery are much shorter and fatter, about 10 μm long and 2.5 μm in diameter at the base [792, p. 6]. Another shape difference between rods and cones is the shape of the synaptic terminals. The terminal of a rod is small and rounded, and is therefore called the *spherule*, while that of a cone is more pyramid-shaped and is called the *pedicle*.

In general, rods are more sensitive to light than cones except in the long-wavelength region of the visible spectrum. Cones are sensitive to the ray direction of the incident light, while rods are not (this is called the Stiles–Crawford effect).[1] The rods respond to light with a slower time course than the cones, i.e. the temporal resolution of the rod's vision is lower than that of the cone. Also, the rod's vision has a lower spatial resolution than that of the cone, because rods' responses are summed over a larger receptive field (which can be as large as 1° of visual angle for the dark-adapted eye). The differences in the spatial, temporal, and spectral responses of the rods and cones will be discussed further later. Here we shall consider the following characteristics of the two types of receptor: (1) the range of operation, (2) the dynamic range of response, (3) the time course of adaptation, (4) the retinal distribution, and (5) the spectral sensitivity.

(1) The range of operation

The range of luminances in which we can see around us spans about 10 log units: from a scene illuminated by star light (about 10^{-6} cd m^{-2}) to that illuminated by the bright sunshine (about 10^4 cd m^{-2}). The vision mediated by the rods operates from the absolute threshold of about 5×10^{-4} scotopic trolands to the rod saturation luminance level around 3000 scotopic trolands, a range of almost 7 log units. The vision mediated by the cones operates, depending on the spectral composition of the light, from about 0.1 scotopic troland up, with a range of more than 7 log units. The operating ranges of the two photoreceptor systems thus overlap each other by a range of about 4 log units.

Roughly speaking, rods are at least about 25 times more sensitive to light than cones [264, p. 87]. In the dark-adapted human eye, absorption of only 2 photons of light by rod cells within an area of 350 rods during 1 ms can lead to our perceptual

---

[1] There are mechanisms that actively realign the cones to point toward the entrance pupil of the eye and the local disarray in pointing direction between cones is very small [805].

detection of the light (see the discussion in [215, p. 25]). In an experiment [1023], it was estimated that the minimum quantal catch by a single cone for detection was near 5 (4–6), and the effective number of illuminated cones was 1 or 2. Other data show that about 20–50 quanta absorbed per rod (dark-adapted) are needed to give a half-maximal response. For cones, it ranges from 600 quanta in turtles to 3000 quanta in primates [264, p. 88]. Therefore, rods are mainly responsible for seeing in dim light (scotopic vision). When dark-adapted, they saturate at luminances that cause more than about 100 photoisomerizations per integration time (about 200 ms) [902, p. 207]. However, the exact luminance level at which rods are completely saturated in their operating range is dependent on the stimulus size, retina location, and the spectral composition of the light. On the other hand, cones seems to be able to continue operate to a very high level of luminance without complete saturation. In summary, rods are able to detect single-photon events, but saturate at the light level at which about 100 photons are absorbed per rod. Cones are not able to detect single-photon events (because the response is too weak to be reliably distinguished from noise), but do not seem to saturate until they are almost completely bleached. The exact mechanisms underlying these behaviors are not completely understood. Interesting discussions can be found in [467, 801, pp. 219–221, 802].

(2) The dynamic range of response to change

By dynamic range, here we mean the ratio of the maximum to the minimum *change* of intensity over which the photoreceptor can operate with a detectable change in output response. This is similar to another term called the dynamic range for a brief flash [802, p. 143]. Obviously, the temporal characteristics of the photoreceptors have to be considered. In fact, the dynamic range of response to change has to be specified as a function of temporal frequency and the adapting luminance level. In typical image viewing conditions, our eyes are constantly moving and each photoreceptor encounters rapid rises or falls in image irradiance when the retina moves across an edge. Although the PSF of the eye optics makes a step edge somewhat smooth on the retina, a dynamic range measure based on a brief flash is still relevant to the photoreceptors' day-to-day operation. To a rough approximation, both rods and cones can respond to a dynamic range of about 100:1 [802, Chapter 7]. Temporally, cones have faster response time than rods.

(3) Adaptation

Adaptation usually refers to the gain control process by which a sensory system adjusts its operating range and response sensitivity. By this definition, the light (or dark) adaptation refers to the visual system's adjustment of its operating point when the overall luminance of the visual field is increased (or decreased). If the luminance change is less than a few log units, the new operating point is usually reached within seconds.

The slower visual adaptation process is dark adaptation. The visual threshold of a dark-adapted eye is elevated by a factor of more than 6 log units immediately after the eye is exposed to an intense illumination for a period of time. As time goes by, the threshold gradually decreases until it again reaches the absolute threshold for the dark-adapted eye. This process of threshold recovery is a typical measure of the dark adaptation. Cones dark-adapt much faster than rods. The dark-adapted cone threshold

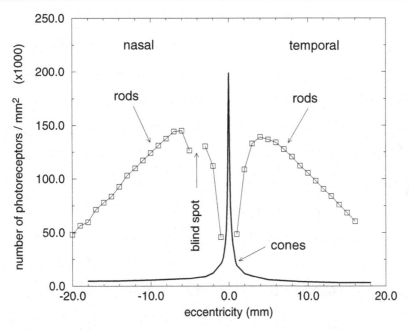

Figure 12.5. Mean cone and rod densities as functions of eccentricity from the fovea along the horizontal meridian of the human retina.

is completely recovered within 15 minutes of light exposure, while it takes longer than 50 minutes for the rods to do so.

(4) Retinal distribution

The average human retina contains 92 ± 15 million rods and 4.6 ± 0.45 million cones [224]. The cones are most densely packed at the center of the fovea where no rod exits. The cone density decreases very quickly outside the fovea. The rods, on the other hand, start to appear at about 1° from the center of the fovea and their density increases and reaches maximum at about 20° and then starts to decrease slowly towards the periphery of the retina (see Fig. 12.5). Peak foveal cone density averages $199\,000 \pm 87\,000$ cones per square millimeter and is highly variable between individuals [224]. The point of the highest cone density can be found in an area as large as $0.032^{\circ 2}$. In the fovea, the average rod-free zone is 1.25° (350 μm) in diameter. The number of cones in the rod-free area is about 7000. The cone density falls off steeply with increasing eccentricity. There is a streak of high cone density along the horizontal meridian. At the same eccentricities, the cone density is 40–45% higher in nasal compared with temporal retina. The highest rod densities are located along an elliptical ring at about the eccentricity of the optic disk.

(5) Spectral sensitivity

The peak sensitivity of the rod occurs at 507 nm (at the cornea). It is the same as the CIE luminous efficiency function for scotopic vision, $V'(\lambda)$. There are three types of cone: one sensitive to the long wavelengths (the L cone), one sensitive to the middle wavelengths (the M cone), and one to the short wavelengths (the S cone). Their

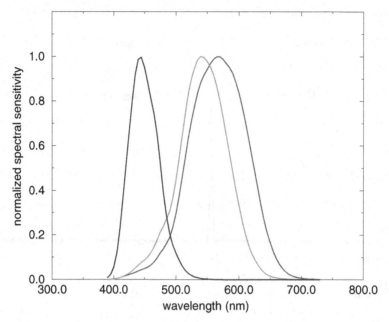

Figure 12.6. Normalized spectral sensitivities of human cones (Stockman–MacLeod–Johnson).

peak sensitivities (at the cornea) occur at 566 nm, 543 nm, and 440 nm, respectively [247]. The spectral sensitivity functions of the rod and the three cones have been estimated by various means. Figure 12.6 shows an estimate of the normalized human cone spectral sensitivities by transient chromatic adaptation, published by Stockman, MacLeod, and Johnson [910]. The numerical values given by these authors were from 390 nm to 730 nm in increments of 5 nm. The frequently used set of cone fundamentals by Smith and Pokorny [885] was determined from the color matching data of color deficient observers. These two sets of cone fundamentals are quite close to each other for calculating the L, M, S cone responses of most broadband spectra. However, they produce significant differences when used for narrow-band spectra. The Smith–Pokorny's fundamentals are based on Judd's modified color matching functions. The Stockman–MacLeod–Johnson cone fundamentals are based on the CIE 1964 10° color matching functions and therefore, have the advantage of building on an international standard. The question of which set of cone fundamentals is best is still being debated.

Photoreceptor response to light

In darkness, the outer segment of a rod or a cone has a high permeability to Na^+ ions, resulting in a steady flow of membrane current coming into the outer segment because the Na^+ ion concentration is higher in the extracellular space. At the inner segment and the synaptic ending, a steady leakage of K^+ ions flow out of the cell, completing the loop of the dark current. However, a Na^+/K^+ exchange pump in the cell membrane continuously works to pump the Na^+ ions out and take the K^+ ions in to maintain a low Na^+ ion concentration and a high K^+ ion concentration inside the cell. As a result of this concentration gradient, rods and cones are polarized in the dark (however, because of the dark current, they are not as polarized as typical neurons which have a resting potential of -70 mV). The dark resting potential of rods is about -37 mV, and that of cones about -46 mV, in the macaque retina. In response to light, the permeability of the outer segment is reduced, resulting in a decrease of the membrane current and an increase of the membrane voltage (hyperpolarization). Intracellular recordings of the photovoltage of rods and cones show that the response are highly variable from cell to cell. The maximum response for rods varies from 13 mV to 35 mV, and that of cones from 5 mV to 11 mV [840]. The mean peak response due to the absorption of a single photon is estimated at 1 mV for rods and 5.2 μV for cones. Intracellular recordings also confirm the following anatomical findings: (1) rods interact with each other only weakly if at all, consistent with the absence of gap junctions between primate rods; (2) cones are observed to receive excitatory input from rods (possible through gap junctions or contacts in synaptic processes). Another important finding from intracellular recordings is that the photovoltage response of both rods and cones as a function of retinal illuminance E can be well described by the Michaelis–Menten function:

$$V_{\text{intra}} = \frac{V_{\max} E}{E + E_0},$$

(12.1)

where $V_{\max}$ is the maximum photovoltage response of a photoreceptor, and E_0 is the retinal illuminance required to evoke the half-maximum response $V = V_{\max}/2$. However, the values $V_{\max}$ and E_0 are highly variable among different rods and cones. The average value of E_0 is 75 photons μm^{-2} for rods and 1430 photons μm^{-2} for cones. (The Michaelis–Menten function was derived by Leonor Michaelis and Maud Menten for their work on enzyme kinetics in 1913.)

Another method of measuring the photovoltage response is through extracellular recordings. This method is easier to do, but the response may be due to more than one photoreceptor, and typically the magnitude of the voltage response is much smaller than in the intracellular recording. The response voltage as a function of retinal illuminance from the extracellular recordings has a slightly different functional form:

$$V_{\text{extra}} = \frac{V_{\max} E^n}{E^n + E_0^n},$$

(12.2)

where $n = 0.74$. Of course, $V_{\max}$ and E_0 here are quite different from those in the intracellular recordings. (This function, similar to the Michaelis–Menten function, was first used by Archibald Hill in 1913 for describing the oxygen-binding of hemoglobin, and the coefficient n is called the Hill coefficient [922, p. 155]. In vision research literature, the Hill function is often called the Michaelis–Menten function or Naka–Rushton function [689].)

Yet another way to measure the photoresponse is to measure the change in the membrane current due to absorption of photons. The advantage of measuring the photocurrent is that it is not affected by interaction or coupling between neighboring cells. The amplitude of the response current of a rod to a single photon is about 1 pA. The response of a cone to a single photon is estimated to be about 30 fA. The rod response rises to a peak in about 200 ms, while the cone response peaks in about 55 ms and follows with an undershoot before returning to the dark level. The response–illuminance relation can be fairly described as an exponential function:

$$i = i_{max}(1 - e^{-kE}), \tag{12.3}$$

where i_{max} is the maximum current response and k is a constant. However, some photoreceptors can be better described by the Michaelis–Menten function or a weighted average of the exponential function and the Michaelis–Menten function [839].

Having reviewed the general characteristics of the photo response of rods and cones, let us examine the underlying mechanisms in more detail. The subject of the light response of photoreceptors has also been reviewed extensively in the literature (e.g., see [90, 589, 655, 802]).

The light-absorbing pigments in the rods and the cones consist of the chromophore (the light-absorbing atom or molecule) 11-*cis* retinal [454], which is embedded in a seven-helix transmembrane protein molecule called opsin. We now know that each type of photoreceptor contains only one type of pigment. It is the slight difference in the amino sequences of the opsin in the pigment that controls the difference in the absorption spectra of the different photoreceptors. As we mentioned before, there are three types of cones: L, M, and S cones. The names red, green, and blue cones are sometimes still used, but are not recommended because they are not individually responsible for producing the perception of red, green, and blue colors. The amino sequences of all four visual pigments (for the rod and L, M, S cones) have been worked out (from their DNA structures).

The outer segment of a rod or a cone contains a stack of roughly 1000–2000 membrane disks. In rods, the interior of the disk is not continuous with the external medium, whereas in cones it can be demonstrated that the disk interior is continuous with the external medium. Each disk contains numerous ($\approx 10^5$) pigment molecules. Light passing through the densely packed stack of disks has a very high probability (about 0.5–0.7 at the peak) of being absorbed by one of the pigment molecules.

So far, the best-studied photoreceptor response to light is that of the rhodopsin in the rod [149]. In the dark, some (fewer than 5%) of the cGMP-gated ion channels in the outer segment membrane are open and there is a steady dark current (Na^+ and Ca^{2+}) flowing from the cell body out to the extracellular space and then into the outer segment. The absorption of a photon by the rhodopsin molecule activates an enzymatic cascade that leads to closure of the channels in the plasma membrane of the outer segment. The cascade is initiated by the photoisomerization (from *cis* to *trans*) of the retinal chromophore of rhodopsin (R). Photo-excited rhodopsin (R*) then activates transducin (T). (The transducin is a G-protein which also plays important roles in many signal transduction processes in other cell functions.) The transducin, in turns, switches on a potent phosphodiesterase (PDE*) that rapidly hydrolyzes cGMP (guanosine 3′,5′ cyclic monophosphate). (Each of these cascaded reactions amplifies the signal a few hundred times. For example, a single R* activates about 500 transducins and the cGMP is hydrolyzed to 1/e of its initial concentration by fully activated PDE in only 0.6 ms.) The light-induced decrease in the cGMP level closes channels, thereby blocking the influx of cations. The absorption of a single photon causes the closure of a few hundred channels. The resulting hyperpolarization of the plasma membrane is transmitted to the synaptic terminal at the other end of the cell. In the dark, there is a constant release of neuro-transmitters to the bipolar cells. The light-induced hyperpolarization decreases the rate of the release and the absorption of photons thus modulates the output of the bipolar cells. The photoreceptor response to light (degree of hyperpolarization) is a graded potential, which is different from the later neural response in pulses of action potentials. Recovery of the dark state is mediated by deactivation of the PDE and activation of guanylate cyclase. The cGMP level is restored, and the membrane channels open again.

The isomerization of 11-*cis* retinal to the all-*trans* form is an efficient process, with a quantum yield of 0.6–0.7. The 11-*cis* retinal is very stable at normal body temperature. Spontaneous isomerization of the retinal chromophore of rhodopsin occurs at the rate of about once in a thousand years. Nature has chosen retinal as the chromophore of rhodopsin because it is unique among biomolecules in having a highly tunable absorption band, a high absorbance coefficient, a high quantum yield of photoisomerization, an extremely low thermal isomerization rate, a large light-induced conformational change, and a reactive group for attachment to opsin.

The transduction mechanism of vertebrate cones is very much like that of rods. The chromophore is again 11-*cis* retinal. The genes for the three human cones have been cloned and sequenced [694]. The deduced amino acid sequences can be folded into the seven-transmembrane helix motif of vertebrate rhodopsins. About 45% of the sequence of each of the cone pigments is identical to that of the rhodopsin. Likewise, the transducin in cones is similar to that in rods. Cones also contain a cGMP PDE that is like that of rods. Finally, the light-sensitive channel in the cone outer segments is gated by cGMP and has many features in common with the channels in rods. Thus, the transduction mechanisms of rods and cones are variations of the same fundamental theme.

The L cone and M cone pigments whose genes are on the X chromosome showed a 95% identity with each other, but only 43% identity with the S cone pigment, whose gene is on a different chromosome [264]. Neitz and Jacobs [703] concluded from their experiments that in color-normal humans: (1) there are discrete variations in both middle- and long-wavelength cone pigments, and (2) most individuals have more than three different cone pigment types. The cone mechanisms variant in Rayleigh color matching are separated by 3 nm. The actual difference in the peak sensitivity wavelengths of these two cone pigments is believed to be 6 nm.

The retina cone mosaic
The cones in the fovea form domains of fairly regular hexagonal arrays [591] (each cone has six nearest neighbors). The cone mosaic is less regular at higher eccentricity. The relative numbers of the L, M, and S cones are less certain, being estimated at roughly 61:31:8. However, high-resolution retinal imaging using adaptive optics shows that the proportion of L to M cones seems to vary significantly from individual to individual [803, 804, 1034]. Furthermore, there are large retinal patches in which either L or M cones are missing. Thus, it appears that the L cones and the M cones are not completely randomly distributed across the fovea. In the center of the fovea (about 20′ in diameter), the S cones are absent [225]. On the foveal slope, the S cone population increases to 12–14% [520, 1032]. Its peak density occurs at about 2° eccentricity. The S cones have longer inner segments and seem to form a

semi-regular array in the retina of the macaque monkey [855]. Within the human fovea, the center-to-center spacing, a, between cones is about 2.6 µm [591]. The Nyquist frequency is $1/\sqrt{3}a$, which is roughly 63 cycles per degree (assuming that 1 mm is 3.5°).

Photoreceptor noise
Retinal photoreceptors generate discrete electrical events in the dark that are indistinguishable from those evoked by light. The rate of these random events is highly dependent on the temperature, strongly suggesting that the noise originates from the thermal isomerizations of the chromophore molecule, 11-*cis* retinal. However, the isomerization seems to be a two-step process. First, the Schiff-base linkage between the chromophore and the protein is deprotonated. Second, the unprotonated form of the photopigment undergoes the thermal isomerization of 11-*cis* retinal to the all-*trans* form [55].

Photoreceptor's synapses with the other neurons
As we mentioned before, the rod and the cone also differ in the shape of their synaptic terminals. The rod spherule has a diameter of about 3 µm and the cone pedicle's diameter is about 8 µm. The rod spherule and the cone pedicle have pits (invaginations) where synaptic contacts with horizontal cells and bipolar cells occur (see Fig. 12.4). The human rod has a single pit which usually has 2–3 lateral processes (from horizontal cells) and 1–5 central ones (from bipolar cells). The cone contains 12–30 pits, each of which has two lateral processes from the horizontal cells and one central process from the bipolar cell (the three-process structure is called a triad). There is also some preliminary evidence that S cone pedicles are different from those of the other two types of cones in that they are smaller, have more synaptic vesicles, deeper invaginations, and basal processes extending into the outer plexiform layer.

Cone–cone and rod–cone interaction
Light microscopy shows that cone pedicles in the human fovea extend basal processes toward each other [14]. Since basal processes have been found to form gap junctions in many other species, this observation is a strong cue that gap junctions do exist between human fovea cones. Although 99% of the area (excluding the basal surface) around the cone pedicle is shielded by glia cell wrappings, as many as 15 gap junctions per pedicle have been reported in the macaque monkey retina [970] and they appear to couple neighboring photoreceptors (both cones and rods) nonselectively [241, p. 111, 970, Fig. 5, 1057].

Except for the gap junctions between rods and cones, and some other possible interaction through horizontal cells, the primary pathways for rods and cones are separate until they merge in the input to ganglion cells [241]. There is anatomical and psychophysical evidence that shows there are two pathways in the human rod visual system. One pathway is from rods to rod bipolar cells, to AII amacrine cells, and then either: (1) to depolarizing cone bipolar cells and ON-ganglion cells by way of gap junctions, or (2) to hyperpolarizing cone bipolar cells and OFF-ganglion cells by way of synapses. The other pathway is through the cone–rod gap junctions and onto the cone bipolar cells and then into the ON- and OFF-ganglion cells. The first pathway is believed to be active mainly at low light levels, while the second pathway is active at higher illuminance levels. Psychophysical data seem to show that there are two rod signals transmitted through the human retina at different speeds.

The first pathway may be the slower one, while the second pathway through cone–rod gap junctions may be the faster one [911].

12.4.2 Horizontal cells

There are at least two types of horizontal cells: H1 and H2 [230]. Evidence seems to indicate that there may be a third type, H3, which is about 30% larger than the traditionally classified H1 cells and contacts 30% more cones [520]. Both H1 and H2 horizontal cells synapse with more than one spectral type of cone in their dendritic fields. H1 cells receive nonopponent additive input from L and M cones, but seem to make only a few (if any) contacts with S cones. H2 cells also receive additive input from L and M cones (but they contact L and M cones sparsely within their dendritic fields), and they seem to make a large number of contacts with S cones, responding to all spectral input with hyperpolarization. H3 cells, on the other hand, seem to avoid any contact with the S cones. It has been proposed [520, p. 69] that H1 cells provide surround response to the luminance channel in the bipolar cells, H2 cells, which make contact with many L and M cones, provide yellow surround (via the cones) to the S cone bipolar cells and ganglion cells, and H2 and H3 horizontal cells could provide color-opponent surrounds for the midget bipolar cells. However, few recordings have been made from human or primate bipolar cells and they did not indicate well-developed surround responses. It is likely that amacrine cells may have a stronger contribution to the formation of the surround responses of the ganglion cells.

The dendrites of a horizontal cell divide repeatedly and their terminals form about 6–12 clusters of contact endings. The coverage of each cluster is roughly the size of a cone pedicle. Since each cone pedicle has 12–30 invaginations and each invagination triad has two processes from the horizontal cells, each cone is contacted by 24–60 horizontal cell dendritic terminals. These contacts come from about 6–8 horizontal cells. Therefore, an individual horizontal cell can make up to 10 contacts with a cone. Since a horizontal cell makes contact with many cones and since its processes in the synaptic triads are in direct contact with the bipolar processes, it is very likely that the function of a horizontal cell is to compute the average response of the surrounding cones to regulate the effect of light response of the center cone on the bipolar cells that are in contact. This center-surround receptive field plays a very important role in the retinal processing of the visual information.

In all species that have been studied, the horizontal cells respond to light (through photoreceptors) with graded potential change (hyperpolarization), similarly to the rods and cones. Mammalian horizontal cell response is hyperpolarization regardless of the wavelength of the incident light. Therefore, color-opponent processing does not seem to occur at this stage.

12.4.3 Bipolar cells

There are many types of bipolar cells in the human retina. Two basic classes are rod bipolar cells and cone bipolar cells. They receive input from rods and cones, respectively. Rod bipolar cells have finer and more bushy dendrites than cone bipolar cells and so far no further division into subclasses has been made [241]. Each rod bipolar cell contacts between 15 and 50 or more rod spherules, depending on eccentricity. All rod bipolar cell axons terminate close to the ganglion cell layer (sublamina b in Fig. 12.4) [126].

Cone bipolar cells can be divided into many subclasses, based on their contacts with the cone pedicles (such as invaginating and flat), the extent of their dendritic field (midget and diffuse), their response polarity (ON and OFF), and their synaptic contacts with the amacrine cells and the ganglion cells (inhibitory or excitatory). Of course, these features are not mutually exclusive and the number of functionally independent classes in the human retina is still not known. The differentiation between midget and diffuse classes is important. A midget bipolar cell makes contact with only one cone pedicle, while a diffuse (or parasol) bipolar cell makes contact with many (usually 5–10) cones. The midget bipolar cells thus preserve a spatial resolution as fine as the individual photoreceptor and they are found mostly in the fovea cone connections. The existence of ON and OFF classes is usually thought to increase the response resolution because they provide a larger dynamic range for signal modulation. ON-bipolar cells respond to a light spot projected onto their receptive field center with depolarization, while the OFF-bipolar cells respond with hyperpolarization. One type of midget bipolar cell has processes invaginated in the cone pedicles, forming the center process of the triad. Evidence shows that the invaginating midget bipolar cells carry the ON-channel. Another class of midget bipolar cells have their dendritic terminals contacting the cone pedicles at flat, basal junctions. These are called the flat midget bipolar cells, and are believed to carry the OFF-channel. From the fovea to the periphery, each midget bipolar cell is shown to have an exclusive contact with a single cone [126] and maybe only one midget ganglion cell. The midget bipolar cells are believed to serve only the L and the M cones.

The diffuse bipolars are also found to have flat and invaginating types. Another possible classification is according to the stratification of the axons in the inner plexiform layer, whether closer to the amacrine (sublamina a) or to the ganglion cells (sublamina b). Such a scheme leads to the classifications DB1–DB6, the six different types of the diffuse bipolar cells in rhesus monkeys [126]. Since the diffuse bipolar cells contact all cones in their dendritic fields, they are not likely to carry chromatic signals [126]. The S cone bipolar cells are morphologically distinct as a separate class [126]. Anther study suggests that the diffuse invaginating bipolar and the differently classified giant bistratified bipolar cells both receive S cone input [634].

Like photoreceptors and horizontal cells, bipolar cells respond to light in their receptive field with graded potential changes. Bipolar cells have center-surround receptive fields, with the excitatory center receiving input directly from the cones, and the inhibitory surround receiving input from the horizontal cells that pool over many cones in the neighborhood. The neural transmitter released by the photoreceptor to the bipolar cells is glutamate. The ON-bipolars respond by depolarizing and the OFF-bipolars by hyperpolarizing. Since both the ON- and the OFF-bipolar cells respond to the same neural transmitter, their response mechanisms must be different. It has been shown that 2-amino-4-phosphonobutyrate (APB) prolongs hyperpolarization in the ON-bipolar cells, making them unresponsive to subsequent light stimuli [834]. (In fact, APB suppresses the maintained as well as the light-driven activity of all ON-ganglion cells in cats [686].) On the other hand, the OFF-bipolar cells are largely unaffected.

Rod bipolar cells appear to depolarize in response to light (the ON cells) [1013]. Behavior studies show that under dark-adapted conditions when only rods are functional, APB blocks monkeys' detection of both light increment and light decrement, confirming that the primate rod bipolar cells are probably all of the ON type [834, p. 89]. Rod bipolar cells terminate in the inner portions (sublamina b) of the inner plexiform layer, just as do cone ON-bipolar cells. However, rod bipolar cells do not seem to contact the ganglion cells directly. Instead they form synaptic contacts with amacrine cells which in turn make excitatory contacts (gap junctions) with ON cone bipolar cells and inhibitory (glycinergic) contacts with OFF-bipolar cells and OFF-ganglion cells [1013]. This is one of the two rod signal pathways that we discussed before. The ON- and OFF-channels remain segregated in the LGN and start to converge in the visual cortex. Current evidence [834] seems to support the proposal that the ON-channel facilitates the detection of light increment and the OFF channel the detection of light decrement.

12.4.4 Amacrine cells

Amacrine cells are located between the bipolar cells and the ganglion cells. They make contact with these two groups of cells and with each other. There are many (as high as 30 according to some classifications) types of amacrine cells and almost every neuro-transmitter found in the brain can be found in some retinal amacrine cells. One of the most common amacrine cell types in the retina is the AII amacrine cell, which plays an important role in linking the rod bipolar cells to the ganglion cells. AII amacrine cells are coupled to each other by gap junctions and form a pool of activity similar to that of horizontal cells. Rod bipolar cells make sign-conserving (excitatory) synapses onto the dendrites of AII amacrine cells which contact ON-cone bipolar cells through gap junctions and make sign-inverting (inhibitory) synapses onto OFF-cone bipolar cells. Thus, AII amacrine cells provide the rod signals with the necessary neural circuits to merge into the ON- and the OFF-pathways of the ganglion cells [802, pp. 131–2]. Four other types of amacrine cell are also discussed in [801, Chapter 11]: ON-starburst, OFF-starburst, dopaminergic, and AI. One of the striking features of starburst amacrine cells is the large coverage factor of their dendritic fields. In primates, their coverage factor is about 10, meaning that each point on the retina is covered by the dendritic field of about 10 starburst amacrine cells. Dopaminergic amacrine cells control the degree to which AII amacrine cells are coupled through gap junctions [802, pp. 247 and 251]. In the dark, AII amacrine cells are strongly coupled, and therefore signals from more rods are pooled together to increase the sensitivity to light. In the light, they are decoupled by the dopaminergic amacrine cells. (From the digital image processing point of view, this provides a convolution mask whose size is dependent on luminance level!)

Electronic microscope study showed that each midget ganglion cell of the human parafoveal retina receives quantitatively as much synaptic input from amacrine cells as from the midget bipolar cell with which it forms exclusive contacts [520, Table 1].

12.4.5 Ganglion cells

Ganglion cells are the cells in the last layer of the retina. Their response to light differs from rods, cones, and bipolar cells, by sending out electrical pulses along their axons to the LGNs. Morphologically, there are at least four types of ganglion cells in the human retina:

midget ganglion cells, small parasol ganglion cells, large parasol ganglion cells, and small bistratified ganglion cells. Their dendritic diameter in fovea retina is 5–9 μm for midget ganglion cells, 10–35 μm for small parasols, and 25–90 μm for large parasols [520, p. 64]. However, there is conflicting evidence that the parasol cells form only a single cluster whose size distribution covers both the small and the large parasol cells as classified by Kolb [226]. The dendritic field size increases with eccentricity. For example, the dendritic diameter of the midget ganglion cells increases tenfold between 2 and 6 mm eccentricity, followed by a smaller increase, reaching 225 μm in the retinal periphery [227]. The midget ganglion cells carry the color-opponent signals to the parvocellular layers of the LGN, the small parasol ganglion cells carry the broad-band, tonic "luminance" signals also to the parvo layer, and the large parasol ganglion cells carry the broad-band, phasic signals to the magnocellular layers of the LGN. The term *tonic* means sustained (or lower temporal frequency) and the term *phasic* means transient (or high temporal frequency).

Midget ganglion cells are also called A cells, Pβ cells, or P cells (because they project to the parvocellular layers of the LGN). Parasol cells are also called B cells, Pα cells, or M cells (because they project to the magnocellular layers of the LGN). The dendritic field of a parasol cell is about four times wider than that of a midget cell. Each midget cell receives its major input from its associated midget bipolar cell in the form of about 50–80 synaptic contacts. It also makes about the same number of contacts with the amacrine cells [521].

Parasol cells whose dendrites stratify in the inner portion (sublamina b) of the inner plexiform layer (IPL) give ON-center responses, and those that stratify in the outer portion of the IPL layer give OFF-center responses. Similarly, midget cells also have ON-center and OFF-center types, depending on where their dendrites stratify in the inner plexiform layer. These four types of cells (midget ON and OFF, parasol ON and OFF) do not seem to receive input from S cones. A separate cell type, called the small bistratified cell, which has dendrites stratified in both the inner and outer portions of the IPL, seems to receive excitatory input from S cones [228]. The inner tier in sublamina b is larger in diameter and more densely branched than the outer tier in sublamina a (see Fig. 12.4). Its dendritic diameter is about 50 μm around the fovea and about 400 μm in the far periphery. The proportion of small bistratified ganglion cells ranges from about 1% of the total ganglion cells in the central retina to about 6–10% at the periphery. The small bistratified ganglion cells and the midget ganglion cells project to the parvocellular layers of the (dorsal) LGN, while the parasol ganglion cells project to the magnocellular layers of the (dorsal) LGN. It should be noted that these projections refer to the majority of the cells that have been studied. The details of the exact number, type, and projection of the many types of ganglion cells are still unknown.

The ON- and OFF-dendritic trees of the midget ganglion cells oppose one another but do not overlap, having a coverage of no greater than 1. The two mosaics have different spatial scales, with the ON-dendritic field being larger than the OFF-dendritic field in an area ratio of about 1.7:1 [227]. It was estimated that 80% are midget ganglion cells and 10% are parasol ganglion cells. The proportion of midget ganglion cells ranges from about 95% of the total ganglion cells in the fovea to about 45% at the periphery. The calculated Nyquist frequencies from the midget cell spacing closely match the measured human achromatic spatial acuity from 6° to 55° eccentricity [227]. Therefore, the visual resolution is limited by the ganglion cell density in this range of eccentricity. (In comparison, in the central vision of the fovea, the visual resolution is limited by the cone density.)

Many ganglion cells have center-surround receptive fields. The ON-cells are excited by illumination in the center and inhibited by illumination in the surround. The response profile is often approximated as the difference between two Gaussian functions. When their receptive fields are uniformly illuminated, the ganglion cells maintain a roughly constant rate of discharge, averaging about 20–30 impulses per second in the macaque retina under 2000 td illumination [964].[2] The peak discharge rate of a ganglion cell is between a few hundred and a thousand impulses per second, and therefore the sustained discharge rate of the ganglion cells is not high enough for decremental modulation. The ON- and OFF-channels thus serve the purpose of encoding the increments and the decrements of light with higher resolution.

In the center-surround receptive fields of ganglion cells, there are variations in the spectral responses in the center and the surround. These cells are called color-opponent cells. Since their properties are almost the same as those cells found in the LGN, and since cells in the LGN are easier to study, most studies on color-opponent properties were performed in the LGN. We will discuss the color-opponent encoding in the next section, where we discuss the structures and properties of the LGN.

Photosensitive ganglion cells

The ganglion cells that we have discussed tend to respond to spatial and/or temporal changes in the visual field. They derive their responses from the light incident on the rods and the cones. However, certain light-related biological responses, such as our internal clock (the circadian clock) and pupil control, are concerned more with the overall illumination level than with the spatial-temporal changes in visual patterns. The ganglion cells we have mentioned so far do not seem to fit this role.

A new class of ganglion cells (on the order of 1% of the total ganglion population) has been found in the mammal retinas. These ganglion cells are sensitive to light and their action spectra (peaked at about 484 nm) are different from those of the rods and the cones [107]. Furthermore, their response kinetics are much slower (on the order of several seconds) than typical ganglions. Their response thresholds are higher (about the illumination by the dawn sky), and their dendritic field sizes are large (about 500 μm in diameter). The photosensitive pigments seem to be distributed over both cell soma and cell dendrites. These ganglion cells are mostly located in the OFF sublayer of the inner plexiform layer. They project to the suprachiasmatic nucleus of the hypothalamus (known to be involved in the circadian clock) and also possibly to the olivary pretectal nucleus which is involved in the pupil control neural circuits [383].

12.5 Lateral geniculate nucleus (LGN)

The ganglion cells in the retina transmit visual signals through the optic nerves that branch out to different areas in the brain. The majority of them terminate at the LGNs in the

---

[2]   The troland (symbol td) is defined in Section 11.4.

thalamus. The human lateral geniculate nucleus has six major layers, each of which can be divided into two sublayers: the principal sublayer and the koniocellular (or the intercalated) sublayer (see Fig. 12.3). Each major layer is about 6–10 cells thick. Although the LGN receives input from both eyes, the signals from the two eyes remain separate in the LGN. Each of the six layers receives input from only one eye. For example, major layers 1, 4, and 6 receive input from only the opposite (contralateral) eye, and major layers 2, 3, and 5 receive input from the eye on the same side as the LGN (see Fig. 12.3). All layers maintain a well-registered map of half the visual field. If cell recordings are made along a perpendicular path through the layers, the receptive fields of all the cells encountered correspond to roughly the same region in the visual field, except areas where there is no correspondence between the two eyes. Cells in layers 1 and 2 are larger in size than those in the other four layers. Therefore, layers 1 and 2 are called the magnocellular layers and the other four layers, the parvocellular layers. The magnocellular neurons (M cells) exhibit transient responses when light stimuli are turned on or off or when they are moved across the visual field. The parvocellular neurons (P cells) respond to prolonged illumination with sustained discharges.

The receptive fields of the P cells and the M cells are center-surround organizations, similar to those of the ganglion cells – so similar that the LGN was once considered as merely a relay station for the ganglion cells. However, the LGN also receive fibers from the cerebral cortex, and from the brainstem. Therefore, the LGN are more than just relay stations. There is evidence that an LGN also functions as an attention filter [862]. The spectral sensitivities of the center and the surround of many LGN cells are the opposite of each other (e.g., the center is more sensitive to long-wavelength light while the surround is more sensitive to middle-wavelength light). Spectrally, there are three types of P cells: broad-band, red–green opponent, and yellow–blue opponent. The M cells do not seem to show any clear chromatic opponency. The color encoding is the subject of discussion shortly.

Based on numerous anatomical, physiological, and psychophysical studies, it appears that P cells and M cells form two distinct visual pathways: the P pathway and the M pathway [599, 1066]. Discrimination of color, fine pattern, and texture require the parvocellular layers, while perception of motion and depth require the magnocellular layers. Immunoreactive staining also reveals that the koniocellular (or intercalated) sublayer cells in each of the six main layers seem to form a distinct third channel (in addition to the P and M channels) that projects to the visual cortex [392, 393, 802]. Retrograde labeling shows that these cells provide input to the cytochrome oxidase-rich blobs in layers 2 and 3 of the primary visual cortex that are known to have mostly cells that process color information.

12.5.1 Color-opponent encoding

Color vision is possible only when photoreceptors of more than one type work together by comparing the information they sense from the incoming spectra. A single type of sensor, such as a rod used in low-light vision, can only signal how much light is coming from a spatial location. A red flower will appear darker than a yellow flower, but not different in other perceptual attributes. When there are two or more types of photoreceptor, such as the L, M, and S cones, working together to compare the separate information they have gathered, spectral attributes can be computed. The L cones have a larger response than the M cones for a red flower, and the opposite may be true for a yellow flower. But how is color information processed and encoded in the various stages along the neural pathways? It turns out that the L, M, and S cone signals are not sent to the brain independently in three separate channels. In fact, one of the major design principles of the neural signal processing is to preserve retinal image contrast, or even enhance the differences spectrally, spatially, and temporally. The three cone signals are compared and combined early on, and by the time they reach the ganglion cells, color seems to be coded in opponent processes. For example, one type of ganglion cell responds to a small spot of long wavelength illuminating the center of the receptive field by increasing the pulse rate, but to a larger spot of middle-wavelength light by decreasing the pulse rate. The long wavelength is excitatory, but the middle wavelength is inhibitory – there is an opposite response for different wavelengths.

There are many types of ganglion and LGN cells. Figure 12.7 shows some of the major types that have been found. The notation used is R, G, B, Y, and W, representing the long wavelength, middle wavelength, short wavelength, long + middle wavelength, and wideband spectra. This notation is how those cells were labeled when they were first found; it might have been better to label them using the L, M, and S notation. However, there are questions about whether these center or surround fields are contributed by one or more types of cones. Therefore, we will tentatively use R, G, B, Y, and W here, with the understanding

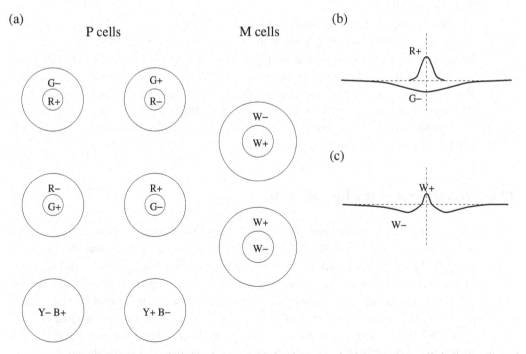

Figure 12.7. Cell types found in the LGN: (a) the six types of color-opponent cells in the P cells and the M cells; (b) a model of the R+ G− receptive field; (c) a model of the center-surround broadband receptive field.

that they are not directly linked to our perception of red, green, blue, yellow, and white. The color-opponent cells are mostly found among the P cells, while the broadband cells are among the M cells. However, it is important to point out that the spectral responses of cells that belong to the same type, say, R+ G−, are not exactly identical. In fact, they tend to vary continuously; so much so that initially there was a lot of difficulty describing what their spectral response characteristics were, other than using vague words such as red, green, yellow, and blue. Fortunately, studies with better control in the spectral composition of the stimuli give us some good ways to described them. One such description is based on a color space called the DKL color space [480], because it was first explicitly expressed in a paper by Derrington, Krauskopf, and Lennie [252], who did an extensive analysis of the spectral responses of the LGN cells, using this color space. The DKL color space consists of one luminance axis and two chromatic axes. The luminance axis represents the CIE photopic luminance. Depending on how the cone sensitivities L and M are scaled, we can write the luminance axis as $w_1 L + w_2 M$. One convention is to scale the cone sensitivities so that the luminance is simply $L + M$. One of the two chromatic axes is defined as the constant S axis. That is, points along this axis have different L and/or M responses, but their S responses are all the same. The other chromatic axis is the constant L and M axis. Points along these axes have different S responses, but they all have the same L and M responses. These two axes are sometimes called the cardinal axes. Derrington, Krauskopf, and Lennie found that most of the LGN cells fall on one of three planes in the DKL space, meaning that substitution of one stimulus by another on the same plane does not change the response of that class of cells.

Although many studies have been done to quantify how color information is encoded in our neural pathways, currently there are still no definitive models that can account for the many varied observations. Specifically, the psychophysical color appearance data are not directly correlated with those that have been measured from neurons. For example, the opponent color processes proposed by Hering [396], and Hurvich and Jameson [436] do not correspond to the DKL color axes. A similar difference exists between spatial frequency channels and the observed neural responses. It seems that the neural correlates with perceptual attributes lie further up in the brain.

12.6   Visual areas in the human brain

The total area of the human cerebral cortex is about 1500–1900 cm^2. About 27% of the area is predominantly for vision, 8% for hearing, 7% for the sense of touch, and 7% for motor control [982]. The large visual cortex area has been found to consist of many subareas, each of which is involved in a different step or specialized processing of visual information. The full complexity is far from clear, but the understanding of the organization of the visual areas has been much refined due to the use of functional magnetic resonance imaging (fMRI) [262, 980, 981, 1007]. The brain cortex is a convoluted three-dimensional surface and therefore is difficult to draw on a flat display. Using computers, it is possible to flatten out the cortical surface (like projecting the earth's surface on a flat map). Figure 12.8 shows a schematic flat map of the right brain cortex and the approximate locations of the various

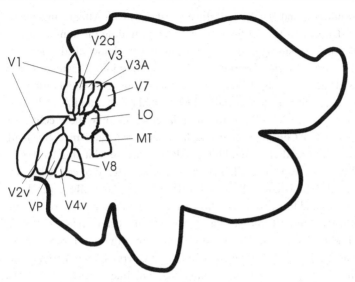

Figure 12.8. Schematic diagram of the flattened map for the right human brain, showing the various visual cortical areas (redrawn from [982]).

visual areas. Most of the areas have not been well studied yet and some of the areas are not named universally (for example, the area MT in the human is tentatively so named here because its response characteristics are similar to the corresponding area in the macaque monkey). Many of the areas, such as V1, V2, V4, and MT, have been studied extensively in the monkey. Area V1 is the primary area to which LGN neurons project. Area MT has been shown to be essential for motion perception. It should be noted that even the size of the well-studied areas can vary from individual to individual by a factor of as much as 2 or more. The boundaries between neighboring areas are often quite subtle and cannot be distinguished with high resolution. Since these areas are partitioned by response characteristics, anatomy, and physiology, some ambiguities and inhomogeneities do exist. Therefore, the map serves only as a rough guide of our current understanding and should not be taken too literally.

The visual cortex studies that will be discussed here were on the macaque monkey, unless the desciption explicitly refers to humans. Differences between the macaque and the human visual areas have only begun to be mapped out by fMRI in recent years. In particular, human V3A is much more sensitive to motion [956], and human V4 seems to be located in a different location [999].

12.6.1 Primary visual cortex

The primary visual cortex (area V1) is about 2 mm thick. The human V1 area is about 20–30 cm^2, which, as a percentage of the total cortex area, is relatively smaller than that of the macaque monkey. The primary visual cortex contains about 200 million cells in each half of the brain. When we compare this with the 1.5 million cells in the LGN, we expect to find that there is a lot of signal processing here. Initially, neuroscientists, who were recording from the neurons in the monkey visual cortex, used diffuse light to illuminate the retina to see if the cells would respond, but the cells did not respond at all. After trying many different types of stimuli, Hubel and Wiesel finally succeeded in finding the stimuli to which these cells would respond very strongly. Although we do not yet know all the details, it seems that the cells in the primary visual cortex may be computing image features such as edges, lines, corners, and ends of a line, etc. (see [418] for a fascinating account of this discovery).

The axons of LGN neurons terminate in the two sublayers, α and β, of layer 4C of the primary visual cortex. The M cells terminate in layer 4Cα, while the P cells terminate in layer 4Cβ (see Fig. 12.3). Cells in layer 4C still have center-surround receptive fields similar to the LGN cells, but instead of responding weakly to a diffuse white light as the LGN cells do, they virtually do not respond at all. This is a continuous trend of cell behavior as we go from the retina to LGN and then to the visual cortex and beyond. Cells respond to more and more specific stimuli and less and less to diffuse light. From layer 4Cα, we find projections to layer 4B, and then from 4B to other visual association cortex areas, such as V5. From layer 4Cβ, we find projections to layers 2 and 3, and from there to layers 5 and 6, and to other visual areas, such as V2, V3, and V4. In the sublayers of layer 4, Hubel and Wiesel found many cells that respond strongly to stimuli that look like edges and lines. They called them simple-cells, because their receptive field structures are simpler than the complex-cells that they found in layers 2, 3, 5, and 6. Almost all cells are orientation selective. They only respond to lines or edges that are oriented in a certain direction and their response amplitudes decrease sharply when the features are oriented about 10–20° off the optimal angle. Figure 12.9 shows three types of receptive field for such simple-cells. The size of a simple-cell receptive field ranges from $\frac{1}{4}°$ near the fovea to 1° at the far periphery. The

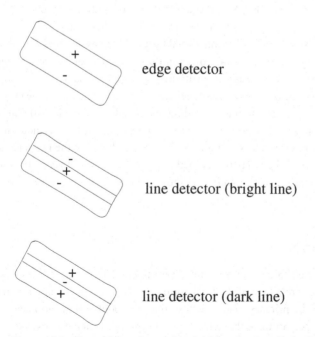

edge detector

line detector (bright line)

line detector (dark line)

Figure 12.9. Three types of receptive field for simple-cells in the primary visual cortex. The "+" means excitatory region and the "−" the inhibitory region.

width of the center bar of a line detector is only a few minutes of arc (Fig. 12.9). To evoke sustained responses from the simple-cells, the line or the edge has to be critically positioned and oriented.

Complex-cells respond to moving lines and edges, and they do not have clear excitatory and inhibitory regions in their receptive fields. They respond to lines and edges moving through their receptive fields with the correct orientations. Complex-cells have larger receptive fields than simple-cells. Near the fovea, the field size is about $\frac{1}{2}° \times \frac{1}{2}°$. The width of the bar in the field is about the same as that of a simple-cell. We still do not know how the complex-cell receptive field is constructed from its input signals.

Another interesting type of cell is the end-stopped cell. Simple-cells and complex-cells respond best to lines that are as long as their receptive fields. End-stopped cells respond best when the line ends in a certain region of its receptive field. If the line is longer, the response weakens or disappears.

All simple-cells, complex-cells, and end-stopped cells are orientation selective, and they are mostly not particularly selective to color changes. That is, for most cells, their receptive fields are the same whether they are mapped out using white light, or colored light. However, a separate group of cells in layers 2 and 3 has a completely different behavior. These cells were identified by staining the cortex for the enzyme cytochrome oxidase. The staining patterns look like dark blobs, patches, or spots. Some cells in the blobs have receptive fields that are similar to those of the LGN color opponent cells. Some others have center-surround receptive fields, but they are different from the color-opponent cells of the LGN. For example, the center is excited by long-wavelength light, but inhibited by middle-wavelength light, while the surround responds in the opposite way. The spatial-opponency and the color-opponency coincide exactly, and these cells are called double-opponent cells. Their receptive field centers are several times larger than those of the color-opponent cells in the LGN. Yet another type of cell has a color-opponent center and a nonchromatically opponent surround [968]. It is also found that within the same blob, cells seem to have the same color opponency. Blobs dedicated to red/green color opponency are about three times more numerous than those dedicated to yellow/blue [968].

With the complicated cell response behaviors described above, we cannot help wondering how so much computation can be accomplished in so few steps along the neural signal processing pathways. What is more amazing is the finding that macaque V1 neurons seem to signal illusory contours [367, 587]. Therefore, not only true edges and lines are detected here, but also the proper completion of contours may be accomplished as early as V1. More data are needed to confirm such complicated behavior. The other aspect that is still not clearly understood is the role of feedforward and feedback gain controls from other precortex and cortex areas to the primary visual cortex. Anatomically, we have found many such neural contacts. Psychophysical evidence is beginning to show that these gain control signals shape the information encoding as early as the primary visual cortex V1 [963].

One other important discovery made by Hubel and Wiesel about the primary visual cortex is the spatial organization of eye-preference and orientation-preference cells. Cells receiving input predominantly from one eye are arranged in a stripe against another stripe that has cells from the other eye. They also found that orientation preference

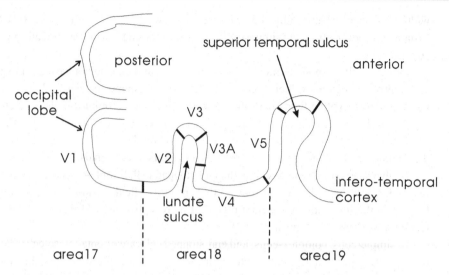

Figure 12.10. A schematic diagram of the visual cortical areas (redrawn from Fig. 17.1 in [52]).

differs by about $10°$ for every 0.05 mm distance parallel to the surface of the cortex. This type of cell organization seems to imply that a spatial point in the visual field is analyzed with respect to all possible orientations in a very small and localized region of V1.

12.6.2   Other cortical areas

The primary cortex area, V1, sends major projections to other cortical areas, such as V2, V3, and V5, and it also sends minor projections to V3A and V4, etc. Figure 12.10 shows a simple sketch of the relative locations of the various cortical areas. These other cortical areas are identified as distinct regions by their connection patterns, topographic organizations, and other physiological properties [981]. The best-studied area among these is V2 [969]. When stained for cytochrome oxidase, V2 shows alternate dark and pale stripes. Two types of stripe can be seen in the dark stripes: thin stripes and thick stripes. Therefore we have three histologically defined structures in the V2 areas and they are found to be connected to the three divisions in V1: the thin stripes are connected to the blobs in V1, the pale stripes to the interblob regions, and the thick stripes to the M-pathway in layer 4B of V1.

From V2, the thin stripes and the pale stripes both project to V4, and the thick stripes project to V3 and V5. The structure of V3 is less studied, but we find that V3 receives major projections from layer 4B in V1 and projects to both V4 and V5. In area V4, we find cells whose responses are more directly related to perceptual attributes of color, such as hue, rather than to wavelength. For example, because of the change of the spectral composition of the illumination, part of a colored object may reflect a different spectrum into the retina, but our perceived color of that object remains the same. Some V4 cells also respond in the same way without being confused by the wavelength changes. In area V5, we find cells that respond to perceived global motion, rather than to the local optical flow. For example, if two gratings are moving in perpendicular directions, we see a combined global motion in the diagonal direction. However, local optical flow analysis shows that each grating is moving in a different direction. Cells in the LGNs respond to the local optical flow vectors, but some cells in V5 respond to the perceived global motion vector, instead. In the still higher cortical areas, cells respond to even more global and three-dimensional concepts, such as surface orientation [971, 979]. These findings suggest that by the time we reach cortical areas V4 and V5, perceptual attributes have been extracted from the raw visual signals sensed by the retina. V4 further projects to the inferior temporal cortex which is known to process information about the "what" aspect of an object, such as the form, shape, and color. V5 further projects to the posterior parietal cortex which is known to process information about the "where" aspect of an object, such as location, and motion. However, it should be pointed out that the functions of the two cortical pathways, one to the inferior temporal cortex and the other to the posterior parietal cortex, are not clearly understood. Instead of the "what" and "where" visual functions, the inferior temporal pathway is said to process perceptual representation and the posterior parietal to process visuomotor control signals [666]. The existence of many pathways to process different aspects of visual perception may explain some very strange behavior in patients who suffer from brain damage in one of the pathways [403, 782].

12.7 Visual perception and the parallel neural pathways

In our discussion of neural structures and connections of the retina and the visual cortex, we have mentioned three main concurrent processing pathways: (1) the P–I pathway (parvo → $4C\beta$ → interblob → pale stripe → V4), (2) the P–B pathway (parvo → $4C\beta$ → blob → thin stripe → V4,V5), and (3) the M pathway (magno → $4C\alpha$ → 4B → thick stripe → V3,V5). Evidence for the existence of such parallel neural pathways comes mainly from the anatomical tracing of neural projections from one area to another, and from the morphological (shape), chemical (staining), and physiological (extra- and intra-cellular recordings) classification of cell types. However, it should be pointed out that the segregations between these pathways are not complete and independent. Lesion studies also indicate that the parvo- and the magno-cells from LGNs may provide input to other pathways than those in the above projections. By measuring the response characteristics of a cell, we cannot say to which pathway it belongs. For example, the P–B pathway is characterized by cells that have high wavelength selectivity, but similar selectivity can also be found in the other two pathways. Similarly, stereo disparity selectivity can be found in both the P–I and M pathways. Table 12.1 shows how cells with various selectivities are found in the different cortical areas and visual pathways of the macaque monkey (which has been shown to have very similar color vision to humans) in terms of percentages. It is therefore not correct to say, for example, that cells in the M pathway do not respond to chromatic signals just because the M pathway seems to be mainly for processing motion information. There are at least two reasons why making such a statement is likely to be misleading: (a) color information may also be useful for computing motion, and (b) the M pathway may be processing more than just motion information. So what is a proper or most likely interpretation of these parallel

Table 12.1. *Selectivities of neurons in various areas in the macaque*

These numbers were complied by DeYoe and Van Essen [253] from different studies. They are meant to provide only an approximate idea of how cells of different selectivities are found. The actual numbers could vary significantly from different studies.

Area	Wavelength	Direction of motion	Orientation	Stereo disparity
V1 blob	65%	little	little	not tested
V1 inter-blob	40%	little	high incidence	high incidence
V1 4B	10%	50%	85%	moderate incidence
V2 thin stripes	85%	5%	20% (varies)	30% (varies)
V2 pale stripes	65% (varies)	0%	20%	20%
V2 thick stripes	15%	20%	50%	70%
V3	15%	40%	70%	40%
V4	50%	5%	50%	40%
MT (V5)	0%	85%	75%	70%

pathways? DeYoe and Van Essen [253] provide a plausible view of such an interpretation as follows.

Vision is concerned with extracting information about three-dimensional objects and environments from two-dimensional retinal images. Visual information is described in our visual system in terms of certain perceptual attributes, such as color (hue, saturation, and lightness), shape, motion, depth, etc. These perceptual attributes have to be computed from two-dimensional retinal images, from which one can compute the sensory cues, such as the gradient of the image irradiances as a measure of local contrast, the density and orientation of local edges as a measure of local textures, and the relative variations of the L, M, and S cone excitations at different spatial positions as a measure of reflectance and illumination changes, etc. To derive the perceptual attributes from the sensory cues is a very complex computational problem [636]. A given sensory cue can be used to help compute many visual attributes and any given visual attribute requires more than one sensory cue for its robust computation.

Knowing that the human brain has localized centers for certain sensory or motor functions allows us to assume that one visual attribute is mainly computed in one localized cortical area. Since the visual attributes are normally quite different from the physical cues that they are computed from, we do not expect that the computations can be accomplished in one step. For example, a white object in the shade may reflect less light than a black object under the sun, but our perceptual attribute, lightness, is more correctly correlated with the actual reflectance of the object, than with the amount of light reflected from the object. In order to compute such a correct visual attribute, it is necessary to group pixels into objects, make an inference about the surface shape, compute the spatial layout, and estimate the illumination distribution. Each of these steps is difficult and may itself require many steps to compute. But, more importantly, the results from each of these steps are also useful for deriving other visual attributes as well. It is true that certain computations use one type of physical cue more heavily than others. For example, motion may not require high-resolution spatial information because the image areas under motion are blurred anyway. To the extent that such demands of low-level image information can be parceled into different spectral–temporal–spatial signal partitions, our neural computations can be processed in

Table 12.2. *The main characteristics of the three visual pathways*

Pathway	Spatial resolution	Temporal resolution	Contrast sensitivity	Color selectivity
P–I	high	low	low	yes
P–B	low	low	high	yes
M	low	high	high	no

parallel, and so we can justify the existence of parallel processing streams. However, the computational results from each intermediate step need to be shared among various processes that eventually lead to different perceptual attributes. We therefore expect that these parallel pathways will diverge and converge, and share information along the progressive stages from the retina to LGN, V1, V2, V3, V4, V5 and beyond. Furthermore, some computations may have to be duplicated among pathways, if sharing is not complete. Viewed from this perspective, it is not surprising if we find wavelength-selective cells, or stereo-selective cells in the motion pathway.

With the above perspective, we can now discuss the general characteristics of the three pathways. Their main characteristics are listed in Table 12.2. The P–I pathway seems to be involved in the perceptual tasks of shape and orientation discrimination and computation. The P–B pathway seems to be computing color perception. The M pathway seems to be involved in movement perception, depth perception, and figure–ground discrimination [599]. These perceptual tasks are found to be highly correlated with the response characteristics of the neurons that are typically found in the associated pathways. (Although most of the anatomical studies were performed on monkeys, there is evidence that the correlation is also the same in humans [599, 977, 1066].) For example, our motion perception is insensitive to color, has high temporal resolution and low spatial resolution, and high contrast sensitivity, all of which are characteristic of the cells found in the M pathway. If we create an equiluminant target of red and green bars drifting across the visual field, we do not see the motion very well, although we are aware of the changing of the position of the red and the green bars. Since the M cells have a broadband sensitivity, they cannot detect the boundary between the equiluminant red and green bars and, therefore, are not able to compute the motion information from them very effectively. On the other hand, the P–I pathway is sensitive to color and it responds to the shape and orientation of the bars. This type of stimulus almost never occurs in nature, and the strange perception of such a dissociation of form and motion perception is a very surprising validation of our anatomical and physiological findings about the parallel visual pathways! We can take advantage of these unique characteristics of our visual perception in many of the color imaging applications.

12.8 Problems

12.1 Describe the main differences in the characteristics between rods and cones, in terms of morphology, cell structure, response dynamic range, light sensitivity, and retinal distribution.

12.2 Let us assume that the photoreceptor response voltage, V, is related to the retina image irradiance, E, by the Hill function:

$$V = \frac{V_m E^n}{E^n + E_0^n}. \tag{12.4}$$

One hypothesis proposed in the literature is that the lightness, L^* in CIELAB, as a function of Y (luminance) is a good fit to the first half of the Hill function. Determine the proper values of V_m, E_0, and n that produce a "best" fit. How do you interpret V_m and E_0 in such a fit?

12.3 The 11-*cis* retinal is very stable at normal body temperature. Spontaneous isomerization of the retinal chromophore of rhodopsin occurs once in a thousand years. However, our retina contains about 92 million rods and each rod contains about 1500 membrane disks, each of which contains about 10^5 rhodopsin molecules. On the average, how many spontaneous isomerizations per second occur in the retina? How do our eyes cope with this noise level?

12.4 Experiments show that the measured color matching functions are slightly different for different observers. Discuss the various factors that might account for such differences.

12.5 The primary pathways for rods and cones remain separate until they merge into the input to ganglion cells. Describe how and where the rod signals merge with the cone signals.

12.6 It is often said that the retina has a mixed signal processing structure, i.e., visual signals are represented in analog and digital forms at different stages of processing. Can you point out which part is analog (graded potential) and which part is digital (pulses of action potential)?

12.7 What are the P-pathway and the M-pathway? What are their possible visual functions?

13 Visual psychophysics

An important part in our study of color imaging science is the subject of image perception. Before we embark on that topic, we need to review some general results from visual psychophysics. In many cases, understanding how we perceive a reproduced image is not sufficient, because we also need to understand how we perceive the original (three-dimensional) scene so that we can make a reasoning about and judgment of the imaging and reproduction processes.

In this chapter, we will discuss the nature of psychophysical measurements and the various psychophysical phenomena in visual perception. Psychophysics is the science of studying the (human) psychological responses to physical stimuli. Since our psychological responses are subject to the influence of many variables, the major problem in psychophysics is to define the physical stimulus carefully so that only the relevant response is measured. The formulation of most psychophysical problems is obviously very difficult and the majority of psychophysical experiments have not succeeded well in this respect. Therefore, most experimental results in psychophysics are not easy to interpret. The dilemma is that, if the stimulating configurations are very specific, we wonder if the results are useful for other configurations. If they are not well controlled, we wonder which factors in the configurations are affecting the responses. Discussions on these concerns and other theoretical issues would take us too far from our main objective here. Our emphasis will be more on experimental observations, rather than theoretical models. If visual perception were better understood, we would be able to present our knowledge in a better organized manner. In fact, there have been many theories and hypotheses that we could have built upon to simplify our presentation, but we feel that at this moment, these theories or models do not have sufficient validity and generality to warrant such a presentation. Therefore, in this chapter we will first present the experimental foundations of certain simple principles regarding visual perception and then we will discuss various aspects of vision that will help our later study of imaging system design and evaluation issues, and also important visual phenomena that will be useful as constraints or guidance when we study the computational models of vision. Hopefully, this emphasis on experimental data and observations will avoid one of the problems in some areas in vision research: too much theorizing and too little study of what is to be explained [290, Preface].

13.1 Psychophysical measurements

Typical responses measured in psychophysical experiments can be classified into seven categories (according to Stevens [904]): (1) Absolute thresholds: what is the minimum strength of a stimulus we can detect? (2) Differential (incremental or decremental) thresholds: what is the minimum change in a stimulus that we can detect? (3) Equality (or matching): which stimuli that differ in certain physical attributes (such as spectral composition in color matching) are perceptually equal? (4) Rank ordering: how is a set of stimuli arranged in order according to some perceptual attribute? (5) Equal interval: what physical stimuli produce equal differences in some perceptual attribute? (6) Equal ratio: what physical stimuli produce equal ratios in some perceptual attribute? (7) The subjective estimation of physical attributes. These seven categories vary greatly in difficulty and reliability. Unfortunately, in color imaging applications, we are often interested in measuring the "higher" level or more subjective responses and hence have to deal with even worse problems in the reliability and interpretation of the measured results. The best strategy is always to formulate the experiments in one of the first four categories, whenever possible. These issues will be discussed in the context of psychometric methods later.

There are three main areas in psychophysics that are of interest to us: (1) How do we quantify psychological responses (measurement scale)? (2) What psychophysical methods are useful for measuring responses (psychometric methods)? (3) How do we interpret psychophysical data for color imaging applications (data interpretation)? The last area covers both error analysis and data extrapolation. Our presentation here is necessarily limited in scope and depth. Readers should consult books and papers that deal with the topics in more details (e.g., [298, 342, 361, 370, 904]).

13.1.1 Measurement scales

In our everyday conversation, it is often easy to say that one color is much brighter than another without being more specific about how much brighter. Brightness perception is one aspect of our sensory processes that we learn to relate and communicate with others without having to define quantitatively. However, if we want to be more precise in quantifying the brightness of an object, we immediately appreciate the basic problems in psychophysical measurements. The first problem is to define the nature of the mapping between numbers and perceived brightness. We assume that such a mapping is possible and the problem is what experimental procedure should be used to derive that mapping. We need a rule (or a process) to assign a number to the perceptual quantity and the rule is called a scale for that quantity. For brightness perception, this rule is called the brightness scale. However, since a scale is determined by an experimental procedure, it may not be unique, and this is a major source of problems when we try to apply psychophysical data to an imaging application.

There are typically four different types of scale that are used in psychophysics. They are the nominal scale, the ordinal scale, the interval scale, and the ratio scale. These scales are defined by their empirical operations. The nominal scale is used only for determination of equality, the ordinal scale, for determination of greater or less, the interval scale, for determination of equality in differences, and the ratio scale, for determination of equality of ratios. We are interested only in the interval scale and the ratio scale. By definition, the interval scale is determined by judging equality of differences, it does not need to have an origin, i.e., zero point. For example, if we take a piece of white paper and a piece of black paper, and we ask an observer to select a piece of gray paper that is equally different from both of them in lightness, we can collect a set of data that tell us what the reflectance factor of the gray paper should be to produce a lightness that is half way between those of the white paper and the black paper. We can then repeat this process to determine other equal-difference points and come up with an interval scale for lightness because it is determined by judgments of equality in differences. In this process, there is no need to assume an origin (i.e., the zero point) because as far as the process is concerned, it is irrelevant. In comparison, the ratio scale requires the existence of a zero point so that it is meaningful to talk about ratios. For example, we can show a piece of dark gray paper A and a piece of light gray paper B, and ask an observer to select a piece of even lighter paper C so that the lightness of B to A is equal to lightness C to B. Again, by repeating this process, we can determine a ratio scale of lightness. In this procedure, we have implicitly assumed that there is something called zero lightness and all other lightness values are measured from that zero point. Thus, it is meaningful to talk about lightness B, lightness A and their ratio. Fortunately, experiments seem to show that these two lightness scales are equivalent (i.e., they can be described by the same mathematical equation, $L = Y^p - c$, where L is the perceived lightness, Y is the luminance of the paper, c is a constant, and p is approximately 1/3 for light surround).

13.1.2 Psychometric methods

Historically, psychometric measurements were produced by assuming that observers used the same criteria for the same task, that they have infinite patience and that they are always consistent from trial to trial. Very soon it was recognized that these assumptions were unrealistic and new methods (or procedures) for psychophysical measurements are developed. However, not every psychometric quantity can be measured by a single efficient and accurate method, and trade-offs between cost, feasibility, time, and accuracy have to be made in choosing a method for a psychophysical experiment. Among the many variations, the following are the most frequently used:

- Method of adjustment
  The observer is provided with a standard stimulus S_s with the task of adjusting a variable stimulus S_v so that S_v appears equal to S_s. S_v is initially set so that it appears very different from S_s.
- Method of limits (method of just noticeable difference)
  In one variation of this method, the variable stimulus S_v is initially set equal to S_s. The observer adjusts S_v in small steps until its difference from S_s is just noticeable. In another variation, the experimenter adjusts the stimulus and the observer indicates its appearance relative to S_s or according to a criterion.
- Method of paired comparison
  Stimuli are presented in pairs and the observer chooses from each pair which one is greater or less than the other in some perceptual attribute.

- Method of constant stimuli

  If a stimulus of constant strength is presented many times, the observer may or may not perceive it the same way every time. In the measurement of an absolute threshold, the same stimulus may or may not be visible or detected every time. If the stimulus is presented 20 times, and the observer reports seeing it 15 times, the probability of detection is estimated at 75%. Now, if seven or more levels of stimulus are mixed in a large number of presentations, with each level repeated many times randomly and intermixed with other levels, we can determine the probability of detection as a function of the stimulus level (called the psychometric function). This type of repeated presentation of a constant stimulus to determine detection probability is called the method of constant stimuli. This method seems to be the most reliable and widely used method for determining thresholds. The method can be combined with the method of paired comparison in which a constant stimulus is paired with many others and repeated many times.

- Method of rating scale

  Each of a set of stimuli is given an absolute rating, with or without comparison with a reference stimulus or reference stimuli. In one form of the method (called magnitude estimation), the observer is given a reference stimulus with an assigned sensory magnitude, say 100. Other stimuli are then presented and the observer is instructed to give an estimate of the corresponding sensory magnitude for each stimulus, with the specific constraint that ratios are to be preserved.

The method of adjustment and the method of limits suffer from lack of control of the criteria used by the observer. Two different observers may use different criteria to judge when the stimuli are equal or just noticeable. Furthermore, these two methods are also shown to produce biased estimates. For example, in the method of adjustment, an observer may stop adjusting prematurely because of frustration, or may overadjust the stimulus control to make sure that some difference can be surely observed. For these reasons, these two methods are not and should not be used when the method of constant stimuli under computer control can be used. Currently, a widely used procedure is multiple alternative forced choice, in which the observer is forced to choose in which of the few time intervals (presented sequentially) or alternative stimuli (presented simultaneously), the desired signal is present. This procedure can be used under computer control to determine some threshold value or some psychometric function very quickly and accurately.

13.1.3 Data interpretation

Because of the subjective nature of many psychophysical measurements, experimental data are often difficult to interpret. Even among experts in psychophysics, opinions vary as to the reliability of different procedures and methods of measurement. For engineers, who are trained to deal with physical measurements, psychophysical data (probably with the exception of visual threshold data) are often questionable. This is completely reasonable and healthy. However, in order to optimize or improve the performance of a color imaging system, we cannot avoid using psychophysical data entirely. Therefore, we have to appreciate their limitations, while taking full advantage of them whenever no reliable alternatives are available. Here we offer several cautions with the hope that if we can use the information correctly, psychophysical data will help us in our engineering design and evaluation.

Cautions in using psychophysical data

There is a tremendous wealth of visual measurement data in the literature. Unfortunately, most of the data are not directly applicable for color imaging applications. The main reason is that most of the data were measured using very restricted viewing conditions (such as no head movements, constant fixation, etc.) and oversimplied visual stimuli (such as uniform background, uniformly illuminated disk, planar color patches, etc.). One of the objectives of this chapter is to present a summary of this wealth of data in such a way that we may know how our visual system responds under the various experimental conditions so that we can use these data strictly for gaining insight into the subjective experience of vision. When applying the knowledge to a typical color imaging application, we have to be prepared to verify the validity of these experimental conclusions for our particular application. For example, the power law is shown, by an abundance of experimental data, to describe the brightness sensation as a function of luminance. However, few of those data were obtained using complex scenes as the targets. We may therefore use the power law relation only as a guide, and we cannot automatically make the assumption that it is also applicable to our image applications. Therefore, the first reason for caution is that visual responses are quite different for different visual stimuli and the experimental data were rarely measured for complex scenes or images.

The second reason for caution in using visual data from the literature is that the visual response measured in the experiments may not be what we want. For example, the brightness scale has been measured by at least three methods: (1) by the method of discrimination (just noticeable difference in brightness), (2) by the method of interval partition (given a black target and a white target, choose a gray target that is equally different from those two targets), and (3) by the method of magnitude estimation (the ratio scale). The trouble is that the results do not generally agree. The question of which data should be used for a given application can be answered only if we know what we are looking for.

The third reason for caution in using visual data from the literature is that observers in psychophysical experiments may use different criteria for responding to the experimental tasks and therefore may produce quite different results for the same task. For example, Bartleson and Breneman [78] found four different types of observers in brightness scaling experiments and each produced a very different brightness vs. luminance function. When the results were pooled together, the final resulting brightness function had a shape that differed from the results of the majority of the observers. Another finding is that each type of observer also differed in their consistency and reliability in making a brightness estimate. The difficulty and the inherent variability in measuring the subjective, perceptual responses to visual stimuli should never be overlooked.

The fourth reason for caution in using the visual data in the literature is that these data were often summarized as a model or a theory. Once such a model or theory is presented and used widely, we often forget the underlying assumptions and the experimental conditions in which the data were measured. A good example is Fechner's hypothesis that brightness scale,

B, is the integral of the just noticeable difference (JND) as a function of luminance level, Y. At high luminance levels, the JND luminance, ΔY, is found to be roughly proportional to the luminance. Therefore, according to Fechner's hypothesis: $\Delta B = k\Delta Y/Y$, and, integrating both sides, we get $B = k \log Y$. Using this brightness function in imaging applications raises very serious questions. First of all, the proportionality constant, k, is not a constant, but varies with luminance level and stimulus configuration. Secondly, the experimental stimuli that were used to determine the JND luminance are quite different from a complex, natural scene. Thirdly, the JND luminance may be related more to the noise in the visual system that makes it impossible to discriminate two similar luminance levels than to the brightness sensation itself. To make the jump from $\Delta Y(\text{JND}) = k'Y$ to $\Delta B = k\Delta Y/Y$ is in fact an assumption, not an experimental conclusion. However, the literature of digital image processing is full of models that take $B = k \log Y$ as the basic relation that relates the brightness to the luminance of the stimulus. This is a most unfortunate mistake made again and again by engineers who are not aware of the assumptions and the conditions of the experiments.

In summary, visual psychophysical data are quite important for us to understand how our visual perception works, but we should always pay attention to the experimental conditions and the type of stimuli used in the experiments. For engineers working on color imaging applications, it is not easy to check the details in these visual experiments. The first question one should ask when presented with some psychophysical "laws" is to ask under what conditions do they apply. For example, Weber's law says that the JND in stimulus intensity ΔI is proportional to the stimulus intensity I. This law is so generally useful in many areas of perception that it is often considered as a summary of facts. In reality, experimental data show that this law is true only over some range of stimulus intensity and even then it is true only for certain stimulus configurations. Before we use Weber's law in our imaging application, we have to know those constraints. When we study the psychophysical literature, we need to make clear distinctions between data, concepts, theories, and models. Weber's law as applied in visual perception is a model of only limited validity.

Physical and psychophysical variables of visual measurements
One of the most important guidelines in using psychophysical data is to systematically check how physical and psychophysical variables are controlled in the experiments that produce the data. This is important because visual performance often changes when one or more of these variables is changed. The seven major variables are: (1) the spectral composition of the stimuli, (2) the spatial layout and modulation of the stimuli (including the target size and the field size), (3) the temporal variation of the stimuli, (4) the luminance level (including achromatic and chromatic adaptation), (5) the noise level, (6) variations between individuals (including age, race, culture, etc.) and (7) the experience and learning effect.

13.2 Visual thresholds

Visual thresholds, which represent our capability to detect the presence of a visual stimulus under various conditions, are the best-studied area in visual psychophysics. Two of the most important visual thresholds are the absolute threshold for detecting the minimum amount of light energy and the contrast threshold for detecting the slight difference between two neighboring luminance levels. The detection of small color differences is also studied in the context of various thresholds, depending on which attribute or physical variable is changed and detected.

13.2.1 Absolute thresholds

Hecht, Shlaer, and Pirenne [387] showed that after complete dark adaption of our eyes, we can detect a flash (0.001 s) of light consisting of 54–148 quanta at the cornea, covering a circular retinal area (20° temporally on the horizontal axis) about 10′ in diameter. Accounting for the loss of light in the optical media of the eye, it was concluded that 5–14 quanta absorbed in rods were required for a human observer to detect such a flash of light 60% of the time. On the other hand, from physiological measurements, we know that a rod can detect a single photon [89]. Therefore, we can infer that the 5–14 quanta needed for detection is our visual system's decision threshold to distinguish a real flash from the response of a rod caused by the spontaneous, thermal decomposition of a single photopigment (rhodopsin) molecule. However, it should be pointed out that visual thresholds are not simply determined by the photochemical processes in the photoreceptors. Other factors are also important [46].

If we measure the absolute threshold with monochromatic light of different wavelengths, we find that rods are most sensitive (in terms of energy) to a wavelength of about 507 nm and the sensitivity (1 divided by the threshold) curve has a shape similar to the CIE $V'(\lambda)$ curve. Cones are most sensitive (in terms of energy) to a wavelength about 555 nm and the sensitivity curve has a shape similar to the CIE $V(\lambda)$ curve. The two sensitivity curves are also shifted vertically at the peaks. Rods are more sensitive than cones by a factor of 7 or more in terms of the number of quanta ($\approx$ 80 quanta for rods and $\approx$ 600 quanta for cones [85, p. 36]).

The chance of our visual system detecting a very weak stimulus is increased if photons are absorbed over a spatially small neighborhood on the retina or in a temporally short time interval. This is called spatial summation or temporal summation, respectively. For example, if two light pulses are separated by an interval less than the temporal summation time, their visual effects sum together additively. If both of them are below threshold, their combined effect may exceed the threshold and become visible (in the proper probability sense). Spatial and temporal summation occurs at and near the absolute threshold. Two empirical laws summarize the observations: Ricco's law of total spatial summation and Bloch's law of complete temporal summation. The area of spatial summation in Ricco's law increases from the fovea to the periphery. In foveal vision, the spatial summation area is about 7 minutes of arc [85, p. 37], while in peripheral vision, it increases from 32 minutes of arc at 7° to about 1°58′ at 35°. Bloch's law holds up to about 100 ms. for both foveal vision and peripheral vision [85, p. 39].

13.2.2 Contrast thresholds

Contrast thresholds of the human visual system are typically measured in three ways: (1) with a circular disk against a uniform background, (2) using bipartite fields of different

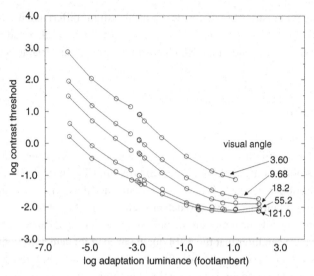

Figure 13.1. Contrast thresholds as a function of the adaptation luminance and the target size. These are measured with a circular disk against a uniform background (stimulus brighter than the background). The target size is expressed as the visual angle in minutes of arc.

luminance, and (3) with sine wave gratings. The results from (1) and (2) are about the same. Contrast thresholds for sine wave gratings are quite different and they are discussed in the next section.

Since visual thresholds depend on target size, viewing distance (visual accommodation), retinal position, eye movement, and time of viewing, these factors need to be controlled in the experiments. When comparing contrast threshold data, it is important to note if these factors are controlled the same way in the experiments. However, for imaging applications, there is usually no constraint in retinal position or viewing time, and data that are collected under these conditions are still quite useful, if not more so. One set of the best-known contrast threshold data was collected by Blackwell [114], who used circular disks of various sizes against a uniform background at different luminance levels. The observers were free to move their eyes and had plenty of time (longer than 15 s) to examine the visual field. Contrast is defined as the absolute luminance difference (between the target and the background) divided by the background luminance. The contrast threshold is defined as the contrast which an average observer will see 50% of the time, after due allowance is made for chance success. It was pointed out that the observers did not feel confident of having seen a stimulus unless the level of probability of detection was greater than 90%. For this level of detection, the threshold value has to be multiplied by a factor of 1.62. Figure 13.1 shows the log threshold contrast as a function of log adaptation luminance and the target size (in minutes of arc) from Blackwell's experiments. It is clear that the curves have two branches separated approximately at 10^{-3} cd m^{-2} (1 footlambert = 3.426 cd m^{-2}). The left-hand branch is believed to be rod-dominated detection and the right-hand branch the cone-dominated one. When the target size is larger, it is easier to detect and the contrast threshold is about 0.76% for the 121′ target at high-luminance adaptation. We can see that for the largest target at high luminance (above 1 cd m^{-2}), the contrast threshold is essentially independent of the background luminance, as predicted by Weber's law that says that the detectable luminance difference is proportional to the mean (or background) luminance. The smallest target size used was 36 minutes of arc because in lower background luminance the visual threshold for a target smaller than this size depends mainly on the product of luminance and target area. In higher luminance (above 1 cd m^{-2}), this critical visual angle is about 1 minute of arc.

In measuring the contrast threshold, we can use a stimulus that is either brighter (increment threshold) or darker (decrement threshold) than the background. Experimental data show that, when the adapting background is brighter than 1 cd m^{-2} and the target size is larger than 100 minutes of arc, the two thresholds are about the same. However, with lower light levels or smaller targets, the decrement threshold is consistently lower than the increment threshold by as much as 20%. A target darker than the background is easier to detect than one that is brighter [750].

13.2.3   *Contrast sensitivity functions (CSFs)*

A sinusoidal signal passing through a linear, shift-invariant system will preserve its sinusoidal waveform, except that its amplitude and phase may be changed. Therefore, if the system response for a sinusoidal input of every frequency is specified (in a so-called system transfer function), we can predict the system response to any type of input signal that can be represented as a sum or integral of sine waves (the Fourier transform theory). Although the human visual system is not a linear, shift-invariant system, visual thresholds to sine wave gratings of different frequencies have been measured for many viewing conditions (luminance levels, noise levels, viewing distances, fields sizes, etc.). Contrast sensitivity is defined as 1 over the contrast threshold. Thus if the contrast threshold is 1%, then the contrast sensitivity is 100. When the contrast sensitivity is measured as a function of spatial frequency under one viewing condition, the resulting function is called a CSF. One may question the usefulness of the contrast sensitivity data because our visual system is not linear and the CSF cannot serve as a system transfer function in a strict sense. However, there are two reasons why CSF data can be useful for some applications: (1) near a fixed operating point, most systems can be approximated as linear systems if the input signal modulation is small (this is a consequence of Taylor series expansion), and (2) the CSF data seem to describe many visual threshold data well. In fact, CSF data have been applied to suprathreshold applications and seem to give reasonable results [234]. An interesting interpretation of the CSF data is to treat them as equivalent-noise in our visual detection process [15].

Luminance CSF

There have been many experimental measurements on our contrast sensitivities [70]. Although they are not always compatible with each other because the experimental conditions were not controlled the same way, detailed analysis of these data allows us to see the general features and the important variables of the CSF data. With normal eye movement, our luminance contrast sensitivity function at high luminance (above 3 cd m^{-2}) is found to be bandpass in shape, peaked at around 2–8 cycles per degree (varies between experiments).

As the luminance decreases, the peak becomes broader and its maximum point gradually shifts to lower frequency. For luminance higher than 50 cd m^{-2}, the CSF remains quite constant. When the stimuli have the same mean luminance, the CSF of a monochromatic luminance grating does not seem to depend on the wavelength [985].

Our contrast sensitivity, S, varies with many physical variables, such as spatial frequency v in cycles per degree, orientation θ, light adaptation level L in candelas per square meter, image area s, in degrees squared, viewing distance d in meters (for the accommodation effect), and retinal eccentricity ϕ in visual degrees. After comparing many published data, Daly [234] proposed the following empirical function for describing the visual contrast sensitivity:

$$S(v, \theta, L, s, d, \phi) = S_0 \cdot \min\left[C\left(\frac{v}{r_d \cdot r_\phi \cdot r_\theta}, L, s \right), C(v, L, s) \right], \quad (13.1)$$

where S_0 is used to adjust the peak sensitivity and the adjustment factors, r_a, r_ϕ, and r_θ are given by

$$r_d = 0.856 \cdot d^{0.14}, \quad (13.2)$$

$$r_\phi = \frac{1}{1 + 0.24\phi}, \quad (13.3)$$

$$r_\theta = 0.11 \cos(4\theta) + 0.89, \quad (13.4)$$

and the real shape of the CSF is given by $C(v, L, s)$:

$$C(v, L, s) = Av\{[3.23(v^2 s)^{-0.3}]^5 + 1\}^{-0.2} e^{-Bv}\sqrt{1 + 0.06e^{Bv}}, \quad (13.5)$$

$$A = 0.801\epsilon \left(\frac{1.7}{L} \right)^{-0.2}, \quad (13.6)$$

$$B = 0.3\epsilon \left(\frac{101}{L} \right)^{0.15}, \quad (13.7)$$

where $\epsilon = 0.9$ for the luminance CSF. Another frequently used model was proposed by Barten and is well described in his book [70]. Both Daly's model and Barten's model seem to fit a large number of experimental data quite well and, therefore, are quite useful for imaging applications where the CSF can serve as a link between image processing and visual perception. For example, the task of fine tuning the JPEG quantization tables benefits from the CSF data [233]. Psychophysical experiments using the DCT basis functions as the stimuli also show a CSF similar, but not identical, to the CSF measured with sinusoidal patterns [756].

Figure 13.2 shows how typical contrast sensitivity varies as a function of spatial frequency and luminance level. The functions are plotted in linear scale and log scale. Three major features are noticeable in the figure: (1) the peak sensitivity is about 200–500 at about 2–5 cycles per degree for daylight luminance; (2) the peak sensitivity increases as the luminance increases until it reaches about 1000 cd m^{-2}; and (3) in the log–log plot, the curves appear to be linear in the very-low- and very-high-frequency regions. Because of (3), a simple CSF model (including temporal frequency) is given by [540, p. 289]:

$$S(v_x, v_t) = S_E \exp[-av_x - bv_t] - S_I \exp[-cv_x - dv_t], \quad (13.8)$$

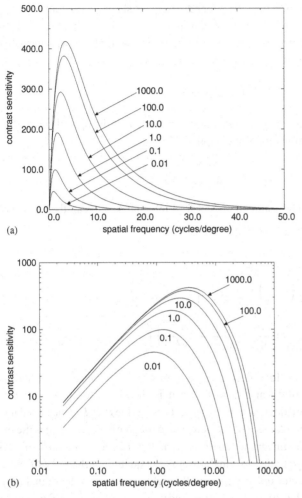

Figure 13.2. Contrast sensitivity functions. In (a) the CSFs are plotted in linear scale, while in (b) they are plotted on a log scale. The numbers are the luminance levels in candelas per square meter.

where a, b, c, and d are model parameters, and v_x and v_t are the spatial and temporal frequencies. The constants S_E and S_I represent the strength of the "excitation" and inhibition" components, in accounting for the center-surround types of receptive field as measured along the visual pathway. It should be pointed out that Daly's model implies that $S(v = 0) = 0$ and we are not able to see the zero frequency, i.e., a uniform field. This seems to agree with the stabilized image experiments. However, this interpretation is not without controversy because one can argue that, even with our eyes closed, we can still notice a difference between light and dark [540, p. 290].

A more theoretically developed contrast sensitivity model was proposed by Barten [70]. This consists of two cascaded stages. The luminance signal entering the eye is first degraded by the optical MTF of the eye (a low-pass filter). It then goes through another degradation due to the neural process of the lateral inhibition, which has the effect of a high-pass filter.

These two stages combine to give the general bandpass shape of the luminance CSF. The model then accounts for the effect of photon noise, the effect of neural noise, the effect of spatial-temporal integration and the psychometric function of the two-alternative forced choice method. The optical MTF of the eye is modeled as:

$$MTF_{\text{optical}}(v) = e^{-2\pi^2\sigma^2 v^2}, \tag{13.9}$$

where v is the spatial frequency. The standard deviation σ of the optical spread function of the eye is modeled as a function of the pupil diameter d:

$$\sigma = \sqrt{\sigma_0^2 + (C_{ab}d)^2}, \tag{13.10}$$

where σ_0 is a constant. The complete model for binocular vision can then be described by the following:

$$S(v) = \frac{e^{-2\pi^2\sigma^2 v^2}}{k\sqrt{\left(\dfrac{2}{TA}\right)\left(\dfrac{1}{\eta p E} + \dfrac{\Phi_0}{1 - e^{-(v/v_0)^2}}\right)}} \tag{13.11}$$

$$A = 1 \bigg/ \sqrt{\left(\frac{1}{X_0^2} + \frac{1}{X_{\text{max}}^2} + \frac{v^2}{N_{\text{max}}^2}\right)\left(\frac{1}{Y_0^2} + \frac{1}{Y_{\text{max}}^2} + \frac{v^2}{N_{\text{max}}^2}\right)}, \tag{13.12}$$

where A is the effective area for object size; k is a constant calculated from the psychometric function of the task involved and in this case it is the signal-to-noise ratio for grating detection; σ is the standard deviation of the optical LSF of the eye; T is the visual integration time [s]; X_0 (Y_0) is the angular size of the object size [degree]; X_{max} (Y_{max}) is the maximum X (Y) angular size of the integration area; N_{max} is the maximum number of cycles over which the eyes can integrate the information; η is the quantum efficiency of the eye; p is the photon conversion factor that depends on the light source; E is the retinal illuminance [td]; Φ_0 is the spectral density of the neural noise; and v_0 is the cut-off frequency of the lateral inhibition. The photon conversion factor p is defined by the number of photons per unit of time, per unit of area, and per unit of luminous flux per angular area entering the eye. Let $P(\lambda)$ be the spectral power distribution of the visual target and $V(\lambda)$ be the photopic luminous efficiency function, then the photon conversion factor, p, can be computed by the equation

$$p = 2.246 \times 10^3 \frac{\int P(\lambda)V(\lambda)\lambda d\lambda}{\int P(\lambda)V(\lambda)d\lambda}, \tag{13.13}$$

where λ is expressed in nanometers and the unit of p is [photons s^{-1} deg^{-1} (photopic td)$^{-1}$]. For example, if $P(\lambda)$ is the same as the spectral power distribution of CIE Illuminant A, $p = 1.285 \times 10^6$ [70, p. 63]. Typical values of the paramters are: $k = 3.0$; $T = 0.1$ s; $\eta = 0.03$; $\sigma_0 = 0.5$ arcmin; $C_{ab} = 0.08$ arcmin mm^{-1}; $X_{\text{max}} = 12°$; $\Phi_0 = 3 \times 10^{-8}$ s deg^2; $N_{\text{max}} = 15$ cycles; and $v_0 = 7$ cycles per degree. This model has been shown to describe many experimental data very well under various experimental conditions [70].

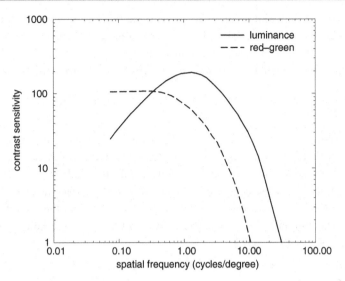

Figure 13.3. Comparison of the luminance CSF and the chrominance CSF. The bandwidths of this set of data seem to be narrower than other measured values. However, the general shapes are consistent in different experimental results.

Chrominance CSF

Measurement of the chrominance CSFs is more difficult to do because of two complications: (1) the detection criteria and (2) the correction for chromatic aberrations. Higher-frequency color gratings can be detected before we can tell their colors. Therefore, we need to define the criteria for the detection threshold. In general, the question is compounded by the fact that pure chrominance (isoluminant) gratings are not easy to produce because they are specific to each individual. The other difficulty is that our eyes have very significant chromatic aberrations. Without correction, we are not sure if the detection is based purely on chrominance variations. These problems have been addressed and the results show that isoluminant red–green and yellow–blue chromatic CSFs have the same low-pass shape (compared with the bandpass shape of the luminance CSF), but the yellow–blue sensitivity is about 0.5 log unit lower than that for red–green [540, p. 215]. It has also been shown that at each spatial frequency color contrast sensitivity declines with eccentricity approximately twice as steeply as luminance contrast sensitivity [685]. Figure 13.3 shows a comparison of the luminance CSF and the chrominance CSF for a typical observer as reported in [684]. The absolute sensitivity and the absolute resolution limit tend to vary from experiment to experiment. The data shown in Fig. 13.3 seem to be on the low side. The reported highest frequencies of the luminance and chrominance CSFs are twice as high as shown here. For example, the red–green isoluminant interference fringes up to 20–25 cycles per degree are still perceptible in some experiments [847].

It should be pointed out that, in color imaging applications, it is not practically possible for color signals to be separated into pure luminance and pure chrominance components and therefore, the precision of the chrominance CSF data is usually not critical. For example, the NTSC YIQ color encoding is far from exact in this respect, but it achieves the major benefit of chrominance bandwidth compression. The same thing can be said about most color image compression algorithms. However, it does not mean that we need not worry about this issue at all [673]. The fact is that the more accurately we encode our color signals, the better the image compression, transmission, or processing results we will achieve.

13.2.4 Photochromatic interval

If a chromatic test spot is presented on a white background, we can detect its presence as a luminance increment although we may not be able to identify its color. The threshold, E_c, for the perception of color is called the chromatic threshold and the threshold, E_a, for detecting luminance difference is called the achromatic threshold. For all visible wavelengths, E_c is greater than E_a [356]. The detection threshold is thus smaller than the identification threshold for color discrimination. The difference between these two thresholds is called the photochromatic interval [2, p. 418].

13.2.5 Thresholds of visual blur

When the retinal image of an object is blurred, it becomes more difficult to detect the presence of the object. The question is: how are our contrast thresholds affected by the image blur [724]? Our minimum angle of resolution is a function of eccentricity [773], but it is on the order of 1 minute of arc in the fovea. This is related to how we should define the depth of field or depth of focus in an optical imaging system and how we can set specifications for image capturing devices.

13.3 Visual adaptation

When the human visual system is first exposed to a new stimulus, its sensitivity to it is initially quite high and then it drops as the time of exposure increases. The adjustment of sensitivity to an external stimulus is called visual adaptation. For example, if we look at a spatial sine wave grating for a long time, our sensitivity to another sine wave grating of the same frequency is decreased. Another type of visual adaptation refers to the adjustment of our visual system to a new operating point. For example, if we enter a dark theater from a bright sunlit street, our eyes cannot see much for the first few minutes. After that, our visual system gradually adjusts its light sensitivity over time. This is called dark adaptation. Visual adaptation is a very important factor to consider in imaging science applications, because the images are often viewed in an environment very different from the one in the original scene. The operating condition for our visual system has changed and the effect of visual adaptation has to be carefully considered.

13.3.1 Achromatic adaptation

The full range of luminance in which our visual system can see is roughly from 10^{-6} cd m^{-2} for the completely dark-adapted eye to 10^6 cd m^{-2} for the completely light-adapted eye [477,

p. 354]. The methods of colorimetry apply strictly to a middle range of about 1000-fold in cone vision. In order for the eyes to function over such a large dynamic range, our visual system adjusts its operating point photochemically and neurophysiologically. Light adaptation refers to the change of visual sensitivity to an increase of background or average luminance of the visual field, while dark adaptation refers to the change in sensitivity in response to a decrease in luminance. By measuring visual thresholds at different times after the light is turned on (off), we can estimate the time course of our light (dark) adaptation. The curve of visual threshold as a function of time in the light (or dark) clearly shows two separate branches. In dark adaptation, the visual threshold is initially determined by the cone vision and after some time by the rod vision. It is found that the rods and cones adapt at different rates: cone adaptation is completed in about 7–15 minutes, while rod adaptation continues for about 1 hour or more [366, p. 86]. In light adaptation, the rods determine the initial threshold elevation. Rods begin to saturate at around 100 scotopic td and the visual threshold is then determined by the cones [53, 153, Chapter 3].

Within a factor of 100 in luminance change for photopic vision, our light or dark adaptation is accomplished relatively fast. The brightness and lightness of the objects appear to be approximately the same after our eyes adapt to the change. For example, if we sit near a window to read a book from morning to noon, we can hardly detect the continuous change in the daylight luminance level. How does the visual system know how much adjustment is needed to maintain the brightness constancy? At a first glance, this seems to be a trivial problem because all the visual system has to do is to use the paper of the book as a reference to adjust its light sensitivity so that the paper will look the same brightness or lightness while the illumination is changing. However, that solution is not very robust since a reference object may not be present all the time. Furthermore, the illumination changes not only in intensity, but also in the direction and distribution of lighting. The so-called invariant reference is actually not easy to track after we turn a page. One can also turn the question around and ask how we know the paper is white in the first place. In any case, our visual system seems to perform much better than this type of solution. It does not matter whether the ratios or the gradients are computed to construct a brightness/lightness description of the scene, the central problem is how to determine an anchor point to which the computed description can be "normalized" so that "white" objects remain "white" almost all the time. This anchoring problem is also one of the most important problems in photofinishing, where the problem is called the density balance problem – how to adjust the print density so that the image will look good.

13.3.2   Chromatic adaptation

If we spend an hour or so reading a book under a fluorescent lamp and then immediately walk to a room illuminated by a tungsten lamp, all objects in the room appear to have a strong orange-red color cast, especially the "white" paper of the book. After a few minutes, the orange-red color cast is greatly reduced and the "white" begins to look reasonably "white" again. This is called chromatic adaptation – our visual system adjusts its color sensitivity (to a certain extent) to the "colored" illumination so that the color appearance of objects is more or less maintained. One of the early models of chromatic adaptation was proposed by von Kries, based on the idea that the three cone systems adjust their individual sensitivities linearly and independently:

$$L' = k_l L, \quad M' = k_m M, \quad S' = k_s S, \tag{13.14}$$

where L, M, S are the cone responses before they are adapted to one illuminant, L', M', S' are cone responses after they are adapted to another illuminant, and k_l, k_m, k_s are three constants. The model is called the von Kries coefficient rule and the transformation from L, M, S to L', M', S' is called the von Kries transformation. But, how does the visual system know how much adjustment is needed to maintain the constant colors, i.e., how do we determine k_l, k_m, k_s from an image? This problem is similar to the anchoring problem in the brightness/lightness computation and it is called the color balance problem in photofinishing. Many studies show that the chromatic adaptation data deviate significantly from the von Kries coefficient rule, especially the S cone response. Furthermore, Helson and Judd [389, 475] observed that, under highly chromatic illuminants, bright objects continue to appear in the same chromatic hue as the illuminant and dark objects appear to have a hue complementary to the illuminant. For example, after adapting to a tungsten light, white paper continues to appear slightly yellow–orange and very dark gray paper appears to be slightly bluish. This effect is called the Helson–Judd effect. Note that this description assumes that there is a "normal" illuminant under which this effect does not exist, otherwise, we cannot define what we mean by highly chromatic illuminants. This "normal" illuminant seems to relate to the so-called "absolute white point", which can be measured in complete dark adaptation by judging which blackbody illuminant requires least luminance to appear white. However, not many data are available on this type of measurement and therefore the concept of the "absolute white point" or the resting adaptation state requires further experimental confirmation.

Many studies have been performed on the general characteristics of our chromatic adaptation. The main empirical observations are:

1. The amount of adaptation is more complete at higher illuminance.
2. There is proportionally less adaptation for the S cones.
3. Linear von Kries transformation can account for the major effect of chromatic adaptation, especially when the proportionality constants k_l, k_m, k_s are calculated with the corresponding grays (instead of whites) under two illuminants [138].
4. A highly chromatic light source will be seen as having a definite hue even when used as the sole source of illumination.
5. The Helson–Judd effect is larger for highly chromatic illumination sources.
6. The resting adaptation state ("absolute white point") varies between individuals, from 4850 K to 7500 K at 16–40 cd m^{-2} for a 5–12° field.
7. Most light when sufficiently intense can be seen as white.
8. Fully dark-adapted eyes can see luminances as low as 10^{-5} cd m^{-2}, but are dazzled by a luminance of only 80 cd m^{-2}.
9. Fully daylight-adapted eyes can see low luminance at about 1 cd m^{-2}, and luminance as high as 300 000 cd m^{-2} without much pain.

It is important to note that although, from an engineering point of view, achromatic adaptation and chromatic adaptation both act to adjust the operating point of the visual system, these two mechanisms alone do not account for our color perception in general. All the evidence suggests that the perceived world is a *reconstructed representation* of the retinal images over time and space. For example, we do not see a blurry peripheral field or black hole(s) created by the absence of photoreceptors in the blind spot. In addition to the adjustment of the operating point, the visual system also has to compute many features to reconstruct the perceived world. The algorithms (or neurons) used in such computations impose their own ways of interpreting what the retinal signals mean. Let us take an optical character recognition (OCR) system as an example. The scanner sensors may adjust their operating point such as their amplifier gain or gray-level lookup tables so that optimum images of the input documents can be captured. The OCR algorithms are ultimately responsible for deciding what characters are on the documents. If the algorithms do not recognize a particular font, it does not matter how well the operating point has been adjusted. Therefore, it is important for us to understand that the function of visual adaptation is not to compute the color of the light source and compensate for the change in illumination. Rather, its function is to adjust the "amplifier gains and biases" for sensing the input signal in the optimal operating range.

Today, we know more about the achromatic and chromatic adaptations than about the algorithms that our brain uses to compute the color perception. However, many of the psychophysical data in this field were measured without strict control of these separate processes. There are experimental tasks that are not sensitive to this type of control, but not all of them are clear cut. Therefore, we need to be careful when using such data.

13.4 Eye movements and visual perception

When we fix our eyes on a definite target in space, our eyes do not stay motionless. A fine tremor of amplitude about $30''$ of arc (roughly the cone-to-cone distance in the fovea) is always present in the eye movements. This small tremor has a temporal frequency in the range 30–80 Hz or higher. The tremor movements are very irregular and appear to be noise-like in recorded eye-movement charts. In addition to the tremor, there are two other types of eye movements: drifts and saccades. Drifts are very slow, low-frequency movements (about 1–4 minutes per second). Saccades are occasional, sharp movements. Involuntary saccades are usually less than 10 minutes of arc. The median intersaccadic interval is about 600 ms and the duration of a saccade is about 70 ms [257, p. 375]. Experimental measurements showed that saccades in the two eyes are highly correlated, in both amplitude and direction. This implies that there is a central action controlling the saccades in both eyes. With the three types of involuntary eye movement, we cannot maintain an exact fixation. The distribution of the direction of gaze is found to be a two-dimensional Gaussian function. The horizontal and vertical standard deviations are usually different and the correlation coefficient is not zero. The size of the standard deviation is on the order of 2–4 minutes of arc over a time interval of 60 s. These measurements are often taken with the head held stationary by some artificial support. Studies show that under natural viewing (without head support), the gaze is more unstable by a factor of 1.5–3 and the mean eye speed is increased by a factor of 2 (from 0.25 to 0.5 degrees per second) [526, p. 81].

In the presence of eye movements, the optical images formed by the eye are moving across the retina. This raises at least two interesting questions: (1) Image motion across retina should create motion blur; why don't we perceive such blur? (2) What happens to our visual perception if we eliminate such motion? The answers to these questions are not complete at this time, but many experiments have revealed important insights into how our visual system works. A simplified answer to the first question is that perception is suppressed during the eye movements and the missing temporal information is interpolated. In order for the interpolation to work, some information about the eye movements has to be provided to the visual processes. It seems that the control center that issues the signals for the eye movements also sends the information to the visual processes for the correction of eye movements. Experimental data show that our contrast threshold is not elevated until image velocity exceeds 2 degrees per second. The answer to the second question turns out to be quite unexpected, and it leads us to very interesting and important discoveries about the mechanisms of visual perception. In summary, when the retinal images are well stabilized, the images tend to disappear or fade out in a few (1–3) seconds to a few minutes, depending on the spatial-spectral composition and the luminance of the stimulus. The color of the stimulus first becomes desaturated and the brightness decreases, and then the structures of the image fade out into a uniform, foggy, dark, gray field. Images that have low-contrast edges fade out sooner than those with high-contrast edges. The perceived dark gray field occasionally becomes completely black for a few seconds and then returns to dark gray. This is called black-out. It is believed that the fade-out phenomenon is due to neurons' complete adaptation to the stationary retinal image, while the black-out phenomenon seems to be caused by a complete loss of vision, as a result of the central visual attention mechanism shutting down all visual processing.

Although several apparatuses [257, Chapter 5] have been developed for producing stabilized images on the retina, this type of experiment is not easy to do (some residual motion still exists in most experiments), thus the total number of observers who have taken part in the experiments is small. Therefore, quantitative data are scarce, but qualitative data are quite revealing and they are all consistent in showing the importance of eye movements on the normal function of vision [257, 758, 1059]. The most compelling evidence from the stabilized image experiments seems to suggest that edges and gradients of the image irradiances are the key features from which our perceived images are constructed. Figure 13.4 shows one of the experiments by Krauskopf [528]. The stimulus was a red central disk surrounded by a green annulus (as seen in (a)). When the boundary between the central disk and the annulus surround is stabilized on the retina, the subject sees a uniform green disk! One can explain such a perception by arguing that, after it is stabilized, the boundary of the central disk disappears. Our visual system does not see the red–green boundary and our perception simply fills in the central disk with the green color. The propagation of information from the edges into the interior region surrounded by the edges is thus called the filling-in process. The basic reasoning behind the explanation is that, without detecting any temporal changes before and after the eye movement, the brain interprets the corresponding image area as uniform and thus whatever is in the surround is used to fill in the center.

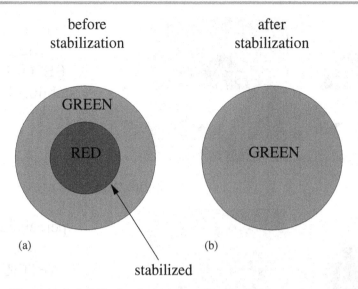

before
stabilization

after
stabilization

(a)   (b)

stabilized

Figure 13.4. Stabilized retinal images. The stimulus is a red central disk surrounded by a green annulus (as seen in (a)). When the boundary between the central disk and the annulus surround is stabilized on the retina, the subject sees a uniform green disk (as shown in (b))!

Although the hypothesis of such a filling-in process is a relatively intuitive explanation in such a simple case, it is not clear how such a process works in a more complicated image where edges cannot always be detected reliably and where the surrounding region is not uniform. For example, a student with a damaged thin stripe in the fovea (burnt by a laser) reported seeing a faint gray line when looking at a bright background [799]. If filling-in works perfectly, this gray line should not be seen at all.[1] In fact, Yarbus [1059, p. 80] described an experiment where the surrounding region of a stabilized disk is a colored checker board pattern (see Fig. 13.5). After its stabilization, the disk faded into a dark gray field and continued to appear that way throughout the experiment. The region corresponding to the stabilized disk was never perceived as filled in from the surrounding region! It is therefore important to remember that as appealing as the concept of filling-in may sound, it is only a grossly oversimplified way to describe a complicated phenomenon that we still do not understand. At this point, it should also be mentioned that the filling-in process has also been used to explain why we do not see a black hole at the blind spot of our retina (even when we close one of our eyes). Again, this has to be taken with much care, because the blind spot has never generated any neural signals, whereas other retinal areas constantly generate temporal varying signals in normal visual viewing. When an image is stabilized on the retina, these other areas generate no responses, which are signals of absence of changes. In comparison, in the blind spot area, there is an absence of signals. These two situations might be interpreted by the brain differently.

One of the many important conclusions from Yarbus' extensive series of studies using stabilized images is that there seem to be two adaptation processes: one fast and the other

---

[1]   However, the filling-in process may take some time to complete [782, p. 99], and it is possible that a faint gray line can be seen, but it may disappear a few moments later.

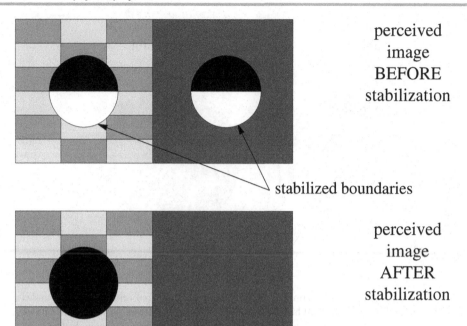

perceived
image
BEFORE
stabilization

stabilized boundaries

perceived
image
AFTER
stabilization

Figure 13.5. Stabilized retinal images. The stimulus is a checker board pattern on the left and a uniform red background on the right. In each half is a circular disk, half white and half black. The boundaries between the circular disks and the backgrounds are stabilized on the retina, while the background patterns are not. The observer fixates at the target so that the disks do not move across the two different backgrounds. When the stimulus is first turned on, the target appears to the observer as the top panel. Within a few seconds, both disks fade out to dark gray. After a few more seconds, the disk against the uniform red background disappears (or becomes part of the red field), but the disk against the checker board pattern remains dark gray.

slow. The "fast" process reaches a steady state in 1–3 seconds, while the "slow" process takes 30–40 seconds or longer [1059, p. 78]. For example, the stabilized part (the background) of the visual field (saturated red) takes only 1–3 seconds to fade out, but the unstabilized part (a moving white disk) continues to change in color appearance from white to cyan for 30 s or longer. This finding is confirmed by many other experiments that measured the adaptation time more directly.

Another very interesting experiment by Piantanida and Gilchrist [346, pp. 26–27] shed more light on how visual perception is encoded. Instead of stabilizing the boundary between the center target and its background, they stabilized the boundary between the background and the surround. Figure 13.6(a) shows the stimulus configuration. The outer borders of the black and white backgrounds were retinally stabilized. The two center squares have the same luminance (middle gray). Figure 13.6(b) shows how the stimulus appears to the subject after the stabilization. The original white and black backgrounds disappear to become a uniform gray. The left center square now appears black and the right center square white, even though they have the same luminance. A simple explanation is that the differences or ratios between the center squares and their backgrounds are encoded. Stabilizing the outer borders of the

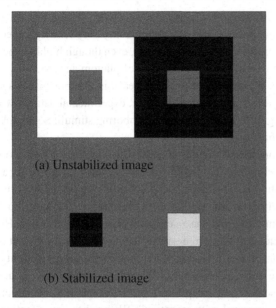

Figure 13.6. (a) The stimulus configuration used in Piantanida and Gilchrist's experiment. The outer borders of the black and white backgrounds were retinally stabilized. (b) Appearance of the stimulus after the borders were stabilized.

backgrounds does not change those unstabilized relations. Here it is clear that the visual system does not simply fill in the backgrounds and use the filled-in value and the luminance of the two center squares to compute their appearances – the differences or ratios are encoded first and they are used by the reconstruction algorithms.

13.5   Perception of brightness and lightness

The computational issues regarding visual perception are enormously complex [10, 337, 339, 346, 636, 802]. Before we discuss the broad and general subject of brightness perception, let us examine how our visual perception behaves in a very simplified visual field. From studying the simple visual stimuli, we hope to gain insight into some of the basic principles of how our visual system works.

In order to simplify our discussion in this section, we will only deal with stimuli that are identical in spectral composition and appear achromatic (meaning that, at a steady state, the stimuli do not appear to have hues, such as red, green, orange, etc.). We will also assume that the stimuli remain constant for the time of viewing. The only variable of the stimuli is the intensity (radiance or luminance).

The first problem we need to deal with is the definition. Unfortunately, this is also one of the most difficult problems in the study of visual perception. This is due to not only the nature of subjective judgment in visual perception, but, more seriously, even the basic categorical delineation of the component percepts is uncertain. For example, the amount of light coming into the eye from a spatial area (the radiance or luminance) can be measured in absolute physical quantities. However, experimental data clearly show that the human visual system cannot judge or estimate this absolute physical quantity very reliably, especially in a complex scene. That is why professional photographers, even though highly experienced in judging photographic lighting, often carry some type of photometer around when they are taking pictures. Therefore, the first basic thing we learn is that our visual system is not designed to be a radiometer or a photometer. However, experimental data show that we are extremely good at detecting differences between neighboring stimuli. So what kinds of perceptual quantity can we define?

Let us start with the sensation caused by light. It appears true to our common experience that, if everything else is kept constant, the more light coming into our eyes from a spatial region, the stronger that sensation is. Therefore, let us define a quantity, called brightness, which corresponds to the strength of our sensation to the intensity of light. So far, the definition of brightness seems intuitive and reasonable, and we will leave it as that. However, we should keep in mind that such a definition presumes that there is an agreement on what the sensation is and that somehow it can be judged internally with some reliability [815]. Both assumptions can become quite questionable when complex comparisons are being made. Also, the history of research on perception is full of debate and confusion about the meaning of "sensation" as opposed to "perception". We need to pay attention to the distinction between the two words here because "sensation" is meant to be more direct and lower-level visual reception, without the contextual, cognitive, high-level interpretation that belongs to "perception". For example, under tungsten lighting, the sensation produced by the light reflected from a piece of paper may be yellowish, but we may perceive it as being a piece of "white" paper. Although we often do not pay attention to the fact that our color sensation of snow in the shade is actually bluish because we perceive it as white, once someone points it out to us, we can indeed see the bluish color in it. Many experiments have shown that we are extremely capable of seeing and interpreting the visual world in its proper context. When we look around, we are seeing not only the objects, their shapes, colors, and textures, but also the general lighting and spatial layout of the room. We see that the objects in the shade appear to have less light reflected from them because they are in the shade, not because they have lower reflectances. This means that experimenters have to ask the right questions to get the right answers. For this reason, *brightness* is used to mean apparent luminance and *lightness*, apparent reflectance [796, 1028]. In many of the older psychophysical studies (say before the 1960s), the difference between these two was not clearly distinguished and the resulting data from different experiments can lead us to very different conclusions.

One related issue regarding to the definition of brightness is the use of the words "dark" and "black". We will use "bright" or "dark" when the sensation of brightness is strong or weak, and reserve "white" and "black" to refer to other perceptual attributes to be discussed later.

13.5.1 *Brightness perception of a uniform visual field (ganzfeld)*

The simplest visual stimulus is a uniform field (usually called a ganzfeld). If the visual field is completely uniform, eye movements do not change the illuminance on any point of the retina, except for the slight change due to the optical nonuniformity of the eye. We therefore expect that, in ganzfeld viewing, similar perceptual phenomena will be observed to those in the stabilized image experiments, and indeed this seems to be the case. When the light in the uniform field is turned on, initially the field appears to be a uniformly bright field of a certain color. Gradually, the color begins to desaturate and darken, and soon the entire visual field looks like a dark gray field (the fade-out phenomenon) [45, 203, 204, 373, 374]. Just like in the viewing of an image stabilized on our retina, the perceived dark gray field occasionally becomes completely black for a few seconds and then returns to dark gray again. When the state of fading out is reached in viewing a ganzfeld, the final, perceived dark gray often differs from complete darkness, in the sense that a certain faint sensation of "brightness" does exist. The strength of this sensation of "brightness", at its steady state, increases slightly with the luminance of the ganzfeld. An easy way to approximate this sensation is to close both eyes in a lighted room. The moment we close our eyes, we see a dark gray field. If we are not sure this dark gray field is a steady state perception, we can continue keeping our eyes closed and watch what changes occur during the dark adaptation. In fact, our eyelids are not sufficiently opaque to keep out all the room light, and therefore we are not undergoing a true dark adaptation. If, without opening our eyes, we now turn off the room light (or have someone else turn off the light for us), we see the dark gray field momentarily becomes much darker and then after a few seconds the field returns to dark gray again and this dark gray appears to be much darker than when the room light was on. Depending on how much residual light remains in the room, the visual field can appear from very dark to completely dark. We therefore come to the conclusion that there is some sensation of light even when the visual field is completely uniform.

13.5.2 Brightness perception of an isolated finite uniform area

If we reduce the size of the uniform field from a ganzfeld to only a small fraction of our visual field (say 5°), we have the stimulus of an isolated patch of light in the dark. Again, when the light is first turned on, the target initially appears brighter and then it becomes a little darker as we look at it for a while (say 2 s or more). However, its brightness remains quite stable. We can give an estimate of its subjective brightness magnitude. If we now turn off the light and let our eyes rest in the dark for 20 s or more, then we turn on the light again but with a different luminance, we can give another estimate of its brightness. By repeating this for many different luminances, we can construct a relation between the perceived brightness magnitude and the luminance. In a long series of experiments, Stevens and his colleagues [905, 906] concluded that this relation can be approximated as a power function with a power of 0.33:

$$B = kY^{0.33}, \qquad (13.15)$$

where B is the perceived brightness, Y is the luminance of the target, and k is a constant. Although results from some other experiments (e.g., [56]) do not always agree with this conclusion, in general, for a dark adapted observer viewing an isolated, medium-sized (1–10°) target against a completely dark background, this seems to be a good approximation, except possibly at the low end of the luminance range, where the brightness seems to be proportional to the luminance.

If the size of the target is reduced below $1°$, the luminance–brightness relation is still a power function, but the power becomes greater than 0.33. For example, when the target is 1.5 minutes of arc, the power becomes 0.51. Similarly when the duration of stimuli is reduced below 1 s, the power also increases. For example, for flashes of 20–200 ms, the power increases to about 0.4. It should be remembered that the psychophysical magnitude estimation often has large variances and the exact functional form of the luminance–brightness relation and its power should be taken only as an approximation.

The above experiments were performed on dark-adapted eyes. What happens to the brightness–luminance relation when the eyes are light-adapted? We still want to measure the brightness of an isolated spot of light without any contrasting background. Therefore, we let the eye adapt to a constant luminance for a long time, and at the moment just before the target is presented, the background light is turned off. Therefore the target is again seen against a dark background, but the eye is in a different adaptation state. The effect of light adaptation on the brightness function can be measured either by magnitude estimation or by interocular matching, with one eye dark-adapted and the other light-adapted. Both procedures produce the same results. The perceived brightness of the central target is still a power function of the target luminance when the eye is light-adapted. However, the power is slightly increased and there is a sharp curvature near the threshold brightness. The following equation can be used to describe the functions:

$$B = k(Y - Y_0)^n \quad \text{for } Y > Y_0. \tag{13.16}$$

Light adaptation lowers the value of k and raises the value of Y_0. The value of n is slightly increased. For example, adaptation to a luminance of 1590 cd m^{-2} raises the value of n from 0.33 to 0.43. The value of Y_0 determined by fitting the data to the equation was found to be the same as the measured threshold brightness for the same level of light adaptation [905, p. VII-12]. Table 13.1 shows the parameter values as determined by Stevens and Stevens [905, p. VII-14].

Table 13.1. *The effect of light adaptation on the parameters of the brightness equation,* $B = k(Y - Y_0)^n$

The numbers are converted from millilamberts and do not represent significant digits.

Adaptation (cd m^{-2})	k	n	Y_0 (cd m^{-2})
0.0 (dark)	10	0.333	2.23×10^{-6}
0.003183	9.6	0.334	0.0003183
0.031830	8.6	0.335	0.0012732
0.318300	7.2	0.342	0.0050928
3.183000	5.5	0.355	0.0251457
31.83000	3.7	0.38	0.1018560
318.3000	2.2	0.41	0.5092800
3183.000	1.0	0.44	5.0291400
31830.00	0.26	0.49	79.893300

13.5.3 Brightness perception of two adjacent uniform areas

The above experiments use isolated spots of light as the stimuli. There is no other light in the visual field to be compared with the test target. The isolated target always appears to be self-luminous and there seems to be only one perceptual attribute involved that varies from dark, through dim, to bright and very bright, and so on. Specifically, dim light is perceived as dim, not gray [1003, p. 312]. When there are two target areas in the visual field, describing the physical stimuli suddenly becomes much more complicated than just a factor of 2, because the sizes, shapes, and relative positions of the targets can be varied. So does the complexity of describing our perception. This may sound odd because we are often told that our color perception involves only three perceptual attributes: hue, saturation, and brightness. With achromatic targets, we should have the brightness attribute as the only variable, and therefore, if there are two targets in the visual field, we should only perceive them as two targets of different brightness and no other new perceptual attributes should arise. However, this does not seem to be the case. First of all, for a single, isolated target, our perception is that the target looks like a light source of some brightness. With two targets, we can begin to see a target as a reflective surface in one situation and as a self-luminous source in another situation, depending on its spatial and luminance relations with the other target. When we see it as a reflective surface, a new perceptual attribute is experienced, that is gray. Evans discussed a series of experiments aimed at clarifying the nature of this attribute in his book [290]. We will come back to this attribute shortly.

One of the early experiments that demonstrated the striking difference between the perception of a single isolated area of light and that of two adjacent areas of light was reported by Gelb [907]. Gelb's original experiments were conducted using spinning disks to vary the equivalent reflectance factors of the test targets. Wallach [1003] described a simpler setup for observing the same effect: if a single piece of "black" (meaning it has a low reflectance factor) paper is suspended in the air and illuminated by intense light in an otherwise dark room, and the arrangement is such that the light beam of the illumination itself is not visible (see, for example, [712, 907] for possible arrangements), the paper, seen by itself, appears "white". If a piece of "white" (high reflectance factor) paper is now placed in front of the "black" paper so that it is also illuminated by the same light, the "black" paper suddenly becomes black. The perception of a single illuminated piece of paper is so different from that of two pieces of paper that the dramatic change in appearance is given a name: the Gelb effect. No less interesting is that when the "white" paper is suddenly removed, the "black" paper may take 5–7 seconds to return to the previous "white" appearance [712, p. 87]. Experiments like this led researchers to distinguish two modes of perception. The perception of a single isolated spot of light is called the aperture mode and that of two or more areas in contact is called the surface mode. There are other modes of color perception, but the important thing is not knowing when to apply different psychophysical laws to these different modes of perception, it is recognition of the fact that color perception as an effort to make sense out of the retinal images uses more attributes than just hue, saturation, and brightness.

Let us first study the case when the two areas of light of different luminances are in contact with each other. The most extensively studied configuration is a central circular disk surrounded by a concentric ring (annulus) of a different luminance. We will call the central disk the target field. In the experiments reported by Stevens and Stevens [905], the central disk is about 2.4° and the annulus about 5.7°. In their experiments, the disk and its annulus are presented at the same time for only about 2 s, with about 10 s between presentations [905, p. VIII-9]. Therefore, the observers did not fully, if at all, adapt to the stimuli. This is a key point to remember when interpreting their results and when comparing them with other experimental results. One may question whether this set of experimental results are useful for our imaging applications. However, there are many interesting qualitative perceptual phenomena that can be seen from the results, and that makes it interesting to examine the data. Another reason is that the data are also consistent with those from some other experiments (e.g., [583]) that allowed continuous viewing and judging.

When the surround is fixed at a certain luminance and the disk is varied from very low luminance to the luminance of the surround, the perceived brightness of the disk again varies as a power function of its luminance, as described by Eq. (13.16), except that the exponent n is increased as a function of the surround luminance:

$$n = 0.45 + 0.4 \log S, \tag{13.17}$$

where S is the luminance of the surround in candelas per square meter. For $S = 100 \, \text{cd m}^{-2}$, the exponent is 2.33 which is very much higher than the 0.33 when no surround is present. Now if the disk luminance is increased beyond that of the surround, its brightness is no longer influenced by the surround and follows about the same relation with the luminance as in the single disk, no surround experiment.

Stevens and Stevens [905] also described an attempt to answer a very important question related to imaging applications. A reflection print contains areas of different reflectances. The question is: if we view the print under various illuminations of different luminances, will the perceived brightness difference between two areas on the print increase with the illumination level or will it remain constant? Our everyday experience indicates that the picture on a reflection print looks more vivid under brighter illumination and indeed this is also true for the simple disk and annulus stimuli. The experimental data suggest a simple relation for describing this phenomenon. Let the surround luminance be S and the disk luminance be ρS, i.e., a fixed fraction ρ of the surround. It was found that the brightness of the disk grows as a power function of the luminance with an exponent m given by:

$$m = 0.33 + 0.04 \log \rho. \tag{13.18}$$

This suggests that a disk with a reflectance smaller than 14% of the surround will look darker as the illuminance increases, because the exponent is negative. On the other hand, a disk with a reflectance greater than 15% of the surround will look brighter as the illuminance increases due to the positive exponent. (The brightness of a disk with a reflectance of about 15% of the surround will remain the same independently of the illuminance.) As a consequence, dark regions become darker and bright regions become brighter when the illuminance is increased, and a reflection print looks more vivid under brighter illumination.

13.5.4 Brightness and lightness perception depends on the perceived spatial layout

The above discussions are mostly centered around very constrained stimuli. These stimuli are so simple that there is virtually no cognitive interpretation involved. The experiments are important only because they provide us with a means of checking out some of the basic operations underlying our visual perception. For example, we learned that the difference between or ratio of luminances of two neighboring regions is more useful information than the absolute luminances [346]. However, we also learned that there is much evidence that our visual perception of complex scenes can be quite different from what the results for simple stimuli would predict. For example, let us pick up a medium gray object and move it around in our visual field. The object looks, as far as we can tell, equally bright whether we see it in front of a bright background or a dark background. This is completely different from what we would see if we viewed a uniformly illuminated disk in front of another uniformly illuminated background disk in a dark room. In a complex scene, our cognitive interpretation does not simply rely on the lower-level data-driven visual processes. More often than not, our higher-level model-driven (or hypothesis-driven) processes determine what we see. In fact, when looking at a familiar object, visual data, such as stereo disparity, are often overridden by our internal model of the object. This strategy of our visual perception is not difficult to understand because, most of the time, visual data are ambiguous and noisy [366, 636]. What is difficult to understand is how our visual system combines and selects what to believe. From this perspective, it is not surprising that our judgment of lightness is dependent on the interpretation of the spatial layout of the scene [9, 345]. In Chapter 17, we will need a model of brightness perception. Since images are mostly of complex scenes and they are often viewed in complex environments, our choice of the psychophysical data to use has to be very selective.

13.6 Trichromatic and opponent-process theories

If the goal of color vision is to distinguish visual stimuli of different spectral compositions (such as telling if a banana is ripe for eating), then the task is truly complicated, not simply because illumination and reflectance are coupled (the same problem exists for brightness and lightness perception), but also because the potential number of spectral compositions is huge. Palmer, Young, and von Helmholtz (see [728]) correctly reasoned that we cannot have infinitely many types of color sensors, one for each spectral composition, and they further proposed that in fact we have only three. Their theory of color vision based on direct sensor outputs from the three types of photoreceptor in our retina is called trichromatic theory. Maxwell's demonstration that most colors we see can be reproduced by additively mixing three primary colors gave further support to trichromatic theory. Of course, modern physiological, anatomical, and psychophysical studies confirm the basic trichromatic nature of our color vision. Most of us indeed have only three types of cone in our retina, and, furthermore, it was argued that even if some of us have more than three cone types (because of mutation and inheritance), our neural signal processing does not provide more than three (luminance and chrominance) channels.

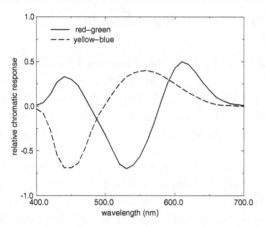

Figure 13.7. The chromatic response functions of the two chromatic opponent processes, red–green and yellow–blue.

However, careful analysis of our color perception (mainly through self-inspection of what one sees) convinced Schopenhauer (1816) and Hering (1870) [396] that our color vision is coded and represented internally as three opponent processes: light–dark (white–black), red–green, and yellow–blue. The two chromatic processes account for the "facts" that our perceived hues can be arranged in a circle and there seem to be four unique hues (red, yellow, green, and blue) that together produce all hues. The achromatic process (light–dark) accounts for bright and dark colors. The term "opponent" further means that white and black, red and green, and yellow and blue cannot be seen in the same color stimulus (i.e., no color should look reddish green or yellowish blue), because they represent the opposite polarities of each of the three processes. Hurvich and Jameson [436] measured the chromatic response functions of the two chromatic processes by using red to cancel green, blue to cancel yellow, and vice versa, in the color of every monochromatic wavelength. This procedure is called hue cancelation and assumes that the chromatic responses of different wavelengths are additive. Figure 13.7 shows the chromatic response functions from their measurements. The wavelengths at which the two chromatic response functions cross zero correspond to the unique hues. The chromatic response functions vary with chromatic adaptation and so do the unique hues.

For a while, there were supporters and opponents of trichromatic theory and opponent-process theory. However, von Kries [163] proposed zone theory in which the color sensing step is by three color cone types and then the sensed color signals are transformed and encoded in opponent processes. This is now a commonly accepted view of our color vision. Although physiological measurements show that there are neurons from the retina to the visual cortex that seem to encode color signals in opponent processes, the data are not quite consistent, nor are they neatly packaged as the opponent-process theory described. Instead, neurons are shown to have so many different spectral response types that interpretations in terms of opponent processes are only conceptual and have no predictive value in neurophysiology.

13.7 Some visual phenomena

In this section, we describe some well-known visual phenomena. Not all of them are important to know for color imaging applications. However, since we understand so little about how our visual perception works, it might be useful to be aware of as many visual phenomena as possible, not only because they provide important clues for our research effort, but also because they impose severe constraints on how our visual model should work.

13.7.1 Brilliance as a separate perceptual attribute

In trying to explain some of his experimental results on color perception, Evans proposed that a new attribute called brilliance should be added to the other four conventional attributes (brightness, lightness, hue, and saturation) in describing our color perception [290]. Reading his long series of experiments in quantifying this new percept is very worthwhile because it reveals to us how little we actually know about our color perception.

It is true that we have only three types of cone (L, M, S) in our retinas, but this does not mean that our perception of color cannot have more than three attributes. The reason is that spatially we have many (L, M, S) responses that can be compared and combined to form new perceptual variables. In fact, intercomparison between neighboring cone responses gives us more reliable color computation than a set of independent and separate, individual cone responses can do, because in each cone response, illumination, reflectance and surface orientation are compounded together. When we compare and combine neighboring cone responses, computation of each of the compounding factors becomes possible. For example, our everyday color perception shows that, in our perceived world, the illumination is always seen as separate from the objects. This will be discussed next. Another example is the perception of white. White is only perceived when other objects are present for comparison. In most cases, we use white simply to mean that we do not perceive any hue and that it is lighter than gray. However, Evans found that, when different amounts of finely ground chalk powder were suspended in transparent glasses filled with water, each looked a different color white [287]. Therefore he concluded that white is not a color attribute *per se*, but an appearance attribute, similar to glossiness and transparency [290, p. 88]. He restricted the meaning of perceived color to those color attributes that can be changed only by changing the energy or the spectral composition reaching the eye from a spatial region. Even in this restricted sense of color perception, he proposed that we need the new variable called brilliance. Let us describe the experiments that led him to this conclusion.

In Evans' experiments, a small circular stimulus ($1–2°$) is seen against a larger, isolated, circular stimulus ($10°$) that appears to be achromatic with $(x, y) = (0.303, 0.326)$ (approximately 7143 K). The luminance and chromaticity of the center stimulus are controlled separately and independently of the larger background stimulus, which is set at a luminance of 318 cd m^{-2}. If we set the luminance and the chromaticity of the center stimulus to be the same as the larger, background stimulus, we cannot distinguish between them.

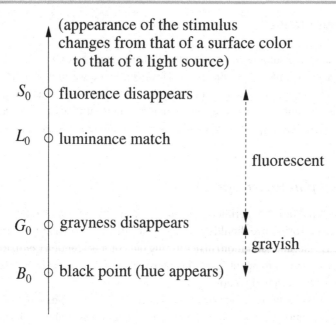

Figure 13.8. The four threshold points in Evans' center-surround experiments.

The perception as a whole is a bright disk, characterized by a single attribute called brightness. If we decrease or increase the luminances of both by equal amounts, the perceived brightness also decreases or increases. If we now fix the luminance of the larger circular disk and reduce the luminance of the center small disk by half, we immediately encounter a new perceptual attribute called grayness – the center disk now appears gray. The center disk also appears darker than the larger disk. This darkness (or lightness) was found to be a separate variable, different from the grayness. The two variables are the same only for achromatic stimuli. If we further decrease the center luminance, its grayness increases and it looks darker and darker, until a point, the *black point* (B_0 in Fig. 13.8), is reached when the center disk looks black. Further decreases in luminance no longer make the center look darker – it remains black. If we change the chromaticity of the center stimulus and repeat the process, it does not matter what the chromaticity of the center is, as its luminance is decreased, a point is always reached when it looks black without any trace of hue.

Evans described the color perception when the luminance of the center stimulus (say 700 nm) is increased from zero until it could not be tolerated by the eyes as follows. When the luminance is much smaller than the surround (say, less than 1/1000), the center stimulus looks black without any hue. As the luminance is increased, a point is reached when a hue starts to appear. This point is called the black point B_0, as we described above. Further increase of the center luminance results in less grayness in the stimulus. A point G_0 is reached when the grayness disappears (for 700 nm, G_0 is about 1/10 of the surround luminance) Further increase in luminance makes the color appear to be fluorescent. Since no actual, physical fluorescence is involved, Evans called this phenomenon "fluorence", and said the stimulus appeared "fluorent". A point L_0 is then reached when the center luminance matches that of the surround. Although no new perception occurs at this point, it is said to be recognizable by skilled and experienced observers. If we continue to increase the center luminance, the strength of fluorence continues to increase and then abruptly decreases and disappears at a point S_0. The appearance of the center stimulus then changes from that of a surface color to that of a light source.

Evans and his coworker measured G_0 for monochromatic light of various wavelengths as the center stimulus. The resulting $G_0(\lambda)$ was found to have a shape almost identical to the purity threshold curve, which is measured by adding monochromatic light to white light to produce a just-noticeable hue. For this reason, Evans suggested that G_0 represents the varying "chromatic strengths" of the different wavelengths. Evans further found that the black point is a constant fraction of G_0, independent of wavelength. With these findings, he then defined G_0 as the point when the "brilliance" of the center is equal to that of the surround. He also pointed out that the chromatic strength is not an inherent characteristic that can be assigned to the individual wavelengths because such a measured function $G_0(\lambda)$ varies with different surround stimuli [290, p. 134]. Although all these experimental results are quite interesting and seem to be of fundamental importance, few follow-up studies are to be found. Interested readers should consult Evans' book [290].

13.7.2 Simultaneous perception of illumination and objects

In analyzing how images are formed on our retinas (or on the film of a camera), we find that the image irradiance is proportional to a product of the light source intensity, the surface reflectance factor, and the surface orientation. The most amazing thing in visual perception is that we see all these three factors *separately* and *simultaneously*! Light that is seen as illuminating the objects is perceived as *separate* from the objects; the surface reflectance factor is perceived as *separate* from the surface shape and the illumination; and the surface orientation (shape) is perceived as *separate* from the reflectance factor and the illumination. There are situations in which these three factors are not perceived correctly and we are surprised. It should be the other way around.

13.7.3 Afterimages

If we look steadily at a saturated, colored target for about 10 s, and then look at a blank sheet of white paper, we will see a pattern with a shape similar to that of the target, but a color complementary to the original target color. This pattern is called the afterimage of the original target. Afterimages that appear to be negative versions of the original are called negative afterimages. For example, the negative afterimage of a red object appears to be cyan, and so on. However, not all afterimages are complementary in color with respect to the original objects. Some afterimages appear to have the same colors as the originals, but often less saturated. These are called positive afterimages. It is also possible to see an afterimage that changes its color appearance over time and does not seem to have a well-defined relationship with the original colors. Negative afterimages often fade and disappear in about 15 s or longer, while positive afterimages seldom last more than 5–10 s.

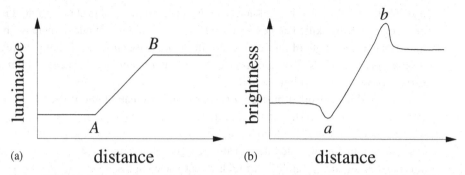

Figure 13.9. (a) A luminance profile across a transition edge and (b) its corresponding profile of the perceived brightness.

13.7.4 The Mach band

Near the transition boundary of two regions of different luminances, we often see dark and bright bands parallel to the boundary. This phenomenon was described and discussed by Mach [624, 784] and the bands are called the Mach bands. Figure 13.9 shows a luminance profile across a transition edge and the corresponding profile of the perceived brightness. The dark band appears in the darker region and the bright band in the lighter region. Both seem to be located at inflection points where the second derivative of the luminance distribution has a local extremum. The dark band seems to occur at the positive second derivative, while the bright band is at the negative second derivative. The second derivatives are good predictors, but they are not always right. Mach bands can be seen over a considerable range of transition width from about 2 to 300′ [257, p. 285]. They do not seem to appear when the edge transition is narrower than 2–4′ [810], even though the second derivative is very high. This is in dispute, because some researchers argue otherwise.

The width of the Mach bands varies from about 1 arcmin to 12 arcmin or more [316], depending on the spatial distribution of luminance. The bright band is often perceived as having a higher overshoot than the undershoot in the dark band. The presence of Mach bands makes the edge transition appear to be sharper than the actual luminance profile. Mach bands appear in images quite frequently. They look quite "real" and can be very difficult to tell from dark and white luminance bands that are actually in the image, such as those created by the adjacency effect in film development or the unsharp masking effect in digital image processing.

When the edge transition is pure luminance, Mach bands have the same hue as the surrounds. If the spectral composition is also changed in the edge transition, the dark band tends to have the complementary hue of the darker region. When the edge transition is pure chrominance (i.e., the edge is an isoluminant edge), the Mach bands are very difficult to see or do not appear at all. This seems to be consistent with the observation that the chromatic CSF is a low-pass filter, rather than a bandpass filter as in the luminance CSF. However, using CSF as an explanation is not justified, because according to that explanation we would not be able to see any uniform areas as such in our perception.

Figure 13.10. The Chevreul effect: uniform-luminance squares do not appear to be uniform when arranged to be adjacent to others.

(a)   (b)

Figure 13.11. Hermann–Hering grids. The dark gray dots seen at the intersections of white lines in (a) are called Hermann grids. The light gray dots seen at the intersections of black lines in (b) are called Hering grids.

13.7.5   The Chevreul effect

When uniform-luminance squares are arranged so that they are adjacent to others (see Fig. 13.10), they do not appear to be uniform. The side that is adjacent to a lighter neighbor appears to be darker than the side that is adjacent to a darker neighbor. This is called the Chevreul effect [178]. Whether this is related to Mach bands is still in debate, because some researchers insisted that Mach bands are not visible near perfectly sharp (narrower than 2′) edges.

13.7.6   Hermann–Hering grids

When white lines intersect on a black background, dark gray dots seem to appear at the junctions. These dots are called Hermann grids [397]. Figure 13.11(a) shows such an example. In Fig. 13.11(b), the black and white are reversed and we can see light gray dots at the junctions of the black lines. There seems to be no gray dot at the fixation point and the dots tend to be more visible away from the fixation point. When the width of the lines is varied, the size of the dots also seems to vary proportionally [1000, p. 160].

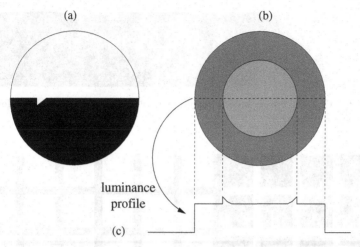

Figure 13.12. The Craik–O'Brien–Cornsweet effect: (a) the reflectance pattern of a circular disk; (b) the appearance of the disk in (a) when it is rotating at high speed; (c) the luminance profile as measured by a photometer with a long integration time (longer than many cycles of the rotation).

13.7.7   The Craik–O'Brien–Cornsweet effect

The importance of luminance changes in determining the perceived brightness or lightness is clearly demonstrated in a phenomenon called the Craik–O'Brien–Cornsweet effect [215, 220, 722]. Figure 13.12 shows one way to generate such a perceptual effect. Figure 13.12(a) shows the reflectance pattern of a circular disk. Note that there is a white notch at the black/white boundary. When the disk is rotating at high speed, it appears, as shown in Fig. 13.12(b), to have a central disk brighter than the rest of the rotating disk. Figure 13.12(c) shows the luminance profile as measured by a photometer with a long integration time (longer than many cycles of the rotation). The abrupt change in luminance profile creates a region that is seen as a brighter disk, although its interior luminance is the same as that outside the region.

13.7.8   Simultaneous contrast and successive contrast

When patterns of different colors are adjacent to each other (especially when one is surrounded by another), the colors appear to be more different than they look when they are seen apart. (However, the actual computation is very complex and the phenomenon may be interpreted quite differently [670, 886].) For example, Fig. 13.13 shows two gray disks of equal luminance, but they appear to be of quite different brightnesses, because one is surrounded by a lighter surround and the other by a darker surround. The brightness simultaneous contrast effect has been studied in detail [388]. For chromatic patterns, if a color A is surrounded by another color B, color A appears to have a color shift in the direction complementary to color B. However, this hue or saturation shift appears to be not as strong as the shift in the brightness or lightness simultaneous contrast effect.

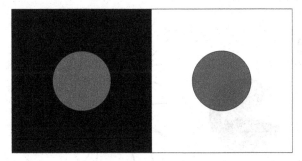

Figure 13.13. The simultaneous contrast effect.

13.7.9 Assimilation

When patterns of different colors are adjacent to each other (such as a square wave grating consisting of alternating green and yellow stripes), the simultaneous contrast effect tends to increase the apparent color differences. However, when one of the color patterns is much finer than the others, its color tends to be pulled toward (rather than pushed away from) the coarser color pattern surrounding it. This effect is called assimilation [436, p. 175]. It is quite sensitive to the relative and the absolute sizes of the color patterns involved. For example, assimilation is mostly seen above 4 cycles per degree for a square wave stimulus [886]. Therefore, we may have to hold the patterns at some further distance away from us to see the effect. It should be noted that the effect occurs while the yellow patterns in the grating mentioned above are still distinctly visible as separate elements. Therefore, it is not optical blur alone that is causing the effect to happen.

13.7.10 Subjective (illusory) contours

When geometric figures in a set are interrupted smoothly, a contour of an object is perceived as if that object is occluding the interrupted figures. It is interesting to note that the region bounded by that subjective contour appears to be brighter than the paper. These subjective contours were systematically studied by Kanizsa [485] and are sometimes called Kanizsa contours. Figure 13.14 shows two examples of such illusory contours. In Fig. 13.14(a), a triangle (brighter than the paper) can be seen, while in Fig.13.14(b), a circular disk can be seen. The end points of the black straight lines generate the subjective contour of a disk slightly brighter than the white background [278]. Psychophysical experiments show that Kanizsa subjective contours can be detected in parallel in the human visual system [238], and therefore they belong to the preattentive early stages in vision. This is consistent with the physiological findings that neurons responding to these subjective contours can be found in the primary visual cortex V1 [367]. What is most instructive is that our visual system takes these contours very seriously. Or, in other words, the subjective contours give us a hint of how contours and regions are formed in our visual perception. Occlusions are very common and it is difficult not to interpret the patterns in Fig. 13.14 as such. From the computation point of view, certain examples of the problem can be solved by analyzing the junction types of the occlusion contours and using other smoothness constraints [827].

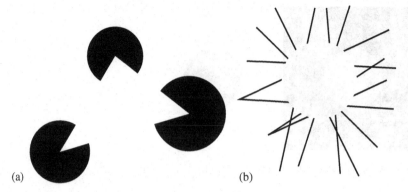

Figure 13.14. Subjective contours can be generated easily in many different ways.

However, a general solution requires a greater understanding of the basic visual processes involved.

13.7.11   The Bezold–Brücke effect

If the spectral composition of a color stimulus is fixed but its radiance is varied, its perceived hue changes. This effect is called the Bezold–Brücke effect [141, 990]. It is usually explained as an effect due to the nonlinearity of the color response [995]. If the color stimuli are monochromatic lights, several experimenters found that there are three wavelengths ($\approx$ 478 nm, 500 nm, 578 nm) that show little or no significant variation in hue when their luminance is varied over a range of 1–2 log units. These are called *invariant hues* (invariant over luminance change). It was also found that the invariant hues also seem to be the same as the *unique hues* in hue cancelation experiments.

13.7.12   The Helmholtz–Kohlrausch effect

Saturated colors look brighter than pastel colors of the same luminance (as determined by the CIE luminosity curve). This effect is called the Helmholtz–Kohlrausch effect [699]. For some colors a factor of 3 reduction of luminance is required to match the luminance of a gray or white stimulus.

13.7.13   The Abney effect

If white light is added to a spectrum color, the latter not only appears desaturated, but also changes its perceived hue. This effect is called the Abney effect [1]. On a CIE chromaticity diagram, adding white light to a spectrum color produces color stimuli whose chromaticities fall on the straight-line segment connecting the white light and the spectrum color. The Abney effect means that these straight lines are not constant hue loci. For most spectrum colors, this is true. However, there are two constant hue loci, Munsell 10Y and 5P at Munsell value 5 under illuminant C, that are nearly straight (see [1053, p. 857]). The significance of these two hues is not clear.

13.7.14 The McCollough effect

If one looks at a horizontal grating of red and black bars and a vertical grating of green and black bars for a period of time (3–6 min), then looks at a grating of white and black bars, the white bars will look cyan (the complementary color of red) if they are horizontal, and magenta (the complementary color of green) if they are vertical. This effect is called the McCollough effect [651]. It belongs to a class of visual effects called the contingent aftereffects [54, p. 183]. One of the most striking things about the McCollough effect is its long lasting period. A few hours after viewing the adapting red and green gratings, one may still see the effect.

13.7.15 The Stiles–Crawford effect

The same amount of light entering the eye through different parts of the pupil and imaged onto the same retina location is perceived as having different brightnesses and colors. This directional sensitivity is called the Stiles–Crawford effect. The effect exists mainly in cones, and is very much reduced in rods. The magnitude of the effect for the central fovea region is about 4:1 when the light ray enters near the center of the pupil and when it enters through the pupil edge ([1053], pp. 424–9). Some of the Stiles–Crawford effect seems to be due to the shape of the cone outersegment, which produces some kind of wave-guide effect to funnel the photons through the layers of disk structures of photopigments.

13.7.16 Small field tritanopia

The number of S cones is only about 5–10% of the total cone population. The S cones are also spaced widely apart. As a consequence, green–blue or red–blue color variations over a small visual angle (less than 10 arcmin) are difficult to discriminate, while red–green variations over as little as 5 arcmin can still be detected. Furthermore, for a small region in the central fovea, no S cones are present and color vision becomes dichromatic [1037].

13.7.17 The oblique effect

Psychophysical experiments showed that the visual detection and discrimination thresholds are often poorer when the stimuli are oriented at 45° from vertical than when horizontal or vertical [99, 159, 769]. This is called the oblique effect.

13.8 Problems

13.1 Describe how the Weber fraction, $\Delta L/L$, varies as a function of the adaptation luminance level and the size of the visual target.

13.2 The CSF is often used to optimize the quantization table used in JPEG compression. A 512×512 image is to be displayed on an area of 20 cm by 20 cm of an ideal CRT monitor (with $MTF = 1.0$ for all frequencies). The average luminance level of the image is 50 cd m^{-2}, and the viewing distance is 25 cm. Determine the optimal quantization table with the quantization interval set at 16 for the peak sensitivity frequency. What are the potential problems with this design method?

13.3 The von Kries transformation is not very accurate, but it accounts for the major effect of chromatic adaptation. The three coefficients are often determined from the light source colors. Experimental data show that the transformation would work even better if the coefficients were determined from the corresponding, perceived grays in both illuminants. How is the Helson–Judd effect related to this finding?

13.4 Are the invariant hues in the Bezold–Brücke effect related to the unique hues (hues that are pure red, pure green, pure blue, and pure yellow) in the opponent processes (see the discussion in [995])?

13.5 The Mach bands are good examples showing that what we see is not a simple point-by-point mapping of the scene luminance. Can you construct a mathematical model of the Mach band perception? Does your model explain why the Mach bands are difficult to see on a sharp edge?

14 Color order systems

Having studied radiometry, colorimetry, and the psychophysics of our visual perception, we now have the appropriate background to study the subject of color order systems. This is a subject that is often discussed on an intuitive level, but the concepts and the logic of color order systems can be much better appreciated if we have a proper knowledge of the physics of color and the psychophysics of human color perception. Therefore, we have delayed discussion of this subject until now. Color order systems are important in applications because they provide some practical solutions for many color problems in our daily life, such as how to specify the paint color we want and how to coordinate the colors of furniture. Color order systems are also quite important for the explicit expression of our theoretical thinking and understanding of how we perceive colors, such as the opponent-color processes.

14.1 Introduction

How many colors can we distinguish? The number is estimated to be more than one million [713]. How do we accurately communicate with each other about a particular color without actually showing a real sample? Obviously our vocabulary of color names is too limited for this purpose. A system is needed to order all possible colors according to certain chosen attributes in a well-defined manner so that any color can be specified by its attributes in the system. In principle, a color order system can be designed purely on a conceptual level [519]. However, for the convenience of practical use, most color systems are implemented as collections of physical color samples. This makes them easy to understand and easy to use, and means it is easy to make approximate interpolation between colors. For example, when selecting the color of paints to use, we have a better appreciation of the colors if we have actual samples to see (of course, we have to be aware of the effects of the illumination). For this reason, the actual physical color samples are as important as the conceptual color order system on which the physical samples are based. In order to distinguish the two, the conceptual system will be referred to as the *color order system* and its physical color samples will be called the *color atlas*.

From the vision point of view, colors are most often perceived as belonging to objects. Their perceived attributes are greatly influenced by their surrounds, surface textures, surface shapes, illumination, and the adaptation state of the observer. It is hard to imagine how colors in all their possible modes of appearance can be systematically ordered.

In fact, without a detailed understanding of the human visual system as a whole, such an attempt is not possible because we do not know what attributes to use for the ordering. A practical approach is to restrict the domain of interest to the colors of uniform, textureless, flat surfaces as viewed against a uniform, textureless, flat, neutral surround, under a standard illumination. In this restricted domain, the spatial and temporal variables are excluded, the quality and quantity of illumination are well controlled, and the adaptation state of the observers is maintained at a "constant", steady state by asking them to move their eyes continuously across the entire visual field. From our understanding of the human visual system, we hope that we have essentially fixed all the visual variables except the spectral variations. With the additional assumption that in photopic vision, only three types of photoreceptor are responsible for vision, we can propose that we need only a three-dimensional solid for ordering all the colors in this restricted domain of interest. However, even within this greatly simplified domain, infinite possible choices exist and other requirements or preferences are needed to specify a color order system [399, 430, 519, 795, 1050].

The basic difference between systems is the attributes they choose to order colors. We will describe only four color order systems to illustrate the diverse views that can be taken to order colors: the Ostwald system, the Munsell system, the natural color system (NCS), and the Optical Society of America (OSA) system. Descriptions of other systems, such as the DIN system and the Coloroid system, can be found in [11, 399, 430, 795]. Among the four systems discussed here, the Munsell system is the most widely used system (especially in the USA and Asia).

14.2   The Ostwald system

Wilhelm Ostwald (1853–1932), a Nobel Laureate in chemistry in 1909, began to work on color intensively after he retired from his career at the University of Leipzig at age of 53 [734]. Within the next 10 years, he developed a color system that became very influential in Germany and many other countries, especially in the field of color harmony, art, and commercial applications.

A question that is often asked in art and commercial applications is: which color combinations have pleasant effects and which do not, i.e., which colors go together in harmony? Ostwald, having constructed his color system in a mathematically elegant manner, proposed a far-reaching "basic law" of color harmony: harmony = order. He suggested that colors that are selected in an orderly sequence from his color system, such as colors of the same dominant wavelength (hue), or colors of the same chromaticity, constitute a pleasing harmony. There are many possible orders in which one can traverse his color solid and Ostwald asserted that the simpler the order, the more convincing is the harmony. Although not everyone agrees with his "basic laws" (see the discussions in [477, pp. 380, 390–6]), many artists and color designers have benefited from his teaching [11, 112, 122]. Unfortunately, in the USA, the Munsell system is most popular and the Ostwald system is relatively unknown in the field of color science. This is mainly due to a number of difficulties in color specifications inherent in the Ostwald system [122] .

14.2.1 The Ostwald color order system

Ostwald formulated his color system based on idealized spectral reflectance curves, the Weber–Fechner law, and Hering's opponent-color processes. He first defined the achromatic colors as generated from spectral reflectance curves that are constant values over the visible wavelength range. The ideal white, W, is from the reflectance curve which is 1.0 for all wavelengths, and the ideal black, B, is from that of zero reflectance. Other achromatic colors come from spectral reflectance curves of constant values between 0 and 1. Ostwald realized that he could arrange the achromatic scale more uniformly by using the Weber–Fechner law. He derived an achromatic scale with ten steps in each logarithmic decade. For example, reflectance factors between 0.01 and 0.1 and between 0.1 and 1.0 span two logarithmic decades. Within each decade, ten quantization steps in the logarithmic scale are used. In terms of linear reflectance value, the quantization divisions between 0.1 and 1.0 are 0.1259 ($= 0.1 \times 10^{0.1}$), 0.1585 ($= 0.1 \times 10^{0.2}$), 0.1995 ($= 0.1 \times 10^{0.3}$), 0.2512, 0.3162, 0.3981, 0.5012, 0.6309, 0.7943.

He then defined full colors, C, as from spectral reflectance curves that have either 0% or 100% reflectances over the visible wavelengths. In the following we will assume that the visible wavelengths are from 360 nm to 830 nm (CIE convention). For a given illuminant, a pair of full colors, complementary to each other, is associated with a wavelength and its complementary wavelength (if it exists). For example, for CIE Illuminant C, the wavelengths 440 nm and 568 nm are complementary to each other (i.e., some additive mixture of the two wavelengths can match Illuminant C). The pair of full colors that is defined by this pair of wavelengths is generated by one spectral reflectance curve that is 1.0 from 440 nm to 568 nm and zero elsewhere, and the other spectral reflectance curve that is zero from 440 nm to 568 nm and 1.0 elsewhere. If a wavelength does not have a complementary wavelength, for example, 550 nm, the pair of full colors is generated by one spectral reflectance factor that is 1.0 from 360 nm to 550 nm and zero elsewhere, and the other spectral reflectance curve that is zero from 360 nm to 550 nm and 1.0 elsewhere. Although this definition of full color covers a relatively large gamut, it can be shown that there are color samples which could be produced by available paint pigments, having colors outside the Ostwald color solid [324].

In the above definition of full colors, the reflectance values are always 0.0 or 1.0. If we scale the spectral reflectance factor of a full color by a factor c and add a constant w to it, so that $c + w \leq 1$, we obtain a spectral reflectance factor that corresponds to some less "saturated" color. Let us define $b = 1 - c - w$. The three numbers, c, w, b, are called the color content, the white content, and the black content of the resulting color. This is a fundamental concept of the Ostwald color system in which every color is specified by its white content, black content, and color content. For any given full color C, any color represented by a point in the triangle determined by W (white), B (black), and C, is said to have the same Ostwald hue. Ostwald called such a triangle, a monochromatic triangle.

Ostwald required that complementary colors were located at the opposite ends of a diameter of the hue circle. Based on Hering's opponent theory, he placed red, yellow, green, and blue at 90° from their two neighbors. He further indicated that other hues should be placed on the hue circle in perceptually equal steps. However, this requirement is generally

believed to be incompatible with the placements of the red, yellow, green, and blue at 90°
intervals because there are more perceptually equal steps in hue between red and blue than
between red and yellow.

The most widely used ideas from the Ostwald color system are his rules of color harmony.
Within each monochromatic triangle, colors that have equal white content, w, are called
isotints, colors that have equal black content, b, are called *isotones*, and colors that have
equal color content, c, are called *isochromes* (also called the shadow series). Colors that
have the same white content as well as black content in different monochromatic triangles
form an *isovalue* series. Ostwald's basic rule for color harmony is to require that colors be
presented in an orderly sequence in his color system. The four isoseries mentioned above
plus the isohue series (colors that are in the same monochromatic triangle) are the five
simple orders that he liked very much and so do many others [112, 734].

14.2.2   The Ostwald color atlas

Since the Ostwald color system is constructed on the physical idealization of spectral
reflectance factors, it is in essence a color order system that exists only in theory. It is in
fact not possible to produce color samples to represent the ideal Ostwald color system (see
the discussion in [358]).

In 1958, the Container Corporation of America (Chicago) published the fourth edition of
its *Color Harmony Manual*, which was based on the theoretical, colorimetric specifications
of the abridged Ostwald color system. It contains 949 color chips. The CIE standard Illuminant C was chosen to be the reference illumination. Ostwald used the notation a, c, e, g, i,
l, n, and p to denote the reflectance factors 0.891 ($= 0.1 \times 10^{0.95}$), 0.562 ($= 0.1 \times 10^{0.75}$),
0.355, 0.224, 0.141, 0.0891, 0.0562, and 0.0355. Within a monochromatic triangle, a color
is denoted by two letters, the first indicating white content, and the second the black content. For example, the color denoted by gc has 0.355 white content and 0.562 black content.
There are 24 hues (monochromatic triangles) in the color solid. Hue number 2 is yellow,
number 14 is blue, number 8 is red, and number 20 is green (seagreen). The colorimetric
measurements of the color chips in the 1942 (first) edition are reported in [358].

14.3   The Munsell system

Since its conception by Munsell in 1905, the Munsell color system has been extended and
refined many times. Efforts to smooth its irregularities and to calibrate it colorimetrically
were completed in 1943 [711]. Since then, the color atlas, the *Munsell Book of Color*, has
been revised to conform fully with the 1943 renotation. It is now the most widely used color
order system and has been incorporated in many national standards [11, p. 114].

14.3.1   The Munsell color order system

The Munsell color order system assumes that the basic attributes of color are its Hue (red
or green), Value (how much light is reflected compared with a white surface), and Chroma

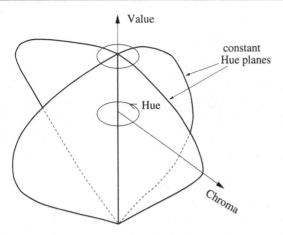

Figure 14.1. A schematic diagram of the Munsell color order system.

(how colorful it is compared with a white surface). Figure 14.1 shows a schematic diagram of the system. Hue is arranged as a circle, Value as the axis perpendicular to the Hue circle, and Chroma as the radial distance from the center of the Hue circle. A color is thus specified by its Hue, and on that Hue plane, it is further specified by its Value, and then by its Chroma. For example, 7.5YR5/4 indicates that the color is on the Hue plane 7.5YR, and its Value is 5.0 and its Chroma is 4.0. The important feature of the Munsell system is the scaling of the attributes. Colors that differ only in one attribute are arranged so that an equal difference in the attribute represents an equal perceptual difference. For example, along the Value attribute, equal steps in Value represents equal perceptual differences in lightness. The same is also done along the Hue circle and the Chroma radial distance. For a given Value and a given Chroma, equal angular distance in Hue is meant to represent equal perceptual difference in Hue. Since the Munsell system arranges colors in equal perceptual intervals on cylindrical coordinates, equal Euclidean distances in the Munsell system do not necessarily represent equal perceptual differences, unless two of the attributes are the same. This is the basic difference between the Munsell system and the OSA color system (to be discussed shortly) in which equal Euclidean distances are meant to represent equal perceptual differences.

14.3.2 The Munsell color atlas

The *Munsell Book of Color* contains painted color samples that are arranged in approximately equal perceptual steps, spanning the lightness, Hue, and Chroma space. The major significance of the Munsell system is the large number of experimental observations (some 3 000 000 color judgments by 40 observers) that were put in to quantify the psychophysical specifications of color perception [711], producing conversion tables between the CIE 1931 tristimulus values and the Munsell surface colors.

There are five principal Hues (red, yellow, green, blue, and purple) and five intermediate Hues (yellow–red, green–yellow, blue–green, purple–blue, and red–purple). Clockwise on the Hue circle, the ten major Hues are: 5R (0°), 5YR (36°), 5Y (72°), 5GY (108°), 5G

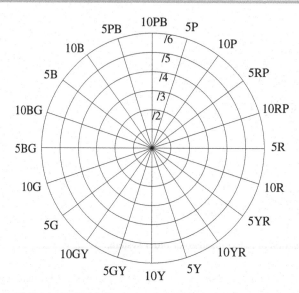

Figure 14.2. The Hue circle of the Munsell color order system.

(144°), 5BG (180°), 5B (216°), 5PB (252°), 5P (288°), and 5RP (324°) (see Fig. 14.2). One Hue step is defined to be 3.6°, resulting in ten Hue steps between the neighboring major Hues. The naming of these Hues starts from the mid-point between the major Hues and is numbered from 0 to 10. For example, the Hue 6R is at 3.6°, 7R at 7.2°, 8R at 10.8°, 9R at 14.4°, 10R at 18° which can also be referred to as 0YR. The next Hue at 21.6°, being closer to the major Hue YR, is named 1YR, and the next Hue at 25.2° is 2YR, and so on. However, the *Munsell Book of Color* does not provide chip samples at every Hue step. Between the neighboring major Hues, only three Hue samples are provided (although in the collection of glossy color chips, supplementary colors of intermediate Hue are also provided for some Chromas and Values). For example, between 5R (0°) and 5YR (36°), color chips of 7.5R (9°), 10R (18°), and 2.5YR (27°) are provided. The collection of color chips thus provides 40 Hues, each representing a perceptually equally-spaced hue, 9° apart.

The Munsell Chroma scale (corresponding to the perceptual attribute of *saturation*) is measured along a Hue radius, starting with zero at the center for neutral black, gray, or white. Munsell color samples are provided at Chroma 1 for the Hues at 18° intervals (5R, 10R, 5YR, and so on), and at Chroma 2, 4, 6, up to the maximum Chroma that can be produced reliably and with certain permanency by the available pigments. The total number of Chroma steps within the theoretical MacAdam limit [617] for all the Hues and Values is estimated as 5836 [713].

The Munsell Value V (corresponding to the perceptual attribute of *lightness*) ranges between 0 and 10 in equal perceptual steps. V can be computed from the luminance reflectance factor, R_Y, under Illuminant C by first normalizing the luminance Y of the sample to Y_w, that of the then white standard MgO (97.5% reflectance) as 100%, i.e., $R_Y = Y/Y_w$, and then finding the solution of the following equation:

$$R_Y = 1.2219V - 0.23111V^2 + 0.23951V^3 - 0.021009V^4 + 0.0008404V^5. \quad (14.1)$$

According to the psychological judgment [713], one Chroma step corresponds to roughly five just-perceptible increments, one Hue step corresponds to roughly two just-perceptible increments, and one value step corresponds to roughly 50 just perceptible increments. The total number of surface colors that may be distinguished under good viewing conditions [713] is thus estimated to be around 7 500 000, which needs about 23 bits in digital representation, provided the ideal quantization of the entire space for surface colors is achieved.

One major complaint about the Munsell color system is that the Munsell Value does not correlate well with the perceived "lightness". In general, color chips that have higher Chromas tend to look lighter than those of lower Chromas but the same Value [1050]. This is a result of the way Value was defined. In the color judgment experiments conducted for the Munsell renotation, the value adjustments were made on the neutral or near-neutral samples with the assumption that the Value of a color is a function of the luminance factor (Y) only, regardless of its chroma (see [711, p. 417]).

14.4 The NCS

In 1964, the Royal Swedish Academy of Engineering Science established the Swedish Colour Centre Foundation. Its initial aim was to create another and better edition of *Hesselgren's Colour Atlas*, based on the Hering–Johansson idea of opponent-color processes. After a long course of study and experiment, it concluded that hue and saturation are not the basic color elements. The NCS was then developed by Hard, Sivik, and their coworkers, based on the concept of specifying a color in terms of relative amounts of the six basic colors perceived to be present. The NCS system does not attempt to scale its color attributes for perceptual uniformity, but the color gradation on any hue plane of its color atlas looks very smooth.

14.4.1 The NCS color order system

Hering [396] proposed that our color perception is based on three opponent processes, i.e., white–black, red–green, and yellow–blue. Our visual sensation of color is the result of the combined perception generated by these three processes. They are opponent in the sense that reddish and greenish sensations cannot be perceived at the same time, nor can yellowish and bluish sensations, and nor can blackish and whitish sensations. Any color can be described by the relative amounts of the responses from these three opponent processes. For example, the sensation of a light purple color comes from some positive response of the red–green process, some negative response of the yellow–blue process, and some positive response from the white–black process [436]. The NCS is developed from this very concept of opponent-color processes, except that whiteness and blackness are allowed to coexist. This coexistence of whiteness and blackness is similar to the concept of gray content proposed by Evans [290]. The six basic colors, white, black, red, green, yellow, and blue, are located at the vertices of three mutually orthogonal axes. On the plane of the two axes representing various hues, a hue circle is drawn through the four basic hues (red, green, yellow, and blue). The color solid thus has the shape of one cone on top of another inverted cone. Since redness and greenness cannot coexist, and yellowness and blueness cannot coexist, any color can have at most four components of the six basic colors in it. A color is thus specified by the relative amounts of the four components in terms of percentages. For example, a color can have 20% whiteness, 30% blackness, 10% yellowness, and 40% redness. The NCS defines Y, R, B, G as the four major hues. All other hues are expressed as the relative percentage of the two neighboring major hues. For the color in the above example, yellowness is $10/(10+40) = 20\%$ and the redness is $40/(10+40) = 80\%$. The hue can thus be denoted by 20Y80R. Since the yellowness and the redness sum up to 100%, we need only write Y80R. The NSC defines chromaticness as the sum of the two major hue components. For the color in the above example, the chromaticness is $10 + 40 = 50$. The complete NCS color specification is "blackness, chromaticness, hue". For the color in the above example, the NCS notation is 3050-Y80R.

14.4.2   The NCS color atlas

Over 60 000 observations made on painted color samples were collected to produce *The NCS Color Atlas*, which contains 1526 color samples in its second edition (1990). Color samples of the same hue are arranged on a page. There are 40 hues in the atlas. Colorimetrically, the NCS unique red, unique green, unique yellow, and unique blue are close to Munsell 5R, 5G, 5Y, and 7.5B, respectively. The NCS blackness, s, can be approximated by the CIE luminance factor Y using the following relation:

$$s = 100 - 156Y/(56 + Y).\qquad(14.2)$$

14.5   The Optical Society of America (OSA) color system

In 1947, the Optical Society of America formed the Committee on Uniform Color Scales [619] to review all available data on subjective magnitudes of color differences and to develop a set of color samples that can be assembled to form uniform color scales of as many varieties as is feasible. The committee conducted color judgment experiments with 76 normal observers, using hundreds of pairs of color differences. By analyzing the data, a set of formulas was constructed so that the Euclidean distance in the resulting color scales represents color difference. After 30 years of work, the *OSA Uniform-Color-Scale Atlas* was produced in 1977. The important features of the OSA color system are: (1) the CIE tristimulus values are linearly transformed to a space that uses estimated cone spectral sensitivities, before any nonlinear approximation to color appearance is done; (2) all the color differences used are about ten times the just-noticeable difference, and therefore the results are not intended for applications involving small color differences.

14.5.1   The OSA color order system

The OSA color system uses the color matching functions, $\bar{r}_{10}(\lambda)$, $\bar{g}_{10}(\lambda)$, and $\bar{b}_{10}(\lambda)$, of the CIE 1964 Supplementary Standard Colorimetric Observer to estimate the cone spectral sensitivities. The cone tristimulus values R_{10}, G_{10}, B_{10} are estimated from the CIE 1964 tristimulus values, X_{10}, Y_{10}, Z_{10}, by the following transformation:

$$R_{10} = 0.799X_{10} + 0.4194Y_{10} - 0.1648Z_{10},$$
$$G_{10} = -0.4493X_{10} + 1.3265Y_{10} + 0.0927Z_{10}, \tag{14.3}$$
$$B_{10} = -0.1149X_{10} + 0.3394Y_{10} + 0.717Z_{10},$$

where X_{10}, Y_{10}, Z_{10} are measured in D_{65} with Y_{10} set to 100 for white. The three coordinates L (lightness), j (yellowness), g (greenness), of the OSA color system are defined as:

$$L = 5.9[\overline{Y}_{10}^{1/3} - 2/3 + 0.042(\overline{Y}_{10} - 30)^{1/3}], \tag{14.4}$$
$$j = C(1.7R_{10}^{1/3} + 8G_{10}^{1/3} - 9.7B_{10}^{1/3}), \tag{14.5}$$
$$g = C(-13.7R_{10}^{1/3} + 17.7G_{10}^{1/3} - 4B_{10}^{1/3}), \tag{14.6}$$

where

$$\overline{Y}_{10} = Y_{10}(4.4934x_{10}^2 + 4.3034y_{10}^2 - 4.276x_{10}y_{10} - 1.3744x_{10} - 2.5643y_{10} + 1.8103), \tag{14.7}$$

$$C = \frac{L}{5.9(\overline{Y}_{10}^{1/3} - 2/3)}. \tag{14.8}$$

The surround used for all the committee's color comparisons was a medium gray with 30% reflectance factor.

14.5.2   The OSA color atlas

The atlas of the OSA uniform color scale arranges color samples in a regular rhombohedral crystal lattice. Each sample is surrounded by 12 equal-distance neighbors. Since the goal was to create a uniform color scale, there are no explicit definitions for saturations or hues. Planar cross-sections of the color solid show the color variations along different directions. A total of 558 cards colored with glossy acrylic paint are available. Of them, 424 form the basic set, and the other 134 color samples are intermediate colors to be inserted in the central region of the color solid to create a denser atlas for the pale colors. The detailed descriptions of the geometry and structure of the atlas can be found in some references (see e.g., [11, 620]).

14.6   Color harmony

In color imaging science, the question of color harmony is rarely raised. However, with the advance of computing technology, color images can now be manipulated easily on a pixel level, and it is likely that certain basic issues in color harmony will arise, especially in image synthesis. As we mentioned earlier, the major theory in color harmony was proposed by Ostwald. The basic idea is that color combinations have to follow certain orderly distributions in color attributes. Five of these orderly distributions are:

- monochromatic triangle: colors of the same dominant wavelength;
- isotints: colors of the same white content and on the same monochromatic triangle;
- isotones: colors of the same black content and on the same monochromatic triangle;
- isochromes (shadow series): colors of the same chromatic content and on the same monochromatic triangle;
- isovalents: colors of the same white, black, and chromatic content.

We all have seen pleasant color combinations in interior decorations, in clothing, in architecture, and in paintings. There seems to be some themes or rules underlying these combinations. Application of these orderly distributions to artistic designs sometimes produces great results [112], but sometimes does not [399]. Studies on color harmony are difficult because of its subjective nature. A summary of Judd's comments on this issue is still most appropriate at this moment: "(1) Color harmony is a matter of likes and dislikes, and emotional responses vary from one person to another, and from time to time with the same person. We get tired of old color combinations. On the other hand, we sometimes learn to appreciate a color combination that we did not like initially. (2) Color harmony depends on the size, shape, design, and geometric construction, as well as on the colors themselves. (3) Color harmony depends on the subjective interpretation of the design by the observer. It is very unlikely that attempts to give simple rules for the construction of color harmonies will be successful in all contexts."

14.7 Problems

14.1 Of the four color order systems discussed in this chapter, which one is actually defined without reference to any visual system?

14.2 Of the four color order systems discussed in this chapter, which one has the property that equal Euclidean distances represent equal color differences?

14.3 Plot the lightness as a function of luminance value in the four color order systems in this chapter. How do they compare with the L^* in CIELAB?

15 Color measurement

Quantitative analysis in color imaging requires measurements of all the relevant characteristics of the scene, the imaging system, and the display devices and media. The major concepts underlying these measurements, such as radiometry, photometry, colorimetry, and scene physics, have been covered in the previous chapters in the book. In this chapter, we will briefly describe how various measurement instruments work and study how color measurements are performed. Various national and international standards have been defined (such as in [39, 444]) and it is important to understand them if accurate, standard measurements are required.

There are three major types of color measurement in color imaging: spectral measurement, colorimetric measurement, and density measurement. In addition to these three types, some applications also require the measurements of spectral distribution as a function of geometrical variables, such as the incident angles and the reflection angles. For example, measurements of the BSRDF of surface materials are often performed for textile, printing, or computer animation applications. Instruments that can make this type of measurement are called gonioreflectometers.

15.1 Spectral measurements

The first step in many color imaging applications is to calibrate the devices that will be used in the application, so that quantitative physical relations can be established between the scenes, the sensors, and the displays. The most detailed description of a color stimulus is its *absolute* spectral power distribution. This is usually measured as spectral radiance or spectral irradiance by an instrument called a spectroradiometer. For many applications, only *relative* spectral power distributions (with respect to some reference objects) are needed. The relative spectral power distribution is measured by an instrument called a spectrophotometer. The names of these two types of instrument are related to the fact that radiometry deals with *absolute* radiant fluxes and photometry deals with *relative* light fluxes (with respect to the human luminous sensitivity).

15.1.1 Spectroradiometer

A spectroradiometer (see Fig. 15.1) consists of four major parts: (1) the collecting optics, (2) the monochromator, (3) the detector, and (4) the readout device. The collecting optics

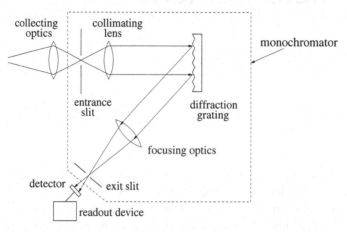

Figure 15.1. The schematic diagram of a spectroradiometer [525].

serves the function of collecting or imaging light from the target and forming a light beam in a proper shape for the monochromator. The monochromator selects and transmits a narrow band of wavelengths (ideally a single wavelength) from the spectrum of the incident light beam. A dispersing element (such as a prism or a diffraction grating) inside the monochromator receives the incident light beam and spreads different wavelengths in different angular directions. The focusing optics is then moved and positioned along the angular spread to focus a narrow portion of the spectrum to pass through the exit slit to the detector. The detector senses the radiant power and outputs an electrical signal to the readout device. Figure 15.1 shows a schematic diagram of a spectroradiometer.

One of the key components in a spectroradiometer is the dispersing element that separates different wavelengths of the incident light. Diffraction gratings are often used for this purpose. The way a diffraction grating works is well described in the literature (e.g., [385, 437, 646, 772]). Basically, periodic micro-structures on the grating surface cause the reflected (or transmitted) light waves to interfere constructively or destructively, depending on the angle of propagation upon reflection or transmission. At any particular angle, a certain wavelength may have the strongest intensity due to constructive interference, while other wavelengths are not completely in phase and are weaker in intensity. This means that wavelength separation is never perfect. This problem is called spectral scattering: unwanted light of neighboring wavelength is scattered or diffracted into the exit slit and mixed with the wavelength of interest. The scattering can come from the grating, mirrors, or the housing of the monochromator. The best way to reduce spectral scattering is to pass the output beam of one monochromator through yet another monochromator (in a setup called a double monochromator). If a single monochromator is used, a method of software correction, deconvolution, can be employed to improve the spectral resoution from the measured data [714, Chapter 8].

If the collecting optics is equipped with a telescope type of imaging lens, the spectroradiometer can be used to measure the spectral radiant power from a spot in the scene. This type of instrument is called a tele-spectroradiometer. It is a most useful instrument for color imaging research because we can use it to measure the spectral radiance from any

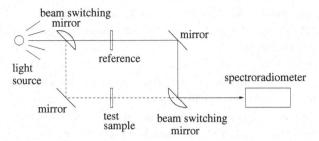

Figure 15.2. The schematic diagram of a spectrophotometer [525].

sample point in the scene under the natural, complex, ambient illumination in which we are interested.

15.1.2 Spectrophotometer

A spectrophotometer is basically a spectroradiometer that has its own light source and is equipped to switch the measurement between two alternative input light beams, one reflected from or transmitted through the test sample and the other reflected from a reference object (a reflection standard) or transmitted through an open gate without the test sample. Figure 15.2 shows a schematic diagram of a spectrophotometer.

15.1.3 Factors to consider

Accurate and precise spectral measurements are relatively difficult to achieve [893]. Measurement errors of 10% are quite common [525, p. 2]. The main reason is that there are many variables in color stimuli and many components in the measuring instrument, each contributing some uncertainty to the final measurement value. There are several important factors that we have to consider when making spectral measurements:

- Sample and standard preparation: the samples to be used in the measurement have to be prepared so that they are representative of their intended use. Any standards to be used should be kept in good condition (no scratches, no dust, no cracks, etc.).
- Instrument preparation: an instrument should be allowed to warm up long enough to reach a stable state. (For some instruments, this may take a long time, e.g., 1 or 2 hours.)
- Direction and position dependency: the response of a measuring instrument to light is often a function of its incident direction and position. An integrating sphere is often quite effective in making the response insensitive to such variations. However, light incident in an integrating sphere is distributed over the whole sphere and only a small portion leaves the output port. The attenuation factor is often larger than two orders of magnitude. Therefore, it is desirable to use a small integrating sphere to reduce the light loss.
- Polarization: most monochromators are sensitive to polarization. For unpolarized color stimuli, this is not a problem. However, for measuring reflection targets, it may be useful

to make sure that the lighting and measuring geometry do not create problems. If the instrument has a diffuser or an integrating sphere in the fore-optics, the measurement will not be sensitive to polarization.

- Spectral scattering: when measuring an incident spectrum at a wavelength λ with an intended spectral wavelength window $\Delta\lambda$, stray light of other wavelengths may be scattered into the detector. This is called spectral scattering. It can cause serious errors if the target wavelength is near a strong spectral peak. The scattered light may be stronger than the spectral light to be measured. In most color imaging applications, spectral functions are quite smooth and therefore their measurements are not as difficult as those with spiky spectral lines. Some exceptions are fluorescent lamps and CRT monitors.
- Wavelength calibration: the monochromator in the spectroradiometer or spectrophotometer spreads different wavelengths out in different directions. An accurate spectral measurement requires an accurate wavelength identification. A small wavelength offset can produce a large error in the calculation of tristimulus values. Fortunately, there are various standard spectral lines that can be used for calibrating the wavelength positions.
- Fluorescence: some materials absorb radiant flux of certain wavelengths and reradiate it at other (usually longer) wavelengths. It is thus very important to characterize the light source of the instrument so that the amount of fluorescence can be quantified [39, ASTM E 991, 431]. If color filters are used, it is important to check to see if they are fluorescent.
- Nonlinearity: the responsivity function of an instrument is often nonlinear, especially when a large dynamic input range is involved. It should be part of the instrument calibration procedure to characterize the nonlinearity in detail.

Although extremely high accuracy of spectral measurements is difficult to achieve, good instrumental repeatability can be obtained to about 0.15 CIELAB units [296]. Ceramic color tiles used as reflectance standards have a stability even better than that.

15.2 Gonioreflectometers

In order to fully characterize the optical properties of a reflecting surface, it is necessary to measure the spectral reflectance factors for all incident angles and reflection angles. An instrument that can systematically vary the lighting and measuring geometry for the measurement of the reflectance factor is called a gonioreflectometer. There are two types of such instrument. For a given incident angle, one type [58, 321] measures one reflecting angle at a time, while the other type [235, 637, 1012] measures a large number of reflecting angles at the same time. The latter type, using optics to form an image of all or half of reflecting beams, is obviously orders of magnitude more efficient, but tends to be less accurate.

In a gonioreflectometer, the spectral information on the surface reflection can be measured by using either a spectroradiometer as the detector [321] or a light source with a

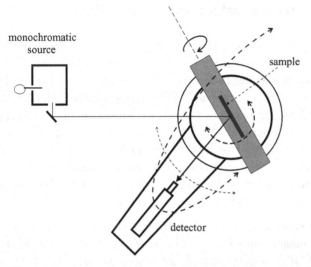

Figure 15.3. Schematic diagram of a gonioreflectometer. Here the light source is a monochromator illuminator and the detector is a simple photodiode detector. Alternatively, the light source may be a white-light source and the detector may be a spectroradiometer.

monochromator [778]. Figure 15.3 shows a schematic diagram of a gonioreflectometer. In order to make full BRDF measurements, the incident angle and the reflection angle each require two degrees of freedom. As a result, the mechanical arrangement of a gonioreflectometer is fairly complicated. Calibration of a gonioreflectometer requires careful alignment of source optics, detector optics, and surface positions. The incident light beam has to be very collimated (parallel rays) so that the incident angle is well defined. The detector should only collect reflected rays from a specified area on the sample surface.

15.3   Measurements with colorimetric filters

From our study of colorimetry, we know that, as far as our color perception is concerned, a color stimulus can be represented by its tristimulus values, regardless of its spectral power distribution. Therefore, most spectral measurements are converted into the CIEXYZ tristimulus values. In many applications, it is necessary only to measure the CIEXYZ tristimulus values or the luminance and chromaticity (Y, x, y), without having to measure the spectral power distribution of the light. In this case, instruments that use colorimetric spectral filters, such as $\bar{x}(\lambda)$, $\bar{y}(\lambda)$, and $\bar{z}(\lambda)$, can be used to make the measurements very efficiently. This type of instrument is called a colorimeter. However, it is very difficult to manufacture color filters that closely approximate the CIE color matching functions, and most colorimeters have limited accuracy. With the fast development of new types of optical filter material, such as the giant birefringent optics (GBO) polymers [1019], it may be possible to have very inexpensive, but very accurate colorimeters in the near future [919]. The major advantage is that tristimulus values can be measured very fast in a very convenient way.

15.4 Computation of tristimulus values from spectral data

As discussed in Section 15.1.3, there are many potential sources of error in spectral measurements. Factors, such as lighting and viewing geometry, polarization, and fluorescence, have to be carefully checked. Other factors, such as wavelength scale, spectral scattering, and zero-offset, are somewhat correctable. One approach for such data correction is to model the errors with simple equations and find the parameters of those equations so that corrected values can be determined [102, 870]. Therefore, the success of this type of correction depends on the validity of the error model and the magnitude of the error.

Once we have obtained reliable spectral data, we can compute the tristimulus values according to their definitions, replacing the integrals with discrete sums. However, there are several situations that may cause problems in many applications:

- When the measurement interval is too large. The process recommended by the CIE for computing the tristimulus values is to use 1 nm interval or 5 nm interval if the spectral function is smooth. If the spectral data are available only for 10 nm or 20 nm intervals, calculation with subsampled color matching functions at such a large wavelength interval often produces very significant numerical errors. The ASTM-recommended method for calculation is to interpolate the wavelength samples that were not measured. The interpolation can be as simple as assuming that the missing wavelength samples have the same values as their nearest measured data points.

- When the measurement range is too small. The CIE-recommended range is from 360 nm to 830 nm. In practice, the CIE color matching functions have very small values below 380 nm and above 780 nm, and that is a very typical range for spectral measurement. Sometimes, spectral measurement data are available for an even smaller range, say 400 nm to 700 nm. The recommended process is to extrapolate the wavelength samples that are not measured, again by assuming they have the same values as the nearest measured data points.

The above situations of working with missing data points are fairly classical problems in signal estimation. Knowledge of the signal itself, such as the bandwidth, can be used to derive more accurate results. For example, if we know that the spectral data were measured with a triangular window which has the half-height width as the wavelength interval, we can work out a set of optimum weights for the illuminant–observer functions (assuming that the reflectance or transmittance factor of all the samples is equally likely to be going up or down in any wavelength interval), and use those optimum weights to calculate the tristimulus values. Experimental data showed that this approach can indeed reduce the computation error very significantly [988].

15.5 Density measurements

Although spectral radiances of color stimuli give us the complete information, it is not always easy or convenient to make such measurements. The instruments are expensive and the procedures time consuming. Fortunately, for many applications, such as photographic imaging and graphic art printing, an alternative color measurement called density can be used with great success. Densities are proportional to log reflectance or log transmittance. They are very effective in modeling the color reproduction processes and are much simpler and less expensive to measure. There are two important reasons why densities are so useful in these applications: (1) they are approximately proportional to the additive sum of dye or ink amounts, when the colorants are substantially transparent, and (2) color cross-talks (such as the interimage effect in color films) through which one color layer affects the formation of another color layer can be approximately modeled by product terms in density. Therefore, a significant portion of color measurement in imaging has been reported in terms of density. However, there is a serious drawback in using densities because they are tied to a particular device and medium. The same density measured on two different media can appear quite different visually. Therefore, use of density as color measurement works best when a single closed system is the target application. There are three major factors that have to be considered in density measurements: (1) aperture, (2) optical geometry, and (3) system spectral response.

In the digitization of a film image, the aperture used by a scanner or a microdensitometer is usually quite small (on the order of 10–20 μm). On the other hand, the characteristic curves of films are often measured with large apertures. In order to reduce the effect of noise and nonuniformity, a minimum aperture area of 7 mm^2 is recommended [924, p. 545]. Also, the measurement should be made at least 1 mm away from the edge of the exposure. To measure the density of half-tone images, the minimum aperture size is dependent on the screen ruling frequency. For example, according to ISO 13655, for a screen frequency of 300 lines per inch, the measurement should use a minimum aperture of 1 mm, and, for a screen of 65 lines per inch, a minimum of 3.5 mm. Typical density measurements are certified only to two decimal places. To measure reliable and traceable density values, physical standards (such as those produced by NIST) should be used frequently to keep the densitometers in good calibration. Instrument-specific calibration procedures are described in the manuals provided with the instruments. A good practical discussion can be found in [928, Chapter 1].

Since how a sample reflects or transmits light depends on how it is illuminated and how the detector collects the light, the illumination (influx) and the light-collection (efflux) geometry for density measurement have to be specified explicitly. The geometric parameters usually involve the cone shape, the solid angle, and the direction of light flux. In a general classification, the cone shape can be specular or diffuse, and the flux direction can be 0° or 45° from the surface normal of the sample being measured. However, the best optical geometry to use should be determined by the particular imaging application. For example, if a photographic print is to be viewed under general office lighting, the influx geometry should be close to diffuse lighting.

The last major factor in density measurement is the system spectral response. Again, the target application should be the dominating decision factor. For example, if a color negative is to be printed by an optical printer, the density should be measured by the combined spectral response function of the printer light source, the color filters, and the color paper spectral sensitivities. The density measured by a system spectral response of a specific printer and paper combination is called the printing density. There are system spectral response functions that are standardized by national and international standards organizations. Density measurements made according to such standards are given special names, such as Status A density, Status M density, and so on. In considering the system spectral response function for measuring densities, we have to understand one very important factor – the position of the peak response for each red, green, and blue channel. The spectral density as a function of the amount of dye in most transparency films can be well approximated by Beer's law, i.e., doubling the amount of dye in a film doubles its spectral density (not spectral transmittance) of each wavelength. However, the (integral) density of a film is actually calculated from the integration of the total transmitted light (not the spectral density) of all wavelengths. Therefore, the (integral) film density measurement is quite sensitive to the peak position of the system spectral response function. As can be seen in the following ISO system spectral responses, these functions are all very-narrow-band filters and often their peak positions are selected to measure commonly used dye or ink materials for a particular application industry. That is the major reason why there are such a plurality of status filters in the standards.

15.5.1 Reflection density, D_ρ and D_R

Let ρ be the reflectance of a reflection color target, then the reflectance density D_ρ is defined as

$$D_\rho = - \log_{10} \rho. \tag{15.1}$$

In the CIE lighting vocabulary, the term reflectance density is intended for a measurement geometry that collects all the reflected light, as specified in the definition of reflectance, ρ. This is to be distinguished from reflectance factor R, in which the measurement geometry is a finite cone. The density defined for the reflectance factor is called the reflectance factor density, D_R:

$$D_R = - \log_{10} R. \tag{15.2}$$

In the literature, the terms reflection density and optical density are also frequently used to mean either the reflectance density or the reflectance factor density. Since an exact specification of any density measurement has to include the illumination geometry, the measurement geometry, the system spectral response, and the aperture, it is generally acceptable to use the term reflection density as a generic term to distinguish it from the transmission density when transmitted light is measured.

Reflection geometry

A typical reflection density measurement uses 0/45 or 45/0 geometry. In order to increase the illumination level on the reflection target, an annular ring-shaped light source is positioned at a 45° angle from the surface normal and the reflected light is collected through a cone centered along the surface normal (0°). Figure 15.4 shows such a configuration. Alternatively, we can also position the light source at the normal and collect the reflected light with an annular aperture.

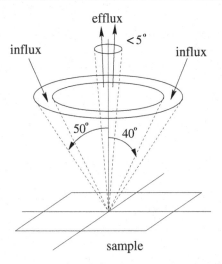

Figure 15.4. Typical geometry for a reflection density measurement.

System spectral responses

The system spectral response function for density measurement is different for different applications. For example, if color negative densities are measured for optical printing purposes, then it makes sense to measure them in terms of how they will be seen by the photographic paper. If we want to measure the reflection density of a black-and-white photograph to be viewed under tungsten illumination (say, CIE Illuminant A), it makes sense to use the product of that illuminant and the CIE photopic luminous efficiency function, $V(\lambda)$, as the system spectral response function. In order to facilitate standard measurements, ISO has defined various system spectral responses for different imaging applications. An excellent description can be found in [924]. The following is a short summary of the most frequently used density types:

- ISO visual density: the system spectral response function is the product of the spectrum of CIE Illuminant A and $V(\lambda)$ (see Fig. 15.5).
- ISO Status A density: this is mostly used for photographic color prints (and color reversal film). The system spectral response functions are specified as Status A red, green, and blue filters (see Fig. 15.5).
- ISO Status T density: this is used for color images from which color separations are to be prepared, as in graphic arts applications. Status T densitometers are recommended for measuring process control parameters in web offset printing in the USA [930, p. 17]. The system spectral response function of Status T density is shown in Fig. 15.7.
- ISO Status E density: this serves the same purpose as the Status T density, except that it is mainly used in Europe.

Sample backing material

Since most reflection print (paper) substrates are not completely opaque, light transmitted through the substrate reflects back to the density measurement instrument if the sample backing material has a high reflectance. ISO 5-4 and ISO 13655 suggest that a black material

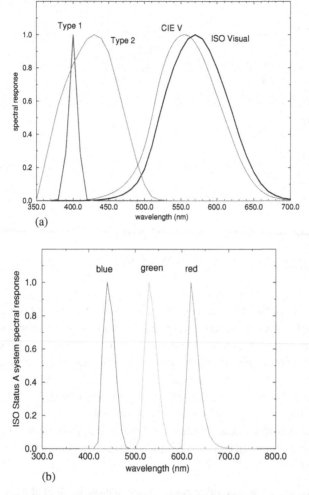

Figure 15.5. System spectral responses for (a) ISO visual density, type 1 and type 2 printing density, and (b) Status A density.

be used for reflection density measurement. The backing material should be spectrally nonselective, diffuse-reflecting, and have an ISO reflection density of 1.50 ± 0.20.

15.5.2 Transmission density

For a color negative film or a color slide film (color reversal film) the developed density is determined by measuring how much light is transmitted through the film in a given measurement condition. The transmittance (for incident radiation of given spectral composition, polarization and geometrical distribution), τ, is defined as the ratio of the transmitted radiant or luminous flux to the incident flux in the given condition. The transmittance density D_τ is defined as

$$D_\tau = -\log_{10} \tau. \tag{15.3}$$

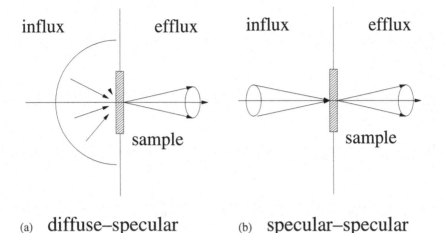

(a) **diffuse–specular**   (b) **specular–specular**

Figure 15.6. Geometry for measuring transmission density. The diffuse–specular geometry in (a) is for measuring diffuse transmission density. The specular–specular geometry in (b) is for measuring projection density.

Similar to reflection density, an exact specification of any transmittance density measurement has to include the illumination geometry, the measurement geometry, the system spectral response, and the aperture. Therefore, it is generally acceptable to use the term transmission density as a generic term (to distinguish it from the reflection density), when transmitted light is measured.

Transmission geometry

The geometry for measuring transmission density refers to the incident light (influx) and the transmitted light (efflux). The influx and the efflux geometry both can be either diffuse or specular (regular). Therefore, there are four combinations: diffuse–diffuse, diffuse–specular $(d/0°)$, specular–diffuse $(0°/d)$, and specular–specular. The type of geometry to use is dependent on the intended application. For example, if a color reversal film (transparency) is to be displayed against a diffuse light source, the influx geometry for density measurement should be diffuse as well. Since the transparency is usually viewed in a surface normal direction, the efflux geometry should be specular. The transmission density measured with such a diffuse–specular geometry is called the diffuse transmission density. (ISO 13655 specifies that the transmittance factor shall be measured with $d/0°$ or $0°/d$ geometry.) On the other hand, if the transparency is to be projected by a slide projector in which light from the projector lamp passes through a condenser lens and forms a radiant cone or beam, the influx geometry for density measurement should be specular. Since the transmitted light is projected and focuses in a cone of radiant flux, the efflux geometry is also specular. Therefore, for such an application, the proper geometry for density measurement is specular–specular, and the density so measured is called the projection transmission density. These two types of measurement geometry are shown in Fig. 15.6. The half-angle of the specular cone should be no larger than 10°.

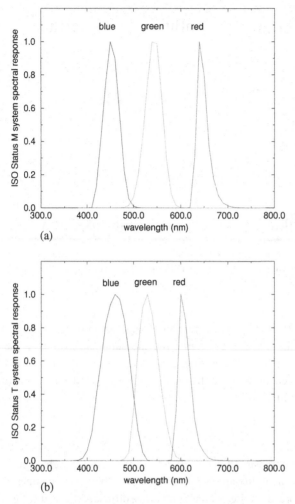

Figure 15.7. System spectral responses for: (a) ISO Status M density and (b) Status T density.

System spectral responses

The following is a short summary of the most frequently used transmission densities:

- ISO Status A density: the three (R, G, B) system spectral responses for color reversal films are the same as defined in the reflection density.
- ISO Status M density: this is for color negative film. The Status M spectral responses were meant for measuring color negative densities for typical optical printers (see Fig. 15.7). However, they are no longer good approximations for most optical printers and color papers. ISO 5-3 further defined two other types of printing density. ISO type 1 printing density is mainly for print films used in micrographics. ISO type 2 printing density is for black-and-white films to be printed on blue-sensitized silver halide black-and-white films or papers (see Fig. 15.5).
- ISO Status T density: the three (R, G, B) system spectral responses for graphic arts applications are the same as defined in the reflection density.

15.6 Error analysis in calibration measurements

When we use an instrument to measure some physical quantity, we often do not obtain the true value of the quantity that we are trying to measure. The difference between the measured value and the true value is called an error. Of course, in most cases, we do not know what the true value is and therefore we do not know the error either. In reality, we can only estimate the error, mostly through repeated measurements.

There are two things that we are particularly concerned with in measurement results: *accuracy* and *precision*. Accuracy is a measure of how close the measured value comes to the true value. Precision is a measure of how reproducible the measurement is. The absolute precision is the magnitude of the uncertainty in the measurement in the same units as the measurement. The relative precision is the uncertainty expressed as a percentage or a fraction of the true value.

Excluding operational errors caused by human mistakes, measurement errors are generally classified into three types: systematic errors, instrumental errors, and statistical errors. Systematic errors are due to system bias or faulty calibration. For example, if a spectrophotometer does not have the correct wavelength scale or alignment, the measured spectral functions will have systematic errors. Instrumental errors are caused by the limited precision of the instrument. For example, a digital meter cannot measure a quantity more precisely than the last significant digit. Electronic noise in the instrument also limits how precisely a quantity can be measured each time. Statistical errors are caused by the statistical distribution of the physical quantity to be measured. For example, the number of photons arriving at a detector within a given time interval is statistical in nature. The reason for making such a classification of errors is that different classes of error have different probability distributions that need to be considered when we analyze the measured data. Systematic errors should be removed by careful calibration of the instrument. In the following discussion, we will assume that systematic errors do not exist. Instrumental errors and statistical errors are called random errors. We will deal only with random errors in this chapter.

15.6.1 Error estimation

In error analysis and device calibration, the desired quantity can only be estimated from the statistical measurement data. If the estimate is given as a single value, it is called a point estimate. If it is a range, it is called an interval estimate. For color calibration, we often use point estimates. It is well known that if a measurement is repeated more times, the averaged value will be closer to the mean of the statistical distribution of the measured data. We say that the sample mean is an estimator of the true mean. An estimator is said to be *unbiased* if the expected value of the estimator is equal to the true value being estimated. For example, the sample mean, $\bar{x} = \sum x_i/n$, is an unbiased estimator of the true mean. On the other hand, the sample variance s' as defined by

$$s' = \frac{1}{n} \sum_{i=1}^{n} (x_i - \bar{x})^2 \tag{15.4}$$

is known to be a biased estimator of the true variance. An unbiased sample variance, s, should be

$$s = \frac{1}{n-1} \sum_{i=1}^{n} (x_i - \bar{x})^2. \tag{15.5}$$

Let x and y be two random variables with a joint probability density function, then we define the variances of x and y and their covariance as $V(x) = \sigma_x^2 = \mathcal{E}[(x - \mathcal{E}[x])^2]$, $V(y) = \sigma_y^2 = \mathcal{E}[(y - \mathcal{E}[y])^2]$, and $C(x, y) = \mathcal{E}[(x - \mathcal{E}[x])(y - \mathcal{E}[y])]$, where $\mathcal{E}[.]$ means the expected value. One can show that $V(ax + by) = a^2 V(x) + b^2 V(y) + 2ab C(x, y)$. When x and y are uncorrelated, i.e., $C(x, y) = 0$, then $V(ax + by) = a^2 V(x) + b^2 V(y)$.

Let $\mathbf{x}$ be an $n \times 1$ random vector, $\mathbf{y}$ be an $m \times 1$ random vector, and A be an $m \times n$ matrix. The variance matrix of $\mathbf{x}$ is defined as $V(\mathbf{x}) = \mathcal{E}[(\mathbf{x} - \mathcal{E}[\mathbf{x}])(\mathbf{x} - \mathcal{E}[\mathbf{x}])^T]$. The covariance matrix of $\mathbf{x}$ and $\mathbf{y}$ is $C(\mathbf{x}, \mathbf{y}) = \mathcal{E}[(\mathbf{x} - \mathcal{E}[\mathbf{x}])(\mathbf{y} - \mathcal{E}[\mathbf{y}])^T]$. If $\mathbf{y} = A\mathbf{x} + \mathbf{b}$, then $V(\mathbf{y}) = A V(\mathbf{x}) A^T$. This is a useful relation because matrices are often used in color transformation from one color vector space to another. Another useful relation is a quadratic form. Let $\mathcal{E}[\mathbf{x}] = \mu$ and $V(\mathbf{x}) = \Phi$, then $\mathcal{E}[\mathbf{x}^T A \mathbf{x}] = \mathrm{tr}(A\Phi) + \mu^T A \mu$, where $\mathrm{tr}(.)$ means trace of a matrix, i.e., the sum of all the diagonal elements. Let us look at an example. Let $\mathbf{x} = (\Delta X, \Delta Y, \Delta Z)$ be the error vector in the tristimulus values. Let Φ be the variance matrix of $\mathbf{x}$ and let the matrix J be defined by

$$\begin{bmatrix} \Delta L^* \\ \Delta a^* \\ \Delta b^* \end{bmatrix} = \begin{bmatrix} \partial L^*/\partial X & \partial L^*/\partial Y & \partial L^*/\partial Z \\ \partial a^*/\partial X & \partial a^*/\partial Y & \partial a^*/\partial Z \\ \partial b^*/\partial X & \partial b^*/\partial Y & \partial b^*/\partial Z \end{bmatrix} \begin{bmatrix} \Delta X \\ \Delta Y \\ \Delta Z \end{bmatrix} = J \begin{bmatrix} \Delta X \\ \Delta Y \\ \Delta Z \end{bmatrix}. \tag{15.6}$$

In calculating the CIELAB color error, $(\Delta E)^2 = (\Delta L^*)^2 + (\Delta a^*)^2 + (\Delta b^*)^2$, caused by a CIEXYZ error, we can express $(\Delta E)^2$ as a quadratic form in $\mathbf{x}$: $(\Delta E)^2 = (J\mathbf{x})^T(J\mathbf{x}) = \mathbf{x}^T J^T J \mathbf{x}$. Therefore, if we assume that $E[\mathbf{x}] = \mathbf{0}$, the variance of the CIELAB error can be calculated as $\mathcal{E}[(\Delta E)^2] = \mathrm{tr}(J^T J \Phi) + E[\mathbf{x}]^T J^T J E[\mathbf{x}] = \mathrm{tr}(J^T J \Phi)$.

15.6.2 Propagation of errors

The uncertainty in directly measured quantities propagates into quantities that are calculated from the directly measured data. This is called the propagation of errors. For example, we can measure the (X, Y, Z) tristimulus values and use them to calculate the CIELAB values. The uncertainty in the former will propagate into the latter. The study of how error propagates through the derived quantities allows us to estimate the magnitude of the final error and to establish a product specification in a controlled way. The other use of error propagation is in digital image processing where the effect of noise has to be analyzed. For example, a color edge detector often requires a statistically determined threshold to reduce the false detection of edges due to noise [567].

Basic analysis of error propagation relies on Taylor series expansion. For a scalar function, f, of a real variable, x, the Taylor series expansion is

$$f(x + a) = f(x) + f'(x)(a) + \frac{1}{2!} f''(x)(a)^2 + \cdots, \tag{15.7}$$

where a is a (small) real number. For a scalar function, f, of an n-dimensional vector, $\mathbf{x}$, the Taylor series expansion becomes:

$$f(\mathbf{x} + \mathbf{a}) = f(\mathbf{x}) + [\nabla f(\mathbf{x})]^{\mathrm{T}}(\mathbf{a}) + \frac{1}{2!}(\mathbf{a})^{\mathrm{T}}\mathbf{H}(f(\mathbf{x}))(\mathbf{a}) + \mathbf{e}(\mathbf{x}, \mathbf{a})\|\mathbf{a}\|^2, \quad (15.8)$$

where $\mathbf{a}$ is a (small) n-dimensional vector, $\nabla f(\mathbf{x})$ is the gradient vector of $f(\mathbf{x})$, $\mathbf{e}(\mathbf{x}, \mathbf{a}) \to \mathbf{0}$ as $\mathbf{a} \to \mathbf{0}$, and $\mathbf{H}$ is the Hessian matrix:

$$\mathbf{H}(f(\mathbf{x})) = \begin{bmatrix} D_{11}^2 f(\mathbf{x}) & D_{12}^2 f(\mathbf{x}) & \cdots & D_{1n}^2 f(\mathbf{x}) \\ D_{21}^2 f(\mathbf{x}) & D_{22}^2 f(\mathbf{x}) & \cdots & D_{2n}^2 f(\mathbf{x}) \\ \vdots & \vdots & & \vdots \\ D_{n1}^2 f(\mathbf{x}) & D_{n2}^2 f(\mathbf{x}) & \cdots & D_{nn}^2 f(\mathbf{x}) \end{bmatrix}, \quad (15.9)$$

where $D_{ij}^2 f(\mathbf{x}) = (\partial^2 f)/(\partial x_i \partial x_j)$. For an m-dimensional vector field, $\mathbf{f}$, of an n-dimensional vector, $\mathbf{x}$, the Taylor series expansion becomes:

$$\mathbf{f}(\mathbf{x} + \mathbf{a}) = \mathbf{f}(\mathbf{x}) + [J(\mathbf{f}(\mathbf{x}))](\mathbf{a}) + \frac{1}{2!}\begin{bmatrix} (\mathbf{a})^{\mathrm{T}}\mathbf{H}(f_1(\mathbf{x}))(\mathbf{a}) \\ (\mathbf{a})^{\mathrm{T}}\mathbf{H}(f_2(\mathbf{x}))(\mathbf{a}) \\ \vdots \\ (\mathbf{a})^{\mathrm{T}}\mathbf{H}(f_m(\mathbf{x}))(\mathbf{a}) \end{bmatrix} + \mathbf{e}(\mathbf{x}, \mathbf{a})\|\mathbf{a}\|^2, \quad (15.10)$$

where $\mathbf{a}$ is a (small) n-dimensional vector, and $J(\mathbf{f}(\mathbf{x}))$, the Jacobian matrix, is now an $m \times n$ matrix:

$$J(\mathbf{f}(\mathbf{x})) = \mathbf{D}(\mathbf{x}) = \begin{bmatrix} D_1 f_1(\mathbf{x}) & D_2 f_1(\mathbf{x}) & \cdots & D_n f_1(\mathbf{x}) \\ D_1 f_2(\mathbf{x}) & D_2 f_2(\mathbf{x}) & \cdots & D_n f_2(\mathbf{x}) \\ \vdots & \vdots & & \vdots \\ D_1 f_m(\mathbf{x}) & D_2 f_m(\mathbf{x}) & \cdots & D_n f_m(\mathbf{x}) \end{bmatrix}, \quad (15.11)$$

where $D_j f_k = \partial f_k/\partial x_j$ is the jth partial derivative of the kth component of $\mathbf{f}$.

Taylor series expansions can also be generalized to matrix functions (see, e.g., [625]), but vector fields are sufficient for most color imaging calculations. When the measured quantity itself is a matrix, such as the Mueller matrix, one should consult publications in those fields [348, 701]. In the analysis of error propagation, the variable a (or the vector $\mathbf{a}$) represents the error, which is often assumed to be normally distributed with zero mean (or zero mean vector) and variance (or covariance matrix) σ^2. The variable x (or the vector $\mathbf{x}$) represents the true value. Thus, $x + a$ (or $\mathbf{x} + \mathbf{a}$) is the measured value. The above expressions can be used to calculate how the errors are propagated from the measurement $x + a$ (or $\mathbf{x} + \mathbf{a}$) to the derived quantity $f(x + a)$ (or $\mathbf{f}(\mathbf{x} + \mathbf{a})$). For example, let $y = x + a$ be the measured value of x, then

$$\mathcal{E}[f(y)] = \mathcal{E}[f(x + a)] = \mathcal{E}[f(x)] + f'(x)\mathcal{E}[a] + \frac{1}{2!}f''(x)\mathcal{E}[a^2] + \cdots$$

$$\approx f(x) + \frac{1}{2!}f''(x)\sigma^2, \quad (15.12)$$

where $\mathcal{E}[.]$ represents the expected value. Therefore, the derived value $f(y)$ is a biased estimator of $f(x)$. To compute the variance of $f(y)$, we have

$$\mathcal{E}[(f(y) - \mathcal{E}[f(y)])^2] \approx \mathcal{E}\left[\left(f(x+a) - f(x) - \frac{1}{2!}f''(x)\sigma^2\right)^2\right]$$

$$\approx [f'(x)]^2\sigma^2 - (f''(x)\sigma^2)^2/4. \qquad (15.13)$$

These simple examples show that the result of the error analysis is not always intuitive and therefore it is important to check out the analytical results when estimation of error is required. The other alternative for error analysis when the analytical calculation is too complex is to do a simulation. One can generate random errors in the measurement data and use them to calculate the derived quantities and their statistical distribution.

15.7 Expression of measurement uncertainty

In our previous discussion on error analysis, we mentioned systematic errors, instrumental errors, and statistical errors. Even after careful correction of all known sources of error (such as systematic errors and instrumental errors), the resulting estimate of the measured value still has some uncertainty component in it. In the literature, measurement uncertainty has not been reported with a clear convention. For example, if a measured weight of an object is reported as 100.37 ± 0.02 g, it is not clear whether 0.02 is the standard deviation, or the 95% confidence interval, or another measure of uncertainty. Furthermore, it is not clear what the assumed underlying distribution is and how the uncertainty or confidence interval is calculated. In order to standardize the evaluation and reporting of measurement uncertainty, the ISO and several other standards bodies issued a guide book, *Guide to the Expression of Uncertainty in Measurement* [448, 941], to facilitate global trade and technology exchange.

ISO's *Guide* distinguishes two types of evaluation of standard uncertainty. Type A evaluation is based on repeated measurements and the resulting empirical distribution. Type B evaluation is based on *a priori* distributions, such as manufacturer's specifications or previous measurements. In Type A evaluation, the estimate of the measured quantity q is given by the sample mean,

$$\bar{q} = \frac{1}{n}\sum_{k=1}^{n} q_k. \qquad (15.14)$$

The uncertainty $u(\bar{q})$ in this estimate is given by

$$u(\bar{q}) = \sqrt{\frac{1}{n(n-1)}\sum_{k=1}^{n}(q_k - \bar{q})^2}, \qquad (15.15)$$

which is the square root of the sample variance divided by the number of samples. The reason for using the square root is that it has the same dimension as the measured quantity. When a measurand Y is not measured directly, but is determined from other independent quantities, $X_1, X_2, \ldots, X_N$, through a functional relationship: $Y = f(X_1, X_2, \ldots, X_N)$, the combined uncertainty in the estimate of Y can be computed from the component uncertainties in X_i as explained in Section 15.6.2.

The recommended procedure for evaluating and expressing uncertainty is summarized in the ISO *Guide* [448, p. 28] document as follows:

1. Express mathematically the relationship between the measurand Y and the input quantities X_i on which Y depends: $Y = f(X_1, X_2, \ldots, X_N)$. The function f should contain every quantity, including all corrections and correction factors, that can contribute a significant component of uncertainty to the result of the measurement.
2. Determine x_i, the estimated value of input quantity X_i.
3. Evaluate the standard uncertainty $u(x_i)$ of each input estimate x_i.
4. Evaluate the covariances associated with any input estimates that are correlated.
5. Calculate the result of the measurement, i.e., the estimate y of the measurand Y, from the functional relationship f using for the input quantities X_i the estimates x_i obtained in step 2.
6. Determine the combined standard uncertainty $u_c(y)$ of the measurement result y from the standard uncertainties and covariances associated with the input estimates. If the measurement determines simultaneously more than one output quantity, calculate their covariances.
7. If it is necessary to give an expanded uncertainty U, whose purpose is to provide an interval $y - U$ to $y + U$ that may be expected to encompass a large fraction of the distribution of values that could reasonably be attributed to the measurand Y, multiply the combined uncertainty $u_c(y)$ by a coverage factor k, typically in the range 2–3, to obtain $U = k u_c(y)$.
8. Report the result of the measurement y together with its combined standard uncertainty $u_c(y)$ or expanded uncertainty U. Describe how y and $u_c(y)$ or U were obtained.

The recommended format for reporting measurement uncertainty has several forms (see [448, p. 26]). For example, the following two statements demonstrate two ways of expressing the measurement uncertainty: "the weight of the object is 100.37 g with a combined standard uncertainty $u_c = 0.02$ g" and "the weight of the object is (100.37 ± 0.06) g, where the number following the symbol $\pm$ is the numerical value of an expanded uncertainty $U = k u_c$, with U determined from a combined uncertainty $u_c = 0.02$ g and a coverage factor $k = 3.0$ based on the t-distribution for $v = 9$ degrees of freedom, and defines an interval estimated to have a level of confindence of 95 percent."

15.8 Problems

15.1 Since light of different polarizations is reflected differently from a smooth surface, how does this difference affect the measurement of the spectral reflectance factor of an object surface? How can we eliminate the polarization sensitivity of a given instrument?

15.2 A color negative film is exposed in a series of neutral density steps. Using densitometer A to measure the D–log H curve of the film, we find that the red, green, and blue curves are parallel. However, when we use densitometer B to measure the curves, they are not parallel. Can you explain why there might be such a difference? Is it always justified to say that densitometer B is not as well calibrated as densitometer A?

15.3 A piece of film has a specular density 1.0; what is its transmittance? Assume that the index of refraction of the film is 1.5. What is the film's internal transmittance value after we correct for the air–film interface reflection?

15.4 Let the Status A red, green, blue densities of an area on a reflection print be D_r, D_g, and D_b. If $D_r = D_g = D_b$, would that area look achromatic?

15.5 Under D_{65}, the tristimulus values, (X,Y,Z), measured from a color target have a mean of (34.0, 29.0, 15.0) and a variance matrix of

$$
\begin{bmatrix}
2.62 & 1.23 & 0.56 \\
1.32 & 2.34 & 1.15 \\
0.61 & 1.29 & 3.87
\end{bmatrix}.
\tag{15.16}
$$

Measurement noise in XYZ causes errors, ΔE, in computed CIELAB values. Calculate the variance of ΔE, i.e., $\mathcal{E}[(\Delta E)^2]$.

16 Device calibration

In conventional photography, from capturing an image on a color negative to getting a color print back from a photofinisher, most consumers do not have to bother with measuring light and color because the entire image chain (from film to reflection print) has been designed to reproduce good tone and color, and the uncontrolled variables left are taken care of by the automatic focus and exposure algorithms in the camera, and automatic color–density balance algorithms in the photofinishing printer. The conventional photographic system is a closed system and no user intervention is required. In electronic imaging, the situation is quite different. Digital cameras, film scanners, paper scanners, color monitors, and color printers are not manufactured to the same system specifications. Therefore, these imaging devices require careful calibration to ensure that they work together to reproduce good color images. Figure 16.1 shows a general block diagram for a color imaging application. The image data from an input device have to be calibrated so that they can be manipulated and processed according to the algorithm specifications. Similarly, the image processing algorithm outputs a digital image in a chosen color metric and that image has to be converted through an output calibration so that the desired color image can be reproduced by the output device.

Let us say, we have a nice color picture (reflection print) of our relatives and friends, and we would like to produce more copies of the picture to send to each of them. We use a scanner to digitize the picture into a digital file which is then sent to a color printer for printing. How do we know if the printed copies will look like the original? We do not, and most likely the copies will not look like the original, unless we carefully control the digitization and printing processes. The scanner digitizes the picture into a stream of digital numbers, one (or three for R,G,B) for each point on the image. The question is: what do those numbers represent? When we send the digital file to the printer, what colors does it produce for those digital numbers? In order to ensure consistent tone and color reproduction, we have to know the correspondence between the colors in the original picture and the numbers that the scanner outputs, and also the correspondence between the numbers we send to the printer and the colors that are printed on the paper by the printer. The task of establishing such correspondences is called device calibration. Color measurements have to be made to calibrate each device.

In this chapter, we will study the general issues in device calibration. The basic mathematic tools are presented and the various methods for color interpolation and approximation are discussed. These tools and methods are applicable to all device calibration tasks and therefore it is beneficial to study them in a general framework. In the next few chapters,

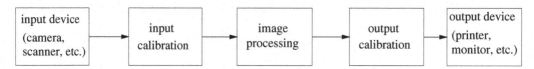

Figure 16.1. A general block diagram for a color imaging application.

we will be studying various image capture and image display devices. Specific calibration problems related to each individual device will be discussed in more detail there.

16.1 Colorimetric calibration

For color imaging applications, device calibration usually involves three processes: (a) device adjustment, (b) target measurement, and (c) signal transformation. The device adjustment process is aimed at setting up the device at the desired operating conditions. For example, a good CRT monitor calibration should include: (a) device adjustment: adjusting the CRT's cut-off bias, gain, dynamic range, color tracking, etc.; (b) target measurement: measuring the luminance and the chromaticity for each of the selected input code values; and (c) signal transformation: constructing lookup tables that map any reproducible color into the digital values that will produce the color on the CRT screen. Device adjustment usually requires professional knowledge and is not commonly performed by users. The remaining processes of target measurement and signal transformation are called device characterization. However, in the color imaging literature, the term "calibration" is loosely used to mean either (a) + (b) + (c), or (b) + (c). In some of the literature, especially in statistics, "calibration" is used to mean (c) alone [140, 640]. For example, given n points, $(x_i, y_i), i = 1, 2, \ldots, n$, where x is the independent variable and y is the dependent variable (or the response to the input x), we can fit a model $y(x)$ to the data points. This model fitting process is called regression (or approximation). For any future x, we can find (or predict) what the response y will be by the regression model $y(x)$. If, instead, we are given a response y and asked to determine what x can produce that response, the problem is called calibration. In the example of a scanner, if we scan a gray scale of known reflectance values x, we can read out the scanner response value y for each reflectance. We can run regression to determine a function $y(x)$. When we examine the digital values in the scanned image, we want to find out what their corresponding reflectances are. This then becomes a calibration problem.

16.1.1 Input calibration

A typical color calibration problem for an input device involves capturing the image of a target of known colors under a known illuminant. For example, the Macbeth ColorChecker has been used as a color target for calibration because all the colors have been measured and the target has been carefully manufactured to conform to the specified measured data [647]. A digital image of the Macbeth ColorChecker taken by a digital camera to be calibrated can be used to establish the correspondence between the measured colors (say, in CIELAB) on the ColorChecker and the digital responses from the camera. The calibration problem then is to determine the color metrics (say, in terms of CIELAB) of an unknown object that corresponds to a future camera (R,G,B) digital response of a pixel of the image of that object. In this example, we can see many difficult problems in calibrating an imaging device:

1. **The spectra sampling problem** If the spectral responsivities of the input device are not a linear combination of the human cone sensitivities, there is no way to calibrate the device so that it will see all colors the same way that an average human observer sees them, unless the input device effectively measures the spectral compositions of the color stimuli, rather than measuring only three (R,G,B) spectral bands. This is called the spectral sampling problem because it is caused by the fact that a three-color imaging device is undersampling the spectral signals.

2. **The scene balance problem** The scene illuminant is usually different from the illuminant used in the calibration. Either the captured image or the calibration table has to be adjusted to compensate for the difference. The questions are whether it is possible to do such an adjustment and how good the adjustment can be. This is called the scene balance problem. The problem is usually addressed in two parts: (a) the brightness (or density) balance problem deals with the fact that the exposure control of an input device varies from image to image, depending how strong the scene illumination is; and (b) the color balance problem deals with the different chromatic shifts due to the difference between the spectral composition of the scene illuminant (including ambient light) and that of the calibration illuminant. In the video imaging applications, the color balance problem is called the white balance problem.

3. **The color interpolation problem** For practical reasons, the number of color targets that are measured is often relatively small compared with the total number of possible colors that can be represented in the input device. For example, a color digital camera usually outputs an image in 8 bits per color per pixel. In theory, there are 16.7 million (2^{24}) representable colors. Although many of them never occur in natural scenes, we cannot realistically measure even a fraction of 1% of that many colors. Therefore, a basic problem in color calibration is the color interpolation (or approximation) problem. We should point out the difference between interpolation and approximation (regression). Interpolation requires that $y_i = y(x_i)$ for all i, where (x_i, y_i) are the measured data points. Therefore, the curve or the model $y(x)$ is forced to pass through all given data points. In approximation or regression, this is not required. In principle, all color measurements contain noise and thus we should always use approximation rather than interpolation. However, approximation requires a good functional model of the color data, and an imaging device is usually too complicated for us to guess a good model. Furthermore, color calibration involves multivariate approximation and interpolation and the data are not very easy to visualize. Forcing a model through the calibration data can produce unexpected large errors. As a result, interpolation is often used in color calibration. When interpolation is used, color measurements are repeated many times and averages are taken as the ground truths.

Figure 16.2 shows a general block diagram for input device calibration. The first step in the calibration is to remove any nonlinearity in sensor response. The image data are

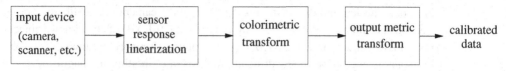

Figure 16.2. A general block diagram for input device calibration.

converted into a metric that is linearly proportional to image irradiance. Removal of sensor nonlinearity is usually done with a one-dimensional lookup table (1-D LUT) for each color channel. With image data in linear space, we can perform the colorimetric transform to put the image data into some kind of colorimetric quantities, such as CIEXYZ or CIELAB. Depending on the desired metrics and accuracy, this step is performed with either a 3×3 matrix or a three-dimensional lookup table (3-D LUT). Finally, the colorimetric image data are mapped into the desired output data metric. For example, if the images are to be viewed on a monitor, the desired output metric is usually sRGB, NTSC or other standard video signal. This step of converting to the desired output metric can be complicated and therefore may need to be carried out in multiple transformations. The general diagram in Fig. 16.2 thus represents conceptual steps rather than implementational steps. Therefore, blocks can be merged or split in any particular implementation. We will see examples of input device calibration in Chapter 19 in which we discuss image capture devices. At this point, we only have to note that the 1-D LUT, the 3-D LUT, and the 3×3 matrix are commonly used building blocks for input device calibration.

16.1.2   Output calibration

Color calibration for output devices presents some different problems. A typical process is to display or print some test colors from a selected set of (R,G,B) numbers sent to the monitor or printer to be calibrated. Again, we have the scene balance problem and the color interpolation problem. The spectral sampling problem now becomes the color matching stability problem for hard-copy output devices. In addition, we also have the color gamut problem. The calibration problems for output devices are as follows:

1. **The color matching stability problem**   The inks or dyes used in a color hard-copy output device reproduce colors (under a given viewing illuminant) by metameric color matching to the original color stimuli. The reproduced colors are not matched to those of the original in terms of spectral composition, but rather in terms of equivalent human cone spectral responses. When the spectral composition of the viewing illuminant is changed (as is often the case in consumer imaging), the reproduced colors no longer match those of the original. Because of this problem, inks and dyes have to be selected to reflect or transmit somewhat broad spectral bands. This does not solve the problem, only makes it less severe. As a consequence, the range of reproducible colors is often quite limited.

2. **The color gamut problem**   The phosphors (in CRT monitors), the color filters (in LCDs), the inks (in inkjet printers) and the dyes (in photographic papers) are almost always much less saturated in the colors they can reproduce than the spectrum colors

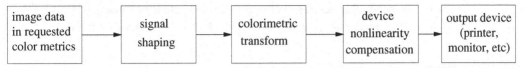

Figure 16.3. A general block diagram for output device calibration.

produced by diffraction gratings or interference. The range (or the volume) of reproducible colors produced by a given output device/medium is called the color gamut of that device. When an input color cannot be reproduced by the output device, it is called an out-of-gamut color. Rendering a color image on an output device requires a systematic algorithm for handling the out-of-gamut colors. The class of algorithms for handling out-of-gamut colors is called the gamut mapping algorithms.

3. **The media-dependency problem** Calibration of hard-copy devices is tied to a specific output medium and how it is processed. For photographic paper, the chemical processes have to be controlled well to make the calibration work. For the same paper and dye, different surface finishes also affect color reproduction. A printer calibrated with one type of paper will not produce good prints on another type of paper.

4. **The viewing condition problem** There are three types of problem in the viewing of a hard-copy reproduction. One is caused by the difference in the measurement geometry and the viewing geometry. For example, most color measurements are performed under 0/45 or 45/0 geometry, but images are rarely viewed with the same type of geometry because the illumination tends to be more diffuse. The second problem is caused by the luminance level difference between the illumination of the original scene and that of the viewing environment. Reflective objects look less colorful when viewed under lower-luminance lighting. The third problem is that the surround of the image also affects the color appearance in the reproduced image.

Figure 16.3 shows a general block diagram for output device calibration. Usually but not always, the first step in the output calibration is to perform signal shaping on the image data. The reason for this is that the relation between the incoming image data and the input data expected by the output device can be highly nonlinear. For example, the incoming image data may be in CIEXYZ, but the printer may be expecting CMYK data. In theory, we can always use a 3-D LUT to achieve such a nonlinear mapping. In reality, computing time and memory cost often force us to use a sparse 3-D LUT and some simple linear interpolation. Any nonlinear relation between the input and the output metrics will cause large errors in linear interpolation from sparse data [486]. The signal shaping step is to use 1-D LUTs to transform the input image data into a shape that is more nearly linear with respect to the output metric. The next step of colorimetric transform is usually done by a 3-D LUT or a 3×3 matrix. The purpose is to convert the image data into the output device's color primaries. Once the image data are in the output color space, it is often necessary to predistort the data to compensate for the nonlinear characteristics of the output device/medium. Again, the general diagram in Fig. 16.3 represents only conceptual steps rather than implementational steps. Therefore, blocks can be merged or split in any particular implementation. We will see examples of output device calibration in Chapter 20 in which we discuss image display devices. At this point, we should notice that a 1-D LUT, a 3-D LUT, and a 3 × 3 matrix are also the building blocks for output device calibration.

16.1.3   Device model versus lookup tables

Before high-capacity computer memory chips became available, most calibrations relied heavily on device models in which the physical behavior of a device is modeled with matrices and simple analytical functions (such as polynomials, logs, and exponentials). The advantage of such an approach is that physical understanding of device behavior is of key importance and therefore calibration is adjusted for different operating conditions with good controls. The disadvantage is that highly nonlinear or complex device behaviors cannot be modeled well with only a few parameters and functions. For example, the interimage effect through which one color channel affects the other color channels in photographic film is quite complicated. Detailed models require tens of parameters and functions, and yet the observed effects cannot be predicted from the complicated models as accurately as some imaging applications would require.

In the last decades, computer memory chips have become inexpensive and they come with high capacity. Lookup tables have become affordable and are the preferred method for device calibration. They often produce more accurate calibration results than device models, especially when complex behaviors are involved. The reason is quite simple: a 3-D LUT with 16 × 16 × 16 grid points has 4096 parameters, more than any complex device models have. One disadvantage is that we now have to measure 4096 data points. Furthermore, if some imaging condition is changed, the whole lookup table has to be measured and constructed from scratch. However, with automated measuring instruments, these two disadvantages are no longer too serious. Therefore, there is a trend to use exclusively larger and denser lookup tables for calibrating all imaging devices.

However, for a given cost and computing resource, relying on larger lookup tables alone is often not the most accurate approach, nor is it the most cost-effective approach. The reason is that, if we want to use a single, large 3-D LUT to handle every type of device calibration, we will need a very large table for a very nonlinear device (such as an inkjet printer). A more efficient way is to use a device model to remove the major nonlinearity before the 3-D LUT is constructed. Therefore, if we use three 1-D LUTs to shape the signals first, we can use a very sparse 3-D LUT and achieve very high color accuracy. In order to arrive at the most efficient lookup table structures, a good device model is extremely valuable. This point is very important and we will give an example to help us appreciate it more.

Let us assume that we need to determine the CMY dye amounts of a photographic reflection print from the (R, G, B) Status A densities that are measured. Since the number of input variables is three, we can simply build a 3-D LUT for this purpose. However, the application requires high accuracy and therefore the 3-D LUT has to be densely populated so that interpolation from it can produce accurate results. It turns out that a simple device model of the photographic color paper can tell us exactly how to use three 1-D LUTs and a 3 × 3 matrix to greatly reduce the size of the 3-D LUT and increase the accuracy of the results.

Let D_r, D_g, and D_b be the Status A densities of a color patch on a photographic color paper, a_c, a_m, and a_y be the amount of cyan, magenta, and yellow dyes, and $C(\lambda)$, $M(\lambda)$, $Y(\lambda)$

be the spectral transmission functions of unit amount of cyan, magenta, and yellow dye, respectively. The spectral transmittance $T(\lambda)$ of the combined dye layers can be computed as

$$T(\lambda) = 10^{-[a_c\,C(\lambda)+a_m\,M(\lambda)+a_y\,Y(\lambda)]}. \tag{16.1}$$

By definition, the spectral transmittance $T(\lambda)$ is related to the spectral transmission density $D_t(\lambda)$ by the following relation:

$$D_t(\lambda) = -\log T(\lambda). \tag{16.2}$$

Now we have to relate the spectral transmission density $D_t(\lambda)$ to the spectral reflection density $D_\rho(\lambda)$ by an empirical function $f(D_t(\lambda))$ that can be determined experimentally. The function $f(D_t(\lambda))$ converts the transmission density D_t of the dyes to the reflection density, D_ρ of the print. (This function is further explained in Section 20.5.5.) We also have to account for the minimum spectral density $D_{min}(\lambda)$ of the paper when no dye is formed. Thus

$$D_\rho(\lambda) = f(D_t(\lambda)) + D_{min}(\lambda). \tag{16.3}$$

Let S_r, S_g, S_b be the system Status A spectral response functions, and ρ_r, ρ_g, ρ_b be the Status A reflectance factors. By the definition of Status A density, we have the following relations:

$$\rho(\lambda) = 10^{-D_\rho(\lambda)},$$

$$\rho_r = \int \rho(\lambda)\,S_r(\lambda)\,d\lambda,$$

$$\rho_g = \int \rho(\lambda)\,S_g(\lambda)\,d\lambda,$$

$$\rho_b = \int \rho(\lambda)\,S_b(\lambda)\,d\lambda,$$

$$D_r = -\log \rho_r,$$

$$D_g = -\log \rho_g,$$

$$D_b = -\log \rho_b.$$

We would like to construct a 3-D LUT that will map D_r, D_g, and D_b to a_c, a_m, and a_y. In order to simplify the above equations to come up with a practical calibration model, we need to remove all the integrals. From Fig. 15.5, we can observe that the spectral bandwidths of the Status A response functions are fairly narrow compared with the general spectral reflectance functions. We can therefore make the following approximations:

$$\rho_r = \int \rho(\lambda)\,S_r(\lambda)\,d\lambda \approx \rho(\lambda_r)S_r(\lambda_r), \tag{16.4}$$

$$\rho_g = \int \rho(\lambda)\,S_g(\lambda)\,d\lambda \approx \rho(\lambda_g)S_g(\lambda_g), \tag{16.5}$$

$$\rho_b = \int \rho(\lambda)\,S_b(\lambda)\,d\lambda \approx \rho(\lambda_b)S_b(\lambda_b), \tag{16.6}$$

where λ_r, λ_g, and λ_b are the peak wavelengths of the spectral sensitivity functions S_r, S_g,

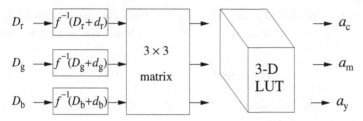

Figure 16.4. A model-based lookup table design for mapping Status A densities to dye amounts.

and S_b, respectively. We can now express the Status A red density D_r as

$$D_r = -\log \rho_r$$
$$D_r \approx -\log[\rho(\lambda_r)S_r(\lambda_r)]$$
$$D_r = -\log \rho(\lambda_r) - \log S_r(\lambda_r)$$
$$D_r = -\log 10^{-D_\rho(\lambda_r)} - \log S_r(\lambda_r)$$
$$D_r = D_\rho(\lambda_r) - \log S_r(\lambda_r)$$
$$D_r = f(D_t(\lambda_r)) + D_{\min}(\lambda_r) - \log S_r(\lambda_r)$$
$$D_r = f(-\log T(\lambda_r)) + D_{\min}(\lambda_r) - \log S_r(\lambda_r)$$
$$D_r = f(a_c C(\lambda_r) + a_m M(\lambda_r) + a_y Y(\lambda_r)) + D_{\min}(\lambda_r) - \log S_r(\lambda_r).$$

Let us define $d_r = \log S_r(\lambda_r) - D_{\min}(\lambda_r)$, $d_g = \log S_g(\lambda_g) - D_{\min}(\lambda_g)$, and $d_b = \log S_b(\lambda_b) - D_{\min}(\lambda_b)$, then

$$\begin{bmatrix} a_c \\ a_m \\ a_y \end{bmatrix} \approx \begin{bmatrix} C(\lambda_r) & M(\lambda_r) & Y(\lambda_r) \\ C(\lambda_g) & M(\lambda_g) & Y(\lambda_g) \\ C(\lambda_b) & M(\lambda_b) & Y(\lambda_b) \end{bmatrix}^{-1} \begin{bmatrix} f^{-1}(D_r + d_r) \\ f^{-1}(D_g + d_g) \\ f^{-1}(D_b + d_b) \end{bmatrix}. \qquad (16.7)$$

The above equation tells us that three 1-D LUTs plus a 3×3 matrix will essentially transform the Status A densities to the three dye amounts. Since the model has made some simplifying assumptions, it cannot be as accurate as required in the application. However, if we follow the 1-D LUTs and the 3×3 matrix with a 3-D LUT, we will be able to get very accurate results. Since the model has removed most of the nonlinearity between the input variables and the output variables, the 3-D LUT does not need many grid points and it serves only to correct local errors caused by the oversimplified device model. Figure 16.4 shows the final lookup table structure for this calibration problem. It requires some more memory space, but gives much better results than a simple 3-D LUT can provide.

16.2   Computational tools for calibration

In the above discussion, we have identified several common building blocks for device calibration. They are: (a) device models (for sensor and display nonlinearity), (b) 3×3 matrices, (c) 1-D LUTs, and (d) 3-D LUTs. In order to construct these common building blocks, we need to study several statistical and computational tools: regression, approximation, interpolation, and constrained optimization. Regression and approximation are used for determining parameters for device models. Approximation and interpolation are used for generating lookup tables and finding the needed unknown values from the known values in the lookup tables. Constrained optimization is used to determine the optimal 3 × 3 matrix for color transformation. These tools will be briefly reviewed here. There are many books and papers on these computational tools and their statistical and mathematical foundations (see, e.g., [110, 140, 175, 239, 256, 545, 552, 601, 640, 748, 812, 1001]). They should be consulted for more detailed studies.

16.2.1 Interpolation

Given a set of data points $(x_i, f(x_i))$, $i = 1, 2, \ldots, N$, where $x_i < x_j$ for all $i < j$, the problem of interpolation is to determine $f(x)$ for any new x value when $x_1 < x < x_N$. The function $f(x)$ is, of course, unknown, but it is known to pass through the given set of data points. Data interpolation serves two purposes in color calibration. It is used in populating a lookup table (off-line) and also in generating pixel values from the lookup table (on-line). Typically, the number of measured data points is much smaller than the number of lookup table entries, which is in turn much smaller than the number of representable colors in a digital image. For example, a typical digital color image has 8 bits per color per pixel, which can represent $256 \times 256 \times 256$ colors. A typical color lookup table contains $33 \times 33 \times 33$ entries. The number of measured color targets is often $9 \times 9 \times 9$, which is a lot of colors to measure. From these measured data points, we have to use interpolation to populate the $(33 \times 33 \times 33)$-entry lookup table. When processing an image, the color of each pixel, one out of the $256 \times 256 \times 256$ colors, has to be calculated by interpolation from the $33 \times 33 \times 33$ lookup table. The first color interpolation for populating the lookup table can be performed off-line, but the second color interpolation for each pixel has to be performed on-line. The off-line interpolation can be sophisticated and slow, but the on-line interpolation needs to be very, very fast, usually using only the simplest linear interpolation. When we discuss methods of interpolation, we have to distinguish between these two different applications.

Univariate interpolation

Univariate interpolation is used in color calibration when each color channel is calibrated independently or when only the luminance channel is calibrated. In most cases, several data points are measured and the goal is to interpolate between them to determine the output response for the unmeasured input. Another application is for generating a tone scale curve from a given set of points with or without the slope specified.

Data interpolation for functions of a single variable is a well-studied subject [237, 239]. Many of these well-known methods can be used in color calibration. When a single-variate lookup table is needed in calibration (for tone scale or curve shaping), the table size is usually small enough (≤ 4096) that a full lookup table is generated off-line. Therefore, the criteria for choosing one interpolation method over the others are mostly based on physical models of the devices, rather than on computational complexity. For example, the luminance as a function of the digital input value of a CRT monitor has been found to follow a certain power

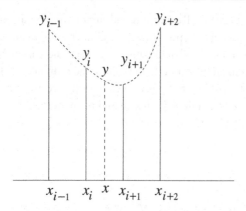

Figure 16.5. Using four data points (x_{i-1}, y_{i-1}), (x_i, y_i), (x_{i+1}, y_{i+1}), and (x_{i+2}, y_{i+2}) to determine a cubic polynomial for interpolating the interval $[x_i, x_{i+1}]$.

function very well. There is no reason, then, to interpolate the table by, say, a cubic spline. On the other hand, the reflectance of an output gray patch as a function of the input digital value of a printer does not seem to follow any particular analytical function. Piecewise cubic interpolation can thus be very well used here.

One of the major concerns in color interpolation is the unpredictable, nonlinear characteristics of an imaging device. It is thus not generally a good idea to use global functions for interpolation. For example, Lagrange interpolation with all the data points included is a very bad choice, because every data point exerts its influence on the entire curve. A preferred method uses only a few neighboring data points for interpolation. In this sense, piecewise cubic interpolation is better than the cubic spline, because the former only uses two neighboring data points on each side for interpolation, whereas the cubic spline involves all the data points.

Piecewise polynomial interpolation

Although it is always possible to find an Nth-degree polynomial function to go through a set of $N + 1$ data points, such a high-degree polynomial often exhibits oscillatory behaviors between data points. Therefore, a global polynomial is rarely a good model for interpolating calibration data. A useful way to use polynomial interpolation is to fit a piecewise low-degree polynomial to each part of the data. For example, one useful polynomial interpolation is the piecewise cubic interpolation. Given a set of data points, $S = \{(x_0, y_0), (x_1, y_1), \ldots, (x_n, y_n)\}$, we would like to interpolate any interval $[x_i, x_{i+1}]$ by a cubic polynomial, $y = ax^3 + bx^2 + cx + d$ (see Fig. 16.5). Since there are four unknowns, we need four data points (x_{i-1}, y_{i-1}), (x_i, y_i), (x_{i+1}, y_{i+1}), and (x_{i+2}, y_{i+2}) to determine the four coefficients, a, b, c, and d:

$$\begin{bmatrix} a \\ b \\ c \\ d \end{bmatrix} = \begin{bmatrix} x_{i-1}^3 & x_{i-1}^2 & x_{i-1} & 1 \\ x_i^3 & x_i^2 & x_i & 1 \\ x_{i+1}^3 & x_{i+1}^2 & x_{i+1} & 1 \\ x_{i+2}^3 & x_{i+2}^2 & x_{i+2} & 1 \end{bmatrix}^{-1} \begin{bmatrix} y_{i-1} \\ y_i \\ y_{i+1} \\ y_{i+2} \end{bmatrix}. \tag{16.8}$$

For the two intervals at the ends, the first four data points and the last four data points can be used. This type of piecewise polynomial interpolation is continuous, but the derivatives at the data points often are not continuous or do not exist. This is not necessarily a concern because there are situations in which the devices to be calibrated may not have sufficiently smooth response functions. Piecewise cubic interpolation is often used in scanner calibration where several neutral (gray) patches of known reflectance are scanned and the complete curves that relate scanner code values to input reflectances are constructed through piecewise cubic interpolation [422]. If the scanner codes are averaged over many pixels in each region of the reflectance target, the resulting curves are often smooth enough for scanner calibration.

Spline interpolation

It is possible to find a piecewise polynomial function for a set of data points such that some of its derivatives are continuous throughout the entire interval covering all the data points. One such example is the spline function of order k, defined as a piecewise polynomial function of degree $k - 1$ on every interval between two consecutive data points with $k - 2$ continuous derivatives at the data points.

Definition Given a strictly increasing sequence of points (called knots) $x_0 < x_1 < \ldots < x_{N-1}$, where $x_0 = a$ and $x_{N-1} = b$, a function $f(x)$, defined on the finite interval $[a, b]$, is called a spline function of order $k > 0$, if: (1) on each interval, $[x_i, x_{i+1}], i = 0, \ldots, N - 2$, $f(x)$ is a polynomial of, at most, degree $k - 1$, and (2) $f(x)$ and its derivatives, up to order $k - 2$, are continuous on $[a, b]$.

A spline function of order 1 is a piecewise constant function, with each interval given by a zeroth degree polynomial (constant). The function itself is not continuous. A spline function of order 2 is a piecewise linear function (linear interpolation) with each interval given by a first degree polynomial. The function is continuous. Although linear interpolation does not produce a smooth curve, it is very fast and often sufficiently accurate. When a large image has to be mapped through a sparsely populated calibration table (especially three- or four-dimensional tables), linear interpolation is often used. The best-known spline function is the spline function of order 4, with each interval given by a third-degree (cubic) polynomial. It is called the cubic spline. It has continuous first and second derivatives over the entire data interval $[a, b]$. It can be shown [545, Theorem 3.7.2] that the family of cubic spline functions over a given set of N knots is a vector space of dimension $N + 2$. Therefore, one can find $N + 2$ basis functions that will span the vector space of cubic spline functions. One particularly useful basis function is the B-spline function (B here means basis), which has a finite support and a bell shape similar to a Gaussian function. If we have one B-spline function at each knot and two more at two artificially introduced knots, we have enough basis functions to span the entire vector space. B-spline functions are useful tools in digital image processing applications, such as image interpolation and edge-detector-based wavelet decomposition.

Multivariate interpolation

Interpolation of a multivariate function is much less well studied [175]. Color interpolation can be seen as a special case in multivariate interpolation. If the measured data are on a regularly spaced Cartesian-product grid (for example, equally-spaced x, y, and z intervals), we can apply the univariate interpolation to each grid axis and then interpolate at the desired point. The real difficulty occurs when the data points are located irregularly in a multi-dimensional space. This case is called interpolation from scattered data [327]. The difficulty lies not only in the lack of well-studied methods, but also in the behaviors of most known methods. It is fair to say that we are still searching for a better solution of multivariate color interpolation, although a number of good methods have been well described [488].

The first step in multivariate interpolation is to select from the given data points which ones to use for interpolation. Once the points are selected, we need an interpolation model to do the calculation. These two steps, the point selection strategy and the data interpolation model, are somewhat coupled, but can also be treated independently.

The commonly used point selection strategies are:

- Select all data points: this is a global interpolation strategy. Every point in the grid affects the interpolation result of every other point. Neural network and global polynomial fitting belong to this strategy.
- Select the nearest neighbors: find the k nearest neighbors and use them to interpolate the point of interest. Although this strategy makes sense physically, it does not guarantee that the convex hull of the k nearest neighbors will include the point to be interpolated.
- Select the vertices of the smallest convex partition: first the entire color space is partitioned into small convex volumes. The vertices of the volume that contains the point of interest are used for interpolation.

Once a set of points has been selected to interpolate the point of interest, we need a data interpolation model. The commonly used data interpolation models are:

- Polynomials: depending on the number of points selected by the point selection strategy, we can fit a multivariate polynomial to the selected points and use it to interpolate. For example, if four noncoplanar points are selected in a three-dimensional color space, a first order polynomial $f(x, y, z) = ax + by + cz + d$ can be used to interpolate a point. The very useful tetrahedral interpolation algorithm uses such a data model.
- Distance-based: the interpolated value is a weighted linear combination of the values of the selected points. The weight assigned to each selected point is a function of its distance to the point to be interpolated. This is a very general class of methods for multivariate interpolation for scattered data [355, 860]. However, it is not widely used in color interpolation, partly because there are other fast and accurate methods, and partly because its underlying physical meaning does not match well how most color imaging devices behave.
- Volume-based: in this data model, the volume of the convex hull of the selected k points is partitioned into k segments, each of which uses the point of interest as one of the vertices. The weight assigned to each of the selected points is proportional to the volume of the segment opposite to it. Figure 16.6 shows an example of such a data model. In fact, it can be shown that such a data model is equivalent to the one used in the popular trilinear interpolation, in which each axis is linearly interpolated in sequence.

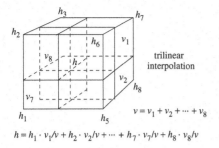

$$v = v_1 + v_2 + \cdots + v_8$$

$$h = h_1 \cdot v_1/v + h_2 \cdot v_2/v + \cdots + h_7 \cdot v_7/v + h_8 \cdot v_8/v$$

Figure 16.6. Example of a volume-based data interpolation model. The volume labeled v_1 is the rectangular volume that has the vertex h_7 and the point of interest, h, as the diagonal vertices. The weight assigned to vertex 1 is v_1 divided by the total volume v.

There are several practical considerations in color interpolation that impose constraints on the choices of the methods of multivariate interpolation:

- **Local adaptivity** As in the univariate color interpolation, device nonlinearity often requires the interpolation to be local. We may use a good physical model to predict the global shape of the multi-dimensional lookup table, but we cannot usually predict how the device might deviate from the ideal model locally. It is therefore important that the interpolation model be adaptive to local changes.
- **Convex inclusion** The neighboring points that are used to interpolate the point of interest are often selected by their distance from the point to be interpolated. This is intuitively a good criterion because points near by will have colors closer to the one we want to determine. However, this criterion alone is not sufficient. It is known that, given a set of points, interpolation at an interior point is much more reliable than extrapolation at an exterior point, especially for regions near the color gamut. Therefore, an important criterion for selecting neighboring points is that the selected points have to form a volume that contains the point to be interpolated. This property is called convex inclusion. Somewhat disappointing is that the point selection strategy that uses the nearest neighbors does not have the convex inclusion property.
- **Invertibility** If we use an interpolation algorithm to create a lookup table that maps a point P_A in color space A to a point P_B in color space B and then use the same algorithm to map P_B back to color space A, will we get back to P_A? If the answer is yes, we say that the interpolation algorithm is invertible. Otherwise, it is not invertible, An invertible algorithm is useful in those applications that require color transformation in both directions.
- **Smoothness** In order to render subtle color variations well, the mapping from one color space to another color space has to be smooth and continuous. For some point selection strategies, the interpolated values are not continuous. For example, let the input color space be partitioned into polyhedra. If two polyhedra that share a face do not share the entire face, there is a potential for discontinuous mapping because points on different sides of the shared face are interpolated by different sets of points. Figure 16.7 shows such an example.

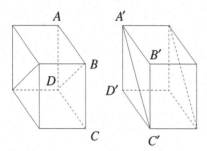

A A'

B

B'

D D'

C C'

Figure 16.7. Example of neighboring polyhedra that do not share a full face. The diagram shows two neighboring cubes drawn separately for a better view, i.e., A and A' are the same point, and so are B and B', C and C', and D and D'. The left-hand cube is partitioned into two prisms and so is the right-hand cube, but the ways they are partitioned are different. As a result, none of the four prisms shares a full face with another.

All the multivariate interpolation methods discussed so far require fair amounts of memory space for lookup table storage and computing power for on-line calculation. One natural question to ask is whether it is possible to combine several 1-D LUTs to do the job of a 3-D LUT. For example, $f(x, y, z) = xyz$ can be represented as $f(x, y, z) = \exp[\ln x + \ln y + \ln z]$. Thus, it is possible to use three 1-D LUTs to transform x, y, and z into $\ln x$, $\ln y$, and $\ln z$. We then add the outputs of the three 1-D LUTs and use the resulting value (properly quantized) as an index to a fourth 1-D LUT to perform the exponential function. Although this example seems to be quite contrived, one amazing result in approximation theory is that it is possible to represent a continuous function of several variables by superpositions and additions of functions of one variable. This was proved by Kolmogorov in 1957. The result can be stated by the following Theorem of Kolmogorov [601, p. 168]:

Theorem of Kolmogorov   *Let $I = [0, 1]$ and A be the n-dimensional cube, $0 \leq x_i \leq 1$, $i = 1, 2, \ldots, n$. There exist n constants, $0 < \lambda_i \leq 1$, $i = 1, 2, \ldots, n$, and $2n + 1$ functions $\phi_j(x)$, $j = 0, 1, \ldots, 2n$, defined on I and with values in I; ϕ_j are strictly increasing. For each continuous function f on A, one can find a continuous function $g(u)$, $0 \leq u \leq n$ such that*

$$f(x_1, \ldots, x_n) = \sum_{j=0}^{2n} g(\lambda_1 \phi_j(x_1) + \cdots + \lambda_n \phi_j(x_n)). \tag{16.9}$$

It is thus theoretically possible to reduce all multi-dimensional lookup tables to some superpositions and additions of 1-D LUTs. The Theorem of Kolmogorov says that one only needs eight 1-D LUTs to represent any 3-D LUT. This has not been done in practice, but it indicates the possibility that most multi-dimensional lookup table designs may benefit from shaping the input variables by 1-D LUTs. Approximation by a function of fewer variables is a topic that has received some careful studies [175, 349] and may someday become quite useful for designing multi-dimensional lookup tables. An alternative method is to perform a three-way decomposition of the 3-D LUT [581], similar to the singular value

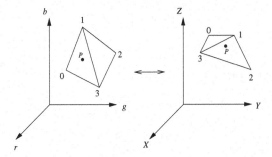

Figure 16.8. The tetrahedral interpolation problem.

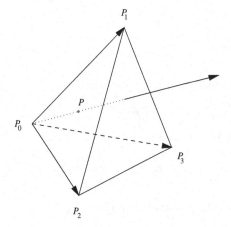

Figure 16.9. The convex inclusion problem.

decomposition of a matrix. However, this may take many components to produce a good approximation.

16.2.2 Tetrahedral interpolation

Having discussed the general issues in multivariate interpolation, we will now present the details of an accurate and efficient method for color interpolation that is frequently used in practical applications. The method is called tetrahedral interpolation [24, 422, 486, 488, 819]. The problem is described in Fig. 16.8. Given a tetrahedron in an (r, g, b) color space and its corresponding tetrahedron in another color space (X, Y, Z), for any point in (X, Y, Z) space, determine if the point is inside the tetrahedron, and if yes, determine its corresponding coordinates in the (r, g, b) color space. To solve these problems, it is convenient to take one of the four vertices (see Fig. 16.9), say vertex P_0, as the origin and treat the edges from P_0 to the other three vertices P_1, P_2, and P_3, as vectors $\overline{P_0P_1}$, $\overline{P_0P_2}$, and $\overline{P_0P_3}$.

How to determine if a point is inside a given tetrahedron? If $\overline{P_0P_1}$, $\overline{P_0P_2}$, and $\overline{P_0P_3}$ are three linearly independent vectors, then for any point P in the space, the vector $\overline{P_0P}$ can be

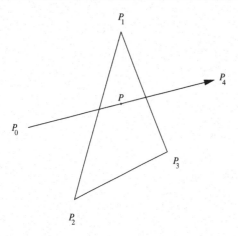

Figure 16.10. Intersection of a vector and a plane.

expressed as a linear sum of the three vectors, $\overline{P_0P_1}$, $\overline{P_0P_2}$, and $\overline{P_0P_3}$:

$$\overline{P_0P} = \alpha\overline{P_0P_1} + \beta\overline{P_0P_2} + \gamma\overline{P_0P_3},$$

$$\begin{bmatrix} X_P - X_0 \\ Y_P - Y_0 \\ Z_P - Z_0 \end{bmatrix} = \begin{bmatrix} X_1 - X_0 & X_2 - X_0 & X_3 - X_0 \\ Y_1 - Y_0 & Y_2 - Y_0 & Y_3 - Y_0 \\ Z_1 - Z_0 & Z_2 - Z_0 & Z_3 - Z_0 \end{bmatrix} \begin{bmatrix} \alpha \\ \beta \\ \gamma \end{bmatrix}.$$

Test for convex inclusion   Point P is inside the tetrahedron if and only if $\alpha \geq 0$, $\beta \geq 0$, $\gamma \geq 0$, and $\alpha + \beta + \gamma \leq 1$, where

$$\begin{bmatrix} \alpha \\ \beta \\ \gamma \end{bmatrix} = \begin{bmatrix} X_1 - X_0 & X_2 - X_0 & X_3 - X_0 \\ Y_1 - Y_0 & Y_2 - Y_0 & Y_3 - Y_0 \\ Z_1 - Z_0 & Z_2 - Z_0 & Z_3 - Z_0 \end{bmatrix}^{-1} \begin{bmatrix} X_p - X_0 \\ Y_p - Y_0 \\ Z_p - Z_0 \end{bmatrix}. \tag{16.10}$$

The above conditions can be proved as outlined below:

1. P_0 and P are on the same side of the plane $P_1P_2P_3 \iff \alpha + \beta + \gamma \leq 1$.
2. P_1 and P are on the same side of the plane $P_0P_2P_3 \iff \alpha \geq 0$.
3. P_2 and P are on the same side of the plane $P_1P_0P_3 \iff \beta \geq 0$.
4. P_3 and P are on the same side of the plane $P_1P_2P_0 \iff \gamma \geq 0$.

What are the (r, g, b) coordinates of an interior point P?   When P is inside the tetrahedron, its (r, g, b) coordinates can be determined from those of the four vertices by:

$$\begin{bmatrix} r_P \\ g_P \\ b_P \end{bmatrix} = \begin{bmatrix} r_1 - r_0 & r_2 - r_0 & r_3 - r_0 \\ g_1 - g_0 & g_2 - g_0 & g_3 - g_0 \\ b_1 - b_0 & b_2 - b_0 & b_3 - b_0 \end{bmatrix} \begin{bmatrix} \alpha \\ \beta \\ \gamma \end{bmatrix} + \begin{bmatrix} r_0 \\ g_0 \\ b_0 \end{bmatrix}. \tag{16.11}$$

In Fig. 16.10, when P_0 and P_4 are on opposite sides of the plane $P_1P_2P_3$, and the vector $\overline{P_0P_4}$ intersects with the triangular face $P_1P_2P_3$ at a point P, what are the (X, Y, Z) and *(r, g, b) coordinates of P?*

$$\begin{bmatrix} \alpha \\ \beta \\ \gamma \end{bmatrix} = \begin{bmatrix} X_1 - X_0 & X_2 - X_0 & X_3 - X_0 \\ Y_1 - Y_0 & Y_2 - Y_0 & Y_3 - Y_0 \\ Z_1 - Z_0 & Z_2 - Z_0 & Z_3 - Z_0 \end{bmatrix}^{-1} \begin{bmatrix} X_4 - X_0 \\ Y_4 - Y_0 \\ Z_4 - Z_0 \end{bmatrix}. \tag{16.12}$$

The conditions for P_0 and P_4 to be on opposite sides of the plane $P_1 P_2 P_3$ and for the vector $\overline{P_0 P_4}$ to intersect the triangular face $P_1 P_2 P_3$ are: $\alpha \geq 0, \beta \geq 0, \gamma \geq 0$, and $\alpha + \beta + \gamma \geq 1$. In this case, the intersection point P can be determined by normalizing α, β, and γ with their sum so that their normalized values sum to 1.

$$\begin{bmatrix} X_P \\ Y_P \\ Z_P \end{bmatrix} = \begin{bmatrix} X_1 - X_0 & X_2 - X_0 & X_3 - X_0 \\ Y_1 - Y_0 & Y_2 - Y_0 & Y_3 - Y_0 \\ Z_1 - Z_0 & Z_2 - Z_0 & Z_3 - Z_0 \end{bmatrix} \begin{bmatrix} \alpha/(\alpha + \beta + \gamma) \\ \beta/(\alpha + \beta + \gamma) \\ \gamma/(\alpha + \beta + \gamma) \end{bmatrix} + \begin{bmatrix} X_0 \\ Y_0 \\ Z_0 \end{bmatrix} \tag{16.13}$$

and

$$\begin{bmatrix} r_P \\ g_P \\ b_P \end{bmatrix} = \begin{bmatrix} r_1 - r_0 & r_2 - r_0 & r_3 - r_0 \\ g_1 - g_0 & g_2 - g_0 & g_3 - g_0 \\ b_1 - b_0 & b_2 - b_0 & b_3 - b_0 \end{bmatrix} \begin{bmatrix} \alpha/(\alpha + \beta + \gamma) \\ \beta/(\alpha + \beta + \gamma) \\ \gamma/(\alpha + \beta + \gamma) \end{bmatrix} + \begin{bmatrix} r_0 \\ g_0 \\ b_0 \end{bmatrix}. \tag{16.14}$$

16.2.3 Regression and approximation

Fitting equations to the measured data is called regression analysis. The equations describe the model of an imaging device. Regression analysis is used to estimate the parameters in the model, the errors of the estimate, and the goodness of fit between the data and the model. If the goodness of fit is not acceptable, one needs to find a new model to describe the data.

Using a family of chosen functions to approximate another unknown or known, but more complicated, function is called approximation. In the theory of approximation, the function to be approximated is known, but may be difficult or time-consuming to calculate. In color imaging applications, the measured data are assumed to come from an unknown function and the task is to approximate it with some function or functions of our choice. The purpose is to use the chosen function(s) to approximate other points of interest that are not measured. The major difference between interpolation and approximation is that the latter does not require the approximation function to pass through the measured data. For our applications, regression analysis is treated as one type of functional approximation.

Linear regression

Given a set of data points (x_i, y_i), $i = 1, 2, \ldots, n$, and a device model $y = f(x) = \sum_{j=1}^{m} u_j \phi_j(x)$, we would like to find the coefficients u_j, $j = 1, 2, \ldots, m$, such that the total error is minimized. This problem is a linear regression problem because $f(x)$ is a linear function of the unknowns u_j, $j = 1, 2, \ldots, m$, although the functions $\phi_j(x)$ in the expansion of $f(x)$ may be nonlinear. For example, a cubic spline can also be cast into linear regression [960]. The most frequently used regression criterion is to minimize the squared errors, χ^2, by setting all the partial derivatives to 0:

$$\chi^2 = \sum_i^n [y_i - f(x_i)]^2 = \sum_i^n \left[y_i - \sum_{j=1}^m u_j \phi_j(x_i) \right]^2,$$

$$\frac{\partial \chi^2}{\partial u_k} = -2 \sum_i^n \left[y_i \phi_k(x_i) - \sum_{j=1}^m u_j \phi_k(x_i) \phi_j(x_i) \right] = 0.$$

Rearranging the terms, we obtain:

$$\sum_{j=1}^m u_j \left[\sum_i^n \phi_1(x_i) \phi_j(x_i) \right] = \sum_i^n y_i \phi_1(x_i),$$

$$\sum_{j=1}^m u_j \left[\sum_i^n \phi_2(x_i) \phi_j(x_i) \right] = \sum_i^n y_i \phi_2(x_i),$$

$$\vdots \qquad\qquad\qquad \vdots$$

$$\sum_{j=1}^m u_j \left[\sum_i^n \phi_m(x_i) \phi_j(x_i) \right] = \sum_i^n y_i \phi_m(x_i).$$

The above equations are called the normal equations and they can be written in a matrix form. Let Φ be an $m \times m$ matrix, where $\Phi_{kj} = \sum_i^n \phi_k(x_i) \phi_j(x_i)$, and $\mathbf{u}$ and $\mathbf{b}$ be $m \times 1$ vector, where the jth component of the vector $\mathbf{u}$ is u_j, and the kth component of the vector $\mathbf{b}$ is $b_k = \sum_i^n y_i \phi_k(x_i)$, then $\Phi \mathbf{u} = \mathbf{b}$, i.e.,

$$\begin{bmatrix} \sum_i^n \phi_1(x_i)\phi_1(x_i) & \sum_i^n \phi_1(x_i)\phi_2(x_i) & \cdots & \sum_i^n \phi_1(x_i)\phi_m(x_i) \\ \sum_i^n \phi_2(x_i)\phi_1(x_i) & \sum_i^n \phi_2(x_i)\phi_2(x_i) & \cdots & \sum_i^n \phi_2(x_i)\phi_m(x_i) \\ \vdots & \vdots & & \vdots \\ \sum_i^n \phi_m(x_i)\phi_1(x_i) & \sum_i^n \phi_m(x_i)\phi_2(x_i) & \cdots & \sum_i^n \phi_m(x_i)\phi_m(x_i) \end{bmatrix} \begin{bmatrix} u_1 \\ u_2 \\ \vdots \\ u_m \end{bmatrix}$$

$$= \begin{bmatrix} \sum_i^n y_i \phi_1(x_i) \\ \sum_i^n y_i \phi_2(x_i) \\ \vdots \\ \sum_i^n y_i \phi_m(x_i) \end{bmatrix}. \tag{16.15}$$

If the matrix Φ is not singular, the coefficient vector $\mathbf{u} = \Phi^{-1}\mathbf{b}$. However, the matrix Φ is often very ill-conditioned (some small perturbation in the data leads to a large change in the solution [960, Lecture 12]) and matrix inversion tends to be numerically unstable. Therefore, the normal equations are usually solved by the singular value decomposition. Before we examine a more general case of the least-squares problem, let us introduce the singular value decomposition and the Moore–Penrose inverse.

Singular value decomposition theorem [625, p. 18]: *Let A be a real $m \times n$ matrix, with rank r. There exist an $m \times r$ matrix U such that $U^T U = I_r$, an $n \times r$ matrix V such that $V^T V = I_r$, and an $r \times r$ diagonal matrix Λ with positive diagonal elements, such that $A = U \Lambda V^T$, where I_r is an $r \times r$ identity matrix.*

(Note that this theorem is stated in a form so that the $r \times r$ diagonal matrix Λ is invertible. This property will be used to find the Moore–Penrose inverse. In most singular value decomposition algorithms, the diagonal matrix is computed as an $m \times n$ matrix. In that case, very small singular values have to be discarded and the matrices made into the form stated here before the Moore–Penrose inverse is computed as $A^+ = V\Lambda^{-1}U^T$. In numerical computation, the rank r of matrix A is defined by the smallest singular value that we decide to keep.)

The Moore–Penrose inverse An $n \times m$ matrix A^+ is called the Moore–Penrose inverse of a real $m \times n$ matrix A if (1) $AA^+A = A$, (2) $A^+AA^+ = A^+$, (3) $(AA^+)^T = AA^+$, and (4) $(A^+A)^T = A^+A$.

The Moore–Penrose inverse of a matrix A can be found by the singular value decomposition. Let $A = U\Lambda V^T$, then $A^+ = V\Lambda^{-1}U^T$. It can be proved that, for each A, A^+ exists and is unique [625, p. 32]. In many applications, A has a full column rank, i.e., rank$(A) = n$, then $(A^TA)^{-1}$ exists and $A^+ = (A^TA)^{-1}A^T$.

The linear regression problem can now be stated in matrix algebra. We would like to approximate an $n \times 1$ vector $\mathbf{y}$ by a linear combination of the column vectors of an $n \times m$ matrix A, i.e., $\mathbf{y} \approx A\mathbf{u}$, so that $(\mathbf{y} - A\mathbf{u})^T(\mathbf{y} - A\mathbf{u})$ is minimized. The vector $\mathbf{y} = [y_1, y_2, \ldots, y_n]^T$ is the "observation" vector and

$$A = \begin{bmatrix} \phi_1(x_1) & \phi_2(x_1) & \cdots & \phi_m(x_1) \\ \phi_1(x_2) & \phi_2(x_2) & \cdots & \phi_m(x_2) \\ \vdots & \vdots & & \vdots \\ \phi_1(x_n) & \phi_2(x_n) & \cdots & \phi_m(x_n) \end{bmatrix} \tag{16.16}$$

is the "design" matrix. The regression model $\mathbf{y} \approx A\mathbf{u}$ means that the dependent (observation) variable, y, is a linear combination of the variables $\phi_1(x)$, $\phi_2(x)$, $\ldots$, $\phi_m(x)$, i.e., $y = u_1\phi_1(x) + u_2\phi_2(x) + \cdots + u_m\phi_m(x)$, and the coefficients are given by the vector $\mathbf{u}$ which is to be determined by the method of least squares. It can be proved that $(\mathbf{y} - A\mathbf{u})^T(\mathbf{y} - A\mathbf{u}) \geq \mathbf{y}^T(I - AA^+)\mathbf{y}$ and the least squares solution for $\mathbf{u}$ is given by $\mathbf{u} = A^+\mathbf{y} + (I - A^+A)\mathbf{c}$, where I is the identity matrix, and $\mathbf{c}$ is an arbitrary constant $n \times 1$ vector [625, p. 232]. In most applications, A has a full column rank, then $A^+ = (A^TA)^{-1}A^T$ and $A^+A = I$. Therefore, $\mathbf{u} = A^+\mathbf{y} = (A^TA)^{-1}A^T\mathbf{y}$. (Note that $A^T\mathbf{y} = \mathbf{b}$, $A^TA = \Phi$, and $\mathbf{u} = \Phi^{-1}\mathbf{b}$.)

A more generalized least squares problem is to allow different weighting factors for the error components, and the weighted square errors become $(\mathbf{y} - A\mathbf{u})^TW(\mathbf{y} - A\mathbf{u})$, where the weight matrix W is assumed to be a symmetric, positive semidefinite $n \times n$ matrix (i.e., $\mathbf{u}^TW\mathbf{u} \geq 0$ for all $\mathbf{u}$). It can be proved that $(\mathbf{y} - A\mathbf{u})^TW(\mathbf{y} - A\mathbf{u}) \geq \mathbf{y}^T(W - WA(A^TWA)^+A^TW)\mathbf{y}$ and the weighted least squares solution is given by $\mathbf{u} = (A^TWA)^+A^TW\mathbf{y} + (I - (A^TWA)^+A^TWA)\mathbf{c}$, where $\mathbf{c}$ is an arbitrary constant $n \times 1$ vector. Again, when A^TWA has a full column rank, $\mathbf{u} = (A^TWA)^{-1}A^TW\mathbf{y}$.

Nonlinear regression

Sometimes, the nonlinear models can be reformulated into linear ones. For example, $y = ax^b$ can be changed to $\log y = \log a + b \log x$. Although linear regression problems are relatively easy to solve, not all models can be cast in that way. For example, the CRT monitor luminance as a function of input code value is well described by a power function: $L = a(v + b)^\gamma$. The parameters, a, b, and γ, cannot be cast into linear coefficients of any chosen function. Standard nonlinear optimization algorithms, such as the Levenberg–Marquardt method [777], can be used. However, as in any nonlinear optimization problem, we have to use a good initial guess and avoid local minima in the optimization process. The other problem is that the valley near the global minimum of the cost function may be very shallow and the algorithm can stop prematurely before it reaches the true minimum. In the case of monitor calibration, most monitors have a gamma value within a certain range, say $2.0 < \gamma < 2.5$, and it is helpful to include a penalty function to prevent the algorithm from being trapped at a gamma value far from 2.2.

Robust regression

The most widely used cost function in regression is the squared errors. The popular least squares regression is mathematically easy to solve and, in the case of Gaussian noise, it is also the maximum likelihood solution. However, it is quite sensitive to outliers. A single outlier in the data may throw the estimates off so far as to make the results useless. The basic problem is that the cost function is proportional to the square of the distance, and therefore, is heavily biased by the outliers. A family of new cost functions has been proposed to reduce the impact of outliers by discounting large deviations. Regression using this type of cost function is called robust regression. The least median of squares (LMS) is found to have many good characteristics. It can tolerate up to almost 50% bad data, because the median is not much affected [812].

However, there is no efficient way to compute the LMS solution. Current algorithms use random sampling of the data to run regressions. If enough different subsets are tried, a good subset will not contain an outlier and thus will produce the LMS. In order to make sure that at least one good subset is included, a sufficiently large number of random samplings have to be tried. That is why the LMS takes much more time to compute. However, for off-line interpolation, the robustness may be worth the effort.

16.2.4 Constrained optimization

In calibrating color imaging devices, we often have to trade color accuracy with cost (hardware, software, or CPU time). Under cost constraints, the color transformation paths can only use a restricted set of processing steps. If there are some signal characteristics that we wish to preserve in the signal processing chain, they have to be imposed as constraints in the system optimization. Therefore, constrained optimization is a very useful computational tool in color calibration. For example, if a dense 3-D LUT is used for color calibration in digital cameras, it is possible to achieve very high color reproduction quality. However, the cost is quite high in many measures: large memory space, long computing time, and tedious calibration procedures. Therefore, almost all digital cameras use 1-D LUTs and 3×3 matrices. When faced with limited signal transformation methods, important color reproduction criteria have to be imposed as constraints. Let us consider the problem of deriving the optimal 3×3 color transformation matrix for a digital camera. For this discussion, we will assume that the output of the digital camera is in CIEXYZ space. Therefore, the function of the 3×3 matrix is to transform the camera (R, G, B) values into CIEXYZ tristimulus values. We can use the camera to take an image of a color calibration target, such as the Macbeth ColorChecker, which has 24 color patches. Since the CIEXYZ values of the color calibration target are known for a given illuminant, we can determine the 3×3 matrix that minimizes the total errors between the transformed and the measured CIEXYZ values. Or, alternatively we can minimize the CIELAB differences. However, if the matrix is determined in this way without any constraint, it is very likely that a neutral object in the (R, G, B) image (say, after color balance, $R = G = B$) may not be reproduced as neutral. When an image is rendered with a slight presence of hue in neutral areas (such as gray or white objects), it becomes quite objectionable. Since preservation of neutrals is one of the most important requirements in color reproduction, a matrix that does not preserve neutrals is usually not an acceptable solution. Therefore, in the minimization of color errors, the matrix elements should be constrained in such a way that neutrals are preserved. The other frequently used constraint is the explicit constraint on skin color reproduction.

General constrained optimization problems have been well studied (see, e.g., [605, 668]). Algorithms appropriate to their intended domain should be used for each application. Here we will present one simple method that allows us to impose linear equality constraints. This is called the method of Lagrange multipliers [108]. We will use it to solve the color transformation matrix problem under the constraint that neutrals be preserved. First let us show that the neutral constraint can be formulated as equality constraints. Under a given illuminant with chromaticity coordinates (x_c, y_c), all neutral objects should have the same chromaticity as that of the illuminant. Let M be the 3×3 color transformation matrix that maps camera (R, G, B) to CIE (X', Y', Z'):

$$\begin{bmatrix} X' \\ Y' \\ Z' \end{bmatrix} = M \begin{bmatrix} R \\ G \\ B \end{bmatrix} = \begin{bmatrix} m_{11} & m_{12} & m_{13} \\ m_{21} & m_{22} & m_{23} \\ m_{31} & m_{32} & m_{33} \end{bmatrix} \begin{bmatrix} R \\ G \\ B \end{bmatrix}. \tag{16.17}$$

We will assume that the camera RGB image has been properly color balanced and $R = G = B$ for neutral colors. A neutral object with $R = G = B = c$ is transformed to (X', Y', Z'), where

$$X' = c(m_{11} + m_{12} + m_{13}),$$
$$Y' = c(m_{21} + m_{22} + m_{23}),$$
$$Z' = c(m_{31} + m_{32} + m_{33}).$$

To preserve the neutral colors, the chromaticity coordinates should be equal to those of the illuminant, i.e.,

$$x' = \frac{X'}{X' + Y' + Z'} = x_c,$$
$$y' = \frac{Y'}{X' + Y' + Z'} = y_c,$$
$$z' = \frac{Z'}{X' + Y' + Z'} = z_c.$$

Since $X'/Y' = x'/y' = x_c/y_c$ and $Z'/Y' = z'/y' = z_c/y_c$, we have

$$y_c(m_{11} + m_{12} + m_{13}) = x_c(m_{21} + m_{22} + m_{23}), \tag{16.18}$$

$$y_c(m_{31} + m_{32} + m_{33}) = z_c(m_{21} + m_{22} + m_{23}). \tag{16.19}$$

Furthermore, the scale of the transformation is specified by conventions. For example, when $R = G = B = 255$ (maximum input value), we want the output luminance Y' to be set at 255 (maximum output value) as well. In that case, $m_{21} + m_{22} + m_{23} = 1$. Therefore,

$$m_{11} + m_{12} + m_{13} = x_c/y_c, \tag{16.20}$$

$$m_{21} + m_{22} + m_{23} = 1, \tag{16.21}$$

$$m_{31} + m_{32} + m_{33} = z_c/y_c. \tag{16.22}$$

The general problem can be stated as follows: Given a set of corresponding color values: $U_i = (R_i, G_i, B_i)^T$, $V_i = (X_i, Y_i, Z_i)^T$, $i = 1, 2, \ldots, n$, find a 3×3 color transformation matrix, M, so that the color errors are minimized in CIELAB space, under the constraint that the neutral colors have to be preserved. Within first-order approximation, the error, $V_i - MU_i = [X_i - X_i', Y_i - Y_i', Z_i - Z_i']^T = [\Delta X_i, \Delta Y_i, \Delta Z_i]^T$ is related to the error $[\Delta L_i^*, \Delta a_i^*, \Delta b_i^*]^T$ by:

$$\begin{bmatrix} \Delta L_i^* \\ \Delta a_i^* \\ \Delta b_i^* \end{bmatrix} = \begin{bmatrix} \partial L^*/\partial X & \partial L^*/\partial Y & \partial L^*/\partial Z \\ \partial a^*/\partial X & \partial a^*/\partial Y & \partial a^*/\partial Z \\ \partial b^*/\partial X & \partial b^*/\partial Y & \partial b^*/\partial Z \end{bmatrix} \begin{bmatrix} \Delta X_i \\ \Delta Y_i \\ \Delta Z_i \end{bmatrix} = J_i \begin{bmatrix} \Delta X_i \\ \Delta Y_i \\ \Delta Z_i \end{bmatrix}$$

$$= J_i(V_i - MU_i). \tag{16.23}$$

We want to find the matrix M that minimizes the following cost function:

$$\chi^2 = \sum_{i=1}^{n} [J_i(V_i - MU_i)]^T [J_i(V_i - MU_i)] - \sum_{j=1}^{3} 2\lambda_j(m_{j1} + m_{j2} + m_{j3} - c_j), \tag{16.24}$$

where $c_1 = x_c/y_c$, $c_2 = 1$, $c_3 = z_c/y_c$, and (x_c, y_c, z_c) are the chromaticity coordinates of the illuminant. Setting the first partial derivative of χ^2 with respect to m_{ij} to zero, we can express the solution in the following matrix form:

$$\frac{\partial \chi^2}{\partial M} = -2 \sum J_i^T J_i V_i U_i^T + 2 \sum J_i^T J_i MU_i U_i^T - 2 \begin{bmatrix} \lambda_1 & \lambda_1 & \lambda_1 \\ \lambda_2 & \lambda_2 & \lambda_2 \\ \lambda_3 & \lambda_3 & \lambda_3 \end{bmatrix} = 0. \tag{16.25}$$

There are nine equations for twelve unknowns (m_{ij}, $i = 1, 2, 3$, $j = 1, 2, 3$, λ_1, λ_2, and λ_3). The other three equations are from the equality constraints: $m_{j1} + m_{j2} + m_{j3} = c_j$, $j = 1, 2, 3$. Therefore the matrix M can be determined. This solution is based on the first order approximation of the CIELAB errors by the (X, Y, Z) errors. If we only want to minimize the total square errors in (X, Y, Z) space, the solution for M is greatly simplified.

Setting all the J_i matrices to the identity matrix, let us reformulate the cost function of Eq. (16.24) by adding an additional cost term: $k \sum_i \sum_j m_{ij}^2$, which penalizes large matrix elements because they often amplify noise. Therefore, we have

$$\chi^2 = \sum_{i=1}^{n}(V_i - MU_i)^{\mathrm{T}}(V_i - MU_i) - \sum_{j=1}^{3} 2\lambda_j(m_{j1} + m_{j2} + m_{j3} - c_j) + k \sum_{i=1}^{3} \sum_{j=1}^{3} m_{ij}^2$$

(16.26)

and in order to find the optimal M, we set the partial derivatives to zero:

$$\frac{\partial \chi^2}{\partial M} = -2 \sum V_i U_i^{\mathrm{T}} + 2 \sum MU_i U_i^{\mathrm{T}} - 2 \begin{bmatrix} \lambda_1 & \lambda_1 & \lambda_1 \\ \lambda_2 & \lambda_2 & \lambda_2 \\ \lambda_3 & \lambda_3 & \lambda_3 \end{bmatrix} + 2kM = 0.$$

(16.27)

Let $P = \sum V_i U_i^{\mathrm{T}}$, $S = \sum U_i U_i^{\mathrm{T}}$, $Q = (S + kI)^{-1}$, and

$$[\lambda] = \begin{bmatrix} \lambda_1 & \lambda_1 & \lambda_1 \\ \lambda_2 & \lambda_2 & \lambda_2 \\ \lambda_3 & \lambda_3 & \lambda_3 \end{bmatrix}.$$

(16.28)

Equation (16.27) becomes

$$M(S + kI) = P + [\lambda],$$

(16.29)

$$M = PQ + [\lambda]Q.$$

(16.30)

We can now solve for $[\lambda]$ in terms of the known data. Let

$$N = \begin{bmatrix} 1 \\ 1 \\ 1 \end{bmatrix}, \quad C = \begin{bmatrix} c_1 & c_1 & c_1 \\ c_2 & c_2 & c_2 \\ c_3 & c_3 & c_3 \end{bmatrix}, \quad \text{and} \quad W = \begin{bmatrix} 1 & 1 & 1 \\ 1 & 1 & 1 \\ 1 & 1 & 1 \end{bmatrix}.$$

(16.31)

Multiplying, from the right, both sides of Eq. (16.30) by W, we have

$$C = MW = PQW + [\lambda]QW = PQW + [\lambda]N^{\mathrm{T}}QN,$$

(16.32)

and therefore, $[\lambda] = (C - PQW)/N^{\mathrm{T}}QN$. Substituting $[\lambda]$ into Eq. (16.30), we have

$$M_0 = PQ + (C - PQW)Q/(N^{\mathrm{T}}QN),$$

(16.33)

where M_0 means the zeroth-order solution of M.

The constrained minimization problem in Eq. (16.24) can also be formulated in a more concise manner by writing the desired matrix M as a 9×1 vector

$\mathbf{u} = [m_{11}, m_{12}, m_{13}, m_{21}, m_{22}, m_{23}, m_{31}, m_{32}, m_{33}]^{\mathrm{T}}$. Let A be a $3n \times 9$ matrix:

$$A = \begin{bmatrix}
R_1 & G_1 & B_1 & 0 & 0 & 0 & 0 & 0 & 0 \\
0 & 0 & 0 & R_1 & G_1 & B_1 & 0 & 0 & 0 \\
0 & 0 & 0 & 0 & 0 & 0 & R_1 & G_1 & B_1 \\
R_2 & G_2 & B_2 & 0 & 0 & 0 & 0 & 0 & 0 \\
0 & 0 & 0 & R_2 & G_2 & B_2 & 0 & 0 & 0 \\
0 & 0 & 0 & 0 & 0 & 0 & R_2 & G_2 & B_2 \\
\vdots & \vdots & \vdots & \vdots & \vdots & \vdots & \vdots & \vdots & \vdots \\
R_n & G_n & B_n & 0 & 0 & 0 & 0 & 0 & 0 \\
0 & 0 & 0 & R_n & G_n & B_n & 0 & 0 & 0 \\
0 & 0 & 0 & 0 & 0 & 0 & R_n & G_n & B_n
\end{bmatrix}, \tag{16.34}$$

$\mathbf{y}$ be a $3n \times 1$ vector: $\mathbf{y} = [X_1, Y_1, Z_1, X_2, Y_2, Z_2, \ldots, X_n, Y_n, Z_n]^{\mathrm{T}}$; F be a 3×9 matrix:

$$F = \begin{bmatrix}
1 & 1 & 1 & 0 & 0 & 0 & 0 & 0 & 0 \\
0 & 0 & 0 & 1 & 1 & 1 & 0 & 0 & 0 \\
0 & 0 & 0 & 0 & 0 & 0 & 1 & 1 & 1
\end{bmatrix}; \tag{16.35}$$

$\mathbf{c}$ be a 3×1 vector: $\mathbf{c} = [c_1, c_2, c_3]^{\mathrm{T}}$ and J be a $3n \times 3n$ matrix:

$$J = \begin{bmatrix}
(J_1)_{11} & (J_1)_{12} & (J_1)_{13} & 0 & 0 & 0 & \cdots & 0 & 0 & 0 & 0 & 0 & 0 \\
(J_1)_{21} & (J_1)_{22} & (J_1)_{23} & 0 & 0 & 0 & \cdots & 0 & 0 & 0 & 0 & 0 & 0 \\
(J_1)_{31} & (J_1)_{32} & (J_1)_{33} & 0 & 0 & 0 & \cdots & 0 & 0 & 0 & 0 & 0 & 0 \\
0 & 0 & 0 & (J_2)_{11} & (J_2)_{12} & (J_2)_{13} & \cdots & 0 & 0 & 0 & 0 & 0 & 0 \\
0 & 0 & 0 & (J_2)_{21} & (J_2)_{22} & (J_2)_{23} & \cdots & 0 & 0 & 0 & 0 & 0 & 0 \\
0 & 0 & 0 & (J_2)_{31} & (J_2)_{32} & (J_2)_{33} & \cdots & 0 & 0 & 0 & 0 & 0 & 0 \\
\vdots & \vdots & \vdots & \vdots & \vdots & \vdots & & \vdots & \vdots & \vdots & \vdots & \vdots & \vdots \\
0 & 0 & 0 & 0 & 0 & 0 & \cdots & 0 & 0 & 0 & (J_n)_{11} & (J_n)_{12} & (J_n)_{13} \\
0 & 0 & 0 & 0 & 0 & 0 & \cdots & 0 & 0 & 0 & (J_n)_{21} & (J_n)_{22} & (J_n)_{23} \\
0 & 0 & 0 & 0 & 0 & 0 & \cdots & 0 & 0 & 0 & (J_n)_{31} & (J_n)_{32} & (J_n)_{33}
\end{bmatrix}.$$

Let $B = J^{\mathrm{T}}J$, then the constrained minimization problem becomes to minimize $(\mathbf{y} - A\mathbf{u})^{\mathrm{T}} B (\mathbf{y} - A\mathbf{u})$ subject to $F\mathbf{u} = \mathbf{c}$. The solution is given by [625, pp. 233–4]: $\mathbf{u} = \mathbf{u}_0 + H^{+}F^{\mathrm{T}}(FH^{+}F^{\mathrm{T}})^{+}(\mathbf{c} - F\mathbf{u}_0) + (I - H^{+}H)\mathbf{q}$, where $H = A^{\mathrm{T}}BA + F^{\mathrm{T}}F$, $\mathbf{u}_0 = H^{+}A^{\mathrm{T}}B\mathbf{y}$ and $\mathbf{q}$ is an arbitrary constant 9×1 vector. Very often in practical applications, $H^{+}H = I$ and the solution for $\mathbf{u}$ is unique.

16.3   Spatial calibration

In addition to the colorimetric calibration discussed in the previous section, color imaging devices, such as cameras, scanners, CRT displays, and printers, also require spatial calibration to characterize their performance in reproducing spatial patterns. Resolution and geometry calibrations are two of the most frequently performed procedures. The former is aimed at measuring how a device reproduces spatial details, and the latter how a device reproduces geometric shapes. The resolution of an imaging device is often defined in several ways, each of which may measure somewhat different characteristics of the system. For example, in one definition, the resolution of an imaging device is the smallest distance between two dots that can be visually resolved. In another definition, two lines are used. In yet another definition, the bandwidth of the system transfer function is used to represent its resolution. All these three definitions attempt to use one number to characterize the system. Here, by resolution calibration, we will mean the measurement of the spatial frequency response function or the MTF of the system. In the case of a nonlinear device, international standards often specify the operating point at which the response function is measured by a low-contrast input signal. Geometric calibration is often more complicated than resolution calibration, especially for image capture devices [331, 449, 590, 966, 1009, 1039]. It is actually an important part of several engineering fields, such as photogrammetery, remote sensing, and computer vision. The complexity increases quickly with the desired accuracy. Fortunately, not all imaging devices require complicated geometric calibrations. For example, color thermal printers usually do not require such a calibration process because the alignment of pixels is often done in the manufacturing of print heads. The geometric calibration will be discussed in Chapter 19 when we deal with different types of imaging device (for example, digital cameras). Here, we discuss the general method for resolution calibration.

16.3.1 Resolution calibration

The system transfer function, $H(\nu_x, \nu_y)$, is related to the PSF, $h(x, y)$, by:

$$H(\nu_x, \nu_y) = \int \int h(x, y)e^{-i2\pi(\nu_x x + \nu_y y)}dxdy \qquad (16.36)$$

The line spread function $l(x)$ is by definition:

$$l(x) = \int h(x, y)dy \qquad (16.37)$$

and its Fourier transform $L(\nu_x)$ is:

$$L(\nu_x) = \int l(x)e^{-i2\pi \nu_x x}dx = \int [\int h(x, y)dy]e^{-i2\pi \nu_x x}dx$$

$$= \int \int h(x, y)e^{-i2\pi \nu_x x}dxdy = H(\nu_x, 0). \qquad (16.38)$$

The edge spread function (ESF), $\epsilon(x, y)$, is the convolution of $h(x, y)$ with an ideal step function, $s(x, y)$, which is equal to zero for all $x < 0$, and 1 for all $x \geq 0$. These expressions are of practical importance because a relatively good knife-edge target is not difficult to create and the image of the ESF of a device can be analyzed to derive the system transfer function of the device. Since it is almost impossible to perfectly align the knife edge along any direction, the image of a slanted edge has to be analyzed. For digital devices, the slanted edge image actually provides good information for estimating the system spatial frequency response (SFR) beyond the Nyquist frequency. The reason is that we have complete knowledge of the signal. Various pixels across the slanted edge provide digital

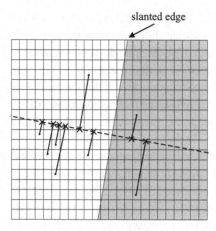

slanted edge

Figure 16.11. By projecting all the pixels onto a line perpendicular to the slanted edge, we can pool them together to form a subpixel sampling of the ESF. The figure shows only the projection of some of the pixels as examples.

samples at many different distances from the edge and, when all of them are projected onto a line perpendicular to the slanted edge (see Fig. 16.11), they can be pooled together to form a subpixel sampling of the ESF,[1] allowing the computation of the spatial frequency response much beyond the Nyquist frequency of the pixel grids. A well-known method for estimating the device SFR from a digital image of a slanted edge [150, 788] relies on taking the first derivative of the ESF to compute the LSF, from which one can compute the device SFR as shown in Eq. (16.38). In order to estimate responses at other spatial frequencies, we have to take images with the knife edge slanted at different orientations.

16.3.2 Line fitting on a digital image

In the slanted edge method for estimating the device SFR, one of the steps is to determine the straight line from a set of edge points on a digital image. Fitting a straight line to a set of points where both coordinates are subject to noise perturbation is different from the case when only the y-coordinate is assumed to have errors. Instead of minimizing the sum of the squares of the y deviations, we now wish to minimize the sum of the squares of the perpendicular distances from the observed points to the line to be determined.

Let the equation of the straight line be $ax + by - c = 0$, where $a^2 + b^2 = 1$. The distance, d_i, from a point (x_i, y_i) to the line is $d_i = |ax_i + by_i - c|$. Given a set of points, (x_i, y_i), $i = 1, 2, 3, \ldots, n$, we would like to determine a, b, and c, so that

$$S = \sum_{i=1}^{n}(ax_i + by_i - c)^2 \tag{16.39}$$

is minimized, subject to the constraint $a^2 + b^2 = 1$. First, we set the first partial derivative

---

[1]   If the slope of the slanted edge is a rational number, the projections form a periodic sampling with a period smaller than the original pixel sampling. If the slope is not a rational number, then projections are not exactly periodic and the between-projection intervals are irregular.

of S with respect to c equal to zero. We obtain:

$$c = a\bar{x} + b\bar{y}, \tag{16.40}$$

where $\bar{x} = (\sum_{i=1}^{n} x_i)/n$ and $\bar{y} = (\sum_{i=1}^{n} y_i)/n$ are the means of x_i and y_i. Therefore, the least square line goes through the center of gravity of the given points. In order to determine a and b, we use the Lagrange multiplier λ to form a new cost function:

$$S_m = \sum_{i=1}^{n} (ax_i + by_i - c)^2 - \lambda(a^2 + b^2 - 1)$$

$$= \sum_{i=1}^{n} [a(x_i - \bar{x}) + b(y_i - \bar{y})]^2 - \lambda(a^2 + b^2 - 1).$$

Setting the first partial derivatives of S_m to zero, we have

$$\begin{bmatrix} \sum_{i=1}^{n}(x_i - \bar{x})^2 & \sum_{i=1}^{n}(x_i - \bar{x})(y_i - \bar{y}) \\ \sum_{i=1}^{n}(x_i - \bar{x})(y_i - \bar{y}) & \sum_{i=1}^{n}(y_i - \bar{y})^2 \end{bmatrix} \begin{bmatrix} a \\ b \end{bmatrix} = \lambda \begin{bmatrix} a \\ b \end{bmatrix}. \tag{16.41}$$

Therefore, $[a, b]^T$ is an eigenvector of the covariance matrix of (x_i, y_i), $i = 1, 2, 3, \ldots, n$. In general, there are two eigenvectors for the covariance matrix. The eigenvector that corresponds to the smaller eigenvalue is the desired solution for a and b. Note that the eigenvector has to be normalized, i.e., $a^2 + b^2 = 1$.

16.4 Problems

16.1 Given the four data points in Table 16.1, we want to find the straight line that best fits the four data points. (a) What is the least square solution if there is no error in x? (b) What is the least squares solution if both x and y have errors?

Table 16.1.

i	1	2	3	4
x_i	0.50	1.00	1.50	2.00
y_i	1.97	3.06	3.74	5.03

16.2 Given the four (r, g, b) and (X, Y, Z) pairs from a printer shown in Table 16.2, use the tetrahedral interpolation to interpolate the (r_p, g_p, b_p) input to the printer so that it will print the color $(X_p, Y_p, Z_p) = (46.6, 31.9, 41.9)$.

Table 16.2.

i	(r_i, g_i, b_i)	(X_i, Y_i, Z_i)
0	(115,104,107)	(45.0,30.0,40.0)
1	(125,104,107)	(49.0,32.0,43.0)
2	(125,114,107)	(48.0,34.0,42.0)
3	(125,104,117)	(47.0,33.0,44.0)

16.3 A 3×3 matrix M is used to transform camera (R,G,B) to CIE (X,Y,Z) under Illuminant D_{65} (chromaticity coordinates: $(x, y) = (0.3127, 0.3290)$), such that

$$\begin{bmatrix} X \\ Y \\ Z \end{bmatrix} = \begin{bmatrix} m_{11} & m_{12} & m_{13} \\ m_{21} & m_{22} & m_{23} \\ m_{31} & m_{32} & m_{33} \end{bmatrix} \begin{bmatrix} R \\ G \\ B \end{bmatrix}. \qquad (16.42)$$

If Y is normalized to 100 when $R = G = B = 255$ and all the neutrals $(R = G = B)$ are to be mapped to the chromaticity coordinates of D_{65}, then what is $m_{11} + m_{12} + m_{13}$?

17 Tone reproduction

17.1 Introduction

Images are often considered as records of the physical scenes that we have seen. Therefore, we wish to have images that reproduce the visual impressions of the original scenes as we remember them. Among the various attributes that contribute to the total visual impression, tone and color are two of the most important factors. Tone reproduction is the process of reproducing the visual brightness/lightness impression of the original scene in an image. Similarly, color reproduction refers to the process of reproducing the visual color impression. Although color perception involves brightness/lightness perception, the two topics will be discussed separately, with the implied, narrower definitions that tone reproduction deals with luminance perception and color reproduction chrominance perception. However, it should be understood that there are interactions and trade-offs between the two processes. The criteria and goals of tone reproduction vary from application to application, and we will mainly be interested in consumer imaging applications.

Since the success of a tone reproduction is finally judged by human observers, there are at least two separate systems involved in a tone reproduction task, i.e., the imaging system and the human visual system. Therefore, it is convenient to divide any tone reproduction into three processes: (1) the subjective process that specifies what a desired reproduction should be in terms of visual impression, (2) the psychophysical (translation) process that converts the perceptual criteria as specified in the subjective process into physically quantifiable criteria, and (3) the objective process that deals with calibrating and controlling image devices to achieve the desired reproduction in terms of physical quantities. It is arguable whether the first subjective process can be or should be separated from the second psychophysical (translation) process. In the existing literature, these two processes are in fact merged into one [470, 704, 706]. However, there are good expository reasons to separate them as we do here. The main reason is that visual impression relies on terms that are not easy to define, but seem to be intuitively clear to us. Therefore, it is very effective to be able to describe the tone reproduction criteria in those terms. The psychophysical process that is supposed to translate these meaningful perceptual terms into physically quantifiable criteria is a much more difficult task. If we separate the two processes, we can better evaluate the cause of the success or failure of the entire tone reproduction. A good example of such a practical use is as follows. When we say that one object appears to be brighter than another object the meaning is quite clear to everyone. Therefore, we can say that we would like to make the reproduced tone scale preserve the brightness of the scene as we see it. This criterion of reproducing the perceived brightness is clearly understandable to us, but to translate the visual impression of brightness into a physically quantifiable measure turns out to be extremely difficult. We can take the position that if we cannot quantify a term, then we should not use that term. Unfortunately, this would make most discussion even more difficult and not necessarily more precise. The question can also be raised as to whether we are hiding all the difficulties in the second process. The answer is that this is not true. For example, the subjective criterion could be changed to reproducing the perceived contrast, and the change would have a pronounced effect on the direction in which we should conduct the psychophysical process. This will be clear in our later discussion.

In the third objective process, we are interested in establishing the relation between the reproduced luminance and the original scene luminance. This relation is often expressed as a curve, called the tone reproduction curve (TRC) or the tone scale curve. For example, we would like to determine the image illuminance on the film or sensor as a function of the scene luminance, the output luminance of the display device as a function of the input image signal, and the illumination flare as a function of viewing luminance. The objective process is quantitative and can be experimentally measured and verified. Tone reproduction that aims at producing artistic expressions of specific moods or feelings is fascinating, but its goal is beyond our current understanding so we cannot deal with it effectively. Other applications, such as scientific imaging, have quite different tone reproduction objectives than that of consumer imaging, but the objective tone reproduction processes underlying all applications are very similar to each other.

In the discussion of tone reproduction, it is convenient to consider monochromatic images (such as black-and-white pictures) as the main subject of study. Tone reproduction of color images will be discussed in the context of color reproduction in the next chapter. Studies show that good tone reproduction for monochromatic images also applies to color images [427]. Although tone reproduction is the most important aspect of making a good image, it is rarely discussed in the digital image processing literature. For many people, the pixel values in a digital image are simply assumed to represent scene radiances at those pixel locations and they are often called the gray levels, implying that when the image is printed on a reflective medium, such as paper, the pixel values are to be printed as reflectance factors. However, a good tone reproduction is much more complicated than this simple intuition implies. First of all, the pixel values are rarely, if ever, proportional to scene radiances, because of the presence of camera flare or scanner flare. Secondly, scene radiances have a much wider dynamic range than most media can render, and a straight one-to-one linear reproduction of scene radiances on a medium is not only impossible, but also undesirable. The reason is that the absolute luminance level of the scene may not be reproducible in the medium, and, even when it is reproducible, it is not really desirable because highlights and shadows will be clipped, without visible details. Even in the very rare cases in which all scene luminances can be reproduced on the medium, it is often found that a straight one-to-one linear reproduction does not produce an image as well as we might think.

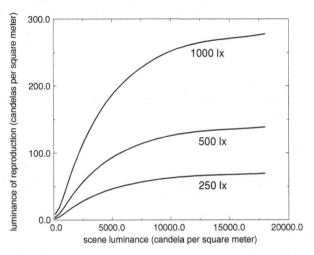

Figure 17.1. TRCs for a reflection print viewed under three different levels of illumination.

17.2 TRCs

We have defined the TRC as the curve that describes the relation between the reproduced luminance and the original scene luminance. Since every imaging system has its own spectral responsivity function, luminance as defined by the CIE luminous efficiency function is not always the most appropriate metric for this purpose. However, luminance is calculated with the human visual sensitivity and is thus quite appropriate for describing the visual impression of the tone reproduction. For this reason, luminance has always been used for this purpose. It should be understood that often the metrics used in a TRC are measured with system or instrument spectral responsivities. In those cases, the TRCs are related to luminances only in a proportional sense for a fixed spectral composition.

There are several ways that we can plot the TRC that relate the reproduced image luminance to the scene luminance. The most direct plot is to show the luminance of reproduction as a function of the scene luminance. Figure 17.1 shows the TRCs of a reflection print viewed under three different illumination levels. There are several drawbacks with TRCs plotted in this way. First, it requires many curves for a single reflection print, one for each illumination level. As we will see shortly, the appearance of a reflection print does not change much over a range of illumination, say, from 250 lx to 1000 lx. Therefore, it is not efficient to use the absolute luminances as the variables. For reflection prints or transparencies, it is more efficient to specify the reproduction luminance on a relative scale. The minimum density reproducible on a medium is often used as the reference. Similarly, the scene luminance is usually specified on a relative scale. For example, the perfect Lambertian surface (reference white) can be used as the reference. Second, the perceived brightness or lightness of an object is not linearly proportional to the luminance. The slope of the curve in a linear–linear plot does not give us information about the perceptual rate of change at any region on the luminance scale. Due to the wide acceptance of Weber's law, log luminance is most frequently used for the luminance scale. It is also well known that the slope in a log luminance vs.

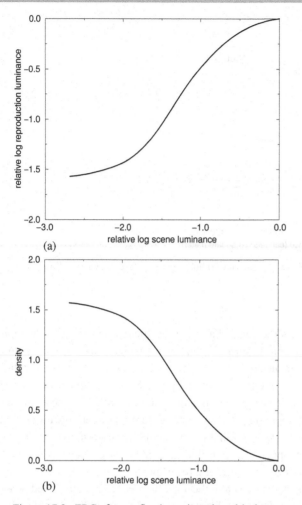

Figure 17.2. TRCs for a reflection print, plotted in log space: (a) the relative log luminance of the reproduction as a function of the relative log luminance of the scene; (b) the density of the reflection print as a function of the relative log luminance of the scene.

log luminance plot correlates very well with perceived contrast. Therefore, the log–log plot is, by far, the most widely-used way to plot the TRC. However, measurements on reproduced hard-copies are usually done with densitometers, and the reproduction luminance is expressed as a density. Here, we have to be aware of the fact that there are several densitometric standards. The one most frequently used for evaluating photographic reflection prints is the Status A density. In most photography or graphic art literature, the TRCs are plotted as density vs. relative log scene luminance. Figure 17.2 shows both types of log–log plot for the same reflection print as used in Fig. 17.1. Figure 17.2(a) is a log luminance vs. log luminance plot and Fig. 17.2(b) is a density vs. log luminance plot. In this case, we have assumed that the minimum density of the paper is 0. In general, the curve in Fig. 17.2(b) will be shifted up by the minimum density of the paper, usually on the order 0.05–0.1. The log–log plot not only looks quite different from the linear–linear plot, but also shows more information that is relevant to our image perception. The nearly straight line portion on the log–log curve (roughly from -1.6 to -1.0 on the x-axis) tells us that within this range of luminance the perceptual contrast is approximately constant. This range corresponds to a scene luminance range 500–2000 cd m^{-2} on the linear–linear plot, occupying only a small fraction of the range on the linear axis.

17.3   The concept of reference white

In our discussion of TRCs, we mentioned that it is useful to deal with relative log luminances, instead of absolute log luminances. In that context, we mentioned the concept of reference white and used it to calculate the relative quantities. For example, in viewing a reflection print, we often use the minimum density of the paper as the reference white. However, the concept is ambiguous in other situations. Some clarification is needed. In viewing the original scene, we mentioned that a perfect (100%) Lambertian reflector (called diffuse white) can be used as the reference white. This in itself is not sufficient because the angle between the reflector and the light source has to be specified too. Furthermore, the reflector may not be uniformly illuminated in every part that is visible to the camera. Obviously, natural scenes may be more complicated than we can define exhaustively. For the purpose of our future discussion, we will assume that there is a main subject in the image and the imaginary, perfect reflector has the same shape and spatial location as the main subject. If the illumination is not uniform, a subjective preference comes in as to how that subject should be produced. The "reference white" is similarly adjusted. For example, if the subject is half in the shade and half in the sun, and the preference is to produce the shaded part properly and let the sunlit part be too light, the reference white should be defined relative to the shaded part.

For viewing a projected transparency image in a darkened room, choosing a reference white is again problematic. If we choose the open-gate (meaning no slide in the projector) luminance of the screen as the reference white, specular highlight in the image cannot be rendered at all. Empirical tests show that the "reference white" in the scene should be produced somewhat darker than the open-gate luminance. Figure 17.3 shows an example of how the reference (diffuse) white of the scene is typically produced for a reflection print and for a transparency. In this example, the scene white is produced at about 0.2 above the minimum density (D_{min}) for the transparency and at about 0.1 above the minimum paper density for the reflection print. However, this placement of scene white is not necessarily optimum for all pictures. There is sufficient variation in the optimum placement that we should not take these numbers literally as recommendations. The inherent difficulty in defining the reference white is only part of the cause for this variation. Scene content, viewing illuminance, and the shape of the TRC also play a role here.

In summary, the concept of reference white is ambiguous for many applications. It can be defined only when the subject is a planar object, uniformly illuminated. In future discussion, the term should be understood with the ambiguity in mind. Whenever the main subject can be assumed to be a uniformly illuminated, planar object, the reference white

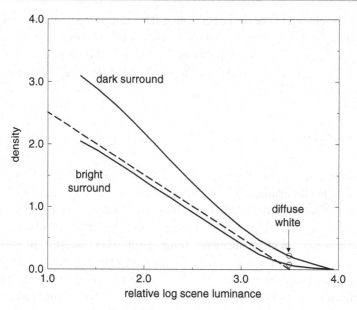

Figure 17.3. The average optimum TRCs for a reflection print (bright surround) and a transparency (dark surround) from empirical studies [706]. Note that the zero density point is the minimum density (D_{min}) reproducible for the intended medium. The diffuse white in both cases is reproduced at some density above D_{min}, so that specular highlight can be rendered with some visible contrast. The dashed line has a slope of 1.0.

can be defined. In other cases, quantitative analysis involving the use of a "reference white" can only be as exact as that term can be defined for the particular imaging condition under discussion.

17.4   Experimental studies of tone reproduction

The early studies on tone reproduction did not attempt to formulate what is to be achieved subjectively in the tone reproduction process. Instead, the experiments produced a large number of images, each through a different TRC, on reflection prints and projected transparencies. The procedure was to ask the observers to select the best reproduction of a given scene and then the corresponding TRC used to generate that picture was analyzed. Although it is not possible to derive truly optimum tone reproduction this way, these experiments were very successful in discovering some of the important factors in the tone reproduction process. Among them are scene content, luminance level, and viewing surround.

Two of these early experiments will be described here because the insights gained from their results are very helpful to our understanding of the dimension of the tone reproduction problem. The first experiment was done by Simonds [880] for reflection prints, and the second experiment by Clark [197] for transparencies. One of the key questions in the design of these experiments is how to systematically generate different TRCs that can be used to produce images for subjective evaluation. At that time, photographic film and paper were the main interests of the organizations where the research was done. It was discovered that the characteristic curves (density as a function of log exposure) of films and papers could be well described by a few (four or five) vectors derived from principal component analysis. This implied that, by properly choosing different films, papers, and processing variations, they could generate various tone reproductions for a given picture.

Simonds used four scenes for his study. Scene A was an indoor wedding portrait with a moderately complex background and its log luminance range was 2.58. Scenes B and C were close-up indoor portraits with uniform walls as the backgrounds, and the log luminance range was 2.20 for both scenes. Scene D was an outdoor picnic scene with direct sunlight and dark shadows, and its log luminance range was 2.70. The luminances of the scenes were measured and recorded by photographic photometry. Various (black-and-white) films, camera exposures, printer flares, (black-and-white) papers, and processings were used to reproduce these four scenes on reflection prints. The reflection densities of these prints were measured using a 45/0 geometry. The negatives were 5 in by 7 in and the prints were 8 in by 10 in. Scenes A, B, and C were printed on Polycontrast Paper with a semi-matte (G) surface. The prints for Scene D were printed on the Polycontrast Paper with a glossy (F) surface, having a higher maximum density than the semi-matte surface paper. Thirty experienced observers ranked the prints in order of subjective quality. The prints were viewed under a bank of fluorescent lights with the illuminance maintained at 861 lx. The mean rank of a print given by the observers was taken as its final quality measure. The mean rank numbers for a given reproduction were linearly transformed to a quality scale Q from 0 to 100, in which 100 means the optimum quality reproduced for that scene. It was found that approximately 10 units on this quality scale represent a quality change which would be discerned and similarly ranked by at least 85% of the observers.

Clark performed a similar experiment for projected transparencies (reversal films). He used only two scenes: Scene 1 was the same as Scene C in Simonds' study and Scene 2 was an outdoor sunlit scene with a brick house, trees, shrubs, a car, and a human subject. The transparencies were printed from 5 in by 7 in negatives by projection onto 3.25 in by 4 in projector slide plates. A wide variety of tone reproductions were generated by varying the exposure and processing, by the choice of the contrast grade of the plates, and by the use of a variety of positive masks. For Scene 1, several negatives were prepared with different negative materials and various levels of exposure and processing, so that more variations of tone reproduction could be obtained. The major difference between this experiment and that by Simonds is that the slides were viewed in a dark surround. The visual angle subtended by the projected image was 35° in diagonal, leaving plenty of peripheral areas dark. From an earlier work by Breneman [136], it was known that an image viewed with a dark surround (as in viewing slides) produces a very different visual impression from that of the same image viewed with a light surround (as in viewing reflection prints). In order to study the effect of the surround, Clark's experiment included a second part study in which the projected image was surrounded with a bright border about one-third of the width of the image. One other factor that was studied in the experiment was the effect of the luminance level of the projected image on its perceived quality. The following paragraphs summarize the main results from these and other experiments [427, 472, 704, 706].

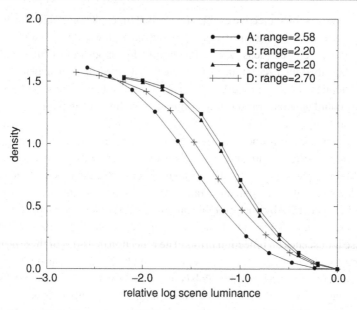

Figure 17.4. The optimum TRCs for the four scenes in Simonds' study on reflection prints.

17.4.1 *Best tone reproduction depends on scene contents*

The optimum TRCs for the four scenes studied by Simonds were different from each other, even for very similar scenes such as Scenes B and C. Figure 17.4 shows the four optimum TRCs as determined in Simonds' experiment. Before we analyze the results, we should notice that all four scenes have wider log luminance dynamic ranges (from 2.20 to 2.70) than those of the papers (from 1.5 to 1.6) used in the study. Therefore, certain parts of the scenes had to be rendered with lower than their original contrast. The question is: how would the observers prefer the highlight and shadow compressed in the tone reproduction? As can be seen in Fig. 17.4, all the preferred tonal compressions in highlights and shadows are gradual. None of the optimum curves showed any steep clipping or cut-off in the highlights and shadows. The other important point to observe is that, when the scene luminance range is larger, the preferred TRC has a smaller mid-tone slope. This means that the observers would rather reduce the reproduction contrast in order to squeeze and render more highlight and shadow detail visible, or the original scene contrast was too harsh due to lighting and the optimum reproduction should render it softer, or both. In all cases, the experimental results seem to indicate that a good tone reproduction should not lose too much highlight or shadow detail, and when loss of detail is not avoidable, the degradation has to be gradual.

Two other important observations can be made from these curves. (1) The same *relative* log scene luminance is not printed at the same reflection density on the print. This means that the maximum scene luminance is a very poor predictor of how light or dark the mid-tone should be printed. (2) All the optimum TRCs deviate from one-to-one reproduction of relative luminance. In fact they all lie below the 45° line through the origin.

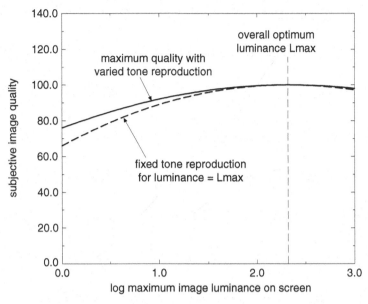

Figure 17.5. The optimum quality of the projected image as a function of the projector luminance for a given scene.

17.4.2 Best tone reproduction depends on luminance levels

Clark's experiment on varying the luminance level of the projected image gave us several very important results. Figure 17.5 summarizes these results. First, he showed that a given transparency (slide) when projected at a very dim luminance level appears to have low visual quality. As the luminance level of the projector is increased, the visual quality improves, until it reaches an optimum and then further increase of the projector luminance begins to degrade the visual quality (see the dashed curve in Fig. 17.5). This means that we should adjust the projector luminance for each slide in order to achieve its optimum visual quality. Second, he showed that of all the TRCs that were used to generate the various projected images from a given scene, there was an optimum projector luminance and film curve combination that gave the overall optimum image quality of that scene (see the solid curve in Fig. 17.5). This means that for a given viewing condition and a given scene, our visual system cannot continue to adapt to the various luminance levels and perceive the projected image with an optimum impression. There is a unique luminance level that is preferred for all possible reproductions of a given scene. However, this optimum luminance level is very broadly tuned, i.e., changing the luminance level by a factor of 2 either way from the optimum does not degrade the perceived image quality much.

17.4.3 Best tone reproduction depends on viewing surrounds

Viewing surrounds have a dramatic impact on how an image is perceived. For each different viewing surround, the optimum TRC of a given scene has to be changed. This is most

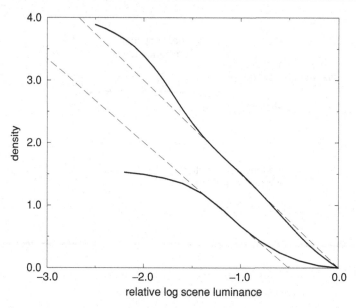

Figure 17.6. Comparison between the optimum TRCs for dark surround and light surround viewing conditions. The upper curve is for the dark viewing surround and the lower curve is for the light surround. The two dashed curves are straight lines with slopes equal to 1.5 (upper) and 1.34 (lower).

clearly seen by comparing the optimum TRCs of the same scene for the dark surround (as in the slide viewing condition) and for the light surround (as in the reflection print viewing condition). Scene C in Simonds' reflection print experiment is the same as Scene 1 in Clark's slide experiment. The optimum tone reproduction curves for these two viewing conditions, as determined by the observers, are shown in Fig. 17.6. The major conclusion is that the optimum slope (also called gamma) of the TRC for the dark surround viewing condition has to be much higher than that for the light surround viewing condition. On the average for many scenes, the optimum gamma is about 1.5 for dark surrounds and 1.0–1.2 for light surrounds [427, 706].

17.4.4 Best tone reproduction renders good black

In printing an image, if the dark area is printed too light, the image looks "smoky" or "foggy". Although the dark area may only occupy a small portion of the image, the "smoky" or "foggy" visual impression is of the entire image! Why should our visual impression (or interpretation) of an image be so dramatically affected by a small portion of the total image area? In most natural viewing conditions, there are always shadows. The illumination in the shadows is much weaker than that of the directly lighted areas. The illuminance ratio of highlight to shadow is often 2:1 or higher. The reflectance factor of a white-looking object is about 0.6 or higher and that of a black-looking object is about 0.06 or lower. Therefore, natural scenes almost always have a luminance range greater than 20:1. In fact, in a study by Jones and Condit [471], the mean luminance range (average in log luminance) of natural scenes was found to be 160:1. The luminance of a scene can be greatly reduced if smoke or fog is present. When an image is printed such that the darkest shadow has a density less than 1.3 (corresponding to a luminance range of less than 20:1), it often gives a visual impression of fog or flare. In digital printing, adjusting the TRC is an easy thing to do, but the shadow has to be rendered as a good black to produce a good image. This is a fairly consistent requirement in tone reproduction.

In an experiment to determine the best control of photographic printing, Jones and Nelson [472] reported that the majority of the negatives they used tended to produce the most preferred print when the minimum density of the negative (the darkest area in the scene) was printed on the shoulder of the D–$\log E$ curve of the paper (at a density of about 1.46–1.49, which is 0.1–0.07 less than the maximum density, $D_{max} = 1.56$, of the paper used in that experiment). Although we have to be cautious about this conclusion because the number of negatives they used was quite small (only 171), and because all the scenes used were front-lighted [472, p. 585], this finding seems to agree with our common experience in printing images. Another interesting aspect of this finding in the Jones and Nelson experiment was that this preference of having good black came at the price of losing highlight details in many of the prints, and yet most observers chose this trade-off very decisively! Those two authors suggested that in making the trade-off between losing the shadow details and losing the highlight details, the observers preferred to preserve the shadow details. In reality, the trade-off is more complicated than that. We also know that most people preferred faces to be reproduced at a density slightly lighter than that of the real facial skins. Typical Caucasian skin has a luminance factor about 37 and the preferred skin reproduction is at a luminance factor of 39. This preference of flesh color reproduction is an additional constraint on tone reproduction other than the trade-off to render the shadow or highlight details.

There is one minor question raised in Jones and Nelson's experiment: why was the preferred black at a density 0.1 less than the paper D_{max}? This question cannot be resolved because the spot size used in these density measurements was not given in the original publication and we can only suspect that there were image details finer than the spot size of the densitometer used. If the negative density was measured with a much smaller spot size (as small as the smallest visible details when the negative is printed on the paper), it is likely that it would have been preferred that the minimum negative density was printed at the paper D_{max}. But, this is not necessarily the right thing to do because a smaller spot will produce high noise in the reading and the absolute minimum density so measured may no longer be reliable.

17.5   Tone reproduction criteria

In the last section we described some of the early efforts to determine the optimum tone reproduction through experimental trials. Although these experiments gave us many useful insights, blind variation of TRCs cannot really give us the *true* optimum results and it would be too expensive to conduct such an exhaustive search experiment for every different viewing condition, and every different camera, flare, film, processing, and printer combination. For these reasons, several attempts have been made to come up with a good theoretical criterion for tone reproduction. Some of these efforts have been to define in perceptual terms what is to be achieved in the ideal tone reproduction. In the early days before digital printing was affordable, the effort was mainly on designing a "system-level" TRC, which could be used as the default tone scale for all images. This is still important in digital printing applications because a good system tone scale can serve as the baseline on which adjustment can be made digitally on an image-by-image basis. As digital printing becomes widely available today, subjective tone reproduction criteria have become much more complicated, because high-speed digital processing can now be used to manipulate spatial details pixel by pixel, which is equivalent to dodging and burning in a photographic dark room, only more efficient and precise. Tone reproduction can no longer be described by a single curve. For this reason, it is important for us to study the subjective criteria for tone reproduction at a conceptual level, rather than at an implementation level. Building upon the perceptual criteria, we can use spatial processing to implement whatever perceptual tone adjustment we desire.

17.5.1 Reproducing relative luminance

Intuitively, if we reproduce the luminance of the scene in the image, the image will look like the scene. However, this is usually not practical for reflection prints because the luminance of an outdoor scene is often much higher than any typical indoor light sources can provide. For projected images from transparencies, viewed in a dark surround, we also found that reproducing the absolute scene luminance does not produce the best visual quality. This, as we will see shortly, is due to the difference in the state of adaptation in our visual system.

For tone reproduction on reflection prints, experiments showed that if we reproduce the *relative* luminance of the scene, the images will look reasonably good, on average. Since reflection prints are viewed in an illuminated surround, this finding seems to imply two things: (1) Our visual system can adapt to different levels of luminance quite well and reproducing the *relative* luminance seems to reproduce the same visual impression. (2) The images as seen on reflection prints are perceived as two-dimensional planar objects, but the visual judgment of reproduction quality does not seem to be affected by this aware-ness. However, these two statements are true only in a limited range. When the luminance difference between the scene and the reproduction is less than a factor of 50 or so, our visual system can adapt well. Beyond that, our visual adaptation does not compensate for the luminance difference as effectively and the relative luminance reproduction criterion no longer works well. Also, when the scene is seen in its full three-dimensional structure, our visual perception can discount the illumination nonuniformity better than when our eyes are looking at a two-dimensional photographic print [285]. In addition, we also mentioned that the relative luminance criterion does not work when the viewing surround is dark. Furthermore, this simple criterion applies mostly to the mid-tone. It does not tell us how to treat the highlights and the shadows in the images. For all these reasons, reproducing relative luminance as a criterion in tone reproduction has been largely replaced by other more comprehensive criteria.

17.5.2 Reproducing relative brightness

One of the most influential criteria ever proposed for subjective tone reproduction is that the relative visual brightness of the scene should be reproduced in the reproduction [76, 77, 704, 706]. The key to implementing this criterion is, of course, to determine the perceived brightness as a function of the luminance for all viewing conditions. This difficult experiment was carefully completed by Bartleson and Breneman in 1967 [75]. This brightness function can be well described by the following equation:

$$\log B = 1.967 + 0.1401(\log L) - \gamma \left(\frac{L}{3.183}\right)^d, \tag{17.1}$$

where $\gamma = 0.99 + 0.318(L_w f)^{0.25}$, $d = -0.0521 - 0.0427(L_w f)^{0.093}$, L_w is the luminance of the scene white in candelas per square meter, f is 1.0 for light surround and 0.1 for dark surround, L is the luminance of a scene element in candelas per square meter, and B is the brightness in subjective units of an arbitrary size. If we examine the above equation, we find that the model was intended for the prediction of brightness under "typical" imaging viewing conditions and not for general-purpose modeling of brightness perception. First, the field size of the image is not a parameter of the equation. Second, the parameter f is an empirical factor and there is no algorithm to calculate its proper value for any given condition. Third, simultaneous contrast cannot be predicted, because the scene structure is not explicitly given as a factor. In spite of these deficiencies, this was the first comprehensive, empirical model derived from complex fields and under typical image viewing conditions, and as such it was extremely useful for imaging applications. Figure 17.7 shows the ideal TRCs that reproduce the relative brightness of the scene on the reflection print and on the transparency for their intended viewing conditions. The most striking feature of Fig. 17.7 is that both curves are nearly straight lines. Our visual system can adapt to the large luminance change from 5000 cd m^{-2} to 300 cd m^{-2} without disturbing our visual perception of the world. This is one of the main reasons why image reproduction is possible at all. Practices in photographic tone reproduction also confirm this finding [146]. According to the Bartleson and Breneman brightness model, the slope for the reflection print should be between 1.1 and 1.2, while that for the transparency (and motion pictures) should be between 1.4 and 1.5. These slopes agree with other experimental results fairly well [76, 197, 248, 706]. Furthermore, the model predicted the optimum tone reproduction at the optimum luminance in Clark's experiments fairly well. However, for luminance levels other than the optimum, the predictions deviate from the experimental data significantly [197, p. 313].

The Bartleson and Breneman brightness model also predicted the optimum luminance level for projected transparency images. In Clark's experiment [197], it was shown that the image quality increases as the projector luminance is increased until an overall optimum luminance is reached. Bartleson and Breneman's brightness model (Eq. (17.1)) showed that, at this overall optimum luminance, the *absolute* brightness is reproduced, whereas in the suboptimum reproduction only the *relative* brightness is reproduced [76, p. 258].

Much research has been done in the last 20 years on color appearance models [292]. Several other brightness models have been proposed. These new models are slightly more specific about visual field size and much more specific about chromatic adaptation.

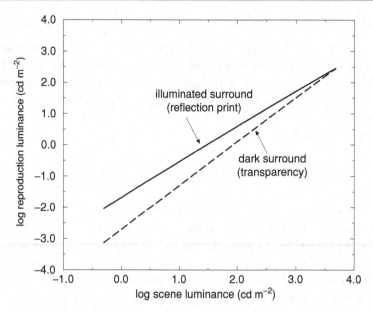

Figure 17.7. Ideal TRCs that reproduce the relative brightness of the scene. The brightness is calculated according to the Bartleson–Breneman brightness model. The luminance of the scene reference
white is $5000 \, cd \, m^{-2}$ and the luminance of the reference white in the reproduction is $300 \, cd \, m^{-2}$. The
solid curve is for the illuminated surround (reflection print viewing condition) and the dashed curve
is for the dark surround (transparency viewing condition). The slope of the solid curve is between 1.1
and 1.2, while that of the dashed curve is between 1.40 and 1.5.

Therefore, we can also use these new brightness models to derive the TRCs. The general
effect of the viewing surround on brightness perception is similar to that of the Bartleson
and Breneman model, and therefore we will not discuss this further here.

Relative brightness as a subjective reproduction criterion is incomplete for several reasons, two of which are: (1) The display media have limited dynamic range and, therefore,
cannot reproduce the relative brightness as required by the criterion. The criterion gives
no guidance as to how the highlight and shadow brightness should be compressed. (2) The
brightness model relies on the "reference white" as the anchor point. The criterion does not
tell us at what density the "reference white" should be reproduced. For reflection prints, it
seems that the paper white can be used as the "reference white". However, doing so will
leave no room for printing the specular highlight, which is brighter than white. Experiments
show that the reference white of the scene should be printed somewhat darker than the paper
white to produce optimum image quality.

17.5.3 Reproducing visual contrast

The above two criteria attempt to reproduce the visual impression as a function of the
scene luminance. The implicit assumption is that the luminance is the only variable and
the scene content was not considered. Of course, this assumption is well known to be
false. The assumption was made for practical reasons because the immediate concern was

the "system" tone reproduction, not the individual images. With the advent of high-speed computing, we may ask if there are other tone reproduction criteria that are more general and more desirable. One of the well-known properties of our visual system is that our perception is correlated more with the contrast signals than with the image irradiance signals. It is the difference between spatially neighboring elements that determines our perception, not the absolute luminances at those elements. If the luminance of each image point is increased by a factor of 10, the image will still look about the same. We know this is more or less true over a limited luminance range. The idea of "reproducing the visual contrast of the scene on the image" is thus a very reasonable tone reproduction criterion. The difficulty is in the implementation.

There are many issues to be addressed in carrying out such a tone reproduction process. First, how do we define the visual contrast of a scene? Second, how does the perceived contrast change with viewing conditions, such as luminance level and surround? Third, how is the quality of the reproduction affected by the unavoidable distortion in contrast reproduction? In spite of these difficulties, early attempts to achieve such a tone reproduction objective seem to show encouraging results [751]. This is an area of active research.

17.5.4 Reproducing maximum visible details

For certain applications, the goal of the tone reproduction is to render the maximum amount of image detail as visible as possible. Strictly, this goal is beyond the scope of our interest here. However, from this goal comes a whole class of tone reproduction methods, called histogram modification. Among their numerous variations, some do produce images of relatively good aesthetic quality. It is likely that reproducing visible details does indeed improve image quality in some way, even though the criterion by itself does not attempt to reproduce the visual impression of what we see in the scene.

None of the tone reproduction criteria we have discussed so far teaches us how to handle images that have a much larger dynamic range than can be rendered on the display media. Most histogram modification methods deal with this problem by allocating the available output dynamic range according to the computed image histogram. Therefore a complete TRC (not just the mid-tone) can be computed. This is one of the main advantages of histogram modification methods and one of the reasons we want to study some of these methods.

As we mentioned before, early experiments showed that the best TRC is scene-dependent. This conclusion is both obvious and surprising. It is obvious because every image has its special content that requires emphasis through different tonal adjustments, and therefore its best TRC is different from that for other images. However, it is also surprising in the sense of what happens if one takes many images of the same scene, but each differs from the next one by a small fraction of the total image area. Let us assume that the lighting does not change during the time. Out of this set, there may be a number of images that have quite different fields of view. If a particular TRC works very well for one of the images, should we not expect that it will also work well for others in this set of images? Our practical experience tells us that the answer is yes, unless the fields of view are illuminated very differently. This agrees with what a subjective criterion (such as reproducing the relative brightness) would predict. Let us express it in a different way. We know that the best tone reproduction is scene-dependent, but we also know that this dependence is related, to a large extent, to the lighting and, to a much smaller degree, to the objects present in the scene. This is why a large number of the pictures taken by consumers are reproduced very well by the fixed system tone reproduction process that exists in the current photographic system. The scenes that are not handled well are mostly those with extreme lighting conditions, such as harsh flash and backlit scenes. This is an important point to keep in mind when we review the various methods of histogram modification. Another thing worth pointing out is that one need not constrain oneself to the use of histogram modification for deriving a tone transformation curve. A simple and effective way to produce a good tone curve for an input image is to extract some histogram features and use those features to adjust the parameters that control the shape of the tone curve [407].

There are two key issues in histogram modification methods: (1) how to sample the image so that the resulting histogram represents more directly what we want to measure; and (2) how to modify the histogram so that the resulting tone reproduction will render the image in the way we desire. Obviously, sampling every pixel in a digital image to form the histogram will make the histogram too sensitive to the scene objects and not sensitive enough to the scene lighting. The best example is an image in which a human subject is standing in front of a uniform wall. The histogram is dominated by the pixels of the wall and almost no useful feature about the scene lighting can be extracted from the histogram. This is one of the main reasons why histogram equalization as originally proposed does not work in general.

One of the new ideas in histogram modification methods is the realization that the input image has to be sampled intelligently to avoid the excessive bias introduced by irrelevant pixels. One of the early attempts was to sample a pixel only when it is sufficiently different from its neighbors in a raster scan order [421]. Other sampling schemes use Laplacian or edge operators [16, 180, 671, 735]. These methods attempt to derive a histogram that represents the log scene luminance distribution of the modulated parts of an image. It is known from experiments on stabilized retinal images that edges are important in our visual perception. Therefore, the luminance histogram of the edges in an image represents a simple extraction of what our visual system sees. From an argument based on the central limit theorem in statistics [16, 790], we can expect that the log scene luminance histograms tend to be normally distributed. Therefore, it is claimed that if a TRC is constructed to transform the input edge histogram into a Gaussian distribution, the image will look esthetically pleasing [16, 180, 671, 735]. One may argue that, since the Gaussian distribution is only a statistical tendency, it is not reasonable to expect that every individual image should have a Gaussian histogram for its edge pixels. Based on thinking along those lines, a flexible algorithm was proposed that modifies the shape of the output target histogram as a function of the input histogram [574]. It seems to produce reasonably good results for most images.

Another variation of histogram modification is to measure the amount of image modulation activity present in an image and form an image activity histogram as a function of the digital code value in the image. The image activity histogram is then used to construct the TRC for that image [572, 576]. The image activity measures can be based on the number of level-crossings, the image gradient, the image Laplacian, or the number of neighboring pixels that have similar gray levels. The focus of attention in this type of approach has shifted from measuring how many pixels have a certain property to measuring how much image activity is present in the image at what tonal range. This shift in attention represents an attempt to construct a histogram that is directly coupled to the main objective of reproducing image details.

17.5.5 Preferred tone reproduction

Black-and-white images produced by professional photographers are often quite striking to look at. The tone reproduction of these images does not seem to follow any of the criteria discussed above. Highlights and shadows are sometimes exaggerated to make the main subject stand out in sharp contrast with the rest of the background, or sometimes softened to express vague or misty impressions. Most often these tonal manipulations are spatially varying, depending on the artistic intent of the images. Although we may not be able to achieve the same artistic expression with an automatic digital image processing algorithm, it is still quite valuable to study how the masters render nature in such magnificent luminance variations that are so, mathematically speaking, unnatural. Perhaps we simply have not yet understood the essence of the nature of our perception that makes those images so touching or so striking.

17.6 Density balance in tone reproduction

The term *density balance* refers to adjusting the overall brightness of a reproduced image. In traditional photographic applications, both reflection prints and transparencies are measured in density, and therefore the brightness adjustment is done by changing the density in the reproductions. For this reason, the term density balance is used for this manipulation. According to our definition of tone reproduction, density balance is part of the tone reproduction process. In a traditional negative–positive photographic system, the shape of the system TRC is fixed. The only variable under standard processing and printing was in exposing the image on the negative film onto the photographic paper. Here, the exposure can be adjusted to make the final image look brighter or darker. The density balance operation is thus also called the printer exposure control. In digital printing, the density balance can occur any time before the digital image is sent to a digital (inkjet, thermal, or laser) printer. If the digital image is in log exposure metric, the density balance is accomplished by simply adding or subtracting a number from every pixel of the image. If the digital image is in a linear exposure metric, a multiplication or division has to be performed. The density balance operation is equivalent to increasing/decreasing the exposure time of the camera or increasing/decreasing the light source intensity in the original scene, both being multiplicative operations in linear luminance metric.

In consumer imaging applications, thousands of prints are made every hour by a photofinishing machine. Density balance has to be performed automatically for each image. Computation of the optimum density balance is the single most important factor in the print quality of a well-exposed negative.

17.7 Tone reproduction processes

Having discussed various tone reproduction criteria, we are now ready to study the tone reproduction process, in which the TRC of an imaging system is derived. Let us take a published case study [573] as an example. In this application, the goal is to derive good TRCs for computed radiography. This example is simpler than the consumer photographic system, but contains all the key elements of a tone reproduction process. Therefore, we will use it to illustrate how we go about designing tone reproduction curves.[1]

The absorption and scattering of x-rays produces a shadow image of the internal structures of an object. This shadow image represents the x-ray transmittances through the object. The mathematical mapping of this invisible x-ray transmittance to the visible film density is called the tone scale of the radiographic system. Since soon after their discovery by Roentgen in 1895, x-rays have been used as a tool for medical diagnosis. Until the 1990s, photographic films have been the dominant sensing (direct, or indirect from phosphor screen) and display media. The characteristic curves of the combined screen/film systems thus determine the tone scale mapping for diagnostic radiography. In computed radiography, an x-ray transmittance image is recorded on a phosphor screen and then a laser scanning system is used to read out the exposure signals which are converted into a digital image. The digital image values are often calibrated so that they are proportional to log exposures of the x-rays on the phosphor screen. In order to view the image, the digital image is often printed on a radiographic film. The film writer is often calibrated in film density. The question is: what is the optimal mapping from the digital image value (in log exposure) to the film density? This is similar to the question in consumer imaging where the relative scene log exposure is mapped to paper density on the reflection print.

As we discussed at the beginning of the chapter, there are three components in a typical tone reproduction process: (1) the subjective criteria that specify a desired reproduction in terms of visual impression, (2) the psychophysical model that translates the perceptual criteria into physically quantifiable criteria, and (3) the objective process that deals with calibrating and controlling image devices to achieve the desired reproduction in terms of physical quantities. Let us discuss these three components one at a time.

The first question is: what is the objective of the TRC? A simple answer for diagnostic radiography is that we wish to optimize the chance for a radiologist to visually detect a tumor. If the TRC is not designed well, the tumor may be more difficult to see in a darker area than in a lighter area, or the reverse. Therefore, a logical objective is to make a tumor equally visible independent of the density of its background. To a first-order approximation, equal thickness increments of a homogeneous object correspond to equal log exposure differences. A given object in the path of x-ray beams will absorb a certain percentage of the x-ray energy independently of what is in front of or behind it. That means that an object (say, a tumor) will roughly create a certain log exposure difference in the image no matter what density the surrounding area has. (This, of course, is only approximately true, because of the scattering and the polychromatic nature of the x-ray source.) Based on this objective, Van Metter [573]

---

[1]   This section is a shortened and modified version of a paper [573] published in *Proceedings of SPIE*, Volume 3036. Readers interested in more details should read the paper.

proposed that the tone reproduction criterion is to produce equal brightness difference for equal log exposure difference.

The second question is: what is the physical correlate of visual brightness? There are many brightness models that we can use to answer this question. However, x-ray image viewing conditions are somewhat different from other image viewing conditions, such as for movies, TVs, or transparencies. It is necessary to verify the performance of each model for such viewing conditions. Seven brightness models and their parametric variations were tested: (1) Hunt's color-appearance model [432], (2) CIELAB L^* [794], (3) Bartleson and Breneman's model [75], (4) the Michaelis–Menten function with a small local support [851], (5) the Michaelis–Menten function with one global adaptation parameter [718], (6) power laws [80, 117, 903], and (7) the logarithmic function (the Weber–Fechner law [906]). Although a number of the models produced reasonable uniformity in brightness contrast, none of them produced truly equal brightness differences across the entire gray scale. The experimental results show that:

1. The logarithmic function and the linear functions are clearly not good, i.e., equal-density or equal-luminance differences do not correspond to equal-brightness differences. For the logarithmic function, the brightness increment is too small at the dark end and too large at the light end. This is the opposite of the linear function: equal-luminance increments produce too small a brightness increment at the light end and too large a brightness increment at the dark end.

2. The power law, $B = L^p - c$, where L is the luminance and B is the brightness, seems to give a fairly uniform brightness scale when p is between 0.2 and 0.3.

3. With proper choice of parameters, Hunt's model and Bartleson and Breneman's model also produce very respectable uniform gray scales, comparable to that from the power law.

4. The Michaelis–Menten function characterizes the rate of biochemical reaction when an enzyme is involved [326, 658, 917]. It also describes very well the physiological response of primate cones [978] and the psychophysical response of human brightness perception [409, 432, 718]. The Michaelis–Menten (or Hill) function

$$B = \frac{B_{\mathrm{m}}L^n}{L^n + L_0^n},$$ (17.2)

where B is the perceived brightness, B_{m} is a scale factor, L is the luminance of the object, and the Hill coefficient $n = 0.7$ seems to give the best uniform gray scale for this particular application. Let L_{a} be the adapting luminance (cd m^{-2}) of the visual field, L_0 can be calculated as

$$L_0 = 12.6 \times L_{\mathrm{a}}^{0.63} + 1.083 \times 10^{-5}.$$ (17.3)

Let L_{w} be the luminance of the reference white (the minimum density area of the x-ray film). Hunt [432] suggested that $L_{\mathrm{a}} = 0.2 \times L_{\mathrm{w}}$.

Among all the brightness models tested, the Michaelis–Menten function (Eq. (17.2)) performs best for the x-ray image viewing applications. Therefore, we will choose it as the brightness model.

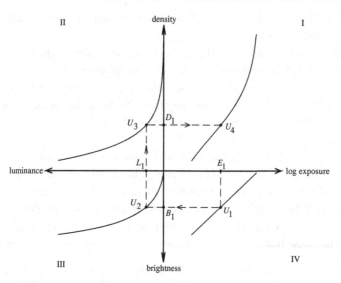

Figure 17.8. An example of a graphic method of deriving a TRC for an x-ray film system. The tone reproduction objective in this system is to produce equal-brightness difference for equal-log-exposure difference.

The third question is: how is the image luminance related to the film density? For x-ray image viewing, the luminance of an image area, L, is related to the film density, D, by

$$L = S \times 10^{-D}, \tag{17.4}$$

where S is the view-box luminance (about 2200–3200 cd m^{-2}).

Having answered all three questions, we can now proceed to complete the entire tone reproduction process. By convention, a tone scale curve is a curve that shows film density, D, as a function of log exposure, log H (see quadrant I in Figure 17.8). If equal log-exposure difference is to be reproduced as equal brightness difference, we can express their relation as

$$B = a \log H + b. \tag{17.5}$$

The parameter a controls the contrast (or gamma) of the tone scale and the parameter b controls the exposure or speed of the film. From the brightness model (Eq. (17.2)) and Eqs. (17.4) and (17.5), we can construct the ideal tone scale curve for any given contrast a and speed b. Figure 17.8 shows an example of such a construction. The first quadrant shows the tone scale curve to be constructed. Quadrant II shows the relationship between the film density and the luminance of an image area as described by Eq. (17.4). Quadrant III shows the relation between luminance and perceived brightness as described by the Michaelis–Menten function (Eq. (17.2)). Quadrant IV shows the linear relation (Eq. (17.5)) as required to achieve Van Metter's objective. A given exposure E_1 defines a point U_1 on the brightness vs. log exposure curve, which in turn defines a brightness point B_1. Point B_1 defines point U_2 on the luminance vs. brightness curve. This in turn defines a luminance point L_1. Point L_1 then defines point U_3 on the luminance vs. density curve. Point U_3 defines a density

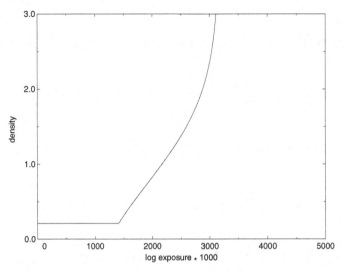

Figure 17.9. An example of a visually optimized tone scale curve.

point D_1. Given density point D_1 at exposure point E_1, a point U_4 is completely defined on the tone scale curve. In a similar fashion, the other points on the tone scale curve can be constructed.

Figure 17.9 shows an example of such a visually optimized tone scale curve. The sharp discontinuities at the toe ($D_{min} = 0.21$) and the shoulder ($D_{max} = 3.0$) are due to the limitations of the display medium (in this case, a film with an assumed minimum density of 0.21 and an assumed maximum density of 3.0). This could create two problems: (1) loss of details in the highlight or shadow because of the sharp truncation, and (2) sensitivity to exposure error. Gentle roll-offs in the toe and shoulder are needed to produce a more pleasing image. Such roll-offs can be constructed from tails of conventional film curves. Green and Saunders described such a family of curves by the following logistic type of function [917, p. 263]:

$$D = D_{min} + \frac{D_{max} - D_{min}}{1 + 10^{\beta(\log H_0 - \log H)}}. \tag{17.6}$$

We can use the above function to generate a smooth toe and a smooth shoulder, and paste them on the visual aim curve in Fig. 17.9 to produce a smooth curve shown in curve (b) of Fig. 17.10, so that the overall TRC will have a gentle roll-off in the shadow and in the highlight, while the mid-tone region is the visually optimized tone curve. In order to produce a smooth tone scale curve, we require that the visual tone scale curve and the Green–Saunders curve be continuous in the first derivative. This is achieved through the following replacement calculation.

Let $D = V(\log H)$ be the visually optimized tone scale curve as determined by Eqs. (17.2), (17.4), and (17.5). Let $D = A(\log H)$ be the aim tone scale curve to be constructed from $D = V(\log H)$ by rolling off the toe and the shoulder.

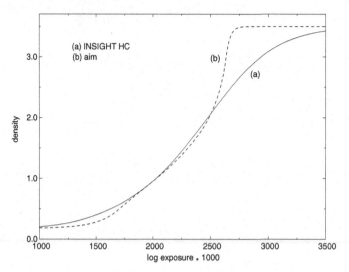

Figure 17.10. Comparison between a visually optimized tone scale curve (b) and the KODAK INSIGHT HC Thoracic Imaging Screen/Film tone scale (a).

Let D_t be the density where $D = A(\log H)$ starts to deviate from the ideal curve, $D = V(\log H)$, at the toe, and G_t be the slope at $D = D_t$:

$$G_t = \left.\frac{dA}{d\log H}\right|_{D=D_t} = \left.\frac{dV}{d\log H}\right|_{D=D_t}. \tag{17.7}$$

Since $D = V(\log H)$ can be numerically generated from Eqs. (17.2), (17.4), and (17.5), G_t can be numerically calculated as well.

Letting $y = 10^{\beta(\log H_0 - \log H)}$, the Green–Saunders equation can be written as

$$D - D_{\min} = \frac{D_{\max} - D_{\min}}{1 + y}. \tag{17.8}$$

Its derivative is

$$\frac{dD}{d\log H} = \frac{(D_{\max} - D_{\min})(\ln 10)\beta y}{(1 + y)^2}. \tag{17.9}$$

Given $D = D_t$, we can solve for y_t from Eq. (17.8):

$$y_t = \frac{D_{\max} - D_{\min}}{D_t - D_{\min}} - 1. \tag{17.10}$$

Knowing G_t and y_t, we can solve for β from Eq. (17.9):

$$\beta = \frac{G_t(1 + y_t)^2}{(D_{\max} - D_{\min})(\ln 10)y_t}. \tag{17.11}$$

Having determined y_t and β, the only unknown left is log H_0, which can be found from:

$$\log H_0 = \log H_t + (\log y_t)/\beta, \tag{17.12}$$

where log H_t is the log exposure that maps to D_t when $D = V(\log H)$ is generated.

Let D_s be the density where $D = A(\log H)$ starts to deviate from the ideal curve, $D = V(\log H)$, at the shoulder, and G_s be the slope at $D = D_s$. The above procedure can also be applied to generate a roll-off shoulder with the Green–Saunders equation.

Figure 17.10 shows an example of an aim tone scale curve generated to match the slope and exposure of the KODAK INSIGHT HC Thoracic Imaging Screen/Film tone scale curve at density 0.9. It can be seen that a higher contrast in the highlight and the shadow is desirable for improving this screen/film system. However, this comes at the price of reducing the exposure latitude of the film.

17.8 Flare correction

In our study of the tone reproduction process for computed radiography, we did not consider the effect of viewing flare because we assumed that the x-ray images are viewed in a dark room. The major effect of viewing flare is to reduce the perceptual contrast in the dark areas in an image, similarly to the effect of camera flare (imaging flare). Since a system tone scale curve cannot correct for localized flare, the best one can do is to assume a uniform flare model and correct for the average effect. For example, let us assume that the ideal camera exposure at a pixel without flare is H and the amount of flare is H_f, then the actual camera exposure $H' = H + H_f$. In a linear–linear plot, the effect of flare is simply an offset. However, we know that a log–log plot is perceptually more meaningful. Therefore, the effect of flare is better shown in a log–log plot as in Figure 17.11. This clearly shows that the slope in the dark areas of an image is greatly reduced, and so is the perceived contrast. Compensation for the imaging flare in a tone reproduction process can be done simply by

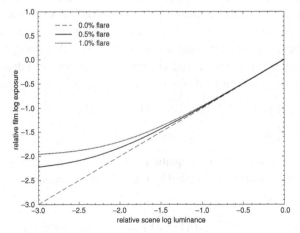

Figure 17.11. The effect of camera flare in a log–log plot. The percentage flare is relative to the reference white at log luminance $= 0$.

relating the real exposure H' to the ideal exposure H, i.e., $H = H' - H_f$. Compensation for the viewing flare is performed at the output end. If the intended output image luminance is L and the viewing flare is L_f, the actual luminance the system should produce is $L' = L - L_f$, so that when the image is viewed, the viewing flare L_f will be added to L' to produce the intended luminance L.

17.9 Gamma correction

The tone scale in digital images that are intended for viewing on a CRT monitor has to be predistorted to compensate for the nonlinear tone reproduction characteristics of a CRT monitor. This process is called gamma correction. The CRT TRC is well described by a power function: $L = A \cdot (V + B)^\gamma$, where L is the luminance on the monitor screen, V is the input value to the monitor (usually normalized to 1 at the peak input), and A and B are two constants. The value of γ varies from monitor to monitor, but is around 2.0–3.0. The standard γ value is assumed to be 2.22 in most international standards. If a monitor is well set up and carefully adjusted, B is usually set to zero, i.e.,

$$L = A \cdot (V)^\gamma = A \cdot V^{2.22}. \tag{17.13}$$

The gamma correction curve is therefore the inverse function of the nonlinear TRC of the CRT monitor, i.e.,

$$V = Y^{1/\gamma} = Y^{0.45}, \tag{17.14}$$

where Y is the image illuminance, which is linearly proportional to scene luminance. With such a gamma correction, Eqs. (17.13) and (17.14) in combination give $L = A \cdot Y$. Although the relative scene luminance is reproduced on the CRT screen, the contrast of the resulting images often appears too low and the colors too dull. There are three possible causes: (1) camera flare, (2) viewing flare, and (3) dim viewing surrounds. In order to compensate for flares, dark areas have to be driven darker than Eq. (17.14) would render them. In order to compensate for dim viewing surrounds, the overall contrast has to be raised. There are several ways to design a better gamma correction curve to accomplish these two goals. One of the most popular methods is to use a linear segment in conjunction with the offset gamma correction. Such a family of curves can be expressed as:

$$V = \begin{cases} (1+\alpha)Y^n - \alpha & \text{for } 1.0 \geq Y \geq Y_0 \\ \beta Y & \text{for } Y_0 > Y \geq 0.0 \end{cases}, \tag{17.15}$$

where α and β are determined so that the two equations have the same first derivative at Y_0 where they meet. The three parameters are related by the following relations:

$$Y_0 = \left[\frac{\alpha}{(1-n)(1+\alpha)} \right]^{1/n}, \tag{17.16}$$

$$\beta = n(1+\alpha)Y_0^{n-1}. \tag{17.17}$$

Empirical evidence shows that this family of functions produces very-high-quality images when α is properly chosen to compensate for the camera flare, viewing flare, and viewing surrounds. The only drawback is that flare compensation and contrast adjustment are coupled in this function. If we want to keep the same highlight contrast and only darken the shadow, another family of curves can be used:

$$V = \begin{cases} Y^n & \text{for } 1.0 \geq Y \geq Y_0 \\ a Y^3 + b Y^2 + c Y & \text{for } Y_0 > Y \geq 0.0 \end{cases}, \tag{17.18}$$

where

$$a = \frac{c Y_0 + (n-2) Y_0^n}{Y_0^3}, \tag{17.19}$$

$$b = \frac{Y_0^n - c Y_0 - a Y_0^3}{Y_0^2}. \tag{17.20}$$

Again, the two curve segments have the same first derivative at Y_0 where they intersect with each other. There are two degrees of freedom here. We can choose a desired slope, c, at the origin and the point of intersection Y_0. These two degrees of freedom are very useful because c also controls the quantization interval in the shadow region, as defined by Y_0. For example, if a gamma correction table is provided to convert an eight-bit input signal to an eight-bit output signal, a straight implementation of Eq. (17.14) will map input code 0 to output code 0, and input code 1 to output code 21, leaving the first 20 code values unused in the output. If we use $c = 6$ and $Y_0 = 0.12$ in Eq. (17.18), input value 1 will be mapped to 6, and the two curves only differ below Y_0. In fact, Eq. (17.18) often produces better images because it compensates camera flare in the dark area. Equation (17.18) can also be used to adjust the overall contrast by choosing a higher n value. Compared with Eq. (17.15), the advantage of using Eq. (17.18) is that the contrast adjustment and flare compensation can be explicitly controlled. The drawback of this family of functions is that the cubic polynomial can produce a nonmonotonic curve and the final curve should be visually examined to see if it is satisfactory.

The viewing conditions for television are also quite unique in that the room is often dim, but not completely dark. Therefore, some ambient flare is always present. The luminance of typical receivers is around 70–200 cd m^{-2}. From our discussions so far, we should be able to develop a good TRC for television. We can take "reproducing the relative brightness" as the objective and use the Bartleson–Breneman brightness model to derive the desired TRC. It is also important to compensate for the viewing flare. By going through this exercise, we will find that the resulting tone scale curve is not too far from the standard curves adopted by various television systems. Let us look at one example of such standards. The international standard (ITU-R BT.709-2) for encoding HDTV luminance channel is specified by the following:

$$V = \begin{cases} 1.099 \, Y^{0.45} - 0.099 & \text{for } 1.0 \geq Y \geq 0.018 \\ 4.50 Y & \text{for } 0.018 > Y \geq 0.0 \end{cases}, \tag{17.21}$$

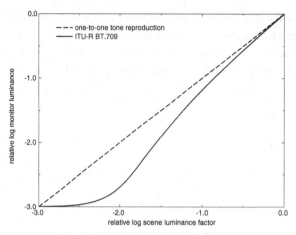

Figure 17.12. The TRC used in the HDTV luminance channel as specified by the international standard (ITU-R BT.709).

If we assume that the video signal is displayed on a CRT monitor with a gamma of 2.22 and a viewing flare of 0.1%, the TRC for the HDTV images can be derived. The result is shown in Figure 17.12. From the figure, it is obvious that the curve has a slope much higher than 1, as is required by the Bartleson–Breneman brightness model.

17.10 Problems

17.1 A scene is reproduced as a reflection print (to be viewed in a light surround) and a transparency (to be viewed in a dark surround). The minimum density of the paper is 0.1 and that of the transparency is 0.2. If the objective of the tone reproduction is to reproduce the relative brightness, we learned from the Bartleson–Breneman brightness model that the reflection print should have a gamma of 1.0 and the transparency should have a gamma of 1.5. We will assume that there is no camera flare, that the TRCs are straight lines, and that the minimum density of each medium serves as the reference white.

(a) If there is no viewing flare and given that an object in the scene is reproduced at density 1.8 on the reflection print, at what density should it be reproduced on the transparency?

(b) Let us assume that the amount of viewing flare is 1% of the reference white. At what density should the object in (a) be printed on the reflection print?

(Hint: The viewing flare is added to whatever light is reflected from the print. The density of a reflection print is measured with a 0/45 geometry and thus is not affected by the *viewing* flare.)

17.2 The maximum luminance of a bright outdoor scene is $30\,000$ cd m^{-2}. We want to make a transparency to be projected on a screen and viewed in a dark room. The maximum luminance produced by the projector on the screen when no film is present is 500 cd m^{-2}. The transparency (slide) film has a maximum density of 3.4 and a minimum density of 0.05. Use the Bartleson–Breneman brightness model to derive a TRC that reproduces the relative brightness of the scene on the projected image. (Relative brightness here means that the brightness of an object in the scene is relative to that of the maximum luminance and the brightness of an object in the projected image is relative to the minimum-density area on the transparency film, i.e., $L_w = 30\,000$ for the scene and $L_w = 500 \times 10^{-0.05}$ for the projected image.) The toe and the shoulder of the TRC are then rolled off at the densities $D_t = 0.5$ and $D_s = 2.9$, using the film equation:

$$D = D_{\min} + \frac{D_{\max} - D_{\min}}{1 + 10^{\beta(\log H - \log H_0)}}.$$

17.3 If a camera has a 3% flare, in theory we can use the following gamma correction function to remove the uniform flare:

$$V = \begin{cases} (Y - 0.03)^{0.45}/(1 - 0.03)^{0.45} & \text{for } 1.0 \geq Y \geq 0.03 \\ 0 & \text{for } 0.03 > Y \geq 0.0 \end{cases}. \qquad (17.22)$$

However, this will leave the first 3% of the code values unused in the input[2] and also create a large quantization gap in the range following the first 3% because the power function has a large slope at $Y = 0.03$. A better alternative is to use either Eq. (17.15) or Eq. (17.18) to approximate Eq. (17.22).

(a) Find the appropriate parameters for Eq. (17.15) to approximate Eq. (17.22).
(b) Find the appropriate parameters for Eq. (17.18) to approximate Eq. (17.22).

---

[2] Since flare is never uniform, these code values are still useful in areas not affected by flare.

18 Color reproduction

18.1 Introduction

The reproduction of colors in many imaging applications requires "faithful reproduction" of the color appearances in the original scenes or objects. Since faithfulness is in the eyes of the beholder, the objective of color reproduction needs careful examination.

For some applications, the objective is easy to define in exact, physical terms, but turns out to be very difficult to achieve: for example, a mail-order catalogue has to reproduce the image of merchandise just as it will look when the customer actually holds it in his hand. The only true solution is to reproduce the spectral reflectance of the object, including the fluorescent property of the original material if any. The Lippman method and the micro-dispersion method [429, pp. 5–8], which come close to reproducing the spectra, are simply too expensive and inconvenient to use.

For some other applications, the objective is very difficult to define in exact, physical terms, and there is no known method of achieving the objective systematically. For example, there is no convenient method of reproducing the wide dynamic luminance range of an outdoor scene on a bright sunny day on a reflection print, which has only a very limited dynamic range. In this case, it is difficult to specify the physical criteria for a good or faithful color reproduction. Furthermore, it is likely that there will not be a reproduction that most people agree to be the best possible reproduction. The subject may well fall into the domain of artistic impression, which is still far beyond our limited understanding. In this chapter, we will study what is known and hope to come up with a systematic solution for practical applications, be it optimal or not.

18.2 Additive and subtractive color reproduction

In a typical natural scene, the reflected spectral radiance at each surface element of an object is determined by the spectral reflectance factor of the surface and the spectral power distribution of the illumination. Therefore, there are very rich varieties of spectral distributions that produce colorful images in our visual perception. In a reproduced image, either hard-copy or soft-copy, we cannot create colors using such rich varieties of spectral compositions. Fortunately, due to the trichromatic nature of our color vision, we can reproduce most colors by using mixtures of a few (≥ 3) primary colors. In general, colors can be reproduced either by using self-emitting light (e.g. in CRT monitors), or by using reflected or transmitted light (e.g. in paintings, prints, and slides). If self-emitting light is used, different colors are often produced by *additively* mixing the chosen primaries, which is similar to what is done in color matching experiments. For example, on a CRT monitor, very small dots of red, green, and blue phosphors are coated on the screen. When the phosphors are excited by more electron current, they generate more red, green, and blue light. Since the phosphor dots are visually unresolvable at a typical viewing distance, the red, green, and blue light is additively mixed (or blurred) on our retina. This type of color reproduction is called additive color reproduction.

When reflected or transmitted light is used for color reproduction, the light sources are often broad-band sources that contain radiant power in all visible wavelengths. Typically these sources appear "white" or nearly so when they are seen directly. In order to produce colors, the spectral composition of the source has to be modified, usually by filtering out some parts of the spectrum more strongly than other parts. For example, if a red color is to be produced, the middle-wavelength and the short-wavelength parts of the source spectrum are often filtered out or subtracted out. Color reproduction by subtracting light energy from a source spectrum is called subtractive color reproduction, and is the basic working principle underlying the majority of color imaging applications. For example, a photographic reflection print uses a cyan dye that absorbs (i.e., subtracts) the long-wavelength light (≈ 600–700 nm), a magenta dye that absorbs the middle-wavelength light (≈ 500–600 nm), and a yellow dye that absorbs the short-wavelength light (≈ 400–500 nm). Light illuminating a reflection print goes through the dyes, is reflected from the diffuse reflection layer coated on the paper support, and goes through the dyes again before passing through the air and entering our eyes. If we want to produce a bright red color, we deposit on the paper no cyan dye, but a lot of magenta and yellow dyes, which absorb most of the light from 400 nm to 600 nm. Similarly, if we want to produce a bright green color, we deposit no magenta dye, but a lot of cyan and yellow dyes, on the paper.

In principle, we can also use additive color reproduction for reflected or transmitted light. For example, if we can lay down nonoverlapping, opaque dots of red, green, and blue inks on paper, color images can be reproduced in a manner similar to that in a CRT monitor. Colors can be varied by changing the relative dot sizes. However, such a scheme has one major difficulty: small dots are difficult to lay down without overlapping. Therefore, most color reproduction for reflected or transmitted light is based on the subtractive method.

18.3 Objectives of color reproduction

As in our discussion of the objectives of tone reproduction, the success of any color reproduction is finally judged by human observers, therefore, it is convenient to also divide any color reproduction into three processes: (1) the subjective color reproduction process that specifies what a desired reproduction should be in terms of visual impression, (2) the psychophysical (translation) process that converts the perceptual criteria as specified in the subjective process into physically quantifiable criteria, and (3) the objective process that deals with calibrating and controlling image devices to achieve the desired reproduction in terms of physical quantities. The major difference between tone and color reproduction objectives is that the former is univariate, while the latter is multivariate. Color reproduction is thus more complicated and even less understood than tone reproduction. Fortunately, we are not as sensitive to deviation from the desired color reproduction as we are to deviation in tone reproduction. In spite of the added complexity, the criteria and objectives for color reproduction can be phrased in a similar list to those for tone reproduction: (a) reproducing the absolute color stimuli (i.e., either the absolute radiant spectral powers, or the absolute colorimetric quantities), (b) reproducing the relative color stimuli (i.e., either the relative radiant spectral powers, or the relative colorimetric quantities), (c) reproducing the color appearances, (d) reproducing color contrasts, (e) reproducing maximum visible color details, and (f) reproducing the preferred colors.

Objectives (a) and (b) do not involve any subjective color reproduction process and therefore are self-evident in what they are trying to achieve. Whether they are practical or desirable depends on the particular application. For example, in copying a reflection color print to the same type of material (including the same dye set or inks), it is both desirable and practical to reproduce the exact spectral compositions in the original. When the media or inks are different, reproducing the relative colorimetric quantities may be both desirable and practical too. However, when the originals (say, natural scenes) and the reproductions (say, photographic prints) are very different in dynamic range, color gamut, and spectral characteristics, reproduction objectives such as (a) and (b) are no longer practical and often not desirable either.

The objectives (d) and (e) are achievable when (a) and (b) are achievable. The interesting cases are when (a) and (b) are not practical or desirable. We can try to achieve (d) and (e) using methods similar to the histogram modification methods in tone reproduction. There are few (if any) serious studies of these two objectives in the literature and we will not discuss them further here. Objectives (c) and (f) have attracted more attention in the past and some of the ideas about them are presented below.

18.3.1 Appearance color reproduction

The basic idea here is similar to the objective of reproducing the relative brightness in tone reproduction. Whatever the color appearances are in the originals, we would like to reproduce them in the reproduction (in the relative sense if the original color appearance cannot be reproduced in absolute magnitude). The key to implementing such a color reproduction objective is an accurate and practical color appearance model that can be used to calculate the color appearances for the input and use them to calculate what the output physical quantities should be so that the input color appearances will be reproduced. Color appearance models have been extensively studied. This subject will be discussed shortly.

18.3.2 Preferred color reproduction

It has been observed in many situations that the most desirable or preferred color reproduction is not necessarily the most faithful reproduction. Typical examples are the colors of grass, sky, and skin. It is not clear whether the preference is due to our memory of the colors of those objects being different from those of the actual physical measurements, or due to some ideal prototype colors that we prefer to see. For example, we may prefer to see our body shape as more like that of a fashion model, although we do not have the illusion that that shape is what we remember of our bodies. In any case, an ideal objective of color reproduction is to reproduce all colors as we prefer to see them.

This objective is difficult to achieve not only because its goal is ambiguous, but also because it is not easy to get good data to aim for. Some of the difficulties are:

1. Experiments only varied the selected colors without changing others. This type of color manipulation is not globally consistent and therefore the results may vary with the color gamut of the reproduction media and the viewing conditions.

2. The physical difference in skin colors for different peoples is relatively large, as the following measurement data (forehead/cheek) [246, 759, 1055] show:

   African: $L^* = 37.6 \pm 1.3$, $a^* = 6.9 \pm 1.4$, $b^* = 10.7 \pm 2.3$;
   Arabian: $L^* = 61.5 \pm 2.3$, $a^* = 5.6 \pm 1.1$, $b^* = 17.3 \pm 1.8$;
   Caucasian: $L^* = 66.3 \pm 2.8$, $a^* = 11.2 \pm 0.9$, $b^* = 12.3 \pm 1.8$;
   Japanese: $L^* = 60.7 \pm 4.37$, $a^* = 10.8 \pm 2.36$, $b^* = 17.1 \pm 2.19$;
   Vietnamese: $L^* = 65.1 \pm 3.1$, $a^* = 5.4 \pm 0.8$, $b^* = 15.4 \pm 1.1$.

3. The preferred color reproduction varies with culture. For example, it has been shown that the preferred skin colors are different in different regions of the world, and possibly at different times. Ancient people preferred lighter skin color (a sign of being rich enough not to have to work out in the sun), while modern people prefer a suntanned skin color (a sign of being rich enough to spend time on the beach). Certain regions of the world prefer a more cyan-blue (cool) color balance, while there are others that prefer a more red–yellow warm color balance.

Bartleson's study [73] on flesh color reproduction showed that the preferred (Caucasian) flesh color reproduction is close to the mean memory color $(x,y) = (0.3548, 0.3441)$ under Illuminant C, which is significantly different from the average natural flesh color, located at about $(x,y) = (0.3786, 0.3463)$ under Illuminant C. The preferred flesh reproduction (about Munsell 7.5YR6.3/3.3) is yellower, lighter, and less saturated than the actual average flesh color (about Munsell 1.5YR5.8/4.3). However, that study was done in the 1950s and may not be representative today. The preferred skin color reproduction also varies with races. Assuming D55, the preferred skin colors in CIELAB are approximately $(a^*,b^*) = (19–27, 21–31)$ for the Japanese, $(16–25, 14–23)$ for Caucasians, and $(20–32, 24–37)$ for blacks. It is also observed that there are considerable variations between individuals. All races seem to like to have skin tone reproduced yellower than it actually is. The empirical observations in preferred color reproduction studies [74, 428] can be summarized as follows:

1. The preferred skin color in reflection prints is more orange–yellow than the actual average skin color. The preferred skin color is quite close to the memory skin color. Reproducing the actual average skin chromaticity on a reflection print is only marginally acceptable. The preferred skin color (luminance factor 39) is also slightly lighter than the average skin (luminance factor 37).

2. The preferred grass color (luminance factor 27) is slightly yellower and lighter than average grass samples (luminance factor 13, 5.6GY/1-4). The preferred grass color is more yellow–green than the memory grass color.

3. The preferred sky color (luminance factor 30) is about the same dominant wavelength as the actual sky, but with higher excitation purity. It is more purple–blue than the memory sky color.

18.4   Psychophysical considerations

In most applications, the objective of color reproduction is mainly to reproduce the color appearance. We have to understand how our perceived color appearances are related to the physical stimuli. Through many elegant demonstrations by numerous color scientists in the past, it has been firmly established that there is no one-to-one correspondence between a physical stimulus and its perceived color. A given light can appear to be red or orange or black or white in color, depending on what else is present in our visual field at that time and what we had been looking at in the previous few minutes or even much longer. (The famous McCollough effect [54, p. 183] can last for a few hours or more.) Color appearance is thus a function of spatial, temporal, as well as spectral variables. Currently we only have a few very limited ideas of how this function behaves. Most of these ideas came from extensive observations and systematic studies under controlled viewing conditions. It is not surprising that they are applicable only in some situations and they are not easy to generalize. However, they currently constitute the bulk of guidelines for color reproduction, and, in a few applications, they are very successful in achieving the objective of reproducing color appearance. In a very real sense, all sciences follow the same path, some further along than others, but none can claim to have the ultimate truth.

The three major factors that affect the color appearance of an image are: (1) the state of adaptation (chromatic as well as achromatic) of the eye(s), (2) the surround of the image, and (3) the method of presentation. The major efforts of color science research have been to quantify these three factors and their effects on color appearance.

18.4.1   The effect of the adaptation state

A dramatic demonstration of the effect of chromatic adaptation on color perception is to go into a room dimly illuminated by tungsten lamps after staying for a long time in a room brightly illuminated by cool-white fluorescent lamps. Initially every thing looks very yellowish. After a few minutes, things gradually begin to look somewhat "normal" again. Of course, they don't look exactly the same as in the other room, no matter how long we remain in the tungsten-illuminated room. Studies show that although chromatic adaptation tends to compensate to a large degree for the changing illumination to achieve "color constancy", things never look exactly the same when they are illuminated with light sources of very different spectral composition.

Among the early efforts to quantify the effect of the adaptation was the determination of corresponding tristimulus values under two different lighting conditions. For example, if an eye is adapted to D65 daylight illumination, light with the CIE tristimulus values (X_1, Y_1, Z_1) appears to be a certain purple color P. If now, the eye is adapted to a tungsten illumination, say the CIE illuminant A, and suppose that light with tristimulus values (X_2, Y_2, Z_2) looks exactly like the same purple color P, then, (X_2, Y_2, Z_2) is said to be the Illuminant A's corresponding tristimulus values of the D_{65}'s (X_1, Y_1, Z_1). Hunt [425, 426] and Burnham, Evans and Newhall [148] determined many such pairs by matching colors between observers who were adapted to different illuminations. It was found that a linear transformation could fit the data very well. For example, the following transformation mapped Illuminant C's tristimulus values (X_c, Y_c, Z_c) to the corresponding values (X_a, Y_a, Z_a) under Illuminant A adaptation:

$$X_a = 0.9132X_c + 0.4222Y_c - 0.1988Z_c + 0.0024, \tag{18.1}$$

$$Y_a = 0.0299X_c + 1.0215Y_c - 0.1020Z_c + 0.0025, \tag{18.2}$$

$$Z_a = 0.0175X_c - 0.1378Y_c + 0.4708Z_c - 0.0019. \tag{18.3}$$

The chromaticity of the Illuminant A used was (0.4475, 0.4084), and that of the Illuminant C was (0.3125, 0.3343). Under both illuminants, the illuminance of the white surrounds was set to 25 foot lamberts (i.e., $85.65\, \mathrm{cd\, m^{-2}}$). Using the linear transformation, the white surface under Illuminant C, $(X_c, Y_c, Z_c) = (23.3697, 25.0, 26.4134)$ was mapped to $(X_a, Y_a, Z_a) = (26.6476, 23.5446, 9.3975)$, which has a luminance smaller than 25 foot lamberts and a chromaticity of (0.4472, 0.3951), slightly different from that of the Illuminant A. Assuming that the difference was real, i.e., larger than the regression error (in this case, this assumption is only marginally true), the same white object looked a little brighter and a little more yellow under tungsten lighting. The phenomenon that a white object takes on the hue of the illuminant is known as the Helson–Judd effect [389, 390, 475], as we mentioned before. (This shows that color constancy is not strictly true.) The Helson–Judd effect also predicts that a dark object will take on a complementary hue, but this is not predicted exactly by the above linear transformation. For example, $(X_c, Y_c, Z_c) = (0.9348, 1.0000, 1.0565)$ is mapped to $(X_a, Y_a, Z_a) = (1.0682, 0.9442, 0.3741)$ which has a luminance of 0.9442 ft lamberts and a chromaticity of (0.4476, 0.3956), not too different from the corresponding chromaticity for the white object. Evidence seems to indicate that linear transformations cannot fully describe the effect of adaptation [79, 432, 475], but they are good approximations if the correct coefficients can be determined [138].

There has been extensive experimental and modeling work on the effect of chromatic adaptation [81, 138, 291, 292, 432, 698, 998]. The chromatic adaptation transforms in the two color appearance models, CIECAM97s and CIECAM02, recommended by the CIE provide us with some standard models for color imaging applications. We will study these two models shortly. However, it should be pointed out that current color appearance models are empirical in nature, do not account for the spatial processing involved in color vision, and the model parameters have to be tuned by trial and error. This unsatisfactory status will hopefully be improved by developing new models that are more based on computational theory and algorithmic design.

Figure 18.1 shows how a typical chromatic adaptation model is applied to find the corresponding tristimulus values from one illuminant to another. The first step is to transform

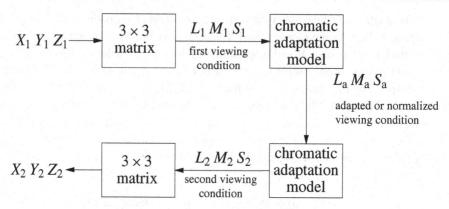

Figure 18.1. Computation of corresponding tristimulus values using a chromatic adaptation model.

the CIEXYZ to the LMS cone excitation space. This step is necessary because it is believed that the nonlinear behavior of cone adaptation can be much more accurately modeled in the cone excitation space. The chromatic adaptation model is then applied to determine the corresponding cone excitations under a different illuminant. Many chromatic adaptation experiments using simple color images showed that in general the von Kries model works reasonably well [79, 132, 133, 138]. One of the surprising findings in Breneman's study [138] of chromatic adaptation using complex images is that the simple von Kries model (described in Section 13.3.2) can account for most of the effect, but the scaling coefficients have to be based on the matching grays, not reference whites, under the two illuminants [138] . Figure 18.2 shows a comparison of von Kries' model predictions based on normalizing to the physical white (Fig. 18.2(a)) and normalizing to the perceived gray (Fig. 18.2(b)). His data showed that the chromaticity coordinates of the perceived gray are different from those of the illuminant. It is clear that the prediction is much more accurate if the von Kries normalization is based on the matching grays (Fig. 18.2(b)) under the two different illuminants.

A reproduction presented under low illuminance gives us a very different visual impression than under high illuminance. The following three effects are well known:

1. Under chromatic illumination (chromaticity very different from D_{55}), when an observer is presented with a series of nonselective reflectance samples, the high-reflectance samples appear to take on the color of the illuminant and the low-reflectance samples appear to have a hue complementary to the illuminant. Only the medium-reflectance samples appear neutral gray.[1] This is called the Helson–Judd effect [389, 390, 475].
2. Light of a given chromaticity appears to be more colorful when its luminance is increased. This is called the Hunt effect [425, 426].
3. The perceived scene contrast increases with luminance. This is called the Stevens effect [906].

---

[1]   This empirical observation seems to contradict the data from Breneman's experiments, in which complex images were used. It is possible that the observers in the two experiments might be answering two different types of question [30]. This shows that our visual perception is much richer than some simple experimental protocols can specify.

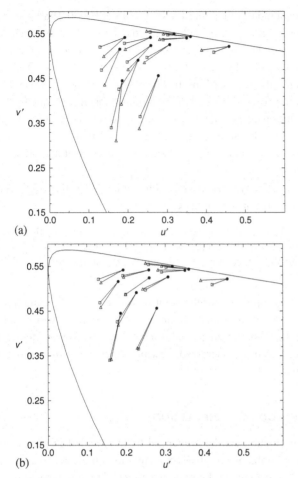

Figure 18.2. Comparison of von Kries' model predictions, using Breneman's experimental data [138]: (a) panel is based on normalizing with respect to the illuminant, and (b) with respect to gray. The luminance level was kept constant at 1500 cd m^{-2}. The solid circles are the chromaticities under illuminant A. The open squares are the matching chromaticities under D$_{65}$ as set by the observers. The open triangles are the model predictions. The prediction errors are the distances between the open squares and the open triangles.

18.4.2 The effect of viewing surrounds

From our discussion on tone reproduction, a dark viewing surround makes the image appear to be of lower contrast than when the same image is viewed with an illuminated surround. Therefore, images to be viewed with dark surrounds have to be prepared with a higher overall gamma (about 1.5). The question is whether the perceived color saturation will be affected by the dark surround as well. Experimental results, using complex stimuli, showed that approximately the same purities were required for equal saturation in light-surround and dark-surround viewing conditions [137]. However, with advances in color appearance modeling, more sophisticated color adjustment can now be done to compensate for the subtle effect (if any) of viewing surrounds [292, 676].

The American National Standards Institute (ANSI) ANSI PH2.30-1989 specifies the standard viewing conditions for graphic arts, with regard to color prints, transparencies, and photomechanical reproductions. The light source should have a spectral power distribution of D50 (or close to it) with CIE (1931) chromaticity coordinates of (0.3457, 0.3586). The surround should be a neutral light gray of Munsell N8/ (60% reflectance factor) with matte finish. The illuminance on the color prints and the photomechanical reproductions should be 2200 ± 470 lx, and the luminance for the transparencies (direct viewing or projection) should be 1400 ± 300 cd m^{-2}. The luminance of the projected image is measured from 50 cm away from the screen which should have a spatial resolution of at least 40 cycles per millimeter.

The following recommendation by some GATF publications (*GATFWORLD*, Volume 2, Issue 6, p. 6, 1990) shows how primitive our state of understanding is:

In the initial evaluation stage, when materials are being selected for reproduction, judgments should be made under the point-of-use illuminating conditions. During the reproduction process, however, standard viewing conditions should be used to improve the consistency and communication between all the parties involved.

It is not clear how we can compensate for the point-of-use illuminating conditions after we have done all the color reproduction process under the standard viewing conditions. Presumably, if the point-of-use illuminating conditions are not convenient to set up for a color reproduction process, using standardized viewing conditions will at least prevent inconsistent conclusions from different parties.

18.4.3   The effect of the method of presentation

Our judgment of color reproduction can be influenced by the method of presentation. A study by Bartleson [72] of the influence of observer adaptation on the acceptance of color prints showed some interesting differences between the effect of a colored background and the effect of a colored illuminant. With a colored background, the observers were more tolerant of color balance errors in the direction of the color of the background, which was uniformly colored. With a complex field as the background (as in typical print viewing at home), the observers were more tolerant of color balance error in the opposite direction to the illuminant color. This experiment showed that tolerance of color errors can be quite context-dependent.

18.5   Color balance

In most color imaging applications, once the imaging chain (from capture to display) has been calibrated for a standard imaging and viewing condition, the first order problem in color reproduction is to reproduce the neutral colors correctly for each input image. This is called the white balance problem in consumer electronic imaging (video camcorders, digital cameras, desktop scanners, etc.). A similar, but more general, problem in photography and graphic arts is called the color balance problem, which tends to also include adjusting some color interaction to make all the colors look right.

The factors that cause a calibrated system to give poor color reproduction vary from system to system, but they can be classified into three main categories:

1. Variations in scene illumination. A calibrated system expects a neutral color to be represented by certain numerical relations in each color channel. For example, the red, green, and blue gray levels of a neutral color are expected to be the same for a calibrated color monitor. The relative gains in the three color channels have to be adjusted in the captured images or in the image capturing devices for different scene illuminations. For example, a tungsten light source has much less spectral power in the short-wavelength region than a daylight source. Therefore, the blue channel gain has to be higher when the image is taken under a tungsten illumination than when it is taken under a daylight illumination. Digital cameras attempt to make such adjustments in the image capturing process, while photographic systems tend to correct the color bias at the printing stage.

2. Variations in image capture processes. Imaging system characteristics often change with temperature, usage, exposure time, aperture size, and luminance levels. These variations can introduce uncontrolled color variations in the image capture stage. For example, underexposed films have lower sensitometrical contrast and underexposed digital camera images exhibit clipping and quantization. These affect color reproduction differently depending on which color channel has the lowest exposure. Other factors are random in nature. CCD sensor characteristics depend on the operating temperature and film sensitometry depends on chemical processing. These factors vary in a more or less uncontrolled manner.

3. Variations in image display processes. The characteristics of display systems and printers are also subject to change with the physical environment and the usage parameters. The output color of an inkjet printer can be affected by the quality of the paper and the ink. Photographic paper processing can change from day to day and batch to batch. The characteristics of a color monitor can be affected by the temperature and the electromagnetic fields in the surrounds. These can all cause shifts in reproduced colors.

For most systems, the dominating factor is the variations in scene illumination. This will be discussed here. It should be noted that the color balance problem is related to the "color constancy" problem in human color vision. The objective is to study how the color variations due to changing illumination can be discounted or compensated for. The fact that our visual system can perceive and discount the illumination variations serves as an existence proof that the problem should be solvable to a large extent. However, as we will see, we are not anywhere near this yet.

18.5.1 Problem formulations

In order to simplify our discussion, let us assume that our color imaging system has three color channels: red, green, and blue. For a given lighting and imaging geometry, we can consider the simplified imaging equations as follows:

$$E_r(x, y) = k \int L(\lambda, x, y)\rho(\lambda, x, y)N(\theta, \phi, x, y)S_r(\lambda)d\lambda, \tag{18.4}$$

$$E_g(x, y) = k \int L(\lambda, x, y)\rho(\lambda, x, y)N(\theta, \phi, x, y)S_g(\lambda)d\lambda, \tag{18.5}$$

$$E_b(x, y) = k \int L(\lambda, x, y)\rho(\lambda, x, y)N(\theta, \phi, x, y)S_b(\lambda)d\lambda, \tag{18.6}$$

where E_r, E_g, and E_b are the image irradiances, $L(\lambda, x, y)$ is the spectral power distribution of the illuminant, $\rho(\lambda, x, y)$ is the spectral reflectance factor of the object point corresponding to the image location (x, y), and $S_r(\lambda)$, $S_g(\lambda)$, and $S_b(\lambda)$ are the red, green, and blue system spectral responsivity functions. The geometric factor $N(\theta, \phi, x, y)$, accounts for the effects of f-number, surface orientation, light source direction, object distance, etc. This system of equations is not completely general (for example, the spectral and the geometrical factors in general are not separable), but is sufficient for our discussion here.

From this set of equations, one can say that the most general problem of color balance is that, given a color image $(E_r(x, y), E_g(x, y), E_b(x, y))$, one would like to estimate $L(\lambda, x, y)$ and $\rho(\lambda, x, y)$. We will call this type of problem formulation the (illuminant) spectra estimation problem. Clearly, the number of unknowns in this formulation far exceeds the number of measured data, and the problem is often solved by assuming that $L(\lambda)$ and $\rho(\lambda)$ are linear combinations of a small number of basis vectors. Such an approach is called the linear model approach.

The color balance problem can and should also be looked at from the utility point of view. The practical purpose of solving the color balance problem is to use the solution to correct the color reproduction of an image which was taken under an unknown illuminant different from the one we will use to view the image, or the one we assume to be the standard illuminant. General color correction can be done through various means of different complexity. For example, scanners often use 3-D LUTs, while digital cameras use 3×3 matrices. However, in correcting for color balance error, 3×3 matrices are probably as complicated as is practicable. Therefore, one can formulate the color balance problem as estimating the optimal 3×3 matrix that will transform the given color image into one that has the best desired color reproduction according to the user's objective. This problem formulation is called the (illuminant) matrix estimation problem. One series of the most critical colors to be balanced correctly is the neutral series (black, gray, to white). Therefore, the estimated matrix should transform the neutral colors under the unknown illuminant to the neutral colors under the desired illuminant.

A simpler formulation of the problem is to estimate only the three channel responses (R_n, G_n, B_n) corresponding to a neutral surface of which $\rho(\lambda) = c$:

$$R_n = kc \int L(\lambda)S_r(\lambda)d\lambda, \tag{18.7}$$

$$G_n = kc \int L(\lambda)S_g(\lambda)d\lambda, \tag{18.8}$$

$$B_n = kc \int L(\lambda)S_b(\lambda)d\lambda. \tag{18.9}$$

It is usually possible to estimate only the ratios between R_n, G_n, and B_n because the image irradiances are scaled by sensor sensitivity, lens transmittance, and other unknown factors, all of which are lumped into the factor k. We will call this type of problem formulation, the (illuminant) chromaticity estimation problem, because the objective is to estimate the illuminant chromaticity, such as $(R_n/G_n, B_n/G_n)$. Even for this simplified problem, it is still fairly easy to see that without additional information or constraints, there is no unique solution to this problem. For example, if we multiply $L(\lambda)$ by a positive function $\beta(\lambda)$ and divide all $\rho(\lambda)$ by the same function $\beta(\lambda)$, we get exactly the same input image $(E_r(x, y), E_g(x, y), E_b(x, y))$, but now the correct answer for (R_n, G_n, B_n) becomes

$$R_n = kc \int [L(\lambda)\beta(\lambda)]S_r(\lambda)d\lambda, \tag{18.10}$$

$$G_n = kc \int [L(\lambda)\beta(\lambda)]S_g(\lambda)d\lambda, \tag{18.11}$$

$$B_n = kc \int [L(\lambda)\beta(\lambda)]S_b(\lambda)d\lambda. \tag{18.12}$$

18.5.2 Color cues

The above discussion makes it clear that the color balance problem is an underdetermined problem with no unique solution. However, this is clearly in contradiction with our day-to-day visual experience. We can often (although not always) perceive and recognize a piece of "white" paper as white, under most natural and man-made light sources. So what is the additional information that we can use to derive an estimate of the light source chromaticity? Different approaches make use of different constraints, prior knowledge, and assumptions. The types of additional information used in the various algorithms can be roughly listed as follows:

- Statistical color properties of natural scenes
  Gray-world assumption: the averaged color of all the pixels in the scene is gray [71, 144, 288, 570].
  The retinex theory: let the maximum, thresholded, normalized ratio in each color channel be r_{max}, g_{max}, and b_{max}, then $(r_{max}, g_{max}, b_{max})$ is perceived as white [434, 546, 648, 650].

- Statistical color distributions of natural scenes
  Randomly sampled color distributions are log-normally distributed and an equal percentile of the red, green, blue histograms is an estimate of neutral at that luminance level [16].
  Using collected color distributions of natural scenes under different illuminants, one can use Bayesian statistics to estimate the most probable illuminant of the given input image [133, 313, 806].

- Statistical color gamut of natural scenes
  It can be shown that the color gamut of a natural scene under any illuminant is a convex set. If we compare the color gamut of an input image taken under an unknown

illuminant with the previously compiled standard color gamut under a standard illuminant, we can compute all the possible linear transforms that can map the input color gamut into the standard gamut. From the feasible set of transforms, we can use some criterion to select the transform that best accounts for the gamut distortion [311, 315, 322].

- Neutral interface reflection (specular highlight)
  The interface reflection component of an inhomogeneous surface has the same spectral composition as the illuminant. Therefore, the chromaticity loci of various surfaces will converge at the illuminant chromaticity [505, 560, 934].

- Natural light sources
  The chromaticity loci of natural light sources are located near those of blackbody radiators [244, 312, 315, 561].

- Eigenvector (linear) models of sources and reflectances:
  It is known that natural daylight spectra can be well approximated by one mean vector and two principal components [476]. It is also known that spectral reflectance functions of common materials and Munsell color chips can be well approximated by one mean vector and 2–6 principal components [200, 630]. Therefore, the illuminant spectral estimation problem can be cast as a problem for estimating the few coefficients of the dominant principal components [270, 629, 825, 939]. In addition, the distribution of the coefficients has a definite structure that can be used to reduce the number of unknowns for estimation [254, 255].

- Machine-learning models:
  If we collect a very large sample of color images taken under various illuminants, we can use them to train a learning machine, such as a neural network, to do the illuminant estimation [332].

18.5.3   Color balance algorithms

Since the introduction of color films in the 1930s, practical color balance algorithms have been developed in the research laboratories of a few photographics companies, mainly for automatic photofinishing printers. With the introduction of consumer digital cameras in the 1980s, many research groups in electronics companies and universities began to work on automatic color balance algorithms. The new research groups brought with them new concepts, more mathematical skills, and better computing facilities and have developed several interesting new algorithms. At the same time, not being familiar with the prior arts, they also reinvented many wheels. Unfortunately, most well-tested algorithms used by consumer products tend to be proprietary and their details are not in the public domain. Even published algorithms have so many important details missing that it is very difficult to verify their claims. Here we only introduce some of the well-known algorithms that represent different major approaches. Since each major algorithm has many possible variations, we recommend that interested readers refer to the references cited.

The integration-to-gray algorithm and its photofinishing applications

The integration-to-gray algorithm works by setting the averaged color of an image to a predefined gray. It is probably the oldest color balance algorithm that is successfully used in consumer photography. Although the idea seems to be too simple to be practically useful, its many modifications have been improved through various heuristics since the 1950s.

In 1946, R.M. Evans filed a patent application for a method for automatic exposure control (color and density balance) in photographic printers for color negative or positive transparency films. The color correction is achieved by "adjusting the intensity of the printing light so that when integrally passed through said transparency, it has the same printing characteristics as light which prints substantially as gray" [288, lines 32–36, column 4]. Realizing that if there is a dominant color in the image, the integration-to-gray method will result in too much correction, he further said in the patent: "It may not always be desirable to effect a correction to an exact neutral gray, but sometimes the correction need only be carried toward the neutral point, or in the direction of gray" [288, lines 15-19, column 4].

The idea was very simple to implement and apparently relatively effective. According to one study, the method produces a "satisfactory" print about 70% of the time [947]. The integration-to-gray method was known in the trade as the large-area transmission density (LATD) method. It quickly became the backbone of many of the color balance algorithms used in printers, digital cameras, and camcorders. Bartleson [71] provided a very detailed review on the development and refinement of the LATD method before 1956. He also elaborated on the optimal correction level that Evans referred to in his patent.

The complexity of the early algorithms was limited by the then available sensors, electronic components, and analog computing machinery. The two major problems of the LATD algorithm were quickly recognized: (1) it fails when the image contains large areas of some saturated color (in the USA, this is called subject failure; in Europe, it is called dominant color); and (2) it is biased toward low-density areas (or underexposed areas). For example, in the negative of a flash picture, the dark background is weighted more heavily than the main subjects in the foreground because the dark area in the scene corresponds to the low-density area on the developed negative film and more light passes through the low-density area, resulting in a greater contribution to the integrated transmittance.

Various solutions have been proposed to reduce the error magnitudes when the above two problems occur. The error in the dominant color (or subject failure) problem is reduced by: (1) using different correction levels: the amount of color correction applied to an image is adjusted based on how much the LATD measure differs from typical values [272, p. 4.17]; (2) excluding highly saturated colors [305] and those colors whose luminance components are outside of the middle range of the luminance signals [345]; (3) sampling along edges in the image [16, 421] or using the weighted average according to spatial contrast [527]; (4) using averages from multiple frames [951]; (5) using between-frame similarity [22, 944]; (6) using color space classification [333]; (7) changing the color balance as a function of over- or under-exposures [272, 946]; and (8) using *a priori* knowledge on light source distribution [561]. The error in the low-density bias problem is reduced by: (1) throwing away underexposed regions [951] and (2) using geometric weighting (the center portion of the image is more likely to contain the main subjects of interest) and other heuristic rules [23, 272].

In addition to the average density, other simple features such as the minimum density, the maximum density, and various other combinations are used in the regression optimization of the algorithm performance [206, 472, 945, 972]. As memory devices become cheaper and computer processors become more and more powerful, algorithms are designed to be more intelligent in an attempt to recognize objects and scene types in the images and adjust color balance accordingly. For example, detecting faces and skins [826, 932] in the images can be used to help produce a pleasing skin tone or correct for the overall lightness of the print. Detection of sky, backlit, flash, snow, or beach scenes allows the color and density balance algorithm to adjust its estimated correction, depending on the scene types.

The retinex algorithm

In 1971, after many years of experiments on human color perception, Land and McCann [546] published a very influential computational theory of color perception, which contains a specific proposal on how human color constancy might work. What lies behind the theory is that the color we perceive at a spatial location is computed from relative comparisons with everything else in the visual field. Therefore, the spectral content, the three cone responses, and the absolute stimulus power by themselves alone do not uniquely determine the color we see [547, 648]. From this perspective, a CIE chromaticity diagram painted with different colors is the worst thing one can show to teach how color vision works.

The retinex theory proposes that the visual system computes three "lightness" images, one from each of the three color channels independently. The red, green, and blue lightness values at each spatial location determine the color we see at that location. There are three key steps in the theory: (1) the relative surface reflectance corresponding to each image location is computed by a threshold and reset operation; (2) the maximum relative reflectance in each color channel is used to normalize all the relative reflectance values in that channel, thus making the maximum relative reflectance in the channel equal to 1; and (3) the normalized reflectance values in each channel are mapped through a nonlinear function to the lightness values of that channel. The threshold and reset operation step to compute the relative reflectance values is based on a simple idea that the local illumination variation is small and therefore if the ratio between the sensor responses from two neighboring pixels is close to 1, it should be reset to 1 to remove the gradual shading created by the illumination. The second step of normalization to maximum channel reflectance is the most daring proposal of the theory. It does not mean that a white object has to be present in the visual field. It asserts that when no white object is present in the scene, the maximum reflectance from each channel is taken by our visual system to be equivalent to the channel reflectance of an object that will be perceived as white. For example, if the maximum red channel reflectance, r_{max}, is from a red object, the maximum green channel reflectance, g_{max}, is from a green object, and the maximum blue channel reflectance, b_{max}, is from a blue object, then the retinex theory asserts that $(r_{max}, g_{max}, b_{max})$ will be perceived as white. The third step of converting the normalized reflectances to the lightness values is less surprising because it is well known that the perceived lightness is a nonlinear function of surface reflectance.

Although, as a computational algorithm, its operations are too simple to deal with natural images, and as a theory of color vision, it fails to explain many important visual phenomena, such as simultaneous contrast and nonlinear chromatic adaptation, the retinex theory had a great impact on the research on color constancy because it emphasizes the importance of edges in color perception, it insists on using the reflectance ratio (not the tristimulus values) as the major predictor for perceived lightness and color, and it pioneers the use of a computational algorithm for predicting visual perception. As a result, it has stimulated many other research projects that eventually go well beyond its original, oversimplified operational description [434, 889]. Many algorithms today claim to be better implementations of retinex theory, but in reality, there have been few experiments [648, 650] aiming at verifying the most important claim in the theory that normalization to the maximum channel reflectance is "the" operation for color constancy.

The chromaticity convergence algorithms

It is a very common perceptual observation that the specular highlight from surface reflection often appears white or desaturated color. An analysis of this observation leads to a simple two-component reflection model that has been described in detail in Section 8.2.3 as the NIR model. Rendering algorithms in computer graphics mix the illuminant color with the object color to produce specular highlights [213]. When such additive mixtures of the illuminant color and the object color are plotted in the CIE 1931 chromaticity diagram, their chromaticity loci form a line segment connecting the chromaticity point of the illuminant and the chromaticity point of the object color. If there are other colored surfaces in the image, the chromaticity diagram has many line segments pointing to a common intersection point which is the illuminant chromaticity point [560]. This method of estimating the light source chromaticity is called the chromaticity convergence algorithm [562].

The simple two-component reflection model that has been used in computer graphics for quite some time was later formulated into a more general model, called the dichromatic reflection model [854], in which the interface reflection component can be spectrally selective, instead of nonselective as assumed by the NIR model. The dichromatic model proved to be an inspiring source for algorithm development. The chromaticity convergence method can be performed in the three-dimensional tristimulus space because the interface reflection and the body reflection can be treated as two three-dimensional vectors and they span a plane. Colors from various points on each surface material populate one plane (in the linear RGB space) and the colors from multiple surfaces fall on many planes with their common intersection line being the illuminant vector [312, 954].

The obvious difficulties of this approach are: (1) There may not be strong enough interface reflection in the image to generate a reliable signal. This does not mean that strong specular highlights have to be visible on object surfaces, because the line segment length in the chromaticity or RGB space is not necessarily proportional to the perceptual strength. (2) There might be incidental color variations that can form chromaticity line segments that are not pointing to the illuminant chromaticity. For example, in the autumn, leaves might have a strong color variation along the yellow–green direction due to varying concentrations of different colored pigments.

The gamut mapping algorithms

Let R, G, B be the color responses of an image capture device, such as a digital camera. Without loss of generality, let us assume that each color channel is represented with only eight-bit precision, i.e., $R,G,B = 0, 1, \ldots, 255$. For any color image captured by the device, it turns out that many of the (R,G,B) values will not occur. The total volume of the (R,G,B) values that occur in an image is called the color gamut of that image. The color gamut of one image is often different from that of another image for various reasons. For example, an image of a forest scene may not have saturated red or blue colors, while an image of Christmas decorations may have a much larger selection of colors. The color gamut can also differ because of the illumination. If an image is taken under tungsten lighting, the whole color gamut will be shifted in the red–orange direction. This color shift occurs for every object in the scene. Assuming that a scene contains a sufficient number of colored objects, intuitively one should be able to make some estimate of the illuminant color by comparing the color gamut of the input image with the canonical gamut[2] under a reference illuminant, say D65. Under tungsten lighting, even the most bluish color cannot have a very high blue value. This is the basic idea behind the gamut mapping algorithm for color constancy [322].

Clearly, there are two obvious difficulties with this approach: one is the statistical validity and the other is the computational cost. If the color gamut of an input image does not have any pixels that have high blue values, is it because there was no bluish object in the scene or is it because the scene was illuminated by tungsten lamps? This type of ambiguity is not unique to this approach, but is inherent in the color balance problem because of its underdetermined nature. In the gamut mapping algorithms, this ambiguity translates into a large set of illuminants that are all compatible with the input color gamut. For linear imaging sensors, the color gamut of an image can be shown to be a convex set. In order to speed up the computation, the input gamut and the canonical gamut are both approximated by their convex hulls and the mapping between the two gamuts is checked only for the vertices of the two polyhedrons. The set of all the linear transforms that can map all the input vertices into the canonical gamut is called the feasible set. We then need a selection criterion to choose the best mapping from the feasible set. For example, we can choose the mapping that maximizes the volume of the transformed gamut or the one that is closest to the natural daylight locus. The question is: how well does it work in practice? As one would expect, the performance of the algorithm is quite sensitive to the choice of the canonical gamut and the criteria it uses to select the best guess from the feasible set. What is surprising is that, from the limited experiments reported, the algorithms can work reasonably well [57, 955].

A different implementation of the gamut mapping idea is to cast the problem into one of illuminant classification [315, 955]. If we compare the input gamut with the gamuts of a set of illuminants we can choose the illuminant which generates the gamut that is most similar to the input gamut. The gamut comparison can be done very quickly by segmenting the input color image into a few tens of color regions and computing the convex inclusion relation only on those few tens of colors.

Bayesian estimation and the color by correlation algorithms

If one examines the color histograms of many images, it becomes quite apparent that not all colors are created equal – some are present more frequently than others. Furthermore,

---

[2]   Unfortunately, there are no safe rules as to how this canonical gamut can be constructed. In practice, it is usually synthesized by whatever color samples are available to the implementer of the algorithm.

as the illuminant changes, the color distribution is shifted and skewed, as we discussed in the gamut mapping algorithms. If we collect the various color distributions under different illuminants, we can use the Bayesian rule to estimate the likelihood that an input image was taken under any illuminant and choose the most likely illuminant as an estimate of the scene illuminant [133]. This is called the Bayesian estimation approach.

A very interesting way of implementing the Bayesian illuminant estimation approach is by a framework called color by correlation [313]. The first thing to notice is that for color balance applications, it seems sufficient to partition natural light sources into about 10–20 different illuminants, depending on the precision required for the estimate. For each of these illuminants, many color images can be taken to compile the probability distribution that a color will occur under an illuminant. A correlation matrix is then put together, in which each column represents one illuminant and each row represents a color. A given element in the correlation matrix thus contains the probability of occurrence of the color represented by that row and under the illuminant represented by that column. An input image is represented as a column vector, with the ith element representing the same color as represented by the ith row in the correlation matrix. If a color is present in the image, the element is set to 1, otherwise, it is set to 0. The input column vector is then correlated with each column of the correlation matrix (element-by-element multiplication and summation) to derive the likelihood of the illuminant corresponding to the column. The operation basically adds up all the probabilities of the colors present in the image. The most likely illuminant is chosen as the illuminant estimate. This color-by-correlation algorihm is very fast and is claimed to be quite accurate. It is very important to note that each color present in an image is only counted once and therefore, this method is not sensitive to large areas of dominant color. A threshold is imposed so that an accidental color pixel will not cause the probability of that color to be added.

18.6 Color appearance models

One of the most intuitive objectives in color reproduction is to reproduce the color appearance. The difficulty of course lies in computing the color appearance from the original and predicting it in the reproduction. An accurate computational theory or algorithm for computing color appearance requires a thorough understanding of how our color perception works. Undoubtedly, this will involve spatial and temporal processing, in addition to spectral processing. Since this is not achievable in the foreseeable future, even an oversimplified color appearance model for uniform color patches in a uniform background is useful for some applications. Several color appearance models for such applications have been proposed and tested. They are well described and compared in the literature (e.g., see [292]).

According to CIE Technical Committee 1-34 (TC1-34), a color appearance model is any model that includes predictors of at least the relative color appearance attributes of lightness, chroma, and hue [292, p. 217]. Since changes in illumination alter most quantities from physical measurements, a basic requirement of any color appearance model is to account for the chromatic adaptation. From this definition, CIELAB is a color appearance model, although a very simple one. Its lightness predictor is L^*. It also has the hue and chroma predictors. It accounts for the chromatic adaptation by normalizing all CIEXYZ values by those of the reference white (X_n, Y_n, Z_n). This is one of the major weaknesses in CIELAB because the normalization is based on the CIE tristimulus values XYZ, which are an arbitrary linear combination of the LMS cone spectral sensitivities. A reasonable chromatic adaptation model should be based directly on the cone spectral sensitivities instead. Furthermore, psychophysical data show that the S cones seem to behave differently from the L and M cones and therefore require a different type of gain adjustment to account for the chromatic adaptation data. The other major deficiency in using CIELAB as a color appearance model is that it does not account for the effect of the viewing surround.

18.6.1   Color appearance attributes

Here we present several terms that are used in color appearance models. They are not easy to define rigorously, but need to be qualitatively described first to avoid unnecessary confusion in future discussion. It should be kept in mind that these concepts are not fundamental in any theoretical sense. However, their definitions are attempts to distinguish several different subtle aspects in color perception that have not been properly discussed in typical engineering treatments of color reproduction. We should try to appreciate what are being described here based on our personal color experiences. One of the central assumptions is that there are two types of judgments in our color perception, absolute and relative, and there are two modes of color perception: unrelated and related. The judgment of an absolute quantity is our visual perception of the absolute physical amount, for example the brightness is our perception of how much light energy or power is radiated to our eyes from an element of the scene. In most cases, the judgment of a relative quantity is relative with respect to a perfect reflecting diffuser (reference white) similarly illuminated. The unrelated mode of color perception is that a color stimulus is perceived as an isolated color, without being associated to any object shape or lighting. The related mode refers to colors that are perceived in relation to others in the visual field, especially as being some properties of object surfaces or volumes. (If you don't feel quite sure if this partition of color perception into two modes makes sense at all, you are not alone. The attempt here is to distinguish the color seen as a property associated with an object from the color seen as a sensation all by itself without being judged relative to those of other objects. For example, object colors are often accompanied by the simultaneous perception of illumination, texture, and shape, while unrelated colors are not perceived as being associated with any physical objects. For now, due to lack of better understanding, we will take these concepts at their proclaimed values in our discussion of color appearance.)

- *Brightness* (absolute): how much light.
- *Lightness* (relative): brightness relative to white.
- *Hue* (absolute): red, yellow, green, blue, purple, etc.
- *Achromatic*: without hue.
- *Colorfulness* (absolute): how much hue. Colorfulness increases with illumination level.

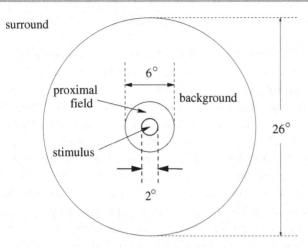

Figure 18.3. Specification of the visual field for a color appearance model.

- *Chroma* (relative): colorfulness relative to the brightness of a white object similarly illuminated. Chroma is not applicable for object surfaces that are not uniformly illuminated. Chroma is approximately constant across different illumination levels.
- *Saturation* (relative): colorfulness relative to its own brightness. Saturation is used for isolated color stimuli (unrelated color) and for describing the color of an object surface which is not uniformly illuminated.

18.6.2 Descriptions of the stimuli and the visual field

The color appearance of a stimulus depends on many factors. In order to predict the appearance of a color stimulus, we have to specify these factors as the input to the color appearance model. The spatial layout specifications in the CIE color appearance model are relatively simple. They include the stimulus, the proximal field, the background, and the surround, as shown in Fig. 18.3. The size of the stimulus is assumed to be roughly 2° visual angle. It is surrounded by a proximal field, then a background field, and then a surround field.

18.6.3 CIECAM97s

Due to popular demand from industry and the universities, CIE planned to recommend a complete version (CIECAMc) and a simple version (CIECAMs) of an interim color appearance model. The complete model has not yet appeared. We will here briefly describe the simple model, i.e., the CIE 1997 Interim Color Appearance Model (Simple Version), abbreviated to CIECAM97s [193]. A more detailed description of the model can be found in [293, 431, Chapter 12]. Color appearance modeling is still an active research area and constant consultation of the color research literature is necessary for anyone planning to work on related problems. In 2003, CIE was still working to approve a draft revised version of its "new" color appearance model called CIECAM02 [676]. However, an even more sophisticated color appearance model for imaging applications is being developed to account for spatial frequency and simultaneous contrast effects [295]. This is definitely a good direction in which to go and we can expect a better model to be available for future color imaging applications.

Before we present the CIECAM97s model, we should give a warning for engineers and scientists who are used to working on firm theoretical foundations. The color appearance model to be discussed will strike you as a mess of empirical equations, with no justification whatsoever. If that is how you feel, again you are certainly not alone. However, these empirical equations did not "come from nowhere". They represent a justifiable effort to summarize a huge amount of experimental data with a few equations. They do not look trustworthy only because it would have taken a few hundred pages to list all the relevant experimental data and to explain how the equations were derived to fit those data. In a sense, this is a desperate effort to make those data useful for people who do not have the time to go through the same derivation process, i.e., for those people who simply want to have a blackbox machine to compute the physical correlates of some of the important perceptual judgments, such as brightness, lightness, hue, chroma, and colorfulness. If you do not have any use for such a blackbox machine, you should feel free to skip this section. However, if you do work in a color imaging related field, you may encounter discussions on this subject from time to time. It is probably useful at least to know what it is trying to do and get some idea about how it works. We need to treat it as work in progress and expect, that as we understand more about how our color vision works, the models will be changed accordingly.

The input data to the model include:

1. the photopic luminance of the adapting field, L_A (cd m^{-2});
2. the tristimulus values of the test sample in the source conditions, XYZ;
3. the tristimulus values of the source white in the source conditions, $X_w Y_w Z_w$;
4. the relative luminance of the source background in the source conditions, Y_b;
5. the impact of background, c;
6. the chromatic induction factor, N_c;
7. the lightness contrast factor, F_{LL};
8. the degree of adaptation, F.

Some of the recommended parameters are given in Table 18.1

The first step is to account for chromatic adaptation. The reference viewing illuminant is chosen to be the equal-energy white. All color appearance attributes are formulated in the reference conditions. The tristimulus values in the application are first transformed into an approximation of cone responses. These responses are then further transformed to the reference viewing conditions by the Bradford chromatic adaptation model. The transformation from CIEXYZ to some intermediate normalized responses R, G, B (in which the

Table 18.1. *Recommended values for some parameters in the CIECAM97s model*

Viewing conditions	c	N_c	F_{LL}	F
average surround, sample > 4°	0.69	1.0	0.0	1.0
average surround	0.69	1.0	1.0	1.0
dim surround	0.59	1.1	1.0	0.9
dark surround	0.525	0.8	1.0	0.9
cut-sheet transparencies	0.41	0.8	1.0	0.9

simple chromatic adaptation model was found to work well) is given by:

$$\begin{bmatrix} R \\ G \\ B \end{bmatrix} = \begin{bmatrix} 0.8951 & 0.2664 & -0.1614 \\ -0.7502 & 1.7135 & 0.0367 \\ 0.0389 & -0.0685 & 1.0296 \end{bmatrix} \begin{bmatrix} X/Y \\ Y/Y \\ Z/Y \end{bmatrix} = M_B \begin{bmatrix} X/Y \\ Y/Y \\ Z/Y \end{bmatrix}. \quad (18.13)$$

Note that each row of the transformation matrix, M_B, sums up to 1. For the CIE tristimulus values (X_{ref}, Y_{ref}, Z_{ref}) of the equal-energy reference illuminant, $X_{\text{ref}} = Y_{\text{ref}} = Z_{\text{ref}}$ and therefore $R_{\text{ref}} = G_{\text{ref}} = B_{\text{ref}} = 1$.

The normalized responses R, G, B are then transformed into the corresponding quantities R_c, G_c, B_c under the reference conditions by the following chromatic adaptation model:

$$R_c = [D(1/R_w) + 1 - D]R, \quad (18.14)$$

$$G_c = [D(1/G_w) + 1 - D]G, \quad (18.15)$$

$$B_c = [\text{sign of } (B)][D(1/B_w^p) + 1 - D]|B|^p, \quad (18.16)$$

$$p = (B_w/1.0)^{0.0834}, \quad (18.17)$$

$$D = F - \frac{F}{1 + 2(L_A^{1/4}) + (L_A^2/300)}, \quad (18.18)$$

where D is the luminance-adjusted degree of chromatic adaptation, computed as a function of luminance level by a user specified parameter F, the degree of chromatic adaptation. Alternatively, if we want to predict the case where the illuminant is completely discounted, we can set $D = 1.0$. If we do not wish to discount the illuminant at all, we can set $D = 0.0$. This parameter accounts for the empirical finding that our visual system seems to be able to estimate the illuminant color, and in color perception, we are able to either consciously discount the illuminant or simply judge it as pure sensation without discounting the illuminant. Note that when $D = 1.0$, the red and the green adaptations are the simple von Kries transform, but the blue adaptation is a nonlinear function.

The following adaptation-related parameters are then calculated by

$$k = \frac{1}{5L_A + 1}, \quad (18.19)$$

$$F_L = 0.2k^4(5L_A) + 0.1(1 - k^4)^2(5L_A)^{1/3}, \quad (18.20)$$

$$N_{bb} = N_{cb} = 0.725 \left(\frac{Y_w}{Y_b}\right)^{0.2}, \quad (18.21)$$

$$z = 1 + F_{LL} \left(\frac{Y_b}{Y_w}\right)^{1/2}, \quad (18.22)$$

and the normalized responses under reference conditions, R_c, G_c, B_c, are now transformed into some approximation of cone responses, R', G', B' as follows:

$$\begin{bmatrix} R' \\ G' \\ B' \end{bmatrix} = \begin{bmatrix} 0.389\,71 & 0.688\,98 & -0.078\,68 \\ -0.229\,81 & 1.183\,40 & 0.046\,41 \\ 0.0 & 0.0 & 1.0 \end{bmatrix} M_B^{-1} \begin{bmatrix} YR_c \\ YG_c \\ YB_c \end{bmatrix} \quad (18.23)$$

$$= M_H M_B^{-1} \begin{bmatrix} YR_c \\ YG_c \\ YB_c \end{bmatrix}. \quad (18.24)$$

We now calculate the adapted responses R'_a, G'_a, B'_a as follows:

$$R'_a = \frac{40(F_L|R'|/100)^{0.73}}{(F_L|R'|/100)^{0.73} + 2} + 1, \tag{18.25}$$

$$G'_a = \frac{40(F_L|G'|/100)^{0.73}}{(F_L|G'|/100)^{0.73} + 2} + 1, \tag{18.26}$$

$$B'_a = \frac{40(F_L|B'|/100)^{0.73}}{(F_L|B'|/100)^{0.73} + 2} + 1, \tag{18.27}$$

The redness–greenness response, a, the yellowness–blueness response, b, and the hue angle, h, are computed as follows:

$$a = R'_a - \left(\frac{12}{11}\right) G'_a + \left(\frac{1}{11}\right) B'_a, \tag{18.28}$$

$$b = \left(\frac{1}{9}\right)(R'_a + G'_a - 2B'_a), \tag{18.29}$$

$$h = \tan^{-1}\left(\frac{b}{a}\right) \quad \text{[degree]}, \tag{18.30}$$

and

$$n = \frac{Y_b}{Y_w}, \tag{18.31}$$

Hue quadrature, H, and eccentricity factor, e, are calculated from the following unique hue data through linear interpolation between the following values for the unique hues:

- red: $h = 20.14°$, $e = 0.8$, $H = 0$ or 400;
- yellow: $h = 90.0°$, $e = 0.7$, $H = 100$;
- green: $h = 164.25°$, $e = 1.0$, $H = 200$; and
- blue: $h = 237.53°$, $e = 1.2$, $H = 300$.

For any color stimulus, we have to first identify the two neighboring unique hues, and note their e, h, and H values. We can then use them to calculate the eccentricity factor and the hue quadrature of the color stimulus with the following formulas:

$$e = e_1 + (e_2 - e_1)(h - h_1)/(h_2 - h_1), \tag{18.32}$$

$$H = H_1 + \frac{100(h - h_1)/e_1}{(h - h_1)/e_1 + (h_2 - h)/e_2}. \tag{18.33}$$

We can now calculate the various appearance attributes as follows:

The achromatic response, A:

$$A = \left[2R'_a + G'_a + \left(\frac{1}{20}\right) B'_a - 2.05\right] N_{bb}. \tag{18.34}$$

Lightness, J:

$$J = 100 \left(\frac{A}{A_w}\right)^{cz}. \tag{18.35}$$

Brightness, Q:

$$Q = \left(\frac{1.24}{c}\right)\left(\frac{J}{100}\right)^{0.67}(A_w + 3)^{0.9}. \tag{18.36}$$

Saturation, s:

$$s = \frac{50(a^2 + b^2)^{1/2}100e(\frac{10}{13})N_c N_{cb}}{R'_a + G'_a + (\frac{21}{20})B'_a}. \tag{18.37}$$

Chroma, C:

$$C = 2.44s^{0.69}\left(\frac{J}{100}\right)^{0.67n}(1.64 - 0.29^n). \tag{18.38}$$

Colorfulness, M:

$$M = CF_L^{0.15}. \tag{18.39}$$

As can be seen in the equations listed above, the computation of CIECAM97s involves many nonlinear functions. Furthermore, the inverse transform from the perceptual attributes to the CIEXYZ is even more complicated. For industrial applications, complex computations are often avoided and, as a result, CIECAM97s has not been as widely used as it was hoped. This prompted the CIE to simplify the model further and the revised color appearance model called CIECAM02 was proposed.

18.6.4 CIECAM02 and revision of CIECAM97s

Soon after the publication of CIECAM97s, various research groups began to find some deficiencies in the model. For example, changes in surround relative luminance produce nonmonotonic changes in appearance because the recommended N_c value for a dim surround ($N_c = 1.1$) is higher than that for the average surround ($N_c = 1.0$) and that for the dark surround ($N_c = 0.8$). This shows the inherent weakness of this type of empirical modeling: too many parameters that are set empirically without a principle to check for global consistency. Another deficiency is that the lightness values, J, are not always 0 for $Y = 0$. Furthermore, it was shown that the chroma scale was expanded at low chroma level. These and other deficiencies are summarized in [294] and they were explicitly addressed when a simplified, revised model was being drafted. The revised model is called CIECAM02 and is currently being tested. The revised parameter values are shown in Table 18.2.

Table 18.2. *Recommended values for some parameters in the CIECAM02 model*

Viewing conditions	c	N_c	F
average surround	0.69	1.0	1.0
dim surround	0.59	0.95	0.9
dark surround	0.525	0.8	0.8

In order to simplify the computations, the original nonlinear chromatic adaptation transform was changed into a linear one, with a new CIEXYZ to RGB transformation matrix.

$$\begin{bmatrix} R \\ G \\ B \end{bmatrix} = \begin{bmatrix} 0.7328 & 0.4296 & -0.1624 \\ -0.7036 & 1.6975 & 0.0061 \\ 0.0030 & 0.0136 & 0.9834 \end{bmatrix} \begin{bmatrix} X \\ Y \\ Z \end{bmatrix} = M_{\text{CAT02}} \begin{bmatrix} X \\ Y \\ Z \end{bmatrix}. \tag{18.40}$$

The responses R, G, B are then transformed into the corresponding quantities R_c, G_c, B_c under the reference conditions by the following chromatic adaptation model:

$$R_c = [D(Y_w/R_w) + 1 - D]R, \tag{18.41}$$

$$G_c = [D(Y_w/G_w) + 1 - D]G, \tag{18.42}$$

$$B_c = [D(Y_w/B_w) + 1 - D]B, \tag{18.43}$$

$$D = F\left(1 - \frac{1}{3.6}e^{-(L_A+42)/92}\right). \tag{18.44}$$

The following adaptation-related parameters are then calculated by:

$$k = \frac{1}{5L_A + 1}, \tag{18.45}$$

$$F_L = 0.2k^4(5L_A) + 0.1(1 - k^4)^2(5L_A)^{1/3}, \tag{18.46}$$

$$n = Y_b/Y_w, \tag{18.47}$$

$$N_{bb} = N_{cb} = 0.725(Y_w/Y_b)^{0.2}, \tag{18.48}$$

$$z = 1.48 + (Y_b/Y_w)^{1/2}, \tag{18.49}$$

and the responses under reference conditions, R_c, G_c, B_c, are now transformed into some approximation of cone responses, R', G', B' as follows:

$$\begin{bmatrix} R' \\ G' \\ B' \end{bmatrix} = \begin{bmatrix} 0.389\,71 & 0.688\,98 & -0.078\,68 \\ -0.229\,81 & 1.183\,40 & 0.046\,41 \\ 0.0 & 0.0 & 1.0 \end{bmatrix} M_{\text{CAT02}}^{-1} \begin{bmatrix} R_c \\ G_c \\ B_c \end{bmatrix} \tag{18.50}$$

$$= M_H M_{\text{CAT02}}^{-1} \begin{bmatrix} R_c \\ G_c \\ B_c \end{bmatrix}. \tag{18.51}$$

We can now calculate the adapted responses R'_a, G'_a, B'_a as follows:

$$R'_a = \frac{400(F_L|R'|/100)^{0.42}}{(F_L|R'|/100)^{0.42} + 27.13} + 0.1, \tag{18.52}$$

$$G'_a = \frac{400(F_L|G'|/100)^{0.42}}{(F_L|G'|/100)^{0.42} + 27.13} + 0.1, \tag{18.53}$$

$$B'_a = \frac{400(F_L|B'|/100)^{0.42}}{(F_L|B'|/100)^{0.42} + 27.13} + 0.1. \tag{18.54}$$

The redness–greenness response, a, the yellowness–blueness response, b, and the hue angle, h, are computed as follows:

$$a = R'_a - \left(\frac{12}{11}\right) G'_a + \left(\frac{1}{11}\right) B'_a, \tag{18.55}$$

$$b = \left(\frac{1}{9}\right)(R'_a + G'_a - 2B'_a), \tag{18.56}$$

$$h = \tan^{-1}\left(\frac{b}{a}\right) \quad \text{[degree]}. \tag{18.57}$$

Hue quadrature, H, is calculated from the following unique hue data through linear interpolation between the following values for the unique hues:

- red: $h = 20.14°$, $e = 0.8$, $H = 0$ or 400;
- yellow: $h = 90.0°$, $e = 0.7$, $H = 100$;
- green: $h = 164.25°$, $e = 1.0$, $H = 200$; and
- blue: $h = 237.53°$, $e = 1.2$, $H = 300$.

The eccentricity factor, e, is calculated by the following formula:

$$e = N_c N_{cb} \frac{12500}{13} \left[3.8 + \cos\left(\frac{\pi}{180}h + 2\right)\right]. \tag{18.58}$$

For any color stimulus, we have to first identify the two neighboring unique hues, and note their e, h, and H values. We can then use them to calculate the hue quadrature of the color stimulus by the following formula:

$$H = H_1 + \frac{100(h - h_1)/e_1}{(h - h_1)/e_1 + (h_2 - h)/e_2}. \tag{18.59}$$

The chroma scale now requires the calculation of a new factor, t,

$$t = \frac{e(a^2 + b^2)^{1/2}}{R'_a + G'_a + 1.05 B'_a}. \tag{18.60}$$

We can now calculate the various appearance attributes as follows:

The achromatic response, A:

$$A = \left[2R'_a + G'_a + \left(\frac{1}{20}\right) B'_a - 0.305\right] N_{bb}. \tag{18.61}$$

Lightness, J:

$$J = 100 \left(\frac{A}{A_w}\right)^{cz}. \tag{18.62}$$

Brightness, Q:

$$Q = \left(\frac{4}{c}\right)\left(\frac{J}{100}\right)^{0.5}(A_w + 4)(F_L)^{0.25}. \tag{18.63}$$

Chroma, C:

$$C = 0.1t^{0.9}\sqrt{J}(1.64 - 0.29^n)^{0.73}. \tag{18.64}$$

Colorfulness, M:

$$M = CF_L^{0.25}. \tag{18.65}$$

Saturation, s:

$$s = 100 \left(\frac{M}{Q}\right)^{0.5}. \tag{18.66}$$

Values computed can be quite different for CIECAM97s and CIECAM02, especially the chroma value C and the hue H. While the lightness, J, has a nominal range of 100, the scale of brightness, Q, is more arbitrary and the large brightness difference in the two models is only a matter of scale. Initial field trials seem to show that CIECAM02 is significantly more accurate and consistent, in addition to being simpler.

18.7 Theoretical color gamut

In developing his color order system, Ostwald defined his full colors (most-saturated colors) as those generated from spectral reflectance curves that have either 0% or 100% reflectance over the visible wavelengths. Schrödinger [842] and then MacAdam [617] showed that this type of spectral reflectance function indeed produces the maximum attainable excitation purity for a given luminance reflectance factor and dominant wavelength, provided that the spectral reflectance factors are restricted to between 0% and 100%. Ostwald's full colors are now called the optimal colors. It is also known that the spectral reflectance factor function of an optimal color has one or at most two transitions in the visible wavelength range. Therefore, there are four types of spectral reflectance factor function [441, 842] as shown in Fig. 18.4. The set of all optimal colors constitutes the theoretical boundary of the volume of colors reproducible by all object surfaces that reflect light diffusely and do not produce fluorescence or other nonlinear optical energy conversion. In the USA, this theoretical

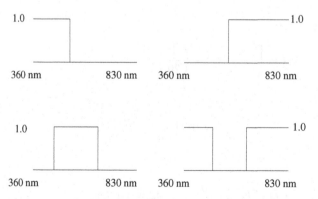

Figure 18.4. The four types of spectral reflectance function for optimal colors.

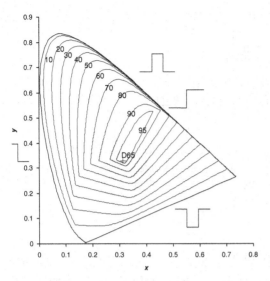

Figure 18.5. Chromaticity loci of optimal color stimuli, under D_{65}, as a function of luminance level $Y = 10, 20, 30, \ldots, 80, 90, 95$. These chromaticity contours are computed with the wavelength resolution interpolated to 0.1 nm.

boundary of color volume is often referred to as the MacAdam limits. Figure 18.5 shows the chromaticity loci of optimal color stimuli under D_{65} illuminant.

It is not difficult to understand qualitatively why the spectral reflectance factor function, $\rho(\lambda)$, of an optimal color has at most two transitions. Let us start with $\rho(\lambda) = 0$ for all λ. Now as an example, given the dominant wavelength at 520 nm and the luminance at $Y = 80$, the optimal color can be determined by first setting $\rho(520 \text{ nm}) = 1$. This is the highest excitation purity possible for that dominant wavelength. Of course, this function does not reflect enough luminance. We can then set either $\rho(519 \text{ nm}) = 1$ or $\rho(521 \text{ nm}) = 1$, depending on which one will result in a chromaticity closer to the dominant wavelength 520 nm. Setting one more wavelength to 1 will slightly increase the luminance, but it will also slightly decrease the excitation purity. If we continue this process of setting the ρ at the neighboring wavelength equal to 1 so that the resulting color has a dominant wavelength always close or equal to 520 nm, we arrive at a spectral reflectance factor function, $\rho(\lambda)$, that produces the desired luminance Y. At that point, all other $\rho(\lambda)$ are at 0. Therefore, we have at most two transitions in the spectrum. The resulting excitation purity is the highest of all other spectral reflectance factor functions because each $\rho(\lambda)$ we set to 1 in the process is also the wavelength closest to 520 nm. From the the chromaticity collinearity property of color mixtures, we know that the resulting chromaticity of the mixture of all the monochromatic stimuli is bounded within the region enclosed by their chromaticity loci, and therefore will be closest to the chromaticity locus of 520 nm. If a chromaticity direction does not have a dominant wavelength, the complementary wavelength, λ_c, has to be used. In this case, we need to start with $\rho(\lambda) = 1$ for all λ and set the $\rho(\lambda_c)$ to 0 as the first step. We then proceed to set neighboring wavelengths to 0 one at a time until the desired luminance is reached. From this discussion, it is also easy to see that the one-transition types of spectral reflection

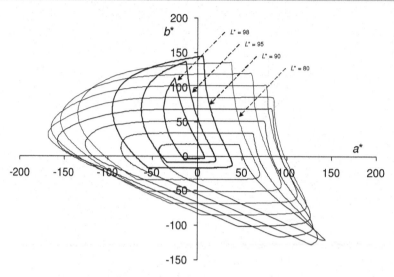

Figure 18.6. CIELAB contours of optimal color stimuli, under D_{65}, as functions of lightness level $L^* = 10, 20, 30, \ldots, 80, 90, 95, 98$. These chromaticity contours are computed with wavelength resolution interpolated to 0.05 nm.

factor function as shown on the top row in Fig. 18.4 are the intermediate type of the bottom two types. The upper half of the chromaticity diagram has the bottom left type, while the lower half has the bottom right type. The top right type happens in the middle of the right half of the chromaticity diagram, and the top left type in the middle of the left half. For example, in Fig. 18.5 under D_{65}, the one-transition type occurs at about 585 nm for $Y = 60$.

If the computation of optimal colors is done by the above procedure using discrete sums, instead of real integrals, through the entire wavelength interval, significant quantization errors are encountered, unless the color matching functions are sampled at a resolution much finer than 1 nm. The contours as shown in Fig. 18.5 are computed with a wavelength resolution interpolated to 0.1 nm. We can also compute the optimal colors in the CIELAB color space. Figure 18.6 shows the theoretical boundary under D_{65}. As will be seen shortly, in a study by Pointer almost all real object colors fell well within this boundary. When the lightness is increased above $L^* = 95$, the theoretical boundary closes in very quickly to the origin. Very bright colors cannot have very high chromas. It is also interesting to note that, at $L^* = 98$, the color boundary is very asymmetric with respect to the origin – yellow colors have much higher chromas than red or blue colors. This is easy to understand because the luminous efficiency function, $V(\lambda) = \bar{y}(\lambda)$, peaks in the "middle" wavelength range.

18.8   Color gamut mapping

Since the optimal colors require (physically impossible) discontinuous transitions between 0% and 100% reflectance values, the volume of real surface colors is actually significantly smaller than the theoretical volume, as has been shown by a number of studies [766]. Figure 18.7 shows the gamut of a large collection of real surface colors plotted in (a^*, b^*).

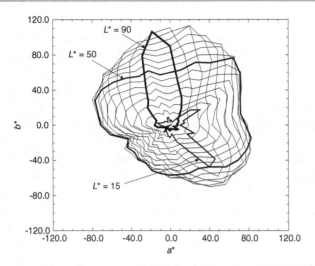

Figure 18.7. The gamut of real surface colors plotted in (a^*, b^*). Each contour represents a constant lightness level, from $L^* = 15$ to $L^* = 90$ in increments of 5. The data were reported by Pointer [766].

We can see that the gamut is not symmetric with respect to neutral and the distribution of lighter color, say $L^* = 90$ (the thickest contour), is completely skewed towards yellow (the 90–100° direction).

An output device, such as a printer or a monitor, can display only a limited set of colors on a given medium, such as paper or a phosphor screen. This set of colors is called the color gamut of the device/medium combination. Any color that is outside this gamut has to be mapped into a displayable color before it can be sent to the device/medium. This process is called color gamut mapping. Various strategies have been proposed to perform such a mapping. Since cost, speed, and quality requirements differ greatly from application to application, we will discuss different color gamut mapping strategies separately for different sets of design considerations. The major questions are: (1) Is the mapping image-dependent [818] or image-independent? (2) Does the mapping require spatial processing or not? Another important factor to consider is whether the evaluation is done by single stimulus (seeing only the reproduction) or pair comparison (seeing both the original and the reproduction).

18.8.1   Selection of color space and metrics

The first step in color gamut mapping is to select a proper color space to represent the color gamut and a good color-difference metric to measure the distance between two colors. Two obvious criteria for the selection of the color space are that it should be perceptually based and it should be as uniform as possible so that color difference is easy to compute. These two selection criteria seem to make sense because an implicit goal of the mapping is to reduce perceptual errors. Therefore, most existing algorithms use CIELAB and CIELUV. However, there are several problems: (1) CIELAB and CIELUV are not truly uniform [191, 450, 612]; (2) spatial variations (luminance and chrominance contrast sensitivities) are not accounted for; (3) effects due to the viewing surround are not accounted for; and

(4) chromatic adaptation is not properly modeled. In order to reduce the nonuniformity, different approaches have been taken. One is to modify the color-difference formula, such as ΔE_{94}^* [191]. Another is to use the Munsell Color System. A third approach is to use color appearance models, such as CIECAM97s [193] or CIECAM02 [676]. Since these models do not account for spatial variations either, spatial processing models have also been used [47, 295, 678, 692, 770, 1052].

Although we may think that the most accurate color appearance model will be the best choice for color gamut mapping, it should be realized that most of the models are dependent on viewing conditions because our color perception is a function of viewing conditions. However, in practical applications, reproduced images, such as color reflection prints, are intended to be viewed under many different and often uncontrolled viewing conditions. The optimality criteria for color gamut mapping for these types of applications should take into account the wide range of viewing conditions.

18.8.2   Computing the device color gamut

After a color space is chosen, we have to determine the color gamut of the output device for our application. For an analog system, such as an optical printer printing on photographic paper, a good approach is to use a physical model of the device/media system. For example, photographic paper can be modeled using the Lambert–Beer law and some empirical relation between reflection density and transmission density, as described in Section 16.1.3. With a proper model, the color gamut can be determined fairly efficiently by searching along surfaces formed by minimum and maximum dye mixtures [440].

For a digital output device, its color gamut can often be determined by printing and measuring color patches that correspond to input combinations with one of the primary colors set to the minimum or the maximum digital value. For example, if a three-color printer can accept RGB values, with 8 bits per color, then color patches that correspond to $(R, G, B) = (0, m, n)$ or $(R, G, B) = (255, m, n)$, $0 \leq m,n \leq 255$, often have colors that are on the boundary of the printer's color gamut. Therefore, the entire color gamut of a printer can be determined by measuring colors produced by such combinations. This is, of course, based on the assumption that the color gamut is a convex volume without holes. In some cases, this may not be true and we must be careful in making such an assumption. It is always necessary to compare the neighboring color combinations to see if monotonicity or convexity is violated. For example, let us assume that a printer is set by the manufacturer to produce brighter colors for larger RGB values. Therefore, we would expect the color patch corresponding to $(R, G, B) = (m, m, m)$ to have a lower reflectance factor than that of $(R, G, B) = (n, n, n)$, if $m \leq n$. However, measured reflectances for some inkjet printers show that this may not always be true.

18.8.3   Image-independent methods for color gamut mapping

Most color gamut mappings are carried out in the output device calibration process. For any input color specified in CIEXYZ or CIELAB, the printer calibration table provides the required RGB values that will print the desired color. When the desired color is

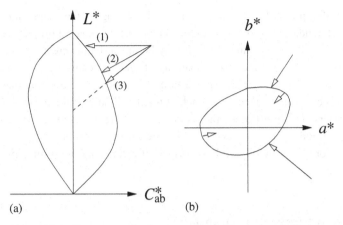

Figure 18.8. Two types of color gamut mapping strategy: (a) three examples of the hard-clipping approach; (b) an example of the soft-compression approach.

outside of the printer color gamut, the color gamut mapping process takes over to find a "closest" in-gamut color to use for printing the desired color. This strategy is called hard-clipping. Alternatively, we can also create a mapping (linear or nonlinear) that shrinks all colors towards neutral so that out-of-gamut colors are compressed into the printable gamut. This is called soft-compression. Figure 18.8 shows typical examples of these two approaches: Fig.18.8(a) shows three commonly used hard-clipping strategies, and Fig. 18.8(b) shows an example of the soft-compression approach in which some out-of-gamut colors are mapped to the gamut boundary and some of the in-gamut colors are mapped inwards away from the boundary. In either case, the color gamut mapping operates on a pixel-by-pixel basis, independently of the image content and without any spatial processing. Extensive studies have shown that neither of these two strategies is uniformly good for all images [677, 857, Chapter 10]. Hard-clipping tends to preserve pleasing color saturation, but lose image details where clipping occurs. Soft-compression preserves some details, but tends to desaturate and noticeably distort many colors. There are many variations in both approaches. The major differences between different algorithms are: (i) the color difference formula used to measure color distances, and (ii) the constraints on the allowable mapping. The former has been discussed in the context of the color space and metric. The latter is often classified [450] in terms of the dimensionality of the constraints: one-, two-, or three-dimensional. For example, the most often used one-dimensional constraint is to pre-serve hue and lightness (as shown by projection (1) in Fig. 18.8(a)). Therefore, the chroma of the out-of-gamut color is reduced to the maximum printable chroma for the same hue and lightness. The allowable mapping is a one-dimensional projection along the chroma direction. This strategy actually works very well for images whose color gamuts are only slightly larger than the printer gamut. Colors maintain their colorfulness and are mostly undistorted. Figure 18.8 also shows two examples of typical two-dimensional constraints (projections (2) and (3) in the figure). One constraint (projection (2)) is to project to the nearest in-gamut color on the constant hue plane. The motivation is to distort out-of-gamut colors as little as possible, according to the defined color distance. However, this approach can make the out-of-gamut colors lighter or darker, depending on the shape and distance of the local gamut boundary. For example, on one hue plane, the nearest projection may be downward, but, on a neighboring hue plane, it may be upward, thus creating noisy luminance fluctuations. In order to reduce the probability of such an occurrence, one strategy is to project towards a medium gray point (projection (3)). It is easy to imagine many other variations around such *ad-hoc* constraints. Each of them will do well for some images and not so well for others. This motivates other strategies that are either image-dependent or spatially-varying, or both. All these new strategies are the subject of quite active research and require a lot more work before we know which directions are the promising ones to pursue in the future.

18.9   Using more than three color channels

Many color reproduction problems can be solved more robustly if we have more than three color channels to use. On the input side, theory says three is enough ONLY if the three spectral sensitivity functions of the imaging system are a linear combination of the three human cone spectral sensitivity functions. Otherwise, there will be metameric problems. Even if metameric problems are not a concern, there are some other potential advantages in having more than three channels. For example, one can make better estimates about the spectral power distribution of the incident light. This potential has been studied before by different groups. The conclusion seems to be that the potential is realizable. Some digital cameras are using sensors that have more than three spectral channels and are claimed to have better color reproduction than those with conventional trichromatic sensors. It is also easy to see that color scanners can beneficially take this path.

On the output side, three channels are not enough, mainly because of the limited color gamut. Black ink expands the color gamut for the dark colors (including gray and black). Other color inks expand the color gamut in different parts of the color space. The other potential benefit for more than three output channels is similar to that of the input side, i.e., the metameric problems. The more channels we use, the more stable the color reproduction will be under different illuminants. In the extreme case, one can reproduce the spectral reflectance of an object.

18.10   Color management systems

In a closed system such as the conventional photographic system, all the components in the imaging chain are made to work with each other. Little intervention is needed to "manage" the color reproduction process. In digital imaging applications, there are many different input and output devices available, each of which might be made by a different manufacturer without conforming to a single standard. One digital camera may use NTSC primaries to specify its output colors, while another camera may use sRGB as output metrics. Similarly, if the same digital image is printed on two printers, the resulting color prints may look very different. In order to solve the problems created by the incompatible color metrics used in the various devices, color management systems are set up to do color conversions between different color metrics so that color imaging devices can talk to each other properly. Furthermore, a color management system has to deal with color conversion from one viewing condition to another, the luminance adjustment when there is a mismatch in the dynamic ranges between two devices, and the interpretation of rendering intent as specified in the device profiles. These issues and solutions of color management systems can be found in a number of books [347, 469].

One solution proposed by the International Color Consortium (ICC) is to use device profiles, which are files that contain device calibration information in a standard data format. Device manufacturers are asked to provide a device profile for each model of imaging device they make. A color management system will then makes color transformations from one device to another, based on the device profile that comes with the imaging device. Therefore, the color management system works like an international bank that may receive a payment in one currency and make a payment in another currency. It works only if there is a table of exchange rates between different currencies, or a table of exchange rates with a common currency.

However, the solution provided by device profiles is not perfect. Some of the main problems are as follows:

- Quantization errors. Color transformations are often performed with a limited number of bits (e.g., 8 bits). Converting from one device-dependent color space to another often involves transformation to an intermediate device-independent color space, such as CIEXYZ or CIELAB. The resulting quantization errors can be quite serious.
- Device stability. A device profile may be generated in the factory when the device is made. However, device characteristics often drift with time, making the original device profile inaccurate.
- Viewing conditions. A device profile may be produced under one viewing condition and the application may use another viewing condition. Although one can use a color appearance model to compensate for the difference, the model may not work well because there is no automatic algorithm for calculating the required parameters for the particular viewing condition.
- Device characteristics. When the characteristics of an output device are very different from those the profile was designed for, the color reproduction may be less than ideal; for example, if the output dynamic range is too small or the viewing flare is larger than expected.
- Ambiguous interpretation. Some color transformation is not one-to-one. For example, RGB to CMYK is not a one-to-one mapping. In such cases, an optimal mapping may not be chosen by a color management system. For example, if certain areas in a color document are to be printed black, a color management system may map the device-dependent RGB to a device-independent CIELAB, and then from there to a printer-dependent CMYK space. The process may cause the printer to print some cyan, magenta, and yellow inks, in addition to black ink, resulting in a muddy black.

18.11 Problems

18.1 We use a digital camera to take a picture of a room and print it using a color printer. We can then compare the color print and the original scene side by side to see how good the color reproduction of our camera and printer as an imaging chain is.

(a) What do you think is a proper color reproduction criterion for this application?
(b) Can we use ΔE in CIELAB for this comparison?
(c) How do we quantify the color reproduction errors in such a situation?

(Hint: Although this scenario sounds simple, as a color reproduction problem, it is actually quite complicated. The purpose of this exercise is to let us think through what we have learned so far and see how we should formulate some kind of solution.)

18.2 We use a scanner to digitize a color print and then print the digitized image using an inkjet printer. We can now compare the original with the scan/print copy in terms of color reproduction.

(a) What do you think is a proper color reproduction criterion for this application?
(b) Can we use ΔE in CIELAB for this comparison?
(c) How do we quantify the color reproduction errors in such a situation?
(d) If the paper white of the original has a low minimum density, say, 0.05, and the paper white of the copy has a higher minimum density, say, 0.15, how do you justify your answers in (a), (b), and (c) ?

18.3 The CIE 1997 Interim Color Appearance Model (CIECAMs) provides a way of computing the lightness, J, of a color sample under a given viewing condition. The L^* in CIELAB is also recommended for computing the lightness of flat color samples in a light-gray–white background. Let us assume that the light source is CIE Illuminant C. Compare the two lightness scales, J and L^*, as functions of luminance Y for neutral gray patches.

19 Color image acquisition

Color images of scenes and objects can be captured on photographic film by conventional cameras, on video tape by video cameras, and on magnetic disk or solid-state memory card by digital cameras. Digital color images can be digitized from film or paper by scanners. In this chapter, we will cover these major color image acquisition devices. Photographic film has the longest history and still offers a convenient, low-cost, high-quality means for capturing color images. For this reason, it is very useful to understand the photographic processes, photographic film and photographic paper, because they are often the sources of many color images that we will encounter. They have some unique properties that influence how film-originated digital color images should be processed by computers. The next in importance is the solid state sensors, of which charge-coupled devices (CCDs) are the most widely used so far, with others (such as complementary metal-oxide–semiconductor (CMOS) sensors) gaining in popularity. Scanners are devices that are used to digitize images from film and paper. They are the main devices for generating high-quality digital color images. Most scanners use CCD sensors, except some high-end graphic arts scanners that use photomultiplier tubes. Digital cameras are becoming more and more competitive with photographic films in terms of image quality and convenience. Most digital cameras today also use CCD sensors. Each of these devices has different characteristics and unique image processing problems. They are discussed separately.

19.1 General considerations for system design and evaluation

Color image acquisition systems are designed under a lot of practical constraints. Many system components are designed and manufactured separately. For example, CCD sensors, zoom lenses, and DSP (digital signal processing) chips are made by different companies. Almost all imaging systems are not optimized on a system design level, but rather the performance is optimized after the components are made and when the system is put together. Therefore, color imaging engineers usually do not have the chance to apply their knowledge and expertise to the system as a whole. However, if every engineer in the imaging field analyzes performance on a system level, we might hope that the components are not too far off from how they should be designed. It is thus very important for us to have a good overall understanding of what the general issues are before we look at each individual image acquisition system in this chapter. Some of these general issues are: (1) spectral sensitivity/responsivity, (2) calibration and linearity, (3) dynamic range and signal-to-noise ratio, (4) signal shaping and quantization, (5) geometrical accuracy, (6) resolution and addressability, (7) image processing algorithms, and (8) output metric conversion. System engineers should study how these different factors may interact with each other before they can lay out a good system hardware and firmware architecture to ensure that the final images from the system are of the best quality possible.

19.1.1   Considerations for input spectral responsivities

For color image acquisition devices, system spectral response functions are important design considerations because they affect the overall system performance in terms of color reproduction, signal-to-noise ratio, and cost. For consumer imaging, the final image quality is judged by human observers. If the spectral responsivity functions of an imaging system are linear transformations of the CIE color matching functions, there will be no difference between what the system sees and what an average human observer sees. This condition is called the Luther condition. Mismatches between the object colors and the reproduced colors may be noticed quite easily, and therefore, within other cost/performance constraints, it is very desirable that the system spectral response functions be as close as possible to the human cone spectral sensitivity functions (or their linear combinations) [709]. However, there are two practical difficulties in doing so: (1) the cost of producing the required color filters is often too high, and (2) the system signal-to-noise performance may be unacceptable. For example, the human L and M cones have a large overlap in their spectral sensitivity functions, making it difficult, without overly magnifying the noise, to convert the L and M cone signals to a color image to be displayed on a color monitor that does not use primaries close to those required by the human LMS cone systems.

In reality, the spectral sensitizing dyes in the films and the color filters in the CCD/CMOS sensors are chosen from only a limited set of choices because the dyes and pigments have to be compatible with other materials in the devices, stable in the finished products, and inexpensive to make. Given that system spectral response functions have to be chosen from a set of available compromises, practical spectral optimization methods have to be developed for each type of image capture device [424, 725, 780, 781, 991, 992, 996, 1046, 1065].

There are two different types of approach one can take for spectral optimization: data-driven and sensor-theoretic. The data-driven approach requires us to compile a large set of color samples or their spectral reflectances that are representative of the intended application. The system spectral functions are then optimized with respect to the color reproduction of those color samples. The main difficulty in this approach is to make sure that the collected color samples are indeed representative. Alternatively, we can only use a number of important colors, such as skin, grass, and sky, for optimization. Colorcheckers that contain these important colors are commercially available because they are so useful for such purposes [647]. The sensor-theoretic approach is to develop a metric that measures the goodness of a set of spectral response functions and then optimizes them with respect to the metric, under all other system constraints. The main difficulty is in the development of a reliable metric for goodness measure. This problem has been studied many times in the past [992]. One possibility is to calculate the angle between the subspace of the LMS cone sensitivity functions and the subspace of the system spectral response functions as the goodness measure [991]. Of course, the sensor-theoretic approach can be cross-validated by the data-driven approach to make sure that the theoretical optimal spectral responses are in fact a good solution for a collection of color samples.

19.1.2 Calibration, linearity, signal shaping, and quantization

The first step in optimizing an image acquisition system is to calibrate the sensor response with respect to the scene radiance. Establishing such an input/output relation is fairly straightforward for systems that do not have any cross-talk between different color channels. However, most image capture devices do have some color cross-talk. For example, the green channel response is also a function of the red and blue channel responses. CCD and CMOS sensors have less color cross-talk, while photographic films have much more. In general, the sensor response as a function of scene radiance is measured at a series of luminance levels for a reference illumination source. This will establish the neutral response function. We then have to model the color cross-talk and use the model to remove the cross-talk as much as possible. Alternatively, this can also be done with a 3-D LUT.

It is also important to correct for sensor nonlinearity and measure the noise as a function of signal level. For many image processing algorithms, there is a preferred color space to work with. Furthermore, the analog sensor signals have to be digitized into digital signals. In order to preserve visible details and reduce visible noise, the best color space for analog to digital conversion is often in some kind of nonlinear visual space, such as L^*. Therefore, some type of signal shaping may be desirable before analog to digital conversion.

19.1.3 Dynamic range and signal-to-noise ratio

There are many different ways to define the dynamic range of an image acquisition system. For our discussion here, we will use a simple conceptual definition. The ratio of the highest scene radiance to the lowest scene radiance whose system responses can be *reliably discriminated* by the image acquisition system is called the dynamic range of the system. Two response levels can be reliably discriminated if they are separated by a multiple of the noise standard deviations. In many cases, the signal-to-noise ratio at a response level is required to be greater than a chosen threshold, e.g., 2. Therefore, the slope of the response versus scene radiance curve should be divided by the noise standard deviation and the ratio should be greater than 2. With this example criterion, the lowest scene radiance whose system response can be reliably discriminated is almost always not zero. A digital camera with a linear 10-bit output does not have a 1023:1 dynamic range as some people would think because the signal-to-noise ratio at an output response of 1 is most likely less than 2.

The reason for characterizing the dynamic range of the system is that when the captured color image is converted into the output metric, the system dynamic range is an important factor in the design of the image processing pipeline and the output metric conversion algorithm, such as tone scale and color gamut mappings.

19.2 Photographic films

Photographic films and papers are the dominant input/output media for high-quality color images. This is due to their excellent image resolution, exposure latitude, compactness, and convenience for image recording and storage. With the advances in solid-state sensors and memory devices, many applications, such as photojournalism, entertainment, and educational videos use electronic imaging devices instead of the conventional photographic films and papers. However, when it comes to consumer photography or high-quality hard-copy output, film and paper are still the media of choice because of their cost, convenience, and quality. Of course, the trend to electronic imaging is quickening its pace and imaging engineers need to learn both systems.

The chemistry of daguerreotype photography was first described in France in 1839 [210, p. 20]. Initially, the single layer emulsion was coated on glass plates. The first commercial color film, 16 mm Kodachrome motion picture film, was introduced in 1935. The image dye couplers for Kodachrome are in the developers. The Kodachrome transparency film consists of five layers: a blue-sensitive layer with a yellow dye to trap the blue light, a clear gelatine layer, a blue-and-green-sensitive layer, a clear gelatin layer, and a blue-and-red sensitive layer at the bottom, coated on a celluloid support. In the following year, Alga announced a reversal film, a negative film, and a motion picture film based on a tripack idea, proposed by Rudolph Fischer in 1912. The tripack films use nondiffusing couplers which are put in the film emulsion layers. By the end of the 1950s, photofinishers were processing color films for consumer imaging. Long years of research in chemistry, physics, photoscience, emulsion coating, and manufacturing technology have made color photography possible for consumer applications. This is one of the major achievements in color imaging history.

19.2.1 The structure of a black-and-white film

Photographic emulsion consists of silver halide crystals dispersed in gelatin. The emulsion is coated on various support media, such as cellulose triacetate. Some sheet film uses polyester (polyethylene terephthalate or PETP). The thickness of an emulsion layer is typically less than 10 μm. The silver halide crystals, usually called grains, are the light-sensitive elements of the emulsion. The shape of the silver halide grains varies from round, triangular, hexagonal, square, to some irregular shapes, with the triangular shape being the most common, accounting for over a third of the population [690]. The size of a silver halide grain is usually measured by its projected area on the film plane. In most emulsions for consumer imaging, the grain size distribution can be well described [690, 691] as a double log-normal distribution:

$$f(a) = A_0 \exp[-K(\ln a/a_0)^2] + A_1 \exp[-K(\ln a/a_1)^2], \qquad (19.1)$$

where a is the grain size, a_0 and a_1 are the two peak grain sizes, A_0 and A_1 are constants, and K is a measure of the spread of the distribution. In general, the contrast (gamma) of a film characteristic curve reduces with the *spread* of the grain size distribution, while the speed of the film increases with the mean grain size. Typical mean grain sizes for the consumer films are on the order of 0.2–0.7 μm^2.

Gelatin is used to prevent silver halide grains from aggregating. It allows each grain to be acted upon by the developer individually. Because of the presence of gelatin, when the emulsion is coated, it is set to a jelly-like layer on the film support and partially dried. The gelatin swells in the developer or other solutions, allowing the chemical agents to penetrate freely to reach all parts of the emulsion. The wonderful physical and chemical properties of gelatin make it an indispensiable ingredient in most photographic films and papers. So far, no other medium has been found that can replace gelatin in this application with the same cost/efficiency performance.

19.2.2   The latent image

Silver halide crystals have various structural defects, such as surface kinks and lattice dislocations, that can serve as traps for electrons or holes. When a photon is absorbed by a silver halide crystal, it can create an electron–hole pair. An electron can be trapped by a silver ion to form a silver atom, resulting in a latent image center, or it can wander around and recombine with a hole, resulting in a loss of detection efficiency. What happens after the photon absorption is not known exactly, but experimental evidence shows that it results in aggregates of silver atoms in a silver halide crystal. The minimum number of silver atoms that will make the grain developable is around 3–6, depending on the developer activity. Most of these clusters, called latent image centers, seem to be quite stable at room temperature, because an exposed film can be kept for quite a long time (years) and still be developable. Although it takes only three or more silver atoms to form a developable latent image center, it usually takes 3–10 times as many photon aborptions to do so because a major fraction of the photon-generated electrons is lost in electron-hole recombinations. There are methods to reduce the recombination rate, but this problem is still an area of active research [93, 377, 937].

The natural spectral absorption of a silver halide grain occurs for wavelengths below 500 nm. In order to make a film sensitive to longer-wavelength light, organic dyes that absorb photons in the desired spectral regions are often used. These dyes adhere to the grain surface and, when they absorb photons, some electrons are elevated to higher-energy states, from where they can be transferred to the conduction band of the silver halide grain, thus contributing to the formation of silver atom aggregates of the grain. These dyes are called the sensitizing dyes (which should be distinguished from the image dyes to be discussed below). These sensitizing dyes are used either to extend the absorption spectra of the black-and-white films above 500 nm, or to synthesize color film emulsion layers that are sensitive to different spectral regions.

19.2.3   Film processing

A developer solution is a reduction agent (electron donor) that reduces silver ions to silver atoms. Photon absorption by the silver halide grain creates clusters of silver atom aggregates that are apparently more susceptible to electron transfer from the developer than other grain locations that have no silver atom aggregates. A typical silver halide grain contains 10^8 silver ions. A latent image center of three or more silver atoms [377] can lead to the reduction of the entire silver halide grain consisting of about 10^8 silver atoms. The signal amplification of the silver halide imaging is thus on the order of 10^6, about the same magnitude as in the human photoreceptors. Photographic developer solutions are reducing agents that act on exposed grains several orders of magnitude faster than the unexposed grains (some of which are also developed).

After the latent image is converted into a silver image, the rest of the undeveloped silver halide grains are dissolved and washed out from the emulsion by a different chemical solution. This process is called fixing. After the fixing, what is left on the emulsion is a negative image, in the sense that, where there was high exposure, there is now a large amount of silver deposit and less light is reflected from or transmitted through the area.

Alternatively, if the developed silver is dissolved and washed away by some chemicals and the undeveloped silver halide grains are then exposed and developed to silver deposits, we have a positive image. This process is then called the reversal processing.

A small proportion of the grains that do not have latent image centers may also be developed, forming a small density across the developed film even where little or no light has irradiated. This small density level is called fog. In addition to the fog density, other ingredients, such as the film support or the colored-coupler in the color film, in the processed film or paper also contribute to the minimum density, D_{min}, that a piece of film or paper has. This density component is called the base density. Therefore, D_{min} is equal to base density plus fog density.

19.2.4   Color photography

Because of the trichromatic nature of human color vision, color photography can use as few as three spectral sensitive emulsion layers to record a color image: one sensitive to the long-wavelength light (red) (also sensitive to blue), one sensitive to the middle-wavelength light (green) (also sensitive to blue), and one sensitive to the short-wavelength light (blue). As discussed before, the spectral selectivity is accomplished by using spectral sensitizing dyes adsorbed onto the silver halide grains. The three layers of emulsions are coated one on top of another, although they are physically separated. The order of the coating is that the red-sensitive layer is deposited first (i.e., at the bottom), the green-sensitive layer is next, a yellow filter is then deposited on top on the green-sensitive layer, and the blue-sensitive layer is finally coated on the top (the exposing side). The reason for this order is that silver halide grains are inherently sensitive to the blue light. The yellow filter below the blue sensitive layer absorbs the blue (short-wavelength) component of the incident light and thus prevents the blue light from exposing the green and red layers below the yellow filter. The green-sensitive layer is coated above the red-sensitive layer because our visual system is more sensitive to sharpness degradation in the middle-wavelength spectral region. The bottom, red-sensitive layer thus suffers more image blurring due to light scattering when passing through the top few layers.

Modern color films can have as many as 15 emulsion layers, each of which has to be coated with less than 0.1 μm error in thickness. For example, a consumer color negative film may contain, from top to bottom, the following layers: (1) overcoat, (2) adsorber layer, (3) ultraviolet filter layer, (4) high-speed (coarse-grain) blue-sensitive emulsion layer,

(5) low-speed (fine grain) blue-sensitive emulsion layer, (6) yellow filter layer, (7) active separating layer, (8) high-speed green-sensitive emulsion layer, (9) low-speed green-sensitive emulsion layer, (10) red filter layer, (11) high-speed red-sensitive emulsion layer, (12) low-speed red-sensitive emulsion layer, (13) antihalation coating, and (14) film base (cellulose acetate). The emulsion thickness of the 35 mm role film is about 23 μm and the film base is about 125 μm.

Although the spectral information is sensed in roughly the three differently-sensitized layers, there remains the question of how one can extract the three color signals from the three layers. There are two major approaches to solving this problem. The first approach is to put image dyes in the developers, with the image dye being formed when the latent image centers are developed. The second approach is to put the image dye precursors into the emulsion layers, with the image dyes being formed when the latent silver image is developed. Kodachrome uses the former, while most others use the latter. Since the Kodachrome processing is much more complicated and less frequently used, we will only discuss the latter approach.

As we described before, the film developing process uses a reducing agent to reduce the silver ions in the exposed grains to silver atoms. In this reaction, the reducing agent is oxidized. If we can put in the emulsion some chemicals that will in turn react with the oxidized developer to form image dyes, we can produce a dye image which is proportional to the silver image. These chemicals are called couplers, because they couple with the oxidized developer to form dyes. The coupler which forms the cyan dye is called the cyan coupler, and similarly we also have the magenta coupler and the yellow coupler.

19.2.5 Subtractive color reproduction in photography

Dyes are light transmitting materials although they absorb part of the spectrum of the incident light. A color negative film or a color transparency (slide) is coated on a transparent support. If we put the negative or the slide on a black background, we will not be able to see the image on the film or the slide. In order to see the image well, we have to view it in front of a light source. This means that the spectral composition of the light source is selectively absorbed (subtracted) by the image dye and removed from our view. In order to produce colored stimuli, certain spectral range(s) of the incident light has (have) to be subtracted more than other spectral range(s). Again, due to the trichromatic nature of our visual system, the number of image dyes used in color photography is usually three. Using three dyes to modify the spectral composition of the transmitted light imposes a constraint on the absorption characteristics of the dyes: an image dye has to absorb certain parts of the spectrum in varying intensity as a function of its concentration, and it has to transmit all other wavelengths freely so that other image dyes can exert their control over the passage of wavelengths in other parts of the spectrum. Thus, the cyan dye should absorb "red" light in an amount varying with its concentration, but it should ideally transmit 100% of the "green" and the "blue" light. Similarly, the magenta dye should absorb some "green" light and transmit all the "red" and the "blue" light. Yellow dye is used to control how much "blue" light passes through and it should let all the "red" and the "green" light pass freely. Subtractive color reproduction in photography thus uses the three dyes to control how much "red", "green", and "blue" light pass through the media. For example, if an image region is to be rendered red, there should be little or no cyan dye, but there should be a lot of magenta and yellow dyes to block the passage of the "green" and the "blue" light. The intensity of the red light can be made stronger or weaker by adjusting the amount of cyan dye on the film or the slide, but, at every intensity, all of the green and the blue light has to be completely removed, otherwise the hue of the red color will shift when its intensity is changed. This analysis has two important consequences: (1) color reproduction in photography is subtractive in nature, and (2) an ideal image dye has to transmit 100% in some parts of the spectrum, and it has to transmit various amounts of light in other parts of the spectrum. This type of ideal dye is thus called a block dye, because its spectral transmission curve must look like a series of blocks, having sharp transitions from 100% transmission to some intermediate transmission value as a function of dye concentration.

Photographic paper also reproduces color by the subtractive process. Image dyes are formed on top of the highly reflective support. Light shining on the paper, with a small fraction of first surface reflection, has to penetrate through the dyes, be reflected from the paper support, and then come back out into the air to reach our eyes. The spectral composition of the reflected light is thus modified by the absorption of the dyes and any color stimuli are thus produced by a subtractive process as we discussed in the case of the negative film or the positive slide.

19.2.6   Color masking

Real dyes differ from the ideal block dye in that they do not transmit or absorb any wavelength of light with 100% efficiency. For example, the ideal cyan dye is supposed to pass all the "green" and "blue" light, but real cyan dyes absorb "blue" light; as much as 10% of the energy absorbed may be from blue light. This secondary absorption creates some complications in color reproduction because we can no longer control the three image dyes independently. If we use a certain amount of cyan dye to control the passage of "red" light to the desired amount, we have to reduce the amount of yellow dye because part of the "blue" light has been absorbed by the cyan dye and we no longer need as much yellow dye to attenuate the "blue" light. The trouble with this unwanted blue absorption by the cyan dye is that its absorption is a function of the cyan dye concentration, and any attempt to correct this problem has to use an image-dependent color mask. Similar dependency occurs between other pairs of image dyes. In order to calculate the correct amounts of the three dyes required to match a target color, an iterative search is often necessary because the underlying relations do not have a closed-form solution. How can we compensate for the unwanted absorption in a photographic emulsion? For color negative film, there is an ingenius solution based on the use of the colored couplers to achieve so called color masking, a simple and yet powerful way to achieve color correction of the unwanted absorption by the real dyes.

Recall that an image dye is formed from the reaction of a coupler with the oxidized developer. Wherever more cyan dye is formed, there is less cyan coupler left. The important thing to take advantage of is that the sum of the amounts of cyan dye and cyan coupler is a constant across the entire film. Therefore, if we can choose a cyan coupler which has exactly the color that is created from the unwanted absorption of the cyan dye, the cast of that color bias will be a constant across the entire image independent of the local "red" exposure. Thus, instead of a transparent cyan coupler, we use a colored cyan coupler to correct the unwanted aborption of the cyan dye. For example, if the cyan dye absorbs some of the "green" and the "blue" light, the colored cyan coupler has to partially absorb the same amount of the "green" and the "blue" light. Similarly, the magenta dye has unwanted absorption in the "red" and "blue" regions, and the magenta coupler is made to partially absorb the "red" and "blue" light. The reason that most color negatives have a strong red–orange color cast is the result of using colored cyan and magenta couplers to correct for the unwanted absorptions. The color cast in the color negative can be easily removed in the printing process by adjusting the color filters used. Colored couplers increase the overall density of the negatives and it takes longer for a printer to print images from the negatives, but the resulting color quality improvement is more than worthwhile.

19.2.7 Sensitometry and densitometry

The film response to light is usually measured in terms of the density due to exposure on the film before development. The density plotted as a function of log exposure is called the characteristic curve of the film (see Fig. 19.1). For a color film, three curves are plotted, one for each color record. The characteristic curve of a film is also called by several other names, such as D–log H curve, D–log E curve,[1] or the H&D curve, named after Hurter and Driffield who first used it to characterize a film. In order to measure the characteristic curve of a film, precise exposures of controlled spectral composition have to be made on the film. Machines made for such a purpose are called sensitometers. After the film is exposed, it is developed using standard chemical processes, and the densities are measured by densitometers, which are instruments designed to measure densities with standard optical geometry and spectral responses.

The light sensitivity of a film is often specified in terms of the photographic speed, which is defined by ISO standards. Figure 19.1 shows how film speeds are measured. For black-and-white negative films, the speed S is defined as $S = 0.80/H_m$, where H_m is the exposure (in lux seconds) at which the film has been developed to a density of 0.10 above the base plus fog density. Because the film characteristic curve changes with the chemical processing used, the speed definition requires that the film be developed so that at an exposure H_n, 1.30 log units above H_m, the film density is 0.90 above the base plus fog density. For color negative films, the speed S is defined as $S = \sqrt{2}/H_m$, where H_m is the geometric mean of H_G and the maximum of H_R, H_G, and H_B (see Fig. 19.1(b)), which are the exposures at which the red, green, and blue densities of the developed film are 0.15 units above the respective base plus fog density for each color channel.

It should be pointed out that film characteristic curves are measured from sensitometric exposure strips, which contain uniform square patches of exposure steps. The densities measured from these steps represent large-uniform-area (macro-)densities, i.e., zero spatial

---

[1] Here E means exposure, but the CIE standard symbol for exposure is H. Therefore, most new literature uses the term D–log H curve, instead of D–log E curve.

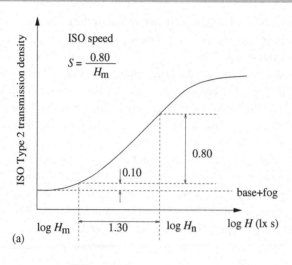

(a)

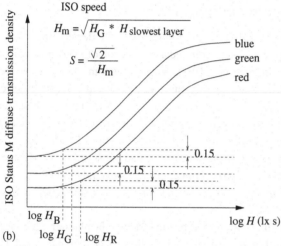

(b)

Figure 19.1. Determination of ISO photographic speeds for (a) black-and-white negative films and (b) color negative films.

frequency. When a picture on a film is digitized, the density of each pixel represents micro-densities. There is a significant difference between the macro-density and the micro-density for two reasons: (1) the aperture size of the film scanner is usually smaller than that used in a densitometer, and, (2) the optical signal modulation (such as an edge) in a natural scene produces a film density modulation that is dependent on spatial frequency as well as chemical processing. Detailed models of micro-densities will be discussed next.

19.3   Color images digitized from photographic films

Color images scanned from photographic films represent a major source of high-quality digital images. There are many factors that affect the correspondence between the image irradiance and the micro-density recorded on the film. We will look at some of the factors and review film models from a signal processing perspective.[2]

Light incident on the photographic film is spread from the point of incidence to the surrounding area by reflection, refraction, diffraction, and scattering. The resulting effect is an additional blur to the input optical image. Because in consumer photography the incident light is incoherent, this stage of image blur is, presumably, a linear process in terms of light intensity. This PSF is called the film's optical PSF.

As film is developed, the reaction products from chemical developing diffuse through the emulsion layers, causing an additional spread of the information contained in the latent image. The reaction-product concentration generated per unit area at each point in the latent image appears to be proportional to the amount of silver being developed at that point. For color films, the color dye image is produced by the coupling of the oxidation product of the developer and the coupler. The diffusion of an oxidation product in the emulsion layer generates a dye cloud in the neighborhood of a silver halide grain. The dye-forming processes, thus, introduce still more image blur. These effects are nonlinear and very complicated. Their detailed mechanisms are not completely clear.

Because of the nonlinear characteristics of the film, the concept of cascading system component MTFs is no longer valid. The analysis of photographic images has therefore taken two different paths.

19.3.1 The effective exposure MTF approach

One approach is to pick an operating point on the film characteristic curve and use the small-signal approximation to analyze the reproduction of image details with very low contrast amplitudes. The advantage of this approach is the preservation of the MTF concept, using linear approximation for a nonlinear system. Clearly, it appears very unlikely that typical consumer images with a dynamic range of 1.5–3 log exposure [471] could be treated this way. Nevertheless, this type of analysis has been used very frequently for practical image evaluation.

Lamberts [543] defined the film MTF concept in terms of effective exposure. An input sine-wave exposure pattern produces a very distorted sine-wave-like density pattern on the developed film. The idea of the effective exposure is to map the peak-to-peak density difference back to the exposure space through the macroscopic D–$\log H$ curve. This has the nice feature that the MTF can now be defined without being affected by macroscopic nonlinearities of the film. However, it should be pointed out that the concept of effective exposure MTF as a computational definition does not really solve the problem of predicting the shape of the output signal from a given input signal.

Despite all the difficulties, Lamberts [544] cascaded the effective exposure MTFs of three successive printings and found that the predicted resultant MTF agreed well with the direct measurement. He also compared the density trace of an edge with that predicted from the cascaded MTFs. They are remarkably close. He claimed that, for printing purposes,

---

[2] The next sections are a slightly modified version of part of a paper [564] published in *Optical Engineering*.

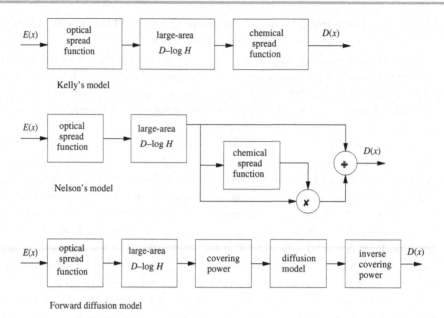

Figure 19.2. Three nonlinear models for the photographic process. Redrawn from [873].

modulations as high as 60–70% could be used and MTF data would still be effective. Furthermore, the correlation between visual perception and computed sharpness from such MTF measurements is quite high. MTFs are now generally measured as part of film evaluation.

19.3.2 The nonlinear model approach

Another approach is to give up the MTF cascading concept and model the photographic process with nonlinear components [277, 498, 499, 705, 731, 873]. Among the various models, Kelly's three-stage model, Nelson's model, and the diffusion model proposed by Ehn and Silevitch (see Fig. 19.2) represent different degrees of mathematical complexity and mixtures of intuition and empiricism. The first model laid the groundwork for the other two, and deserves a detailed discussion here.

In Kelly's three-stage model [498, 499], the effect of the photographic process in the film is modeled as a light diffusion/scattering stage (linear in exposure space), followed first by a nonlinear transformation from exposure space to density space, and then by another chemical diffusion stage (which is assumed to be linear in density space). The second-stage nonlinear transformation curves are derived from the conventional sensitometric measurements that produce the film D–log H characteristic curves. The light diffusion/scattering stage has been studied by many people [329, 829] (also see [731] for other references). According to Kelly's experiment (see [499, p. 327]), the best one-parameter function to describe the PSF is the Sayanagi model [829]:

$$h_s(r) = \frac{1}{2\pi\sigma_s^2} \exp(-r/\sigma_s), \tag{19.2}$$

which has the following Fourier transform:

$$H_s(v) = [1 + (2\pi\sigma_s v)^2]^{-\frac{3}{2}}. \tag{19.3}$$

Frieser's model using the following LSF is also favored by many other researchers:

$$l_f(r) = \frac{1}{2\sigma_f} \exp(-r/\sigma_f); \tag{19.4}$$

it has the following Fourier transform:

$$H_f(v) = [1 + (2\pi\sigma_f v)^2]^{-1}. \tag{19.5}$$

For a typical color negative film, the constant σ_s is about 2–3 μm for the yellow layer, 3–4 μm for the magenta, and 7–8 μm for the cyan. The constant σ_f is about 1.22 times the corresponding σ_s.

The third stage, chemical diffusion, has been modeled as a high-pass unsharp masking filter in density space. The mechanism is usually described as follows [498, 705]. The chemical concentrations during film development vary throughout the emulsion as functions of local exposure levels. Since the developer is more nearly exhausted where the density is greatest, and vice versa, the developer-concentration distribution is tone-reversed with respect to the density image. On the other hand, the reaction products that tend to slow down the development have higher concentrations in the high-density region. Fresh developer and the reaction products will thus diffuse in opposite directions across the boundary of regions of different densities. The net result is to make the density higher on the high-density side and lower on the low-density side. The effect is therefore called the adjacency effect (for a detailed review of other factors, see [67]). Nelson [705] studied this effect, and proposed a formula to predict, for the one-dimensional case only, the final density level $D_c(x)$ as a function of the density $D(x)$ that would have been produced according to the large-area sensitometric D–$\log E$ curves. He called $D(x)$ the *nominal density* at position x. Nelson's semi-empirical formula is as follows:

$$D_c(x) = D(x) + BD^2(x) - D(x) \int_{-\infty}^{\infty} b(\xi)D(x - \xi)d\xi, \tag{19.6}$$

where $b(\xi)$ is the chemical LSF, and

$$B = \int_{-\infty}^{\infty} b(\xi)d\xi. \tag{19.7}$$

The above formula assumes that the relation between density, D, and mass of silver per unit area, M, is linear for the particular film and development combination involved. If this is not true, the mass of silver per unit area should be used instead of the density, because the chemical concentration of the reaction products is proportional to the former, not the latter. An empirical relation between these two quantities was given as

$$M = PD^n, \tag{19.8}$$

where P is the reciprocal of the covering power of silver at a density of 1.0, and n usually lies between 0.5 and 1.0. When n is not equal to 1, the following formula should be used in place of Eq. (19.6):

$$M_c(x) = M(x) + \frac{B}{P}M^2(x) - \frac{M(x)}{P}\int_{-\infty}^{\infty} b(\xi)M(x-\xi)d\xi. \tag{19.9}$$

The usual procedure is to determine P and n in Eq. (19.8), then substitute PD^n for M in Eq. (19.9) to obtain the following formula:

$$D_c^n(x) = D^n(x) + BD^{2n}(x) - D^n(x)\int_{-\infty}^{\infty} b(\xi)D^n(x-\xi)d\xi. \tag{19.10}$$

According to Nelson's experiments, the discrepancies between the predicted and measured densities were generally less than 0.04 at density levels above 2.0 and less than 0.03 or 0.02 at lower densities.

To determine the chemical LSF, a knife edge is exposed by x-ray on the film to be measured (it is assumed that x-ray suffers only a negligible amount of optical blur). The density variation across the edge is then traced by a microdensitometer. If the nominal density on the low-density side is D_1 for $x < 0$ and on the high-density side D_2 for $x > 0$, then $b(x)$ can be determined according to the following formula:

$$b(x) = -\frac{nD^{n-1}}{D_x^n(D_2^n - D_1^n)}\frac{dD}{dx}, \tag{19.11}$$

where $D_x = D_2$ for $x > 0$, and $D_x = D_1$ for $x < 0$. It is usually more reliable to determine $b(x)$ from the high-density side [401], because the signal-to-noise ratio is higher.

Measurement data showed that the chemical LSF could be well described by the following functions:

$$b(x) = K_1 \exp(-x/\sigma_1) + K_2 \exp(-x/\sigma_2). \tag{19.12}$$

For a typical film, $\sigma_1 \approx 10$ μm and $\sigma_2 \approx 60$ μm (both numbers seem to be quite insensitive to change in development time). The numbers K_1 and K_2, on the other hand, vary significantly when the development time is changed, although their ratio seems to stay the same for the same film. A typical ratio of K_1/K_2 is about 6.0. It should be pointed out that these numbers are all dependent on the developer composition and agitation, development time and temperature, and photographic emulsion type.

The chemical LSF as defined in Eq. (19.10) has a different meaning from what is usually called the LSF in optics. Also, if Eq. (19.10) is sufficiently correct, the chemical diffusion effect is not linear either in density or in silver mass. Again, the usual approach is to use the small-signal approximation here. The difference now is that the system is linearized in the density or the silver mass space. Kriss, Nelson, and Eisen [532] derived the following MTF expression for this stage:

$$MTF(v) = \frac{1 + D^n[B - \beta(v)]}{1 + S_i^2 D^n[B - \beta(v)]}, \tag{19.13}$$

where

$$\beta(v) = \int_{-\infty}^{\infty} \cos(vx)b(x)dx. \tag{19.14}$$

Apparently, the MTF depends on the average density level D and the input modulation level S_i. This makes it much less useful for predicting the shape of the output signal.

It should be noted that Nelson's model is derived from the adjacency effect in black-and-white films. Experimental results [464, 593] showed that the model has to be modified to describe the image-enhancing effects in color films. The effects of the various chemicals (e.g., DI(A)R and image coupler) on the chemical LSF are density-dependent. To what degree one can continue using Nelson's model in color films without introducing too much error is a question to be answered by experiment.

Both Kelly's three-stage model and Nelson's model used empirical forms for the chemical spread function. Ehn and Silevitch modeled the film adjacency effects from a more fundamental formulation, which started with the diffusion equations relating the concentration of developer and the concentration of reaction products that inhibit development to the rate of change in the mass of silver developed per unit area. Their results show that Nelson's model can be derived from the diffusion model when the density fluctuation is not too large. However, the chemical spread function is now density-dependent. The full expression of the relation between M and M_c is too complicated to describe here. Silevitch, Gonsalves, and Ehn [873] later simplified it to the following form:

$$M_c(x) = M(x)\frac{1 - \exp[-A + \kappa b(x) * *M(x)]}{1 - \exp[-A + \kappa M(x)]}, \tag{19.15}$$

where A and κ are constants, $b(x)$ is the chemical LSF, and $**$ represents convolution. Although the diffusion model is more appealing, there have been many fewer measurements on these model parameters than on those of Nelson's model. The complexity of Eq. (19.15) also presents a problem in estimating the unknowns.

19.3.3 Interimage effects

In a multi-layer film, such as Kodacolor and Ektachrome, exposure and development in one of the layers influence the degree of development in the adjacent layers. The resulting dye image of the adjacent layer is a function of the exposure occurring in both layers. Such an effect is called an *inter*layer interimage effect [60, 379], while the influence on the neighboring region in the same layer is called an *intra*layer interimage effect. These interimage effects are often used to reduce granularity, enhance sharpness, and boost color saturation in color films. From the digital image processing point of view, these effects make the film a less desirable medium for image signal recording, because they introduce very complicated nonlinear cross-talk, spatially and spectrally, into the recorded image irradiance signals. However, films offer very high image resolution and very wide exposure latitude (range of exposures over which a photographic film can produce acceptable prints), still unmatched by electronic imaging.

Although intralayer interimage effects can be modeled by the equations described in the previous section, there is no good physical model available for interlayer interimage effects. Most models [379] consider only the influence of the points directly above and below the layer of interest. The point-based model is useful only in determining the final dye density in a large uniform area. A region-based model is needed to predict the detail in the final dye image.

The densities, D_c, used in the above equations are the so-called analytical densities, which are the densities of the individual layers. In practice, densities of a developed color film are measured with all the layers contributing (the so-called integral densities). The relations between the integral density D_f and the analytical density D_c are often described by the following linear equations:

$$D_{f,i}^n = \sum_{j=1}^{k} a_{ij} D_{c,j}^n + b_i \quad \text{for } i = 1, \ldots, k, \tag{19.16}$$

where i and j denote the different layers of a color film. A point-based model of the interimage effect can thus be written as

$$D_{f,i}^n = \sum_{j=1}^{k} c_{ij} D_j^n + \sum_{j=1}^{k} \sum_{l=1}^{j} d_{ijl} D_j^n D_l^n + g_i \quad \text{for } i = 1, \ldots, k. \tag{19.17}$$

Using this empirical model, one can convert the so-called nominal densities D_i to the integral film densities $D_{f,i}$ by a 3×10 matrix. This is the current practice of film unbuilding, assuming $n = 1$.

19.4 Film calibration

Photographic films serve as high-quality sensing and storage devices. They are relatively inexpensive and have very fine resolution. An ASA-100 35-mm color negative has an area of 24 mm by 36 mm and its resolution is about equivalent to a 2000×3000 pixel digital camera. Therefore, photographic film remains a very good source of high-quality color images. Film scanners are often used to convert the film images into digital form. The calibration of a film scanner is more complicated than a desktop reflection scanner for two reasons: (a) film is a complex, nonlinear device, and (b) the dynamic range of a film is much higher – roughly about 1000:1, compared with 100:1 for reflection print.

Two major steps in calibrating a film scanner are the removal of the film interimage effect (color cross-talk in film development), and the film D–$\log H$ curve. The film interimage effect can be removed more accurately through a 3-D LUT or less accurately by a 3×10 matrix (including the R, G, B linear terms, the square terms, R^2, G^2, B^2, and the product terms, RG, RB, GB, and a constant term) [443]. Since the interimage effect can be modeled better in film density, the input and output variables in the lookup table or color matrix should be set up in film density. There is also the adjacency effect (which also occurred in the chemical processing of film) which can only be removed approximately by "inverse" filtering in density domain. This is time consuming and rarely done because the adjacency effect actually makes the image look sharper. Let us assume that we want to calibrate a film scanner so that the output codes represent log exposure on the film. A typical calibration will consist of the following steps:

1. The scanner CCD sensor measures scanner transmittance. Since the scanner spectral responsivity functions may not be the same as the standard system response filters (such as Status A for reversal films or Status M for negative films), a 3-D LUT or 3 × 3 matrix is used to convert the scanner transmittance into the transmittance that would have been measured by a standard densitometer.
2. The transmittance is converted into density by 1-D LUTs because the interimage is better modeled in density.
3. The film interimage effect is removed by a 3-D LUT or a 3 × 10 matrix.
4. The 1-D LUTs (inverse D–log H) are used to map the interimage-removed film density to log exposure.

The most expensive step is generating data for the interimage lookup table or matrix. It requires an instrument (sensitometer) that can generate controlled exposures on the film to be calibrated. For consumer applications, photofinishing scanning services usually are equipped to do this step. Therefore, reasonable calibration can be expected when films are scanned by photofinishers. Potential film scanner problems are lamp stability, dusty mirrors, infrared heat absorption, CFA (color filter array) organic dye fading, and dichroic filter fading. Because film scanners have to handle a high dynamic range, often a preliminary low-resolution scan is performed to collect data needed to choose the proper neutral density filter before the final scan is performed.

The above calibration procedure for film digitization is obviously an oversimplified solution to a potentially complicated problem. It is instructive to consider the problem mathematically. Let $F_r(\lambda)$, $F_g(\lambda)$, and $F_b(\lambda)$ be the spectral sensitivity functions of the film. The first complication is that they are also functions of exposure but, over a small exposure range, we can assume that they are not. The definitions of film exposures, H_r, H_g, and H_b, are

$$H_r = \int L(\lambda)F_r(\lambda)d\lambda, \tag{19.18}$$

$$H_g = \int L(\lambda)F_g(\lambda)d\lambda, \tag{19.19}$$

$$H_b = \int L(\lambda)F_b(\lambda)d\lambda, \tag{19.20}$$

where $L(\lambda)$ is the spectral image exposure of the film. When color films are exposed and processed, the resulting (Status A or Status M) densities, D_r, D_g, D_b, are formed as functions of exposures:

$$D_r = f_r(H_r, H_g, H_b), \tag{19.21}$$
$$D_g = f_g(H_r, H_g, H_b), \tag{19.22}$$
$$D_b = f_b(H_r, H_g, H_b). \tag{19.23}$$

There are two main reasons why each color density depends on all three color exposures: (1) the spectral energy intended for one color layer is absorbed by another color layer (punch-through), and (2) the density developed in one color layer is affected by the density developed in other layers (interimage effect). The functions, f_r, f_g, and f_b, are nonlinear and have the general shape of the typical D–log H curve when two of the variables are held constant. The last set of equations needed is the relations between scanner density and the standard density (Status A or Status M). Let $A_r(\lambda)$, $A_g(\lambda)$ and $A_b(\lambda)$ be the system spectral responsivity functions (including the densitometer light source) for the standard density, and $S_r(\lambda)$, $S_g(\lambda)$ and $S_b(\lambda)$ be the scanner spectral responsivity functions (including the scanner light source). Let $T(\lambda)$ be the spectral transmittance of the film, and D_r^s, D_g^s, D_b^s be the scanner densities. We have:

$$D_r = -\log\left[\int T(\lambda)A_r(\lambda)\mathrm{d}\lambda\right], \tag{19.24}$$

$$D_g = -\log\left[\int T(\lambda)A_g(\lambda)\mathrm{d}\lambda\right], \tag{19.25}$$

$$D_b = -\log\left[\int T(\lambda)A_b(\lambda)\mathrm{d}\lambda\right], \tag{19.26}$$

$$D_r^s = -\log\left[\int T(\lambda)S_r(\lambda)\mathrm{d}\lambda\right], \tag{19.27}$$

$$D_g^s = -\log\left[\int T(\lambda)S_g(\lambda)\mathrm{d}\lambda\right], \tag{19.28}$$

$$D_b^s = -\log\left[\int T(\lambda)S_b(\lambda)\mathrm{d}\lambda\right]. \tag{19.29}$$

From Eqs. (19.18)–(19.29), we can see that the film calibration is a complex problem. The calibration procedure we outlined before is thus an engineering approximation. If we compare the equations with the procedure, we can see how the various approximations are made. In some applications, film data may not be available. Empirical data-driven calibration procedures, such as neural network and 3-D LUTs, can also be used very successfully [336, 443].

19.5 Solid-state sensors and CCD cameras

In the last two decades, great progress has been made in the development of solid-state sensors. Among them, the undisputed leader has been the CCD sensor in the area of high-resolution and low-noise sensors [461, 948]. However, CMOS sensors are becoming more popular because it is easier to use the existing CMOS integrated circuit technology to build camera-on-a-chip and because the CMOS sensors have lower power consumption [325, 1047]. Still another type of sensor uses amorphous silicon to build the sensor on top of a dedicated signal processing IC. This type of vertically integrated sensor is called the thin-film-on-ASIC (TFA) sensor [606, 607]. More interestingly, it is possible to change the spectral sensitivity of a pixel electonically on this type of sensor [890]. Another new type of CMOS sensor [616, 656] takes advantage of the fact that light of different wavelengths has different absorption depths in silicon (the longer the wavelength, the deeper it penetrates), and therefore, a vertical pixel can be contructed so that "red", "green", and "blue" image information is captured at the same location of the image plane, but in different depth layers, thus elimating the need for color filters and color interpolation from an *RGB* mosaic. Solid-state sensors are a very active research area and the number of commercially successful sensor types is increasing over time. We will focus our discussion on CCD sensors and their applications in most detail because so far they are the most widely used high-performance sensors, but CMOS sensors are quickly becoming important players.

A CCD camera is different from a film camera in that a CCD is used as the image sensor and an electronic memory device for image storage. Some CCD cameras also have an electronic shutter, instead of the mechanical one in the film cameras. CCD sensors have discrete sensing elements (pixels) and the image exposure at each element is often digitized into discrete numbers by an analog-to-digital converter. Therefore, the images acquired by CCD cameras are often in digital form, which is very convenient for further computer processing.

19.5.1 CCD devices

CCDs are capacitors connected together so that the electrical charges on each capacitor can be transferred from or to its neighboring capacitors under the control of spatially and temporally varying electrical potentials [850]. Typical capacitors used are the metal-oxide–semiconductor (MOS) capacitors, each unit of which consists of a metal conductor (gate) on top of a silicon oxide layer (an insulator), beneath which is a p-type silicon substrate. If a positive voltage (relative to the substrate) is applied to the gate, a depletion region will develop in the substrate directly under the silicon oxide layer. In the depletion region, holes (positive charges) are expelled, forming a potential well where the electrons can accumulate. These electrons can be moved around from one capacitor to another by changing the electrical potentials in the gates. In this sense, the charges among the capacitors are coupled, and therefore, this device with all the connected capacitors is said to be charge-coupled. Initially, CCD devices were used as delay lines because we can shift the charges from one capacitor to another under electrical control.

The silicon substrate has an energy bandgap of about 1.1 eV and a photon in the visible wavelength (700 nm corresponds to 1.77 eV, and 400 nm, 3.10 eV) can be readily absorbed by it. If a photon of sufficient energy hits the silicon (ideally in the depletion region), it can create a hole and electron pair. The electrons are attracted to and kept in the potential well, while the holes are swept away to the ground electrodes connected to the substrate. As a consequence, the number of electrons accumulated in the potential well is proportional to the number of photons illuminating the capacitor. CCD devices thus can be made to function as image sensors. Since the charges created by the photons can be easily transferred to the neighboring capacitors under electrical control, the detectors, the signal transfer mechanisms, and the read-out amplifiers can all be fabricated on a single piece of silicon, making CCD imagers very compact, efficient, and mass producible. Digital cameras using CCD sensors have quickly become popular color image acqusition devices.

19.5.2 CCD sensor architectures

The charge transfer mechanism in a CCD array is based on spatially and temporally changing the voltages on the electrodes on the MOS capacitors. We can build multielectrodes on a

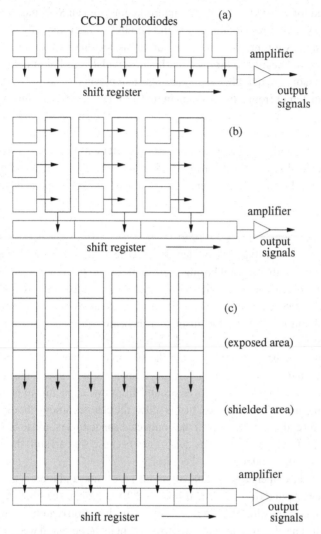

Figure 19.3. Schematic diagram of three types of CCD architecture: (a) linear array, (b) interline transfer, and (c) frame transfer.

single pixel and manipulate the voltages of the electrodes so that the charges are transferred in the desired direction to the neighboring pixel. The arrangement of the electrodes for a pixel is repeated for every pixel. A group of electrodes that receive the same clock signal (control voltage) is called a phase. Most CCD sensors use two-phase, three-phase, or four-phase transfer structures.

CCD sensors are roughly divided into four architectures: (1) linear arrays; (2) interline transfer arrays; (3) frame transfer arrays; and (4) time-delay and intregration (TDI). Figure 19.3 shows schematic diagrams of the first three types of archtectures. The fourth architecture is not usually used in color imaging and will not be discussed here. Sometimes it is also desirable to mix two types of design to achieve a certain system performance requirement. For example, a frame–interline transfer CCD architecture [948, p. 119] can be used so that each vertical line is transferred to an interline shift register and then each vertical shift register is transferred to a full frame storage, which is then read out externally. Linear arrays are mostly used in scanners where high-resolution linear arrays can be used without high cost. Interline transfer arrays have the advantage of a fast read-out rate, but the sensor area occupies only about half of the exposed image area, i.e., the fill-factor is low. If the interline shift registers are shielded from light, the exposure time can be controlled electronically without a mechanical shutter. In comparison, frame transfer arrays have high fill-factors (100% is possible), but suffer from a slow read-out rate.

19.5.3 CCD noise characteristics

The noise in a CCD camera comes from: (a) the photon statistics, (b) the CCD array itself, (c) the on-chip amplifier, (d) the off-chip amplifier(s), (e) the ADC, (f) electrical interference, and (g) the signal processing steps [461]. Each of these noise sources can be further analyzed in terms of different physical factors. The major effect of noise is to reduce the usable dynamic range and to degrade the image quality. Therefore, it is important to understand the causes and how to quantitatively measure the characteristics of the noise. A very good analysis of CCD noise can be found in [461], on which our dicussion will be based.

Noise from photon statistics
Photons arrive at the sensors at random, following a Poisson distribution. The variance of the distribution, σ_p^2, is equal to the mean number of photons per unit time, Φ_p. Since image exposure on the sensor plane is often given in units of radiant energy, we have to convert an energy exposure into the number of photons for each wavelength.

Noise from the CCD array
* **Transfer noise**
  As a charge packet is moved from pixel to pixel, some charges are left behind and some charges are left over by the previous pixels. These charges contribute to the noise added to the current pixel. This noise is called transfer noise. The other noise component that is associated with charge transfer is the spurious charges generated when the clock is switched to the noninverted state to transfer the charges to the neighboring pixel. The holes that are trapped on the $Si–SiO_2$ interface are forced out with sufficient energy to generate additional electron–hole pairs when colliding with silicon atoms. One way to deal with the spurious charges is to shape the electrical waveform of the clock signal so that the accelerating force is reduced.
* **Dark current**
  During the exposure time (integration time), thermal agitation can generate electrons, some of which accumulate in the potential well. This is called the dark current. The longer the integration time, the more thermal electrons the potential well collects. The number of collected thermal electrons is almost proportional to the length of the integration time, although the relation is not strictly a linear one [850, pp. 134–136].

The average dark current i_d generated in a pixel is a sensitive function of the temperature T:

$$i_d = CAT^{1.5} \exp[-E_g/(2kT)] \tag{19.30}$$

where C is a constant, A is the pixel area (cm^2), k is the Boltzmann constant, and E_g is silicon bandgap energy which is given in eV by:

$$E_g = 1.1557 - \frac{7.021 \times 10^{-4}T^2}{1108 + T}. \tag{19.31}$$

Simple calculation shows that when the CCD is cooled from 25 °C to 17 °C, the dark current is reduced by a factor of 2. (Note: 25 °C = 298.16 K.) At lower temperatures, the reduction of the dark current is even more dramatic for the same size temperature decrement.

Occasionally some isolated pixels on a CCD sensor generate an unusually high dark current compared with the average of other pixels. These abnormal pixels are called dark spikes (note that these pixels look bright on the image). It seems that silicon lattice defects in a high electric field tend to generate these dark spikes.

- **Fixed pattern noise**

Fixed pattern noise refers to the variation in the CCD output pixel values when the sensor is uniformly illuminated. However, several factors contribute to the total pixel-to-pixel variations. For example, due to differences in the pixel area in manufacturing, nonuniformity of silicon doping, nonuniformity of substrate thickness, and differences in oxide–substrate surface structure, etc., the quantum efficiency, the spectral responsivity, the dark current, and the voltage offset can vary from pixel to pixel. These variations are properties of each pixel and therefore are called fixed pattern noise. Fortunately, this type of noise can be corrected to a certain degree by taking several kinds of calibration image and performing signal processing to normalize a flat field image.

A simple procedure, called flat-fielding, to correct the fixed pattern noise is to take three kinds of calibration frame of the image: the offset frame $I_o(x, y)$, the dark current frame $I_d(x, y)$, and the response frame $I_r(x, y)$ [791, p. 194]. The offset frame is taken with light blocked off the CCD sensor and using very short exposure time t_o, so that the dark current does not have time to build up. The dark current frame is also taken in the dark, but with a long exposure time t_d, so that the dark current can accumulate to very significant levels. The response frame is taken with a uniform illumination and some normal exposure time t_r. Any image $I(x, y)$ that is captured with exposure time t can be processed to produce a corrected output image, $I_c(x, y)$, by

$$I_c(x, y) = a \frac{[I(x, y) - I_o(x, y)] - (t/t_d)[I_d(x, y) - I_o(x, y)]}{[I_r(x, y) - I_o(x, y)] - (t_r/t_d)[I_d(x, y) - I_o(x, y)]}, \tag{19.32}$$

where a is a constant scaling factor. It should be pointed out that the dark current noise is assumed to be proportional to the exposure (integration) time. The other assumption is that the illumination of the response frame is assumed to have the same spectral composition as that of the image frame (because the CCD response is a function of wavelength). This, of course, cannot be true in typical color imaging applications.

Therefore, the gain correction does not work as precisely as it should in theory. To be effective, each of the calibration frames should be the average of many frames taken under the same conditions.

- **High-energy radiation**
Cosmic rays are contantly bombarding the earth's surface. At sea level, the cosmic ray event rate is about 0.025 cm^{-2} s^{-1}. Therefore, in an hour of use, a 1 cm^2 sensor can be hit by high-energy radiation particles about 90 times.

Noise from the amplifiers
Both the on-chip and off-chip amplifiers generate noise due to the following sources: thermal noise, shot noise, and flicker $(1/f)$ noise:

- **Thermal noise**
From Nyquist's theorem of thermal noise [721, 1070, p. 64], the average available thermal noise power (meaning that the maximum power that can be delivered to an external load) within a frequency interval is given by

$$P_{av} = \left[\frac{1}{2}h\nu + \frac{h\nu}{\exp(h\nu/kT) - 1}\right]\Delta\nu, \qquad (19.33)$$

where $k = 1.38 \times 10^{-23}$ J K^{-1} is Boltzmann's constant, ν is the frequency and $\Delta\nu$ is the bandwidth, which is often written as $B = \Delta\nu$. When $h\nu/kT \ll 1$, i.e., when the frequency is not too high and the temperature is not too low,

$$P_{av} \approx kTB. \qquad (19.34)$$

Across a resistor of resistance R at a constant temperature T, the noise power can be expressed in equivalent (open-circuit) mean-square noise voltage, v_n^2, from the relation $P_{av} = (1/4)v_n^2/R$ (the maximum available power that can be delivered to an external load is an external resistance of R) and therefore, we arrive at the familiar formula for thermal noise (also called Johnson noise):

$$v_n^2 = 4kTRB. \qquad (19.35)$$

For example, a 1 MΩ resistor at room temperature (≈ 293 K) has a noise voltage about 12.7 μV when measured with a bandwidth of 10 kHz. The amplitude distribution of the noise voltage is a Gaussian distribution with a zero mean and a standard deviation of v_n. It should be noted that, as long as $h\nu/kT \ll 1$, thermal noise is independent of frequency. In this sense it is often treated as white noise.

Thermal noise associated with resistors used in the amplifier circuits is an important source of noise, especially in the on-chip amplifier, where charge packets are read out and converted into output voltages. There are a number of different designs of the output stage of a CCD. One common circuit uses a diode as a capacitor, C_s, called the sense node, which is reset to a reference voltage at the begining of each pixel read-out cycle. The charge packet of the current pixel is then dumped into the capacitor and the voltage change due to this charge is sensed by a source-follower amplifier with very-high-input impedance (usually a MOS field-effect transistor (MOSFET)). There are two sources of thermal noise in this output stage: (1) the reset noise from the resistance of the reset transistor (usually a MOSFET functions as a switch) and (2) the source-follower noise from its output resistance. The reset transistor, when switched on, has a very low resistance and allows a quick setting of the reference voltage to the sense node capacitor. Because of the thermal noise in the transistor channel resistance, the actual voltage that is finally reset on the capacitor is the reference voltage plus or minus some random fluctuation. Fortunately, when the reset transistor is switched off for charge readout, its resistance is very high and therefore the time constant (RC) of the capacitor voltage variation is very long. This allows multiple readings of the sense capacitor voltage. By sensing that voltage once before and once after the sensor charge is dumped to the capacitor and taking the difference between these two readings, we can essentially remove the fluctuation of the reference voltage due to the reset transistor resistance. This is called correlated double sampling, and is so effective in removing the reset noise that this noise component is now so small as to be neglected. There are several methods of implementing the correlated double sampling, each having a different frequency response and signal-to-noise ratio [652].

- **Shot noise**
  In a semiconductor device, an electric current is the flow of discrete charge particles (electrons or holes). The discrete nature of the flow produces statistical fluctuations, resulting in noise similar to that due to photon statistics. However, this is much reduced in a metal conductor because, in metals, electrons are strongly coupled over a long distance.
- **Flicker** $(1/f)$ **noise** The source of flicker noise is not well understood. The noise power is inversely proportional to the frequency and therefore it is also called the $1/f$ noise. The flicker noise generally increases with increasing current through an electronic device [791, p. 68]. At very high frequency, this component becomes quite small, compared with the thermal noise which remains relatively independent of frequency as long as $h\nu/kT \ll 1$.

Noise from the analog-to-digital converter

The noise from an analog to digital converter comes from the nonideal behavior of the converter and the quantization step. An analog to digital converter has several types of error that contribute to the noise, among which are: offset error, scale error, and nonlinearity error [414, p. 614]. As a result, an analog signal can be quantized into a wrong digital value. For example, because of the local nonlinearity, some digital codes may never be produced (missing codes). The noise from an ideal quantizer (such as 47.3 quantized to 47) is a uniform distribution with the step size ΔQ as its width. The equivalent noise variance is $\Delta Q/12$. Because of the nonlinearity error of an ADC, some codes occur more often than others for a uniform analog input voltage distribution.

Noise from the electrical interference

Electrical interference noise can be picked up from clock signals, AC power supplies, and radiated electromagnetic fields. This type of noise can be very time consuming to track down. Good circuit and timing designs are most important. The CCD, amplifiers, and driver circuits should be well shielded. For CCD camera users, these problems are presumably

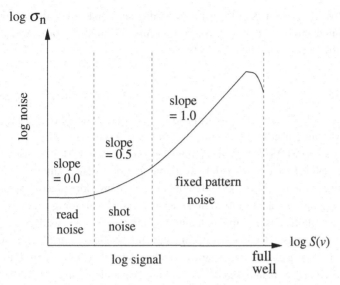

Figure 19.4. An example of a photon transfer curve.

solved by the camera manufacturers, but we should be aware of this possible noise source in case it arises in places where the interference noise might be large.

Photon transfer curve

A very useful way to characterize the performance of a CCD sensor is to measure its photon transfer curve [460], which shows the output noise, $\sigma_n^2(S)$, as a function of output signal level, $S(v)$, where v is the digital output value for a given exposure level. The photon transfer curves are a very important tool because they can tell us many of the sensor parameters, such as the read noise, the full well capacity, and the interacting quantum efficiency, etc.

For a given area on the sensor (say, a 20×20 pixel area), the signal level $S(v)$ is the average digital output code value[3] of the (400) pixels in the area. The exposure time of the camera is systematically changed to vary the signal level $S(v)$, and the output noise level $\sigma_n^2(S)$ is calculated as the variance of the (400) pixels in the area. In order to cover the full range of possible exposures, the exposure time is changed in log steps. The photon transfer curve is often plotted with $\log \sigma_n(S)$ as a function of $\log S(v)$. Figure 19.4 shows an example of the photon transfer curve of a CCD sensor. There are three regions on the curve, characterized by slopes of roughly 0, 0.5, and 1.0. In the read-noise-dominated region, the output noise is independent of the signal level and the slope is nearly 0. In the shot-noise- (Poisson-noise-)dominated region, the noise standard deviation is proportional to the square root of the signal and therefore the slope is about 0.5. In the pattern-noise-dominated region (caused by the fact that each pixel has a slightly different gain factor), the output noise is almost proportional to the signal and the slope is about 1.0. In many cases, it is desirable to exclude the noise introduced by the pixel-to-pixel variation on the CCD sensor,

---

[3]   The output code is assumed to be linearly proportional to image irradiance. Therefore, all gamma correction or tone scale curves should be removed before the measurements are made. It is also important to make sure that the CCD sensor is operating in its linear response range.

the difference between two frames of the same exposure can be taken to calculate the noise variance. Assuming that the noise of the two frames is uncorrelated, the variance calculated from the frame difference should be divided by 2.

19.5.4   CMOS sensors

CMOS sensors use photodiodes [596, 1060, pp. 367–76] or photogates [116, 513] for photon detection, similar to those used in CCD sensors. While CCD sensors use n-channel metal–oxide–semiconductor (NMOS) integrated circuit (IC) processes, CMOS sensors mainly use CMOS processes that have been widely available for solid state memory ICs, such as dynamic random access memory (DRAM). This means that many more functional electronic circuits, such as the amplifier, analog-to-digital converter, and local storage memory, can be integrated onto the CMOS sensor chips, reducing the number of chips needed to construct a digital camera. Furthermore, CCD sensors consume much more power (due to their need of very-high-speed shifting clocks), have slower readout rates (because charge transfer is a slower analog readout process), and require higher voltage supplies than CMOS sensors do. For example, power consumption by CCD sensors is typically 5–10 times that by CMOS sensors. CCD sensors run on 15 V supplies, while CMOS sensors may run on 3.3 V or lower. The fast readout rate of CMOS sensors makes it possible to capture as many as 10 000 frames per second at 352×288 pixels per frame [513]. The price we pay for integrating many more transistors into a CMOS sensor pixel is that much of the surface area is then taken up by the extra circuits and the fraction of the area available for light collection (called the fill-factor) is much smaller than that of a CCD sensor. The fill-factor of a CMOS sensor is typically between 20 and 30%. It is even smaller if more-complicated pixels are used. In comparison, CCD sensors typically have fill-factors higher than 50% to close to 100%. Currently, CMOS sensors tend to have lower quantum efficiency, higher noise, and more pixel cross-talk than the high-end CCD sensors [116].

CMOS sensor architecture
In CCD sensors, photon-generated electron charges are transferred from one pixel location to the next pixel location many times before they reach the readout amplifier and are converted to voltage signals. In CMOS sensors, photon-generated charges are converted to voltages or currents at each pixel [534]. The electrical signal from each pixel can be individually selected through the row select and the column select address decoders (see Fig. 19.5). Typically, a row is selected and each column pixel is read out one at a time (or in parallel). Then the next row is selected and so on, until the entire image is completely read out.

There are many types of CMOS sensor design. Among them, the pixel block in Fig. 19.5 varies greatly in complexity. The simplest pixel structure contains only a photodiode and its parasitic capacitance, as shown in Fig. 19.6(a). This is also called the passive pixel sensor (PPS). Most CMOS sensors include an amplifier in each pixel block to increase the signal amplitude before it is sent to the column processing for digitization, as shown in Fig. 19.6(b). Since the amplifier is implemented with transistors (an active element in electronics), this type of design is called an active pixel sensor (APS). More-complicated pixel block designs have been developed to reduce noise, increase quantum efficiency, and speed up readout

pixel block

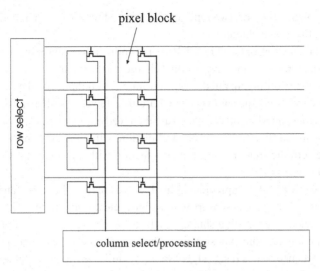

Figure 19.5. A functional block diagram of a typical CMOS sensor architecture.

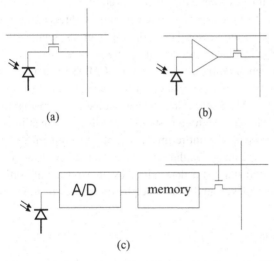

Figure 19.6. Three examples of the pixel block used in CMOS sensors: (a) the simplest pixel has only a photodiode and its own parasitic capacitance; (b) a more advanced pixel block has an amplifier to boost the signal; and (c) a complicated pixel block may have an analog to digital converter (A/D) to convert the photodiode voltage to a digital value and store that digital value in a local memory.

rate [12, 176, 439, 534, 858]. We can even go one step further to include an analog-to-digital converter and a local storage memory in each pixel block to convert the pixel image irradiance signal into digital form and store it in the local memory, as shown in Fig. 19.6(c).

19.5.5 Exposure control for CCD and CMOS sensors

Conventional film cameras use mechanical shutters to control the exposure time. In addition to mechanical shutters, digital cameras can also use the built-in electronic shutters on some of the CCD or CMOS image sensors. Two types of electronic shutter have often been used: the rolling shutter and the global shutter.

In an interline CCD image sensor (see Fig. 19.3(b)), the entire image sensor is reset before the beginning of an exposure, to remove any residual charges in the photodiodes. Each pixel then starts to integrate the photon-generated charges from its photodiode. At the end of the exposure time, the integrated charges at every pixel are transferred simultaneously to the neighboring, light-shielded, interline pixels, which are then read out sequentially. Therefore, a digital camera using an interline CCD sensor can function without a mechanical shutter. In certain cases, the electronic shutter is used in conjunction with a mechanical shutter to achieve better exposure control.

Some CMOS image sensors also implement light-shielded areas on the sensor and therefore can function as the interline CCD sensors with a global electronic shutter [273, 1011]. Most CMOS image sensors use a rolling shutter. Each row of the sensor is reset one after another sequentially, and after some exposure time, the integrated charges in each row are read out in the same sequence as it is reset. Therefore, it is similar to the focal-plane shutter in the film camera described in Section 10.4.3. A rolling shutter, like the focal-plane shutter, tends to create distortion in the image of a moving object. An additional constraint in CMOS sensors with a rolling shutter is that the exposure time can only be integer multiples of the time it takes to read out a row on the sensor. For flickering sources, such as fluorescent lamps, dark bands can appear in the images for certain shutter speeds.

A special problem arises when photoflash is needed for a CMOS imager with a rolling shutter, because the flash duration is often very short (a few tens of a microsecond to less than 1 ms). The operation of the CMOS sensor has to be modified to ensure that each pixel is exposed to the flash light. The operation consists of the following steps in sequence: (1) the sensor is reset row by row for the entire image; (2) at the completion of the reset operation, the flash is fired; (3) the image on the sensor is then read out row by row. The time interval between step (1) and step (3) is determined by an exposure algorithm to get the proper exposure time for the background where the photoflash may be too weak.

19.5.6 CCD/CMOS camera systems

Having discussed the noise and performance issues in CCD/CMOS sensors, we now turn to CCD/CMOS digital cameras. In addition to image sensing, there are many other functions that a digital camera has to perform so that good color images can be acquired efficiently and reliably. As the number of pixels keeps on increasing, the image processing functions have to be performed very fast. In many cases, parallel and pipeline hardware is used for speed [3]. The basic functions of a digital camera are listed as follows:

1. Optical image formation
    Typical CCD sensors used in consumer digital cameras are much smaller (about 1/2.5 to 2/3 of an inch in diagonal) than a frame of a 35 mm color film (24 mm by 36 mm). Furthermore, the rays falling on the sensor need to be as perpendicular to the sensor surface as possible to avoid color cross-talk. Oblique rays, especially of long wavelengths, are often absorbed near or beyond the pixel boundary and the photocarriers

they generate tend to diffuse and be collected by neighboring pixels [551]. In addition, the cameras are often mass produced and the optical elements have to be cheap and their optical performance has to be tolerant of manufacturing errors. Therefore, the optical design is particularly demanding [492, 1027].

2. Exposure control

Although high-quality CCD sensors when cooled to low temperatures can have a very large dynamic range, typical consumer digital cameras operated at room temperature have a narrower exposure latitude than color negative films. Therefore it is important to use the right exposure when taking a picture with a digital camera. Exposure can be controlled using the shutter speed and/or the aperture size. In general, it is desirable to keep the shutter speed high to minimize motion blur due to camera shake or object motion. It is also desirable to use a small aperture to have a longer depth of field and less lens aberration. Therefore, some trade-off has to be made in exposure control. If there is enough light, the shutter speed need not be made shorter than necessary and the aperture can be reduced more. Similarly, we do not want to make the aperture too small because lens diffraction degrades the image quality, and we may increase the exposure time a little more.

Most exposure control algorithms measure the weighted average luminance of the scene to determine a proper exposure. Exactly how that weighted average is calculated is often classified as proprietary information. A simple but relatively effective algorithm can be developed as follows. An image database on the order of several thousands of images is collected, with the optimal (aim) exposure for each image determined manually by displaying each image with many exposure variations. In order to predict a proper exposure for an image, the image is divided into many sections and several statistical descriptors, such as the average, the minimum, and the maximum luminance of each section, are calculated. These descriptors and their combinations are then used in a statistical regression against the manual aims to determine the optimal weighting coefficients for each descriptor. Of course, the results depend on the image database used and therefore it is important to collect the images according to the targeted consumer image population.

3. Focus control

In order to capture images in a fast changing scene, automatic focus control is needed to bring the object of interest quickly into good focus. There are two major classes of approach to automatic focus control: (1) the direct ranging approach works by measuring object distances with infrared (or visible light) triangulation or with ultrasound reflection; and (2) the maximum contrast approach works by taking images at several focus positions, calculating image contrast for each position, and determining the focus position that will produce the maximum image contrast.

4. CFA interpolation

A single-chip CCD camera can take color images by sequentially capturing the image with different color filters. Obviously, this is not applicable if objects move between shots. Therefore, a CCD sensor is coated with different color filters at the pixel sites, so that each pixel senses the image signal within only one of the spectral bands. This is similar to our retinas which have L, M, and S cones, occupying different spatial

R	G	R	G	R
G	B	G	B	G
R	G	R	G	R
G	B	G	B	G
R	G	R	G	R

Figure 19.7. An example of a Bayer CFA.

locations on the retina and sensing different spectral bands. In our retinas, the cone mosaic is somewhat random in both spatial and spectral distributions. It has been argued that the random mosaic helps to reduce visible aliasing. Although it appears that, in the fovea, the eye optics sufficiently blurs the retinal image so that luminance aliasing is not a real concern, it is still not clear how our visual system manages to reconstruct seemingly artifact-free visual images from the color mosaic of cones. For single-chip cameras, several CFA patterns have been used [88, 207, 749]. Some use "primary" color filters, such as red, green, and blue, while others use "complementary" color filters, such as cyan, magenta, and yellow filters. Wide-band (white) filters are also used in conjunction with color filters to measure the luminance signal. A simple and very popular color filter array is the Bayer pattern (see Fig. 19.7) which uses two green pixels for one red pixel and one blue pixel. No matter what CFAs are used, the output images have to be reconstructed so that at each pixel location there are red, green, and blue values, or alternatively one luminance and two chrominance values as required in some video signal representations.

Because color interpolation from the CFA signals often produces undesirable color artifacts, much research has been done to develop good algorithms [4, 5, 6, 7, 19, 20, 205, 207, 328, 372, 506, 783, 967, 1051, 1069]. Unfortunately, many of the high-performing algorithms used in consumer digital cameras are not disclosed in the published literature.

5. Signal processing
Raw image signals captured by the sensors are processed so that sensor defects are corrected, missing color signals interpolated, control signals generated, and output images converted into the desired output formats.

There are two types of signal processing in a digital camera. One generates system control signals, such as automatic focus adjustment, automatic exposure control, and automatic color (white) balance. The other processes control the acquired image signals to produce the output images. System control signals can be calculated from the measurements by separate devices, such as infrared range sensors, or can be calculated from the image signals themselves, such as the exposure control. The many steps of signal

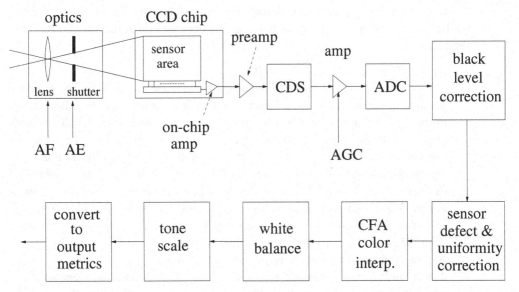

Figure 19.8. A block diagram of typical signal processing steps in a single-chip CCD digital camera where AF, AE, AGC, CDS, and CFA stand for autofocus, autoexposure, automatic gain control, correlated double sampling, and color filter array.

processing typically include: (1) input signal shaping; (2) analog-to-digital conversion; (3) pixel-offset correction; (4) pixel-gain correction; (5) pixel-defect correction; (6) CFA interpolation; (7) exposure (density) balance; (8) color (white) balance; (9) color correction (3 × 3 matrix); (10) output signal shaping. There are many possible variations in the sequence of these signal processing steps. In addition, lens fall-off correction, denoising, contrast enhancement, edge sharpening, and chroma adjustment are operations that are routinely implemented in most image processing pipelines. Figure 19.8 shows an example of a simplified signal processing chain.

6. Image verification

In most digital cameras, images are played back on a small on-camera LCD display soon after they are captured. This provides an easy way to verify the image composition. The possibility also exists of using the display device to check the accuracy of exposure control and white balance. However, this does not seem to have been exploited so far. If focus error is large, the display can also show the problem so that the image can be taken again.

7. Image compression

In film cameras, films serve as both sensors and storage. In digital cameras, images are stored on memory cards or magnetic disks. Images are often compressed to reduce the storage space required.

19.5.7 CCD/CMOS camera calibrations

The calibration of a CCD camera includes the characterization of the camera output as a function of the input scene radiance, the measurement of noise as a function of exposure, the image resolution, and the geometric distortion of image formation. The noise measurement has been discussed previously. We will discuss the other aspects of the camera calibration issues here:

1. Optoelectronic conversion function (OECF)

   The camera OECF of a digital camera is defined as the output digital number as a function of the input scene log luminance. It is important to note that the meaning of the digital number is not specified in the definition. However, the OECF allows us to go back to the scene log luminance and therefore serves as the main calibration function of the camera. If we measure the output digital number as a function of the log exposure at the focal plane (instead of the scene log luminance), the relation is called the focal plane OECF. Since camera flare distribution is scene-dependent, in general it is not possible to derive the camera OECF from the focal plane OECF or vice versa. The measurement of a camera OECF is specified by international standards (ISO 14524, [516]), regarding the test targets to be used, the illumination (luminance, spectral composition, and lighting geometry), and the imaging geometry. Since most digital cameras have automatic exposure control which depends on scene structure, it is important to understand that, given a luminance level of a scene (however it is measured), we cannot assume that a camera OECF measured at the same luminance level can be used directly without verification.

2. SFR

   If the image formation process of a digital camera can be approximated as a linear, shift-invariant system, its system transfer function is a very useful measure for characterizing its spatial imaging performance. There are many ways to measure the system transfer function of an imaging system. For example, if sine-wave targets are available for many spatial frequencies, we can take images of these targets and measure the amplitudes and phases of the sine-wave images to estimate the system transfer function. However, accurate sine-wave targets are difficult to make. Therefore, other targets such as square-wave and knife-edge targets are often used [445, 533, 788]. ISO 12233 recommended using a slanted edge target to determine a camera's SFR. The mathematical basis of such measurements is presented in Section 16.3.1.

3. Geometric calibration

   The goal of the geometric calibration of a digital camera is to determine the geometric mapping from the object space to the image space as observed on the image captured by the camera. To achieve a reasonable accurary, this calibration can be a fairly complicated process [331, 900, 966, 1039]. We will present the basic principles involved in the process.

   From Chapter 9, we learn that in the ideal mapping of Gaussian optics, the object coordinates are related to the image coordinates by a perspective transformation. From Eq. (9.15),

$$y' = \frac{fy}{z - z_0},$$

where $z_0 = z_F$, we can see that, for a rotationally symmetric system, if the object focal point, F, is used as the center of projection, the image coordinate y' is inverted (because

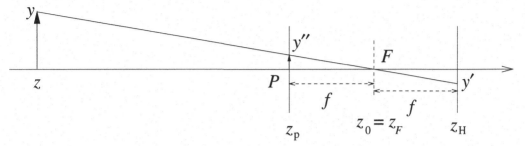

Figure 19.9. A simple diagram for calculating image coordinates from object coordinates. Note that the point at z_F is the object focal point, F, and the point at $z_H = z_F + f$ is the object principal point. In many applications, a plane at $z_p = z_F - f$ is used to intercept the projection at y'' which has the same sign as the object coordinate y. This plane is called the plane of projection.

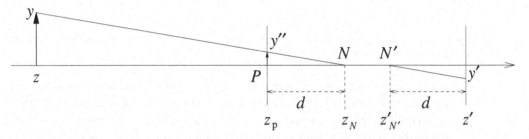

Figure 19.10. An alternative camera model using nodal points. The image coordinate y' is determined by the intersection of the ray emerging from the image nodal point with the image plane located at z'. The distance d between the image nodal point N' and the image plane at z' depends on where the camera is focused. For convenience in many applications, a plane at $z_p = z_N - d$ is used to intercept the projection at y'' which has the same sign as the object coordinate y. This plane is called the plane of projection.

$z - z_0$ is usually negative) and proportional to the object coordinate y. Therefore, a very simple diagram (see Fig. 19.9) can be drawn to help us visualize the geometry of optical image formation. In computer vision applications, the plane located at $z_p = z_0 - f$ is often used for calculating the image coordinate y'' by projecting the object point through the object focal point F at $z_0 = z_F$. It is important to keep in mind that neither z_p nor z_H represents the image plane, which should be calculated from Eq. (9.16). This diagram is a convenient tool, good only for computing the lateral image coordinates (x', y'), but not the image location z'. Therefore, this model can be used to calculate the image coordinates only when the object is in focus. An alternative camera model (see Fig. 19.10) uses the object nodal point, N, as the center of projection. The ray then emerges in the image space from the image nodal point, N', in the same direction. The intersection of the ray with the image plane at z' determines the image coordinate y'. The distance d between the image nodal point N' and the image plane at z' is now a variable that depends on where the camera is focused. Again for convenience, the plane located at $z_p = z_N - f$ is often used for calculating the image coordinate y'' by projecting the object point through the object nodal point N at z_N. The focal point model and the nodal point model (both are called pinhole camera models) are both

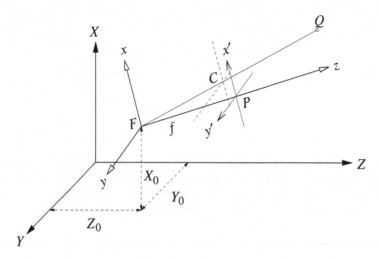

Figure 19.11. The relation between the world coordinates (X, Y, Z), camera coordinates (x, y, z), and image coordinates (x', y', z').

used in the literature, and sometimes there is some confusion about the meaning of the parameters. For example, the distance between the center of projection (perspective center) and the plane of projection is fixed (f) in the focal point model, but variable (d) for the nodal point model. Since the focal point of a camera is not difficult to determine in the laboratory and since it is convenient to have a fixed distance between the perspective center and the plane of projection, the focal point model is more frequently used.

In order to discuss the problem of camera geometric calibration, a more general setting for the coordinate systems is needed. Figure 19.11 shows the relation between the world coordinates (X, Y, Z), camera coordinates (x, y, z), and image coordinates (x', y', z'). The perspective center F is located at (X_0, Y_0, Z_0). The transformation from the world coordinates (X, Y, Z) to the camera coordinates (x, y, z) can be expressed as a translation followed by a rotation (or, alternatively, a rotation followed by a translation):

$$
\begin{bmatrix} x \\ y \\ z \end{bmatrix} = \begin{bmatrix} a_{11} & a_{12} & a_{13} \\ a_{21} & a_{22} & a_{23} \\ a_{31} & a_{32} & a_{33} \end{bmatrix} \begin{bmatrix} X - X_0 \\ Y - Y_0 \\ Z - Z_0 \end{bmatrix} = A \begin{bmatrix} X - X_0 \\ Y - Y_0 \\ Z - Z_0 \end{bmatrix}. \tag{19.36}
$$

The rotational matrix A is an orthogonal matrix (i.e., $AA^T = A^T A = I$). The image coordinates (x', y') can be calculated by projecting (x, y, z) to the projection plane:

$$
x' = \left(\frac{f}{z}\right) x = f \frac{a_{11}(X - X_0) + a_{12}(Y - Y_0) + a_{13}(Z - Z_0)}{a_{31}(X - X_0) + a_{32}(Y - Y_0) + a_{33}(Z - Z_0)}, \tag{19.37}
$$

$$
y' = \left(\frac{f}{z}\right) y = f \frac{a_{21}(X - X_0) + a_{22}(Y - Y_0) + a_{23}(Z - Z_0)}{a_{31}(X - X_0) + a_{32}(Y - Y_0) + a_{33}(Z - Z_0)}. \tag{19.38}
$$

The above equations are true for an ideal imaging system. In practice, there are several types of distortion in a camera. The main ones are lens distortion and decentering distortion [331]. Lens distortion is a result of lens aberration (such as W_{311}) and decentering distortion is a result of misalignment of the optical components along the system optical axis. The ideal image coordinates (x', y') are related to the distorted image coordinates (x'_d, y'_d) by

$$x' = x'_d + \delta x' + \Delta x',$$
$$y' = y'_d + \delta y' + \Delta y',$$

where $\delta x'$ and $\delta y'$ are due to lens distortion, and $\Delta x'$ and $\Delta y'$ are due to decentering distortion.

The lens distortion is often modeled as the radial distortion:

$$\delta r = K_1 r^3 + K_2 r^5 + K_3 r^7 + \cdots, \tag{19.39}$$

where $r = \sqrt{x'^2_d + y'^2_d}$. Projecting the radial distortion to the x'- and y'- axes, we can express them as:

$$\delta x' = \left(\frac{x'_d}{r}\right) \delta r = K_1 x'_d r^2 + K_2 x'_d r^4 + \cdots, \tag{19.40}$$

$$\delta y' = \left(\frac{y'_d}{r}\right) \delta r = K_1 y'_d r^2 + K_2 y'_d r^4 + \cdots. \tag{19.41}$$

The decentering distortion [330] is modeled with a radial component, Δ_r, and a tangential component Δ_t. When they are projected to the x'- and y'-axes, they can be approximated as

$$\Delta x' = \alpha(r^2 + 2x'^2_d) + 2\beta x'_d y'_d, \tag{19.42}$$
$$\Delta y' = \beta(r^2 + 2y'^2_d) + 2\alpha x'_d y'_d, \tag{19.43}$$

where α and β are parameters to be determined in the calibration. In the above derivation, we have assumed that the optical axis of the camera intersects the plane of projection at point P, which is assumed to be the origin of the image coordinates. Ideally, P is located at the center of the image as captured by the CCD camera. However, this is often found not to be true. There are many methods [1039] of determining the point P and they often do not give the same results. Therefore, it is important to use the method that is most relevant to the specific application at hand. In many applications, P is chosen to be the point that will give the minimum radial distortion. Finally, the image coordinates have to be converted into pixel locations for a digital camera [966]. This simple process requires scaling and quantization.

Typically camera calibration involves taking images of test targets of a set of spatial points with known spatial coordinates. Given the set of corresponding points $(x'_d, y'_d)_i$ and $(X, Y, Z)_i, i = 1, 2, \ldots, m$, we can use constrained nonlinear optimization methods to determine the best set of parameters (i.e., A, X_0, Y_0, Z_0, f, K_1, K_2, K_3, etc.) under the constraint that $AA^T = I$, so that the squared errors between the predicted coordinates and the measured coordinates are minimized [449, 590, 1022]. However, such a global optimization may not always give good calibration parameters because:

(1) nonlinear optimization methods require good starting points; and (2) the effect of error in one parameter can be cancelled by the error in another parameter. Therefore, it is often more desirable to calibrate some parameters by special procedures (see, e.g., [487, 627, 900]).

19.6 Scanners

Scanners are often used to convert an analog original into a digital image. The original can be a reflection print or a transmission film (color negative or reversal). There are four main types of scanner: handheld, sheetfed, flatbed, and drum scanners. Some scanners are built specifically for scanning photographic films and some for scanning documents. Here we will first briefly describe some film scanners,[4] and then we will focus on desktop (reflection) scanners.

Several types of scanner are commonly used for digitizing film images [639, 663]. They can be roughly classified according to the relative scanning motion between the light beam, the film, and the sensor. In type I the light beam and the sensor are stationary, and the film is moved through them in a selected path pattern. In type II the light beam is moving, but the film and the sensor are stationary. In type III the light beam, the film, and the sensor are all stationary. These scanner types have different optical and mechanical designs. Microdensitometers, drum scanners, and flatbed scanners are all examples of type I instruments. The basic components of these scanners are: (1) the illuminating (influx) optics, (2) the film-moving stage (sample plane), and (3) the light-collecting (efflux) optics.

The micro-densitometer is a good example of a film scanner. It has been the main workhorse for digitizing very-high-quality, very-high-resolution color images from photographic films. A typical microdensitometer consists of a tungsten lamp as the light source, a source condenser, a source aperture, an influx ocular, an influx objective, the film plane, an efflux objective, an efflux ocular, a sensor aperture, a sensor condenser, and a light sensor (e.g., photomultiplier tube) (see Fig. 19.12). The influx ocular and objective function as a microscope in a reverse direction, forming a reduced image of the source aperture on the film plane, while the efflux objective and ocular function as a microscope, forming, on the sensor aperture, an enlarged transmittance image of the area of the film illuminated by the image of the source aperture. The irradiated region, the specimen (sample), and the detected region are actually on the same plane. They are drawn separately because they are three important parameters that need to be considered separately in the performance analysis [928].

The optical characteristics of the micro-densitometer have been studied quite extensively (see, e.g., [232, Chapter 9, 928], and references cited therein). The instrument is quite sensitive to alignment errors and changes in other parameters [987]. Although many problems (e.g. the partial coherence problem and the conditions for linearity [927]) are fairly well understood and the manufacturers often provide a few guidelines for selecting proper settings, the operation of such a scanner requires careful setup and calibration. If the instrument is

---

[4]   This section is a modified version of part of a paper [564] published in *Optical Engineering*.

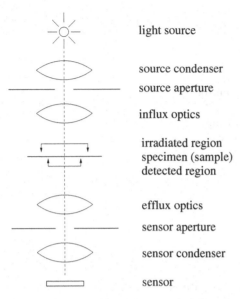

light source

source condenser

source aperture

influx optics

irradiated region
specimen (sample)
detected region

efflux optics

sensor aperture

sensor condenser

sensor

Figure 19.12. Schematic diagram of a micro-densitometer. (Redrawn from [928, Fig. 2.1].)

configured and operated properly, the system transfer function, $M(\nu)$, can be well described [232] by the following equation:

$$M(\nu_x, \nu_y) = F(\nu_x, \nu_y)A(\nu_x, \nu_y), \tag{19.44}$$

where $F(\nu_x, \nu_y)$ is the OTF of the efflux optics, and $A(\nu_x, \nu_y)$ is the Fourier transform of the scanning aperture. This formula has been shown to agree very well with experimental data [458]. The sampling aperture is the smaller of the source aperture and the sensor aperture as they are projected to the sample plane. Good-quality microscope lenses are used in the micro-densitometers, and they often approach the diffraction-limited system. Therefore, to determine $F(\nu_x, \nu_y)$, it is necessary only to know the f/number or the numerical aperture of the efflux lens, which is typically the limiting micro-densitometer optical performance. A numerical aperture of $NA = 0.25$ will have a cut-off frequency of $2(NA)/\lambda$ which, at $\lambda = 500$ nm, is 1000 cycles per millimeter, a resolution far above typical films. It should be pointed out that this assumes that the instrument is operated at a scanning speed such that the bandwidth of the electronic circuits in the instrument does not degrade the sampled signals being measured.

A CRT flying spot scanner is an example of a type II device. In the typical configuration, a scanning spot is generated on the surface of a CRT and a lens system images the light spot onto the film. The transmitted light from the film is then imaged to a sensor. To calculate the system transfer function, one can still use Eq. (19.44) with proper functions in place. One major difference is that the light spot on the CRT generally has a Gaussian-shaped intensity distribution. If the effective scanning aperture (or sampling aperture) is small compared with the Gaussian spot, one can approximate the aperture function as a uniform distribution. Otherwise, it has to be approximated as a truncated Gaussian function. An additional problem with a flying spot scanner is that the light spot is now moving relatively

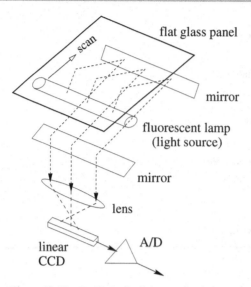

Figure 19.13. A schematic diagram of a desktop flatbed scanner.

fast compared with the mechanical motion of the type I scanner, and the motion blur may have to be considered.

Finally, a CCD area array film scanner (for an example, see [663]) is an example of a type III scanner. The mechanical structure of this kind of scanner is probably the simplest of the three types. Light projected through the film is imaged onto a CCD sensor. The cell size of the sensor relative to the image determines the scanning aperture. The optical system used to form the image determines the optical transfer function. Equation (19.44) can now be used to compute the system response function. Because of the amount of light needed for the sensor, the lens must not be too small, and therefore its OTF has to be considered in computing the total response. Additional problems associated with CCD sensors are lateral charge diffusion [411] and charge transfer efficiency [460].

With the increased availability of personal computers, desktop scanners have also become affordable and popular. The image quality achievable in these inexpensive scanners has also improved a lot. The basic structure of a flatbed desktop color scanner consists of a light source, a (mechanical or optical) scanning mechanism,[5] color filters, light-sensors, and analog-to-digital converter. The original is laid flat on a glass panel and an illuminated line is scanned through the original as the reflected or transmitted light is sensed and digitized. Figure 19.13 shows a simplified schematic diagram of a typical desktop scanner. Almost all desktop flatbed scanners use linear CCD arrays as the sensors. The physical size of the CCD is smaller than the full page width. The scanner optics reduces the physical image size to that of the CCD. Some scanners use contact image sensors that are the same physical size as the area that is scanned. Although this eliminates the need for a lengthy optical path, the self-focus lenses on a contact image sensor are often inefficient in light collection and provide only limited depth of field. Some color scanners may scan an original in three

---

[5]   It is also possible to use optics and a two-dimensional CCD area sensor to capture the whole image at once without having to scan the original.

passes, each with a different color filter inserted between the light and the sensor. Other single-pass color scanners use a trilinear CCD array sensor which has three rows of CCD linear arrays, each with a different built-in color filter on top on the CCD.

19.6.1 Scanner performance and calibration

In order to get the best digitization of an image, we often have to evaluate the performance of a scanner. The items for evaluation include: (1) the uniformity of illumination; (2) the amount of scanner flare; (3) the spatial frequency response (MTF); (4) resolution scaling (method of interpolation from fewer dots per inch to more dots per inch); (5) image noise; (6) gray-scale reproducibility; (7) color reproducibility; and (8) color registration.

The dark current (offset) nonuniformity and the pixel photoresponse (gain) nonuniformity can be corrected by analog or digital compensation. If this is not done correctly by the manufacturer, the user can generate a correction mask by scanning a uniform white target and a uniform black target. Scanner flare is quite difficult to correct because it is image dependent. A crude correction can be made by increasing the slope of the TRC in the dark area. The scanner MTF can be measured by scanning a slanted edge target, computing first the ESF and then the LSF, and finally taking the Fourier transform of the LSF to obtain the scanner MTF perpendicular to the edge direction [788]. Color registation can also be checked by scanning a slanted edge target and comparing the edge transition point for each color record.

19.7 A worked example of 3 × 3 color correction matrix

There are two commonly used tools in device color calibration: the color correction matrix and the 3-D LUT. In this section, we will work out a numerical example of how to derive a 3 × 3 color correction matrix for an image acquisition system, such as a digital camera or a home desktop scanner. Since the spectral response functions of most image capture devices are not any linear combinations of the CIE color matching functions, we cannot expect that a 3 × 3 matrix will accurately transform the device-dependent RGB color space to a device-independent color space, such as CIEXYZ. Furthermore, the light source of the scene or the light source used in a desktop scanner is often very different from that required by most viewing standards. The 3 × 3 matrix is charged with the task of providing a best approximation for correcting the difference both in spectral responses and in illuminants. This being impossible, we should not be surprised when errors for some colored objects become very large. However, using a 3 × 3 matrix for color correction is very cost effective to implement and very fast to compute (compared with 3-D LUTs and the associated multivariate interpolations). In practice, color correction by a 3 × 3 matrix is sufficiently accurate for many digital camera and other desktop applications. We will discuss the matrix approach here for the scanner calibration and the 3-D LUT approach later for the printer calibration. If we want more accurate scanner color calibration, we could also use the 3-D LUT approach here. For the color correction matrix, we can use the Macbeth ColorChecker, which has 18 color patches and 6 gray patches from black to white. For the

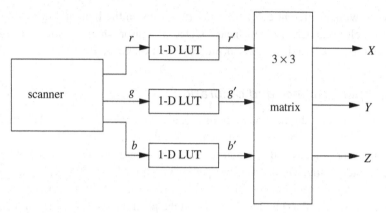

Figure 19.14. A block diagram of scanner calibration using a color correction matrix.

3-D LUT, we would then certainly need to measure more than just 24 color patches as in the ColorChecker. The graphics art standard target IT8.7/2 or Kodak Q-60R can be used for this purpose.

Figure 19.14 shows a block diagram of scanner calibration using a color correction matrix. The scanner output code values (r, g, b) are mapped through three 1-D LUTs into scanner reflectance values (r', g', b'). This step is used to remove any response nonlinearity in the scanner. A 3×3 color correction matrix is then used to transform the scanner reflectance values (r', g', b') into a device-independent color space, such as the CIE XYZ tristimulus values. Alternatively, other device-dependent or device-independent color spaces can be used, but the basic algorithm for deriving the matrix is similar.

There are two types of scanner: reflection and transmission. The transmission scanner is usually used for scanning reversal (slide) films or color negative films. In this example, we will further restrict our attention to reflection scanners. The calibration of a transmission scanner for photographic films is more complicated and has been discussed earlier in this chapter. Scanner calibration using a color correction matrix proceeds as follows. A Macbeth ColorChecker (as described in [647]) is scanned on the reflection scanner. A software program is written that can detect the horizontal and vertical blacklines in the Macbeth ColorChecker. Each of the 24 color and gray patches can be extracted automatically. Several pixels around the boundary of each patch are discarded and the pixel values of the central region of a patch are averaged, thus producing relatively noise-free scanner codes for each patch. Table 19.1 shows the averaged (r, g, b) code values for the 24 color patches of the Macbeth ColorChecker from the output of a desktop reflection scanner. The bottom row is a gray scale from white to black. The usefulness of Macbeth ColorCheckers is that they are made to reproduce the same spectral reflectances and therefore, for noncritical applications, users can rely on the published data without measuring them. Of course, the target can fade and its surface can be contaminated by dust. Therefore, the actual spectral reflectances should be measured for each target when resources permit. From the measured spectral reflectances, we can compute the CIE tristimulus values of all the color patches under a given illuminant. Table 19.2 shows the results of such measurements and calculation for CIE illuminant D50.

Table 19.1. *The averaged (r,g,b) code values for the 24 color patches of the Macbeth ColorChecker from the output of a desktop reflection scanner. The order is the same as the physical target from top to bottom and left to right*

(64.2,37.8,32.1)	(175.2,112.0,89.3)	(57.0,75.9,120.9)	(50.8,63.8,31.2)	(97.0,87.0,154.5)	(97.3,177.4,129.8)
(179.8,73.2,27.9)	(41.6,46.9,125.7)	(158.2,42.8,57.6)	(47.4,29.7,67.4)	(129.2,171.4,36.2)	(206.7,127.6,32.1)
(24.4,28.0,101.6)	(51.1,111.1,34.8)	(130.6,26.4,27.5)	(251.2,194.2,29.5)	(148.4,48.1,114.7)	(37.9,82.4,110.9)
(254.7,254.7,254.8)	(201.7,204.8,204.0)	(128.0,129.6,132.2)	(73.7,75.6,76.1)	(39.0,41.1,42.7)	(18.9,21.3,21.8)

Table 19.2. *The CIE XYZ tristimulus values for the 24 color patches of the Macbeth ColorChecker under illuminant D_{50}. The order is the same as the physical target from top to bottom and left to right*

(12.05 10.33 4.82)	(41.31 35.98 19.50)	(16.92 18.36 25.14)	(11.17 14.10 4.75)	(25.04 23.76 33.95)	(31.14 42.54 34.69)
(42.82 32.72 4.19)	(11.49 10.88 26.94)	(30.50 19.88 9.71)	(8.82 6.40 11.14)	(36.48 44.73 7.94)	(50.82 45.75 6.35)
(8.00 6.56 24.33)	(14.20 21.66 7.38)	(20.92 11.75 3.43)	(61.58 62.14 7.14)	(31.39 20.43 23.40)	(13.56 19.47 30.33)
(86.79 90.05 74.15)	(57.02 59.09 48.14)	(34.78 36.20 29.78)	(19.00 19.79 16.03)	(8.62 9.00 7.24)	(2.92 3.01 2.41)

Table 19.3. *The averaged scanner code values for each gray patch*

Reflectance factor %	Red	Green	Blue
3.1	18.9	21.3	21.8
9.0	39.0	41.1	42.7
19.8	73.7	75.6	76.1
36.2	128.0	129.6	132.2
59.1	201.7	204.8	204.0
90.0	254.7	254.7	254.8

The first step is to find the three 1-D LUTs that characterize the scanner response as a function of the target reflectance. The bottom six patches of the Macbeth ColorChecker are different shades of gray, with almost flat spectral reflectance functions. Table 19.3 shows the averaged scanner r, g, b code values for each gray patch. Figure 19.15 shows a plot of the data. The measured data points are the circles and the continuous curves are the natural cubic spline interpolation through the data (i.e., with second derivatives set to zero at the two end points). There are several things that should be noted: (1) the scanner reponse seems to saturate at the high end, and (2) the curves do not seem to go through the origin. The question is: how do we know if spline interpolation is the right thing to do? This is not an easy question to answer. If we inspect the figure, we can see that the scanner response to the first five gray patches is quite linear. We might as well fit a straight line to the first five points and clip the line at $y = 255$, the maximum possible output value. The answer has to come from an understanding of the device physics of the scanner. Our justification is that the scanner uses a CCD linear array that has an anti-blooming control, which starts to kick in before the sensor is saturated and therefore tends to create a smooth nonlinear curve at the upper end of the response curve. Therefore, a spline interpolation is more likely to be

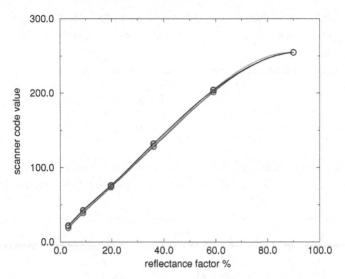

Figure 19.15. The scanner response curves. The circles are the averaged red, green, and blue scanner codes plotted against the reflectance factors of the gray patches. The curves are from the natural cubic spline interpolation through the data points. The red, green, and blue curves are almost on top of each other because scanners are adjusted to give equal r, g, b responses to gray.

closer to the truth than a straight line with clipping. However, this may not always be true for all scanners. One way to find out is to have reflection targets that have a finer increment in reflectance factor. The question of why the curves do not seem to go through the origin is even more troublesome. There are several possible causes, but a likely cause is flare, the stray light scattered into the sensor by other brighter regions adjacent to the patch being measured.

Adjusting the scanner operating point
In the above example, the upper end of the scanner response curve is reaching the saturation level of the sensor. Typically, CCD sensors are quite linear and the nonlinear response regions are to be avoided. This can be adjusted by shortening the exposure time in the scanning. There will be fewer photons captured and the response is proportionally reduced. However, if the region of interest in the original picture is already on the dark side, shortening the exposure time will also reduce the signal-to-noise ratio in the region of interest in the digitized image. This may be quite undesirable, especially if the digitized image is made even lighter by digital image processing, because the noise will become very visible. Therefore, using a long exposure time and a nonlinear calibration curve is justified for low-key pictures. Whenever the exposure time is adjusted for an application, the scanner response curve has to be calibrated for that exposure setting. The important lesson here is that understanding device characteristics is often helpful for making good engineering trade-offs.

Dealing with scanner flare
Good scanner design, like good camera design, always calls for careful flare control. Most camera interiors are black and baffles are used in the lens barrel. The cost pressure of a

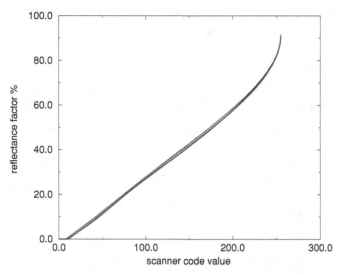

Figure 19.16. The scanner calibration table. For a given scanner code value, we can determine the input reflectance factor from the table.

desktop scanner often forces a manufacturer to save on material cost and, as a result, scanner interiors are not all black, some even have white or shiny parts. The flare problem is often quite severe in desktop scanners [302] and its measurement requires special test targets. The major problem caused by flare is the reduction of image contrast in the dark areas of an image. This is not easy to deal with because the flare is dependent on local image details and the exact solution calls for some kind of deconvolution,[6] which is time consuming and noise sensitive. One corrective measure is to treat the scanner flare as a uniform flare and then use a tone scale curve with a very steep shadow slope to make dark regions darker and higher contrast.

Computing the scanner calibration lookup table
Figure 19.15 shows the scanner code value as a function of reflectance factor. What we want is really the inverse function: given a scanner code vaue, we want to know what the reflectance factor is. This inverse function, the calibration table for the scanner, can be easily computed from Fig. 19.15 by cubic interpolation and extrapolation. Figure 19.16 shows such a calibration table.

Computing the scanner color correction matrix
Having determined the scanner calibration tables for gray scales, we have to face the color correction problem. Before we can calibrate for scanner color transformation, we have to map all our measured scanner (r, g, b) data through the three 1-D LUTs to arrive at the (r', g', b') scanner reflectance values, as shown in Table 19.4.

---

[6] Basically, the flare is measured as a PSF and some constrained inverse filtering can be used to restore the flare-free image.

Table 19.4. *The (r',g',b') code values for the 24 color patches of the Macbeth ColorChecker as the results of mapping data in Table 19.1 through the scanner calibration curves shown in Fig. 19.16.*

(16.91, 7.92, 5.51)	(51.06, 30.55, 22.83)	(14.34, 19.42, 31.98)	(12.44, 15.91, 5.18)	(27.19, 22.66, 41.63)	(26.96, 50.10, 34.61)
(52.17, 18.91, 4.10)	(9.73, 10.30, 33.09)	(46.33, 9.16, 12.91)	(11.56, 5.14, 16.30)	(36.47, 48.98, 6.70)	(61.12, 35.92, 5.38)
(4.36, 4.50, 26.74)	(12.20, 29.90, 5.97)	(37.87, 4.02, 3.91)	(75.37, 55.82, 4.66)	(42.87, 10.85, 30.34)	(8.53, 21.42, 29.38)
(88.98, 88.88, 89.33)	(59.00, 58.47, 57.61)	(36.09, 35.71, 35.29)	(19.73, 19.39, 19.07)	(8.80, 8.85, 8.55)	(2.79, 2.97, 2.57)

Table 19.5. ΔE *errors in the scanner calibration using a color correction matrix.*

Patch #	Measured $L^*a^*b^*$	Approx. $L^*a^*b^*$	ΔE
1	(38.43, 15.37, 16.20)	(39.01, 19.55, 17.41)	4.393
2	(66.50, 21.30, 18.54)	(67.04, 19.32, 18.95)	2.093
3	(49.93, −4.26, −20.97)	(49.71, −6.04, −23.79)	3.340
4	(44.38, −16.51, 26.83)	(44.74, −12.98, 26.31)	3.580
5	(55.85, 9.31, −24.95)	(56.78, 10.42, −23.96)	1.760
6	(71.24, −33.01, 0.52)	(70.85, −30.47, 6.51)	6.524
7	(63.93, 36.92, 63.72)	(60.70, 35.40, 58.27)	6.517
8	(39.38, 7.34, −42.31)	(39.41, 8.14, −42.24)	0.797
9	(51.70, 48.85, 18.67)	(53.07, 51.42, 17.85)	3.024
10	(30.40, 25.28, −22.65)	(33.07, 23.91, −24.17)	3.364
11	(72.71, −20.77, 61.26)	(71.74, −23.15, 59.70)	3.009
12	(73.38, 18.60, 69.00)	(71.36, 17.88, 66.69)	3.154
13	(30.78, 16.42, −52.52)	(27.41, 14.57, −53.09)	3.889
14	(53.66, −36.24, 30.63)	(55.36, −39.72, 37.90)	8.241
15	(40.82, 55.54, 28.64)	(45.34, 56.29, 37.72)	10.176
16	(82.99, 3.90, 82.16)	(81.83, 6.75, 82.65)	3.114
17	(52.32, 49.47, −13.67)	(53.73, 47.98, −13.62)	2.050
18	(51.23, −29.79, −27.42)	(48.90, −24.04, −21.74)	8.415
19	(96.02, −0.08, 0.04)	(95.40, −1.46, −2.50)	2.949
20	(81.34, 0.10, 0.63)	(80.95, −1.06, −1.02)	2.053
21	(66.67, −0.44, 0.07)	(66.27, −0.81, −0.97)	1.180
22	(51.60, −0.43, 0.66)	(51.16, −0.46, −0.54)	1.274
23	(35.98, −0.51, 0.71)	(35.57, −1.04, −0.16)	1.098
24	(20.08, 0.31, 0.59)	(19.58, −2.09, 1.53)	2.627

From the CIEXYZ values of the Macbeth ColorChecker in Table 19.2 and the (r', g', b') scanner reflectance values in Table 19.4, we can determine a 3×3 color transformation matrix to convert scanner (r', g', b') to CIEXYZ, such that the total CIELAB ΔE error is minimized, subject to the constraint that neutral colors $(r' = g' = b' = 100)$ are mapped to the reference white under the chosen illuminant, D50 $(X_n = 96.4306, Y_n = 100.0, Z_n = 82.3924)$. The optimal matrix determined by a conjugate gradient search is:

$$M = \begin{bmatrix} 0.639101 & 0.215884 & 0.096116 \\ 0.318735 & 0.641256 & 0.036091 \\ -0.002456 & 0.054175 & 0.797830 \end{bmatrix}. \tag{19.45}$$

The performance of such a simple calibration process using three 1-D LUTs and one 3×3 matrix can be roughly estimated by comparing the measured (L^*, a^*, b^*) values of the

24 patches with their approximated (L^*, a^*, b^*) from the calibration. Table 19.5 shows the resulting calibration ΔE errors for the 24 patches. The mean ΔE is 3.69, but the maximum ΔE is as high as 10.18 for the red patch (#15). It should be noted that the patches from (#19) to (#24) are known to be neutral, but the calibrated (L^*, a^*, b^*)s for (#19), (#20), and (#24) have quite a noticeable color shift. These errors can be traced back to the calibration curves constructed by the cubic spline. We can see from Table 19.4 that the (r', g', b') values for these three patches have significant deviations from the neutral (i.e., $r' = g' = b'$). Since our visual perception is quite sensitive to neutral errors and they can be very objectionable, we have to be very careful when constructing the three 1-D LUTs. Depending on how objectionable the resulting neutral errors are, we may or may not choose to go back and adjust the calibration curves and recompute the matrix to reduce the neutral errors.

This example clearly shows that in order to achieve a good scanner calibration, we have to pay special attention to the gray-scale measurements. The example clearly shows that a 3-D LUT has to be used to reduce the maximum color error.

19.8 Problems

19.1 Why should we use cyan, magenta, and yellow dyes as the subtractive primaries?

19.2 Design a set of block dyes that will give the maximum color gamut for a color reversal film, using CIE illuminant A as the light source.

19.3 On a Bayer CFA, a blue pixel is immediately surrounded by four green pixels. One method for interpolating the green signal at the blue pixel is to use the average of the medians of the four green neighbors. For example, if the four green pixels have the values 63, 80, 84, 85, the average of the medians, 80 and 84, is 82. This median filter approach is less sensitive to noise and also has the advantage of preserving a high-contrast edge. However, the computation tends to be more costly than other methods. Design a fast method for computing the average of medians. How many comparison operations are needed for each pixel?

19.4 You have a color digital camera and a Macbeth ColorChecker. You would like to convert a color image taken by the camera into a black-and-white image which would approximate an image taken by a camera with a spectral response function identical to the CIE luminous efficiency function, $V(\lambda)$. Given that you know the luminance value of each color patch on the ColorChecker, how do you do the calibration and conversion?

19.5 Let there be m color samples with spectral reflectance factors $\rho_i(\lambda)$, $i = 1, 2, \ldots, m$, and the spectral power distribution of the illumination $L(\lambda)$. An imaging system with spectral response functions $R(\lambda)$, $G(\lambda)$, and $B(\lambda)$ is used to take an image of all the m color samples. The pixel values corresponding to each of the color samples are (r_i, g_i, b_i), $i = 1, 2, \ldots, m$. Assuming that the pixel values are proportional to the image irradiance and that we are only interested in spectral samples at every 10 nm from 400 nm to 700 nm (inclusive):

(a) How can we determine the spectral response functions, $R(\lambda)$, $G(\lambda)$, and $B(\lambda)$, from these pixel values: (r_i, g_i, b_i), $i = 1, 2, \ldots, m$?

(b) What is the minimum number, m, of color samples needed for the determination?

19.6 In calibrating a digital camera, we use three 1-D LUTs and a 3×3 matrix to convert camera (R, G, B) to CIE (X, Y, Z).

(a) What are the three 1-D LUTs for?

(b) What is the 3×3 matrix for?

(c) Under what conditions will this type of calibration give exact results for all color stimuli?

(d) Can we use a 3-D LUT for this calibration? What are the advantages and disadvantages of the 3-D LUT approach over that using 1-D LUTs and a 3×3 matrix?

20 Color image display

Color images can be displayed in many different kinds of devices: CRT monitors [160], liquid-crystal displays (LCDs) [491], plasma display panels (PDPs), field-emission displays (FEDs) [451], organic light-emitting diodes (OLEDs) [865], and other eletroluminescent displays (ELDs) that receive electronic signals and produce color images on the display screen. The images are transient in the sense that they last not much longer than the electric signals. They are called soft-copies. In comparison, color images that are printed on reversal films (slides) and papers, by photographic processes, inject printing, thermal dye transfer, and offset printing, last much longer after the printing is completed. These are called hard-copies.

Color images displayed as soft-copies are almost exclusively based on additive color reproduction, in which colors are produced by additive mixtures of three or more primary colored lights (usually red, green, and blue). In comparison, color images produced by hard-copy devices mostly use subtractive color reproduction, in which part of the light spectrum is selectively removed from the illumination on the hard-copy. For example, cyan ink removes mainly the long-wavelength part of the illuminant spectrum. The more cyan ink is deposited on a paper, the less "red" light is reflected from the print. Different colors are produced by controlling the amounts of cyan ink, magenta ink, yellow ink, and black ink (to produce very dark colors).

Therefore, there are two major topics in our study of color image displays. The first is the device or the medium itself, and the second is the method of color reproduction for that display. The basic principles in additive and subtractive color reproductions are the same, independently of the devices. In this chapter, we will discuss the two most important soft-display devices, CRT monitors and the LCD monitors, and the two most important hard-copy printing technologies: continuous tone printing (such as photographic paper and dye transfer) and half-tone printing (such as inkjet and lithographic offset printing).

20.1 CRT monitors

Since its invention in 1897 by Ferdinand Braun [864], the CRT has been greatly improved and become the most widely used image display device today. Figure 20.1 shows a schematic diagram of a typical CRT, which consists of an electron beam-forming and accelerating subsystem, a beam deflection subsystem, a metal mask, and a phosphor screen, all contained in a vacuum tube. A CRT image display works by producing and focusing an electron beam

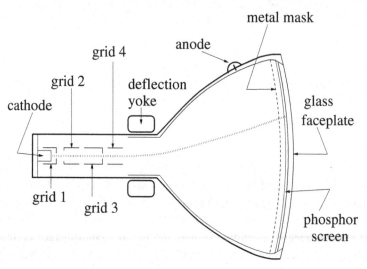

Figure 20.1. Schematic diagram of a typical CRT.

which is deflected by an externally-controlled electromagnetic field into a raster scanning motion. The motion energy of the electron beam is converted into visible light when it hits the phosphor screen behind the glass faceplate of the CRT. The cathode is heated to generate thermal electrons, which are accelerated by the positive voltages at grid 2 and grid 3, and the high anode voltage. The voltage on grid 1 is usually negative relative to the cathode and is used to modulate the electron beam current. Video signals can be connected to the cathode (cathode drive) or to grid 1 (grid drive). The electron beam is focused by grids 2, 3, and 4, and deflected into scanning motion across the CRT screen by the magnetic deflection yokes (coils). The design and manufacturing of the focusing, the deflection, and the alignment of the electron beam in a CRT are quite complicated [97, 938, 1026, Chapters 6–8] and it is only through mass production that we can make CRTs as affordable as they are today.

   Modern color CRTs for typical consumer television sets or monitors are usually shadow-mask (dot-mask or slot-mask) tubes or parallel-stripe (aperture grille) tubes. The dot mask and the aperture grille mask are shown in Fig. 20.2. In the shadow-mask design, in order to prevent the electrons from hitting the phosphor dots of the unintended color, a phosphor dot is often made smaller than the beam cross-section with the space between dots coated with black graphite (black matrix). The black matrix is to prevent external light (coming through the faceplate) reflecting back to the monitor front surface. One of the drawbacks of the shadow screen is the low electron beam efficiency (only about 9% for each gun) because most of the electrons are screened out by the mask. It is also difficult to align the phosphor dots with the mask holes very precisely and therefore high-resolution CRTs are much more difficult to manufacture. In comparison, the parallel-stripe mask design has a higher electron beam efficiency and is easier to align for high resolution. Another type of mask is called the slot mask, which is similar to the dot mask, but instead of circular dots, it uses vertical slots. Slot masks have an electron beam efficiency between that of the dot mask and that of the aperture grille mask.

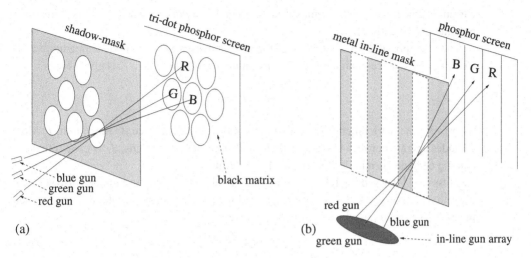

Figure 20.2. Schematic diagrams of typical masks used in color CRTs: (a) the shadow mask (dot mask) invented in 1949; (b) the parallel-stripe (aperture grille) mask with in-line guns.

There are two types of electron gun: the delta gun and the in-line gun. The in-line gun arranges the three electron beams on the horizontal axis. With this arrangement, a deflection yoke can be designed that maintains dynamic convergence over the full face of the tube without the need for correcting waveforms [97, p. 12.16]. Because of this advantage of a simplified deflection circuit, in-line guns are used for most commercial televisions.

The glass bulb (tube) used in a CRT is usually opaque to x-rays and visible light. The mask is made of metal and, as the CRT is warmed up, the mask bulges (the thermal expansion can be caused by the heat generated by electrons hitting the mask). This can cause misalignment between the holes in the mask and the phosphor dots and the resulting mislanding of electrons is called doming. The aperture grille mask is usually restrained with thin wires (called damper wires) to maintain its shape. The phosphor layer is coated with a thin aluminum film so that accumulated electrons on the phosphor layer can be conducted away.

20.1.1 Cathode current as a function of drive voltage

The maximum current density achievable by the cathode is limited by the space-charge and by the cathode temperature. The electron cloud that escapes from the cathode surface has negative charges, which increases the energy required for additional electrons to escape from the cathode surface. For a planar diode, the space-charge-limited current density J_s follows Child's law [179]:

$$J_s = \frac{4}{9}\epsilon_0 \left(\frac{2e}{m}\right)^{\frac{1}{2}} \frac{V^{\frac{3}{2}}}{L^2},\tag{20.1}$$

where ϵ_0 is the permittivity of free space, e and m are the charge and mass of the electron, V is the anode voltage relative to the cathode, and L is the anode-to-cathode distance. In a CRT, grid 1 is maintained at a nonpositive potential relative to the cathode so that no current is drawn to grid 1. The maximum current density occurs when grid 1 is at the same potential as the cathode.

The other possible limiting factor of the current density is the cathode temperature T. If we neglect the space-charge effect, the maximum current density, J_T, is given by

$$J_T = \frac{4\pi m e}{h^3} k^2 T^2 \exp\left(-\frac{e\phi}{kT}\right), \tag{20.2}$$

where $e\phi$ is the work function (about 1–2 eV) of the cathode surface at temperature T. Most cathodes operate between 900 and 1100 K, and, in most CRT designs, J_T is greater than J_s, making cathode current density space-charge-limited.

Moss [681] derived the following empirical relation between the cathode current I_c and the grid drive voltage V_d for the space-charge-limited emission at the cathode surface when the grid 2 voltage is fixed relative to the cathode:

$$I_c = K V_d^3 V_o^{-3/2}, \tag{20.3}$$

where K is a constant, V_o is the absolute value of the cut-off voltage of grid 1, and V_d is positive-going drive signal applied to the negative grid voltage, $-V_o$. Moss also observed that when V_d is greater than about seven-tenths of V_o, the cathode current is better described by the following relation:

$$I_c = K V_d^{3.5} V_o^{-2}. \tag{20.4}$$

If the drive signal is applied to the cathode, instead of to grid 1, then the grid 2 voltage relative to the cathode will vary with the drive signal and the above relation has to be modified (see [97, p. 12.12]).

In practice, the relation between the cathode current and the drive signal (measured above cut-off) is often described as a power function with an exponent that varies from device to device. Over a considerable range of the cathode current, the phosphor luminous output is linearly proportional to the cathode current, and the relation between the phosphor luminance and the signal voltage is also approximated by the power function. The reported exponents for color CRTs vary from about 1.5 to 3.0 ([895, p. 107] reported a range from 2.6 and 3.0). However, the power function is a good model only when the cut-off voltage is subtracted from the applied signal. It is not known if all the reported values were determined with the proper offset subtracted, and therefore the typical value of the exponent of a CRT cannot be accurately estimated from these reported data. NTSC has used 2.2 as its standard gamma and there are informal measurement reports that agree with this value.

20.1.2   Conversion of electron motion energy into light

The electrons are accelerated to an energy level of 15–30 keV when they hit the phosphor screen in a color CRT. In addition to being reflected, scattered, and absorbed, the incident electrons also impart sufficient energy to other electrons so that they are "kicked out" of the phosphor solid surface. These electrons are called the secondary electrons. These secondary electrons can affect the electric potential around the phosphor surface and reduce the light output. In order to prevent such a problem, a thin (150–300 nm) film of aluminum is deposited on the surface of the phosphor screen. This metal coating is thin enough to allow most of the incident high-energy electrons to go through. It also functions as a mirror, reflecting back to the glass side roughly 80–90% of the light emitted to the gun side.

The incident electrons that penetrate into the phosphor lose their energy by interacting with the electrons and nuclei of the phosphor powders. The depth of penetration is approximately a power function of the electron energy [382, p. 295]. For the electron energy between 15 and 30 keV typical of a CRT, the penetration depth is usually less than the average size of phosphor particles, 3–12 μm. A typical screen thickness is about 2–4 particles. This depth is determined to optimize the luminescence efficiency [154]. When the energy of the incident electrons falls below a threshold level, the light output is reduced to zero. Well above the threshold, the screen luminescence intensity is approximately proportional to the energy of the incident electrons. The brightness achievable is limited by several factors: saturation of the activator centers and reduction in efficiency at higher operating temperatures.

20.1.3 CRT phosphors and cathodoluminescence

The primary electrons in the phosphor solid, by ionizing the host atoms, generate electrons and holes of several tens of electron volts. These secondary carriers in turn lose their energy to create phonons. The end products of the whole process are pairs of electrons and holes, and phonons. Cathodoluminescence is the result of the radiative recombination of electron–hole pairs. The exact process of the recombination is different for different phosphor materials.

For example, in commonly used phosphors such as ZnS:Cu,Al (green) and ZnS:Ag,Cl (blue), the donors (Al or Cl) may capture migrated electrons, and the acceptors (Cu or Ag) may capture holes. The luminescence results from the combination of the donor–acceptor pairs. Because the donor and the acceptor are separated by some distance, r, in the phosphor material, and because the electron–hole recombination changes the final electric charge of the donor and the acceptor, the radiated light energy depends on the distribution of r, the distance between the donors and the acceptors. Furthermore, since the Cu and Ag receptor levels have a strong electron–phonon coupling, the emission spectrum corresponding to each donor–acceptor pair has a varying energy spread due to vibrational energy coupling even at a very low temperature. The emission spectrum of these two phosphors thus exhibits a broad, smooth peak, whose position changes as a function of the excitation intensity and the time after excitation [284, 382].

In the phosphors containing rare-earth or transition-metal ions, such as Eu^{3+}, Ce^{3+}, and Mn^{2+}, the radiative recombination occurs in well-localized luminescent centers (e.g., an intraatom transition), so the emission spectrum usually consists of very sharp spectral lines. The frequently used phosphor Y_2O_2S:Eu (red) is one such example. Its emission spectrum consists of a main line at 626 nm and sublines around 590 nm and 710 nm.

One of the important characteristics of phosphors is the persistence time. Typical phosphors used in TVs and monitors have a persistence time (peak to 1/10) from a few tens of microseconds to about a millisecond.

Phosphor intensity saturation

Over a large range of current density, the phosphor luminescent intensity is a linear function of the current density. However, at very high current density, the phosphor luminescent efficiency actually decreases (sometimes to nearly zero). Although there are several hypotheses, there is still no clear understanding of the true mechanism underlying the intensity saturation behavior of most phosphors. In certain cases, a trace amount of some impurity prevents the saturation, e.g., adding a small amount of Tb^{3+} to $Y_2O_2S:Eu$.

Phosphor and glass aging

Even though a CRT can be used for thousands of hours, the accumulated time of electron bombardment for each phosphor particle is quite short because within each sweep of a scan line, the particle is only exposed momentarily. For example, for each 1000 hours of operation, the integrated time that an individual picture element is bombarded is only about 30 seconds. In the case in which the deflection signal is stopped, a hole can be burnt in the phosphor screen within a few seconds. The luminescent efficiency of a phosphor decreases when it is used for longer [160]. The exact causes or mechanisms for the phosphor aging are different for different phosphor materials.

The other factor that affects the light output of a CRT is the aging of the faceplate. The glass faceplate of a CRT turns brown after exposure to high-energy electrons. The aging of the phosphor and the faceplate, together with the changing characteristics of other electric components in the CRT, make it necessary to calibrate a color monitor periodically over its lifetime.

20.1.4   CRT tone transfer curve

A digital code value sent to a color monitor is first converted to an analog electrical signal by a digital-to-analog converter. The output from the digital-to-analog converter is then amplified by the video amplifier. The amplified video signal is then applied to the cathode (or the first grid) of the CRT. This amplified drive signal controls the electron beam current density which in turn determines the luminescent intensity of the phosphor light output. The relation between the digital code value and the amplified video signal is usually linear with a certain amount of distortion. The relation between the luminances (L_r, L_g, L_b) and the digital code values (r, g, b) is found to be well described by the following empirical formula [83, 103]:

$$\begin{aligned}
L_r &= L_{r,max}(a_r r + c_r)^{\gamma_r} + f_r, \\
L_g &= L_{g,max}(a_g g + c_g)^{\gamma_g} + f_g, \\
L_b &= L_{b,max}(a_b b + c_b)^{\gamma_b} + f_b.
\end{aligned} \qquad (20.5)$$

Since most monitors are used with existing room lighting, the total luminance coming from a CRT screen is the sum of the emitted luminance from the CRT phosphor and the reflected flare light from the faceplate. Therefore, we have to add a constant flare component to the above CRT tone transfer models. It is also true that an input of $R = G = B = 0$ (black-level) to a CRT monitor does not make the monitor completely dark. The black-level emissions have to be carefully corrected to produce accurate dark colors [105].

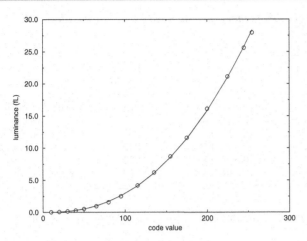

Figure 20.3. The CRT model (solid curve) and the measured data (circles).

Figure 20.3 shows a typical example of the accuracy of the model compared with the measured data (the subject is a SONY-17E10 monitor). The circles are the measured data and the solid curve is the model resulting from the least-square fit. It should be pointed out that measurement of the radiance (luminance) at low signal levels is a very time-consuming process with very low precision. In fact, in a US Patent [83], it is proposed that the model is used to extrapolate at the low end of the curve after the higher radiance levels have been measured with an instrument.

20.1.5 CRT colorimetry

CRT monitors are often used to display color images for the purpose of image preview or color proofing before the images are printed on a hard-copy device. Often, we expect the printed color images to look the same as when they are displayed on the CRT monitors. In order to use CRT monitors as a fast proofing device, we have to calibrate them first. The most important step is to determine the CRT tone transfer curve. Once that is done, we need to work on the chromatic part of the calibration. Since color reproduction on a CRT is achieved by additive color mixing, any in-gamut color can be produced by a linear combination of the three phosphor primaries. Therefore, only a 3×3 matrix is needed to transform CIEXYZ values into tristimulus values based on the monitor phosphor primaries, as described in Section 6.4. This matrix can be measured directly from the monitor with a colorimetric instrument, or, alternatively, it can be determined from the manufacturer's data of the chromaticities of the three phosphor primaries and the white balance of the monitor (see the formulas in Section 6.4).

Unfortunately, there are many different phosphors that are used in CRTs and even phosphors that are designated with the same name (such as P22) can have different chromaticities. Table 20.1 shows some examples of these variations. The P numbers in Table 20.1 (P22) have been used by the Electronics Industries Association (EIA) of the USA since 1945. A new international designation system, the Worldwide Phosphor Type Designation System

Table 20.1. *Examples of phosphors that are designated as P22 by the Electronic Industries Association*

Emission peak (nm)	Emission color	Chromaticity (x,y)	EIA designation	Chemical composition
450	blue	(0.146, 0.061)	P22	ZnS:Ag (pigmented)
530	yellowish green	(0.282, 0.620)	P22	ZnS:Cu, Al
530	yellowish green	(0.321, 0.613)	P22	(ZnCd)S:Cu, Al
535	yellowish green	(0.306, 0.602)	P22	ZnS:Au, Cu, Al
619	red	(0.664, 0.331)	P22	YVO$_4$:Eu
626	red	(0.640, 0.352)	P22	Y$_2$O$_2$S:Eu (pigmented)

Table 20.2. *The chromaticity coordinates of CRT phosphors for the various standards and monitors*

Monitor	(x_r, y_r)	(x_g, y_g)	(x_b, y_b)
NTSC	(0.670, 0.330)	(0.210, 0.710)	(0.140, 0.080)
SMPTE C	(0.630, 0.340)	(0.310, 0.595)	(0.155, 0.070)
ITU-R BT.709	(0.640, 0.330)	(0.300, 0.600)	(0.150, 0.060)
EBU	(0.640, 0.330)	(0.290, 0.600)	(0.150, 0.060)
Sony(20/20)	(0.625, 0.340)	(0.280, 0.595)	(0.155, 0.070)
Hitachi	(0.595, 0.354)	(0.308, 0.585)	(0.160, 0.084)
Barco	(0.618, 0.350)	(0.280, 0.605)	(0.152, 0.063)
Tektronics	(0.610, 0.340)	(0.280, 0.590)	(0.152, 0.063)

(WTDS), was established in 1982. A listing of the various registered phosphors can be found in reference books (for example, [866, Chapter 6]).

Although different national and international standards attempt to define standard phosphors, few if any CRT monitors have the standard phosphors, as can be seen in Table 20.2.

CRT colorimetric calibration

The calibration of a CRT color monitor requires careful adjustments of the electronic circuits that control the convergence and the deflection of the electronic beams, the CRT cut-off voltage, the luminance dynamic range, and the color tracking (i.e., the chromaticity for any input $r = g = b$ should stay the same). Once these aspects of circuit adjustment are dealt with, the monitor can be calibrated to produce a desired color within its color gamut by a 3×3 matrix followed by three 1-D LUTs, as shown in Fig. 20.4. The desired color is often specified in CIEXYZ tristimulus values. The 3×3 matrix rotates the color primaries to those of the CRT phosphors. The three 1-D LUTs are used to predistort the signals to compensate for the CRT nonlinearity. For example, if the phosphor luminance L vs. code value V relation of the monitor is described by $L = a(V + c)^\gamma$, the three 1-D LUTs have the functional form $V = (L/a)^{1/\gamma} - c$.

Assuming that there is no cross-talk between the red, green, and blue channels, we can measure the maximum tristimulus values of each phosphor when its digital value is set at the maximum and the other two color channels are set to zero. Let $(X_R, Y_R, Z_R), (X_G, Y_G, Z_G)$,

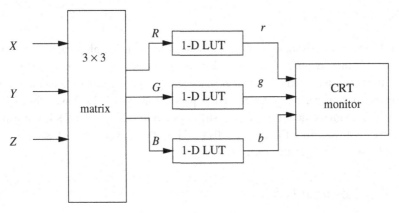

Figure 20.4. Block diagram of CRT calibration.

and (X_B, Y_B, Z_B), be the tristimulus values of the red, green, and blue phosphors, respectively. Then for any CRT tristimulus values, (R, G, B), the tristimulus values (X, Y, Z) of the color displayed on the CRT screen can be calculated as

$$\begin{bmatrix} X \\ Y \\ Z \end{bmatrix} = \begin{bmatrix} X_R & X_G & X_B \\ Y_R & Y_G & Y_B \\ Z_R & Z_G & Z_B \end{bmatrix} \begin{bmatrix} R \\ G \\ B \end{bmatrix} \qquad (20.6)$$

and

$$\begin{bmatrix} R \\ G \\ B \end{bmatrix} = \begin{bmatrix} X_R & X_G & X_B \\ Y_R & Y_G & Y_B \\ Z_R & Z_G & Z_B \end{bmatrix}^{-1} \begin{bmatrix} X \\ Y \\ Z \end{bmatrix}. \qquad (20.7)$$

In the above matrix transformation, we can scale the (R, G, B) tristimulus values to any convenient range, as long as we also scale the matrix elements inversely, so that the equation still holds. The actual code values (r, g, b) that are sent to the color monitor can be looked up from the three 1-D LUTs using (R, G, B) as indices as shown in Fig. 20.4.

CRT spatial calibration
CRT spatial calibration includes measurements of the convergence, the geometric distortion, the nonuniformity, and the MTF, etc. These calibration tasks usually require special-purpose instruments. Interested readers should consult publications in this field (e.g., [160, 496, 554, 621]). If high accuracy is not needed, the MTF of a CRT display can be estimated with the slanted-edge method using a high-resolution digital camera [961]. It is useful to know that the PSF of a monochromatic CRT display is close to a Gaussian function and the 50% spot width is roughly equal to the line spacing [376].

It should be pointed out that CRT monitors cannot be treated as devices that produce each pixel independently of each other. There are several causes for this spatial interaction [754, 755], other than the blurring due to overlapping spots: (1) insufficient video bandwidth in its electronic driving circuits, (2) imperfect DC restoration, and (3) inadequate voltage regulation.

20.2 LCDs

Two of the major disadvantages of CRT monitors are their big physical size and the large power source they require. Flat panel displays using low-voltage, small-power sources have distinct advantages where physical space and weight matter most, such as in portable computers. Among the many types of flat panel displays, LCDs have gained the most popularity. The image quality of LCDs still lags behind that of the CRT, but it has been drastically improved since the early 2000s [491]. In this section, we will study how LCDs work and some of their characteristics.

20.2.1 Properties of liquid crystals

When a solid melts and becomes a liquid, the spatial relations among molecules become randomized and any long-range order in the solid disappears as a consequence. However, when the molecules of a substance are much more elongated in one or two directions, like in a rod or a disk, the long-range order may be partially maintained in a liquid state for some temperature range, because the molecules have lower free energy when they are arranged so that their long axes are parallel to each other. This type of substance is called a liquid crystal [209, 217, Chapter 13, 541]. The elongated molecules also interact with light anisotropically. The index of refraction for light propagating in the direction of the long axis of the molecules is different from that for light propagating in a direction perpendicular to this axis. A substance whose index of refraction depends on the direction of light propagation is said to be birefringent. Liquid crystal materials are birefringent. Furthermore, when elongated molecules are placed in an electric field, they are polarized. The molecules rotate to rearrange their orientation (being in the liquid state, there is little resistance to this type of motion) so that the dipole moments are aligned with the external field. The induced orientation change will also change the optical transmission of the material. This is one way liquid-crystal devices work in electronic displays.

There are three different anisotropic phases in liquid crystals: nematic, smectic, and cholesteric [31, 209, 442, 504]. In the nematic phase, molecules are roughly aligned in their orientations, but their relative positions are random (see Fig. 20.5). In the smectic phase, molecules are also ordered spatially (in a plane-layer type of structure). The smectic phase is also further classified into A, B, C, D, E, F, and G phases. Figure 20.5 shows the smectic A (director n perpendicular to the layer plane) and smectic C phases (n is oblique to the layer plane). In the cholesteric phase, the orientation of molecules rotates spirally from plane to plane. Most LCDs use the twisted nematic (TN) phase and some use the smectic C phase with polar molecules (ferroelectric liquid crystal, FLC). A typical response time of a TN-LCD is about 2 ms, while that of a polymer stabilized FLCD can be 40 μs [517], or even faster with other types of LCD [1002].

20.2.2 The structures of LCDs and how they work

Research and development of LCDs are still very active and good progress in technology and manufacturing is being made every year. We will only discuss, as an example, the operating

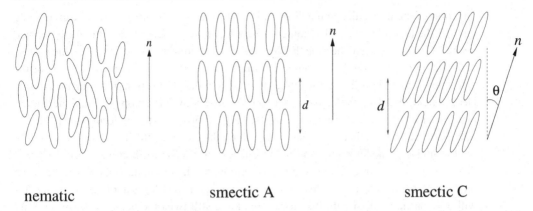

nematic   smectic A   smectic C

Figure 20.5. Examples of different phases in liquid crystals.

principles of the thin-film transistor (TFT), active matrix (AM), TN-LCD, because it is currently the most widely used LCD. Figure 20.6 shows a basic TN liquid crystal cell [679]. In Fig. 20.6(a) without any externally applied electric field, the liquid crystal molecules orient themselves to the glass plates that confine them. Note that the molecules near the top glass plate are oriented in one direction and those near the bottom plate in a direction orthogonal to that of the top plate. The orientation of the molecules in between the two plates gradually twists between the two. Therefore, this is called the twisted nematic liquid crystal. On the surfaces of the top and bottom glass plates are polarizer plates, each polarized to the

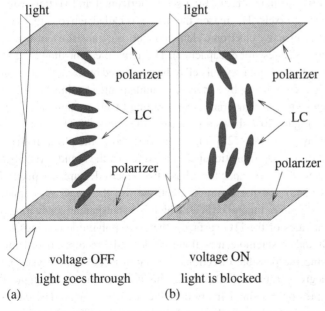

Figure 20.6. The polarized light is: (a) transmitted or (b) blocked, depending on the externally applied voltage.

direction of the molecules immediately adjacent to it. An unpolarized light beam passing through the top polarizer will become polarized, and this polarization is gradually twisted by the LC molecules. By the time the light reaches the bottom glass plate, it has the correct polarization to go through the bottom polarizer plate and emerge on the other side of the cell. Therefore, light is transmitted when the cell is in the off position (meaning no external electric field). If a large voltage (say 10 V) is applied between the top plate and the bottom plate, an electric field is present in the cell (see Fig. 20.6(b)) and the molecules are polarized into electrical dipoles that align themselves along the electric field. The polarization of the light beam is now no longer twisted and when the light reaches the bottom polarizer plate, it does not have the correct polarization to pass through. Therefore, the light is blocked when the voltage is on. It turns out that, if a smaller voltage (say 4 V) is applied, the molecules will only partially align with the electric field and still twist the polarization of the light somewhat to allow partial transmission of the light through the bottom of the cell. By controlling the cell voltage, we can therefore control how much light is transmitted through the TN liquid crystal cell. (This way of using DC voltage differences to drive the LCD is called direct drive. Over a wide range of AC frequencies, TN liquid crystal also responds to the root-mean-square (RMS) of the voltage difference. Most TN-LCD drivers are now based on these characteristics.) What we have just discussed is called the normally-white mode. We can also arrange the bottom polarizer to make it parallel with the top polarizer to obtain a normally-black mode, because then the beam is twisted to orthogonal polarization and cannot pass through without external voltage applied to the cell.

The basic cell we described above can function as a pixel. If we have an array of pixels and can apply the image signals as voltages to each pixel individually, we then have a liquid-crystal image display. The most successful method for addressing each pixel in an LCD is by an AM drive, which is basically a set of horizontal and vertical voltage lines forming a grid pattern of pixels. The reason the matrix is called active is that at each grid (pixel) location there is an active electronic element (such as a transistor), instead of merely a passive element (such as a resistor or capacitor). The active element allows the transfer of the signal at each pixel to the liquid crystal cell to be controlled by a small addressing clock signal. This is usually accomplished by a transistor, implemented by thin-film deposition of differently-doped semiconductor materials. The resulting LCDs are thus called TFT-LCDs (the AM is implied). Figure 20.7 shows a schematic diagram of a TFT-LCD with a CFA for color image display [249, 680, 728]. Figure 20.7(a) shows the physical structure and Fig. 20.7(b) shows the equivalent functional circuit. Note that the liquid crystal here serves as the dielectric material of the capacitor whose two electrodes are the pixel electrode (on the lower glass plate) and the common electrode (on the upper glass plate). Both electrodes are made of indium tin oxide (ITO) which is a transparent conducting material. On the liquid crystal sides of the ITO surfaces, there are polyimide coatings, which are robbed to align the liquid crystal molecules along the desired directions. In order to operate smoothly (by reducing the possible directions of rotation), the liquid-crystal molecules are tilted at a few degrees from the ITO planes. This is called the pretilt angle. The TFT is opaque and occupies only a small fraction of the total pixel area. The data signal is transferred to the pixel electrode from the data line through the TFT. The voltage between the pixel electrode and the common electrode creates the electrical field that is applied to the

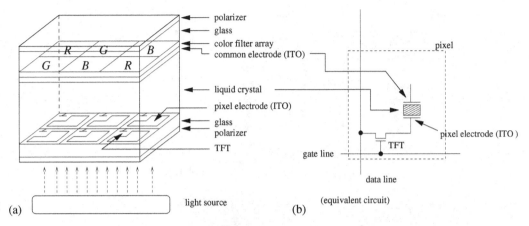

Figure 20.7. A schematic diagram of an AM LCD using TFTs (a) physical structure, (b) equivalent functional circuit.

liquid crystal molecules to change the light-transmitting property. The R, G, B color filters modify the output spectra to produce the desired color stimulus at a spatial location on an image.

There are several types of material that have been used to make the TFTs. Amorphous (noncrystal) silicon has been the most widely used material because it does not require high-temperature processes. However, its mobility is low (therefore giving slow response time) and it is sensitive to light (thus it requires the light shield). Polysilicon material has high mobility, but usually requires high-temperature processes and/or special glass plates. However, low-temperature, polysilicon (LTPS) transistors have been successfully manufactured into very good quality displays.

One of the major operational differences between a CRT and an LCD is the duration of the dwell time which is the length of time a pixel is illuminating in each refresh cycle. In the AM LCD, each pixel is addressed once per field or frame and the luminance of the pixel stays constant until it is addressed again. In order to avoid DC voltage build-up, the polarity of the driving voltage of an LCD cell is often alternated at line rate or field rate. This still makes the dwell time of an LCD pixel orders of magnitude longer than that of a CRT pixel. As a consequence, flickering is generally not a problem in an LCD.

One of the major deficiencies of the TN-LCD as described above is the narrowness of the viewing angle, typically 40° vertically and 90° horizontally. This is caused partially by the polarizers but mainly by the angular transmittance of the liquid crystal cell being a sensitive function of angle between the light beam direction and the orientations of the liquid crystal molecules. The viewing angle can be greatly increased by various methods, such as optical film, multidomains, in-plane switching, and axially symmetric aligned micro-cell mode [542]. These methods have different advantages and shortcomings. For example, the in-plane switching method is one of the early successful methods, but it suffers from having a lower aperture ratio and slower response time. Figure 20.8 shows how the in-plane switching LCD works. It is possible to extend the viewing angle to 140° both vertically and horizontally by this method [523].

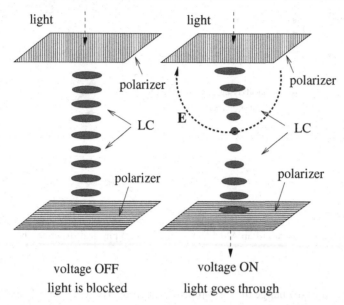

Figure 20.8. A simplified diagram of the principle of the in-plane switching mechanism. Note that the electric field **E** is controlled to steer the direction of the liquid crystal molecules in the same plane as the layered structures.

20.2.3 LCD calibration

Since LCDs also use additive color reproduction, the basic color calibration procedure for an LCD is the same as that for a CRT monitor. However, a good calibration of an LCD is more difficult to achieve than that of a CRT monitor for many reasons [293, 848, 856, 876, 933, 1049, 1061]. Chief among them are:

- Often there is light leakage in the OFF state of an LCD [293].
- The color and brightness in an LCD vary as functions of viewing angle and ambient light.
- The voltage-to-luminance transfer function for LCDs is strongly dependent on material and cell structural parameters.
- Measuring instruments may be sensitive to polarization errors.
- The chromaticity of an LCD varies with luminance (probably due to light leakage [293]).
- There is cross-talk between neighboring pixels in an LCD (as well as in a CRT).
- The device characteristics of an LCD vary with temperature.
- The fluorescent lamps used in an LCD as light sources require narrow-band spectral measurements.
- The ambient light is reflected by an LCD surface in a more complex manner than by a CRT surface. Depending on the depth and angle of the light reflection, the spectral composition of the reflected ambient light can be modified in a way difficult to model [218].

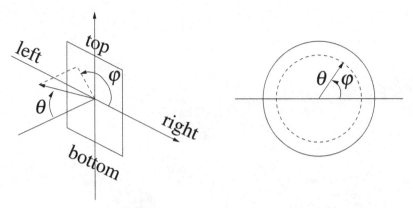

Figure 20.9. Coordinate framework for the polar diagram of an LCD angular measurements.

Several experimental measurements of the BRDF of LCD surfaces [91, 497] show that much of the ambient light is reflected as a haze component, i.e., the image is not as sharp as a specular reflection, and not as uniform as from a Lambertian surface either.

The electrooptical transfer curve of an LCD, the voltage–luminance curve, has an s-shape that is quite different from that of a CRT monitor. The toe and the shoulder of the s-curve are often not symmetric, with one much steeper than the other (see, for example, [856, Fig. 7]). The red, green, and blue electrooptical transfer curves of an LCD also tend to differ more from each other, resulting in neutral color shift as a function of input code values. Because the luminance and chromaticity of a pixel vary dramatically as a function of viewing angle, the calibration of an LCD usually requires measurements at various angles. The convention is to plot the angular variation of the measured data on a polar diagram, where the radius vector represents the inclination angle θ and the polar angle represents the azimuth angle ϕ, both being defined with respect to the LCD plane (Fig. 20.9). There are two methods for making measurements of the angular distribution: the goniometric method and the conoscopic method [848]. The goniometric method uses precisely machined equipment to rotate the LCD and measure its light output with a photometer, a colorimeter, or a spectroradiometer. The conoscopic method uses an optical system to map the angular distribution to be measured into a spatial image. Therefore, the conoscopic method is much faster.

20.3 PDPs

Light produced by gas discharge has been well studied. Fluorescent lamps and neon lamps are well-known light sources based on gas discharge. However, high-luminance and high-resolution display panels based on gas discharge were introduced to the consumer electronics market in the early 2000s. Judging from their excellent image quality, we can expect that they will become more widely used for high-quality color displays.

Basically, a PDP works with a neon light at each pixel. A pixel cell is filled with inert gas between two electrodes, one of which is transparent to light. When the voltage between

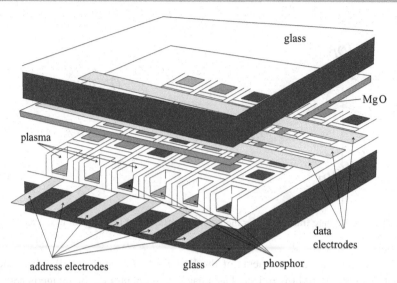

Figure 20.10. An example of the basic structure of a color PDP.

the two electrodes of the gas-filled cell is increased, the current increases at a very small rate and begins to saturate at a very low level. As the voltage increases further and further, a point is reached when the electrons gain enough energy to ionize other gas atoms (such as neon) during collisions, and the freed electrons can further ionize other atoms, and the current starts to increase at an exponential rate. Eventually a current level is reached at which it can sustain itself while the voltage remains at about the same level. If there are no external current-limiting circuits, it is very difficult to control the operating point of this gas plasma (ionized atoms and electrons). When the current is further increased beyond this level, the voltage across the gas gap actually decreases (a negative resistance). At this operating point, the gas plasma glows with light [1018]. The spectral emission is a characteristic of the gas composition. For example, the red–orange glow seen on some PDPs is due to neon gas. This is vaguely called the "primary color" of the gas. Different types of gas have different electron orbital energy levels and the emitted wavelengths correspond to the energy differences between orbitals. By using different gas compositions, different color primaries can be generated for a color PDP. Some of the light emitted by the gaseous discharge is in the ultraviolet range and can be used to excite phosphors which in turn emit photons of different wavelengths, the same mechanism as is used in fluorescent lamps. By using different phosphors, different color primaries can be produced. Color PDPs may use one of these two methods to produce different colors at different pixel cells. Figure 20.10 shows an example of the basic structure of a color PDP.

Color PDPs have several advantages over CRTs and other flat panel display devices. Since there is not much pressure difference between the inside and the outside of the panel, PDPs do not require thick glass plates like CRTs. While the response time of an LCD is on the order on 10^{-3} s, the PDP response time is on the order of 10^{-6} s. Another advantage is that PDPs can be made fairly large (40–50 in) because the capacitance between electrodes is not large and the required driving circuits can be readily achieved. The level of luminance (500 cd m^{-2}) and luminous efficiency (2–3 1m W^{-1}) of the modern PDPs are as good as those of CRTs [974]. With contrast ratios approaching 500:1, the images of commercially available color PDPs are of very high quality (they look very colorful and very sharp).

20.4 Electroluminescent displays

There are many new types of color display that are self-emissive. Most of them rely on energy transformation from externally supplied power into photons. Luminescence is the nonthermal emission of photons by a material when it is excited by some form of external energy. For example, chemical reactions supply the external energy for chemiluminescence, mechanical disruptions that for triboluminescence, and electron motion energy that for cathodoluminescence (as used in CRTs). The type of luminescence we are interested in this section is electroluminescence which converts electric energy into light, mainly through electric fields.

20.4.1   OLED and PLED

In Section 7.2.5, we mentioned LEDs as promising light sources [843, 1073]. Typical LEDs are made from inorganic semiconductor materials, such as silicon and gallium crystals. In order to make a high-resolution color display, we have to put tens of thousands of LEDs together to form a useful display panel. Such displays for outdoor viewing do exist, but they are too large and too expensive for indoor use. In the 1960s, organic electroluminescent materials were discovered and extensively studied (e.g., [375, 771]). However, it was not until the 1980s that modern thin-film deposition techniques and new organic materials were used to produce practical electroluminescent cells [935] that had the potential to be manufactured into image displays. These are called OLEDs. The organic materials used at that time were not usually large (molecular weight less than 3000). In the late 1980s, some organic conjugated polymers with a molecular weight greater than 10 000 were found to be electroluminescent [151]. LEDs made of organic polymers are now called polymer light-emitting diodes (PLEDs) or light-emitting polymers (LEPs) to differentiate them from the small-molecule OLEDs. The discovery that certain conjugated polymers can become electroluminescent was a remarkable event. Many varieties have been found since then. The physics of semiconductor devices made of conjugated polymers has been reviewed in [49, pp. 186–213, 364, 865].

Figure 20.11 shows examples of the basic structure of a cell in an LEP and a cell in an OLED display device. It should be noted that there are many different variations in the basic structures for practical OLED displays. The general design criteria [931, pp. 294–5] for OLED devices are: (1) thin layers to lower bias voltages; (2) low injection barriers for electrons and holes; and (3) proper bandgaps for the desired colors. Functionally, it is convenient to imagine that there are five layers between the cathode and the anode: an electron injection layer, an electron transport layer, a light-emissive layer (where electrons and holes are combined to emit photons), a hole transport layer, and a hole injection layer. Typically the total thickness of the five layers is less than a micrometer which is made possible by the good insulating properties of the organic light-emitting layer. However, good insulators resist hole and/or electron injection from the metal electrodes. One of the

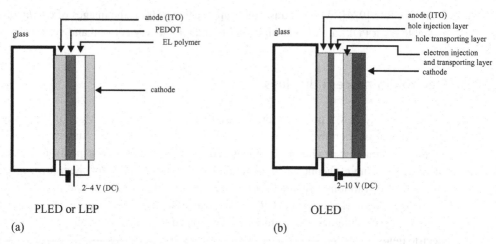

Figure 20.11. Examples of the basic structure of a cell of: (a) an LEP display [555] and (b) a cell of a (small-molecule) OLED display.

major inventions in this field was the development of materials for hole/electron injection layers that allow efficient injection of electrons and holes. Holes and electrons will not have a good chance to recombine and produce photons if they pass by each other too fast or do not have properly matched energies or quantum states. Therefore, the transport layers were developed to increase the efficiency of photon-producing hole–electron recombination. In practice, the electron injection layer and the electron transport layer are often combined into one layer and the light-emissive layer can be in the hole–electron transport layer. The structures for small-molecule OLED cells and those for LEP cells are quite similar, but the latter tend to require fewer layers than the former.

The spectral emission bandwidth of organic molecules is usually around 50–70 nm at the half-height amplitude. The color gamut can be made larger by sharpening the emission peak. Very high luminous efficiencies have been achieved with these OLEDs, roughly on the order of 10–40 lm W^{-1} in the green [415]. Operating voltages are low, on the order of 3–10 V, because the organic emissive layer is very thin, on the order of 50–200 nm. The manufacturing processes of the low-molecular OLED and the polymer OLED are quite different. Color displays using either type of OLED have been demonstrated. They are very bright (they can be greater than 50 000 cd m^{-2}), have long lifetimes (longer than 10 000 hours), have wide viewing angles (greater than 160°), and fast response time (less than 10^{-6} s). As manufacturing processes are perfected and quantities grow, the OLED color displays may become one of the dominant color image display devices for many applications.

20.5 Printing technologies

Before personal computers were widely used, office printing relied on typewriters, daisy-wheels, or dot-matrix printers that used a type bar or stylus to strike the print medium

printing technologies

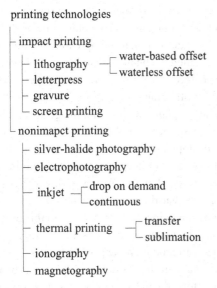

Figure 20.12. Various types of printing technologies.

(paper) to produce output documents. These printing processes are known as impact print-ing. Traditional commercial printing processes, such as letterpress, gravure, lithography, flexography, and screen printing, rely on separate carriers called plates to transfer images or documents to a blanket and then to impress them on the output medium (paper). These are the conventional impact printing processes, and are generally known as plate printing. Other printing technologies, such as electrophotography, inkjet, and thermal dye transfer, are called nonimpact printing or plateless printing [719]. Figure 20.12 shows a list of cur-rent printing technologies. The printing industry is a very large industry and many different printing technologies are used to produce documents and hard-copy images [8, 216, 511]. Here we briefly describe some of the technologies commonly used for printing color im-ages. The main purpose is to introduce the working principles of each technology so that we can have at least some basic understanding of the physical processes when dealing with the potential color imaging science problems associated with each printing technology. Readers who are interested in more detailed information should consult books on these technologies (e.g., [8, 484, 511, 719]).

20.5.1 Offset lithography

Offset lithography is the most widely used printing process because of its speed, quality, and cost-effectiveness. The word, lithography, comes from the Greek words *lithos* (stone) and *graphein* (to write). The process was first invented by etching the documents or the images on a stone plate, applying greasy ink to it, and then impressing the inked and water-wetted plate to the paper. Today, the plate is made of metal or other materials that can be mounted on a cylinder. However, direct printing from the plate to paper does not give very good images because, in order to be durable in shape, the plate has to be made of a hard (though possibly thin and flexible) material (such as aluminum) which does not transfer or impress inks to paper very well. In 1903, Ira Rubel built a lithographic machine in which the plate image was impressed on a rubber-covered cylinder that in turn impressed the image on the paper [199]. The rubber-covered cylinder is called the blanket cylinder and the plate image is said to be offset to the blanket cylinder before it is transferred to the paper. Therefore, the combined printing process is called offset lithography.

On a lithographic plate, the image areas are coplanar with the nonimage areas. The basic working principle of lithography is that the image areas on the plate are ink-accepting and the nonimage areas are ink-repellent. For example, in water-based lithography, the image areas are hydrophobic (i.e., water repellent), and the nonimage areas are hydrophilic. Greasy inks are thus adsorbed only onto the image areas. However, new waterless offset printing technology uses silicon-layer coated plates so that the nonimage areas are ink-repellent [511, p. 211]. The image areas are formed by removing the silicon layer. In this process, no water is needed to wet the nonimage areas. The plates used in offset lithography printing are thin (up to 0.3 mm) and therefore are easy to mount on the plate cylinders.

The lithographic process is inherently binary in the sense that the amount of ink per unit area is not controlled in gradation. Therefore, the half-toning process is always used in offset lithography. Typically four color plates (CMYK) are prepared by using different color filters and screens of different angles to produce half-tone images. There are many books and papers on the science and practice of color separations and proofing [142, 310, 1065].

20.5.2   Letterpress

In the letterpress process, the image areas on the plate are raised above the nonimage areas. A layer of ink of uniform thickness is applied to the image areas, usually all raised to the same height, with a roller. The inked plate is then pressed and transferred to the surface of the print substrate (e.g., paper). Letterpress printing used to be the dominant printing technology for printing books and has been used for hundreds of years. Plates for letterpress printing were traditionally made of rigid materials, predominantly alloys of lead, tin, and other metals. Most letterpress plates today use flexible materials, such as rubber or photopolymers. This is called flexography. Unlike traditional letterpress printing, flexogaphy requires relatively low pressure between the plate cylinder and the substrate. Therefore, it can be used to print on very thin, flexible film, rough-surfaced packaging materials, and fabrics [511, p. 397].

20.5.3   Gravure

In the gravure printing process, the image areas on the plate are recessed below the nonimage plate areas. They are engraved into the plate surface. The recessed image areas can be of different depths (continuous tone) or the same depth (half-tone). The ink applied to the plate is trapped into the recessed areas while the ink adhered to the nonimage areas of the plate is wiped out by a doctor blade. The plate is then pressed on the printing substrate and the ink is transferred to the substrate. The print quality of the gravure process is excellent. Due to the high cost of plate making, it is often used only for very-long-run jobs (e.g., more than a million copies), such as weekly news magazines and packaging boxes.

20.5.4 Screen printing

In the screen printing process, the ink is forced through a screen onto the printing substrate. The screen is a fine mesh made of plastic or metal fibers. The stencil covers the entire screen mesh and is not permeable to the ink. The stencil on the image areas is then removed to expose the open mesh of the screen. The ink is applied to the stencil-screen and the ink is forced through the image areas. For very-high-resolution screen printing, the stencil is formed with screen emulsions with photopolymers. The film emulsion can be hardened by ultraviolet exposure and the nonexposed film areas can be removed by a jet of water. Therefore, the image areas can be written with optical resolution. The advantage of screen printing is that many kinds of ink with the most varied properties can be used and the thickness of the ink layer can be high (20–100 µm) compared with that of the offset printing (0.5–2 µm) [511, p. 58].

20.5.5 Silver halide photography

Photographic papers

Photographic papers have long been the high-quality output media of choice, because they offer excellent continuous-tone reproduction, very good color reproduction, reasonably high sharpness, and very low cost. Photographic papers are basically photographic emulsions coated on paper supports. A black-and-white paper consists of a protective overcoat, an emulsion layer, a diffuse reflection layer, a paper base and an antistatic coating. The emulsion layer is about 8 µm, and the paper base is about 220 µm. Color negative paper (to print from color negative film) has many more layers: (1) protective layer, (2) interlayer with ultraviolet absorber, (3) red-sensitive cyan layer, (4) interlayer, (5) green-sensitive magenta layer, (6) interlayer, (7) blue-sensitive yellow layer, (8) diffuse reflection layer, (8) paper base (cellulose fibers), and (9) antistatic layer. Color negative paper is mostly coated with silver chloride emulsions that do not have intrinsic blue sensitivity, and therefore, the blue-sensitive yellow layer can be placed at the bottom. The total thickness of the emulsions is about 10 µm (not much thicker than the black-and-white photographic paper emulsions). The thickness of the paper base is about 230 µm. Light going through the cyan, magenta, and yellow dye layers is reflected back to the air (through the dye layers again) by the diffuse reflection layer which can be treated to produce a variety of good-looking surfaces, such as matte, silk, glossy, or fine-grain luster surfaces with random textures. Two major types of diffuse reflection coating are used for photographic paper: resin (polyethylene) coated paper and baryta (barium sulfate) coated paper. The resin coating consists of mainly polyethylene mixed with titanium dioxide, toning pigments, and optical brighteners to achieve the desired neutral tone of the paper. The baryta coating consists of white pigment (barium sulfate), toning dyes, optical brightener, and binder (gelatin).

Color reversal paper is used to print from color reversal film (slide). The emulsion is usually silver bromide that has intrinsic blue sensitivity and the blue-sensitive yellow layer is placed on the top with a yellow filter layer beneath it. It is also different from color negative paper because it goes through a black-and-white processing first. A positive image is then formed on the unexposed silver halide grains.

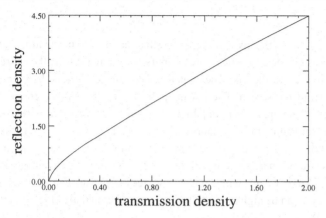

Figure 20.13. An example of the reflection density as a function of transmission density, $D_\rho = f(D_t)$.

The spectral composition of the light reflected from color paper can be computed fairly well from the amounts of dyes and their spectral transmittance functions. If multiple reflections between the air–emulsion interface and the emulsion-paper coating are neglected, the reflection density is approximately twice the dye transmission density because most reflected light goes through the dye layers twice. However, multiple reflections account for a significant portion of the total reflected light [386, 867, 1035] and the reflection density $D_\rho(\lambda)$ is a nonlinear function, $D_\rho(\lambda) = f(D_t(\lambda))$, of the transmission density $D_t(\lambda)$, both being functions of wavelength. Of course, this nonlinear relation is dependent on the illumination and viewing geometry. Figure 20.13 shows an example of such a nonlinear relation. Note that when the transmission density is larger, the effect of multiple reflections is smaller, and the reflection density increases linearly at a rate approximately twice that of the transmission density because the reflected light passes through the dyes twice. Using this measurable nonlinear function [761], the reflection densities can be calculated from the dye amounts analytically as discussed in Section 16.1.3.

The density range of a good glossy color paper is from a minimum density of 0.05–0.1 to a maximum density of 2.2–2.4, measured by 0/45 reflection densitometers. This represents a dynamic range of about 160:1. In typical print viewing environments, such as the office or home, the illumination is more diffuse (thus creating more viewing flare) and the available dynamic range is often less than 50:1. The average gradient of color negative paper (i.e., the average slope of the D–logH curve) is about 1.7–1.8 so that the images recorded on color negative films (average gradient about 0.63) can be printed to a final contrast of about 1.1–1.2. The average gradient of color reversal paper is much lower because color reversal films have a higher gradient of 1.3–1.5.

Color reversal films
Color reversal films (slides) are often viewed in a dark surround. Their density range is from a minimum density of 0.1–0.2 to a maximum density of 3.0–3.5, measured by 0/0 transmission densitometers. The projector, ambient light, and screen flares often reduce the available dynamic range to about 300:1. Because of the effect of the dark surround

viewing on our brightness perception, it was found that films with a gamma higher than 1.0 produce higher-quality images. Therefore, color reversal films usually have a gamma of 1.3–1.5. Another factor related to image quality is the screen luminance level. In general, image quality increases with the screen luminance, up to a certain level (typically from 70 to 100 cd m^{-2}, depending on the TRC), then it falls off gradually. It seems that, when our eyes are adapted to the dark surround, the optimum operating range of our visual system is only partially determined by the screen and therefore very high screen luminance may push the image beyond the optimum visual range.

Similarly to the model of the reflection density, the spectral transmission $T(\lambda)$ of a color reversal film can be calculated from the amounts of dye, a_c, a_m, and a_y:

$$T(\lambda) = b(\lambda)10^{-[a_c\, C(\lambda)+a_m\, M(\lambda)+a_y\, Y(\lambda)]},$$

where $b(\lambda)$ is the spectral transmission functions of the film base, and $C(\lambda)$, $M(\lambda)$, and $Y(\lambda)$ are the spectral transmission densities of a unit amount of cyan, magenta, and yellow dye, respectively.

20.5.6 Electrophotography (xerography)

Copiers and laser printers use a process called electrophotography to produce (or reproduce) texts and images. An electrophotographic process forms a latent image by exposing a photoconductor film with the input image. The latent image is formed as an electrostatic charge pattern on the photoconductor. It is then developed by dusting electrostatically charged toner powder on it. The toner powder is then transferred to and fused with paper to produce a printed page. Copiers use reflected light from the originals and laser printers use lasers to form the latent image on the photoconductor. The six major steps in electrophotography are [334, 832]:

1. Charge: the photoconductor is uniformly (+) charged in the dark.
2. Expose: the image is exposed onto the photoconductor by optical lenses (copier) or by laser beams (laser printer), producing an electrostatic latent image. The areas of the photoconductor that receive more light are discharged more because the charges are conducted away.
3. Develop: the toner powder (oppositely charged −) is dusted on the photoconductor. Photoconductor areas that were exposed to more light have less (+) charges and therefore attract less (−) toner powder. Areas that were exposed to less light have more (+) charges and attract more (−) charged toner. The latent electrostatic image is thus said to be developed with the toner powder.
4. Transfer: the developed toner image is then transferred to the receiving substrates, such as paper.
5. Fuse: the toner powder is then fused to the receiving substrate by heat and pressure to produce the output hard-copy.
6. Clean: the photoconductor is then discharged and cleaned for the next job.

In the laser printer, because of the large white area on a printed page, it is more efficient to write and discharge the text area. The development process needs to be reversed. The photoconductor is first uniformly (−) charged in the dark. The laser discharges the black text areas and the negatively charged toner powder is repelled from the unexposed areas and only attaches to the discharged text areas. In color copiers or color laser printers, the process is repeated three (CMY) or four (CMYK) times to produce a color copy.

The electrophotographic process is inherently high contrast because it is difficult to control gentle gradation of toner powder as it is developed on the photoconductor and transferred to the paper. For this reason, the half-toning process is used to produce images. There is a trade-off between different half-tone patterns for producing sharp, high-contrast texts or for producing gray-scale images.

20.5.7 Inkjet printing

Inkjet printing has become one of the main printing technologies in homes and offices. Its major advantages are its simplicity, low-cost, and truly nonimpact nature, which allows it to be used to print on many different substrates in varying shapes and at varying traveling speed. With advances in ink formulation and high-resolution addressability [553], the inkjet output images are approaching or sometimes exceeding the perceived sharpness and color gamut of photographic prints. Currently, the major disadvantages of inkjet printing are its speed and image stability. The speed is a difficult problem because inks have to be liquid in the print heads and dry out very fast on the substrates before they are overprinted by other inks. In addition, heavily colored pages tend to curl and wrinkle.

Inkjet printing works by squirting very tiny ink droplets through very fine nozzles and directing the droplets to adhere to the output media to form an image. If the stream of ink droplets is produced continuously and directed to or away from the medium substrate, depending on whether an image dot is to be printed or not, then the technology is called continuous inkjet printing. Ink droplets that are directed away and not used, are recirculated to the ink supply. The ink droplets are electrically charged and their directions are controlled by electrically controlled deflection plates. The ink recirculation is an inconvenience, but the electrical driving force allows the ink droplets to be delivered over a longer distance. Therefore, it is mainly used in industrial applications, such as printing labels or bar-codes. In most home and office inkjet printers, a burst of inkjet droplets is produced only when it is needed. This eliminates the necessity of the electronic deflection mechanism and the recirculation loop. This is called on-demand inkjet printing. Without the electrical driving force, the substrate has to be placed near the print head and this process is not useful for some industrial applications.

There are two widely used types of print heads that produce streams of ink droplets. One is based on piezo crystals that expand or contract depending on the electric voltages applied to them. This electronically-controlled mechanical force is used to squirt the ink through the nozzles. The other type of print head uses heating elements to rapidly heat up the ink to produce "bubbles" that expand and force the ink droplets to be squirted out of the nozzle. Therefore, this type of inkjet printer is called a bubble jet printer.

The inks used in inkjet printers have to satisfy many requirements and research to produce better inks is still very active [502]. There are three basic types of ink that are currently used: aqueous, solvent, and phase change. Aqueous inks use water-soluble or water-miscible dyes (or pigments in dispersion). Solvent inks are used when the substrates, such as metals or plastics, are hydrophobic or when a very fast drying time is required. Phase change inks are referred to as solid inks or hot-melt inks. They are similar to crayons. At room temperature, they are solid, and they melt quickly when heated.

20.5.8 Thermal printing

Thermal printing uses heat to initiate chemical reactions in the receiver sheet or to initiate diffusion processes to transfer dyes from the dye sheets to the receiver sheet, forming printed images. There are several different types of thermal printing. They can be classified into two main categories: direct thermal and thermal transfer [130]. Direct thermal printing uses a heated stylus or print head directly in contact with coated paper to write an image either through the removal of an opaque top layer on the coated paper or through the initiation of a chemical reaction in the coated paper. This category of printing is very low cost but does not produce good image quality. The other category of thermal printing, thermal transfer, is capable of creating very-high-quality color prints at a very reasonable speed.

Thermal transfer printing uses heat to melt or sublimate colorants contained in a dye sheet (or donor sheet) and transfer them to a receiver sheet. There are two major technologies in thermal transfer printing: the thermal-melt transfer and the dye-diffusion thermal transfer (D2T2) [511, Chapter 5.6]. In the thermal-melt transfer (or the thermal-wax transfer) technology, the color layer of the dye sheet consists of wax (paraffin) or other material that has a low melting temperature, with colorants dissolved or dispersed in it. The receiver is often plain paper. The melted wax along with the colorants is transferred and absorbed onto the paper. This transfer process cannot be controlled to produce gray levels reliably because the transfer tends to be all or nothing. Therefore, half-toning has to be used, although the dot size can be varied by carefully controlling the amount of heat applied (called VDT – variable dot thermal transfer). In contrast, the dye-diffusion thermal transfer technology works by heating up and sublimating the dyes in a dye sheet and, through contact and pressure, pushing the dyes into the receiver sheet, leaving behind the binder in the dye sheet. The penetration proceeds by dye diffusion in the receiver material. This technology can produce continuous tone images because the amount of dye transferred at a pixel is proportional to the amount of heat energy applied to that pixel location (about 64 or more gray levels can be produced reliably). We will therefore discuss dye-diffusion thermal transfer technology in more detail.

In dye-diffusion thermal transfer (D2T2) printing, the dye sheets are produced as rolls. A color image is printed three (CMY) or four (CMYK) times, each time with a separate dye sheet of a different color dye. The C, M, and Y dye sheets are thus arranged as sequential panels in a trichromatic unit. Some dye sheets also have a clear panel that provides a protective overcoat of the finished color print. Each color panel is slightly larger than the maximum print area on the receiver. A dye sheet usually consists of four layers: the dye/binder layer, the subcoat layer, the base support layer (e.g., polyester), and the backcoat layer. The function of the subcoat is to facilitate the adhesion of the dye layer to the base support layer, which provides the necessary tensile strength for the dye sheets and the thermal conductivity to transport the thermal energy from the printhead to the dye layer.

Since the base support may not be able to stand the high temperature of the printhead, the backcoat is to maintain the thermal stability of the dye sheet.

The receiver of the dye-diffusion thermal transfer printing typically consists of three main layers: the release layer on the top, the dye receiving layer in the middle, and the base support at the bottom. The release layer is to prevent the fusion between the dye sheet and the receiver sheet. The dye receiving layer is a clear polymer that is receptive to the dyes. The base support layer can be white paper (for a reflection print) or clear polyester (for an overhead transparency).

20.6   Half-toning

From the above discussion, we have learnt that many important display and printing technologies, such as offset lithography, electrophotography, and inkjet printing, cannot reliably produce many shades of gray. Yet, most of the books and magazines that we see every day are printed with such technologies. Theoretically, it is possible to vary the thickness of ink layers to produce different shades of gray. In practice, the control has to be so precise that the printing process would become so slow and so expensive that few people could afford to use it. If we require that only two levels of gray (black and white) be printed, the process becomes so fast and so economical that it dominates the color image printing market in its sheer volume. But how can a good color image with many shades of hue, chroma, and lightness be produced by a bi-level printing process? First, three colored inks (cyan, magenta, and yellow) and a black are used to produce colors. Second, the appearance of different shades of color is produced by printing small dots of cyan, magenta, yellow, and black inks on a piece of white paper. These dots are so small that they are not visually resolvable at a normal viewing distance. By controlling the fraction of area covered by the ink dots, we can produce different shades of a color. For example, if half of a paper area is covered by black ink, the integrated reflectance of that area will be 0.5. If only one third of a paper area is covered, then the integrated reflectance is one-third.[1] This method (or process) of controlling the black-to-white area ratios to produce the appearance of different shades of gray is called half-toning. The three key factors that make half-toning work are the capability to produce small dots (the smaller the better), the capability to distribute the dots over a small area precisely (the more precisely the better), and the capability to control the ink deposition on the dots. All three capabilities have been greatly enhanced in the last few decades, with a dramatic increase of color image quality in the printed hard-copies. We will first discuss the half-toning process for monochromatic images and then we will show how color images can be printed by half-toning.

20.6.1   Photomechanical half-tone screens and screen angles

Before digital half-toning was made available by high-precision scanners/printers and high-speed computers, half-tone printing was (and sometimes still is) done by using half-tone

---

[1]   In this analysis, we have assumed that the area covered by the ink has a zero reflectance. This is an oversimplified assumption to make the explanation easy.

screens to create the half-tone patterns of a given image. A set of horizontal black lines and a set of vertical black lines form a mechanical screen of regular grids. This screen is placed in front of a high-contrast photographic film. The original image is projected through the screen and the film is located a short distance from the true focused plane to create a slightly out-of-focus image on the film. The amount of light that falls on a grid point on the film is proportional to the radiance from the original (positive) image. Because the film is a high-contrast film, stronger light makes a larger area developable and thus produces a larger dot on the developed film. The film thus contains many dots of various sizes, each proportional to the local radiance of the original image and is used to etch the printing plate. The positioning of the screen and the film relative to the original image has a major impact on the quality of the resulting half-tone image. It takes a lot of experience and skill to perfect this art. In 1953, the contact screen was invented. This is a half-tone screen made from photographic film. The screen is placed in contact with the film to make the exposure, thus eliminating the need for careful adjustment of the screen-to-film distance. The modulated light from the original image (a print or a film) passes through the contact screen to expose the contacted film, creating half-tone dots of varying size as functions of the original image brightness or density. This film with the half-tone dots is then used to make the plate for the printing machine. Contact screens are now mass produced in many different varieties of dot shape, density profile, and density scale.

To produce a half-tone color print, four half-tone images (called color separations) are prepared, one for each of the four color inks (CMYK). Each color separation is produced by placing a red, green, or blue color filter or a combination of color filters (for K) in the light path of the original image and the contact screen. Panchromatic black-and-white films are used for the screened color separations, which are used to produce the color separation plates. In order to reduce visibility of the screen and the unwanted moiré patterns, the screen angle for each color separation is offset from the others. The yellow separation is at $0°$, the cyan at $15°$, the black at $45°$ and the magenta at $75°$. This standard arrangement is based on the observation that the human visual system is most sensitive to horizontal and vertical gratings, and least sensitive to $45°$ gratings. The yellow screen, having the least luminance contrast with the paper white, is thus chosen to be at the most sensitive orientation. The four color separation half-tone images are then overprinted on the output medium to form the final color image. The exact ink lay down sequence is not standardized because it depends on the interaction characteristics (ink trapping) of the four inks.

20.6.2 Screen ruling, addressability, resolution, and gray levels

Because of the historical evolution of printing technology, the uses and meanings of several terms are easy to confuse. Here let us introduce some terms. Both the mechanical screen and the photographic contact screen are specified by the number of lines per unit length, such as lines per inch (*lpi*), or lines per centimeter (*lpcm*). This is called the screen frequency (or the screen ruling). By convention, only the white lines (the transparent lines) are counted. Thus, a screen frequency of 150 lines per inch is equivalent to 300 pixels per inch. Since the shadow of the black lines is actually exposed by the light through the transparent lines due to the focus blur and diffraction, an analog dot can be larger than the width of a white line. These analog screens produce half-tone dots that are not as precise as those in modern digital half-tone printing. Most digital printers, such as inkjet and laser printers, are specified by the number of dots per unit length (e.g., dots per inch, i.e., *dpi*). It is usually assumed that the dots are equal in size and uniformly spaced. The only control is to turn them on or off. For many digital half-toning algorithms (such as the threshold-array-based ordered dithering), different shades of gray are produced by using $N \times N$ dots as a *half-tone cell*. If $N = 4$, then 16 possible shades of gray (plus white) can be represented by a half-tone cell. If the grids are square, the conversion between lpi and dpi is simple: lpi = dpi/N. However, many printers today are capable of producing variable-size dots and maybe variable ink thickness. The relation between lpi and dpi then becomes complicated. Furthermore, for some half-toning algorithms (such as error diffusion and other stochastic screening), there is no regular half-tone cell structure and the dpi frequency is the one that is applicable.

The above discussion assumes that the device outputs square or hexagonal grids, but many digital printers are line oriented devices. For example, a laser printer may scan a line and then move to the next line. On a given line, the pixel frequency is usually very high and can be changed by changing the clock rate. This is called the fast-scan direction. The other direction, from one line to the next line, is called the slow-scan (or the process) direction. Thus, on a given line, the distance between two neighboring, addressable pixel locations may be much smaller than the line-to-line distance, and may be smaller than the minimum dot size that the printer can print. This type of printer is said to have very high addressability. The base resolution of the printer is defined to be the frequency that is most difficult to change. In this example, it is usually the line-to-line frequency. This shows that without a proper printer model, it may not be possible to design a proper half-toning algorithm.

20.6.3   Digital half-toning

In the traditional analog (photomechanical) half-toning, the original analog image is converted by a screen to a half-tone image on a film which is then transferred to a printing plate. In digital half-toning, the original image is often digital with 8-bit or more gray levels (either digitized from film or directly captured by digital cameras) and it is thresholded into a binary, half-tone, digital image which is then sent to a printer. The conversion from a many-bit digital image to a 1-bit binary digital image is called digital half-toning. The basic principle is to place binary dots spatially in a way that creates the illusion of continuous-tone images. For this reason, digital half-toning is also called spatial dithering. It should be pointed out that the number of pixels of the binary output image may or may not be the same as that of the input digital image. Good surveys of and introductions to digital half-toning can be found in the literature (e.g., [17, 143, 483, 976]).

Important factors to consider
Our initial discussion of how half-toning works relies on the simple intuition that if we vary the ratio of the black area to the white area within each microscopic half-tone cell, the human

visual system will locally integrate (or blur) a small area covered with many cells to create the perception of a continuous-tone image. This intuition is true only when the half-tone cell is truly invisible, and it does not matter how the half-tone cell is rendered. When this is not true, the half-tone texture pattern can interfere with our perception of the image we want to see, and then it becomes very important how we control the half-tone pattern to please the eye. Therefore, when we study the vast literature on half-toning techniques, we need to know the spatial resolution that the half-toning technique was good for, because one algorithm may work well for low-resolution images, but may produce unacceptable artifacts for higher-resolution images [516].

Since the main objective of half-tone printing is to (fool and) please the eye, it is obvious that we need to know how the eye can be pleased. A human visual model thus should be a basic component in the design of a good half-toning algorithm [746, 925, 1010]. However, our knowledge of human visual perception is far from complete and it is not always foolproof for any existing visual model to predict what is visible and what is pleasing. For example, our visual sensitivity to the grouping of dots into lines and curves is rarely considered in the existing visual models.

The second key component in the design of a half-toning algorithm is the device/media model [746]. If we are going to produce some dot patterns with a particular device on a particular medium, we have to know how those dot patterns will actually be rendered physically: for example, the printer may not be able to place two neighboring dots at precisely the relative locations that we ask for; a dot when printed on the paper may not have the exact size and shape we ask for; the light reflected from an area of the printed page to the user's eyes may not have the spectral radiance that we ask for, etc. A phenomenum called dot gain is a good example. When a small dot of ink is printed on a piece of paper, its effect on the reflectance cannot be calculated from its area alone. It also depends on how the paper substrate scatters the light under and around the dot. The net effect of light scattering from an isolated dot on the reflectance is to make the dot appear larger. The ratio of the effective dot size to the requested dot size is called the dot gain. This should be part of the device/media model that is considered when designing and implementing any half-toning algorithm. In reality, the device/media model is often considered to be a calibration issue and is dealt with independently from the algorithm design. Obviously, this is often a matter of necessity for practical applications, but certainly a good algorithm design should take as many device/media characteristics into consideration as possible.

The third key component to consider in half-toning design is the model of computational architecture that is to be used to perform the algorithms. Often, the most difficult part is to take care of the long-distance interaction, such as the forming of false contours. Algorithms based on small local windows are often inadequate, unless iterative processing is used to refine the dot patterns repeatedly. Practical implementations cannot afford time-consuming calculation, nor can they afford very large buffer size.

The fourth component to consider is the system calibration and optimization model. It is often assumed that we can design the device hardware, the half-toning algorithm, the media, and the human visual model independently of each other. In reality we may be forced to perform each design in parallel or we may have no control over how other components are designed, but the end product has to be calibrated and optimized. If any of the model parameters cannot be measured or controlled, we have a serious problem in ensuring the final image quality.

From the above discussion, it is clear that in our job as imaging engineers we cannot have a preconceived notion that we can have one or two best half-toning algorithms in our tool box and hope to deal with all applications with the same tricks every time. There is no substitute for a good understanding of how the intended system will work. In reading the following brief introduction to the various terms and techniques in half-toning, we will find that most ideas are based on some oversimplified human visual models, device/media models and computational models. We should try to mentally make those simple assumptions as explicit as possible so that we can understand their fundamental limitations.

Clustered-dot and dispersed-dot

Historically, the black-to-white area ratios are controlled by varying the size of the dot. The entire image area is divided into regularly spaced half-tone cells of equal area. A black dot is printed in the center of each cell. If the image area is light, a small dot (or no dot at all) is printed in the cell. If the image area is dark, a large black dot is printed in the cell. The size of the black dot relative to the cell area determines the integrated reflectance of that cell. In digital half-toning, each half-tone cell is further divided into many smaller printer cells, each of which can be either ON (black) or OFF (white). To simulate a large dot in a half-tone cell we have to turn on many printer cells, and to simulate a smaller dot we turn on fewer printer cells. If those printer cells are turned on as a cluster (i.e., the ON printer cells are neighbors of each other), it is called the clustered-dot pattern. If the half-tone cell size is visually resolvable, the clustered-dot patterns are visible as half-tone noise. For example, newspaper images are often produced at 70 dots per inch and the half-tone pattern is easily visible. Modern digital half-toning methods [550] often break up the single black dot into many smaller dots and distribute them evenly in a half-tone cell. This is called dispersed-dot and the appearance of the resulting image at the same half-tone cell size is much smoother looking and is more pleasing to look at. Of course, this requires that the printer and the paper can render the smaller, dispersed dots precisely.

Random dither

The simplest way to convert a gray-level image to a binary image is to apply a threshold to the gray levels. This creates sharp contours and does not produce the illusion of a continuous-tone image. One of the oldest algorithms in digital half-toning is to add a random noise to the input image signal and then apply a fixed threshold to convert it to a binary output. This is called the method of *random dither*. Usually the method does not produce high-quality half-tone images because the random dither contains noise in all spatial frequencies and our visual perception does not like the low-frequency mottles associated with the random dither.

Although random dither is not a very powerful method in half-toning, it is useful in other applications when contours caused by quantization need to be made less visible in gray-level images. For example, density balance operations on 8-bit color images often create quantization contours in the final prints. Adding a small amount of noise and requantizing the image signal is quite effective in making the contouring artifacts much less visible.

input image				threshold array				output image		
6	4	2		7	8	9		0	0	0
7	5	3		6	1	2		1	1	1
8	6	4		5	4	3		1	1	1

Figure 20.14. An example of ordered dither using a spiral-dot screen.

Ordered dither

In contrast to random dither, *ordered dither* uses a deterministic, periodic, two-dimensional, threshold array to generate a binary image from a gray-level image. For example, if the dimension of the threshold array is $N \times N$, the input image is divided into nonoverlapping, consecutive blocks, each of which is $N \times N$ pixels. Each pixel of the input image is then compared with the corresponding value in the threshold array, and the pixel is set to 0 or 1. Figure 20.14 shows a simple example of how ordered dither works. The numbers in the thresold array can represent either the actual thresholds or the order in which a dot is turned on. Here we treat them as the actual thresholds. The threshold array is repeated over the entire input image and therefore the output binary image contains a fundamental frequency with a period of the size of the threshold array. In this example, a 3×3 threshold array is used, and the fundamental frequency is very high if the dot size is small. However, it can only represent ten levels of gray (including the case when the output is all zeros). In order to increase the number of representable levels of gray, the size of the threshold array has to be increased, resulting in a lower fundamental frequency, which can become very visible and annoying. The threshold array used in this example is called a spiral-dot screen. This is an example of a clustered-dot, ordered dither screen. It is called "clustered-dot" because, for any given uniform gray-level input, the output dots are all clustered. The clustered-dot screen tends to generate a lower-frequency dither noise because small dots are clustered together to become a large dot in a uniform-gray area. If we order the threshold values in the threshold array so that dots turned on at a given gray level are located far away from each other, we obtain a dispersed-dot screen. Figure 20.15 shows an example of the threshold array of a dispersed-dot screen. A systematic design method for the dispersed-dot screen was invented in 1973 by Bayer [87]. Examples of screen design can be found in many articles and books (e.g., [482] and [976]).

Error diffusion

Both the clustered-dot and the dispersed-dot ordered dithers are point operations, each pixel is compared with a value in the threshold array, independently of what the neighboring pixel values are. A completely different approach is to use neighborhood operations. This type of approach tends to be more computationally intensive, but can produce much better looking half-tone images. One very successful method is called the error diffusion method.

2	16	3	13	2
10	6	11	7	10
4	14	1	15	4
12	8	9	5	12
2	16	3	13	2

Figure 20.15. An example of the threshold array of a dispersed-dot screen. The dashed square represents a half-tone cell.

The basic idea behind the error diffusion algorithms is that, when quantizing a gray-level pixel into a binary black or white dot, an error in brightness at that image point is created. This error can be compensated by turning the neighboring pixels in the direction that will cancel the current error when all the reflectances in the neighborhood are integrated by our visual system. Therefore, there are three key components in designing an error diffusion algorithm: an error measure, a neighborhood to diffuse the error to, and a method for distributing the errors. Figure 20.16 shows a conceptual block diagram of the error diffusion algorithm. When the error diffusion algorithm was first invented by Floyd and Steinberg [319], they used the gray value difference between the input pixel value and the thresholded output pixel value as the error measure. The error is diffused to the four nearest "future" neighbors in the raster scan order with different weighting factors. Since then, many variations on the three key components have been proposed and tested with improved results [483, 516]. Images rendered by the error diffusion algorithms are generally quite good, but using a fixed threshold to calculate the error has the potential of creating a false contour in a uniform area when the distributed and accumulated error suddenly exceeds the threshold and requests the algorithm to produce a dot in the output.

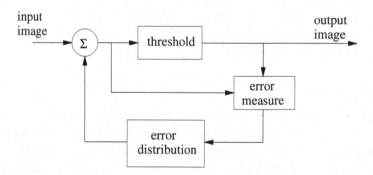

Figure 20.16. A conceptual block diagram of the error diffusion algorithm.

Color half-toning

For display or printing devices where binary output levels are used, we control the perceived gray level of an area by changing the percentage of the area that is covered by black dots. In order to produce a color image on such devices, different colored dots are displayed or printed together to give a visual impression of a color image. Usually, we use dots of only three (CMY) or four (CMYK) primary colors or process inks. We obtain different colors by varying the percentage of the areas printed by these process inks. For example, the color turquoise can be printed using 80% cyan dots, 7% magenta dots, and 20% yellow dots. However, these numbers alone do not mean much for many reasons. For example, the spectral characteristics of the three process inks on the intended paper have to be measured and the printing sequence (e.g., cyan ink is printed first, then magenta, and then yellow) needs to be specified. Colorimetric specifications are thus described in standards, such as SWOP (Specifications for Web Offset Publications) [930].

There are many uncontrollable factors that affect the output color reproduction of a half-toning process. Chief among them is the stochastic distribution of the colored dots. We do not know how much of the area printed with cyan ink will be overprinted by the magenta ink and the yellow ink. The effect of printing one process ink over another is printer- and setup-dependent, and has to be treated as a parameter to be measured for each application. The effect shows up in two ways: (1) the ink trapping problem: the amount of the second process ink printed depends on the amount of overlap area with the first process ink that has been printed on the paper; and (2) the failure of density additivity: the combined spectral density may not be equal to the density sum of the two inks. If the effects are consistent throughout a press run, they can be treated as parameters to be measured.

The basic question in color half-toning is the following: given a set of percentage dot areas for the process inks, can we predict what color will be printed? Or in a reverse sense, given the CIEXYZ tristimulus values, what percentage dot areas should we specify for each process ink to produce that color? Several attempts have been made to analyze the color reproduction in color half-toning. The best-known model is the *Neugebauer equations*, which was extended from Demichel's model by Neugebauer. Let c, m, y, and k be the fractional areas covered by cyan, magenta, yellow, and black process inks, respectively, i.e., $0 \leq c, m, y, k \leq 1$. Assuming that each ink is printed randomly independently of each other, then any half-tone color area consists of combinations of the following components:

- the unprinted white paper:

$$a_1 \cdot \beta_1(\lambda) = (1 - c)(1 - m)(1 - y)(1 - k) \cdot \beta_1(\lambda);$$

- the individual process inks:

$$a_2 \cdot \beta_2(\lambda) = c(1 - m)(1 - y)(1 - k) \cdot \beta_2(\lambda),$$
$$a_3 \cdot \beta_3(\lambda) = (1 - c)m(1 - y)(1 - k) \cdot \beta_3(\lambda),$$
$$a_4 \cdot \beta_4(\lambda) = (1 - c)(1 - m)y(1 - k) \cdot \beta_4(\lambda),$$
$$a_5 \cdot \beta_5(\lambda) = (1 - c)(1 - m)(1 - y)k \cdot \beta_5(\lambda);$$

- the two-color overlaps:

$$a_6 \cdot \beta_6(\lambda) = cm(1-y)(1-k) \cdot \beta_6(\lambda),$$
$$a_7 \cdot \beta_7(\lambda) = c(1-m)y(1-k) \cdot \beta_7(\lambda),$$
$$a_8 \cdot \beta_8(\lambda) = c(1-m)(1-y)k \cdot \beta_8(\lambda),$$
$$a_9 \cdot \beta_9(\lambda) = (1-c)my(1-k) \cdot \beta_9(\lambda),$$
$$a_{10} \cdot \beta_{10}(\lambda) = (1-c)m(1-y)k \cdot \beta_{10}(\lambda),$$
$$a_{11} \cdot \beta_{11}(\lambda) = (1-c)(1-m)yk \cdot \beta_{11}(\lambda);$$

- the three-color overlaps:

$$a_{12} \cdot \beta_{12}(\lambda) = cmy(1-k) \cdot \beta_{12}(\lambda),$$
$$a_{13} \cdot \beta_{13}(\lambda) = cm(1-y)k \cdot \beta_{13}(\lambda),$$
$$a_{14} \cdot \beta_{14}(\lambda) = c(1-m)yk \cdot \beta_{14}(\lambda),$$
$$a_{15} \cdot \beta_{15}(\lambda) = (1-c)myk \cdot \beta_{15}(\lambda);$$

- the four-color overlap: $a_{16} \cdot \beta_{16}(\lambda) = cmyk \cdot \beta_{16}(\lambda),$

where a_i and $\beta_i(\lambda)$, $i = 1, 2, \ldots, 16$, are the fractional area and spectral reflectance factor of each idealized color element. The spectral reflectance factor $\beta(\lambda)$, of the color area can thus be expressed as

$$\beta(\lambda) = \sum_{i=1}^{16} a_i \beta_i(\lambda). \tag{20.8}$$

Several implicit assumptions have been made in this model. (1) It is assumed that the fractional areas of the process inks c, m, y, and k are printed as requested. This is shown to be unrealistic. The dot areas are often different (almost always larger) than requested. As we mentioned before, this dot area magnification in the printing process is called *dot gain*. There are two main reasons for this gain [32, 33]: physical and optical. The physical gain comes from the fact that, when ink is printed on paper, it spreads out slightly. The reason for the optical gain is that light illuminating the area outside the dot boundary can be scattered through the paper into the dot and come out from the dot and vice versa. As a consequence, the coefficients a_i have to be determined from the spectral measurement data, rather than calculated. (2) It is assumed that the spectral reflectance factor does not depend on the size of the overlapped area of different inks. In reality, a tiny overlap area is likely to reflect light differently from a large overlap area. This means that it is not possible to decompose the total areal spectral reflectance factor into a linear combination of 16 spectral functions.

In general, modeling any color half-toning process requires estimates of the parameters in many empirical equations. It can be used to optimize or simulate a product being developed. In practice, modeling is often not used in printer calibration because of the large number of parameters that need to be estimated. Instead, we often use 1-D LUTs to shape the signals, apply matrices to rotate color primaries, and then rely on 3-D LUTs to achieve the desired color mapping. This is discussed in the next section.

Digital screen angles

Conventional photomechanical screens can be arranged at any angle to produce the color separations. However, digital screens are inherently constrained by their raster pixel layout. Imagine drawing a straight-line segment on a square grid pattern at an arbitray angle. It is clear that it is not possible to always have the two end points falling exactly on the grid points. The implication is that if a digital half-toning algorithm uses a half-tone cell as the basic unit, the cell cannot be oriented at an arbitrary angle and still have its corners falling on the pixel grids. The only allowable angles are those with slopes that are ratios of integer numbers. Therefore, this type of screen is called a rational tangent screen. If we combine several half-tone cells into a supercell, it is possible to produce an approximation of an arbitrary angle, but not all the half-tone cells will have the same shape or the same number of dots. These and other angled screens can be designed by several methods developed in the 1980s [335, 405, 808].

20.7 Printer calibration

Compared with CRT monitors, printers are much more complicated to model. Even when models do exist, their accuracies are often less than desirable. The trend is to use 3-D LUTs for printer calibration. There are many ways to construct 3-D LUTs [422, 482, 488] and many ways to structure the signal transformation paths. Here we will present a method for calibrating a digital color printer that expects (R, G, B) as input code values, where R, G, and B are integers and $0 \leq R, G, B \leq 255$. A digital color image to be printed by the printer can be specified in a device-independent color space, such as CIEXYZ or CIELAB. The problem of printer calibration is to establish a signal transformation path that converts the input image into printer (R, G, B) code values so that when the image is printed, the color at each pixel on the print is as close to that specified in the original device-independent color space as possible. What is meant by "as close as possible" should be defined by the user for each application. In many cases, CIELAB ΔE errors are minimized for a selected set of colors.

Since a high-resolution, digital color image usually consists of millions of pixels, the color transformation of each pixel from CIEXYZ or CIELAB to printer (R, G, B) has to be performed very fast and very efficiently. If the 3-D LUT is completely dense, i.e., it contains one entry for every possible input color, the only operation needed is to use the input color as an index to locate the desired output value(s): a memory-read operation. However, this is not yet practical because it would require a lookup table as large as 2^{24} memory locations for each output color channel. Therefore a sparse lookup table is often used. For example, $8 \times 8 \times 8$, $17 \times 17 \times 17$, and $31 \times 31 \times 31$ are typical sizes of 3-D LUTs. An input color is thus interpolated from the table. This is called *forward interpolation*. In order to be efficient, the table is set up on a regular grid so that no search is required to find the neighborhood points that are to be used for interpolation. Trilinear interpolation is often used for this purpose because it is easy to perform and can be made fast by clever tricks. The major issue of calibration is how to set up such a multi-dimensional lookup table on a regular grid that needs to be indexed by the device-independent color coordinates in which the input image is represented. For example, if the input image is in CIELAB, we need to set up a 3-D LUT that will map CIELAB to printer (R,G,B) values. The indices to the table are on a regular grid in CIELAB space. Before the calibration is done, we can only produce color patches from the printer by specifying the printer (R,G,B) values. We can then measure the CIELAB values of each color patch for which we know what printer (R,G,B) values were used to print it. Therefore, we have a set of (R,G,B) versus CIELAB data points, $(L^*,a^*,b^*) = f(R,G,B)$, in which the (R,G,B) values are regularly spaced, but the CIELAB values, (L^*,a^*,b^*), are not. In order to set up a lookup table, $(R,G,B) = h(L^*,a^*,b^*)$, that has regularly spaced CIELAB grid points, we have to interpolate the (R,G,B) values from the measured data set, $(L^*,a^*,b^*) = f(R,G,B)$. This is called *backward interpolation*, because (R,G,B) are known values on a regular grid and (L^*,a^*,b^*) are measured values. The backward interpolation can be done off-line. Therefore complexity is not a concern and the priority is the accuracy.

20.7.1 Calibration of RGB printers

In the following, we will focus our discussion on one procedure that uses a tetrahedral interpolation to set up a regular-grid 3-D LUT off-line (backward interpolation), and then uses a trilinear interpolation for each pixel on-line (forward interpolation). We can always use other types of interpolation algorithm if we desire to do so. The procedure is applicable to most applications and therefore there is no loss in generality in the discussion.

The first issue to notice is that the functions $(R,G,B) = h(L^*,a^*,b^*)$, for which the 3-D LUT represents a set of discrete samples, can be quite nonlinear. Since we are going to use a trilinear interpolation on this table, the error can be quite large where the functions deviate from linearity locally. The color error is particularly noticeable for neutral colors. A good way to reduce such errors is to reduce the nonlinearity in the mapping to be accomplished by the 3-D LUT. This can be achieved by using 1-D LUTs and 3×3 matrices to shape and mix the input signals (L^*,a^*,b^*) so that they are more linearly related to the intended output space, the printer (R,G,B) . In this example, there are two important observations: (1) (L^*,a^*,b^*) represents a luminance–chrominance representation, while (R,G,B) does not; and (2) (R,G,B) may be nonlinear functions of reflectance factors on the color print. In many printers, (R,G,B) are adjusted to print from gamma-corrected video signals and therefore are not linear functions of reflectance factors or CIEXYZ. Furthermore, video monitor primaries are quite different from CIEXYZ primaries. From these two observations, we know that we need one 3×3 matrix A to transform (L^*,a^*,b^*) to $(X',Y',Z') \approx ((X/X_n)^{1/3}, (Y/Y_n)^{1/3}, (Z/Z_n)^{1/3})$, three 1-D LUTs, F, to transform (X',Y',Z') to (X,Y,Z), and three more 1-D LUTs, P, to account for the nonlinearity in the printer (R,G,B) . After all these transformations, we arrive at an (R',G',B') space that is approximately linear with the printer (R,G,B) . A 3-D LUT to map (R',G',B') to (R,G,B) at this stage is able to take care of the remaining deviations that have not been accounted for in the previous color transformations. The complete calibration steps are shown in Fig. 20.17. It should be pointed out that a calibration structure as complete as Fig. 20.17 is not always used in practice because it may be too slow or cost too much to implement. Therefore, for some applications, the entire calibration is often done by a single 3-D LUT. However, it is important to remember that signal shaping by 1-D LUTs and color

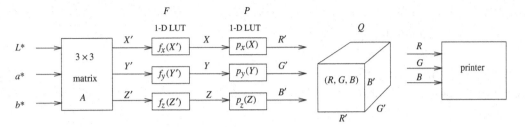

Figure 20.17. An example of printer calibration from CIELAB to RGB.

transformation by 3×3 matrices are very effective means for reducing nonlinearity in the color mapping and should be used wherever they are practical.

In Fig. 20.17, the matrix A and the 1-D LUTs, F, are determined from the definition of CIELAB. The calibration task is to determine the three 1-D LUTs, P, and the 3-D LUT, Q, for the targeted printer/medium. Let us summarize the basic steps in printer calibration as follows:

1. Use the printer to print a set of color patches corresponding to some selected input color values. For example, for an 8-bit/color/pixel printer, an input pixel contains three numbers: (R, G, B) where $0 \le R, G, B \le 255$. Let us select (R_i, G_j, B_k), $i, j, k = 1, 2, \ldots, m$, $R_1 = G_1 = B_1 = 0$, and $R_m = G_m = B_m = 255$. It is important to include 0 and 255 in the combinations so that the printer color gamut can be determined. It is also desirable to print a gray scale of many neutral steps, (R_l, G_l, B_l), $l = 1, \ldots, n$. This will be useful for deriving the 1-D LUTs, P, for correcting the printer RGB nonlinearity.

2. Measure the spectral reflectance factors and calculate the colorimetric data for the printed color patches under the desired viewing illuminant: (X_i, Y_j, Z_k) corresponding to (R_i, G_j, B_k), $i, j, k = 1, 2, \ldots, m$, and (X_l, Y_l, Z_l) corresponding to the gray scale: (R_l, G_l, B_l), $l = 1, \ldots, n$.

3. Use the gray-scale data, (X_l, Y_l, Z_l), $l = 1, \ldots, n$, to derive the 1-D LUTs, P. For example, we can fit piecewise cubic polynomial functions, $p_r(R)$, $p_g(G)$, and $p_b(B)$, to the data such that $p_r(R_l) = X_l$, $p_g(G_l) = Y_l$, and $p_b(B_l) = Z_l$, for $l = 1, \ldots, n$. Then the three 1-D LUTs, P, in Fig. 20.17, are simply the inverse functions: $p_x = p_r^{-1}$, $p_y = p_g^{-1}$, and $p_z = p_b^{-1}$. (Note that these three 1-D LUTs essentially convert the XYZ tristimulus values of the neutral grays into a linear function of printer RGB values. However, for some printers, $R = G = B$ does not print neutral grays. In that case, we have to find the RGB values that will print to grays so that the three 1-D LUTs can be used to linearize the neutral axis in the following 3-D LUT.)

4. Map (X_i, Y_j, Z_k), $i, j, k = 1, 2, \ldots, m$, through the 1-D LUTs, P, to (R_i', G_j', B_k'), i.e., $R_i' = p_x(X_i)$, $G_j' = p_y(Y_j)$, and $B_k' = p_z(Z_k)$. We now have a data set: $(R_i, G_j, B_k) \rightarrow (R_i', G_j', B_k')$, $i, j, k = 1, 2, \ldots, m$.

5. Construct the 3-D LUT, $Q : (R', G', B') \rightarrow (R, G, B)$, from the data $(R_i, G_j, B_k) \rightarrow (R_i', G_j', B_k')$, $i, j, k = 1, 2, \ldots, m$, by backward tetrahedral interpolation. This set of data has a regular grid in (R, G, B), but it is irregular in (R', G', B').

The last step of constructing the 3-D LUT, $Q : (R', G', B') \rightarrow (R, G, B)$, is a complicated step. We now explain this step in more detail. The data set, $(R_i, G_j, B_k) \rightarrow$

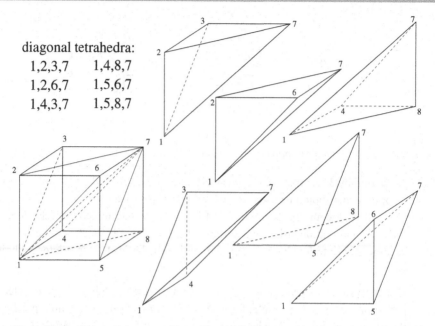

diagonal tetrahedra:
  1,2,3,7   1,4,8,7
  1,2,6,7   1,5,6,7
  1,4,3,7   1,5,8,7

Figure 20.18. Diagonal decomposition of a cube into six tetrahedra.

(R_i', G_j', B_k'), i, j, $k = 1, 2, \ldots, m$, is a big cube in (R, G, B), which has $m \times m \times m$ grid points with known (R', G', B') values. Therefore, we can consider the data set as consisting of $m \times m \times m$ small cubes, with all the eight vertices of each cube known. Each small cube can be partitioned into six tetrahedra as shown in Fig. 20.18. There are many ways to decompose a cube into nonoverlapping tetrahedra. We will call the partition shown in Fig. 20.18 the diagonal partition. It has been shown to produce quite accurate color interpolation results compared with other partitions [488]. Let us denote the resulting tetrahedra as T_s, $s = 1, 2, \ldots, 6m^3$.

Our goal at this step is to construct the 3-D LUT, $Q : (R', G', B') \rightarrow (R, G, B)$. Let us assume that it will be a $21 \times 21 \times 21$ LUT. The range of (R', G', B') can be scaled to $0 \leq R', G', B' \leq 100$. Therefore, the sampling interval is 5.0 on each of the (R', G', B') axes: (R_u', G_v', B_w'), $u, v, w = 1, 2, \ldots, 21$. We need to determine the corresponding (R_u, G_v, B_w). This can be done for each (R_u', G_v', B_w') by searching through all the tetrahedra T_s, $s = 1, 2, \ldots, 6m^3$ to find the one that contains (R_u', G_v', B_w'). The four vertices of that tetrahedron are then used to compute the corresponding (R_u, G_v, B_w). This has been discussed in the context of multivariate interpolation methods in Section 16.2.2. If no tetrahedron can be found that contains a color (R_u', G_v', B_w'), then this color is outside of the printer color gamut. Several gamut mapping strategies can be used. This is discussed in Section 18.8 on color gamut mapping.

20.7.2   Four-color printing

Three-color printing using CMY inks cannot produce many of the commonly seen dark colors because of the unwanted absorption in each of the CMY inks, the limited ink trapping, and the interface reflection at the ink layers. For example, a three-color reproduction on grossy paper with high-quality inks can have a density range of only about 1.5. Furthermore, high-density dark grays tend to be unstable (i.e., they deviate significantly from neutral when the viewing illuminant is changed). These problems can be solved to a large degree by adding black ink. The printable color gamut is greatly increased by the black ink. For example, the reproducible density range can be extended to about 2.0.

In three-color printing, there is only one combination of the three colorants (or inks) that will match the color (say, CIEXYZ) of the original under a given illuminant. If we now add a fourth colorant (or ink), there are many combinations that will produce the same match. The question is: which of the many combinations should be used to match the desired color? In many cases, black ink is used for neutral grays so that they are more stable against illuminant changes. In other cases, the black ink is the least expensive of the inks, and therefore it is profitable to use as much black ink as possible to replace color inks when a color match is realizable. These two cases happen frequently and they have special names: undercolor removal (UCR) and gray component replacement (GCR). UCR reduces the amounts of CMY ink to make room for the black ink. It is applied only to the neutral areas in the image. GCR is similar to undercolor removal, but is applied to all color areas. The process colors (CMY) are usually replaced by the black ink so that the gray component in the color is mostly reproduced by the black ink. The current recommended safe range of GCR to use is between 50% and 80% [930, p. 31], i.e., 50% to 80% of the gray component normally produced by the CMY inks is removed and an equivalent amount of the black ink is added. It is important that the percentage of color inks after GCR should not be too small, otherwise the color will appear less glossy and less stable. In some other cases, UCR and GCR are required because of physical constraints of the printing processes. For example, in high-speed wet printing, there is not enough time to wait for one ink to dry before another ink is printed. Therefore, as little total ink as possible should be used. Another application is when too much ink overprinting creates an ink-trapping problem, i.e., too much of one ink prevents more than a certain amount of another ink being printed over it. It is fairly typical that the maximum total amount of inks to be printed cannot exceed some percentage of the dot area, usually around 240–300%, depending on the size of the colored area.

The additional degree of freedom in choosing how much black ink to use for certain colors thus demands a strategy in color reproduction. Several commonly used strategies are:

- Maximum black: black is substituted for the three colors up to the point where one of the colors is completely replaced.
- Minimum black: no black is used except for the areas where the dark colors cannot be produced by the three process colors.
- Minimum dot area: black is substituted for the process color that has the minimum dot area.
- Smoothest transition: use the amount of the black ink that results in the spectral reflectance curve changing as little as possible from the neighboring colors in a chosen color space. This requires an off-line global optimization in the 3-D LUT to ensure that the black ink usage changes smoothly from color to color [423].

20.8 Problems

20.1 Use Eq. (8.55) to derive the relation, $D_\rho = f(D_t)$, that expresses the reflection density, D_ρ, as a function of transmission density D_t.

20.2 A color imaging application requires a reflection print to be scanned and the scanned image displayed on a CRT monitor.

(a) Draw a block diagram showing the building blocks necessary to calibrate the whole imaging chain from the scanner to the CRT monitor so that the (X, Y, Z) tristimulus values in the reflection print can be fairly well reproduced on the CRT screen. The only building blocks that you can use are 1-D LUTs and 3×3 matrices. You have to specify the input and the output variables for each block and briefly explain the physical meaning of each variable.

(b) Since the reflection print is typically viewed in a light surround and the CRT monitor is viewed in a dark surround, explain which blocks you would modify to compensate for the visual effect due to the difference in the viewing surround.

20.3 If you want to scan an image on a reflection print and post it on the web, what do you have to do to make sure that your image will look good on most computer monitors?

20.4 The NTSC chromaticity transformation between the phosphor primaries and the CIEXYZ primaries is given in Table 20.3.

Table 20.3.

Stimulus	r	g	b	x	y	z
red phosphor	1	0	0	0.67	0.33	0.00
green phosphor	0	1	0	0.21	0.71	0.08
blue phosphor	0	0	1	0.14	0.08	0.78
white (Illuminant C)	1/3	1/3	1/3	0.3101	0.3162	0.3737

The ITU-R BT.709-2 HDTV chromaticity transformation between the phosphor primaries and the CIEXYZ primaries is given in Table 20.4.

Table 20.4.

Stimulus	r	g	b	x	y	z
red phosphor	1	0	0	0.64	0.33	0.03
green phosphor	0	1	0	0.30	0.60	0.10
blue phosphor	0	0	1	0.15	0.06	0.79
White (D_{65})	1/3	1/3	1/3	0.3127	0.3290	0.3583

Determine the 3×3 matrix to transform the NTSC RGB signals to the ITU-R BT.709-2 HDTV RGB signals. (Since the reference whites in both standards, Illuminant C and D_{65}, are fairly close to each other in this problem, use the CIELAB type of "normalization to white" to find the corresponding tristimulus values for the two illuminants, i.e., $X_{709}/X_{D_{65}} = X_{NTSC}/X_C$. In general, if the two illuminants are quite different, a chromatic adaptation model (such as the Bradford transformation) has to be used to find the corresponding tristimulus values.)

20.5 The error measure and the error distribution are two important components in the error diffusion method for half-toning. What kind of error measure can we use and what are the computations involved for the error distribution? For example, can we use ΔE in CIELAB as the error measure ? If so, how do we distribute the error?

20.6 In most half-toning algorithms, the percentage dot area requested is assumed to be what is actually printed. In practice, this is not strictly true. This difference between what is specified and what is actually printed is called the dot gain, and can be caused by ink spread, optical diffusion, and ink transfer problems. Given a half-toning algorithm, how do you take care of the dot gain problem?

21 Image quality

The performance of a color imaging system is often evaluated by the image quality it can deliver to the user. Image quality can be evaluated physically (objective image quality) or psychophysically (subjective or perceptual image quality) or both. In this chapter, we will discuss some of the metrics and procedures that are used in image quality measurements. Objective image quality measures, such as resolving power, noise power spectrum, detective quantum efficiency (DQE), and system MTF, are well defined and can often be measured consistently [64]. However, they may not be directly correlated with the perceived image quality. Therefore psychophysical procedures are used to construct metrics that relate to the subjective image quality. Given our inadequate understanding of image perception, one may even argue that the definitive quality evaluation can only be done by human observers looking at images and making judgments. Therefore, the subjective quality rating is the only reliable metric for image quality. Although this statement is true, it does not help us much in developing better imaging systems because human judgment is too time-consuming, costly, and not always consistent. Objective image quality metrics are needed for many product optimizations and simulations.

In the past (before 1970), image quality was often measured on a system level. With the advance and availability of digital imaging devices, quality metrics for individual digital images have also been developed. These image-dependent image quality measures are becoming more and more important because they can be used to detect and correct problems before images are displayed or printed. An automatic correction algorithm for individual images requires a reliable image quality metric that can be computed from a digital image [489, 672].

21.1 Objective image quality evaluation

The design and manufacturing of imaging devices often require making trade-offs between various desirable features. For example, a lens designer would like to minimize all lens aberrations at all wavelengths, but that would increase the cost of lenses beyond what is affordable. Therefore, the question of what constitute the most desirable or optimal trade-offs arises. The lens is only one component of an imaging system. The design and manufacturing of the other components in the system also require similar trade-offs. If the entire imaging system (from capture to display) is designed by a single manufacturer, all the components can be optimized together. However, this is almost never the case. As a consequence, many component-specific image quality metrics have been developed. These component-specific image quality metrics are very useful for component designers, but may not be as useful for system engineers or consumers, because some of the parameters cannot be measured conveniently or because the metrics are less correlated with perceptual image quality. In this section, we will discuss only the more generally applicable, system-oriented quality metrics. A color imaging system is often evaluated in terms of optical image quality, detector efficiency, tone reproduction, color reproduction, image structure (including resolving power, MTF, and noise), and system stability. It should be pointed out that image quality evaluation is always related to what we plan to do with the images [61, 62, 63], especially in the fields of medical imaging, remote sensing, and pattern recognition. Here we are mainly interested in consumer imaging and the task is not well defined, other than for people's enjoyment and saving for memory.

21.1.1 Detector efficiency

The quality of image sensors, such as CCDs or photographic films, can be measured in several ways. For detectors that produce countable events in response to the incident photons, the detector efficiency is often measured in terms of the responsive quantum efficiency (RQE). In the case of a CCD sensor, the RQE can be defined as the number of collected electrons divided by the number of incident photons. RQE is a function of wavelength and, for some high-energy photons, it can be greater than 1 because a photon may generate more than one electron. Typically the RQE of CCD sensors can be as low as a few percent from 400 nm to 450 nm and as high as or higher than 50% from 650 nm to 700 nm. The efficiency of a solid-state detector (such as CCD or CMOS) also depends on the imaging geometry because most sensors are also direction sensitive [166]. A similar definition can be applied to photomultiplier tubes, in which one photon usually produces many electrons through stages of amplification.

The RQE is not easy to define if the response of the detector cannot be quantified in countable events. Furthermore, it does not say how noise is transfered by the detector. If a detector is noisy, it cannot be an efficient detector because it will be difficult to distinguish between two different levels of the input signal. For this reason, another type of quantum efficiency, the DQE, is more widely used to characterize detector performance. DQE is defined as the output signal-to-noise ratio divided by the input signal-to-noise ratio. In most cases, the DQE is less than 100% because invariably noise is added by the detector in the sensing or amplification processes. For example, a typical DQE of photographic films is usually less than 1% [232, p. 29]. Clearly, DQE is a function of many variables, such as spatial frequency, wavelength, etc.

21.1.2 Spatial frequency analysis

How well an imaging system captures details can be analyzed in many ways. For example, we can measure the light distribution of the image of a point, a line, or a knife-edge.

Alternatively, we can also measure the minimum resolvable distance of two point sources. However, the most widely used method for system analysis is spatial frequency analysis. There are several related functions in this type of analysis. They are all based on the idea of measuring the system output in response to a sinusoidal input as a function of spatial frequency.

- The OTF [354, 882, 887]: this is defined for the optical image forming components. The function is normalized to 1.0 at zero frequency. Both the amplitude and phase responses as functions of input spatial frequency are specified.
- The system transfer function: this is a general term, applied to all linear, shift-invariant systems. It describes the output amplitude and phase as a function of the input sinusoidal signal at various frequencies.
- The MTF: this is the amplitude response part of a system transfer function. It is often assumed that the phase response is a linear function.
- The contrast transfer function (CTF): this term is occasionally used in imaging applications. Contrast is often defined as the ratio of the difference to the sum of the maximum and the minimum signal amplitude (called the Michelson contrast). The CTF is the output contrast divided by the input contrast as a function of spatial frequency. The main difference between the CTF and the MTF is that the definition of contrast usually requires that a DC level is specified to be greater than or equal to the minimum of the signal, i.e., the modulation cannot drive the signal to negative because an image signal cannot have a negative amount of light.
- The SFR function: this term is used to denote the MTF in the spatial domain, as opposed to the temporal domain.

The sinusoidal functions are eigenfunctions of linear, shift-invariant systems, i.e., if the input is a sinusoidal function, the output is also a sinusoidal function of the same frequency, although the amplitude or phase may be different from that of the input. Fourier analysis allows us to represent any square-integrable function as sums or integrals of sinusoidal functions. If we can characterize how a system responds to any sinusoidal function by a system transfer function $H(\omega_x, \omega_y)$, where ω_x and ω_y are the angular frequencies for the x and y spatial variables, we can compute the Fourier transform $G(\omega_x, \omega_y)$ of the output function $g(x, y)$ for any square-integrable input function $f(x, y)$ by transforming the input signal into its spatial frequency representation, $F(\omega_x, \omega_y)$, and

$$G(\omega_x, \omega_y) = H(\omega_x, \omega_y)F(\omega_x, \omega_y). \tag{21.1}$$

It turns out that an optical imaging system can be approximated (in the limit of paraxial approximation) as a linear, shift-invariant system for a small region around the optical axis on an image plane [354, Chapter 6]. Use of Fourier analysis in optics was popularized by Duffieux in 1946 [267]. OTFs were calculated for lens aberrations by Hopkins [410]. The applications of the Fourier method to imaging system analysis were extensively demonstrated by Schade [830, 831]. Since almost all practical imaging systems are not linear, shift-invariant systems, spatial frequency analysis is not a complete measure of the system characteristics. In order to characterize the optical image quality of an imaging system, many OTFs have to be measured along different angles and at different positions on the image planes. It is also important to measure the OTF as a function of distance from the ideal image plane to get a measure of the depth of focus for the camera. If we choose a spatial frequency and plot the system response as a function of distance, we will obtain a function, called the "through-focus transfer function". For digital cameras, the OTF can be measured by the slanted edge method [788]. There are two reasons for applying frequency analysis to nonlinear systems: (1) theoretically, when the signal amplitude is small around a fixed operating point of a nonlinear system, linear analysis can be a good approximation; (2) empirically, the results from cascading frequency response functions of nonlinear systems seem to be quite useful in predicting some attributes of the final image quality, such as the sharpness of reflection prints from color negative films. Until better metrics can be formulated and verified, spatial frequency analysis will continue to be used as a convenient (although not complete), objective, image quality measure.

Other, simpler measures of optical image quality are also commonly used. For example, a lens may be designed to produce at an image plane the maximum Strehl intensity [124, p. 462] (i.e., the image irradiance, normalized to the ideal diffraction-limited case, at the peak of the PSF). A system may be characterized by its highest cut-off frequency, or the half-height frequency, where the OTF is equal to 1/2 of the DC level. Yet another measure is to use the maximum number of line pairs per millimeter that can be resolved on an image.

21.1.3 Image noise

Image noise is a complex pattern of variation in space (mostly two-dimensional) and time (as in video sequences). Random field models [983] are often used to characterize image noise. These models are usually valid over only a limited spatial and time scales. The characteristics of image noise, therefore, should be specified with the spatial and time scales in which the measurements are made. This is true even if the model is a fractal model, because we have not found any model that is valid over all scales.

In the simple case, we will treat image noise as a scalar random field $I(x, y)$ of two spatial variables, x and y, corresponding to the two Cartesian spatial coordinate axes. For color images, a vector random field model has to be used. This will be discussed later.

A random field is completely specified when all its joint probability density functions $p(x_1, y_1, \ldots, x_n, y_n)$ are known for any arbitrary set of points (x_i, y_i), $i = 1, 2, \ldots, n$, and for all integer $n \geq 1$. A random field is *homogeneous* (or stationary) if all the joint probability functions are invariant to translations, *isotropic* if invariant to rotation, and *ergodic* if all probability functions can be determined from a single realization of the random field (e.g., the ensemble mean can be calculated from the mean of all locations of a single realization). A random field is a Gaussian random field if all its joint probability density functions are (multivariate) Gaussian distributions. In practice, it is obviously not feasible to characterize a random field by determining all the joint probability density functions. The most widely used characteristics are the second order statistics, such as covariance functions, correlation functions, and power spectra. Gaussian random fields are often used as models because they are completely determined by their means and autocorrelation functions.

Let $t_1 = (x_1, y_1)$ and $t_2 = (x_1, y_1)$ be two locations in a random field I, $\mu_1 = E[I(t_1)]$ and $\mu_2 = E[I(t_2)]$ be the mean values at t_1 and t_2, and σ_1 and σ_2 be the standard deviations at t_1 and t_2. The covariance of the values of a random field, I, at t_1 and t_2 is called the covariance function (of t_1 and t_2):

$$C(t_1, t_2) = E[(I(t_1) - \mu_1)(I(t_2) - \mu_2)], \tag{21.2}$$

and the correlation function is defined as

$$\rho(t_1, t_2) = \frac{C(t_1, t_2)}{\sigma_1 \sigma_2}. \tag{21.3}$$

First, we note that $C(t_1, t_2) = C(t_2, t_1)$ and $\rho(t_1, t_2) = \rho(t_2, t_1)$. For a homogeneous random field, the covariance function and the correlation function are invariant to translations and therefore depend only on the relative location: $\tau = (\tau_x, \tau_y) = (x_1 - x_2, y_1 - y_2)$ between the two locations, i.e., $C(t_1, t_2) = C(\tau)$ and $\rho(t_1, t_2) = \rho(\tau)$. The *autocorrelation function*, $R_{II}(t_1, t_2)$, is defined as

$$R_{II}(t_1, t_2) = E[I(t_1)I(t_2)]. \tag{21.4}$$

Again, for a homogeneous random field, $R_{II}(t_1, t_2) = R_{II}(\tau)$. For two random fields, $I(x, y)$ and $J(x, y)$, we can define the cross-correlation function, R_{IJ}, as

$$R_{IJ}(t_1, t_2) = E[I(t_1)J(t_2)]. \tag{21.5}$$

Noise power spectra

For a square-integrable, deterministic signal $f(x, y)$, its Fourier transform $F(\omega_x, \omega_y)$ tells us the amplitude and phase of each spatial frequency $\omega = (\omega_x, \omega_y)$ component in the signal. The Fourier amplitude squared, $\|F(\omega_x, \omega_y)\|^2$, is proportional to the signal power in that frequency (ω_x, ω_y). Therefore, $\|F(\omega_x, \omega_y)\|^2$ is called the power spectrum of the signal $f(x, y)$. As we mentioned before, the advantage of analyzing signals in the frequency domain is that, for linear, shift-invariant systems, the output signals can be completely described by the system transfer functions. It is desirable to see if we can also characterize noise fields by their spectral contents. This is indeed feasible and we can characterize the system response to noise fields by the same system transfer functions we use to compute the system responses to any arbitrary signals [744]. The frequency analysis of noise is based on the concept of the noise power spectra [113, 353, 745].

In the Fourier analysis of a random noise, there are two problems that need to be solved: (1) noise by its very nature does not decay to zero at infinity and therefore is not strictly square-integrable; (2) for each finite-area realization of a noise field, a straight Fourier transform produces only a very unreliable estimate of the noise power spectrum. The signal collected from a finite area represents a truncation of the original random field and therefore its Fourier transform is the desired spectrum convolved with a sinc function. Furthermore, any single realization of the random field is only a random sample from the ensemble.

One way to solve the first problem is by defining the power spectrum $S_{II}(\omega_x, \omega_y)$ of a homogeneous random field, $I(x, y)$, as the Fourier transform of its autocorrelation function,

$R_{II}(\tau_x, \tau_y)$, which usually decays very fast and thus is square-integrable.

$$S_{II}(\omega_x, \omega_y) = \int_{-\infty}^{\infty} R_{II}(\tau_x, \tau_y) e^{-i(\omega_x \tau_x + \omega_y \tau_y)} d\tau_x d\tau_y. \tag{21.6}$$

It can be shown that this definition also holds true for square-integrable, deterministic signals, and the new definition is equivalent to the original concept of power spectra [113, pp. 83–88]. Wiener [1030, 1031] and Khinchine [503] established the relationship between the autocorrelation function and the spectral density function (the power spectrum). For this reason, power spectra are often called Wiener spectra. Another way to solve the first problem (see, e.g., [353, p. 70]) is to define the power spectrum of a random field as the limit of the expected value of the average power over a finite area as the area goes to infinity.

The second problem is solved by using windows to reduce the leakage of energy of a frequency into its neighboring frequencies, and by averaging many finite areas of one or more realizations to reduce the variance in the estimate (assuming that the random field is ergodic). Alternatively, the autocorrelation is computed from the data and its Fourier transform is computed as the power spectrum. The variance in the estimate of the noise power spectrum can be reduced by multiplying the autocorrelation function by a smooth window function.

It is interesting to note that increasing the area of the noise field used to do the Fourier transform does not reduce the variance of the estimate. The extra data just increase the resolution of the estimate. An effective way to reduce the variance is to do a moving average to smooth the computed spectrum. This essentially trades the extra resolution in the estimate to get a more accurate estimate of the power (see, e.g., [777, pp. 549–58]). Therefore the data field is divided into overlapping or nonoverlapping segments. The FFT is used to compute the Fourier transform of each segment. The square of the Fourier transform is then taken to obtain the power spectrum of each segment. Finally, the power spectra of all the segments are summed and averaged to obtain the final estimate of the noise power spectrum.

For two random fields, $I(x, y)$ and $J(x, y)$, we can define the cross-power spectrum, $S_{IJ}(\omega_x, \omega_y)$, as

$$S_{IJ}(\omega_x, \omega_y) = \int_{-\infty}^{\infty} R_{IJ}(\tau_x, \tau_y) e^{-i(\omega_x \tau_x + \omega_y \tau_y)} d\tau_x d\tau_y. \tag{21.7}$$

Let $I(x, y)$ and $J(x, y)$ be the input and output random fields of a linear shift-invariant system with a system transfer function of $H(\omega_x, \omega_y)$. It can then be proved [744, p. 312] that:

$$S_{JJ}(\omega_x, \omega_y) = \|H(\omega_x, \omega_y)\|^2 \cdot S_{II}(\omega_x, \omega_y), \tag{21.8}$$

$$S_{JJ}(\omega_x, \omega_y) = H(\omega_x, \omega_y) \cdot S_{IJ}(\omega_x, \omega_y), \tag{21.9}$$

$$S_{IJ}(\omega_x, \omega_y) = H^*(\omega_x, \omega_y) \cdot S_{II}(\omega_x, \omega_y), \tag{21.10}$$

where $H^*(\omega_x, \omega_y)$ is the complex conjugate of $H(\omega_x, \omega_y)$. The first of these three relations shows that the power of the input noise at a given frequency is amplified by the linear system to produce the power of the output noise, just as is done to any deterministic signal. One can therefore input a noise field to a linear system and measure its output noise field to derive the system transfer function.

A homogeneous random field, $I(x, y)$, is called white noise if $R_{II}(\tau_x, \tau_y) = \delta(\tau_x) \cdot \delta(\tau_y)$. The power spectrum of white noise is a constant for all spatial frequencies. The color analogy here is that the equal-energy spectrum in optical radiation appears to be white. Similarly, if the noise power spectrum has more energy in the high frequencies than in the low frequencies, it is called blue noise.

RMS noise and granularity

A simpler measure of image noise is the standard deviation of the measured signal when the image is a flat field from a uniform exposure. This measure is called the RMS noise in electronic imaging and the RMS granularity in photography. In most imaging systems, RMS noise is a function of signal level, aperture size, and the metric used in the measurement. Therefore, it is important to report noise levels with these parameters and other measurement conditions explicitly stated.

A particularly well-studied image noise is the RMS granularity of photographic films and papers [21, 849, 1074]. Photographic images are formed by metallic silver particles in black-and-white films and papers, and by dye clouds in color films and papers. In a uniformly exposed flat field, these silver specks or dye clouds are randomly distributed, but their sizes are much too small (on the order of 0.1–2 μm) to be discerned or resolved by our vision. The perceived mottled granular patterns on the photographic images are caused by image density fluctuation due to the random distribution of these silver particles and dye clouds. Photographic noise is usually measured in terms of density and, for a flat field, it is well approximated as a Gaussian noise in that metric. If the silver or dye "grain" size is much smaller than the area of the measurement aperture, Selwyn [849] derived a relation between the RMS granularity σ_D and the aperture size A (area). For a black-and-white film,

$$A \cdot \sigma_D^2 \approx \text{constant.} \tag{21.11}$$

This relation does not work well for some color materials, prints from negatives, and radiographic films. Therefore, it is always necessary to specify the aperture size when reporting the film granularity. For example, Kodak has chosen to use a circular aperture 48 μm in diameter to measure the granularity values for most Kodak films. Furthermore, noise is a function of signal level. In silver-image films or color reversal films, granularity increases with mean density. In color negative films, granularity increases with density in the low-density areas and then stays constant or decreases as density increases. Kodak has chosen to measure granularity at a diffuse density of 1.0. Typically film granularity is from about 0.005 to 0.05. It is important to note that equal granularity is not equally visible on a reflection print because density is not a perceptually uniform lightness scale. It requires a much larger density difference in the dark area than in the light area to make an edge visible. The just-noticeable difference (JND) in granularity was found to be about 6% for a uniform field of density 1.0, and can be as much as 16–30% for complex scenes [1075], due to visual masking from image signals.

21.2 Subjective image quality evaluation

In color imaging applications, it is often desirable to evaluate subjective image quality for a given system performance. For example, when a new photographic film is developed, the manufacturer would like to know if the new film delivers better image quality than a competing film. A digital camera manufacturer would like to know if a new CFA interpolation algorithm works better than the old one. In general, image quality questions are very difficult to answer reliably for several reasons: (1) Most image quality improvements are incremental and therefore not obviously perceptible. (2) Improvements are often made at the sacrifice of some other image attributes and whether the results are perceived as improvements can be a matter of preference. A good example is image sharpening which makes the image look sharper, but also makes the noise more visible. There is no question that most people prefer sharper images, but they differ a lot in terms of how much noise they are willing to tolerate. (3) There is a learning effect that can go either way. The new "look" of a processed image can be initially perceived to be objectionable, and yet gradually becomes acceptable or even preferred. This learning effect can go the other way too. The new "look" can be perceived initially as a great improvement, but gradually become regarded as less desirable. (4) Image quality evaluation is often performed by third-party observers (people who did not take the pictures and do not know the subjects in the pictures). Their judgments of image quality can be quite different from those of first-party observers. (5) Image quality judgments are affected by the judgment attitudes and strategies induced by the experimental protocols and procedures [251, 343], such as the influence of context and the influence of instructions. (6) Reliable evaluation of system performance requires a large sample of images. Most imaging systems make compromises in cost/performance trade-offs. A system may do an excellent job in certain imaging situations, but fail miserably for other imaging situations. For example, a camera may give an excellent exposure for a frontlit scene, but a poor exposure for a backlit scene. Without proper statistical sampling in "photographic space" (all the possible situations in which the imaging system may be used to take pictures), it is impossible to thoroughly evaluate the system performance. We will return to this topic later in the chapter.

There are many image attributes that affect the overall image quality. The problem of image quality evaluation can thus be seen as projecting a multi-dimensional space into a one-dimensional space. For example, contrast, sharpness, noise, tone reproduction, and color reproduction are five of the most studied attributes. For digital images, artifacts of digital processing also add many more dimensions to the problem. Whether it is possible to give a numerical quality to each image is something that we all have to keep in mind when we deal with image quality issues. Another problem of image quality evaluation is the question of methodology [281]. Psychophysical methods that are successfully used for measuring the detection threshold and the discrimination threshold are not always applicable to image quality evaluation, and, when they are, it is often too time consuming to conduct experiments with those methods. One frequently used method in image quality evaluation is that of numerical category scaling. For example, image quality is rated from 1 to 10 and the task of an observer is to assign a quality number to each image. It is important to understand that we should not assume the numerical categories to be equally distanced.

In fact, observers may scale things differently in different parts of the scale. Numerical category scaling is easy and fast, but its validity is based on the assumption that observers can indeed evaluate all the attributes of an image and consistently produce a numerical value to represent the combined impact of all the attributes. Fortunately cross-comparison with other nonnumerical methods (such as judging which one is better in a pair comparison [875]) seems to show that the results from the method of numerical category scaling seem to be consistent with those from other, more time-consuming methods. In summary, perceptual evaluation of image quality can be done with statistical validity, but the reliability differs from task to task. In particular, if many attributes are varied at the same time, the results tend to be more noisy. In the next few sections, we will discuss the effect of varying one attribute at a time. We will then discuss some attempts that have been made to evaluate the impact on the total image quality of a combination of many varying attributes.

21.2.1 Contrast

When black letters are printed on a piece of white paper, the "contrast" of the printed page is perceived to be high. The contrast in this case is correlated with the reflectance ratio between the letters and the paper. When a dark room is illuminated by a small point source, the "contrast" of the scene is also perceived to be high. Here, the contrast is produced by comparison of the luminances in the shadow and in the highlight. In addition to reflectance and lighting, contrast can also be produced by color differences. Ideally, we would like to conclude that reflectance contrast, illumination contrast, and color contrast are the three main physical correlates of our perceived contrast of a scene or its image. However, we do not have sufficient knowledge of how various physical (contrast) events are combined and perceived as the perceptual attribute that we call image contrast. Perceptually, we seem to be able to visually parse the scene into reflectance, illumination, and color variations; it is unlikely that our visual system does this parsing for the sole purpose of computing the perceived scene contrast. A more likely scenario is that the perceptual contrast is a by-product of other visual computations, such as edge detection, contour integration, and shape from shading, etc.

Although we are quite ignorant about how our perceptual contrast is computed from an image, we do know a number of physical variables that we can use to manipulate it, such as sharpness and chroma [156]. The best-known variable is called gamma, the slope of the TRC when the log output luminance is plotted as a function of log input luminance. The results from several experiments [811] can be summarized as follows:

- The perceived image contrast increases with gamma, but it reaches a maximum at a gamma of 3–5, depending on the scene.
- The optimum gamma (the one that gives the best image quality) is dependent on scene type and viewing conditions.
- When image quality is plotted as a function of perceived image contrast, image quality is a convex function of perceived image contrast. It reaches a peak when the perceived contrast is about 6 on a scale of 1–10. Surprisingly, this does not seem to be scene-dependent.

21.2.2 Sharpness

The intuitive meaning of image sharpness is associated with how clearly and distinctly a physical object in the image can be seen. Step edges and fine textures are often the objects used to judge image sharpness. In the ideal world of geometrical optics, a step edge is reproduced as a step edge, and any deviation from that constitutes a blur, i.e., a degradation of sharpness. In practice, depending on the viewing conditions, our visual system cannot perceive a blur which is less than certain threshold value. For example, the minimum detectable blur on a knife edge (transition width) is about 25 sec to 1 minute of are, under foveal inspection (presumably for longer than 1 s) [378, 1017, 1024]. However, when the exposure time is reduced to 30 ms, the blur threshold increases by a factor of 2–4 [1024]. Physical sharpness, such as is characterized by the spread of the PSF or the system MTF, is found to correlate quite well with perceptual sharpness. This has been studied extensively and several sharpness measures have been proposed. Among them are edge gradients [400, 493], various acutances (e.g., system modulation transfer (SMT) acutance [221], cascaded modulation transfer (CMT) acutance [340] and a modulation transfer (AMT) acutance [222]), the subjective quality factor (SQF) [357], the square-root integral (SQRI) method [69], the sharpness factor (SF), and the perceived information capacity (PIC) [455]. Given their purely empirical nature, the predictive power of these sharpness measures is surprisingly good. Reviews and comparisons of the various metrics can be found in a number of references [455, 533, 707]. We will briefly mention some of these sharpness measures to gain some insights into these empirical findings.

1. Acutance: $A_c = \overline{G_x^2}\Delta D$, where $\overline{G_x^2}$ is the average density gradient squared and ΔD is the density difference between two sides of the image of a knife-edge.

2. CMT acutance:

$$CMTA = 125 - 20\log[200/(\int E_c(\omega)M(\omega)d\omega)]^2, \tag{21.12}$$

where $E_c(\omega)$ is the eye function approximated as a Gaussian function with $\sigma = 26.7$ cycles per degree and $M(\omega)$ is the cascaded system transfer function.

3. AMT acutance:

$$AMTA = 100 + 66\log[(\int E_a(\omega)M(\omega)d\omega)/(\int E_a(\omega)d\omega)], \tag{21.13}$$

where $E_a(\omega)$ is the eye function, approximated as a Gaussian function with $\sigma = 13$ cycles per degree and $M(\omega)$ is the cascaded system transfer function.

4. Perceived information capacity:

$$PIC = k_1 \left\{ \int \ln\left[1 + \frac{S(\omega)M_{eye}^2(\omega)}{N(\omega)M_{eye}^2(\omega) + N_{eye}(\omega)}\right]\frac{d\omega}{\omega} \right\}^{0.5} + k_2, \tag{21.14}$$

where $S(\omega)$ is the signal power spectrum multiplied by the squares of the system MTF, $M_{eye}(\omega)$ and $N_{eye}(\omega)$ are the eye "MTF" and the equivalent eye noise power spectrum, and $N(\omega)$ is the system noise power spectrum.

Several interesting observations can be made from this long series of studies:

- The logarithm of the integrated area of the CSF[1]-weighted MTF of an imaging system is found to be linearly correlated with the subjective sharpness, especially when the system noise is low or not perceptible.
- When the noise is high, the system's signal-to-noise ratio seems to predict the perceived sharpness better.
- With digital image processing, it is now possible to enhance images with MTFs greater than 1 and in almost any arbitrary shape. None of the existing sharpness measures has been tested thoroughly for this type of MTF manipulation. It is often assumed that image quality increases with sharpness. This cannot be true if the existing sharpness measures are used because certain MTF manipulations make images look quite unnatural, and their quality is actually degraded, although their computed sharpness is higher.

The perception of image sharpness is coupled with the perception of image contrast. For a given system gamma, the perceived sharpness increases with the cut-off frequency. As gamma is increased, the perceived sharpness for a given cut-off frequency is also increased until the gamma value reaches 0.8 or higher, then it becomes insensitive to further gamma change [811, p. 49].

21.2.3 Graininess and noise perception

The perception of image noise depends on the image details, the illumination, and the color of the target, etc., in addition to the granularity, the lightness, the covariance matrix of the color records, and the noise power spectrum. Graininess is the term used to describe the perceived noisy fluctuation related to granularity. It is important to point out that both luminance noise and chrominance noise contribute to the perceived image noise [820].

The following numerical results are for a 560 μm diameter aperture, 2500 lx illuminance, D_{50}, with Status A densitometry. The noise power spectra were well described by: $\ln N(\nu) = \text{constant} - 0.5\nu$ (cycles per millimeter). The psychophysical relationship between graininess and granularity is found to be the same for targets of different chromaticity. For the interval scale experiment, one level of mean density of 0.95 was used. For the ratio scale experiment, three density levels at 0.43, 0.95, and 1.41 were used. The data were normalized with an empirical formula to equivalent graininess at density 0.9.

- Noise power spectrum: assuming that the noise is a stationary random field, the Fourier transform of its autocorrelation function is the noise power spectrum.
- Granularity: the objective measurement of the local density variation, such as the standard deviation or the RMS granularity.
- Graininess: the subjective perception of a random pattern of brightness or color fluctuation.
- Visual granularity: $\sigma_v = [(0.3\sigma_r)^2 + (0.5\sigma_g)^2 + (0.2\sigma_b)^2]^{1/2}$.

---

[1] (Luminance) contrast sensitivity function.

- Graininess (interval scale): $G_{interval} = 6.0 \log \sigma_v - 2.6$.
- Graininess (ratio scale): $G_{ratio} = 0.06\sigma_v^2$.
- Graininess (ratio scale) decreases linearly when the print density increases for constant granularity.

21.2.4   Tonal reproduction

An image on a CRT screen or on a reflection print can look too light or too dark, too harsh or too flat, and sometimes too dull or too foggy. These are called tone reproduction errors. Obviously, in addition to measurable physical deviations from the intended reproduction, these errors also involve psychophysical judgments. We still do not know why an image looks too dark or too light. It is not clear to us how our visual perception decides on this judgment. From a technical point of view, the question is, what should be regarded as the most accurate or the most pleasing reproduction aim for a given scene or a given image?

If the goal is to duplicate a print original with another print, we can take any deviation from the original as reproduction error, and the error can be quantified with the average ΔE in CIELAB space. However, even in this simple case, it is not clear if error in one tonal region, say the shadow of the main subject, should be regarded as equally serious as error in another tonal region, say the main subject. If the original is not a print, but a natural scene, then the tone reproduction error becomes even more complicated to evaluate. In fact, the tone reproduction of many beautiful photographic prints by great photographers, such as Ansel Adams, is often quite different from the orignal scene, no matter how we scale the scene luminances.

For practical purposes, tone reproduction error is often evaluated by the variables in the mechanism used by an imaging system for tone reproduction. For example, in a negative–positive photographic system, the tone reproduction process is controlled by the D–$\log H$ curve of the negative film, the chemical processing, and the D–$\log H$ curve of the paper. Since the shape of the D–$\log H$ curve of a silver halide medium does not vary much (by design), the tone reproduction errors are often classified into three types: (1) exposure (density) error, (2) contrast (gamma) error, and (3) D_{min} and D_{max} errors. An exposure error by the camera or by the printer is translated into a density error in the final print and therefore is called a density error. The consequence of a density error is that the images look too light or too dark. A density error greater than 0.2–0.3 is considered as unacceptable in density balance. In consumer photofinishing, a density balance error greater than 2 buttons is considered as unacceptable. Since a density button corresponds to 0.075 log exposure on paper [214, p. 152], a 2-button error can translate into a 0.3 density error or higher in the mid-tone, depending on the gamma of the paper used. A contrast error is often due to chemical processing or film/paper keeping (or storage) problems. Contrast errors greater than $\pm20\%$ are generally considered unacceptable, but the decision is quite dependent on the scene contents and the lighting contrast. The consequence of a contrast error is that images look too harsh (highlight washed out and shadow without details) or too flat. D_{min} or D_{max} errors are usually caused by camera flare, printer flare, chemical processing errors, or film/paper keeping problems. As a consequence, the images look flat or foggy.

In electronic imaging systems, equivalent types of tone reproduction error also exist. Furthermore, due to limited bit-depth, tonal quantization errors can sometimes be clearly seen, especially after image compression. On a pixel level, errors due to color matrixing and edge enhancement are also visible in some image areas. In general, tone reproduction errors can be measured in terms of ΔL^* in CIELAB on a pixel-by-pixel basis, or on an image-by-image basis. However, certain quantization errors are much more objectionable than the mere ΔL^* error can tell us.

21.2.5 Color reproduction

When we look at a photographic print, we often notice that the colors are not reproduced correctly. How do we do that? One simple explanation is that we compare the reproduced colors with what we remember. This explanation is not without difficulty because experiments show that we do not remember the color of any particular object very well. The typical color of a class of objects, such as bananas, may not be the same as the particular object we are seeing in the image. Another explanation is that we can tell color balance error by noting that a white object is not reproduced as white. The question is how do we know that that object, if unfamiliar, is actually white? Of course, these types of question are related to the so-called color constancy problem and we do not currently have a good answer to any of these questions. However, experiments show that we are indeed fairly capable of computing illumination, reflectance, and shape from an image. This has different implications for soft-copy viewing and hard-copy viewing. In the case of soft-copy viewing in a dark room, our visual system computes the neutral point from the image on the screen and the computation is relatively independent of the white point of the soft display. In the case of hard-copy viewing in a complex surround, our visual system computes the neutral point from the image and the complex surround, and the computed neutral point is often very close to the color of the illumination. Therefore, we are much less sensitive to color balance error when viewing a soft display in a dark room than when viewing a hard-copy in a bright, complex surround.

In an effort to quantify the quality of color reproduction, Pointer [767, 768] proposed a metric called the color reproduction index (CRI). The basic idea is to compute the weighted sum of differences in *color appearance* between the original and the reproduced colors. The key point here is in the term *color appearance*. CIELAB can be used to calculate the color reproduction errors, but it does not properly account for visual adaptation and viewing surrounds. The basic computational steps for the CRI are as follows:

1. Define the reference and test situations.
2. Compute the colorimetric data.
3. Compute color appearance data.
4. Compute the weights.
5. Compute the hue indices.
6. Compute the lightness indices.
7. Compute the chroma indices.
8. Scale and combine the indices.

Experimental results [42] showed that acceptability versus overall CRI is both scene- and hue-dependent. It is clear that any attempt to quantify color reproduction errors has to take the main subject matter into account. A fixed weighting scheme cannot do a proper job.

In consumer photofinishing, a color balance error greater than 2 buttons is considered to be unacceptable. The color button here corresponds to 0.05 log exposure on paper [214, p. 152]. Since most photographic color papers have very nonlinear D–$\log H$ curves, a 2-button error in color exposure will introduce varying amounts of color shift in highlight, mid-tone, and shadow. In the mid-tone areas, the color error can translate into a 0.1 density error or higher, depending on the gamma of the paper used. The other complication is that we are more sensitive to green–magenta error than to yellow–blue error, and therefore, the acceptable color balance error should be hue-dependent. Alternatively, the color error should be specified in a perceptually more uniform color metric, such as CIELAB. In summary, the 2 button criterion gives us an empirical rule of thumb, which is based on a long history of photofinishing. However, this criterion is not generalizable to other color imaging applications because the photographic system is a closed system and the color button correction cannot be easily translated to other systems.

21.2.6 Combined effects of different image attributes

Psychophysical image quality evaluation is often performed by varying only one perceptual attribute, while keeping all others as constant as possible. Hopefully, such a well-controlled experiment may provide us with more reliable data for deriving the physical correlate of the perceptual attribute under manipulation. Of course, this is not always possible because we may not know enough about the interaction between one attribute and another. For example, sharpness and contrast are two perceptual attributes that seem to interact with each other when some physical parameters, such as gamma, are changed.

When the effect of varying any individual image attribute is known, we would like to be able to predict the combined effect of co-varying some of the attributes. Such a prediction is often based on a combination model. The general finding in this area is that the worse attribute often determines the total image quality [494]. For example, if an image is out of focus, and its sharpness attribute is the worst of all the attributes, the image quality is low, no matter how good its color and tone reproduction might be. Among different mathematical functions, the following l^p-norm-like function seems to fit experimental data reasonably well:

$$Q = [a_1 A_1^p + a_2 A_2^p + \cdots + a_n A_n^p]^{1/p} + b, \qquad (21.15)$$

where A_i, $i = 1, 2, \ldots, N$, are the individual image attributes, and Q is the combined image quality. The parameters, p, b, and a_i, $i = 1, \ldots, N$, are determined from data fitting. The constant term b can be considered as an offset term for the image quality measure and the mathematical expression is essentially the same as the l^p norm in vector space, or the Minkowski distance. However, this type of function implies that the image quality is a monotonic function of each image attribute. This has been found to be false. In general, image quality peaks at a medium level of some perceived image attributes, such as contrast, sharpness, and colorfulness [156, 304, 463]. Different types of function have been proposed to model such nonmonotonic dependence [282].

Let us look at one example of such a study on the combination model. In combining the influence of sharpness and graininess, Bartleson [82] found that $p = -3.4$ seemed to fit his experimental data well. It should be pointed out that these were purely empirical curve fittings and the exponents may vary widely for different sets of data. In fact, for each print, different parameters are needed. The value $p = -3.4$ was for the average of the set of prints used in the experiment. The same expression is also found to describe the combined effect of various perceptual impairments on image quality. Image quality degradations (blurring and distortion) caused by artifacts are called perceptual impairments. Several studies [250, 717] have shown that, in image coding, the total perceptual impairment I due to impairments I_i in different image attributes can be combined in Minkowski distance:

$$I^p = \sum_{i=1}^{N} I_i^p \tag{21.16}$$

where p is a parameter determined by experiments.

21.2.7 Multi-dimensional modeling of image quality

The above discussion on various image quality attributes, such as sharpness, contrast, noise, etc., is based on the assumption that observers have an intuitive understanding of the aspect of image quality they are asked to judge. This assumption seems safe, but is by no means obvious. In fact, these image attributes are often found to be mutually interacting. For example, when the contrast of an image is increased, most observers also indicate an increase in the sharpness. This raises some serious questions: (1) What do we mean by an image attribute? Is clearness an image attribute? How about conspicuousness? (2) Do the observers know what they are judging? Because of concerns like these over the effectiveness of any "preconceived" attributes to represent the subjective image quality, we should ask if it is possible to model the multi-dimensional nature of image quality in a different way. The answer is yes. One of the frequently used tools in such a formulation is called multi-dimensional scaling.

Multidimensional scaling [123, 219, 240] is a statistical method for analyzing distance or proximity data to extract their inherent or latent dimensions and structures. For example, given the distances between each pair in a set of 12 cities in the USA, a multi-dimensional scaling program can figure out that the 12 cities are located on a two-dimensional space and reconstruct a map of their relative locations.

If we can conduct a psychophysical experiment to estimate the quality distances among a set of images, we can use multi-dimensional scaling techniques to extract the relevant attributes of this set of images, without predefining what image quality attributes to use, as required in the approach discussed in the previous section. Of course, the results depend on what physical parameters are used to generate such a set of images. For example, we can take a reference image and add various amounts of white noise to it. We can also change its gamma to various values. Such variations of noise and gamma generate a set of images that can be used for quality distance judgements. From the pair-wise distance (dis-similarity) measures, we can then use multi-dimensional scaling to figure out which combinations of noise and gamma can serve as the efficient measure of image quality. Experiments that use stimuli generated from combinations of physical parameters without predefined image attributes have been conducted to establish physical descriptors for psychophysical attributes [641, 753]. This type of approach is inherently more satisfactory than predefining each image quality attribute and then combining their contribution with a Minkowski distance. However, this is generally useful only if most relevant physical parameters are considered in generating the experimental images.

21.3 Photographic space sampling

Image quality performance evaluation is a complex process, not only because image quality is a subjective judgment, but also because system performance requires statistical validation with proper sampling in the "photographic space", i.e., the frequency distribution of image taking as a function of photographic variables [303, 846]. Many of the algorithms in a digital camera, such as autoexposure and auto-white-balance, are statistical in nature. Certain types of scene can make an algorithm fail frequently because those scenes do not follow the assumptions that the algorithm makes when computing its output values. If a digital camera produces too many bad pictures in a field test, it does not necessarily mean that the camera has poor quality performance. It could be a result of taking too many pictures of the same type of scene that happens to be inconsistent with the assumptions on which the algorithms are based. A simple example is that if the autowhite-balance algorithm is based on the assumption that an image always integrates to gray, then any scene that has a dominant subject color is likely to cause a significant error in the color balance of the image of that scene. Modern auto-white-balance algorithms are much more sophisticated than the simple integrate-to-gray algorithm, but they are all based on some variations of the same basic assumption.

Once we understand the subjective and the statistical nature of the image quality performance evaluation, it is important for us to follow some agreed process to approach the problem in order to arrive at a repeatable and reliable result. Since the performance of algorithms is highly dependent on the type of scene that are being imaged, a reliable evaluation has to cover enough varieties of scene type to be statistically valid. The following is an attempt to provide a partial check list for testing each of the major functions of a camera or other image capture device.

- Autoexposure: the following scene types can be used for evaluation: (1) back-lit, (2) front-lit with close-up objects, (3) side-lit with strong shadow and highlight, (4) mixed illumination (e.g., outdoor scenes with some buildings in the sun and others in the shade), (5) main subject wearing white clothing, (6) main subject wearing dark clothing, (7) dark surrounds, (8) bright surrounds, (9) busy background, (10) uniform background, (11) main subject in the center, (12) main subject off-center, (13) main subject half in the shade and half in the sun, (14) snow or beach scenes, (15) document images, (16) event images (graduation, birthday, reunion, etc), (17) location images (amusement parks, mountains, stores, shopping malls, office buildings), (18) baby and small child images.

- Auto-white-balance: the following scene types can be used for evaluation: (1) scenes under different illuminations, such as tungsten light, at different times of the day, under fluorescent light, (2) scenes that have dominant colors, such as large areas of green grass, blue sky, or red carpet as the background, (3) scenes with mixed illuminants, (4) scenes that have bright saturated colors, (5) event images (parties, dinners).

- Autofocus: the following scene types can be used for evaluation: (1) scenes with objects located at varying distances, (2) scenes that have busy textures at distances other than that of the main subject, (3) scenes that have two main subjects, located on either sides of the center of the image, (4) baby and small child images, (5) event images, (6) location images.

- Tone reproduction: the following scene types can be used for evaluation: (1) scenes that have very subtle and gradual shadings, such as cloudless sky or uniform walls, (2) scenes that have very wide luminance dynamic ranges, such as some objects illuminated by bright sunlight and others in deep shadow, (3) overcast days, (4) snow or beach scenes, (5) flash-in-the-face scenes, (6) event images, (7) location images (street scenes, mountains, office scenes, amusement parks), (8) home life images.

- Color reproduction: the following scene types can be used for evaluation: (1) scenes that have a Macbeth ColorChecker, (2) scenes that have large skin areas, such as a close-up portrait, (3) people scenes, (4) home life images, (5) location images (restaurants, stores, parks, etc), (6) scenes with blue sky and green grass, (7) scenes that show fruit.

- Edge enhancement: the following scene types can be used for evaluation: (1) scenes that have busy textures, such as those that show hair and grass, (2) scenes that have high-contrast and low-contrast edges, (3) close-up portraits, (4) snow scenes, (5) beach and water scenes, (6) scenes that have objects at varying distances, (7) scenes of building, (8) natural scenes (such as mountains, lakes, etc.), (9) scenes with blue sky and white clouds, (10) scenes with gradual and subtle shading, (11) scenes with high-spatial-frequency patterns.

- Noise suppression: the following scene types can be used for evaluation: (1) scenes that are underexposed, (2) scenes that have fine textures, such as those that show hair, grass, or a water surface, (3) portraits, (4) scenes with edges in various directions, (5) scenes with wide dynamic luminance range, (6) scenes with stripe structures, such as shirts with grid patterns, (7) scenes with people at varying distances.

- Image compression: the following scene types can be used for evaluation: (1) scenes that have subtle shading and high-contrast diagonal edges, (2) close-up portraits, (3) scenes that have fine textures, such as those that show hair and grass, (4) scenes with people at varying distances.

21.4   Factors to be considered in image quality evaluation

Image quality evaluation studies are costly and time-consuming to conduct and their results can have a major impact on business decisions. Therefore it is very important to clearly define the objective, the method, the procedure, and the control. Expertise is required in the following areas: psychophysics, marketing, imaging science, and system engineering. Image quality evaluation studies differ from other marketing or psychophysical studies. Here, we will discuss some of the issues in observer screening and the planning of experiments.

21.4.1 Observer screening

From many previous studies, it is known that consumer preferences in image attributes vary with culture, race, region, experience, and expectation. For example, Asian consumers prefer more saturated colors than western consumers do. Caucasian consumers prefer more tanned skin colors than Asians. Also, some consumers have little tolerance of image blur or color error, but others are more sensitive to noise. Some people's preference for high or low contrast is found to be very strong, and they are not willing to compromise much. In order to get a reliable evaluation of image quality performance, it is desirable to have as large a group of observers with as diversified preferences as possible. However, this is not always practical. A good compromise is to prescreen candidates to make sure that diverse preferences are indeed represented in the small group of image judges we have for the evaluation tasks.

21.4.2 Planning of experiments

1. Pilot test and formal test: since a complete run of the process takes a lot of time and effort, it is recommended that the process should be conducted in two stages: a pilot test and a formal test. In the pilot test, the number of images and the variety of scene types can be greatly reduced. The main purpose of the pilot test is to see if there are obvious image quality problems before the formal test is run.
2. Selection of judges: the judges should be people who are not directly working on the engineering issues. Because people tend to have different preferences, the more judges the better. For practical reasons, 3–5 judges of diverse backgrounds and preferences should be acceptable.
3. Selection of scenes: for a pilot test, the number of images can be as few as four or five, one for each of the most common types of scene. For a formal test, the number of scenes should be on the order of 100 or more. The most critical aspect is the varieties of scene. Variations and combinations of the following variables should be included: lighting, dynamic range, busyness, location, subject distance, color distribution, and luminance level, etc.
4. Double-blind test procedure: the identities of the cameras or algorithms of all images should be recorded but hidden from both the observers and those who are conducting the experiments. The presentation sequence of images should be randomized.
5. Presentation of stimuli: either hard-copy or soft-copy can be used. Images of the same scene should be presented at the same time for side-by-side comparison. If hard-copies are used, the viewing surround should be medium gray and the illumination close to D_{65} (or D_{50}). If a color monitor is used, the white point should be adjusted to D_{65} (or D_{50}), and the ambient light should be shielded from the monitor screen.

6. Image resolution: Digital images can be compressed, subsampled, and displayed at various resolutions. Therefore, it is important that a fair comparison is made at the same resolution, compression ratio, and viewing distance. For example, if a camera offers three different compression ratios, only images of the same compression ratio should be compared.

7. Calibration: The printers or monitors that are used for image display should be properly calibrated. Viewing flare should be minimized. Most digital camera outputs are calibrated to the sRGB standard and the printer/monitor should also be calibrated to the same color space. If a candidate test model uses a different color space, its images should be calibrated separately.

21.5 Image fidelity and difference evaluation

In color imaging applications, it is often necessary to determine if two versions of an image are visibly different. For example, if one image is compressed and then decompressed by an image compression algorithm, we would like to know if it is visibly different from the original image without compression. This question is important because we would like to compress an image as much as possible without visibly distorting the image. An automated computer program that can predict visible differences between two versions of the same image would be very useful for optimizing image compression parameters.

In the past, mean-square errors have been used to quantify image distortions. However, the results were not satisfactory for two main reasons: (1) the metrics used were not perceptually based; (2) perceptible errors are frequency- and context-dependent. For the example, the differential threshold is greatly elevated near the edges [595]. In particular, contrast sensitivity and visual masking play a very important role in determining if a given error is visible or not. These two aspects will be discussed in the following sections. One simple way [234] to demonstrate how inadequate the mean-square errors are in predicting visual differences is to map an image through a straight-line tone scale curve with the slope adjusted about 5% higher or lower than 1.0. This slope adjustment is slightly less than the average threshold and most people cannot detect the difference between the contrast adjusted image and the original. However, the mean-square errors between these two images are very high, compared with the distortions introduced by typical image compression algorithms.

In order to evaluate whether a certain image difference is perceptible or not, it is necessary to make sure that all image quantities are calibrated and the intended rendering and viewing conditions are explicitly specified. These are not always known in advance. In the case of unknown conditions, a conservative estimate has to be stated to make the evaluation results meaningful. For example, the viewing distance of the rendered images is often unconstrained. We may have to specify the shortest reasonable viewing distance in calculating the visual thresholds. In the following discussions, we will assume that the images, the rendering paths, and the display media have been specified and calibrated, so that colorimetric or radiometric quantities can be derived.

21.5.1 Perceptible color differences

One simplified method for evaluating image differences is to calculate the mean-square errors in perceptually uniform color space, such as CIELAB or CIELUV. The deficiency of such a method is that spatial variations are not accounted for. For this reason, there have been efforts [1067, 1068] to incorporate the luminance and chrominance contrast sensitivity functions. The basic idea is to transform an input color image into the opponent color processes, filter the luminance and chrominance channels with psychophysically measured contrast sensitivity functions, and then transform the filtered opponent color processes to CIELAB space to calculate the image differences. The filtering operation accounts for the low visibility of high-frequency chromatic variations. However, visual masking is not accounted for. The other major deficiency is that the viewing conditions, such as light/dark surrounds, are not considered. The advantage of such a simplified method is its speed.

Empirical studies [824, 914] on using color-difference formulas, such as CIELAB, CIE94, and CIEDE2000, as a measure of perceptible image difference reach some tentative conclusions:

1. When the observers make overall judgments of image difference, scene content has some, but not a very strong, effect on perceptibility tolerances for pictorial images.
2. CIELAB ΔE is adequate for estimating perceptibility tolerances, but varying the weight of the lightness difference in CIE94 and CIEDE2000 significantly improves the predictive performance. In general, the lightness difference is less perceptible.
3. Acceptability tolerances are not linearly scaled values of perceptibility tolerances.
4. Color charts cannot be assumed to be good simulators of a pictorial image with respect to perceptibility thresholds.

Incorporating the contrast sensitivity functions as filters has been shown to produce more-accurate predictions [1068]. In order to further improve the predictive performance, we need to model the human visual perception in more detail as will be discussed next.

21.5.2 Visible difference prediction

In order to better predict visible differences, we need to consider many other behaviors of the human visual system that have been observed in psychophysical experiments [115, 892, 1006, 1014]: visual nonlinearity, visual masking, visual adaptation, subthreshold summation, frequency- and orientation-selective channels, etc. However, our understanding of these behaviors is far from complete and most visual models available today are empirical rather than based on a computational theory [636] or mechanisms. Therefore, the only way to verify the available models [234, 604, 943, 1014] is to see how well they predict the visible differences between two images. It turns out that these empirical models work reasonably well for typical image viewing conditions, such as light surround, high luminance level, and normal viewing distances (10–20 inches). Typical processing steps in these models may include the following modules:

1. eye optics and cone nonlinearity;
2. opponent processing;

3. spatial frequency channels;
4. image and noise masking;
5. probability summation for detection threshold.

Readers are encouraged to consult the original papers, such as Daly's "Visible difference predictor" [234], for the details of the model implementation. A fundamental difficulty in all the contrast-sensitivity-based models is that when the luminance of a large uniform area is changed, the models predict visible differences only around the boundaries of the area, rather than over the whole area. The problem is that contrast sensitivity functions are not system transfer functions, and the image we "see" is in fact only a percept reconstructed from the image features our low-level vision extracts from the scene. For example, we never see a black spot in our visual field corresponding to the blind spot ($5° \times 7°$) on our retinas, even when we close one eye and stare steadily at the scene. Any model that relies only on contrast sensitivity functions to predict perceptual differences cannot account for the object-oriented nature of our perception.

21.6 Problems

21.1 The RMS granularity, $\sigma_D = 0.04$, of a black-and-white film is measured with a 24 μm aperture. However, if the standard aperture for reporting RMS granularity is 48 μm, use Selwyn's relation to convert the σ_D to the standard aperture.

22 Basic concepts in color image processing

Digital image processing is a field that has diverse applications, such as remote sensing, computer vision, medical imaging, computer graphics, graphic arts, pattern recognition, and industrial inspection. There have been many books that cover the general topics of digital image processing in varying depths and applications (e.g., [86, 165, 262, 351, 363, 456, 457, 594, 752, 776, 807, 841]). Readers are encouraged to consult these books for various operations and algorithms for digital image processing. Most of the books deal with monochromatic images. When dealing with color images, there are several concepts that are inherently quite different. For example, if we treat the *RGB* signals at a pixel as a three-dimensional vector, a color image becomes a vector field, while a monochromatic image is a scalar field. Typical operations, such as the gradient of an image, have to be thought over again because simply repeating the same scalar operation three times is often not the best thing to do. Another important reason for much of the required rethinking is that our visual perception of a color image is usually described in terms of luminance–chrominance color attributes, not *RGB* color channels. A color image simply provides much more information than a monochromatic image about the scene, its material properties and its illumination. We have to think and rethink about how to extract the additional information more effectively for the applications we have in mind. In this chapter, we will study some basic issues and explore some new concepts for formulating old problems which we might have encountered when working on monochromatic image processing.

22.1 General considerations

In every image processing task, the most important job is always problem formulation. If the problem is not formulated well, the solution is often less than desirable. Let us take image sharpening as an example. Many engineers immediately go to the textbooks and the published literature to see what kinds of algorithm there are, and pick up the one that they like best according to whatever criteria they have. Often, they choose some variation of an adaptive unsharp masking algorithm [1064] because it is widely used and they have seen many impressive images in the published papers. They then spend a lot of effort coding it up and trying it out by systematically adjusting the important parameters. Although most adaptive unsharp masking algorithms are quite acceptable for many applications, few engineers actually think through their justification and compare them with other image sharpening algorithms, such as multiscale contrast enhancement [997], edge shaping [549], or curvelet transform [897, 898]. It is often observed that, over the lifetime of an algorithm research project, less than 5% of the time is spent on problem formulation, 30% on coding and debugging, and the rest on modifying the codes to fix the "minor" failures or the "occasional" image artifacts created by the algorithm. In fact, it might be more profitable to spend more than 20% of the time on problem formulation. In the case of image sharpening, the unsharp masking approach attempts to raise the slope of edge transitions at the risk of distorting the edge profiles with overshoots. Furthermore, the unsharp masking operation is a second-order derivative and therefore quite sensitive to image noise. Before we rush to implement the algorithm, we should seriously consider other appoaches that do not create overshoots and are not as sensitive to image noise.

In general, after going through a careful thought process to formulate the problem, we have to study the following four basic questions that face every color image processing problem:

1. Which scene model is the most adequate for this problem?
    Almost all color image processing algorithms make some assumptions about the physical scenes. However, few algorithm developers attempt to make those assumptions explicit and examine their scene models to see if the models are adequate for their problem domain. For example, many CFA interpolation algorithms assume that color ratios are invariant over an object surface. This means that specular highlight is not processed correctly.

2. Which image capture model is most appropriate for this problem?
    Images captured by different types of device may have very different signal and noise characteristics. An algorithm needs to fully utilize such system-specific prior knowledge. Furthermore, different image capture devices may be calibrated for different output metrics. For example, some engineers process a color image without knowing how the image was calibrated. When the homomorphic transform [909] was first proposed for image dynamic range compression in 1972, a common mistake was to assume that the image value is linearly proportional to image irradiance. At that time, most images were scanned from photographic films and they were calibrated in film density or in relative log scene exposure. Today, almost all color images from digital cameras are in gamma-corrected sRGB space. A very widely-used image manipulation tool provides a function for increasing the brightness of an image by adding a constant value to all the pixels. This function should be used only when the image is calibrated in log exposure or film density. Many users do not realize this and simply use this operation on sRGB images.

3. Which color space is best for this problem?
    There are many color spaces that we can choose to process an image, but in most cases, there are only one or two choices that are suitable for the problem. For example, if the problem is to perform image segmentation, it does not make sense to use CIELAB as the color space because the problem concerns the scene physics, not the human psychophysics.

4.   Which objective function is most useful for this problem?
     In developing a color image processing algorithm, the problem is often formulated as
     an optimization process. Therefore, it is important to choose an objective function that
     is useful in achieving our goals. Otherwise, the optimal solution will not give us the
     optimal results. For example, in color reproduction, if we take the sum of CIELAB ΔE
     over all pixels as an objective function to minimize, we may expend a lot of effort, but
     the results may be less than desirable because the user's attention may be focused only
     on the face of the main subject.

22.2   Color spaces and signal representations

Use of color information in machine vision and image processing has raised questions about
the "best" color space for a particular task. That is, how do we represent the color information
so that the task can be implemented efficiently? For example, if we would like to detect and
locate faces in images using skin color as one of the features, what is a good color space to do
skin color detection? One can argue that since all color spaces are transformations of each
other, it does not matter which color space is used. Mathematically speaking, this may be
true. In practice, a poor choice of color space can increase the complexity of processing and
sometimes obscure useful features. An analogy is the time domain versus frequency domain
representations. They are mathematically equivalent, but some tasks can be performed more
efficiently in the frequency domain, and others in the time domain. However, there are more
issues to be considered in choosing an efficient color representation than choosing a time
or frequency representation.

In most cases, the "best" color space depends on the intended application. For example,
if we want to quantify how a trade-mark is reproduced in an image, a perceptually uniform
color space such as CIELAB or the Munsell system is the most useful. On the other hand,
if our job is to adjust the color balance of an image, some kind of log exposure space is
a good choice because the adjustment can be done by simple subtraction or addition of
constants. In this case, CIELAB is very inconvenient to use because changing (X_n, Y_n, Z_n)
for all pixels involves a lot of computation. Yet for other applications, the color space may
be fixed by the requirement of the imaging chain. For example, NTSC TV (video) signals
are broadcast in a standard YIQ encoding. In the receiver, image processing circuits are
often designed to receive YIQ or gamma-corrected *RGB* space. To do otherwise requires
extra hardware and increase product cost.

Conventional color spaces [430] were defined either for colorimetry (such as CIEXYZ)
or for perceptual comparison (such as CIELAB, the Munsell system, and the Natural Color
System). Although these color systems provide good specifications of color information,
they are not necessarily suitable for machine vision and image processing applications. For
example, the CIE (x,y) chromaticity is known to be singular for zero input values, making
it very sensitive to noise for dark image regions [501]. Other systems that use hue angles
as one of the attributes are very unstable for the less saturated colors. A more theoretically-
oriented approach has been proposed that uses the eigenvectors of the covariance of the color
signals [145, 727, 776]. This is a good idea for data compression because the eigenvectors

tend to decorrelate the color components. However, it is not clear how one can estimate the "true" covariance of the natural color variations. We will come back to this subject shortly.

In this section, we will first discuss the general issues that one has to consider when choosing a color space. In the next section, we will then develop a good color space for image segmentation based on the discussion here. In order to restrict the scope of the discussion, we will assume that the vision or imaging system has three color channels that sense three independent spectral signals from a natural scene. Following conventions in consumer applications, we will designate the three color signals as the red, green, and blue signals which simply indicates their relative sensitivities to the long, medium, and short wavelengths. These spectral bands are often about 100 nm wide (say 400–500 nm, 500–600 nm, and 600–700 nm). There are also systems which use color filters that are broader in spectral transmittance, such as yellow, cyan, and magenta, to collect more light in each channel. These "complementary" color signals are then converted into red, green, and blue for further color processing.

In processing digital color images, the first thing we should find out is what the numbers mean, i.e., the signal calibration. For example, we should know if the digital numbers are proportional to the scene radiances (linear), or the log scene radiances (log), or the gamma-corrected scene radiances (video). Although these are the three metrics that are most directly tied to the original scenes, there are other media- or perception-related metrics that are also very widely used. For example, images that are digitized from photographic films are often calibrated in terms of film density or printing density. Images that are used in graphic arts are often calibrated in reflection density or CMYK ink coverage. Images that are captured by digital cameras may have been rendered with nonstandard gamma correction curves [177]. Ideally we should also find out the spectral responsivity function of the device/medium that is used to capture the original image and, if possible, the signal processing (chemical, or electronic) that was applied to the captured image. Unfortunately, this information is often not available and can be very difficult or expensive to determine. The next best thing is to have companion images that include certain calibration targets (such as the Macbeth ColorChecker [647], IT8 or ISO 12641 targets [446]) on them. However, it is not unusual for there to be no calibration information related to the image at all. In such cases, the statistical or physical properties of the image may be used for automatic rendering or classification of the unkown images [300, 368, 575, 597]. Alternatively, some careful comparisons of the digital values corresponding to various objects in the image may give a clue as to which of the possible metrics is most likely to be the correct one.

Once we know the metric of the digital images, we have to consider three issues before we decide how to transform our color signals to a best representation for the task in hand. These three issues are: (a) signal characteristics, (b) noise statistics, and (c) system constraints.

22.2.1 Signal characteristics

In order to effectively represent the color signals for our task, it is very important to understand the characteristics of the signal with which we are dealing. For example, color images of presentation graphics (such as pie charts, bar graphs, etc.) are very different from those of natural scenes. Presentation graphics are full of saturated colors, high-contrast edges, and uniform areas with little image noise. The major concern here is to make sure that they are easy to read and give good visual impressions. For this type of image, it may be desirable to represent color signals in perceptual spaces so that visual contrast and color preference can be manipulated directly. On the other hand, for color images of natural scenes, the representation issues are more complicated. Here we list some of the key factors that need to be considered:

1. Effect of light source variation

   Daylight, tungsten lamps, fluorescent lamps, and electronic flashes are the four major types of light source for color imaging. They differ greatly in their spectral power distributions. Daylight is the dominant natural light source in outdoor scenes, but its spectral composition varies with location, weather conditions, and the time of the day. Fortunately, the variation can be approximated by two eigenvectors and a mean vector as specified in the CIE daylight illuminants. Its chromaticity locus (daylight locus) is almost parallel to that of the blackbody radiator at different temperatures. Object surfaces of a natural scene are mainly illuminated by various mixtures of two major components of daylight sources: sunlight and skylight. If we compute the eigenvectors of the covariance matrix of the red, green, and blue signals of a natural scene, the exact results vary from scene to scene. However, one of the eigenvectors is most often in the general direction of yellow–blue. The most probable cause is that yellow–blue is the direction of the additive mixture of yellow sunlight and blue skylight. Surfaces of different orientations relative to the sun are illuminated by mixtures of the two components in varying amounts, and therefore the reflected light of a homogeneous curved surface tends to have a wider spread of color in the yellow–blue direction than any other direction. Furthermore, objects in shadow are mainly illuminated by the skylight, and those under the sun by the sunlight. Therefore, the chromaticity distribution of a natural scene is often elongated along the sunlight–skylight direction. In addition to the global lighting variation, virtually every object surface is illuminated by light of different spectral compositions, due to mutual reflections among surfaces. This variation is multiplicative in scene spectral radiances or integrated radiances [563]. Any color signal representation for natural scenes should account for the multiplicative color variation of different illuminations.

2. Effect of reflectance variation

   There are many more dark colors than bright colors in natural scenes. Studio photos may have dominant groups of white objects in the scene, but they are not typical in consumer photos or outdoor scenes. If we plot the reflectance distribution of natural objects, it is not a symmetric or uniform distribution. In fact, various studies have shown that the average reflectance is between 14 and 20%. If a linear metric is used to represent color signals (such as the 12-bit digital output of an analog-to-digital converter that is used to digitize the analog output of a CCD sensor), we will expend many of the bits in the high-reflectance region, where only a relatively small percentage of pixels occur. The number of bits used in a logarithmic metric may be more proportional to the number of objects in natural scenes, therefore many dark objects can be distinguished.

3. Effect of surface orientation and texture

Object surfaces reflect light differently in different directions. Variation of the surface orientation creates shading and shadows, and the effect is again multiplicative in scene radiances. Another effect of surface orientation on reflection is in the spectral composition. For surfaces, such as paint, plastic, and plant leaves, that are colored by pigments or dye particles embedded in transparent media, their light reflection consists of an interface reflection component (often nonselective) and a body reflection component (selective reflection). The two reflection components mix additively in varying proportions depending on the lighting and viewing geometry [560, 563]. The other effect is due to dust on object surfaces. Dust usually scatters light in a spectrally nonselective manner, resulting in an illuminant-like component that adds to the reflected light. That is why surface colors look more saturated after rain because the rain washes away the dust and greatly reduces the surface scattering. Here, the nonselective reflection component is additive in spectral composition.

4. Effect of scale and size

When images are formed in the image region corresponding to object boundaries optical blur integrates light from different object surfaces in the scene. This also happens in image regions of textures with different color elements. Grass and tree leaves are good examples. The light mixes additively before it is sensed and recorded in the color image.

From the above discussion, we can see that representing color signals in logarithmic metrics (such as log exposure) allows us to easily make adjustments for the multiplicative processes, such as light source variation and reflection distribution. On the other hand, representing color signals in linear metrics (such as exposure) allows us to deal easily with reflective color mixtures (interface and body reflections) and optical blur in the imaging process. However, neither logarithmic metrics nor linear metrics approximate perceptual brightness well. If we choose to use perceptual metrics, such as CIELAB, we lose the advantages we just mentioned. It is clear that the best color space to use depends on the application.

22.2.2   Noise statistics

Different image capture processes introduce different types of noise. Photographic films introduce grain noise, which is approximately normally distributed in film density. CCD sensors introduce dark noise due to the dark current, which is additive in image irradiance, and also pattern noise due to gain variation from pixel to pixel, which is multiplicative in image irradiance. Photon flux noise due to random quantum arrival and absorption is often characterized by a Poisson distribution. It is also additive in image irradiance. When we represent color signals, the effect of noise statistics has to be considered. If we are processing film-originated images, noise is distributed more symmetrically in logarithmic metrics. If we are processing CCD images, noise is more symmetric in a linear metric. Noise should also be considered for specific tasks to be accomplished. For example, if we would like to detect chromatic edges, the CIE (x, y) chromaticity coordinates will not be a good color space for such a purpose because the chromatic edge signal is very sentive to noise corruption in the low-light region where the (x, y) chromaticity representation has a singularity at zero. Similarly, a logarithmic metric has the same problem. As a result, color signals are best represented in a space that eliminates any such singularity [566].

22.2.3 System constraints

Cost, response time, throughput, memory size, hardware architecture, and compatibility with standards are typical system constraints that imaging scientists and engineers have to deal with when working out a practical solution. One of the major considerations is the number of bits that can be used in representing color signals. For example, a digital image is often coded with 8 bits per color per pixel. This is a very serious constraint for certain applications. For example, tone scale manipulation is difficult because stretching a tonal range may create contours in the rendered images. When choosing a color space, we have to match the digital representation to the driver signal spaces in the output device.

22.3 Color image segmentation

When we look at the world around us, our visual system readily parses the retinal images into objects and their spatial layouts. Because this is done so fast and effortlessly by our visual perception, we are often led to believe that this can also be done by a computer as a processing step preceding all other, higher-level cognitive interpretations. This step of parsing and grouping of image regions into perceptually or physically meaningful objects is called image segmentation. However, we soon find that this is probably the most difficult problem in vision. Many years of research have not resulted in much progress in the algorithms for, or the understanding of, image segmentation.

If we examine the problem further, we realize that too many of our ideas are simply too naive. The first misleading idea is that physical objects are well-defined entities and therefore, we should be able to segment the image into objects. However, this is not true. Let us consider the following questions. Is a nose an object? Is a face an object? Is a head an object? Or is an entire human being an object? How about the clothing on our body? A second misleading idea is that the color of an object is uniform and therefore it can be used to segment the image into different regions of objects. Again, this is not true, not only because surfaces rarely have uniform BRDFs, but also because they are almost never uniformly illuminated. A third misleading idea is that an object has boundaries that are distinguishable from the background. The reality is that object boudaries may be distinct physically, but they may not be detectable in the image. There are many other difficult questions like these that make image segmentation a very unrealistic goal unless we define the problem in a more manageable manner. The most important thing to clarify is that perfect segmentation in terms of grouping pixels into semantically meaningful entities (such as sky, trees, houses, roads, people, etc.) is ill defined and not achievable from a purely bottom-up, data-driven approach without using some top-down, model-driven processes. On the other hand, using colors, edges, and textures, we can often accomplish a useful partition of an image into regions that other processes can further analyze (e.g., [610, 611, 894]). For example, we can locate regions that have skin-like colors and then look for other face features in those regions. This type of low-level region partitioning will be the subject of our discussion here [571, 609]. In particular, we will examine a case in which we would like to see how we can do such a primitive image segmentation based on a color feature.[1] An input color image is partitioned into nonverlapping regions, each corresponding to a "different color". In order to quantify what we mean by "different colors", we have to define a color space to specify colors, and a distance metric to measure color differences.

22.3.1   Color space for image segmentation

As we discussed previously, the choice of a proper color space is very important and should be tightly coupled to the goal of the application. In order to make the relevant considerations more specific, we will assume that the images are digitized from photographic films. For image segmentation, our goal is to separate image regions corresponding to different physical objects (or more accurately, surfaces of different material). We are not concerned about visual color differences. Neither do we wish to convert the spectral responsivities of the imaging system to a particular standard. The sole criterion of a good color space is its usefulness in simplifying the algorithm complexity and in achieving a good image segmentation. After specifying the criteria for color space selection, we compare two major candidate spaces. We then design a physics-based distance metric for partitioning the color space according to the nearest local maximum in the color histogram.

It should be emphasized that, in all our considerations regarding various choices, the relations between the physical processes and the measured color signals should always guide our designs. Without understanding this basic rule, one may wonder why we may overlook so many well-documented color spaces and search for yet another color space. For example, dust on object surfaces usually scatters light in a spectrally nonselective manner, resulting in an illuminant-like component in addition to the reflected light. This natural cause of color variations should be discounted in the segmentation algorithm. A color space that highly distorts this signature will either degrade the algorithm performance or increase the complexity of the clustering procedures. The selection of a color space has to be based on these basic, physical considerations.

Among the factors that we mentioned in Section 22.2, we will briefly consider the following four: (1) the statistical distribution of color signals; (2) the effect of noise in color coordinates; (3) the effect of light source variations; and (4) the effect of reflectance variations.

Regarding the statistical distribution of color signals, it has been argued that the logarithm of image irradiance has a more symmetric distribution than the image irradiance itself [575, 790]. For a highly skewed signal distribution, a uniform quantization in irradiance results in too few steps in the densely populated irradiance range and too many steps in the sparsely populated range. By taking the logarithm of the image irradiance, this problem is greatly reduced. Therefore, to represent the luminance variation well, log exposure is a better metric to use than exposure.

---

[1]   This section is a shortened and slightly modified version of a paper published in *Journal of the Society of Photographic Science and Technology of Japan* [571]. Interested readers should read the paper for more details and the related application.

When considering the effect of noise in color coordinates, we have to remember that noise in the color signals broadens a single point in a color space into a volume. If noise is isotropic in the chosen color space, the volume is a sphere around the true color point. Partitioning in such a space will have an equal probability of error in all directions. Noise in images from film origination is additive and more symmetric in density space (proportional to log exposure) than in exposure space.

Regarding the effect of light source variations, we should first note that the spectral composition of the light reflected from an object surface changes under different illuminations. For different color spaces, the change of color coordinates takes place in different forms. For a given set of objects, some color spaces preserve the geometric relations (such as angle and distance) between the different colors better than other spaces, when the objects are illuminated with different light sources. For example, in the CIE chromaticity diagram, changing the illuminant (say, from illuminant A to D65) will cause a large geometrical distortion in the relative positions of the chromaticity coordinates. For image segmentation, it is desirable to use a color space that preserves the geometric relations under different illuminations, so that the segmentation results are less dependent on the illumination.

With regard to the effect of reflectance variations, we need to consider the fact that the radiance and spectral content of the light reflected from an object surface depend on the lighting and viewing geometry. As the surface orientation changes, the diffuse (body reflection) component of the light reflected from an object often varies in radiance but not in chromaticity [560, 562, 563]. This is one of the reasons why we see a uniformly-painted, curved object as having gradual shading but constant "color". The specular reflection (interface reflection), on the other hand, often dilutes the saturation of the object color. A color space that provides simple geometric relations for additive mixtures of light is a better choice for segmentation because it is easier to design the segmentation metric to accommodate the desaturation effect of object colors due to the specular reflection.

22.3.2 Comparison of linear and logarithmic spaces

The four factors discussed above do not by themselves uniquely define the possible choices of color spaces. We have to establish other desirable features before we can finally narrow down the choices to a few candidate spaces for comparison. The first feature is that the color space should have a luminance component[2] that represents the intensity variation of the light. If the light illuminating a surface is stronger or weaker because of a change in lighting geometry such as surface orientation, we would like to be able to easily discount that variation in our segmentation. Furthermore, if this intensity variation affects *only* the luminance component, we can simply give less weight to the luminance component without having to simultaneously adjust the other two chrominance components. Thus the second feature is that the two chrominance components should be intensity-invariant.

Among the few color spaces that possess the two desirable features, we will mainly compare two of the most popular: the linear (Y, x, y) and the logarithmic (L, s, t) spaces.

---

[2] The luminance here relates to the magnitude of radiant exposure. It is not meant to be the luminance as defined in photometry.

Comparison between these two spaces is done according to the four factors listed in the previous section.

Let r, g, b be the three (red, green, blue) color signals (image irradiances or exposures), and R, G, B be the logarithms of r, g, b, respectively. For images scanned from film, integral densities are the quantities that can be conveniently measured. In order to get the log exposure, we have to convert the film density through the D–$\log H$ curves. Films all have D–$\log H$ curves that have very small slopes around the film $D_{\min}$ and $D_{\max}$, where a small density variation is thus translated into a large difference in log exposure. In order to avoid greatly amplifying noise around these toe and shoulder density ranges, we convert the film density to "equivalent" log exposure by dividing the density by the average gamma of the film. We will refer to the "equivalent" log exposure simply as the log exposure.

The two color spaces are defined as follows:

$$Y = \alpha r + \beta g + \gamma b,$$
$$x = \frac{r}{r+g+b}, \tag{22.1}$$
$$y = \frac{g}{r+g+b}$$

and

$$L = \frac{1}{\sqrt{3}}(R + G + B) = \frac{1}{\sqrt{3}}(\log r + \log g + \log b),$$
$$s = \frac{1}{\sqrt{2}}(R - B) = \frac{1}{\sqrt{2}}(\log r - \log b), \tag{22.2}$$
$$t = \frac{1}{\sqrt{6}}(R - 2G + B) = \frac{1}{\sqrt{6}}(\log r - 2\log g + \log b).$$

Both spaces consist of one "luminance" component and two "chrominance" components. Furthermore, the chrominance components in both spaces are intensity-invariant, i.e., they remain constant when the light source intensity is changed by any arbitrary, nonzero factor. Both spaces have singularity points that can be dealt with by setting small values to some constant. In photographic applications, these singularity points are not of any practical importance, because films have minimum densities that serve as the threshold for small signal values. The (Y, x, y) space is similar to the CIE luminance–chromaticity space [1053]. The (L, s, t) space is traditionally called the T-space in photographic applications. Similar spaces had been used before [727], but it is not clear if the RGB in those spaces are linear or log. The use of log exposure instead of film density makes the segmentation algorithm independent of film gamma.

The chromatic axes for the (L, s, t) space are chosen so that the s component approximately represents the illuminant variations (daylight to tungsten light). The three components are mutually orthogonal and are normalized to have unit vector length. The normalization to unity is to make the noise variances of the three components approximately equal. (In practice, there is more noise in the blue signal, and it may be desirable to adjust the coefficients accordingly.) Other considerations, such as aligning the color vectors with the principal components of the covariance matrix of the color signals, or with the opponent processes of human color encoding, lead to coefficients similar to those in (L, s, t) space [565, 569].

The first consideration, of the statistical distribution of color signals, favors the use of (L, s, t) space because both theory [790] and empirical data [16, 735] show that the statistical distribution of color signals is more symmetrical in log space than in linear space.

For images originated from film, the second consideration, of noise, favors the (L, s, t) space because film grain noise, is more symmetrically distributed in log exposure space. (However, the choice for images captured with CCD sensors is not as easy because the CCD noise distribution is more symmetric in the linear exposure space [566].)

To evaluate the effects of light source and reflectance variations on the color coordinates, we have chosen eight spectral samples recommended by the CIE for evaluating the color rendering power of different illuminants [620]. Skin and a green plant leaf are also included because of their frequent appearance in consumer images, making a total of ten samples of varying hues and saturations. The relative spectral reflectance curves are shown in Fig. 7.7 As can be seen, these ten samples represent wide variations of different spectral reflectances.

For the effect of illuminant variation, the comparison is done by plotting the color coordinates of these ten samples under D_{65} and tungsten illuminants (the tungsten illuminant is a blackbody radiator at 2856 K) and checking the distortions with and without a von Kries type color normalization ([1053, p. 431]). We use a consumer color negative film as the hypothetical image sensing and recording medium, whose spectral sensitivities are shown in Fig. 22.1. Figure 22.2 shows the color coordinates, in the two color spaces, of the ten samples under the two illuminants. As can be clearly seen, the ten points undergo a fairly simple translational shift in the (s, t) space, but a highly complex distortion in the (x, y) space.

For the effect of specular reflection, the (x, y) chromaticity space is known to be quite simple: the color coordinates of additive mixtures of the diffuse and specular components of the reflected light fall on a straight line. This is a very good property for image segmentation because it is very simple to define a distance metric in the space to discount the color desaturation effect due to specular reflection. Mathematically, one can prove that the collinear property does not hold in the (s, t) space. However, the deviation from that

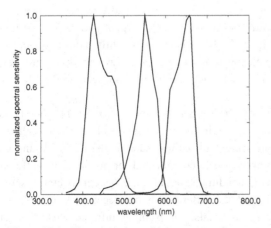

Figure 22.1. The spectral sensitivity curves of a consumer color negative film.

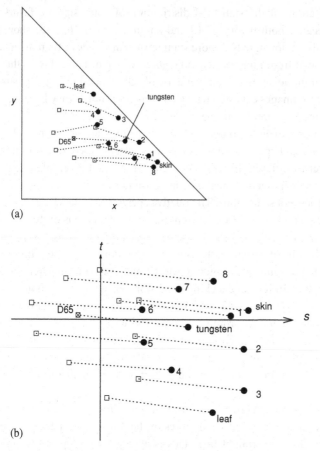

(a)

(b)

Figure 22.2. The color coordinates of reflectance samples under different illuminants: (a) is the CIE chromaticity diagram; (b) the (s, t) chromaticity diagram.

property becomes large only when the color is very saturated. If we add a specular reflection component of 10% to the ten samples, i.e., we increase the spectral reflectance value 0.1 at all wavelengths, their color coordinates are shifted convergently to the illuminant point in both spaces, as can be seen in Fig. 22.3. (Note that the large shift in the color coordinates of the green leaf is due to its relatively low reflectance at most wavelengths before the specular component is added.) Even in the (s, t) space, the lines do not seem to deviate much from the illuminant point.

Judging from the above comparison, we conclude that the (L, s, t) space is the better choice for segmenting images of film origin. We have not considered the so-called uniform color spaces or others based on perceptual scaling, such as the CIELUV and CIELAB, for two reasons. (1) They are unnecessarily complicated for images from different imaging systems. Not only the viewing conditions, but also the system spectral responsivities, have to be specified. (2) The perceptual difference is not necessarily a better metric for separating two physically different materials. For example, infrared sensing is very good for segmenting hot objects from cold ones, without any corresponding visual perception signals.

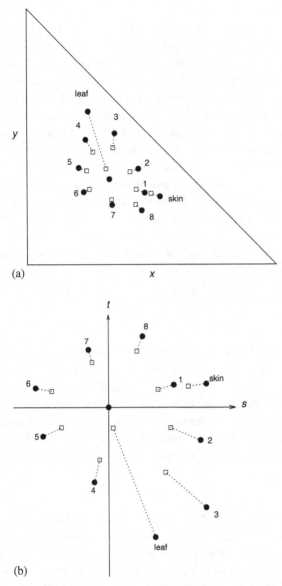

(a)

(b)

Figure 22.3. The color coordinates of reflectance samples with and without 10% specular (interface) reflection component: (a) the CIE chromaticity diagram; (b) the (s,t) chromaticity diagram.

22.3.3 Method for partitioning the color space

Once we have decided on a proper color space to use for image segmentation, we can compute the color histogram of the input image. The following describes a method of color image segmentation by color histogram partitioning. Segmentation by partitioning the color space is a vector quantization technique. However, the primary concern of segmentation is not coding efficiency, but rather the separation of image regions that correspond to physically different objects. The optical properties of the surface material and the light reflection processes are the key considerations.

General outline of the method

The algorithm proposed here is called "k-mode clustering". A three-dimension color histogram in (L, s, t) space is formed from the input color image. In order to minimize the size of the histogram, we can experiment with many combinations of quantization intervals for L, s, and t. It is found that suitable values are 0.08 for L and 0.02 for s and t. It should be pointed out that the quantization levels are related to the image digitization and the color distance metric. The values used were empirically determined from images that had been digitized to 8 bits in 0.01 log exposure with a gamma of 0.63–0.8. For a gamma of 0.63, typical of consumer color negative films, a digital increment of 1 in the green code value corresponds to an increment of 0.00916 in L, 0.0112 in s, and 0.01296 in t. It is better to choose quantization intervals greater than these minimum increments so that the histogram dose not have gaps due to image digitization. Using the selected quantization intervals, it is found that 32 bins for the L-axis and 100 bins for the s- and t-axes are sufficient to cover most color gamuts in the film.

The three-dimensional color histogram is first smoothed by a $3 \times 3 \times 3$ convolution kernel with the following coefficients:

$$\begin{matrix} 0 & 1 & 0 \\ 1 & 2 & 1 \\ 0 & 1 & 0 \end{matrix} \qquad \begin{matrix} 1 & 2 & 1 \\ 2 & 4 & 2 \\ 1 & 2 & 1 \end{matrix} \qquad \begin{matrix} 0 & 1 & 0 \\ 1 & 2 & 1 \\ 0 & 1 & 0 \end{matrix}. \qquad (22.3)$$

The smoothed image is divided by 28, the sum of all the coefficients in the smoothing kernel. The local maxima (peaks) in the smoothed histogram are then detected. All the peaks that contain more than one pixel are chosen (i.e., if a peak contains only one pixel, it is considered as noise). We then partition the entire color space into separate volumes (one for each peak) such that each point in a volume has a shorter distance to the peak in that volume than to any other peaks. The distance metric will be discussed below. Each pixel in the input image is then labeled according to the volume that contains its color.

22.3.4 The distance metric

Let us consider a curved surface of an object. Because the angle between the surface normal and the light source direction varies along the surface, the reflected radiance changes accordingly, creating gradual shading. A segmentation algorithm should avoid segmenting the image region of the shaded surface into many pieces due to their difference in luminance. If one carries the argument further, one may conclude that luminance should not be used at all, because it will fragment the image region that corresponds to a curved surface. However, there are good reasons to incorporate luminance in the color segmentation:

- Colors that are similar in chrominance but quite different in luminance are not uncommon in images, e.g., hair and skin, brown paint and red brick, gray sky and white snow, etc. Although the hue and saturation may not be identical, digitization and image noise reduce our capability to differentiate them purely on chrominance alone.
- A uniform, curved surface, half in the shade and half in the sun, is illuminated by light of different spectral content in the two halves. They literally have two different colors and will be segmented into two halves on chrominance alone. Introducing the luminance attribute in the segmentation does not further degrade the results in this

case. In fact, surface areas that differ much in luminance are almost always illuminated by light of different spectral contents.

It is true that introducing luminance into the segmentation increases the risk of breaking up an image region that corresponds to one object surface, but empirical results show that this is a risk well worth taking.

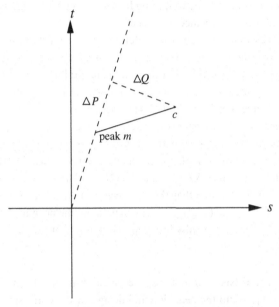

Figure 22.4. The decomposition of the distance into a "saturation" component, ΔP, and a "hue" component, ΔQ. Point c represents a color in (s, t) space and m represents the center of a color cluster (i.e., a local peak in the three-dimensional color histogram).

In the color space, a color segmentation algorithm attempts to partition the whole space into volumes that hopefully correspond to colors of different objects. The metric for partitioning should thus be coarser in the luminance component than in the chrominance components. Furthermore, the metric should also be coarser in color saturation than in hue, in order to reduce the effect of specular reflection.

If "hue" and "saturation" are to be used by the distance metric, we will need an estimate of the neutral point in the chrominance space. Methods for estimating the neutral point have been discussed in Section 18.5 and we will not discuss them here. Suffice it to say that a rough estimate, such as the average of the whole image, is often better than taking a default value. Moreover, the distance measure should not be too sensitive to the error in estimating the neutral point. From the above considerations and experiments on many images, the following distance metric was found to be quite satisfactory:

$$\text{distance}(c, m) = 2.0 * (\Delta L)^2_{c-m} + 0.5 * (\Delta P)^2_{c-m} + (\Delta Q)^2_{c-m}, \qquad (22.4)$$

where $(\Delta L)_{c-m}$, $(\Delta P)_{c-m}$, and $(\Delta Q)_{c-m}$ are the differences, between a color c and a peak m, in luminance, "saturation", and "hue", respectively, *after* they have been quantized into histogram bins (see Fig. 22.4). It should be noted that the above coefficients are dependent on the quantization intervals used in forming the three-dimensional color histogram. The definitions of $(\Delta P)_{c-m}$ and $(\Delta Q)_{c-m}$ are as follows. If we connect each peak with the neutral point, we form one radial line for each peak. The distance from any point, c, to a peak, m, is decomposed into two components: one parallel and the other perpendicular to the radial line of that peak. The parallel component is $(\Delta P)_{c-m}$ and the perpendicular, $(\Delta Q)_{c-m}$. Remember that the luminance quantization is much coarser than that of the two chrominance components (0.08 vs. 0.02). The weighting factor 2.0 of $(\Delta L)^2_{c-m}$ in Eq. (22.4) still greatly reduces the effect of the luminance difference.

There are a few alternatives that one can use to define "hue" and "saturation". For example, one can use hue angle and relative saturation. We have chosen not to use hue angle, because it is very sensitive to the estimation error in the neutral point, and not to use relative saturation, because, in principle, the (L, s, t) space does not have a finite support. This is not to say that the distance metric in Eq. (22.4) is best in any sense. We have not been able to formulate its definition on a firmer theoretical ground.

As readers may have noticed, the distance metric in Eq. (22.4) is not symmetric with respect to c and m, i.e., if c, instead of m, is the peak, the two components, $(\Delta P)_{m-c}$ and $(\Delta Q)_{m-c}$, are, in general, different from $(\Delta P)_{c-m}$ and $(\Delta Q)_{c-m}$. The reason we chose to define the metric as shown in Fig. 22.4, rather than the other way, is mainly for computational speed. In order to compute $(\Delta P)_{c-m}$ and $(\Delta Q)_{m-c}$, one can prestore the normalized vectors from the neutral point to all the peaks (typically less than 64 in number).

Remarks

An image segmentation algorithm based on color space partitioning has been described above. Much thought has been put into the selection and design of the color space with a proper distance metric, all based on considerations of the physical principles underlying the color imaging processes. The algorithm was designed to be simple and fast, while tolerating some potential segmentation errors that could only be dealt with by reasoning in both the spatial and color domains at the same time [609]. For example, boundary pixels should be classified with a higher probability of being in one of the neighboring segments, rather than equally likely to be in all the segments, near or far. Another obvious improvement can be achieved by using edge detection results [566] for delineating the segment boundaries.

22.4 Color gradient

Color changes from one point to another in an image. For many applications, it is desirable to detect such color changes, so that image operations can be adjusted accordingly. For example, in smoothing out image noise, we would also like to preserve the sharpness of edges. The change in color (vector) is called the color gradient. It is a measure similar to the luminance (scalar) gradient (in irradiance) for a monochromatic image. Let us look at how we can define the color gradient as a generalization of the luminance gradient.[3]

---

[3]   This and the following sections are a shortened and modified version of a paper published in *IEEE Transactions on Signal Processing* [567]. Readers interested in more details should consult the paper.

A monochromatic image, $f(x, y)$, is a scalar field defined on a two-dimensional domain. A color image, $\mathbf{f}(x, y) = [r(x, y), g(x, y), b(x, y)]^T$, is a vector field, again defined on a two-dimensional domain. Of course, images can be formed in more than two-dimensional space (such as MRI volume scan images), and the attributes can be more than just three colors. In general, an image can be defined as a vector field which maps an n-dimensional (spatial) space to an m-dimensional (color or attribute) space. The derivatives of a vector field (the vector gradient) can be defined as follows.

Let $\mathbf{f}: \mathbf{S} \to \mathbf{R}^m$ be a vector field, $V_{n \to m}$, defined on $\mathbf{S}$, a subset of $\mathbf{R}^n$. Let f_k denote the kth component of $\mathbf{f}$. If $\mathbf{f}$ is a three-color image, then f_1, f_2, and f_3 represent the red, green, and blue components of the image. It can be shown [28, pp. 269–273] that the first order Taylor expansion takes the form:

$$\mathbf{f}(\mathbf{x} + \mathbf{a}) = \mathbf{f}(\mathbf{x}) + [\mathbf{f}'(\mathbf{x})](\mathbf{a}) + \|\mathbf{a}\| \mathbf{e}(\mathbf{x}, \mathbf{a}), \tag{22.5}$$

where $\mathbf{a}$, $\mathbf{x}$ are $n \times 1$ vectors, $\mathbf{e}$ is an $m \times 1$ vector, $\mathbf{e}(\mathbf{x}, \mathbf{a}) \to \mathbf{0}$ as $\mathbf{a} \to \mathbf{0}$, and $\mathbf{f}'(\mathbf{x})$ is an $m \times n$ matrix $\mathbf{D}(\mathbf{x})$:

$$\mathbf{f}'(\mathbf{x}) = \mathbf{D}(\mathbf{x}) = \begin{bmatrix} D_1 f_1(\mathbf{x}) & D_2 f_1(\mathbf{x}) & \cdots & D_n f_1(\mathbf{x}) \\ D_1 f_2(\mathbf{x}) & D_2 f_2(\mathbf{x}) & \cdots & D_n f_2(\mathbf{x}) \\ \vdots & \vdots & & \vdots \\ D_1 f_m(\mathbf{x}) & D_2 f_m(\mathbf{x}) & \cdots & D_n f_m(\mathbf{x}) \end{bmatrix}, \tag{22.6}$$

where $D_j f_k = (\partial f_k / \partial x_j)$ is the jth partial derivative of the kth component of $\mathbf{f}$.

If one travels out from the point $\mathbf{x}$ with a unit vector $\mathbf{u}$ in the spatial domain, $d = \sqrt{\mathbf{u}^T \mathbf{D}^T \mathbf{D} \mathbf{u}}$ is the corresponding distance traveled in the color (attribute) domain. It can be proved (see, e.g., [26, pp. 453–6]) that the vector that maximizes d is the eigenvector of the matrix $\mathbf{D}^T \mathbf{D}$ that corresponds to its largest eigenvalue. The square root of the largest eigenvalue and its corresponding eigenvector are, for a vector field, the equivalents of the gradient magnitude and the gradient direction of a scalar field. We will call them the gradient of a vector field, or the vector gradient. Numerically, it is often better to use singular value decomposition to determine these quantities because it is more stable [323]. The largest singular value of the matrix $\mathbf{D}$ is then the gradient magnitude, and the direction of the corresponding right singular vector is the gradient direction.

22.5   Color edge detection

Edge detection is a very widely used operation in image processing and computer vision, but what do we mean by edges? A general definition may be that they correspond to reflectance, illumination, or object boundaries. However, even this general definition does not completely describe our intuitive concept of edges. For example, most people will agree that a nose is an object on our face (that is why it has a name). How do we define the boundary of the nose on a face? Careful thinking along these lines tells us that as long as our mathematical definition of edges does not cover our intuitive concept of edges, we cannot expect to develop a "perfect" edge detector. In fact, we may begin to question whether we are asking the right questions. Having pointed out the negative aspects of this topic, we should also look at some of the positive things that we have learned from many years of research in edge detection.

At least, three definitions of edges for monochromatic images have been proposed: (a) edges are where the rate of change in image irradiance is a local maximum along the gradient direction (e.g., [161, 380, 635]); (b) edges are where the scene radiances (or their derivatives) are discontinuous (e.g., [559]); and (c) edges are boudaries where the statistical distribution of image irradiances changes from one side to another (e.g., [417, 419, 524]). All these three definitions are quite reasonable, but they lead to different methods and thus different results of edge detection. Here we will use definition (a) and show how we can generalize it to color images.

The most straightforward generalization of color edge detection is to treat each color independently. Edges are detected in each of the three color components and then combined together to give a final edge map according to some proposed rules [245, 435, 710, 798]. A typical color gradient is computed as the square root of the sum of the squares of the three scalar gradient mangnitudes: $\sqrt{\|\nabla r\|^2 + \|\nabla g\|^2 + \|\nabla b\|^2}$. As for the direction of a color edge, the rule chooses either the direction that corresponds to the maximum component or a weighted average of the three gradient directions. Instead of separately computing the scalar gradient for each color component, we can treat a color image as a vector field and compute the vector gradient of the vector field to detect the local maximum gradient [259, 567, 720]. It will be shown shortly that the vector gradient approach is slightly less sensitive to noise than the approach that uses the sum of the squares of the scalar gradients.

22.5.1   Derivative of a color image

We will now give a closed form expression for a vector gradient of a color image $V_{2\rightarrow3}$ that maps a two-dimensional (spatial) space (x, y) to a three-dimensional (color) space (r, g, b). The matrix $\mathbf{D}$ can be written as

$$\mathbf{D} = \begin{bmatrix} \partial r/\partial x & \partial r/\partial y \\ \partial g/\partial x & \partial g/\partial y \\ \partial b/\partial x & \partial b/\partial y \end{bmatrix}. \tag{22.7}$$

Let us define the following variables to simplify the expression of the final solution:

$$p = \left(\frac{\partial r}{\partial x}\right)^2 + \left(\frac{\partial g}{\partial x}\right)^2 + \left(\frac{\partial b}{\partial x}\right)^2, \tag{22.8}$$

$$t = \left(\frac{\partial r}{\partial x}\right)\left(\frac{\partial r}{\partial y}\right) + \left(\frac{\partial g}{\partial x}\right)\left(\frac{\partial g}{\partial y}\right) + \left(\frac{\partial b}{\partial x}\right)\left(\frac{\partial b}{\partial y}\right), \tag{22.9}$$

$$q = \left(\frac{\partial r}{\partial y}\right)^2 + \left(\frac{\partial g}{\partial y}\right)^2 + \left(\frac{\partial b}{\partial y}\right)^2. \tag{22.10}$$

The matrix $\mathbf{D}^T\mathbf{D}$ becomes

$$\mathbf{D}^T\mathbf{D} = \begin{bmatrix} p & t \\ t & q \end{bmatrix}, \tag{22.11}$$

and its largest eigenvalue λ is

$$\lambda = \frac{1}{2}\left[p + q + \sqrt{(p+q)^2 - 4(pq - t^2)}\right]. \tag{22.12}$$

The gradient direction requires a little careful examination. In the general case, the direction is along the vector $[t, \lambda - p]^T$, which is the eigenvector corresponding to the eigenvalue λ. However, if $t = 0$ and $\lambda = p$, then $[t, \lambda - p]^T$ becomes a zero vector, and we have to use $[\lambda - q, t]^T$. The remaining case to be considered is when both vectors are zero vectors. In this case, $\mathbf{u}^T\mathbf{D}^T\mathbf{Du}$ is locally a spherical surface, and all vector directions are equivalent.

It is interesting to note that

$$pq - t^2 = \left(\frac{\partial r}{\partial x}\frac{\partial g}{\partial y} - \frac{\partial g}{\partial x}\frac{\partial r}{\partial y}\right)^2 + \left(\frac{\partial g}{\partial x}\frac{\partial b}{\partial y} - \frac{\partial b}{\partial x}\frac{\partial g}{\partial y}\right)^2 + \left(\frac{\partial b}{\partial x}\frac{\partial r}{\partial y} - \frac{\partial r}{\partial x}\frac{\partial b}{\partial y}\right)^2. \tag{22.13}$$

Therefore, $pq - t^2 \geq 0$, and $p + q \geq \lambda$. Since

$$p + q = \left(\frac{\partial r}{\partial x}\right)^2 + \left(\frac{\partial r}{\partial y}\right)^2 + \left(\frac{\partial g}{\partial x}\right)^2 + \left(\frac{\partial g}{\partial y}\right)^2 + \left(\frac{\partial b}{\partial x}\right)^2 + \left(\frac{\partial b}{\partial y}\right)^2 \tag{22.14}$$

$$= \|\nabla r\|^2 + \|\nabla g\|^2 + \|\nabla b\|^2, \tag{22.15}$$

it follows that sum of the squares of scalar gradients $p + q$ is always greater than or equal to λ, the vector gradient squared. This is true even for the case of a general vector field, $\mathbf{V}_{n \to m}$, as can be seen by the following simple proof. The sum of the squares of scalar gradients is the trace of the matrix $\mathbf{D}^T\mathbf{D}$. Since $\mathbf{D}^T\mathbf{D}$ is symmetric and positive semi-definite, it has all real, nonnegative eigenvalues. The trace of $\mathbf{D}^T\mathbf{D}$ is also equal to the sum of its eigenvalues. Since the eigenvalues are all nonnegative, the trace is at least as large as the largest eigenvalue. But the largest eigenvalue is the square of the magnitude of the vector gradient. Therefore the vector gradient squared is never larger than the sum of the squares of scalar gradients, and can be as small as $1/n$ of the latter.

In summary, when using the vector gradient in boundary detection, the vector gradient is about the same as the scalar gradient for the signal, but its value becomes smaller than the scalar gradient for the noise. The effect is a net increase in the signal-to-noise ratio for edge detection. This gain comes from the fact that signals of different color components are more correlated than noise. We can therefore conclude that, for a typical color image, the vector gradient is less sensitive to noise than the scalar gradient.

22.5.2 Statistics of noise in a boundary detector

To characterize the noise behavior in a boundary detector, we have to limit our discussion to two-dimensional images to reduce the complexity of the solutions. The images can have an arbitrary number of attributes (colors). Noise is assumed to be identically and independently distributed in all the attribute components. We also have to choose a particular form of boundary detector in order to analyze the noise statistics. For this purpose, a simplified version of Canny's edge detector [161] is implemented with the following steps:

1. The input image is smoothed by a Gaussian filter with standard deviation of σ_b.
2. Partial derivatives with respect to x and y are computed by the following two masks:

$$
\begin{array}{ccc}
-1 & 0 & 1 \\
-1 & 0 & 1, \\
-1 & 0 & 1
\end{array}
\qquad
\begin{array}{ccc}
1 & 1 & 1 \\
0 & 0 & 0. \\
-1 & -1 & -1
\end{array}
\tag{22.16}
$$

3. The amplitudes and directions of gradients are computed from the partial derivatives.
4. The points that are the local gradient maxima along their gradient directions are marked as candidate boundary points.
5. The candidate boundary points that have gradient amplitudes greater than a low threshold, T_l, and are connected to at least one point that has a gradient amplitude greater than a high threshold, T_h, are marked as the boundary points. This is Canny's thresholding with hysteresis [161, p. 54].

The choice of the two thresholds, T_l and T_h, is important for the boundary detector. Too low a threshold will produce too many false edges, while too high a threshold will throw away too many true edges. In order to quantify the trade-off, we have to characterize the noise behavior of the boundary detector. In the following, we will assume that the noise at each point of the image is stationary, white (independent), Gaussian noise $N(x, y)$, with mean $= 0$ and variance $= \sigma_n^2$. We also assume that all the attributes have the same amount of noise. If this is not true, each attribute has to be weighted with the inverse of its noise standard deviation before it is combined with other attributes.

After the image smoothing in step 1, the smoothed noise $P(x, y)$ is no longer white. Its autocorrelation function $R_P(m, n)$ can be approximated as follows [567]:

$$
R_P(m, n) = E[P(m, n)P(0, 0)] \approx \frac{\sigma_n^2}{4\pi\sigma_b^2} \exp\left(-\frac{m^2 + n^2}{4\sigma_b^2}\right).
\tag{22.17}
$$

This approximation is very good for $\sigma_b \geq 1.0$ pixel, but quickly becomes unacceptable when σ_b is less than 0.7. In practice, for σ_b less than 1.0 pixel, the discrete Gaussian mask becomes a very undersampled representation of a Gaussian filter, and should not be used without careful analysis. The partial derivatives $P_x = \partial P/\partial x$ and $P_y = \partial P/\partial y$ of $P(x, y)$, as computed by step 2, can be shown to be independent of each other, and their variances are given by:

$$
\sigma_d^2 = \sigma_{P_x}^2 = \sigma_{P_y}^2 = 6R_P(0, 0) + 8R_P(1, 0) - 2R_P(2, 0) - 8R_P(2, 1) - 4R_P(2, 2).
\tag{22.18}
$$

Substituting Eq. (22.17) into Eq. (22.18), we arrive at the following relation:

$$
\sigma_d^2 \approx \frac{\sigma_n^2}{4\pi\sigma_b^2}(6 + 8c - 2c^4 - 8c^5 - 4c^8),
\tag{22.19}
$$

where $c = \exp[-1/(4\sigma_b^2)]$. When σ_b is large, $c \approx 1 - 1/(4\sigma_b^2)$, and

$$
\sigma_d \approx \frac{3\sigma_n}{\sqrt{2\pi}\sigma_b^2}.
\tag{22.20}
$$

Smoothing with a Gaussian filter of size σ_b thus reduces the noise standard deviation of the partial derivative by a factor of approximately $1/\sigma_b^2$. If we increase the size of the smoothing filter by a factor of 2, the noise is reduced by a factor of 4. Equations (22.19) and (22.20) are the quantitative relations we need to determine how much smoothing we need for step boundary detection. Since the partial derivatives, such as P_x and P_y, are linear combinations of Gaussian random variables, they are themselves normally distributed. We now have all the information needed to derive the distribution of the scalar gradient.

Let the amplitude r_s of the scalar gradient of a vector field, $V_{n\to m}$, which maps $(x_1, \ldots, x_n)$ to $(u_1, \ldots, u_m)$, be defined as

$$r_s = \sqrt{\sum_{i=1}^{n} \sum_{j=1}^{m} \left(\frac{\partial u_j}{\partial x_i} \right)^2}. \tag{22.21}$$

The distribution of r_s^2 is a χ^2 distribution, and the distribution of r_s is

$$p(r_s) = \frac{1}{2^{k/2-1}\Gamma(k/2)\sigma_d} \left(\frac{r_s}{\sigma_d} \right)^{k-1} \exp\left(-\frac{r_s^2}{2\sigma_d^2} \right) \quad \text{for } r_s \geq 0, \tag{22.22}$$

where $k = mn$ and σ_d^2 is the variance of the partial derivative, which, for $n = 2$, can be computed by Eq. (22.18). The peak of the distribution occurs at $r_s = \sqrt{k-1}\sigma_d$.

Let r_v be the amplitude of the vector gradient of a vector field, $V_{2\to m}$, which maps (x_1, x_2) to $(u_1, \ldots, u_m)$. The statistical distribution of r_v turns out to be too complicated for us to find a closed form expression. We therefore search for an empirical equation to describe it. First, we show that in Eq. (22.12), the value of $(pq - t^2)$ is statistically a fraction of $(p+q)^2$:

$$E[pq - t^2] = \frac{1}{2}E\left[\sum_{i=1}^{m} \sum_{j=1,j\neq i}^{m} \left(\frac{\partial u_i}{\partial x_1}\frac{\partial u_j}{\partial x_2} - \frac{\partial u_j}{\partial x_1}\frac{\partial u_i}{\partial x_2} \right)^2 \right]$$

$$= \frac{1}{2}\sum_{i=1}^{m} \sum_{j=1,j\neq i}^{m} \left\{ E\left[\left(\frac{\partial u_i}{\partial x_1}\frac{\partial u_j}{\partial x_2} \right)^2 \right] - 2E\left[\frac{\partial u_i}{\partial x_1}\frac{\partial u_j}{\partial x_2}\frac{\partial u_j}{\partial x_1}\frac{\partial u_i}{\partial x_2} \right] \right.$$

$$\left. + E\left[\left(\frac{\partial u_j}{\partial x_1}\frac{\partial u_i}{\partial x_2} \right)^2 \right] \right\}$$

$$= \frac{1}{2}\sum_{i=1}^{m} \sum_{j=1,j\neq i}^{m} (\sigma_d^4 - 0 + \sigma_d^4)$$

$$= m(m-1)\sigma_d^4. \tag{22.23}$$

Since $p + q = \sum_{i=1}^{m}[(\partial u_i/\partial x_1)^2 + (\partial u_i/\partial x_2)^2]$ has a χ^2 distribution with $2m$ degrees of freedom, its mean is $2m\sigma_d^2$ and its variance is $4m\sigma_d^4$. We have

$$E[(p+q)^2] = 4m\sigma_d^4 + (2m\sigma_d^2)^2 = 4m(m+1)\sigma_d^4. \tag{22.24}$$

The expected value of $4(pq - t^2)$ is the fraction $(m-1)/(m+1)$ of the expected value of $(p+q)^2$. For $m = 3$, this fraction is 0.5. Now we can roughly rewrite Eq. (22.12) in the following way:

$$r_v = \sqrt{\lambda} = \left\{ \frac{1}{2} \left[p + q + \sqrt{(p+q)^2 - 4(pq - t^2)} \right] \right\}^{1/2}$$

$$\approx \frac{\sqrt{p+q}}{\sqrt{2}} \left(1 + \sqrt{1 - \frac{m-1}{m+1}} \right)^{1/2}$$

$$= \frac{r_s}{\sqrt{2}} \left(1 + \sqrt{\frac{2}{m+1}} \right)^{1/2}. \tag{22.25}$$

Assuming that the above approximation is true for all integer values of m, the surprising conclusion is that, even by measuring more and more attributes, the spread of the noise vector gradient cannot be reduced beyond $1/\sqrt{2}$ of that of the noise scalar gradient, and the return diminishes fairly quickly. For $m = 2$, $r_v \approx 0.953 r_s$, and for $m = 3$, $r_v \approx 0.924 r_s$. Therefore, we might expect that the amplitude of the vector gradient, r_v, would have a distribution very similar in shape to that of the scalar gradient, r_s, with the scale reduced by a fraction. Experimental results confirm that this is indeed a very good approximation. Thus, we have a numerically predictable advantage of reduced noise sensitivity when we use the vector gradient instead of the scalar gradient. However, the advantage is not large.

22.5.3   Detection of a step boundary

As we discussed in the above, a step boundary in an image corrupted with Gaussian white noise can be effectively detected by prefiltering the noise before computing the image gradient. Prefiltering is done by using a low-pass Gaussian filter. Smoothing with a low-pass filter has two major effects on the computation of gradient:

* It reduces the noise amplitude more than the signal amplitude, and thus increases the signal-to-noise ratio in the computation of gradient amplitude.
* It reduces the noise-induced angular spread in the gradient direction, and produces a more reliable estimate of directional angle.

Gradient amplitude
A two-dimensional step edge with step size A, after smoothing by a Gaussian filter of size σ_b, becomes a blurred edge with the following profile:

$$f(x) = \frac{A}{\sqrt{2\pi}\,\sigma_b} \int_{-\infty}^{x} \exp\left(\frac{-t^2}{2\sigma_b^2} \right) dt. \tag{22.26}$$

Its gradient amplitude is

$$\|\nabla f(x)\| = \frac{A}{\sqrt{2\pi}\,\sigma_b} \exp\left(\frac{-x^2}{2\sigma_b^2} \right). \tag{22.27}$$

The maximum gradient of a step edge is thus reduced by a factor proportional to σ_b^{-1} after the smoothing. For the noise, the reduction factor is proportional to σ_b^{-2} (as shown in Eq. (22.20)). Therefore, in principle, it is possible to apply a proper smoothing filter to increase the signal-to-noise ratio to any desirable amount for detecting an ideal step boundary (even if the step signal is arbitrarily small compared with the noise!). In practice, one never has an ideal step edge with an infinite extent of flat regions on both sides of the edge. Furthermore, extensive Gaussian smoothing distorts the underlying edge structures in image irradiances, especially around the corners. The smallest size of the smoothing kernel which gives an acceptable performance requirement in terms of detection errors is always preferred over a larger smoothing-kernel size. For ideal step edges, we know the statistical distributions of both the pure noise and the signal-plus-noise, therefore it is possible to calculate the statistical errors in this simple case of edge detection [567].

Gradient direction

Another interesting effect of the smoothing is on the distribution of the directional angle of the gradient. We will first derive the angular distribution of the gradient directions along a step boundary for the special case ($m = 1$) in which the vector field has only one color (e.g., a monochromatic image). It is shown that the angular spread is reduced as the amount of smoothing is increased. We then look at the case in which there are three colors in the vector field ($m = 3$). The distributions show the same trend of reduced angular spread for increased smoothing. Furthermore, for the same amount of smoothing, increasing m, the number of colors, also reduces the angular spread.

For a vector field $V_{2 \to 1}$, the vector gradient is the same as the scalar gradient. Assume that a step boundary with step size A is oriented vertically and the additive Gaussian white noise has a standard deviation of σ_n. Let the smoothed image be E and its partial derivatives E_x and E_y. As we mentioned before, E_x and E_y are independent Gaussian random fields with the same standard deviation, σ_d. The mean of E_y is zero, while that of E_x is given by

$$\mu = \frac{3A}{\sqrt{2\pi}\sigma_b}\left[1 + \exp\left(\frac{-1}{2\sigma_b^2}\right)\right].$$

The angular distribution of the gradient direction along the step boundary can be determined by performing a change of variables to polar coordinates and integrating out the variable of radial distance. After lengthy but straightforward manipulations, the resulting distribution is found to be

$$p_{2\pi}(\theta) = \frac{e^{-s^2}}{\sqrt{2\pi}}\left\{\frac{1}{\sqrt{2\pi}} + \frac{1}{\sqrt{2}}(s\cos\theta)[1 + \mathrm{erf}(s\cos\theta)]e^{s^2\cos^2\theta}\right\}, \qquad (22.28)$$

where $s = \mu/(\sqrt{2}\sigma_d)$, $0 \le \theta < 2\pi$, and the error function, erf, is defined as

$$\mathrm{erf}(x) = \frac{2}{\sqrt{\pi}}\int_0^x e^{-t^2}\,dt. \qquad (22.29)$$

Since we treat the directional angle θ as equivalent to $\theta + \pi$, we have to modify the range of the distribution to that of $-\pi/2$ to $\pi/2$ (or 0 to π):

$$p_\pi(\theta) = \frac{e^{-s^2}}{\sqrt{\pi}}\left[\frac{1}{\sqrt{\pi}} + (s\cos\theta)\mathrm{erf}(s\cos\theta)e^{s^2\cos^2\theta}\right]. \qquad (22.30)$$

For example, let us look at the case of a vector field with three colors ($m = 3$). Since the distribution of the directional angle is too complicated for us to derive a closed form expression, we can use the same function ω in Eq. (22.30) to approximate the angular distribution of the vector gradient of an m-color vector field by defining s to be

$$s = \sqrt{\sum_{i=1}^{m} s_i^2} = \sqrt{\sum_{i=1}^{m} \frac{\mu_i^2}{2\sigma_{d_i}^2}}. \tag{22.31}$$

Numerical experiments showed that this approximation seems to be quite reasonable [567].

22.6   Statistics of directional data

A line segment in space can be directed or undirected. For example, a vector has a definite direction and it is directed. On the other hand, a line segment in a triangle is undirected. In dealing with color images or vector fields, we often encounter some statistics of vectorial data (directed line) and axial data (undirected line). Both vectorial data and axial data deal with orientations of lines, and we will call them directional data. For example, color hue angles are vectorial data, while edge directions are axial data. Certain denoising algorithms assume that the hue angle is a smooth function within an object surface. Since noise will perturb the hue angle, the algorithms have to model the hue angle distribution as a function of noise. We have to deal with the statistics of directional data. The most important difference in dealing with directional data is that the distribution has to be periodic. Therefore, the very useful Gaussian distribution is no longer valid for directional data. Many of the familiar concepts that we have learned about nondirectional data have to be modified to deal with directional data. For example, our familiar way of expressing a histogram as a linear array has to be changed into a pie chart, a fan diagram, or a rose diagram in which the radial length is proportional to the number of data points in the given direction. Taking an average of directional data becomes a modulo π or 2π operation. Fortunately, there are very good books on this unfamiliar topic [318, 633, 1016].

22.6.1   Representation and descriptive measures

How do we define the mean and the variance of directional data? Before we answer that question, we need to define how we represent directional data. Directional data are represented with unit vectors. When we use Cartesian coordinates, a two-dimensional unit vector can be written as $\mathbf{U} = [x, y]^T$, where $x^2 + y^2 = 1$, and a three-diemnsional unit vector can be written as $\mathbf{U} = [x, y, z]^T$, where $x^2 + y^2 + z^2 = 1$. The cosine of the angle between two unit vectors, $\mathbf{U}$ and $\mathbf{V}$, is given by the inner product of the two vectors: $\cos \theta = \mathbf{U} \cdot \mathbf{V}$. The x, y, and z are also called the direction cosines because they are the inner products of the unit vector and each of the X-, Y-, and Z-axes. Let $[x_i, y_i, z_i]^T$, $i = 1, 2, \ldots, n$, be a set of unit vectors, and

$$\mathbf{R} = \left[\sum_{i=1}^{n} x_i, \sum_{i=1}^{n} y_i, \sum_{i=1}^{n} z_i \right]^T. \tag{22.32}$$

The vector **R** is called the resultant vector of the set. The mean direction of the set of unit vectors is simply the direction of the resultant vector. Let r be the length of the resultant vector. If most of the vectors are clustered around the mean direction, r will have a value close to n. If most of the vectors are spread out, r will be a small number. Therefore, r is a measure of the concentration (or dispersion) of the distribution of the directional data. The spherical variance is thus defined as $s = (n - r)/n$.

In a spherical coordinate system (see Fig. 8.2), a direction is specified with two angles: (θ, ϕ), with $x = \sin\theta\cos\phi$, $y = \sin\theta\sin\phi$, $z = \cos\theta$. However, the quantity $d\theta d\phi$ used in probability integration does not represent an elemental area. An elemental area dA on the unit sphere is $\sin\theta d\theta d\phi$. This means that the factor $\sin\theta$ often appears in the probability density function (pdf) of a distribution of directional data. Let us derive the pdf of the uniform distribution on the unit sphere as an example. Let $g(\theta, \phi)dA$ be an elemental probability. By the definition of a uniform distribution on the unit sphere, $g(\theta, \phi) = 1/(4\pi)$. Therefore, the pdf, $f(\theta, \phi)$, of a uniform distribution on the unit sphere is

$$f(\theta, \phi)d\theta d\phi = g(\theta, \phi)dA = \frac{\sin\theta}{4\pi}d\theta d\phi, \tag{22.33}$$

$$f(\theta, \phi) = \frac{\sin\theta}{4\pi}, \quad 0 \le \theta \le \pi, \quad 0 \le \phi < 2\pi. \tag{22.34}$$

22.6.2 Model distributions for directional data

Since the Gaussian distribution is so useful for nondirectional data, we may ask if there is an equivalent distribution for directional data. Theoretically, the answer is no, in the sense that no directional distribution has been found to have all the properties of the Gaussian distribution, such as the maximum likelihood estimation, the central-limit theorem, and the additive property (the sum of two Gaussian variables is also a Gaussian variable). However, in a two-dimensional space, two angular distributions come very close to the Gaussian distribution. They are (1) the wrapped normal distribution, and (2) the von Mises distribution. The pdf of the wrapped normal distribution with zero mean is defined as

$$f(\theta) = \frac{1}{\sigma\sqrt{2\pi}}\sum_{k=-\infty}^{\infty}\exp\left[-\frac{1}{2}\frac{(\theta + 2\pi k)^2}{\sigma^2}\right], \quad 0 \le \theta < 2\pi. \tag{22.35}$$

The pdf of the von Mises distribution is defined as

$$g(\theta; \mu_0, \kappa) = \frac{1}{2\pi I_0(\kappa)}e^{\kappa\cos(\theta - \mu_0)}, \quad 0 \le \theta < 2\pi, \quad \kappa > 0, \quad 0 \le \mu_0 < 2\pi, \tag{22.36}$$

where $I_0(\kappa)$ is the modified Bessel function of the first kind and order zero. The mean direction is μ_0 and the directional concentration is specified by κ. Each of these two distributions has some of the properties possessed by the Gaussian distribution, and together they have most of the properties. Furthermore, for any given wrapped normal distribution, one can always find a von Mises distribution that can approximate it very well [901]. Since the von Mises distribution is much easier to analyze, it is often used as the "circular normal distribution", especially when the distribution has a narrow spread.

For spherical data (i.e., in a three-dimensional space), the von Mises distribution is generalized to a distribution called the Fisher distribution. Let $\mathbf{U}_0$ (with angle μ_0) be the mean direction vector of a von Mises distribution, and κ be the directional concentration. For a unit vector $\mathbf{U}$ in direction θ, the probability density function of the von Mises distribution is

$$g(\theta) = \frac{1}{2\pi I_0(\kappa)} e^{\kappa \cos(\theta - \mu_0)} = \frac{1}{2\pi I_0(\kappa)} e^{\kappa \mathbf{U} \cdot \mathbf{U}_0}. \tag{22.37}$$

Therefore, the von Mises distribution can be generalized to the spherical data simply by using, in the exponent, the inner product of a three-dimensional unit vector and the mean unit vector of the distribution. Let $\mathbf{U} = [\sin\theta \cos\phi, \sin\theta \sin\phi, \cos\theta]^{\mathrm{T}}$ and $\mathbf{U}_0 = [\sin\theta_0 \cos\phi_0, \sin\theta_0 \sin\phi_0, \cos\theta_0]^{\mathrm{T}}$, we have

$$\mathbf{U} \cdot \mathbf{U}_0 = \sin\theta \sin\theta_0 \cos(\phi - \phi_0) + \cos\theta \cos\theta_0. \tag{22.38}$$

Let (θ_0, ϕ_0) be the mean direction, the resulting function is called the Fisher distribution:

$$f(\theta, \phi) = \frac{\kappa}{4\pi \sinh \kappa} e^{\kappa[\sin\theta \sin\theta_0 \cos(\phi - \phi_0) + \cos\theta \cos\theta_0]} \sin\theta, \tag{22.39}$$

where $0 \le \theta \le \pi$, $0 \le \phi < 2\pi$, $\kappa > 0$, $0 \le \theta_0 \le \pi$, and $0 \le \phi_0 < 2\pi$. Let the north pole be the mean directional vector, i.e., $\theta_0 = 0$, then

$$f(\theta, \phi) = \frac{\kappa}{4\pi \sinh \kappa} e^{\kappa \cos\theta} \sin\theta. \tag{22.40}$$

In fact, the von Mises distribution and the Fisher distribution can be generalized to a hypersphere of dimension m, and the resulting distribution is called the Langevin distribution [318]. The general form is simpler if we again assume that the mean directional vector is the north pole of the hypersphere. The pdf of the hyperspherical directional distribution [633, p. 247, 1015, 1016] of polar angles $\theta_1, \theta_2, \ldots, \theta_{m-1}$ can be expressed as

$$f(\theta_1, \theta_2, \ldots, \theta_{m-1}) = \frac{\kappa^{\frac{m}{2}-1}}{(2\pi)^{\frac{m}{2}} I_{\frac{m}{2}-1}(\kappa)} e^{\kappa \cos\theta_1} (\sin\theta_1)^{m-2} \cdots \sin\theta_{m-2}, \tag{22.41}$$

where $0 \le \theta_i \le \pi$, $i = 1, \ldots, m-2$; $0 \le \theta_{m-1} < 2\pi$; $\kappa > 0$; and I_p is the modified Bessel function of order p.

Another frequently used distribution is the Watson distribution which has two modes on the opposite ends of a diameter. The pdf of the Watson distribution is:

$$w(\theta, \phi) = \frac{1}{4\pi \int_0^1 \exp(\kappa t^2) dt} e^{\kappa[\sin\theta \sin\theta_0 \cos(\phi - \phi_0) + \cos\theta \cos\theta_0]^2} \sin\theta, \tag{22.42}$$

where $0 \le \theta \le \pi$, $0 \le \phi < 2\pi$, $\kappa > 0$, $0 \le \theta_0 \le \pi$, and $0 \le \phi_0 < 2\pi$. When $\theta_0 = 0$, the pdf is simplied to

$$w(\theta, \phi) = \frac{1}{4\pi \int_0^1 \exp(\kappa t^2) dt} e^{\kappa \cos^2\theta} \sin\theta. \tag{22.43}$$

22.7 Denoising

Image noise comes from several sources, such as the photon statistics, sensor noise, amplifier noise, and quantization noise. Some of them are signal-independent, and some are not. Basic methods for dealing with signal-dependent noise are of two types. The first approach scales the signal plus noise so that the noise variance becomes constant for all levels. The second approach uses a lookup table to adjust the noise threshold at different signal levels [566].

Noise makes image details difficult to see and it also interferes with computer image analysis. Many algorithms have been proposed to reduce the undesirable presence of noise through digital image processing. In order to reduce noise, we need to ask ourselves: how can we tell the signal from the noise? Most of the existing algorithms rely on three assumptions about noise: (1) image noise is less correlated than the image signal from pixel to pixel (spatial correlation), and between color channels (color correlation); (2) image noise is more objectionable in high spatial frequencies; and (3) image noise has a lower contrast amplitude than that of the image signal. The validity of these assumptions depends on the noise source, image rendering, and image viewing. But, the important thing to remember is that all these three criteria require more quantitative specification before they can be useful in practical applications.

One important observation is that our visual system can tell the image noise from the image signal when looking at the image as a whole, correctly interpreting objects and textures. However, if we only cut out a small part of an image, say a 5 pixel by 5 pixel window, we are not much better than a computer at telling the noise and the signal apart. However, that is typically the neighborhood size used by many denoising algorithms. Our visual perception seems to rely on a much larger context and global inference to distinguish noise from signal. Thus we should not expect any denoising algorithms to perform well for images that have low signal-to-noise ratios. However, when the image signal is much stronger than the noise, some algorithms can do a fairly good job in cleaning up the images. Although denoising problems can often be formulated as finding a minimum mean-squared-error estimate of the noise-free image, such as the Wiener filtering [27, 457, 776], the resulting image often looks soft and blurry. In general, methods (e.g., [535, 577, 688]) that pay careful attention to preserving edge sharpness by adaptive processing tend to produce much better looking images.

Edge-preserving smoothing algorithms are based on the idea of choosing the proper neighboring pixels to do the averaging, so that the smoothing operation does not run across edges. For example, an elongated bar mask can be rotated with the current pixel as the center, and the mask that has the least variance is selected for averaging with the current pixel [688]. An alternative implementation is to select only a given fraction of nearest gray-level pixels in a neighborhood window for averaging. We can imagine that many other variations can be implemented along these lines. This class of algorithm often performs quite well, except in texture regions. Therefore, the variance of the neighborhood is often used to adjust how much smoothing should be used [577]. A new type of filter, called the bilateral filter, has greatly, improved the performance of the edge-preserving smoothing approach [953]. With conventional filters, the filter weights spatially nearby pixels more than the faraway pixels.

The bilateral filter further varies a neighboring pixel's weighting according to how close its brightness value is to that of the center pixel. If the value of a neighboring pixel is closer to the center pixel value, it is weighted more than a value that is farther away. Therefore, the filter weighting is in both the spatial domain and the image exposure domain. The bilateral filter is a very effective noise smoother without blurring high-contrast edges. However, it still blurs fine textures.

Another class of noise smoothing algorithm is based on signal transforms, such as singular value decomposition [568], wavelet [260, 530], curvelet [897, 898], or polynomials [299]. The basic idea is that these transforms tend to represent correlated image signals better than the uncorrelated noise. Therefore, a simple discrimination between signal and noise can be made from the magnitude of the transform coefficient. The main thrust of the curvelet methods [897, 898] is that image structures, such as edges and curves, can be modeled in many directions and many scales, allowing a better discrimination of signal from noise.

The denoising algorithms discussed so far apply equally well to monochromatic images and color images. However, if we treat color images as vector fields, there are several possible ways to generalize some classical denoising algorithms to color images. For example, the vector median filter [40] is generalized from the scalar median filter for removing the impulsive noise. The median vector $\mathbf{X}_{\text{median}}$ of a set of vectors, $Q = \{\mathbf{X}_i : i = 1, 2, \ldots, n\}$, is the vector that minimizes the sum of all distances between the vector and all other vectors in the set:

$$\mathbf{X}_{\text{median}} = \min_{X \in Q} \sum_{i=1}^{n} ||\mathbf{X}_i - \mathbf{X}||. \tag{22.44}$$

When the vector is a scalar, the definition becomes the same as the scalar median. In higher dimensions, the definition of the median vector depends on the definition of the vector norm (or the distance between two vectors). The choice of an effective norm and a fast way to search for the median are required for practical applications [59]. Since a vector has a length and a direction, we can also perform color noise filtering with vector directional filters [958, 959]. The idea is that on a smooth surface, the direction of a color vector should also very smoothly. We can use the spherical variance as defined in Section 22.6.1 to form a vectorized version of the sigma filter [578]. A different definition of the angular spread is as follows [959]. Let $Q = \{\mathbf{X}_i : i = 1, 2, \ldots, n\}$ be a set of color vectors and $A(\mathbf{X}_i, \mathbf{X}_j)$ be the angle between the vectors $\mathbf{X}_i$ and $\mathbf{X}_j$. Define an angular spread s_i associated with a vector $\mathbf{X}_i$ as

$$s_i = \sum_{j=1}^{n} A(\mathbf{X}_i, \mathbf{X}_j) \quad \text{where} \quad A(\mathbf{X}_i, \mathbf{X}_j) = \cos^{-1} \left(\frac{\mathbf{X}_i \cdot \mathbf{X}_j}{||\mathbf{X}_i|| ||\mathbf{X}_j||} \right). \tag{22.45}$$

We can then choose the vector that has the minimum angular spread as the filtered output. This is similar to the idea of the spherical median as defined in [318, p. 111], except that the spherical median is not constrained to be one of the vectors in the set. The spherical median has several robustness properties similar to those of the linear median [317]. We can also order the vectors in Q according to its angular spread and choose to average the lowest k vectors as the output.

It should be pointed out that color vectors can and should be expressed in different color spaces, depending on the application. For denoising purposes, we should consider perceptual color spaces, such as CIELAB and CIELUV. We can also transform the color image into luminance–chrominance vectors and work on the hue angle as a function of image location, i.e., a hue field. A noise-corrupted pixel is more likely to have a hue angle significantly different from its neighbors. Therefore color denoising can be done by suppressing random variations in a smooth hue region while preserving the sharp boundaries between the smooth regions [96].

Appendix Extended tables

A.1 CIE 1931 color matching functions and corresponding chromaticities

λ (nm)	$\bar{x}(\lambda)$	$\bar{y}(\lambda)$	$\bar{z}(\lambda)$	$x(\lambda)$	$y(\lambda)$
360	0.000 129 900 0	0.000 003 917 000	0.000 606 100 0	0.175 56	0.005 29
365	0.000 232 100 0	0.000 006 965 000	0.001 086 000	0.175 16	0.005 26
370	0.000 414 900 0	0.000 012 390 00	0.001 946 000	0.174 82	0.005 22
375	0.000 741 600 0	0.000 022 020 00	0.003 486 000	0.174 51	0.005 18
380	0.001 368 000	0.000 039 000 00	0.006 450 001	0.174 11	0.004 96
385	0.002 236 000	0.000 064 000 00	0.010 549 99	0.174 01	0.004 98
390	0.004 243 000	0.000 120 000 0	0.020 050 01	0.173 80	0.004 92
395	0.007 650 000	0.000 217 000 0	0.036 210 00	0.173 56	0.004 92
400	0.014 310 00	0.000 396 000 0	0.067 850 01	0.173 34	0.004 80
405	0.023 190 00	0.000 640 000 0	0.110 200 0	0.173 02	0.004 78
410	0.043 510 00	0.001 210 000	0.207 400 0	0.172 58	0.004 80
415	0.077 630 00	0.002 180 000	0.371 300 0	0.172 09	0.004 83
420	0.134 380 0	0.004 000 000	0.645 600 0	0.171 41	0.005 10
425	0.214 770 0	0.007 300 000	1.039 050 1	0.170 30	0.005 79
430	0.283 900 0	0.011 600 00	1.385 600 0	0.168 88	0.006 90
435	0.328 500 0	0.016 840 00	1.622 960 0	0.166 90	0.008 55
440	0.348 280 0	0.023 000 00	1.747 060 0	0.164 41	0.010 86
445	0.348 060 0	0.029 800 00	1.782 600 0	0.161 11	0.013 79
450	0.336 200 0	0.038 000 00	1.772 110 0	0.156 64	0.017 71
455	0.318 700 0	0.048 000 00	1.744 100 0	0.150 99	0.022 74
460	0.290 800 0	0.060 000 00	1.669 200 0	0.143 96	0.029 70
465	0.251 100 0	0.073 900 00	1.528 100 0	0.135 50	0.039 88
470	0.195 360 0	0.090 980 00	1.287 640 0	0.124 12	0.057 80
475	0.142 100 0	0.112 600 0	1.041 900 0	0.109 60	0.086 84
480	0.095 640 00	0.139 020 0	0.812 950 1	0.091 29	0.132 70
485	0.057 950 01	0.169 300 0	0.616 200 0	0.068 71	0.200 72
490	0.032 010 00	0.208 020 0	0.465 180 0	0.045 39	0.294 98
495	0.014 700 00	0.258 600 0	0.353 300 0	0.023 46	0.412 70
500	0.004 900 000	0.323 000 0	0.272 000 0	0.008 17	0.538 42
505	0.002 400 000	0.407 300 0	0.212 300 0	0.003 86	0.654 82
510	0.009 300 000	0.503 000 0	0.158 200 0	0.013 87	0.750 19
515	0.029 100 00	0.608 200 0	0.111 700 0	0.038 85	0.812 02
520	0.063 270 00	0.710 000 0	0.078 249 99	0.074 30	0.833 80
525	0.109 600 0	0.793 200 0	0.057 250 01	0.114 16	0.826 21
530	0.165 500 0	0.862 000 0	0.042 160 00	0.154 72	0.805 86
535	0.225 749 9	0.914 850 1	0.029 840 00	0.192 88	0.781 63

(cont.)

(cont.)

λ (nm)	$\bar{x}(\lambda)$	$\bar{y}(\lambda)$	$\bar{z}(\lambda)$	$x(\lambda)$	$y(\lambda)$
540	0.290 400 0	0.954 000 0	0.020 300 00	0.229 62	0.754 33
545	0.359 700 0	0.980 300 0	0.013 400 00	0.265 78	0.724 32
550	0.433 449 9	0.994 950 1	0.008 749 999	0.301 60	0.692 31
555	0.512 050 1	1.000 000 0	0.005 749 999	0.337 36	0.658 85
560	0.594 500 0	0.995 000 0	0.003 900 000	0.373 10	0.624 45
565	0.678 400 0	0.978 600 0	0.002 749 999	0.408 73	0.589 61
570	0.762 100 0	0.952 000 0	0.002 100 000	0.444 06	0.554 72
575	0.842 500 0	0.915 400 0	0.001 800 000	0.478 78	0.520 20
580	0.916 300 0	0.870 000 0	0.001 650 001	0.512 49	0.486 59
585	0.978 600 0	0.816 300 0	0.001 400 000	0.544 79	0.454 43
590	1.026 300 0	0.757 000 0	0.001 100 000	0.575 15	0.424 23
595	1.056 700 0	0.694 900 0	0.001 000 000	0.602 93	0.396 50
600	1.062 200 0	0.631 000 0	0.000 800 000 0	0.627 04	0.372 49
605	1.045 600 0	0.566 800 0	0.000 600 000 0	0.648 23	0.351 40
610	1.002 600 0	0.503 000 0	0.000 340 000 0	0.665 76	0.334 01
615	0.938 400 0	0.441 200 0	0.000 240 000 0	0.680 08	0.319 75
620	0.854 449 9	0.381 000 0	0.000 190 000 0	0.691 51	0.308 34
625	0.751 400 0	0.321 000 0	0.000 100 000 0	0.700 61	0.299 30
630	0.642 400 0	0.265 000 0	0.000 049 999 99	0.707 92	0.292 03
635	0.541 900 0	0.217 000 0	0.000 030 000 00	0.714 03	0.285 93
640	0.447 900 0	0.175 000 0	0.000 020 000 00	0.719 03	0.280 94
645	0.360 800 0	0.138 200 0	0.000 010 000 00	0.723 03	0.276 95
650	0.283 500 0	0.107 000 0	0.000 000 000 000	0.725 99	0.274 01
655	0.218 700 0	0.081 600 00	0.000 000 000 000	0.728 27	0.271 73
660	0.164 900 0	0.061 000 00	0.000 000 000 000	0.729 97	0.270 03
665	0.121 200 0	0.044 580 00	0.000 000 000 000	0.731 09	0.268 91
670	0.087 400 00	0.032 000 00	0.000 000 000 000	0.731 99	0.268 01
675	0.063 600 00	0.023 200 00	0.000 000 000 000	0.732 72	0.267 28
680	0.046 770 00	0.017 000 00	0.000 000 000 000	0.733 42	0.266 58
685	0.032 900 00	0.011 920 00	0.000 000 000 000	0.734 05	0.265 95
690	0.022 700 00	0.008 210 000	0.000 000 000 000	0.734 49	0.265 61
695	0.015 840 00	0.005 723 000	0.000 000 000 000	0.734 59	0.265 41
700	0.011 249 16	0.004 102 000	0.000 000 000 000	0.734 69	0.265 31
705	0.008 110 916	0.002 929 000	0.000 000 000 000	0.734 69	0.265 31
710	0.005 790 346	0.002 091 000	0.000 000 000 000	0.734 69	0.265 31
715	0.004 109 457	0.001 484 000	0.000 000 000 000	0.734 69	0.265 31
720	0.002 899 327	0.001 047 000	0.000 000 000 000	0.734 69	0.265 31
725	0.002 049 190	0.000 740 000 0	0.000 000 000 000	0.734 69	0.265 31
730	0.001 439 971	0.000 520 000 0	0.000 000 000 000	0.734 69	0.265 31
735	0.000 999 949 3	0.000 361 100 0	0.000 000 000 000	0.734 69	0.265 31
740	0.000 690 078 6	0.000 249 200 0	0.000 000 000 000	0.734 69	0.265 31
745	0.000 476 021 3	0.000 171 900 0	0.000 000 000 000	0.734 69	0.265 31
750	0.000 332 301 1	0.000 120 000 0	0.000 000 000 000	0.734 69	0.265 31
755	0.000 234 826 1	0.000 084 800 00	0.000 000 000 000	0.734 69	0.265 31
760	0.000 166 150 5	0.000 060 000 00	0.000 000 000 000	0.734 69	0.265 31
765	0.000 117 413 0	0.000 042 400 00	0.000 000 000 000	0.734 69	0.265 31
770	0.000 083 075 27	0.000 030 000 00	0.000 000 000 000	0.734 69	0.265 31
775	0.000 058 706 52	0.000 021 200 00	0.000 000 000 000	0.734 69	0.265 31
780	0.000 041 509 94	0.000 014 990 00	0.000 000 000 000	0.734 69	0.265 31
785	0.000 029 353 26	0.000 010 600 00	0.000 000 000 000	0.734 69	0.265 31

(cont.)

(cont.)

λ (nm)	$\bar{x}(\lambda)$	$\bar{y}(\lambda)$	$\bar{z}(\lambda)$	$x(\lambda)$	$y(\lambda)$
790	0.000 020 673 83	0.000 007 465 700	0.000 000 000 000	0.734 69	0.265 31
795	0.000 014 559 77	0.000 005 257 800	0.000 000 000 000	0.734 69	0.265 31
800	0.000 010 253 98	0.000 003 702 900	0.000 000 000 000	0.734 69	0.265 31
805	0.000 007 221 456	0.000 002 607 800	0.000 000 000 000	0.734 69	0.265 31
810	0.000 005 085 868	0.000 001 836 600	0.000 000 000 000	0.734 69	0.265 31
815	0.000 003 581 652	0.000 001 293 400	0.000 000 000 000	0.734 69	0.265 31
820	0.000 002 522 525	0.000 000 910 930 0	0.000 000 000 000	0.734 69	0.265 31
825	0.000 001 776 509	0.000 000 641 530 0	0.000 000 000 000	0.734 69	0.265 31
830	0.000 001 251 141	0.000 000 451 810 0	0.000 000 000 000	0.734 69	0.265 31

A.2   CIE 1964 10-degree color matching functions

λ (nm)	$\bar{x}_{10}(\lambda)$	$\bar{y}_{10}(\lambda)$	$\bar{z}_{10}(\lambda)$
360	0.1222E-06	0.13398E-07	0.535027E-06
365	0.91927E-06	0.10065E-06	0.402830E-05
370	0.59586E-05	0.6511E-06	0.261437E-04
375	0.33266E-04	0.3625E-05	0.14622E-03
380	0.159952E-03	0.17364E-04	0.704776E-03
385	0.66244E-03	0.7156E-04	0.00292780
390	0.0023616	0.2534E-03	0.0104822
395	0.0072423	0.7685E-03	0.032344
400	0.0191097	0.0020044	0.0860109
405	0.043400	0.004509	0.197120
410	0.084736	0.008756	0.389366
415	0.140638	0.014456	0.656760
420	0.204492	0.021391	0.972542
425	0.264737	0.029497	1.28250
430	0.314679	0.038676	1.55348
435	0.357719	0.049602	1.79850
440	0.383734	0.062077	1.96728
443	0.388396	0.069764	2.01740
445	0.386726	0.074704	2.02730
450	0.370702	0.089456	1.99480
455	0.342957	0.106256	1.90070
460	0.302273	0.128201	1.74537
465	0.254085	0.152761	1.55490
470	0.195618	0.185190	1.31756
475	0.132349	0.219940	1.03020
480	0.080507	0.253589	0.772125
485	0.041072	0.297665	0.570060
490	0.016172	0.339133	0.415254
495	0.005132	0.395379	0.302356
500	0.003816	0.460777	0.218502
505	0.015444	0.531360	0.159249
510	0.037465	0.606741	0.112044

(cont.)

(cont.)

λ (nm)	$\bar{x}_{10}(\lambda)$	$\bar{y}_{10}(\lambda)$	$\bar{z}_{10}(\lambda)$
515	0.071358	0.685660	0.082248
520	0.117749	0.761757	0.060709
525	0.172953	0.823330	0.043050
530	0.236491	0.875211	0.030451
535	0.304213	0.923810	0.020584
540	0.376772	0.961988	0.013676
545	0.451584	0.982200	0.007918
550	0.529826	0.991761	0.003988
555	0.616053	0.999110	0.001091
557	0.651901	1.000000	0.000407
560	0.705224	0.997340	0.000000
565	0.793832	0.982380	0.0
570	0.878655	0.955552	0.0
575	0.951162	0.915175	0.0
580	1.01416	0.868934	0.0
585	1.07430	0.825623	0.0
590	1.11852	0.777405	0.0
595	1.13430	0.720353	0.0
600	1.12399	0.658341	0.0
605	1.08910	0.593878	0.0
610	1.03048	0.527963	0.0
615	0.950740	0.461834	0.0
620	0.856297	0.398057	0.0
625	0.754930	0.339554	0.0
630	0.647467	0.283493	0.0
635	0.535110	0.228254	0.0
640	0.431567	0.179828	0.0
645	0.343690	0.140211	0.0
650	0.268329	0.107633	0.0
655	0.204300	0.081187	0.0
660	0.152568	0.060281	0.0
665	0.112210	0.044096	0.0
670	0.0812606	0.0318004	0.0
675	0.0579300	0.0226017	0.0
680	0.0408508	0.0159051	0.0
685	0.0286230	0.0111303	0.0
690	0.0199413	0.0077488	0.0
695	0.0138420	0.0053751	0.0
700	0.00957688	0.00371774	0.0
705	0.00660520	0.00256456	0.0
710	0.00455263	0.00176847	0.0
715	0.00314470	0.00122239	0.0
720	0.00217496	0.84619E-03	0.0
725	0.00150570	0.58644E-03	0.0
730	0.00104476	0.40741E-03	0.0
735	0.727450E-03	0.284041E-03	0.0
740	0.508258E-03	0.198730E-03	0.0
745	0.356380E-03	0.139550E-03	0.0
750	0.250969E-03	0.98428E-04	0.0

A.3   Cone fundamentals

λ (nm)	Stockman–MacLeod–Johnson [910]			De Marco–Pokorny–Smith [247]		
	$L(\lambda)$	$M(\lambda)$	$S(\lambda)$	$L(\lambda)$	$M(\lambda)$	$S(\lambda)$
390	0.000314	0.000253	0.007874			
395	0.000903	0.000751	0.022845			
400	0.002231	0.001929	0.057372	0.002655	0.0028229	0.10768
405	0.004782	0.004334	0.126067	0.0043826	0.0047486	0.17946
410	0.008758	0.008461	0.239001	0.0068892	0.0076700	0.28485
415	0.013198	0.013932	0.380189	0.010833	0.012424	0.45258
420	0.017474	0.020497	0.527594	0.015822	0.018901	0.65924
425	0.022004	0.028721	0.669885	0.019967	0.025365	0.81312
430	0.026946	0.038788	0.802971	0.023314	0.031709	0.90754
435	0.032569	0.050687	0.918333	0.026833	0.039462	0.97713
440	0.038362	0.063562	0.986734	0.030096	0.047706	1.0000
445	0.043451	0.075701	0.996093	0.032371	0.055456	0.97017
450	0.048798	0.087882	0.950167	0.034307	0.063547	0.91046
455	0.055144	0.100879	0.884097	0.036796	0.073070	0.85005
460	0.065163	0.119674	0.812456	0.041195	0.085998	0.79913
465	0.078614	0.144411	0.746105	0.050228	0.10675	0.77451
470	0.096872	0.176482	0.651178	0.062656	0.13009	0.68910
475	0.119179	0.212178	0.528810	0.079771	0.15739	0.58169
480	0.137626	0.237739	0.394276	0.10189	0.18879	0.46772
485	0.161808	0.270770	0.288270	0.12799	0.22358	0.36158
490	0.187629	0.304089	0.209363	0.16199	0.26703	0.27638
495	0.232167	0.362660	0.156819	0.20635	0.32389	0.21151
500	0.296688	0.447920	0.119042	0.26285	0.39624	0.16357
505	0.373938	0.545381	0.089433	0.33706	0.49056	0.12802
510	0.459198	0.646845	0.062116	0.42302	0.59483	0.095566
515	0.546764	0.744046	0.043301	0.51989	0.70561	0.067565
520	0.635770	0.833106	0.029424	0.61674	0.80775	0.047387
525	0.710559	0.899705	0.019445	0.70010	0.88440	0.034711
530	0.776068	0.946455	0.012829	0.77322	0.94098	0.025602
535	0.836951	0.984238	0.008492	0.83367	0.97750	0.018168
540	0.882673	0.999540	0.005610	0.88336	0.99658	0.012414
545	0.915799	0.994947	0.003735	0.92308	0.99910	0.008255
550	0.941673	0.977462	0.002505	0.95381	0.98652	0.005453
555	0.967832	0.954553	0.001692	0.97743	0.96103	0.003647
560	0.987643	0.918544	0.001151	0.99332	0.92249	0.002533
565	0.998160	0.867561	0.000788	0.99976	0.87024	0.001839
570	0.998849	0.803156	0.000544	0.99737	0.80635	0.001444
575	0.986961	0.726273	0.000377	0.98555	0.73228	0.001258
580	0.968278	0.644763	0.000263	0.96453	0.65073	0.001160
585	0.950824	0.566370	0.000185	0.93356	0.56418	0.001001
590	0.925337	0.487528	0.000131	0.89420	0.47699	0.000812
595	0.886135	0.409072	0.000093	0.84818	0.39346	0.000741
600	0.836180	0.335120	0.000066	0.79460	0.31763	0.000610
605	0.777678	0.268473	0.000048	0.73544	0.25012	0.000478
610	0.711541	0.210329	0.000035	0.67030	0.19331	0.000312
615	0.638852	0.161287	0.000025	0.60183	0.14701	0.000240
620	0.563508	0.121927	0.000018	0.53006	0.11015	0.000198
625	0.489666	0.092598	0.000013	0.45397	0.080815	0.000132
630	0.415432	0.069279	0.000010	0.37994	0.058332	0.000090

(*cont.*)

(cont.)

λ (nm)	Stockman–MacLeod–Johnson [910]			De Marco–Pokorny–Smith [247]		
	$L(\lambda)$	$M(\lambda)$	$S(\lambda)$	$L(\lambda)$	$M(\lambda)$	$S(\lambda)$
635	0.339782	0.049283	0.000007	0.31482	0.041757	0.000067
640	0.271456	0.034119	0.000005	0.25642	0.029558	0.000052
645	0.214289	0.023201	0.000004	0.20415	0.020664	0.000038
650	0.166150	0.015678	0.000003	0.15903	0.014430	0.000025
655	0.126125	0.010927	0.000002	0.12186	0.010063	0.000019
660	0.094037	0.007697	0.000002	0.091421	0.006990	0.000014
665	0.069040	0.005343	0.000001	0.066972	0.004849	0.000010
670	0.049934	0.003692	0.000001	0.048166	0.003329	0.000007
675	0.035563	0.002542	0.000001	0.034975	0.0023257	0.000005
680	0.025061	0.001748	0.000001	0.025667	0.001641	0.000004
685	0.017555	0.001206	0.000000	0.018022	0.001111	0.000003
690	0.012229	0.000833	0.000000	0.012422	0.000750	0.000002
695	0.008488	0.000573	0.000000	0.008662	0.000516	0.000001
700	0.005872	0.000395	0.000000	0.006210	0.000368	0.000000
705	0.004050	0.000273	0.000000			
710	0.002793	0.000189	0.000000			
715	0.001930	0.000132	0.000000			
720	0.001335	0.000092	0.000000			
725	0.000925	0.000065	0.000000			
730	0.000642	0.000046	0.000000			

A.4 Judd's modified $V_M(\lambda)$ (CIE 1988) and scotopic $V'(\lambda)$ (CIE 1951)

λ (nm)	$V_M(\lambda)$	$V'(\lambda)$	λ (nm)	$V_M(\lambda)$	$V'(\lambda)$
380	0.20000E-03	0.000589	385	0.39556E-03	0.001108
390	0.80000E-03	0.002209	395	0.15457E-02	0.00453
400	0.28000E-02	0.00929	405	0.46562E-02	0.01852
410	0.74000E-02	0.03484	415	0.11779E-01	0.0604
420	0.17500E-01	0.0966	425	0.22678E-01	0.1436
430	0.27300E-01	0.1998	435	0.32584E-01	0.2625
440	0.37900E-01	0.3281	445	0.42391E-01	0.3931
450	0.46800E-01	0.455	455	0.52122E-01	0.513
460	0.60000E-01	0.567	465	0.73900E-01	0.620
470	0.90980E-01	0.676	475	0.11260	0.734
480	0.13902	0.793	485	0.16930	0.851
490	0.20802	0.904	495	0.25860	0.949
500	0.32300	0.982	505	0.40730	0.998
510	0.50300	0.997	515	0.60820	0.975
520	0.71000	0.935	525	0.79320	0.880
530	0.86200	0.811	535	0.91485	0.733
540	0.95400	0.650	545	0.98030	0.564
550	0.99495	0.481	555	1.00000	0.402
560	0.99500	0.3288	565	0.97860	0.2639
570	0.95200	0.2076	575	0.91540	0.1602
580	0.87000	0.1212	585	0.81630	0.0899
590	0.75700	0.0655	595	0.69490	0.0469

(cont.)

(cont.)

λ (nm)	$V_M(\lambda)$	$V'(\lambda)$	λ (nm)	$V_M(\lambda)$	$V'(\lambda)$
600	0.63100	0.03315	605	0.56680	0.02312
610	0.50300	0.01593	615	0.44120	0.01088
620	0.38100	0.00737	625	0.32000	0.00497
630	0.26500	0.003335	635	0.21700	0.002235
640	0.17500	0.001497	645	0.13820	0.001005
650	0.10700	0.000677	655	0.81600E-01	0.000459
660	0.61000E-01	0.0003129	665	0.44580E-01	0.0002146
670	0.32000E-01	0.0001480	675	0.23200E-01	0.0001026
680	0.17000E-01	0.0000715	685	0.11920E-01	0.0000501
690	0.82100E-02	0.00003533	695	0.57230E-02	0.00002501
700	0.41020E-02	0.00001780	705	0.29290E-02	0.00001273
710	0.20910E-02	9.14E-06	715	0.14840E-02	6.60E-06
720	0.10470E-02	4.78E-06	725	0.74000E-03	3.482E-06
730	0.52000E-03	2.546E-06	735	0.3611E-03	1.870E-06
740	0.24920E-03	1.379E-06	745	0.17190E-03	1.022E-06
750	0.12000E-03	7.60E-07	755	0.84800E-04	5.67E-07
760	0.60000E-04	4.25E-07	765	0.42400E-04	3.196E-07
770	0.30000E-04	2.413E-07	775	0.21200E-04	1.829E-07
780	0.14990E-04	1.390E-07			

A.5 Standard illuminants

λ (nm)	A	B	C	D_{65}
360	6.14462	9.600	12.90	46.6383
365	6.94720	12.40	17.20	49.3637
370	7.82135	15.20	21.40	52.0891
375	8.76980	18.80	27.50	51.0323
380	9.79510	22.40	33.00	49.9755
385	10.8996	26.85	39.92	52.3118
390	12.0853	31.30	47.40	54.6482
395	13.3543	36.18	55.17	68.7015
400	14.7080	41.30	63.30	82.7549
405	16.1480	46.62	71.81	87.1204
410	17.6753	52.10	80.60	91.4860
415	19.2907	57.70	89.53	92.4589
420	20.9950	63.20	98.10	93.4318
425	22.7883	68.37	105.80	90.0570
430	24.6709	73.10	112.40	86.6823
435	26.6425	77.31	117.75	95.7736
440	28.7027	80.80	121.50	104.865
445	30.8508	83.44	123.45	110.936
450	33.0859	85.40	124.00	117.008
455	35.4068	86.88	123.60	117.410
460	37.8121	88.30	123.10	117.812
465	40.3002	90.08	123.30	116.336
470	42.8693	92.00	123.80	114.861
475	45.5174	93.75	124.09	115.392
480	48.2423	95.20	123.90	115.923
485	51.0418	96.23	122.92	112.367
490	53.9132	96.50	120.70	108.811

(cont.)

(cont.)

λ (nm)	A	B	C	D$_{65}$
495	56.8539	95.71	116.90	109.082
500	59.8611	94.20	112.10	109.354
505	62.9320	92.37	106.98	108.578
510	66.0635	90.70	102.30	107.802
515	69.2525	89.65	98.81	106.296
520	72.4959	89.50	96.90	104.790
525	75.7903	90.43	96.78	106.239
530	79.1326	92.20	98.00	107.689
535	82.5193	94.46	99.94	106.047
540	85.9470	96.90	102.10	104.405
545	89.4124	99.16	103.95	104.225
550	92.9120	101.00	105.20	104.046
555	96.4423	102.20	105.67	102.023
560	100.000	102.80	105.30	100.000
565	103.582	102.92	104.11	98.1671
570	107.184	102.60	102.30	96.3342
575	110.803	101.90	100.15	96.0611
580	114.436	101.00	97.80	95.7880
585	118.080	100.07	95.43	92.2368
590	121.731	99.20	93.20	88.6856
595	125.386	98.44	91.22	89.3459
600	129.043	98.00	89.70	90.0062
605	132.697	98.08	88.83	89.8026
610	136.346	98.50	88.40	89.5991
615	139.988	99.06	88.19	88.6489
620	143.618	99.70	88.10	87.6987
625	147.235	100.36	88.06	85.4936
630	150.836	101.00	88.00	83.2886
635	154.418	101.56	87.86	83.4939
640	157.979	102.20	87.80	83.6992
645	161.516	103.05	87.99	81.8630
650	165.028	103.90	88.20	80.0268
655	168.510	104.59	88.20	80.1207
660	171.963	105.00	87.90	80.2146
665	175.383	105.08	87.22	81.2462
670	178.769	104.90	86.30	82.2778
675	182.118	104.55	85.30	80.2810
680	185.429	103.90	84.00	78.2842
685	188.701	102.84	82.21	74.0027
690	191.931	101.60	80.20	69.7213
695	195.118	100.38	78.24	70.6652
700	198.261	99.10	76.30	71.6091
705	201.359	97.70	74.36	72.9790
710	204.409	96.20	72.40	74.3490
715	207.411	94.60	70.40	67.9765
720	210.365	92.90	68.30	61.6040
725	213.268	91.10	66.30	65.7448
730	216.120	89.40	64.40	69.8856
735	218.920	88.00	62.80	72.4863
740	221.667	86.90	61.50	75.0870
745	224.361	85.90	60.20	69.3398
750	227.000	85.20	59.20	63.5927
755	229.585	84.80	58.50	55.0054
760	232.115	84.70	58.10	46.4182

The chromaticity coordinates in the table below are based on 5 nm intervals from 380 nm to 780 nm. For D_{55}, D_{65}, and D_{75}, the (x, y) chromaticity coordinates are computed from the CIE daylight chromaticity equations for $T_c = 5503$ K, 6504 K, and 7504 K respectively.

Illuminant	(x, y)	(x_{10}, y_{10})
A	(0.4476, 0.4074)	(0.4512, 0.4059)
C	(0.3101, 0.3162)	(0.3104, 0.3191)
D_{50}	(0.3457, 0.3586)	(0.3478, 0.3595)
D_{55}	(0.3324, 0.3475)	(0.3341, 0.3488)
D_{65}	(0.3127, 0.3291)	(0.3138, 0.3310)
D_{75}	(0.2990, 0.3150)	(0.2997, 0.3174)

A.6   CIE daylight vectors

λ (nm)	$S_0(\lambda)$	$S_1(\lambda)$	$S_2(\lambda)$	λ (nm)	$S_0(\lambda)$	$S_1(\lambda)$	$S_2(\lambda)$
300.0	0.04	0.02	0.0	305.0	3.02	2.26	1.0
310.0	6.0	4.5	2.0	315.0	17.8	13.45	3.0
320.0	29.6	22.4	4.0	325.0	42.45	32.2	6.25
330.0	55.3	42.0	8.5	335.0	56.3	41.3	8.15
340.0	57.3	40.6	7.8	345.0	59.55	41.1	7.25
350.0	61.8	41.6	6.7	355.0	61.65	39.8	6.0
360.0	61.5	38.0	5.3	365.0	65.15	40.2	5.7
370.0	68.8	42.4	6.1	375.0	66.1	40.45	4.55
380.0	63.4	38.5	3.0	385.0	64.6	36.75	2.1
390.0	65.8	35.0	1.2	395.0	80.3	39.2	0.05
400.0	94.8	43.4	−1.1	405.0	99.8	44.85	−0.8
410.0	104.8	46.3	−0.5	415.0	105.35	45.1	−0.6
420.0	105.9	43.9	−0.7	425.0	101.35	40.5	−0.95
430.0	96.8	37.1	−1.2	435.0	105.35	36.9	−1.9
440.0	113.9	36.7	−2.6	445.0	119.75	36.3	−2.75
450.0	125.6	35.9	−2.9	455.0	125.55	34.25	−2.85
460.0	125.5	32.6	−2.8	465.0	123.4	30.25	−2.7
470.0	121.3	27.9	−2.6	475.0	121.3	26.1	−2.6
480.0	121.3	24.3	−2.6	485.0	117.4	22.2	−2.2
490.0	113.5	20.1	−1.8	495.0	113.3	18.15	−1.65
500.0	113.1	16.2	−1.5	505.0	111.95	14.7	−1.4
510.0	110.8	13.2	−1.3	515.0	108.65	10.9	−1.25
520.0	106.5	8.6	−1.2	525.0	107.65	7.35	−1.1
530.0	108.8	6.1	−1.0	535.0	107.05	5.15	−0.75
540.0	105.3	4.2	−0.5	545.0	104.85	3.05	−0.4
550.0	104.4	1.9	−0.3	555.0	102.2	0.95	−0.15
560.0	100.0	0.0	0.0	565.0	98.0	−0.8	0.1
570.0	96.0	−1.6	0.2	575.0	95.55	−2.55	0.35
580.0	95.1	−3.5	0.5	585.0	92.1	−3.5	1.3
590.0	89.1	−3.5	2.1	595.0	89.8	−4.65	2.65
600.0	90.5	−5.8	3.2	605.0	90.4	−6.5	3.65
610.0	90.3	−7.2	4.1	615.0	89.35	−7.9	4.4
620.0	88.4	−8.6	4.7	625.0	86.2	−9.05	4.9

(*cont.*)

(cont.)

λ (nm)	$S_0(\lambda)$	$S_1(\lambda)$	$S_2(\lambda)$	λ (nm)	$S_0(\lambda)$	$S_1(\lambda)$	$S_2(\lambda)$
630.0	85.0	−9.5	5.1	635.0	84.55	−10.2	5.9
640.0	85.1	−10.9	6.7	645.0	83.5	−10.8	7.0
650.0	81.9	−10.7	7.3	655.0	82.25	−11.35	7.95
660.0	82.6	−12.0	8.6	665.0	83.75	−13.0	9.2
670.0	84.9	−14.0	9.8	675.0	83.1	−13.8	10.0
680.0	81.3	−13.6	10.2	685.0	76.6	−12.8	9.25
690.0	71.9	−12.0	8.3	695.0	73.1	−12.65	8.95
700.0	74.3	−13.3	9.6	705.0	75.35	−13.1	9.05
710.0	76.4	−12.9	8.5	715.0	69.85	−11.75	7.75
720.0	63.3	−10.6	7.0	725.0	67.5	−11.1	7.3
730.0	71.7	−11.6	7.6	735.0	74.35	−11.9	7.8
740.0	77.0	−12.2	8.0	745.0	71.1	−11.2	7.35
750.0	65.2	−10.2	6.7	755.0	56.45	−9.0	5.95
760.0	47.7	−7.8	5.2	765.0	58.15	−9.5	6.3
770.0	68.6	−12.2	7.4	775.0	66.8	−10.8	7.1
780.0	65.0	−10.4	6.8	785.0	65.5	−10.5	6.9
790.0	66.0	−10.6	7.0	795.0	63.5	−10.15	6.7
800.0	61.0	−9.7	6.4	805.0	57.15	−9.0	5.95
810.0	53.3	−8.3	5.5	815.0	56.1	−8.8	5.8
820.0	58.9	−9.3	6.1	825.0	60.4	−9.55	6.3
830.0	61.9	−9.8	6.5				
840.0	61.7	−8.6	7.4				
850.0	61.2	−7.3	7.8				
860.0	60.4	−6.1	8.0				
870.0	60.1	−4.8	8.6				
880.0	54.7	−4.4	3.6				
890.0	51.7	−3.7	1.4				
900.0	50.5	−2.7	1.0				
910.0	47.3	−2.3	−1.7				
920.0	43.8	−2.1	−4.9				
930.0	41.4	−2.8	−8.0				
940.0	44.9	−1.9	−4.2				
950.0	51.7	−3.0	−3.0				

A.7 Pointer's gamut of real surfaces

Pointer [766] computed CIELAB data for a large collection of spectral reflectance measurements of real object surfaces. The color gamut boundary is expressed in terms of the CIELAB chroma for each lightness (in increments of 5) and hue angle (in increments of 10°). The table shows the CIELAB chroma as a function of hue angle and lightness:

Hue/L^*	15	20	25	30	35	40	45	50	55	60	65	70	75	80	85	90
0	10	30	43	56	68	77	79	77	72	65	57	50	40	30	19	8
10	15	30	45	56	64	70	73	73	71	64	57	48	39	30	18	7
20	14	34	49	61	69	74	76	76	74	68	61	51	40	30	19	9
30	35	48	59	68	75	82	84	83	80	75	67	56	45	33	21	10
40	27	40	53	66	79	90	94	93	88	82	72	60	47	35	22	10

(cont.)

(cont.)

Hue/L^*	15	20	25	30	35	40	45	50	55	60	65	70	75	80	85	90
50	10	21	34	45	60	75	90	100	102	99	88	75	59	45	30	15
60	4	15	26	37	48	59	70	82	93	103	106	98	85	66	45	23
70	5	15	25	36	46	56	67	76	85	94	102	108	103	82	58	34
80	6	15	24	32	40	48	55	64	72	82	94	105	115	115	83	48
90	4	12	20	28	36	44	53	60	68	75	83	90	98	106	111	90
100	9	16	23	30	37	45	51	58	65	72	80	86	94	100	106	108
110	9	18	27	35	44	52	59	66	74	82	87	92	95	100	96	84
120	4	14	23	32	41	49	57	64	71	78	84	90	94	95	83	50
130	5	18	30	40	48	56	64	70	77	82	85	88	89	84	64	35
140	7	20	32	42	52	60	69	76	82	87	89	90	83	71	54	30
150	7	21	34	45	57	68	75	81	84	84	83	80	72	58	44	20
160	8	24	36	48	58	68	76	82	85	83	78	69	59	49	34	15
170	13	25	36	47	57	65	70	75	76	75	71	65	57	45	30	15
180	10	25	38	48	57	64	69	71	72	69	64	59	51	41	29	16
190	7	19	30	40	48	55	59	62	62	60	55	49	41	32	23	13
200	5	19	29	37	42	45	46	46	45	43	39	35	30	22	14	7
210	0	12	17	26	34	43	49	51	54	50	46	40	32	24	14	4
220	2	12	20	28	35	40	45	48	51	49	45	38	32	23	15	6
230	10	20	29	36	42	46	49	51	52	50	45	39	32	24	15	7
240	8	16	26	34	41	47	49	50	50	47	42	36	29	21	12	4
250	9	21	32	40	49	54	55	55	52	48	43	36	29	21	13	4
260	12	24	34	41	46	51	55	56	51	46	40	33	27	20	13	6
270	14	31	42	50	55	60	60	57	50	45	39	33	26	20	13	6
280	10	29	45	55	60	61	60	57	53	46	40	34	25	18	11	4
290	20	40	60	69	71	69	65	58	50	43	36	29	24	18	12	5
300	30	55	72	81	79	72	64	57	50	42	35	30	24	17	12	5
310	62	76	85	88	85	80	71	62	55	47	41	34	27	20	14	6
320	60	71	79	84	85	86	82	74	66	57	48	40	31	24	16	8
330	20	50	72	86	89	89	86	80	72	63	54	45	36	27	18	9
340	26	49	63	73	82	87	87	83	78	71	62	51	40	28	16	4
350	15	37	52	65	73	79	82	84	79	73	63	53	40	30	17	6

Glossary

Most of the following terms and definitions are from *International Lighting Vocabulary*, CIE Publication No. 17.4. Others are from various standard documents, such as ISO, ANSI, CGATS, etc.

Abney's law
An empirical law stating that, if two stimuli, A and B, are perceived to be of equal brightness and two other color stimuli, C and D, are perceived to be of equal brightness, the additive mixtures of A with C and B with D will also be perceived to be of equal brightness. The validity of this law depends strongly on the observation conditions.

absorption
Transformation of radiant energy to a different form of energy by interaction with matter.

adapted white
Color stimulus that an observer who is adapted to the viewing environment would judge to be perfectly achromatic and to have a luminance factor of unity. The adapted white usually varies within a scene.

additive mixture of color stimuli
Mixture of color stimuli acting in such a manner that they enter the eye simultaneously or in rapid succession and are incident on the same area of the retina, or are incident in the form of mosaic which the eye cannot resolve.

aliasing
Output image artifacts that occur in a sampled imaging system for input images having significant energy at frequencies greater than the Nyquist frequency of the system.

alychne
Plane in color space representing the locus of colors of zero luminance. This plane passes through the black point (usually the origin of the system); it intersects any linear chromaticity diagram in a straight line which is also called an alychne.

aperture color
Color perceived as nonlocated in depth such as that perceived as filling a hole in a screen.

Bezold–Brücke phenomenon
Change in the hue of the perceived color with a change in luminance level within the range of photopic vision.

brightness
Attribute of visual sensation according to which an area appears to emit more or less light.

candela (cd)
SI unit of luminous intensity, in a given direction of a source that is emitting monochromatic radiant energy of frequency 540×10^{12} Hz (555.016 nm in air) and whose radiant intensity in that direction is $1/683$ W sr^{-1}.

candela per square meter (cd m^{-2})
SI unit of luminance.

cathodoluminescence
Luminescence caused by the impact of electrons on certain types of luminescent materials, such as the coating on a television screen.

chroma
Attribute of visual sensation which permits a judgement to be made of the amount of pure chromatic color present, irrespective of the amount of achromatic color. Note: in a series of perceived colors of constant saturation, the chroma increases with the luminosity.

chromatic adaptation
Adaptation by stimuli in which the dominant effect is that of different relative spectral distributions.

CIE standard illuminants
Standard illuminant A, 2855.6 K
Standard illuminant B, 4874 K (direct sunlight)
Standard illuminant C, 6774 K
Standard illuminant D$_{65}$, 6504 K

CIE standard photometric observer
Ideal observer having a relative spectral responsivity curve that conforms to the $V(\lambda)$ function for photopic vision or to the $V'(\lambda)$ function for scotopic vision, and that complies with the summation law implied in the definition of the luminous flux.

coherent radiation
Monochromatic radiation whose electromagnetic oscillations maintain constant phase differences from one position to another.

color (perceived)
Attribute of visual perception consisting of any combination of chromatic and achromatic content. This attribute can be described by chromatic color names such as yellow, orange, brown, red, green, blue, pink, purple, etc., or by achromatic color names such as white, gray, black, etc., and be qualified by bright, dim, light, dark, etc., or by combinations of such names. Perceived color depends on the spectral distribution of the color stimulus, on the size, shape, structure and surround of the stimulus area, on the state of adaptation of the observer's visual system, and on the observer's experience of the prevailing and similar situations of observation.

color atlas
Collection of color samples used for evaluating colors by visual matching.

color equation

$$C(\mathbf{C}) \equiv R(\mathbf{R}) + G(\mathbf{G}) + B(\mathbf{B})$$

color gamut
Volume in a color space, consisting of all those colors that are either (1) present in a specific scene, artwork, print, or some form of reproduction, or (2) capable of being produced or created using a particular output device and/or medium.

colorimeter
Instrument for measuring the tristimulus values or the chromaticity coordinates of a color stimulus.

colorimetry
Measurement of colors based on a set of conventions. If the eye is used to make a quantitative comparison of colors, it is called visual colorimetry. If physical devices are used for the comparison, it is physical colorimetry.

color matching functions
Tristimulus values of monochromatic stimuli of equal radiant power.

color rendering
Mapping of image data representing the colorimetric coordinates of the elements of a scene or original to image data representing the colorimetric coordinates of the elements of a reproduction.

color space
Manifold of three dimensions for the geometrical representation of colors.

color temperature
Temperature of the full radiator which emits radiation of the same chromaticity as the radiation considered. (See, also, correlated color temperature.)

contrast sensitivity
Reciprocal of the minimum relative luminance difference perceptible: $S_c = L/\Delta L$.

correlated color temperature
The color temperature corresponding to the point on the Planckian locus which is nearest to the point representing the chromaticity of the illuminant considered on an agreed uniform-chromaticity-scale diagram.

diffraction
Deviation of the direction of the propagation of a radiation, determined by the wave nature of radiation and occurring when the radiation passes the edge of an obstacle.

diffusion
Change of the spatial distribution of a beam of radiation when it is deflected in many directions by a surface or by a medium without change of frequency of the monochromatic components of which the radiation is composed.

equi-energy spectrum, equi-energy white
Spectrum in which the spectral concentration of energy evaluated on a wavelength basis is constant throughout the visible region.

flare

Unintended stray light added to an image.

fluorescence

Photoluminescence in which the emitted optical radiation results from direct transitions from the photoexcited energy level to a lower level, usually taking less than 10^{-8} s.

footcandle

Unit of illuminance: lumen per square foot. 1 footcandle = 10.76 lux.

fovea; fovea centralis

Central part of the retina, thin and depressed, which contains almost exclusively cones and is the site of the most distinct vision. It subtends an angle of about 0.026 rad or 1.5°.

foveola

Central region of the fovea which contains only cones. It subtends about 1°.

Helmholtz–Kohlrausch phenomenon

Change in brightness of perceived color produced by increasing the purity of a color stimulus while keeping its luminance constant within the range of photopic vision.

hue

Attribute of visual sensation which has given rise to color names, such as blue, green, yellow, red, purple, etc.

hyperfocal distance

Focus distance of a camera lens that offers the greatest depth of field.

incandescence

Emission of visible radiation by thermal excitation

infrared radiation

Radiation with a wavelength greater than that of visible light and shorter than 1 mm. IR-A: 780–1400 nm, IR-B: 1.4–3 μm, IR-C: 3 μm to 1 mm.

interflection (interreflection)

General effect of the reflections of radiation between several reflecting surfaces.

irradiance (at a point of a surface) E_e

Quotient of the radiant flux $d\Phi_e$ incident on an element of the surface containing the point, by the area of that element.

$$E_e = \frac{d\Phi_e}{dA} \quad [\text{W m}^{-2}].$$

Equivalent definition: integral taken over the hemisphere visible from the given point of the expression $L_e \cdot \cos\theta \cdot d\Omega$, where L_e is the radiance at the given point in the various directions of the incident elementary beams of solid angle $d\Omega$, and θ is the angle between any of these beams and the normal to the surface at the given point. The following integration is over 2π sr.

$$E_e = \int_{2\pi\,\text{sr}} L_e \cdot \cos\theta \cdot d\Omega \quad [\text{W m}^{-2}].$$

lightness (of a related color)
The brightness of an area judged relative to the brightness of a similarly illuminated area that appears to be white or highly transmitting.

lumen
SI unit of luminous flux: luminous flux emitted within unit solid angle (1 sr) by a point source having a uniform luminous intensity of 1 cd.

luminance factor
See radiance factor.

luminescence
Emission of optical radiation by a material as the result of energy excitation other than the normal thermal agitation. For example, luminescence caused by optical radiation is called photoluminescence. If it is caused by x-rays or other radio-active high-energy radiation, it is called radioluminescence. If it is caused by an electric field, it is called electroluminescence. Luminescence caused by energy released by a chemical reaction is called chemilumines-cence. Luminescence caused by the impact of electrons on certain types of materials is called cathodoluminescence.

luminous efficacy
Quotient of luminous flux by the corresponding radiant flux. In the English language the term efficiency has been reserved for a dimensionless quantity (i.e. a ratio) which cannot exceed unity (100%). If the quantity has dimensions (i.e. it is a quotient) the term used is efficacy.

Luther condition
When the spectral responsivity functions of a trichromatic imaging system are a linear transformation of the CIE color matching functions (or the human cone spectral sensitivity functions), the system is said to satisfy the Luther condition.

lux (lx)
Unit of illuminance: 1 lux = 1 lumen per square meter.

metameric color stimuli
Spectrally different radiations that produce the same color under the same viewing conditions.

monochromatic radiation
Radiation characterized by a single frequency. In practice, radiation of a very small range of frequencies which can be described by stating a single frequency.

Nyquist frequency
Frequency equal to 0.5 times the inverse of the sampling interval.

object color
Color perceived to belong to an object.

optical radiation
Electromagnetic radiation at wavelengths between the region of transition to x-rays ($\lambda \approx$ 1 nm) and the region of transition to radio waves ($\lambda \approx$ 1 mm).

optoelectronic conversion function (OECF)
Relationship between the input log exposure (luminance) and the output digital levels for an optoelectronic image capture system. If the exposure is measured at the focal plane, it is called the focal plane OECF. If the input is log scene luminance, it is called the camera OECF.

perfect reflecting (transmitting) diffuser
Ideal uniform diffuser with a reflectance (transmittance) equal to 1.

phosphorescence
Photoluminescence delayed by storage of energy in an intermediate energy level. The delay time is usually longer than 10^{-8} s.

photometer
Instrument for measuring photometric quantities.

photometry
Measurement of quantities referring to radiation evaluated according to the visual effect which it produces, as based on certain conventions.

photopic vision
Vision by the normal eye when it is adapted to levels of luminance of at least several candelas per square meter.

primary light source
Surface or object emitting light produced by the transformation of energy

radiance (in a given direction, at a point of a real or imaginary surface) L_e
Quantity defined by the formula

$$L_e = d^2\Phi/(d\Omega dA \cos\theta) \quad [\text{W m}^{-2} \text{ sr}^{-1}],$$

where $d^2\Phi$ is the radiant flux transmitted by an elementary beam passing through the given point and propagating in the solid angle $d\Omega$ containing the given direction; dA is the area of a section of that beam containing the given point; θ is the angle between the normal to that section and the direction of that beam.

radiance (luminance) factor (at a point on the surface of a non-self-radiating body, in a given direction, under specified conditions of irradiation (illumination)) β
Ratio of radiance (luminance) of the body to that of a perfect reflecting or transmitting diffuser identically irradiated (illuminated).

radiant exitance (at a point of a surface) M_e
Quotient of the radiant flux $d\Phi_e$ leaving an element of the surface containing the point, by the area of that element:

$$M_e = \frac{d\Phi_e}{dA} \quad [\text{W m}^{-2}].$$

Equivalent definition: integral, taken over the hemisphere visible from the given point, of the expression $L_e \cos\theta d\Omega$, where L_e is the radiance at the given point in the various directions of the incident elementary beams of solid angle $d\Omega$, and θ is the angle between any of these beams and the normal to the surface at the given point:

$$M_e = \int_{2\pi\,\text{sr}} L_e \cos\theta\, d\Omega \quad [\text{W m}^{-2}].$$

radiant exposure (at a point of a surface, for a given duration) H_e
Quotient of dQ_e, radiant energy incident on an element of the surface containing the point over the given duration Δt, by the area dA of that element.

$$H_e = \frac{dQ_e}{dA} = \int_{\Delta t} E_e dt \quad [\text{W s m}^{-2}].$$

radiant flux; radiant power (Φ_e, Φ, P)
Power emitted, transmitted, or received in the form of radiation.

radiant intensity (of a source in a given direction) (I_e, I)
Quotient of the radiant flux $d\Phi_e$ leaving the source and propagated in the element of solid angle $d\Omega$ containing the given direction, by the element of solid angle.

$$I_e = \frac{d\Phi_e}{d\Omega} \quad [\text{W sr}^{-1}].$$

radiometry
Measurement of the quantities associated with radiation.

Rayleigh scattering (in a medium)
Diffusion of radiation in the course of its passage through a medium containing particles the size of which is small compared with the wavelength of the radiation.

reflectance factor (at a point on the surface, for the part of the reflected radiation contained in a given cone with its apex at the point on the surface, and for incident spectral composition and geometric distribution)
Ratio of the radiant flux reflected in the directions delimited by the cone to that reflected in the same directions by a perfect reflecting diffuser identically irradiated. Note: if the solid angle of the cone approaches zero, then the reflectance factor approaches the radiance factor. If the solid angle of the cone approaches 2π, then the reflectance factor approaches the reflectance.

reflectance (optical) density D_ρ
Logarithm to base 10 of the reciprocal of the reflectance. $D_\rho = -\log_{10}\rho$.

reflection
Return of radiation by a surface without change of frequency of the monochromatic components of which the radiation is composed. "Regular reflection": reflection without diffusion in accordance with the laws of optical reflection as in a mirror. "Diffuse reflection": diffusion by reflection in which, on the macroscopic scale, there is no regular reflection. "Retro-reflection": reflection in which radiation is returned in directions close to the direction from which it came, this property being maintained over wide variations of the direction of the incident radiation.

reflectivity ρ_∞
Reflectance of a layer of material of such a thickness that there is no change of reflectance with increase in thickness.

refractive index
Ratio of the velocity of light in vacuum to the phase velocity of that in a medium.

related color
Color perceived to belong to an area or object in relation to other perceived colors in the visual field.

relative responsivity $\hat{s}$
Ratio of the responsivity $s(X)$ when the detector input is X to the responsivity $s(N)$ when the detector input is the reference irradiation $N : \hat{s} = s(X)/s(N)$.

relative spectral responsivity $\hat{s}(\lambda)$
Ratio of the spectral responsivity $s(\lambda)$ of the detector at wavelength λ to a given reference value $s_m : \hat{s}(\lambda) = s(\lambda)/s_m$.

responsivity s
Quotient of the detector output Y by the detector input $X : s = Y/X$. Note: if the detector output is Y_0 when there is no input, and is Y_1 when the input is X, then $s = (Y_1 - Y_0)/X$.

retro-reflecting material
Material in which is incorporated a large number of very small elements which, by refraction and reflection, produce the phenomenon of retro-reflection when they become the surface as the material wears. (See, also, reflection.)

saturation
Attribute of visual sensation which permits a judgement to be made of the proportion of pure chromatic color in the total sensation.

scotopic vision
Vision by the normal eye when it is adapted to levels of luminance of less than some hundredths of a candela per square meter.

secondary light source
Surface or object which is not self-emitting but receives light and redirects it, at least in part, by reflection or transmission.

sensation
Element of mental content of a sense impression which cannot be analyzed further.

spectral distribution X_λ (of a radiant, luminous or photon quantity $X(\lambda)$)
Quotient of the radiant or luminous or photon quantity $dX(\lambda)$ contained in an elementary range of $d\lambda$ of wavelength at the wavelength λ, by that range.

$$X_\lambda = \frac{dX(\lambda)}{d\lambda}.$$

spectral luminous efficiency ($V(\lambda)$ for photopic vision or $V'(\lambda)$ for scotopic vision)
Ratio of the radiant flux at wavelength λ_m to that at wavelength λ such that both radiations

produce equally intense luminous sensations under specified photometric conditions and λ_m is chosen so that the maximum value of this ratio is equal to 1.

spectral responsivity $s(\lambda)$

Quotient of the detector output $dY(\lambda)$ by the monochromatic detector input $dX(\lambda) = X_\lambda(\lambda)d\lambda$:

$$s(\lambda) = \frac{dY(\lambda)}{dX(\lambda)}.$$

spectroradiometer

Instrument for measuring the spectral concentration of radiant energy or power.

spectrophotometer

Instrument for measuring the ratio of two spectral radiometric quantities.

Stiles–Crawford effect

Decrease of the brightness of a light stimulus with the position of entry of the light pencil through the pupil. This is called the Stiles–Crawford effect of the first kind. If the variation is in hue and saturation instead of in brightness, it is called the Stiles–Crawford effect of the second kind.

Talbot's law

If a point of the retina is excited by a light stimulus undergoing periodic variations in magnitude at a frequency exceeding the fusion frequency, the visual sensation produced is identical to that produced by a steady stimulus whose magnitude is equal to the mean magnitude of the variable stimulus taken over one period.

tone reproduction

Relationship of the luminance (luminance factor, L^*, log luminance, density) in a scene or original to the luminance (luminance factor, L^*, log luminance, density) in a reproduction. Tone reproduction is usually used to describe an imaging system (such as a system consisting of a digital camera and a digital printer).

tonescale

Tonescale is a rule of mapping between two numerical representations of photometric quantities (such as luminance, luminance factor, L^*, and density). For example, the tonescale of a printer means the mapping of the input digital values (representing some recorded photometric quantities of an image) to the photometrically measured values of the printed output. Tonescale is usually used to describe an imaging device (such as a printer or a film).

transmission

Passage of radiation through a medium without change of frequency of the monochromatic components of which the radiation is composed.

transmittance (for incident radiation of given spectral composition, polarization and geometrical distribution) τ

Ratio of the transmitted radiant or luminous flux to the incident flux in the given conditions.

transmittance (optical) density D_τ

Logarithm to base 10 of the reciprocal of the transmittance. $D_\tau = -\log_{10}\tau$.

trichromatic system

System of color specification based on the possibility of matching a color stimulus by the additive mixture of three suitably chosen reference stimuli.

tristimulus values of a color stimulus

Amounts of the three reference color stimuli (primaries), in a given trichromatic system, required to match the color of the stimulus considered. For example, if a color stimulus $(\mathbf{C})$ is matched by the three primaries $(\mathbf{R})$, $(\mathbf{G})$, and $(\mathbf{B})$, as expressed by $(\mathbf{C}) \equiv R(\mathbf{R}) + G(\mathbf{G}) + B(\mathbf{B})$, then R, G, B are the tristimulus values of the color $(\mathbf{C})$.

troland

Unit used for expressing the magnitude of the external light stimulus applied to the eye. When the eye is viewing a surface of uniform luminance, the number of trolands is equal to the product of the area in square millimeters of the limiting pupil and the luminance of the surface in candelas per square meter. Note: in computing retinal illuminance, absorption and reflection losses and the dimension of the particular eye under consideration must be taken into account. If all the corrections are negligible, 1 troland produces a retinal illuminance of approximately 0.002 lm m^{-2}.

ultraviolet radiation

Radiation with a wavelength less than that of visible light and longer than 1 nm.

uniform color space

Color space in which the distance between any two colors is intended to represent a measure of the perceived difference between the corresponding colors.

unrelated color

Color perceived to belong to an area with completely dark surroundings.

veiling glare

Light reflected from an imaging medium that has not been modulated by the means used to produce the image.

viewing flare

Veiling glare that is observed in a viewing environment, but not accounted for in radiometric measurements made using the prescribed measurement geometry and calibration conditions.

visible radiation

Any optical radiation capable of causing visual sensation directly. The lower limit is generally taken to be between 360 nm and 400 nm, and the upper limit between 760 nm and 830 nm.

wave number (σ)

The reciprocal of the wavelength $[\text{m}^{-1}]$.

References

[1] W. Abney, "On the changes in hue of spectrum colours by dilution with white light," *Proceedings of the Royal Society (London)*, **A83**, 120–124, 1910.

[2] W. Abney, *Researches in Colour Vision and the Trichromatic Theory*, London: Longmans, Green, 1913.

[3] K. Adachi, T. Nishimura, and K. Iwabe, "Parallel signal processing system for a super high-resolution digital camera," in *Proc. IS&T's 2003 PICS Conference*, 340–344, 2003.

[4] J.E. Adams, Jr., "Interaction between color plane interpolation and other image processing functions in electronic photography," *SPIE Proceedings*, **2416**, 144–151, 1995.

[5] J.E. Adams, Jr., "Design of practical color filter array interpolation algorithms for digital cameras," *SPIE Proceedings*, **3028**, 117–125, 1997.

[6] J.E. Adams, Jr., "Design of practical color filter array interpolation algorithms for digital cameras, Part 2," *Proc. IEEE International Conference on Image Processing*, Chicago, **1**, 488–492, 1998.

[7] J. Adams, K. Parulski, and K. Spaulding, "Color processing in digital cameras," *IEEE Micro*, **18**, 6, 20–30, 1998.

[8] M.J. Adams and P.A. Dolin, *Printing Technology*, 5th edition, Clifton Park, NY: Delmar Publishers, 2002.

[9] E.H. Adelson, "Perceptual organization and the judgement of brightness," *Science*, **262**, 2042–2044, 1993.

[10] E.H. Adelson, "Lightness perception and lightness illusions," in *The Cognitive Neurosciences*, edited by M. Gazzaniga, pp. 339–351, Cambridge, MA: MIT Press, 2000.

[11] G.A. Agoston, *Color Theory and Its Application in Art and Design*, 2nd edition, Berlin: Springer-Verlag, 1987.

[12] G. Agranov, V. Berezin, and R.H. Tsai, "Crosstalk and microlens study in a color CMOS image sensor," *IEEE Transactions on Electron Devices*, **50**, 1, 4–11, 2003.

[13] M. Aguilar and W.S. Stiles, "Saturation of the rod mechanism of the retina at high levels of stimulation," *Optica Acta*, **1**, 59–65, 1954.

[14] P.K. Ahnelt and R. Pflug, "Telodendrial contacts between foveolar cone pedicles in the human retina," *Experientia*, **42**, 298–300, 1986.

[15] A.J. Ahumada and A.B. Watson, "Equivalent-noise model for contrast detection and discrimination," *Journal of the Optical Society of America*, A, **2**, 7, 1133–1139, 1985.

[16] J.S. Alkofer, *Tone Value Sample Selection in Digital Image Processing Method Employing Histogram Normalization*, US Patent 4,654,722, March 31, 1987.

[17] J.P. Allebach, (editor), *Selected Papers on Digital Halftoning*, Bellingham WA: SPIE Press, 1999.

[18] E. Allen, "Colorant formulation and shading," in *Optical Radiation Measurements*, Volume 2, *Color Measurement*, edited by F. Grum and C.J. Bartleson, New York, NY: Academic Press, 1980.

[19] D. Alleysson, S. Süsstrunk, and J. Hérault, "Color demosaicing by estimating luminance and opponent chromatic signals in the Fourier domain," *Proc. IS&T/SID 10th Color Imaging Conference*, 331–336, 2002.

[20] D. Alleysson, S. Süsstrunk, and J. Marguier, "Influence of spectral sensitivity functions on color demosaicing," *Proc. IS&T/SID 11th Color Imaging Conference*, 351–357, 2003.

[21] J.H. Altman, "The measurement of RMS granularity," *Applied Optics*, **3**, 35–38, 1964.

[22] T. Amano, *Method of Determining Exposure Amounts in Photographic Printing*, US Patent 3,873,201, March 25, 1975.

[23] T. Amano and R. Andoh, *Process of and System for Printing in Color Photography*, US Patent 3,888,580, June 10, 1975.

[24] I. Amidror, "Scattered data interpolation methods for electronic imaging systems: a survey," *Journal of Electronic Imaging*, **11**, 2, 157–176, 2002.

[25] R. Anderson, "Matrix description of radiometric quantities," *Applied Optics*, **30**, 7, 858–867, 1991.

[26] T.W. Anderson, *An Introduction to Multivariate Statistical Analysis*, 2nd edition, New York, NY: John Wiley & Sons, Inc., 1984.

[27] H.C. Andrews and B.R. Hunt, *Digital Image Restoration*, Englewood Cliffs, NJ: Prentice-Hall, 1977.

[28] T.M. Apostol, *Calculus*, Volume II, 2nd edition, pp. 269–271, New York, NY: John Wiley & Sons, Inc., 1969.

[29] R.A. Applegate and V. Lakshminarayanan, "Parametric representation of Stiles–Crawford functions: normal variation of peak location and directionality," *Journal of the Optical Society of America*, A, **10**, 7, 1611–1623, 1993.

[30] L.E. Arend and A. Reeves, "Simultaneous colour constancy," *Journal of the Optical Society of America*, A, **3**, 10, 1743–1751, 1986.

[31] D. Armitage, "Liquid-crystal display device fundamentals," in *Electro-Optical Displays*, edited by M.A. Karim, New York, NY: Marcel Dekker, 1992.

[32] J.S. Arney and M. Alber, "Optical effects of ink spread and penetration on halftones printed by thermal ink jet," *Journal of Imaging Science and Technology*, **42**, 4, 331–334, 1998.

[33] J.S. Arney and E. Pray, "Kubelka–Munk theory and the Yule–Nielsen effect on halftones," *Journal of Imaging Science and Technology*, **43**, 4, 365–370, 1999.

[34] P. Artal, J. Santamaria, and J. Bescos, "Retrieval of wave aberration of human eyes from actual point-spread-function data," *Journal of the Optical Society of America*, A, **5**, 8, 1201–1206, 1988.

[35] P. Artal, "Calculations of two-dimensional foveal retinal images in real eyes," *Journal of the Optical Society of America*, A, **7**, 8, 1374–1381, 1990.

[36] P. Artal, M. Ferro, I. Miranda, and R. Navarro, "Effects of aging in retinal image quality," *Journal of the Optical Society of America*, A, **10**, 7, 1656–1662, 1993.

[37] P. Artal and R. Navarro, "Monochromatic modulation transfer function of the human eye for different pupil diameters: an analytical expression," *Journal of the Optical Society of America*, **11**, 1, 246–249, 1994.

[38] N.W. Ashcroft and N.D. Mermin, *Solid State Physics*, Fort Worth, TX: Saunders, 1976.

[39] ASMT (American Society for Testing and Materials), *ASTM Standards on Color and Apearance Measurement*, 3rd Edition, Philadelphia, PA: ASTM, 1991.

[40] J. Astola, P. Haavisto, and Y. Neuvo, "Vector median filters, *Proceedings of the IEEE*, **78**, 678–689, 1990.

[41] D.A. Atchison, W.N. Charman, and R.L. Woods, "Subjective depth-of-focus of the human eye," *Optometry and Visual Science*, **74**, 511–520, 1997.

[42] G.G. Attridge, C. Leverton, M.R. Pointer, and R.E. Jacobson, "Measured colour difference and the acceptability of colour prints," *The Journal of Photographic Science*, **44**, 14–17, 1996.

[43] P.W. Atkins, *Molecules*, Scientific American Library, New York, NY: W.H. Freeman, 1987.

[44] P.W. Atkins, *Physical Chemistry*, 5th edition, New York, NY: W.H. Freeman, 1994.

[45] L.L. Avant, "Vision in the Ganzfeld," *Psychological Bulletin*, **64**, 4, 246–258, 1965.

[46] H.D. Baker, "The instantaneous threshold and early dark adaptation," *Journal of the Optical Society of America*, **43**, 9, 798–803, 1953.

[47] R. Bala, R. DeQueiroz, R. Eschbach, and W. Wu, "Gamut mapping to preserve spatial luminance variations," *Journal of Imaging Science and Technology*, **45**, 5, 436–443, 2001.

[48] R.M. Balboa, C.W. Tyler, and N.M. Grzywacz, "Occlusions contribute to scaling in natural images," *Vision Research*, **41**, 955–964, 2001.

[49] P. Ball, *Designing the Molecular World*, Princeton, NJ: Princeton University Press, 1994.

[50] P. Bamberg and S. Sternberg, *A Course in Mathematics for Students of Physics: 1*, Cambridge: Cambridge University Press, 1988.

[51] P. Bamberg and S. Sternberg, *A Course in Mathematics for Students of Physics: 2*, Cambridge: Cambridge University Press, 1990.

[52] R. Barker, *Neuroscience: An Illustrated Guide*, New York, NY: Ellis Horwood, 1991.

[53] E. Barlow, "Dark and light adaptation," in *Handbook of Sensory Physiology*, VII/4, Visual Psychophysics, edited by D. Jameson and L.M. Hurvich, Berlin: Springer-Verlag, 1972.

[54] H.B. Barlow and J.D. Mollon, (eds.), *The Senses*, Cambridge: Cambridge University Press, 1982.

[55] R.B. Barlow, R.R. Birge, E. Kaplan, and J.R. Tallent, "On the molecular origin of photoreceptor noise", *Nature*, **366**, 64–66, 1993.

[56] R.B. Barlow, Jr., and R.T. Verrillo, "Brightness sensation in a Ganzfeld," *Vision Research*, **16**, 1291–1297, 1976.

[57] K. Barnard, *Practical Colour Constancy*, Ph.D. thesis, Simon Fraser University, School of Computing, 1999.

[58] P.Y. Barnes, E.A. Early, and A.C. Parr, *NIST Measurement Services: Spectral Reflectance*, NIST Special Publication 250-48, National Institute of Standards and Technology, Gaithersburg, MD, March 1998.

[59] M. Barni, F. Buti, F. Fartolini, and V. Cappellini, "A quasi-Euclidean norm to speed up vector median filtering," *IEEE Transactions on Image Processing*, **9**, 10, 1704–1709, 2000.

[60] C.R. Barr, J.R. Thirtle, and P.W. Vittum, "Development inhibitor releasing (DIR) couplers in color photography," *Photographic Science and Engineering*, **13**, 2, 74–80 (the typographical errors were corrected on pages 214–217), 1969.

[61] H.H. Barrett, "Objective assessment of image quality: effects of quantum noise and object variability," *Journal of the Optical Society of America*, A, **7**, 7, 1266–1278, 1990.

[62] H.H. Barrett, J.L. Denny, R.F. Wagner, and K.J. Meyers, "Objective assessment of image quality. II. Fisher information, Fourier crosstalk, and figures of merit for task performance," *Journal of the Optical Society of America*, A, **12**, 5, 834–852, 1995.

[63] H.H. Barrett, C.K. Abbey, and E. Clarkson, "Objective assessment of image quality. III. ROC metrics, ideal observers, and likelihood-generating functions," *Journal of the Optical Society of America*, A, **15**, 6, 1520–1536, 1998.

[64] H.H. Barrett and K.J. Meyers, *Foundations of Image Science*, New York, NY: John Wiley & Sons, 2004.

[65] D.E. Barrick, "Relationship between slope probability density function and the physical optics integral in rough surface scattering," *Proc. IEEE.* **56**, 1728–1729, 1968 (correction in **57**, 256, 1969).

[66] D.E. Barrick, "Rough surfaces," in *Radar Cross-Section Handbook*, edited by G.T. Ruck, D.E. Barrick, W.D. Stuart and C.K. Krichbaum, New York, NY: Plenum Press, 1970.

[67] R.S. Barrows and R.N. Wolfe, "A review of adjacency effects in silver photographic images," *Photographic Science and Engineering*, **15**, 6, 472–479, 1971.

[68] G.S. Barsh, "What controls variations in human skin color?" *PLoS Biology*, (http://biology.plosjournals.org), **1**, 1, 19–22, 2003.

[69] P.G.J. Barten, "Evaluation of subjective image quality with the square-root integral method," *Journal of the Optical Society of America*, A, **7**, 10, 2024–2031, 1990.

[70] P.G.J. Barten, *Contrast Sensitivity of the Human Eye and Its Effects on Image Quality*, SPIE Optical Engineering Press, Bellingham, WA, 1999.

[71] C.J. Bartleson and R.W. Huboi, "Exposure determination methods for color printing: The concept of optimum correction level," *Journal of the Society of Picture and Television Engineering*, **65**, 205–215, April 1956.

[72] C.J. Bartleson, "Influence of observer adaptation on the acceptance of color prints," *Photographic Science and Engineering*, **2**, 1, 32–39, 1958.

[73] C.J. Bartleson, "Some observations on the reproduction of flesh colors," *Photographic Science and Engineering*, **3**, 3, 114–117, 1959.

[74] C.J. Bartleson and C.P. Bray, "On the preferred reproduction of flesh, blue-sky, and green-grass colors," *Photographic Science and Engineering*, **6**, 1, 19–25, 1962.

[75] C.J. Bartleson and E.J. Breneman, "Brightness perception in complex fields," *Journal of the Optical Society of America*, **57**, 7, 953–957, 1967.

[76] C.J. Bartleson and E.J. Breneman, "Brightness reproduction in the photographic process", *Photographic Science and Engineering*, **11**, 254–262, 1967.

[77] C.J. Bartleson, "Criterion for tone reproduction," *Journal of the Optical Society of America*, **58**, 7, 992–995, 1968.

[78] C.J. Bartleson and E.J. Breneman, "Differences among responses of observers in scaling brightness," *Color 73*, pp. 398–400, 1973.

[79] C.J. Bartleson, "A review of chromatic adaptation," in *Color 77*, edited by F.W. Billmeyer, Jr., and G. Wyszecki, pp. 63–96, Bristol: Adam Hilger, 1978.

[80] C.J. Bartleson, "Colorimetry," in *Optical Radiation Measurements*, Volume 2, edited by F. Grum and C.J. Bartleson, New York, NY: Academic Press, 1980.

[81] C.J. Bartleson, "On chromatic adaptation and persistence," *Color Research and Application*, **6**, 3, 153–160, 1981.

[82] C.J. Bartleson, "The combined influence of sharpness and graininess on the quality of colour prints," *The Journal of Photographic Science*, **30**, 33–38, 1982.

[83] R.E. Bartow, W.K. Darrow, and W.T. Hartmann, *CRT Device Light Versus Input Signal Characteristic Function*, US Patent 4,862,265, Aug. 29, 1989.

[84] M. Bass (ed.), *Handbook of Optics*, Volumes I and II, New York, NY: McGraw-Hill, 1995.

[85] E. Baumgardt, "Threshold quantal problems," in *Handbook of Sensory Physiology*, VII/4, Visual Psychophysics, edited by D. Jameson and L.M. Hurvich, Berlin: Springer-Verlag, 1972.

[86] G.A. Baxes, *Digital Image Processing: Principles and Applications*, New York, NY: John Wiley and Sons, 1994.

[87] B.E. Bayer, "An optimum method for two-level rendition of continuous-tone pictures," *IEEE International Conference on Communications*, **1**, 26.11–26.15, 1973.

[88] B.E. Bayer, *Color Imaging Array*, US Patent 3,971,065, July 20, 1976.

[89] D.A. Baylor, T.D. Lamb, and K.-W. Yau, "Responses of retinal rods to single photons," *Journal of Physiology*, **288**, 613–634, 1979.

[90] D.A. Baylor, "Photoreceptor signals and vision," *Investigative Ophthalmology and Visual Science*, **28**, 1, 34–49, 1987.

[91] M.E. Becker, "Evaluation and characterization of display reflectance," *SID 97 Digest*, 827–830, 1997.

[92] P. Beckmann and A. Spizzichino, *The Scattering of Electromagnetic Waves from Rough Surfaces*, New York, NY: Pergamon, 1963.

[93] J. Belloni, M. Treguer, H. Remita, and R.R. De Heyzer, "Enhanced yield of photoinduced electrons in doped silver halide crystals," *Nature*, **402**, 865–867, 1999.

[94] A.G. Bennett and R.B. Rabbetts, *Clinical Visual Optics*, 2nd edition, London: Butterworths, 1989.

[95] J.M. Bennett, and L. Mattsson, *Introduction to Surface Roughness and Scattering*, Washington, DC: Optical Society of America, 1989.

[96] O. Ben-Shahar and S.W. Zucker, "Hue field and color curvatures: a perceptual organization approach to color image denoising," in *Proc. 2003 IEEE Computer Society Conference on Computer Vision and Pattern Recognition*, Volume II, pp. 713–720, 2003.

[97] K.B. Benson (ed.), *Television Engineering Handbook*, New York, NY: McGraw-Hill Book Company, 1986.

[98] M.J. Beran and G.B. Parrent, Jr., *Theory of Partial Coherence*, Englewood Cliffs, NJ: Prentice-Hall, 1964.

[99] M.A. Berkley, F. Kitterle, and D.W. Watkins, "Grating visibility as a function of orientation and retinal eccentricity," *Vision Research*, **15**, 239–244, 1975.

[100] S.M. Berman, G. Fein, D.J. Jewett, and F. Ashford, "Luminance controlled pupil size affects Landolt C test performance," *Journal of the Illuminating Engineering Society*, **22**, 2, 150–165, 1993.

[101] S.M. Berman, D.J. Jewett, B.R. Benson, and T.M. Law, "Despite different wall colors, vertical scotopic illuminance predicts pupil size," *Journal of the Illuminating Engineering Society*, **26**, 2, 59–64, 1997.

[102] R.S. Berns and K.H. Petersen, "Empirical modeling of systematic spectrophotometric error," *COLOR Research and Application*, **13**, 243–256, 1988.

[103] R. Berns, R. Motta, and M. Gorzynski, "CRT Colorimetry. Part I: Theory and Practice," *COLOR Research and Application*, **18**, 5, 299–314, 1993. R. Berns, M. Gorzynski, and R. Motta, "'CRT Colorimetry. Part II: Metrology," *COLOR Research and Application*, **18**, 5, 315–325, 1993.

[104] R.S. Berns, *Billmeyer and Saltzman's Principles of Color Technology*, 3rd edition, New York, NY: John Wiley and Sons, 2000.

[105] R.S. Berns, S.R. Fernandez, and L. Taplin, "Estimating black-level emissions of computer-controlled displays," *COLOR Research and Application*, **28**, 5, 379–383, 2003.

[106] M.J. Berry, D.K. Warland, and M. Meister, "The structure and precision of retinal spike trains," *Proc. of National Academy of Science*, **94**, 5411–5416, 1997.

[107] D.M. Berson, F.A. Dunn, and M. Takao, "Phototransduction by retinal ganglion cells that set the circadian clock," *Science*, **295**, 1070–1073, 2002.

[108] D.P. Bertsekas, *Nonlinear Programming*, Belmont, MA: Athena Scientific, 1999.

[109] E.I. Betensky, "Photographic lenses," Chapter 1 in *Applied Optics and Optical Engineering*, Vol. VIII, edited by R.R. Shannon and J.C. Wyant, pp. 1–30, New York, NY: Academic Press, Inc., 1980.

[110] P.R. Bevington, *Data Reduction and Error Analysis for Physical Sciences*, New York, NY: McGraw-Hill, 1969.

[111] F.W. Billmeyer and M. Saltzman, *Principles of Color Technology*, 2nd edition, New York, NY: John Wiley & Sons, Inc., 1981.

[112] F. Birren, "Application of the Ostwald color system to the design of consumer goods," *Journal of the Optical Society of America*, **34**, 7, 396–399, 1944.

[113] R.B. Blackman and J.W. Tukey, *The Measurement of Power Spectra*, New York, NY: Dover, 1959.

[114] H.R. Blackwell, "Contrast thresholds of the human eye," *Journal of the Optical Society of America*, **36**, 11, 624–643, 1946.

[115] C. Blakemore (ed.), *Vision: Coding and Efficiency*, Cambridge: Cambridge University Press, 1990.

[116] A.J. Blanksby and M.J. Loinaz, "Performance analysis of a color CMOS photogate image sensor," *IEEE Transactions on Electron Devices*, **47**, 1, 55–64, 2000.

[117] H. W. Bodmann, P. Haubner, and A. M. Marsden, "A unified relationship between brightness and luminance", *CIE Proceedings*, Kyoto Session, pp. 99–102, 1979.

[118] K.R. Boff, L. Kaufman, and J.P. Thomas, *Handbook of Perception and Human Performance*, Volume I, *Sensory Processes and Perception*, New York, NY: John Wiley and Sons, 1986.

[119] K.R. Boff, L. Kaufman, and J.P. Thomas, *Handbook of Perception and Human Performance*, Volume II, *Cognitive Processes and Performance*, New York, NY: John Wiley and Sons, 1986.

[120] C.F. Bohren and D.R. Huffman, *Absorption and Scattering of Light by Small Particles*, New York, NY: John Wiley and Sons, 1983.

[121] C.F. Bohren, "Scattering by particles," in *Handbook of Optics*, Volume I, edited by M. Bass, New York, NY: McGraw-Hill, 1995.

[122] M.E. Bond and D. Nickerson, "Color-order system, Munsell and Ostwald," *Journal of the Optical Society of America*, **32**, 709–719, 1942.

[123] I. Borg and P. Groenen, *Modern Multidimensional Scaling: Theory and Applications*, New York, NY: Springer, 1997.

[124] M. Born and E. Wolf, *Principles of Optics*, 6th (corrected) edition, Oxford: Pergamon Press, 1983.

[125] M. Born and E. Wolf, *Principles of Optics*, 7th (expanded) edition, Cambridge: Cambridge University Press, 1999.

[126] B.B. Boycott and H. Wassle, "Morphological classification of bipolar cells of the primate retina," *European Journal of Neuroscience*, **3**, 1069–1088, 1991.

[127] R.W. Boyd, *Radiometry and the Detection of Optical Radiation*, New York, NY: John Wiley & Sons, Inc., 1983.

[128] R.N. Bracewell, *The Fourier Transform and Its Applications*, 2nd edition, New York, NY: McGraw-Hill, 1986.

[129] R.N. Bracewell, *The Fourier Transform and Its Applications*, 3rd edition, Boston, MA: McGraw-Hill, 2000.

[130] R. Bradbury, "Thermal printing," Chapter 6 in *Chemistry and Technology of Printing and Imaging Systems*, edited by P. Gregory, London: Blackie Academic and Professional, 1996.

[131] D. Bradley, "Plastics that play on light," *Science*, **261**, 1272–1273, 1993.

[132] D.H. Brainard and B.A. Wandell, "Asymmetric color matching: how color appearance depends on the illuminant," *Journal of the Optical Society of America*, A, **9**, 9, 1433–1448, 1992.

[133] D.H. Brainard and W.T. Freeman, "Bayesian color constancy," *Journal of the Optical Society of America*, A, **14**, 7, 1393–1411, 1997.

[134] D.H. Brainard, A. Roorda, Y. Yamauchi, J.B. Calderone, A.B. Metha, M. Neitz, J. Meitz, D.R. Williams, and G.H. Jacobs, "Functional consequences of individual

variation in relative L and M cone numerosity," *Journal of the Optical Society of America*, A, **17**, 607–614, 2000.

[135] D.A. Brannan, M.F. Esplen, and J.J. Gray, *Geometry*, Cambridge: Cambridge University Press, 1999.

[136] E.J. Breneman, "The effect of level of illuminance and relative surround luminance on the appearance of black-and-white photographs," *Photographic Science and Engineering*, **6**, 3, 172–179, 1962.

[137] E.J. Breneman, "Perceived saturation in complex stimuli viewed in light and dark surrounds," *Journal of the Optical Society of America*, **67**, 5, 657–662, 1977.

[138] E.J. Breneman, "Corresponding chromaticities for different states of adaptation to complex visual fields," *Journal of the Optical Society of America*, A, **4**, 6, 1115–1129, 1987.

[139] P. Brou, T.R. Sciascia, L. Linden, and J.Y. Lettvin, "The colors of things," *Scientific American*, **255**, 3, 84–91, 1986.

[140] P.J. Brown, *Measurement, Regression, and Calibration*, Oxford: Clarendon Press, 1993.

[141] E. Brücke, "Über einige Empfindungen im Gebiet der Sehnerven," *Sitzungsberichte der Akademie der Wissenschaften Wien*, **77**, 39–71, 1878.

[142] M. Bruno, *Principles of Color Proofing*, Salem, NH: Gama Communications, 1986.

[143] O. Bryngdahl, T. Scheermesser, and F. Wyrowski, "Digital halftoning: synthesis of binary images," in *Progress in Optics*, Volume XXXIII, edited by E. Wolf, pp. 389–463, Amsterdam: North-Holland, 1994.

[144] G. Buchsbaum, "A spatial processor model for object colour perception," *Journal of the Franklin Institute*, **310**, 1, 1–26, 1980.

[145] G. Buchsbaum and A. Gottschalk, "Trichromacy, opponent colours coding, and optimum color information transmission in the retina," *Proceedings of the Royal Society of London*, B, **220**, 89–113, 1983.

[146] J.D. Buhr and H.D. Franchino, *Color Image Reproduction of Scenes with Preferential Tone Mapping*, US Patent 5,390,036, Feb. 14, 1995.

[147] C. Buil, *CCD Astronomy: Construction and Use of an Astronomical CCD Camera*, translated and adapted from French by E. Davoust and B. Davoust, Richmond, VA: Willmann-Bell, 1991.

[148] R.W. Burnham, R.M. Evans, and S.M. Newhall, "Prediction of color appearance with different adaptation illuminations," *Journal of the Optical Society of America*, **47**, 1, 35–42, 1957.

[149] M.E. Burns and D.A. Baylor, "Activation, deactivation, and adaptation in vertebrate photoreceptor cells," *Annual Reviews: Neurosciences*, **24**, 779–805, 2001.

[150] P.D. Burns, "Slanted-edge MTF for digital camera and scanner analysis," in *Proc. IS&T's 2000 PICS Conference*, 135–138, 2000.

[151] J.H. Burroughes, D.D.C. Bradley, A.R. Brown, R.N. Marks, K. Mackay, R.H. Friend, P.L. Burn, and A.B. Holmes, "Light-emitting diodes based on conjugated polymers," *Nature*, **347**, 539–541, 1990.

[152] G.J. Burton and I.R. Moorhead, "Color and spatial structure in natural scenes," *Applied Optics*, **26**, 1, 157–170, 1987.

[153] P. Buser and M. Imbert, *Vision*, translated by R.H. Kay, Cambridge, MA: MIT Press, 1992.

[154] W. Busselt and R. Raue, "Optimizing the optical properties of TV phosphor screens," *Journal of the Electrochemical Society*, **135**, 3, 764–771, 1988.

[155] H. Bustard and R. Smith, "Investigation into the scattering of light by human hair," *Applied Optics*, **24**, 30, 3485–3491, 1991.

[156] A.J. Calabria and M.D. Fairchild, "Perceived image contrast and observer preference I. The effects of lightness, chroma, and sharpness manipulations on contrast perception," *Journal of Imaging Science and Technology*, **47**, 6, 479–493, 2003. "Perceived image contrast and observer preference II. Empirical modeling of perceived image contrast and observer preference data," *Journal of Imaging Science and Technology*, **47**, 6, 494–508, 2003.

[157] F.W. Campbell and D.G. Green, "Optical and retinal factors affecting visual resolution," *Journal of Physiology* (London), **181**, 576–593, 1965.

[158] F.W. Campbell and R.W. Gubisch, "Optical quality of the human eye," *Journal of Physiology*, **186**, 558–578, 1966.

[159] F.W. Campbell, J.J. Kulikowski, and J. Levinson, "The effect of orientation on the visual resolution of gratings," *Journal of Physiology*, **187**, 427–436, 1966.

[160] K. Campton, *Image Performance in CRT Displays*, Bellingham, WA: SPIE Press, 2003.

[161] J.F. Canny, *Finding Edges and Lines in Images*, MIT. Artificial Intelligence Laboratory, Cambridge, MA, AI TR 720, 1983. (Also, "A computational approach to edge detection," *IEEE Transactions on Pattern Analysis and Machine Intelligence*, **8**, 6, 679–698, 1986.)

[162] F.E. Carlson and C.N. Clark, "Light sources for optical devices," in *Applied Optics and Optical Engineering*, Volume I, edited by R. Kingslake, pp. 43–109, New York, NY: Academic Press, 1965.

[163] C.R. Carvonius, "Not seeing eye to eye," *Nature*, **370**, 259–260, 1994.

[164] J. Castanet and J.-P. Ortonne, "Hair melanin and hair color," in *Formation and Structure of Human Hair*, edited by P. Jolles, H. Zhan, and H. Hocker, pp. 209–225, Basel: Birkhäuser Verlag, 1997.

[165] K.R. Castleman, *Digital Image Processing*, Upper Saddle River, NJ: Prentice Hall, 1996.

[166] P.B. Catrysse and B.A. Wandell, "Optical efficiency of image sensor pixels," *Journal of the Optical Society of America*, A, **19**, 8, 1610–1620, 2002.

[167] L.M. Chalupa and J.S. Werner, (eds.), *The Visual Neurosciences*, Cambridge, MA: MIT Press, 2004.

[168] S. Chandrasekhar, *Radiative Transfer*, New York, NY: Dover, 1960.

[169] W.N. Charman and J. Tucker, "Dependence of accommodation response on the spatial frequency spectrum of the observed object," *Vision Research*, **17**, 129–139, 1977.

[170] W.N. Charman and H. Whitefoot, "Pupil diameter and the depth-of-field of the human eye as measured by laser speckle," *Optica Acta*, **24**, 12, 1211–1216, 1977.

[171] W.N. Charman and J. Tucker, "Accommodation as a function of object form," *American Journal of Optometry*, **55**, 84–92, 1978.

[172] W.N. Charman and J. Tucker, "Accommodation and color," *Journal of the Optical Society of America*, **68**, 4, 459–471, 1978.

[173] W.N. Charman, "The retinal image in the human eye," in *Progress in Retinal Research*, Volume 2, pp. 1–50, Oxford: Pergamon Press, 1982.

[174] W.N. Charman (ed.), *Vision and Visual Dysfunction*, Volume 1, *Visual Optics and Instrumentation*, Boca Raton, FL: CRC Press, 1991.

[175] E.W. Cheney, *Multivariate Approximation Theory: Selected Topics*, Philadelphia, PA: Society for Industrial and Applied Mathematics, 1986.

[176] H.-Y. Cheng and Y.-C. King, "A CMOS image sensor with dark-current cancellation and dynamic sensitivity operations," *IEEE Transactions on Electron Devices*, **50**, 1, 91–95, 2003.

[177] T.L.V. Cheung and S. Westland, "Accurate estimation of the non-linearity of input–output response for color digital cameras," in *Proc. IS&T's 2003 PICS Conference*, 366–369, 2003.

[178] M.E. Chevreul, *De la loi de contraste simultane des couleurs*, Paris: Leo Laget, 1969. (Original work published in 1839.)

[179] C.D. Child, "Discharge from hot CAO," *Physical Review* (series I), **32**, 5, 492–511, 1911.

[180] R. Chung, "A statistical method for image classification and tone reproduction determination," *Journal of Applied Photographic Engineering*, **3**, 2, 74–81, 1977.

[181] E.L. Church, "Comments on the correlation length," *Proceedings of SPIE*, **680**, 102–111, 1986.

[182] E.L. Church and P.Z. Takacs, "Surface scatttering," in *Handbook of Optics*, Volume I, edited by M. Bass, New York, NY: McGraw-Hill, 1995.

[183] CIE, ISO/CIE 10527, (CIE S002-1986), *Colorimetric Observers*, Vienna: CIE Central Bureau, 1991.

[184] CIE, Publication CIE 13.3, *Method of Measuring and Specifying Colour Rendering Properties of Light Sources*, Vienna: CIE Central Bureau.

[185] CIE, Publication CIE 41, *Light as a True Visual Quantity: Principles of Measurement*, Vienna: CIE Central Bureau, 1978.

[186] CIE, Publication CIE 15.2, *Colorimetry*, 2nd edition, Vienna: CIE Central Bureau, 1986.

[187] CIE, Publication CIE 17.4, *International Lighting Vocabulary*, 4th edition, Vienna: CIE Central Bureau, 1987.

[188] CIE, Publication CIE 81, *Mesopic Photometry: History, Special Problems, and Practical Solutions*, Vienna: CIE Central Bureau, 1989.

[189] CIE, Publication CIE 85, *Solar Spectral Irradiance*, Vienna: CIE Central Bureau, 1989.

[190] CIE, Publication CIE 86, *CIE 1988 2° Spectral Luminous Efficiency Function for Photopic Vision*, Vienna: CIE Central Bureau, 1990.

[191] CIE, Publication CIE 116, *Industrial Colour-Difference Evaluation*, Vienna: CIE Central Bureau, 1995.

[192] CIE, Publication CIE 127, *Measurement of LEDs*, Vienna: CIE Central Bureau, 1997.

[193] CIE, Publication CIE 131, *The CIE 1997 Interim Colour Appearance Model (Simple Version), CIECAM97s*, Vienna: CIE Central Bureau, 1998.

[194] CIE, Publication CIE 142, *Improvement to Industrial Colour-Difference Evaluation*, Vienna: Central Bureau of the CIE, 2001.

[195] The Camera and Imaging Product Association, *Sensitivity of Digital Cameras*, CIPA DC-004, July 27, 2004.

[196] K.J. Ciuffreda, "Accommodation and its anomalies," in *Visual Optics and Instrumentation*, edited by W.N. Charman, pp. 231–279, Boca Raton, FL: CRC Press, 1991.

[197] L.D. Clark, "Mathematical prediction of photographic picture from tone-reproduction data," *Photographic Science and Engineering*, **11**, 5, 306–315, 1967.

[198] R.N. Clark, *Visual Astronomy of the Deep Sky*, New York, NY: Cambridge University Press, 1990.

[199] J.E. Cogoli, *Photo-Offset Fundamentals*, 5th edition, Encino, CA: Glencoe Publishing, 1986.

[200] J. Cohen, "Dependency of the spectral reflectance curves of the Munsell color chips," *Psychonomic Science*, **1**, 369–370, 1964.

[201] J.B. Cohen and W.E. Kappauf, "Metameric color stimuli, fundamental metamers, and Wyszecki's metameric black," *American Journal of Psychology*, **95**, 4, 537–564, 1982.

[202] J.B. Cohen and W.E. Kappauf, "Color mixture and fundamental metamers: Theory, algebra, geometry, application," *American Journal of Psychology*, **98**, 2, 171–259, 1985.

[203] W. Cohen, "Spatial and textural characteristics of the Ganzfeld," *The American Journal of Psychology*, **70**, 3, 403–410, 1957.

[204] W. Cohen, "Color-perception in the chromatic Ganzfeld," *The American Journal of Psychology*, **71**, 2, 390–394, 1958.

[205] D.R. Cok, *Signal Processing Method and Apparatus for Sampled Image Signals*, US Patent 4,630,307, December 16, 1986.

[206] D.R. Cok, *Apparatus and Accompanying Methods for Achieving Automatic Color Balancing in a Film to Video Transfer System*, US Patent 4,945,406, July 31, 1990.

[207] D.R. Cok, "Reconstruction of CCD images using template matching," *Final Programs and Advanced Printing of Papers of IS&T's 47th Annual Conference*, Volume II, 380–385, 1994.

[208] E. Collett, *Polarized Light: Fundamentals and Applications*, New York, NY: Marcel Dekker, 1993.

[209] P.J. Collings and M. Hird, *Introduction to Liquid Crystals Chemistry and Physics*, London: Taylor and Francis, 1997.

[210] D. Collins, *The Story of Kodak*, New York, NY: Harry N. Abrams, Inc., 1990.

[211] A.H. Compton, "The spectrum of scattered X-rays," *Physical Review*, **22**, 409–413, 1923.

[212] H.R. Condit, "Natural Sources", Section 1.3 in *Handbook of Photographic Science and Engineering*, 2nd edition, edited by C.N. Proudfoot, Springfield, VA: The Society for Imaging Science and Technology, 1997.

[213] R.L. Cook and K.E. Torrance, "A reflectance model for computer graphics," *ACM Transactions on Graphics*, **1**, 1, 7–24, 1982.

[214] J.H. Coote, *Photofinishing Techniques and Equipment*, London: The Focal Press, 1970.

[215] T.N. Cornsweet, *Visual Perception*, Orlando, FL: Academic Press, 1970.

[216] F. Cost, *Pocket Guide to Digital Printing*, Albany, NY: Delmar Publishers, 1997.

[217] R. Cotterill, *The Cambridge Guide to the Material World*, Cambridge: Cambridge University Press, 1985.

[218] W. Cowan, "Displays for vision research," in *Handbook of Optics*, Volume I, edited by M. Bass, New York, NY: McGraw-Hill, 1995.

[219] T.F. Cox and M.A.A. Cox, *Multidimensional Scaling*, 2nd edition, Boca Raton, FL: Chapman & Hall/CRC, 2000.

[220] K.J.W. Craik, *The Nature of Psychology. A Selection of Papers, Essays and Other Writings by the Late K.J.W. Craik*, edited by S.L. Sherwood, Cambridge: Cambridge University Press, 1966.

[221] E.M. Crane, "An objective method for rating picture sharpness: SMT acutance," *Journal of the Society of Motion Picture and Television Engineering*, **73**, 643–647, 1964.

[222] E.M. Crane, "Acutance and granulance," *Proceedings of SPIE*, **310**, 125–132, 1981.

[223] H.D. Crane, J.D. Peter, and E. Martinez-Uriegas, *Method and Apparatus for Decoding Spatiochromatically Multiplexed Color Image Using Predetermined Coefficients*, US Patent 5,901,242, May 4, 1999.

[224] C.A. Curcio, K.R. Sloan, R.E. Kalina, and A.E. Hendrickson, "Human photoreceptor topography," *The Journal of Comparative Neurology*, **292**, 497–523, 1990.

[225] C.A. Curcio, K. Allen, K.R. Sloan, C.L. Lerea, J.B. Hurley, I.B. Klock, and A.H. Milam, "Distribution and morphology of human cone photoreceptors stained with anti-blue opsin," *The Journal of Comparative Neurology*, **312**, 610–624, 1991.

[226] D.M. Dacey, "Dendritic field size and morphology of midget and parasol ganglion cells of the human retina," *Proceedings of the National Academy of Science*, **89**, 9666–9670, 1992.

[227] D.M. Dacey, "The mosaic of midget ganglion cells in the human retina," *The Journal of Neuroscience*, **13**, 12, 5334–5355, 1993.

[228] D.M. Dacey and B.B. Lee, "The 'blue-on' opponent pathway in primate retina originates from a distinct bistratified ganglion cell type," *Nature*, **367**, 731–735, 1994.

[229] D.M. Dacey, "Circuitry for color coding in the primate retina," *Proceedings of the National Academy of Science, USA*, **93**, 582–588, 1996.

[230] D.M. Dacey, L.C. Diller, J. Verweij, and D.R. Williams, "Physiology of L- and M-cone inputs to H1 horizontal cells in the primate retina," *Journal of the Optical Society of America*, A, **17**, 589–596, 2000.

[231] D.M. Dacey, "Parallel pathways for spectral coding in primate retina," *Annual Reviews: Neurosciences*, **23**, 743–775, 2000.

[232] J.C. Dainty and R. Shaw, *Image Science*, London: Academic Press, 1974.

[233] S. Daly, "Application of a noise-adaptive contrast sensitivity function to image data compression," *Optical Engineering*, **29**, 8, 977–987, 1992.

[234] S. Daly, "The visible differences predictor: An algorithm for the assessment of image fidelity," in *Digital Images and Human Vision*, edited by A.B. Watson, pp. 179–206, Cambridge, MA: MIT Press, 1993.

[235] K.J. Dana and J. Wang, "Device for convenient measurement of spatially varying bidirectional reflectance," *Journal of the Optical Society of America*, A, **21**, 1, 1–12, 2004.

[236] H.J.A. Dartnall, J.K. Bowmaker, and J.D. Mollon, "Human visual pigments: microspectral photometric results from the eyes of seven persons," *Proceedings of the Royal Society of London*, B, **220**, 115–130, 1983.

[237] A. Davies and P. Samuels, *An Introduction to Computational Geometry for Curves and Surfaces*, Oxford: Clarendon, 1996.

[238] G. Davis and J. Driver, "Parallel detection of Kanizsa subjective figures in the human visual system," *Nature*, **371**, 791–793, 1994.

[239] P.J. Davis, *Interpolation and Approximation*, New York, NY: Dover, 1975.

[240] M.L. Davison, *Multidimensional Scaling*, Melbourne, FL: Krieger, 1993.

[241] N.W. Daw, R.J. Jensen and W.J. Brunken, "Rod pathways in mammalian retinae," *Trends in Neuroscience*, **13**, 3, 110–115, 1990.

[242] R.J. Deeley, N. Drasdo and W.N. Charman, "A simple parametric model of the human ocular modulation transfer function," *Ophthalmic and Physiological Optics*, **11**, 91–93, 1991.

[243] S.G. de Groot and J.W. Gebhard, "Pupil size as determined by adapting luminance," *Journal of the Optical Society of America*, **42**, 492–495, 1952.

[244] P.B. Delahunt and D.H. Brainard, "Does human color constancy incorporate the statistical regularity of natural daylight?", *Journal of Vision*, **4**, 57–81, 2004. (http://journalofvision.org/4/2/1)

[245] C.J. Delcroix and M.A. Abidi, "Fusion of edge maps in color images," *Proceedings of SPIE*, **1001**, 545–554, 1988.

[246] F. Deleixhe-Mauhin, J.M. Krezinski, G. Rorive, G.E. Pierard, "Quantification of skin color in patients undergoing maintenance hemodialysis," *Journal of the American Academy of Dermatology*, **27**, 6, 1, 950–953, 1992.

[247] P. DeMarco, J. Pokorny, and V.C. Smith, "Full-spectrum cone sensitivity functions for X-chromosome-linked anomalous trichromats," *Journal of the Optical Society of America*, A, **9**, 9, 1465–1476, 1992.

[248] L.E. De Marsh, "Optimum telecine transfer characteristics," *Journal of the Society of Motion Picture and Television Engineering*, **81**, 784–787, 1972.

[249] W. den Boer, F.C. Luo, and Z. Yaniv, "Microelectronics in active-matrix LCDs and image sensors," in *Electro-Optical Displays*, edited by M.A. Karim, New York, NY: Marcel Dekker, 1992.

[250] H. de Ridder, "Minkowski-metrics as a combination rule for digital-image-coding impairments," *Proceedings of SPIE*, **1616**, 16–26, 1992.

[251] H. de Ridder, "Psychophysical evaluation of image quality: from judgement to impression," *Proceedings of SPIE*, **3299**, 252–263, 1998.

[252] A.M. Derrington, J. Krauskopf, and P. Lennie, "Chromatic mechanisms in lateral geniculate nucleus of macaque," *Journal of Physiology*, **357**, 241–265, 1984.

[253] E.A. DeYoe and D.C. Van Essen, "Concurrent processing streams in monkey visual cortex," *Trends in Neurosciences*, **11**, 5, 219–226, 1988.

[254] J.M. DiCarlo and B.A. Wandell, "Illuminant estimation: beyond the bases," in *Proc. the 8th IS&T Color Imaging Conference*, 91–96, 2000.

[255] J.M. DiCarlo and B.A. Wandell, "Spectral estimation theory: beyond linear but before Bayesian," *Journal of the Optical Society of America*, A, **20**, 7, 1261–1270, 2003.

[256] P. Dierckx, *Curve and Surface Fitting with Splines*, Oxford: Clarendon Press, 1993.

[257] R.W. Ditchburn, *Eye-Movements and Visual Perception*, Oxford: Clarendon Press, 1973.

[258] R.W. Ditchburn, *Light*, New York, NY: Dover, 1991. (Original text published in 1961.)

[259] S. Di Zenzo, "A note on the gradient of a multi-image," *Computer Vision, Graphics, and Image Processing*, **33**, 116–125, 1986.

[260] D.L. Donoho and I.M. Johnstone, "Wavelet shrinkage: Asymptopia?" *Journal of the Royal Statistical Society*, B, **57**, 2, 301–369, 1995.

[261] A. Doroszkowski, "Paints," in *Technological Applications of Dispersions*, edited by R.B. McKay, New York, NY: Marcel Dekker, 1994.

[262] E.R. Dougherty, *Digital Image Processing Methods*, New York, NY: Marcel Dekker, 1994.

[263] R.F. Dougherty, V.M. Koch, A.A. Brewer, B. Fischer, J. Modersitzki, and B.A. Wandell, "Visual field representations and locations of visual areas V1/2/3 in human visual cortex," *Journal of Vision*, **3**, 586–598, 2003. (http://journalofvision.org/3/10/1)

[264] J.E. Dowling, *The Retina: An Approachable Part of the Brain*, Cambridge, MA: The Belknap Press of Harvard University Press, 1987.

[265] N. Drasdo and C.W. Fowler, "Nonlinear projection of the retinal image in a wide-angle schematic eye," *British Journal of Ophthalmology*, **58**, 709–714, 1974.

[266] R.O. Dror, A.S. Willsky, and E.H. Adelson, "Statistical characterization of real-world illumination," *Journal of Vision*, **4**, 821–837, 2004. (http://journalofvision.org/4/9/11)

[267] P.M. Duffieux, *The Fourier Transform and Its Applications to Optics*, 2nd edition, New York, NY: John Wiley & Sons, 1983. (Original text published in 1946.)

[268] S.Q. Duntley, "The optical properties of diffusing materials," *Journal of the Optical Society of America*, **32**, 2, 61–70, 1942.

[269] D.B. Dusenbery, *Sensory Ecology*, New York, NY: W.H. Freeman, 1992.

[270] M. D'Zmura and G. Iverson, "Color constancy. I. Basic theory of two-stage linear recovery of spectral descriptions for lights and surfaces," and "Color constancy. II. Results for two-stage linear recovery of spectral descriptions for lights and surfaces," *Journal of the Optical Society of America*, A, **10**, 10, 2148–2165, and 2166–2180, 1993.

[271] Eastman Kodak Company, *Encyclopedia of Practical Photography*, Vol. 12 (Shutter), Garden City, NY: American Photographic Book Publishing Company, 1979.

[272] Eastman Kodak Company, *Advanced Color Printing Technology for Photofinishers and Professional Finishers*, Rochester, NY: Eastman Kodak Company, 1979.

[273] Eastman Kodak Company, *Shutter Operations for CCD and CMOS Image Sensors*, Application Note MTD/PS-0259, Eastman Kodak Company, Rochester, NY, October 23, 2001.

[274] E.A. Edwards and S.Q. Duntley, "Pigment and color in living human skin," *American Journal of Anatomy*, **65**, 1–33, 1939.

[275] E.A. Edwards and S.Q. Duntley, "Analysis of skin pigment changes after exposure to sunlight," *Science*, **90**, 235–237, 1939.

[276] W.G. Egan and T.W. Hilgeman, *Optical Properties of Inhomogeneous Materials*, New York, NY: Academic Press, 1979.

[277] D.C. Ehn and M.B. Silevitch, "Diffusion model for the adjacency effect in viscous development," *Journal of the Optical Society of America*, **64**, 5, 667–676, 1974.

[278] W. Ehrenstein, *Probleme der ganzheitspsychologischen Wahrnehmungslehre*, Leipzig: J.A. Barth, 1954.

[279] N.R. Eldred, *Chemistry for the Graphic Arts*, 2nd edition, Pittsburgh, PA: Graphic Arts Technical Foundation, 1992.

[280] J.M. Elson, "Theory of light scattering from a rough surface with an inhomgeneous dielectric permittivity," *Physical Review*, B, **30**, 5460–5480, 1984.

[281] P.G. Engeldrum, "Psychometric scaling: avoiding the pitfalls and hazards," in *Proc. IS&T's 2001 PICS Conference*, 101–107, 2001.

[282] P.G. Engeldrum, "Extending image quality models," in *Proc. IS&T's 2002 PICS Conference*, 65–69, 2002.

[283] J.M. Enoch and F.L. Tobey, Jr. (eds.), *Vertebrate Photoreceptor Optics*, Berlin: Springer-Verlag, 1981.

[284] K. Era, S. Shionoya, and Y. Washizawa, "Mechanism of broad-band luminescences in ZnS phosphors," *Journal of Physics and Chemistry of Solids*, **29**, 1827, 1968.

[285] R.M. Evans and J. Klute, "Brightness constancy in photographic reproduction," *Journal of the Optical Society of America*, **34**, 533–540, 1944.

[286] R.M. Evans, *An Introduction to Color*, New York, NY: John Wiley and Sons, Inc., 1948.

[287] R.M. Evans, "On some aspects of white, gray, and black," *Journal of the Optical Society of America*, **39**, 9, 774–779, 1949.

[288] R.M. Evans, *Method for Correcting Photographic Color Prints*, US Patent 2,571,697, Oct. 16, 1951. (The patent application was filed on June 20, 1946.)

[289] R.M. Evans, W.T. Hanson, and W.L. Brewer, *Principles of Color Photography*, New York, NY: John Wiley and Sons, Inc., 1953.

[290] R.M. Evans, *The Perception of Color*, New York, NY: Wiley, 1974.

[291] M.D. Fairchild and P. Lennie, "Chromatic adaptation to natural and incandescent illuminants," *Vision Research*, **32**, 11, 2077–2085, 1992.

[292] M.D. Fairchild, *Color Appearance Models*, Reading, MA: Addison-Wesley, 1997.

[293] M.D. Fairchild and D.R. Wyble, *Colorimetric Characterization of the Apple Studio Display (Flat Panel LCD)*, Munsell Color Science Laboratory Technical Report, Center for Imaging Science, Rochester Institute of Technology, July, 1998.

[294] M.D. Fairchild, "A revision of CIECAM97s for practical applications," *COLOR Research and Application*, **26**, 418–427, 2001.

[295] M.D. Fairchild and G.M. Johnson, "Image appearance modeling," *Proceedings of SPIE*, **5007**, 149–160, 2003.

[296] H.S. Fairman, and H. Hemmendinger, "Stability of ceramic color reflectance standard," *COLOR Research and Application*, **23**, 6, 408–415, 1998.

[297] D.S. Falk, D.R. Brill, and D.G. Stork, *Seeing the Light*, New York, NY: John Wiley & Sons, 1986.

[298] J.C. Flamagne, "Psychophysical measurement and theory," in *Handbook of Perception and Human Performance*, Volume 1, edited K.R. Boff, L. Kaufman, and J.P. Thomas, New York, NY: John Wiley & Sons, 1986.

[299] J. Fan and I. Gijbels, *Local Polynomial Modelling and Its Applications*, London: Chapman and Hall, 1996.

[300] H. Farid, "Blind inverse gamma correction," *IEEE Transactions on Image Processing*, **10**, 10, 1428–1433, 2001.

[301] P.A. Farrant, *Color in Nature*, London: Blandford, 1997.

[302] J.E. Farrell and B.A. Wandell, "Scanner linearity," *Journal of Electronic Imaging*, **2**, 3, 225–230, 1993.

[303] T.W. Faulkner and T.M. Rice, "The use of photographic space in the development of the disc photographic system," in *Proceedings of the Journal of Applied Photographic Engineering, 36th Annual Meeting*, **9**, 2, 52–57, 1983.

[304] E.A. Fedorovskaya, H. De Ridder, and F.J.J. Blommaert, "Chroma variations and perceived quality of color images of natural scenes," *COLOR Research and Application*, **22**, 96, 1997.

[305] B. Fergg, W. Zahn, and W. Knapp, *Automatic Color Printing Apparatus*, US Patent 4,101,217, July 18, 1978.

[306] R.P. Feynman, R.B. Leighton, and M.L. Sands, *The Feynman Lectures in Physics*, Volumes I, II, and III, Reading, MA: Addison-Wesley, 1965.

[307] R.P. Feynman, *QED: The Strange Theory of Light and Matter*, Princeton, NJ: Princeton University Press, 1985.

[308] D.J. Field, "Relations between the statistics of natural images and the response properties of cortical cells," *Journal of the Optical Society of America*, A, **4**, 12, 2379–2394, 1987.

[309] G.G. Field, *Color and Its Reproduction*, Pittsburgh, PA: Graphic Arts Technical Foundation, 1988.

[310] G.G. Field, *Tone and Color Correction*, Pittsburgh, PA: Graphic Arts Technical Foundation, 1991.

[311] G.D. Finlayson and S.D. Hordley, "Improving Gamut mapping color constancy," *IEEE Transactions on Image Processing*, **9**, 10, 1774–1783, 2000.

[312] G.D. Finlayson and G. Schaefer, "Convex and non-convex illuminant constraints for dichromatic colour constancy," *Proc. Conf. on Computer Vision and Pattern Recognition*, **I**, 598–604, 2001.

[313] G.D. Finlayson, S.D. Hordley, and P.M. Hubel, "Color by correlation: a simple, unifying framework for color constancy," *IEEE Transactions on Pattern Analysis and Machine Intelligence*, **23**, 11, 1209–1221, 2001.

[314] G.D. Finlayson and S.D. Hordley, "Color constancy at a pixel," *Journal of the Optical Society of America*, A, **18**, 2, 253–264, 2001.

[315] G.D. Finlayson, S.D. Hordley, and I. Tastl, "Gamut constrained illuminant estimation," *Proceedings of the Ninth IEEE International Conference on Computer Vision*, 792–799, 2003.

[316] A. Fiorentini, "Mach band phenomena," in *Handbook of Sensory Physiology*, Volume VII/4, edited by D. Jameson and L.M. Hurvich, pp. 188–201, Berlin: Springer-Verlag, 1972.

[317] N.I. Fisher, "Spherical median," *Journal of the Royal Statistical Society*, B, **47**, 2, 342–348, 1985.

[318] N.I. Fisher, T. Lewis, and B.J.J. Embleton, *Statistical Analysis of Spherical Data*, Cambridge: Cambridge University Press, 1987.

[319] R.W. Floyd and L. Steinberg, "An adaptive algorithm for spatial grayscale," *Proceedings of the Society for Information Display*, **17**, 2, 75–77, 1976.

[320] J.D. Foley, A. van Dam, S.K. Feiner, and J.F. Hughes, *Computer Graphics Principles and Practice*, 2nd edition, pp. 568–573, Reading, MA: Addison-Wesley Publishing Company, 1990.

[321] S.C. Foo, *A Gonioreflectometer for Measuring the Bidirectional Reflectance of Material for Use in Illumination Computation*, Master Thesis, Cornell University, 1997.

[322] D.A. Forsyth, "A novel algorithm for color constancy," *International Journal of Computer Vision*, **5**, 1, 5–36, 1990.

[323] G.E. Forsythe, M.A. Malcolm, and C.B. Moler, *Computer Methods for Mathematical Computations*, Chapter 9, Englewood Cliffs, NJ: Prentice-Hall, 1977.

[324] C.E. Foss, D. Nickerson, and W.C. Granville, "Analysis of the Ostwald color system," *Journal of the Optical Society of America*, **34**, 7, 361–381, 1944.

[325] E.R. Fossum, "CMOS image sensor: Electronic camera-on-a-chip," *IEEE Transactions on Electron Devices*, **44**, 10, 1689–1698, 1997.

[326] R. L. Foster, *The Nature of Enzymology*, New York, NY: Halsted Press, 1980.

[327] R. Franke, "Scattered data interpolation: Tests of some methods," *Mathematics of Computation*, **38**, 157, 181–200, 1982.

[328] W.T. Freeman, *Method and Apparatus for Reconstructing Missing Color Samples*, US Patent 4,663,655, 1987.

[329] H. Frieser, "Spread function and contrast transfer function of photographic layers," *Photographic Science and Engineering*, **4**, 6, 324–329, 1960.

[330] J. Fryer and D. Brown, "Lens distortion for close-range photogrammetry," *Photogrammetric Engineering and Remote Sensing*, **52**, 1, 51–58, 1986.

[331] J.G. Fryer, "Camera calibration in non-topographic photogrammetry," in *Non-Topographic Photogrammetry*, 2nd edition, edited by H.M. Karara, Falls Church, VA: American Society for Photogrammetry and Remote Sensing, 1989.

[332] B.V. Funt, V. Cardei, and K. Barnard, "Learning color constancy," *Proc. IS&T/SID 4th Color Imaging Conference*, 58–60, 1996.

[333] M. Fürsich and H. Treiber, B. Fergg, G. Findeis, and W. Zahn, *Method of Copying Color Exposures*, US Patent 4,566,786, January 28, 1986.

[334] R.S. Gairns, "Electrophotography," Chapter 4 in *Chemistry and Technology of Printing and Imaging Systems*, edited by P. Gregory, London: Blackie Academic and Professional, 1996.

[335] W. Gall and K. Wellendorf, *Production of Screen Printing Blocks*, US Patent 4,499,489, February 12, 1985.

[336] A. Gatt, J. Morovic, and L. Noriega, "Colorimetric characterization of negative film for digital cinema post-production," in *Proc. IS&T/SID Eleventh Color Imaging Conference*, 341–345, 2003.

[337] K.R. Gegenfurtner and L.T. Sharpe (eds.), *Color Vision: From Genes to Perception*, Cambridge: Cambridge University Press, 2000.

[338] W.S. Geisler, "Physical limits of acuity and hyperacuity," *Journal of the Optical Society of America*, A, **1**, 775–782, 1984.

[339] W.S. Geisler and B.J. Super, "Perceptual organization of two-dimensional images," *Psychological Review*, **107**, 677–708, 2000.

[340] R.G. Gendron, "An improved objective method for rating picture sharpness: CMT acutance," *Journal of the Society of Motion Picture and Television Engineering*, **82**, 1009–1012, 1973.

[341] A. Gerrard and J.M. Burch, *Introduction to Matrix Methods in Optics*, New York, NY: Dover, 1994. (Original text published in 1975.)

[342] G.A. Gescheider, *Psychophysics: Method, Theory, and Application*, 2nd edition, Hillsdale, NJ: Lawrence Erlbaum Associates, 1985.

[343] G.A. Gescheider, "Psychophysical scaling," *Annual Review of Pschology*, **39**, 169–200, 1988.

[344] A.L. Gilchrist, "Perceived lightness depends on perceived spatial arrangement," *Science*, **195**, 185–187, 1977.

[345] A.L. Gilchrist, S. Delman, and A. Jacobsen, "The classification and integration of edges as critical to the perception of reflectance and illumination," *Perception and Psychophysics*, **33**, 425–436, 1983.

[346] A.L. Gilchrist (editor), *Lightness, Brightness, and Transparency*, Hillsdale, NJ: Lawrence Erlbaum Associates, 1994.

[347] E.J. Giorgianni and T.E. Madden, *Digital Color Management*, Reading, MA: Addison-Wesley, 1997.

[348] D.H. Goldstein and R.A. Chipman, "Error analysis of a Mueller matrix polarimeter," *Journal of the Optical Society of America*, A, **7**, 693–700, 1990.

[349] M. Golomb, "Approximation by functions of fewer variables," in *On Numerical Approximation*, edited by R.E. Langer, pp. 275–327, Madison, WI: The University of Wisconsin Press, 1959.

[350] G.H. Golub and C.F. van Loan, *Matrix Computations*, p. 139, Baltimore, MD: The Johns Hopkins University Press, 1983.

[351] R.C. Gonzalez and R.E. Woods, *Digital Image Processing*, Reading, MA: Addison-Wesley, 1992.

[352] J.W. Goodman, *Introduction to Fourier Optics*, New York, NY: McGraw-Hill Book Company, 1968.

[353] J.W. Goodman, *Statistical Optics*, New York, NY: John Wiley & Sons, 1985.

[354] J.W. Goodman, *Introduction to Fourier Optics*, 2nd edition, New York, NY: McGraw-Hill Book Company, 1996.

[355] W.J. Gordon and J.A. Wixom, "Shepard's method of metric interpolation to bivariate and multivariate interpolation," *Mathematics of Computation*, **32**, 141, 253–264, 1978.

[356] C.H. Graham and Y. Hsia, "Saturation and the foveal achromatic interval," *Journal of the Optical Society of America*, **59**, 993–997, 1969.

[357] E.M. Granger and K.N. Cupery, "An optical merit function (SQF), which correlates with subjective image judgements," *Photographic Science and Engineering*, **16**, 3, 221–230, 1972.

[358] W.C. Granville and E. Jacobson, "Colorimetric specification of the Color Harmony Manual from spectrophotometric measurements," *Journal of the Optical Society of America*, **34**, 7, 382–395, 1944.

[359] H.G. Grassman, "Theory of compound colors," English translation collected in *Sources of Color Science*, edited by D.L. MacAdam, Cambridge MA: MIT Press, 1970, pp. 53–60.

[360] L.S. Gray, B. Winn, and B. Gilmartin, "Accommodative microfluctuations and pupil diameter," *Vision Research*, **33**, 15, 2083–2090, 1993.

[361] D.R. Green and J.A. Swets, *Signal Detection Theory and Psychophysics*, Los Altos, CA: Peninsula Publishing, 1988.

[362] P.J. Green and L.W. MacDonald (eds.), *Colour Engineering*, Chichester: John Wiley and Sons, 2002.

[363] W.B. Green, *Digital Image Processing: A System Approach*, 2nd edition, New York, NY: Van Nostrand Reinhold, 1989.

[364] N.C. Greenham and R.H. Friend, "Semiconductor device physics of conjugated polymers," *Solid State Physics*, **49**, 1–149, 1995.

[365] A.R. Greenleaf, *Photographic Optics*, New York, NY: MacMillan Company, 1950.

[366] R.L. Gregory, *Eye and Brain*, 3rd edition, Princeton, NJ: Princeton University Press, 1990.

[367] D.H. Grosof, R.M. Shapley, and M.J. Hawken, "Macaque V1 neurons can signal illusory contours", *Nature*, **366**, 550–552, 1993.

[368] M.D.Grossberg and S.K. Nayar, "Modeling the space of camera response functions," *IEEE Transactions on Pattern Analysis and Machine Intelligence*, **25**, 10, 1272–1282, 2004.

[369] F. Grum and R.J. Becherer, *Optical Radiation Measurements*, Volume I, *Radiometry*, New York, NY: Academic Press, 1979.

[370] J.P. Guilford, *Psychometric Methods*, 2nd edition, New York, NY: McGraw-Hill, 1954.

[371] V.W. Guillemin and S. Sternberg, *Symplectic Techniques in Physics*, Cambridge: Cambridge University Press, 1984.

[372] B.K. Gunturk, Y. Altunbasak, and R.M. Mersereau, "Color plane interpolation using alternating projection," *IEEE Transactions on Image Processing*, **11**, 9, 997–1013, 2002.

[373] M. Gur, "Color and brightness fade-out in the Ganzfeld is wavelength dependent," *Vision Research*, **29**, 10, 1335–1341, 1989.

[374] M. Gur, "Perceptual fade-out occurs in the binocularly viewed Ganzfeld," *Perception*, **20**, 645–654, 1991.

[375] E.F. Gurnee and R.T. Fernandez, *Organic Electroluminescent Phosphors*, US Patent 3,172,862, March 9, 1965.

[376] J. Hagerman, "Optimum spot size for raster-scanned monochrome CRT displays," *Journal of the Society of Information Display*, **1/3**, 367–369, 1993.

[377] R. Hailstone, "Making every photon count," *Nature*, **402**, 23, 856–857, 1999.

[378] J.R. Hamerly and C.A. Dvorak, "Detection and discrimination of blur in edges and lines," *Journal of the Optical Society of America*, **71**, 448–452, 1981.

[379] W.T. Hanson Jr. and C.A. Horton, "Subtractive color reproduction: interimage effects," *Journal of the Optical Society of America*, **42**, 9, 663–669, 1952.

[380] R.M. Haralick, "Edge and region analysis for digital image data," *Computer Vision, Graphics, and Image Processing*, **12**, 60–73, 1980.

[381] W.A. Harrison, *Solid State Theory*, New York, NY: Dover, 1979.

[382] T. Hase, T. Kano, E. Nakazawa, and H. Yamamoto, "Phosphor materials for cathode-ray tubes," *Advances in Electronics and Electron Physics*, **79**, 271–373, 1990.

[383] S. Hattar, H.-W. Liao, M. Takao, D.M. Berson, and K.-W. Yau, "Melanopsin-containing retinal ganglion cells: architecture, projections, and intrinsic photosensitivity," *Science*, **295**, 1065–1070, 2002.

[384] X.D. He, K.E. Torrance, F.X. Sillion, and D.P. Greenberg, "A comprehensive physical model of light reflection," *Computer Graphics* (SIGGRAPH '91 Conference Proceedings) **25**, 4, 175–186, 1991.

[385] E. Hecht, *Optics*, 2nd edition, Reading, MA: Addison-Wesley Publishing Company, 1987.

[386] M. Hebert and R.D. Hersch, "Classical print reflection models: a radiometric approach," *Journal of Imaging Science and Technology*, **48**, 4, 363–374, 2004.

[387] S. Hecht, S. Shlaer, and M.H. Pirenne, "Energy, quanta, and vision," *Journal of General Physiology*, **25**, 819–840, 1942.

[388] E.G. Heinemann, "Simultaneous brightness induction," in *Handbook of Sensory Physiology*, VII/4, *Visual Psychophysics*, edited by D. Jameson and L.M. Hurvich, pp. 146–169, Berlin: Springer-Verlag, 1972.

[389] H. Helson, "Fundamental principles in color vision. I. The principle governing changes in hue, saturation, and lightness of non-selective samples in chromatic illumination," *Journal of Experimental Psychology*, **23**, 439–471, 1938.

[390] H. Helson, *Adaptation-Level Theory*, New York, NY: Harper and Row, 1964.

[391] B. Henderson and G.F. Imbusch, *Optical Spectroscopy of Inorganic Solids*, Oxford: Clarendon Press, 1989.

[392] S.H.C. Hendry and T. Yoshioka, "A neurochemically distinct third channel in the Macaque dorsal lateral geniculate nucleus," *Science*, **264**, 575–577, 1994.

[393] S.H.C. Hendry and R.C. Reid, "The koniocellular pathway in primate vision," *Annual Reviews: Neurosciences*, **23**, 127–153, 2000.

[394] M. Henle, *Modern Geometry: The Analytic Approach*, Upper Saddle River, NJ: Prentice Hall, 1997.

[395] R.T. Hennessy, T. Iida, K. Shina, and H.W. Leibowitz, "The effect of pupil size on accommodation," *Vision Research*, **16**, 587–589, 1976.

[396] E. Hering, *Outlines of a Theory of the Light Sense*, translation by L.M. Hurvich and D. Jamesin, Cambridge, MA: Harvard University Press, 1964. (Originally published in 1920.)

[397] L. Hermann, "Eine Erscheinung des simultanen Kontrastes," *Pflügers Archiv für die gesamte Physiologie*, **3**, 13–15, 1870.

[398] E.H. Hess, "Attitude and pupil size," *Scientific American*, **212**, 4, 44–54, 1965.

[399] S. Hesselgren, "Why color order systems," *Color Research and Application*, **9**, 4, 220–228, 1984.

[400] G.C. Higgins and L.A. Jones, "The nature and evaluation of the sharpness of photographic images," *Journal of the SMPTE*, **58**, 277–290, 1952.

[401] G.C. Higgins, "Methods for analyzing the photographic system, including the effects of nonlinearity and spatial frequency response," *Photographic Science and Engineering*, **15**, 2, 106–118, 1971.

[402] F.B. Hildebrand, *Advanced Calculus for Applications*, 2nd edition, Englewood Cliffs, NJ: Prentice-Hall, 1976.

[403] D.D. Hoffman, *Visual Intelligence*, New York, NY: W.W. Norton and Company, 1998.

[404] H. Hogrefe and C. Kunz, "Soft x-ray scattering from rough surfaces: experimental and theoretical analysis," *Applied Optics*, **26**, 14, 2851–2859, 1987.

[405] T.M. Holladay, "An optimum algorithm for halftone generation for displays and hardcopies," *Proceedings of the Society for Information Display*, **21**, 2, 185–192, 1980.

[406] A. Holloway, *The Handbook of Photographic Equipment*, pp. 11, 21, New York, NY: Alfred A. Knopf, Inc., 1981.

[407] J.M. Holm, *Pictorial Digital Image Processing Incorporating Adjustments to Compensate for Dynamic Range Differences*, US Patent 6,628,823, September 30, 2003.

[408] R.T. Holm, "Convention confusion," in *Handbook of Optical Constants of Solids II*, pp. 21–55, edited by E.D. Palik, San Diego, CA: Academic Press, 1991.

[409] D. C. Hood, T. Ilves, E. Maurer, B. Wandell, and E. Buckingham, "Human cone saturation as a function of ambient intensity: A test of models of shifts in the dynamic range," *Vision Research*, **18**, 983–993, 1978.

[410] H.H. Hopkins, "The frequency response of a defocused optical system," *Proceedings of the Royal Society of London*, A, **231**, 91–103, 1955.

[411] G.R. Hopkinson, "Analytic modeling of charge diffusion in charge-coupled-device imagers," *Optical Engineering*, **26**, 8, 766–772, 1987.

[412] B.K.P. Horn and R.W. Sjoberg, "Calculating the reflectance map," *Applied Optics*, **18**, 11, 1770–1779, 1979.

[413] B.K.P. Horn, "Exact reproduction of colored images," *Computer Vision, Graphics, and Image Processing*, **26**, 135–167, 1984.

[414] P. Horowitz and W. Hill, *The Art of Electronics*, 2nd edition, Cambridge: Cambridge University Press, 1989.

[415] W.E. Howard, "Better displays with organic films," *Scientific American*, **290**, 2, 76–81, 2004.

[416] J. Huang and D. Mumford, "Statistics of natural images and models," in *Proc. IEEE Computer Society Conference on Computer Vision and Pattern Recognition*, **1**, 541–547, 1999.

[417] J.S. Huang and D.H. Tseng, "Statistical theory of edge detection," *Computer Vision, Graphics, and Image Processing*, **43**, 337–346, 1988.

[418] D.H. Hubel, *Eye, Brain, and Vision*, Scientific American Library, New York, NY: W.H. Freeman, 1988.

[419] M.H. Hueckel, "An operator which locates edges in digitized pictures," *Journal of the Association for Computing Machinery*, **18**, 1, 113–125, 1971.

[420] M.E. Hufford and H.T. Davis, "The diffraction of light by a circular opening and the Lommel wave theory," *Physical Review*, **33**, 589–597, 1929.

[421] J. Hughes and J.K. Bowker, "Automatic color printing techniques," *Image Technology*, 39–43, April/May 1969.

[422] P.-C. Hung, "Colorimetric calibration in electronic imaging devices using a look-up-table model and interpolation," *Journal of Electronic Imaging*, **2**, 1, 53–61, 1993.

[423] P.-C. Hung, "Smooth colorimetric calibration technique utilizing the entire color gamut of CMYK printers," *Journal of Electronic Imaging*, **3**, 4, 415–424, 1994.

[424] P.-C. Hung, "Camera sensitivity evaluation and primary optimization considering color constancy," *Proc. IS&T/SID Tenth Color Imaging Conference*, 127–132, 2002.

[425] R.W.G. Hunt, "The effects of daylight and tungsten light-adaptation on color perception," *Journal of the Optical Society of America*, **40**, 6, 362–371, 1950.

[426] R.W.G. Hunt, "Light and dark adaptation and the perception of color," *Journal of the Optical Society of America*, **42**, 190–199, 1952.

[427] R.W.G. Hunt, I.T. Pitt, and P.C. Ward, "The tone reproduction of colour photographic materials," *The Journal of Photographic Science*, **17**, 198–204, 1969.

[428] R.W.G. Hunt, I.T. Pitt, and L.M. Winter, "The preferred reproduction of blue sky, green grass and Caucasian skin," *The Journal of Photographic Science*, **22**, 144–150, 1974.

[429] R.W.G. Hunt, *The Reproduction of Colour in Photography, Printing, and Television*, 4th edition, pp. 441–442, Tolworth: Fountain Press, 1987.

[430] R.W.G. Hunt, *Measuring Colour*, Chichester: Ellis Horwood Limited, 1987; 2nd edition, 1991.

[431] R.W.G. Hunt, *Measuring Colour*, 3rd edition, Kingston-upon-Thames: Fountain Press, 1998.

[432] R.W.G. Hunt, "Revised colour-appearance model for related and unrelated colours," *COLOR Research and Application*, 16, **3**, 146–165, 1991.

[433] R.W.G. Hunt, *The Reproduction of Colour in Photography, Printing, and Television*, 5th edition, Tolworth: Fountain Press, 1995.

[434] A. Hurlbert, "Formal connections between lightness algorithms," *Journal of the Optical Society of America*, A, **3**, 10, 1684–1693, 1986. "Synthesizing a color algorithm from examples," *Science*, **239**, 482–485, 1988.

[435] A. Hurlbert, *The Computation of Color*, Ph.D. Thesis, Department of Brain and Cognitive Science, Massachusetts Institute of Technology, Cambridge, MA, September 1989.

[436] L.M. Hurvich, *Color Vision*, Sunderland, MA: Sinauer Associates Inc., 1981.

[437] M.C. Hutley, *Diffraction Gratings*, London: Academic Press, 1982.

[438] J.K. IJspeert, T.J.T.P. van den Berg, and H. Spekreijse, "An improved mathematical description of the foveal visual point spread function with parameters for age, pupil size, and pigmentation," *Vision Research*, **33**, 1, 15–20, 1993.

[439] I. Inoue, N. Tanaka, H. Yamashita, T. Yamaguchi, H. Ishiwata, and H. Ihara, "Low-leakage-current and low-operating-voltage buried photodiode for a CMOS imager," *IEEE Transactions on Electron Devices*, **50**, 1, 43–47, 2003.

[440] M. Inui, "A fast algorithm for computing the colour gamuts of subtractive colour mixtures," *The Journal of Photographic Science*, **38**, 163–164, 1990.

[441] M. Inui, "A fast algorithm computing optimal colors" (in Japanese), *Journal of the Sciety of Photographic Science and Technology of Japan*, **57**, 6, 420–423, 1994.

[442] A. Ishihara, *Condensed Matter Physics*, New York, NY: Oxford University Press, 1991.

[443] A. Ishii, "Color management technology for digital film mastering," in *Proc. IS&T/SID Eleventh Color Imaging Conference*, 319–325, 2003.

[444] ISO (International Organization for Standardization), *Photography – Density Measurements*, Part 1, *Terms, Symbols and Notations*, ISO 5/1-1984(E/F/R); Part 2, *Geometric Conditions for Transmission Density*, ISO 5-2:1991(E); Part 3, *Spectral Conditions*, ISO 5/3-1984(E); Part 4, *Geometric Conditions for Reflection Density*, ISO 5/4-1983(E).

[445] ISO (International Organization for Standardization), *Photography – Electronic Still Picture Cameras – Resolution Measurements*, ISO 12233:2000, 2000.

[446] ISO (International Organization for Standardization), *Graphic Tecnology – Prepress Digital Data Exchange – Colour Targets for Input Scanner Calibration*, ISO 12641:1997, 1997.

[447] ISO (International Organization for Standardization), *Photography – Electronic Still Picture Cameras – Methods for Measuring Opto-electronic Conversion Functions (OECFs)*, ISO 14524:2000, 2000.

[448] ISO (International Organization for Standardization), *Guide to the Expression of Uncertainty in Measurement*, 1995.

[449] M. Ito and A. Ishii, "A non-iterative procedure for rapid and precise camera calibration," *Pattern Recognition*, **27**, 2, 301–310, 1994.

[450] M. Ito and N. Katoh, "Three-dimensional gamut mapping using various color difference formulae and color spaces," *Proceedings of SPIE*, **3648**, 83–95, 1999.

[451] S. Itoh and M. Tanaka, "Current status of field-emission displays," *Proceedings of the IEEE*, **90**, 4, 514–520, 2002.

[452] N.G. Jablonski and G. Chaplin, "Skin deep," *Scientific American*, **287**, 4, 74–81, 2002.

[453] J.D. Jackson, *Classical Electrodynamics*, 2nd edition, New York, NY: John Wiley & Sons, 1975.

[454] G.H. Jacobs and M.P. Rowe, "Evolution of vertebrate colour vision," *Clinical and Experimental Optometry*, **87**, 4–5, 206–216, 2004.

[455] R.E. Jacobson, "An evaluation of image quality metrics," *The Journal of Photographic Science*, **43**, 7–16, 1995.

[456] B. Jähne, *Digital Image Processing: Concepts, Algorithms, and Scientific Applications*, 4th edition, Berlin: Springer-Verlag, 1997.

[457] A.K. Jain, *Fundamentals of Digital Image Processing*, Englewood Cliffs, NJ: Prentice-Hall, 1989.

[458] J. Jakubowski, "Scanner performance from edge slope and cutoff frequencies," *Optical Engineering*, **35**, 7, 1993–2004, 1996. Errata: **36**, 8, 2361, 1997.

[459] T.H. James (ed.), *The Theory of the Photographic Process*, 4th edition, New York, NY: Macmillan, 1977.

[460] J.R. Janesick, T. Elliott, S. Collins, M.M. Blouke, and J. Freeman, "Scientific charge-coupled devices," *Optical Engineering*, **26**, 8, 692–714, 1987.

[461] J.R. Janesick, *Scientific Charge-Coupled Devices*, Bellingham, WA: SPIE Press, 2001.

[462] J.R. Janesick, "Lux transfer: Complementary metal oxide semiconductors versus charge-coupled devices," *Optical Engineering*, **41**, 6, 1203–1215, 2002.

[463] R. Janssen, *Computational Image Quality*, Bellingham, WA: SPIE Press, 2001.

[464] J.R. Jarvis, "The calculation of sharpness parameters for color negative materials incorporating DIR coupler," in *Photographic and Electronic Image Quality*, Royal Photographic Symposium, University of Cambridge, September 1984, pp. 10–20, 1984.

[465] J.A.M. Jennings and W.N. Charman, "An analytical approximation for the modulation transfer function of the eye," *British Journal of Physiological Optics*, **29**, 64–72, 1974.

[466] H.W. Jensen, S.R. Marschner, M. Levoy, and P. Hanrahan, "A practical model for subsurface light transport," *ACM Proceedings of SIGGRAPH 2001*, 511–518, 2001.

[467] J. Jin, G.J. Jones, and M.C. Cornwall, "Movement of retinal along cone and rod photoreceptors," *Visual Neuroscience*, **11**, 389–399, 1994.

[468] C.A. Johnson, "Effects of luminance and stimulus distance on accommodation and visual resolution," *Journal of the Optical Society of America*, **66**, 138–142, 1976.

[469] T. Johnson, *Colour Management in Graphic Arts and Publishing*, Leatherhead: Pira International, 1996.

[470] L.A. Jones, "The evaluation of negative film speeds in terms of print quality," *Journal of the Franklin Institute*, **227**, 3, 297–354 and 497–544, 1939.

[471] L.A. Jones and H.R. Condit, "The brightness scale of exterior scenes and the computation of correct photographic exposure," *Journal of the Optical Society of America*, **31**, 651–678, 1941.

[472] L.A. Jones and C.N. Nelson, "The control of photographic printing be measured characteristics of the negative," *Journal of the Optical Society of America*, **32**, 558–619, 1942.

[473] L.A. Jones and H.R. Condit, "Sunlight and skylight as determinants of photographic exposure. Part I," *Journal of the Optical Society of America*, **38**, 123–178, 1948; Part II, **39**, 94–135, 1949.

[474] P.R. Jones, "Evolution of halftoning technology in the United States patent literature," *Journal of Electronic Imaging*, **3**, 3, 257–275, 1994.

[475] D.B. Judd, "Hue, saturation, and lightness of surface colors with chromatic illumination," *Journal of the Optical Society of America*, **30**, 2–32, 1940.

[476] D.B. Judd, D.L. MacAdam, G.W. Wyszecki, "Spectral distribution of typical daylight as a function of correlated color temperature," *Journal of the Optical Society of America*, 54, 1031–1040, 1964.

[477] D.B. Judd and G. Wyszecki, *Color in Business, Science, and Industry*, 3rd edition, New York, NY: John Wiley and Sons, 1975.

[478] G. Kaiser, *A Friendly Guide to Wavelets*, Boston, MA: Birkhäuser, 1994.

[479] P.K. Kaiser, "Photometric measurements," Chapter 11 in *Optical Radiation Measurements*, Volume 5, edited by C.J. Bartleson and F. Grum, Orlando, FL: Academic Press, 1984.

[480] P.K. Kaiser and R.M. Boynton, *Human Color Vision*, 2nd edition, Washington, DC: Optical Society of America, 1996.

[481] K. Kanamori, "Interpolation errors on gray gradations caused by the three-dimensional lookup table method," *Journal of Electronic Imaging*, 10, 2, 431–444, 2001.

[482] K. Kanatani, *Geometric Computation for Machine Vision*, Oxford: Clarendon Press, 1993.

[483] H.R. Kang, *Color Technology for Electronic Imaging Devices*, Bellingham, WA: SPIE Press, 1997.

[484] H.R. Kang, *Digital Color Halftoning*, Bellingham, WA: SPIE Press, 1999.

[485] G. Kanizsa, "Margini quasi-percettivi in campi con stimolazione omogenea," *Rivisita di Psicologia*, 49, 7–30, 1955.

[486] M. Kaplan, "Monte Carlo calculation of light distribution in an integrating cavity illuminator," *Proceedings of SPIE*, 1448, 206–217, 1991.

[487] H.M. Karara (ed.), *Non-Topographic Photogrammetry*, 2nd edition, Falls Church, VA: American Society for Photogrammetry and Remote Sensing, 1989.

[488] J.M. Kasson, S.I. Nin, W. Plouffe, and J.L. Hafner, "Performing color space conversions with three-dimensional linear interpolation," *Journal of Electronic Imaging*, 4, 3, 226–250, 1995.

[489] J. Katajamäki and H. Saarelma, "Objective quality potential measures of natural color images," *Journal of Imaging Science and Technology*, 42, 3, 250–263, 1998.

[490] A.H. Katz, "Camera shutters," *Journal of the Optical Society of America*, 39, 1, 1–21, 1949.

[491] H. Kawamoto, "The history of liquid-crystal displays," *Proceedings of the IEEE*, 40, 4, 460–500, 2002.

[492] S. Kawamura, "Capturing images with digital still cameras," *IEEE Micro*, 18, 6, 14–19, 1998.

[493] V. Kayargadde and J.-B. Martens, "Estimation of edge parameters and image blur using polynomial transforms," *CVGIP: Graphic Models and Image Processing*, 56, 6, 442–461, 1994.

[494] B.W. Keelan, *Handbook of Image Quality*, New York, NY: Marcel Dekker, 2002.

[495] K. Keller (ed.), *Science and Technology of Photography*, Weinheim: VCH, 1993.

[496] P.A. Keller, *Electronic Display Measurement: Concepts, Techniques and Instrumentation*, New York, NY: John Wiley & Sons, 1997.

[497] E.F. Kelley and G.R. Jones, "Utilizing the bi-directional reflection distribution function to predict reflections from FPDs," *SID 97 Digest*, 831–834, 1997.

[498] D.H. Kelly, "Systems analysis of the photographic process. I. A three-stage model," *Journal of the Optical Society of America*, **50**, 3, 269–276, 1960.

[499] D.H. Kelly, "Systems analysis of the photographic process. II. Transfer function measurements," *Journal of the Optical Society of America*, **51**, 3, 319–330, 1961.

[500] D.H. Kelly, *Visual Science and Engineering: Models and Applications*, New York, NY: Marcel Dekker, 1994.

[501] J.R. Kender, "Instabilities in color transformations," in *Proc. IEEE Conference on Pattern Recognition and Image Processing*, Troy, NY: Rensselaer Polytechnical Institute, pp. 266–274, 1977.

[502] R.W. Kenyon, "Ink jet printing," in *Chemistry and Technology of Printing and Imaging Systems*, edited by P. Gregory, London: Blackie Academic and Professional, 1996.

[503] I.A. Khinchine, *Mathematical Foundations of Statistical Mechanics*, New York, NY: Dover, 1949.

[504] I.-C. Khoo, *Liquid Crystals: Physical Properties and Nonlinear Optical Phenomena*, New York, NY: John Wiley & Sons, 1995.

[505] J.-Y. Kim, Y.-S. Seo, and T.-H. Ha, "Estimation of illuminant chromaticity from single color image using perceived illumination and highlight," *Journal of Imaging Science and Technology*, **45**, 3, 274–282, 2001.

[506] R. Kimmel, "Demosaicing: image reconstruction from CCD samples," *IEEE Transactions on Image Processing*, **8**, 1221–1228, 1999.

[507] R. Kingslake, "Illumination in optical images," in *Applied Optics and Optical Engineering*, Vol. II, p.195, New York, NY: Academic Press, 1965.

[508] R. Kingslake, *Lens Design Fundamentals*, San Diego, CA: Academic Press, 1978.

[509] R. Kingslake, *Optics in Photography*, Bellingham, WA: SPIE Optical Engineering Press, 1992.

[510] M. Klien and I.W. Kay, *Electromagnetic Theory and Geometrical Optics*, New York, NY: Wiley(Interscience), 1965.

[511] H. Kipphan (ed.), *Handbook of Print Media*, Berlin: Springer, 2001.

[512] M.V. Klein and T.E. Furtak, *Optics*, 2nd edition, New York, NY: John Wiley and Sons, 1986.

[513] S. Kleinfelder, S.H. Lim, X. Liu, and A. El Gamal, "A 10000 frames/s CMOS digital pixel sensor," *IEEE Journal of Solid-State Circuits*, **36**, 12, 2049–2059, 2001.

[514] J.A. Kneisly, III., "Local curvature of wavefronts in an optical system," *Journal of the Optical Society of America*, **54**, 229–235, 1964.

[515] K. Knoblauch, F. Vital-Durand, and J.L. Barbur, "Variation of chromatic sensitivity across the life span," *Vision Research*, **41**, 23–36, 2001.

[516] D.E. Knuth, "Digital halftones by dot diffusion," *ACM Transactions on Graphics*, **6**, 4, 245–273, 1987.

[517] S. Kobayashi, "An LCD in the multimedia network age: polymer stabilized FLCD," *Proceedings of the 18th International Display Research Conference, Asia Display '98*, 11–14, 1998.

[518] Kodak Limited, *The Complete Kodak Book of Photography*, Ann Arbor, MI: Lowe & B. Hould Publishers, 1994.

[519] J.J. Koenderink, "Color atlas theory," *Journal of the Optical Society of America*, A, **4**, 7, 1314–1321, 1987.

[520] H. Kolb, "Anatomical pathways for color vision in the human retina," *Visual Neuroscience*, **7**, 61–74, 1991.

[521] H. Kolb and L. Dekorver, "Midget ganglion cells of the parafovea of human retina: a study by electron microscopy and serial section reconstructions," *The Journal of Comparative Neurology*, **303**, 617–636, 1991.

[522] H. Kondo, Y. Chiba, and T. Yoshida, "Veiling glare in photographic systems," *Optical Engineering*, **21**, 2, 343–346, 1982.

[523] K. Kondo, K. Kinugawa, N. Konishi, and H. Kawakami, "Wide-viewing-angle displays with in-plane switching mode of nematic LCs addressed by 13.3-in. XGA TFTs," *SID 96 Digest*, 81–84, 1996.

[524] S. Konishi, A.L. Yuille, J.M. Coughlan, and S.C. Zhu, "Statistical edge detection: learning and evaluating edge cues," *IEEE Transactions on Pattern Analysis and Machine Intelligence*, **25**, 1, 57–74, 2003.

[525] H.J. Kostkowski, *Reliable Spectroradiometry*, La Plata, MD: Spectroradiometry Consulting, 1997.

[526] E. Kowler, "The stability of gaze and its implication for vision," in *Eye Movements*, edited by R.H.S. Carpenter, Boca Raton, FL: CRC Press, 1991.

[527] W. Kraft and W.R. von Stein, *Exposure Control Process and Photographic Color Copying Apparatus*, US Patent 5,016,043, May 14, 1991.

[528] J. Krauskopf, "Effect of retinal image stabilization on the appearance of heterochromatic targets," *Journal of the Optical Society of America*, **53**, 741–744, 1963.

[529] Y.A. Kravtsov and L.A. Apresyan, "Radiative transfer: new aspects of the old theory," in *Progress in Optics*, Volume XXXVI, edited by E. Wolf, Amsterdam: Elsevier, 1996.

[530] H. Krim, D. Tucker, S. Mallat, and D. Donoho, "On denoising and best signal representation," *IEEE Transactions on Information Theory*, **45**, 7, 2225–2238, 1999.

[531] E.L. Krinov, *Spectral Reflectance Properties of Natural Formations*, translated by G. Belkov, National Research Council of Canada, Technical Translation TT-439, 1953.

[532] M.A. Kriss, C.N. Nelson, and F.C. Eisen, "Modulation transfer function in photographic systems containing development adjacency effects," *Photographic Science and Engineering*, **18**, 2, 131–138, 1974.

[533] M.A. Kriss, "Image Structure," in *The Theory of the Photographic Process*, 4th edition, edited by T.H. James, pp. 547–552, New York, NY: Macmillan Publishing Co., 1977.

[534] A.I. Krymski, N.E. Bock, N. Tu, D. Van Blerkom, and E.R. Fossum, "A high-speed, 240–frames/s. 4.1-Mpixel CMOS sensor," *IEEE Transactions on Electron Devices*, **50**, 1, 130–135, 2003.

[535] D.T. Kuan, A.A. Sawchuk, T.C. Strand, and P. Chavel, "Adaptive noise smoothing filter for image with signal-dependent noise," *IEEE Transactions on Pattern Analysis and Machine Intelligence*, **7**, 165–177, 1985.

[536] P. Kubelka and F. Munk, "Ein Beitrag zur Optik der Farbanstriche," *Z. Techn. Physik*, **12**, 593–601, 1931.

[537] P. Kubelka, "New contributions to the optics of intensely light-scattering materials, Part I," *Journal of the Optical Society of America*, **38**, 49, 1067, 1948.

[538] P. Kubelka, "New contributions to the optics of intensely light-scattering materials, Part II. Nonhomogeneous layers," *Journal of the Optical Society of America*, **44**, 330, 1954.

[539] R.G. Kuehni, *Color: An Introduction to Practice and Principles*, New York, NY: John Wiley & Sons, 1997.

[540] J.J. Kulikowski, V. Walsh, and I.J. Murray (eds.), *Vision and Visual Dysfunction*, Volume 5, *Limits of Vision*, Boca Raton, FL: CRC Press, 1991.

[541] S. Kumar, *Liquid Crystals: Experimental Study of Physical Properties and Phase Transitions*, New York, NY: Cambridge University Press, 2001.

[542] Y. Kume, N. Yamada, S. Kozaki, H. Kisishita, F. Funada, and M. Hijikigawa, "Advanced ASM mode: Improvement of display performance by using a negative-dielectric liquid crystal," *SID 98 Digest*, 1089–1092, 1998.

[543] R.L. Lamberts, "Measurement of sine-wave response of a photographic emulsion," *Journal of the Optical Society of America*, **49**, 5, 425–428, 1959.

[544] R.L. Lamberts, "Sine-wave response techniques in photographic printing," *Journal of the Optical Society of America*, **51**, 9, 982–987, 1961.

[545] P. Lancaster and K. Šalkauskas, *Curve and Surface Fitting*, London: Academic Press, 1986.

[546] E.H. Land and J.J. McCann, "Lightness and retinex theory," *Journal of the Optical Society of America*, **61**, 1–11, 1971.

[547] E.H. Land, "The retinex theory of color vision," *Scientific American*, **237**, 6, 108–129, 1977.

[548] M.S. Langer, "Large-scale failures of $f-\alpha$ scaling in natural image spectra," *Journal of the Optical Society of America*, A, **17**, 1, 28–33, 2000.

[549] G.N. LaRossa and H.-C. Lee, *Digital Image Processing Method for Edge Shaping*, US Patent 6,611,627, August 26, 2003.

[550] D.L. Lau, R. Ulichney, and G.R. Arce, "Blue- and green-noise halftoning models," *IEEE Signal Processing Magazine*, 28–38, July 2003.

[551] J.P. Lavine, E.A. Trabka, B.C. Burkey, T.J. Tredwell, E.T. Nelson, and C. Anagnostopoulos, "Steady-state photocarrier collection in silicon imaging devices," *IEEE Transactions on Electron Devices*, **30**, 9, 1123–1134, 1983.

[552] C.L. Lawson and R.J. Hanson, *Solving Least Squares Problems*, Englewood Cliffs, NJ: Prentice-Hall, 1974. (Reprinted with corrections and a new appendix by SIAM, Philadelphia, 1995.)

[553] H.P. Le, "Progress and trends in ink-jet printing technology," *Journal of Imaging Science and Technology*, **42**, 1, 49–62, 1998.

[554] J.C. Leachtenauer, *Electronic Image Display: Equipment Selection and Operation*, Bellingham, WA: SPIE Press, 2003.

[555] M. Leadbeater, "Polymers shine the light," *SPIE's OE Magazine*, 14–17, June 2002.

[556] B.B. Lee, J. Pokorny, V.C. Smith, P.R. Martin, and A. Valbergt, "Luminance and chromatic modulation sensitivity of macaque ganglion cells and human observers," *Journal of the Optical Society of America*, A, **7**, 12, 2223–2236, 1990.

[557] B.B. Lee, D.M. Dacey, V.C. Smith, and J. Pokorny, "Horizontal cells reveal cone type-specific adaptation in primate retina," *Proc. of National Academy of Science, USA*, **96**, 25, 14611–14616, 1999.

[558] C. Lee, M. Eden, and M. Unser, "High-quality image resizing using oblique projection operators," *IEEE Transactions on Image Processing*, **7**, 5, 679–692, 1998.

[559] D. Lee, "Coping with discontinuities in computer vision: their detection, classification, and measurement," *IEEE Transactions on Pattern Analysis and Machine Intelligence*, **12**, 4, 321–344, 1990.

[560] H.-C. Lee, "Method for computing the scene-illuminant chromaticity from specular highlights," *Journal of the Optical Society of America*, A, **3**, 10, 1694–1699, 1986.

[561] H.-C. Lee, *Digital Color Image Processing Method Employing Constrained Correction of Color Reproduction Function*, US Patent, 4,663,663, May 5, 1987.

[562] H.-C. Lee, *Estimating the Illuminant Color from the Shading of a Smooth Surface*, MIT AI Memo 1068, Massachusetts Institute of Technology, Cambridge, MA, August 1988.

[563] H.-C. Lee, E.J. Breneman, and C.P. Schulte, "Modeling light reflection for computer color vision," *IEEE Transactions on Pattern Analysis and Machine Intelligence*, **12**, 4, 402–409, 1990.

[564] H.-C. Lee, "A review of image-blur models in a photographic system using the principles of optics," *Optical Engineering*, **29**, 5, 405–421, 1990.

[565] H.-C. Lee, "A computational model for opponent color encoding," in *Advanced Printing of Conference Summaries, SPSE's 43rd Annual Conference*, Rochester, New York, May 1990, pp. 178–181, 1990.

[566] H.-C. Lee, "Chromatic edge detection: Idealization and reality," *International Journal of Imaging Systems and Technology*, **2**, 251–266, 1990.

[567] H.-C. Lee and D.R. Cok, "Detecting boundaries in a vector field," *IEEE Transactions on Signal Processing*, **39**, 5, 1181–1194, 1991.

[568] H.-C. Lee, H.-J. Lee, H. Kwon, and J. Liang, *Noise Suppression Algorithm Using Singular Value Decomposition*, US Patent 5,010,504, April 23, 1991.

[569] H.-C. Lee, "A physics-based color encoding model for images of natural scenes," in *Proceedings of the Conference on Modern Engineering and Technology*, Electro-Optics Session, Taipei, Taiwan, Dec. 6–15, pp. 25–52, 1992.

[570] H.-C. Lee and R.M. Goodwin, "Colors as seen by humans and machines," in *Final Program and Advance Printing Papers of the IS&T's 47th Annual Conference*, 401–405, 1994.

[571] H.-C. Lee, "Color image quantization based on physics and psychophysics," *Journal of the Society of Photographic Science and Technology of Japan*, **59**, 1, 212–225, 1996.

[572] H.-C. Lee, L.L. Barski, and R.A. Senn, *Automatic Tone Scale Adjustment Using Image Activity Measures*, US Patent 5,633,511, May 27, 1997.

[573] H.-C. Lee, S. Daly, and R.L. Van Metter, "Visual optimiztion of radiographic tone scale," *Proceedings of SPIE*, **3036**, 118–129, 1997.

[574] H.-C. Lee and H. Kwon, *Method for Estimating and Adjusting Digital Image Contrast* US Patent 5,822,453, October 13, 1998.

[575] H.-C. Lee, "Internet Color Imaging," *Proceedings of SPIE*, **4080**, 122–135, 2000.

[576] H.-C. Lee, *Tone Scale Processing Based on Image Modulation Activity*, US Patent No. 6,717,698, Apr. 6, 2004.

[577] J.-S. Lee, "Refined filtering of image noise using local statistics," *Computer Graphics and Image Processing*, **15**, 380–389, 1981.

[578] J.-S. Lee, "Digital image smoothing and the sigma filter," *Computer Vision, Graphics, and Image Processing*, **24**, 2, 255–269, 1983.

[579] J.S. Lee, J. Shah, M.E. Jernigan, and R.I. Hornsey, "Characterization and deblurring of lateral crosstalk in CMOS image sensors," *IEEE Transactions on Electron Devices*, **50**, 12, 2361–2368, 2003.

[580] Y. Le Grand and S.G. El Hage, *Physiological Optics*, Berlin: Springer-Verlag, 1980.

[581] D. Leibovici and R. Sabatier, "A singular value decomposition of a k-way array for a principal component analysis of multiway data, PTA-k," *Linear Algebra and Its Applications*, **269**, 307–329, 1998.

[582] H. Leibowitz, "The effect of pupil size on visual acuity for photometrically equated test fields at various levels of luminance," *Journal of the Optical Society of America*, **42**, 6, 416–422, 1952.

[583] H. Leibowitz, N.A. Myers, and P. Chinetti, "The role of simultaneous contrast in brightness constancy," *Journal of Experimental Psychology*, **50**, 1, 15–18, 1955.

[584] H.W. Leibowitz and D.A. Owens, "New evidence for the intermediate position of relaxed accommodation," *Documenta Ophthalmologica*, **46**, 133–147, 1978.

[585] P. Lennie, "Parallel visual pathways: a review," *Vision Research*, **20**, 561–594, 1980.

[586] P. Lepoutre, *The Structure of Paper Coatings: An Update*, Atlanta, GA: TAPPI Press, 1989.

[587] A.G. Leventhal, Y. Wang, M.T. Schmolesky, and Y. Zhou, "Neural correlates of boundary perception," *Visual Neroscience*, **15**, 1107–1118, 1998.

[588] L. Levi and R.H. Austing, "Tables of the modulation transfer function of a defocused perfect lens," *Applied Optics*, **7**, 5, 967–974, 1968.

[589] A. Lewis and L.V. Del Priore, "The biophysics of visual photoreception," *Physics Today*, 38–46, January, 1988.

[590] M. Li and J.-M. Lavest, "Some aspects of zoom lens camera calibration," *IEEE Transactions on Pattern Analysis and Machine Intelligence*, **18**, 11, 1105–1110, 1996.

[591] J. Liang, D.R. Williams, and D.T. Miller, "Supernormal vision and high-resolution retinal imaging through adaptive optics," *Journal of the Optical Society of America*, A, **14**, 11, 2873–2883, 1997.

[592] S. Liebes, Jr., "Brightness – On the ray invariance of B/n^2," *American Journal of Physics*, **37**, 9, 932–934, 1969.

[593] W. Liekens, "A modified chemical spread function concept for the prediction of densities in fine detail in photographic images," in *Photographic Image Quality*, Royal Photographic Symposium, Oxford, September pp. 8–14, 1980.

[594] J.S. Lim, *Two-Dimensional Signal and Image Processing*, Englewood Cliffs, NJ: Prentice-Hall, 1990.

[595] J.O. Limb, "Distortion criteria of the human viewer," *IEEE Transactions on System, Man, and Cybernetics*, **9**, 12, 778–793, 1979.

[596] C.-S. S. Lin, M.P. Mathur, and M.-C. F. Chang, "Analytical charge collection and MTF model for photodiode-based CMOS imagers," *IEEE Transactions on Electron Devices*, **49**, 5, 754–761, 2002.

[597] S. Lin, J. Gu, S. Yamazaki, H.-Y. Shum, "Radiometric calibration from a single image," in *Proc. IEEE Computer Society Conference on Computer Vision and Pattern Recognition*, 938–945, 2004.

[598] R.G. Littlejohn and R. Winston, "Corrections to classical radiometry," *Journal of the Optical Society of America*, A, **10**, 9, 2024–2037, 1993.

[599] M.S. Livingstone and D.H. Hubel, "Segregation of form, color, movement, and depth: anatomy, physiology, and perception," *Science*, **240**, 740–749, 1988.

[600] N.A. Logan, "Survey of some early studies of the scattering of plane waves by a sphere," *Proceedings of the IEEE*, **53**, 773, 1965.

[601] G.G. Lorentz, *Approximation of Functions*, 2nd edition, New York, NY: Chelsea, 1986.

[602] R. Loudon, *The Quantum Theroy of Light*, Oxford: Oxford University Press, 1983.

[603] O. Lowenstein and I.E. Loewenfeld, "The pupil," in *The Eye*, Volume 3, 2nd edition, edited by H. Davson, New York, NY: Academic Press, 1969.

[604] J. Lubin, "A visual discrimination model for imaging systems design and evaluation," in *Visual Models for Target Detection and Recognition*, edited by E. Peli, pp. 245–283 Singapore: World Scientific, 1995.

[605] D.G. Luenberger, *Optimization by Vector Space Methods*, New York, NY: John Wiley & Sons, 1969.

[606] T. Lule, M. Wagner, M. Verhoeven, H. Keller, and M. Bohm, "100,000-pixel, 120-dB imager in TFA technology," *IEEE Journal of Solid-State Circuits*, **35**, 5, 732–739, 2000.

[607] T. Lule, S. Benthien, H. Keller, F. Mutze, P. Rieve, K. Seibel, M. Sommer, and M. Bohm, "Sensitivity of CMOS based imagers and scaling perspectives," *IEEE Transactions on Electron Devices*, **47**, 11, 2110–2122, 2000.

[608] R.K. Luneburg, *Mathematical Theory of Optics*, Berkeley, CA: University of California Press, 1964.

[609] J. Luo, R.T. Gray, and H.-C. Lee, "Towards physics-based segmentation of photographic color images," in *Proc. International Conference on Image Processing*, **3**, 58–61, 1997.

[610] J. Luo and A. Singhal, "On measuring low-level saliency in photographic images," in *Proc. IEEE Conference on Computer Vision and Pattern Recognition*, **1**, 84–89, 2000.

[611] J. Luo and S.P. Etz, "A physical model-based approach to detecting sky in photographic images," *IEEE Transactions on Image Processing*, **11**, 3, 201–212, 2002.

[612] M.R. Luo and B. Rigg, "BFD(l:c) colour difference formula" (Part 1 and Part 2), *Journal of the Society of Dyers and Colourists*, 126–132, 1987.

[613] M.R. Luo, G. Cui, and B. Rigg, "The development of CIE2000 colour-difference formula: CIEDE2000," *COLOR Research and Application*, **26**, 5, 340–350, 2001.

[614] S.M. Luria and D.F. Neri, "Individual differences in luminous efficiency measured by flicker photometry", *COLOR Research and Application*, **11**, 1, 72–75, 1986.

[615] D.K. Lynch and W. Livingston, *Color and Light in Nature*, Cambridge CA: Cambridge University Press, 1995.

[616] R.F. Lyon and P.M. Hubel, "Eyeing the camera: Into the next century," in *Proceedings IS&T/SID Tenth Color Imaging Conference*, 349–355, 2002.

[617] D.L. MacAdam, "Maximum visual efficiencies of colored materials," *Journal of the Optical Society of America*, **25**, 361–367, 1935.

[618] D.L. MacAdam, "Visual sensitivities to color differences in daylight," *Journal of the Optical Society of America*, **32**, 247, 1942.

[619] D.L. MacAdam, "Uniform color scales," *Journal of the Optical Society of America*, **64**, 1691–1702, 1974.

[620] D.L. MacAdam, *Color Measurement*, Heidelberg: Springer-Verlag, 1985.

[621] L.W. MacDonald and A.C. Lowe (eds.), *Display Systems: Design and Applications*, Chichester: John Wiley & Sons, 1997.

[622] L.W. MacDonald and M.R. Luo (eds.), *Colour Imaging: Vision and Technology*, Chichester: John Wiley and Sons, 2000.

[623] L.W. MacDonald and M.R. Luo (eds.), *Colour Image Science: Exploiting Digital Media*, Chichester: John Wiley and Sons, 2002.

[624] E. Mach, "Über die Wirkung der räumlichen Verteilung des Lichtreizes auf die Netzhaut. I. *Sitzungsberichte der mathematisch-naturwissenschaftlichen Classe der Kaiserlichen Akademie der Wissenschaften*, **52 II**, 303–322, 1865.

[625] J.R. Magnus and H. Neudecker, *Matrix Differential Calculus with Applications in Statistics and Econometrics*, Chichester: John Wiley & Sons, 1988.

[626] V.N. Mahajan, *Aberration Theory Made Simple*, Bellingham WA: SPIE Optical Engineering Press, 1991.

[627] D. Malacara (ed.), *Optical Shop Testing*, New York, NY: John Wiley and Sons, 1978.

[628] S.G. Mallat, *A Wavelet Tour of Signal Processing*, 2nd edition, Orlando, FL: Academic Press, 1999.

[629] L. Maloney and B. Wandell, "Color constancy: a method for recovering surface spectral reflectance," *Journal of the Optical Society of America*, A, **3**, 1, 29–33, 1986.

[630] L.T. Maloney, "Evaluation of linear models of surface spectral reflectance with small number of parameters," *Journal of the Optical Society of America*, A, **3**, 1673–1683, 1986.

[631] L. Mandel and E. Wolf, *Optical Coherence and Quantum Optics*, New York: Cambridge University Press, 1995.

[632] S. Marcos, E. Moreno, and R. Navarro, "The depth-of-field of the human eye from objective and subjective measurements," *Vision Research*, **39**, 2039–2049, 1999.

[633] K.V. Mardia, *Statistics of Directional Data*, London: Academic Press, 1972.

[634] A.P. Mariani, "Bipolar cells in monkey retina selective for cones likely to be blue-sensitive," *Nature*, **308**, 184–186, 1984.

[635] D.C. Marr and E. Hildreth, "Theory of edge detection," *Proceedings of the Royal Society of London*, B, **207**, 187–217, 1980.

[636] D. Marr, *Vision: A Computational Investigation into the Human Representation and Processing of Visual Information*, San Francisco, CA: W.H. Freeman, 1982.

[637] S.R. Marschner, S.H. Westin, E.P.F. Lafortune, and K.E. Torrance, "Image-based bidirectional reflectance distribution function measurement," *Applied Optics*, 39, 16, 2592–2600, 2000.

[638] S.R. Marschner, H.W. Jensen, M. Cammarano, S. Worley, and P. Hanrahan, "Light scattering from human hair fibers," *ACM Transactions on Graphics*, **22**, 3, 780–791, 2003.

[639] G.F. Marshall, "Scanning devices and systems," *Applied Optics and Optical Engineering*, **VI**, 203–262, 1980.

[640] H. Martens and T. Næs, *Multivariate Calibration*, Chichester: John Wiley and Sons, 1989.

[641] J.-B. Martens, "Multidimensional modeling of image quality," *Proceedings of the IEEE*, **90**, 1, 133–153, 2002.

[642] J.-B. Martens, *Image Technology Design: A Perceptual Approach*, Boston, MA: Kluwer, 2003.

[643] S. Martin, "Glare characteristics of lenses and optical instruments in the visible region," *Optica Acta*, **19**, 6, 499–513, 1972.

[644] R.H. Masland and E. Raviola, "Confronting complexity: strategy for understanding the microcircuitry of the retina," *Annual Reviews: Neurosciences*, **23**, 249–284, 2000.

[645] S. Matsuda and T. Nitoh, "Flare as applied to photographic lenses," *Applied Optics*, **11**, 8, 1850–1856, 1972.

[646] D. Maystre, "Rigorous vector theories of diffraction gratings," *Progress in Optics*, Volume XXI, edited by E. Wolf, pp. 1–67, Amsterdam: North-Holland Publishing Company, 1984.

[647] C.S. McCamy, H. Marcus, and J.G. Davidson, "A color-rendition chart," *Journal of Applied Photographic Engineering*, **11**, 3, 95–99, 1976.

[648] J.J. McCann, S.P. McKee, and T.H. Taylor, "Quantitative studies in retinex theory: a comparison between theoretical predictions and observer responses to the color Mondrian experiments," *Vision Research*, **16**, 445–458, 1976.

[649] J.J. McCann, "Capturing a black cat in shade: past and present of Retinex color appearance model, " *Journal of Electronic Imaging*, **13**, 1, 36–47, 2004.

[650] J.J. McCann, "Color constancy: small overall and large local changes," *Proceedings of SPIE*, **1666**, 310–320, 1992.

[651] C. McCollough, "Color adaptation of edge detectors in the human visual system," *Science*, **149**, 1115–1116, 1965.

[652] T.W. McCurnin, L.C. Shooley, and G.R. Sims, "Charge-coupled device signal processing models and comparisons," *Journal of Electronic Imaging*, **2**, 2, 100–107, 1993.

[653] R. McDonald (ed.), *Colour Physics for Industry*, 2nd edition, Bradford: The Society of Dyers and Colourists, 1997.

[654] K. McLaren, *The Colour Science of Dyes and Pigments*, 2nd edition, Bristol: Adam Hilger Ltd, 1986.

[655] P.A. McNaughton, "Light response of vertebrate photoreceptors", *Physiological Reviews*, **70**, 3, 847–883, 1990.

[656] R.B. Merrill, *Vertical Color Filter Detector Group and Array*, US Patent 6,632,701, October 14, 2003.

[657] J. Meyer-Arendt, *Introduction to Classical and Modern Optics*, 2nd edition, Englewood Cliffs, NJ: Prentice-Hall, 1984.

[658] L. Michaelis and M. Menten, "Die kinetik der invertinwerkung," *Biochemische Zeitschrift*, **49**, 333, 1913.

[659] D.D. Michaels, *Visual Optics and Refraction*, 3rd, St. Louis, MO: The C.V. Mosby Company, 1985.

[660] A.A. Michelson and F.G. Pease, "Measurement of the diameter of α Orionis with the interferometer," *Astrophysical Journal* **53**, 249–259, 1921.

[661] A.A. Michelson, *Studies in Optics*, New York, NY: Dover, 1995. (Original text published in 1927.)

[662] G. Mie, "Beitrage zur Optik trüber Medien speziell kolloidaler Metallösungen," *Annalen der Physik*, **25**, 377–445, 1908.

[663] J.R. Milch, "Image scanning and digitization," Chapter 10 in *Imaging Processes and Materials*, edited by J. Sturge, V. Walworth, and A. Shepp, New York, NY: Van Nostrand Reinhold, 1989.

[664] M. Millodot and J. Sivak, "Influence of accommodation on the chromatic aberration of the eye," *British Journal of Physiological Optics*, **28**, 169–174, 1973.

[665] M. Millodot, "Image formation in the eye," in *The Senses*, edited by H.B. Barlow and J.D. Mollon, London: Cambridge University Press, 1982.

[666] A.D. Milner and M.A. Goodale, *The Visual Brain in Action*, Oxford: Oxford University Press, 1995.

[667] M. Minnaert, *Light and Color in the Outdoors*, translated by L. Seymour, New York, NY: Springer-Verlag, 1993.

[668] K.V. Mital, *Optimization Methods in Operations Research and Systems Analysis*, New Delhi: Wiley Eastern Limited, 1977.

[669] S. Mitton (ed.), *The Cambridge Encyclopedia of Astronomy*, New York, NY: Crown Publishers, 1977.

[670] E. Miyahara, V.C. Smith, and J. Pokorny, "The consequences of opponent rectification: the effect of surround size and luminance on color appearance," *Vision Research*, **41**, 859–871, 2001.

[671] Y. Miyake, "Tone correction of color picture by histogram modification," *Nippon Shashin Sakhaishi*, **48**, 2, 94–101, 1980.

[672] Y. Miyake, *Analysis and Evaluation of Digital Color Images*, Tokyo, Japan University of Tokyo Press, 2000.

[673] Y. Miyake, T. Ishihara, K. Ohishi, and N. Tsumura, "Measurement and modeling for the two dimensional MTF of human eye and its application for digital color reproduction," in *Proc. IS&T/SID Ninth Color Imaging Conference*, 153–157, 2001.

[674] P. Moon and D.E. Spencer, *The Photic Field*, Cambridge, MA: The MIT Press, 1981.

[675] J. Morgan, *Introduction to Geometrical and Physical Optics*, pp. 114–121, New York, NY: McGraw-Hill Book Company, 1953.

[676] N. Moroney, M.D. Fairchild, R.W.G. Hunt, C.J Li, M.R. Luo, and T. Newman, "The CIECAM02 color appearance model", *Proc. of the IS&T/SID 10th Color Imaging Conference*, Scottsdale, 23–27, 2002.

[677] J. Morovic and M.R. Luo, "Evaluating gamut mapping algorithms for universal applicability," *COLOR Research and Application*, **26**, 1, 85–203, 2001.

[678] J. Morovic and Y. Wang, "A multi-resolution full-colour spatial gamut mapping algorithm," in *Proc. IS&T/SID Eleventh Color Imaging Conference*, 282–287, 2003.

[679] S. Morozumi, "Active-matrix thin-film transistor liquid-crstal displays," in *Advances in Electronics and Electron Physics*, Volume 77, pp. 1–82, New York, NY: Academic Press, 1990.

[680] S. Morozumi, "Issues in manufacturing active-matrix LCDs," in *SID Seminar Lecture Notes*, Volume II, Seminar F3, 1–58, 1992.

[681] H. Moss, *Narrow Angle Electron Guns and Cathode Ray Tubes*, Supplement 3 of Advances in Electronics and Electron Physics series, New York, NY: Academic Press, 1968.

[682] P. Mouroulis and J. Macdonald, *Geometrical Optics and Optical Design*, New York, NY: Oxford University Press, 1997.

[683] P.S. Mudgett and L.W. Richards, "Multiple scattering calculations for technology," *Applied Optics*, **10**, 7, 1485–1502, 1971.

[684] K.T. Mullen, "The contrast sensitivity of human colour vision to red/green and blue/yellow chromatic gratings," *Journal of Physiology (London)*, **359**, 381–400, 1985.

[685] K.T. Mullen, "Colour vision as a post-receptoral specialization of the central visual field," *Vision Research*, **31**, 1, 119–130, 1991.

[686] F. Müller, H. Wässle, and T. Voigt, "Pharmacological modulation of the rod pathway in the cat retina," *Journal of Neural Physiology*, **59**, 1657–1672, 1988.

[687] J.B. Murdoch, *Illumination Engineering – From Edison's Lamp to the Laser*, New York, NY: Macmillan Publishing Company, 1985.

[688] M. Nagao and T. Matsuyama, "Edge preserving smoothing," *Computer Graphics and Image Processing*, **9**, 394–407, 1979.

[689] K.I. Naka and W.A. Rushton, "S-potentials from luminosity units in the retina of fish (Cyprinidae)," *Journal of Physiology (London)*, **185**, 587–599, 1966.

[690] K. Nakamura, "Grain distribution and sensitivity characteristics of photographic black and white films," *Journal of Imaging Technology*, **11**, 17–21, 1985.

[691] K. Nakamura, "Grain distribution of color negative films," *Journal of Imaging Technology*, **12**, 6–10, 1986.

[692] S. Nakauchi, S. Hatanaka, and S. Usui, "Color gamut mapping based on a perceptual image difference measure," *COLOR Research and Application*, **24**, 4, 280–291, 1999.

[693] K. Nassau, *The Physics and Chemistry of Color*, New York, NY: John Wiley and Sons, Inc., 1983.

[694] J. Nathans, D. Thomas, and D.S. Hogness, "Molecular genetics of human color vision: The genes encoding blue, green, and red pigments," *Science*, 232, 193, 1986.

[695] R. Navarro, P. Artal, and D.R. Williams, "Modulation transfer of the human eye as a function of retinal eccentricity," *Journal of the Optical Society of America*, A, **10**, 2, 201–212, 1993.

[696] S.K. Nayar, K. Ikeuchi, and T. Kanade, "Surface reflection: physical and geometrical perspectives," *IEEE Transactions on Pattern Analysis and Machine Intelligence*, **13**, 7, 611–634, 1991.

[697] S.K. Nayar and M. Oren, "Visual appearance of matte surfaces," *Science*, **267**, 1153–1156, 1995.

[698] Y. Nayatani, K. Takahama, H. Sobagaki, and K. Hashimoto, "Color-appearance model and chromatic-adaptation," *Color Research and Application*, **15**, 210–221, 1990.

[699] Y. Nayatani, H. Sobagaki, and K. Hashimoto, "Existence of two kinds of representations of the Helmholtz–Kohlrausch effect. I. The experimental confirmation," *Color Research and Application*, **19**, 4, 246–261, 1994.

[700] NBS (The US National Bureau of Standards), *Self Study Manual on Optical Radiation Measurements*, Part I, NBS Technical Note No. 910–1, 1976; No. 910–2, 1978; and No. 910–3, 1977.

[701] S.-M. F. Nee, "Error analysis for Mueller matrix measurement," *Journal of the Optical Society of America*, A, **20**, 8, 1651–1657, 2003.

[702] J. Neitz and G.H. Jacobs, "Polymorphism of long-wavelength cone in normal human colour vision," *Nature*, **323**, 623–625, 1986.

[703] J. Neitz and G.H. Jacobs, "Polymorphism in normal human color vision and its mechanism," *Vision Research*, **30**, 4, 621–636, 1990.

[704] C.N. Nelson, "The theory of tone reproduction," in *The Theory of the Photographic Process*, 3rd edition, edited by T.H. James, pp. 464–498, New York, NY: Macmillan Publishing Co., 1966.

[705] C.N. Nelson, "Prediction of densities in fine detail in photographic images," *Photographic Science and Engineering*, **15**, 1, 82–97, 1971.

[706] C.N. Nelson, "Tone and color reproduction," in *The Theory of the Photographic Process*, 4th edition, edited by T.H. James, pp. 547–552, New York, NY: Macmillan Publishing Co., 1977.

[707] C.N. Nelson and G.C. Higgins, "Image Sharpness," in *Advances in the Psychophysical and Visual Aspects of Image Evaluation*, edited by R.P. Dooley, pp. 72–75, Springfield, VA: The Society of Photographic Scientists and Engineers, 1977.

[708] A.N. Netravali and B.G. Haskell, *Digital Pictures: Representation and Compression*, New York, NY: Plenum Press, 1988.

[709] H.E. Neugebauer, "Quality factor for filters whose spectral transmittances are different from color mixture curves, and its application to color photography," *Journal of the Optical Society of America*, **46**, 821–824, 1956.

[710] R. Nevatia, "A color edge detector and its use in scene segmentation," *IEEE Transactions on Systems, Man, and Cybernetics*, **7**, 820–826, 1977.

[711] S.M. Newhall, "Final report of the O.S.A. subcommittee on the spacing of the Munsell Colors," *Journal of the Optical Society of America*, **33**, 7, 385–418, 1943.

[712] L.J. Newson, "Some principles governing changes in the apparent lightness of test surfaces isolated from their normal backgrounds," *The Quarterly Journal of Experimental Psychology*, **10**, 82–95, 1958.

[713] D. Nickerson and S.M. Newhall, "A psychological color solid," *Journal of the Optical Society of America*, **33**, 7, 419–422, 1943.

[714] F.E. Nicodemus (ed.), *Self-Study Manual on Optical Radiation Measurements*, Part I – *Concepts*, Gairthersburg, MD: National Bureau of Standards (now, National Institute of Standards and Technology): Chapters 1–3, March 1976; Chapters 4–5, February 1978; Chapter 6, June 1977; Chapters 7–9, June 1979; Chapter 10, March 1983; Chapter 11, April 1984; Chapter 12, April 1985.

[715] F.E. Nicodemus, J.C. Richmond, J.J. Hsia, I.W. Ginsberg, and T. Limperis, *Geometrical Considerations and Nomenclature for Reflectance*, Gairthersburg, MD: National Bureau of Standards (US), Monograph 160, October 1977.

[716] Nihon Shikisaigakkai [The Color Science Association of Japan], *Handbook of Color Science*, 2nd edition (in Japanese), Tokyo: Tokyo University Press, 1998.

[717] M.R.M. Nijenhuis and F.J.J. Bloommaert, "Perceptual error measure for sampled and interpolated images," *Journal of Imaging Science and Technology*, *41*, 3, 249–258, 1997.

[718] R.A. Normann, B.S. Baxter, H. Ravindra, and P.J. Anderton, "Photoreceptor contribution to contrast sensitivity: Applications in radiological diagnosis," *IEEE Transactions on System, Man, and Cybernetics*, **13**, 5, 944–953, 1983.

[719] G.A. Nothmann, *Nonimpact Printing*, Pittsburgh, PA: Graphic Arts Technical Foundation, 1989.

[720] C.L. Novak and S.A. Shafer, "Color edge detection," in *Image Understanding Research at CMU*, Proc. DARPA Image Understanding Workshop, Los Angeles, Feb. 1987, edited by T. Kanade, pp. 35–37, Los Altos, CA: Morgan Kaufmann Publishers, Inc., 1987.

[721] H. Nyquist, "Thermal agitation of electrical charge in conductors," *Physical Review*, **32**, 110–113, 1928.

[722] V. O'Brien, "Contour perception, illusion and reality," *Journal of the Optical Society of America*, **48**, 112–119, 1958.

[723] J.A. Ogilvy, *Theory of Wave Scattering from Rondom Rough Surfaces*, Bristol: Institute of Physics Publishing, 1991.

[724] K.N. Ogle, "Blurring of the retinal image and contrast thresholds in the fovea," *Journal of the Optical Society of America*, **50**, 4, 307–315, 1960.

[725] N. Ohta, "Optimization of spectral sensitivities," *Photographic Science and Engineering*, **27**, 193–201, 1983.

[726] N. Ohta, *Introduction to Color Reproduction Technology*, Tokyo: Corona Publishing, 1997.

[727] Y. Ohta, T. Kanade, and T. Sakai, "Color information for region segmentation," *Computer Graphics and Image Processing*, **13**, 221–241, 1980.

[728] W.C. O'Mara, *Liquid Crystal Flat Panel Displays: Manufacturing, Science, and Technology*, New York, NY: Van Nostrand Reinhold, 1993.

[729] E.L. O'Neil, *Introduction to Statistical Optics*, New York, NY: Dover, 1992.

[730] B. O'Neill, *Elementary Differential Geometry*, San Diego, CA: Academic Press, 1966.

[731] S. Ooue, "The photographic image," in *Progress in Optics*, Volume VII, edited by E. Wolf, pp. 300–358, Amsterdam: North-Holland Publishing Company, 1969.

[732] M. Oren and S.K. Nayar, "Generalization of Lambert's reflectance model," *Proceedings of ACM SIGGRAPH 1994*, pp. 239–246, 1994.

[733] D.C. O'Shea, *Elements of Modern Optical Design*, New York, NY: John Wiley and Sons, 1985.

[734] W. Ostwald, *The Color Primer*, English translation edited by F. Birren, New York, NY: Van Nostrand Reinhold Company, 1969.

[735] Y. Ovchinnikov, I. Fainberg, R. Litvan, I. Solntsev, and N. Avatkova, "A new approach to programming in photomechanical reproduction," in *Proc. of the 12th International Conference of Printing Research Institutes*, Versailles, France, edited by W. Banks, pp. 160–163, Guildford: IPC Science and Technology Press, 1974.

[736] R.D. Overheim and D.L. Wagner, *Light and Color*, New York, NY: John Wiley and Sons, 1982.

[737] D.A. Owens, "A comparison of accommodative responsiveness and contrast sensitivity for sinusoidal gratings," *Vision Research*, **20**, 159–167, 1980.

[738] D.A. Owens, "The resting state of the eyes," *American Scientist*, **72**, 378–387, 1984.

[739] E.D. Palik (ed.), *Handbook of Optical Constants of Solids*, Orlando, FL: Academic Press, 1985.

[740] E.D. Palik (ed.), *Handbook of Optical Constants of Solids II*, Orlando, FL: Academic Press, 1991.

[741] J.M. Palmer, *Lens Aberration Data*, New York, NY: American Elsevier Publishing Company, 1971.

[742] S. Pancharatnam, "Partial polarisation, partial coherence, and their spectral description for polychromatic light – Part I", *Proceedings of the Indian Academy of Sciences*, **57**, 4, 218–230, 1963, " – Part II", 231–243, *ibid*. Both papers are collected in *Selected Papers on Interferometry*, edited by P. Hariharan, SPIE Milestone Series, Volume MS28, Bellingham, WA: SPIE Optical Engineering Press, 1991.

[743] A. Papoulis, *The Fourier Integral and Its Applications*, New York, NY: McGraw-Hill, 1962.

[744] A. Papoulis, *Signal Analysis*, New York, NY: McGraw-Hill, 1977.

[745] A. Papoulis, *Probability, Random Variables, and Stochastic Processes*, New York, NY: McGraw-Hill, 1991.

[746] T.N. Pappas, J.P. Allebach, and D.L. Neuhoff, "Model-based digital halftoning," *IEEE Signal Processing Magazine*, 14–27, July 2003.

[747] J.P.S. Parkkinen, J. Hallikainen, and T. Jaaskelainen, "Characteristic spectra of Munsell colors," *Journal of the Optical Society of America*, A, **6**, 2, 318–322, 1989.

[748] J.R. Partington, *Interpolation, Identification, and Sampling*, Oxford: Clarendon Press, 1997.

[749] K.A. Parulski, "Color filters and processing alternatives for one-chip cameras," *IEEE Transactions on Electron Devices*, **32**, 8, 1381–1389, 1985.

[750] A.S. Patel and R.W. Jones, "Increment and decrement visual thresholds," *Journal of the Optical Society of America*, **58**, 5, 696–699, 1968.

[751] S.N. Pattanaik, J.A. Ferwerda, M.D. Fairchild, and D.P. Greenberg, "A multiscale model of adaptation and spatial vision for realistic image display," *Proc. ACM SIGGRAPH 1998*, 287–298, 1998.

[752] T. Pavlidis, *Algorithms for Graphics and Image Processing*, Rockville, MD: Computer Science Press, 1982.

[753] F. Pellaacini, J.A. Ferwerda, and D.P. Greenberg, "Toward a psychophysically-based light reflection model for image synthesis," *Proc. ACM SIGGRAPH 2000*, 55–64, 2000.

[754] D.G. Pelli and L. Zhang, "Accurate control of contrast on microcomputer display," *Vision Research*, **31**, 1337–1350, 1991.

[755] D.G. Pelli, "Pixel independence: Measuring spatial interactions on a CRT display," *Spatial Vision*, **10**, 4, 443–446, 1997.

[756] H. Peterson, A.J. Ahumada, and A.B. Watson, "An improved detection model for DCT coefficient quantization," *Proceedings of SPIE*, **1913**, 191–201, 1993.

[757] B.T. Phong, "Illumination for computer generated images," *Communications of ACM*, **18**, 6, 311–317, 1975.

[758] T. Piantanida and J. Larimer, "The impact of boundaries on color: Stabilized image studies," *Journal of Imaging Technology*, **15**, 2, 58–63, 1989.

[759] G.E. Pierard, C. Pierard-Franchimont, F. Laso Dosal, T. Ben Mosbah, J. Arrese-Estrada, A. Rurangirwa, A. Dowlati, and M. Vardar, "Pigmentary changes in skin senescence," *Journal of Applied Cosmetology*, **9**, 57–63, 1991.

[760] E.R. Pike and S. Sarkar, *The Quantum Theory of Radiation*, Oxford: Clarendon Press, 1995.

[761] J. E. Pinney and W. F. Voglesong, "Analytical Densitometry of Reflection Color Print Materials," *Photographic Science and Engineering*, **6**, 6, 367–370, 1962.

[762] F.H.G. Pitt and E.W.H. Selwyn, "Colour of outdoor photographic subjects," *The Photographic Journal*, **78**, 115–121, 1938.

[763] M. Planck, "Distribution of energy in the spectrum," *Annals of Physics*, **4**, 3, 553–563, 1901.

[764] W.T. Plummer, "Photographic shutters: better pictures with a reconsideration of shutter efficiency," *Applied Optics*, **16**, 7, 1914–1917, 1977.

[765] T. Poggio and F. Girosi, "Regularization algorithms for learning that are equivalent to multilayer networks," *Science*, **247**, 4945, 978–982, 1990.

[766] M.R. Pointer, "The gamut of real surface colours," *Color Research and Application*, **5**, 145, 1980.

[767] M.R. Pointer, "Measuring colour reproduction," *The Journal of Photographic Science*, **34**, 81–90, 1986.

[768] M.R. Pointer, "A colour reproduction index," in *Proceedings of the 2nd IS&T/SID Color Imaging Conference*, 180–182, 1994.

[769] F.J.A.M. Poirier and R. Gurnsey, "The effects of eccentricity and spatial frequency on the orientation discrimination asymmetry," *Spatial Vision*, **11**, 4, 349–366, 1998.

[770] A.B. Poirson and B.A. Wandell, "The appearance of colored patterns: pattern–color separability," *Journal of the Optical Society of America*, **A, 10**, 2458–2471, 1993.

[771] M. Pope, H.P. Kallmann, and P.J. Magnante, "Electroluminescence in organic crystals," *Journal of Chemical Physics*, **38**, 2042–2043, 1963.

[772] E. Popov, "Light diffraction by relief gratings: a macroscopic and microscopic view," *Progress in Optics*, vol. XXXI, edited by E. Wolf, pp. 139–187, Amsterdam: North-Holland, 1993.

[773] Z. Popovic and J. Sjöstrand, "Resolution, separation of retinal ganglion cells, and cortical magnification in humans," *Vision Research*, **41**, 1313–1319, 2001.

[774] M.I. Posner and M.E. Raichle, *Images of Mind*, Scientific American Library, New York, NY: W.H. Freeman, 1994.

[775] C. Poynton, *Digital Video and HDTV: Algorithms and Interfaces*, San Francisco, CA: Morgan Kaufmann, 2003.

[776] W.K. Pratt, *Digital Image Processing*, 2nd edition, New York, NY: John Wiley & Sons, 1991.

[777] W.H. Press, B.P. Flannery, S.A. Teukolsky, and W.T. Vetterling, *Numerical Recipes in C*, 2nd edition, Cambridge: Cambridge University Press, 1992.

[778] J.E. Proctor and P.Y. Barnes, "NIST high accuracy reference reflectometer-spectrophotometer," *Journal of Research of the National Institute of Standards and Technology*, **101**, 5, 619–627, 1996.

[779] C.N. Proudfoot (ed.), *Handbook of Photographic Science and Engineering*, 2nd edition, Springfield, VA: The Society for Imaging Science and Technology, 1997.

[780] S. Quan, N. Ohta, and N. Katoh, "Optimization of camera spectral sensitivities," in *Proc. IS&T/SID Eighth Color Imaging Conference*, 273–278, 2000.

[781] S. Quan, N. Ohta, R.S. Berns, and N. Katoh, "Optima design of camera spectral sensitivity functions based on practical filter components," in *Proc. IS \ & T/SID 9th Color Imaging Conference*, 326–331, 2001.

[782] V.C. Ramachandran and S. Blakeslee, *Phantoms in the Brain*, New York, NY: Quill William Morrow, 1998.

[783] R. Ramanath, W.E. Snyder, G.L. Bilbro, and W.A. Sander III, "Demosaicking methods for Bayer color arrays," *Journal of Electronic Imaging*, **11**, 3, 306–315, 2002.

[784] F. Ratliff, *Mach Bands: Quantitative Studies on Neural Networks in the Retina*, San Francisco, CA: Holden-Day, 1965.

[785] S. Ray, *Camera Systems*, London: Focal Press, 1983.

[786] S.F. Ray, *Applied Photographic Optics*, 3rd edition, Oxford: Focal Press, 2002.

[787] K. Ražnjević, *Physical Quantities and the Units of the International System (SI)*, New York, NY: Begell House, 1995.

[788] S.E. Reichenbach, S.K. Park, and R. Narayanswamy, "Characterizing digital image acquisition devices," *Optical Engineering*, **30**, 2, 170–177, 1991.

[789] S. O. Rice, "Reflection of electromagnetic waves from slightly rough surfaces," *Communications on Pure and Applied Mathematics*, **4**, 351–378, 1951.

[790] W.A. Richards, "Lightness scale from image intensity distribution," *Applied Optics*, **21**, 14, 2569–2582, 1982.

[791] G.H. Rieke, *Detection of Light: From the Ultraviolet to the Submillimeter*, Cambridge: Cambridge University Press, 1994.

[792] H. Ripps and R.A. Weale, "The Visual Photoreceptors," in *The Eye*, Volume 2A, 2nd edition, edited by H. Davson, New York, NY: Academic Press, 1976.

[793] C.R. Robbins, *Chemical and Physical Behavior of Human Hair*, 3rd edition, New York, NY: Springer-Verlag, 1994.

[794] A.R. Robertson, "The CIE 1976 color-difference formulae," *Color Research and Application*, **2**, 1, 7–11, 1977.

[795] A.R. Robertson, "Colour order systems: an introductory review," *Color Research and Application*, **9**, 4, 234–240, 1984.

[796] R. Robilotto and Q. Zaidi, "Limits of lightness identification for real objects under natural viewing conditions," *Journal of Vision*, **4**, 779–797, 2004. (http://journalofvision.org/4/9/9)

[797] A.H. Robins, *Biological Perspectives on Human Pigmentation*, Cambridge: Cambridge University Press, 1991.

[798] G.S. Robinson, "Color edge detection," *Optical Engineering*, **16**, 479–484, 1977.

[799] K. Robinson, "Laser safety: Powerful tool need powerful protection," *Photonics Spectra*, 92–100, October 1998.

[800] R.L. Rockhill, T. Euler, and R.H. Masland, "Spatial order within but not between types of retinal neurons," *Proceedings of the National Academy of Science, USA*, **97**, 5, 2303–2307, 2000.

[801] R.W. Rodieck, "The primate retina," in *Comparative Primate Biology*, Vol. 4, *Neurosciences*, pp. 203–278, New York, NY: Alan R. Liss Inc., 1988.

[802] R.W. Rodieck, *The First Steps in Seeing*, Sunderland, MA: Sinauer Associates, 1998.

[803] A. Roorda and D.R. Williams, "The arrangement of the three cone classes in the living human eye," *Nature*, **397**, 520–522, 1999.

[804] A. Roorda, A.B. Metha, P. Lennie, and D.R. Williams, "Packing arrangement for the three cone classes in primate retina," *Vision Research*, **41**, 1291–1306, 2001.

[805] A. Roorda and D.R. Williams, "Optical fiber properties of individual human cones," *Journal of Vision*, **2**, 404–412, 2002.

[806] C. Rosenberg, M. Hebert, and S. Thrun, "Color constancy using KL-divergence," *Proc. 8th IEEE International Conference on Computer Vision*, 239–246, 2001.

[807] A. Rosenfeld and A.C. Kak, *Digital Picture Processing*, 2nd edition, New York, NY: Academic Press, 1982.

[808] G. Rosenfeld, *Screened Image Reproduction*, US Patent 4,456,924, June 26, 1984.

[809] K. Rosenhauer and K. Rosenbruch, "Flare and optical transfer function," *Applied Optics*, **7**, 2, 283–287, 1968.

[810] J. Ross, M.C. Morrone, and D.C. Burr, "The conditions under which Mach bands are visible," *Vision Reseach*, **29**, 6, 699–715, 1989.

[811] J.A.J. Roufs, "Perceptual image quality: concept and measurement," *Philips Journal of Research*, **47**, 1, 35–62, 1992.

[812] P.J. Rousseeuw and A.M. Leroy, *Robust Regression and Outlier Detection*, New York, NY: John Wiley & Sons, 1987.

[813] D.L. Ruderman, "Origins of scaling in natural images," *Vision Research*, **37**, 23, 3385–3395, 1997.

[814] J.C. Russ, *The Image Processing Handbook*, Boca Raton, FL: CRC Press, 1992.

[815] M.D. Rutherford and D.H. Brainard, "Lightness constancy: a direct test of the illumination-estimation hypothesis," *Psychological Science*, **13**, 2, 142–149, 2002.

[816] A. Safir, L. Hyams, and J. Philpot, "The retinal directional effect: a model based on the Gaussian distribution of cone orientations," *Vision Research*, **11**, 819–831, 1971.

[817] K. Sagawa and Y. Takahashi, "Spectral luminous efficiency as a function of age," *Journal of the Optical Society of America*, A, **18**, 11, 2659–2667, 2001.

[818] R. Saito and H. Kotera, "Image-dependent three-dimensional gamut mapping using gamut boundary descriptor," *Journal of Electronic Imaging*, **13**, 3, 630–638, 2004.

[819] T. Sakamoto and A. Itooka, *Linear Interpolator for Color Correction*, US Patent 4,275,413, June 23, 1981.

[820] K. Sakatani and T. Itoh, "Color noise analysis," *Proc. IS&T's 1999 PICS Conference*, 241–246, 1999.

[821] T.O. Salmon and L. Thibos, "Comparison of the eye's wave-front aberration measured psychophysically and with the Shack-Hartmann wave-front sensor," *Journal of the Optical Society of America*, A, **15**, 9, 2457–2465, 1998.

[822] T.O. Salmon, *Cornea Contribution to the Wavefront Aberration of the Eye*, Ph.D. Dissertation, Indiana University School of Optometry, 1999.

[823] C.L. Sanders, "Color preferences for natural objects," *Illumination Engineering*, **54**, 452–456, 1959.

[824] C. Sano, T. Song, and M.R. Luo, "Colour differences for complex images," in *Proceedings IS&T/SID Eleventh Color Imaging Conference*, 121–126, 2003.

[825] G. Sapiro, "Color and illuminant voting," *IEEE Transactions on Pattern Analysis and Machine Intelligence*, **21**, 11, 1210–1215, 1999.

[826] Y. Satoh, Y. Miyake, H. Yaguchi, and S. Shinohara, "Facial pattern detection and color correction from negative color film," *Journal of Imaging Technology*, **16**, 2, 80–84, 1990.

[827] E. Saund, "Perceptual organization of occluding contours generated by opaque surfaces," *Proc. of IEEE Computer Society Conference on Computer Vision and Pattern Recognition*, **2**, 624–630, 1999.

[828] J.L. Saunderson, "Calculation of the color of pigmented plastics," *Journal of the Optical Society of America*, **32**, 727–736, 1942.

[829] K. Sayanagi, "On the light distribution in the photographic image," *Journal of the Optical Society of America*, **47**, 6, 566–567, 1957.

[830] O.H. Schade, "Image gradation, graininess and sharpness in television and motion-picture systems," *Journal of the Society of Motion Picture and Television Engineers*, (This is a four-part article.) Part I: **56**, 2, 137–177, 1951; Part II: **58**, 3, 181–222, 1952; Part III: **61**, 8, 97–164, 1953; Part IV: **64**, 11, 593–617, 1955.

[831] O.H. Schade, Sr., "An evaluation of photographic image quality and resolving power," *Journal of the Society of Motion Picture and Television Engineers*, **73**, 2, 81–119, 1964.

[832] L.B. Schein, *Electrophotography and Development Physics*, Morgan Hill, CA: Laplacian Press, 1996.

[833] P. Scheunders, "An orthogonal wavelet representation of multivalued images," *IEEE Transactions on Image Processing*, **12**, 6, 718–725, 2003.

[834] P.H. Schiller, "The ON and OFF channels of the visual system," *Trends in Neurosciences*, **15**, 3, 86–92, 1992.

[835] D. Schmidt and P. Bachmann, *Circuit Apparatus for Automatic Correction of TV Color Balance*, US Patent 5,040,054, August 13, 1991.

[836] J.M. Schmitt, G.X. Zhou, and E.C. Walker, "Multilayer model of photon diffusion in skin," *Journal of the Optical Society of America*, A, **7**, 11, 2141–2153, 1990.

[837] J.L. Schnapf, T.W. Kraft, and D.A. Baylor, "Spectral sensitivity of human cone photoreceptors," *Nature*, **325**, 439–441, 1987.

[838] J.L. Schnapf, T.W. Kraft, B.J. Nunn, and D.A. Baylor, "Spectral sensitivity of primate photoreceptors," *Visual Neuroscience*, **1**, 255–261, 1988.

[839] J.L. Schnapf, B.J. Nunn, M. Meister, and D.A. Baylor, "Visual transduction in cones of the monkey *Macaca fascicularis*," *Journal of Physiology*, **427**, 681–713, 1990.

[840] D.M. Schneeweiss and J.L. Schnapf, "Photovoltage of rods and cones in the Macaque retina," *Science*, **268**, 1053–1056, 1995.

[841] W.F. Schreiber, *Fundamentals of Electronic Imaging Systems*, 2nd edition, Berlin: Springer-Verlag, 1991.

[842] E. Schrödinger, "Theorie der Pigmente von gröster Leuchtkraft," *Annalen der Physik*, **62**, 603–622, 1920.

[843] E.F. Schubert, *Light-Emitting Diodes*, Cambridge: Cambridge University Press, 2003.

[844] A. Schuster, "Radiation through a foggy atmosphere," *Astrophysical Journal*, **21**, 1, 1–22, 1905.

[845] A. Schwarz, "Camera shutters," *Applied Optics and Optical Engineering*, edited by R. Kingslake, Vol. IV, pp. 95–125 New York, NY: Academic Press, 1967.

[846] R.K. Segur, "Using photographic space to improve the evaluation of consumer cameras," in *Proc. IS&T's 2000 PICS Conference*, 221–224, 2000.

[847] N. Sekiguchi, *Contrast Sensitivity for Isoluminant Interference Fringes in Human Foveal Vision*, Ph.D. Dissertation, Department of Psychology, University of Rochester, 1992.

[848] L. Selhuber and A. Parker, "Optical characterisation of LCDs: pitfalls and solutions," in *Display Systems: Design and Application*, edited by L.W. MacDonald and A.C. Lowe, Chichester: John Wiley & Sons, 1997.

[849] E.W.H. Selwyn, "A theory of graininess," *Photographic Journal*, **75**, 571–580, 1935.

[850] C.H. Sequin and M.F. Tompsett, *Charge Transfer Device*, New York, NY: Academic Press, 1975.

[851] M. I. Sezan, K. L. Yip and S. Daly, "Uniform perceptual quantization: Applications to digital radiography," *IEEE Transactions on System, Man, and Cybernetics*, **17**, 4, 622–634, 1987.

[852] R.V. Shack, "The influence of image motion and shutter operation on the photographic transfer function," *Applied Optics*, **3**, 10, 1171–1181, 1964.

[853] J.F. Shackelford, *Introduction to Materials Science for Engineers*, 4th edition, Upper Saddle River, NJ: Prentice Hall, 1996.

[854] S.A. Shafer, "Using color to separate reflection components," *Color Research and Application*, **10**, 4, 210–218, 1985.

[855] M.B. Shapiro, S.J. Schein, and F.M. De Monasterio, "Regularity and structure of the spatial pattern of blue cones of macaque retina," *Journal of the American Statistical Association*, **80**, 803–812, 1985.

[856] G. Sharma, "LCDs versus CRTs – color-calibration and gamut considerations," *Proceedings of the IEEE*, **90**, 4, 605–622, 2002.

[857] G. Sharma (ed.), *Digital Color Imaging Handbook*, Boca Raton, FL: CRC Press, 2002.

[858] I. Shcherback and O. Yadid-Pecht, "Photoresponse analysis and pixel shape optimization for CMOS active pixel sensors," *IEEE Transactions on Electron Devices*, **50**, 1, 12–18, 2003.

[859] R.A. Shelby, D.R. Smith, and S. Schultz, "Experimental verification of a negative index of refraction," *Science*, **292**, 5514, 77–79, 2001.

[860] D. Shepard, "A two-dimensional interpolation function for irregularly spaced data," *Proc. 23rd National Conference of ACM*, 517–524, 1968.

[861] P.D. Sherman, *Colour Vision in the Nineteenth Century*, Chapter 6 Bristol: Adam Hilger Ltd, 1981.

[862] S.M. Sherman and C. Koch, "The control of retinogeniculate transmission in the mammalian lateral geniculate nucleus," *Experimental Brain Research*, **63**, 1–20, 1986.

[863] S.K. Shevell (ed.), *The Science of Color*, 2nd edition (Optical Society of America), Amsterdam: Elsevier, 2003.

[864] G. Shiers, "Ferdinand Braun and the cathode-ray tube," *Scientific American*, **230**, 3, 92–101, March 1974.

[865] J. Shinar (ed.), *Organic Light-Emitting Devices: A Survey*, New York, NY: Springer-Verlag, 2003.

[866] S.H. Shionoya and W.M. Yen (eds.), *Phosphor Handbook*, Boca Raton, FL: CRC Press, 1999.

[867] J.D. Shore and J.P. Spoonhower, "Reflection density in photographic color prints: generalizations of the Williams-Clapper transform," *Journal of Imaging Science and Technology*, **45**, 5, 484–488, 2001.

[868] R.A. Shore, B.J. Thompson, and R.E. Whitney, "Diffraction by apertures illuminated with partially coherent light," *Journal of the Optical Society of America*, **56**, 6, 733–738, 1966.

[869] J.B. Shumaker, *Self-Study Manual on Optical Radiation Measurements*. Part I Concepts, Chapter 6, Distribution of Optical Radiation with Respect to Polarization, Washington, DC: National Bureau of Standards (now NIST), 1977.

[870] J.B. Shumaker, *Self-Study Manual on Optical Radiation Measurements*. Part I Concepts, Chapter 8, Deconvolution, Washington, DC: National Bureau of Standards (now NIST), 1979.

[871] W.A. Shurcliff, *Polarized Light: Production and Use*, Cambridge, MA: Harvard University Press, 1962.

[872] R. Siegel and J.R. Howell, *Thermal Radiation Heat Transfer*, 2nd edition, Washington, DC: Hemisphere Publishing, 1981.

[873] M.B. Silevitch, R.A. Gonsalves, and D.C. Ehn, "Prediction and removal of adjacency effects from photographic images," *Photographic Science and Engineering*, **21**, 1, 7–13, 1977.

[874] S. Silver, "Microwave aperture antennas and diffraction theory," *Journal of the Optical Society of America*, **52**, 131, 1962.

[875] D.A. Silverstein and J.E. Farrell, "Efficient method for paired comparison," *Journal of Electronic Imaging*, **10**, 2, 394–398, 2001.

[876] L.D. Silverstein, "Color in electronic displays," in *SID Seminar Lecture Notes*, **II**, Seminar F5, 1–75, 1997.

[877] J.W. Simmons and M.J. Guttmann, *States, Waves and Photons: A Modern Introduction to Light*, Reading, MA: Addison-Wesley, 1970.

[878] H. Simon, *The Splendor of Iridescence*, New York, NY: Dodd, Mead and Company, 1971.

[879] E.P. Simoncelli and B.A. Olshausen, "Natural image statistics and neural representation," *Annual Reviews: Neurosciences*, **24**, 1193–1216, 2001.

[880] J.L. Simonds, "A quantitative study of the influence of tone-reproduction factors on picture quality," *Photographic Science and Engineering*, **5**, 5, 270–277, 1961.

[881] E.M. Slayter and H.S. Slayter, *Light and Electron Microscopy*, Cambridge: Cambridge University Press, 1992.

[882] G.G. Slyusarev, *Aberration and Optical Design Theory*, 2nd edition, translated by Major J.H. Dixon, Bristol: Adam Hilger Ltd., 1984.

[883] B.G. Smith, "Geometrical shadowing of a random rough surface," *IEEE Transactions on Antennas and Propagation*, **15**, 5, 668–671, 1967.

[884] G. Smith and D.A. Atchison, *The Eye and Visual Optical Instruments*, Cambridge: Cambridge University Press, 1997.

[885] V.C. Smith, and J. Pokorny, "Spectral sensitivity of the foveal cone photopigments between 400 and 500 nm," *Vision Research*, **15**, 161–171, 1975.

[886] V.C. Smith, P.Q. Jin, and J. Pokorny, "The role of spatial frequency in color induction," *Vision Research*, **41**, 1007–1021, 2001.

[887] W.J. Smith, *Modern Optical Engineering*, 3rd edition, New York, NY: McGraw-Hill Book Company, 2000.

[888] W.R. Smythe, *Static and Dynamic Electricity*, 3rd edition, New York, NY: McGraw-Hill, 1969.

[889] R. Sobol, "Improving the Retinex algorithm for rendering wide dynamic range photographs," *Journal of Electronic Imaging*, **13**, 1, 65–74, 2004.

[890] M. Sommer, P. Rieve, M. Verhoeven, M. Bohm, B. Schneider, B. van Uffel, and F. Librecht, "First multispectral diode color imager with three color recognition and color memory in each pixel," in *Proceedings of the 1999 IEEE Workshop on Charged-Coupled Devices and Advanced Image Sensors*, pp. 187–190. Piscataway, NY: The IEEE, 1999.

[891] J.M. Soto-Crespo, M. Nieto-Vesperinas, and A.T. Friberg, "Scattering from slightly rough random surfaces: a detailed study on the validity of the small perturbation method," *Journal of the Optical Society of America*, A, **7**, 7, 1185–1201, 1990.

[892] L. Spillmann and J.S. Werner (eds.), *Visual Perception: The Neurophysiological Foundations*, San Diego, CA: Academic Press, 1990.

[893] D.L. Spooner, "Why do measured values taken with different color instruments usually differ?" in *Proc. 2nd IS&T/SID Color Imaging Conference*, 159–164, 1994

[894] N. Sprague and J. Luo, "Clothed people detection in still images," in *Proc. 16th International Conference on Pattern Recognition*, Volume 3, 585–589, 2002.

[895] W.N. Sproson, *Colour Science in Television and Display Systems*, Bristol: Adam Hilger Ltd, 1983.

[896] R.F. Stamm, M.L. Garcia, and J.J. Fuchs, "The optical properties of human hair I. fundamental considerations and goniophotometer curves," *Journal of the Society of Cosmetic Chemists*, **28**, 571–600, 1977.

[897] J.-L. Starck, E.J. Candés, and D.L. Donoho, "The curvelet transform for image denoising," *IEEE Transactions on Image Processing*, **11**, 6, 670–684, 2002.

[898] J.-L. Starck, F. Murtagh, E.J. Candés, and D.L. Donoho, "Gray and color image contrast enhancement by the curvelet transform," *IEEE Transactions on Image Processing*, **12**, 6, 706–717, 2003.

[899] O.N. Stavroudis, *The Optics of Rays, Wavefronts, and Caustics*, New York, NY: Academic Press, 1972.

[900] G.P. Stein, *Internal Camera Calibration Using Rotation and Geometric Shapes*, Master Thesis, Dept. of Electrical Engineering and Computer Science, Massachusetts Institute of Technology, Cambridge, MA, 1993.

[901] M.A. Stephens, "Random walk on a circle," *Biometrika*, **50**, 385–390, 1963.

[902] P. Sterling, "Retina," in *The Synaptic Organization of the Brain*, edited by G.M. Shepherd, New York, NY: Oxford University Press, 1990.

[903] J. C. Stevens and S. S. Stevens, "Brightness function: Effects of adaptation," *Journal of the Optical Society of America*, **53**, 3, 375–385, 1963.

[904] S.S. Stevens (ed.), *Handbook of Experimental Psychology*, New York, NY: John Wiley & Sons, 1951.

[905] S.S. Stevens and J.C. Stevens, *The Dynamics of Visual Brightness*, Psychophysical Project Report PPR-246, Harvard University, Cambridge, MA., August 1960.

[906] S.S. Stevens, "To honour Fechner and repeal his law," *Science*, **133**, 80–86, 1961.

[907] E.C. Stewart, "The Gelb effect," *Journal of Experimental Psychology*, **57**, 4, 235–242, 1959.

[908] W.S. Stiles, "The luminous efficiency of monochromatic rays entering the eye pupil at different points and a new color effect," *Proceedings of the Royal Society of London*, B, **123**, 90–118, 1937.

[909] T.G. Stockham Jr., "Image processing in the context of a visual model," *Proceedings of the IEEE*, **60**, 828–842, July 1972.

[910] A. Stockman, D.I.A. MacLeod, and N.E. Johnson, "Spectral sensitivities of the human cones," *Journal of the Optical Society of America*, A, **10**, 12, 2491–2521, 1993.

[911] A. Stockman, L.T. Sharpe, K. Rüther, and K. Nordby, "Two signals in the human rod visual system: A model based on electrophysiological data," *Visual Neuroscience*, **12**, 951–970, 1995.

[912] A. Stogryn, "Electromagnetic scattering by random dielectric constant fluctuations in a bounded medium," *Radio Science*, **9**, 5, 509–518, 1974.

[913] G.G. Stokes, "On the composition and resolution of streams of polarized light from different sources," *Transactions of the Cambridge Philosophical Society*, **9**, 399–416, 1852.

[914] M. Stokes, M.D. Fairchild, and R.S. Berns, "Colorimetrically quantified visual tolerances for pictorial images," *1992 TAGA Proceedings* (Technical Association of the Graphic Arts), **2**, 757–777, 1992.

[915] P.A. Stokseth, "Properties of a defocused optical system," *Journal of the Optical Society of America*, **59**, 10, 1314–1321, 1969.

[916] J.C. Stover, *Optical Scattering: Measurement and Analysis*, New York, NY: McGraw-Hill, 1990.

[917] G. Strang, *Calculus*, pp. 263 and 265, Wellesley, MA: Wellesley-Cambridge Press, 1991.

[918] A. Streitwieser, Jr. and C.H. Heathcock, *Introduction to Organic Chemistry*, New York, NY: Macmillan, 1976.

[919] R. Strharsky and J. Wheatley, "Polymer optical interference filters," *Optics and Photonics News*, **13**, 11, 34–40, 2002.

[920] L. Stroebel, J. Compton, I. Current, and R. Zakia, *Photographic Materials and Processes*, Boston, MA: Focal Press, 1986.

[921] J.W. Strutt (Lord Rayleigh), "On the light from the sky, its polarization and colour," *Philosophical Magazine*, **XLI**, 107–120, 274–279, 1871.

[922] L. Stryer, *Biochemistry*, 3rd edition, New York, NY: W.H. Freeman, 1988.

[923] J. Sturge, V. Walworth, and A. Shepp (eds.), *Imaging Processes and Materials*, New York, NY: Van Nostrand Reinhold, 1989.

[924] T. Suga, "Methods for measuring properties of silver halide products," in *Handbook of Photographic Science and Engineering*, 2nd edition, edited by C.N. Proudfoot, Springfield, VA: The Society for Imaging Science and Technology, 1997.

[925] J. Sullivan, L. Ray, and R. Miller, "Design of minimum visual modulation halftone patterns," *IEEE Transactions on Systems, Man, and Cybernetics*, **21**, 1, 33–38, 1991.

[926] C.C. Sung and W.D. Eberhardt, "Scattering of an electromagnetic wave from a very rough semi-infinite dielectric plane (exact treatment of the boundary conditions)," *Journal of Applied Physics*, **49**, 3, 994–1001, 1978.

[927] R.E. Swing, "Microdensitometer optical performance: scalar theory and experiment," *Optical Engineering*, 15, 6, 559–577, 1976.

[928] R.E. Swing, *An Introduction to Microdensitometer*, Bellingham, WA: SPIE Optical Engineering Press, 1998.

[929] E. Switkes, M.J. Mayer, and J.A. Sloan, "Spatial frequency analysis of the visual environment: Anisotropy and the carpentered environment hypothesis," *Vision Research*, **18**, 1393–1399, 1978.

[930] SWOP, *Specifications for Web Offset Publications*, 8th edition, New York, NY: SWOP Inc., 1997.

[931] S.M. Sze, *Semiconductor Devices, Physics and Technology*, New York, NY: John Wiley & Sons, 2002.

[932] K. Takahashi, T. Akimoto, and S. Watanabe, *Method of Detecting Flesh Color in Color Originals*, US Patent 4,203,671, May 20, 1980.

[933] N. Tamura, N. Tsumura, and Y. Miyake, "Masking model for accurate colorimetric characterization of LCD," in *Proceedings of the IS&T/SID Tenth Color Imaging Conference*, 312–316, 2002.

[934] R.T. Tan, K. Nishino, and K. Ikeuchi, "Illumination chromaticity estimation using inverse-intensity chromaticity space," in *Proc. IEEE Conference on Computer Vision and Pattern Recognition*, **I**, 673–680, 2003.

[935] C.W. Tang and S.A. Van Slyke, "Organic electroluminescent diodes," *Applied Physics Letters*, **51**, 913–915, 1987.

[936] T. Tani, *Photographic Sensitivity: Theory and Mechanisms*, New York, NY: Oxford University Press, 1995.

[937] T. Tani, "A review of the mechanism of photographic sensitivity and roles of silver clusters," *Journal of Imaging Science and Technology*, **48**, 3, 278–284, 2004.

[938] L.E. Tannas, Jr. (ed.), *Flat-Panel Displays and CRTs*, New York, NY: Van Nostrand Reinhold, 1985.

[939] B. Tao, I. Tastl, and N. Katoh, "Illumination detection in linear space," in *Proceedings of the IS&T/SID Eighth Color Imaging Conference*, 172–177, 2000.

[940] S. Tatsuoka, "Optical flare of photographic lenses," *Journal of Applied Physics, Japan*, **35**, 9, 649–655, 1966.

[941] B.N. Taylor and C.E. Kuyatt, *Guidelines for Evaluating and Expressing the Uncertainty of NIST Measurement Results*, NIST Technical Note 1297, January 1993.

[942] B.N. Taylor, *Guide for the Use of the International System of Units (SI)*, NIST special publication 811, 1995 edition, April 1995.

[943] C.C. Taylor, Z. Pizlo, and J. P. Allebach, "Perceptually relevant image fidelity," *Proceedings of SPIE*, **3299**, 110–118, 1998.

[944] T. Terashita, *Exposure Control Method*, US Patent 4,397,545, August 9, 1983.

[945] T. Terashita, *Methods of Locating Abnormal Originals*, US Patent 4,416,539, November 22, 1983.

[946] T. Terashita, *Methods of Setting Conditions in Photographic Printing*, US Patent 4,603,969, August 5, 1986.

[947] T. Terashita, *Photographic Printer*, US Patent 4,707,119, November 17, 1987.

[948] A.J.P. Theuwissen, *Solid-State Imaging with Charge-Coupled Devices*, Dordrecht: Kluwer Academic, 1995.

[949] H.S. Thompson, "The pupil," in *Adler's Physiology of the Eye*, 9th edition, edited by W.H. Hart Jr., St. Louis, MO: Mosby-Year Book, 1992.

[950] E.I. Thorsos and D.R. Jackson, "Studies of scattering theory using numerical methods," *Waves in Random Media*, **3**, S165–S190, 1991.

[951] S. Thurm, K. Bunge, and G. Findeis, *Method of and Apparatus for Determining the Copying Light Amounts for Copying from Color Originals*, US Patent 4,279,502, July 21, 1981.

[952] R.J.D. Tilley, *Colour and the Optical Properties of Materials*, Chichester: John Wiley & Sons, 2000.

[953] C. Tomasi and R. Manduchi, "Bilateral filtering for gray and color images," in *Proceedings of the 6th International Conference on Computer Vision*, 839–846, 1998.

[954] S. Tominaga and B.A. Wandell, "Standard surface-reflectance model and illuminant estimation," *Journal of the Optical Society of America*, A, **6**, 4, 576–584, 1989.

[955] S. Tominaga and B.A. Wandell, "Natural scene-illuminant estimation using the sensor correlation," *Proceedings of the IEEE*, **90**, 1, 42–56, 2002.

[956] R.B.H. Tootell, J.D. Mendola, N.K. Hadjikhani, P.J. Ledden, A.K. Liu, J.B. Reppas, M.I. Sereno, and A.M. Dale, "Functional analysis of V3A and related areas in human visual cortex," *The Journal of Neuroscience*, **17**, 7060–7078, 1997.

[957] K.E. Torrance and E.M. Sparrow, "Theory for off-specular reflection from roughened surfaces," *Journal of the Optical Society of America*, **57**, 9, 1105–1114, 1967.

[958] P. E. Trahanias and A.N. Venetsanopoulos, "Vector directional filters: A new class of multichannel image processing filters," *IEEE Transactions on Image Processing*, **2**, 528–534, 1993.

[959] P. E. Trahanias, D. G. Karakos, and A.N. Venetsanopoulos, "Directional processing of color images: Theory and experimental results," *IEEE Transactions on Image Processing*, **5**, 868–880, 1996.

[960] L.N. Trefethen and D. Bau, III, *Numerical Linear Algebra*, SIAM, Philadelphia, 1997.

[961] S. Triantaphillidou and R.E. Jacobson, "A simple method for the measurement of modulation transfer functions of displays," in *Proceedings of the IS&T's 2000 PICS Conference*, 139–144, 2000.

[962] R.C. Tripathi and B.J. Tripathi, "Anatomy, orbit and adnexa of the human eye," in *The Eye*, Volume 1a, edited by H. Davson, Orlando, FL: Academic Press, 1984.

[963] Y. Trotter and S. Celebrini, "Gaze direction controls response gain in primary visual-cortex neurons," *Nature*, **398**, 239–242, 1999.

[964] J.B. Troy and B.B. Lee, "Steady discharges of macaque retinal ganglion cells," *Visual Neuroscience*, **11**, 111–118, 1994.

[965] H.J. Trussell, "Applications of set theoretic methods to color systems," *COLOR Research and Application*, **16**, 1, 31–41, 1991.

[966] R.Y. Tsai, "A versatile camera calibration technique for high-accuracy 3-D machine vision metrology using off-the-shelf TV cameras and lenses," *IEEE Journal of Robotics and Automation*, **3**, 4, 323–344, 1987.

[967] P.-S. Tsai, T. Acharya, and A.K. Ray, "Adaptive fuzzy color interpolation," *Journal of Electronic Imaging*, **11**, 3, 293–305, 2002.

[968] D.Y. Ts'o and C.D. Gilbert, "The organization of chromatic and spatial interactions in the primate striate cortex," *The Journal of Neuroscience*, **8**, 5, 1712–1727, 1988.

[969] D.Y. Ts'o, A. Wang Roe, and C.D. Gilbert, "A hierarchy of the functional organization for color form and disparity in primate visual area V2," *Vision Research*, **41**, 1333–1349, 2001.

[970] Y. Tsukamoto, P. Masarachia, S. Schein, and P. Sterling, "Gap junctions between the pedicles of macaque foveal cones," *Vision Research*, **32**, 10, 1809–1815, 1992.

[971] K.-I.Tsutsui, H. Sakata, T. Naganuma, and M. Taira, "Neural correlates for perception of 3D surface orientation from texture gradient," *Science*, **298**, 5592, 409–412, 2002.

[972] C.M. Tuttle, "Photoelectric photometry in the printing of amateur negatives," *Journal of Franklin Institute*, **224**, 315–337, 1937.

[973] K. Uchikawa, H. Uchikawa, and P.K. Kaiser, "Luminance and saturation of equally bright colors," *Color Research and Application*, **9**, 1, 5–14, 1984.

[974] H. Uchike and T. Hirakawa, "Color plasma displays," *Proceedings of the IEEE*, **90**, 4, 533–539, 2002.

[975] K. Ukai, "Spatial pattern as a stimulus to the pupillary system," *Journal of the Optical Society of America*, A, **2**, 7, 1094–1100, 1985.

[976] R. Ulichney, *Digital Halftoning*, Cambridge, MA: The MIT Press, 1987.

[977] L.M. Vaina, "Functional segregation of color and motion processing in the human visual cortex: clinical evidence," *Cerebral Cortex*, **4**, 5, 555–572, 1994.

[978] J.M. Valeton and D. van Norren, "Light adaptation of primate cones: an analysis based on extracellular data," *Vision Research*, **23**, 12, 1539–1547, 1983.

[979] W. Vanduffel, D. Fize, H. Peuskens, K. Denys, S. Sunaert, J.T. Todd, and G.A. Orban, "Extracting 3D from motion:differences in human and monkey intraparietal cortex," *Science*, **298**, 5592, 413–415, 2002.

[980] D.C. Van Essen and H.A. Drury, "Structural and functional analyses of human cerebral cortex using a surface-based map," *The Journal of Neuroscience*, **17**, 7079–7102, 1997.

[981] D.C. Van Essen, J.W. Lewis, H.A. Drury, N. Hadjikhani, R.B.H. Tootell, M. Bakircioglu, and M.I. Miller, "Mapping visual cortex in monkeys and humans using surface-based atlases," *Vision Research*, **41**, 1359–1378, 2001.

[982] D.C. Van Essen, "Organization of visual areas in macaque and human cerebral cortex," in *The Visual Neurosciences*, edited by L.M. Chalupa and J.S. Werner, Cambridge, MA: MIT Press, 2004.

[983] E. Vanmarcke, *Random Fields: Analysis and Synthesis*, Cambridge, MA: The MIT Press, 1983.

[984] A. van Meeteren, "Calculations on the optical modulation transfer function of the human eye for white light," *Optica Acta*, **21**, 5, 395–412, 1974.

[985] F.L. Van Nes and M.A. Bouman, "Spatial modulation transfer in the human eye," *Journal of the Optical Society of America*, **57**, 401–406, 1967.

[986] R. Varma, J.M. Tielsch, H.A. Quigley, *et al.*, "Race-, age-, gender-, and refractive error-related differences in the normal optic disc," *Archives of Ophthalmology*, **112**, 1068–1076, 1994.

[987] F.O.C.A. Veau, *Optimization of the Modulation Transfer Fuction of a Joyce Loebl Microdensitometer*, Master Thesis, School of Physics, University of Melbourne, Australia, 1971.

[988] W.H. Venable, "Accurate tristimulus values from spectra data," *Color Research and Application*, **14**, 5, 260, 1989.

[989] H.G. Völz, *Industrial Color Testing: Fundamentals and Techniques*, Weinheim: VCH, Germany, 1995.

[990] W. Von Bezold, *Die Farbenlehre*, Braunschweig: Westerman, 1874.

[991] P.L. Vora and H.J. Trussell, "Measure of goodness of a set of color-scanning filters," *Journal of the Optical Society of America*, A, **10**, 7, 1499–1508, 1993.

[992] P.L. Vora, "Inner products and orthogonality in color recording filter design," *IEEE Transactions on Image Processing*, **10**, 4, 632–642, 2001.

[993] J.J. Vos, J. Walraven, and A. van Meeteren, "Light profiles of the foveal image of a point source," *Vision Research*, **16**, 215–219, 1976.

[994] J.J. Vos, "Disability glare – a state of the art report", *CIE-Journal*, **3**, 39–53, 1984.

[995] J.J. Vos, "Are unique and invariant hues coupled?" *Vision Research*, **26**, 337, 1986.

[996] M.J. Vrhel and H.J. Trussell, "Optimal color filters in the presence of noise," *IEEE Transactions on Image Processing*, **4**, 6, 814–823, 1995.

[997] P. Vuylsteke and E. Schoeters, "Multiscale image contrast amplification," *Proceedings of SPIE*, **2167**, 551–560, 1994.

[998] A.R. Wade and B.A. Wandell, "Chromatic light adaptation measured using functional magnetic resonance imaging," *The Journal of Neuroscience*, **22**, 18, 8148–8157, 2002.

[999] A.R. Wade, A.A. Brewer, J.W. Rieger, and B.A. Wandell "Functional measurements of human ventral occipital cortex: retinotopy and colour," *Philosophical Transactions of the Royal Society of London*, B, **357**, 963–973, 2002.

[1000] N. Wade, *Visual Allusions: Pictures of Perception*, Hove: Lawrence Erlbaum Associates, 1990.

[1001] G. Wahba, *Spline Models for Observational Data*, Society for Industrial and Applied Mathematics, Philadelphia, PA, 1990.

[1002] D.M. Walba, "Fast ferroelectric liquid-crystal electrooptics," *Science*, **270**, 250–251, 1995.

[1003] H. Wallach, "Brightness constancy and the nature of achromatic colors," *Journal of Experimental Psychology*, **38**, 310–324, 1948.

[1004] G. Walsh, W.N. Charman, and H.C. Howland, "Objective technique for the determination of monochromatic aberrations of the human eye," *Journal of the Optical Society of America*, A, **1**, 9, 987–992, 1984.

[1005] B.A. Wandell, "The synthesis and analysis of color images," *IEEE Transactions on Pattern Analysis and Machine Intelligence*, **9**, 1, 2–13, 1987.

[1006] B.A. Wandell, *Foundations of Vision*, Sunderland, MA: Sinauer Associates, 1995.

[1007] B.A. Wandell and A.R. Wade, "Functional imaging of the visual pathways," *Neurologic Clinics of North America*, **21**, 417–443, 2003.

[1008] H. Wang, "Influence of black-target size and detection aperture on veiling-glare measurements," *Optical Engineering*, **33**, 11, 3818–3825, 1994.

[1009] L.-L. Wang and W.-H. Tsai, "Camera calibration by vanishing lines for 3–D computer vision," *IEEE Transactions on Pattern Analysis and Machine Intelligence*, **13**, 4, 370–376, 1991.

[1010] M. Wang and K.J. Parker, "Prediction of the texture visibility of color halftone patterns," *Journal of Electronic Imaging*, **11**, 2, 195–205, 2002.

[1011] M. Wäny and G.P. Israel, "CMOS Image sensor with NMOS-only global shutter and enhanced responsivity," *IEEE Transactions on Electron Devices*, **50**, 1, 57–62, 2003.

[1012] G.J. Ward, "Measuring and modeling anisotropic reflection," *Computer Graphics*, **26**, 2, 265–272, 1992. (*Proceedings of ACM SIGGRAPH 1992*.)

[1013] H. Wässle, M. Yamashita, U. Greferath, U. Grünert, and F. Müller, "The rod bipolar cell of the mammalian retina," *Visual Neural Science*, **7**, 99–112, 1991.

[1014] A.B. Watson (ed.), *Digital Images and Human Vision*, Cambridge, MA: MIT Press, 1993.

[1015] G.S. Watson and E.J. Williams, "On the construction of significance tests on the circle and the sphere," *Biometrika*, **43**, 344–352, 1956.

[1016] G.S. Watson, *Statistics on Spheres*, New York, NY: John Wiley, 1983.

[1017] R.J. Watt and M. Morgan, "The recognition and representation of edge blur," *Vision Research*, **23**, 1465–1477, 1983.

[1018] L.F. Weber, *Plasma Displays*, Seminar Lecture Notes, M-8, 1–36, Santa Ana, CA: Society for Information Display, 1994.

[1019] M.F. Weber, C.A. Stover, L.R. Gilbert, T.J. Nevitt, and A.J. Ouderkirk, "Giant birefringent optics in multilayer polymer mirrors," *Science*, **287**, 2451–2456, 2000.

[1020] V.R. Weidner and J.J. Hsia, "Reflection properties of pressed polytetrafluoroethylene powder," *Journal of the Optical Society of America*, **71**, 7, 856–861, 1981.

[1021] W.T. Welford, *Aberrations of Optical Systems*, Bristol: Adam Hilger Ltd, 1986.

[1022] J. Weng, P. Cohen, and M. Herniou, "Camera calibration with distortion models and accuracy evaluation," *IEEE Transactions on Pattern Analysis and Machine Intelligence*, **14**, 10, 965–980, 1992.

[1023] M.F. Wesner, J. Pokorny, S.K. Shevell, and V.C. Smith, "Foveal cone detection statistics in color-normals and dichromats," *Vision Research*, **31**, 6, 1021–1037, 1991.

[1024] G. Westheimer, "Sharpness discrimination for foveal targets," *Journal of the Optical Society of America*, A, **8**, 4, 681–685, 1991.

[1025] G. Westheimer, "Optics in vision," in *Visual Science and Engineering*, edited by D.H. Kelly, New York, NY: Marcel Dekker, Inc., 1994.

[1026] J.C. Whitaker, *Electronic Displays*, New York, NY: McGraw-Hill, 1994.

[1027] G. Whiteside, E. Betensky, D. Butler, Y. Chao, and J. Van Tassell, "Image acquisition module with all plastic optics," *Proc. IS&T's PICS Conference*, pp. 70–75, Savannah, Georgia, April 1999.

[1028] P. Whittle, "The psychophysics of contrast brightness," and "Contrast brightness and ordinary seeing," in *Lightness, Brightness, and Transparency*, edited by A.L. Gilchrist, Hillsdale, NJ: Lawrence Erlbaum, 1994.

[1029] H. Widdel and D.L. Post (eds.), *Color in Electronic Displays*, New York, NY: Plenum Press, 1992.

[1030] N. Wiener, "Generalized harmonic analysis," *Acta Mathematica*, **55**, 117–258, 1930.

[1031] N. Wiener, *Extrapolation, Interpolation and Smoothing of Stationary Time Series*, Cambridge, MA: MIT Press, 1949.

[1032] D.R. Williams, D.I.A. MacLeod, and M. Hayhoe, "Foveal tritanopia," *Vision Research*, **21**, 1341–1356, "Punctate sensitivity of the blue-sensitive mechanisms," *Vision Research*, **21**, 1357–1375, 1981.

[1033] D.R. Williams, "Topography of the foveal cone mosaic in the living human eye," *Vision Research*, **28**, 433–454, 1988.

[1034] D.R. Williams and A. Roorda, "The trichromatic cone mosaic in the human eye," in *Color Vision: From Genes to Perception*, edited by K.R. Gegenfurtner and L.T. Sharpe, pp. 113–122, Cambridge: Cambridge University Press, 2000.

[1035] F. C. Williams and F. R. Clapper, "Multiple internal reflections in photographic color prints," *Journal of the Optical Society of America*, **43**, 7, 595–599, 1953.

[1036] S.J. Williamson and H.Z. Cummins, *Light and Color in Nature and Art*, New York, NY: John Wiley and Sons, 1983.

[1037] E.N. Willmer and W.D. Wright, "Colour sensitivity of the fovea centralis," *Nature*, **156**, 119–121, 1945.

[1038] F.M. Willmouth, "Transparency, translucency, and gloss," Chapter in *Optical Properties of Polymers*, edited by G.H. Meeten, 5 London: Elsevier Applied Science Publishers, 1986.

[1039] R.G. Willson, *Modeling and Calibration of Zoom Lenses*, Ph.D. Thesis, Robotics Institute, Carnegie Mellon University, Pittsburg, PA, 1994.

[1040] M.C.K. Wiltshire, "Bending light the wrong way," *Science*, **292**, 5514, 60–61, 2001.

[1041] E. Wolf, "Coherence and radiometry," *Journal of the Optical Society of America*, **68**, 1, 6–17, 1978.

[1042] J.M. Wolfe and D.A. Owens, "Is accommodation colorblind? Focusing chromatic contours," *Perception*, **10**, 53–62, 1981.

[1043] W.L. Wolfe, "Radiometry," in *Applied Optics and Optical Engineering*, Vol. VIII, pp. 117–170, New York, NY: Academic Press, 1980.

[1044] W.L. Wolfe, *Introduction to Radiometry*, Bellingham, WA: SPIE Press, 1998.

[1045] L.B. Wolff, "Diffuse-reflectance model for smooth dielectric surfaces," *Journal of the Optical Society of America*, A, **11**, 11, 2956–2968, 1994.

[1046] M. Wolski, C.A. Bouman, J.P. Allebach, and E. Walowit, "Optimization of sensor response functions for colorimetry of reflective and emissive objects," *IEEE Transactions on Image Processing*, **5**, 507–517, 1996.

[1047] H.-S. Wong, "Technology and device scaling considerations for CMOS imagers," *IEEE Transactions on Electron Devices*, **43**, 12, 2131–2142, 1996.

[1048] E.A. Wood, *Crystals and Light*, New York, NY: Dover, 1977.

[1049] S.L. Wright, K. Ho, and A. Lien, "Status of TFTLCD color and metrology," in *Proc. IS&T/SID Eighth Color Imaging Conference*, 301–304, 2000.

[1050] W.D. Wright, "The basic concepts and attributes of colour order systems," *COLOR Research and Application*, **9**, 4, 229–233, 1984.

[1051] X. Wu and N. Zhang, "Primary-consistent soft-decision color demosaicking for digital cameras." *IEEE Transactions on Image Processing*, **13**, 9, 1263–1274, 2004.

[1052] S. Wuerger, A.B. Watson, and A.J. Ahumada Jr., "Toward a standard observer for spatio-chromatic detection," *Proceedings of the SPIE*, **4662**, 159–172, 2002.

[1053] G. Wyszecki and W.S. Stiles, *Color Science*, 2nd edition, New York, NY: John Wiley and Sons, 1982.

[1054] J.M. Yaeli, "Stray light measurement for imaging systems," *Optical Engineering*, **27**, 1, 86–87, 1988.

[1055] Y. Yamamoto, "Colorimetric evaluation of skin color in the Japanese," *Plastic and Reconstructive Surgery*, **96**, 1, 139–145, 1995.

[1056] L. Yang and B. Kruse, "Revised Kubelka–Munk theory. I. Theory and application," *Journal of the Optical Society of America*, **21**, 10, 1933–1941, 2004.

[1057] X.L. Yang and S.M. Wu, "Modulation of rod-cone coupling by light," *Science*, **244**, 352–354, 1989.

[1058] T. Yano and K. Hashimoto, "Preference for Japanese complexion color under illumination," *Color Research and Application*, **22**, 4, 269–274, 1997.

[1059] A.L. Yarbus, *Eye Movements and Vision*, translated by B. Haigh, New York, NY: Plenum Press, 1967.

[1060] A. Yariv, *Optical Electronics*, New York, NY: CBS College Publishing, Holt, Rinehart and Winston, 1985.

[1061] Y. Yoshida and Y. Yamamoto, "Color calibration of LCDs," in *Proc. IS&T/SID 10th Color Imaging Conference*, 305–311, 2002.

[1062] R.S.L. Young and M. Alpern, "Pupil responses to foveal exchange of monochromatic lights," *Journal of the Optical Society of America*, **70**, 6, 697–706, 1980.

[1063] K.C. Yow and R. Cipolla, "Feature-based human face detection," *Image and Vision Computing*, **15**, 9, 713–735, 1997.

[1064] J.A.C. Yule, "Unsharp masks and a new method of increasing definition in prints," *Photographic Journal*, **84**, 321–327, 1944.

[1065] J.A.C. Yule, *Principles of Color Reproduction*, New York, NY: Wiley, 1967.

[1066] S. Zeki, *A Vision of the Brain*, Oxford: Blackwell Scientific Publications, 1993.

[1067] X. Zhang and B. Wandell, "A spatial extension of CIELAB for digital color image reproduction," *SID Digest*, **27**, 731–734, 1996.

[1068] X. Zhang and B. Wandell, "Color image fidelity metrics evaluated using image distortion maps," *Signal Processing*, **70**, 201–214, 1998.

[1069] W. Zhu, K. Parker, and M.A. Kriss, "Color filter arrays based on mutually exclusive blue noise patterns," *Journal of Visual Communication and Image Representation*, **10**, 245–267, 1999.

[1070] A. van der Ziel, *Noise in Solid State Devices and Circuits*, New York, NY: John Wiley and Sons, 1986.

[1071] H. Zollinger, *Color Chemistry*, 2nd edition, Weinheim: VCH Publishers, 1991.

[1072] G. Zorpette, "Let there be light," *IEEE Spectrum*, **39**, 9, 70–74, September, 2002.

[1073] A. Zukauskas, M.S. Shur, and R. Caska, *Introduction to Solid-State Lighting*, New York, NY: John Wiley & Sons, 2002.

[1074] D.M. Zwick, "Colour granularity and graininess," *Journal of Photographic Science*, **11**, 269–275, 1963.

[1075] D. Zwick and D.L. Brothers, Jr., "RMS granularity: determination of just-noticeable differences," *Photographic Science and Engineering*, **19**, 4, 235–238, 1975.

Index